Mirrors & Windows

Connecting with Literature

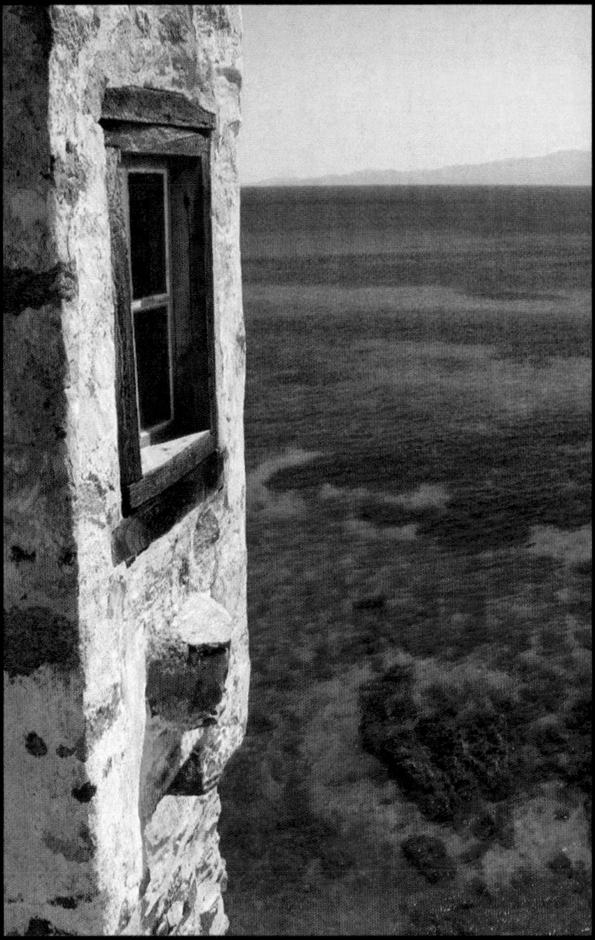

Level II

EMC Publishing®

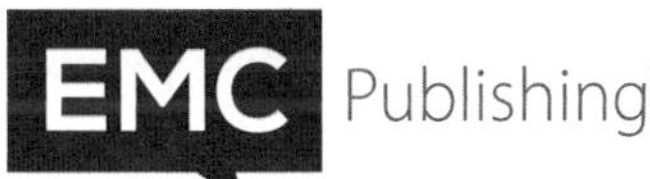

ST. PAUL

Staff Credits

Managing Editor: Brenda Owens
Editor: Nancy Papsin
Associate Editor: Carley Bomstad
Editorial Assistants: Erin Saladin, Lindsay Ryan
Permissions Coordinator: Lindsay Ryan
Photo Researcher: Brendan Curran
Marketing Director: Peter Hodges
Cover Designer: Leslie Anderson
Text Designer: Ronan Design
Page Layout Designers: Jack Ross, Matthias Frasch
Production Director: Deanna Quinn
Production Specialist: Petrina Nyhan, Tammy Norstrem
Project Manager: Sara Dovre Wudali, Buuji, Inc.
Editorial Development and Production: Nieman Inc.
ATE Composition: Parkwood Composition

Literary Acknowledgments: Literary Acknowledgments appear following the Glossary of Vocabulary Words. We have made every effort to trace the ownership of all copyrighted material and to secure permission from copyright holders. In the event of any question arising as to the use of any material, we will be pleased to make the necessary corrections in future printings. Thanks are due to the authors, publishers, and agents for permission to use the materials indicated.

Art and Photo Credits: Art and Photo Credits appear following the Literary Acknowledgments.

ISBN 978-0-82198-147-4 (print)
ISBN 978-0-82197-825-2 (eBook Version 1.0)

875 Montreal Way
St. Paul, MN 55102
E-mail: educate@emcp.com
Web site: www.emcp.com

Printed in the United States of America

21 20 19 18 17 16 15   1 2 3 4 5 6 7 8 9 10

Grade 7 California Common Core State Standards for English Language Arts

The California Common Core State Standards provide the foundation for instruction to ensure that all students master the skills needed to succeed in college and future careers. The English Language Arts Standards are divided into four strands: Reading, Writing, Speaking and Listening, and Language. These four learning strands and skill areas align with the College and Career Readiness (CCR) Anchor Standards for English Language Arts.

College and Career Readiness Anchor Standards

Reading: Literature and Informational Texts

- Key Ideas and Details
- Craft and Structure
- Integration of Knowledge and Ideas
- Range of Reading and Level of Complexity

Writing

- Text Types and Purposes
- Production and Distribution of Writing
- Research to Build and Present Knowledge
- Range of Writing

Speaking and Listening

- Comprehension and Collaboration
- Presentation of Knowledge and Ideas

Language

- Conventions of Standard English
- Knowledge of Language
- Vocabulary Acquisition and Use

The following grade-specific standards define what you need to know and do by the end of Grade 7.

Reading: Literature

Key Ideas and Details

1. Cite several pieces of textual evidence to support analysis of what the text says explicitly as well as inferences drawn from the text.
2. Determine a theme or central idea of a text and analyze its development over the course of the text; provide an objective summary of the text.
3. Analyze how particular elements of a story or drama interact (e.g., how setting shapes the characters or plot).

Craft and Structure

4. Determine the meaning of words and phrases as they are used in a text, including figurative and connotative meanings; analyze the impact of rhymes and other repetitions of sounds (e.g., alliteration) on a specific verse or stanza of a poem or section of a story or drama. **(See grade 7 Language standards 4–6 for additional expectations.) CA**
5. Analyze how a drama's or poem's form or structure (e.g., soliloquy, sonnet) contributes to its meaning.
6. Analyze how an author develops and contrasts the points of view of different characters or narrators in a text.

Integration of Knowledge and Ideas

7. Compare and contrast a written story, drama, or poem to its audio, filmed, staged, or multimedia version, analyzing the effects of techniques unique to each medium (e.g., lighting, sound, color, or camera focus and angles in a film).
8. (Not applicable to literature.)
9. Compare and contrast a fictional portrayal of a time, place, or character and a historical account of the same period as a means of understanding how authors of fiction use or alter history.

Range of Reading and Level of Text Complexity

10. By the end of the year, read and comprehend literature, including stories, dramas, and poems, in the grades 6–8 text complexity band proficiently, with scaffolding as needed at the high end of the range.

Reading: Informational Text

Key Ideas and Details

1. Cite several pieces of textual evidence to support analysis of what the text says explicitly as well as inferences drawn from the text.
2. Determine two or more central ideas in a text and analyze their development over the course of the text; provide an objective summary of the text.
3. Analyze the interactions between individuals, events, and ideas in a text (e.g., how ideas influence individuals or events, or how individuals influence ideas or events).

Craft and Structure

4. Determine the meaning of words and phrases as they are used in a text, including figurative, connotative, and technical meanings; analyze the impact of a specific word choice on meaning and tone. **(See grade 7 Language standards 4–6 for additional expectations.)** CA
5. Analyze the structure an author uses to organize a text, including how the major sections contribute to the whole and to the development of the ideas.
   a. **Analyze the use of text features (e.g., graphics, headers, captions) in public documents.** CA
6. Determine an author's point of view or purpose in a text and analyze how the author distinguishes his or her position from that of others.

Integration of Knowledge and Ideas

7. Compare and contrast a text to an audio, video, or multimedia version of the text, analyzing each medium's portrayal of the subject (e.g., how the delivery of a speech affects the impact of the words).
8. Trace and evaluate the argument and specific claims in a text, assessing whether the reasoning is sound and the evidence is relevant and sufficient to support the claims.
9. Analyze how two or more authors writing about the same topic shape their presentations of key information by emphasizing different evidence or advancing different interpretations of facts.

Range of Reading and Level of Text Complexity

10. By the end of the year, read and comprehend literary nonfiction in the grades 6–8 text complexity band proficiently, with scaffolding as needed at the high end of the range.

b. Apply grade 7 Reading standards to literary nonfiction (e.g. "Trace and evaluate the argument and specific claims in a text, assessing whether the reasoning is sound and the evidence is relevant and sufficient to support the claims").

Range of Writing

10. Write routinely over extended time frames (time for research, reflection, and revision) and shorter time frames (a single sitting or a day or two) for a range of discipline-specific tasks, purposes, and audiences.

Speaking and Listening

Comprehension and Collaboration

1. Engage effectively in a range of collaborative discussions (one-on-one, in groups, and teacher-led) with diverse partners on grade 7 topics, texts, and issues, building on others' ideas and expressing their own clearly.
   a. Come to discussions prepared, having read or researched material under study; explicitly draw on that preparation by referring to evidence on the topic, text, or issue to probe and reflect on ideas under discussion.
   b. Follow rules for collegial discussions, track progress toward specific goals and deadlines, and define individual roles as needed.
   c. Pose questions that elicit elaboration and respond to others' questions and comments with relevant observations and ideas that bring the discussion back on topic as needed.
   d. Acknowledge new information expressed by others and, when warranted, modify their own views.
2. Analyze the main ideas and supporting details presented in diverse media and formats (e.g., visually, quantitatively, orally) and explain how the ideas clarify a topic, text, or issue under study.
3. Delineate a speaker's argument and specific claims, **and attitude toward the subject**, evaluating the soundness of the reasoning and the relevance and sufficiency of the evidence. CA

Presentation of Knowledge and Ideas

4. Present claims and findings **(e.g., argument, narrative, summary presentations)**, emphasizing salient points in a focused, coherent manner with pertinent

Reading: Informational Text

Key Ideas and Details

1. Cite several pieces of textual evidence to support analysis of what the text says explicitly as well as inferences drawn from the text.
2. Determine two or more central ideas in a text and analyze their development over the course of the text; provide an objective summary of the text.
3. Analyze the interactions between individuals, events, and ideas in a text (e.g., how ideas influence individuals or events, or how individuals influence ideas or events).

Craft and Structure

4. Determine the meaning of words and phrases as they are used in a text, including figurative, connotative, and technical meanings; analyze the impact of a specific word choice on meaning and tone. **(See grade 7 Language standards 4–6 for additional expectations.) CA**
5. Analyze the structure an author uses to organize a text, including how the major sections contribute to the whole and to the development of the ideas.
    a. **Analyze the use of text features (e.g., graphics, headers, captions) in public documents. CA**
6. Determine an author's point of view or purpose in a text and analyze how the author distinguishes his or her position from that of others.

Integration of Knowledge and Ideas

7. Compare and contrast a text to an audio, video, or multimedia version of the text, analyzing each medium's portrayal of the subject (e.g., how the delivery of a speech affects the impact of the words).
8. Trace and evaluate the argument and specific claims in a text, assessing whether the reasoning is sound and the evidence is relevant and sufficient to support the claims.
9. Analyze how two or more authors writing about the same topic shape their presentations of key information by emphasizing different evidence or advancing different interpretations of facts.

Range of Reading and Level of Text Complexity

10. By the end of the year, read and comprehend literary nonfiction in the grades 6–8 text complexity band proficiently, with scaffolding as needed at the high end of the range.

Writing

Text Types and Purposes

1. Write arguments to support claims with clear reasons and relevant evidence.
   - **a.** Introduce claim(s), acknowledge **and address** alternate or opposing claims, and organize the reasons and evidence logically. CA
   - **b.** Support claim(s) **or counterarguments** with logical reasoning and relevant evidence, using accurate, credible sources and demonstrating an understanding of the topic or text. CA
   - **c.** Use words, phrases, and clauses to create cohesion and clarify the relationships among claim(s), reasons, and evidence.
   - **d.** Establish and maintain a formal style.
   - **e.** Provide a concluding statement or section that follows from and supports the argument presented.
2. Write informative/explanatory texts to examine a topic and convey ideas, concepts, and information through the selection, organization, and analysis of relevant content.
   - **a.** Introduce a topic **or thesis statement** clearly, previewing what is to follow; organize ideas, concepts, and information, using strategies such as definition, classification, comparison/contrast, and cause/effect; include formatting (e.g., headings), graphics (e.g., charts, tables), and multimedia when useful to aiding comprehension. CA
   - **b.** Develop the topic with relevant facts, definitions, concrete details, quotations, or other information and examples.
   - **c.** Use appropriate transitions to create cohesion and clarify the relationships among ideas and concepts.
   - **d.** Use precise language and domain-specific vocabulary to inform about or explain the topic.
   - **e.** Establish and maintain a formal style.
   - **f.** Provide a concluding statement or section that follows from and supports the information or explanation presented.
3. Write narratives to develop real or imagined experiences or events using effective technique, relevant descriptive details, and well-structured event sequences.
   - **a.** Engage and orient the reader by establishing a context and point of view and introducing a narrator and/or characters; organize an event sequence that unfolds naturally and logically.

b. Use narrative techniques, such as dialogue, pacing, and description, to develop experiences, events, and/or characters.

c. Use a variety of transition words, phrases, and clauses to convey sequence and signal shifts from one time frame or setting to another.

d. Use precise words and phrases, relevant descriptive details, and sensory language to capture the action and convey experiences and events.

e. Provide a conclusion that follows from and reflects on the narrated experiences or events.

Production and Distribution of Writing

4. Produce clear and coherent writing in which the development, organization, and style are appropriate to task, purpose, and audience. (Grade-specific expectations for writing types are defined in standards 1–3 above.)

5. With some guidance and support from peers and adults, develop and strengthen writing as needed by planning, revising, editing, rewriting, or trying a new approach, focusing on how well purpose and audience have been addressed. (Editing for conventions should demonstrate command of Language standards 1–3 up to and including grade 7.)

6. Use technology, including the Internet, to produce and publish writing and link to and cite sources as well as to interact and collaborate with others, including linking to and citing sources.

Research to Build and Present Knowledge

7. Conduct short research projects to answer a question, drawing on several sources and generating additional related, focused questions for further research and investigation.

8. Gather relevant information from multiple print and digital sources, using search terms effectively; assess the credibility and accuracy of each source; and quote or paraphrase the data and conclusions of others while avoiding plagiarism and following a standard format for citation.

9. Draw evidence from literary or informational texts to support analysis, reflection, and research.

   a. Apply grade 7 Reading standards to literature (e.g., "Compare and contrast a fictional portrayal of a time, place, or character and a historical account of the same period as a means of understanding how authors of fiction use or alter history").

b. Apply grade 7 Reading standards to literary nonfiction (e.g. "Trace and evaluate the argument and specific claims in a text, assessing whether the reasoning is sound and the evidence is relevant and sufficient to support the claims").

Range of Writing

10. Write routinely over extended time frames (time for research, reflection, and revision) and shorter time frames (a single sitting or a day or two) for a range of discipline-specific tasks, purposes, and audiences.

Speaking and Listening

Comprehension and Collaboration

1. Engage effectively in a range of collaborative discussions (one-on-one, in groups, and teacher-led) with diverse partners on grade 7 topics, texts, and issues, building on others' ideas and expressing their own clearly.
   a. Come to discussions prepared, having read or researched material under study; explicitly draw on that preparation by referring to evidence on the topic, text, or issue to probe and reflect on ideas under discussion.
   b. Follow rules for collegial discussions, track progress toward specific goals and deadlines, and define individual roles as needed.
   c. Pose questions that elicit elaboration and respond to others' questions and comments with relevant observations and ideas that bring the discussion back on topic as needed.
   d. Acknowledge new information expressed by others and, when warranted, modify their own views.
2. Analyze the main ideas and supporting details presented in diverse media and formats (e.g., visually, quantitatively, orally) and explain how the ideas clarify a topic, text, or issue under study.
3. Delineate a speaker's argument and specific claims, **and attitude toward the subject**, evaluating the soundness of the reasoning and the relevance and sufficiency of the evidence. **CA**

Presentation of Knowledge and Ideas

4. Present claims and findings **(e.g., argument, narrative, summary presentations)**, emphasizing salient points in a focused, coherent manner with pertinent

descriptions, facts, details, and examples; use appropriate eye contact, adequate volume, and clear pronunciation. CA

a. **Plan and present an argument that: supports a claim, acknowledges counterarguments, organizes evidence logically, uses words and phrases to create cohesion, and provides a concluding statement that supports the argument presented. CA**

5. Include multimedia components and visual displays in presentations to clarify claims and findings and emphasize salient points.
6. Adapt speech to a variety of contexts and tasks, demonstrating command of formal English when indicated or appropriate. (See grade 7 Language standards 1 and 3 for specific expectations.)

Language

Conventions of Standard English

1. Demonstrate command of the conventions of standard English grammar and usage when writing or speaking.
   a. **Explain the function of phrases and clauses in general and their function in specific sentences.**
   b. Choose among simple, compound, complex, and compound-complex sentences to signal differing relationships among ideas.
   c. Place phrases and clauses within a sentence, recognizing and correcting misplaced and dangling modifiers.
2. Demonstrate command of the conventions of standard English capitalization, punctuation, and spelling when writing.
   a. Use a comma to separate coordinate adjectives (e.g., *It was a fascinating, enjoyable movie* but not *He wore an old[,] green shirt*).
   b. Spell correctly.

Knowledge of Language

3. Use knowledge of language and its conventions when writing, speaking, reading, or listening.
   a. **Choose language that expresses ideas precisely and concisely, recognizing and eliminating wordiness and redundancy.**

Vocabulary Acquisitions and Use

4. Determine or clarify the meaning of unknown and multiple-meaning words and phrases based on grade 7 reading and content, choosing flexibly from a range of strategies.
   a. Use context (e.g., the overall meaning of a sentence or paragraph; a word's position or function in a sentence) as a clue to the meaning of a word or phrase.
   b. Use common, grade-appropriate Greek or Latin affixes and roots as clues to the meaning of a word (e.g., *belligerent*, *bellicose*, *rebel*).
   c. Consult general and specialized reference materials (e.g., dictionaries, glossaries, thesauruses), both print and digital, to find the pronunciation of a word or determine or clarify its precise meaning or its part of speech **or trace the etymology of words. CA**
   d. Verify the preliminary determination of the meaning of a word or phrase (e.g., by checking the inferred meaning in context or in a dictionary).
5. Demonstrate understanding of figurative language, word relationships, and nuances in word meanings.
   a. Interpret figures of speech (e.g., literary, biblical, and mythological allusions) in context.
   b. Use the relationship between particular words (e.g., synonym/antonym, analogy) to better understand each of the words.
   c. Distinguish among the connotations (associations) of words with similar denotations (definitions) (e.g., *refined*, *respectful*, *polite*, *diplomatic*, *condescending*).
6. Acquire and use accurately grade-appropriate general academic and domain-specific words and phrases; gather vocabulary knowledge when considering a word or phrase important to comprehension or expression.

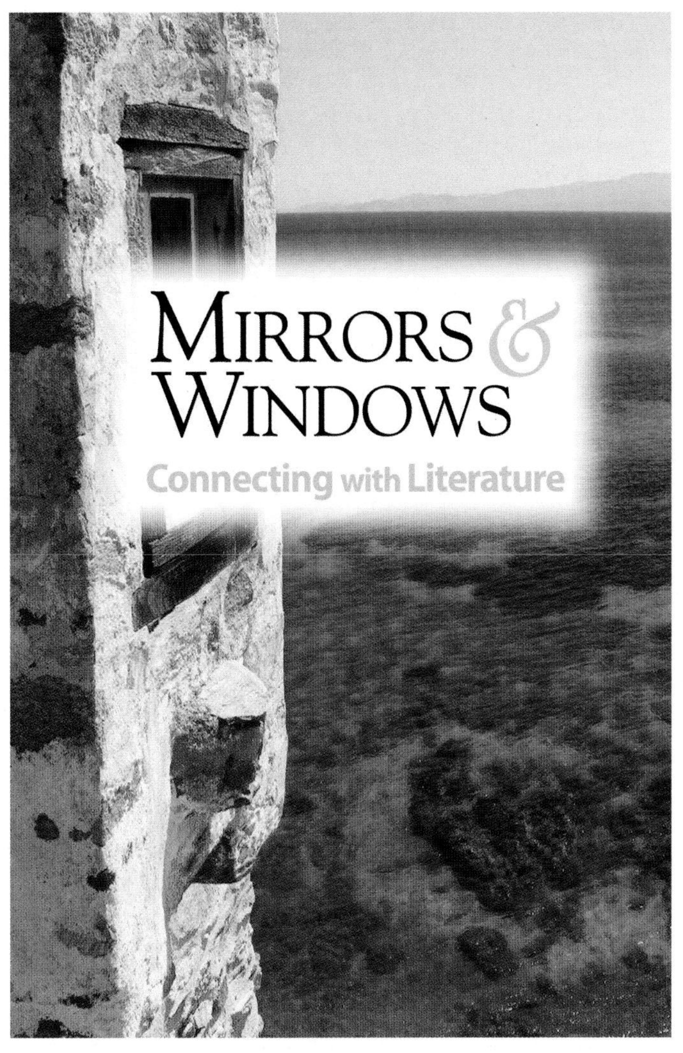

"The whole purpose of education is to turn mirrors into windows."

— Sydney J. Harris

Consultants, Reviewers, and Focus Group Participants

Tracy Pulido
Language Arts Instructor
West Valley High School
Fairbanks, Alaska

Jean Martorana
Reading Specialist/English Teacher
Desert Vista High School
Phoenix, Arizona

Cindy Johnston
English Teacher
Argus High School
Ceres, California

Susan Stoehr
Language Arts Instructor
Aragon High School
San Mateo, California

John Owens
Reading Specialist
St. Vrain Valley Schools
Longmont, Colorado

Fred Smith
Language Arts Instructor
St. Bernard High School
Uncasville, Connecticut

Penny Austin-Richardson
English Department Chair
Seaford Senior High School
Seaford, Delaware

Cecilia Lewis
Language Arts Instructor
Mariner High School
Cape Coral, Florida

Jane Feber
Teacher
Mandarin Middle School
Jacksonville, Florida

Dorothy Fletcher
Language Arts Instructor
Wolfson Senior High School
Jacksonville, Florida

Tamara Doehring
English/Reading Teacher
Melbourne High School
Melbourne, Florida

Patti Magee
English Instructor
Timber Creek High School
Orlando, Florida

Margaret J. Graham
Language Arts/Reading Teacher
Elizabeth Cobb Middle School
Tallahassee, Florida

Elizabeth Steinman
English Instructor
Vero Beach High School
Vero Beach, Florida

Wanda Bagwell
Language Arts Department Chair
Commerce High School
Commerce, Georgia

Betty Deriso
Language Department Chairperson
Crisp County High School
Cordele, Georgia

Dr. Peggy Leland
English Instructor
Chestatee High School
Gainsville, Georgia

Matthew Boedy
Language Arts Instructor
Harlem High School
Harlem, Georgia

Patty Bradshaw
English Department Chair
Harlem High School
Harlem, Georgia

Dawn Faulkner
English Department Chair
Rome High School
Rome, Georgia

Carolyn C. Coleman
AKS Continuous Improvement Director
Gwinnett County Public Schools
Suwanee, Georgia

Elisabeth Blumer Thompson
Language Arts Instructor
Swainsboro High School
Swainsboro, Georgia

Toi Walker
English Instructor
Northeast Tifton County High School
Tifton, Georgia

Jeanette Rogers
English Instructor
Potlatch Jr.-Sr. High School
Potlatch, Idaho

Gail Taylor
Language Arts Instructor
Rigby High School
Rigby, Idaho

Carey Robin
Language Arts Instructor
St. Francis College Prep
Brookfield, Illinois

Patricia Meyer
English Department Chair
Glenbard East High School
Lombard, Illinois

Liz Rebmann
Language Arts Instructor
Morton High School
Morton, Illinois

Helen Gallagher
English Department Chair
Main East High School
Park Ridge, Illinois

Rosemary Ryan
Dean of Students
Schaumburg High School
Schaumburg, Illinois

Donna Cracraft
English Department Co-Chair/IB Coordinator
Pike High School
Indianapolis, Indiana

Consultants, Reviewers, and Focus Group Participants (cont.)

K. C. Salter
Language Arts Instructor
Knightstown High School
Knightstown, Indiana

Lisa Broxterman
Language Arts Instructor
Axtell High School
Axtell, Kansas

Shirley Wells
Language Arts Instructor
Derby High School
Derby, Kansas

Karen Ann Stous
Speech & Drama Teacher
Holton High School
Holton, Kansas

Martha-Jean Rockey
Language Arts Instructor
Troy High School
Troy, Kansas

Shelia Penick
Language Arts Instructor
Yates Center High School
Yates Center, Kansas

John Ermilio
English Teacher
St. Johns High School
Shrewsbury, Massachusetts

James York
English Teacher
Waverly High School
Lansing, Michigan

Mary Spychalla
Gifted Education Coordinator
Valley Middle School
Apple Valley, Minnesota

Shari K. Carlson
Advanced ILA Teacher
Coon Rapids Middle School
Coon Rapids, Minnesota

Rebecca Benz
English Instructor
St. Thomas Academy
Mendota Heights, Minnesota

Michael F. Graves
Professor Emeritus
University of Minnesota
330A Peik Hall
Minneapolis, Minnesota

Kathleen Nelson
English Instructor
New Ulm High School
New Ulm, Minnesota

Adonna Gaspar
Language Arts Teacher
Cooper High School
Robbinsdale, Minnesota

Sara L. Nystuen
English Department Chair; AP Instructor
Concordia Academy
Roseville, Minnesota

Tom Backen
English Teacher
Benilde-St. Margaret's School
St. Louis Park, Minnesota

Daniel Sylvester
Jr. High English & American Experience Teacher
Benilde-St. Margaret's School
St. Louis Park, Minnesota

Jean Borax
Literacy Coach
Harding High School
St. Paul, Minnesota

Erik Brandt
English Teacher
Harding High School
St. Paul, Minnesota

Kevin Brennan
High School English Teacher
Cretin-Derham Hall
St. Paul, Minnesota

Anna Newcombe
English Instructor
Harding High School
St. Paul, Minnesota

Rosemary Ruffenach
Language Arts Teacher, Consultant, and Writer
St. Paul, Minnesota

Nancy Papsin
English Teacher/Educational Consultant
White Bear Lake, Minnesota

Shannon Umfleet
Communication Arts Instructor
Northwest High School
Cedar Hill, Missouri

Ken Girard
Language Arts Instructor
Bishop LeBlond High School
St. Joseph, Missouri

Jessica Gall
Language Arts Instructor
Fremont High School
Fremont, Nebraska

Michael Davis
Language Arts Instructor
Millard West High School
Omaha, Nebraska

Lisa Larnerd
English Teacher
Basic High School
Henderson, Nevada

Jo Paulson
Title I Reading Teacher
Camino Real Middle School
Las Cruces, New Mexico

Stacy Biss
Language Arts Instructor
Hackensack High School
Hackensack, New Jersey

J. M. Winchock
Reading Specialist, Adult Literacy Instructor
Hillsborough High School
Hillsborough, New Jersey

Consultants, Reviewers, and Focus Group Participants (cont.)

Matthew Cahn
Department of English & Related Arts Supervisor
River Dell High School
Oradell, New Jersey

Jean Mullooly
Language Arts Instructor
Holy Angels High School
Trenton, New Jersey

Fenice Boyd
Assistant Professor, Learning and Instruction
State University of New York at Buffalo
Buffalo, New York

Michael Fedorchuk
Assistant Principal
Auburn High School
Auburn, New York

Robert Balch
English Instructor
Beacon High School
Beacon, New York

Rene A. Roberge
Secondary English/AP English Instructor
Hudson Falls High School
Hudson Falls, New York

Melissa Hedt
Literacy Coach
Asheville Middle School
Asheville, North Carolina

Jane Shoaf
Educational Consultant
Durham, North Carolina

Kimberly Tufts
Department Chair for ELA
Cranberry Middle School
Elk Park, North Carolina

Cheryl Gackle
English Instructor
Kulm High School
Kulm, North Dakota

Barbara Stroh
English Department Chair
Aurora High School
Aurora, Ohio

Mary Jo Bish
Language Arts Instructor
Lake Middle School
Millbury, Ohio

Judy Ellsesser-Painter
Language Arts Instructor
South Webster High School
South Webster, Ohio

Adele Dahlin
English Department Chair
Central Catholic High School
Toledo, Ohio

Joshua Singer
English Instructor
Central Catholic High School
Toledo, Ohio

Debbie Orendorf
Language Arts Instructor
Berlin Brothers Valley High School
Berlin, Pennsylvania

Dona Italiano
English Teacher/Language Arts Coordinator
Souderton Area High School
Souderton, Pennsylvania

Tina Parlier
Secondary English Instructor
Elizabethton High School
Elizabethton, Tennessee

Wayne Luellen
English Instructor
Houston High School
Germantown, Tennessee

Ed Farrell
Senior Consultant
Emeritus Professor of English Education
University of Texas at Austin
Austin, Texas

Terry Ross
Secondary Language Arts Supervisor
Austin Independent School District
Austin, Texas

Angelia Greiner
English Department Chair
Big Sandy High School
Big Sandy, Texas

Sharon Kremer
Educational Consultant
Denton, Texas

E. J. Brletich
Supervisor of English/Language Arts
Spotsylvania City School
Fredericksburg, Virginia

Jeffrey Golub
Educational Consultant
Bothell, Washington

Clifford Aziz
Language Arts Instructor
Washington High School
Tacoma, Washington

Becky Palmer
Reading Teacher
Madison Middle School
Appleton, Wisconsin

Mary Hoppe
English Teacher
Bonduel High School
Bonduel, Wisconsin

Lou Wappel
English, Humanities & Guidance Instructor
St. Lawrence Seminary High School
Mount Calvary, Wisconsin

Gregory R. Kier
Language Arts Instructor
East Elementary School
New Richmond, Wisconsin

CONTENTS IN BRIEF

Unit 1 Fiction Meeting the Unexpected 3

Introduction to Fiction 4

Understanding Plot 6

Fiction Close Reading Model 8

Understanding Characters 17

Understanding Setting 29

Unit 2 Fiction Learning Values 139

Understanding Point of View 140

Understanding Theme 153

Unit 3 Nonfiction Experiencing the World 253

Introduction to Nonfiction 254

Nonfiction Close Reading Model 256

Understanding the Essay 281

Unit 4 Nonfiction Responding to Nature 375

Introduction to Informational Text and Visual Media 376

Unit 5 Poetry Appreciating Life 461

Introduction to Poetry 462

Understanding Imagery and Figurative Language 464

Poetry Close Reading Model 465

Understanding Sound Devices 473

Unit 6 Poetry Searching Beneath the Surface 537

Understanding Meaning in Poetry 538

Unit 7 Drama Facing Challenges 607

Introduction to Drama 608

Drama Close Reading Model 610

Unit 8 Folk Literature Seeking Wisdom 723

Introduction to Folk Literature 724

Folk Literature Close Reading Model 726

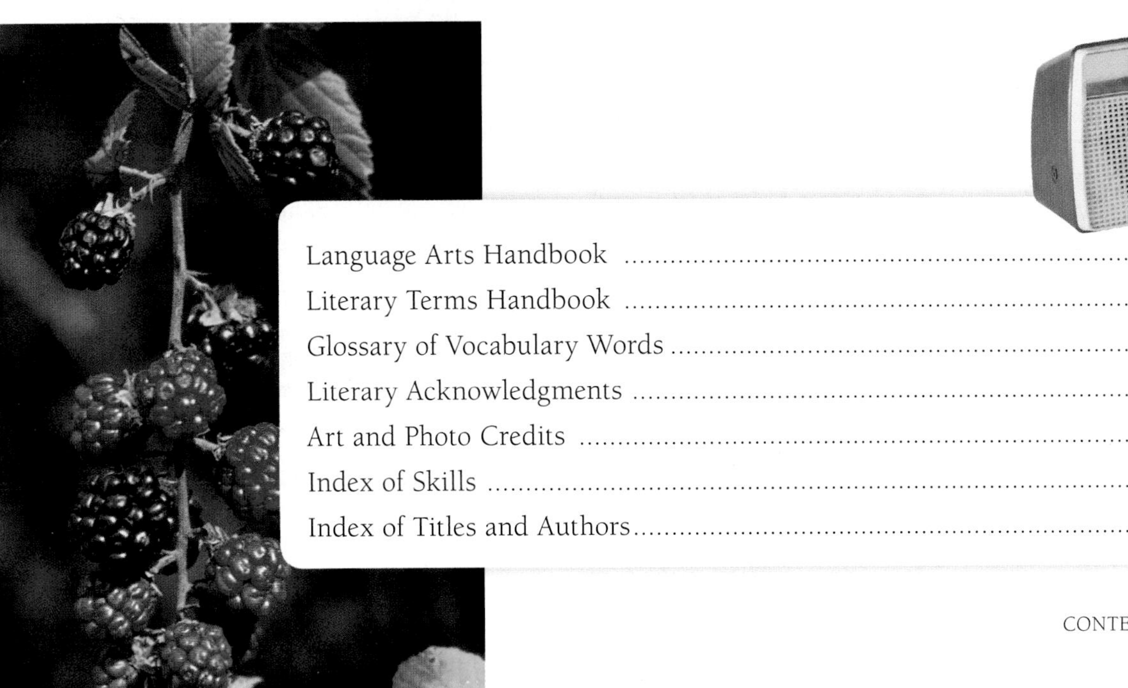

Language Arts Handbook 834

Literary Terms Handbook 940

Glossary of Vocabulary Words 950

Literary Acknowledgments 954

Art and Photo Credits 959

Index of Skills 965

Index of Titles and Authors 972

Unit 1 Fiction Meeting the Unexpected 3

Introduction to Fiction 4

GUIDED READING

Understanding Plot 6

Fiction Close Reading Model 8

O. Henry — **After Twenty Years** — SHORT STORY 9

VOCABULARY & SPELLING Denotation and Connotation 16

Understanding Characters 17

Patricia McKissack — **The 11:59** — SHORT STORY 18

INFORMATIONAL TEXT CONNECTION Text-to-Text

Patricia and Fredrick McKissack — *from* **A Long Hard Journey: The Story of the Pullman Porter** — ESSAY 26

Understanding Setting 29

Lensey Namioka — **The Inn of Lost Time** — SHORT STORY 30

GRAMMAR & STYLE Subject-Verb Agreement 48

DIRECTED READING

Tomás Rivera — **The Portrait** — SHORT STORY 49

GRAMMAR & STYLE Pronoun-Antecedent Agreement 56

Ernest Hemingway — **A Day's Wait** — ANCHOR TEXT/SHORT STORY 57

INFORMATIONAL TEXT CONNECTION Text-to-Text

NASA — **Mars Climate Orbiter Team Finds Likely Cause of Loss** — PRESS RELEASE 61

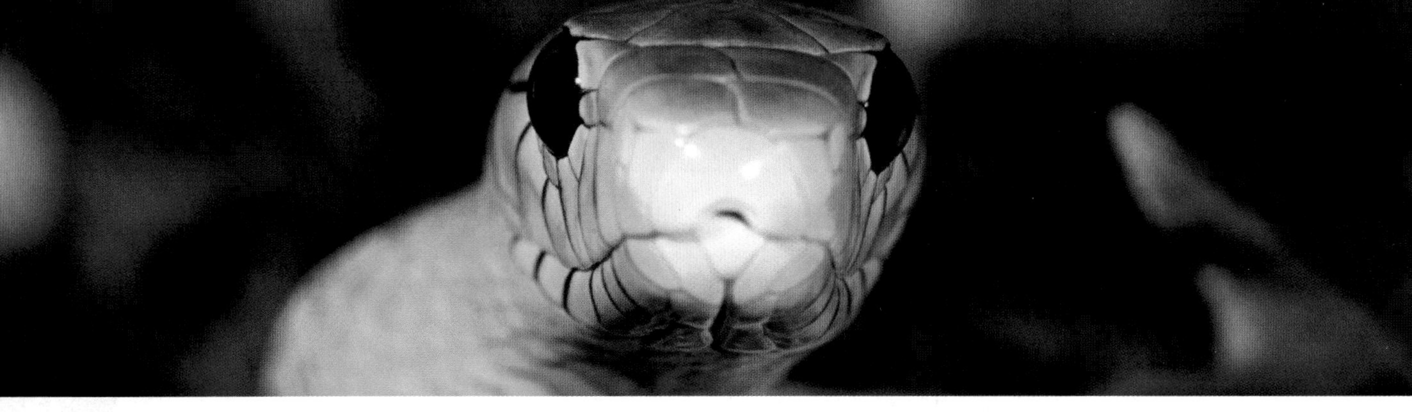

Author	Title	Genre	Page
Toni Cade Bambara	**The War of the Wall**	SHORT STORY	63
	History Connection *Civil Rights*		69
	GRAMMAR & STYLE Nominative and Objective Pronouns		72
Ray Bradbury	**The Foghorn**	SHORT STORY	73
	Science Connection *Sea Creatures*		79
	INFORMATIONAL TEXT CONNECTION Text-to-Text		
David Macaulay	**The Aqualung**	VISUAL MEDIA	83
	COMPARING TEXTS		
Rudyard Kipling	**Rikki-Tikki-Tavi**	SHORT STORY	85
Roald Dahl	**The Green Mamba**	AUTOBIOGRAPHY	98

INDEPENDENT READING

Author	Title	Genre	Page
Leslie Marmon Silko	**Uncle Tony's Goat**	SHORT STORY	105
Joan Aiken	**The Serial Garden**	SHORT STORY	111

FOR YOUR READING LIST 125

WRITING WORKSHOP
Informative Writing: Responding to a Short Story 126

SPEAKING & LISTENING WORKSHOP
Giving and Actively Listening to Oral Summaries 132

TEST PRACTICE WORKSHOP
Writing Skills: Literary Response 134
from **The Snow Goose,** by Paul Gallico 134
Revising and Editing Skills 135
Reading Skills 136
The Dinner Party, by Mona Gardner 136

Unit 2 Learning Values 139
Fiction

GUIDED READING

Understanding Point of View **140**

Cherylene Lee | **Hollywood and the Pits** | SHORT STORY | 141
Science Connection *Geologic Time* 148

Understanding Theme **153**

Marta Salinas | **The Scholarship Jacket** | SHORT STORY | 154
GRAMMAR & STYLE Comma Use 162

DIRECTED READING

Piri Thomas | **Amigo Brothers** | ANCHOR TEXT/SHORT STORY | 163
INFORMATIONAL TEXT CONNECTION **Text-to-Text**
Walter Dean Myers | *from* **The Greatest: Muhammad Ali** | BIOGRAPHY | 173
VOCABULARY & SPELLING Prefixes, Roots, and Suffixes 176

Sandra Cisneros | **Four Skinny Trees** | SHORT STORY | 177
Gish Jen | **The White Umbrella** | SHORT STORY | 181
GRAMMAR & STYLE Independent and Dependent Clauses 190

COMPARING TEXTS

Joseph Bruchac	**Jed's Grandfather**	SHORT STORY	191
Edna St. Vincent Millay	**The Courage That My Mother Had**	LYRIC POEM	197
Borden Deal	**Antaeus**	SHORT STORY	199
	History Connection *Victory Gardens*		203
	LITERATURE CONNECTION **Text-to-Text**		
Lucille Clifton	**in the inner city**	LYRIC POEM	210
Gary Soto	**Seventh Grade**	SHORT STORY	212
	GRAMMAR & STYLE Consistent Verb Tense		219

INDEPENDENT READING

Cynthia Rylant	**Papa's Parrot**	SHORT STORY	220
Anne McCaffrey	**The Smallest Dragonboy**	SHORT STORY	224

FOR YOUR READING LIST 237

WRITING WORKSHOP
Narrative Writing: Writing a Short Story 238

SPEAKING & LISTENING WORKSHOP
Giving and Actively Listening to Literary Presentations 246

TEST PRACTICE WORKSHOP
Writing Skills: Literary Response 248
Revising and Editing Skills 249
Reading Skills 250
The Ground Is Always Damp, by Luci Tapahonso 250

Unit 3 Experiencing the World 253
Nonfiction

Introduction to Nonfiction 254

GUIDED READING

Nonfiction Close Reading Model 256

Annie Dillard — *from* **An American Childhood** — MEMOIR 257

GRAMMAR & STYLE Phrases 264

Milton Meltzer — **Elizabeth I** — BIOGRAPHY 265

Cultural Connection *The Renaissance* 272

PRIMARY SOURCE CONNECTION Text-to-Text

Queen Elizabeth I — *from* **Queen Elizabeth's Speech to Her Last Parliament** — SPEECH 277

Written with a Diamond on Her Window at Woodstock — POEM 278

Written in Her French Psalter — POEM 278

from **Letter to Mary, Queen of Scots, 1586** — LETTER 278

VOCABULARY & SPELLING Greek, Latin, and Anglo-Saxon Roots 280

Understanding the Essay 281

Julia Alvarez — **Names/Nombres** — PERSONAL ESSAY 282

Geography Connection *The Dominican Republic* 285

LITERATURE CONNECTION Text-to-Text

Janet S. Wong — **Face It** — LYRIC POEM 289

Louis L'Amour — **The Eternal Frontier** — ARGUMENTATIVE ESSAY 291

GRAMMAR & STYLE Sentence Types 296

DIRECTED READING

Arthur Ashe — *from* **Off the Court** — ANCHOR TEXT/AUTOBIOGRAPHY 297

INFORMATIONAL TEXT CONNECTION Text-to-Text

Arthur Ashe — **A Black Athlete Looks at Education** — EDITORIAL 310

Bill Cosby — **Was Tarzan a Three-Bandage Man?** — PERSONAL ESSAY 312

History Connection *Jackie Robinson* 314

Amy Tan — **Fish Cheeks** — PERSONAL ESSAY 317

GRAMMAR & STYLE Fragments and Run-on Sentences 321

COMPARING TEXTS

Jerry Izenberg	**A Bittersweet Memoir**	BIOGRAPHY	322
W. P. Kinsella	**Searching for January**	SHORT STORY	333
Jim Haskins	**Madam C. J. Walker**	BIOGRAPHY	340
	LITERATURE CONNECTION **Text-to-Text**		
Faith Ringgold	**The Sunflower Quilting Bee at Arles**	STORY QUILT	348

INDEPENDENT READING

Ernesto Galarza	*from* **Barrio Boy**	MEMOIR	352
James Thurber	**The Night the Bed Fell**	PERSONAL ESSAY	356

FOR YOUR READING LIST 361

WRITING WORKSHOP
Informative Writing: Cause-and-Effect Essay 362

SPEAKING & LISTENING WORKSHOP
Giving and Actively Listening to Informative Presentations 368

TEST PRACTICE WORKSHOP
Writing Skills: Informative Essay 370
from **Alone Across the Arctic,** by Pam Flowers 370
Revising and Editing Skills 371
Reading Skills 372
from **Flying,** by Reeve Lindbergh 372

Unit 4 Nonfiction Responding to Nature

Introduction to Informational Text and Visual Media 376

GUIDED READING

Robert Jastrow **The Size of Things** SCIENTIFIC ESSAY 378
LITERATURE CONNECTION Text-to-Text
Pattiann Rogers **Achieving Perspective** LYRIC POEM 386
GRAMMAR & STYLE Adjective and Adverb Clauses 389
David Allen Sibley *from* **The Sibley Guide To Birds** VISUAL MEDIA 390
INFORMATIONAL TEXT CONNECTION Text-to-Text
John James Audubon *from* **Wild Turkey** ESSAY 394

DIRECTED READING

Al Gore **Ships in the Desert** ANCHOR TEXT/ESSAY 396
Science Connection *Global Warming* 400
INFORMATIONAL TEXT CONNECTION Text-to-Text
Chief Dan George **I Am a Native of North America** PERSONAL ESSAY 403
GRAMMAR & STYLE Simple and Compound Subjects 407

COMPARING TEXTS

Author	Title	Genre	Page
Diane Ackerman	**Mute Dancers: How to Watch a Hummingbird**	SCIENTIFIC ESSAY	408
William Saroyan	**The Hummingbird That Lived Through Winter**	SHORT STORY	412
Jennifer Armstrong	**The Face of the Deep Is Frozen**	HISTORICAL ESSAY	415
	LITERATURE CONNECTION Text-to-Text		
Robert Frost	**Fire and Ice**	LYRIC POEM	421
	VOCABULARY & SPELLING Context Clues		423
Mee Vang	**Hmong Storycloth**	VISUAL MEDIA	424
	PRIMARY SOURCE CONNECTION Text-to-Text		
Maijue Xiong	**An Unforgettable Journey**	AUTOBIOGRAPHY	426
Arthur Rothstein	**Dust Bowl Photographs**	VISUAL MEDIA	432
	INFORMATIONAL TEXT CONNECTION Text-to-Text		
Margaret Bourke-White	**Dust Changes America**	ESSAY	436
	History Connection *The New Deal*		438

INDEPENDENT READING

Author	Title	Genre	Page
Lewis Thomas	**Death in the Open**	SCIENTIFIC ESSAY	440
Tim Flannery & Peter Schouten	**Astonishing Animals**	VISUAL MEDIA	443

FOR YOUR READING LIST 447

WRITING WORKSHOP
Descriptive Writing: Descriptive Essay 448

VIEWING WORKSHOP
Critical Viewing 454

TEST PRACTICE WORKSHOP
Writing Skills: Descriptive Essay 456
Revising and Editing Skills 457
Reading Skills 458
from **Beastly Behaviors,** by Janine Benyus 458

Unit 5 Appreciating Life
Poetry

Unit 5 Appreciating Life — Poetry 461

Introduction to Poetry 462

GUIDED READING

Understanding Imagery and Figurative Language 464

Poetry Close Reading Model 465

Pat Mora	**Gold**	LYRIC POEM	466
May Swenson	**Feel Like a Bird**	LYRIC POEM	469

Understanding Sound Devices 473

Lewis Carroll	**Father William**	HUMOROUS POEM	475
	Cultural Connection *Wonderland*		478
	GRAMMAR & STYLE Personal and Possessive Pronouns		480
Galway Kinnell	**Blackberry Eating**	LYRIC POEM	481
	VOCABULARY & SPELLING Synonyms and Antonyms		484

DIRECTED READING

Henry Wadsworth Longfellow	**The Village Blacksmith**	NARRATIVE POEM	485
	GRAMMAR & STYLE Nouns: Proper, Plural, Possessive, and Collective		490
Langston Hughes	**Mother to Son**	LYRIC POEM	491
Diana Rivera	**Under the Apple Tree**	ANCHOR TEXT/LYRIC POEM	495
	INFORMATIONAL TEXT CONNECTION Text-to-Text		
Michael Pollan	*from* **The Botany of Desire**	ESSAY	498
	GRAMMAR & STYLE Reflexive and Intensive Pronouns		501
Claude McKay	**The Tropics in New York**	LYRIC POEM	502

COMPARING TEXTS

Naoshi Koriyama	**Unfolding Bud**	LYRIC POEM	505
Eve Merriam	**How to Eat a Poem**	LYRIC POEM	508
Matsuo Bashō, Yosa Buson, and Kobayashi Issa Translated by Robert Hass	**Haiku**	HAIKU	510

INFORMATIONAL TEXT CONNECTION Text-to-Text

Steven Harvey	*from* **Lost in Translation**	ESSAY	513
E. E. Cummings	**the sky was**	CONCRETE POEM	515

INDEPENDENT READING

Eve Merriam	**Two People I Want to Be Like**	LYRIC POEM	518
Walt Whitman	**Miracles**	LYRIC POEM	520
Gogisgi	**Early Song**	LYRIC POEM	522

FOR YOUR READING LIST 523

WRITING WORKSHOP
Informative Writing: Compare-and-Contrast Essay 524

SPEAKING & LISTENING WORKSHOP
Giving and Actively Listening to Informative Presentations 530

TEST PRACTICE WORSHOP
Writing Skills: Informative Essay 532
Song, by Robert Browning 532
The Gardener (LXXXV), by Rabindranath Tagore 532
Revising and Editing Skills 533
Reading Skills 534
Silver, by Walter de la Mare 534

Unit 6 Searching Beneath the Surface 537
Poetry

GUIDED READING

Understanding Meaning in Poetry 538

Carl Sandburg **Theme in Yellow** LYRIC POEM 539

GRAMMAR & STYLE Simple, Compound, Complex, and Compound-Complex Sentences 543

Robert Frost **Once by the Pacific** LYRIC POEM 544

DIRECTED READING

COMPARING TEXTS

Edgar Allan Poe **Annabel Lee** NARRATIVE POEM 547

Cultural Connection *Gothic Literature* 550

Alfred Noyes **The Highwayman** NARRATIVE POEM 551

Elizabeth Bishop **The Filling Station** LYRIC POEM 557

VOCABULARY & SPELLING Figurative Language 561

Phil George **Name Giveaway** ANCHOR TEXT/LYRIC POEM 562

PRIMARY SOURCE CONNECTION **Text-to-Text**

Ah-nen-la-de-ni *from* **An Indian Boy's Story** MEMOIR 564

VOCABULARY & SPELLING Spelling by Syllables 567

Dudley Randall	**Ancestors**	LYRIC POEM	568
	GRAMMAR & STYLE Simple, Complete, and Compound Predicates		571
Naomi Shihab Nye	**The Lost Parrot**	NARRATIVE POEM	572
Janice Mirikitani	**For My Father**	NARRATIVE POEM	576
	History Connection *Japanese Internment*		578
Janet S. Wong	**Money Order**	NARRATIVE POEM	580
	Sisters	LYRIC POEM	582

INDEPENDENT READING

Emily Dickinson	**I'm Nobody**	LYRIC POEM	584
Lorna Dee Cervantes	**Refugee Ship**	LYRIC POEM	586
Wendy Rose	**Loo Wit**	LYRIC POEM	588
	Science Connection *Mount Saint Helens*		590
Robert Frost	**The Pasture**	LYRIC POEM	591

FOR YOUR READING LIST 593

WRITING WORKSHOP
Narrative Writing: Personal Narrative 594

SPEAKING & LISTENING WORKSHOP
Giving and Actively Listening to Narrative Presentations 600

TEST PRACTICE WORKSHOP
Writing Skills: Personal Essay 602
Revising and Editing Skills 603
Reading Skills 604
from **The Song of Hiawatha,** by Henry Wadsworth Longfellow 604

Unit 7 Drama Facing Challenges 607

Introduction to Drama **608**

GUIDED READING

Drama Close Reading Model **610**

Neil Simon **A Defenseless Creature** DRAMA 611

GRAMMAR & STYLE Verbals: Participles, Gerunds, and Infinitives 622

DIRECTED READING

Israel Horovitz **A Christmas Carol: Scrooge and Marley, Act 1** ANCHOR TEXT/DRAMA 623

History Connection *Industry and Reform* 634

INFORMATIONAL TEXT CONNECTION **Text-to-Text**

Daniel Pool *from* **What Jane Austen Ate and Charles Dickens Knew** ESSAY 642

Israel Horovitz **A Christmas Carol: Scrooge and Marley, Act 2** DRAMA 645

PRIMARY SOURCE CONNECTION **Text-to-Text**

John Leech *from* **A Christmas Carol** ILLUSTRATIONS 665

VOCABULARY & SPELLING Using Dictionaries and Thesauruses 668

Paul Zindel **Let Me Hear You Whisper** DRAMA 669

INFORMATIONAL TEXT CONNECTION **Text-to-Text**

Natalie Rosinsky *from* **Going Ape Over Language** ARTICLE 683

COMPARING TEXTS

William Shakespeare	**St. Crispian's Day Speech**	DRAMATIC MONOLOGUE	687
Alfred, Lord Tennyson	**The Charge of the Light Brigade**	NARRATIVE POEM	690
	Cultural Connection *Crimean War*		691
	GRAMMAR & STYLE Punctuation: Dashes, Semicolons, and Colons		693

INDEPENDENT READING

Rod Serling	**The Monsters Are Due on Maple Street**	SCREENPLAY	694

FOR YOUR READING LIST 709

WRITING WORKSHOP
Argumentative Writing: Argumentative Essay 710

SPEAKING & LISTENING WORKSHOP
Giving and Actively Listening to Argumentative Presentations 716

TEST PRACTICE WORKSHOP
Writing Skills: Argumentative Essay 718
from **Braille: The Early Life of Louis Braille,** by Lola H. and Coleman A. Jennings 718
Revising and Editing Skills 719
Reading Skills 720
from **The Ugly Duckling,** by A. A. Milne 720

Unit 8 Seeking Wisdom 723
Folk Literature

Introduction to Folk Literature 724

GUIDED READING

Folk Literature Close Reading Model 726

Author	Title	Genre	Page
Anonymous Retold by Ingri and Edgar Parin d'Aulaire	**Persephone and Demeter**	GREEK MYTH	727
Anonymous Retold by Judith Gleason	**Eshu**	YORUBAN FOLK TALE	733

DIRECTED READING

Author	Title	Genre	Page
Anonymous Retold by Geraldine Harris	**The Secret Name of Ra**	EGYPTIAN MYTH	738
	History Connection *Ancient Egypt*		741
Translated by John A. Wilson	LITERATURE CONNECTION Text-to-Text *from* **Akhenaton's Hymn to the Sun**	HYMN	743
	VOCABULARY & SPELLING Homographs, Homophones, and Homonyms		746
Norah Roper with Alice Lee Marriott	**Tsali of the Cherokees**	ANCHOR TEXT/ORAL HISTORY	747
	Social Studies Connection *Indian Removal*		751
Christine Graf	INFORMATIONAL TEXT CONNECTION Text-to-Text **Moving West: A Native American Perspective**	MAGAZINE ARTICLE	755
Anonymous Retold by Laurence Yep	**We Are All One**	CHINESE FOLK TALE	757
	GRAMMAR & STYLE Misplaced Modifiers		764
Aesop's Fables Retold by James Reeves and Joseph Jacobs	**Ant and Grasshopper** **The Fox and the Crow** **The Lion and the Statue**	GREEK FABLES	765
Anonymous Retold by Olivia E. Coolidge	**Phaëthon, Son of Apollo**	GREEK MYTH	770
	Science Connection *Solar Models*		773

GRAMMAR & STYLE Dangling Modifiers 776

COMPARING TEXTS

Author	Title	Genre	Page
Anonymous Retold by Joseph Campbell with Bill Moyers	**The Instruction of Indra**	HINDU MYTH	777
R. K. Narayan	**Such Perfection**	SHORT STORY	782
Anonymous Retold by Carolyn Swift	**Amaterasu**	JAPANESE MYTH	786
	Cultural Connection *Shintoism*		789
Anonymous Retold by Judith Ortiz Cofer	**Aunty Misery**	PUERTO RICAN FOLK TALE	792

INDEPENDENT READING

Author	Title	Genre	Page
Anonymous Retold by Rudolfo A. Anaya	**The Force of Luck**	SOUTHWESTERN FOLK TALE	796
Anonymous Retold by Zora Neale Hurston	**How the Snake Got Poison**	AFRICAN-AMERICAN FOLK TALE	803
James Thurber	**The Rabbits Who Caused All the Trouble**	FABLE	805
Michael Thompson and Jacob Warrenfeltz	**Rabbit and the Tug of War**	GRAPHIC TALE	807
Gail Carson Levine	*from* **Ella Enchanted**	NOVEL	815

FOR YOUR READING LIST 819

WRITING WORKSHOP
Informative Writing: Research Report 820

SPEAKING & LISTENING WORKSHOP
Giving and Actively Listening to Research Presentations 828

TEST PRACTICE WORKSHOP
Writing Skills: Research Report 830
Revising and Editing Skills 831
Reading Skills 832
from **Why the Owl Has Big Eyes** 832

LANGUAGE ARTS RESOURCES

Language Arts Handbook 834

Reading Strategies & Skills

1.1 The Reading Process 834
1.2 Using Reading Strategies 836
1.3 Using Reading Skills 839

Vocabulary & Spelling

2.1 Using Context Clues 850
2.2 Breaking Words Into Base Words, Word Roots, Prefixes, and Suffixes 851
2.3 Using a Dictionary 855
2.4 Exploring Word Origins and Word Families 855
2.5 Understanding Multiple Meanings 856
2.6 Understanding Denotation and Connotation 856
2.7 Spelling 857

Grammar & Style

3.1 The Sentence 866
3.2 The Parts of Speech 869
3.3 Nouns 869
3.4 Pronouns 870
3.5 Verbs 873
3.6 Complements 875
3.7 Agreement 876
3.8 Modifiers 878
3.9 Prepositions and Conjunctions 879
3.10 Interjections 880
3.11 Phrases 880
3.12 Clauses 882
3.13 Common Usage Problems 882
3.14 Commonly Misused Words 885
3.15 Punctuation 890
3.16 Capitalization 896
3.17 Writing Effective Sentences 898

Writing

4.1 The Writing Process 902
4.2 Modes and Purposes of Writing 911

Research & Documentation

5.1 Research Skills 912
5.2 Internet Research 915

5.3 Media Literacy 916
5.4 Evaluating Sources 917
5.5 Documenting Sources 918

Applied English

6.1 Workplace and Consumer Documents 923
6.2 Writing a Step-by-Step Procedure 923
6.3 Writing a Business Letter 923
6.4 Writing a Proposal 924
6.5 Writing a Public Service Announcement 925

Speaking & Listening

7.1 Verbal and Nonverbal Communication 926
7.2 Listening Skills 927
7.3 Collaborative Learning and Communication 928
7.4 Asking and Answering Questions 929
7.5 Conducting an Interview 929
7.6 Public Speaking 930
7.7 Oral Interpretation 931
7.8 Telling a Story 932
7.9 Participating in a Debate 933
7.10 Preparing a Multimedia Presentation 934

Test-Taking Skills

8.1 Preparing for Tests 935
8.2 Strategies for Taking Standardized Tests 935
8.3 Answering Objective Questions 936
8.4 Answering Multiple-Choice Questions 936
8.5 Answering Reading Comprehension Questions 937
8.6 Answering Synonym and Antonym Questions 937
8.7 Answering Sentence Completion Questions 937
8.8 Answering Constructed-Response Questions 937
8.9 Answering Essay Questions 938

Literary Terms Handbook 940
Glossary of Vocabulary Words 940
Literary Acknowledgments 953
Art and Photo Credits 959
Index of Skills 965
Index of Titles and Authors 972

LANGUAGE ARTS WORKSHOPS

Grammar & Style

Subject -Verb Agreement 48
Pronoun-Antecedent Agreement 56
Nominative and Objective Pronouns 72
Comma Use 162
Independent and Dependent Clauses 190
Consistent Verb Tense 219
Phrases 264
Sentence Types 296
Fragments and Run-on Sentences 321
Adjective and Adverb Clauses 389
Simple and Compound Subjects 407
Personal and Possessive Pronouns 480
Nouns: Proper, Plural, Possessive, and Collective 490
Reflexive and Intensive Pronouns 501
Simple, Compound, Complex, and Compound-Complex Sentences 543
Simple, Complete, and Compound Predicates 571
Verbals: Participles, Gerunds, and Infinitives 622
Punctuation: Dashes, Semicolons, and Colons 693
Misplaced Modifiers 764
Dangling Modifiers 776

Vocabulary & Spelling

Denotation and Connotation 16
Prefixes, Roots, and Suffixes 176
Greek, Latin, and Anglo-Saxon Roots 280
Context Clues 423
Synonyms and Antonyms 484
Figurative Language 561
Spelling by Syllables 567
Using Dictionaries and Thesauruses 668
Homographs, Homophones, and Homonyms 746

Speaking & Listening

Giving and Actively Listening to Oral Summaries 132
Giving and Actively Listening to Literary Presentations 246
Giving and Actively Listening to Informative Presentations 368
Giving and Actively Listening to Informative Presentations 530
Giving and Actively Listening to Narrative Presentations 600
Giving and Actively Listening to Argumentative Presentations 716
Giving and Actively Listening to Research Presentations 828

Writing

Informative Writing (Responding to a Short Story)	126
Narrative Writing (Writing a Short Story)	238
Informative Writing (Cause-and-Effect Essay)	362
Informative Writing (Compare-and-Contrast Essay)	524
Narrative Writing (Personal Narrative)	594
Argumentative Writing (Argumentative Essay)	710
Informative Writing (Research Report)	806

Viewing

Critical Viewing	454

Test Practice

Writing Skills	
Literary Response	134
Literary Response	248
Informative Essay	370
Descriptive Essay	456
Informative Essay	532
Personal Essay	602
Argumentative Essay	718
Research Report	819
Revising and Editing Skills	135, 249, 371, 457, 533, 603, 719, 831
Reading Skills	136, 250, 372, 458, 534, 604, 720, 832

INDEPENDENT READINGS

Fiction

Uncle Tony's Goat, Leslie Marmon Silko 105
The Serial Garden, Joan Aiken 111
Papa's Parrot, Cynthia Rylant 220
The Smallest Dragonboy, Anne McCaffrey 224

Nonfiction

from **Barrio Boy,** Ernesto Galarza 352
The Night the Bed Fell, James Thurber 356
Death in the Open, Lewis Thomas 440
Astonishing Animals, Tim Flannery and Peter Schouten 443

Poetry

Two People I Want to Be Like, Eve Merriam 518
Miracles, Walt Whitman 520
Early Song, Gogisgi 522
I'm Nobody, Emily Dickinson 584
Refugee Ship, Lorna Dee Cervantes 586
Loo Wit, Wendy Rose 588
The Pasture, Robert Frost 591

Drama

The Monsters Are Due on Maple Street, Rod Serling 694

Oral Tradition

The Force of Luck, Rudolfo A. Anaya 796
How the Snake Got Poison, Zola Neale Hurston 803
The Rabbits Who Caused All the Trouble, James Thurber 805
Rabbit and the Tug of War, Michael Thompson and Jacob Warrenfeltz 807
from **Ella Enchanted,** Gail Carson Levine 815

TO THE STUDENT

"The whole purpose of education is to turn mirrors into windows."

— Sydney J. Harris

Think about when you were young and about to start school for the first time. When you stood in front of the mirror, your view was focused on your own reflection and limited by your own experience. Then the windows of learning began to open your mind to new ideas and new experiences, broadening both your awareness and your curiosity.

As you discovered reading, you learned to connect with what you read and to examine your own ideas and experiences. And the more you read, the more you learned to connect with the ideas and experiences of other people from other times and other places. Great literature provides *mirrors* that help you reflect on your own world and *windows* that lead you into new worlds. This metaphor for the reading experience expresses the power of words to engage and transform you.

EMC's literature program, *Mirrors and Windows: Connecting with Literature*, provides opportunities for you to explore new worlds full of people, cultures, and perspectives different from your own. This book contains stories, essays, plays, and poems by outstanding authors from around the globe. Reading these selections will expand your appreciation of literature and your world view. Studying them will help you examine universal themes such as honesty, integrity, and justice and common emotions such as fear, pride, and belonging. You may already have thought about some of these ideas and feelings yourself.

As you read the selections in this book, try to see yourself in the characters, stories, and themes. Also try to see yourself as a citizen of the world—a world from which you have much to learn and to which you have much to offer.

Unit 1

Meeting the Unexpected

Fiction

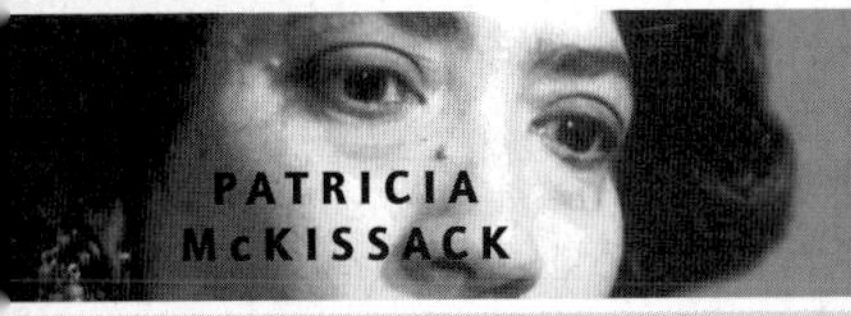

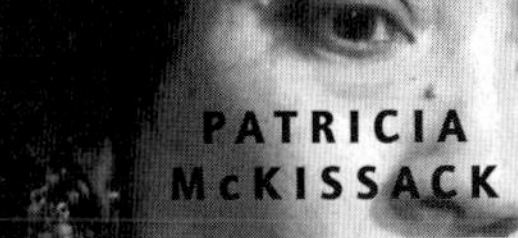

"You been here now for three months, Johnny, so I better prepare you. About this time of year," he said, studying the murk and fog, "something comes to visit the lighthouse."

—RAY BRADBURY, "The Foghorn"

When have you encountered something you didn't expect? What did you learn from the experience? In his short story "The Foghorn," writer Ray Bradbury describes how two lighthouse keepers encounter a strange sea creature that is lured by the sound of their foghorn. As you read the short stories in the unit, imagine how you might feel if confronted with the unusual, unexplainable, or surprising events that they describe.

Introduction to Fiction

"Fear quickened his step. Reaching his small apartment, he hurried up the steps. His heart pounded in his ear, and his left arm tingled. He had an idea, and there wasn't a moment to waste."

—PATRICIA McKISSACK, "The 11:59"

How does this passage make you feel? Does it make you eager to know what will happen next? By creating feelings of expectation, fictional stories can hook readers, making them want to learn more about the characters and what happens to them. A story also provides readers with a window into the fictional lives, thoughts, and experiences of its characters. The very broad category of literature known as **fiction** includes any work of prose (writing other than poetry and drama) that tells an invented or imaginary story.

Types of Fiction

Short Stories and Novels

The two main forms of fiction are the short story and the novel. The **short story** is a brief prose narrative, or story, that usually presents only a single plot, one or two main characters, and one important setting. A **novel** is a long work of prose fiction. Novels often have several plots, many major and minor characters, and numerous settings.

Popular Fiction and Literary Fiction

Another way of dividing fiction is into popular fiction and literary fiction. **Popular fiction** includes subgenres such as mystery, suspense and thriller, horror, science fiction, fantasy, romance, and Western. The works of writers in this book such as Ray Bradbury (famous for his science fiction and fantasy fiction) and Roald Dahl (famous for his fantasy stories) are examples of popular fiction.

Literary fiction does not fit into one of these categories. Writers in this book such as Ernest Hemingway, O. Henry, Sandra Cisneros, and Toni Cade Bambara are considered writers of literary fiction. The dividing line between popular and literary fiction is not clear-cut. For example, some writers of literary fiction, such as Rudyard Kipling, are also well known for their works of popular or imaginative fiction.

Types of Popular Fiction

Here are some of the most widely read types of popular fiction and their common formulas or elements.

- **Mystery:** The main character usually takes on a detective role and tries to uncover clues to a crime or some baffling event.
- **Horror:** Ghosts, monsters, or other dangerous characters may lurk within these stories, whose purpose is to provide a good fright.
- **Science Fiction:** Often the setting is outer space, but it doesn't need to be, as long as advanced technology is a strong element in the story.
- **Fantasy:** Often confused with science fiction, fantasy relies on magic and magical beings instead of technology. Fantasy is often set in another age or world.
- **Westerns:** The setting is important here–the West. The main character is usually a cowboy, often fighting for survival against the wilderness or evildoers.

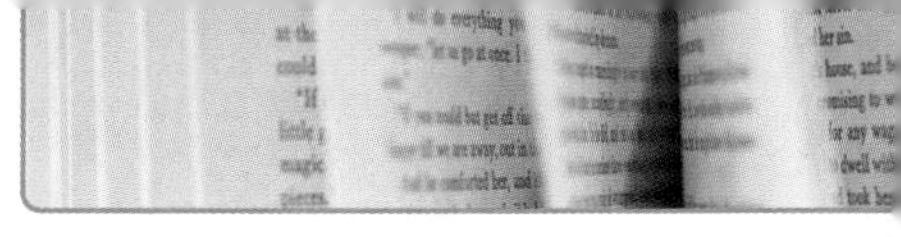

Elements of Fiction

A piece of fiction is made up of various elements that make it work. Some of these elements include plot, characters, setting, point of view, and theme.

Plot

The plot of a work of fiction is the series of events related to a central conflict, or struggle. The plot typically introduces a conflict, develops it, and eventually resolves it.

Characters

The **characters** are the individuals who take part in the action of a story. The **protagonist** is the most important character in the story. This character is sometimes opposed by an **antagonist,** who is in conflict with the protagonist. In Tomás Rivera's "The Portrait" (page 49), Don Mateo is the protagonist and the portrait salesman is his antagonist.

Major characters play significant roles in the action, and **minor characters** play lesser roles. In Patricia McKissack's "The 11:59" (page 18), Lester Simmons is a major character because the story concentrates on him almost completely. His friends at the shoeshine stand are minor characters because they are only briefly introduced.

Setting

The **setting** of a story is the time, place, and environment in which the events take place. The setting can include the following elements:

- geographic location
- specific sites (such as a building or room)
- time period
- cultural, social, or economic conditions

Setting is important in helping to establish mood, or the emotion created in the reader by part, or all, of the story. The setting of Lensey Namioka's "The Inn of Lost Time" (page 30) includes both the geographic location of Japan and the eighteenth century—the time period in which the story takes place.

Point of View

Point of view is the vantage point from which the story is told—in other words, who is telling the story.

- In *first-person* point of view, the story is told by someone who participates in or witnesses the action; this person, called the *narrator*, uses words such as *I* and *we*.
- In *third-person* point of view, the narrator usually stands outside the action and observes. The narrator uses words such as *he, she, it,* and *they*.
- In a *third-person omniscient* point of view, the thoughts of all the characters are revealed. Piri Thomas's "Amigo Brothers" (page 163) is told from a third-person omniscient point of view.
- In a *third-person limited* point of view, the thoughts of only the narrator or a single character are revealed. Gary Soto's "Seventh Grade" (page 212) is told from a third-person limited point of view.

Theme

The **theme** is the central idea about life that is revealed through a literary work. A *stated theme* is presented directly, but an *implied theme* must be inferred by the reader. Many works of fiction do not have a stated theme but rather have one or more implied themes. A story may also have a stated theme and an implied theme. A stated theme of "The Scholarship Jacket" (page 154) is that earning something is different from buying something. An implied theme is that it is important to stand up for what you believe.

Literary Element

Understanding Plot

What Is Plot?

When you describe the events that take place in a story, you are describing the plot. The **plot** is a series of related events that drive a short story or novel. The most exciting element of fiction for many readers is the plot, which can keep them guessing what will happen next. What do you think will happen next to Ichabod Crane in the passage on this page from "The Legend of Sleepy Hollow"?

The Elements of Plot

The typical plot contains the following elements: **exposition, rising action, climax, falling action,** and **resolution.** The diagram below shows how these elements shape the development of the plot of Ernest Hemingway's "A Day's Wait" (page 57).

Plot Diagram

Exposition
One morning, the narrator's son Schatz wakes with a headache and looks ill.

Rising Action
The narrator calls a doctor, who takes Schatz's temperature and prescribes flu medicine.

Climax
The narrator comes home to find Schatz causing a commotion. He refuses to let anyone into his room and asks his father how long he has to live.

Falling Action
It is revealed that Schatz doesn't understand the difference between Celsius and Fahrenheit. He thought his fever was much higher than it actually was.

Resolution
Schatz is relieved to learn that he is not going to die and is able to relax after a day of stress.

All of the stories of ghosts and goblins that he had heard in the afternoon, now came crowding upon his recollection. The night grew darker and darker....

—WASHINGTON IRVING, "The Legend of Sleepy Hollow"

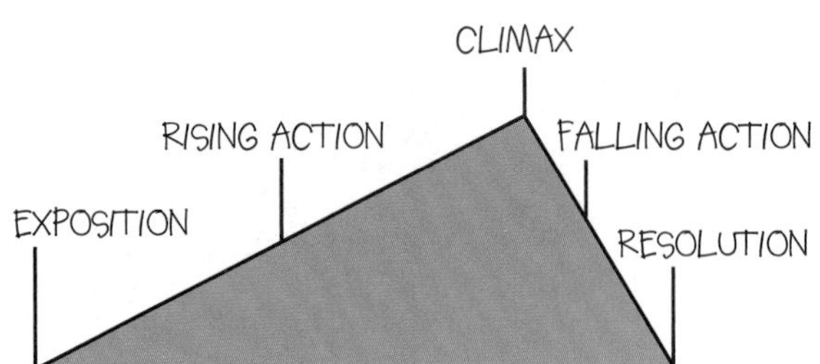

Plot and Conflict

A plot revolves around some type of **conflict,** or struggle. Usually, throughout the course of a story, a central conflict is introduced, developed, and resolved. In units 1 and 2, you will read stories in which characters encounter different kinds of conflict.

External and Internal Conflicts

There are two basic types of conflict, external and internal. An *external conflict* is a struggle that takes place between a character and some outside force. These outside forces are of three principal types:

- another character, or **antagonist** (see Understanding Characters, page 17)
- nature
- society

Conflict with Another Character In Tomás Rivera's "The Portrait" (page 49), the main character, Don Mateo, speaks of confronting the portrait salesman who has taken advantage of him.

> I just grabbed him right then and there. Poor guy couldn't even talk. He was all scared. And I told him that I wanted that portrait of my son....

Conflict with Nature In Ray Bradbury's "The Foghorn" (page 73), the struggle is between the main characters and a force of nature, a strange sea creature attracted by the sound of the foghorn.

Conflict with Society One of the main characters in Borden Deal's "Antaeus" (page 199) is a boy who has his plans to make a roof garden shattered by the building's owner.

> We had grown up aware of adult authority, of policemen and night watchmen and teachers, and this man sounded like all the others. But it was a new thing to T. J.

The other principal type of conflict is *internal conflict,* a struggle that goes on within the main character. In Gish Jen's "The White Umbrella" (page 181), the main character struggles with her own anxiety about fitting in and feeling accepted.

> I stared at the umbrella. I wanted to open it, twirl it around by its slender silver handle; I wanted to dangle it from my wrist on the way to school the way the other girls did.

Plot and Organization

A story has to have a beginning and an end. A story's plot, therefore, is often organized by time. Some stories may present a single day in a character's life, or even an hour, whereas others may span many years. O. Henry's "After Twenty Years" (page 9) takes place in one evening. The events recalled in Cherylene Lee's "Hollywood and the Pits" (page 141) occupy a decade.

Many stories are told in **chronological order,** that is, the events are presented in the order in which they occur in time. Sometimes writers play with time. They use **flashbacks** to tell about something that happened in the past. In Lensey Namioka's "The Inn of Lost Time" (page 30), the narrator begins in the present and then goes back into the past.

> It happened about seven years ago, when I was a green, inexperienced youngster not quite eighteen years old.

Writers use flashbacks to help develop relationships between characters, advance the plot, or add an element of mystery or expectation to a developing narrative.

Another way in which writers play with time is through the use of **foreshadowing,** giving hints or clues about what is going to happen in the future. In Joseph Bruchac's "Jed's Grandfather" (page 191), the main character's dreams suggest coming difficulties.

> He was in the boat, dark water widening between them. The old man stood there on The Island, unaware of the great dark wave coming at him from behind. His eyes were on Jed, but Jed couldn't call out. He couldn't move his arms.

Fiction Close Reading Model

BEFORE READING

Build Background
You need to apply two types of background to read fiction effectively. One type is the story's literary and historical context. Read the **Build Background** and **Meet the Author** features to get this information. The other type of background is the personal knowledge and experience you bring to your reading.

Set Purpose
A fiction writer presents characters and actions to say something about life. Read **Set Purpose** to decide what you want to get out of the story.

Analyze Literature
A fiction writer uses literary techniques, such as plot and setting, to create meaning. The **Analyze Literature** feature draws your attention to a key literary element in the story.

Use Reading Skills
The **Use Reading Skills** feature will show you skills to help you get the most out of your reading. Learn how to apply skills such as determining author's purpose and using context clues. Identify a graphic organizer that will help you apply the skill before and while you read.

DURING READING

Use Reading Strategies
- **Ask questions** about things that seem significant or interesting.
- **Make predictions** about what's going to happen next. As you read, gather more clues to confirm or change your prediction.
- **Visualize** the story. Form pictures in your mind to help you see the characters, actions, and settings.
- **Make inferences,** or educated guesses, about what is not stated directly.
- **Clarify,** or check that you understand, what you read. Reread any difficult parts.

Analyze Literature
What literary elements stand out? Are the characters vivid and interesting? Is there a strong central conflict? As you read, consider how these elements affect your enjoyment and understanding of the story.

Make Connections
Notice where connections can be made between the story and your life or the world outside the story. What feelings or thoughts do you have while reading the story?

AFTER READING

Find Meaning
Recall the important details of the story, such as the sequence of events and characters' names. Use this information to **interpret,** or explain, the meaning of the story.

Make Judgments
- **Analyze** the text by examining details and deciding what they contribute to the meaning.
- **Evaluate** the text by making judgments about how the author creates meaning.

Analyze Literature
Review how the use of literary elements increases your understanding of the story. For example, if the author uses dialogue, how does it help to shape the story's meaning?

Extend Understanding
Go beyond the text by exploring the story's ideas through writing or other creative projects.

After Twenty Years

A Short Story by O. Henry

Build Background

Literary Context O. Henry is best known for his use of the ironic, or surprise, ending. His work has been translated into many languages and has been adapted for movies and television. Since 1919 when it was first given, the O. Henry Award has been one of the most coveted prizes for short story writing.

Reader's Context Can you predict what your friends will be like twenty years from now?

Set Purpose

Skim and scan the story for unfamiliar terms. Also, pay attention to words that are defined in footnotes. Based on these words, try to predict what the story will be about.

Analyze Literature

Plot A **plot** is a series of events related to a central **conflict,** or struggle. A plot usually involves the introduction of the conflict, the events that lead to the **climax**—the point of highest tension in the story—and the **resolution,** the point at which the central conflict is resolved. As you read "After Twenty Years," identify the conflict and make predictions about how the conflict will be resolved.

Use Reading Skills

Analyze Cause and Effect A *cause* is an action or event that results in another event. An *effect* is what happens as the result of an event or action. Analyzing cause-and-effect relationships can help you understand how the events in a story are related. As you read "After Twenty Years," use a chart to keep track of causes and effects.

Cause	Effect
The weather is chilly, rainy, and windy.	The streets are nearly empty.

Meet the Author

O. Henry (1862–1910) is the pseudonym of William Sydney Porter, an American short story writer. After working for several years as a bank teller, Porter was convicted of embezzlement. Although it was likely an accounting error, Porter served three years. In prison he began writing short stories using the pen name O. Henry. Upon his release, he moved to New York City.

Preview Vocabulary

ha•bit•u•al (hʉ´ bi ch [ə] wel) *adj.*, behaving in a certain manner by habit

in•tri•cate (in´ tri kət) *adj.*, elaborate

swag•ger (swa´ gər) *n.*, walk with an insolent air; strut

staunch•est (stônch´ est) *adj.*, most loyal or committed

e•go•tism (ē´ gə' ti zəm) *n.*, large sense of self-importance; conceit

A Short Story by O. Henry

After Twenty Years

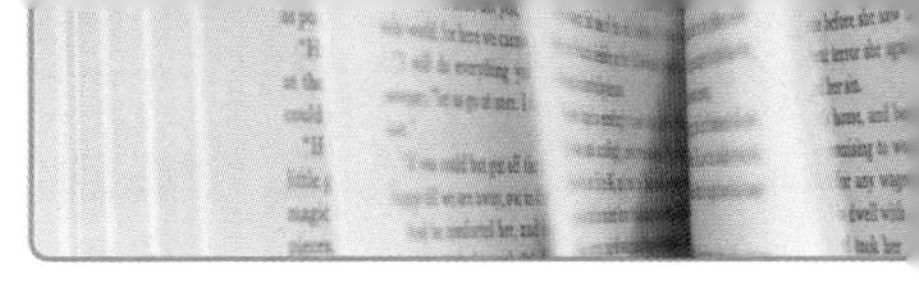

"I'm just waiting for a friend. It's an appointment made twenty years ago."

The policeman on the beat[1] moved up the avenue impressively. The impressiveness was habitual and not for show, for spectators were few. The time was barely ten o'clock at night, but chilly gusts of wind with a taste of rain in them had well nigh depeopled the streets.

ha•bit•u•al (hə´ bi ch [ə] wel) *adj.*, behaving in a certain manner by habit

Trying doors as he went, twirling his club with many intricate and artful movements, turning now and then to cast his watchful eye down the pacific thoroughfare, the officer, with his stalwart form and slight swagger, made a fine picture of a guardian of the peace. The vicinity was one that kept early hours. Now and then you might see the lights of a cigar store or of an all-night lunch counter, but the majority of the doors belonged to business places that had long since been closed.

in•tri•cate (in´ tri kət) *adj.*, elaborate

swag•ger (swa´ gər) *n.*, walk with an insolent air; strut

DURING READING

Analyze Literature
Plot What do the setting details suggest about possible conflicts in the story?

When about midway of a certain block, the policeman suddenly slowed his walk. In the doorway of a darkened hardware store a man leaned with an unlighted cigar in his mouth. As the policeman walked up to him, the man spoke up quickly.

"It's all right, officer," he said reassuringly. "I'm just waiting for a friend. It's an appointment made twenty years ago. Sounds a little funny to you, doesn't it? Well, I'll explain if you'd like to make certain it's all straight. About that long ago there used to be a restaurant where this store stands—'Big Joe' Brady's restaurant."

"Until five years ago," said the policeman. "It was torn down then."

The man in the doorway struck a match and lit his cigar. The light showed a pale, square-jawed face with keen eyes and a little white scar near his right eyebrow. His scarf pin was a large diamond, oddly set.

DURING READING

Use Reading Strategies
Make Inferences What do these details suggest to you about the man in the doorway?

"Twenty years ago tonight," said the man, "I dined here at 'Big Joe' Brady's with Jimmy Wells, my best chum and the finest chap in the world. He and I were raised here in New York, just like two

1. **beat.** Area regularly patrolled by a policeman

(Opposite page) ***Small Town at Night After Snowstorm,*** c. 1930. Charles Ephraim Burchfield.

brothers, together. I was eighteen and Jimmy was twenty. The next morning I was to start for the West to make my fortune. You couldn't have dragged Jimmy out of New York; he thought it was the only place on earth. Well, we agreed that night that we would meet here again exactly twenty years from that date and time, no matter what our conditions might be or from what distance we might have to come. We figured that in twenty years each of us ought to have our destiny worked out and our fortunes made, whatever they were going to be."

DURING READING

Use Reading Skills
Analyze Cause and Effect Why is the man waiting in the doorway?

"It sounds pretty interesting," said the policeman. "Rather a long time between meets, though, it seems to me. Haven't you heard from your friend since you left?"

"Well, yes, for a time we corresponded,"[2] said the other. "But after a year or two we lost track of each other. You see, the West is a pretty big proposition, and I kept hustling around over it pretty lively. But I know Jimmy will meet me here if he's alive, for he always was the truest, staunchest old chap in the world. He'll never forget. I came a thousand miles to stand in this door tonight, and it's worth it if my old partner turns up."

DURING READING

Use Reading Skills
Analyze Cause and Effect Why did the two friends lose contact?

staunch•est (stônch´ est) *adj.*, most loyal or committed

"A man gets in a groove in New York. It takes the West to put a razor edge on him."

The waiting man pulled out a handsome watch, the lids of it set with small diamonds.

"Three minutes to ten," he announced. "It was exactly ten o'clock when we parted here at the restaurant door."

"Did pretty well out West, didn't you?" asked the policeman.

"You bet! I hope Jimmy has done half as well. He was a kind of plodder,[3] though, good fellow as he was. I've had to compete with

DURING READING

Use Reading Strategies
Make Predictions Will the man's old partner show up? If so, will the man really think it was worth the effort?

---

2. **corresponded.** Communicated by letter
3. **plodder.** One who works slowly and monotonously; a drudge

some of the sharpest wits going to get my pile. A man gets in a groove in New York. It takes the West to put a razor edge on him."

The policeman twirled his club and took a step or two.

"I'll be on my way. Hope your friend comes around all right. Going to call time on him sharp?"[4]

"I should say not!" said the other. "I'll give him half an hour at least. If Jimmy is alive on earth, he'll be here by that time. So long, officer."

"You've changed lots, Jimmy."

"Good night sir," said the policeman, passing on along his beat, trying doors as he went.

There was now a fine, cold drizzle falling, and the wind had risen from its uncertain puffs into a steady blow. The few foot passengers astir in that quarter hurried dismally and silently along with coat collars turned high and pocketed hands. And in the door of the hardware store the man who had come a thousand miles to fill an appointment, uncertain almost to absurdity, with the friend of his youth, smoked his cigar and waited.

About twenty minutes he waited, and then a tall man in a long overcoat, with collar turned up to his ears, hurried across from the opposite side of the street. He went directly to the waiting man.

"Is that you, Bob?" he asked, doubtfully.

"Is that you, Jimmy Wells?" cried the man in the door.

"Bless my heart!" exclaimed the new arrival, grasping both the other's hands with his own. "It's Bob, sure as fate. I was certain I'd find you here if you were still in existence. Well, well, well!—twenty years is a long time. The old restaurant's gone, Bob; I wish it had lasted, so we could have had another dinner there. How has the West treated you, old man?"

"Bully; it has given me everything I asked it for. You've changed lots, Jimmy. I never thought you were so tall by two or three inches."

---

4. call time on him sharp. Leave if he doesn't arrive exactly on time

DURING READING

Use Reading Strategies
Make Predictions Now that the two men have met, what do you think will happen next?

e•go•tism (ē´ gə' ti zəm) *n.*, large sense of self-importance; conceit

"Oh, I grew a bit after I was twenty."

"Doing well in New York, Jimmy?"

"Moderately. I have a position in one of the city departments. Come on, Bob; we'll go around to a place I know of and have a good long talk about old times."

The two men started up the street, arm in arm. The man from the West, his egotism enlarged by success, was beginning to outline the history of his career. The other, submerged in his overcoat, listened with interest.

At the corner stood a drugstore, brilliant with electric lights. When they came into this glare, each of them turned simultaneously[5] to gaze upon the other's face.

The man from the West stopped suddenly and released his arm.

"You're not Jimmy Wells," he snapped. "Twenty years is a long time, but not long enough to change a man's nose from a Roman to a pug."[6]

"It sometimes changes a good man into a bad one," said the tall man. "You've been under arrest for ten minutes, 'Silky' Bob. Chicago thinks you may have dropped over our way and wires[7] us she wants to have a chat with you. Going quietly, are you? That's sensible. Now, before we go to the station, here's a note I was asked to hand to you. You may read it here at the window. It's from Patrolman Wells."

The man from the West unfolded the little piece of paper handed him. His hand was steady when he began to read, but it trembled a little by the time he had finished. The note was rather short.

Bob: I was at the appointed place on time. When you struck the match to light your cigar, I saw it was the face of the man wanted in Chicago. Somehow I couldn't do it myself, so I went around and got a plainclothes man to do the job.

Jimmy

✣

DURING READING

Analyze Literature
Plot In what way did the setting affect the resolution?

---

5. **simultaneously.** At the same time
6. **Roman to a pug.** Two distinctly shaped noses
7. **wires.** Communicates by telegram

What circumstances might cause you to do what Jimmy Wells did? What are the limits of loyalty?

Find Meaning

1. (a) How does the narrator describe the policeman? (b) What does this description suggest about this character?
2. Why does the man in the doorway feel it is necessary to explain his presence to the policeman?
3. (a) What are the most important details of the setting? (b) Why are these details important?

Make Judgments

4. What does the waiting man's description of Jimmy Wells as a "plodder" suggest about his attitude toward his friend?
5. Is it surprising that the waiting man traveled a thousand miles for the meeting? Explain.
6. What overall message, or theme, do you think O. Henry wanted to convey in "After Twenty Years"?

Analyze Literature

Plot Did you predict the climax and the resolution of the story? Use a plot diagram to identify the exposition, climax, and resolution of "After Twenty Years."

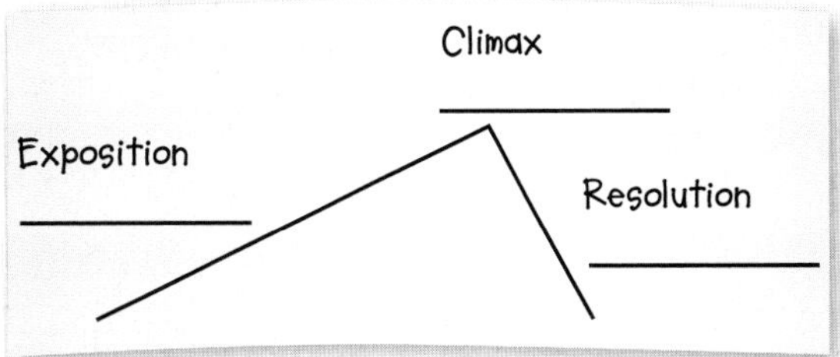

Extend Understanding

Writing Options

Creative Writing Imagine that you are Jimmy Wells writing to your former friend after Bob has been sent to jail. Write a **letter** explaining how you feel about what you had to do. Offer to support Bob in turning his life around.

Informative Writing The plainclothes policeman tells Bob that twenty years is long enough to change "a good man into a bad one." Using your cause-and-effect chart, write a short **essay** in which you analyze the causes and effects that brought Bob to justice in "After Twenty Years."

Collaborative Learning

Investigate Police Work With a partner, research how detective work has evolved over the past century. Pay particular attention to how communication, scientific advances, and computers have affected the way detectives work. Prepare a chart or a poster that lists the five most important changes you find.

Critical Literacy

Conduct an Interview Work with a partner to role-play a reporter interviewing the character "Silky" Bob. Find out why he entered a life of crime. Before you begin, work together to prepare a basic time line of Bob's life. Then create a list of questions for the reporter to ask. Take turns playing the reporter's role. Afterward, compare the notes taken by each reporter.

Go to **www.mirrorsandwindows.com** for more.

Vocabulary & Spelling

Denotation and Connotation

The light showed a pale, square-jawed face with keen eyes and a little white scar near his right eyebrow.

—O. HENRY, "After Twenty Years"

In the passage above, O. Henry describes a man standing in a doorway. In addition to their dictionary meanings, some of the words he uses also have emotional associations.

Every word has a **denotation,** or dictionary definition. In the passage above, *keen* denotes being "extremely sensitive in perception." *Keen* also has **connotations,** or emotional associations, suggesting sharpness and accuracy.

EXAMPLE

unhappy

blue

depressed

desolate

In this example, each word denotes sadness, but each connotes a different level of sadness. You might think of these words as **synonyms,** or words that have basically the same meaning. However, these are **near synonyms,** words that have slightly different meanings.

EXAMPLES

cheap / inexpensive

miserly / frugal

wasteful / generous

In these examples, each pair of words denotes the same meaning. However, one word has positive connotations, and the other negative connotations. *Inexpensive, frugal,* and *generous* are positive, while *cheap, miserly,* and *wasteful* are negative.

Vocabulary Practice

For each of the following words, choose a word with a more positive connotation.

1. nosy
2. bland
3. strange
4. picky
5. lazy

Identify the denotation of each of the following words from "After Twenty Years." Then note whether each word has a positive, neutral, or negative connotation.

6. habitual
7. intricate
8. swagger
9. egotism
10. beat

Spelling Practice

Words with Double Letters

Words with double letters can pose a spelling challenge because you may hear only one occurrence of the letter's sound. To prevent spelling mistakes for these words, you will need to memorize how the words look. For some words, the doubling is caused by a prefix or suffix being added, such as in the word "misspell." Try to figure out which words have doubling caused by affixes (prefixes and suffixes). This list of words from "After Twenty Years" gives examples of words with double letters.

announced	correspond	opposite
appointment	dismally	passengers
beginning	hurried	reassuringly
brilliant	impressive	success
collar	officer	suddenly

Literary Element

Understanding Characters

What Are Characters?

What does this photograph tell you about its subjects? It presents each person visually, but it also suggests something about their personalities. Consider these two people's poses, their facial expressions, and how they are sitting in relation to each other. In this portrait, the photographer has created characters. Writers also create characters. A **character** is an imaginary person or animal who takes part in the action of a literary work.

Characterization and Motivation

In the passage to the right, how is the character of Lester Simmons created? **Characterization** is the act of creating or describing a character. Writers create characters using three major techniques:

- Showing what characters say, do, or think
- Showing what other characters (and the narrator) say or think about them
- Describing what physical features, dress, and personality the characters display

In real life, people do not act for no reason at all. Something—a need, a desire, a feeling, or some other force—causes them to act. Characters respond in the same way. A **motivation** is a force that moves a character to think, feel, or behave in a certain way. Motivation can be either *internal* (from within a character) or *external* (from an outside source).

Types of Characters

The main character in a literary work is called the **protagonist.** A character who struggles against the main character is called an **antagonist.** Characters can also be classified as major characters or minor characters. **Major characters** are ones who play important roles in a work. **Minor characters** are ones who play less important roles.

Another way to classify characters is by how fully they are developed by the writer. A *flat character* is one-dimensional, exhibiting only a single quality or trait. A *round character* is three-dimensional and seems to have all the complexities of an actual human being.

Finally, characters can be distinguished by whether they develop in the course of a literary work or remain the same. A *static character* does not change in the course of a work. A *dynamic character* changes as a result of the story's events.

Lester Simmons was a thirty-year retired Pullman car porter—had his gold watch to prove it. "Keeps perfect train time," he often bragged. "Good to the second."

—PATRICIA McKISSACK, "The 11:59"

GUIDED READING

The 11:59

A Short Story by Patricia McKissack

Build Background

Historical Context The Pullman sleeping car was introduced in 1865 to provide train passengers with comfortable sleeping quarters for overnight trips. Pullman porters tended to the sleeping quarters, carried luggage, and assisted passengers. For nearly a century, these porters were almost exclusively African American.

Reader's Context What if you had only a few more hours to live? What would you do or think about in those last few hours?

Set Purpose

Preview the title of the story. Then read to determine what significance the title has for the story's main character.

Analyze Literature

Character Writers make careful choices about how they describe a story's **main character,** or **protagonist.** The changes that a character undergoes during a story can help to reveal the writer's message, or theme, to the reader. As you read "The 11:59," pay attention to how the writer presents the main character and think about what you learn from his behavior and feelings.

Use Reading Skills

Take Notes When you read a short story, it can be helpful to take notes. Writing down the names of the main characters and their traits, details of the story's setting and conflict, and the outcome of the events described can all help you better understand what you have read. As you read "The 11:59," take notes in a chart like the one below.

Characters	Setting	Conflict
Lester Simmons		

Meet the Author

Patricia McKissack (b. 1944) is an award-winning writer of fiction and nonfiction for young readers. She grew up in Nashville, Tennessee, in the 1940s and 1950s and attended Tennessee State University. After graduation, she married a longtime friend, Fredrick McKissack; started a family; and continued her education, earning a master's degree in 1975. In the 1980s, she and her husband began to write books for children and young adults.

Preview Vocabulary

mea • ger (mē´ gər) *adj.*, lacking in quantity or quality

chide (chīd) *v.*, express mild disapproval

mes • mer • ize (mez´ mə rīz') *v.*, fascinate, spellbind

wor • ri • some (wʉr´ ē səm) *adj.*, causing worry

spec • ter (spek´ tər) *n.*, spirit or ghost

The 11:59

A Short Story by Patricia McKissack

Ticktock, ticktock.

Lester Simmons was a thirty-year retired Pullman car porter—had his gold watch to prove it. "Keeps perfect train time," he often bragged. "Good to the second."

Daily he went down to the St. Louis Union Station and shined shoes to help supplement[1] his meager twenty-four-dollar-a-month Pullman retirement check. He ate his evening meal at the porter house on Compton Avenue and hung around until late at night talking union, playing bid whist,[2] and spinning yarns with those who were still "travelin' men." In this way Lester stayed in touch with the only family he'd known since 1920.

DURING READING
Use Reading Skills
Take Notes What trait do you notice about Lester right away?

mea•ger (mē´ gər) *adj.*, lacking in quantity or quality

DURING READING
Analyze Literature
Character What can you tell about Lester based on how he spends his time?

1. **supplement.** Add to
2. **bid whist.** Card game played with partners

There was nothing the young porters liked more than listening to Lester tell true stories about the old days, during the founding of the Brotherhood of Sleeping Car Porters, the first black union in the United States. He knew the president, A. Philip Randolph, personally, and proudly boasted that it was Randolph who'd signed him up as a union man back in 1926. He passed his original card around for inspection. "I knew all the founding brothers. Take Brother E. J. Bradley. We hunted many a day together, not for the sport of it but for something to eat. Those were hard times, starting up the union. But we hung in there so you youngsters might have the benefits you enjoy now."

The rookie porters always liked hearing about the thirteen-year struggle between the Brotherhood and the powerful Pullman Company, and how, against all odds, the fledgling[3] union had won recognition and better working conditions.

Everybody enjoyed it too when Lester told tall tales about Daddy Joe, the porters' larger-than-life hero. "Now y'all know the first thing a good Pullman man is expected to do is make up the top and lower berths[4] for the passengers each night."

chide (chīd) *v.*, express mild disapproval

"Come on, Lester," one of his listeners chided. "You don't need to describe our jobs for us."

DURING READING

Analyze Literature
Character What does the dialogue between Lester and the younger porters suggest about Lester's character?

DURING READING

Analyze Literature
Character Is Daddy Joe a flat, one-dimensional character or a round, fully developed character?

"Some of you, maybe not. But some of you, well—" he said, looking over the top of his glasses and raising an eyebrow at a few of the younger porters. "I was just setting the stage." He smiled good-naturedly and went on with his story. "They tell me Daddy Joe could walk flatfooted down the center of the coach and let down berths on both sides of the aisle."

Hearty laughter filled the room, because everyone knew that to accomplish such a feat, Daddy Joe would have to have been superhuman. But that was it: To the men who worked the sleeping cars, Daddy Joe was no less a hero than Paul Bunyan was to the lumberjacks of the Northwestern forests.

"And when the 11:59 pulled up to his door, as big and strong as Daddy Joe was..." Lester continued solemnly. "Well, in the end even he couldn't escape the 11:59." The old storyteller eyed one of the rookie porters he knew had never heard the frightening tale about the porters' Death Train. Lester took joy in mesmerizing his young listeners with all the details.

mes • mer • ize (mez´ mə rīz') *v.*, fascinate, spellbind

3. fledgling. Inexperienced
4. berths. Places for sleeping

"Any porter who hears the whistle of the 11:59 has got exactly twenty-four hours to clear up earthly matters. He better be ready when the train comes the next night..." In his creakiest voice, Lester drove home the point. "All us porters got to board that train one day. Ain't no way to escape the final ride on the 11:59."

Silence.

"Lester," a young porter asked, "you know anybody who ever heard the whistle of the 11:59 and lived to tell—"

"Not a living soul!"

Laughter.

"Well," began one of the men, "wonder will we have to make up berths on *that* train?"

"If it's an overnight trip to heaven, you can best be believing there's bound to be a few of us making up the berths," another answered.

"Shucks," a card player stopped to put in. "They say even up in heaven *we* the ones gon' be keeping all that gold and silver polished."

"Speaking of gold and silver," Lester said, remembering. "That reminds me of how I gave Tip Sampson his nickname. Y'all know Tip?"

There were plenty of nods and smiles.

The memory made Lester chuckle. He shifted in his seat to find a more comfortable spot. Then he began. "A woman got on board the *Silver Arrow* in Chicago going to Los Angeles. She was dripping in finery—had on all kinds of gold and diamond jewelry, carried twelve bags. Sampson knocked me down getting to wait on her, figuring she was sure for a big tip. That lady was worrisome! Ooowee! 'Come do this. Go do that. Bring me this.'

"Ain't no way to escape the final ride on the 11:59."

DURING READING

Analyze Character
Character What do you think Lester's co-workers thought of him during his career?

DURING READING

Use Reading Skills
Context Clues What is *finery*? Use context clues in the surrounding text to determine the meaning of the word. What clues help you determine the words meaning?

wor•ri•some (wʉr´ ē səm) *adj.*, causing worry

Sampson was running over himself trying to keep that lady happy. When we reached L.A., my passengers all tipped me two or three dollars, as was customary back then.

"When Sampson's Big Money lady got off, she reached into her purse and placed a dime in his outstretched hand. A *dime!* Can you imagine? *Ow!* You should have seen his face. And I didn't make it no better. Never did let him forget it. I teased him so—went to calling him Tip, and the nickname stuck."

> **DURING READING**
>
> **Analyze Literature**
> **Character** What character traits does Lester reveal about himself in telling how he gave Tip his nickname? Explain.

Laughter.

"I haven't heard from ol' Tip in a while. Anybody know anything?"

"You haven't got word, Lester? Tip boarded the 11:59 over in Kansas City about a month ago."

> **DURING READING**
>
> **Use Reading Strategies**
> **Make Predictions** What might this reference to Tip foreshadow?

"Sorry to hear that. That just leaves me and Willie Beavers, the last of the old, old-timers here in St. Louis."

Lester looked at his watch—it was a little before midnight. The talkfest had lasted later than usual. He said his good-byes and left, taking his usual route across the Eighteenth Street bridge behind the station.

In the darkness, Lester looked over the yard, picking out familiar shapes—the *Hummingbird*, the *Zephyr.* He'd worked on them both. Train travel wasn't anything like it used to be in the old days—not since people had begun to ride airplanes. "Progress," he scoffed. "Those contraptions will never take the place of a train. No sir!"

Suddenly he felt a sharp pain in his chest. At exactly the same moment he heard the mournful sound of a train whistle, which the wind seemed to carry from some faraway place. Ignoring his pain, Lester looked at the old station. He knew nothing was scheduled to come in or out till early morning. Nervously he lit a match to check the time. 11:59!

"No," he said into the darkness. "I'm not ready. I've got plenty of living yet."

Fear quickened his step. Reaching his small apartment, he hurried up the steps. His heart pounded in his ear, and his left arm tingled. He had an idea, and there wasn't a moment to waste. But his own words haunted him. *Ain't no way to escape the final ride on the 11:59.*

"But I'm gon' try!" Lester spent the rest of the night plotting his escape from fate.

"I won't eat or drink anything all day," he talked himself through his plan. "That way I can't choke, die of food poisoning, or cause a cooking fire."

Lester shut off the space heater to avoid an explosion, nailed shut all doors and windows to keep out intruders, and unplugged every electrical appliance. Good weather was predicted, but just in case a freak storm came and blew out a window, shooting deadly glass shards in his direction, he moved a straight-backed chair into a far corner, making sure nothing was overhead to fall on him.

"I'll survive," he said, smiling at the prospect of beating Death. "Won't that be a wonderful story to tell at the porter house?" He rubbed his left arm. It felt numb again.

Lester sat silently in his chair all day, too afraid to move. At noon someone knocked on his door. He couldn't answer it. Footsteps... another knock. He didn't answer.

A parade of minutes passed by, equally measured, one behind the other, ticking...ticking...away...The dull pain in his chest returned. He nervously checked his watch every few minutes.

Ticktock, ticktock.

Time had always been on his side. Now it was his enemy. Where had the years gone? Lester reviewed the thirty years he'd spent riding the rails. How different would his life have been if he'd married Louise Henderson and had a gallon of children? What if he'd taken that job at the mill down in Opelika? What if he'd followed his brother to Philly? How different?

Ticktock, ticktock.

So much living had passed so quickly. Lester decided if he had to do it all over again, he'd stand by his choices. His had been a good life. No regrets. No major changes for him.

Ticktock, ticktock.

The times he'd had—both good and bad—what memories. His first and only love had been traveling, and she was a jealous companion. Wonder whatever happened to that girl up in Minneapolis? Thinking about her made him smile. Then he laughed. That *girl* must be close to seventy years old by now.

Ticktock, ticktock.

Daylight was fading quickly. Lester drifted off to sleep, then woke from a nightmare in which, like Jonah, he'd been swallowed by an enormous beast.[5] Even awake he could still hear its heart beating... *ticktock, ticktock*...But then he realized he was hearing his own heartbeat.

Lester couldn't see his watch, but he guessed no more than half an hour had passed. Sleep had overtaken him with such little

DURING READING

Use Reading Skills
Take Notes What is this story's conflict? What do you think the outcome will be?

DURING READING

Analyze Literature
Character What is Lester's motivation for refusing to answer the door?

DURING READING

Make Connections
How does Lester's judgment about his life affect your feelings about what is happening to him?

---

5. Jonah...beast. Refers to the biblical story of Jonah and the whale resistance. Would Death, that shapeless shadow, slip in that easily? Where was he lurking? *Yea, though I walk through the valley of the shadow of death, I will fear no evil*...The Twenty-third Psalm was the only prayer Lester knew, and he repeated it over and over, hoping it would comfort him.

Lester rubbed his tingling arm. He could hear the blood rushing past his ear and up the side of his head. He longed to know what time it was, but that meant he had to light a match—too risky. What if there was a gas leak? The match would set off an explosion. "I'm too smart for that, Death," he said.

"I'm too smart for that, Death..."

Ticktock, ticktock.

It was late. He could feel it. Stiffness seized his legs and made them tremble. How much longer? he wondered. Was he close to winning?

Then in the fearful silence he heard a train whistle. His ears strained to identify the sound, making sure it *was* a whistle. No mistake. It came again, the same as the night before. Lester answered it with a groan.

Ticktock, ticktock.

He could hear Time ticking away in his head. Gas leak or not, he had to see his watch. Striking a match, Lester quickly checked the time. 11:57.

Although there was no gas explosion, a tiny explosion erupted in his heart.

Ticktock, ticktock.

Just a little more time. The whistle sounded again. Closer than before. Lester struggled to move, but he felt fastened to the chair. Now he could hear the engine puffing, pulling a heavy load. It was hard for him to breathe, too, and the pain in his chest weighed heavier and heavier.

Ticktock, ticktock.

Time had run out! Lester's mind reached for an explanation that made sense. But reason failed when a glowing phantom dressed in the porters' blue uniform stepped out of the grayness of Lester's confusion.

"It's *your* time, good brother." The specter spoke in a thousand familiar voices.

spec•ter (spek´ tər) *n.*, spirit or ghost

Freed of any restraint now, Lester stood, bathed in a peaceful calm that had its own glow. "Is that you, Tip?" he asked, squinting to focus on his old friend standing in the strange light.

"It's me, ol' partner. Come to remind you that none of us can escape the last ride on the 11:59."

"I know. I know," Lester said, chuckling. "But man, I had to try."

Tip smiled. "I can dig it. So did I."

"That'll just leave Willie, won't it?"

"Not for long."

"I'm ready."

Lester saw the great beam of the single headlight and heard the deafening whistle blast one last time before the engine tore through the front of the apartment, shattering glass and splintering wood, collapsing everything in its path, including Lester's heart.

When Lester didn't show up at the shoeshine stand two days running, friends went over to his place and found him on the floor. His eyes were fixed on something quite amazing—his gold watch, stopped at exactly 11:59. ✤

> **DURING READING**
>
> **Analyze Literature**
>
> **Character** Based on what you know about Lester, is his acceptance of his fate surprising? Explain.

Lester tells Tip he "had to try" to fight off Death. Have you ever clung to something you knew you would lose? How can clinging to hope help us come to terms with the inevitable?

Find Meaning

1. (a) How does Lester spend his evenings after he retires from his job as a Pullman porter? (b) Why does he spend his evenings in this way?

2. (a) What physical symptoms does Lester feel during his last day alive? (b) What do you think is happening to Lester?

3. (a) What time is on Lester's watch when his friends find him two days later? (b) Why does his watch read that time?

Make Judgments

4. (a) What does the reader learn about the lives of porters and their relationships with one another from this story? (b) What things did the porters share that reinforced their bonds with one another?

5. (a) How does Lester's mood change when he first hears the 11:59? (b) What does this mood change tell you about Lester's personality?

6. (a) How does Lester feel when he sees who the porter on the 11:59 is? (b) What does the manner in which they talk tell you about Lester's mood or attitude?

INFORMATIONAL TEXT ▶▶ CONNECTION

In "The 11:59," Patricia McKissack tells a fictional story about a Pullman porter, weaving in details about the porters' struggle to build a union. The following excerpt is from *A Long Hard Journey: The Story of the Pullman Porter,* by **Patricia** and **Fredrick McKissack.** Their book focuses on the Pullman porters' fight to build a union. The McKissacks have written many histories, biographies, and fictional works about African Americans.

from A Long Hard Journey: The Story of the Pullman Porter

An Essay by Patricia and Fredrick McKissack

Railroading has an unusual number of "firsts," making it difficult to target a single invention, event, or date as the *beginning* of American railroads. The earliest mention of an American-built, steam-propelled carriage was in 1804, developed by a Philadelphian, Oliver Evans. The Mohawk & Hudson Line boasted that in 1826, theirs was the first chartered American railroad. However, in 1825 Colonel John Stevens's steam-powered, rack-rail engine with wooden cogged wheels was the first machine to carry passengers on wooden cogged tracks in the United States. John B. Javis's first use of the steam locomotive in the Western Hemisphere made passenger travel faster and more comfortable and opened the way for the Baltimore & Ohio, the first American chartered passenger line.

As eastern railroads expanded westward toward the Mississippi River, the demand for better overnight accommodations increased. On September 1, 1859, a new chapter in railroad history began when George Mortimer Pullman's first sleeping car made its debut[1] run between Bloomington, Illinois, and Chicago.

The original Pullman car was described as a "primitive thing," but shortly after the Civil War, George Pullman developed a sleeping car that was unrivaled in design and service. Giving each traveler pampered treatment—making him feel special—was the Pullman hallmark. But George Pullman didn't give the personalized service for which his name became synonymous. Thousands of porters helped make the legendary Pullman service a reality.

Beginning in 1867, Pullman staffed his earliest cars with the former genteel servants of the Plantation South. His decisions to hire ex-slaves set a business precedent and for nearly a century *all* Pullman porters were black. These emancipated[2] slaves repaid Pullman with loyalty and dedicated service. Grateful for the opportunity to stand proudly beside other working people, the early porters worked willingly and joyfully, graciously receiving passengers, carrying their

1. **debut.** First
2. **emancipated.** Freed

luggage, making up the berths, serving beverages and food, keeping the guests happy—and all with a smile. These men did their jobs so well they became known as the "Ambassadors of Hospitality."

Seventy years later, the gratitude had worn thin. The new generation of free-born, more informed porters was not satisfied with the Pullman Company's long hours, low wages, and unfair company policies. Their smiles changed to pleas in the beginning, then shouts of protest. Unable to get the powerful Pullman Company to negotiate in good faith, the porters united under the leadership of A. Philip Randolph, and in 1925, against all odds, they formed the first black-controlled union: the Brotherhood of Sleeping Car Porters.

The Brotherhood was the largest representative of black workers in America. It was also the first union admitted to the American Federation of Labor (AFL)[3] as a full member, and the first black union to negotiate a contract with a major corporation.

The porters' struggle for recognition and fair treatment is a classic David-and-Goliath story. A handful of black workers squared off against one of American history's corporate mega-giants and won. ✣

3. **American Federation of Labor (AFL).** Federation of labor unions founded in 1886

TEXT ←TO→ TEXT CONNECTION

Both Patricia McKissack's story and the excerpt from Patricia and Fredrick McKissack's book give information about the Pullman porters. Compare and contrast the kinds of information each selection presents. What do the details about Lester's life and death reveal about the Pullman porters? Summarize the texts in ways that maintain meaning and logical order.

AFTER READING

Analyze Literature

Character Writers use a variety of techniques to create characters to whom readers can relate and who can convey lessons about life. Use a chart to analyze how the author creates the character of Lester in "The 11:59." Then analyze, in one or two sentences, how the reader is made to feel about Lester at the end of the story.

Lester's Character

Habits/Behaviors	Relationships with Others
hard worker	friendly

Extend Understanding

Writing Options

Creative Writing Imagine that Lester beat the 11:59. Write a brief **dialogue** in which Lester tells the other porters about how he outsmarted Death. Review Lester's story about Tip and the wealthy lady and try to duplicate Lester's storytelling style. With a partner, read aloud your dialogue for the class.

Narrative Writing When friends gather at a funeral, they often take turns telling stories and sharing memories of the departed. Write a **paragraph** about Lester's life and personality that you might share at Lester's funeral with his friends from the porter house. Include an example or an anecdote to illustrate a memorable character trait. Share your work with the class.

Collaborative Learning

Create a Chart With a partner, skim and scan "The 11:59" to find as many examples of foreshadowing as you can. List each example in the left column of a two-column chart. In the right column, explain what the example foreshadows. When you finish, compare your chart with your classmates' charts and identify similarities and differences.

Lifelong Learning

Create a Time Line Imagine that you have been asked to direct a video documentary. Use the library or the Internet to research the history of the Pullman porters. Take careful notes and be sure to write down dates of events. Then use your notes to create an illustrated time line of the most important events in the history of the Pullman porters. Present your time line to the class and explain how your video will treat each event.

Go to **www.mirrorsandwindows.com** for more.

Literary Element

Understanding Setting

What Is Setting?

Where was this photograph taken? What details in the photograph help you answer this question? These details relate to the setting of the picture. In the same way, writers use the details of setting to tell a reader when and where the events of a story are taking place. The **setting** of a literary work is the time and place in which it happens.

Setting in Fiction

Writers create setting in many different ways. Setting can be revealed through imagery in descriptive passages, but it can also be developed through action and dialogue. In fiction, setting is often revealed by descriptions of the following:

- seasons and weather
- landscapes, cities, and towns
- buildings and vehicles
- furniture and clothing

Setting and Community

Setting can also be revealed by how characters talk and behave. For example, in the following passage from "Uncle Tony's Goat" (page 105), how does the author use details of setting to tell the reader about the community that inhabits that setting?

> My sister helped out around the house mostly, and I was supposed to carry water from the hydrant and bring in kindling. I helped my father look after the horses and pigs, and Uncle Tony milked the goats and fed them.

Setting and Mood

Setting is an important element in the creation of **mood,** the feeling or emotion created by a literary work. How would you describe the mood generated by the details of setting in the passage from "The Inn of Lost Time"?

> *The sun was just beginning to set. We passed a bamboo grove, and in the low evening light the thin leaves turned into little golden knives. I saw a gilded clump of bamboo shoots. The sight made me think of the delicious dish they would make when boiled in soy sauce.*
>
> *We hurried forward. To our delight we soon came to a clearing with a thatched house standing in the middle. The fragrant smell of rice was now so strong that we were certain a meal was being prepared inside.*
>
> —LENSEY NAMIOKA, "The Inn of Lost Time"

The Inn of Lost Time

A Short Story by Lensey Namioka

GUIDED READING

Build Background

Historical Context In feudal Japan (1100s to 1800s), the country was broken up into many domains, each held by a lord, or land baron. The feudal lord's land was protected by samurai, members of the warrior class, who were the only people allowed to carry weapons. This story takes place during the 1700s, a period of famine and civil wars. Many landowners could no longer afford to keep their samurai, and these master-less samurai, or ronin, wandered the countryside looking for work.

Reader's Context Do you ever say things like "I can't wait until I'm older"? What if you could skip years of your life?

Set Purpose

Skim the text and predict what effect the setting of the story will have on the plot. Read to find out if your prediction is accurate.

Analyze Literature

Setting In addition to physical descriptions of time and place, **setting** also includes the broader cultural, social, and historical background in which a story's characters live and interact. As you read "The Inn of Lost Time," record the setting details that the writer presents and consider the effect that the setting has on the characters and the plot.

Use Reading Skills

Sequence of Events As you read "The Inn of Lost Time," use a time line to track the sequence of events. Begin by recording the first events mentioned in the story. Complete the time line by adding the events that occur before and after these events. Look for signal words such as *before*, *after*, *then*, *while*, and *later*.

Preview Vocabulary

rapt (rapt) *adj.*, mentally engrossed or absorbed

des•o•late (de´ sə lət) *adj.*, lonely, sad

poi•gnant (poi´ nyənt) *adj.*, deeply affecting or touching; somber

rav•en•ous (ra´ və nəs) *adj.*, very eager for food

com•pen•sate (käm´ pən sāt') *v.*, balance, offset, repay

Meet the Author

Lensey Namioka was born in 1929 in Beijing, China. Her family moved to the United States when she was nine. Namioka taught mathematics before her interest in the history of her husband's family led her to write about feudal Japan. Zenta and Matsuzo, the ronin in "The Inn of Lost Time," appear in several of her historical mystery novels.

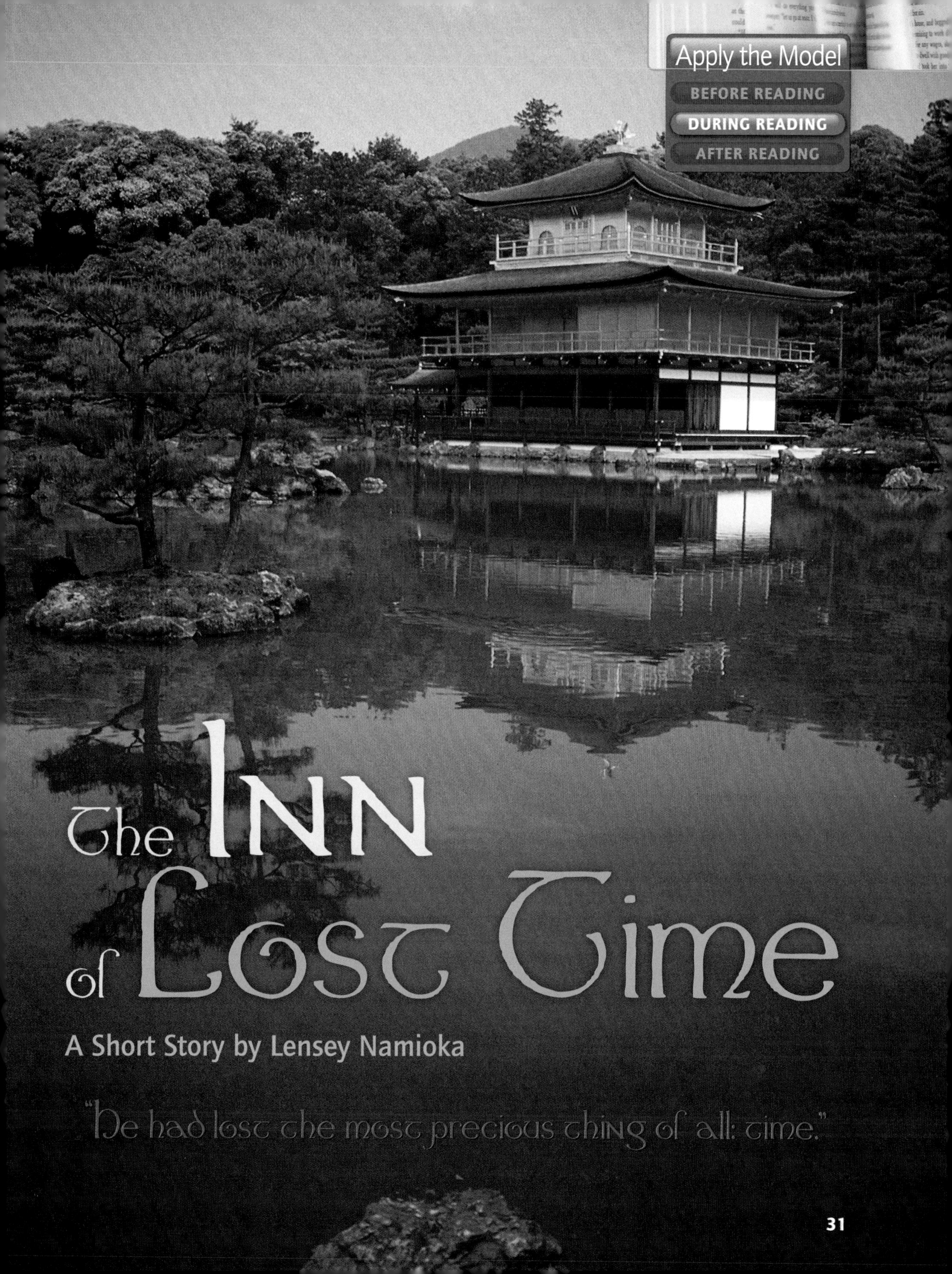

Apply the Model

BEFORE READING

DURING READING

AFTER READING

The Inn of Lost Time

A Short Story by Lensey Namioka

"He had lost the most precious thing of all: time."

"Will you promise to sleep if I tell you a story?" said the father. He pretended to put on a stern expression.

"Yes! Yes!" the three little boys chanted in unison. It sounded like a nightly routine.

The two guests smiled as they listened to the exchange. They were wandering ronin, or unemployed samurai, and they enjoyed watching this cozy family scene.

The father gave the guests a helpless look. "What can I do? I have to tell them a story, or these little rascals will give us no peace." Clearing his throat, he turned to the boys. "All right. The story tonight is about Urashima Taro."

Instantly the three boys became still. Sitting with their legs tucked under them, the three little boys, aged five, four, and three, looked like a descending row of stone statuettes. Matsuzo, the younger of the two ronin, was reminded of the wayside half-body statues of Jizo, the God of Travelers and Protector of Children.

Behind the boys the farmer's wife took up a pair of iron chopsticks and stirred the ashes of the fire in the charcoal brazier.[1] A momentary glow brightened the room. The lean faces of the two ronin, lit by the fire, suddenly looked fierce and hungry.

DURING READING

Analyze Literature

Setting What do the details tell you about where the ronin are and when this scene takes place?

The farmer knew that the two ronin were supposed to use their arms in defense of the weak. But in these troubled times, with the country torn apart by civil wars, the samurai didn't always live up to their honorable code.

Then the fire died down again and the subdued red light softened the features of the two ronin. The farmer relaxed and began his story.

The tale of Urashima Taro is familiar to every Japanese. No doubt the three little boys had heard their father tell it before—and more than once. But they listened with rapt attention.

rapt (rapt) *adj.*, mentally engrossed or absorbed

Urashima Taro, a fisherman, rescued a turtle from some boys who were battering it with stones. The grateful turtle rewarded Taro by carrying him on his back to the bottom of the sea, where he lived happily with the Princess of the Underseas. But Taro soon became homesick for his native village and asked to go back on land. The princess gave him a box to take with him but warned him not to peek inside.

When Taro went back to his village, he found the place quite changed. In his home he found his parents gone and living there was

1. **brazier.** Pan for holding burning coals

another old couple. He was stunned to learn that the aged husband was his own son whom he had last seen as a baby. Taro thought he had spent only a pleasant week or two undersea with the princess. On land, seventy-two years had passed! His parents and most of his old friends had long since died.

Desolate, Taro decided to open the box given him by the princess. As soon as he looked inside he changed in an instant from a young man to a decrepit[2] old man of more than ninety.

des•o•late (de´ sə lət) *adj.*, lonely, sad

At the end of the story the boys were close to tears. Even Matsuzo found himself deeply touched. He wondered why the farmer had told his sons such a poignant bedtime story. Wouldn't they worry all evening instead of going to sleep?

poi•gnant (poi´ nyənt) *adj.*, deeply affecting or touching; somber

But the boys recovered quickly. They were soon laughing and jostling each other, and they made no objections when their mother shooed them toward bed. Standing in order of age, they bowed politely to the guests, and then lay down on the mattresses spread out for them on the floor. Within minutes the sound of their regular breathing told the guests that they were asleep.

DURING READING
Analyze Literature
Setting Based on the details in this passage, what can you infer about the farmer's house?

Zenta, the older of the two ronin, sighed as he glanced at the peaceful young faces. "I wish I could fall asleep so quickly. The story of Urashima Taro is one of the saddest that I know among our folk tales."

The farmer looked proudly at his sleeping sons. "They're stout lads. Nothing bothers them much."

The farmer's wife poured tea for the guests and apologized. "I'm sorry this is only poor tea made from coarse leaves."

Zenta hastened to reassure her. "It's warm and heartening on a chilly autumn evening."

"You know what I think is the saddest part of the Urashima Taro story?" said Matsuzo, picking up his cup and sipping the tea. "It's that Taro lost not only his family

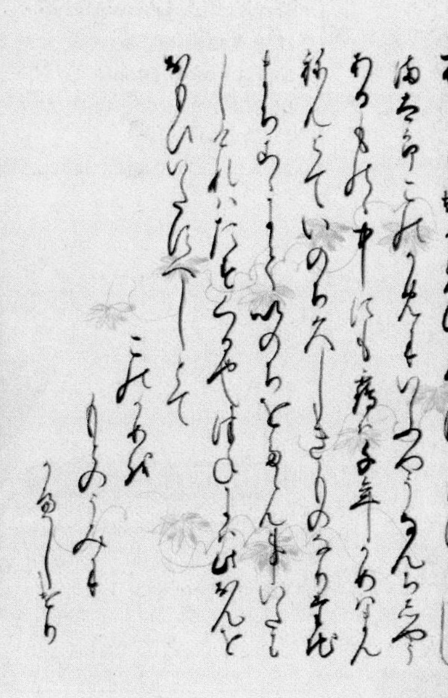

Urashima Taro (manuscript illustration), 1688–1704. Unknown artist.

2. **decrepit.** Broken down; weak

and friends, but a big piece of his life as well. He had lost the most precious thing of all: time."

The farmer nodded agreement. "I wouldn't sell even one year of my life for money. As for losing seventy-two years, no amount of gold will make up for that!"

Zenta put his cup down on the floor and looked curiously at the farmer. "It's interesting that you should say that. I had an opportunity once to observe exactly how much gold a person was willing to pay for some lost years of his life." He smiled grimly. "In this case the man went as far as one gold piece for each year he lost."

"That's bizarre!" said Matsuzo. "You never told me about it."

"It happened long before I met you," said Zenta. He drank some tea and smiled ruefully.[3] "Besides, I'm not particularly proud of the part I played in that strange affair."

"Let's hear the story!" urged Matsuzo. "You've made us all curious."

The farmer waited expectantly. His wife sat down quietly behind her husband and folded her hands. Her eyes looked intently at Zenta.

"Very well, then," said Zenta. "Actually, my story bears some resemblance to that of Urashima Taro..."

DURING READING

Use Reading Skills

Sequence of Events When did the events of Zenta's story take place?

It happened about seven years ago, when I was a green, inexperienced youngster not quite eighteen years old. But I had had a good training in arms, and I was able to get a job as a bodyguard for a wealthy merchant from Sakai.

As you know, wealthy merchants are relatively new in our country. Traditionally the rich have been noblemen, landowners, and warlords with thousands of followers. Merchants, considered as parasites[4] in our society, are a despised class. But our civil wars have made people unusually mobile and stimulated trade between various parts of the country. The merchants have taken advantage of this to conduct businesses on a scale our fathers could not imagine. Some of them have become more wealthy than a warlord with thousands of samurai under his command.

DURING READING

Analyze Literature

Setting What do these details reveal about the Japanese society that serves as a background for the story?

The man I was escorting,[5] Tokubei, was one of this new breed of wealthy merchants. He was trading not only with outlying provinces

---

3. **ruefully.** In a regretful way
4. **parasites.** People who make a habit of taking advantage of others
5. **escorting.** Accompanying; guiding

but even with the Portuguese from across the sea. On this particular journey he was not carrying much gold with him. If he had, I'm sure he would have hired an older and more experienced bodyguard. But if the need should arise, he could always write a message to his clerks at home and have money forwarded to him. It's important to remember this.

The second day of our journey was a particularly grueling one, with several steep hills to climb. As the day was drawing to its close, we began to consider where we should spend the night. I knew that within an hour's walking was a hot-spring resort known to have several attractive inns.

But Tokubei, my employer, said he was already very tired and wanted to stop. He had heard of the resort, and knew the inns there were expensive. Wealthy as he was, he did not want to spend more money than he had to.

While we stood talking, a smell reached our noses, a wonderful smell of freshly cooked rice. Suddenly I felt ravenous. From the way Tokubei swallowed, I knew he was feeling just as hungry.

rav•en•ous (ra´ və nəs) *adj.*, very eager for food

We looked around eagerly, but the area was forested and we could not see very far in any direction. The tantalizing smell seemed to grow and I could feel the saliva filling my mouth.

"There's an inn around here, somewhere," muttered Tokubei. "I'm sure of it."

We followed our noses. We had to leave the well-traveled highway and take a narrow, winding footpath. But the mouth-watering smell of the rice and the vision of fluffy, freshly aired cotton quilts drew us on.

DURING READING

Analyze Literature
Setting How does the imagery in this passage explain why Tokubei and Zenta leave the highway to search for an unknown inn?

The sun was just beginning to set. We passed a bamboo grove, and in the low evening light the thin leaves turned into little golden knives. I saw a gilded clump of bamboo shoots. The sight made me think of the delicious dish they would make when boiled in soy sauce.

We hurried forward. To our delight we soon came to a clearing with a thatched house standing in the middle. The fragrant smell of rice was now so strong that we were certain a meal was being prepared inside.

Standing in front of the house was a pretty girl beaming at us with a welcoming smile. "Please honor us with your presence," she said, beckoning.

There was something a little unusual about one of her hands, but, being hungry and eager to enter the house, I did not stop to observe closely.

DURING READING

Analyze Literature
Setting What is odd about the location of the inn? Why isn't Zenta suspicious?

You will say, of course, that it was my duty as a bodyguard to be suspicious and to look out for danger. Youth and inexperience should not have prevented me from wondering why an inn should be found hidden away from the highway. As it was, my stomach growled, and I didn't even hesitate but followed Tokubei to the house.

Before stepping up to enter, we were given basins of water to wash our feet. As the girl handed us towels for drying, I saw what was unusual about her left hand: she had six fingers.

Tokubei had noticed it as well. When the girl turned away to empty the basins, he nudged me. "Did you see her left hand? She had—" He broke off in confusion as the girl turned around, but she didn't seem to have heard.

The inn was peaceful and quiet, and we soon discovered the reason why. We were the only guests. Again, I should have been suspicious. I told you that I'm not proud of the part I played.

Tokubei turned to me and grinned. "It seems that there are no other guests. We should be able to get extra service for the same amount of money."

The girl led us to a spacious room which was like the principal chamber of a private residence. Cushions were set out for us on the floor and we began to shed our traveling gear to make ourselves comfortable.

The door opened and a grizzled-haired man entered. Despite his vigorous-looking[6] face his back was a little bent and I guessed his age to be about fifty. After bowing and greeting us he apologized in advance for the service. "We have not always been innkeepers here," he said, "and you may find the accommodations lacking. Our good intentions must make up for our inexperience. However, to compensate for our inadequacies,[7] we will charge a lower fee than that of an inn with an established reputation."

com • pen • sate (käm´ pən sāt') *v.*, balance, offset, repay

Tokubei nodded graciously, highly pleased by the words of our host, and the evening began well. It continued well when the girl came back with some flasks of wine, cups, and dishes of salty snacks.

While the girl served the wine, the host looked with interest at my swords. From the few remarks he made, I gathered that he was a former samurai, forced by circumstances to turn his house into an inn.

---

6. vigorous. Lively; energetic
7. inadequacies. Shortcomings

Having become a bodyguard to a tight-fisted merchant, I was in no position to feel superior to a ronin turned innkeeper. Socially, therefore, we were more or less equal.

We exchanged polite remarks with our host while we drank and tasted the salty snacks. I looked around at the pleasant room. It showed excellent taste, and I especially admired a vase standing in the alcove.

My host caught my eyes on it. "We still have a few good things that we didn't have to sell," he said. His voice held a trace of bitterness. "Please look at the panels of these doors. They were painted by a fine artist."

Tokubei and I looked at the pair of sliding doors. Each panel contained a landscape painting, the right panel depicting a winter scene and the left one the same scene in late summer. Our host's words were no idle[8] boast. The pictures were indeed beautiful.

Tokubei rose and approached the screens for a closer look. When he sat down again, his eyes were calculating. No doubt he was trying to estimate what price the paintings would fetch.

After my third drink I began to feel very tired. Perhaps it was the result of drinking on an empty stomach. I was glad when the girl brought in two dinner trays and a lacquered container of rice. Uncovering the rice container, she began filling our bowls.

Again I noticed her strange left hand with its six fingers. Any other girl would have tried to keep that hand hidden, but this girl made no effort to do so. If anything, she seemed to use that hand more than her other one when she served us. The extra little finger always stuck out from the hand, as if inviting comment.

The hand fascinated me so much that I kept my eyes on it, and soon forgot to eat. After a while the hand looked blurry. And then everything else began to look blurry. The last thing I remembered was the sight of Tokubei shaking his head, as if trying to clear it.

When I opened my eyes again, I knew that time had passed, but not how much time. My next thought was that it was cold. It was not only extremely cold but damp.

When I opened my eyes again, I knew that time had passed, but not how much time.

I rolled over and sat up. I reached immediately for my swords and found them safe on the ground beside me. On the ground? What was I doing on the ground? My last memory was of staying at an inn with a merchant called Tokubei.

8. idle. Without worth or basis in fact

DURING READING

Use Reading Skills

Sequence of Events Zenta has three drinks and the girl serves the rice. What happens after that?

The thought of Tokubei put me into a panic. I was his bodyguard, and instead of watching over him, I had fallen asleep and had awakened in a strange place.

I looked around frantically and saw that he was lying on the ground not far from where I was. Had he been killed?

I got up shakily, and when I stood up my head was swimming. But my sense of urgency gave some strength to my legs. I stumbled over to my employer and to my great relief found him breathing—breathing heavily, in fact.

When I shook his shoulder, he grunted and finally opened his eyes. "Where am I?" he asked thickly.

It was a reasonable question. I looked around and saw that we had been lying in a bamboo grove. By the light I guessed that it was early morning, and the reason I felt cold and damp was because my clothes were wet with dew.

"It's cold!" said Tokubei, shivering and climbing unsteadily to his feet. He looked around slowly, and his eyes became wide with disbelief. "What happened? I thought we were staying at an inn!"

His words came as a relief. One of the possibilities I had considered was that I had gone mad and that the whole episode with the inn was something I had imagined. Now I knew that Tokubei had the same memory of the inn. I had not imagined it.

But why were we out here on the cold ground, instead of on comfortable mattresses in the inn?

DURING READING

Make Connections

What assumption would you make if you found yourself in this situation?

"They must have drugged us and robbed us," said Tokubei. He turned and looked at me furiously. "A fine bodyguard you are!"

There was nothing I could say to that. But at least we were both alive and unharmed. "Did they take all your money?" I asked.

Tokubei had already taken his wallet out of his sash and was peering inside. "That's funny! My money is still here!"

This was certainly unexpected. What did the innkeeper and his strange daughter intend to do by drugging us and moving us outside?

At least things were not as bad as we had feared. We had not lost anything except a comfortable night's sleep, although from the heaviness in my head I had certainly slept deeply enough—and long enough too. Exactly how much time had elapsed[9] since we drank wine with our host?

All we had to do now was find the highway again and continue

9. elapsed. Passed

our journey. Tokubei suddenly chuckled. "I didn't even have to pay for our night's lodging!"

As we walked from the bamboo grove, I saw the familiar clump of bamboo shoots, and we found ourselves standing in the same clearing again. Before our eyes was the thatched house. Only it was somehow different. Perhaps things looked different in the daylight than at dusk.

But the difference was more than a change of light. As we approached the house slowly, like sleepwalkers, we saw that the thatching was much darker. On the previous evening the thatching had looked fresh and new. Now it was dark with age. Daylight should make things appear brighter, not darker. The plastering of the walls also looked more dingy.[10]

DURING READING

Analyze Literature

Setting What is different about the outside of the house?

Tokubei and I stopped to look at each other before we went closer. He was pale, and I knew that I looked no less frightened. Something was terribly wrong. I loosened my sword in its scabbard.

We finally gathered the courage to go up to the house. Since Tokubei seemed unable to find his voice, I spoke out. "Is anyone there?"

After a moment we heard shuffling footsteps and the front door slid open. The face of an old woman appeared. "Yes?" she inquired. Her voice was creaky with age.

What set my heart pounding with panic, however, was not her voice. It was the sight of her left hand holding on to the frame of the door. The hand was wrinkled and crooked with the arthritis of old age—and it had six fingers.

I heard a gasp beside me and knew that Tokubei had noticed the hand as well.

The door opened wider and a man appeared beside the old woman. At first I thought it was our host of the previous night. But this man was much younger, although the resemblance was strong. He carried himself straighter and his hair was black, while the innkeeper had been grizzled and slightly bent with age.

"Please excuse my mother," said the man. "Her hearing is not good. Can we help you in some way?"

Tokubei finally found his voice. "Isn't this the inn where we stayed last night?"

The man stared. "Inn? We are not innkeepers here!"

"Yes, you are!" insisted Tokubei. "Your daughter invited us in and

---

10. dingy. Dirty or discolored; showing signs of wear or neglect

served us with wine. You must have put something in the wine!"

The man frowned. "You are serious? Are you sure you didn't drink too much at your inn and wander off?"

"No, I didn't drink too much!" said Tokubei, almost shouting. "I hardly drank at all! Your daughter, the one with six fingers in her hand, started to pour me a second cup of wine..." His voice trailed off, and he stared again at the left hand of the old woman.

"I don't have a daughter," said the man slowly. "My mother here is the one who has six fingers in her left hand, although I hardly think it polite of you to mention it."

Urashima on the Turtle,
1882. Yoshitoshi.

"I've lost fifty years! Fifty years of my life went by while I slept at this accursed inn!"

"I'm getting dizzy," muttered Tokubei and began to totter.

"I think you'd better come in and rest a bit," the man said to him gruffly. He glanced at me. "Perhaps you wish to join your friend. You don't share his delusion[11] about the inn, I hope?"

"I wouldn't presume to contradict my elders," I said carefully. Since both Tokubei and the owner of the house were my elders, I wasn't committing myself. In truth I didn't know what to believe, but I did want a look at the inside of the house.

The inside was almost the same as it was before but the differences were there when I looked closely. We entered the same room with the alcove and the pair of painted doors. The vase I had admired was no longer there, but the doors showed the same landscapes painted by a master. I peered closely at the pictures and saw that the colors looked faded. What was more, the left panel, the one depicting a winter scene, had a long tear in one corner. It had been painstakingly mended, but the damage was impossible to hide completely.

Tokubei saw what I was staring at and he became even paler. At this stage we had both considered the possibility that a hoax of some sort had been played on us. The torn screen convinced Tokubei that our host had not played a joke: the owner of a valuable painting would never vandalize it for a trivial reason.

As for me, I was far more disturbed by the sight of the sixth finger on the old woman's hand. Could the young girl have disguised

DURING READING

Analyze Literature
Setting What detail in the house convinces Tokubei that the host is not just playing a joke? Explain.

11. delusion. Incorrect perception of reality

herself as an old crone? She could put rice powder in her hair to whiten it, but she could not transform her pretty straight fingers into old fingers twisted with arthritis. The woman here with us now was genuinely old, at least fifty years older than the girl.

It was this same old woman who finally gave us our greatest shock. "It's interesting that you should mention an inn, gentlemen," she croaked. "My father used to operate an inn. After he died, my husband and I turned this back into a private residence. We didn't need the income, you see."

"Your...your...f-father?" stammered Tokubei.

"Yes," replied the old woman. "He was a ronin, forced to go into innkeeping when he lost his position. But he never liked the work. Besides, our inn had begun to acquire an unfortunate reputation. Some of our guests disappeared, you see."

Even before she finished speaking, a horrible suspicion had begun to dawn on me. Her father had been an innkeeper, she said, her father who used to be a ronin. The man who had been our host was a ronin turned innkeeper. Could this mean that this old woman was actually the same person as the young girl we had seen?

I sat stunned while I tried to absorb the implications. What had happened to us? Was it possible that Tokubei and I had slept while this young girl grew into a mature woman, got married, and bore a son, a son who was now an adult? If that was the case, then we had slept for fifty years!

The old woman's next words confirmed my fears. "I recognize you now! You are two of the lost guests from our inn! The other lost ones I don't remember so well, but I remember you because your disappearance made me so sad. Such a handsome youth, I thought, what a pity that he should have gone the way of the others!"

A high wail came from Tokubei, who began to keen[12] and rock himself back and forth. "I've lost fifty years! Fifty years of my life went by while I slept at this accursed inn!"

The inn was indeed accursed. Was the fate of the other guests similar to ours? "Did anyone else return as we did, fifty years later?" I asked.

The old woman looked uncertain and turned to her son. He frowned thoughtfully. "From time to time wild-looking people have come to us with stories similar to yours. Some of them went mad with the shock."

DURING READING

Use Reading Skills

Sequence of Events What sequence of events is suggested to Zenta by the old woman's words?

---

12. keen. Lament or complain loudly

Tokubei wailed again. "I've lost my business! I've lost my wife, my young and beautiful wife! We had been married only a couple of months!"

A gruesome chuckle came from the old woman. "You may not have lost your wife. It's just that she's become an old hag like me!"

That did not console Tokubei, whose keening became louder. Although my relationship with my employer had not been characterized by much respect on either side, I did begin to feel very sorry for him. He was right: he had lost his world.

As for me, the loss was less traumatic.[13] I had left home under extremely painful circumstances, and had spent the next three years wandering. I had no friends and no one I could call a relation. The only thing I had was my duty to my employer. Somehow, some way, I had to help him.

"They would wake up twenty, thirty, or even fifty years later."

"Did no one find an explanation for these disappearances?" I asked. "Perhaps if we knew the reason why, we might find some way to reverse the process."

The old woman began to nod eagerly. "The priestess! Tell them about the shrine priestess!"

"Well," said the man, "I'm not sure if it would work in your case...."

"What? What would work?" demanded Tokubei. His eyes were feverish.

"There was a case of one returning guest who consulted the priestess at our local shrine," said the man. "She went into a trance and revealed that there was an evil spirit dwelling in the bamboo grove here. This spirit would put unwary[14] travelers into a long, unnatural sleep. They would wake up twenty, thirty, or even fifty years later."

"Yes, but you said something worked in his case," said Tokubei.

The man seemed reluctant to go on. "I don't like to see you cheated, so I'm not sure I should be telling you this."

"Tell me! Tell me!" demanded Tokubei. The host's reluctance only made him more impatient.

DURING READING

Analyze Literature
Setting What do the details about the evil spirit reveal about people's beliefs in this time and place?

"The priestess promised to make a spell that would undo the work of the evil spirit," said the man. "But she demanded a large sum of money, for she said that she had to burn some very rare and costly incense before she could begin the spell."

---

13. traumatic. Shocking
14. unwary. Easily fooled

At the mention of money Tokubei sat back. The hectic flush died down on his face and his eyes narrowed. "How much money?" he asked.

The host shook his head. "In my opinion the priestess is a fraud[15] and makes outrageous claims about her powers. We try to have as little to do with her as possible."

"Yes, but did her spell work?" asked Tokubei. "If it worked, she's no fraud!"

"At least the stranger disappeared again," cackled the old woman. "Maybe he went back to his own time. Maybe he walked into a river."

Tokubei's eyes narrowed further. "How much money did the priestess demand?" he asked again.

"I think it was one gold piece for every year lost," said the host. He hurriedly added, "Mind you, I still wouldn't trust the priestess."

"Then it would cost me fifty gold pieces to get back to my own time," muttered Tokubei. He looked up. "I don't carry that much money with me."

"No, you don't," agreed the host.

Something alerted me about the way he said that. It was as if the host knew already that Tokubei did not carry much money on him.

Meanwhile Tokubei sighed. He had come to a decision. "I do have the means to obtain more money, however. I can send a message to my chief clerk and he will remit[16] the money when he sees my seal."

"Your chief clerk may be dead by now," I reminded him.

"You're right!" moaned Tokubei. "My business will be under a new management and nobody will even remember my name!"

"And your wife will have remarried," said the old woman, with one of her chuckles. I found it hard to believe that the gentle young girl who had served us wine could turn into this dreadful harridan.[17]

"Sending the message may be a waste of time," agreed the host.

"What waste of time!" cried Tokubei. "Why shouldn't I waste time? I've wasted fifty years already! Anyway, I've made up my mind. I'm sending that message."

"I still think you shouldn't trust the priestess," said the host.

That only made Tokubei all the more determined to send for the money. However, he was not quite resigned to the amount. "Fifty

DURING READING

Use Reading Strategies
Clarify The Latin phrase *carpe diem* applies to this story. Identify the meaning of this foreign phrase and explain how it fits with this section of the story.

---

15. fraud. One who cheats or deceives
16. remit. Send (money)
17. harridan. Ill-tempered woman

gold pieces is a large sum. Surely the priestess can buy incense for less than that amount?"

"Why don't you try giving her thirty gold pieces?" cackled the old woman. "Then the priestess will send you back thirty years, and your wife will only be middle-aged."

While Tokubei was still arguing with himself about the exact sum to send for, I decided to have a look at the bamboo grove. "I'm going for a walk," I announced, rising and picking up my sword from the floor beside me.

The host turned sharply to look at me. For an instant a faint, rueful smile appeared on his lips. Then he looked away.

Outside, I went straight to the clump of shoots in the bamboo grove. On the previous night—or what I perceived as the previous night—I had noticed that clump of bamboo shoots particularly, because I had been so hungry that I pictured them being cut up and boiled.

The clump of bamboo shoots was still in the same place. That in itself proved nothing, since bamboo could spring up anywhere, including the place where a clump had existed fifty years earlier. But what settled the matter in my mind was that the clump looked almost exactly the way it did when I had seen it before, except that every shoot was about an inch taller. That was a reasonable amount for bamboo shoots to grow overnight.

DURING READING

Use Reading Skills

Sequence of Events What inconsistency does Zenta discover in the old woman's story of lost time?

Overnight. Tokubei and I had slept on the ground here overnight. We had not slept here for a period of fifty years.

Once I knew that, I was able to see another inconsistency: the door panels with the painted landscapes. The painting with the winter scene had been on the right last night and it was on the left this morning. It wasn't simply a case of the panels changing places, because the depressions in the panel for the handholds had been reversed. In other words, what I saw just now was not a pair of paintings faded and torn by age. They were an entirely different pair of paintings.

But how did the pretty young girl change into an old woman? The answer was that if the screens could be different ones, so could the women. I had seen one woman, a young girl, last night. This morning I saw a different woman, an old hag.

The darkening of the thatched roof? Simply blow ashes over the roof. The grizzled-haired host of last night could be the same man who claimed to be his grandson today. It would be a simple matter for a young man to put gray in his hair and assume a stoop.

And the purpose of the hoax? To make Tokubei send for fifty pieces of gold, of course. It was clever of the man to accuse the shrine priestess of fraud and pretend reluctance to let Tokubei send his message.

I couldn't even feel angry toward the man and his daughter—or mother, sister, wife, whatever. He could have killed me and taken my swords, which he clearly admired. Perhaps he was really a ronin and felt sympathetic toward another one.

When I returned to the house, Tokubei was looking resigned. "I've decided to send for the whole fifty gold pieces." He sighed.

"Don't bother," I said. "In fact we should be leaving as soon as possible. We shouldn't even stop here for a drink, especially not of wine."

Tokubei stared. "What do you mean? If I go back home, I'll find everything changed!"

"Nothing will be changed," I told him. "Your wife will be as young and beautiful as ever."

"I don't understand," he said. "Fifty years..."

"It's a joke," I said. "The people here have a peculiar sense of humor, and they've played a joke on us."

Tokubei's mouth hung open. Finally he closed it with a snap. He stared at the host, and his face became first red and then purple. "You—you were trying to swindle me!" He turned furiously to me. "And you let them do this!"

"I'm not letting them," I pointed out. "That's why we're leaving right now."

"Are you going to let them get away with this?" demanded Tokubei. "They might try to swindle someone else!"

"They only went to this much trouble when they heard of the arrival of a fine fat fish like you," I said. I looked deliberately at the host. "I'm sure they won't be tempted to try the same trick again."

"And that's the end of your story?" asked Matsuzo. "You and Tokubei just went away? How did you know the so-called innkeeper wouldn't try the trick on some other luckless traveler?"

Zenta shook his head. "I didn't know. I merely guessed that once the trick was exposed, they wouldn't take the chance of trying it again. Of course I thought about revisiting the place to check if the people there were leading an honest life."

"Why didn't you?" asked Matsuzo. "Maybe we could go together. You've made me curious about that family now."

"Then you can satisfy your curiosity," said Zenta, smiling. He

DURING READING

Use Reading Skills
Sequence of Events How does this paragraph signal a shift from the flashback to the "frame" story?

held his cup out for more tea, and the farmer's wife came forward to pour.

Only now she used both hands to hold the pot, and for the first time Matsuzo saw her left hand. He gasped. The hand had six fingers.

"Who was the old woman?" Zenta asked the farmer's wife.

> **DURING READING**
>
> **Analyze Literature**
> **Setting** Where are Zenta and Matsuzo staying now?

"She was my grandmother," she replied. "Having six fingers is something that runs in my family."

At last Matsuzo found his voice. "You mean this is the very house you visited? This is the inn where time was lost?"

"Where we thought we lost fifty years," said Zenta. "Perhaps I should have warned you first. But I was almost certain that we'd be safe this time. And I see that I was right."

He turned to the woman again. "You and your husband are farmers now, aren't you? What happened to the man who was the host?"

"He's dead," she said quietly. "He was my brother, and he was telling you the truth when he said that he was a ronin. Two years ago he found work with another warlord, but he was killed in battle only a month later."

Matsuzo was peering at the pair of sliding doors, which he hadn't noticed before. "I see that you've put up the faded set of paintings. The winter scene is on the left side."

> **DURING READING**
>
> **Use Reading Skills**
> **Sequence of Events** What happened to their host after Zenta and Tokubei's visit to the inn?

The woman nodded. "We sold the newer pair of doors. My husband said that we're farmers now and that people in our position don't need valuable paintings. We used the money to buy some new farm implements."

She took up the teapot again. "Would you like another cup of tea?" she asked Matsuzo.

Staring at her left hand, Matsuzo had a sudden qualm. "I—I don't think I want any more."

Everybody laughed. ✣

What if you could sell ten years of your life? What amount, if any, would make it worthwhile to lose the possibilities those years might hold for you? What do you think time is worth?

Find Meaning

1. (a) What do Zenta and Tokubei notice that is unusual about the girl at the inn? (b) Why do you suppose the girl, and later the old woman, makes no effort to hide her left hand?
2. (a) While Tokubei and the host are arguing about whether Tokubei should send for money, what does Zenta decide to do, and how does the host respond? (b) Why does a rueful smile appear on the host's lips?

Analyze Literature

Setting Setting often has an effect on plot. Use a Venn diagram to list the details that describe the inn when Zenta and Tokubei arrive and "after fifty years," when they awaken from their drugged sleep. What details are the same? What details are different? How do these details influence the plot?

Make Judgments

3. (a) What words, behaviors, and gestures demonstrate Tokubei's attitude about money? (b) How do these attitudes affect his response when he learns about the hoax?
4. (a) Why do you think the innkeeper decides to try to swindle the two travelers? (b) Do you think he feels guilty? Explain.
5. Why do you think Zenta is more forgiving of the innkeeper and his family than Tokubei is?

Extend Understanding

Writing Options

Creative Writing Imagine that you are Tokubei and that you have decided to make a police report. Write a **descriptive paragraph** to help the police make an identification of the innkeepers. Include character traits as well as physical descriptions. Support your statements with evidence from the story.

Informative Writing Consider how Zenta's story would be different if the "frame" story featuring Zenta, Matsuzo, and the farmer's family were removed. Write a short **literary analysis** of "The Inn of Lost Time" in which you examine how the author's use of flashback helps increase suspense. Include a thesis and support.

Collaborative Learning

Hold a Discussion With a partner, discuss how you might react if you realized that a great deal of time had passed while you slept or had been unconscious as a result of an accident or illness. Would you be upset? frightened? confused? Write a few sentences to summarize your feelings.

Critical Literacy

Write Questions Prepare a set of questions that you would ask Tokubei to prompt him to tell his version of the story. Read aloud your questions to the class and invite volunteers to supply Tokubei's answers.

MW Go to **www.mirrorsandwindows.com** for more.

Grammar & Style

Subject-Verb Agreement

Identifying Subject-Verb Agreement

The sun was just beginning to set.

—LENSEY NAMIOKA, "The Inn of Lost Time"

In the sentence above, the subject *sun* is singular. A verb must agree with the subject in number. Number refers to whether the subject is singular or plural. If the subject is plural, the verb must also be plural. If the subject is singular, the verb must also be singular. Then the singular subject *sun* needs the singular verb *was*.

> EXAMPLE
>
> *The <u>inn</u> in the woods <u>was</u> dark in the evening.*

In this example, the subject and verb are separated by a prepositional phrase. The prepositional phrase *in the woods* modifies the subject, *inn*. The subject is singular, so the verb, *was*, is also singular. If you are not sure of the subject-verb agreement in a sentence with a prepositional phrase, try rewriting the sentence without the phrase.

Fixing Subject-Verb Agreement

> INCORRECT
>
> *One of the innkeepers give the ronin a dinner of rice and vegetables.*

In the sentence above, the verb *give* agrees with *innkeepers*, the noun it follows. However, *innkeepers* is not the subject. *Innkeepers* is part of the prepositional phrase *of the innkeepers*. The subject is *one*, which is singular. The verb *give* is plural. To fix the sentence, change the verb to *gives*, the singular form. Note that the singular form of many verbs ends in an *-s*.

> INCORRECT
>
> *Tokubei want to discover what happened as he slept.*

In this example, the subject *Tokubei* is singular, but the verb *want* is plural. To fix the sentence, change the verb to *wants*, the singular form.

Sentence Improvement

For each of the following sentences, select the word that best completes the sentence. Then rewrite the sentences on a separate sheet of paper.

1. Wealthy (merchant / merchants) usually complain more than others.
2. The farmer's (tale / tales) about Urashima Taro is famous.
3. (Zenta / The two ronin) waits for the end of the story.
4. The (innkeeper / innkeepers) were not telling the truth.
5. (Tokubei / The innkeepers) is suspicious of the situation.
6. The painted (screen / screens) seem different from the night before.
7. That inn by the two pine trees (are / is) very old.
8. The travelers in the bamboo grove (pass / passes) the inn.
9. Inside of the inn, the guests (are / is) sleeping.
10. The (guest / guests) on the path were very hungry.

THE PORTRAIT

A Short Story by Tomás Rivera

BEFORE READING

Build Background

Literary Context Mexican-American literature is sometimes referred to as Chicano literature. A main subject of Chicano literature is the experiences of newcomers to the United States. Mexican-American writers, such as Tomás Rivera, often describe the many challenges and pleasures associated with straddling two different cultures.

Reader's Context Imagine that you have a treasured photograph of a well-loved pet, friend, or relative whom you will never see again. What might cause you to trust that photograph with a stranger?

Set Purpose

Preview the title and skim the first page of text. Make a prediction about the story's conflict and its resolution. Then read to determine if your prediction is accurate. You may change your prediction as you gain new information from the story.

Analyze Literature

Plot A **plot** is a series of events related to a central problem, or **conflict.** A typical plot begins with the introduction of the conflict, followed by events that lead to the **climax,** which is the point of highest tension or excitement in the story. The **resolution** is the point at which the central conflict is resolved. As you read "The Portrait," identify the central conflict, climax, and resolution.

Use Reading Skills

Analyze Cause and Effect When you analyze cause and effect, you look for a logical relationship between a cause or several causes and one or more effects. Sometimes signal words such as *because, since*, and *therefore* signal cause-and-effect relationships. Keeping track of what happens in a story can help you better understand the story events. As you read "The Portrait," use a chart to keep track of causes and effects.

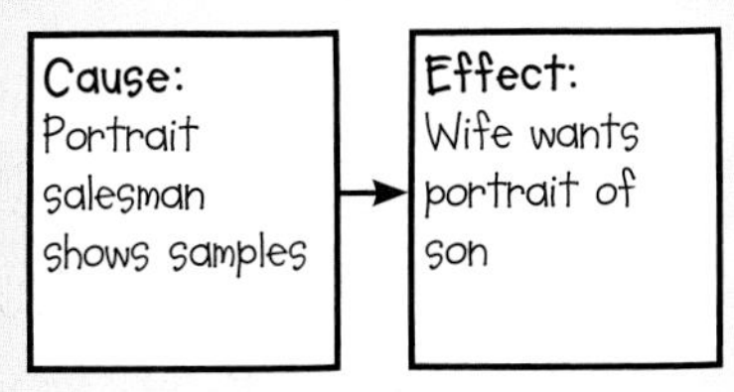

Meet the Author

Tomás Rivera (1935–1984) was the son of migrant farm workers, but he went on to earn a Ph.D. in Romance Languages and Literature. Rivera's published work includes novels, short stories, poetry, and essays, written in English and Spanish. His fiction is known for its realistic portrayal of the enduring spirit and strong family and community ties of Mexican-American migrant workers.

Private First Class Eugene A. Obregon was awarded the Medal of Honor in Korea for giving his life to save a fellow soldier.

THE PORTRAIT

A Short Story by Tomás Rivera

As soon as the people returned from up north the portrait salesmen began arriving from San Antonio. They would come to rake in.[1] They knew that the workers had money and that was why, as Dad used to say, they would flock in. They carried suitcases packed with samples and always wore white shirts and ties; that way they looked more important and the people believed everything they would tell them and invite them into their homes without giving it much thought. I think that down deep they even longed for their children to one day be like them. In any event, they would arrive and make their way down the dusty streets, going house to house carrying suitcases full of samples.

I remember once I was at the house of one of my father's friends when one of these salesmen arrived. I also remember that that particular one seemed a little frightened and timid. Don Mateo asked him to come in because he wanted to do business.

It's the only picture we have of him.

"Good afternoon, traveler. I would like to tell you about something new that we're offering this year."

"Well, let's see, let's see..."

"Well, sir, see, you give us a picture, any picture you may have, and we will not only enlarge it for you but we'll also set it in a wooden frame like this one and we'll shape the image a little, like this—three dimensional, as they say."

"And what for?"

"So that it will look real. That way...look, let me show you...see? Doesn't he look real, like he's alive?"

"Man, he sure does. Look, vieja.[2] This looks great. Well, you know, we wanted to send some pictures to be enlarged...but now, this must cost a lot, right?"

"No, I'll tell you, it costs about the same. Of course, it takes more time."

"Well, tell me, how much?"

"For as little as thirty dollars we'll deliver it to you done with inlays[3] just like this, one this size."

"Boy, that's expensive! Didn't you say it didn't cost a lot more? Do you take installments?"

"Well, I'll tell you, we have a new manager and he wants everything in cash. It's very fine work. We'll make it look like real. Shaped like that, with inlays...take a look. What do you think? Some fine work, wouldn't you say? We can have it all finished for you in a month. You just tell us what color you want the clothes to be and we'll come by with it all finished one day when you least expect, framed and all. Yes, sir, a month at the longest. But like I say, this man, who's the new manager, he wants the full payment in cash. He's very demanding, even with us."

"Yes, but it's much too expensive."

"Well, yes. But the thing is, this is very fine work. You can't say you've ever seen portraits done like this, with wood inlays."

"No, well, that's true. What do you think, vieja?"

"Well, I like it a lot. Why don't we order one? And if it turns out good...my Chuy...may he rest in peace. It's the only picture we have of him. We took it right before he left for Korea. Poor m'ijo,[4] we never saw him again. See...this is his picture. Do

1. **rake in.** Make lots of money
2. ***vieja.*** Old woman; wife (Spanish)
3. **inlays.** Material set into a surface in pieces to form a design
4. ***m'ijo.*** My son (Spanish; a contraction of *mi hijo*)

you think you can make it like that, make it look like he's alive?"

"Sure, we can. You know, we've done a lot of them in soldier's uniforms and shaped it, like you see in this sample, with inlays. Why, it's more than just a portrait. Sure. You just tell me what size you want and whether you want a round or square frame. What do you say? How should I write it down?"

"What do you say, vieja, should we have it done like this one?"

"Well, I've already told you what I think. I would like to have m'ijo's picture fixed up like that and in color."

"All right, go ahead and write it down. But you take good care of that picture for us because it's the only one we have of our son grown up. He was going to send us one all dressed up in uniform with the American and Mexican flags crossed over his head, but he no sooner got there when a letter arrived telling us that he was lost in action.[5] So you take good care of it."

"Don't you worry. We're responsible people. And we understand the sacrifices that you people make. Don't worry. And you just wait and see, when we bring it, you'll see how pretty it's gonna look. What do you say, should we make the uniform navy blue?"

"But he's not wearing a uniform in that picture."

"No, but that's just a matter of fixing it up with some wood fiber overlays. Look at these. This one, he didn't have a uniform on but we put one on him. So what do you say? Should we make it navy blue?"

And two more weeks had passed by the time they made the discovery.

"All right."

"Don't you worry about the picture."

And that was how they spent the entire day, going house to house, street by street, their suitcases stuffed with pictures. As it turned out, a whole lot of people had ordered enlargements of that kind.

"They should be delivering those portraits soon, don't you think?"

"I think so, it's delicate work and takes more time. That's some fine work those people do. Did you see how real those pictures looked?"

"Yeah, sure. They do some fine work. You can't deny that. But it's already been over a month since they passed by here."

"Yes, but from here they went on through all the towns picking up pictures...all the way to San Antonio for sure. So it'll probably take a little longer."

"That's true, that's true."

And two more weeks had passed by the time they made the discovery. Some very heavy rains had come and some children, who were playing in one of the tunnels leading to the dump, found a sack full of pictures, all worm-eaten and soaking wet. The only reason that they could tell that these were pictures was because there were a lot of them and most of them the same size and with faces that could just barely be made out. Everybody caught on right away. Don Mateo was so angry that he took off to San Antonio to find the so and so who had swindled them.

---

5. lost in action. Killed in battle

"Well, you know, I stayed in Esteban's house. And every day I went with him to the market to sell produce. I helped him with everything. I had faith that I would run into that son of a gun some day soon. Then, after I'd been there for a few days, I started going out to the different barrios[6] and I found out a lot that way. It wasn't so much the money that upset me. It was my poor vieja, crying and all because we'd lost the only picture we had of Chuy. We found it in the sack with all the other pictures but it was already ruined, you know."

"I see, but tell me, how did you find him?"

"Well, you see, to make a long story short, he came by the stand at the market one day. He stood right in front of us and bought some vegetables. It was like he was trying to remember who I was. Of course, I recognized him right off. Because when you're angry enough, you don't forget a face. I just grabbed him right then and there. Poor guy couldn't even talk. He was all scared. And I told him that I wanted that portrait of my son and that I wanted it three dimensional and that he'd best get it for me or I'd let him have it. And I went with him to where he lived. And I put him to work right then and there. The poor guy didn't know where to begin. He had to do it all from memory."

> **"Well, to be honest, I don't remember too well how Chuy looked."**

"And how did he do it?"

"I don't know. I suppose if you're scared enough, you're capable of doing anything. Three days later he brought me the portrait all finished, just like you see it there on that table by the Virgin. Now tell me, how do you like the way my boy looks?"

"Well, to be honest, I don't remember too well how Chuy looked. But he was beginning to look more and more like you, isn't that so?"

"Yes, I would say so. That's what everybody tells me now. That Chuy's a chip off the old block and that he was already looking like me. There's the portrait. Like they say, one and the same." ✣

---

6. ***barrios.*** Neighborhoods (Spanish)

How satisfying did you find the ending of the story? If knowing the truth about something would make you unhappy, would you want to know the truth, or would you rather not know but remain happy? What do you think is more important: truth or happiness?

Find Meaning

1. Why do the portrait salesmen dress the way they do?
2. (a) Who is Chuy? (b) Why is Chuy's photograph so important to Don Mateo and his wife?
3. (a) Why does Don Mateo travel to San Antonio? (b) What does he do there?

Make Judgments

4. What is your opinion of what the salesman says about his manager? Why might he say this?
5. After Don Mateo gives the photograph of his son to the salesman, what clues help you to predict what will happen next?
6. (a) How does the portrait salesman manage to create the new portrait? (b) Do you think the salesman should have simply refunded the money? Explain.

Analyze Literature

Plot In a plot, once the conflict is identified, the events build in intensity until the action reaches the climax, the moment at which the outcome of the conflict is decided. Then the resolution concludes the story. On a plot diagram, indicate the climax and the resolution of "The Portrait." Explain at what points you verified or changed your predictions about the outcome of the story.

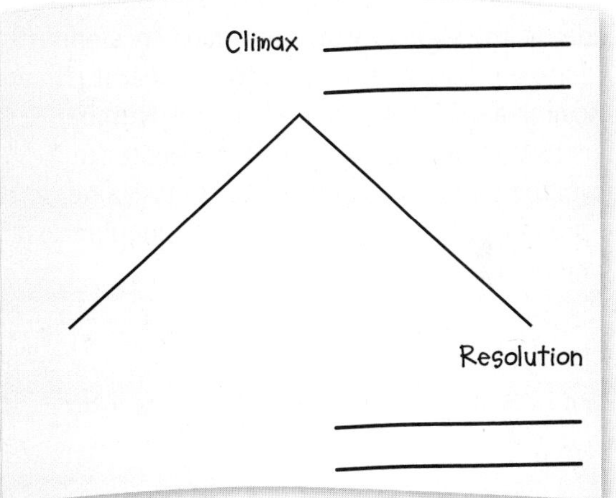

Extend Understanding

Writing Options

Creative Writing Write a **news report** for a local radio station about the incidents described in the story. Remember that a good news report begins with an attention-grabbing first line. Be sure to answer the questions of *who, what, where, when, why,* and *how*. Present your news report to the class.

Narrative Writing In a brief **story summary,** describe the problem faced by Don Mateo in the story and the steps he takes to solve the problem. Also consider the problem that the portrait salesman has when Don Mateo wants him to create the portrait of Chuy from memory. How does he solve the problem? Does the story end happily for Don Mateo? Explain.

Collaborative Learning

List Setting Details In small groups, discuss the setting of "The Portrait." Create a list of details from the story that helped you determine the time period and the locations. Use this list to analyze how both time and place influence the theme or message of the selection. Present your conclusions to the class.

Lifelong Learning

Research the Internet Use the Internet to gather information about Hispanic Americans who served in the Korean War (1950–1953). Find out about Hispanic-American recipients of the Medal of Honor, and create a "Wall of Honor" for them in the classroom.

 Go to **www.mirrorsandwindows.com** for more.

Grammar & Style

Pronoun-Antecedent Agreement

Gender Agreement

Don Mateo was so angry that he took off to San Antonio....

—TOMÁS RIVERA, "The Portrait"

Pronouns must agree with their antecedents. That means pronouns must have the same number and gender as the word or words they refer to. **Gender** is the form a pronoun takes to show whether it is masculine, feminine, or gender neutral. **Number** refers to the singular or plural. In the sentence above, the antecedent *Don Mateo* is masculine, so the pronoun used is *he. Don Mateo* is singular, so the pronoun is also singular.

EXAMPLE

Don Mateo went to the market. It was crowded with people.

In this example, the pronoun *it* is gender neutral. Use *it* when the antecedent is not a person.

Unclear Antecedents

Make sure that the antecedent of each pronoun is clear and does not seem to refer to more than one pronoun. Also, avoid the pronouns *that, this, it,* and *which* when the antecedent is unclear.

EXAMPLE

Many families were confused and angry. <u>This</u> was understandable.

Clarify by restating the antecedent.

EXAMPLE

Many families were confused and angry. <u>Their feelings were</u> understandable.

A pronoun may sometimes seem to refer to multiple antecedents. In the following example, the antecedent of the pronoun *he* is unclear.

EXAMPLE

After Don Mateo visited Esteban, he was pleased.

Reword the sentence or remove the pronoun to correct this problem.

EXAMPLE

Don Mateo was pleased after visiting Esteban.

Sentence Improvement

For each of the following sentences, select the best revision of the underlined portion.

1. <u>Vieja was unhappy. She cried all day.</u>
A. Vieja was unhappy. It cried all day.
B. Vieja was unhappy. They cried all day.
C. Vieja was unhappy. We cried all day.
D. NO CHANGE

2. The townspeople found the rotting bag beneath a bridge. <u>They were sitting in a puddle of water.</u>
A. It was sitting in a puddle of water.
B. He was sitting in a puddle of water.
C. She was sitting in a puddle of water.
D. NO CHANGE

3. Don Mateo and Esteban were angry with the salesman. <u>He couldn't understand why the portrait would cost so much.</u>
A. Esteban couldn't understand why the portrait would cost so much.
B. She couldn't understand why the portrait would cost so much.
C. It couldn't understand why the portrait would cost so much.
D. NO CHANGE

A Day's Wait

A Short Story by Ernest Hemingway

ANCHOR TEXT

DIRECTED READING

BEFORE READING

Build Background

Cultural Context The metric system was introduced in France in the 1790s in order to standardize units of measurement, which varied widely from country to country and even from town to town. In 1875, many countries, including the United States, signed the *Treaty of the Meter*, establishing the International Bureau of Weights and Measures. English-speaking countries have lagged in adopting the metric system. The United Kingdom did not begin to use metric units until 1965.

Reader's Context When has misinformation or lack of information caused you to be frightened of something?

Set Purpose

One way writers develop their characters is through dialogue. As you read "A Day's Wait," examine how the dialogue influences character development.

Analyze Literature

Conflict The plot of a story centers on a **conflict,** or struggle, that the main character has with internal or external forces. An *internal conflict* involves the character's struggle with emotions such as fear or love. An *external conflict* involves a struggle with outside forces such as nature, another character, or society. As you read "A Day's Wait," examine the conflict and try to determine if it is internal or external. Record your answers.

Use Reading Skills

Draw Conclusions

When you draw conclusions, you use evidence from the text to support your ideas about characters, conflicts, and other literary elements. As you read "A Day's Wait," use a two-column chart to record details from this story. List details about the characters in the left- hand column and your conclusions about them in the right.

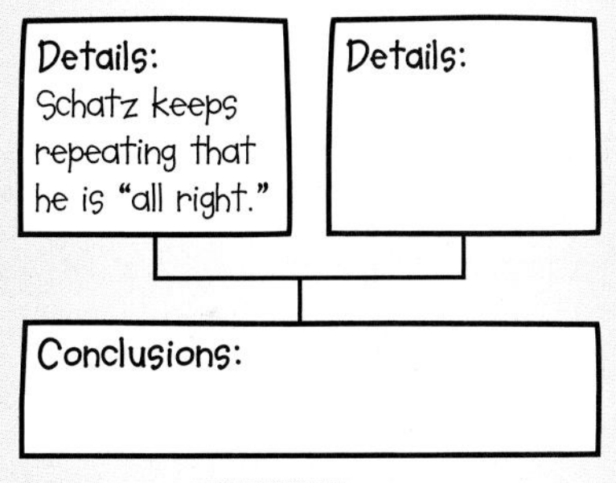

Meet the Author

Ernest Hemingway (1899–1961) is considered one of the greatest fiction writers of the twentieth century. His stories and novels, written in a distinctively spare and terse prose style, often reflect his lifelong love of hunting, fishing, and outdoor adventure. During World War I, an eye problem prevented him from joining the U.S. Army, so he served with an ambulance unit. He was wounded in the war and was awarded the Italian Silver Medal for Valor. Hemingway received a Pulitzer Prize in 1953 and the Nobel Prize for Literature in 1954.

Preview Vocabulary

in•flu•en•za (in' flu['] en´ zə) *n.*, viral disease characterized by fever, muscular aches, and respiratory distress

ep•i•dem•ic (e' pə de´ mik) *n.*, outbreak of contagious disease that spreads rapidly

flush (fləsh) *adj.*, having a red color to the skin

A Day's Wait

A Short Story by Ernest Hemingway

He came into the room to shut the windows while we were still in bed and I saw he looked ill. He was shivering, his face was white, and he walked slowly as though it ached to move.

"What's the matter, Schatz?"

"I've got a headache."

"You better go back to bed."

"No. I'm all right."

"You go to bed. I'll see you when I'm dressed."

But when I came downstairs he was dressed, sitting by the fire, looking a very sick and miserable boy of nine years. When I put my hand on his forehead I knew he had a fever.

"You go up to bed," I said, "you're sick."

"I'm all right," he said.

When the doctor came he took the boy's temperature.

"What is it?" I asked him.

"One hundred and two."

Downstairs, the doctor left three different medicines in different colored capsules with instructions for giving them. One was to bring down the fever, another a purgative, the third to overcome an acid condition. The germs of influenza can only exist in an acid condition, he explained. He seemed to know all about influenza and said there was nothing to worry about if the fever did not go above one hundred and four degrees. This was a light epidemic of flu and there was no danger if you avoided pneumonia.[1]

Back in the room I wrote the boy's temperature down and made a note of the time to give the various capsules.

"Do you want me to read to you?"

---

1. **pneumonia.** Disease marked by inflammation of the lungs

in • flu • en • za (in' flu['] en´ zə) *n.*, viral disease characterized by fever, muscular aches, and respiratory distress

ep • i • dem • ic (e' pə de´ mik) *n.*, outbreak of contagious disease that spreads rapidly

"All right. If you want to," said the boy. His face was very white and there were dark areas under his eyes. He lay still in the bed and seemed very detached from what was going on.

I thought perhaps he was a little lightheaded...

I read aloud from Howard Pyle's *Book of Pirates;* but I could see he was not following what I was reading.

"How do you feel, Schatz?" I asked him.

"Just the same, so far," he said.

I sat at the foot of the bed and read to myself while I waited for it to be time to give another capsule. It would have been natural for him to go to sleep, but when I looked up he was looking at the foot of the bed, looking very strangely.

"Why don't you try to go to sleep? I'll wake you up for the medicine."

"I'd rather stay awake."

After a while he said to me, "You don't have to stay in here with me, Papa, if it bothers you."

"It doesn't bother me."

"No, I mean you don't have to stay if it's going to bother you."

I thought perhaps he was a little lightheaded and after giving him the prescribed capsules at eleven o'clock I went out for a while. It was a bright, cold day, the ground covered with a sleet that had frozen so that it seemed as if all the bare trees, the bushes, the cut brush and all the grass and the bare ground had been varnished with ice. I took the young Irish setter for a little walk up the road and along a frozen creek, but it was difficult to stand or walk on the glassy surface and the red dog slipped and slithered and I fell twice, hard, once dropping my gun and having it slide away over the ice.

We flushed[2] a covey of quail under a high clay bank with overhanging brush and I killed two as they went out of sight over the top of the bank. Some of the covey lit[3] in trees but most of them scattered into brush piles and it was necessary to jump on the ice-coated mounds of brush several times before they would flush. Coming out while you were poised unsteadily on the icy, springy brush they made difficult shooting, and I killed two, missed five and started back pleased to have found a covey close to the house and happy there were so many left to find on another day.

At the house they said the boy had refused to let anyone come into the room.

"You can't come in," he said. "You mustn't get what I have."

"Something like a hundred," I said.

I went up to him and found him in exactly the position I had left him, white-faced, but with the tops of his cheeks flushed by the fever, staring still as he had stared at the foot of the bed.

I took his temperature.

"What is it?"

"Something like a hundred," I said. It was one hundred and two and four tenths.

"It was a hundred and two," he said.

"Who said so?"

---

2. **flushed.** Frightened a game bird from cover
3. **covey lit.** Flock of birds came to rest

> **flush** (fləsh) *adj.*, having a red color to the skin

"The doctor."

"Your temperature is all right," I said. "It's nothing to worry about."

"I don't worry," he said. "but I can't keep from thinking."

"Don't think," I said. "Just take it easy."

"I'm taking it easy," he said and looked straight ahead. He was evidently holding tight on to himself about something.

"Take this with water."

"Do you think it will do any good?"

"Of course it will."

I sat down and opened the *Pirate* book and commenced[4] to read, but I could see he was not following, so I stopped.

"About what time do you think I'm going to die?" he asked.

"What?"

"About how long will it be before I die?"

"You aren't going to die. What's the matter with you?"

"Oh, yes, I am. I heard him say a hundred and two."

"People don't die with a fever of one hundred and two. That's a silly way to talk."

"I know they do. At school in France the boys told me you can't live with forty-four degrees. I've got a hundred and two."

He had been waiting to die all day, ever since nine o'clock in the morning.

"You poor Schatz," I said. "Poor old Schatz. It's like miles and kilometers. You aren't going to die. That's a different thermometer. On that thermometer thirty-seven is normal. On this kind it's ninety-eight."

"Are you sure?"

"Absolutely," I said. "It's like miles and kilometers. You know, like how many kilometers we make when we drive seventy miles in the car?"

"Oh," he said.

But his gaze at the foot of the bed relaxed slowly. The hold over himself relaxed too, finally, and the next day it was very slack and he cried very easily at little things that were of no importance. ✣

---

4. **commenced.** Began

How would you feel at the end of the story if you were Schatz? What advice would you give him or his father to help them avoid future misunderstandings? How does communication play a vital role in solving and preventing problems?

Find Meaning

1. (a) What kind(s) of conflict can be found in this story? (b) What is the most important conflict in the story? Why?
2. (a) Why does the father go hunting instead of staying by his son's bedside? (b) How do you think the boy felt when his father went out?
3. (a) What causes the boy to think he is going to die? (b) Does his reaction seem reasonable? Why or why not?

Make Judgments

4. (a) At the beginning of the story, why does Schatz keep insisting that he's "all right"? (b) What does this behavior suggest about his character?
5. The narrator often refers to his son as "the boy." What does this imply about their relationship?

INFORMATIONAL TEXT ▶▶ CONNECTION

In "A Day's Wait," a young boy's misunderstanding about a thermometer reading causes him to believe that he is about to die, and he spends an entire day in extreme, but needless, anxiety. The following selection is a press release from the National Aeronautics and Space Administration (NASA) that describes how a misunderstanding about units of measure affected a Mars space mission.

Mars Climate Orbiter Team Finds Likely Cause of Loss

A Press Release by NASA

A failure to recognize and correct an error in a transfer of information between the Mars Climate Orbiter spacecraft team in Colorado and the mission navigation team in California led to the loss of the spacecraft last week, preliminary findings by NASA's Jet Propulsion Laboratory internal peer review[1] indicate.

"People sometimes make errors," said Dr. Edward Weiler, NASA's Associate Administrator for Space Science. "The problem here was not the error, it was the failure of NASA's systems engineering,[2] and the checks and balances in our processes to detect the error. That's why we lost the spacecraft."

The peer review preliminary findings indicate that one team used English units (e.g., inches, feet and pounds) while the other used metric units for a key spacecraft operation. This information was critical to the maneuvers[3] required to place the spacecraft in the proper Mars orbit.

"Our inability to recognize and correct this simple error has had major implications," said Dr. Edward Stone, director of the Jet Propulsion Laboratory. "We have underway a thorough investigation to understand this issue."

Two separate review committees have already been formed to investigate the loss of Mars Climate Orbiter: an internal JPL peer group and a special review board of JPL and outside experts. An independent NASA failure review board will be formed shortly.

"Our clear short-term goal is to maximize the likelihood of a successful landing of the Mars Polar Lander on December 3," said Weiler. "The lessons from these reviews will be applied across the board in the future."

Mars Climate Orbiter was one of a series of missions in a long-term program of Mars

1. **peer review.** Process of subjecting work to the scrutiny of experts
2. **systems engineering.** Overall planning, design, and specifications for a project
3. **maneuvers.** Controlled movements

exploration managed by the Jet Propulsion Laboratory for NASA's Office of Space Science, Washington, DC. JPL's industrial partner is Lockheed Martin Astronautics, Denver, CO. JPL is a division of the California Institute of Technology, Pasadena, CA. ✣

Both Hemingway's story and NASA's press release focus on mistakes related to units of measurement. In each selection, how do different measurement systems create problems? What is similar about the mistakes that are made? What is different?

AFTER READING

Analyze Literature

Conflict Identifying cause-and-effect relationships in a story helps you understand what happened and why. A *cause* is an event or action that brings about an *effect,* or outcome. Use a chart to analyze the cause and the effect of the conflict in "A Day's Wait." Then summarize the cause-and-effect relationship in a brief statement.

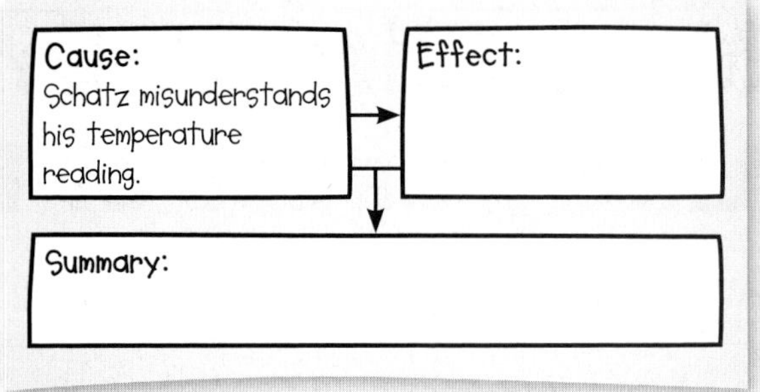

Extend Understanding

Writing Options

Creative Writing Write a **letter** to a friend in which you give a real or fictional account of a misunderstanding that caused you to experience anxiety. Use the first-person point of view, and include a summary of how the experience changed you.

Argumentative Writing Write an **editorial** for your local newspaper stating why all schools and industries in the United States should use metric measurements instead of the measurement system currently used in the United States. State your position in the topic sentence. Then argue for your position, including at least three reasons for your position. Organize your reasons by order of importance, and provide examples or supporting facts. Conclude your editorial by restating your position.

Critical Literacy

Create a Chart Create a chart for Schatz that shows the Fahrenheit equivalents for Celsius temperatures from 36 to 44 degrees. You can use library resources to research Fahrenheit and Celsius conversion formulas, or you can find a converter on the Internet, such as the one provided by the National Weather Service.

Media Literacy

Conduct Internet Research Perform key word searches with a search engine or an electronic library database to locate information about a problem or confusing situation caused by unit conversion. Summarize the information in one or two paragraphs, and present it to the class.

Go to **www.mirrorsandwindows.com** for more.

The War of the Wall

A Short Story by Toni Cade Bambara

BEFORE READING

Build Background

Cultural Context Outdoor urban murals, or paintings on walls, emerged as a form of public art in the United States during the 1960s and 1970s. Urban murals have the potential to bring together communities through the expression of common interests and values. The themes often relate to the community in which the mural is located. The images often include cultural and religious symbols, historical events, contemporary events, and historical and contemporary leaders and personalities.

Reader's Context Where do you and your friends or family like to gather to relax and have fun? How would you feel if a stranger started to make a major change in that place?

Set Purpose

Paying attention to what the characters say, do, and think can help you understand why they feel or behave a certain way. Read to determine how the characters' needs, desires, or feelings affect their motivations.

Analyze Literature

Dialect A **dialect** is a version of a language spoken by people of a particular place, time, or group. Writers use dialect to develop characters, to establish setting, and to create a mood. As you read "The War of the Wall," think about what the characters' dialect tells you about them and what it adds to the atmosphere, or mood, of the story.

Use Reading Skills

Analyze Cause and Effect In fiction, sometimes one event explains *why* another event takes place. The event that explains why is a *cause;* the event that results is an *effect.* Understanding cause-and-effect relationships can help you grasp the meaning of a story. Sometimes a single cause has several effects, and an effect can have several causes. As you read "The War of the Wall," use a chart to keep track of causes and effects.

Cause:		Effect:
A stranger is painting the wall that is the neighborhood's gathering place.	→	The narrator is angry.

DIRECTED READING

Meet the Author

Toni Cade Bambara (1939–1995) was deeply influenced by the Harlem, New York community where she spent the first years of her life. She published her first short story shortly after college. As a college professor, writer, social activist, and filmmaker, Bambara worked throughout her life to fight oppression and injustice. The themes of family and community are woven throughout Bambara's work.

Preview Vocabulary

mas • ter • piece (mas´ tər pēs') *n.*, artist's greatest work

trance (tran[t]s) *n.*, state of detachment from one's physical surroundings

lib • er • a • tion (li' bə rā´ shən) *n.*, state of being free or of achieving civil rights

The War of the Wall

A Short Story
by Toni Cade Bambara

Me and Lou had no time for courtesies. We were late for school. So we just flat out told the painter lady to quit messing with the wall. It was our wall, and she had no right coming into our neighborhood painting on it. Stirring in the paint bucket and not even looking at us, she mumbled something about Mr. Eubanks, the barber, giving her permission. That had nothing to do with it as far as we were concerned. We've been pitching pennies against that wall since we were little kids. Old folks have been dragging their chairs out to sit in the shade of the wall for years. Big kids have been playing handball against the wall since so-called integration[1] when the crazies 'cross town poured cement in our pool so we couldn't use it. I'd sprained my neck one time boosting my cousin Lou up to chisel Jimmy Lyons's name into the wall when we found out he was never coming home from the war in Vietnam to take us fishing.

"If you lean close," Lou said, leaning hipshot against her beat-up car, "you'll get a whiff of bubble gum and kids' sweat. And that'll tell you something—that this wall belongs to the kids of Taliaferro Street." I thought Lou sounded very convincing. But the painter lady paid us no mind. She just snapped the brim of her straw hat down and hauled her bucket up the ladder.

"You're not even from around here," I hollered up after her. The license plates on her old piece of car said "New York." Lou dragged me away because I was about to grab hold of that ladder and shake it. And then we'd really be late for school.

When we came from school, the wall was slick with white. The painter lady was running string across the wall and taping it here and there. Me and Lou leaned against the gumball machine outside the pool hall and watched. She had strings up and down and back and forth. Then she began chalking them with a hunk of blue chalk.

So we just flat out told the painter lady to quit messing with the wall.

The Morris twins crossed the street, hanging back at the curb next to the beat-up car. The twin with the red ribbons was hugging a jug of cloudy lemonade. The one with yellow ribbons was holding a plate of dinner away from her dress. The painter lady began snapping the strings. The blue chalk dust measured off halves and quarters up and down and sideways too. Lou was about to say how hip it all was, but I dropped my book satchel on his toes to remind him we were at war.

Some good aromas were drifting our way from the plate leaking pot likker[2] onto the Morris girl's white socks. I could tell from where I stood that under the tinfoil was baked ham, collard greens, and candied yams. And knowing Mrs. Morris, who sometimes bakes for my mama's restaurant, a slab of buttered cornbread was probably up

1. integration. Ending of segregation, or the separation of races
2. pot likker. Cooking juices

under there too, sopping up some of the pot likker. Me and Lou rolled our eyes, wishing somebody would send us some dinner. But the painter lady didn't even turn around. She was pulling the strings down and prying bits of tape loose.

Side Pocket came strolling out of the pool hall to see what Lou and me were studying so hard. He gave the painter lady the once-over, checking out her paint-spattered jeans, her chalky T-shirt, her floppy-brimmed straw hat. He hitched up his pants and glided over toward the painter lady, who kept right on with what she was doing.

"Watcha got there, sweetheart?" he asked the twin with the plate.

"Suppah," she said all soft and countrylike.

"For her," the one with the jug added, jerking her chin toward the painter lady's back.

Still she didn't turn around. She was rearing back on her heels, her hands jammed into her back pockets, her face squinched up like the masterpiece she had in mind was taking shape on the wall by magic. We could have been gophers crawled up into a rotten hollow for all she cared. She didn't even say hello to anybody. Lou was muttering something about how great her concentration was. I butt him with my hip, and his elbow slid off the gum machine.

"Good evening," Side Pocket said in his best ain't-I-fine voice. But the painter lady was moving from the milk crate to the step stool to the ladder, moving up and down fast, scribbling all over the wall like a crazy person. We looked at Side Pocket. He looked at the twins. The twins looked at us. The painter lady was giving a show. It was like those old-timey music movies where the dancer taps on the tabletop and then starts jumping all over the furniture, kicking chairs over and not skipping a beat. She didn't even look where she was stepping. And for a minute there, hanging on the ladder to reach a far spot, she looked like she was going to tip right over.

"Ahh," Side Pocket cleared his throat and moved fast to catch the ladder. "These young ladies here have brought you some supper."

"Ma'am?" The twins stepped forward. Finally the painter turned around, her eyes "full of sky," as my grandmama would say.

We could have been gophers crawled up into a rotten hollow for all she cared.

Then she stepped down like she was in a trance. She wiped her hands on her jeans as the Morris twins offered up the plate and the jug. She rolled back the tinfoil, then wagged her head as though something terrible was on the plate.

"Thank your mother very much," she said, sounding like her mouth was full of sky too. "I've brought my own dinner along." And then, without even excusing herself, she went back up the ladder, drawing on the wall in a wild way. Side Pocket whistled one of

mas•ter•piece (mas´ tər pēs') *n.*, artist's greatest work

trance (tran[t]s) *n.*, state of detachment from one's physical surroundings those oh-brother breathy whistles and went back into the pool hall. The Morris twins shifted their weight from one foot to the other, then crossed the street and went home. Lou had to drag me away, I was so mad. We couldn't wait to get to the firehouse to tell my daddy all about this rude woman who'd stolen our wall.

All the way back to the block to help my mama out at the restaurant, me and Lou kept asking my daddy for ways to run the painter lady out of town. But my daddy was busy talking about the trip to the country and telling Lou he could come too because Grandmama can always use an extra pair of hands on the farm.

Later that night, while me and Lou were in the back doing our chores, we found out that the painter lady was a liar. She came into the restaurant and leaned against the glass of the steam table, talking about how starved she was. I was scrubbing pots and Lou was chopping onions, but we could hear her through the service window. She was asking Mama was that a ham hock in the greens, and was that a neck bone in the pole beans, and were there any vegetables cooked without meat, especially pork.

"I don't care who your spiritual leader is," Mama said in that way of hers. "If you eat in the community, sistuh, you gonna eat pig by-and-by, one way or t'other."

Me and Lou were cracking up in the kitchen, and several customers at the counter were clearing their throats, waiting for Mama to really fix her wagon for not speaking to the elders when she came in. The painter lady took a stool at the counter and went right on with her questions. Was there cheese in the baked macaroni, she wanted to know? Were there eggs in the salad? Was it honey or sugar in the iced tea? Mama was fixing Pop Johnson's plate. And every time the painter lady asked a fool question, Mama would dump another spoonful of rice on the pile. She was tapping her foot and heating up in a dangerous way. But Pop Johnson was happy as he could be. Me and Lou peeked through the service window, wondering what planet the painter lady came from. Who ever heard of baked macaroni without cheese, or potato salad without eggs?

"Do you have any bread made with unbleached flour?" the painter lady asked Mama. There was a long pause, as though everybody in the restaurant was holding their breath, wondering if Mama would dump the next spoonful on the painter lady's head. She didn't. But when she set Pop Johnson's plate down, it came down with a bang. When Mama finally took her order, the starving lady all of a sudden couldn't make up her mind whether she wanted a vegetable plate or fish and a salad. She finally settled on the broiled trout and a tossed salad. But just when Mama reached for a plate to serve her, the painter lady leaned over the counter with her finger all up in the air.

"Excuse me," she said. "One more thing." Mama was holding the plate like a Frisbee, tapping that foot, one hand on her hip. "Can I get raw beets in that tossed salad?"

"You will get," Mama said, leaning her face close to the painter lady's, "whatever Lou back there tossed. Now sit down." And the painter lady sat back down on her stool and shut right up.

All the way to the country, me and Lou tried to get Mama to open fire on the painter lady. But Mama said that seeing as how she was from the North, you couldn't expect her to have any manners. Then Mama said she was sorry she'd been so impatient with the woman because she seemed like a decent person and was simply trying to stick to a very strict diet. Me and Lou didn't want to hear that. Who did that lady think she was, coming into our neighborhood and taking over our wall?

"Wellllll," Mama drawled, pulling into the filling station so Daddy could take the wheel, "it's hard on an artist, ya know. They can't always get people to look at their work. So she's just doing her work in the open, that's all."

Me and Lou definitely did not want to hear that. Why couldn't she set up an easel downtown or draw on the sidewalk in her own neighborhood? Mama told us to quit fussing so much; she was tired and wanted to rest. She climbed into the back seat and dropped down into the warm hollow Daddy had made in the pillow.

All weekend long, me and Lou tried to scheme up ways to recapture our wall. Daddy and Mama said they were sick of hearing about it. Grandmama turned up the TV to drown us out. On the late news was a story about the New York subways. When a train came roaring into the station all covered from top to bottom, windows too, with

All weekend long, me and Lou tried to scheme up ways to recapture our wall.

writings and drawings done with spray paint, me and Lou slapped five. Mama said it was too bad kids in New York had nothing better to do than spray paint all over the trains. Daddy said that in the cities, even grown-ups wrote all over the trains and buildings too. Daddy called it "graffiti." Grandmama called it a shame.

We couldn't wait to get out of school on Monday. We couldn't find any black spray paint anywhere. But in a junky hardware store downtown we found a can of white epoxy paint, the kind you touch up old refrigerators with when they get splotchy and peely. We spent our whole allowance on it. And because it was too late to use our bus passes, we had to walk all the way home lugging our book satchels and gym shoes, and the bag with the epoxy. When we reached the corner of Taliaferro and Fifth, it looked like a block party or something. Half the neighborhood was gathered on the sidewalk in front of the wall. I looked at Lou, he looked at me. We both looked at the bag with the epoxy and wondered how we were going to work our scheme. The painter lady's car was nowhere in sight. But there were too many people standing around to do anything. Side Pocket and his buddies were leaning on their cue sticks, hunching each other. Daddy was there with a lineman he catches a ride with on Mondays. Mrs. Morris had her arms flung around the shoulders of the twins on either side of her. Mama was talking with some of her customers, many of them with napkins still at the throat. Mr. Eubanks came out of the barbershop, followed by a man in a striped poncho, half his face shaved, the other half full of foam.

"She really did it, didn't she?" Mr. Eubanks huffed out his chest. Lots of folks answered right quick that she surely did when they saw the straight razor in his hand.

Mama beckoned us over. And then we saw it. The wall. Reds, greens, figures outlined in black. Swirls of purple and orange. Storms of blues and yellows. It was something. I recognized some of the faces right off. There was Martin Luther King, Jr. And there was a man with glasses on and his mouth open like he was laying down a heavy rap. Daddy came up alongside and reminded us that was Minister Malcolm X. The serious woman with a rifle I knew was Harriet Tubman because my grandmama has pictures of her all over the house. And I knew Mrs. Fannie Lou Hamer 'cause a signed photograph of her hangs in the restaurant next to the calendar.

Then I let my eyes follow what looked like a vine. It trailed past a man with a horn, a woman with a big white flower in her hair, a handsome dude in a tuxedo seated at a

HISTORY ▶▶ CONNECTION

Civil Rights Throughout the first half of the twentieth century, African Americans struggled against restrictive segregation laws. In spite of the 1954 Supreme Court ruling against segregation in public schools, segregation and discrimination persisted. The Civil Rights era of the 1960s was inspired by leaders such as Martin Luther King, Jr., who encouraged blacks and whites to engage in demonstrations, sit-ins, and "freedom rides" in order to achieve integration and voting rights for African Americans. Why might it be important to remember these historical events?

piano, and a man with a goatee[3] holding a book. When I looked more closely, I realized that what had looked like flowers were really faces. One face with yellow petals looked just like Frieda Morris. One with red petals looked just like Hattie Morris. I could hardly believe my eyes.

...as though he'd been waiting all his life to give this lesson.

"Notice," Side Pocket said, stepping close to the wall with his cue stick like a classroom pointer. "These are the flags of liberation," he said in a voice I'd never heard him use before. We all stepped closer while he pointed and spoke. "Red, black and green," he said, his pointer falling on the leaflike flags of the vine. "Our liberation flag. And here, Ghana, there Tanzania. Guinea-Bissau, Angola, Mozambique."[4] Side Pocket sounded very tall, as though he'd been waiting all his life to give this lesson.

Mama tapped us on the shoulder and pointed to a high section of the wall. There was a fierce-looking man with his arms crossed against his chest guarding a bunch of children. His muscles bulged, and he looked a lot like my daddy. One kid was looking at a row of books. Lou hunched me 'cause the kid looked like me. The one that looked like Lou was spinning a globe on the tip of his finger like a basketball. There were other kids there with microscopes and compasses. And the more I looked, the more it looked like the fierce man was not so much guarding the kids as defending their right to do what they were doing.

Then Lou gasped and dropped the paint bag and ran forward, running his hands over a rainbow. He had to tiptoe and stretch to do it, it was so high. I couldn't breathe either. The painter lady had found the chisel marks and had painted Jimmy Lyons's name in a rainbow.

"Read the inscription,[5] honey," Mrs. Morris said, urging little Frieda forward. She didn't have to urge much. Frieda marched right up, bent down, and in a loud voice that made everybody quit oohing and ahhing and listen, she read,

To the People of Taliaferro Street
I Dedicate This Wall of Respect
Painted in Memory of My Cousin
Jimmy Lyons ✤

---

3. **goatee.** Small beard on the chin, sometimes trimmed into a point
4. **Ghana, Tanzania, Guinea-Bissau, Angola, Mozambique.** African countries that were once under European domination
5. **inscription.** Message written or carved on a surface

lib•er•a•tion (li′ bə rā′ shən) *n.*, state of being free or of achieving civil rights

Have you ever made a snap judgment about someone and later regretted it? Are snap judgments more often positive or negative? What are some of the factors that lead people to make snap judgments about others?

AFTER READING

Find Meaning

1. (a) What is the setting of the story? (b) What details provide clues about the time and place?
2. (a) How do the children of Taliaferro Street feel about the wall? Explain. (b) Why are they angry with the painter?
3. (a) What do the narrator and Lou decide to do in order to "recapture" their wall? (b) What causes them to change their plan?

Make Judgments

4. (a) What words would you use to describe the painter's behavior? (b) Why do you think the author portrayed the painter in this way?
5. (a) Are the adults as angry with the painter as the children are? Explain. (b) What might explain their attitude?
6. (a) How does the narrator's attitude toward the painter change? (b) What lesson might be learned from the narrator's experience?

Analyze Literature

Dialect Writers use dialect to create a realistic mood, or atmosphere, in a story. In "The War of the Wall," the narrator uses dialect in telling the story as well as in the dialogue. Scan the story for examples of dialect. Use a chart to record examples of dialect and to describe the mood or feeling the dialect creates. Discuss how the use of dialect heightens the conflict with the painter.

Dialect Examples	Effect on Mood
"If you eat in the community, sistuh, you gonna eat pig by-and-by, one way or t'other."	

Extend Understanding

Writing Options

Creative Writing Tone is a speaker's emotional attitude toward the subject. Use the narrator's dialect to write the **dialogue** that the narrator and Lou might have had as they planned the wall's "recapture." Remember that they "slapped five" after they saw the spray-painted subway trains. Try to capture that attitude, or tone, in your dialogue. With a partner, read aloud your dialogue for the class.

Informative Writing Write a brief **research essay** that explains, for teenagers from another country, the Civil Rights era that is reflected in this story. Connect the historical and cultural setting to examples from the story. Be sure to cite the sources from which you draw your information.

Lifelong Learning

Write a Biography Research the life of one of the people depicted in the mural, using both primary sources (firsthand accounts such as letters and diaries) and secondary sources (descriptions or explanations of primary sources such as encyclopedias and textbooks). Write a brief biography to be placed in a classroom resource center.

Media Literacy

Analyze Urban Murals Use the Internet to locate at least three images of urban murals like the one in the story. With these images, prepare an actual or virtual slide show for your classmates in which you evaluate and analyze the images, describe the artists' purposes, and state your own opinion.

 Go to **www.mirrorsandwindows.com** for more.

Grammar & Style

Nominative and Objective Pronouns

Nominative Pronouns

I recognized some of the faces right off.

—TONI CADE BAMBARA, "The War of the Wall"

In the sentence above, the pronoun *I* is the subject of the verb *recognized*. When a pronoun is the subject of a verb, you use the **nominative** case of the pronoun. The nominative case includes *I, you, he, she, it, we,* and *they*.

Sometimes the subject of a verb is compound. This can be confusing. If you are not sure which pronoun to use, try each part of the sentence separately.

EXAMPLE

Lou and (me / I) bought white paint to cover the mural.

Look closely at the sentence to choose the correct pronoun. The nominative pronoun will still be correct without the word *Lou. Me bought white paint* is incorrect, so the pronoun must be *I*.

When a pronoun or noun appears after a linking verb and refers back to the subject of the sentence, it is called a **predicate nominative.**

EXAMPLE

The painter lady is she.

In the above example, the predicate nominative is *she*, and the subject of the sentence is *painter lady*. Remember to use nominative pronouns after linking verbs.

Objective Pronouns

Lou had to drag me away...

—TONI CADE BAMBARA, "The War of the Wall"

In this sentence, the pronoun *me* is the object of the verb *drag*. What was dragged away? *Me*. When the verb acts upon an object, you use the **objective** case of the pronoun. The objective case includes *me, you, him, her, it, us,* and *them*.

EXAMPLE

Mama told Lou and (me / I) to stop fussing so much.

As above, if you are not sure which pronoun to use, try each part of the sentence separately.

The objective pronoun will still be correct if you remove the word *Lou. Mama told I to stop fussing so much* is incorrect. The correct pronoun must be *me*.

Like the subject of a sentence, the object can sometimes be compound. If you are not sure which pronoun to use, try each part of the sentence separately.

Sentence Improvement

For each of the following sentences, choose the correct pronoun in parentheses.

1. The children couldn't believe that (her / she) refused Mrs. Morris's hospitality.
2. (We / us) told (her / she) about the painter lady's rudeness.
3. The artist is probably (her / she).
4. We wanted (he / him) to help run the painter lady out of town, but Daddy refused.
5. The mural included paintings of Daddy and (I / me).
6. Mama and (me / I) were amazed by all the pictures on the wall.

The Foghorn

A Short Story by Ray Bradbury

BEFORE READING

Build Background

Historical Context Lighthouses date back to ancient Egypt, where beacon fires were kept lit to guide ships. The first lighthouse in the United States was built in 1716. Early lighthouses used candles, fires, and oil lamps to create light. In the late 1800s, electricity was first used. Early audio warnings included bells, whistles, cannons, and rockets. Steam-powered foghorns began to be widely used in the 1860s. With the increased use of electricity and radar in the twentieth century, the need for lighthouses declined.

Reader's Context If you feared that you might be the last person in the world, what would you do to try to find another human being?

Set Purpose

Preview the title of the story and think about what you can infer about the setting. Where are foghorns most commonly used? Read to determine what role the foghorn plays in the story.

Analyze Literature

Mood The **mood** of a story is the emotional response that it evokes in the reader. Writers use a variety of techniques to create mood, including word choice and setting details. As you read "The Foghorn," make a list of words and details that create feelings and emotions for you.

Use Reading Skills

Use Context Clues

Preview the vocabulary words from this story as they are used in the sentences below. Try to unlock the meaning of each word using the context clues provided.

1. Before you turn in your research paper, verify the facts to make sure they are accurate.
2. The archaeologists are searching for clues about the ancient primeval world of the dinosaurs.
3. Don't worry—if you fail this test, it's nothing to brood about.

Preview Vocabulary

ver•i•fy (ver´ ə fī') *v.*, test or check for correctness

pri•me•val (prī mē´ vəl) *adj.*, from the earliest ages

brood (brüd) *v.*, dwell on a gloomy subject; worry

DIRECTED READING

Meet the Author

Ray Bradbury (1920–2012) has won countless awards for his science fiction and fantasy. In 1934, Bradbury's family moved from Illinois to Los Angeles, California, where, as a high school student, he first became interested in writing. His short stories and novels are poetic and fanciful, but they address serious themes such as the value of individuality and modern society's overdependence on technology.

The Foghorn

A Short Story by Ray Bradbury

"One night, years ago, I was here alone, when all of the fish of the sea surfaced out there."

Out there in the cold water, far from land, we waited every night for the coming of the fog, and it came, and we oiled the brass machinery and lit the fog light up in the stone tower. Feeling like two birds in the gray sky, McDunn and I sent the light touching out, red, then white, then red again, to eye the lonely ships. If they did not see our light, then there was always our Voice, the great deep cry of our Fog Horn. It shuddered through the rags of mist to startle the gulls away like decks of scattered cards and make the waves turn high and foam.

"It's a lonely life, but you're used to it now, aren't you?" asked McDunn.

"Yes," I said. "You're a good talker, thank the Lord."

"Well, it's your turn on land tomorrow," he said, smiling, "to dance with the ladies."

"What do you think, McDunn, when I leave you out here alone?"

"On the mysteries of the sea." McDunn lit his pipe. It was a quarter past seven on a cold November evening, the heat on, the light switching its tail in two hundred directions, the Fog Horn bumbling in the high throat of the tower. There wasn't a town for a hundred miles down the coast, just a road, which came lonely through dead country to the sea, with few cars on it, a stretch of two miles of cold water out to our rock, and rare few ships.

"The mysteries of the sea," said McDunn thoughtfully. "You know, the ocean's the biggest snowflake ever? It rolls and swells a thousand shapes and colors, no two alike. Strange. One night, years ago, I was here alone, when all of the fish of the sea surfaced out there. Something made them swim in and lie in the bay, sort of trembling. They stared up at the tower light going red, white, red, white across them so I could see their funny eyes. I turned cold. They were like a big peacock's tail, moving out there until midnight. Then, without so much as a sound, they slipped away. The million of them was gone. I kind of think maybe, in some sort of way, they came all those miles to worship. Strange. But think how the tower must look to them, standing seventy feet above the water, the God-light flashing out from it, and the tower declaring itself with a monster voice. They never came back, those fish, but don't you think for a while they thought they were in the Presence?"

I shivered. I looked out at the long gray lawn of the sea stretching away into nothing and nowhere.

"Oh, the sea's full." McDunn puffed his pipe nervously, blinking. He had been nervous all day and hadn't said why. "For all our engines and so-called submarines, it'll be ten thousand centuries before we set foot on the real bottom of the sunken lands, in the fairy kingdoms there, and know real terror. Think of it. It's still the year 300,000 Before Christ down under there. While we've paraded around with trumpets, lopping off each other's countries and heads, they have been living beneath the sea twelve miles deep and cold in a time as old as the beard of a comet."

"Yes, it's an old world."

"Come on. I got something special I been saving up to tell you."

We ascended the eighty steps, talking and taking our time. At the top, McDunn switched off the room lights so there'd be no reflection in the plate glass. The great eye of the light was humming, turning easily in its oiled socket. The Fog Horn was blowing steadily, once every fifteen seconds.

"Sounds like an animal, don't it?" McDunn nodded to himself. "A big lonely animal crying in the night. Sitting here on the edge of ten billion years calling out to the Deeps, I'm here, I'm here, I'm here. And the Deeps do answer, yes, they do. You been here now for three months, Johnny, so I better prepare you. About this time of year," he said, studying the murk and fog, "something comes to visit the lighthouse."

"The swarms of fish like you said?"

"No, this is something else. I've put off telling you because you might think I'm daft.[1] But tonight's the latest I can put it off, for if my calendar's marked right from last year, tonight's the night it comes. I won't go into detail; you'll have to see it yourself. Just sit down there. If you want, tomorrow you can pack your duffel and take the motorboat into land and get your car parked there at the dinghy pier[2] on the cape and drive on back to some little inland town and keep your lights burning nights. I won't question or blame you. It's happened three years now, and this is the only time anyone's been here with me to verify it. You wait and watch."

Half an hour passed with only a few whispers between us. When we grew tired waiting, McDunn began describing some of his ideas to me. He had some theories about the Fog Horn itself.

"About this time of year," he said, studying the murk and fog, "something comes to visit the lighthouse."

"One day many years ago a man walked along and stood in the sound of the ocean on a cold sunless shore and said, 'We need a voice to call across the water, to warn ships. I'll make one. I'll make a voice like all of time and all of the fog that ever was; I'll make a voice that is like an empty bed beside you all night long, and like an empty house when you open the door, and like trees in autumn with no leaves. A sound like the birds flying

1. **daft.** Insane; crazy
2. **dinghy pier.** Docking place for small boats

ver•i•fy (ver´ ə fī') *v.*, test or check for correctness

The head rose a full forty feet above the water on a slender and beautiful dark neck.

south, crying, and a sound like November wind and the sea on the hard, cold shore. I'll make a sound that's so alone that no one can miss it, that whoever hears it will weep in their souls, and hearths will seem warmer, and being inside will seem better to all who hear it in the distant towns. I'll make me a sound and an apparatus and they'll call it a Fog Horn and whoever hears it will know the sadness of eternity and the briefness of life.'"

The Fog Horn blew.

"I made up that story," said McDunn quietly, "to try to explain why this thing keeps coming back to the lighthouse every year. The Fog Horn calls it, I think, and it comes...."

"But—" I said.

"Sssst!" said McDunn. "There!" He nodded out to the Deeps.

Something was swimming toward the lighthouse tower.

It was a cold night, as I have said; the high tower was cold, the light was coming and going, and the Fog Horn, calling and calling through the raveling mist. You couldn't see far and you couldn't see plain, but there was the deep sea moving on its way about the night earth, flat and quiet, the color of gray mud, and here were the two of us alone in the high tower, and there, far out at first, was a ripple, followed by a wave, a rising, a bubble, a bit of froth. And then, from the surface of the cold sea came a head, a large head, dark-colored, with immense eyes, and then a neck. And then—not a body—but more neck and more! The head rose a full forty feet above the water on a slender and beautiful dark neck. Only then did the body, like a slender little island of black coral and shells and crayfish, drip up from the subterranean. There was a flicker of tail. In all, from head to tip of tail, I estimated the monster at ninety or a hundred feet.

I don't know what I said. I said something.

"Steady, boy, steady," whispered McDunn.

"It's impossible!" I said.

"No, Johnny, *we're* impossible. *It's* like it always was ten million years ago. *It* hasn't changed. It's *us* and the land that've changed, become impossible. Us!"

It swam slowly and with a great dark majesty out in the icy waters, far away. The fog came and went about it, momentarily erasing its shape. One of the monster eyes caught and held and flashed back our immense light, red, white, red, white, like a disk held high and sending a message in primeval code. It was as silent as the fog through which it swam.

"It's a dinosaur of some sort!" I crouched down holding to the stair rail.

"Yes, one of the tribe."

"But they died out!"

pri•me•val (prī mē´ vəl) *adj.*, from the earliest ages

"No, only hid away in the Deeps. Deep, deep down in the deepest Deeps. Isn't *that* a word now, Johnny, a real word, it says so much: the Deeps. There's all the coldness and darkness and deepness in a word like that."

"What'll we do?"

"Do? We got our job, we can't leave. Besides, we're safer here than in any boat trying to get to land. That thing's as big as a destroyer and almost as swift."

"But here, why does it come *here*?"

The next moment I had my answer.

The Fog Horn blew.

And the monster answered.

A cry came across a million years of water and mist. A cry so anguished[3] and alone that it shuddered in my head and my body. The monster cried out at the tower. The Fog Horn blew. The monster roared again. The Fog Horn blew. The monster opened its great toothed mouth and the sound that came from it was the sound of the Fog Horn itself. Lonely and vast and far away. The sound of isolation, a viewless sea, a cold night, apartness. That was the sound.

"Now," whispered McDunn, "do you know why it comes here?"

---

3. anguished. Feeling great suffering or pain

I nodded.

"All year long, poor monster there thousand miles at sea, and twenty miles deep maybe, biding its time, perhaps it's a million years old, this one creature. Think of it, waiting a million years. Could *you* wait that long? Maybe it's the last of its kind. I sort of think that's true. Anyway, here come men on land and build this lighthouse, five years ago. And set up their Fog Horn and sound it and sound it out toward the place where you bury yourself in sleep and sea memories of a world where there were thousands like yourself, but now you're alone, all alone in a world not made for you, a world where you have to hide.

"But the sound of the Fog Horn comes and goes, comes and goes, and you stir from the muddy bottom of the Deeps, and your eyes open like the lenses of two-foot cameras and you move, slow, slow, for you have the ocean sea on your shoulders, heavy. But that Fog Horn comes through a thousand miles of water, faint and familiar, and the furnace in your belly stokes up, and you begin to rise, slow, slow. You feed yourself on great slakes of cod and minnow, on rivers of jellyfish, and you rise slow through the autumn months, through September when the fogs started, through October with more fog and the horn still calling you on, and then, late in November, after pressurizing yourself day by day, a few feet higher every hour, you are near the surface and still alive. You've got to go slow; if you surfaced all at once you'd explode. So it takes you all of three months to surface, and then a number of days to swim through the cold waters to the lighthouse. And there you are, out there, in the night, Johnny, the biggest monster in creation. And here's the lighthouse calling to you, with a long neck like your neck sticking way up out of the water, and a body like your body, and, most important of all, a

SCIENCE ▶▶ CONNECTION

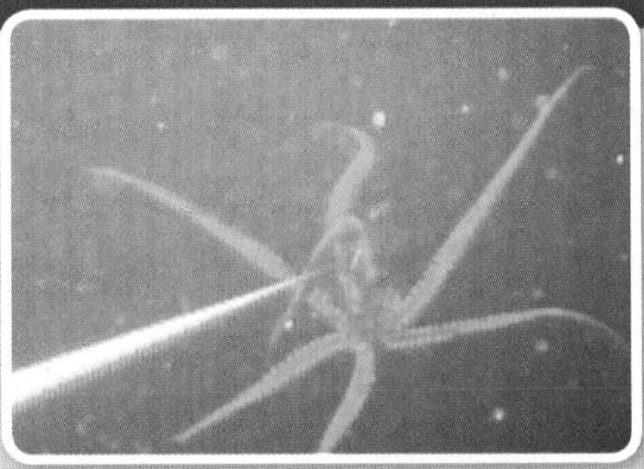

Sea Creatures Many ancient tales and legends describe gigantic sea creatures that rise up from the deep, capsizing ships and terrifying mariners. In September 2004, Japanese scientists snapped rare photographic images of a real-life gigantic deep-sea creature—the giant squid. This cephalopod, with a beaked head and long tentacles, is one of the world's largest animals, growing to forty-six feet long. Live giant squid have rarely been sighted in the wild. Knowing that sperm whales are predators of giant squid, researchers from the Ogasawara Whale Watching Association in Japan tracked sperm whales in the North Pacific Ocean and used a baited fishing line to attract the squid. As the squid's tentacles wrapped around the bait and became snagged on the hook, the scientists took more than five hundred photographs. When the squid escaped, it left behind a tentacle that measured eighteen feet long. How likely is it that other strange creatures may be living at the bottom of the sea, undiscovered by humans?

(Opposite page) ***The Loch Ness Monster,*** c. 1935. Gino d'Achille. Private collection.

voice like your voice. Do you understand now, Johnny, do you understand?"

The Fog Horn blew.

The monster answered.

I saw it all, I knew it all—the million years of waiting alone, for someone to come back who never came back. The million years of isolation at the bottom of the sea, the insanity of time there, while the skies cleared of reptile-birds, the swamps dried on the continental lands, the sloths and saber-tooths[4] had their day and sank in tar pits, and men ran like white ants upon the hills.

The Fog Horn blew.

"Last year," said McDunn, "that creature swam round and round, round and round, all night. Not coming too near, puzzled, I'd say. Afraid, maybe. And a bit angry after coming all this way. But the next day, unexpectedly, the fog lifted, the sun came out fresh, the sky was as blue as a painting. And the monster swam off away from the heat and the silence and didn't come back. I suppose it's been brooding on it for a year now, thinking it over from every which way."

The monster was only a hundred yards off now, it and the Fog Horn crying at each other. As the lights hit them, the monster's eyes were fire and ice, fire and ice.

"That's life for you," said McDunn. "Someone always waiting for someone who never comes home. Always someone loving some thing more than that thing loves them. And after a while you want to destroy whatever that thing is, so it can't hurt you no more."

The monster was rushing at the lighthouse.

The Fog Horn blew.

"Let's see what happens," said McDunn.

He switched the Fog Horn off.

The ensuing minute of silence was so intense that we could hear our hearts pounding in the glassed area of the tower, could hear the slow greased turn of the light.

The monster stopped and froze. Its great lantern eyes blinked. Its mouth gaped. It gave a sort of rumble, like a volcano. It twitched its head this way and that, as if to seek the sounds now dwindled off into the fog. It peered at the lighthouse. It rumbled again. Then its eyes caught fire. It reared up, threshed the water, and rushed at the tower, its eyes filled with angry torment.

"McDunn!" I cried. "Switch on the horn!"

McDunn fumbled with the switch. But even as he flicked it on, the monster was rearing up. I had a glimpse of its gigantic paws, fishskin glittering in webs between the finger-like projections, clawing at the tower. The huge eyes on the right side of its anguished head glittered before me like a

As the lights hit them, the monster's eyes were fire and ice, fire and ice.

4. **saber-tooths.** Prehistoric tigers with large teeth

brood (brüd) *v.*, dwell on a gloomy subject; worry

The monster gasped and cried. The tower was gone.

cauldron into which I might drop, screaming. The tower shook. The Fog Horn cried, the monster cried. It seized the tower and gnashed[5] at the glass, which shattered in upon us.

McDunn seized my arm. "Downstairs!"

The tower rocked, trembled, and started to give. The Fog Horn and the monster roared. We stumbled and half fell down the stairs. "Quick!"

We reached the bottom as the tower buckled down toward us. We ducked under the stairs into the small stone cellar. There were a thousand concussions as the rocks rained down. The Fog Horn stopped abruptly. The monster crashed upon the tower. The tower fell. We knelt together, McDunn and I, holding tight, while our world exploded.

Then it was over, and there was nothing but darkness and the wash of the sea on the raw stones.

That and the other sound.

"Listen," said McDunn quietly. "Listen."

We waited a moment. And then I began to hear it. First a great vacuumed sucking of air, and then the lament,[6] the bewilderment, the loneliness of the great monster, folded over and upon us, above us, so that the sickening reek of its body filled the air, a stone's thickness away from our cellar. The monster gasped and cried. The tower was gone. The light was gone. The thing that had called to it across a million years was gone. And the monster was opening its mouth and sending out great sounds. The sounds of a Fog Horn, again and again. And ships far at sea, not finding the light, not seeing anything, but passing and hearing late that night, must've thought: There it is, the lonely sound, the Lonesome Bay horn. All's well. We've rounded the cape.

And so it went for the rest of that night. The sun was hot and yellow the next afternoon when the rescuers came out to dig us from our stoned-under cellar.

"It fell apart, is all," said Mr. McDunn gravely. "We had a few bad knocks from the waves and it just crumbled." He pinched my arm.

There was nothing to see. The ocean was calm, the sky blue. The only thing was a great algaic[7] stink from the green matter that covered the fallen tower stones and the shore rocks. Flies buzzed about. The ocean washed empty on the shore.

The next year they built a new lighthouse, but by that time I had a job in the little town and a wife and a good small warm house that glowed yellow on autumn nights, the doors locked, the chimney puffing smoke. As for McDunn, he was master of the new lighthouse, built to his own specifications, out of steel-reinforced concrete. "Just in case," he said.

The new lighthouse was ready in November. I drove down alone one evening late and parked my car and looked across the

---

5. gnashed. Struck with the teeth

6. lament. Loud mourning; wailing

7. algaic. Made up of algae, or simple water organisms

gray waters and listened to the new horn sounding, once, twice, three, four times a minute far out there, by itself.

The monster?

It never came back.

"It's gone away," said McDunn. "It's gone back to the Deeps. It's learned you can't love anything too much in this world. It's gone into the deepest Deeps to wait another million years. Ah, the poor thing! Waiting out there, and waiting out there, while man comes and goes on this pitiful little planet. Waiting and waiting."

I sat in my car, listening. I couldn't see the lighthouse or the light standing out in Lonesome Bay. I could only hear the Horn, the Horn, the Horn. It sounded like the monster calling.

I sat there wishing there was something I could say.

The sea creature in "The Foghorn" waited thousands of years in hopes of seeing others of its kind. How long would you be willing to wait for something you really wanted? When might it be best to abandon a goal?

Find Meaning

1. (a) Where do the narrator and McDunn work? (b) Why do you think the narrator says he is thankful that McDunn is so talkative?

2. (a) As the creature comes into view, how does McDunn answer Johnny's exclamation, "It's impossible"? (b) What does McDunn mean by his response?

3. (a) What does the sea creature do to the foghorn and the lighthouse? (b) What do you think causes the sea creature to react in this way?

Make Judgments

4. (a) What words would you use to describe the character of McDunn? (b) Why do you think the author chose to have McDunn tell the story about the night that all the fish of the sea surfaced?

5. (a) What attitude does McDunn have toward the sea creature? (b) What might explain this attitude?

6. (a) What are some examples of the author's use of repetition in the story? (b) What effect does each example create?

INFORMATIONAL TEXT ▶▶ CONNECTION

In "The Foghorn," an ancient sea creature has existed for centuries in the ocean, unknown to the humans who now populate the earth and try to penetrate the ocean's mysteries. The aqualung, which is described in the following selection from **David Macaulay's** book, *The New Way Things Work,* was developed as a tool to help scientists explore the underwater world and learn about the creatures that live there. Before you read "The Aqualung," preview the title and the diagram. What do you expect to learn from reading this selection?

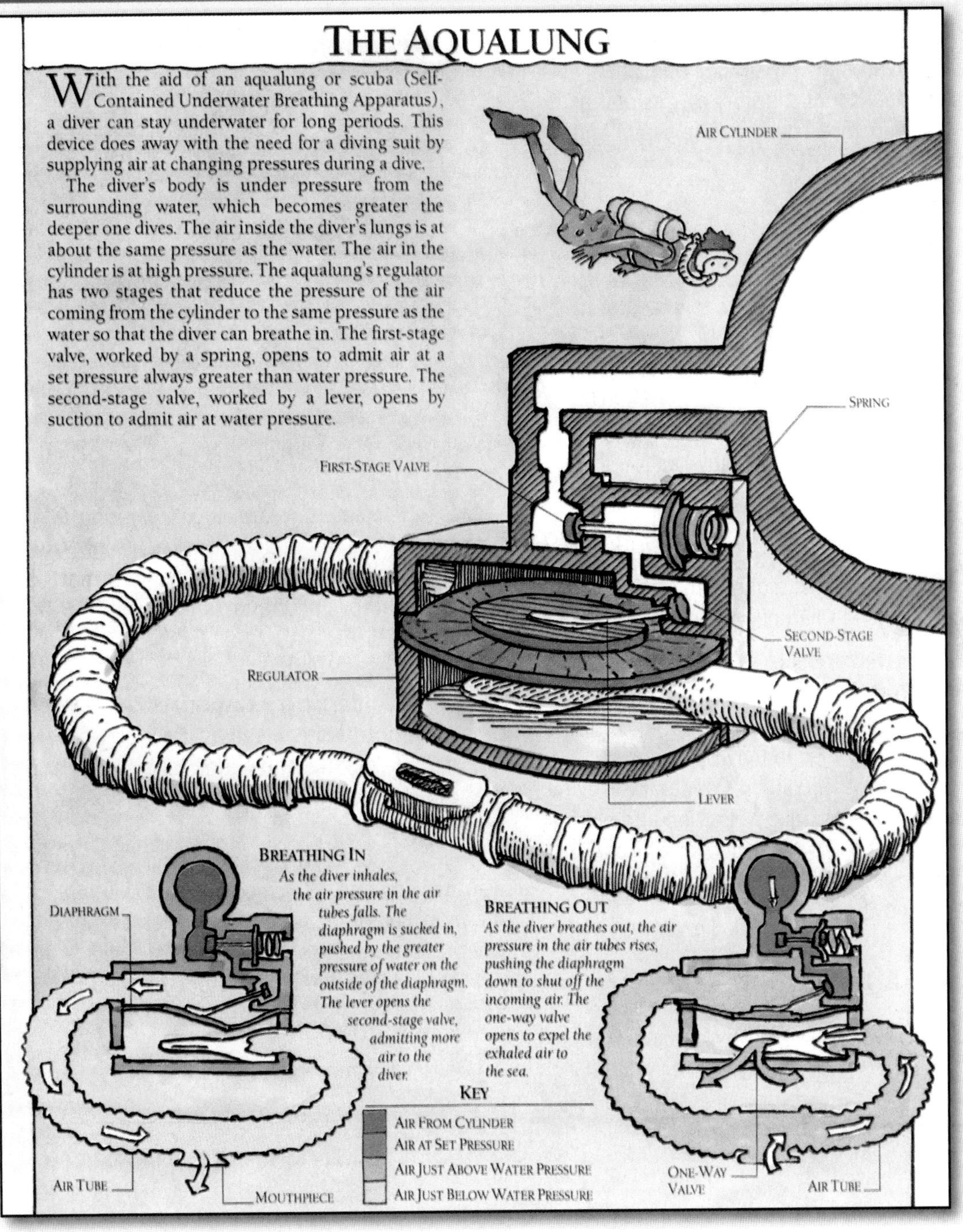

THE AQUALUNG

With the aid of an aqualung or scuba (Self-Contained Underwater Breathing Apparatus), a diver can stay underwater for long periods. This device does away with the need for a diving suit by supplying air at changing pressures during a dive.

The diver's body is under pressure from the surrounding water, which becomes greater the deeper one dives. The air inside the diver's lungs is at about the same pressure as the water. The air in the cylinder is at high pressure. The aqualung's regulator has two stages that reduce the pressure of the air coming from the cylinder to the same pressure as the water so that the diver can breathe in. The first-stage valve, worked by a spring, opens to admit air at a set pressure always greater than water pressure. The second-stage valve, worked by a lever, opens by suction to admit air at water pressure.

TEXT TO TEXT CONNECTION

In "The Foghorn," McDunn imagines what life must be like at the bottom of the ocean. He says, "For all our engines and so-called submarines, it'll be ten thousand centuries before we set foot on the real bottom of the sunken lands...." After reading "The Aqualung," do you agree with McDunn? Why or why not?

AFTER READING

Analyze Literature

Mood Use a cluster chart to organize the words and details that created emotional responses for you as you read the story. Think about the various emotions that the story evokes and in one or two sentences, describe the overall mood of the story.

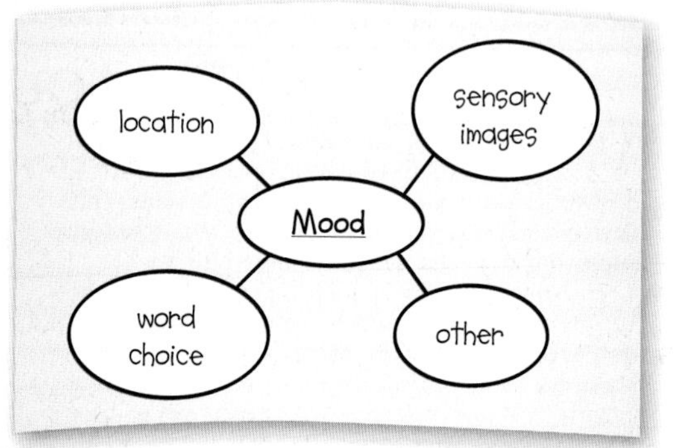

Extend Understanding

Writing Options

Creative Writing Since Johnny has found a job in the town, McDunn needs a new assistant lighthouse keeper. Write a **job description** for the position. Remember that you want to attract applicants who will get along with McDunn and who will not mind the lonely location.

Argumentative Writing How reliable is Johnny's version of what happened? In one column of a two-column chart, list details from the story showing that Johnny is a reliable narrator; in the other column, list details showing that he is unreliable. Take a position and write a short **paragraph** in which you explain to a group of researchers why they should or should not try to find the sea creature.

Collaborative Learning

Re-create a Scene In small groups, review "The Foghorn" and discuss the descriptions in the story. As a group, choose one of the author's scenes to re-create in a drawing, a painting, a stage scene, or an audio recording. Think about the sights, sounds, and sensations that make the author's descriptions effective.

Media Literacy

Research Underwater Creatures A number of legendary creatures, such as the Loch Ness Monster, are reportedly living in lakes, rivers, and seas around the world. Use the Internet to research these creatures. Keep a log with information about each creature and the websites you visit. Which creature do you find the most believable? Why? Finally, assess whether the websites you viewed used the correct level of formality and tone on their pages and explain how they might improve.

Go to **www.mirrorsandwindows.com** for more.

Comparing Texts

Rikki-Tikki-Tavi

A Short Story by Rudyard Kipling

The Green Mamba

An Autobiography by Roald Dahl

BEFORE READING

Build Background

Scientific Context Both Rudyard Kipling's "Rikki-tikki-tavi" and Roald Dahl's "The Green Mamba" present encounters with dangerous snakes. Of the more than 2,700 species of snakes on Earth, about 375 are poisonous, including the green mamba, the cobra, and the krait.

Reader's Context Who is the most courageous person you've ever met? What do you think made that person so brave?

Set Purpose

Look at the illustrations on page 93 and page 103. What different feelings do you get from each image? As you read the story and autobiography, note how each work deals with the different feelings aroused by the presence of danger.

Compare Literature: Personification

Personification is a figure of speech in which something not human, such as an animal, object, or idea, is described as if it were human. To understand the technique of personification, use a chart to record the different characteristics given to the snakes in each work.

"Rikki-tikki-tavi"	"The Green Mamba"
Nag—wicked, cold-hearted, able to speak	

Meet the Authors

Rudyard Kipling (1865–1936) was born in India and cared for by a native nurse, who told him Indian legends. "Rikki-tikki-tavi" is a story in one of his most popular works, *The Jungle Book*.

Roald Dahl (1916–1990) lived a life of adventure before becoming a writer. His first job involved traveling across what was then the British colony of Tanganyika and is today the independent country of Tanzania. During World War II, he was a fighter pilot with the Royal Air Force until injuries forced him to take a desk job.

Preview Vocabulary

cul•ti•vat•ed (kʉl´ tə vāt' əd) *adj.*, prepared for growing plants

cow•er (kaů´ [ə]r) *v.*, shrink and tremble as from anger, threats, or blows

prov•i•dence (präv ´ əd əns) *n.*, valuable gift; godsend

for•lorn (fər lôrn´) *adj.*, sad; lonely; hopeless

ma•nip•u•late (mə nip´ yə lāt) *v.*, treat or operate with the hands in a skillful manner

Rikki-Tikki-Tavi, 1937. Andre Collot. Bibliotheque Nationale, Paris.

Rikki-Tikki-Tavi

A Short Story by Rudyard Kipling

This is the story of the great war that Rikki-tikki-tavi fought single-handed, through the bathrooms of the big bungalow in Segowlee cantonment.[1] Darzee, the tailorbird, helped him, and Chuchundra, the muskrat, who never comes out into the middle of the floor but always creeps round by the wall, gave him advice; but Rikki-tikki did the real fighting.

He was a mongoose, rather like a little cat in his fur and his tail but quite like a weasel in his head and his habits. His eyes and the end of his restless nose were pink; he could

1. **Segowlee cantonment.** Living quarters for British troops in the town of Segowlee in India

scratch himself anywhere he pleased with any leg, front or back, that he chose to use; he could fluff up his tail till it looked like a bottlebrush, and his war cry as he scuttled through the long grass was *Rikk-tikk-tikki-tikki-tchk!*

One day, a high summer flood washed him out of the burrow where he lived with his father and mother and carried him, kicking and clucking, down a roadside ditch. He found a little wisp of grass floating there and clung to it till he lost his senses. When he revived, he was lying in the hot sun in the middle of a garden path, very draggled indeed, and a small boy was saying: "Here's a dead mongoose. Let's have a funeral."

It is the hardest thing in the world to frighten a mongoose....

"No," said his mother; "let's take him in and dry him. Perhaps he isn't really dead."

They took him into the house, and a big man picked him up between his finger and thumb and said he was not dead but half choked; so they wrapped him in cotton wool and warmed him over a little fire, and he opened his eyes and sneezed.

"Now," said the big man (he was an Englishman who had just moved into the bungalow), "don't frighten him, and we'll see what he'll do."

It is the hardest thing in the world to frighten a mongoose, because he is eaten up from nose to tail with curiosity. The motto of all the mongoose family is "Run and find out," and Rikki-tikki was a true mongoose. He looked at the cotton wool, decided that it was not good to eat, ran all round the table, sat up and put his fur in order, scratched himself, and jumped on the small boy's shoulder.

"Don't be frightened, Teddy," said his father. "That's his way of making friends."

"Ouch! He's tickling under my chin," said Teddy.

Rikki-tikki looked down between the boy's collar and neck, snuffed at his ear, and climbed down to the floor, where he sat rubbing his nose.

"Good gracious," said Teddy's mother, "and that's a wild creature! I suppose he's so tame because we've been kind to him."

"All mongooses are like that," said her husband. "If Teddy doesn't pick him up by the tail or try to put him in a cage, he'll run in and out of the house all day long. Let's give him something to eat."

They gave him a little piece of raw meat. Rikki-tikki liked it immensely, and when it was finished, he went out into the veranda and sat in the sunshine and fluffed up his fur to make it dry to the roots. Then he felt better.

"There are more things to find out about in this house," he said to himself, "than all my family could find out in all their lives. I shall certainly stay and find out."

He spent all that day roaming over the house. He nearly drowned himself in the bathtubs, put his nose into the ink on a writing table, and burnt it on the end of the big man's cigar, for he climbed up in the big man's lap to see how writing was done. At nightfall he ran into Teddy's nursery to watch how kerosene lamps were lighted, and when Teddy went to bed, Rikki-tikki climbed up too; but he was a restless companion, because he had to get up and attend to every noise all through the night and find out what made it. Teddy's mother and father came in, the last thing, to look at their boy, and Rikki-tikki was awake on the pillow. "I don't like that," said Teddy's mother; "he may bite the child." "He'll do no such thing," said the father. "Teddy's safer with that little beast than if he had a bloodhound to watch him. If a snake came into the nursery now—"

But Teddy's mother wouldn't think of anything so awful.

Early in the morning, Rikki-tikki came to early breakfast in the veranda riding on Teddy's shoulder, and they gave him banana and some boiled egg; and he sat on all their laps one after the other, because every well-brought-up mongoose always hopes to be a house mongoose someday and have rooms to run about in; and Rikki-tikki's mother (she used to live in the General's house at Segowlee) had carefully told Rikki what to do if ever he came across white men.

"Be careful. I am Death!"

Then Rikki-tikki went out into the garden to see what was to be seen. It was a large garden, only half cultivated, with bushes, as big as summer houses, of Marshal Niel roses; lime and orange trees; clumps of bamboos; and thickets of high grass. Rikki-tikki licked his lips. "This is a splendid hunting ground," he said, and his tail grew bottlebrushy at the thought of it, and he scuttled up and down the garden, snuffing here and there till he heard very sorrowful voices in a thorn bush.

It was Darzee, the tailorbird, and his wife. They had made a beautiful nest by pulling two big leaves together and stitching them up the edges with fibers and had filled the hollow with cotton and downy fluff. The nest swayed to and fro as they sat on the rim and cried.

"What is the matter?" asked Rikki-tikki.

"We are very miserable," said Darzee. "One of our babies fell out of the nest yesterday and Nag ate him."

"H'm!" said Rikki-tikki, "that is very sad—but I am a stranger here. Who is Nag?"

Darzee and his wife only cowered down in the nest without answering, for from the thick grass at the foot of the bush there came a low hiss—a horrid, cold sound that made Rikki-tikki jump back two clear feet. Then inch by inch out of the grass rose up the head and spread hood of Nag, the big black cobra, and he was five feet long from tongue to tail. When he had lifted one third of himself clear of the ground, he stayed balancing to and fro exactly as a dandelion tuft balances in the wind, and he looked at Rikki-tikki with the wicked snake's eyes that never change their expression, whatever the snake may be thinking of.

"Who is Nag?" said he. "*I* am Nag. The great God Brahm[2] put his mark upon all our people, when the first cobra spread his hood to keep the sun off Brahm as he slept. Look, and be afraid!"

He spread out his hood more than ever, and Rikki-tikki saw the spectacle mark on the back of it that looks exactly like the eye part of a hook-and-eye fastening. He was afraid for the minute; but it is impossible for a mongoose to stay frightened for any length of time, and though Rikki-tikki had never met a live cobra before, his mother had fed him on dead ones, and he knew that all a grown mongoose's business in life was to fight and eat snakes. Nag knew that too, and

---

2. **Brahm.** Short for *Brahma,* the creator of the universe according to Hindu religion

cul•ti•vat•ed (kʉl´ tə vāt' id) *adj.,* prepared for growing plants

cow•er (kaů´ [ə]r) *v.,* shrink and tremble as from anger, threats, or blows

at the bottom of his cold heart, he was afraid.

"Well," said Rikki-tikki, and his tail began to fluff up again, "marks or no marks, do you think it is right for you to eat fledglings out of a nest?"

Nag was thinking to himself and watching the least little movement in the grass behind Rikki-tikki. He knew that mongooses in the garden meant death sooner or later for him and his family, but he wanted to get Rikki-tikki off his guard. So he dropped his head a little and put it on one side.

"Let us talk," he said. "You eat eggs. Why should not I eat birds?"

"Behind you! Look behind you!" sang Darzee.

Rikki-tikki knew better than to waste time in staring. He jumped up in the air as high as he could go, and just under him whizzed by the head of Nagaina, Nag's wicked wife. She had crept up behind him as he was talking, to make an end of him; and he heard her savage hiss as the stroke missed. He came down almost across her back, and if he had been an old mongoose, he would have known that then was the time to break her back with one bite; but he was afraid of the terrible lashing return stroke of the cobra. He bit, indeed, but did not bite long enough, and he jumped clear of the whisking tail, leaving Nagaina torn and angry.

"Wicked, wicked Darzee!" said Nag, lashing up as high as he could reach toward the nest in the thorn bush; but Darzee had built it out of reach of snakes, and it only swayed to and fro.

Rikki-tikki felt his eyes growing red and hot (when a mongoose's eyes grow red, he is angry), and he sat back on his tail and hind legs like a little kangaroo, and looked all round him, and chattered with rage. But Nag and Nagaina had disappeared into the grass. When a snake misses its stroke, it never says anything or gives any sign of what it means to do next. Rikki-tikki did not care to follow them, for he did not feel sure that he could manage two snakes at once. So he trotted off to the gravel path near the house and sat down to think. It was a serious matter for him. If you read the old books of natural history, you will find they say that when the mongoose fights the snake and happens to get bitten, he runs off and eats some herb that cures him. That is not true. The victory is only a matter of quickness of eye and quickness of foot—snake's blow against the mongoose's jump—and as no eye can follow the motion of a snake's head when it strikes, this makes things much more wonderful than any magic herb. Rikki-tikki knew he was a young mongoose, and it made him all the more pleased to think that he had managed to escape a blow from behind. It gave him confidence in himself, and when Teddy came running down the path, Rikki-tikki was ready to be petted. But just as Teddy was stooping, something wriggled a little in the dust and a tiny voice said: "Be careful. I am Death!" It was Karait, the dusty brown snakeling that lies for choice on the dusty earth; and his bite is as dangerous as the cobra's. But he is so small that nobody thinks of him, and so he does the more harm to people.

Rikki-tikki's eyes grew red again, and he danced up to Karait with the peculiar rocking, swaying motion that he had inherited from his family. It looks very funny, but it is so perfectly balanced a gait that you can fly off from it at any angle you please; and in dealing with snakes this is an advantage. If Rikki-tikki had only known, he was doing a much more dangerous thing than fighting Nag, for Karait is so small and can turn so quickly that unless Rikki bit him close to the back of the head, he would get the return stroke in his eye or his lip. But Rikki did not know; his eyes were all red, and he rocked back and forth, looking for a good place to hold. Karait struck out, Rikki jumped sideways and tried to run in, but the wicked little dusty gray head lashed within a fraction of his shoulder, and he had to jump over the body, and the head followed his heels close.

Teddy shouted to the house: "Oh, look here! Our mongoose is killing a snake," and Rikki-tikki heard a scream from Teddy's mother. His father ran out with a stick, but by the time he came up, Karait had lunged out once too far, and Rikki-tikki had sprung, jumped on the snake's back, dropped his head far between his forelegs, bitten as high up the back as he could get hold, and rolled away. That bite paralyzed Karait, and Rikki-tikki was just going to eat him up from the tail, after the custom of his family at dinner, when he remembered that a full meal makes a slow mongoose, and if he wanted all his strength and quickness ready, he must keep himself thin. He went away for a dust bath under the castor-oil bushes, while Teddy's father beat the dead Karait. "What is the use of that?" thought Rikki-tikki; "I have settled it all"; and then Teddy's mother picked him up from the dust and hugged him, crying that he had saved Teddy from death, and Teddy's father said that he was a providence, and Teddy looked on with big, scared eyes. Rikki-tikki was rather amused at all the fuss, which, of course, he did not understand. Teddy's mother might just as well have petted Teddy for playing in the dust. Rikki was thoroughly enjoying himself.

That night at dinner, walking to and fro among the wineglasses on the table, he might have stuffed himself three times over with nice things; but he remembered Nag and Nagaina, and though it was very pleasant to be patted and petted by Teddy's mother and to sit on Teddy's shoulder, his eyes would get red from time to time, and he would go off into his long war cry of *Rikk-tikk-tikki-tikki-tchk!*

Teddy carried him off to bed and insisted on Rikki-tikki's sleeping under his chin. Rikki-tikki was too well bred to bite or scratch, but as soon as Teddy was asleep, he went off for his nightly walk round the house, and in the dark he ran up against Chuchundra, the muskrat, creeping round by the wall. Chuchundra is a brokenhearted little beast. He whimpers and cheeps all night, trying to make up his mind to run into the middle of the room; but he never gets there.

"Don't kill me," said Chuchundra, almost weeping. "Rikki-tikki, don't kill me!"

"Do you think a snake killer kills muskrats?" said Rikki-tikki scornfully.

"Those who kill snakes get killed by snakes," said Chuchundra, more sorrowfully than ever. "And how am I to be sure that Nag won't mistake me for you some dark night?"

"There's not the least danger," said Rikki-tikki, "but Nag is in the garden, and I know you don't go there."

prov•i•dence (präv´ əd əns) *n.*, valuable gift; godsend

"My cousin Chua, the rat, told me—" said Chuchundra, and then he stopped.

"Told you what?"

"H'sh! Nag is everywhere, Rikki-tikki. You should have talked to Chua in the garden."

"I didn't—so you must tell me. Quick, Chuchundra, or I'll bite you!"

Chuchundra sat down and cried till the tears rolled off his whiskers. "I am a very poor man," he sobbed. "I never had spirit enough to run out into the middle of the room. H'sh! I mustn't tell you anything. Can't you *hear*, Rikki-tikki?"

Rikki-tikki listened. The house was as still as still, but he thought he could just catch the faintest *scratch-scratch* in the world—a noise as faint as that of a wasp walking on a windowpane—the dry scratch of a snake's scales on brickwork.

"Those who kill snakes get killed by snakes...."

"That's Nag or Nagaina," he said to himself, "and he is crawling into the bathroom sluice.[3] You're right, Chuchundra; I should have talked to Chua."

He stole off to Teddy's bathroom, but there was nothing there, and then to Teddy's mother's bathroom. At the bottom of the smooth plaster wall there was a brick pulled out to make a sluice for the bathwater, and as Rikki-tikki stole in by the masonry curb where the bath is put, he heard Nag and Nagaina whispering together outside in the moonlight.

"When the house is emptied of people," said Nagaina to her husband, "*he* will have to go away, and then the garden will be our own again. Go in quietly, and remember that the big man who killed Karait is the first one to bite. Then come out and tell me, and we will hunt for Rikki-tikki together."

"But are you sure that there is anything to be gained by killing the people?" said Nag.

"Everything. When there were no people in the bungalow, did we have any mongoose in the garden? So long as the bungalow is empty, we are king and queen of the garden; and remember that as soon as our eggs in the melon bed hatch (as they may tomorrow), our children will need room and quiet."

"I had not thought of that," said Nag. "I will go, but there is no need that we should hunt for Rikki-tikki afterward. I will kill the big man and his wife, and the child if I can, and come away quietly. Then the bungalow will be empty, and Rikki-tikki will go."

Rikki-tikki tingled all over with rage and hatred at this, and then Nag's head came through the sluice, and his five feet of cold body followed it. Angry as he was, Rikki-tikki was very frightened as he saw the size of the big cobra. Nag coiled himself up, raised his head, and looked into the bathroom in the dark, and Rikki could see his eyes glitter.

"Now, if I kill him here, Nagaina will know; and if I fight him on the open floor, the odds are in his favor. What am I to do?" said Rikki-tikki-tavi.

Nag waved to and fro, and then Rikki-tikki heard him drinking from the biggest water jar that was used to fill the bath. "That is good," said the snake. "Now, when Karait was killed, the big man had a stick. He may have that stick still, but when he comes in to bathe in the morning, he will not have a stick. I shall wait here till he comes. Nagaina—do you hear me?—I shall wait here in the cool till daytime."

---

3. sluice. Valve through which water is run

There was no answer from outside, so Rikki-tikki knew Nagaina had gone away. Nag coiled himself down, coil by coil, round the bulge at the bottom of the water jar, and Rikki-tikki stayed still as death. After an hour he began to move, muscle by muscle, toward the jar. Nag was asleep, and Rikki-tikki looked at his big back, wondering which would be the best place for a good hold. "If I don't break his back at the first jump," said Rikki, "he can still fight; and if he fights—O Rikki!" He looked at the thickness of the neck below the hood, but that was too much for him; and a bite near the tail would only make Nag savage.

"It must be the head," he said at last, "the head above the hood; and when I am once there, I must not let go."

...a hot wind knocked him senseless and red fire singed his fur.

Then he jumped. The head was lying a little clear of the water jar, under the curve of it; and as his teeth met, Rikki braced his back against the bulge of the red earthenware to hold down the head. This gave him just one second's purchase,[4] and he made the most of it. Then he was battered to and fro as a rat is shaken by a dog—to and fro on the floor, up and down, and round in great circles, but his eyes were red and he held on as the body cartwhipped over the floor, upsetting the tin dipper and the soap dish and the flesh brush, and banged against the tin side of the bath. As he held, he closed his jaws tighter and tighter, for he made sure he would be banged to death, and for the honor of his family, he preferred to be found with his teeth locked. He was dizzy, aching, and felt shaken to pieces, when something went off like a thunderclap just behind him; a hot wind knocked him senseless and red fire singed his fur. The big man had been wakened by the noise and had fired both barrels of a shotgun into Nag just behind the hood.

Rikki-tikki held on with his eyes shut, for now he was quite sure he was dead; but the head did not move, and the big man picked him up and said: "It's the mongoose again, Alice; the little chap has saved *our* lives now." Then Teddy's mother came in with a very white face and saw what was left of Nag, and Rikki-tikki dragged himself to Teddy's bedroom and spent half the rest of the night shaking himself tenderly to find out whether he really was broken into forty pieces, as he fancied.

When morning came, he was very stiff but well pleased with his doings. "Now I have Nagaina to settle with, and she will be worse than five Nags, and there's no knowing when the eggs she spoke of will hatch. Goodness! I must go and see Darzee," he said.

Without waiting for breakfast, Rikki-tikki ran to the thorn bush, where Darzee was singing a song of triumph at the top of his voice. The news of Nag's death was all over the garden, for the sweeper had thrown the body on the rubbish heap.

"Oh, you stupid tuft of feathers!" said Rikki-tikki angrily. "Is this the time to sing?"

"Nag is dead—is dead—is dead!" sang Darzee. "The valiant Rikki-tikki caught him by the head and held fast. The big man brought the bang-stick, and Nag fell in two pieces! He will never eat my babies again."

"All that's true enough, but where's

---

4. purchase. Firm hold

(Opposite page) ***Rikki-Tikki-Tavi*** (illustration), 1937. Louis Joseph Soulas. Bibliotheque Nationale, Paris.

Nagaina?" said Rikki-tikki, looking carefully round him.

"Nagaina came to the bathroom sluice and called for Nag," Darzee went on; "and Nag came out on the end of a stick—the sweeper picked him up on the end of a stick and threw him upon the rubbish heap. Let us sing about the great, the red-eyed Rikki-tikki!" and Darzee filled his throat and sang.

"If I could get up to your nest, I'd roll your babies out!" said Rikki-tikki. "You don't know when to do the right thing at the right time. You're safe enough in your nest there, but it's war for me down here. Stop singing a minute, Darzee."

"For the great, beautiful Rikki-tikki's sake I will stop," said Darzee. "What is it, O Killer of the terrible Nag?"

"Where is Nagaina, for the third time?"

"On the rubbish heap by the stables, mourning for Nag. Great is Rikki-tikki with the white teeth."

"Bother my white teeth! Have you ever heard where she keeps her eggs?"

"In the melon bed, on the end nearest the wall, where the sun strikes nearly all day. She hid them there weeks ago."

"And you never thought it worthwhile to tell me? The end nearest the wall, you said?"

"Rikki-tikki, you are not going to eat her eggs?"

"Not eat exactly; no. Darzee, if you have a grain of sense, you will fly off to the stables and pretend that your wing is broken and let Nagaina chase you away to the bush. I must get to the melon bed, and if I went there now, she'd see me."

Darzee was a featherbrained little fellow who could never hold more than one idea at a time in his head, and just because he knew that Nagaina's children were born in eggs like his own, he didn't think at first that it was fair to kill them. But his wife was a sensible bird, and she knew that cobra's eggs meant young cobras later on; so she flew off from the nest and left Darzee to keep the babies warm and continue his song about the death of Nag. Darzee was very like a man in some ways.

She fluttered in front of Nagaina by the rubbish heap and cried out, "Oh, my wing is broken! The boy in the house threw a stone at me and broke it." Then she fluttered more desperately than ever.

Nagaina lifted up her head and hissed, "You warned Rikki-tikki when I would have killed him. Indeed and truly, you've chosen a bad place to be lame in." And she moved toward Darzee's wife, slipping along over the dust.

"The boy broke it with a stone!" shrieked Darzee's wife.

"Well! It may be some consolation to you when you're dead to know that I shall settle accounts with the boy. My husband lies on the rubbish heap this morning, but before night the boy in the house will lie very still. What is the use of running away? I am sure to catch you. Little fool, look at me!"

Darzee's wife knew better than to do *that*, for a bird who looks at a snake's eyes gets so frightened that she cannot move. Darzee's wife fluttered on, piping sorrowfully and never leaving the ground, and Nagaina quickened her pace.

Rikki-tikki heard them going up the path from the stables, and he raced for the end of the melon patch near the wall. There, in the warm litter above the melons, very cunningly hidden, he found twenty-five eggs about the size of a bantam's eggs but with whitish skins instead of shells.

"I was not a day too soon," he said, for he could see the baby cobras curled up inside the skin, and he knew that the minute they were hatched, they could each kill a man or a mongoose. He bit off the tops of the eggs as

fast as he could, taking care to crush the young cobras, and turned over the litter from time to time to see whether he had missed any. At last there were only three eggs left, and Rikki-tikki began to chuckle to himself, when he heard Darzee's wife screaming:

"Rikki-tikki, I led Nagaina toward the house, and she has gone into the veranda, and—oh, come quickly—she means killing!"

Rikki-tikki smashed two eggs, and tumbled backward down the melon bed with the third egg in his mouth, and scuttled to the veranda as hard as he could put foot to the ground. Teddy and his mother and father were there at early breakfast, but Rikki-tikki saw that they were not eating anything. They sat stone still, and their faces were white. Nagaina was coiled up on the matting by Teddy's chair, within easy striking distance of Teddy's bare leg, and she was swaying to and fro, singing a song of triumph.

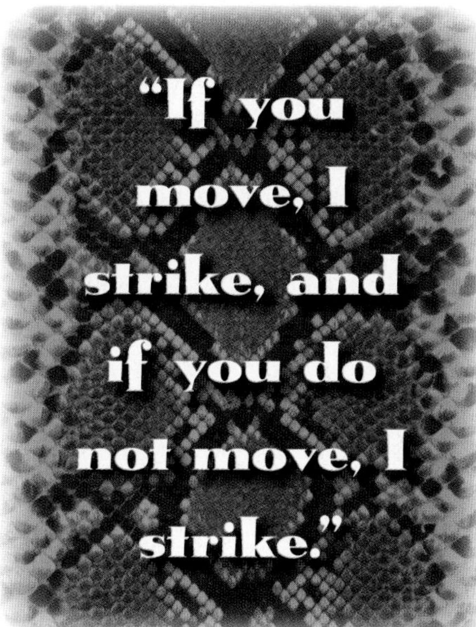

"Son of the big man that killed Nag," she hissed, "stay still. I am not ready yet. Wait a little. Keep very still, all you three! If you move, I strike, and if you do not move, I strike. Oh, foolish people, who killed my Nag!"

Teddy's eyes were fixed on his father, and all his father could do was to whisper, "Sit still, Teddy. You mustn't move. Teddy, keep still."

Then Rikki-tikki came up and cried: "Turn round, Nagaina; turn and fight!"

"All in good time," said she, without moving her eyes. "I will settle my account with *you* presently. Look at your friends, Rikki-tikki. They are still and white. They are afraid. They dare not move, and if you come a step nearer, I strike."

"Look at your eggs," said Rikki-tikki, "in the melon bed near the wall. Go and look, Nagaina!"

The big snake turned half round and saw the egg on the veranda. "Ah-h! Give it to me," she said.

Rikki-tikki put his paws one on each side of the egg, and his eyes were blood-red. "What price for a snake's egg? For a young cobra? For a young king cobra? For the last—the very last of the brood? The ants are eating all the others down by the melon bed."

Nagaina spun clear round, forgetting everything for the sake of the one egg; and Rikki-tikki saw Teddy's father shoot out a big hand, catch Teddy by the shoulder, and drag him across the little table with the teacups, safe and out of reach of Nagaina.

"Tricked! Tricked! Tricked! *Rikk-tck-tck!*" chuckled Rikki-tikki. "The boy is safe, and it was I—I—I that caught Nag by the hood last night in the bathroom." Then he began to jump up and down, all four feet together, his head close to the floor. "He threw me to and fro, but he could not shake me off. He was dead before the big man blew him in two. I did it! *Rikki-tikki-tck-tck!* Come then, Nagaina. Come and fight with me. You shall not be a widow long."

Nagaina saw that she had lost her chance of killing Teddy, and the egg lay between Rikki-tikki's paws. "Give me the egg, Rikki-tikki. Give me the last of my eggs, and I will go away and never come back," she said, lowering her hood.

"Yes, you will go away, and you will never come back; for you will go to the rubbish heap with Nag. Fight, widow! The big man has gone for his gun! Fight!"

Rikki-tikki was bounding all round Nagaina, keeping just out of reach of her stroke, his little eyes like hot coals. Nagaina gathered herself together and flung out at him. Rikki-tikki jumped up and backwards. Again and again and again she struck, and each time her head came with a whack on the matting of the veranda and she gathered herself together like a watch spring. Then Rikki-tikki danced in a circle to get behind her, and Nagaina spun round to keep her head to his head, so that the rustle of her tail on the matting sounded like dry leaves blown along by the wind.

He had forgotten the egg. It still lay on the veranda, and Nagaina came nearer and nearer to it, till at last, while Rikki-tikki was drawing breath, she caught it in her mouth, turned to the veranda steps, and flew like an arrow down the path, with Rikki-tikki behind her. When the cobra runs for her life, she goes like a whiplash flicked across a horse's neck. Rikki-tikki knew that he must catch her or all the trouble would begin again. She headed straight for the long grass by the thorn bush, and as he was running, Rikki-tikki heard Darzee still singing his foolish little song of triumph. But Darzee's wife was wiser. She flew off her nest as Nagaina came along and flapped her wings about Nagaina's head. If Darzee had helped, they might have turned her, but Nagaina only lowered her hood and went on. Still, the instant's delay brought Rikki-tikki up to her, and as she plunged into the rat hole where she and Nag used to live, his little white teeth were clenched on her tail and he went down with her—and very few mongooses, however wise and old they may be, care to follow a cobra into its hole. It was dark in the hole, and Rikki-tikki never knew when it might open out and give Nagaina room to turn and strike at him. He held on savagely and stuck out his feet to act as brakes on the dark slope of the hot, moist earth. Then the grass by the mouth of the hole stopped waving, and Darzee said: "It is all over with Rikki-tikki! We must sing his death song. Valiant Rikki-tikki is dead! For Nagaina will surely kill him underground."

So he sang a very mournful song that he made up on the spur of the minute, and just as he got to the most touching part, the grass quivered again, and Rikki-tikki, covered with dirt, dragged himself out of the hole leg by leg, licking his whiskers. Darzee stopped with a little shout. Rikki-tikki shook some of the dust out of his fur and sneezed. "It is all over," he said. "The widow will never come out again." And the red ants that live between the grass stems heard him and began to troop down one after another to see if he had spoken the truth.

Rikki-tikki curled himself up in the grass and slept where he was—slept and slept till it was late in the afternoon, for he had done a hard day's work.

"Now," he said, when he awoke, "I will go back to the house. Tell the Coppersmith, Darzee, and he will tell the garden that Nagaina is dead."

The Coppersmith is a bird who makes a noise exactly like the beating of a little hammer on a copper pot, and the reason he is always making it is because he is the town crier to every Indian garden and tells all the news to everybody who cares to listen. As Rikki-tikki went up the path, he heard his "attention" notes like a tiny dinner gong and then the steady "*Ding-dong-tock!* Nag is *dead—dong!* Nagaina is dead! Ding-dong-tock!" That set all the birds in the garden

singing and the frogs croaking, for Nag and Nagaina used to eat frogs as well as little birds.

When Rikki got to the house, Teddy and Teddy's mother (she looked very white still, for she had been fainting) and Teddy's father came out and almost cried over him; and that night he ate all that was given him till he could eat no more and went to bed on Teddy's shoulder, where Teddy's mother saw him when she came to look late at night.

> **"Just think, he saved all our lives."**

"He saved our lives and Teddy's life," she said to her husband. "Just think, he saved all our lives."

Rikki-tikki woke up with a jump, for the mongooses are light sleepers.

"Oh, it's you," he said. "What are you bothering for? All the cobras are dead; and if they weren't, I'm here."

Rikki-tikki had a right to be proud of himself, but he did not grow too proud, and he kept that garden as a mongoose should keep it, with tooth and jump and spring and bite, till never a cobra dared show its head inside the walls. ✣

Is Rikki-tikki-tavi "brave" in killing the snakes, or is he just doing what a mongoose does? Is courage more like an instinct we are born with or like a habit we can learn?

Find Meaning

1. (a) In "Rikki-tikki-tavi," what is the motto of the mongoose family? (b) What does this motto tell you about Rikki-tikki?
2. (a) What is the plan Nag and Nagaina come up with to regain the garden as their territory? (b) Why would the plan get rid of Rikki-tikki?

Make Judgments

3. (a) What different battles does Rikki-tikki fight? (b) In your opinion, in which of these battles does the mongoose show the greatest courage? Explain your answer.
4. (a) How do animals and people respond to Rikki-tikki? (b) How do these responses help shape the character of the mongoose?

The Green Mamba

An Autobiography by Roald Dahl

Oh, those snakes! How I hated them! They were the only fearful thing about Tanganyika, and a newcomer very quickly learned to identify most of them and to know which were deadly and which were simply poisonous. The killers, apart from the black mambas, were the green mambas, the cobras and the tiny little puff adders that looked very much like small sticks lying motionless in the middle of a dusty path, and so easy to step on.

> "There's a green mamba in your living room!"

One Sunday evening I was invited to go and have a sundowner[1] at the house of an Englishman called Fuller who worked in the Customs office[2] in Dar es Salaam. He lived with his wife and two small children in a plain white wooden house that stood alone some way back from the road in a rough grassy piece of ground with coconut trees scattered about. I was walking across the grass toward the house and was about twenty yards away when I saw a large green snake go gliding straight up the veranda[3] steps of Fuller's house and in through the open front door. The brilliant yellowy-green skin and its great size made me certain it was a green mamba, a creature almost as deadly as the black mamba, and for a few seconds I was so startled and dumbfounded and horrified that I froze to the spot. Then I pulled myself together and ran round to the back of the house shouting, "Mr. Fuller! Mr. Fuller!"

1. **sundowner.** Evening refreshment
2. **Customs office.** Government agency that controls taxes on imports and exports
3. **veranda.** Open-air porch, usually with a roof

Mrs. Fuller popped her head out of an upstairs window. "What on earth's the matter?" she said.

"You've got a large green mamba in your front room!" I shouted. "I saw it go up the veranda steps and right in through the door!"

"Fred!" Mrs. Fuller shouted, turning round. "Fred! Come here!"

Freddy Fuller's round red face appeared at the window beside his wife. "What's up?" he asked.

"There's a green mamba in your living room!" I shouted.

Without hesitation and without wasting time with more questions, he said to me, "Stay there. I'm going to lower the children down to you one at a time." He was completely cool and unruffled.[4] He didn't even raise his voice.

A small girl was lowered down to me by her wrists and I was able to catch her easily by the legs. Then came a small boy. Then Freddy Fuller lowered his wife and I caught her by the waist and put her on the ground. Then came Fuller himself. He hung by his hands from the windowsill and when he let go he landed neatly on his two feet.

We stood in a little group on the grass at the back of the house and I told Fuller exactly what I had seen.

The mother was holding the two children by the hand, one on each side of her. They didn't seem to be particularly alarmed.

"What happens now?" I asked.

"Go down to the road, all of you," Fuller said. "I'm off to fetch the snake-man." He trotted away and got into his small ancient black car and drove off. Mrs. Fuller and the two small children and I went down to the road and sat in the shade of a large mango tree.

"Who is this snake-man?" I asked Mrs. Fuller.

"He is an old Englishman who has been out here for years," Mrs. Fuller said. "He actually *likes* snakes. He understands them and never kills them. He catches them and sells them to zoos and laboratories all over the world. Every native for miles around knows about him and whenever one of them sees a snake, he marks its hiding place and runs, often for great distances, to tell the snake-man. Then the snake-man comes along and captures it. The snake-man's strict rule is that he will never buy a captured snake from the natives."

"Why not?" I asked.

"To discourage them from trying to catch snakes themselves," Mrs. Fuller said. "In his early days he used to buy caught snakes, but so many natives got bitten trying to catch them, and so many died, that he decided to put a stop to it. Now any native who brings in a caught snake, no matter how rare, gets turned away."

"That's good," I said.

"What is the snake-man's name?" I asked.

"Donald Macfarlane," she said. "I believe he's Scottish."

"Is the snake in the house, Mummy?" the small girl asked.

"Yes, darling. But the snake-man is going to get it out."

"He'll bite Jack," the girl said.

"Oh, my God!" Mrs. Fuller cried, jumping to her feet. "I forgot about Jack!" She began calling out, "Jack! Come here, Jack! Jack!... Jack!...Jack!"

The children jumped up as well and all of them started calling to the dog. But no dog came out of the open front door.

---

4. unruffled. Poised; calm

"He's bitten Jack!" the small girl cried out. "He must have bitten him!" She began to cry and so did her brother, who was a year or so younger than she was. Mrs. Fuller looked grim.

"Jack's probably hiding upstairs," she said. "You know how clever he is."

Mrs. Fuller and I seated ourselves again on the grass, but the children remained standing. In between their tears they went on calling to the dog.

"Would you like me to take you down to the Maddens' house?" their mother asked.

"No!" they cried. "No, no, no! We want Jack!"

"Here's Daddy!" Mrs. Fuller cried, pointing at the tiny black car coming up the road in a swirl of dust. I noticed a long wooden pole sticking out through one of the car windows.

The children ran to meet the car. "Jack's inside the house and he's been bitten by the snake!" they wailed. "We know he's been bitten! He doesn't come when we call him!"

Mr. Fuller and the snake-man got out of the car. The snake-man was small and very old, probably over seventy. He wore leather boots made of thick cowhide and he had long gauntlet-type gloves[5] on his hands made of the same stuff. The gloves reached above his elbows. In his right hand he carried an extraordinary implement, an eight-foot-long wooden pole with a forked end. The two prongs of the fork were made, so it seemed, of black rubber, about an inch thick and quite flexible, and it was clear that if the fork was pressed against the ground the two prongs would bend outward, allowing the neck of the fork to go down as close to the ground as necessary. In his left hand he carried an ordinary brown sack.

It lay there like a long, beautiful, deadly shaft of green glass, quite motionless, perhaps asleep.

Donald Macfarlane, the snake-man, may have been old and small but he was an impressive-looking character. His eyes were pale blue, deep-set in a face round and dark and wrinkled as a walnut. Above the blue eyes, the eyebrows were thick and startlingly white, but the hair on his head was almost black. In spite of the thick leather boots, he moved like a leopard, with soft slow catlike strides, and he came straight up to me and said, "Who are you?"

"He's with Shell,"[6] Fuller said. "He hasn't been here long."

"You want to watch?" the snake-man said to me.

"Watch?" I said, wavering. "Watch? How do you mean watch? I mean where from? Not in the house?"

"You can stand out on the veranda and look through the window," the snake-man said.

"Come on," Fuller said. "We'll both watch."

"Now don't do anything silly," Mrs. Fuller said.

The two children stood there forlorn and miserable, with tears all over their cheeks.

The snake-man and Fuller and I walked over the grass toward the house, and as we approached the veranda steps the snake-man

---

5. gauntlet-type gloves. Protective gloves
6. Shell. Shell Oil, the company Dahl flew for

for•lorn (fər lôrn´) *adj.*, sad; lonely; hopeless

whispered, "Tread softly on the wooden boards or he'll pick up the vibration. Wait until I've gone in, then walk up quietly and stand by the window."

The snake-man went up the steps first and he made absolutely no sound at all with his feet. He moved soft and catlike onto the veranda and straight through the front door and then he quickly but very quietly closed the door behind him.

I felt better with the door closed. What I mean is I felt better for myself. I certainly didn't feel better for the snake-man. I figured he was committing suicide. I followed Fuller onto the veranda and we both crept over to the window. The window was open, but it had a fine mesh mosquito netting all over it. That made me feel better still. We peered through the netting.

The living room was simple and ordinary, coconut matting on the floor, a red sofa, a coffee table and a couple of armchairs. The dog was sprawled on the matting under the coffee table, a large Airedale with curly brown and black hair. He was stone dead.

The snake-man was standing absolutely still just inside the door of the living room. The brown sack was now slung over his left shoulder and he was grasping the long pole with both hands, holding it out in front of him, parallel to the ground. I couldn't see the snake. I didn't think the snake-man had seen it yet either.

A minute went by...two minutes...three... four...five. Nobody moved. There was death in that room. The air was heavy with death and the snake-man stood as motionless as a pillar of stone, with the long rod held out in front of him.

And still he waited. Another minute...and another...and another.

And now I saw the snake-man beginning to bend his knees. Very slowly he bent his knees until he was almost squatting on the floor, and from that position he tried to peer under the sofa and the armchairs.

And still it didn't look as though he was seeing anything.

Slowly he straightened his legs again, and then his head began to swivel around the room. Over to the right, in the far corner, a staircase led up to the floor above. The snake-man looked at the stairs, and I knew very well what was going through his head. Quite abruptly, he took one step forward and stopped.

Nothing happened.

A moment later I caught sight of the snake. It was lying full-length along the skirting[7] of the right-hand wall, but hidden from the snake-man's view by the back of the sofa. It lay there like a long, beautiful, deadly shaft of green glass, quite motionless, perhaps asleep. It was facing away from us who were at the window, with its small triangular head resting on the matting near the foot of the stairs.

I nudged Fuller and whispered, "It's over there against the wall." I pointed and Fuller saw the snake. At once, he started waving both hands, palms outward, back and forth across the window, hoping to get the snake-man's attention. The snake-man didn't see him. Very softly, Fuller said, "Pssst!" and the snake-man looked up sharply. Fuller

7. skirting. Baseboard

pointed. The snake-man understood and gave a nod.

Now the snake-man began working his way very very slowly to the back wall of the room so as to get a view of the snake behind the sofa. He never walked on his toes as you or I would have done. His feet remained flat on the ground all the time. The cowhide boots were like moccasins, with neither soles nor heels. Gradually, he worked his way over to the back wall, and from there he was able to see at least the head and two or three feet of the snake itself.

But the snake also saw him. With a movement so fast it was invisible, the snake's head came up about two feet off the floor and the front of the body arched backwards, ready to strike. Almost simultaneously, it bunched its whole body into a series of curves, ready to flash forward.

The snake-man was just a bit too far away from the snake to reach it with the end of his pole. He waited, staring at the snake, and the snake stared back at him with two small malevolent[8] black eyes.

Then the snake-man started speaking to the snake. "Come along, my pretty," he whispered in a soft wheedling[9] voice. "There's a good boy. Nobody's going to hurt you. Nobody's going to harm you, my pretty little thing. Just lie still and relax..." He took a step forward toward the snake, holding the pole out in front of him.

What the snake did next was so fast that the whole movement couldn't have taken more than a hundredth of a second, like the flick of a camera shutter. There was a green flash as the snake darted forward at least ten feet and struck at the snake-man's leg.

The sack started jumping about as though there were fifty angry rats inside it....

Nobody could have got out of the way of that one. I heard the snake's head strike against the thick cowhide boot with a sharp little crack, and then at once the head was back in that same deadly backward-curving position, ready to strike again.

"There's a good boy," the snake-man said softly. "There's a clever boy. There's a lovely fellow. You mustn't get excited. Keep calm and everything's going to be all right." As he was speaking, he was slowly lowering the end of the pole until the forked prongs were about twelve inches above the middle of the snake's body. "There's a lovely fellow," he whispered. "There's a good kind little chap. Keep still now, my beauty. Keep still, my pretty. Keep quite still. Daddy's not going to hurt you."

I could see a thin dark trickle of venom running down the snake-man's right boot where the snake had struck.

The snake, head raised and arcing[10] backwards, was as tense as a tight-wound spring and ready to strike again. "Keep still, my lovely," the snake-man whispered. "Don't move now. Keep still. No one's going to hurt you."

Then *wham*, the rubber prongs came down right across the snake's body, about midway along its length, and pinned it to the floor. All I could see was a green blur as the snake thrashed around furiously in an effort to free itself. But the snake-man kept up the

8. **malevolent.** Having or showing hatred
9. **wheedling.** Coaxing; flattering
10. **arcing.** Following a curved course

pressure on the prongs and the snake was trapped.

What happens next? I wondered. There was no way he could catch hold of that madly twisting flailing length of green muscle with his hands, and even if he could have done so, the head would surely have flashed around and bitten him in the face.

Holding the very end of the eight-foot pole, the snake-man began to work his way round the room until he was at the tail end of the snake. Then, in spite of the flailing and the thrashing, he started pushing the prongs forward along the snake's body toward the head. Very very slowly he did it, pushing the rubber prongs forward over the snake's flailing body, keeping the snake pinned down all the time and pushing, pushing, pushing the long wooden rod forward millimeter by millimeter. It was a fascinating and frightening thing to watch, the little man with white eyebrows and black hair carefully manipulating his long implement and sliding the fork ever so slowly along the length of the twisting snake toward the head. The snake's body was thumping against the coconut matting with such a noise that if you had been upstairs you might have thought two big men were wrestling on the floor.

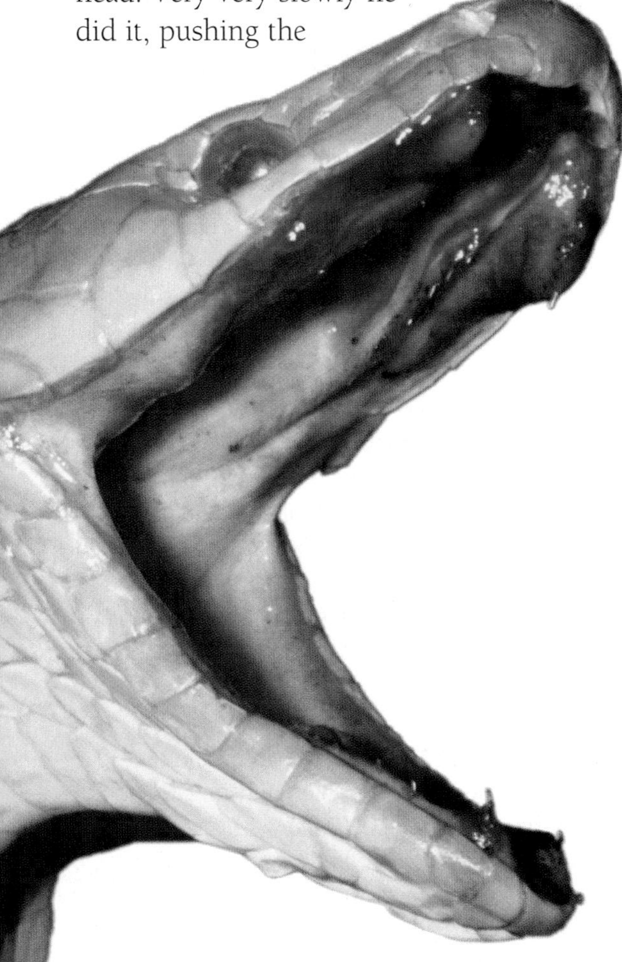

Then at last the prongs were right behind the head itself, pinning it down, and at that point the snake-man reached forward with one gloved hand and grasped the snake very firmly by the neck. He threw away the pole. He took the sack off his shoulder with his free hand. He lifted the great, still twisting length of the deadly green snake and pushed the head into the sack. Then he let go the head and bundled the rest of the creature in and closed the sack. The sack started jumping about as though there were fifty angry rats inside it, but the snake-man was now totally relaxed and he held the sack casually in one hand as if it contained no more than a few pounds of potatoes. He stooped and picked up his pole from the floor, then he turned and looked toward the window where we were peering in.

"Pity about the dog," he said. "You'd better get it out of the way before the children see it." ✣

ma•nip•u•late (mə nip´ yə lāt) *v.*, treat or operate with the hands in a skillful manner

Who do you think shows more courage—the snake-man or Rikki-tikki-tavi? How is their behavior in the presence of danger similar? How is it different?

Comparing Texts

AFTER READING

Find Meaning

1. (a) How does Mr. Fuller respond to the news that the snake has entered his living room? (b) Based on his actions, how do you think Mr. Fuller feels about the snake?
2. (a) How do the children and Mrs. Fuller respond when they realize the dog is still in the house? (b) What role does the dog play in the story?
3. What is the snake-man's attitude toward the snake? Explain.

Make Judgments

4. (a) What words and phrases does the narrator use to describe the green mamba and its actions? (b) What effect does he create with his descriptions of the snake?
5. (a) What words and phrases does the narrator use to describe the snake-man and his actions? (b) What is the effect of his characterization of the snake-man?

Compare Literature

Personification When a writer uses personification, he or she gives human intelligence, emotions, abilities, and other traits to non-human characters. Review the characteristics of the snakes in "Rikki-tikki-tavi" and "The Green Mamba" that you recorded in your chart to answer the following questions.

1. How does the author personify Karait, Nag, and Nagaina in "Rikki-tikki-tavi"?
2. Does the author personify the snake in "The Green Mamba"? Explain your answer.
3. Which snakes—those in "Rikki-tikki-tavi" or the green mamba—do you find more frightening? Why do you feel this way?

Extend Understanding

Writing Options

Creative Writing Imagine that the snake-man was writing a **letter** to a friend who also studies snakes describing the events in "Rikki-tikki-tavi." Keep in mind the attitude toward snakes he shows in "The Green Mamba" in creating his version of the story of Rikki-tikki's battles with Karait, Nag, and Nagaina.

Informative Writing Write a brief **compare-and-contrast essay** examining the similarities and differences between the settings, characters, and themes of "Rikki-tikki-tavi" and "The Green Mamba." You may organize your essay either by examining all three elements first in one work and then in the other or by discussing each literary element in turn. Share your work with the class.

Collaborative Learning

Hold a Panel Discussion Use "Rikki-tikki-tavi" and "The Green Mamba" as jumping-off points in a discussion about what personal characteristics enable individuals to perform well in a crisis. Keep a list of such traits as you discuss them, and at the conclusion, vote to determine which are the three most important characteristics.

Media Literacy

Conduct Internet Research Use the Internet to research information for a comparison study of the western green mamba *(Dendroaspis viridis)* and the king cobra *(Ophiophagus hannah)*. Find out facts about their size, appearance, habitat, range, and habits. Determine which of the two snakes represents a greater danger to human beings.

Go to **www.mirrorsandwindows.com** for more.

INDEPENDENT READING

UNCLE TONY'S GOAT

A Short Story
by Leslie Marmon Silko

"Something will get hurt. Maybe even one of you."

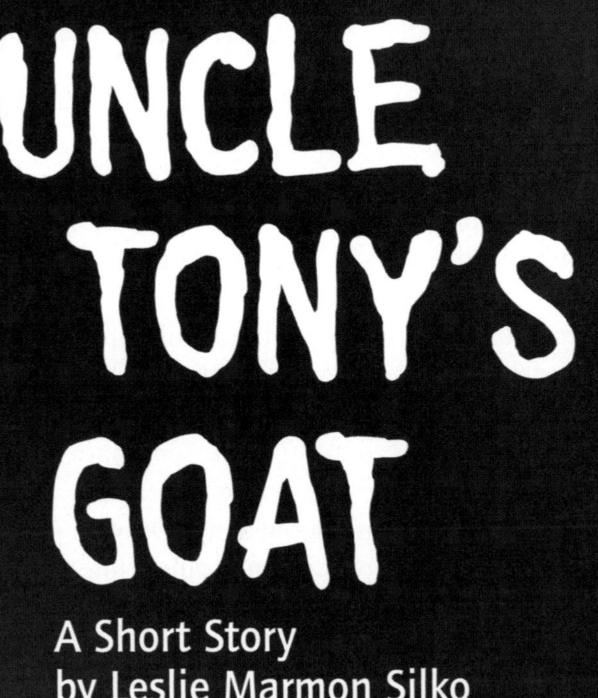

We had a hard time finding the right kind of string to use. We knew we needed gut to string our bows the way the men did, but we were little kids and we didn't know how to get any. So Kenny went to his house and brought back a ball of white cotton string that his mother used to string red chili with. It was thick and soft and it didn't make very good bowstring. As soon as we got the bows made we sat down again on the sand bank above the stream and started skinning willow twigs for arrows. It was past noon, and the tall willows behind us made cool shade. There were lots of little minnows that day, flashing in the shallow water, swimming back and forth wildly like they weren't sure if they really wanted to go up or down the stream; it was a day for minnows that we were always hoping for—we could have filled our rusty coffee cans and old pickle jars full. But this was the first time for making bows and arrows, and the minnows weren't much different from the sand or the rocks now. The secret is the arrows. The ones we made were crooked, and when we shot them they didn't go straight—they flew around in arcs and curves; so we crawled through the leaves and branches, deep into the willow groves, looking for the best, the straightest willow branches. But even after we skinned the sticky wet bark from them and whittled the knobs off, they still weren't

Although she is of mixed ancestry—Laguna Pueblo, Mexican, and European—**Leslie Marmon Silko** has always identified most closely with the Native American part of her background. Born in 1948, she was raised on the Laguna Pueblo reservation where she grew up hearing traditional stories. She draws on her Native American heritage in her writing, which includes poetry, novels, short stories, essays, articles, and film scripts. Her story "Uncle Tony's Goat" grew out of a late-night telephone conversation with an old friend and fellow Pueblo Indian, the poet Simon Ortiz, who told her a story about a mean billy goat.

straight. Finally we went ahead and made notches at the end of each arrow to hook in the bowstring, and we started practicing, thinking maybe we could learn to shoot the crooked arrows straight.

We left the river each of us with a handful of damp, yellow arrows and our fresh-skinned willow bows. We walked slowly and shot arrows at bushes, big rocks, and the juniper tree that grows by Pino's sheep pen. They were working better just like we had figured; they still didn't fly straight, but now we could compensate[1] for that by the way we aimed them. We were going up to the church to shoot at the cats old Sister Julian kept outside the cloister.[2] We didn't want to hurt anything, just to have new kinds of things to shoot at.

The billy goat never forgot the bows and arrows....

But before we got to the church we went past the grassy hill where my uncle Tony's goats were grazing. A few of them were lying down chewing their cud[3] peacefully, and they didn't seem to notice us. The billy goat was lying down, but he was watching us closely like he already knew about little kids. His yellow goat eyes didn't blink, and he stared with a wide, hostile[4] look. The grazing goats made good deer for our bows. We shot all our arrows at the nanny goats and their kids; they skipped away from the careening[5] arrows and never lost the rhythm of their greedy chewing as they continued to nibble the weeds and grass on the hillside. The billy goat was lying there watching us and taking us into his memory. As we ran down the road toward the church and Sister Julian's cats, I looked back, and my uncle Tony's billy goat was still watching me.

My uncle and my father were sitting on the bench outside the house when we walked by. It was September now, and the farming was almost over, except for bringing home the melons and a few pumpkins. They were mending ropes and bridles and feeling the afternoon sun. We held our bows and arrows out in front of us so they could see them. My father smiled and kept braiding the strips of leather in his hand, but my uncle Tony put down the bridle and pieces of scrap leather he was working on and looked at each of us kids slowly. He was old, getting some white hair—he was my mother's oldest brother, the one that scolded us when we told lies or broke things.

"You'd better not be shooting at things," he said, "only at rocks or trees. Something will get hurt. Maybe even one of you."

We all nodded in agreement and tried to hold the bows and arrows less conspicuously[6] down at our sides; when he turned back to his work we hurried away before he took the bows away from us like he did the time we made the slingshot. He caught us shooting rocks at an old wrecked car; its windows were all busted out anyway, but he took the slingshot away. I always wondered what he did with it and with the knives we made ourselves out of tin cans. When I was much older I asked my mother, "What did he ever do with those knives and slingshots he took

1. **compensate.** Offset or counterbalance an effect
2. **cloister.** Convent, or residence of nuns
3. **cud.** Partially digested food chewed a second time by cows, goats, and other grazing animals
4. **hostile.** Unfriendly
5. **careening.** Moving wildly; uncontrolled
6. **conspicuously.** In a very noticeable way

away from us?" She was kneading[7] bread on the kitchen table at the time and was probably busy thinking about the fire in the oven outside. "I don't know," she said; "you ought to ask him yourself." But I never did. I thought about it lots of times, but I never did. It would have been like getting caught all over again.

The goats were valuable. We got milk and meat from them. My uncle was careful to see that all the goats were treated properly; the worst scolding my older sister ever got was when my mother caught her and some of her friends chasing the newborn kids. My mother kept saying over and over again, "It's a good thing I saw you; what if your uncle had seen you?" and even though we kids were very young then, we understood very well what she meant.

The billy goat never forgot the bows and arrows, even after the bows had cracked and split and the crooked, whittled arrows were all lost. This goat was big and black and important to my uncle Tony because he'd paid a lot to get him and because he wasn't an ordinary goat. Uncle Tony had bought him from a white man, and then he'd hauled him in the back of the pickup all the way from Quemado.[8] And my uncle was the only person who could touch this goat. If a stranger or one of us kids got too near him, the mane[9] on the billy goat's neck would stand on end and the goat would rear up on his hind legs and dance forward trying to reach the person with his long, spiral horns. This billy goat smelled bad, and none of us cared if we couldn't pet him. But my uncle took good care of this goat. The goat would let Uncle Tony brush him with the horse brush and scratch him around the base of his horns. Uncle Tony talked to the billy goat—in the morning when he unpenned the goats and in the evening when he gave them their hay and closed the gate for the night. I never paid too much attention to what he said to the billy goat; usually it was something like "Get up, big goat! You've slept long enough," or "Move over, big goat, and let the others have something to eat." I think Uncle Tony was proud of that billy goat.

"Get up, big goat!"

We all had chores to do around home. My sister helped out around the house mostly, and I was supposed to carry water from the hydrant[10] and bring in kindling. I helped my father look after the horses and pigs, and Uncle Tony milked the goats and fed them. One morning near the end of September I was out feeding the pigs their table scraps and pig mash;[11] I'd given the pigs their food, and I was watching them squeal and snap at each other as they crowded into the feed trough. Behind me I could hear the milk squirting into the eight-pound lard pail that Uncle Tony used for milking.

When he finished milking he noticed me standing there; he motioned toward the goats still inside the pen. "Run the rest of them out," he said as he untied the two milk goats and carried the milk to the house.

I was seven years old, and I understood that everyone, including my uncle, expected me to handle more chores; so I hurried over to the goat pen and swung the tall wire gate

7. kneading. Pressing or squeezing with the hands
8. Quemado. Town in west central New Mexico
9. mane. Hair growing about the neck of some animals
10. hydrant. Pipe that discharges water
11. mash. Animal feed

open. The does and kids came prancing out. They trotted daintily past the pigpen and scattered out, intent on finding leaves and grass to eat. It wasn't until then I noticed that the billy goat hadn't come out of the little wooden shed inside the goat pen. I stood outside the pen and tried to look inside the wooden shelter, but it was still early and the morning sun left the inside of the shelter in deep shadow. I stood there for a while, hoping that he would come out by himself, but I realized that he'd recognized me and that he wouldn't come out. I understood right away what was happening and my fear of him was in my bowels and down my neck; I was shaking.

Finally my uncle came out of the house; it was time for breakfast. "What's wrong?" he called out from the door.

"The billy goat won't come out," I yelled back, hoping he would look disgusted and come do it himself.

"Get in there and get him out," he said as he went back into the house.

I looked around quickly for a stick or broom handle, or even a big rock, but I couldn't find anything. I walked into the pen slowly, concentrating on the darkness beyond the shed door; I circled to the back of the shed and kicked at the boards, hoping to make the billy goat run out. I put my eye up to a crack between the boards, and I could see he was standing up now and that his yellow eyes were on mine.

My mother was yelling at me to hurry up, and Uncle Tony was watching. I stepped around into the low doorway, and the goat charged toward me, feet first. I had dirt in my mouth and up my nose and there was blood running past my eye; my head ached. Uncle Tony carried me to the house; his face was stiff with anger, and I remembered what he'd always told us about animals; they won't bother you unless you bother them first. I didn't start to cry until my mother hugged me close and wiped my face with a damp wash rag. It was only a little cut above my eyebrow, and she sent me to school anyway with a Band-Aid on my forehead.

Uncle Tony locked the billy goat in the pen. He didn't say what he was going to do with the goat, but when he left with my father to haul firewood, he made sure the gate to the pen was wired tightly shut. He looked at the goat quietly and with sadness; he said something to the goat, but the yellow eyes stared past him.

"What's he going to do with the goat?" I asked my mother before I went to catch the school bus.

"He ought to get rid of it," she said. "We can't have that goat knocking people down for no good reason."

I didn't feel good at school. The teacher sent me to the nurse's office and the nurse made me lie down. Whenever I closed my eyes I could see the goat and my uncle, and I felt a stiffness in my throat and chest. I got off the school bus slowly, so the other kids would go ahead without me. I walked slowly and wished I could be away from home for a while. I could go over to Grandma's house, but she would ask me if my mother knew where I was and I would have to say no, and she would make me go home first to ask. So I walked very slowly, because I didn't want to see the black goat's hide hanging over the corral fence.

When I got to the house I didn't see a goat hide or the goat, but Uncle Tony was on his horse and my mother was standing beside the horse holding a canteen and a flour sack bundle tied with brown string. I was frightened at what this meant. My uncle looked down at me from the saddle.

"The goat ran away," he said. "Jumped out of the pen somehow. I saw him just as he went over the hill beyond the river. He stopped at the top of the hill and he looked back this way."

Uncle Tony nodded at my mother and me and then he left; we watched his old roan gelding[12] splash across the stream and labor up the steep path beyond the river. Then they were over the top of the hill and gone.

Uncle Tony was gone for three days. He came home early on the morning of the fourth day, before we had eaten breakfast or fed the animals. He was glad to be home, he said, because he was getting too old for such long rides. He called me over and looked closely at the cut above my eye. It had scabbed over good, and I wasn't wearing a Band-Aid any more; he examined it very carefully before he let me go. He stirred some sugar into his coffee.

"That miserable goat," he said. "I followed him for three days. He was headed south, going straight to Quemado. I never could catch up to him." My uncle shook his head. "The first time I saw him he was already in the piñon[13] forest, halfway into the mountains already. I could see him most of the time, off in the distance a mile or two. He

12. **roan gelding.** Reddish brown male horse that has been neutered

13. **piñon.** Small evergreen

would stop sometimes and look back." Uncle Tony paused and drank some more coffee. "I stopped at night. I had to. He stopped too, and in the morning we would start out again. The trail just gets higher and steeper. Yesterday morning there was frost on top of the blanket when I woke up and we were in the big pines and red oak leaves. I couldn't see him any more because the forest is too thick. So I turned around." Tony finished the cup of coffee. "He's probably in Quemado by now."

I looked at him again, standing there by the door, ready to go milk the nanny goats.

"There wasn't ever a goat like that one," he said, "but if that's the way he's going to act, O.K. then. That stubborn goat was just too mean anyway."

He smiled at me and his voice was strong and happy when he said this. ✣

What do you find most appealing about animals? What do you find most frightening? How do you think the experience of living with animals enriches people's lives?

Analyze and Extend

1. (a) How does the narrator respond to animals at the beginning of the story? (b) How does this reaction change?
2. (a) What does Uncle Tony value about the goat? (b) How does he view the animal at the end of the story?
3. What lesson do you think this experience teaches the narrator?

Creative Writing Imagine that the narrator of "Uncle Tony's Goat" keeps a diary. Re-create the major events of the story as **diary entries.** Adopt an appropriate style in your entries. (Remember that the narrator is seven years old.) You might want to add illustrations to your entries, showing how the narrator sees Uncle Tony, the goat, and other characters in the story.

Collaborative Learning Work with a small group of fellow students to discuss the outcome of the story. Consider the following questions: Why do you think the story ended the way it did? If you had been writing the story, how would you have ended it? How would you describe the ending of the story?

 Go to **www.mirrorsandwindows.com** for more.

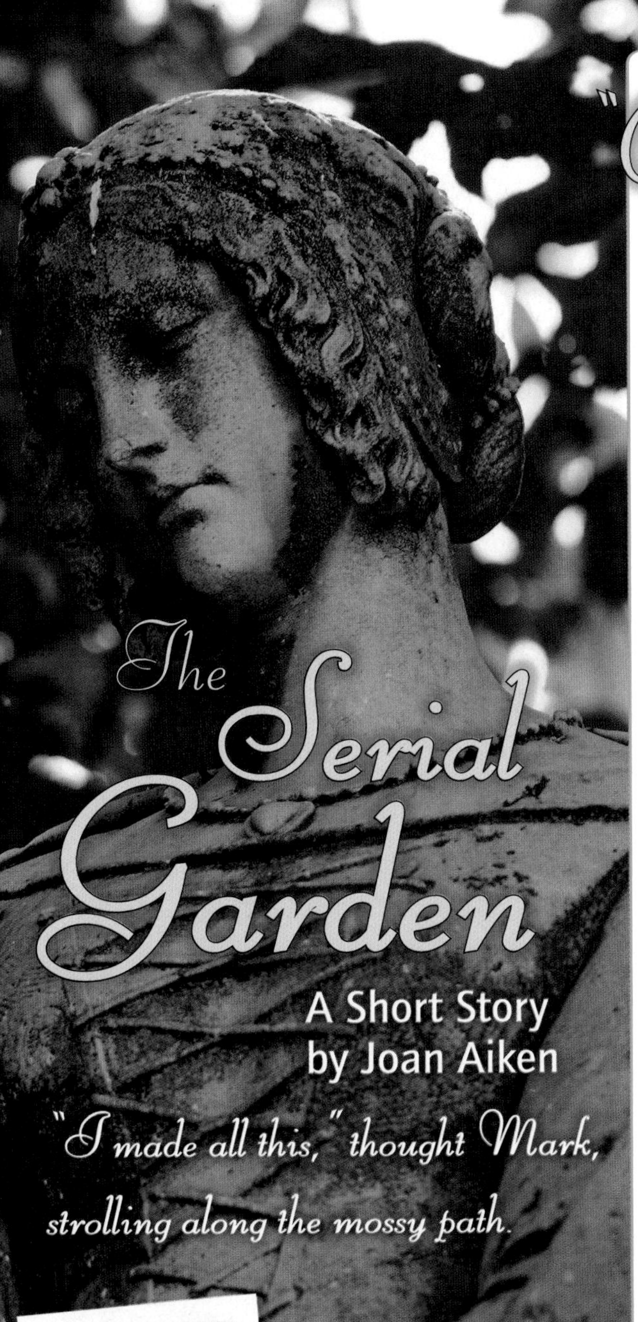

"Cold rice pudding for breakfast?" said Mark, looking at it with disfavor.

"Don't be fussy," said his mother. "You're the only one who's complaining." This was unfair, for she and Mark were the only members of the family at table, Harriet having developed measles while staying with a school friend, while Mr. Armitage had somehow managed to lock himself in the larder.[1] Mrs. Armitage never had anything but toast and marmalade for breakfast anyway.

Mark went on scowling at the chilly-looking pudding. It had come straight out of the fridge, which was not in the larder.

"If you don't like it," said Mrs. Armitage, "unless you want Daddy to pass your corn flakes through the larder ventilator,[2] flake by flake, you'd better run down to Miss Pride and get a small packet of cereal. She opens at eight; Hickmans doesn't open till nine. It's no use waiting till the blacksmith comes to let your father out; I'm sure he won't be here for hours yet."

There came a gloomy banging from the direction of the larder, just to remind them that Mr. Armitage was alive and suffering in there.

"*You're* all right," shouted Mark heartlessly as he passed the larder door.

---

1. **larder.** Pantry
2. **ventilator.** Device used to bring in fresh air and drive out foul air; fan

Joan Aiken (1924–2004) grew up telling stories. Born in Sussex, England, she exchanged tales with her brother about imaginary lands. She was fascinated by mysterious happenings and loved to read stories by Charles Dickens, Rudyard Kipling, Edgar Allan Poe, and Jane Austen. In "The Serial Garden," she presents a new approach to a familiar theme of fantasy literature, the alternative world. Instead of falling down a rabbit hole into Wonderland like Alice, young Mark Armitage gains entry to his fantasy world by assembling the cutouts on the back of a box of breakfast cereal.

"There's nothing to stop *you* having cornflakes. Oh, I forgot, the milk's in the fridge. Well, have cheese and pickles then. Or treacle tart."[3]

Even through the zinc grating[4] on the door, he could hear his father shudder at the thought of treacle tart and pickles for breakfast. Mr. Armitage's imprisonment was his own fault, though; he had sworn that he was going to find out where the mouse got into the larder if it took him all night, watching and waiting. He had shut himself in, so that no member of the family should come bursting in and disturb his vigil.[5] The larder door had a spring catch that sometimes jammed; it was bad luck that this turned out to be one of the times.

Mark ran across the fields to Miss Pride's shop at Sticks Corner and asked if she had any corn flakes.

"Oh, I don't think I have any left, dear," Miss Pride said woefully. "I'll have a look....I think I sold the last packet a week ago Tuesday."

"What about the one in the window?"

"That's a dummy, dear."

Miss Pride's shop window was full of nasty, dingy old cardboard cartons with nothing inside them, and several empty display stands that had fallen down and never been propped up again. Inside the shop were a few small, tired-looking tins and jars, which had a worn and scratched appearance as if mice had tried them and given up. Miss Pride herself was small and wan,[6] with yellowish gray hair; she rooted rather hopelessly in a pile of empty boxes. Mark's mother never bought any groceries from Miss Pride's if she could help it, since the day when she had found a label inside the foil wrapping of a cream cheese saying, "This cheese should be eaten before May 11, 1899."

"No corn flakes I'm afraid, dear."

"Any wheat crispies? Puffed corn? Rice nuts?"

"No, dear. Nothing left, only Brekkfast Brikks."

"Never heard of *them,*" said Mark doubtfully.

"Or I've a jar of Ovo here. You spread it on bread. That's nice for breakfast," said Miss Pride, with a sudden burst of salesmanship. Mark thought the Ovo looked beastly, like yellow paint, so he took the packet of Brekkfast Brikks. At least it wasn't very big.... On the front of the box was a picture of a fat, repulsive, fair-haired boy, rather like the chubby Augustus, banging on his plate with his spoon.

"They look like tiny doormats," said Mrs. Armitage, as Mark shoveled some Brikks into the bowl.

"They taste like them, too. Gosh," said Mark, "I must hurry or I'll be late for school. There's rather a nice cutout garden on the back of the packet, though; don't throw it away when it's empty, Mother. Goodby, Daddy," he shouted through the larder door; "hope Mr. Ellis comes soon to let you out." And he dashed off to catch the school bus.

At breakfast next morning Mark had a huge helping of Brekkfast Brikks and persuaded his father to try them.

"They taste just like esparto grass,"[7] said Mr. Armitage fretfully.[8]

---

3. treacle tart. Pastry with a sweet molasses filling
4. zinc grating. Metal framework on a door
5. vigil. Watchful wakefulness during the usual hours of sleep
6. wan. Pale; sickly
7. esparto grass. Coarse grass used to make rope
8. fretfully. Irritably

"Yes, I know, but do take some more, Daddy. I want to cut out the model garden; it's so lovely."

"Rather pleasant, I must say. It looks like an eighteenth-century German engraving," his father agreed. "It certainly was a stroke of genius putting it on the packet. No one would ever buy these things to eat for pleasure. Pass me the sugar, please. And the cream. And the strawberries."

It was the half-term holiday, so after breakfast Mark was able to take the empty packet away to the playroom and get on with the job of cutting out the stone walls, the row of little trees, the fountain, the yew arch,[9] the two green lawns, and the tiny clumps of brilliant flowers. He knew better than to "stick tabs in slots and secure with paste," as the directions suggested; he had made models from packets before and knew they always fell to pieces unless they were firmly bound together with transparent sticky tape.

It was a long, fiddling, pleasurable job.

Nobody interrupted him. Mrs. Armitage cleaned the playroom only once every six months or so, when she made a ferocious descent on it and tidied up the tape recorders, roller skates, meteorological sets, and dismantled railway engines, and threw away countless old magazines, stringless tennis rackets, abandoned paintings, and unsuccessful models. There were always bitter complaints from Mark and Harriet; then they forgot and things piled up again till next time.

As Mark worked, his eye was caught by a verse on the outside of the packet:

"Brekkfast Brikks to start the day
Make you fit in every way.
Children bang their plates with glee
At Brekkfast Brikks for lunch and tea!
Brekkfast Brikks for supper too
Give peaceful sleep the whole night
through."

"Blimey," thought Mark, sticking a cedar tree into the middle of the lawn and then bending a stone wall round at dotted lines A, B, C, and D. "I wouldn't want anything for breakfast, lunch, tea, and supper, not even Christmas pudding. Certainly not Brekkfast Brikks."

He propped a clump of gaudy scarlet flowers against the wall and stuck them in place.

The words of the rhyme kept coming into his head as he worked, and presently he found that they went rather well to a tune that was running through his mind, and he began to hum, and then to sing. Mark often did this when he was alone and busy.

"Brekkfast Brikks to sta-art the day,
Ma-ake you fi-it in every way—

"Blow, where did I put that little bit of sticky tape? Oh, there it is.

"Children bang their pla-ates with glee
At Brekkfast Brikks for lunch and tea

"Slit gate with razor blade, it says; but it'll have to be a penknife.

---

9. yew arch. Gateway in a garden made out of yew branches. A yew is an evergreen bush.

"Brekkfast Brikks for supper toohoo
Give peaceful sleep the whole night
throughoo....

"Hullo. That's funny," said Mark.

It was funny. The openwork iron gate he had just stuck in position now suddenly towered above him. On either side, to right and left, ran the high stone wall, stretching away into foggy distance. Over the top of the wall he could see tall trees, yews and cypresses and others he didn't know.

"Well, that's the neatest trick I ever saw," said Mark. "I wonder if the gate will open."

He chuckled as he tried it, thinking of the larder door. The gate did open, and he went through into the garden.

One of the things that had already struck him as he cut them out was that the flowers were not at all in the right proportions. But they were all the nicer for that. There were huge, velvety violets and pansies the size of saucers; the hollyhocks were as big as dinner plates and the turf was sprinkled with enormous daisies. The roses, on the other hand, were miniature, no bigger than cuffbuttons. There were real fish in the fountain, bright pink.

"I made all this," thought Mark, strolling along the mossy path to the yew arch. "Won't Harriet be surprised when she sees it. I wish she could see it now. I wonder what made it come alive like that."

He passed through the yew arch as he said this, and discovered that on the other side there was nothing but gray, foggy blackness. This, of course, was where his cardboard garden had ended. He turned through the archway and gazed with pride at a border of huge, scarlet tropical flowers that were perhaps supposed to be geraniums but certainly hadn't turned out that way.

"I know! Of course, it was the rhyme, the rhyme on the packet."

He recited it. Nothing happened. "Perhaps you have to sing it," he thought and (feeling a little foolish) he sang it through to the tune that fitted so well. At once, faster than blowing out a match, the garden drew itself together and shrank into its cardboard again, leaving Mark outside.

"What a marvelous hiding place it'll make when I don't want people to come bothering," he thought. He sang the spell once more, just to make sure that it worked, and there was the mossy wall, the stately iron gate, and the treetops. He stepped in and looked back. No playroom to be seen, only gray blankness.

At that moment he was startled by a tremendous clanging, the sort of sound the Trump of Doom[10] would make if it was a dinner bell. "Blow," he thought. "I suppose that's lunch." He sang the spell for the fourth time; immediately he was in the playroom, and the garden was on the floor beside him, and Agnes was still ringing the dinner bell outside the door.

"All right, I heard," he shouted. "Just coming."

He glanced hurriedly over the remains of the packet to see if it bore any mention of the fact that the cutout garden had magic properties. It did not. He did, however, learn that this was Section Three of the Beautiful Brekkfast Brikk Garden Series, and that Sections One, Two, Four, Five, and Six would be found on other packets. In case of difficulty in obtaining supplies, please write to Fruhstucksgeschirrziegelsteinindustrie (Great Britain), Lily Road, Shepherds Bush.

"Elevenpence a packet," Mark murmured to himself, going to lunch with unwashed hands. "Five elevens are thirty-five. Thirty-five pennies are—no, that's wrong. Fifty-five pence are four-and-sevenpence. Father, if I mow the lawn and carry coal every day for a month, can I have four shillings[11] and sevenpence?"

"You don't want to buy another space gun, do you?" said Mr. Armitage looking at him suspiciously. "Because one is quite enough in this family."

"No, it's not for a space gun, I swear."

"Oh, very well."

"And can I have the four-and-seven now?"

Mr. Armitage gave it reluctantly. "But that lawn has to be like velvet, mind," he said. "And if there's any falling off in the coal supply, I shall demand my money back."

"No, no, there won't be," Mark promised in reply. As soon as lunch was over, he dashed down to Miss Pride's. Was there a chance that she would have sections One, Two, Four, Five, and Six? He felt certain that no other shop had even heard of Brekkfast Brikks, so she was his only hope, apart from the address in Shepherds Bush.

"Oh, I don't know, I'm sure," Miss Pride said, sounding very doubtful—and more than a little surprised. "There might just be a couple on the bottom shelf—yes, here we are."

They were sections Four and Five, bent and dusty, but intact, Mark saw with relief. "Don't you suppose you have any more anywhere?" he pleaded.

"I'll look in the cellar but I can't promise. I haven't had deliveries of any of these for a long time. Made by some foreign firm they were; people didn't seem very keen on them," Miss Pride said aggrievedly.[12] She opened a door revealing a flight of damp stone stairs. Mark followed her down them like a bloodhound on the trail.

The cellar was a fearful confusion of mildewed, tattered, and toppling cartons, some full, some empty. Mark was nearly knocked cold by a shower of pilchards[13] in tins, which he dislodged onto himself from the top of a heap of boxes. At last Miss Pride, with a cry of triumph, unearthed a little cache[14] of Brekkfast Brikks, three packets

10. Trump of Doom. Trumpet blast believed to announce the end of the world

11. shillings. Former British coins, each worth twelve pennies (or pence)

12. aggrievedly. In an annoyed way

13. pilchards. Small fish of the herring family

14. cache. Secret, hidden supply

"There, isn't that a piece of luck now!"

which turned out to be the remaining sections, Six, One, and Two.

"There, isn't that a piece of luck now!" she said, looking quite faint with all the excitement. It was indeed rare for Miss Pride to sell as many as five packets of the same thing at one time.

Mark galloped home with his booty and met his father on the porch. Mr. Armitage let out a groan of dismay.

"I'd almost rather you'd bought a space gun," he said. Mark chanted in reply:

"Brekkfast Brikks for supper too
Give peaceful sleep the whole night
through."

"I don't want peaceful sleep," Mr. Armitage said. "I intend to spend tonight mousewatching again. I'm tired of finding footprints in the Stilton."[15]

During the next few days, Mark's parents watched anxiously to see, Mr. Armitage said, whether Mark would start to sprout esparto grass instead of hair. For he doggedly ate Brekkfast Brikks for lunch, with soup, or sprinkled over his pudding; for tea, with jam; and for supper, lightly fried in dripping, not to mention, of course, the immense helpings he had for breakfast, with sugar and milk.

Mr. Armitage, for his part, soon gave out; he said he wouldn't taste another Brekkfast Brikk even if it were wrapped in an inch-thick layer of *paté de foie gras.*[16] Mark regretted that Harriet, who was a handy and uncritical eater, was still away, convalescing from her measles with an aunt.

In two days, the second packet was finished (sundial, paved garden, and espaliers).[17] Mark cut it out, fastened it together, and joined it onto Section Three with trembling hands. "Would the spell work for this section, too?" He sang the rhyme in rather a quavering voice, but luckily the plywood door was shut, and there was no one to hear him. Yes! The gate grew again above him, and when he opened it and ran across the lawn through the yew arch, he found himself in a flagged[18] garden full of flowers like huge blue cabbages.

Mark stood hugging himself with satisfaction and then began to wander about smelling the flowers, which had a spicy perfume most unlike any flower he could think of. Suddenly he pricked up his ears. Had he caught a sound? There! It was like somebody crying and seemed to come from the other side of the hedge. He ran to the next opening and looked through. Nothing; only gray mist and emptiness. But, unless he had imagined it, just before he got there, he thought his eye had caught the flash of white-and-gold draperies swishing past the gateway.

15. Stilton. Strongly flavored British cheese
16. ***paté de foie gras.*** Puréed goose livers (French)
17. espaliers. Trees trained to grow on a trellis, or framework
18. flagged. Paved with flagstones

"Do you think Mark's all right?" Mrs. Armitage said to her husband next day. "He seems to be in such a dream all the time."

"Boy's gone clean off his rocker, if you ask me," grumbled Mr. Armitage. "It's all these doormats he's eating. Can't be good to stuff your insides with moldy jute.[19] Still, I'm bound to say he's cut the lawn very decently and seems to be remembering the coal. I'd better take a day off from the office and drive you over to the shore for a picnic; sea air will do him good."

Mrs. Armitage suggested to Mark that he should slack off on the Brekkfast Brikks, but he was so horrified that she had to abandon the idea. But, she said, he was to run four times round the garden every morning before breakfast. Mark almost said, "Which garden?" but stopped just in time. He had cut out and completed another large lawn, with a lake and weeping willows; and on the far side of the lake he had a tantalizing glimpse of a figure dressed in white and gold who moved away and was lost before he could get there.

After munching his way through the fourth packet, he was able to add on a broad grass walk bordered by curiously clipped trees. At the end of the walk, he could see the white-and-gold person, but when he ran to the spot, no one was there—the walk ended in the usual gray mist.

When he had finished and had cut out the fifth packet (an orchard), a terrible thing happened to him. For two days he could not remember the tune that worked the spell. He tried other tunes, but they were no use. He sat in the playroom singing till he was hoarse or silent with despair. Suppose he never remembered it again?

His mother shook her head at him that evening and said he looked as if he needed a dose. "It's lucky we're going to Shinglemud Bay for the day tomorrow," she said. "That ought to do you good."

"Oh, *blow.* I'd forgotten about that," Mark said. "Need I go?"

His mother stared at him in utter astonishment.

But in the middle of the night he remembered the right tune, leaped out of bed in a tremendous hurry, and ran down to the playroom without even waiting to put on his dressing gown and slippers.

The orchard was most wonderful, for instead of mere apples, its trees bore oranges, lemons, limes and all sorts of tropical fruits whose names he did not know, and there were melons and pineapples growing, and plantains[20] and avocados. Better still, he saw the lady in her white and gold waiting at the end of an alley and was able to draw near enough to speak to her.

"Who are you?" she asked. She seemed very much astonished at the sight of him.

"My name's Mark Armitage," he said politely. "Is this your garden?"

Close to, he saw that she was really very grand indeed. Her dress was white

19. jute. Strong rope made from plant fibers
20. plantains. Banana-like fruit

satin embroidered with pearls, and swept the ground; she had a gold scarf and her hair, dressed high and powdered, was confined in a small, gold-and-pearl tiara. Her face was rather plain, pink with a long nose, but she had a kind expression and beautiful gray eyes.

"Indeed it is," she announced with hauteur.[21] "I am Princess Sophia Maria Louisa of Saxe-Hoffenpoffen-und-Hamster. What are you doing here, pray?"

"Well," Mark explained cautiously, "it seemed to come about through singing a tune."

"Indeed. That is most interesting. Did the tune, perhaps, go like this?"

The princess hummed a few bars.

"That's it! How did you know?"

"Why, you foolish boy, it was I who put the spell on the garden, to make it come alive when the tune is played or sung."

"I say!" Mark was full of admiration. "Can you do spells as well as being a princess?"

She drew herself up. "Naturally! At the court of Saxe-Hoffenpoffen, where I was educated, all princesses were taught a little magic, not so much as to be vulgar, just enough to get out of social difficulties."

"Jolly useful," Mark said. "How did you work the spell for the garden, then?"

"Why, you see," (the princess was obviously delighted to have somebody to talk to; she sat on a stone seat and patted it, inviting Mark to do likewise) "I had the misfortune to fall in love with Herr Rudolf, the court Kapellmeister,[22] who taught me music. Oh, he was so kind and handsome! And he was most talented, but my father, of

---

21. hauteur. Disdainful pride; snobbery
22. Kapellmeister. Conductor of a choir or an orchestra in Germany

> *"Can you do spells as well as being a princess?"*

course, would not hear of my marrying him because he was only a common person."

"So what did you do?"

"I arranged to vanish, of course. Rudi had given me a beautiful book with many pictures of gardens. My father kept strict watch to see I did not run away, so I used to slip between the pages of the book when I wanted to be alone. Then, when we decided to marry, I asked my maid to take the book to Rudi. And I sent him a note telling him to play the tune when he received the book. But I believe that spiteful Gertrud must have played me false and never taken the book, for more than fifty years have now passed and I have been here all alone, waiting in the garden, and Rudi has never come. Oh, Rudi, Rudi," she exclaimed, wringing her hands and crying a little, "where can you be? It is so long—so long!"

"Fifty years," Mark said kindly, reckoning that must make her nearly seventy. "I must say you don't look it."

"Of course I do not, dumbhead. For me, I make it that time does not touch me. But tell me, how did you know the tune that works the spell? It was taught me by dear Rudi."

"I'm not sure where I picked it up," Mark confessed. "For all I know it may be one of the Top Ten. I'll ask my music teacher; he's sure to know. Perhaps he'll have heard of your Rudolf too."

Privately Mark feared that Rudolf might very well have died by now, but he did not like to depress Princess Sophia Maria by such a suggestion, so he bade her a polite good night, promising to come back as soon as he could with another section of the garden and any news he could pick up.

He planned to go and see Mr. Johansen, his music teacher, next morning, but he had forgotten the family trip to the beach. There was just time to scribble a hasty post card to the British office of Fruhstucksgeschirrziegelsteinindustrie, asking them if they could inform him from what source they had obtained the pictures used on the packets of Brekkfast Brikks. Then Mr. Armitage drove his wife and son to Shinglemud Bay, gloomily prophesying wet weather.

In fact, the weather turned out fine, and Mark found it quite restful to swim and play beach cricket and eat ham sandwiches and lie in the sun. For he had been struck by a horrid thought: suppose he should forget the tune again when he was inside the garden—would he be stuck there, like Father in the larder? It was a lovely place to go and wander at will, but somehow he didn't fancy spending the next fifty years there with Princess Sophia Maria. Would she oblige him by singing the spell if he forgot it, or would she be too keen on company to let him go? He was not inclined to take any chances.

It was late when they arrived home, too late, Mark thought, to disturb Mr. Johansen, who was elderly and kept early hours. Mark ate a huge helping of sardines on Brekkfast Brikks for supper—he was dying to finish Section Six—but did not visit the garden that night.

Next morning's breakfast (Brikks with hot milk for a change) finished the last packet—and just as well, for the larder mouse, which Mr. Armitage still had not caught, was discovered to have nibbled the bottom left-hand corner of the packet, slightly damaging an ornamental grotto[23] in a grove of lime trees. Rather worried about this, Mark decided to make up the last section straightaway, in case the magic had been affected. By now he was becoming very skillful at the tiny, fiddling task of cutting out the little tabs and slipping them into the little slots; the job did not take long to finish. Mark attached Section Six to Section Five and then, drawing a deep breath, sang the incantation[24] once more. With immense relief, he watched the mossy wall and rusty gate grow out of the playroom floor; all was well.

He raced across the lawn, round the lake, along the avenue, through the orchard, and into the lime grove. The scent of the lime flowers was sweeter than a cake baking.

Princess Sophia Maria came towards him from the grotto, looking slightly put out.

"Good morning!" she greeted Mark. "Do you bring me any news?"

"I haven't been to see my music teacher yet," Mark confessed. "I was a bit anxious because there was a hole—"

"Ach, yes, a hole in the grotto! I have just been looking. Some wild beast must have made its way in, and I am afraid it may come again. See, it has made tracks like those of a big bear." She showed him some enormous footprints in the soft sand of the grotto floor. Mark stopped up the hole with prickly branches and promised to bring a dog when he next came, though he felt fairly sure the mouse would not return.

"I can borrow a dog from my teacher—he has plenty. I'll be back in an hour or so—see you then," he said.

"*Auf Wiedersehen,*[25] my dear young friend."

Mark ran along the village street to Mr. Johansen's house, Houndshaven Cottage. He knew better than to knock at the door because Mr. Johansen would be either practicing his violin or out in the barn at the back, and in any case the sound of barking was generally loud enough to drown any noise short of gunfire.

Besides giving music lessons at Mark's school, Mr. Johansen kept a guest house for dogs whose owners were abroad or on holiday. He was extremely kind to the guests and did his best to make them feel at home in every way, finding out from their owners what were their favorite foods, and letting them sleep on his own bed, turn about. He spent all his spare time with them, talking to them and playing either his violin or long-playing records of domestic sounds likely to appeal to the canine fancy—such as knives being sharpened, cars starting up, and children playing ball games.

Mark could hear Mr. Johansen playing Brahms's lullaby in the barn, so he went out there; the music was making some of the more susceptible inmates feel homesick: howls, sympathetic moans, and long, shuddering sighs came from the numerous comfortably carpeted cubicles all the way down the barn.

Mr. Johansen reached the end of the piece as Mark entered. He put down his fiddle and smiled welcomingly.

---

23. grotto. Cavelike house or shrine
24. incantation. Magic spell
25. *Auf Wiedersehen.* Goodbye (German)

"...if I whistle a tune to you, can you write it down for me?"

"*Ach, how gut!* It is the young Mark."

"Hullo, sir."

"You know," confided Mr. Johansen, "I play to many audiences in my life all over the world, but never anywhere do I get such a response as from zese dear doggies—it is really remarkable. But come in, come into ze house and have some coffee cake."

Mr. Johansen was a gentle, white-haired, elderly man; he walked slowly with a slight stoop and had a kindly, sad face with large, dark eyes. He looked rather like some sort of dog himself, Mark always thought, perhaps a collie or a long-haired dachshund.

"Sir," Mark said, "if I whistle a tune to you, can you write it down for me?"

"Why, yes, I shall be most happy," Mr. Johansen said, pouring coffee for both of them.

So Mark whistled his tune once more; as he came to the end, he was surprised to see the music master's eyes fill with tears, which slowly began to trickle down his thin cheeks.

"It recalls my youth, zat piece," he explained, wiping the tears away and rapidly scribbling crotchets and minims[26] on a piece of music paper. "Many times I am whistling it myself—it is wissout doubt from me you learn it—but always it is reminding me of how happy I was long ago when I wrote it."

"You *wrote* that tune?" Mark said, much excited.

"Why yes. What is so strange in zat? Many, many tunes haf I written."

"Well—" Mark said, "I won't tell you just yet in case I'm mistaken—I'll have to see somebody else first. Do you mind if I dash off right away? Oh, and might I borrow a dog—preferably a good ratter?"

"In zat case, better have my dear Lotta—alzough she is so old she is ze best of zem all," Mr. Johansen said proudly. Lotta was his own dog, an enormous, shaggy, lumbering animal, with a tail like a palm tree and feet the size of electric polishers; she was reputed to be of incalculable age; Mr. Johansen called her his strudel-hound. She knew Mark well and came along with him quite biddably,[27] though it was rather like leading a mammoth.

Luckily, his mother, refreshed by her day at the sea, was heavily engaged with Agnes the maid in spring cleaning. Furniture was being shoved about, and everyone was too busy to notice Mark and Lotta slip into the playroom.

A letter addressed to Mark lay among the clutter on the table; he opened and read it while Lotta foraged happily among the piles of magazines and tennis nets and cricket bats and rusting electronic equipment, managing to upset several things and increase the general state of huggermugger in the room.

Dear Sir, (the letter said—it was from Messrs. Digit, Digit, & Rule, a firm of chartered accountants)—We are in receipt of your inquiry as to the source of pictures on packets of Brekkfast Brikks. We are pleased to inform you that these were reproduced from the illustrations of a little-known 18th-century German work, *Steinbergen's Gartenbuch.* Unfortunately, the only known remaining copy of this book

26. crotchets and minims. Musical notation
27. biddably. Obediently

was burnt in the disastrous fire that destroyed the factory and premises of Mssrs. Fruhstucksgeschirrziegelsteinindustrie two months ago. The firm has now gone into liquidation and we are winding up their effects.

Yours faithfully,

P. J. Zero, Gen. Sec.

"*Steinbergen's Gartenbuch,*" Mark thought. "That must have been the book that Princess Sophia Maria used for the spell—probably the same copy. Oh, well, since it's burned, it's lucky the pictures were reproduced on the Brekkfast Brikks packets. Come on, Lotta, let's go and find a nice princess then. Good girl! Rats! Chase 'em!"

He sang the spell, and Lotta, all enthusiasm, followed him into the garden.

They did not have to go far before they saw the princess—she was sitting sunning herself on the rim of the fountain. But what happened then was unexpected. Lotta let out the most extraordinary cry—whine, bark, and howl all in one—and hurled herself towards the princess like a rocket.

"Hey! Look out! Lotta! *Heel!*" Mark shouted in alarm. But Lotta, with her great paws on the princess's shoulders, had about a yard of salmon-pink tongue out, and was washing the princess's face all over with frantic affection.

The princess was just as excited. "Lotta, Lotta! She knows me; it's dear Lotta; it must be! Where did you get her?" she cried to Mark, hugging the enormous dog, whose tail was going round faster than a turbo prop.

"Why, she belongs to my music master, Mr. Johansen, and it's he who made up the tune," Mark said.

The princess turned quite white and had to sit down on the fountain's rim again.

"*Johansen?* Rudolf Johansen? My Rudi! At last! After all these years! Oh, run, run, and fetch him immediately, please! Immediately!"

Mark hesitated a moment.

"Please make haste!" she besought him. "Why do you wait?"

"It's only—well, you won't be surprised if he's quite *old,* will you? Remember he hasn't been in a garden keeping young like you."

"All that will change," the princess said confidently. "He has only to eat the fruit of the garden. Why, look at Lotta—when she was a puppy, for a joke I gave her a fig from this tree, and you can see she is a puppy still, though she must be older than any other dog in the world! Oh, please hurry to bring Rudi here."

"Why don't you come with me to his house?"

"That would not be correct etiquette," she said with dignity. "After all, I *am* royal."

"Okay," said Mark. "I'll fetch him. Hope he doesn't think I'm crackers."

"Give him this." The princess took off a locket on a gold chain. It had a miniature of a romantically handsome young man with dark, curling hair. "My Rudi," she explained fondly. Mark could just trace a faint resemblance to Mr. Johansen.

He took the locket and hurried away. At the gate, something made him look back: the princess and Lotta were sitting at the edge of the fountain, side by side. The princess had an arm round Lotta's neck; with the other hand she waved to him, just a little.

"Hurry!" she called again.

Mark made his way out of the house, through the spring-cleaning chaos, and flew down the village to Houndshaven Cottage. Mr. Johansen was in the house this time, boiling up a noisome[28] mass of meat and bones for the dogs' dinner. Mark said nothing at all, just handed him the locket. He took one look at it and staggered, putting his hand to his heart; anxiously, Mark led him to a chair.

"Are you all right, sir?"

"Yes, yes! It was only ze shock. Where did you get ziss, my boy?"

So Mark told him.

Surprisingly, Mr. Johansen did not find anything odd about the story; he nodded his head several times as Mark related the various points.

"Yes, yes, her letter, I have it still—" he pulled out a worn little scrap of paper, "but ze *Gartenbuch* it reached me never. Zat wicked Gertrud must haf sold it to some bookseller who sold it to Fruhstucksgeschirrziegelsteinindustrie. And so she has been waiting all zis time! My poor little Sophie!"

"Are you strong enough to come to her now?" Mark asked.

"*Natürlich!* But first we must give ze dogs zeir dinner; zey must not go hungry."

So they fed the dogs, which was a long job, as there were at least sixty and each had a different diet, including some very odd preferences like Swiss roll spread with

"*Yes, yes, her letter, I have it still—*"

Marmite and yeast pills wrapped in slices of caramel. Privately, Mark thought the dogs were a bit spoiled, but Mr. Johansen was very careful to see that each visitor had just what it fancied.

"After all, zey are not mine! Must I not take good care of zem?"

At least two hours had gone by before the last willow-pattern plate was licked clean and they were free to go. Mark made rings round Mr. Johansen all the way up the village; the music master limped quietly along, smiling a little; from time to time he said, "Gently, my friend. We do not run a race. Remember, I am an old man."

That was just what Mark did remember. He longed to see Mr. Johansen young and happy once more.

The chaos in the Armitage house had changed its location: the front hall was now clean, tidy, and damp; the rumpus of vacuuming had shifted to the playroom. With a black hollow of apprehension in his middle, Mark ran through the open door and stopped, aghast. All the toys, tools, weapons, boxes, magazines, and bits of machinery had been rammed into the cupboards; the floor where his garden had been laid out was bare. Mrs. Armitage was in the playroom taking down the curtains.

"Mother! Where's my Brekkfast Brikks garden?"

28. noisome. Offensive to the sense of smell

"Oh, darling, you didn't want it, did you? It was all dusty; I thought you'd finished with it. I'm afraid I've burned it in the furnace. Really you *must* try not to let this room get into such a clutter; it's perfectly disgraceful. Why, hullo, Mr. Johansen," she added in embarrassment. "I didn't see you. I'm afraid you've called at the worst possible moment. But I'm sure you'll understand how it is at spring-cleaning time."

She rolled up her bundle of curtains, glancing worriedly at Mr. Johansen; he looked rather odd, she thought. But he gave her his tired, gentle smile and said, "Why, yes, Mrs. Armitage, I understand, I understand very well. Come, Mark. We have no business here, you can see."

Speechlessly, Mark followed him. What was there to say?

"Never mind," Mrs. Armitage called after Mark. "The Rice Nuts pack has a helicopter on it."

Every week in The Times newspaper you will see this advertisement:

> **BREKKFAST BRIKKS PACKETS.**
> £100 offered for any in good condition, whether empty or full.

So, if you have any, you know where to send them.

But Mark is growing anxious; none have come in yet, and every day Mr. Johansen seems a little thinner and more elderly. Besides, what will the princess be thinking? ✤

What is your favorite alternative world in literature or films? What qualities of this world make it particularly appealing to you? Why do you think literature that depicts fantasy worlds—from Homer's *Odyssey* to J. K. Rowling's Harry Potter series—has such a widespread appeal?

Analyze and Extend

1. What does Mark's reaction to his discovery of the garden suggest about his personality?
2. How do the everyday settings of the story affect your perception of the garden?
3. This story could have ended with Rudolf and the princess living happily ever after. Is the actual ending stronger or weaker than a typical "fairy tale" ending? Explain.

Informative Writing One definition of fantasy is "the plausible impossible," that is, it makes things that actually couldn't happen seem possible and real. Write a brief **essay** analyzing how Joan Aiken makes her alternative world seem real. State your main idea in your thesis, focusing on one or two literary elements that made this fantasy world believable. Support your thesis with examples from the story.

Collaborative Learning Working with other students, create an advertising jingle like the Brekkfast Brikks song. The jingle should promote a food or product that is generally not considered tasty or exciting. What descriptive words or associations would you use to make the product more appealing to consumers?

Go to **www.mirrorsandwindows.com** for more.

For Your Reading List

A Wrinkle in Time
by Madeleine L'Engle

In this Newbery Award–winning classic, high school student Meg Murry is worried about her father, who has been missing for a year. One stormy night, the mysterious Mrs. Whatsit arrives at the Murrys' door with important news. Mrs. Whatsit tells the family that they must journey through a tesseract, a kind of wrinkle in time, to save Mr. Murry.

Tuck Everlasting
by Natalie Babbitt

Ten-year-old Winnie Foster hates her strict and smothering life. One day she sets off into the woods to get away from everything. Instead of solitude, Winnie finds the Tuck family living there. Winnie wonders why anyone would choose to be so isolated, so the family lets her in on their secret. The deep woods are not safe, though, and soon Winnie must rescue her friends from the law.

The Devil's Arithmetic
by Jane Yolen

During the Jewish holiday of Passover, twelve-year-old Hannah Stern is chosen to open the door during the Seder, to symbolically welcome the prophet Elijah to the family meal. When she opens the door, Hannah suddenly finds herself in Poland in 1942, where everyone thinks she is Chaya Abramowicz.

Bradbury Stories: 100 of His Most Celebrated Tales
by Ray Bradbury

Ray Bradbury has written a wide variety of stories, from horror and fantasy to realistic fiction and humorous anecdotes. What characterizes all of Bradbury's fiction is a natural-born storyteller's delight in the creation of wonder. Selected by the writer, this recent collection includes many of Bradbury's best-known fiction, including "The Flying Machine" and excerpts from *The Martian Chronicles*.

Eragon
by Christopher Paolini

Eragon, a farm boy living in a world much like medieval Europe, finds a magical blue stone that turns out to be a dragon's egg. When the egg hatches, an evil king comes looking for the baby dragon, burning down Eragon's farm and killing his uncle. Thus begins a series of adventures that involve immortal elves, mining dwarves, a wizard, and a magical red sword.

Zazoo
by Richard Mosher

Swimming in her quiet canal, Zazoo spies Marius, a bird-watching boy on a bike. When he asks for information about her quiet French village, she grows curious and begins asking her own questions. Zazoo slowly uncovers the story of her adoptive grandfather's early life. She learns of the "Awful Time" during World War II. But as the story is revealed, old pains are healed and new romance sparked.

Writing Workshop

Informative Writing

Responding to a Short Story

- **Assignment:** Write a response to a short story I have read.
- **Goal:** Present a clear and engaging response to a story or an aspect of a story.
- **Strategy:** Organize my main points and support them with evidence from the story.
- **Writing Rubric:** My response to literature should include the following:
  - a compelling introduction that clearly states my response
  - a clear organizational pattern
  - textual evidence that supports my main ideas
  - varied sentences to engage the reader
  - a conclusion that sums up my response

Reading and Writing

In this unit, you read short stories about the unexpected, including a criminal who runs out of time, time catching up to a Pullman porter, and lost time at a mysterious inn. How did you respond to each of these stories?

As you read a story, you react to it, forming opinions about the characters, setting, plot, and the story as a whole. Perhaps you liked a story in the unit because you could relate to a character or could visualize the setting described. In this workshop, you will learn how to write a **response to a piece of literature.** In a response to literature, you not only tell how you reacted to a selection, you explain your reaction with specific details and examples from the text. The following summary includes a description of your assignment, your goals, strategies, and a writing rubric, that is, a set of standards by which you can judge how well you completed your assignment. You will use this rubric in drafting and revising your response.

What Great Writers Do

Ray Bradbury is the author of many novels and short stories. In the following excerpt, Bradbury discusses how he came to embrace his unique literary tastes. When writing a response essay, why is it important to express your own opinions?

In October 1929 I looked at that one comic strip, with its view of the future, and I thought, "That's where I belong." I started to collect Buck Rogers comic strips. And everybody in the fifth grade made fun of me. I continued to collect them for about a month, and then I listened to the critics. And I tore up my comic strips. That's the worst thing I ever did. Two or three days later, I broke down. I was crying, and I said to myself, "Why am I crying? Whose funeral am I going to? Who died?" And the answer was, "Me." I'd torn up the future.

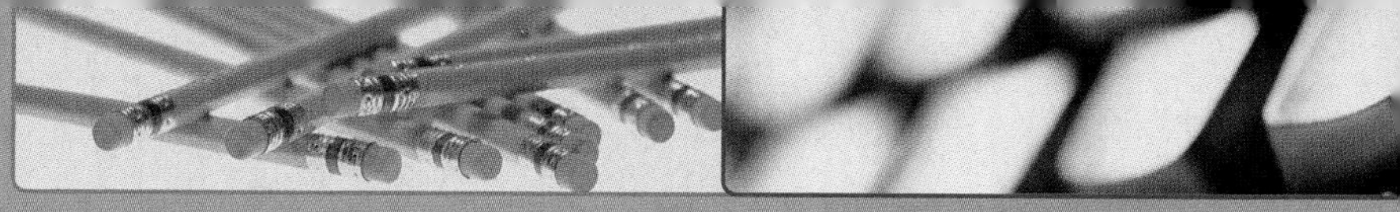

1. PREWRITE

Narrowing Your Topic

Think of the stories from the unit that stand out in your mind. Which stories surprised you? Which were the most interesting or changed your perspective on something? Perhaps there was a particular character or other aspect of the story that influenced your reaction. As you consider stories to write about, make sure the one you choose will give you enough to discuss.

Gathering Details

Once you have chosen a story to write about, gather specific details from the story that caused you to react the way you did. As you draft, you will use these details to support your ideas. One way to gather and organize details about a character or main idea is by using a cluster chart.

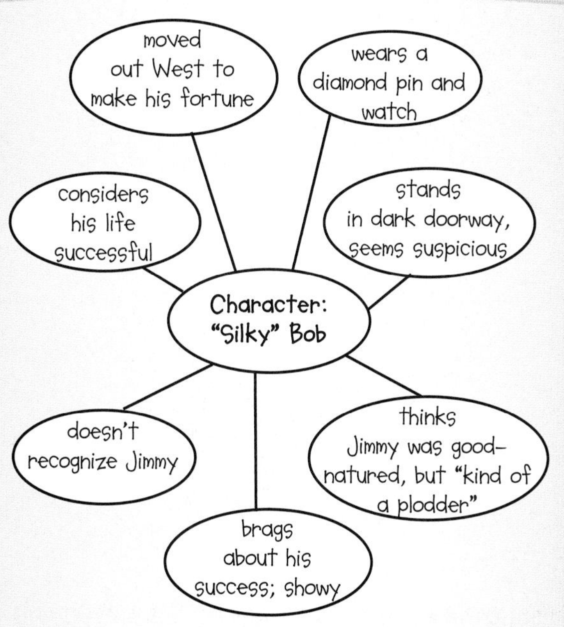

Deciding on Your Purpose

Now that you have gathered details, ask yourself questions to help you decide on your thesis, or the point you want to make about the story. Ask questions about the parts of the story that most affected your reaction to it.

1. What is my opinion of the main characters?
2. What do the characters learn?
3. Is the setting important? Why?
4. Which events were most interesting or surprising?
5. What was the message, or theme, of the story?

In your thesis, give your response to the story and tell which parts of the story created this effect. In the sample below, the writer felt the story was suspenseful and surprising due to the realistic descriptions.

The realistic descriptions made this story suspenseful and surprising to me because they reveal who each character really is, despite how the characters see themselves.

2. DRAFT

Organizing Ideas

Once you have created a thesis and have gathered enough ideas to write about, decide how to organize your ideas. Choose an **organizational pattern** that will help you convey your ideas clearly and effectively. To emphasize your strongest points, organize them by **order of importance.** That is, place your most important point either first or last for the most impact.

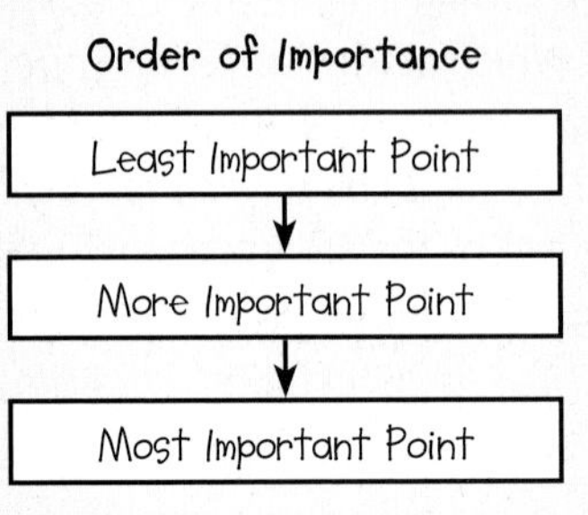

Putting Your Thoughts on Paper

Your essay should have three main parts: an introduction, body paragraphs, and a conclusion. In your introduction, summarize the basic plot of the story and include your thesis. In your body paragraphs, organize your main points by order of importance. Remember that each paragraph should focus on one main idea about the story that in turn supports your thesis. These main ideas will be stated in each paragraph's **topic sentence.** Support each main idea with specific details, examples, and quotations from the story. Then explain how these details support your main ideas. The last paragraph, or **conclusion,** should sum up your main points and restate your thesis. Before drafting, create a plan to identify the main parts of your response.

Intro

- Identify the story "After Twenty Years" by O. Henry.
- Summarize the important parts of the story.
- Include my thesis statement.

Body

- State my least important point and support it.
- State my more important point and support it.
- State my most important point and support it.

Conclusion

- Sum up my main points.
- Restate my thesis.

Use your plan as a guide. You may want to write from beginning to end to create your first draft, and reread and revise only after you have finished the first draft. Or you may want to write each paragraph, then reread to revise it point by point.

Audience and Tone

As you write, keep in mind who will read your response. This is your **audience.** Your audience could be your teacher or your classmates, for example. Make sure you give enough background information so your audience can understand your response. If your audience has also read the story, only summarize the main parts. Use your introduction to "hook," or engage, your audience.

Your **tone** is your attitude toward the subject you are writing about. Your tone tells the reader how you feel about the story, characters, or other subjects you discuss. The tone you take can be formal or informal, and it can show attitudes such as sympathy, humor, disgust, and admiration. Your response should sound natural, but not too casual.

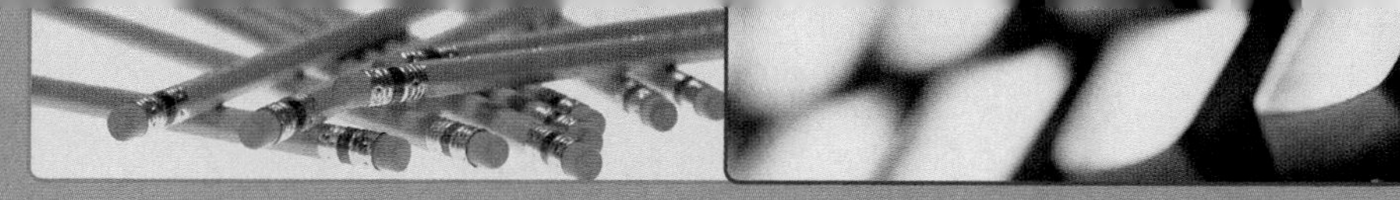

3. REVISE

Evaluating Your Draft

Now that your draft is complete, look over your own paper for strengths and weaknesses. To get the best evaluation of your writing, however, conduct a **peer review.** Exchange papers with a classmate and discuss ways you can improve your paper.

Below is part of a draft of a response to literature. The annotations to the right indicate the reasons for the changes marked in the draft.

Revising Checklist

- ☐ Does the introduction state the thesis?
- ☐ Is the response clearly organized?
- ☐ Are the main ideas supported with specific details and examples?
- ☐ Does the conclusion sum up the thesis and main points?

Friends who meet again after several years are often shocked at how different their lives are. In "After Twenty Years" by O. Henry, ~~is a story about~~ two friends~~. They~~ meet again after twenty years~~.~~, *under surprising circumstances.* The friends, Bob and Jimmy, are scheduled to meet at a restaurant where they had dinner twenty years ago. *The realistic descriptions made this story suspenseful and surprising to me because they reveal who each character really is, despite how the characters see themselves.*

Add a hook and interesting details to engage your reader.

In your thesis, specify what parts of the story made you respond the way you did.

The dark, shadowy setting of the story suggests that appearances may not be what they seem. When the police officer sees Bob, he is in a dark doorway. Neither man seems to recognize the other in the darkness.

Make sure each body paragraph has a topic sentence.

The suspense and unexpected twist in "After Twenty Years" make this an engaging story. ~~Also, the story reminds me of the "Inn of Lost Time."~~ The realistic descriptions gradually reveal the true qualities of each character, whether the characters see that truth or not.

Delete any details that are off topic.

4. EDIT AND PROOFREAD

Focus: Sentence Variety

Including a variety of sentences in your response will make your writing more interesting. As you revise your draft, check that the length and type of your sentences vary. If you have several short, choppy sentences in a row, combine some of them with conjunctions to create complex sentences. Use transitions to connect ideas.

> Yet, Jimmy sees through Bob's bragging. Jimmy feels loyalty toward his old friend. He cannot arrest him himself.

> Yet, *though* Jimmy sees through Bob's bragging, Jimmy feels loyalty toward his old friend, *and* he cannot arrest him himself.

If many of your sentences start or end the same way, revise them to add variety. Add introductory phrases, or change the order of the clauses.

Focus: Commonly Confused Words

Some words can be confusing when you are writing. Review words such as *were* and *we're, its* and *it's,* and *affect* and *effect* as you revise. If you are confused as to which word to use, look up the word in a dictionary.

> In the story, it's "barely 10 o'clock at night," and the street is "depeopled."

If you substitute the words *it is* for the contraction *it's,* you will notice that the correct word was used. The word *its* is the possessive form of the word *it.*

Proofreading

Proofreading for Errors When you proofread, you look for mistakes in the mechanics of your writing. Now is the time to correct mistakes in spelling, punctuation, and capitalization. Use proofreader's marks to highlight any errors you find. (See the Language Arts Handbook, section 4.1, for a list of proofreader's marks.)

5. PUBLISH AND PRESENT

Final Draft

Clean Copy Now that you have revised, edited, and proofread your paper, make a clean copy for presentation. Handwritten papers should be neat and legible. If you are working with a word processing program, double-space the lines of text and use a readable typeface. Follow your teacher's presentation guidelines before submitting your work.

Student Model

After Twenty Years
by Sonia Mendoza

Friends who meet again after several years are often shocked at how different their lives are. In "After Twenty Years" by O. Henry, two friends meet again after twenty years, under surprising circumstances. The friends, Bob and Jimmy, are scheduled to meet at a restaurant where they had dinner twenty years ago. A man calls Bob's name and Bob believes the man is Jimmy. When they reach better light, however, Bob realizes his perceptions have been wrong. The realistic descriptions made this story suspenseful and surprising to me because they reveal who each character really is, despite how the characters see themselves.

Names the story and its author

Summarizes the important points of the story

Presents a clear thesis statement that responds to one aspect of the story

The dark, shadowy setting of the story suggests that appearances may not be what they seem. In the story, it's "barely 10 o'clock at night," and the street is "depeopled." When the police officer sees Bob, he is in a dark doorway. Neither man seems to recognize the other in the darkness. The few people out are unrecognizable with their "coat collars turned high." When the man claiming to be Jimmy arrives, he has his "collar turned up to his ears," suggesting he, too, may not be who he seems.

The descriptions of Jimmy reveal he is impressive and observant, despite what others might think. He sees Bob immediately, even though Bob is standing in a dark doorway, and Bob doesn't recognize him. When Bob talks about Jimmy, he says he was "a kind of plodder, though good-natured fellow." The detail suggests that Bob is not impressed by Jimmy's humble traits. As Bob brags about life out West, Jimmy doesn't seem interested in such showy success. Yet, though Jimmy sees through Bob's bragging, Jimmy feels loyalty toward his old friend, and he cannot arrest him himself.

The descriptions of Bob add suspense to the story, and they reveal that he cannot see himself or others for who they really are. "Silky" Bob is sure his life has turned out better than Jimmy's. After growing up in New York, he moved out West to make his fortune. There, Bob says, "I've had to compete with some of the sharpest wits to get my pile." His pile, it seems, included a life of crime. Yet, though Bob has "keen eyes," he is never able to see himself and his success for what it really is until he is arrested as a criminal.

Is organized in a clear, logical way

Includes clear topic sentences for body paragraphs

Supports the thesis by providing clear explanations

Supports main ideas with specific details and quoted evidence from the story

The suspense and unexpected twist in "After Twenty Years" make this an engaging story. The realistic descriptions gradually reveal the true qualities of each character, whether the characters see that truth or not.

Sums up the main points without repeating the thesis exactly

Speaking & Listening Workshop

Giving and Actively Listening to Oral Summaries

Imagine a friend has asked you to describe a movie you have just seen or a story you have read recently. What information would you give your friend? Would you talk just about the plot? Or would you describe the setting and the characters? An effective oral summary should discuss all of these elements. An **oral summary** is a presentation that conveys the plot, setting, characters, and other elements of a literary work through spoken words rather than writing.

In this workshop you will learn how to plan and deliver an oral summary of a short story. You will also learn how to listen effectively to someone else's presentation. This workshop includes a rubric, a set of standards to use in evaluating either your own presentation or someone else's.

Planning an Oral Summary

Choose a Story Many short stories would make good subjects for an oral summary. Here are a few points to keep in mind when choosing a story for an oral summary.

- Pick a story that you feel strongly about, since you will communicate your own enthusiasm—or lack of it—to your audience.
- Don't pick a story that is so long and complicated that your presentation becomes bogged down in too many plot details and you lose your audience's attention.
- Don't pick a story that is so brief that your presentation will seem skimpy.

Identify Your Audience How you develop your oral summary will depend on who your audience is. Is the audience familiar with the short story? Will you need to provide any background information? Be prepared to answer questions from your audience.

Summarize the Plot Once you have selected the story for your oral presentation, make sure that you know the plot thoroughly. The best way to do this is to create a plot summary. In preparing your summary, include all the main events of the narrative, but avoid unimportant details. Use brief key words and phrases to remind yourself of key plot elements. If you had decided to base your presentation on "The Serial Garden," for example, your key word plot summary might look like this:

- Mark assembles model garden on cereal box
- transports himself into enchanted garden
- meets princess who created garden
- she loved court music teacher
- vanished into garden to await him
- plan failed; still waiting
- he is Mark's music teacher
- Mark tries to reunite the two; plan fails
- mother destroys cardboard model

Use Sensory Details In addition to presenting the plot of the short story you have chosen, your oral summary should help your audience *imagine* it. To do this, use sensory details, or descriptive words that appeal to the five senses. Sensory details will help your audience imagine the setting and characters and can be created through word choice. For example, if you wanted to convey the setting of the enchanted garden in "The Serial Garden," you might use words that suggest rich, glowing color, such as *golden* or *emerald.* To help your audience see the princess, you might use phrases such as "dressed in white satin," "covered with jewels," "pink-faced," or "long-nosed." As with the plot summary, use key words and phrases to remind you of sensory details.

Rehearse Your Summary Once you have prepared the materials for your oral summary, try practicing your presentation in front of a mirror, or use a video recorder to monitor your communication and delivery. Make sure to self-correct any errors in pronunciation or delivery. Remember that if you have practiced and are prepared, your presentation will go smoothly.

Evaluating Your Presentation

Before you deliver your oral summary to an audience, work with a partner to evaluate it. As with the revision of a piece of writing, a peer reviewer can help you improve your presentation. Respond to your reviewer's feedback on what you did well and on what could be improved. If you are asked to be a peer reviewer, remember to listen attentively and provide constructive feedback, which means that you should be respectful and polite whether you give criticism or praise. Whether you work alone or with a peer reviewer, use the rubric on this page to evaluate your oral summary.

Delivering Your Oral Summary

Nonverbal communication is an important part of listening and speaking. As you deliver your oral summary, remember to make eye contact with the audience. Try to stand still and avoid any movements that can distract your listeners. Adjust the pacing of your delivery, and vary the tone and volume of your voice to keep your audience focused and interested.

Listening Actively Just as it is important to be an effective speaker, it is also necessary to be an effective listener. To listen effectively, maintain eye contact with the speaker. Remain silent during the presentation, and ask questions when appropriate.

Speaking Rubric

Your oral summary will be evaluated on the following elements:

Content

- ☐ clear presentation of main details of the plot
- ☐ sensory details that convey setting and characters

Delivery and Presentation

- ☐ appropriate volume
- ☐ appropriate pacing
- ☐ effective nonverbal expression

Listening Rubric

As a peer reviewer or audience member, you should do the following:

- ☐ listen quietly and attentively
- ☐ maintain eye contact with speaker
- ☐ ask appropriate questions
- ☐ (as peer reviewer) provide constructive feedback

Writing Skills

Literary Response

Read the following short excerpt and the writing assignment that follows. Before you begin writing, think carefully about what task the assignment is asking you to perform. Then create an outline to help guide your writing.

from *The Snow Goose* by Paul Gallico

One November afternoon, three years after Rhayader had come to the Great Marsh, a child approached the lighthouse studio by means of the sea wall. In her arms she carried a burden.

She was no more than twelve, slender, dirty, nervous and timid as a bird, but beneath the grime as eerily beautiful as a marsh faery. She was pure Saxon, large-boned, fair, and a head to which her body was yet to grow, and deep-set, violet-colored eyes.

She was desperately frightened of the ugly man she had come to see, for legend had already begun to gather about Rhayader, and the native wild-fowlers hated him for interfering with their sport.

But greater than her fear was the need of that which she bore. For locked in her child's heart was the knowledge, picked up somewhere in the swampland, that this ogre who lived in the lighthouse had magic that could heal injured things.

She had never seen Rhayader before and was close to fleeing in panic at the dark apparition that appeared at the studio door, drawn by her footsteps—the black head and beard, the sinister hump, and the crooked claw.

She stood there staring, poised like a disturbed marsh bird for instant flight.

But his voice was deep and kind when he spoke to her.

"What is it, child?"

She stood her ground and then edged timidly forward. The thing she carried in her arms was a large white bird, and it was quite still. There were stains of blood on its whiteness and on her kirtle where she had held it to her.

The girl placed it in his arms. "I found it, sir. It's hurted. Is it still alive?"

Assignment: What methods of characterization does the author use to develop the two characters in this passage? Plan and write several paragraphs in which you explain how the use of characterization helps the reader to understand the girl's motivation for approaching the man in the lighthouse. What about the old man assists her in overcoming her own fears? Include evidence from this passage in your response.

Revising and Editing Skills

For each of the following questions, choose the *best* revision of the underlined portion of the sentence. If you feel that the underlined portion should not be changed, choose option (A), which repeats the phrasing of the original. Record your answers on a separate sheet of paper.

1. Because we studied so hard, were much happier than the rest of the class.
   A. were much happier than
   B. were much happier, than
   C. were much happier; than
   D. we're much happier than
   E. your much happier than

2. John and he went to visit their grandparents in Arkansas over winter break.
   A. John and he went to visit their
   B. John and him went to visit their
   C. Him and John went to visit their
   D. John and he went to visit they're
   E. Him and John went to visit they are

3. The senator, along with his supporters, were unhappy with the outcome of the election.
   A. senator, along with his supporters, were
   B. senator, along with his supporters, was
   C. senator, along with him supporters, were
   D. senator, along with his supporters, are
   E. senator along with his supporters were

4. Thanks to Johnny, were nearly done with the project.
   A. were nearly done with
   B. were done nearly with
   C. we is nearly done with
   D. we was nearly done with
   E. we're nearly done with

5. Sarah and Haifa were not going to bring their clubs to the course.
   A. were not going to bring their clubs
   B. isn't going to bring their clubs
   C. we're not going to bring their clubs
   D. is not going to bring their clubs
   E. have not bring their clubs

6. The principal is him.
   A. The principal is him.
   B. The principal was him.
   C. The principal were him.
   D. The principal is he.
   E. The principal were he.

7. Monica was unsympathetic to Marie and I.
   A. was unsympathetic to Marie and I.
   B. is unsympathetic to Marie and I.
   C. was unsympathetic to Marie and me.
   D. unsympathetically was to Marie and I.
   E. were unsympathetic to Marie and me.

8. Juan and Tony could not avoid their homework, no matter how hard he tried.
   A. no matter how hard he tried.
   B. no matter how hard we tried.
   C. No matter how hard he tried.
   D. no matter how hard us tried.
   E. no matter how hard they tried.

9. Allen, as well as Allen's three sisters, are going to attend the afternoon's events.
   A. are going to attend
   B. were going to attend
   C. we're going to attend
   D. is going to attend
   E. have attended

10. Were not supposed to use water during the drought.
    A. Were not supposed to use water
    B. We're not supposed to use water
    C. Were is supposed to use water
    D. Were not supposing to use water
    E. Not supposed to use water

Reading Skills

Carefully read the following passage. Then, on a separate piece of paper, answer each question.

"The Dinner Party" by Mona Gardner

The country is India. A colonial official and his wife are giving a large dinner party. They are seated with their guests—army officers and government attachés and their wives, and a visiting American naturalist—in their spacious dining room, which has a bare marble floor, open rafters and wide glass doors opening onto a veranda.

A spirited discussion springs up between a young girl who insists that women have outgrown the jumping-on-a-chair-at-the-sight-of-a-mouse era and a colonel who says that they haven't.

"A woman's unfailing reaction in any crisis," the colonel says, "is to scream. And while a man may feel like it, he has that ounce more of nerve control than a woman has. And that last ounce is what counts." The American does not join in the argument but watches the other guests. As he looks, he sees a strange expression come over the face of the hostess. She is staring straight ahead, her muscles contracting slightly. With a slight gesture she summons the native boy standing behind her chair and whispers to him. The boy's eyes widen: he quickly leaves the room.

Of the guests, none except the American notices this or sees the boy place a bowl of milk on the veranda just outside the open doors.

The American comes to with a start. In India, milk in a bowl means only one thing—bait for a snake. He realizes there must be a cobra in the room. He looks up at the rafters—the likeliest place—but they are bare. Three corners of the room are empty, and in the fourth the servants are waiting to serve the next course. There is only one place left—under the table.

His first impulse is to jump back and warn the others, but he knows the commotion would frighten the cobra into striking. He speaks quickly, the tone of his voice so arresting that it sobers everyone.

"I want to know just what control everyone at this table has. I will count to three hundred—that's five minutes—and not one of you is to move a muscle. Those who move will forfeit fifty rupees. Ready!" The twenty people sit like stone images while he counts. He is saying, "...two hundred and eighty..." when, out of the corner of his eye, he sees the cobra emerge and make for the bowl of milk. Screams ring out as he jumps to slam the veranda doors safely shut.

"You were right, Colonel!" the host exclaims. "A man has just shown us an example of perfect control."

"Just a minute," the American says, turning to his hostess. "Mrs. Wynnes, how did you know that cobra was in the room?" A faint smile lights up the woman's face as she replies: "Because it was crawling across my foot."

1. Based on the context, which of the following is the *best* definition of the word *spacious* in line 3?
   A. big and open
   B. uncomfortable
   C. quiet
   D. very small
   E. crooked

2. Lines 1 through 16 can *best* be described as the
   A. exposition.
   B. climax.
   C. climax and falling action.
   D. falling action.
   E. resolution.

3. Based on the context, which of the following is the *best* definition of the word *forfeit* in line 29?
   A. to bet
   B. to take
   C. to consider
   D. to taper off
   E. to lose

4. What motivates the naturalist to ask the dinner guests to enter into a contest?
   A. He wants to alert the guests to the presence of a snake.
   B. He wants to closely watch the hostess.
   C. He wants to test the colonel's theory.
   D. He wants to win fifty rupees.
   E. He wants to keep everyone completely still.

5. The protagonist of this passage is
   A. the naturalist.
   B. the colonel.
   C. the colonial official.
   D. the boy.
   E. the snake.

6. Which of the following *best* describes the central conflict of this passage?
   A. Members of a dinner party are arguing over a colonel's claim that women are less courageous than men.
   B. People at a dinner party use a snake to solve a dispute.
   C. People at a dinner party are engaged in a contest to see who can hold still the longest.
   D. A cobra has crawled into a dinner party, but those who have noticed cannot alert the rest of the party safely.
   E. A servant at a dinner party attempts to murder the guests as they eat.

7. The conflict in this passage is primarily
   A. internal.
   B. external.
   C. indirect.
   D. resolution.
   E. falling action.

8. The setting of this passage is best described as a
   A. small house.
   B. veranda.
   C. living room.
   D. dining room.
   E. garden.

Unit 2

Learning Values

Fiction

SANDRA CISNEROS

GARY SOTO

CHERYLENE LEE

"But T. J. kept the vision bright within us, his words shrewd and calculated toward the fulfillment of his dream; and he worked harder than any of us. He seemed driven toward a goal that we couldn't see...."

—BORDEN DEAL, "Antaeus"

How do you respond when faced with a challenge? In "Antaeus," T. J. is a newcomer to the city. Though he struggles at first, he is able to excite his friends with his dream of creating a roof garden. As you read the unit, consider how you approach difficult situations. Do you always stay true to your values?

Literary Element

Understanding Point of View

What Is Point of View?

Each of these photographs shows the same subject–a man motorcycling down a rural road. What is different about them? The main difference is the point of view. One photograph shows the motorcyclist from the point of view of another person; the other shows the scene from the point of view of the motorcyclist himself. Point of view is an important element in fiction as well as photography.

Point of View in Fiction

Each of the passages to the right gives an account of a story's main character observing something. Who is the narrator in each? In other words, who is telling the story? How do you know? The vantage point from which a writer presents the events and characters of a story is called the **point of view.**

First-Person Point of View In "Hollywood and the Pits," the story is told from a *first-person point of view.* In other words, the narrator is a character in the story and describes the events. You can tell that a story is told from a first-person point of view because the narrator uses such pronouns as *I* and *we.* In a story told from the first-person point of view, the information must be limited to what the character experiences or knows. A story told in first person often has a heightened intensity, however, because the narrator is experiencing the events that he or she describes.

Third-Person Point of View In the passage from "Jed's Grandfather," the story is told from a *third-person point of view.* In this case, the narrator is usually not a character. The third-person point of view is indicated by the narrator's use of such pronouns as *he, she, it,* and *they.* If a story is told from a *third-person omniscient* ("all-knowing") point of view, the narrator is able to relate everything about all the characters–their experiences, thoughts, and feelings. In a *third-person limited* point of view, the narrator chiefly presents the perspective of only one character.

I breathed, ate, slept, dreamed about the La Brea Tar Pits. I spent summer days working the archaeological dig, and in dreams saw the bones glistening....

—CHERYLENE LEE, "Hollywood and the Pits"

Gulls began swooping down in front of them. They were grey and white. From their yellow beaks came those raucous squawks which seemed to Jed to be the one thing which linked them to the rock they flew up from.

—JOSEPH BRUCHAC, "Jed's Grandfather"

Hollywood and the Pits

A Short Story by Cherylene Lee

Apply the Model

BEFORE READING

DURING READING

AFTER READING

GUIDED READING

Build Background

Scientific Context The La Brea Tar Pits are a major tourist attraction in Los Angeles, California. They began to form nearly 40,000 years ago, when the area was home to such animals as saber-toothed cats, ground sloths, and mammoths. The "tar" is really asphalt, which seeps out of petroleum deposits. Animals entered a watering hole and were trapped by tar under the water. The remains of the animals churn in the tar.

Reader's Context How is becoming a teenager like falling into tar? Do parents really remember what growing up is like?

Set Purpose

Before you begin reading, skim the story for unfamiliar terms. Make a list of terms you need to look up.

Analyze Literature

Point of View A story's **point of view** reflects the vantage point of the narrator. With the *first-person point of view,* the narrator is part of the action, but with the *third-person point of view,* the narrator observes the action. "Hollywood and the Pits" uses both points of view. As you read, think about how the alternating points of view influence the mood, the plot, and your understanding of the main character.

Use Reading Skills

Analyze Cause and Effect You can keep track of causes and effects in this story by creating a cause-effect chart. As you read, create a cause-effect chart like the one below.

Cause: Narrator begins to grow up.	→	Effect:

Preview Vocabulary

ob • sessed (əb sest´) *adj.,* preoccupied

dub (dʉb) *v.,* give a nickname

bar • rage (bə räzh´) *n.,* outpouring of many things at once

pred • a • tor (pred´ ə tər) *n.,* animal that gets food by capturing and eating other animals

scav • en • ger (scav´ ən jər) *n.,* animal that gets food by eating the dead bodies of other animals

Meet the Author

Cherylene Lee (b. 1954) grew up in Los Angeles, California, and appeared in television shows, movies, and stage plays when she was a child. In college, she studied paleontology—fossils and prehistoric life—and geology—Earth's structure. Today she writes stories, poems, and plays. She is best known for her plays, including one set at the La Brea Tar Pits called *Mixed Messages.*

Hollywood and the Pits

A Short Story by Cherylene Lee

I lost myself there and found something else.

1968, when I was fifteen, the pit opened its secret to me. I breathed, ate, slept, dreamed about the La Brea Tar Pits. I spent summer days working the archaeological dig, and in dreams saw the bones glistening, the broken pelvises, the skulls, the vertebrae[1] looped like a woman's pearls hanging on an invisible cord. I welcomed those dreams. I wanted to know where the next skeleton was, identify it, record its position, discover whether it was whole or not. I wanted to know where to dig in the coarse, black, gooey sand. I lost myself there and found something else.

My mother thought something was wrong with me. Was it good for a teenager to be fascinated by death? Especially animal death in the Pleistocene?[2] Was it normal to be so obsessed by a sticky brown hole in the ground in the center of Los Angeles? I don't know if it was normal or not, but it seemed perfectly logical to me. After all, I grew up in Hollywood, a place where dreams and nightmares can often take the same shape. What else would a child actor do?

"Thank you very much, dear. We'll be letting you know."

ob•sessed (əb sest´) *adj.,* preoccupied

DURING READING

Analyze Literature
Point of View Is the narrator part of the action? What else can you tell about the narrator so far?

1. **the broken pelvises, the skulls, the vertebrae.** Bones from the hip, head, and spine (backbone)
2. **Pleistocene.** Geologic epoch that spans 10,000 to 1.6 million years ago

I knew what that meant. It meant I would never hear from them again. I didn't get the job. I heard that phrase a lot that year.

I walked out of the plush office, leaving behind the casting director, producer, director, writer, and whoever else came to listen to my reading for a semiregular role on a family sitcom. The carpet made no sound when I opened and shut the door.

I passed the other girls waiting in the reception room, each poring over her script. The mothers were waiting in a separate room, chattering about their daughters' latest commercials, interviews, callbacks, jobs. It sounded like every Oriental[3] kid in Hollywood was working except me.

My mother used to have a lot to say in those waiting rooms. Ever since I was three, when I started at the Meglin Kiddie Dance Studio, I was dubbed "The Chinese Shirley Temple"—always the one to be picked at auditions and interviews, always the one to get the speaking lines, always called "the one-shot kid," because I could do my scenes in one take—even tight close-ups.[4] My mother would only talk about me behind my back because she didn't want me to hear her brag, but I knew that she was proud. In a way I was proud too, though I never dared admit it. I didn't want to be called a showoff. But I didn't exactly know what I did to be proud of either. I only knew that at fifteen I was now being passed over at all these interviews when before I would be chosen.

dub (dʉb) *v.*, give a nickname

My mother looked at my face hopefully when I came into the room. I gave her a quick shake of the head. She looked bewildered.[5] I felt bad for my mother then. How could I explain it to her? I didn't understand it myself. We left, saying polite good-byes to all the other mothers.

We didn't say anything until the studio parking lot, where we had to search for our old blue Chevy among rows and rows of parked cars baking in the Hollywood heat.

"How did it go? Did you read clearly? Did you tell them you're available?"

"I don't think they care if I'm available or not, Ma."

"Didn't you read well? Did you remember to look up so they could see your eyes? Did they ask you if you could play the piano? Did you tell them you could learn?"

The barrage of questions stopped when we finally spotted our

bar•rage (bə räzh´) *n.*, outpouring of many things at once

3. **Oriental.** Old term for Asian
4. **tight close-ups.** Film shots in which a performer's face fills the camera lens
5. **bewildered.** Puzzled

car. I didn't answer her. My mother asked about the piano because I lost out in an audition once to a Chinese girl who already knew how to play.

My mother took off the towel that shielded the steering wheel from the heat. "You're getting to be such a big girl," she said, starting the car in neutral. "But don't worry, there's always next time. You have what it takes. That's special." She put the car into forward and we drove through a parking lot that had an endless number of identical cars all facing the same direction. We drove back home in silence.

To me the applause sometimes sounded like static, sometimes like distant waves.

In the La Brea Tar Pits many of the excavated bones belong to juvenile[6] *mammals. Thousands of years ago thirsty young animals in the area were drawn to watering holes, not knowing they were traps. Those inviting pools had false bottoms made of sticky tar, which immobilized its victims and preserved their bones when they died. Innocence trapped by ignorance. The tar pits record that well.*

I suppose a lot of my getting into show business in the first place was a matter of luck—being in the right place at the right time. My sister, seven years older than me, was a member of the Meglin Kiddie Dance Studio long before I started lessons. Once during the annual recital held at the Shrine Auditorium, she was spotted by a Hollywood agent who handled only Oriental performers. The agent sent my sister out for a role in the CBS *Playhouse 90* television show *The Family Nobody Wanted.* The producer said she was too tall for the part. But true to my mother's training of always having a positive reply, my sister said to the producer, "But I have a younger sister..." which started my show-biz career at the tender age of three.

DURING READING

Use Reading Skills
Analyze Cause and Effect What launched the narrator's Hollywood career?

My sister and I were lucky. We enjoyed singing and dancing, we were natural hams, and our parents never discouraged us. In fact they were our biggest fans. My mother chauffeured us to all our dance lessons, lessons we begged to take. She drove us to interviews, took us to studios, went on location with us, drilled us on our lines, made sure we kept up our schoolwork and didn't sass back the tutors hired by studios to teach us for three hours a day. She never complained about being a stage mother. She said that we made her proud.

My father must have felt pride too, because he paid for a choreographer to put together our sister act: "The World Famous

6. juvenile. Young

Lee Sisters," fifteen minutes of song and dance, real vaudeville[7] stuff. We joked about that a lot, "Yeah, the Lee Sisters—Ug-Lee and Home-Lee," but we definitely had a good time. So did our parents. Our father especially liked our getting booked into Las Vegas at the New Frontier Hotel on the Strip. He liked to gamble there, though he said the craps tables in that hotel were "cold," not like the casinos in downtown Las Vegas, where all the "hot" action took place.

In Las Vegas our sister act was part of a show called "Oriental Holiday." The show was about a Hollywood producer going to the Far East, finding undiscovered talent, and bringing it back to the U.S. We did two shows a night in the main showroom, one at eight and one at twelve, and on weekends a third show at two in the morning. It ran the entire summer, often to standing-room-only audiences—a thousand people a show.

Our sister act worked because of the age and height difference. My sister then was fourteen and nearly five foot two; I was seven and very small for my age—people thought we were cute. We had song-and-dance routines to old tunes like "Ma, He's Making Eyes at Me," "Together," and "I'm Following You," and my father hired a writer to adapt the lyrics to "I Enjoy Being a Girl," which came out "We Enjoy Being Chinese." We also told corny jokes, but the Las Vegas audience seemed to enjoy it. Here we were, two kids, staying up late and jumping around, and getting paid besides. To me the applause sometimes sounded like static, sometimes like distant waves. It always amazed me when people applauded. The owner of the hotel liked us so much, he invited us back to perform in shows for three summers in a row. That was before I grew too tall and the sister act didn't seem so cute anymore.

Cherylene Lee (left) and her sister performing on television in 1959.

Many of the skeletons in the tar pits are found incomplete—particularly the skeletons of the young, which have only soft cartilage connecting the bones. In life the soft tissue allows for growth, but in death it dissolves quickly. Thus the skeletons of young animals are more apt to be scattered, especially the vertebrae protecting the spinal cord. In the tar pits, the central ends of many vertebrae are found unconnected to any skeleton. Such bone fragments are shaped like valentines, disks that are slightly lobed—heart-shaped shields that have lost their connection to what they were meant to protect.

DURING READING

Make Connections
What does the tone of this writing remind you of? Explain.

---

7. vaudeville. Theatrical variety show

I never felt my mother pushed me to do something I didn't want to do. But I always knew if something I did pleased her. She was generous with her praise, and I was sensitive when she withheld it. I didn't like to disappoint her.

I took to performing easily, and since I had started out so young, making movies or doing shows didn't feel like anything special. It was part of my childhood—like going to the dentist one morning or going to school the next. I didn't wonder if I wanted a particular role or wanted to be in a show or how I would feel if I didn't get in. Until I was fifteen, it never occurred to me that one day I wouldn't get parts or that I might not "have what it takes."

When I was younger, I got a lot of roles because I was so small for my age. When I was nine years old, I could pass for five or six. I was really short. I was always teased about it when I was in elementary school, but I didn't mind because my height got me movie jobs. I could read and memorize lines that actual five-year-olds couldn't. My mother told people she made me sleep in a drawer so I wouldn't grow any bigger.

But when I turned fifteen, it was as if my body, which hadn't grown for so many years, suddenly made up for lost time. I grew five inches in seven months. My mother was amazed. Even I couldn't get used to it. I kept knocking into things, my clothes didn't fit right, I felt awkward and clumsy when I moved. Dumb things that I had gotten away with, like paying children's prices at the movies instead of junior admission, I couldn't do anymore. I wasn't a shrimp or a small fry any longer. I was suddenly normal.

Before that summer my mother had always claimed she wanted me to be normal. She didn't want me to become spoiled by the attention I received when I was working at the studios. I still had chores to do at home, went to public school when I wasn't working, was punished severely when I behaved badly. She didn't want me to feel I was different just because I was in the movies. When I was eight, I was interviewed by a reporter who wanted to know if I thought I had a big head.

"Sure," I said.

"No you don't," my mother interrupted, which was really unusual, because she generally never said anything. She wanted me to speak for myself.

I didn't understand the question. My sister had always made fun of my head. She said my body was too tiny for the weight—I looked like a walking Tootsie Pop. I thought the reporter was making the same observation.

"She better not get that way," my mother said fiercely. "She's not any different from anyone else. She's just lucky and small for her age."

The reporter turned to my mother, "Some parents push their children to act. The kids feel like they're used."

"I don't do that—I'm not that way," my mother told the reporter.

But when she was sitting silently in all those waiting rooms while I was being turned down for one job after another, I could almost feel her wanting to shout, "Use her. Use her. What is wrong with her? Doesn't she have it anymore?" I didn't know what I had had that I didn't seem to have anymore. My mother had told the reporter that I was like everyone else. But when my life was like everyone else's, why was she disappointed?

DURING READING

Make Connections
What feeling do you think the author wants to convey by this comparison to a Tootsie Pop?

DURING READING

Make Connections
Why might most parents have mixed feelings about whether a child should be "normal"?

The churning action of the La Brea Tar Pits makes interpreting the record of past events extremely difficult. The usual order of deposition[8]—the oldest on the bottom, the youngest on the top—loses all meaning when some of the oldest fossils can be brought to the surface by the movement of natural gas. One must look for an undisturbed spot, a place untouched by the action of underground springs or natural gas or human interference. Complete skeletons become important, because they indicate areas of least disturbance. But such spots of calm are rare. Whole blocks of the tar pit can become displaced,[9] making false sequences of the past, skewing the interpretation for what is the true order of nature.

That year before my sixteenth birthday, my mother seemed to spend a lot of time looking through my old scrapbooks, staring at all the eight-by-ten glossies of the shows that I had done. In the summer we visited with my grandmother often, since I wasn't working and had lots of free time. I would go out to the garden to read or sunbathe, but I could hear my mother and grandmother talking.

"She was so cute back then. She worked with Gene Kelly when she was five years old. She was so smart for her age. I don't know what's wrong with her."

"She's fifteen."

DURING READING

Use Reading Skills
Analyze Cause and Effect Why does the narrator's mother spend so much time reviewing the past?

---

8. **order of deposition.** Sequence in which layers of sediment are left behind when water flows over an area and then recedes
9. **Whole blocks of the tar pit can become displaced.** Tar is warm enough to flow very slowly, and whole sections can move from one place to another.

"She's too young to be an ingénue[10] and too old to be cute. The studios forget so quickly. By the time she's old enough to play an ingénue, they won't remember her."

"Does she have to work in the movies? Hand me the scissors."

My grandmother was making false eyelashes using the hair from her hairbrush. When she was young she had incredible hair. I saw an old photograph of her when it flowed beyond her waist like a cascading black waterfall. At seventy, her hair was still black as night, which made her few strands of silver look like shooting stars. But her hair had thinned greatly with age. It sometimes fell out in clumps. She wore it brushed back in a bun with a hairpiece for added fullness. My grandmother had always been proud of her hair, but once she started making false eyelashes from it, she wasn't proud of the way it looked anymore. She said she was proud of it now because it made her useful.

SCIENCE ▶▶ CONNECTION

Geologic Time Evidence in rocks indicates that Earth is more than four billion years old. Scientists use big categories to measure this much time. The largest category of geologic time is the *era*. We are in the Cenozoic Era, which began sixty-five million years ago, after dinosaurs became extinct. An era is divided into *periods*, and periods are split into *epochs*. We live in the Quaternary Period, which started less than two million years ago. The La Brea Tar Pits formed during the last part of the Pleistocene Epoch of the Quaternary Period, approximately forty-thousand years ago. In terms of geologic time, would you say this is recently, or very long ago?

It was painstaking work—tying knots into strands of hair, then tying them together to form feathery little crescents. Her glamorous false eyelashes were much sought after. Theatrical makeup artists waited months for her work. But my grandmother said what she liked was that she was doing something, making a contribution, and besides it didn't cost her anything. No overhead. "Till I go bald," she often joked.

She tried to teach me her art that summer, but for some reason strands of my hair wouldn't stay tied in knots.

"Too springy," my grandmother said. "Your hair is still too young." And because I was frustrated then, frustrated with everything about my life, she added, "You have to wait until your hair falls out, like mine. Something to look forward to, eh?" She had laughed and patted my hand.

---

10. ingénue. Inexperienced young woman

My mother was going on and on about my lack of work, what might be wrong, that something she couldn't quite put her finger on. I heard my grandmother reply, but I didn't catch it all: "Movies are just make-believe, not real life. Like what I make with my hair that falls out—false. False eyelashes. Not meant to last."

The remains in the La Brea Tar Pits are mostly of carnivorous animals. Very few herbivores are found—the ratio is five to one, a perversion of the natural food chain.[11] *The ratio is easy to explain. Thousands of years ago a thirsty animal sought a drink from the pools of water only to find itself trapped by the bottom, gooey with subterranean oil. A shriek of agony from the trapped victim drew flesh-eating predators, which were then trapped themselves by the very same ooze which provided the bait. The cycle repeated itself countless times. The number of victims grew, lured by the image of easy food, the deception of an easy kill. The animals piled on top of one another. For over ten thousand years the promise of the place drew animals of all sorts, mostly predators and scavengers—dire wolves,*[12] *panthers, coyotes, vultures—all hungry for their chance. Most were sucked down against their will in those watering holes destined to be called the La Brea Tar Pits in a place to be named the City of Angels, home of Hollywood movie stars.*

pred • a • tor (pred´ ə tər) *n.,* animal that gets food by capturing and eating other animals

scav • en • ger (scav´ ən jər) *n.,* animal that gets food by eating the dead bodies of other animals

DURING READING

Use Reading Skills
Analyze Cause and Effect Why are there so many predator and scavenger remains in the tar pits?

I spent a lot of time by myself that summer, wondering what it was that I didn't have anymore. Could I get it back? How could I if I didn't know what it was?

That's when I discovered the La Brea Tar Pits. Hidden behind the County Art Museum on trendy Wilshire Boulevard, I found a job that didn't require me to be small or cute for my age. I didn't have to audition. No one said, "Thank you very much, we'll call you." Or if they did, they meant it. I volunteered my time one afternoon, and my fascination stuck—like tar on the bones of a saber-toothed tiger.

My mother didn't understand what had changed me. I didn't understand it myself. But I liked going to the La Brea Tar Pits. It meant I could get really messy and I was doing it with a purpose. I didn't feel awkward there. I could wear old stained pants. I could wear T-shirts with holes in them. I could wear disgustingly filthy sneakers and it was all perfectly justified. It wasn't a costume for a

11. perversion of the natural food chain. Plant-eaters (herbivores) usually greatly outnumber meat-eaters (carnivores); a perversion reverses this relationship.

12. dire wolves. Members of an extinct species of California wolf *(Canis dirus)*

role in a film or a part in a TV sitcom. My mother didn't mind my dressing like that when she knew I was off to the pits. That was okay so long as I didn't track tar back into the house. I started going to the pits every day, and my mother wondered why. She couldn't believe I would rather be groveling in tar than going on auditions or interviews.

While my mother wasn't proud of the La Brea Tar Pits (she didn't know or care what a fossil was), she didn't discourage me either. She drove me there, the same way she used to drive me to the studios.

"Wouldn't you rather be doing a show in Las Vegas than scrambling around in a pit?" she asked.

"I'm not in a show in Las Vegas, Ma. The Lee Sisters are retired." My older sister had married and was starting a family of her own.

"But if you could choose between..."

"There isn't a choice."

"You really like this tar-pit stuff, or are you just waiting until you can get real work in the movies?"

I didn't answer.

My mother sighed. "You could do it if you wanted, if you really wanted. You still have what it takes."

I didn't know about that. But then, I couldn't explain what drew me to the tar pits either. Maybe it was the bones, finding out what they were, which animal they belonged to, imagining how they got there, how they fell into the trap. I wondered about that a lot.

DURING READING

Use Reading Strategies
Make Inferences How has the narrator's relationship with her mother changed by this point in the plot?

At the La Brea Tar Pits, everything dug out of the pit is saved—including the sticky sand that covered the bones through the ages. Each bucket of sand is washed, sieved, and examined for pollen grains, insect remains, any evidence of past life. Even the grain size is recorded—the percentage of silt to sand to gravel that reveals the history of deposition, erosion, and disturbance. No single fossil, no one observation, is significant enough to tell the entire story. All the evidence must be weighed before a semblance of truth emerges.

The tar pits had its lessons. I was learning I had to work slowly, become observant, to concentrate. I learned about time in a way that I would never experience—not in hours, days, and months, but in thousands and thousands of years. I imagined what the past must have been like, envisioned Los Angeles as a sweeping basin, perhaps slightly colder and more humid, a time before people and studios arrived. The tar pits recorded a warming trend; the kinds of animals found there reflected the changing climate. The ones unadapted disappeared. No trace of their kind was found in the area. The ones adapted to warmer weather left a record of bones in the pit. Amid that collection of ancient skeletons, surrounded by evidence of death, I was finding a secret preserved over thousands and thousands of years. There was something cruel about natural selection[13] and the survival of the fittest. Even those successful individuals that "had what it took" for adaptation still wound up in the pits.

I never found out if I had what it took, not the way my mother meant. But I did adapt to the truth: I wasn't a Chinese Shirley Temple any longer, cute and short for my age. I had grown up. Maybe not on a Hollywood movie set, but in the La Brea Tar Pits. ✣

13. natural selection. Process in which individuals and groups best adjusted to the environment survive and reproduce

DURING READING

Use Reading Skills
Analyze Cause and Effect Why does the narrator prefer the tar pits to a career in show business?

DURING READING

Use Reading Skills
Analyze Cause and Effect How have the La Brea Tar Pits helped the narrator gain perspective on her life?

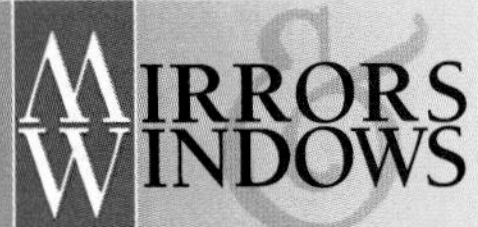

At one point, the narrator says, "I didn't know what I had had that I didn't seem to have anymore." Do you ever feel like you've changed, but people close to you don't seem to notice? Why might this be a common feeling?

Apply the Model

BEFORE READING

DURING READING

AFTER READING

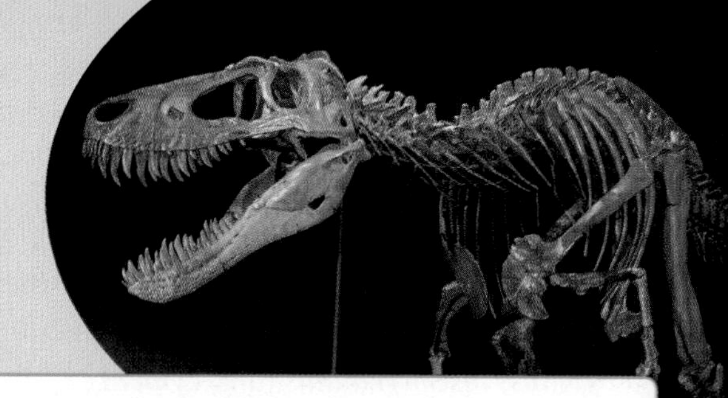

Find Meaning

1. (a) How did the narrator's experiences at auditions change? (b) How well does the narrator understand why her experiences are different?
2. How does the narrator's mother act toward the narrator?

Make Judgments

3. (a) What inspired the narrator to volunteer at the La Brea Tar Pits? (b) How did volunteering there change her outlook on life?
4. (a) What kinds of animals were drawn to the tar pits? (b) How might they resemble people?
5. Which part of her life do you think the narrator has enjoyed the most? Why?

Analyze Literature

Point of View Summarize how Cherylene Lee's use of both first-person and third-person points of view affects the mood and plot of "Hollywood and the Pits." Make a graphic organizer like this one so you can record your key impressions.

	First-Person Narrator (Hollywood)	Third-Person Narrator (The Pits)
How this influences the plot	Presents an internal conflict	Presents an external conflict
How this influences the mood		

Extend Understanding

Writing Options

Creative Writing Imagine that you are creating a time capsule in your backyard. What objects would you include? Write a **journal entry** in which you describe these things and your reasons for including them. When you are finished, share your entry with the class.

Informative Writing How would you describe this story to a friend? Write a three-paragraph **literary response** that describes the conflicts the narrator and her mother experience. Identify each conflict as internal or external and use examples from the story. In your final sentences, tell how the plot resolves each of the conflicts. Make certain you summarize the story in a way that maintains logical order.

Collaborative Learning

Infer the Author's Purpose In a small group, discuss why the story includes the scientific information on the tar pits. What might the tar pits represent? Take notes on your discussion, and then summarize the group's thoughts in one or two paragraphs.

Media Literacy

Dig for Details Use the Internet to find information on an archaeological site in or near your state. Then write a letter to the site director with two or three questions about the site. For example, ask about the fossils scientists have discovered there.

Go to **www.mirrorsandwindows.com** for more.

Literary Element

Understanding Theme

What Is Theme?

What is the main point being made in the passage below from *Peter Pan*, J. M. Barrie's most famous work? In answering this question, you are identifying the theme. A **theme** is the central idea of a literary work.

Themes and Topics

The theme is not the same as the topic. A topic is the subject of a literary work, that is, what it is about. For example, the topic of this novel is Peter Pan's adventures in Neverland. The theme is a general observation based on that topic. Literary works can share the same topic but have different themes. For example, you might have two stories that are both on the topic of sports. One story's theme might be stated: "Sports are a wonderful way to get some exercise and make friends." The other story's theme might be stated: "Sports are overrated; I prefer a good book." The topic is the same, but the themes are very different.

Stated and Implied Themes

Sometimes the central idea of a literary work is presented directly. This is called a *stated theme.* More often, however, the theme of a literary work is not presented directly and must be inferred by the reader. This is an *implied theme.* For example, the theme in the passage from *Peter Pan* is "growing up is both natural and something to be desired." Some works can have both a stated theme and an implied theme—or even several themes—either stated or implied.

Maude Adams as Peter Pan, c. 20th century. Sigismond de Ivanowski.

That was the last time the girl Wendy ever saw him. For a little longer she tried for his sake not to have growing pains; and she felt she was untrue to him when she got a prize for general knowledge. But the years came and went without bringing the careless boy; and when they met again Wendy was a married woman, and Peter was no more to her than a little dust in the box in which she had kept her toys. Wendy was grown up. You need not be sorry for her.

—J. M. BARRIE, *Peter Pan*

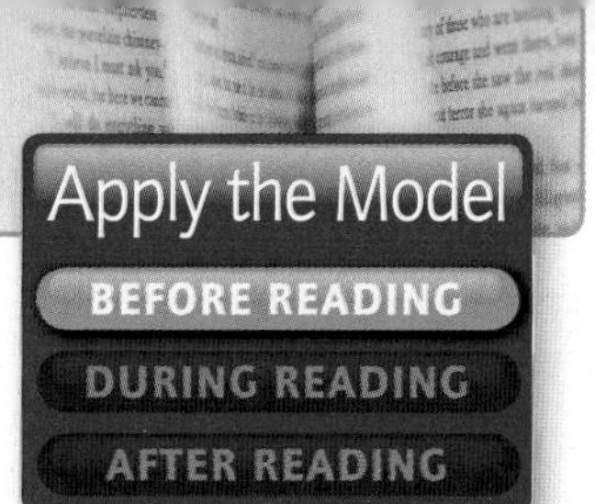

THE SCHOLARSHIP JACKET

A Short Story by Marta Salinas

GUIDED READING

Build Background

Cultural Context The term *valedictorian* comes from the Latin *vale dicere*, which means, literally, "to say farewell." The *valedictorian* makes the valedictory speech, which in turn means "a speech of farewell." A valedictorian is not necessarily the top academic achiever. Many people argue that schools should choose a top student for more than academic achievement—for well-rounded combinations of schoolwork, athletic ability, social skills, and creative talents instead.

Reader's Context When have you felt passed over for recognition that you deserved?

Set Purpose

Based on the title and information in Build Background, predict what this story will be about. Then read to find out how well you predicted the story's theme.

Analyze Literature

Theme The **theme** of a story is the main message the author wants to express. To determine the theme, read the story and then think about it for a while. Ask yourself questions such as: Of all the ideas in this story, what could I say in one sentence that would sum up the author's main point? Write your answer in your notebook.

Use Reading Skills

Context Clues Preview the vocabulary words from this selection as they are used below. Try to unlock the meaning of each word using context clues in the sentences.

1. I was so nervous for my interview that I absentmindedly got on the wrong train.
2. Our meeting at the music store was unplanned, a complete coincidence.
3. When he saw the broken glass, his eyes opened wide and his jaw dropped in dismay.
4. Arlis was so withdrawn, she had turned to face the wall and did not respond to the nurse.

Meet the Author

Marta Salinas is best known for being an environmental activist. In and around McFarland, California, a "cancer cluster" developed when Salinas's children were young. She became a community organizer and spoke out about potential pesticide poisoning. As a result, the U.S. Environmental Protection Agency conducted a detailed study of the area. Salinas has written articles for California newspapers and magazines, as well as this story.

Preview Vocabulary

ab • sent • mind • ed • ly (ab′ sənt mīn′ dəd lē) *adv.*, lost in thought; unaware

co • in • ci • dence (kō in[t]′ sə dən[t]s) *n.*, chance occurrence

dis • may (dis mā′) *n.*, sudden loss of courage; shock

with • drawn (wit͟h drôn′) *adj.*, introverted; unresponsive

THE SCHOLARSHIP JACKET

A Short Story
by Marta Salinas

Why did they have to change the rules just when it was my turn to win the jacket?

The small Texas school that I attended carried out a tradition every year during the eighth grade graduation; a beautiful gold and green jacket, the school colors, was awarded to the class valedictorian, the student who had maintained the highest grades for eight years. The scholarship jacket had a big gold *S* on the left front side and the winner's name was written in gold letters on the pocket.

My oldest sister Rosie had won the jacket a few years back and I fully expected to win also. I was fourteen and in the eighth grade. I had been a straight A student since the first grade, and the last year I had looked forward to owning that jacket. My father was a farm laborer who couldn't earn enough money to feed eight children, so when I was six I was given to my grandparents to raise. We couldn't participate in sports at school because there were registration fees, uniform costs, and trips out of town; so even though we were quite agile and athletic, there would never be a sports school jacket for us. This one, the scholarship jacket, was our only chance.

DURING READING

Analyze Literature
Theme Why won't the narrator get a school jacket for sports?

In May, close to graduation, spring fever struck, and no one paid any attention in class; instead we stared out the windows and at each other, wanting to speed up the last few weeks of school. I despaired every time I looked in the mirror. Pencil thin, not a curve anywhere, I was called "Beanpole" and "String Bean" and I knew that's what I looked like. A flat chest, no hips, and a brain, that's what I had. That really isn't much for a fourteen-year-old to work with, I thought, as I absentmindedly wandered from my history class to the gym. Another hour of sweating in basketball and displaying my toothpick legs was coming up. Then I remembered my P.E. shorts were still in a bag under my desk where I'd forgotten them. I had to walk all the way back and get them. Coach Thompson was a real bear if anyone wasn't dressed for P.E. She had said I was a good forward and once she even tried to talk Grandma into letting me join the team. Grandma, of course, said no.

ab • sent • mind • ed • ly
(ab' sənt mīn´ dəd lē)
adv., lost in thought; unaware

I was almost back at my classroom's door when I heard angry voices and arguing. I stopped. I didn't mean to eavesdrop;[1] I just hesitated, not knowing what to do. I needed those shorts and I was going to be late, but I didn't want to interrupt an argument between my teachers. I recognized the voices: Mr. Schmidt, my history teacher, and Mr. Boone, my math teacher. They seemed to be arguing about me. I couldn't believe it. I still remember the shock

1. **eavesdrop.** Secretly listen to someone else's private conversation

that rooted me flat against the wall as if I were trying to blend in with the graffiti written there.

"I refuse to do it! I don't care who her father is, her grades don't even begin to compare to Martha's. I won't lie or falsify records. Martha has a straight A plus average and you know it." That was Mr. Schmidt and he sounded very angry. Mr. Boone's voice sounded calm and quiet.

"Look, Joann's father is not only on the Board, he owns the only store in town; we could say it was a close tie and—"

The pounding in my ears drowned out the rest of the words, only a word here and there filtered through. "...Martha is Mexican.... resign....won't do it...." Mr. Schmidt came rushing out, and luckily for me went down the opposite way toward the auditorium, so he didn't see me. Shaking, I waited a few minutes and then went in and grabbed my bag and fled from the room. Mr. Boone looked up when I came in but didn't say anything. To this day I don't remember if I got in trouble in P.E. for being late or how I made it through the rest of the afternoon. I went home very sad and cried into my pillow that night so grandmother wouldn't hear me. It seemed a cruel coincidence that I had overheard that conversation.

The next day when the principal called me into his office, I knew what it would be about. He looked uncomfortable and unhappy. I decided I wasn't going to make it any easier for him so I looked him straight in the eye. He looked away and fidgeted with the papers on his desk.

"Martha," he said, "there's been a change in policy this year regarding the scholarship jacket. As you know, it has always been free." He cleared his throat and continued. "This year the Board decided to charge fifteen dollars—which still won't cover the complete cost of the jacket."

I stared at him in shock and a small sound of dismay escaped my throat. I hadn't expected this. He still avoided looking in my eyes.

"So if you are unable to pay the fifteen dollars for the jacket, it will be given to the next one in line."

Standing with all the dignity I could muster,[2] I said, "I'll speak to my grandfather about it, sir, and let you know tomorrow." I cried on the walk home from the bus stop. The dirt road was a quarter of a mile from the highway, so by the time I got home, my eyes were red and puffy.

DURING READING

Analyze Literature
Theme What does Mr. Schmidt refuse to do?

co•in•ci•dence (kō in[t]´ sə dən[t]s) *n.*, chance occurrence

DURING READING

Analyze Literature
Theme How does the narrator know what the principal wants?

dis•may (dis mā´) *n.*, sudden loss of courage; shock

---

2. muster. Call forth; collect

"Where's Grandpa?" I asked Grandma, looking down at the floor so she wouldn't ask me why I'd been crying. She was sewing on a quilt and didn't look up.

"I think he's out back working in the bean field."

I went outside and looked out at the fields. There he was. I could see him walking between the rows, his body bent over the little plants, hoe in hand. I walked slowly out to him, trying to think how I could best ask him for the money. There was a cool breeze blowing and a sweet smell of mesquite[3] in the air, but I didn't appreciate it. I kicked at a dirt clod. I wanted that jacket so much. It was more than just being a valedictorian and giving a little thank you speech for the jacket on graduation night. It represented eight years of hard work and expectation. I knew I had to be honest with Grandpa; it was my only chance. He saw me and looked up.

DURING READING

Analyze Literature
Theme Why is being honest the narrator's only chance?

He waited for me to speak. I cleared my throat nervously and clasped my hands behind my back so he wouldn't see them shaking. "Grandpa, I have a big favor to ask you," I said in Spanish, the only language he knew. He still waited silently. I tried again. "Grandpa, this year the principal said the scholarship jacket is not going to be

3. mesquite. Small tree or shrub with sweet pods and fragrant wood

free. It's going to cost fifteen dollars and I have to take the money in tomorrow, otherwise it'll be given to someone else." The last words came out in an eager rush. Grandpa straightened up tiredly and leaned his chin on the hoe handle. He looked out over the field that was filled with the tiny green bean plants. I waited, desperately hoping he'd say I could have the money.

He turned to me and asked quietly, "What does a scholarship jacket mean?"

I answered quickly; maybe there was a chance. "It means you've earned it by having the highest grades for eight years and that's why they're giving it to you." Too late I realized the significance of my words. Grandpa knew that I understood it was not a matter of money. It wasn't that. He went back to hoeing the weeds that sprang up between the delicate little bean plants. It was a time consuming job; sometimes the small shoots were right next to each other. Finally he spoke again.

"Then if you pay for it, Marta,[4] it's not a scholarship jacket, is it? Tell your principal I will not pay the fifteen dollars."

I walked back to the house and locked myself in the bathroom for a long time. I was angry with grandfather even though I knew he was right, and I was angry with the Board, whoever they were. Why did they have to change the rules just when it was my turn to win the jacket?

It was a very sad and withdrawn girl who dragged into the principal's office the next day. This time he did look me in the eyes.

"What did your grandfather say?"

I sat very straight in my chair.

"He said to tell you he won't pay the fifteen dollars."

The principal muttered something I couldn't understand under his breath, and walked over to the window. He stood looking out at something outside. He looked bigger than usual when he stood up; he was a tall gaunt[5] man with gray hair, and I watched the back of his head while I waited for him to speak.

"Why?" he finally asked. "Your grandfather has the money. Doesn't he own a small bean farm?"

I looked at him, forcing my eyes to stay dry. "He said if I had to pay for it, then it wouldn't be a scholarship jacket," I said and stood up to leave. "I guess you'll just have to give it to Joann." I hadn't

He turned to me and asked quietly, "What does a scholarship jacket mean?"

with•drawn (wi<u>th</u> drôn′) *adj.,* introverted; unresponsive

DURING READING

Analyze Literature

Theme What does it mean that the principal meets her eyes today and not yesterday?

---

4. Marta. The narrator is called *Martha* at school and *Marta* at home.

5. gaunt. Very thin and angular

meant to say that; it had just slipped out. I was almost to the door when he stopped me.

"Martha—wait."

I turned and looked at him, waiting. What did he want now? I could feel my heart pounding. Something bitter and vile tasting was coming up in my mouth; I was afraid I was going to be sick. I didn't need any sympathy speeches. He sighed loudly and went back to his big desk. He looked at me, biting his lip, as if thinking.

DURING READING

Use Reading Skills
Context Clues Based on context clues, what does *vile* mean?

"Okay. We'll make an exception in your case. I'll tell the Board, you'll get your jacket."

I could hardly believe it. I spoke in a trembling rush. "Oh, thank you sir!" Suddenly I felt great. I didn't know about adrenalin[6] in those days, but I knew something was pumping through me, making me feel as tall as the sky. I wanted to yell, jump, run the mile, do something. I ran out so I could cry in the hall where there was no one to see me. At the end of the day, Mr. Schmidt winked at me and said, "I hear you're getting a scholarship jacket this year."

His face looked as happy and innocent as a baby's, but I knew better. Without answering I gave him a quick hug and ran to the bus. I cried on the walk home again, but this time because I was so happy. I couldn't wait to tell Grandpa and ran straight to the field. I joined him in the row where he was working and without saying anything I crouched down and started pulling up the weeds with my hands. Grandpa worked alongside me for a few minutes, but he didn't ask what had happened. After I had a little pile of weeds between the rows, I stood up and faced him.

"The principal said he's making an exception for me, Grandpa, and I'm getting the jacket after all. That's after I told him what you said."

Grandpa didn't say anything, he just gave me a pat on the shoulder and a smile. He pulled out the crumpled red handkerchief that he always carried in his back pocket and wiped the sweat off his forehead.

"Better go see if your grandmother needs any help with supper."

I gave him a big grin. He didn't fool me. I skipped and ran back to the house whistling some silly tune. ✣

---

6. adrenalin. Hormone that gives a person a burst of energy

When has an older person stepped into a situation to stand up for you? Do you think it's always a good thing, or should adults let young people fend for themselves?

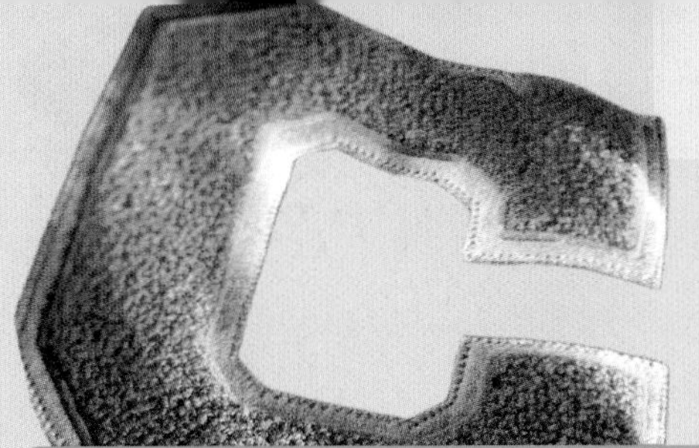

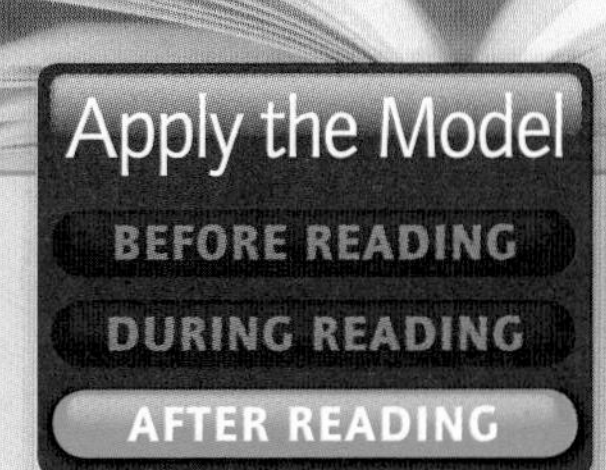

Find Meaning

1. (a) What does the scholarship jacket reward? (b) Why would the school give it to someone who does not meet the usual criteria?
2. (a) Why can't the narrator participate in sports? (b) Why does the narrator want the scholarship jacket so much?
3. Which teacher supports the narrator? Why?

Make Judgments

4. Compare Mr. Schmidt and Mr. Boone. Who do you think is the better person? Why?
5. Compare the actions of the principal and the narrator's grandfather. Who acts more responsibly? Explain.
6. (a) Why does the narrator finally get the scholarship jacket? (b) What does this suggest the theme of the story could be?

Analyze Literature

Theme Review your answers to the During Reading questions on the pages of the "The Scholarship Jacket." Using those responses, make a theme map to determine the story's theme or themes. Draw a large circle labeled "Theme(s)," and then put smaller circles around it. Write details from the story in the smaller circles. Then fill in the center circle.

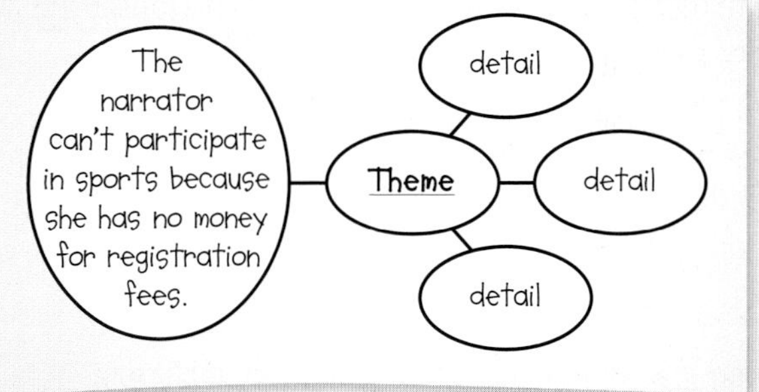

Extend Understanding

Writing Options

Creative Writing Take the role of the narrator in "The Scholarship Jacket" and prepare a one-paragraph **acceptance speech** with a clear main idea. Your speech should cover several key points that support your main idea.

Informative Writing Imagine you have agreed to read this story aloud to a class of fifth graders. Before you start, help them anticipate the story's overall message. Use your theme map to draft an **informative paragraph** in which you explain the story's theme. Support your explanation with evidence from the story.

Lifelong Learning

Find Famous Awards Use the Internet to research the history of a famous award, such as the Nobel Prize for Literature or the Academy Award for directing a movie. Create a list of the criteria used to pick the winners. Prepare a poster of your list.

Collaborative Learning

Communicate by Computer In a small group, discuss what caused Martha, the principal, Mr. Boone, and Mr. Schmidt to make the decisions they made. Consider motivations such as pride, prejudice, and self-respect. Create a list of these reasons, and exchange it electronically with another small group.

 Go to **www.mirrorsandwindows.com** for more.

Grammar & Style

Comma Use

Commas and Compound Sentences

I had been a straight A student since the first grade, and the last year I had looked forward to owning that jacket.

—MARTA SALINAS, "The Scholarship Jacket"

In this compound sentence, two independent, or main, clauses are joined by the coordinating conjunction *and*. (Other coordinating conjunctions are *but, or, nor, for*, and *yet*.) Because these clauses are long, you should use a comma before the conjunction. When the two independent clauses are very short, you can sometimes omit the comma.

EXAMPLE

Martha is a good student and she wants to win the jacket.

Even if a compound sentence is short, include a comma if the sentence would be confusing without it. In the first of the two examples, the sentence sounds odd. Add a comma to make it clear.

EXAMPLES

Martha weeds but her Grandpa works too.

Martha weeds, but her Grandpa works too.

Commas in a Series

You should always use commas to separate items in a series. Three or more words make a series.

EXAMPLE

Martha says that she has good grades, good attendance, and a good attitude.

It is not necessary to use commas if the items in the series are linked by conjunctions.

EXAMPLE

Martha says that she has good grades and good attendance and a good attitude.

Sentence Improvement

For each of the following sentences, select the response that indicates the *best* revision.

1. Martha asks for fifteen dollars but Grandpa refuses to give the money to her.
- **A.** Martha asks for fifteen dollars, but Grandpa refuses to give the money to her.
- **B.** Martha asks for fifteen dollars but, Grandpa refuses to give the money to her.
- **C.** Martha asks for fifteen dollars, but, Grandpa refuses to give the money to her.
- **D.** NO CHANGE

2. Martha spoke with her teachers her grandpa and her grandma.
- **A.** Martha spoke with her teachers her grandpa, and her grandma.
- **B.** Martha spoke with her teachers and her grandpa and her grandma.
- **C.** Martha spoke with her teachers, her grandpa her grandma.
- **D.** NO CHANGE

3. Martha's family couldn't afford registration fees uniform costs and trips out of town.
- **A.** Martha's family couldn't afford registration fees, uniform costs and trips out of town.
- **B.** Martha's family couldn't afford registration fees uniform costs, and trips out of town.
- **C.** Martha's family couldn't afford registration fees, uniform costs, and trips out of town.
- **D.** NO CHANGE

ANCHOR TEXT

Amigo Brothers

A Short Story
by Piri Thomas

DIRECTED READING

BEFORE READING

Build Background

Literary Context Writers create characters in three principal ways. They can show what a character says, does, and thinks. They can show what other characters say about a character. Also, they can describe a character's physical traits. Piri Thomas develops the characters in "Amigo Brothers" in these three ways.

Reader's Context Have you ever had to compete against a friend? How did it affect your relationship?

Set Purpose

Preview the story by reading the first three paragraphs. How are the two main characters similar? How are they different? Do you think their relationship will change during the story?

Analyze Literature

Point of View This story is written from the *third-person point of view,* which means the narrator is not part of the action. A third-person narrator can be omniscient or limited. An *omniscient* narrator knows everything about the characters and the plot. A *limited third-person* narrator knows only some things, such as what anyone observing the characters and situation could see. As you read, think about whether the narrator of "Amigo Brothers" is omniscient or limited. Record your thoughts.

Use Reading Skills

Draw Conclusions The plot of "Amigo Brothers" depends on the characters' competing motivations. Both friends want to win a boxing match, but they don't want to hurt each other. To determine the overall message of the story, keep track of the characters' motivations and actions as well as the key points in the plot. Use a drawing conclusions log like the one below to take notes as you read.

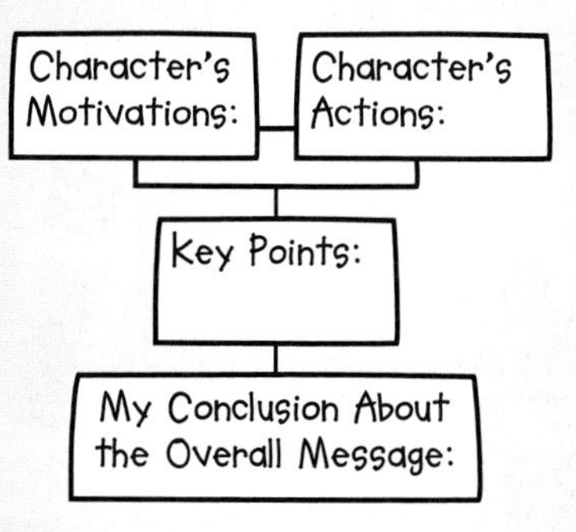

Meet the Author

Piri Thomas (1928–2011) grew up in Spanish Harlem, part of New York City. As a youth, he was a gang member and spent time in prison. He wrote an autobiography called *Down These Mean Streets* in which he tried to persuade other gang members to change. Thomas was known for reaching out to youth at risk for problems with drugs and crime.

Preview Vocabulary

dev•a•stat•ing (de´ və stā' tiŋ) *adj.,* overwhelming

war•y (wer´ ē) *adj.,* cautious

dis•pel (di spel´) *v.,* break up; make vanish

flail (flāl) *v.,* swing

surge (sʉrj) *v.,* rise and move forward

The Big Fight, c. 20th century. P. J. Crook. Private collection.

Amigo Brothers

A Short Story by Piri Thomas

Antonio knew the dynamite that was stored in his amigo brother's fist.

Antonio Cruz and Felix Vargas were both seventeen years old. They were so together in friendship that they felt themselves to be brothers. They had known each other since childhood, growing up on the lower east side of Manhattan in the same tenement building[1] on Fifth Street between Avenue A and Avenue B.

Antonio was fair, lean, and lanky, while Felix was dark, short, and husky. Antonio's hair was always falling over his eyes, while Felix wore his black hair in a natural Afro style.

Each youngster had a dream of someday becoming lightweight champion of the world. Every chance they had the boys worked out, sometimes at the Boys Club on 10th Street and Avenue A and sometimes at the pro's gym on 14th Street. Early morning sunrises would find them running along the East River Drive, wrapped in sweat shirts, short towels around their necks, and handkerchiefs Apache style around their foreheads.

While some youngsters were into street negatives, Antonio and Felix slept, ate, rapped, and dreamt positive. Between them, they had a collection of *Fight* magazines second to none, plus a scrapbook filled with torn tickets to every boxing match they had ever attended, and some clippings of their own. If asked a question about any given fighter, they would immediately zip out from their memory banks divisions, weights, records of fights, knock-outs, technical knock-outs,[2] and draws or losses.

Each had fought many bouts[3] representing their community and had won two gold-plated medals plus a silver and bronze medallion. The difference was in their style. Antonio's lean form and long reach made him the better boxer, while Felix's short and muscular frame made him the better slugger. Whenever they had met in the ring for sparring sessions,[4] it had always been hot and heavy.

Now, after a series of elimination bouts,[5] they had been informed that they were to meet each other in the division finals that were scheduled for the seventh of August, two weeks away—the winner to represent the Boys Club in the Golden Gloves Championship Tournament.

The two boys continued to run together along the East River Drive. But even when joking with each other, they both sensed a wall rising between them.

One morning less than a week before their bout, they met as usual for their daily work-out. They fooled around with a few jabs at the air, slapped skin, and then took off, running lightly along the dirty East River's edge.

Antonio glanced at Felix who kept his eyes purposely straight ahead, pausing from time to time to do some fancy leg work while throwing one-twos followed by upper cuts to an imaginary jaw. Antonio then beat the air with a barrage of body blows and short <u>devastating</u> lefts with an overhand jaw-breaking right. After a mile or so, Felix puffed and said, "Let's stop a while, bro. I think we both got something to say to each other." Antonio nodded. It was not natural to be acting as though nothing unusual was happening when two ace-boon buddies were going to be blasting each other within a few short days.

They rested their elbows on the railing separating them from the river. Antonio

---

1. **tenement building.** Large residential rental building in a city
2. **technical knock-outs.** Fights that are stopped when a referee decides one boxer is too badly hurt to continue
3. **bouts.** Athletic matches
4. **sparring sessions.** Informal matches in which boxers practice being on the offense and the defense
5. **elimination bouts.** Series of contests in which only the winner of each contest continues in the competition

dev•a•stat•ing (de´ və stā' tiŋ) *adj.*, overwhelming

wiped his face with his short towel. The sunrise was now creating day.

Felix leaned heavily on the river's railing and stared across to the shores of Brooklyn. Finally, he broke the silence.

"Man, I don't know how to come out with it."

Antonio helped. "It's about our fight, right?"

"Yeah, right." Felix's eyes squinted at the rising orange sun.

"I've been thinking about it too, *panín.*[6] In fact, since we found out it was going to be me and you, I've been awake at night, pulling punches on you, trying not to hurt you."

"Same here. It ain't natural not to think about the fight. I mean, we both are *cheverote*[7] fighters and we both want to win. But only one of us can win. There ain't no draws[8] in the eliminations."

Felix tapped Antonio gently on the shoulder. "I don't mean to sound like I'm bragging, bro. But I wanna win, fair and square."

Antonio nodded quietly. "Yeah. We both know that in the ring the better man wins. Friend or no friend, brother or no..."

Felix finished it for him. "Brother. Tony, let's promise something right here. Okay?"

"If it's fair, *hermano,*[9] I'm for it." Antonio admired the courage of a tugboat pulling a barge five times its welterweight size.

"It's fair, Tony. When we get into the ring, it's gotta be like we never met. We gotta be like two heavy strangers that want the same thing and only one can have it. You understand, don'tcha?"

"*Sí,* I know." Tony smiled. "No pulling punches. We go all the way."

"Yeah, that's right. Listen, Tony. Don't you think it's a good idea if we don't see each other until the day of the fight? I'm going to stay with my Aunt Lucy in the Bronx.[10] I can use Gleason's Gym for working out. My manager says he got some sparring partners with more or less your style."

---

6. ***panín*** (pä nēn´). Pal (Spanish)
7. ***cheverote*** (shev´ ər ōt). Great (Spanish)
8. **draws.** Ties
9. ***hermano*** (hər män´ ō). Brother (Spanish)
10. **the Bronx.** Part of New York City just north of Manhattan

Tony scratched his nose pensively.[11] "Yeah, it would be better for our heads." He held out his hand, palm upward. "Deal?"

"Deal." Felix lightly slapped open skin.

"Ready for some more running?" Tony asked lamely.

"Naw, bro. Let's cut it here. You go on. I kinda like to get things together in my head."

"You ain't worried, are you?" Tony asked.

"No way, man." Felix laughed out loud. "I got too much smarts for that. I just think it's cooler if we split right here. After the fight, we can get it together again like nothing ever happened."

The amigo brothers were not ashamed to hug each other tightly.

"Guess you're right. Watch yourself, Felix. I hear there's some pretty heavy dudes up in the Bronx. *Suavecito,*[12] okay?"

"Okay. You watch yourself too, *sabe?*"[13]

Tony jogged away. Felix watched his friend disappear from view, throwing rights and lefts. Both fighters had a lot of psyching up to do before the big fight.

The days in training passed much too slowly. Although they kept out of each other's way, they were aware of each other's progress via the ghetto grapevine.

The evening before the big fight, Tony made his way to the roof of his tenement. In the quiet early dark, he peered over the ledge. Six stories below the lights of the city blinked and the sounds of cars mingled with the curses and the laughter of children in the street. He tried not to think of Felix, feeling he had succeeded in psyching his mind. But only in the ring would he really know. To spare Felix hurt, he would have to knock him out, early and quick.

Up in the South Bronx, Felix decided to take in a movie in an effort to keep Antonio's face away from his fists. The flick was *The Champion* with Kirk Douglas, the third time Felix was seeing it.

---

11. pensively. Thoughtfully
12. *suavecito* (swäv´ a sē' tō). Smooth; take it easy (Spanish)
13. *Sabe?* (sä bā´). Understand? (Spanish)

The champion was getting hit hard. He was saved only by the sound of the bell.

Felix became the champ and Tony the challenger.

The movie audience was going out of its head. The challenger, confident that he had the championship in the bag, threw a left. The champ countered with a dynamite right.

Felix's right arm felt the shock. Antonio's face, superimposed on the screen, was hit by the awesome blow. Felix saw himself in the ring, blasting Antonio against the ropes. The champ had to be forcibly restrained. The challenger was allowed to crumble slowly to the canvas.

When Felix finally left the theatre, he had figured out how to psyche himself for tomorrow's fight. It was Felix the Champion vs. Antonio the Challenger.

He walked up some dark streets, deserted except for small pockets of wary-looking kids wearing gang colors. Despite the fact that he was Puerto Rican like them, they eyed him as a stranger to their turf. Felix did a fast shuffle, bobbing and weaving, while letting loose a torrent of blows that would demolish whatever got in its way. It seemed to impress the brothers, who went about their own business.

Finding no takers, Felix decided to split to his aunt's. Walking the streets had not relaxed him, neither had the fight flick. All it had done was to stir him up. He let himself quietly into his Aunt Lucy's apartment and went straight to bed, falling into a fitful sleep with sounds of the gong for Round One.

Antonio was passing some heavy time on his rooftop. How would the fight tomorrow affect his relationship with Felix? After all, fighting was like any other profession. Friendship had nothing to do with it. A gnawing doubt crept in. He cut negative thinking real quick by doing some speedy fancy dance steps, bobbing and weaving like mercury.[14] The night air was blurred with perpetual motions of left hooks and right crosses. Felix, his *amigo* brother, was not going to be Felix at all in the ring. Just an opponent with another face. Antonio went to sleep, hearing the opening bell for the first round. Like his friend in the South Bronx, he prayed for victory, via a quick clean knock-out in the first round.

Large posters plastered all over the walls of local shops announced the fight between Antonio Cruz and Felix Vargas as the main bout.

The fight had created great interest in the neighborhood. Antonio and Felix were well liked and respected. Each had his own loyal following. Antonio's fans counted on his boxing skills. On the other side, Felix's admirers trusted in his dynamite-packed fists.

Felix had returned to his apartment early in the morning of August 7th and stayed there, hoping to avoid seeing Antonio. He turned the radio on to *salsa* music sounds and then tried to read while waiting for word from his manager.

The fight was scheduled to take place in Tompkins Square Park.[15] It had been decided that the gymnasium of the Boys Club was not large enough to hold all the people who were sure to attend. In Tompkins Square Park, everyone who wanted could view the fight, whether from ringside or window fire escapes or tenement rooftops.

The morning of the fight Tompkins Square was a beehive of activity with numerous workers setting up the ring, the seats, and the guest speakers' stand. The scheduled bouts began shortly after noon and the park had begun filling up even earlier.

---

14. mercury. Metal that is liquid at room temperature

15. Tompkins Square Park. Only large open space on Manhattan's lower east side

war • y (wer´ ē) *adj.*, cautious

The local junior high school across from Tompkins Square Park served as the dressing room for all the fighters. Each was given a separate classroom with desk tops, covered with mats, serving as resting tables. Antonio thought he caught a glimpse of Felix waving to him from a room at the far end of the corridor. He waved back just in case it had been him.

The fighters changed from their street clothes into fighting gear. Antonio wore white trunks, black socks, and black shoes. Felix wore sky blue trunks, red socks, and white boxing shoes. Each had dressing gowns to match their fighting trunks with their names neatly stitched on the back.

The loudspeakers blared into the open windows of the school. There were speeches by dignitaries, community leaders, and great boxers of yesteryear. Some were well prepared, some improvised on the spot. They all carried the same message of great pleasure and honor at being part of such a historic event. This great day was in the tradition of champions emerging from the streets of the lower east side.

Interwoven with the speeches were the sounds of the other boxing events. After the sixth bout, Felix was much relieved when his trainer Charlie said, "Time change. Quick knock-out. This is it. We're on."

Waiting time was over. Felix was escorted from the classroom by a dozen fans in white T-shirts with the word FELIX across their fronts.

Antonio was escorted down a different stairwell and guided through a roped-off path.

As the two climbed into the ring, the crowd exploded with a roar. Antonio and Felix both bowed gracefully and then raised their arms in acknowledgment.

Antonio tried to be cool, but even as the roar was in its first birth, he turned slowly to meet Felix's eyes looking directly into his. Felix nodded his head and Antonio responded. And both as one, just as quickly, turned away to face his own corner.

Bong—bong—bong. The roar turned to stillness.

"Ladies and Gentlemen. *Señores y Señoras.*"

The announcer spoke slowly, pleased at his bilingual efforts.

"Now the moment we have all been waiting for—the main event between two fine young Puerto Rican fighters, products of our lower east side. In this corner, weighing 134 pounds, Felix Vargas. And in this corner, weighing 133 pounds, Antonio Cruz. The winner will represent the Boys Club in the tournament of champions, the Golden Gloves. There will be no draw. May the best man win."

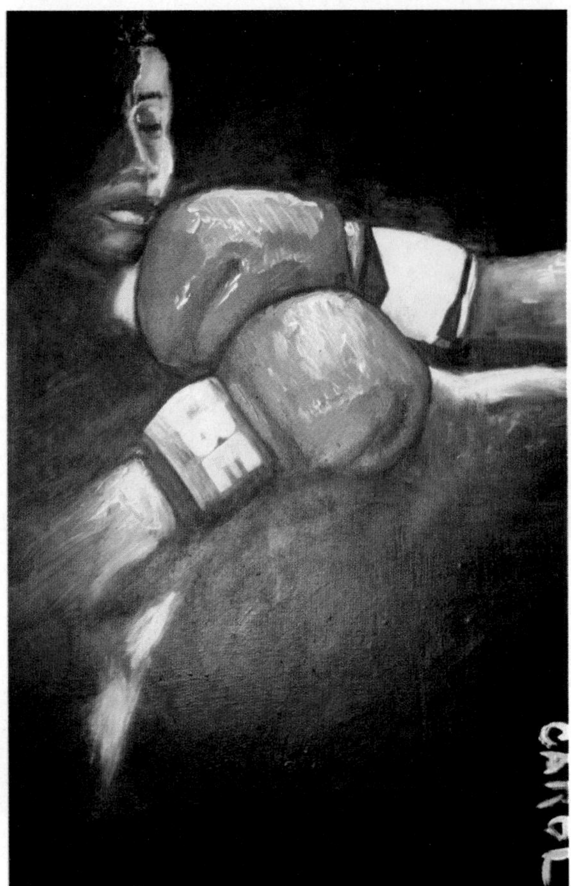

Boxer Right, c. 20th century. Carol Tatham. Private collection.

The cheering of the crowd shook the window panes of the old buildings surrounding Tompkins Square Park. At the center of the ring, the referee was giving instructions to the youngsters.

"Keep your punches up. No low blows. No punching on the back of the head. Keep your heads up. Understand. Let's have a clean fight. Now shake hands and come out fighting."

Both youngsters touched gloves and nodded. They turned and danced quickly to their corners. Their head towels and dressing gowns were lifted neatly from their shoulders by their trainers' nimble fingers. Antonio crossed himself.[16] Felix did the same.

BONG! BONG! ROUND ONE. Felix and Antonio turned and faced each other squarely in a fighting pose. Felix wasted no time. He came in fast, head low, half hunched toward his right shoulder, and lashed out with a straight left. He missed a right cross as Antonio slipped the punch and countered with one-two-three lefts that snapped Felix's head back, sending a mild shock coursing through him. If Felix had any small doubt about their friendship affecting their fight, it was being neatly dispelled.

Antonio danced, a joy to behold. His left hand was like a piston pumping jabs one right after another with seeming ease. Felix bobbed and weaved and never stopped boring in.[17] He knew that at long range he was at a disadvantage. Antonio had too much reach on him. Only by coming in close could Felix hope to achieve the dreamed-of knockout.

Antonio knew the dynamite that was stored in his *amigo* brother's fist. He ducked a short right and missed a left hook. Felix trapped him against the ropes just long enough to pour some punishing rights and lefts to Antonio's hard midsection. Antonio slipped away from Felix, crashing two lefts to his head, which set Felix's right ear to ringing.

Bong! Both *amigos* froze a punch well on its way, sending up a roar of approval for good sportsmanship.

Felix walked briskly back to his corner. His right ear had not stopped ringing. Antonio gracefully danced his way toward his stool none the worse, except for glowing glove burns, showing angry red against the whiteness of his midribs.

"Watch that right, Tony." His trainer talked into his ear. "Remember Felix always goes to the body. He'll want you to drop your hands for his overhand left or right. Got it?"

16. **crossed himself.** Made a gesture to invoke religious protection
17. **boring in.** Making one's way steadily against resistance

dis•pel (di spel´) *v.*, break up; make vanish

Antonio nodded, spraying water out between his teeth. He felt better as his sore midsection was being firmly rubbed.

Felix's corner was also busy.

"You gotta get in there, fella." Felix's trainer poured water over his curly Afro locks. "Get in there or he's gonna chop you up from way back."

Bong! Bong! Round two. Felix was off his stool and rushed Antonio like a bull, sending a hard right to his head. Beads of water exploded from Antonio's long hair.

Antonio, hurt, sent back a blurring barrage of lefts and rights that only meant pain to Felix, who returned with a short left to the head followed by a looping right to the body. Antonio countered with his own flurry, forcing Felix to give ground. But not for long.

Felix bobbed and weaved, bobbed and weaved, occasionally punching his two gloves together.

Antonio waited for the rush that was sure to come. Felix closed in and feinted[18] with his left shoulder and threw his right instead. Lights suddenly exploded inside Felix's head as Antonio slipped the blow and hit him with a pistonlike left catching him flush on the point of his chin.

Bedlam[19] broke loose as Felix's legs momentarily buckled. He fought off a series of rights and lefts and came back with a strong right that taught Antonio respect.

Antonio danced in carefully. He knew Felix had the habit of playing possum[20] when hurt, to sucker[21] an opponent within reach of the powerful bombs he carried in each fist.

A right to the head slowed Antonio's pretty dancing. He answered with his own left at Felix's right eye that began puffing up within three seconds.

Antonio, a bit too eager, moved in too close and Felix had him entangled into a rip-roaring, punching toe-to-toe slugfest that brought the whole Tompkins Square Park screaming to its feet.

Rights to the body. Lefts to the head. Neither fighter was giving an inch. Suddenly a short right caught Antonio squarely on the chin. His long legs turned to jelly and his arms flailed out desperately. Felix, grunting like a bull, threw wild punches from every direction. Antonio, groggy, bobbed and weaved, evading most of the blows. Suddenly his head cleared. His left flashed out hard and straight catching Felix on the bridge of his nose.

Felix lashed back with a haymaker,[22] right off the ghetto streets. At the same instant, his eye caught another left hook from Antonio. Felix swung out trying to clear the pain. Only the frenzied screaming of those along ringside let him know that he had dropped Antonio. Fighting off the growing haze, Antonio struggled to his feet, got up, ducked, and threw a smashing right that dropped Felix flat on his back.

Felix got up as fast as he could in his own corner, groggy but still game.[23] He didn't even hear the count. In a fog, he heard the roaring of the crowd, who seemed to have gone insane. His head cleared to hear the bell sound at the end of the round. He was very glad. His trainer sat him down on the stool.

In his corner, Antonio was doing what all fighters do when they are hurt. They sit and smile at everyone.

The referee signaled the ring doctor to check the fighters out. He did so and then gave his okay. The cold water sponges brought clarity to both *amigo* brothers. They were rubbed until their circulation ran free.

---

18. feinted. Pretended to aim at one place and then hit elsewhere
19. bedlam. Loud confusion
20. playing possum. Pretending to be dead by lying motionless
21. sucker. Deceive; lure under false pretenses
22. haymaker. Powerful blow
23. still game. Still willing to compete

flail (flāl) *v.*, swing

Bong! Round three—the final round. Up to now it had been tic-tac-toe, pretty much even. But everyone knew there could be no draw and this round would decide the winner.

This time, to Felix's surprise, it was Antonio who came out fast, charging across the ring. Felix braced himself but couldn't ward off the barrage of punches. Antonio drove Felix hard against the ropes.

The crowd ate it up. Thus far the two had fought with *mucho corazón*.[24] Felix tapped his gloves and commenced his attack anew. Antonio, throwing boxer's caution to the winds, jumped in to meet him.

Both pounded away. Neither gave an inch and neither fell to the canvas. Felix's left eye was tightly closed. Claret red blood poured from Antonio's nose. They fought toe-to-toe.

The sounds of their blows were loud in contrast to the silence of a crowd gone completely mute. The referee was stunned by their savagery.

Bong! Bong! Bong! The bell sounded over and over again. Felix and Antonio were past hearing. Their blows continued to pound on each other like hailstones.

Finally the referee and the two trainers pried Felix and Antonio apart. Cold water was poured over them to bring them back to their senses.

They looked around and then rushed toward each other. A cry of alarm surged through Tompkins Square Park. Was this a fight to the death instead of a boxing match?

The fear soon gave way to wave upon wave of cheering as the two *amigos* embraced.

No matter what the decision, they knew they would always be champions to each other.

BONG! BONG! BONG! "Ladies and Gentlemen. *Señores* and *Señoras*. The winner and representative to the Golden Gloves Tournament of Champions is..."

The announcer turned to point to the winner and found himself alone. Arm in arm the champions had already left the ring. ✤

---

24. ***mucho corazón*** (mů chō´ kôr ō zōn´). Big heart; much courage (Spanish)

surge (surj) *v.*, rise and move forward

Who do you know who has the courage to "go all out" in a competition? Have you ever seen a winning competitor who seemed out of control? Are winners always people who keep themselves under control?

Find Meaning

1. What makes Antonio and Felix such good friends?

2. (a) How are the *amigo* brothers different in physique and style? (b) How are they similar?

3. (a) What were the friends' goals for the final fight? (b) Based on these goals, what did they have to do to prepare?

4. During training, Felix decides to see a movie called *The Champion.* How does seeing the movie help him prepare for the fight?

Make Judgments

5. (a) Although Felix and Antonio decide to act as if they never met, do you think they really acted that way in the ring? (b) Did the friends meet their goals for the fight? Explain your answer.

6. How long do you think Felix and Antonio can continue being best friends? Why?

In "Amigo Brothers," Piri Thomas presents two boxers in heated competition. The following is an excerpt from *The Greatest: Muhammad Ali*, a biography by **Walter Dean Myers.** Myers (1937–2014) was born in West Virginia but soon moved to New York City. Myers conducted extensive research for his nonfiction writing. As you read, imagine Antonio and Felix experiencing what Myers describes.

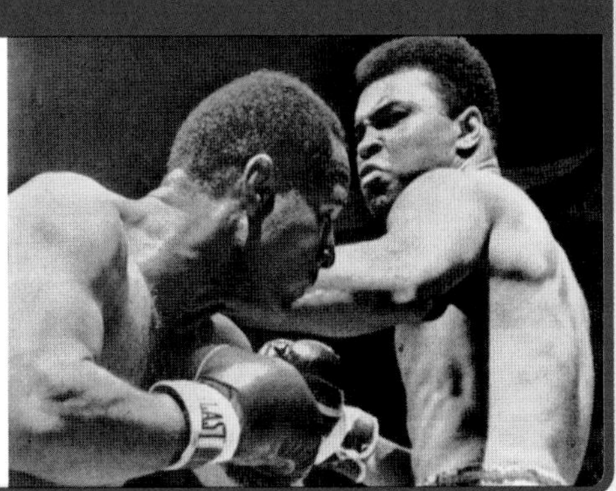

from The Greatest: Muhammad Ali

A Biography by Walter Dean Myers

Each time a fighter steps into the ring he knows there will be a cost. For the glory of the possible win there will be a price measured in units of pain. He will have an idea, if he is honest with himself, of just how much pain he will have to endure on a given night, how much blood he will lose, and just how long it will take for his body to recover from the inevitable battering. Every fight hurts. Every fight damages the body. Some damage the soul.

Fights are often decided in the dressing room as the fighter extends his imagination to the glare of ringside. The image of the impending[1] battle flickers through his mind, and he visualizes himself winning, punishing his opponent more than he is punished. He sees himself using his style, using those tools most comfortable to him, to control the fight. Muhammad Ali could see himself moving quickly, throwing out lightning jabs, leaning back, just out of the reach of the desperate hooks. He saw himself frustrating his opponent, imposing his will on the fight. But even if he was convinced that he could win the fight, convinced beyond the hype and the false bravado[2] he offered to the press, he must still have assessed how much suffering he could bear to carry it off.

When the pain comes, it can be excruciating.[3] A two hundred-pound heavyweight at the top of his form can deliver a devastating blow. A good single blow to the face can break the neck of an ordinary person. Those watching on television or at ringside can scream at a fighter who lies helplessly against the ropes or who has stumbled heavily to the canvas, to get back into the fight. But few fight fans have ever been hit with even a glancing blow from a real fighter. They don't know the courage it takes to continue when the body is screaming to give it up.

Body punches bruise the muscles that help a fighter turn and lift his arms. They push the ribs out of shape; they bruise and tear the internal organs. Hours after the fight

1. **impending.** Upcoming
2. **false bravado.** Pretend display of courage
3. **excruciating.** Sharp; nearly intolerable

the torn tissue and bleeding show up as a bloody tint in the urine.

A fighter's head throbs. Cuts are alive with pain as they are slammed again and again or as a glove is scraped across the exposed nerves. Forehead cuts bleed into the eyes and give color to the violence. Fighters hurt. They survive by accepting the agony of fighting as a way of life.

In the top ranks there are trainers and doctors at ringside, and other doctors to examine and care for the boxer. At the lower end of the spectrum there is less medical attention, less time to heal between fights, less money for good treatment.

Whether the medical treatment received before and after a fight is good or bad, the damage to the body is still done. Mostly, the body is forgiving. It will usually heal. The major physical problems that fighters encounter are with the eyes and with the brain. Physicians have long studied the effects of fighting, and especially of taking blows to the head. Some feel that boxing can be made safer. Others disagree: They feel that as long as the aim of professional fighting is to do damage to the head and body, it will be a dangerous sport. Just how destructive is fighting to the human body? Doctors debate, but fighters know. ✣

TEXT TO TEXT CONNECTION

Myers writes that a fighter "visualizes himself winning, punishing his opponent more than he is punished." Compare Myers's description of a fight with the way Thomas describes the fight between Felix and Antonio. Based on what Myers writes, do you think Thomas gives a realistic portrayal of a boxing match? Explain.

AFTER READING

Analyze Literature

Point of View In what ways does the third-person narrator in "Amigo Brothers" help advance the story's plot? For example, how does the narrator's omniscient point of view affect your understanding of the characters' motivations, actions, and personalities? Put your ideas in a two-column chart.

Detail of Omniscient Narration	Effect on My Understanding
"Antonio and Felix slept, ate, rapped, and dreamt positive."	Even though Antonio and Felix are surrounded by negative influences, they stay positive.

Extend Understanding

Writing Options

Creative Writing Imagine that your class is creating a short scene about what happens to Antonio and Felix immediately after the fight. Decide in your mind who you would have act the part of each fighter. Then write a five- to ten-line **dialogue** between Antonio and Felix. Refer to the story for examples of how the two friends talk to each other. When you are done, consider sharing dialogues with a friend and reading them aloud.

Informative Writing Using your drawing conclusions log, examine how the characters' motivations and actions lead to the resolution of the plot. Synthesize your work into a four-paragraph **informative essay** that maintains the meaning and logical order of the selection. Create a thesis statement and use two or three examples from the text to form paragraphs supporting your thesis.

Collaborative Learning

Write a Script When radio or television stations broadcast sporting events, they often have a color commentator. This person describes the action and talks during lulls, giving statistics and other background information to keep listeners interested. Have members of your group skim the story. Then work together to write a short color commentary script for a specific part of the fight. Read your script aloud in class.

Media Literacy

Conduct Internet Research Using the Internet, research the history of the Golden Gloves tournament. Investigate the various weight divisions and the age restrictions. Using the official competition website, create a list of some famous winners, including the years they won. Choose two of these people. Then do further Internet research to write a brief summary of their later achievements. Put your information into two profiles that you can display and discuss in class.

Go to **www.mirrorsandwindows.com** for more.

Vocabulary & Spelling

Prefixes, Roots, and Suffixes

They were so together in friendship that they felt themselves to be brothers.

—PIRI THOMAS, "Amigo Brothers"

Many words are formed by adding prefixes and suffixes to base words. In the sentence above, the word *friendship* is an example of a word formed by the addition of a suffix. The suffix *-ship*, meaning "state of," added to the root, or base word *friend*, creates *friendship*, meaning "the state of friendship."

A **root** or **base word** is a word to which a prefix or suffix is added. A **prefix** is a letter or group of letters added to the beginning of a base word to change its meaning. A **suffix** is a letter or group of letters added to the end of a base word to change its meaning.

EXAMPLES

inter + woven = interwoven

mid + section = midsection

light + ly = lightly

power + ful = powerful

Below are some common word parts and their origins.

Prefix	Meaning	Origin
auto-	"self"	Greek
bi-	"two"	Latin
micro-	"small"	Greek
mid-	"middle"	Anglo-Saxon
super-	"above, over"	Latin
un-	"not"	Anglo-Saxon

Suffix	Meaning	Origin
-able	"capable of being"	Latin
-cracy	"form of government"	Greek
-ic	"like, having the nature of"	Latin & Greek
-ist	"one who"	Latin
-ful	"full of"	Anglo-Saxon
-ness	"state or quality of"	Anglo-Saxon
-ship	"state of"	Anglo-Saxon

Root	Meaning	Origin
aud	"sound"	Anglo-Saxon
cine	"motion"	Latin
graph	"write"	Greek
junct	"join"	Latin
nym	"name"	Greek
psych	"of the mind"	Greek

Vocabulary Practice

Identify the roots, prefixes, and suffixes for each of the following academic terms along with their origin and meaning. Write the meaning of each term in your own words. Use a dictionary if you need help.

1. psychology
2. cryptographer
3. antonym
4. superimpose
5. bilingual
6. topography

Spelling Practice

Words with Prefixes, Roots, or Suffixes

Being able to recognize common prefixes, roots, and suffixes will help to make you a better speller because you will know how to spell the affix (prefix or suffix) or the root when you hear it. Some affixes you will recognize immediately, such as adding *s* or *es* to the end of a noun to make it plural; others are less common. Examine this list of words to determine which affixes and root words have been used. Remember that most word parts come from Latin, Greek, or Anglo-Saxon origins. For more information, refer to the Language Arts Handbook 2.2, Breaking Words Into Base Words, Word Roots, Prefixes, and Suffixes.

approval	desperately	occasionally
audience	dispelled	perpetual
analogy	elimination	succeeded
circulation	geometry	technical
commence	imaginary	
confident	immediately	

FOUR SKINNY TREES

A Short Story by Sandra Cisneros

BEFORE READING

Build Background

Literary Context "Four Skinny Trees" is from the book *The House on Mango Street,* which was first published in 1984. Cisneros began writing the pieces in the book when she was studying poetry as a graduate student. Poets use language in special ways so that its sound reflects its meaning. Although *The House on Mango Street* is called a novel, the book's structure and voice reflect Cisneros's training as a poet.

Reader's Context How are trees like people? Have you ever imagined that a tree, a flower, or another growing thing had a personality?

Set Purpose

Look at how long this selection is. It has four paragraphs. As a short story, it is very short. Read to find out how a person can tell an entire story in a prose piece of this length.

Analyze Literature

Description Writing that portrays a character, object, or scene is **description.** In this kind of writing, **sensory details** and precise language create vivid mental pictures, or **imagery.** Descriptions often contain **figurative language,** such as **personification.** "Four Skinny Trees" describes trees as if they are human, an example of personification. As you read, take time to let the sensory details and figurative language have an effect on you.

Use Reading Skills

Identify Main Idea To identify the main idea, or theme, of a piece of fiction, examine details such as characters' thoughts and actions, the author's choice of words, the point of view from which the story is told, and the main conflict. To determine the main idea of "Four Skinny Trees," use a main idea map like the one below. List details in the outer ovals and the main idea in the center.

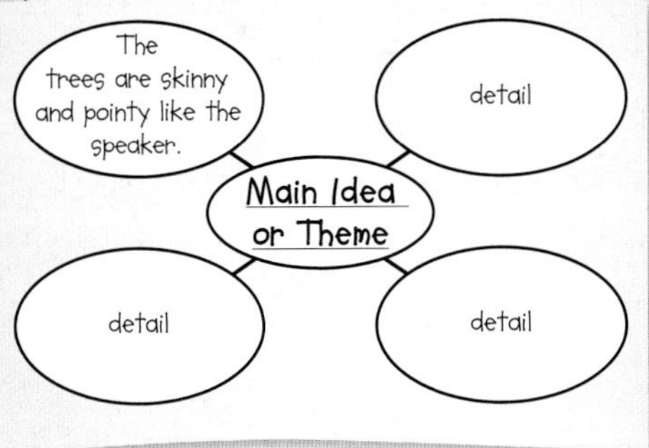

Meet the Author

Sandra Cisneros (b. 1954) grew up in Chicago with six brothers. Her father was Mexican and her mother was Mexican American. After finishing graduate school, she worked as a teacher and poet in schools. *The House on Mango Street* is her most popular book, but she has published another novel as well as short stories, poems, and a bilingual children's book. She lives in San Antonio, Texas, today.

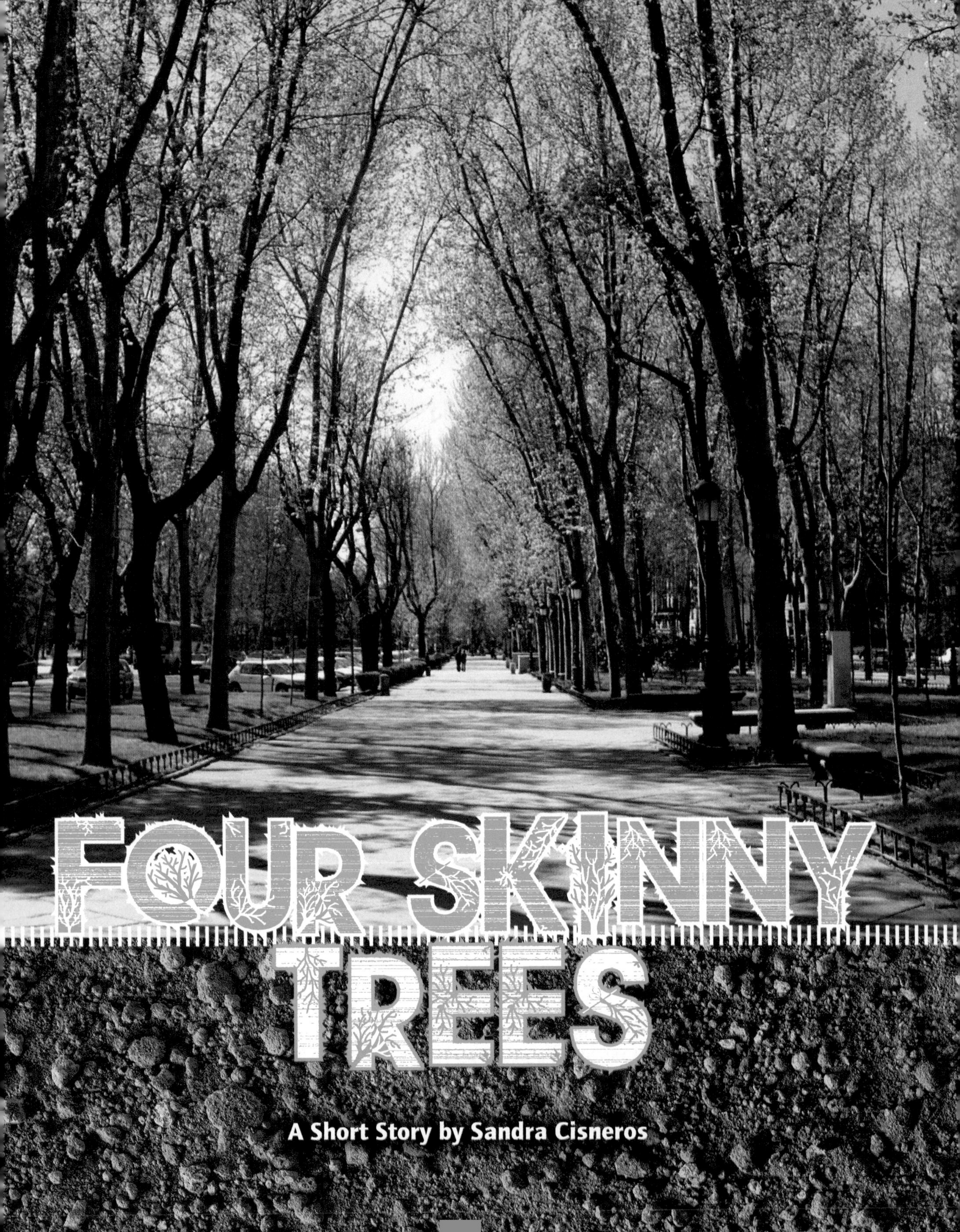

FOUR SKINNY TREES

A Short Story by Sandra Cisneros

They are the only ones who understand me. I am the only one who understands them. Four skinny trees with skinny necks and pointy elbows like mine. Four who do not belong here but are here. Four raggedy excuses planted by the city. From our room we can hear them, but Nenny[1] just sleeps and doesn't appreciate these things.

Their strength is secret. They send ferocious roots beneath the ground. They grow up and they grow down and grab the earth between their hairy toes and bite the sky with violent teeth and never quit their anger. This is how they keep.

Let one forget his reason for being, they'd all droop like tulips in a glass, each with their arms around the other. Keep, keep, keep, trees say when I sleep. They teach.

When I am too sad and too skinny to keep keeping, when I am a tiny thing against so many bricks, then it is I look at trees. When there is nothing left to look at on this street. Four who grew despite concrete. Four who reach and do not forget to reach. Four whose only reason is to be and be. ✣

---

1. **Nenny.** Narrator's younger sister, who shares her room

Think about the things you always see when you look out the window at home. What do you feel especially close to? What is one thing you see that could symbolize your life? Can a nonhuman object ever completely represent a human being?

AFTER READING

Find Meaning

1. (a) Physically, how do the trees resemble the narrator? (b) How do the trees resemble the narrator emotionally?
2. Who put the trees where they are, and why?
3. What doesn't Nenny appreciate?
4. (a) What would cause all the trees to droop? (b) Why aren't the trees drooping now?

Make Judgments

5. Find an example of personification in the first paragraph. What quality does it give to the trees?
6. (a) What does anger do for the trees? (b) What does the narrator mean by the word *keep?*
7. (a) How does the narrator feel in the last paragraph? (b) How do the trees affect the narrator's feelings?

Analyze Literature

Description Sensory details affect a story's mood. Select two descriptions from "Four Skinny Trees" that put a vivid picture in your mind. Read them aloud if you like. Evaluate how the descriptions sound and what they mean. Put your ideas in a chart. Then name a mood that is created by the combination of these images.

Description	Image	Meaning
Grab the earth between their hairy toes	Animal feet squeezing wet soil	Wild and strong, not tame and gentle

Extend Understanding

Writing Options

Creative Writing Close your eyes and picture the view from your favorite window. It can be a window at home, a car window, or any other window with a view. Then imagine that you want to re-create the view for someone else. Write a short **descriptive essay** about the scene you see. Use precise words and sensory details, and use figurative language if possible.

Informative Writing Reread "Four Skinny Trees" to analyze the narrator's emotions. To begin, connect the narrator and her emotions to your own experiences. Write a two-paragraph **literary response.** Using examples from the story, tell how the narrator's emotions impressed you. Try to relate her emotions to her circumstances or the setting.

Collaborative Learning

Give Complex Instructions With a partner, take turns giving oral instructions to perform specific tasks, answer questions, or solve problems. Set at time limit for each speaker and switch when your time is up. Focus your instructions on researching or analyzing the selection or its theme.

Lifelong Learning

Describe a Tree Using the Internet, the library, or a phone call to your local park district, find out which trees grow naturally in your area. Then choose one type of tree and find out more about it. Write a short description of the tree, using sensory details to create a vivid image.

Go to **www.mirrorsandwindows.com** for more.

The White Umbrella

A Short Story by Gish Jen

BEFORE READING

DIRECTED READING

Build Background

Literary Context In a traditional plot, the central conflict is resolved after the climax of the story. Gish Jen's stories don't always have a resolution. Instead, her characters live with tensions that are part of ongoing relationships. Jen has said, "Opposites don't fight each other, but belong together and can intensify each other, and are simply in the nature of the world."

Reader's Context Imagine a teacher asking you to give a reason for what one of your parents is doing right now. What would you say?

Set Purpose

Read the opening scene of the story, the first eight paragraphs. Based on this exchange, try to predict what the theme—the central idea—of the story is going to be.

Analyze Literature

Mood The **mood** of a work of fiction is the way the author wants you to feel as you read it. The setting, descriptive language, and sensory details all affect a story's mood. As you read "The White Umbrella," try to pay attention to your own feelings about the story and the characters, especially the narrator. When you have finished reading, see if you can summarize the mood of the story in a single word.

Use Reading Skills

Compare and Contrast The main character in this story is the narrator. As you read, pay attention to her personality. Use a character chart like the one below to record your first impressions of her. Then, at the end of the story, think about the narrator's personality again. Write down your impressions. How are they similar to and different from your first impressions?

Narrator	Behavior Toward Other People	Internal State
proud	bossy toward her sister	embarrassed to be poor

Meet the Author

Gish Jen (b. 1956) grew up in the New York City area. In college she considered being a lawyer or a doctor, and then she went to business school. She left business school and has been writing ever since. Her works explore identity and the American dream. Many of her stories and novels are about multigenerational, multiethnic families whose members must cope with how they feel about their heritage.

Preview Vocabulary

cred•i•bil•i•ty (kre' də bi´ lə tē) *n.*, believability; ability to inspire belief

stu•pen•dous (stü pen´ dəs) *adj.*, marvelous; awe-inspiring

scep•ter (sep´ tər) *n.*, tall staff or baton that a ruler carries as a symbol of authority

rev•e•la•tion (re' və lā´ shən) *n.*, act of revealing or showing, usually something astonishing or enlightening

The White Umbrella

A Short Story by Gish Jen

"This is the most beautiful umbrella I have ever seen," I said.

When I was twelve, my mother went to work without telling me or my little sister.

"Not that we need the second income." The lilt of her accent drifted from the kitchen up to the top of the stairs, where Mona and I were listening.

"No," said my father, in a barely audible voice. "Not like the Lee family."

The Lees were the only other Chinese family in town. I remembered how sorry my parents had felt for Mrs. Lee when she started waitressing downtown the year before; and so when my mother began coming home late, I didn't say anything and tried to keep Mona from saying anything either.

"But why shouldn't I?" she argued. "Lots of people's mothers work."

"Those are American people," I said.

"So what do you think we are? I can do the pledge of allegiance with my eyes closed."

Nevertheless, she tried to be discreet;[1] and if my mother wasn't home by 5:30, we would start cooking by ourselves, to make sure dinner would be on time. Mona would wash the vegetables and put on the rice; I would chop.

For weeks we wondered what kind of work she was doing. I imagined that she was selling perfume, testing dessert recipes for the local newspaper. Or maybe she was working for the florist. Now that she had learned to drive, she might be delivering boxes of roses to people.

"I don't think so," said Mona as we walked to our piano lesson after school. "She would've hit something by now."

A gust of wind littered the street with leaves.

"Maybe we better hurry up," she went on, looking at the sky."It's going to pour."

"But we're too early." Her lesson didn't begin until 4:00, mine until 4:30, so we usually tried to walk as slowly as we could. "And anyway, those aren't the kind of clouds that rain. Those are cumulus clouds."

We arrived out of breath and wet.

"Oh, you poor, poor dears," said old Miss Crosman. "Why don't you call me the next time it's like this out? If your mother won't drive you, I can come pick you up."

"No, that's okay," I answered. Mona wrung her hair out on Miss Crosman's rug. "We just couldn't get the roof of our car to close, is all. We took it to the beach last summer and got sand in the mechanism." I pronounced this last word carefully, as if the credibility of my lie depended on its middle syllable. "It's never been the same." I thought for a second. "It's a convertible."

"Well then make yourselves at home." She exchanged looks with Eugenie Roberts, whose lesson we were interrupting. Eugenie smiled good-naturedly. "The towels are in the closet across from the bathroom."

Huddling at the end of Miss Crosman's nine foot leatherette couch, Mona and I watched Eugenie play. She was a grade ahead of me and, according to school rumor, had a boyfriend in high school. I believed it....She had auburn hair, blue eyes, and, I noted with a particular pang, a pure white folding umbrella.

"I can't see," whispered Mona.

"So clean your glasses."

"My glasses *are* clean. You're in the way."

I looked at her. "They look dirty to me."

"That's because *your* glasses are dirty."

Eugenie came bouncing to the end of her piece.

"Oh! Just stupendous!" Miss Crosman hugged her, then looked up as Eugenie's

---

1. **discreet.** Using good judgment, especially when deciding how much to say

cred•i•bil•i•ty (kre' də bi´ lə tē) *n.*, believability; ability to inspire belief

stu•pen•dous (stü pen´ dəs) *adj.*, marvelous; awe-inspiring

mother walked in. "Stupendous!" she said again. "Oh! Mrs. Roberts! Your daughter has a gift, a real gift. It's an honor to teach her."

Mrs. Roberts, radiant with pride, swept her daughter out of the room as if she were royalty, born to the piano bench. Watching the way Eugenie carried herself, I sat up and concentrated so hard on sucking in my stomach that I did not realize until the Robertses were gone that Eugenie had left her umbrella. As Mona began to play, I jumped up and ran to the window, meaning to call to them—only to see their brake lights flash then fade at the stop sign at the corner. As if to allow them passage, the rain had let up; a quivering sun lit their way.

The umbrella glowed like a scepter on the blue carpet while Mona, slumping over the keyboard, managed to eke out a fair rendition[2] of a cat fight. At the end of the piece, Miss Crosman asked her to stand up.

"Stay right there," she said, then came back a minute later with a towel to cover the bench. "You must be cold," she continued. "Shall I call your mother and have her bring over some dry clothes?"

"No," answered Mona. "She won't come because she..."

"She's too busy," I broke in from the back of the room.

"I see." Miss Crosman sighed and shook her head a little. "Your glasses are filthy, honey," she said to Mona. "Shall I clean them for you?"

Sisterly embarrassment seized me. Why hadn't Mona wiped her lenses when I told her to? As she resumed abuse of the piano, I stared at the umbrella. I wanted to open it, twirl it around by its slender silver handle; I wanted to dangle it from my wrist on the

---

2. **rendition.** Performance

scep•ter (sep´ tər) *n.*, tall staff or baton that a ruler carries as a symbol of authority way to school the way the other girls did. I wondered what Miss Crosman would say if I offered to bring it to Eugenie at school tomorrow. She would be impressed with my consideration for others; Eugenie would be pleased to have it back; and I would have possession of the umbrella for an entire night. I looked at it again, toying with the idea of asking for one for Christmas. I knew, however, how my mother would react.

"Things," she would say. "What's the matter with a raincoat? All you want is things, just like an American."

Sitting down for my lesson, I was careful to keep the towel under me and sit up straight.

I stared at the umbrella. I wanted to open it, twirl it around by its slender silver handle....

"I'll bet you can't see a thing either," said Miss Crosman, reaching for my glasses. "And you can relax, you poor dear....This isn't a boot camp."[3]

When Miss Crosman finally allowed me to start playing, I played extra well, as well as I possibly could. See, I told her with my fingers. You don't have to feel sorry for me.

"That was wonderful," said Miss Crosman. "Oh! Just wonderful."

An entire constellation rose in my heart.

"And guess what," I announced proudly. "I have a surprise for you."

Then I played a second piece for her, a much more difficult one that she had not assigned.

"Oh! That was stupendous," she said without hugging me. "Stupendous! You are a genius, young lady. If your mother had started you younger, you'd be playing like Eugenie Roberts by now!"

I looked at the keyboard, wishing that I had still a third, even more difficult piece to play for her. I wanted to tell her that I was the school spelling bee champion, that I wasn't ticklish, that I could do karate.

"My mother is a concert pianist," I said.

She looked at me for a long moment, then finally, without saying anything, hugged me. I didn't say anything about bringing the umbrella to Eugenie at school.

The steps were dry when Mona and I sat down to wait for my mother.

"Do you want to wait inside?" Miss Crosman looked anxiously at the sky.

"No," I said. "Our mother will be here any minute."

"In a while," said Mona.

"Any minute," I said again, even though my mother had been at least twenty minutes late every week since she started working.

According to the church clock across the street we had been waiting twenty-five minutes when Miss Crosman came out again.

"Shall I give you ladies a ride home?"

"No," I said. "Our mother is coming any minute."

"Shall I at least give her a call and remind her you're here? Maybe she forgot about you."

"I don't think she *forgot,*" said Mona.

"Shall I give her a call anyway? Just to be safe?"

"I bet she already left," I said. "How could she forget about us?"

Miss Crosman went in to call.

"There's no answer," she said, coming back out.

"See, she's on her way," I said.

"Are you sure you wouldn't like to come in?"

---

3. boot camp. Camp for military basic training, usually perceived as being surprisingly tough

"No," said Mona.

"Yes," I said. I pointed at my sister. "She meant yes too. She meant no, she wouldn't like to go in."

Miss Crosman looked at her watch. "It's 5:30 now, ladies. My pot roast will be coming out in fifteen minutes. Maybe you'd like to come in and have some then?"

"My mother's almost here," I said. "She's on her way."

We watched and watched the street. I tried to imagine what my mother was doing; I tried to imagine her writing messages in the sky, even though I knew she was afraid of planes. I watched as the branches of Miss Crosman's big willow tree started to sway; they had all been trimmed to exactly the same height off the ground, so that they looked beautiful, like hair in the wind.

It started to rain.

"Miss Crosman is coming out again," said Mona.

"Don't let her talk you into going inside," I whispered.

"Why not?"

"Because that would mean Mom isn't really coming any minute."

"But she isn't," said Mona. "She's *working*."

"Shhh! Miss Crosman is going to hear you."

"She's working! She's working! She's working!"

I put my hand over her mouth, but she licked it, and so I was wiping my hand on my wet dress when the front door opened.

"We're getting even *wetter*," said Mona right away. "Wetter and wetter."

"Shall we all go in?" Miss Crosman pulled Mona to her feet. "Before you young ladies catch pneumonia? You've been out here an hour already."

"We're *freezing*." Mona looked up at Miss Crosman. "Do you have any hot chocolate? We're going to catch *pneumonia*."

"I'm not going in," I said. "My mother's coming any minute."

"Come on," said Mona. "Use your *noggin*."[4]

"Any minute."

"Come on, Mona," Miss Crosman opened the door. "Shall we get you inside first?"

"See you in the hospital," said Mona as she went in. "See you in the hospital with *pneumonia*."

I stared out into the empty street. The rain was pricking me all over; I was cold; I wanted to go inside. I wanted to be able to let myself go inside. If Miss Crosman came out again, I decided, I would go in.

She came out with a blanket and the white umbrella.

I could not believe that I was actually holding the umbrella, opening it. It sprang up by itself as if it were alive, as if that were what it wanted to do—as if it belonged in my hands, above my head. I stared up at the network of silver spokes, then spun the umbrella around and around and around. It was so clean and white that it seemed to glow, to illuminate everything around it. "It's beautiful," I said.

Miss Crosman sat down next to me, on one end of the blanket. I moved the umbrella over so that it covered that too. I could feel the rain on my left shoulder and shivered. She put her arm around me.

"You poor, poor dear."

I knew that I was in store for another bolt of sympathy, and braced myself by staring up into the umbrella.

"You know, I very much wanted to have children when I was younger," she continued.

"You did?"

She stared at me a minute. Her face looked dry and crusty, like day-old frosting.

---

4. noggin. Head

"I did. But then I never got married."

I twirled the umbrella around again.

"This is the most beautiful umbrella I have ever seen," I said. "Ever, in my whole life."

"Do you have an umbrella?"

"No. But my mother's going to get me one just like this for Christmas."

"Is she? I tell you what. You don't have to wait until Christmas. You can have this one."

"But this one belongs to Eugenie Roberts," I protested. "I have to give it back to her tomorrow in school."

"Who told you it belongs to Eugenie? It's not Eugenie's. It's mine. And now I'm giving it to you, so it's yours."

"It is?"

She hugged me tighter. "That's right. It's all yours."

"It's mine?" I didn't know what to say. "Mine?" Suddenly I was jumping up and down in the rain. "It's beautiful! Oh! It's beautiful!" I laughed.

Miss Crosman laughed too, even though she was getting all wet.

"Thank you, Miss Crosman. Thank you very much. Thanks a zillion. It's beautiful. It's *stupendous!*"

I could not believe that I was actually holding the umbrella, opening it.

"You're quite welcome," she said.

"Thank you," I said again, but that didn't seem like enough. Suddenly I knew just what she wanted to hear. "I wish you were my mother."

Right away I felt bad.

"You shouldn't say that," she said, but her face was opening into a huge smile as the lights of my mother's car cautiously turned the corner. I quickly collapsed the umbrella and put it up my skirt, holding onto it from the outside, through the material.

"Mona!" I shouted into the house. "Mona! Hurry up! Mom's here! I told you she was coming!"

Then I ran away from Miss Crosman, down to the curb. Mona came tearing up to my side as my mother neared the house. We both backed up a few feet so that in case she went onto the curb, she wouldn't run us over.

"But why didn't you go inside with Mona?" my mother asked on the way home. She had taken off her own coat to put over me and had the heat on high.

"She wasn't using her noggin," said Mona, next to me in the back seat.

"I should call next time," said my mother. "I just don't like to say where I am."

That was when she finally told us that she was working as a check-out clerk in the A&P.[5] She was supposed to be on the day shift, but the other employees were unreliable, and her boss had promised her a promotion if she would stay until the evening shift filled in.

For a moment no one said anything. Even Mona seemed to find the revelation disappointing.

5. A&P. Grocery store

rev•e•la•tion (re' və lā´ shən) *n.*, act of revealing or showing, usually something astonishing or enlightening

"A promotion already!" she said, finally.

I listened to the windshield wipers.

"You're so quiet." My mother looked at me in the rear view mirror. "What's the matter?"

"I wish you would quit," I said after a moment.

She sighed. "The Chinese have a saying: one beam cannot hold the roof up."

"But Eugenie Roberts's father supports their family."

She sighed once more. "Eugenie Roberts's father is Eugenie Roberts's father," she said.

As we entered the downtown area, Mona started leaning hard against me every time the car turned right, trying to push me over. Remembering what I had said to Miss Crosman, I tried to maneuver the umbrella under my leg so she wouldn't feel it.

"What's under your skirt?" Mona wanted to know as we came to a traffic light. My mother, watching us in the rear view mirror again, rolled slowly to a stop.

"What's the matter?" she asked.

"There's something under her skirt," said Mona, pulling at me. "Under her skirt."

Meanwhile, a man crossing the street started to yell at us. "Who do you think you are, lady?" he said. "You're blocking the whole crosswalk."

We all froze. Other people walking by stopped to watch.

"Didn't you hear me?" he went on, starting to thump on the hood with his fist. "Don't you speak English?"

My mother began to back up, but the car behind us honked. Luckily, the light turned green right after that. She sighed in relief.

"What were you saying, Mona?" she asked.

We wouldn't have hit the car behind us that hard if he hadn't been moving too but as it was, our car bucked violently, throwing us all first back and then forward.

"Uh oh," said Mona when we stopped. "Another accident."

I was relieved to have attention diverted from the umbrella. Then I noticed my mother's head, tilted back onto the seat. Her eyes were closed.

"Mom!" I screamed. "Mom! Wake up!"

She opened her eyes. "Please don't yell," she said. "Enough people are going to yell already."

"I thought you were dead," I said, starting to cry. "I thought you were dead."

She turned around, looked at me intently, then put her hand to my forehead.

"Sick," she confirmed. "Some kind of sick is giving you crazy ideas."

As the man from the car behind us started tapping on the window, I moved the umbrella away from my leg. Then Mona and my mother were getting out of the car. I got out after them; and while everyone else was inspecting the damage we'd done, I threw the umbrella down a sewer. ✤

When have you felt two emotions, like shame and anger, at the same time? What kinds of things make people feel conflicting emotions?

AFTER READING

Find Meaning

1. (a) Which of the narrator's parents is the focus of the story? (b) Why doesn't the narrator want other people to know about her parents?
2. (a) What are some lies the narrator tells to the piano teacher? (b) Why does she lie?
3. (a) How does the piano teacher show her sympathy for the narrator? (b) How does the narrator respond to the piano teacher?
4. How is the narrator feeling when her mother arrives at the piano teacher's house?

Make Judgments

5. How does the narrator change over the course of the story? What aspects of her personality stay the same?
6. What does the white umbrella represent to the narrator when she sees it at Miss Crosman's house?
7. Why does the narrator throw away the umbrella?

Analyze Literature

Mood Description helps establish the mood of a story. Review the part of the story when both girls are waiting for their mother after the piano lesson, before Mona goes inside. Look for sensory details and pay attention to the narrator's thoughts. Put those things in the outer circles of a cluster chart. Then write one or two words in the center circle that capture the mood.

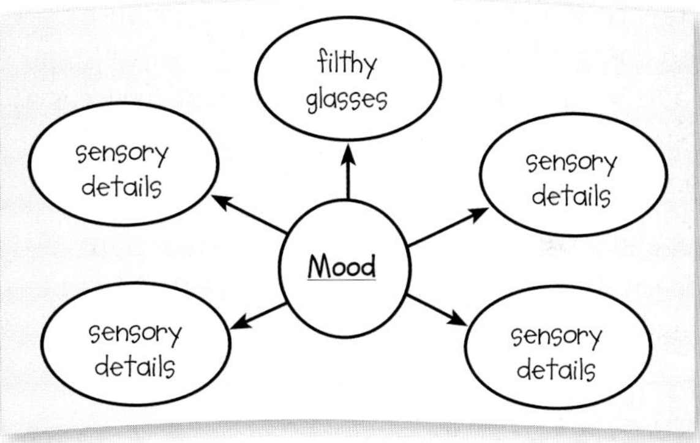

Extend Understanding

Writing Options

Creative Writing Imagine that you are the narrator of "The White Umbrella." Write a **diary entry** about why you threw the umbrella down the sewer. Use the diary to work through your motivations. In other words, try to explain your actions to yourself. At the end of the entry, write one sentence that summarizes why you threw away the umbrella.

Informative Writing Write an **informative paragraph** about the tone of "The White Umbrella." Tone is the writer's attitude toward his or her subject. It can be funny, sad, or serious, for example. Introduce your paragraph with a topic sentence that names the overall tone of the story. Give examples of how the writer creates this tone. Conclude by stating how the tone might affect a reader's response.

Collaborative Learning

Relate Mood to Point of View With a partner, talk about how the first-person point of view affects the mood of "The White Umbrella." Ask each other such questions as: How do the narrator's feelings about her family affect the mood? How do her feelings about herself affect the mood? Write a sentence that relates the mood to the first-person point of view.

Lifelong Learning

Explore a Symbol In Chinese culture, the umbrella has a long history as a cultural symbol and a practical device. Learn more about China's relationship with the umbrella. Use reference books or Internet search engines. Search with terms such as *umbrella*, *China*, and *history*. Use visual aids to present your findings to the class.

Go to **www.mirrorsandwindows.com** for more.

Grammar & Style

Independent and Dependent Clauses

When I was twelve, my mother went to work without telling me or my little sister.

—GISH JEN, "The White Umbrella"

An **independent** (or main) clause has a subject and a predicate and can function as a complete sentence. A **dependent** (or subordinate) clause also has a subject and a predicate but cannot stand alone. In the passage above, *When I was twelve* is a dependent clause. It cannot stand by itself as a complete sentence.

Dependent clauses can function as several parts of speech. Two common types of dependent clauses are adverb and adjective clauses.

Adverb Clauses

An **adverb clause** is a dependent clause that functions as an adverb. Like adverbs, adverb clauses answer such questions as when, where, why, and how an action took place. In the passage above, for example, the dependent clause modifies the verb *went* and tells when this action occurred.

EXAMPLE

She ran to the window, so that she could see the street.

In this example, the dependent clause *so that she could see the street* modifies the verb *ran* and tells why the action took place.

Adjective Clauses

An **adjective clause** is a dependent clause that functions as an adjective. Like adjectives, adjective clauses modify nouns or pronouns.

EXAMPLE

The narrator's family lives in a town that has only one other Chinese family.

In this example, the adjective clause *that has only one other Chinese family* modifies the noun *town.*

EXAMPLE

They who arrive first will get the best seats.

In this example, the adjective clause *who arrive first* modifies the pronoun *they.*

Identifying Clauses

For each of the following sentences, identify the independent and dependent clauses.

1. As Eugenie and her mother left, the rain stopped falling.
2. She wanted the white umbrella that Eugenie had left behind.
3. Miss Crosman praised Eugenie because she played so well.
4. The two girls stood where the rain was falling.
5. The narrator played a piano piece that she had not been assigned.
6. She held the umbrella as if it belonged to her.
7. As the man crossed the street, he yelled at us.
8. Miss Crosman sat down on the couch where the narrator was sitting.
9. The girls' mother arrived after her shift at the grocery store was through.
10. When their mother was late, the girls would start dinner.

Comparing Texts

Jed's Grandfather

A Short Story by Joseph Bruchac

The Courage That My Mother Had

A Lyric Poem by Edna St. Vincent Millay

BEFORE READING

Build Background

Literary Context The setting of a literary work—place and time—almost always contributes to its meaning. Bruchac's story has both a real setting and a dream setting, both of which help the reader understand the characters and what happens in the plot. Millay's poem mentions a place, New England, in describing a person.

Reader's Context Think of elderly relatives you have known. What do you admire about them? Have they ever been ill? How did this make you feel?

Set Purpose

Read the first three paragraphs of "Jed's Grandfather," and then read the title of Edna St. Vincent Millay's poem. Try to think of what both writers seem to value about people. Then read both works to find out if these values stay consistent throughout the texts.

Compare Literature:

Tone The writer's or speaker's attitude toward his or her subject is the **tone.** Word choice is a key tool for creating tone: How a writer says things implies how he or she feels. To help you detect tone, consider the words the author uses along with the connotations of those words. Use a three-column chart like this to compare the tone of each piece.

	Bruchac	Millay
Details	pancakes don't taste right	
Tone		

Meet the Authors

Joseph Bruchac (b. 1942) was raised by his grandparents in the Adirondack Mountains of New York. By heritage he is part Native American (Abenaki), and he draws on that heritage in his writing and storytelling.

Edna St. Vincent Millay (1892–1950) grew up on the coast of Maine. Her parents divorced when she was eight, after which she and her sisters lived with their mother, a nurse. Millay wrote poetry and plays almost all of her life.

Preview Vocabulary

trough (trôf) *n.,* long, shallow container

kind•ling (kin´ [d] liŋ) *n.,* material used to start a fire, often dry sticks

teth•er (te´ t͟hər) *n.,* rope or chain that allows an animal to move in a limited area

Jed's Grandfather

A Short Story by Joseph Bruchac

Jed slowly worked the handle of the backyard pitcher pump. He watched the water lap from side to side in waves as he tilted the bucket back and forth. The patterns of the dream were still going through his head. They hadn't been washed away with the first splash of water from the trough, water so cold that a paper-thin layer of ice still had to be brushed away these early spring mornings. Washing his face usually cleared whatever cobwebs of sleep still clung to his face and his thoughts, but it hadn't happened this morning. The dream was still with him.

The swallows had flown up now. The red sun was a finger's width above the hill. He looked up and watched the swallows darting, stitching the face of the sky the way his mother's needle covered a piece of cloth. The other birds, shorter-winged, fluttered in groups, as if afraid to fly by themselves the way the swallows did. The swallows were the adventurous ones. He remembered how his grandfather first pointed out to him the way a swallow can dart down to the surface of a lake and scoop up a mouthful of water without landing. They had watched swallows

trough (trôf) *n.,* long, shallow container

doing that, drinking from the pond below the house that day last blueberry season[1] when Grandfather rowed him out to The Island.

Usually the sight of the swallows in the morning sky would drive everything else out of his thoughts. He'd arch his back, lift his chin, hold out his arms, hearing his Grandfather's soft voice guiding him. "You want to be a swallow, Jeddy? You can do it. Just feel the wind under ye. That's it."

That wouldn't work this morning. The dream was too strong. He was in the boat, dark water widening between them. The old man stood there on The Island, unaware of the great dark wave coming at him from behind. His eyes were on Jed, but Jed couldn't call out. He couldn't move his arms. He wanted to turn into a swallow, fly out and rescue him, but he was paralyzed. Then the water between them began to open like a crack in the earth...

Washing his face usually cleared whatever cobwebs of sleep still clung to his face and his thoughts, but it hadn't happened this morning.

"Jed!" It was his mother's voice. Jed looked up. The bucket was filled and overflowing around his feet. A chicken was scurrying around the edge of the spreading water, now and then lifting a foot and shaking it as the water touched it. Jed carried the bucket into the kitchen.

His parents were at the table. Jed bent his arms and arched his back, hefting the bucket up onto the sink shelf.

"You're getting stronger every day, son," his father said, thin hand around a steaming mug. Behind him the wood stove crackled, a sound Jed had always loved. The steam from his father's coffee rose through the cold morning air of the kitchen. Jed could smell the coffee. It was a good smell, just as good but not quite the same as that smell when he ground the beans in the coffee mill with its blue enamel sides. But even the good smell of the coffee couldn't drive away the dream. It was there, between him and the things which were good and pleasant in his life, there the way a thick fog comes between a boat and the land. He was on the boat. He didn't know which way was home.

Jed's mother smiled at him, wiped her hands on her apron. It was the first time he had really noticed the way his mother always wiped her hands on her apron before she spoke when they were at the table. She used the same care with her words that she did in making their food. All around Jed were familiar things, things known and loved, but he was seeing them for the first time...the small crystal dog in the east window where a bull's-eye pane of glass split the sun like a prism and painted a rainbow on the wall near the stairs...the woodbox with its splintery top which sometimes snagged his left thumb when he went for an armful of kindling...the rocking chair which always caught the last rays of the setting sun, the chair which was empty now...

"He just takes after his..." his mother was saying. She stopped in mid-sentence. Jed finished the sentence in his own mind. *He takes after his grandfather*. Jed's father was a good man, hard-working, but he never had the strength of his wife's people, the Sabaels. That was why he worked as a clerk at the

1. **blueberry season.** July and August

kind•ling (kin´ [d] liŋ) *n.*, material used to start a fire, often dry sticks store in town three miles from the farm. It was Jed's grandfather, straight as an ash,[2] who always did the work around the farm. Jed was only ten, but he was already as strong as his father.

"Jed," his mother said, her hands smoothing her apron, "you aren't eating."

The pancakes were dry in his mouth. He knew they were good. They were the pancakes his mother was famous for at church socials. They were light and smelled of the goodness of a summer wheatfield, but he couldn't taste them. Instead he tasted the moist air within the fog, felt the pressure of the building storm throb around his temples as the great dark wave lifted.

Jed's father was saying something to his mother. What was it? Starving himself? Jed hadn't heard the words for sure over the roaring of the wave.

"Are you sure?" his mother said.

"You're his daughter," Jed's father answered. He spoke in the same quiet voice Jed heard him use when he answered a customer who asked what to buy to get rid of potato bugs or whether the percale was what she really wanted for her money's worth.

Jed's mother rose and walked over to the stove. She took the plate which had been warming there and covered it with a cloth. She put the cloth-covered plate, some silverware and a stoppered bottle into a basket. Jed recognized the basket. It was one Grandfather made. He remembered the sounds of the mallet as his grandfather pounded the side of the felled ash tree to break loose the withes[3] he'd trim to size. His grandfather had shown him the steps many times, shown him by doing. He felt as if the way of making a basket was woven into him the way the pattern of a web is woven into a spider's limbs. It was a craft passed down for more generations than the Sabaels could count, passed down before Jed's father's people had stepped from their ships onto these shores. For a moment the thought of Grandfather's sure hands weaving a basket drove away the dream. Then the pounding of the mallet became the pounding of whitecaps against the side of the boat and he saw the old man's figure made small by the lifting darkness.

"Take this down to the Little House, Jed," his mother said. She was holding the basket out to him. Jed looked up into her eyes for a moment and then reached out his hand.

"Come," the old man called out, making that simple word one of many meanings.

No smoke was rising from the chimney. Had it been rising it would have traced a perfect line up the face of the mountains and sky above Indian Lake. That was the way smoke rose on spring mornings such as this from the small one-roomed house his grandfather had built where the field fell away, green becoming the grey of stone, then the blue of water. A small boat was tied to a pole that jutted out of the water. The boat moved with the water the way a horse moves when tied to a rail...not pulling hard enough to break free, hardly even putting a strain on its <u>tether</u>, but showing in its motion how anxious it is to be on its way. The boat was still there. But there was no smoke.

Jed drew in a breath, feeling it catch in his stiff throat. But before he could speak he heard his grandfather's voice.

---

2. ash. Tree with thin bark and bendable wood

3. withes. Thin, bendable branches or twigs

teth • er (te´ <u>th</u>ər) *n.,* rope or chain that allows an animal to move in a limited area

"Come," the old man called out, making that simple word one of many meanings. It meant he knew who was there. It meant Jed was welcome. It meant something else, too. It was like the words in the old language his grandfather seldom spoke, the language few people knew he knew. Jed pulled gently at the locust[4] post which held up the small open gate. It creaked as he pulled at it, but the old wood was still firm. A locust post can stay in the ground a hundred years and still bend any nail you're fool enough to try to drive into it. A hundred years.

Jed went in. Joseph Sabael was sitting on the edge of his cot. There was a blanket around his shoulders and he was wearing his woolens,[5] but his feet were bare. There was no rug on the floor, no fire in the stove. It was cold in the Little House, but not as cold as Jed had thought it would be. There was a faint odor in the air, one Jed had not really noticed before. It confused him.

"That's just how the cancer smells, Jeddy," his grandfather said. "Don't pay it no mind. It's just as natural as anything else."

Jed looked at him. Joseph Sabael had always been a tall man, but never one whose frame put on bulk. His shoulders had been broad, but not heavy. His arms had always been long and sinewy[6] like the others in the town who worked the land or the big woods, not the ham-thick sort of arm which turned to softness with age. Like an ash tree's limbs, that was how his grandfather's arms had seemed. But now there was a different look to the old man. His eyes had fallen back into their sockets and one could see the bones beneath the skin in his arms. As he sat hands clasping the blanket about him, it seemed as if his shoulders were folding in around his chest. Jed held out the basket.

4. locust. Tree with hard, stiff wood
5. woolens. Warm underclothing
6. sinewy. Tough and stringy

"Mama sent you this," he said.

"I be glad she let you come," Grandfather said. He didn't reach out his hands for the basket.

"I wasn't sure I wanted to until now," Jed said. He heard his own voice as if it were the voice of a stranger.

His grandfather nodded. Very slowly, he got up from the bed. It seemed to Jed as if he were watching something happen as strange and wonderful, as magical as a tree uprooting itself and stepping across the woodlot.[7] Joseph Sabael walked very slowly to the back door of the Little House. Jed opened it for him. Together they stepped out into the light from the open water, a light which made Jed's eyes squint against the brightness of it all. His grandfather sat down carefully in the rough wooden chair which faced The Island. Again Jed smelled that strange odor, but now he knew what it was and he was not confused. It was his grandfather's death.

Gulls began swooping down in front of them. They were grey and white. From their yellow beaks came those raucous squawks which seemed to Jed to be the one thing which linked them to the rock they flew up from. Those voices, rough and filled with the earth, were all that kept the gulls from flying up and up forever until they blended with the sky.

His grandfather made a small motion with his hand and Jed opened the basket. He removed the cloth from the plate. The heat rose up to touch the back of his hand. With his fingers he broke the pancakes up into small pieces. Then, piece by piece, he tossed them up into the air. Swooping, diving, squabbling in mid-air, the gulls caught them all. Not one piece touched the waveless lake. ✣

7. **woodlot.** Place where people grow trees to use for fuel, building, and paper

What has Jed inherited from his grandfather? Have you inherited anything similar from one of your grandparents? How can a person be sure to receive knowledge from previous generations?

Find Meaning

1. (a) What kinds of birds does Jed observe in the story? (b) Which kind of bird would Jed like to be, and why?
2. (a) What are two different smells Jed experiences in the story? (b) What do these smells represent?
3. What role does the boat play in Jed's dream and in his real life?
4. Who in the story is starving himself?

Make Judgments

5. (a) What kind or kinds of strength does Jed's grandfather have? (b) How does this strength affect Jed?
6. Near the end of the story, as his grandfather stands, "It seemed to Jed as if he were watching something happen as strange and wonderful, as magical as a tree uprooting itself and stepping across the woodlot." What do you think this image suggests about Jed's thoughts and feelings?
7. (a) How does Jed's lingering dream make him feel? (b) What happens in the story that frees Jed from the feeling of the dream?

The Courage That My Mother Had

A Lyric Poem by
Edna St. Vincent Millay

The courage that my mother had
Went with her, and is with her still:
Rock from New England quarried;[1]
Now granite in a granite[2] hill.

The golden brooch[3] my mother wore
She left behind for me to wear;
I have no thing I treasure more:
Yet, it is something I could spare.

Oh, if instead she'd left to me
The thing she took into the grave!—
That courage like a rock, which she
Has no more need of, and I have. ✣

1. **quarried.** Excavated; dug
2. **granite.** Very hard igneous rock
3. **brooch.** Piece of jewelry worn as a pin near the neck

If you had to pick just one thing to inherit from your mother or father, what would it be? Is it right to want to inherit something in particular?

Comparing Texts

AFTER READING

Find Meaning

1. To what does the speaker compare her mother's courage in the first stanza?

2. (a) What does the speaker have that belonged to her mother? (b) How valuable is it?

3. What does the speaker want that she does not have?

Make Judgments

4. (a) How does gold compare to rock? (b) Which would the speaker rather have?

5. Why does the speaker want her mother's courage?

6. (a) If the speaker could talk to her mother, what do you think the speaker would say? (b) What would her mother say?

Compare Literature

Tone Both of these writers chose their words carefully.The connotations of some of those words influence the tone of each work. Refer to the chart in which you recorded the tone in "Jed's Grandfather" and "The Courage That My Mother Had" to answer the questions on the right.

1. What words used to describe Jed's dream most influence the story's tone?

2. How do the words *rock, granite,* and *courage* contribute to the tone and theme of the poem?

Extend Understanding

Writing Options

Creative Writing Write a short **poem** that you could show to your own parents. Use either Bruchac's story or Millay's poem as inspiration. The poem should be about something you would like to inherit from a grandparent, an aunt or uncle, or one of your parents. Try to use at least one symbol in the poem, but no more than three. Draft your poem; then revise it to remove unnecessary words. When you think you are done, give it a title.

Informative Writing Write a paragraph in the form of a **compare-and-contrast essay** in which you compare and contrast the feelings of the speaker in Millay's poem with Jed's feelings for his grandfather. Use what you have determined about the tone of each piece as a foundation for describing these feelings. After you have synthesized these two selections into the essay, summarize the texts in a way that maintains their meaning and logical order.

Collaborative Learning

Study Native Languages Joseph Bruchac has spent much of his life learning about his Abenaki heritage. The Abenaki language is an Algonquian language. These were the languages of the native people who met the first North American colonists. In a small group, find out more about the native people from this linguistic family. Make brief summaries of what you learned and present your findings to the class.

Lifelong Learning

Dream Research Use resources in your school or public library to find out how Native Americans felt and thought about dreams. Find a resource that is authoritative and reliable. You may have to start by researching Native American folklore. When you know something about the role of dreams in Native American traditions, write a short paragraph about it. In a second paragraph, compare what you learned to the way your own culture views dreams today.

Go to **www.mirrorsandwindows.com** for more.

Antaeus

A Short Story by Borden Deal

DIRECTED READING

BEFORE READING

Build Background

Historical Context During the Great Depression of the 1930s, the farm economy collapsed in much of the South. When the United States entered World War II in 1941, many farm laborers had already moved to the cities to look for work. The war industries, such as steel making and ammunition production, drew even more workers to the cities. "Antaeus" is set in a city during World War II.

Reader's Context What connects you to the place you live? If you moved, could you reproduce that feeling somewhere else?

Set Purpose

Preview "Antaeus" by reading the first paragraph. Use the paragraph to predict the story's plot and theme.

Analyze Literature

Conflict The **plot** in a work of fiction usually develops because of a **conflict,** or struggle. A conflict can be *internal,* within a single character. A conflict can also be *external,* between a character and an outside force. As you read, identify the main character and the type of conflict. Record the development of the plot through this main conflict.

Use Reading Skills

Context Clues Preview the vocabulary words as they appear in the sentences below. Try to unlock the meaning of each word using the context clues in the sentences.

1. From the highest tower, the queen could see all of her land, the full extent of her domain.
2. The cat slept so deeply in the sunlight that its feet did not even twitch; its body was totally inert.
3. The child flourished with good food and loving care, growing five inches in one summer.

Meet the Author

Borden Deal (1922–1985) grew up in Mississippi as part of a farming family. His family lost its land in the Great Depression, and his father died when he was sixteen. Deal worked as a firefighter, on a showboat, and in the U.S. Navy. He began publishing novels in his mid-thirties, writing about life and culture in the South. Often, his novels and stories focus on the connections people have to the land and how these connections shape their identities.

Preview Vocabulary

do•main (dō mān´) *n.,* land that a person owns; rightful territory

la•bo•ri•ous (lə bōr´ ē əs) *adj.,* produced by hard work

in•ert (i nurt´) *adj.,* still; unmoving

des•e•crate (des´ i krāt') *v.,* treat with disrespect

flour•ish (flur´ ish) *v.,* grow luxuriously

Antaeus

A Short Story by Borden Deal

Tenement Flats (Family Flats), c. 1934. Millard Sheets. Smithsonian American Art Museum, Washington, DC.

I remember the first day I took T. J. up there to meet the gang.

This was during the wartime, when lots of people were coming North for jobs in factories and war industries, when people moved around a lot more than they do now, and sometimes kids were thrown into new groups and new lives that were completely different from anything they had ever known before. I remember this one kid, T. J. his name was, from somewhere down South, whose family moved into our building during that time. They'd come North with everything they owned piled into the back seat of an old-model sedan that you wouldn't expect could make the trip, with T. J. and his three younger sisters riding shakily on top of the load of junk.

Our building was just like all the others there, with families crowded into a few rooms, and I guess there were twenty-five or thirty kids about my age in that one building. Of course, there were a few of us who formed a gang and ran together all the time after school, and I was the one who brought T. J. in and started the whole thing.

The building right next door to us was a factory where they made walking dolls. It was a low building with a flat, tarred roof that had a parapet[1] all around it about head-high, and we'd found out a long time before that no one, not even the watchman, paid any attention to the roof because it was higher than any of the other buildings around. So my gang used the roof as a headquarters. We could get up there by crossing over to the fire escape from our own roof on a plank and then going on up. It was a secret place for us, where nobody else could go without our permission.

I remember the day I first took T. J. up there to meet the gang. He was a stocky, robust kid with a shock of white hair, nothing sissy about him except his voice; he

1. **parapet.** Low wall around the edge of a roof or platform

talked in this slow, gentle voice like you never heard before. He talked different from any of us and you noticed it right away. But I liked him anyway, so I told him to come on up.

We climbed up over the parapet and dropped down on the roof. The rest of the gang were already there.

"Hi," I said. I jerked my thumb at T. J. "He just moved into the building yesterday."

He just stood there, not scared or anything, just looking, like the first time you see somebody you're not sure you're going to like.

"Hi," Blackie said. "Where are you from?"

"Marion County," T. J. said.

We laughed. "Marion County?" I said. "Where's that?"

He looked at me for a moment like I was a stranger, too. "It's in Alabama," he said, like I ought to know where it was.

"What's your name?" Charley said.

"T. J.," he said, looking back at him. He had pale blue eyes that looked washed-out but he looked directly at Charley, waiting for his reaction. He'll be all right, I thought. No sissy in him, except that voice. Who ever talked like that?

"T. J.," Blackie said. "That's just initials. What's your real name? Nobody in the world has just initials."

"I do," he said. "And they're T. J. That's all the name I got."

His voice was resolute with the knowledge of his rightness, and for a moment no one had anything to say. T. J. looked around at the rooftop and down at the black tar under his feet. "Down yonder where I come from," he said, "we played out in the woods. Don't you-all have no woods around here?"

"Naw," Blackie said. "There's the park a few blocks over, but it's full of kids and cops and old women. You can't do a thing."

T. J. kept looking at the tar under his feet. "You mean you ain't got no fields to raise nothing in?...no watermelons or nothing?"

"Naw," I said scornfully. "What do you want to grow something for? The folks can buy everything they need at the store."

He moved his foot against the black tar. "We could make our own field right here," he said softly, thoughtfully.

He looked at me again with that strange, unknowing look. "In Marion County," he said, "I had my own acre of cotton and my own acre of corn. It was mine to plant and make ever' year."

He sounded like it was something to be proud of, and in some obscure way it made the rest of us angry. Blackie said, "Who'd want to have their own acre of cotton and corn? That's just work. What can you do with an acre of cotton and corn?"

T. J. looked at him. "Well, you get part of the bale offen your acre,"[2] he said seriously. "And I fed my acre of corn to my calf."

We didn't really know what he was talking about, so we were more puzzled than angry; otherwise, I guess, we'd have chased him off the roof and wouldn't let him be part of our gang. But he was strange and different, and we were all attracted by his stolid[3] sense of rightness and belonging, maybe by the strange softness of his voice

2. **you get part of the bale offen your acre.** When T. J. farmed someone else's land, he shared the crop with the owner and was able to keep part of it for himself.

3. **stolid.** Unemotional

contrasting our own tones of speech into harshness.

He moved his foot against the black tar. "We could make our own field right here," he said softly, thoughtfully. "Come spring we could raise us what we want to—watermelons and garden truck[4] and no telling what all."

"You'd have to be a good farmer to make these tar roofs grow any watermelons," I said. We all laughed.

But T. J. looked serious. "We could haul us some dirt up here," he said. "And spread it out even and water it, and before you know it, we'd have us a crop in here." He looked at us intently. "Wouldn't that be fun?"

"They wouldn't let us," Blackie said quickly.

"I thought you said this was you-all's roof," T. J. said to me. "That you-all could do anything you wanted to up here."

"They've never bothered us," I said. I felt the idea beginning to catch fire in me. It was a big idea, and it took a while for it to sink in; but the more I thought about it, the better I liked it. "Say," I said to the gang. "He might have something there. Just make us a regular roof garden, with flowers and grass and trees and everything. And all ours, too," I said. "We wouldn't let anybody up here except the ones we wanted to."

"It'd take a while to grow trees," T. J. said quickly, but we weren't paying any attention to him. They were all talking about it suddenly, all excited with the idea after I'd put it in a way they could catch hold of it. Only rich people had roof gardens, we knew, and the idea of our own private domain excited them.

"We could bring it up in sacks and boxes," Blackie said. "We'd have to do it while the folks weren't paying any attention to us, for we'd have to come up to the roof of our building and then cross over with it."

"Where could we get the dirt?" somebody said worriedly.

"Out of those vacant lots over close to school," Blackie said. "Nobody'd notice if we scraped it up."

I slapped T. J. on the shoulder. "Man, you had a wonderful idea," I said, and everybody grinned at him, remembering that he had started it. "Our own private roof garden."

He grinned back. "It'll be ourn," he said. "All ourn." Then he looked thoughtful again.

HISTORY ▶▶ CONNECTION

Victory Gardens During World War I and World War II, the U.S. government asked citizens to grow their own fruits and vegetables at home. This allowed the government to send canned and preserved food overseas to feed the troops. City people planted in yards and vacant lots and on rooftops. Neighbors cooperated to maintain community food supplies. During World War II, more than twenty million of these "victory gardens" helped people on the home front feel they were contributing to the war effort. Considering the story's setting, what do you think about T. J. and the gang's roof garden? Explain.

4. **garden truck.** Vegetables grown for market

do•main (dō mān´) *n.*, land that a person owns; rightful territory

"Maybe I can lay my hands on some cotton seed, too. You think we could raise us some cotton?" We'd started big projects before at one time or another, like any gang of kids, but they'd always petered out for lack of organization and direction. But this one didn't; somehow or other T. J. kept it going all through the winter months. He kept talking about the watermelons and the cotton we'd raise, come spring, and when even that wouldn't work, he'd switch around to my idea of flowers and grass and trees, though he was always honest enough to add that it'd take a while to get any trees started. He always had it on his mind, and he'd mention it in school, getting them lined up to carry dirt that afternoon, saying in a casual way that he reckoned a few more weeks ought to see the job through.

Our little area of private earth grew slowly. T. J. was smart enough to start in one corner of the building, heaping up the carried earth two or three feet thick so that we had an immediate result to look at, to contemplate with awe. Some of the evenings T. J. alone was carrying earth up to the building, the rest of the gang distracted by other enterprises or interests, but T. J. kept plugging along on his own, and eventually we'd all come back to him again, and then our own little acre would grow more rapidly.

He was careful about the kind of dirt he'd let us carry up there, and more than once he dumped a sandy load over the parapet into the areaway below because it wasn't good enough. He found out the kinds of earth in all the vacant lots for blocks around. He'd pick it up and feel it and smell it, frozen though it was sometimes, and then he'd say it was good growing soil or it wasn't worth anything, and we'd have to go on somewhere else.

Thinking about it now, I don't see how he kept us at it. It was hard work, lugging paper sacks and boxes of dirt all the way up the stairs of our own building, keeping out of the way of the grown-ups so they wouldn't catch on to what we were doing. They probably wouldn't have cared, for they didn't pay much attention to us, but we wanted to keep it secret anyway. Then we had to go through the trap door to our roof, teeter[5] over a plank to the fire escape, then climb two or three stories to the parapet, and drop them down onto the roof. All that for a small pile of earth that sometimes didn't seem worth the effort. But T. J. kept the vision bright within us, his words shrewd and calculated toward the fulfillment of his dream; and he worked harder than any of us. He seemed driven toward a goal that we couldn't see, a particular point in time that

5. teeter. Wobble

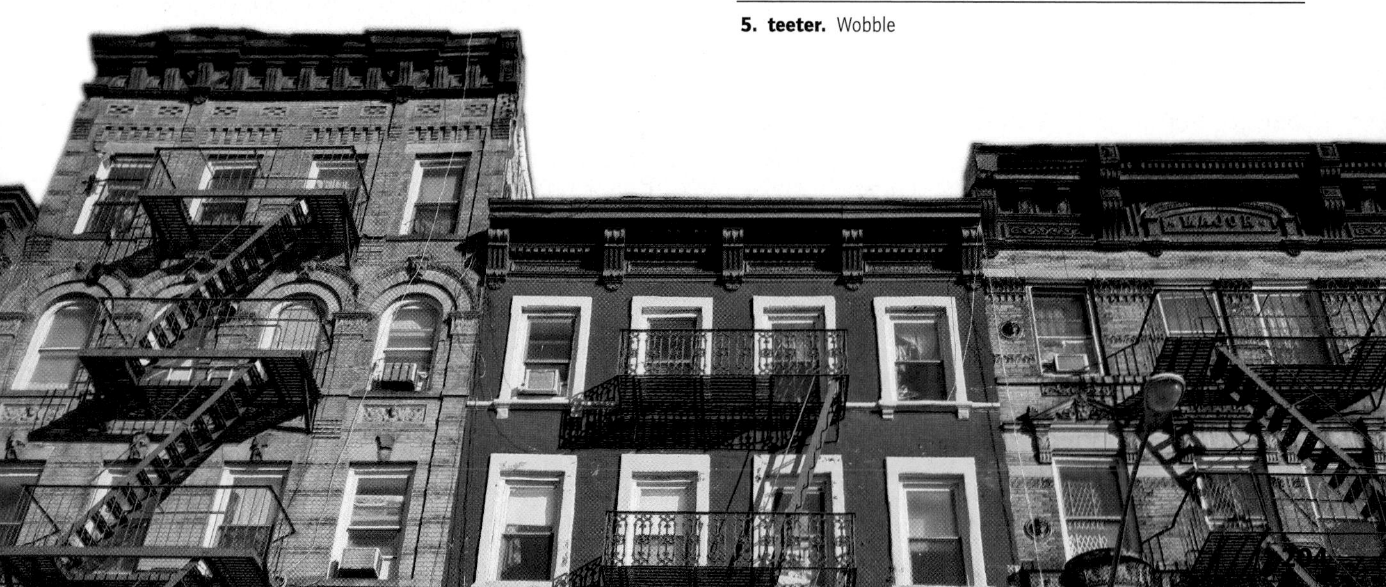

would be definitely marked by signs and wonders that only he could see.

The laborious earth just lay there during the cold months, inert and lifeless, the clods lumpy and cold under our feet when we walked over it. But one day it rained, and afterward there was a softness in the air, and the earth was live and giving again with moisture and warmth.

That evening T. J. smelled the air, his nostrils dilating with the odor of the earth under his feet. "It's spring," he said, and there was a gladness rising in his voice that filled us all with the same feeling. "It's mighty late for it, but it's spring. I'd just about decided it wasn't never gonna get here at all."

We were all sniffing at the air, too, trying to smell it the way that T. J. did, and I can still remember the sweet odor of the earth under our feet. It was the first time in my life that spring and spring earth had meant anything to me. I looked at T. J. then, knowing in a faint way the hunger within him through the toilsome winter months, knowing the dream that lay behind his plan. He was a new Antaeus,[6] preparing his own bed of strength.

"Planting time," he said. "We'll have to find us some seed."

"What do we do?" Blackie said. "How do we do it?"

"First we'll have to break up the clods," T. J. said. "That won't be hard to do. Then we plant the seed, and after a while they come up. Then you got you a crop." He frowned. "But you ain't got it raised yet. You got to tend it and hoe it and take care of it, and all the time it's growing and growing, while you're awake and while you're asleep. Then you lay it by when it's growed[7] and let it ripen, and then you got you a crop."

"There's these wholesale seed houses over on Sixth," I said. "We could probably swipe some grass seed over there."

T. J. looked at the earth. "You-all seem mighty set on raising some grass," he said. "I ain't never put no effort into that. I spent all my life trying not to raise grass."

"But it's pretty," Blackie said. "We could play on it and take sunbaths on it. Like having our own lawn. Lots of people got lawns."

"You-all seem mighty set on raising some grass," he said.

"Well," T. J. said. He looked at the rest of us, hesitant for the first time. He kept on looking at us for a moment. "I did have it in mind to raise some corn and vegetables. But we'll plant grass."

He was smart. He knew where to give in. And I don't suppose it made any difference to him, really. He just wanted to grow something, even if it was grass.

"Of course," he said. "I do think we ought to plant a row of watermelons. They'd be mighty nice to eat while we was a-laying on that grass."

We all laughed. "All right," I said. "We'll plant us a row of watermelons."

Things went very quickly then. Perhaps half the roof was covered with the earth, the half that wasn't broken by ventilators,[8] and

6. **Antaeus.** Mythological giant who gained strength from touching Earth. Hercules defeated Antaeus by holding him off the ground until he weakened and died.
7. **Then you lay it by when it's growed.** To lay by a crop is to tend to it for the last time before harvesting. After laying by, a farmer leaves the crop to mature on its own.
8. **ventilators.** Mechanisms, such as ducts or fans, for getting rid of old air and bringing fresh air into a building

la • bo • ri • ous (lə bōr´ ē əs) *adj.*, produced by hard work

in • ert (i nʉrt´) *adj.*, still; unmoving

we swiped pocketfuls of grass seed from the open bins in the wholesale seed house, mingling among the buyers on Saturdays and during the school lunch hour. T. J. showed us how to prepare the earth, breaking up the clods and smoothing it and sowing the grass seed. It looked rich and black now with moisture, receiving of the seed, and it seemed that the grass sprang up overnight, pale green in the early spring.

We couldn't keep from looking at it, unable to believe that we had created this delicate growth. We looked at T. J. with understanding now, knowing the fulfillment of the plan he had carried alone within his mind. We had worked without full understanding of the task, but he had known all the time.

We couldn't keep from looking at it, unable to believe that we had created this delicate growth.

We found that we couldn't walk or play on the delicate blades, as we had expected to, but we didn't mind. It was enough just to look at it, to realize that it was the work of our own hands, and each evening, the whole gang was there, trying to measure the growth that had been achieved that day.

One time a foot was placed on the plot of ground, one time only, Blackie stepping onto it with sudden bravado. Then he looked at the crushed blades and there was shame in his face. He did not do it again. This was his grass, too, and not to be desecrated. No one said anything, for it was not necessary.

T. J. had reserved a small section for watermelons, and he was still trying to find some seed for it. The wholesale house didn't have any watermelon seed, and we didn't know where we could lay our hands on them. T. J. shaped the earth into mounds, ready to receive them, three mounds lying in a straight line along the edge of the grass plot.

We had just about decided that we'd have to buy the seed if we were to get them. It was a violation of our principles, but we were anxious to get the watermelons started. Somewhere or other, T. J. got his hands on a seed catalog and brought it one evening to our roof garden.

"We can order them now," he said, showing us the catalog. "Look!"

We all crowded around, looking at the fat, green watermelons pictured in full color on the pages. Some of them were split open, showing the red, tempting meat, making our mouths water.

"Now we got to scrape up some seed money," T. J. said, looking at us. "I got a quarter. How much you-all got?"

We made up a couple of dollars among us and T. J. nodded his head. "That'll be more than enough. Now we got to decide what kind to get. I think them Kleckley Sweets. What do you-all think?"

He was going into esoteric[9] matters beyond our reach. We hadn't even known there were different kinds of melons. So we just nodded our heads and agreed that yes, we thought the Kleckley Sweets too.

"I'll order them tonight," T. J. said. "We ought to have them in a few days."

"What are you boys doing up here?" an adult voice said behind us.

It startled us, for no one had ever come up here before, in all the time we had been using the roof of the factory. We jerked around and saw three men standing near the

9. esoteric. Understood by only a small group of people

des•e•crate (des´ i krāt') *v.*, treat with disrespect

trap door at the other end of the roof. They weren't policemen, or night watchmen, but three men in plump business suits, looking at us. They walked toward us.

"What are you boys doing up here?" the one in the middle said again.

We stood still, guilt heavy among us, levied by the tone of voice,[10] and looked at the three strangers.

The men stared at the grass flourishing behind us. "What's this?" the man said. "How did this get up here?"

"Sure is growing good, ain't it?" T. J. said conversationally. "We planted it."

The men kept looking at the grass as if they didn't believe it. It was a thick carpet over the earth now, a patch of deep greenness startling in the sterile industrial surroundings.

"Yes, sir," T. J. said proudly. "We toted that earth up here and planted that grass." He fluttered the seed catalog. "And we're just fixing to plant us some watermelon."

The man looked at him then, his eyes strange and faraway. "What do you mean, putting this on the roof of my building?" he said. "Do you want to go to jail?"

T. J. looked shaken. The rest of us were silent, frightened by the authority of his voice. We had grown up aware of adult authority, of policemen and night watchmen and teachers, and this man sounded like all the others. But it was a new thing to T. J.

"Well, you wasn't using the roof," T. J. said. He paused a moment and added shrewdly, "So we just thought to pretty it up a little bit."

---

10. levied by the tone of voice. Judged by the attitude more than by words

flour • ish (flʉr´ ish) *v.*, grow luxuriously

"And sag it so I'd have to rebuild it," the man said sharply. He started turning away, saying to another man beside him, "See that all that junk is shoveled off by tomorrow."

"Yes, sir," the man said.

T. J. started forward. "You can't do that," he said. "We toted it up here, and it's our earth. We planted it and raised it and toted it up here."

The man stared at him coldly. "But it's my building," he said. "It's to be shoveled off tomorrow."

"It's our earth," T. J. said desperately. "You ain't got no right!"

The men walked on without listening and descended clumsily through the trap door. T. J. stood looking after them, his body tense with anger, until they had disappeared. They wouldn't even argue with him, wouldn't let him defend his earth rights.

He turned to us. "We won't let 'em do it," he said fiercely. "We'll stay up here all day tomorrow and the day after that, and we won't let 'em do it."

We just looked at him. We knew that there was no stopping it.

He saw it in our faces, and his face wavered for a moment before he gripped it into determination. "They ain't got no right," he said. "It's our earth. It's our land. Can't nobody touch a man's own land."

We kept looking at him, listening to the words but knowing that it was no use. The adult world had descended on us even in our richest dream, and we knew there was no calculating the adult world, no fighting it, no winning against it.

We started moving slowly toward the parapet and the fire escape, avoiding a last look at the green beauty of the earth that T. J. had planted for us, had planted deeply in our minds as well as in our experience. We filed slowly over the edge and down the steps to the plank, T. J. coming last, and all of us could feel the weight of his grief behind us.

"Wait a minute," he said suddenly, his voice harsh with the effort of calling.

We stopped and turned, held by the tone of his voice, and looked up at him standing above us on the fire escape.

"We can't stop them?" he said, looking down at us, his face strange in the dusky light. "There ain't no way to stop 'em?"

"No," Blackie said with finality. "They own the building."

We stood still for a moment, looking up at T. J., caught into inaction by the decision working in his face. He stared back at us, and his face was pale and mean in the poor light, with a bald nakedness in his skin like cripples have sometimes.

"They ain't gonna touch my earth," he said fiercely. "They ain't gonna lay a hand on it! Come on."

He turned around and started up the fire escape again, almost running against the effort of climbing. We followed more slowly, not knowing what he intended to do. By the time we reached him, he had seized a board and thrust it into the soil, scooping it up and flinging it over the parapet into the areaway below. He straightened and looked at us.

"They can't touch it," he said. "I won't let 'em lay a dirty hand on it!"

We saw it then. He stooped to his labor again, and we followed, the gusts of his anger moving in frenzied labor among us as we scattered along the edge of the earth, scooping it and throwing it over the parapet, destroying with anger the growth we had nurtured with such tender care. The soil carried so laboriously upward to the light and the sun cascaded swiftly into the dark areaway, the green blades of grass crumpled and twisted in the falling.

It took less time than you would think; the task of destruction is infinitely easier than that of creation. We stopped at the end, leaving only a scattering of loose soil, and when it was finally over, a stillness stood among the group and over the factory building. We looked down at the bare sterility of black tar, felt the harsh texture of it under the soles of our shoes, and the anger had gone out of us, leaving only a sore aching in our minds, like overstretched muscles.

T. J. stood for a moment, his breathing slowing from anger and effort, caught into the same contemplation of destruction as all of us. He stooped slowly, finally, and picked up a lonely blade of grass left trampled under our feet and put it between his teeth, tasting it, sucking the greenness out of it into his mouth. Then he started walking toward the fire escape, moving before any of us were ready to move, and disappeared over the edge.

We followed him, but he was already halfway down to the ground, going on past the board where we crossed over, climbing down into the areaway. We saw the last section swing down with his weight, and then he stood on the concrete below us, looking at the small pile of anonymous earth scattered by our throwing. Then he walked across the place where we could see him and disappeared toward the street without glancing back, without looking up to see us watching him.

They did not find him for two weeks.

Then the Nashville police caught him just outside the Nashville freight yards. He was walking along the railroad track, still heading South, still heading home.

As for us, who had no remembered home to call us, none of us ever again climbed the escapeway to the roof. ✣

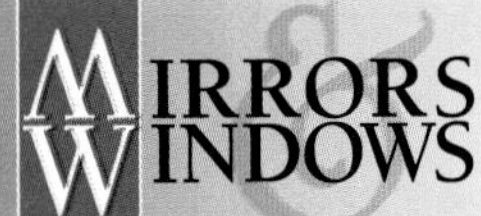

How does it feel to plant a garden, write a poem, play music, or create a work of art? What is so special about the feeling a person gets from growing plants or making something beautiful?

Find Meaning

1. (a) What brings T. J. and his family to the North? (b) Why does the narrator's gang let T. J. in?
2. Why does T. J. want to grow crops?
3. (a) How does the gang manage to plant the grass? (b) How does T. J.'s project affect the gang?

Make Judgments

4. If no one knew they were using the roof, why does the gang keep their project a secret?
5. (a) Once grass is growing, the narrator says about the gang and T. J., "We had worked without full understanding of the task, but he had known all the time." What does the narrator mean by "full understanding"? (b) Why hadn't the gang understood this before?
6. Why does T. J. destroy the garden himself?

LITERATURE ▶▶ CONNECTION

"Antaeus" reveals some deep differences between city and country living. In the following poem, the speaker highlights some differences between two parts of a city. **Lucille Clifton** (1936–2010) was born in a small town near Buffalo, New York. She was a university professor in Maryland and published many poetry collections, children's books, and a memoir. Her African-American heritage and her own family inspired many of her works. Read the poem for insight into what "home" means to someone living in a city.

in the inner city

A Lyric Poem by Lucille Clifton

in the inner city
or
like we call it
home
we think a lot about uptown[1]
and the silent nights
and the houses straight as
dead men
and the pastel[2] lights
and we hang on to our no place
happy to be alive
and in the inner city
or
like we call it
home ✣

1. **uptown.** Residential part of a city away from the center, usually considered safer and more well off than the inner city
2. **pastel.** Pale, light color

TEXT ◀TO▶ TEXT CONNECTION

"Antaeus" and "in the inner city" both deal with contrasts. The poem's speaker contrasts the inner city "home" with uptown, while the story's narrator contrasts city life with T. J.'s dreams. How does the speaker compare the inner city to uptown? What do T. J.'s dreams tell you about day-to-day life in the city?

AFTER READING

Analyze Literature

Conflict The conflict in "Antaeus" is between T. J. and an outside force. It is an external conflict. Identify the main conflict using a cause-and-effect chart. List at least three causes and effects from the story. Then, based on your cause-and-effect examples, state what you think is the story's main conflict.

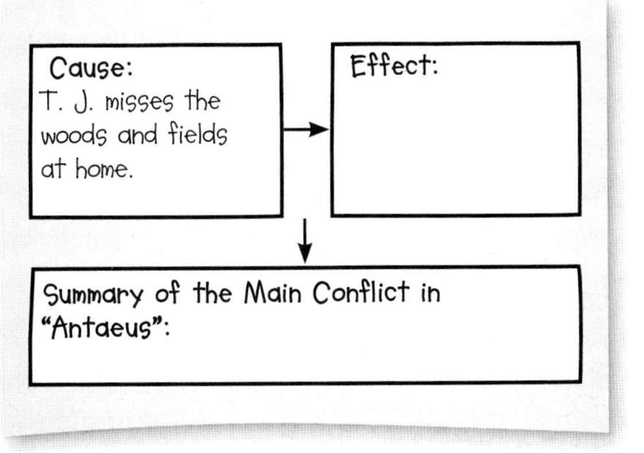

Extend Understanding

Writing Options

Creative Writing Imagine that you are the narrator of "Antaeus." T. J. has been brought back to the city, and you want to help him plant a garden. You decide to formally request use of the factory roof for a victory garden. Write a **business letter** to the factory owner. Follow the instructions for writing a business letter in Language Arts Handbook 6.3, on pages 909–910 of this textbook. In the body of your letter, use evidence to support arguments in favor of growing a garden in this space.

Informative Writing Write a short **literary response** that evaluates the ending of "Antaeus." Name the main conflict in the story and give an example from the text to illustrate it. Then state how the ending resolves the conflict. Finish by showing how T. J. and the gang would have been better off if they had been able to keep their garden.

Collaborative Learning

Discuss Motivation A motivation is a force that moves a character to think, feel, or behave in a certain way. In a small group, discuss T. J.'s motivation. Why did he want crops? Why did he join the narrator's gang? Why did he agree to plant grass? And why did he destroy the garden and leave the city? When your group has reached a consensus on answers to these questions, have a volunteer write one or two sentences summarizing T. J.'s motivation.

Critical Literacy

Explore an Allusion The title of Deal's story is a literary allusion, an indirect reference to something that explains or enriches the story. Use a library or the Internet to find out about the myth of Antaeus. Compare Antaeus and T. J. Make a poster that explains how they are similar and how they are different.

Go to **www.mirrorsandwindows.com** for more.

Seventh Grade

A Short Story by Gary Soto

DIRECTED READING

BEFORE READING

Build Background

Literary Context As a young man, Gary Soto was impressed with writers who used everyday language to write about real places and common experiences. In his own writing, Soto draws from his experiences growing up Mexican American in California's Central Valley. From writing poetry in college, he turned to autobiographical essays and finally to fiction for adults and young people.

Reader's Context Think back to your first day of school this year. What hopes and plans did you have for the months ahead?

Set Purpose

Skim the first two paragraphs of the story. Based on the title and those paragraphs, predict how likely it is that Victor will succeed. Read the story to find out if your prediction is correct.

Analyze Literature

Character A story always has a **main character**–in this case, Victor–and usually one or more **minor characters.** Sometimes a character is *static,* meaning that he or she doesn't change over the course of the story. Other times, a character is dynamic. From the beginning of the story to the end, a *dynamic* character has experiences that change his or her personality and behavior. As you read, pay attention to how Victor's character changes.

Use Reading Skills

Sequence of Events
Most stories are told in chronological order. This means that the events are told in the order in which they occurred. The events can happen within a character's mind or in the setting of the story. Write down the sequence of events in a story using a time line. As you read, follow Victor through his day from beginning to end and record the key events on your time line.

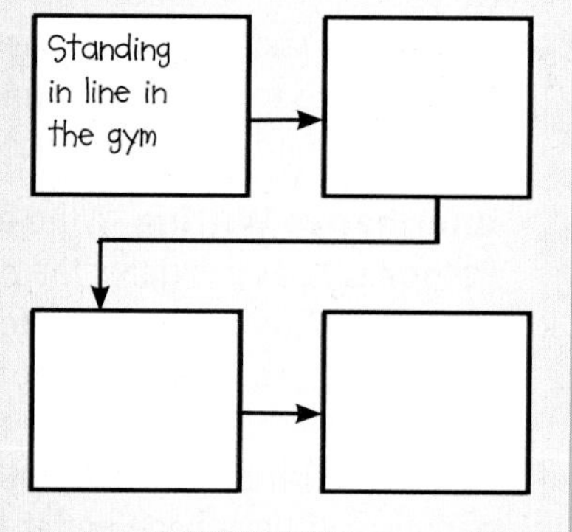

Meet the Author

Gary Soto was born in 1952 and raised in Fresno, California. He did not do well in school, but he loved the school library. Today he is both a poet and a novelist, and he writes for young people and adults. He travels widely to connect with readers. He is also a Young People's Ambassador for the United Farm Workers of America, a large labor union. During many appearances he introduces students to the union's history and activities.

Preview Vocabulary

scowl (skaů[ə]l) *v.,* lower the eyebrows, as if squinting or frowning

fe • roc • i • ty (fə räs´ ət ē) *n.,* fierceness or intensity

con • vic • tion (kən vik´ shən) *n.,* belief; self-confidence; boldness

trudge (trʉj) *v.,* walk heavily; plod

Teresa is going to be my girl this year....

Seventh Grade

A Short Story by Gary Soto

On the first day of school, Victor stood in line half an hour before he came to a wobbly card table. He was handed a packet of papers and a computer card on which he listed his one elective, French. He already spoke Spanish and English, but he thought some day he might travel to France, where it was cool; not like Fresno,[1] where summer days reached 110 degrees in the shade. There were rivers in France and huge churches, and fair-skinned people everywhere, the way there were brown people all around Victor.

Michael thinks making a face makes him handsome.

Besides, Teresa, a girl he had liked since they were in catechism classes[2] at Saint Theresa's, was taking French, too. With any luck they would be in the same class. Teresa is going to be my girl this year, he promised himself as he left the gym full of students in their new fall clothes. She was cute. And good in math, too, Victor thought as he walked down the hall to his homeroom. He ran into his friend, Michael Torres, by the water fountain that never turned off.

They shook hands, *raza*-style,[3] and jerked their heads at one another in a *saludo de vato.*[4] "How come you're making a face?" asked Victor.

"I ain't making a face, *ese.* This is my face." Michael said his face had changed during the summer. He had read a *GQ* magazine[5] that his older brother had borrowed from the Book Mobile and noticed that the male models all had the same look on their faces. They would stand, one arm around a beautiful woman, and scowl. They would sit at a pool, their rippled stomachs dark with shadow, and scowl. They would sit at dinner tables, cool drinks in their hands, and scowl.

"I think it works," Michael said. He scowled and let his upper lip quiver. His teeth showed along with the ferocity of his soul. "Belinda Reyes walked by a while ago and looked at me," he said.

Victor didn't say anything, though he thought his friend looked pretty strange. They talked about recent movies, baseball, their parents, and the horrors of picking grapes in order to buy their fall clothes. Picking grapes was like living in Siberia,[6] except hot and more boring.

"What classes are you taking?" Michael said, scowling.

"French. How 'bout you?"

"Spanish. I ain't so good at it, even if I'm Mexican."

"I'm not either, but I'm better at it than math, that's for sure."

A tinny, three-beat bell propelled students to their homerooms. The two friends socked each other in the arm and went their ways, Victor thinking, man, that's weird. Michael thinks making a face makes him handsome.

On the way to his homeroom, Victor tried a scowl. He felt foolish, until out of the corner of his eye he saw a girl looking at him. Umm, he thought, maybe it does work. He scowled with greater conviction.

1. **Fresno.** Inland city in California's major agricultural region
2. **catechism classes.** Religious instruction
3. ***raza*-style.** In the style of Mexicans or Mexican Americans
4. ***saludo de vato*** (sä lüd´ ō də vä tō´). Greeting between friends (Spanish)
5. ***GQ* magazine.** Fashion and style magazine for men
6. **Siberia.** Vast area of northern Asia with a harsh environment where the Soviet Union used to send prisoners

scowl (skaů[ə]l) *v.*, lower the eyebrows, as if squinting or frowning

fe•roc•i•ty (fə räs´ ət ē) *n.*, fierceness or intensity

con•vic•tion (kən vik´ shən) *n.*, belief; self-confidence; boldness7. *Bonjour.* Good day (French)

In homeroom, roll was taken, emergency cards were passed out, and they were given a bulletin to take home to their parents. The principal, Mr. Belton, spoke over the crackling loudspeaker, welcoming the students to a new year, new experiences, and new friendships. The students squirmed in their chairs and ignored him. They were anxious to go to first period. Victor sat calmly, thinking of Teresa, who sat two rows away, reading a paperback novel. This would be his lucky year. She was in his homeroom, and would probably be in his English and math classes. And, of course, French.

The bell rang for first period, and the students herded noisily through the door. Only Teresa lingered, talking with the homeroom teacher.

"So you think I should talk to Mrs. Gaines?" she asked the teacher. "She would know about ballet?"

"She would be a good bet," the teacher said. Then added, "Or the gym teacher, Mrs. Garza."

Victor lingered, keeping his head down and staring at his desk. He wanted to leave when she did so he could bump into her and say something clever.

He watched her on the sly. As she turned to leave, he stood up and hurried to the door, where he managed to catch her eye.

He wanted to leave when she did so he could bump into her and say something clever.

She smiled and said, "Hi, Victor."

He smiled back and said, "Yeah, that's me." His brown face blushed. Why hadn't he said, "Hi, Teresa," or "How was your summer?" or something nice?

As Teresa walked down the hall, Victor walked the other way, looking back, admiring how gracefully she walked, one foot in front of the other. So much for being in the same class, he thought. As he trudged to English, he practiced scowling.

In English they reviewed the parts of speech. Mr. Lucas, a portly man, waddled down the aisle, asking, "What is a noun?"

"A person, place, or thing," said the class in unison.

"Yes, now somebody give me an example of a person—you, Victor Rodriguez."

"Teresa," Victor said automatically. Some of the girls giggled. They knew he had a crush on Teresa. He felt himself blushing again.

"Correct," Mr. Lucas said. "Now provide me with a place."

Mr. Lucas called on a freckled kid who answered, "Teresa's house with a kitchen full of big brothers."

trudge (trʉj´) *v.*, walk heavily; plod

After English, Victor had math, his weakest subject. He sat in the back by the window, hoping that he would not be called on. Victor understood most of the problems, but some of the stuff looked like the teacher made it up as she went along. It was confusing, like the inside of a watch.

Mr. Bueller, wrinkling his face in curiosity, asked him to speak up.

After math he had a fifteen-minute break, then social studies, and, finally, lunch. He bought a tuna casserole with buttered rolls, some fruit cocktail, and milk. He sat with Michael, who practiced scowling between bites.

Girls walked by and looked at him.

"See what I mean, Vic?" Michael scowled. "They love it."

"Yeah, I guess so."

They ate slowly, Victor scanning the horizon for a glimpse of Teresa. He didn't see her. She must have brought lunch, he thought, and is eating outside. Victor scraped his plate and left Michael, who was busy scowling at a girl two tables away.

The small, triangle-shaped campus bustled with students talking about their new classes. Everyone was in a sunny mood. Victor hurried to the bag lunch area, where he sat down and opened his math book. He moved his lips as if he were reading, but his mind was somewhere else. He raised his eyes slowly and looked around. No Teresa.

He lowered his eyes, pretending to study, then looked slowly to the left. No Teresa. He turned a page in the book and stared at some math problems that scared him because he knew he would have to do them eventually. He looked to the right. Still no sign of her. He stretched out lazily in an attempt to disguise his snooping.

Then he saw her. She was sitting with a girlfriend under a plum tree. Victor moved to a table near her and daydreamed about taking her to a movie. When the bell sounded, Teresa looked up, and their eyes met. She smiled sweetly and gathered her books. Her next class was French, same as Victor's.

They were among the last students to arrive in class, so all the good desks in the back had already been taken. Victor was forced to sit near the front, a few desks away from Teresa, while Mr. Bueller wrote French words on the chalkboard. The bell rang, and Mr. Bueller wiped his hands, turned to the class, and said, *"Bonjour."*[7]

"Bonjour," braved a few students.

"Bonjour," Victor whispered. He wondered if Teresa heard him. Mr. Bueller said that if the students studied hard, at the end of the year they could go to France and be understood by the populace.

One kid raised his hand and asked, "What's 'populace'?"

"The people, the people of France."

Mr. Bueller asked if anyone knew French. Victor raised his hand, wanting to impress Teresa. The teacher beamed and said, *"Très bien. Parlez-vous français?"*[8]

Victor didn't know what to say. The teacher wet his lips and asked something else in French. The room grew silent. Victor felt all eyes staring at him. He tried to bluff his way out by making noises that sounded French.

"La me vave me con le grandma," he said uncertainly.

Mr. Bueller, wrinkling his face in curiosity, asked him to speak up.

Great rosebushes of red bloomed on Victor's cheeks. A river of nervous sweat ran

---

7. ***Bonjour.*** Good day (French)
8. ***Très bien. Parlez-vous français?*** Very good. Do you speak French? (French)

down his palms. He felt awful. Teresa sat a few desks away, no doubt thinking he was a fool. Without looking at Mr. Bueller, Victor mumbled, "Frenchie oh wewe gee in September."

Mr. Bueller asked Victor to repeat what he had said.

"Frenchie oh wewe gee in September," Victor repeated.

Mr. Bueller understood that the boy didn't know French and turned away. He walked to the blackboard and pointed to the words on the board with his steel-edged ruler.

"*Le bateau,*" he sang.

"*Le bateau,*" the students repeated.

"*Le bateau est sur l'eau,*"[9] he sang.

"*Le bateau est sur l'eau.*"

Victor was too weak from failure to join the class. He stared at the board and wished he had taken Spanish, not French. Better yet, he wished he could start his life over. He had never been so embarrassed. He bit his thumb until he tore off a sliver of skin.

The bell sounded for fifth period, and Victor shot out of the room, avoiding the stares of the other kids, but had to return for his math book. He looked sheepishly at the teacher, who was erasing the board, then widened his eyes in terror at Teresa who stood in front of him. "I didn't know you knew French," she said. "That was good."

Mr. Bueller looked at Victor, and Victor looked back. Oh please, don't say anything, Victor pleaded with his eyes. I'll wash your car, mow your lawn, walk your dog—anything! I'll be your best student and I'll clean your erasers after school.

Mr. Bueller shuffled through the papers on his desk. He smiled and hummed as he sat down to work. He remembered his college years when he dated a girlfriend in borrowed cars. She thought he was rich

Oh please, don't say anything, Victor pleaded with his eyes.

because each time he picked her up he had a different car. It was fun until he had spent all his money on her and had to write home to his parents because he was broke.

Victor couldn't stand to look at Teresa. He was sweaty with shame. "Yeah, well, I picked up a few things from movies and books and stuff like that." They left the class together. Teresa asked him if he would help her with her French.

"Sure, anytime," Victor said.

"I won't be bothering you, will I?"

"Oh no, I like being bothered."

"*Bonjour,*" Teresa said, leaving him outside her next class. She smiled and pushed wisps of hair from her face.

"Yeah, right, *bonjour,*" Victor said. He turned and headed to his class. The rose-bushes of shame on his face became bouquets of love. Teresa is a great girl, he thought. And Mr. Bueller is a good guy.

He raced to metal shop. After metal shop there was biology, and after biology a long sprint to the public library, where he checked out three French textbooks.

He was going to like seventh grade. ✤

---

9. ***Le bateau est sur l'eau.*** The boat is on the water. (French)

Have you ever tried to change your look? How much effort should people expend trying to impress each other?

AFTER READING

Find Meaning

1. (a) What does Michael Torres do on the first day of school that surprises Victor? (b) How does Victor respond to Michael?
2. What is Victor's big goal for this school year?
3. (a) When do "great rosebushes of red" bloom on Victor's cheeks? (b) What do the rosebushes represent?

Make Judgments

4. (a) How does Mr. Bueller, the French teacher, treat Victor? (b) What do Victor and Mr. Bueller have in common?
5. (a) When Victor first tries scowling, how does he feel? (b) Does Victor's scowling attract Teresa? If not, how does he get her attention?
6. Which character in the story—Victor, Michael, or Teresa—changes the most? Explain.

Analyze Literature

Character Analyze Victor to find out how he changes during the story. Use a character chart and the time line you created earlier to track Victor's progress. In the left column, write the events you included on your time line. In the right column, write one or two words that describe how Victor feels during each event. When you are done, use one sentence to summarize the main change in Victor.

Event	How Victor Feels
standing in line in the gym	optimistic

Summary Sentence:

Extend Understanding

Writing Options

Creative Writing With a classmate, draft a story about Victor's second day of school. Write a very **short story,** no longer than two paragraphs, to use as a starting point. Think about your own day at school for some ideas. Use the third-person point of view. With your partner, practice reading the story aloud. When you finish, present your story to the class.

Informative Writing Mentally review your own experiences in seventh grade, especially the first day. Then write an **informative essay** to compare your experiences with Victor's. In just one or two paragraphs, draft a thesis statement, a body with examples, and a conclusion. When you are done, trade your essay with a classmate. You and your partner should provide feedback about each other's essays.

Lifelong Learning

Get Romantic French and Spanish are both called "Romance languages." What does this mean? Use a dictionary or encyclopedia to find out. As part of your research, identify at least one other Romance language. Then choose one simple English word, like *school* or *sleep,* and find the word for it in French, Spanish, or another Romance language or languages. Make a chart of the words you have translated.

Critical Literacy

Ask the Author Think over the story of Victor and his first day of school. Then compose a list of questions you would like to ask Gary Soto about how he wrote the story. Start by jotting down any questions that are already in your mind. Then organize your questions and make sure you ask at least one question about the characters and one question about the sequence of events. When you are done, trade the list with a partner and compare your questions.

Go to **www.mirrorsandwindows.com** for more.

Grammar & Style

Consistent Verb Tense

The bell sounded for fifth period, and Victor shot out of the room, avoiding the stares of the other kids, but had to return for his math book.

—GARY SOTO, "Seventh Grade"

In this passage, each of the verbs–*sounded, shot,* and *had*–is in the past tense. When actions take place at the same time, the verbs that express these actions should be in the same tense. Good writers maintain a consistent verb tense in their writing.

INCORRECT

Last summer I took a long bicycle trip and enjoy the outdoors.

In this example, the first verb, *took*, is in the past tense, and the second verb, *enjoy*, is in the present tense. To correct this, make both verbs the same tense.

CORRECT

Last summer I took a long bicycle trip and enjoyed the outdoors.

When writing a literary analysis or other literary essay, maintain the present tense. Because the author is writing to a present reader in the present moment, you should refer to characters, settings, plots, and the author in the present tense.

CORRECT

Victor is both a believable and interesting character.

When you are writing a narrative essay, be sure to maintain a consistent tense between paragraphs.

CORRECT

I walked to the store to purchase a loaf of bread for my grandmother.

I felt happy that I could help.

Most often, personal narratives and short stories are written in the past tense. When describing something habitual or universally true, however, use the present tense.

CORRECT

Victor studied for the test. He wasn't too worried. Victor usually gets straight As.

Sentence Improvement

For each of the following sentences, select the correct form of the verb in parentheses.

1. Last night I went to the movies and (see / saw) a Japanese samurai film.
2. Washington Irving was the author of many short stories, including "Rip Van Winkle," which he (writes / wrote) about a sleepy New Englander.
3. When Hannibal's troops (had crossed / cross) the Alps, they rested briefly before marching southward into Italy.
4. In Soto's story, Victor is a seventh-grader who (decides / decided) to take French.
5. She (turns / turned) off the television set and went to bed.

Papa's Parrot

A Short Story by Cynthia Rylant

Though his father was fat and merely owned a candy and nut shop, Harry Tillian liked his papa. Harry stopped liking candy and nuts when he was around seven, but, in spite of this, he and Mr. Tillian had remained friends and were still friends the year Harry turned twelve.

For years, after school, Harry had always stopped in to see his father at work. Many of Harry's friends stopped there, too, to spend a few cents choosing penny candy from the giant bins or to sample Mr. Tillian's latest batch of roasted peanuts. Mr. Tillian looked forward to seeing his son and his son's friends every day. He liked the company.

When Harry entered junior high school, though, he didn't come by the candy and nut shop as often. Nor did his friends. They were older and they had more spending money. They went to a burger place. They played video games. They shopped for records. None of them were much interested in candy and nuts anymore.

A new group of children came to Mr. Tillian's shop now. But not Harry Tillian and his friends.

The year Harry turned twelve was also the year Mr. Tillian got a parrot. He went to a pet store one day and bought one for more money than he could really afford. He brought the parrot to his shop, set its cage near the sign for maple clusters, and named it Rocky.

Cynthia Rylant was born in Hopewell, Virginia, in 1954. Only a few years later, though, Rylant moved to a small town in the Appalachian Mountains. Due to her family's isolated and impoverished circumstances, she did not see a children's book until the age of twenty-three, and was unaware that such books existed. Today, Rylant is widely known for her works aimed at younger readers, including picture books and nonfiction. Rylant's 1992 novel *Missing May* won the Newbery Award.

Harry thought this was the strangest thing his father had ever done, and he told him so, but Mr. Tillian just ignored him.

Rocky was good company for Mr. Tillian. When business was slow, Mr. Tillian would turn on a small color television he had sitting in a corner, and he and Rocky would watch the soap operas. Rocky liked to scream when the romantic music came on, and Mr. Tillian would yell at him to shut up, but they seemed to enjoy themselves.

The year Harry turned twelve was also the year Mr. Tillian got a parrot.

The more Mr. Tillian grew to like his parrot, and the more he talked to it instead of to people, the more embarrassed Harry became. Harry would stroll past the shop, on his way somewhere else, and he'd take a quick look inside to see what his dad was doing. Mr. Tillian was always talking to the bird. So Harry kept walking.

At home things were different. Harry and his father joked with each other at the dinner table as they always had—Mr. Tillian teasing Harry about his smelly socks; Harry teasing Mr. Tillian about his blubbery stomach. At home things seemed all right.

But one day, Mr. Tillian became ill. He had been at work, unpacking boxes of caramels, when he had grabbed his chest and fallen over on top of the candy. A customer had found him, and he was taken to the hospital in an ambulance.

Mr. Tillian couldn't leave the hospital. He lay in bed, tubes in his arms, and he worried about his shop. New shipments of candy and nuts would be arriving. Rocky would be hungry. Who would take care of things?

Harry said he would. Harry told his father that he would go to the store every day after school and unpack boxes. He would sort out all the candy and nuts. He would even feed Rocky.

So, the next morning, while Mr. Tillian lay in his hospital bed, Harry took the shop key to school with him. After school he left his friends and walked to the empty shop alone. In all the days of his life, Harry had never seen the shop closed after school. Harry didn't even remember what the CLOSED sign looked like. The key stuck in the lock three times, and inside he had to search all the walls for the light switch.

The shop was as his father had left it. Even the caramels were still spilled on the floor. Harry bent down and picked them up one by one, dropping them back in the boxes. The bird in its cage watched him silently.

Harry opened the new boxes his father hadn't gotten to. Peppermints. Jawbreakers. Toffee creams. Strawberry kisses. Harry traveled from bin to bin, putting the candies where they belonged.

"Hello!"

Harry jumped, spilling a box of jawbreakers.

"Hello, Rocky!"

Harry stared at the parrot. He had

forgotten it was there. The bird had been so quiet, and Harry had been thinking only of the candy.

"Hello," Harry said.

"Hello, Rocky!" answered the parrot.

Harry walked slowly over to the cage. The parrot's food cup was empty. Its water was dirty. The bottom of the cage was a mess.

Harry carried the cage into the back room.

"Hello, Rocky!"

"Is that all you can say, you dumb bird?" Harry mumbled. The bird said nothing else.

Harry cleaned the bottom of the cage, refilled the food and water cups, and then put the cage back in its place and resumed sorting the candy.

"Where's Harry?"

Harry looked up.

"Where's Harry?"

Harry stared at the parrot.

"Where's Harry?"

Chills ran down Harry's back. What could the bird mean? It was something from "The Twilight Zone."[1]

"Where's Harry?"

Harry swallowed and said, "I'm here. I'm here, you stupid bird."

---

1. **The Twilight Zone.** Long-running science fiction television program that aired in the 1960s

"You stupid bird!" said the parrot.

Well, at least he's got one thing straight, thought Harry.

"Miss him! Miss him! Where's Harry? You stupid bird!"

Harry stood with a handful of peppermints.

"What?" he asked.

"Where's Harry?" said the parrot.

"I'm *here,* you stupid bird! I'm here!" Harry yelled. He threw the peppermints at the cage, and the bird screamed and clung to its perch.

Harry sobbed, "I'm here." The tears were coming.

"I'm here. I'm here, you stupid bird."

Harry leaned over the glass counter. "Papa." Harry buried his face in his arms.

"Where's Harry?" repeated the bird.

Harry sighed and wiped his face on his sleeve. He watched the parrot. He understood now: someone had been saying, for a long time, "Where's Harry? Miss him."

Harry finished his unpacking and then swept the floor of the shop. He checked the furnace so the bird wouldn't get cold. Then he left to go visit his papa. ✤

Have you ever regretted losing touch with a family member? Have you ever wished you could be more open with your parents or better understand how they saw the world? Why do you think it is important for people to remain in touch with their loved ones?

Analyze and Extend

1. (a) Why did Harry and his friends stop going to Mr. Tillian's candy shop? (b) How do you think this made Mr. Tillian feel?
2. Do you think Mr. Tillian genuinely enjoyed his relationship with the parrot, or was he simply using the parrot as a replacement for his son? Explain.
3. Is Harry a static character, which is a character that remains essentially the same, or a dynamic character, which is a character that changes through the course of the story? Explain your answer.

Creative Writing Imagine that you are Harry. The events described in this story have already taken place and you have gone home after visiting your father. Write a **journal entry** to summarize the events that took place, and explain how they made you feel. Try to capture the style in which Harry would write.

Lifelong Learning Research the ability of parrots to mimic human speech. Then research other mimics in nature. Compare the different kinds of animal mimicry. Use a graphic organizer or an outline to organize your information. Present your findings to the class.

Go to **www.mirrorsandwindows.com** for more.

INDEPENDENT READING

The Smallest Dragonboy

A Short Story by Anne McCaffrey

Although Keevan lengthened his walking stride as far as his legs would stretch, he couldn't quite keep up with the other candidates. He knew he would be teased again.

Just as he knew many other things that his foster mother told him he ought not to know, Keevan knew that Beterli, the most senior of the boys, set that spanking pace just to embarrass him, the smallest dragonboy. Keevan would arrive, tail fork-end of the group, breathless, chest heaving, and maybe get a stern look from the instructing wingsecond.

Dragonriders, even if they were still only hopeful candidates for the glowing eggs which were hardening on the hot sands of the Hatching Ground cavern, were expected to be punctual and prepared. Sloth[1] was not tolerated by the weyrleader of Benden Weyr. A good record was especially important now. It was very near hatching time, when the baby dragons would crack their mottled shells and stagger forth to choose their lifetime companions. The very thought of that glorious moment made Keevan's breath catch in his throat. To be chosen—to be a dragonrider! To sit astride the neck of the winged beast with the jeweled eyes: to be his friend in telepathic communion[2] with him for

1. **sloth.** Laziness
2. **telepathic communion.** Ability to share thoughts with another mind without speaking

Anne McCaffrey (1926–2011) is known for her many works of science fiction and fantasy. However, she is best known for her Dragonriders of Pern series. This series focuses on the planet Pern, which is populated with dragons and magic as well as high technology and other science fiction elements. Her first short story in the Dragonriders series, "Weyr Search," was awarded the prestigious Hugo Award in 1968, making McCaffrey the first female winner of a Hugo Award for fiction. There are about twenty Dragonrider books, including two collections of short stories.

life; to be his companion in good times and fighting extremes; to fly effortlessly over the lands of Pern! Or, thrillingly, *between* to any point anywhere on the world! Flying *between* was done on dragonback or not at all, and it was dangerous.

Keevan glanced upward, past the black mouths of the weyr caves in which grown dragons and their chosen riders lived, toward the Star Stones that crowned the ridge of the old volcano that was Benden Weyr. On the height, the blue watch dragon, his rider mounted on his neck, stretched the great transparent pinions[3] that carried him on the winds of Pern to fight the evil Thread[4] that fell at certain times from the sky. The many-faceted rainbow jewels of his eyes glistened momentarily in the greeny sun. He folded his great wings to his back, and the watchpair resumed their statuesque[5] pose of alertness.

Then the enticing[6] view was obscured as Keevan passed into the Hatching Ground cavern. The sands underfoot were hot, even through heavy wher-hide boots. How the bootmaker had protested having to sew so small! Keevan was forced to wonder again why being small was reprehensible.[7] People were always calling him "babe" and shooing him away as being "too small" or "too young" for this or that. Keevan was constantly working, twice as hard as any other boy his age, to prove himself capable. What if his muscles weren't as big as Beterli's? They were just as hard. And if he couldn't overpower anyone in a wrestling match, he could outdistance everyone in a footrace.

"Maybe if you run fast enough," Beterli had jeered on the occasion when Keevan had been goaded to boast of his swiftness, "you could catch a dragon. That's the only way you'll make a dragonrider!"

"You just wait and see, Beterli, you just wait," Keevan had replied. He would have liked to wipe the contemptuous[8] smile from Beterli's face, but the guy didn't fight fair even when the wingsecond was watching. "No one knows what Impresses[9] a dragon!"

"As we well know, there are only forty eggs and seventy-two candidates."

"They've got to be able to *find* you first, babe!"

Yes, being the smallest candidate was not an enviable position. It was therefore imperative[10] that Keevan Impress a dragon in his first hatching. That would wipe the smile off every face in the cavern, and accord him the respect due any dragonrider, even the smallest one.

Besides, no one knew exactly what Impressed the baby dragons as they struggled from their shells in search of their lifetime partners.

"I like to believe that dragons see into a

---

3. **pinions.** Outer parts of a bird's wings
4. **Thread.** Spore from outer space that feeds on living things and that the dragonriders fight
5. **statuesque.** Statuelike; unmoving
6. **enticing.** Tempting
7. **reprehensible.** Unacceptable; deserving condemnation
8. **contemptuous.** Showing contempt or scorn
9. **Impresses.** Dragonriders become telepathically connected to their dragons through *Impression.*
10. **imperative.** Very important

man's heart," Keevan's foster mother, Mende, told him. "If they find goodness, honesty, a flexible mind, patience, courage—and you've that in quantity, dear Keevan—that's what dragons look for. I've seen many a well-grown lad left standing on the sands, Hatching Day, in favor of someone not so strong or tall or handsome. And if my memory serves me" (which it usually did—Mende knew every word of every Harper's tale worth telling, although Keevan did not interrupt her to say so), "I don't believe that F'lar, our weyrleader, was all that tall when bronze Mnementh chose him. And Mnementh was the only bronze dragon of that hatching."

Dreams of Impressing a bronze were beyond Keevan's boldest reflections, although that goal dominated the thoughts of every other hopeful candidate. Green dragons were small and fast and more numerous. There was more prestige[11] in Impressing a blue or a brown than a green. Being practical, Keevan seldom dreamed as high as a big fighting brown, like Canth, F'nor's fine fellow, the biggest brown on all Pern. But to fly a bronze? Bronzes were almost as big as the queen, and only they took the air when a queen flew at mating time. A bronze rider could aspire to become weyrleader! Well, Keevan would console himself, brown riders could aspire to become wingseconds, and that wasn't bad. He'd even settle for a green dragon: they were small, but so was he. No matter! He simply had to Impress a dragon his first time in the Hatching Ground. Then no one in the weyr would taunt him anymore for being so small.

"Shells," thought Keevan now, "but the sands are hot!"

"Impression time is imminent, candidates," the wingsecond was saying as everyone crowded respectfully close to him. "See the extent of the striations[12] on this promising egg." The stretch marks *were* larger than yesterday.

Everyone leaned forward and nodded thoughtfully. That particular egg was the one Beterli had marked as his own, and no other candidate dared, on pain of being beaten by Beterli on the first opportunity, to approach it. The egg was marked by a large yellowish splotch in the shape of a dragon backwinging to land, talons outstretched to grasp rock. Everyone knew that bronze eggs bore distinctive markings. And naturally, Beterli, who'd been presented at eight Impressions already and was the biggest of the candidates, had chosen it.

"I'd say that the great opening day is almost upon us," the wingsecond went on, and then his face assumed a grave expression. "As we well know, there are only forty eggs and seventy-two candidates." Some of you may be disappointed on the great day. That doesn't necessarily mean you aren't dragonrider material, just that *the* dragon for you hasn't been shelled. You'll have other hatchings, and it's no disgrace to be left behind an Impression or two. Or more."

Keevan was positive that the wingsecond's eyes rested on Beterli, who'd been stood off at so many Impressions already. Keevan tried to squinch[13] down so the wingsecond wouldn't notice him. Keevan had been reminded too often that he was eligible to be a candidate by one day only. He, of all the hopefuls, was most likely to be

---

11. prestige. Honor
12. striations. Grooves
13. squinch. Crouch down

left standing on the great day. One more reason why he simply had to Impress at his first hatching.

"Now move about among the eggs," wingsecond said. "Touch them. We don't know that it does any good, but it certainly doesn't do any harm."

Some of the boys laughed nervously, but everyone immediately began to circulate among the eggs. Beterli stepped up officiously to "his" egg, daring anyone to come near it. Keevan smiled, because he had already touched it...every inspection day ...as the others were leaving the Hatching Ground, when no one could see him crouch and stroke it.

Keevan had an egg he concentrated on too, one drawn slightly to the far side of the others. The shell bore a soft greenish blue tinge with a faint creamy swirl design. The consensus[14] was that this egg contained a mere green, so Keevan was rarely bothered by rivals. He was somewhat perturbed then to see Beterli wandering over to him.

"I don't know why you're allowed in this Impression, Keevan. There are enough of us without a babe," Beterli said, shaking his head.

"I'm of age." Keevan kept his voice level, telling himself not to be bothered by mere words.

"Yah!" Beterli made a show of standing on his toe tips. "You can't even see over an egg; Hatching Day, you better get in front or the dragons won't see you at all. 'Course, you could get run down that way in the mad scramble. Oh, I forget, you can run fast, can't you?"

"You'd better make sure a dragon sees *you,* this time, Beterli," Keevan replied. "You're almost overage, aren't you?"

Beterli flushed and took a step forward, hand half-raised. Keevan stood his ground, but if Beterli advanced one more step, he would call the wingsecond. No one fought on the Hatching Ground. Surely Beterli knew that much.

Fortunately, at that moment the wingsecond called the boys together and led them from the Hatching Ground to start on evening chores.

There were "glows" to be replenished in the main kitchen caverns and sleeping cubicles, the major hallways, and the queen's apartment. Firestone sacks had to be filled against Thread attack, and black rock brought to the kitchen

14. consensus. Agreement among a group

hearths. The boys fell to their chores, tantalized by the odors of roasting meat. The population of the weyr began to assemble for the evening meal, and the dragonriders came in from the Feeding Ground or their sweep checks.

It was the time of day Keevan liked best: once the chores were done, before dinner was served, a fellow could often get close to the dragonriders and listen to their talk. Tonight Keevan's father, K'last, was at the main dragonrider table. It puzzled Keevan how his father, a brown rider and a tall man, could *be* his father—because he, Keevan, was so small. It obviously never puzzled K'last when he deigned to notice his small son: "In a few more turns, you'll be as tall as I am—or taller!"

K'last was pouring Benden drink all around the table. The dragonriders were relaxing. There'd be no Thread attack for three more days, and they'd be in the mood to tell tall tales, better than Harper yarns, about impossible maneuvers they'd done a-dragonback. When Thread attack was closer, their talk would change to a discussion of tactics of evasion, of going *between,* how long to suspend there until the burning but fragile Thread would freeze and crack and fall harmlessly off dragon and man. They would dispute the exact moment to feed firestone to the dragon so he'd have the best flame ready to sear Thread midair and render it harmless to ground—and man—below. There was such a lot to know and understand about being a dragonrider that sometimes Keevan was overwhelmed. How would he ever be able to remember everything he ought to know at the right moment? He couldn't dare ask such a question; this would only have given additional weight to the notion that he was too young yet to be a dragonrider.

"Having older candidates makes good sense," L'vel was saying, as Keevan settled down near the table. "Why waste four to five years of a dragon's fighting prime until his rider grows up enough to stand the rigors?" L'vel had Impressed a blue of Ramoth's first clutch.[15] Most of the candidates thought L'vel was marvelous because he spoke up in front of the older riders, who awed them. "That was well enough in the Interval when you didn't need to mount the full weyr complement to fight Thread. But not now. Not with more eligible candidates than ever. Let the babes wait."

"Any boy who is over twelve turns has the right to stand in the Hatching Ground," K'last replied, a slight smile on his face. He never argued or got angry. Keevan wished he were more like his father. And oh, how he wished he were a brown rider! "Only a dragon...each particular dragon...knows what he wants in a rider. We certainly can't tell. Time and again the theorists," and K'last's smile deepened as his eyes swept those at the table, "are surprised by dragon choice. *They* never seem to make mistakes, however."

"Now, K'last, just look at the roster this Impression. Seventy-two boys and only forty eggs. Drop off the twelve youngest, and there's still a good field for the hatchlings to choose from. Shells! There are a couple of weyrlings unable to see over a wher egg much less a dragon! And years before they can ride Thread."

"True enough, but the weyr is scarcely under fighting strength, and if the youngest Impress, they'll be old enough to fight when

15. clutch. Group of eggs

the oldest of our current dragons go *between* from senility."

"Half the weyrbred lads have already been through several Impressions," one of the bronze riders said then. "I'd say drop some of *them* off this time. Give the untried a chance."

"Only a dragon... each particular dragon... knows what he wants in a rider."

"There's nothing wrong in presenting a clutch with as wide a choice as possible," said the weyrleader, who had joined the table with Lessa, the weyrwoman.

"Has there ever been a case," she said, smiling in her odd way at the riders, "where a hatchling didn't choose?"

Her suggestion was almost heretical[16] and drew astonished gasps from everyone, including the boys.

F'lar laughed. "You say the most outrageous things, Lessa."

"Well, *has* there ever been a case when a dragon didn't choose?"

"Can't say as I recall one," K'last replied.

"Then we continue in this tradition," Lessa said firmly, as if that ended the matter.

But it didn't. The argument ranged from one table to the other all through dinner, with some favoring a weeding out of the candidates to the most likely, lopping off those who were very young or who had multiple opportunities to Impress. All the candidates were in a swivet,[17] though such a departure from tradition would be to the advantage of many. As the evening progressed, more riders were favoring eliminating the youngest and those who'd passed four or more Impressions unchosen. Keevan felt he could bear such a dictum if only Beterli was also eliminated. But this seemed less likely than that Keevan would be tuffed out, since the weyr's need was for fighting dragons and riders.

By the time the evening meal was over, no decision had been reached, although the weyrleader had promised to give the matter due consideration.

He might have slept on the problem, but few of the candidates did. Tempers were uncertain in the sleeping caverns next morning as the boys were routed out of their beds to carry water and black rock and cover the "glows." Mende had to call Keevan to order twice for clumsiness.

"Whatever is the matter with you, boy?" she demanded in exasperation when he tipped black rock short of the bin and sooted up the hearth.

"They're going to keep me from this Impression."

"What?" Mende stared at him. "Who?"

"You heard them talking at dinner last night. They're going to tuff the babes from the hatching."

Mende regarded him a moment longer before touching his arm gently. "There's lots of talk around a supper table, Keevan. And it cools as soon as the supper. I've heard the same nonsense before every hatching, but nothing is ever changed."

---

16. heretical. Something that goes against established thought or tradition

17. swivet. State of confusion

"There's always a first time," Keevan answered, copying one of her own phrases.

"That'll be enough of that, Keevan. Finish your job. If the clutch does hatch today, we'll need full rock bins for the feast, and you won't be around to do the filling. All my fosterlings make dragonriders."

"The first time?" Keevan was bold enough to ask as he scooted off with the rockbarrow.

Perhaps, Keevan thought later, if he hadn't been on that chore just when Beterli was also fetching black rock, things might have turned out differently. But he had dutifully trundled[18] the barrow to the outdoor bunker for another load just as Beterli arrived on a similar errand.

"Heard the news, babe?" asked Beterli. He was grinning from ear to ear, and he put an

18. trundled. Moved something slowly

unnecessary emphasis on the final insulting word.

"The eggs are cracking?" Keevan all but dropped the loaded shovel. Several anxieties flicked through his mind then; he was black with rock dust—would he have time to wash before donning the white tunic of candidacy? And if the eggs were hatching, why hadn't the candidates been recalled by the wingsecond?

"Naw! Guess again!" Beterli was much too pleased with himself.

With a sinking heart Keevan knew what the news must be, and he could only stare with intense desolation at the older boy.

"C'mon! Guess, babe!"

"I've no time for guessing games," Keevan managed to say with indifference. He began to shovel black rock into his barrow as fast as he could.

"I said, 'guess.'" Beterli grabbed the shovel.

"And I said I'd no time for guessing games."

Beterli wrenched the shovel from Keevan's hands. "Guess!"

"I'll have the shovel back, Beterli." Keevan straightened up, but he didn't come up to Beterli's bulky shoulder. From somewhere, other boys appeared, some with barrows, some mysteriously alerted to the prospect of a confrontation among their numbers.

"Babes don't give orders to candidates around here, babe!"

"Hatching?" he cried.

Someone sniggered and Keevan knew, incredibly, that he must've been dropped from the candidacy.

He yanked the shovel from Beterli's loosened grasp. Snarling, the older boy tried to regain possession, but Keevan clung with all his strength to the handle, dragged back and forth as the stronger boy jerked the shovel about.

With a sudden, unexpected movement, Beterli rammed the handle into Keevan's chest, knocking him over the barrow handles. Keevan felt a sharp, painful jab behind his left ear, an unbearable pain in his right shin, and then a painless nothingness.

Mende's angry voice roused him, and startled, he tried to throw back the covers, thinking he'd overslept. But he couldn't move, so firmly was he tucked into his bed. And then the constriction of a bandage on his head and the dull sickishness in his leg brought back recent occurrences.

"Hatching?" he cried.

"No, lovey," said Mende, and her voice was suddenly very kind, her hand cool and gentle on his forehead. "Though there's some

Dragons and other beasts, 1390–1430. Boucicault Master. Bibliotheque Nationale, Paris.

as won't be at any hatching again." Her voice took on a stern edge.

Keevan looked beyond her to see the weyrwoman, who was frowning with irritation.

"Keevan, will you tell me what occurred at the black-rock bunker?" Lessa asked, but her voice wasn't angry.

He remembered Beterli now and the quarrel over the shovel and...what had Mende said about some not being at any hatching? Much as he hated Beterli, he couldn't bring himself to tattle on Beterli and force him out of candidacy.

"Come, lad," and a note of impatience crept into the weyrwoman's voice. "I merely want to know what happened from you, too. Mende said she sent you for black-rock. Beterli—and every weyrling in the cavern—seems to have been on the same errand. What happened?"

"Beterli took the shovel. I hadn't finished with it."

"There's more than one shovel. What did he *say* to you?"

"He'd heard the news."

"What news?" The weyrwoman was suddenly amused.

"That...that...there'd been changes."

"Is that what he said?"

"Not exactly."

"What did he say? C'mon, lad. I've heard from everyone else, you know."

"He said for me to guess the news."

"And you fell for that old gag?" The weyrwoman's irritation returned.

"Consider all the talk last night at supper, Lessa," said Mende. "Of course the boy would think he'd been eliminated."

"In effect, he is, with a broken skull and leg." She touched his arm, a rare gesture of sympathy in her. "Be that as it may, Keevan, you'll have other Impressions. Beterli will not. There are certain rules that must be observed by all candidates, and his conduct proves him unacceptable to the weyr."

She smiled at Mende and then left.

"I'm still a candidate?" Keevan asked urgently.

"Well, you are and you aren't, lovey," his foster mother said. "Is the numb weed working?" she asked, and when he nodded, she said, "You just rest. I'll bring you some nice broth."

At any other time in his life, Keevan would have relished such cosseting,[19] but he lay there worrying. Beterli had been dismissed. Would the others think it was his fault? But everyone was there! Beterli provoked the fight. His worry increased, because although he heard excited comings and goings in the passageway, no one tweaked back the curtain across the sleeping alcove he shared with five other boys. Surely one of them would have to come in sometime. No, they were all avoiding him. And something else was wrong. Only he didn't know what.

Mende returned with broth and beachberry bread.

"Why doesn't anyone come see me, Mende? I haven't done anything wrong, have I? I didn't ask to have Beterli tuffed out."

Mende soothed him, saying everyone was busy with noontime chores and no one was mad at him. They were giving him a chance to rest in quiet. The numb weed made him drowsy, and her words were fair enough. He

---

19. cosseting. Protecting

permitted his fears to dissipate. Until he heard the humming. It started low, too low to be heard. Rather he felt it in the broken shin bone and his sore head. And thought, at first, it was an effect of the numb weed. Then the hum grew, augmented[20] by additional sources. Two things registered suddenly in Keevan's groggy mind: The only white candidate's robe still on the pegs in the chamber was his; and dragons hummed when a clutch was being laid or being hatched. Impression! And he was flat abed.

Bitter, bitter disappointment turned the warm broth sour in his belly. Even the small voice telling him that he'd have other opportunities failed to alleviate[21] his crushing depression. *This* was the Impression that mattered! This was his chance to show *everyone* from Mende to K'last to L'vel and even the weyrleaders that he, Keevan, was worthy of being a dragonrider.

He twisted in bed, fighting against the tears that threatened to choke him. Dragonmen don't cry! Dragonmen learn to live with pain....

Pain? The leg didn't actually pain him as he rolled about on his bedding. His head felt sort of stiff from the tightness of the bandage. He sat up, an effort in itself since the numb weed made exertion difficult. He touched the splinted leg, but the knee was unhampered. He had no feeling in his bone, really. He swung himself carefully to the side of his bed and slowly stood. The room wanted to swim about him. He closed his eyes, which made the dizziness worse, and he had to clutch the bedpost.

Gingerly he took a step. The broken leg dragged. It hurt in spite of the numb weed, but what was pain to a dragonman?

No one had said he couldn't go to the Impression. "You are and you aren't," were Mende's exact words.

Clinging to the bedpost, he jerked off his bedshirt. Stretching his arm to the utmost, he jerked his white candidate's tunic from the peg. Jamming first one arm and then the other into the holes, he pulled it over his head. Too bad about the belt. He couldn't wait. He hobbled to the door, hung on to the curtain to steady himself. The weight on his leg was unwieldy. He'd not get very far without something to lean on. Down by the bathing pool was one of the long crooknecked poles used to retrieve clothes from the hot washing troughs. But it was down there, and he was on the level above. And there was no one nearby to come to his aid: everyone

20. augmented. Amplified
21. alleviate. Relieve

would be in the Hatching Ground right now, eagerly waiting for the first egg to crack.

The humming increased in volume and tempo, an urgency to which Keevan responded, knowing that his time was all too limited if he was to join the ranks of the hopeful boys standing about the cracking eggs. But if he hurried down the ramp, he'd fall flat on his face.

He could, of course, go flat on his rear end, the way crawling children did. He sat down, the jar sending a stab of pain through his leg and up to the wound on the back of his head. Gritting his teeth and blinking away the tears, Keevan scrabbled down the ramp. He had to wait a moment at the bottom to catch his breath. He got to one knee, the injured leg straight out in front of him. Somehow, he managed to push himself erect, though the room wanted to tip over his ears. It wasn't far to the crooked stick, but it seemed an age before he had it in his hand.

Then the humming stopped!

Keevan cried out and began to hobble frantically across the cavern, out to the bowl of the weyr. Never had the distance between the living caverns and the Hatching Ground seemed so great. Never had the weyr been silent, breathless. As if the multitude of people and dragons watching the hatching held every breath in suspense. Not even the wind muttered down the steep sides of the bowl. The only sounds to break the stillness were Keevan's ragged breathing and the thump thud of his stick on the hard-packed ground. Sometimes he had to hop twice on his good leg to maintain his balance. Twice he fell into the sand and had to pull himself up on the stick, his white tunic no longer spotless. Once he jarred himself so badly he couldn't get up immediately.

Then he heard the first exhalation of the crowd, the oohs, the muted cheer, the susurrus[22] of excited whispers. An egg had cracked, and the dragon had chosen his rider. Desperation increased Keevan's hobble. Would he never reach the arching mouth of the Hatching Ground?

An egg had cracked, and the dragon had chosen his rider.

Another cheer and an excited spate of applause spurred Keevan to greater effort. If he didn't get there in moments, there'd be no unpaired hatchling left. Then he was actually staggering into the Hatching Ground, the sands hot on his bare feet.

No one noticed his entrance or his halting progress. And Keevan could see nothing but the backs of the white-robed candidates, seventy of them ringing the area around the eggs. Then one side would surge forward or back and there'd be a cheer. Another dragon had been Impressed. Suddenly a large gap appeared in the white human wall, and Keevan had his first sight of the eggs. There didn't seem to be *any* left uncracked, and he could see the lucky boys standing beside wobble-legged dragons. He could hear the unmistakable plaintive[23] crooning of hatchlings and their squawks of protest as they'd fall awkwardly in the sand.

---

22. susurrus. Whispering sound
23. plaintive. Sounding sad

Suddenly he wished that he hadn't left his bed, that he'd stayed away from the Hatching Ground. Now everyone would see his ignominious[24] failure. He scrambled now as desperately to reach the shadowy walls of the Hatching Ground as he had struggled to cross the bowl. He mustn't be seen.

He didn't notice, therefore, that the shifting group of boys remaining had begun to drift in his direction. The hard pace he had set himself and his cruel disappointment took their double toll of Keevan. He tripped and collapsed sobbing to the warm sands. He didn't see the consternation in the watching weyrfolk above the Hatching Ground, nor did he hear the excited whispers of speculation.[25] He didn't know that the weyrleader and weyrwoman had dropped to the arena and were making their way toward the knot of boys slowly moving in the direction of the archway.

"Never seen anything like it," the weyrleader was saying. "Only thirty-nine riders chosen. And the bronze trying to leave the Hatching Ground without making Impression!"

"A case in point of what I said last night," the weyrwoman replied, "where a hatchling makes no choice because the right boy isn't there."

"There's only Beterli and K'last's young one missing. And there's a full wing of likely boys to choose from...."

"None acceptable, apparently. Where is the creature going? He's not heading for the entrance after all. Oh, what have we there, in the shadows?"

Keevan heard with dismay the sound of voices nearing him. He tried to burrow in to the sand. The mere thought of how he would be teased and taunted now was unbearable.

Don't worry! Please don't worry! The thought was urgent, but not his own.

Someone kicked sand over Keevan and butted roughly against him.

"Go away. Leave me alone!" he cried.

Why? was the injured-sounding question inserted into his mind. There was no voice, no tone, but the question was there, perfectly clear, in his head.

Incredulous, Keevan lifted his head and stared into the glowing jeweled eyes of a small bronze dragon. His wings were wet; the tips hung drooping to the sand. And he sagged in the middle on his unsteady legs, although he was making a great effort to keep erect.

Keevan dragged himself to his knees, oblivious to the pain of his leg. He wasn't even aware that he was ringed by the boys passed over, while thirty-one pairs of resentful eyes watched him Impress the dragon. The weyrleaders looked on, amused and surprised at the draconic choice, which could not be forced. Could not be questioned. Could not be changed.

Why? asked the dragon again. *Don't you like me?* His eyes whirled with anxiety, and his tone was so piteous that Keevan staggered forward and threw his arms around the dragon's neck, stroking his eye ridges, patting the damp, soft hide, opening the fragile-looking wings to dry them, and assuring the hatchling wordlessly over and over again that he was the most perfect, most beautiful, most beloved dragon in the entire weyr; in all the weyrs of Pern.

"What's his name, K'van?" asked Lessa,

---

24. ignominious (ig′ nə mi′ nē əs). Shameful
25. speculation. Theory

smiling warmly at the new dragonrider. K'van stared up at her for a long moment. Lessa would know as soon as he did. Lessa was the only person who could "receive" from all dragons, not only her own Ramoth. Then he gave her a radiant smile, recognizing the traditional shortening of his name that raised him forever to the rank of dragonrider.

My name is Heath, thought the dragon mildly and hiccuped in sudden urgency: *I'm hungry.*

"Dragons are born hungry," said Lessa, laughing. "F'lar, give the boy a hand. He can barely manage his own legs, much less a dragon's."

K'van remembered his stick and drew himself up. "We'll be just fine, thank you."

"You may be the smallest dragonrider ever, young K'van, but you're the bravest," said F'lar.

And Heath agreed! Pride and joy so leaped in both chests that K'van wondered if his heart would burst right out of his body. He looped an arm around Heath's neck and the pair—the smallest dragonboy, and the hatchling who wouldn't choose anybody else—walked out of the Hatching Ground together forever. ❖

When have you felt as if you were not ready for something important, like the first day of school or some other life-changing event? Were your feelings justified? Why might it not be helpful for people, like Keevan in "The Smallest Dragonboy," to worry too much about whether or not they are ready for life-changing experiences?

Analyze and Extend

1. Why do you think Beterli treated Keevan the way he did?
2. (a) What motivated Keevan to leave his bed and go to the Hatching Ground after breaking his leg? (b) What do you think would have happened if he had stayed in bed?
3. List examples of the various elements of fantasy in the story. How do these elements affect the characters? How do they affect the plot?

Argumentative Writing Using your library, locate a recent book review in a local or national newspaper or magazine. Read the review, noting the tone and the reviewer's main idea. Then write your own two-paragraph book review of "The Smallest Dragonboy." Give your opinion and present evidence, including paraphrases and direct quotations, in support of it. At the start of your review, be sure to give a brief summary of "The Smallest Dragonboy." When you are done, present your review using gestures as well as the proper speaking rate, volume, and eye contact.

Collaborative Learning An epic tale is a long story, often told in verse. In the English epic *Beowulf,* the title character battles a fierce fire-breathing dragon. With a partner, research and describe the conventions of epic tales and determine whether "The Smallest Dragonboy" contains any similar elements.

 Go to **www.mirrorsandwindows.com** for more.

For Your Reading List

The Outcasts of 19 Schuyler Place
by E. L. Konigsburg

After being ejected from summer camp, Margaret Rose Kane moves in with her two great uncles, Alex and Morris. However, controversy is brewing in the neighborhood over the three massive, colorful, and strange towers her uncles have been building in their backyard. Can Margaret save her uncles' giant works of art?

Holes
by Louis Sachar

In this Newbery Award winning novel, Stanley Yelnats—whose name reads the same both backward and forward—has been sent to Camp Green Lake to be rehabilitated for a crime he did not commit. In a dried-up Texas lake, the campers of Camp Green Lake are forced every day to dig hole after hole after hole. Stanley soon learns that the camp is not all it at first appears.

Pictures of Hollis Woods
by Patricia Reilly Giff

Hollis Woods wants a loving family but can't seem to stop running away from foster homes. Eventually she finds Josie, a retired teacher, who shares Hollis's love of art. Sadly, Josie seems to be losing her memory, while Hollis still misses the Regans, her last foster family. As the story progresses, the reason for Hollis's departure from the Regan household is slowly revealed.

Al Capone Does My Shirts
by Gennifer Choldenko

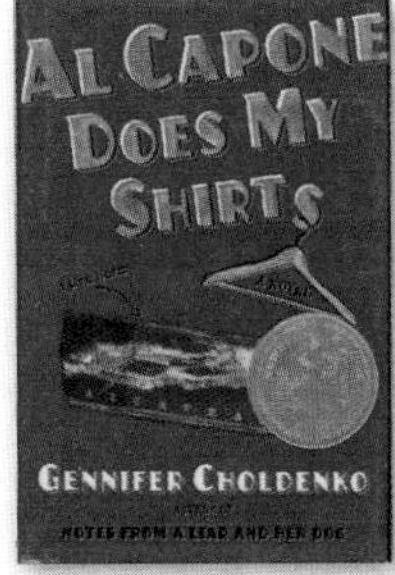

After Moose Flanagan's father takes a job as a prison guard, the Flanagan family is forced to move to Alcatraz Island. Moose must cope with his new environment, help take care of his sister, and deal with the warden's daughter Piper, who always seems to be scheming.

Romiette and Julio
by Sharon Draper

In an Internet chat room, Romiette Cappelle meets Julio Montague. Soon they discover that they attend the same high school and start seeing each other, ignoring both their parents' prejudices and threats from a local gang violently opposed to interracial dating. A retelling of Shakespeare's Romeo and Juliet, the novel brings readers the play's romance and feuding, but with a happier ending.

The Chosen
by Chaim Potok

Reuven and Danny, two boys growing up in Brooklyn, New York, meet by accident during a softball game. As they become friends, they must learn to negotiate the differences in their families' religious practices as well as confusion, love, loss, and other trials of adolescence. Eventually, the differences between the characters open each of them to new worlds.

Writing Workshop

Narrative Writing

Writing a Short Story

Assignment: Write a short story that develops believable characters, setting, and plot.

Goal: Create a story that is interesting and enjoyable for my audience.

Strategy: Create well-developed characters and a detailed setting. Create a plot in which a conflict rises to a climax and is resolved at the end.

Writing Rubric: My short story should include the following:

- complex and believable characters
- a vivid setting
- a logically organized plot that includes a conflict, exposition, rising action, climax, falling action, and resolution
- a consistent point of view

Reading and Writing

You have read stories about values in the unit from such writers as Joseph Bruchac, Sandra Cisneros, and Gary Soto. These selections feature the basic elements of short stories: character development, setting, conflict, plot structure, and dialogue. You will from time to time be asked to write a short story on a particular topic or to develop a character and a believable plot.

In this workshop you will learn how to write a **short story.** You may want to begin this assignment by determining the kind of characters you would like to develop and how you might make these characters believable and complex. Decide how important your setting will be to your story. Consider what conflicts your characters might face and how they could resolve those conflicts through a series of events. Keep in mind that a good story is entertaining, thought provoking, and interesting to its readers. Look at the following writing rubric. This set of standards will help you judge whether or not you have achieved your goal of writing a successful short story. You will use this rubric in both drafting and revising your story.

What Great Writers Do

Walter Dean Myers was a great lover of writing. Here is what he had to say about his approach to writing and revising fiction.

When I work, what I'll do is outline the story first. That forces me to do the thinking. I cut out pictures of all my characters and my wife puts them into a collage, which goes on the wall above the computer. When I walk into the room I can see the characters, and I just get very close to them. I rush through a first draft, and then I go back and rewrite, because I can usually see what the problems are going to be ahead of me. Rewriting is more fun for me than writing is.

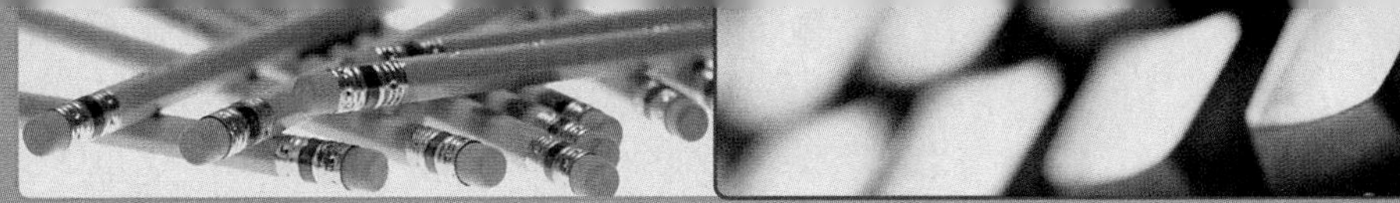

1. PREWRITE

Choosing Your Topic

Planning the Parts of Your Story The topic of your story is who and what you will write about. You may want to begin developing your story by using the *who, when, where, what,* and *how* method.

Who? Do you have a character in mind? What would this character be like? Consider what beliefs, qualities, or problems this character would have.

When and Where? When and where your story takes place is its setting. Think about how important your setting will be. Is it just background, or does it play a strong role in the conflict and its resolution? For instance, consider a story that takes place in an old castle in the 1900s as opposed to a bustling street in present-day New York. No matter which setting you choose, be sure it fits the characters and events in your story.

What? Once you have a main character in mind, decide what will happen to him or her. What conflict will your character face? Maybe the conflict is one you have personally experienced or imagined. The conflict can be with another character, with a situation or outside force (such as nature or society), or within the character's mind.

How? The plot, or series of events, will grow out of the conflict. After the conflict is introduced, the conflict develops with each event until it reaches a climax or turning point. After the climax, the conflict must be resolved in a satisfactory way.

Gathering Details

Now concentrate on the details of the characters, setting, and plot. Use your imagination, but let these ideas guide you:

1. Develop your characters through descriptive details, action, and dialogue.
2. Describe the setting in vivid detail.
3. Bring the conflict to a climax or turning point, and then resolve it by the story's end.
4. Decide on point of view—first-person, third-person limited, or third-person omniscient—and maintain that point of view throughout the story.

To help you keep track of your characters, setting, and plot, use a story map. Here is how one student approached writing his short story.

Characters
James, age 12
Zack, age 12
Zack's mom

Setting
School gym, after school for intramural game of volleyball (present day)

Conflict
Teams are being formed for intramural volleyball. Zack is small for his age, and he wants badly to play on any team, but especially with the Tigers. James, Zack's best friend, makes the team, but Zack doesn't.

The writer used a cluster chart to further develop each character. Keep track of a character's traits by clustering them into categories including physical traits, personality, feelings, and goals.

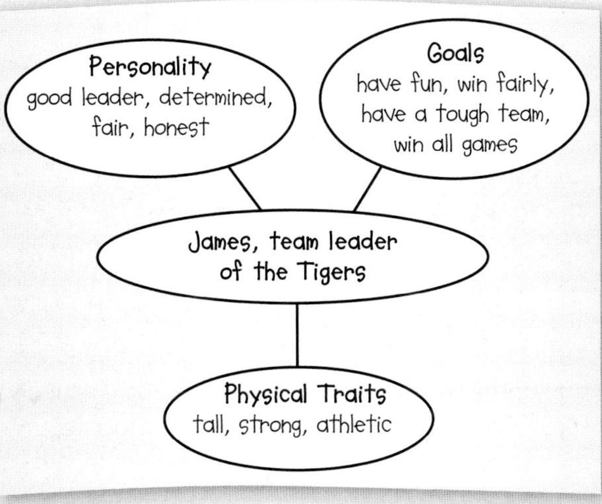

2. DRAFT

Organizing Ideas

Once you have gathered details about the story, plan how the plot will develop. Often, the most logical and effective way to organize stories is by the order the events occurred, or **chronological order.** Study the main parts of a story and what is introduced or developed in each.

Beginning

1. **Exposition:** introduces the main characters, setting, and conflict

Middle

2. **Rising Action:** develops the conflict through a series of events
3. **Climax or Turning Point:** creates the point of highest tension or excitement

End

4. **Resolution:** resolves the conflict

Putting Your Thoughts on Paper

When writing your first draft, organize your characters, setting, conflict, and plot in a logical plan like that shown here. At this stage, focus mainly on developing the conflict. Try to outline the series of events that will lead to the turning point, and, finally, the resolution of your story. Don't worry if you don't have all the events determined before you begin writing. More ideas will come once you begin drafting, but use your plan as a starting point.

1. **Exposition**

Characters: James, Zack, Zack's mom
Setting: present day, during volleyball tryouts
Conflict: James and Zack are great friends, but James is a better athlete.

2. **Rising Action**
    1. James makes the team, but Zack does not.
    2. Zack tries out for a different team.
    3. Zack makes the team.

3. **Climax or Turning Point**

Zack's first game is against James and the Tigers. Everyone is surprised at how well Zack plays.

4. **Resolution**

Zack's team loses, but not before he receives praise from his good friend, James.

Making Connections

The Right Tone As you draft, pay attention to the tone of your writing. Your **tone,** or attitude toward your subject, should be more natural and informal in a short story than in most other types of writing, such as essays. Make sure your dialogue sounds true to the character and to the way people actually speak. Try reading parts of your story—especially the dialogue—out loud to see if it sounds smooth and natural.

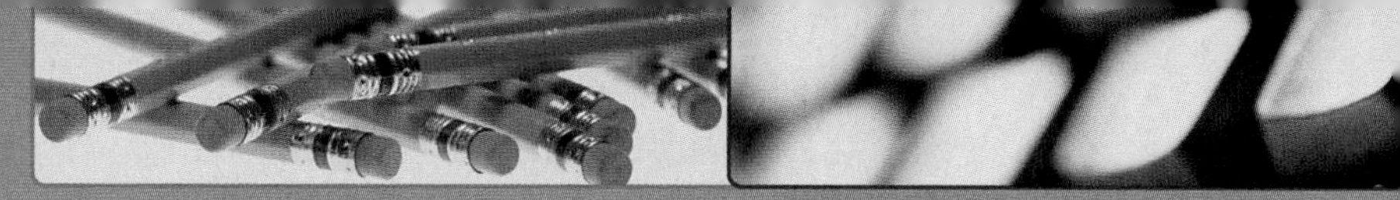

3. REVISE

Evaluating Your Draft

As you reread your draft, look for areas to improve. You may want to exchange papers and do a **peer review.** Evaluate each other's work and discuss ideas for revision. Use the checklist as a guide.

Below is a draft of the first part of the short story, "A Chance to Play." Changes have been made within the body of the text and reasons for the changes are given on the right.

Revising Checklist

- ☐ Are the characters well-developed and introduced at the beginning?
- ☐ Is the setting described in detail?
- ☐ Is the story organized logically?
- ☐ Is the dialogue natural and effective?
- ☐ Is there a consistent point of view?

"James McDermott!" I heard the coach call off the next name on the list. James, who was sitting next to me, tightened his laces one last time and stood up. "Good luck," I said as he gave me a thumbs-up and ran over to the coach standing by the volleyball net. *The gym echoed with shouts and the squeak of sneakers against the floor as players practiced serving and setting.*

Introduce the setting in the exposition. Use sensory details to make the setting vivid.

James had always been good at sports, especially volleyball, for as long as I had known him. I never let him know how I secretly wished I could be like him. It seemed like he and everyone else in the seventh grade was growing taller and stronger, but I was still as short and small as I had always been. *I wanted to try out for volleyball, but even James took one look at me and said, "Maybe volleyball just isn't for you." That hurt, coming from my best friend, but he never lied to me before and was always the kindest guy I had ever known.*

Introduce the conflict within the first few paragraphs.

After a few moments James came back with a smile on his face.

"Did you make it?" I asked.

"Yeah, they said no one else could spike the ball like me." James grabbed his stuff and we went out into the parking lot.

4. EDIT AND PROOFREAD

Focus: Maintaining a Consistent Point of View

Point of view is the perspective from which an author presents the action and characters in a story. If the person who experiences the action tells the story, it is being told from the *first-person point of view.* If the narrator is outside of the action, then the story is being told from the *third-person point of view.* If the narrator is all-knowing and can tell the reader about any and every character's thoughts, ideas, feelings, and actions, then the story is being told from the *third-person omniscient point of view.*

Whatever point of view you choose, maintain that point of view throughout the story. Check your writing carefully to be sure your point of view is consistent. If you decide your story would be better told from a different point of view, be sure to go back and make that change throughout.

> I was just so sick of thinking about how I could never be as good as James. ~~Zack~~ *I* turned on some music, and for a while ~~he~~ *I* was finally able to stop thinking about volleyball and the other kids until my mom called me down for dinner.

Focus: Punctuating Dialogue

Recall the rules for punctuating dialogue:

1. Enclose direct speech within quotation marks.
2. Place any commas or end punctuation of a direct quotation inside the quotation marks.
3. When a speech tag comes before the speaker's words, use a comma after the speech tag. Begin the words of the speaker with a capital letter.
4. When a speech tag comes after the speaker's words, use a comma after the speaker's words.
5. Start a new paragraph when the speaker changes.

> "What's your name?" one of the girls sitting next to me asked.
>
> "Z-Zack," I stuttered.

Embedded Quotations When a speaker quotes what another character said, use embedded quotations. Place the character's direct speech in double quotation marks and the words the character is quoting in single quotation marks.

> "He told me, 'Maybe volleyball just isn't for you.' But it's not just volleyball. It always seems like everything goes his way."

Proofreading

Proofreading for Errors Proofread your story for mechanical errors. Use proofreader's marks to correct mistakes. (See the Language Arts Handbook, section 4.1, for a list of proofreader's marks.)

5. PUBLISH AND PRESENT

Final Draft

Presentation Make a clean final version of your story. Handwritten stories should be neat and legible. Typed stories should be double-spaced and in a standard typeface. Check your teacher's guidelines before submitting your paper.

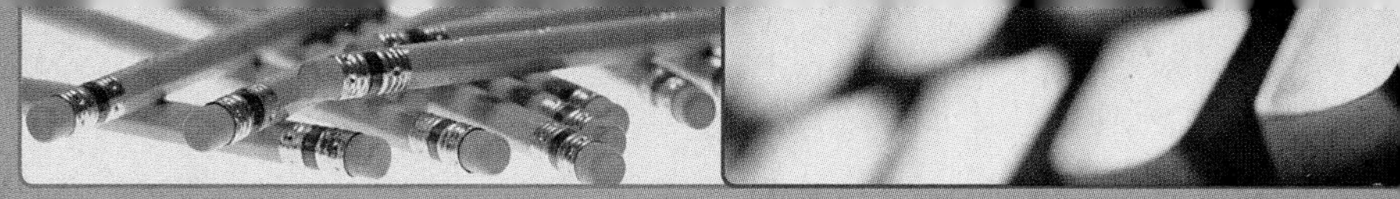

Student Model

A Chance to Play
by John McCombs

"James McDermott!" I heard the coach call off the next name on the list. James, who was sitting next to me, tightened his laces one last time and stood up. "Good luck," I said as he gave me a thumbs-up and ran over to the coach standing by the volleyball net. The gym echoed with shouts and the squeak of sneakers against the floor as players practiced serving and setting.

James had always been good at sports, especially volleyball, for as long as I had known him. I never let him know how I secretly wished I could be like him. It seemed like he and everyone else in the seventh grade was growing taller and stronger, but I was still as short and small as I had always been. I wanted to try out for volleyball, but even James took one look at me and said, "Maybe volleyball just isn't for you." That hurt, coming from my best friend, but he never lied to me before and was always the kindest guy I had ever known.

Introduces the main characters and the conflict

Introduces and describes the setting in vivid detail

After a few moments James came back with a smile on his face.

"Did you make it?" I asked.

"Yeah, they said no one else could spike the ball like me." James grabbed his stuff and we went out into the parking lot. "Coach said practices start next week. This year's team is going to be great," James said as we sat down on a bench.

"Yeah, I just wish I could be a part of it," I said without really thinking about my words.

Suddenly I saw my mom pull up in her red car and I walked over and got in without saying a word.

"So did James make the team?" my mom asked.

"Yeah," I replied. "They said he was the best."

"That's wonderful, I'm sure his parents are proud of him."

Introduces the first event and begins the rising action

I didn't say anything.

"Is something wrong?" my mom asked.

"I just wish that I could be as athletic as James." I fiddled with the radio station. "He told me, 'Maybe volleyball just isn't for you.' But it's not just volleyball. It always seems like everything goes his way."

"That's no way to talk. James just has different gifts than you do."

When we finally got home, I went up to my room and lay down on my bed. I was just so sick of thinking about how I could never be as good as James. I turned on some music, and for a while I was finally able

Develops the conflict and adds suspense

Student Model CONTINUED

Develops the conflict and adds suspense

to stop thinking about volleyball and the other kids until my mom called me down for dinner.

As we ate dinner, my mom slid a piece of paper across the table.

"What's this?" I asked as I skimmed the page.

"It's an after-school program at the community center for boys and girls who want to play volleyball. I thought that since you can't play for the Tigers, maybe you'd want to play for another team."

"When are tryouts?" I asked my mom.

"This weekend, do you want to go?"

Before I could answer, my eyes stopped on one little piece of text.

"What is it?" my mom asked.

"They play in the same league as the Tigers. I'll be playing against my own school!" I couldn't believe it.

"Well, that's great; you'll get to play against your friends."

The idea of playing against the Tigers didn't excite me one bit. They were the best in the city, and I didn't want to look stupid in front of all my friends. Still, I decided to try out since playing on a team was a dream of mine, and I might finally get the chance.

That Saturday, my mom drove me over to the community center. They had the whole gym set up for tryouts. I sat down on a bench with a few other kids and waited for my name to be called.

Uses natural, believable dialogue to develop the characters

"What's your name?" one of the girls sitting next to me asked.

"Z-Zack," I stuttered. She laughed a little.

"Are you nervous?" she asked.

"Yeah, just a little."

"Don't worry; I'm sure you'll make it. By the way, my name is Chris."

Before I could say anything else, I heard someone yell out, "Zack Atkinson!"

I stood up slowly. My legs were shaking.

"Good luck," Chris said as I walked over to the coach.

The coach threw the ball in the air, and I stuck my hands out as it came down. The ball bounced off the side of my hand. I wanted to disappear.

"Hey, Zack, just relax. Trust me, you'll get it," the coach said as he grabbed another ball.

Maintains a consistent point of view

This time as he threw the ball in the air I calmed down and was able to return it to him. I felt so good; I couldn't believe I actually returned it. The tryouts went on until I was finally the one serving.

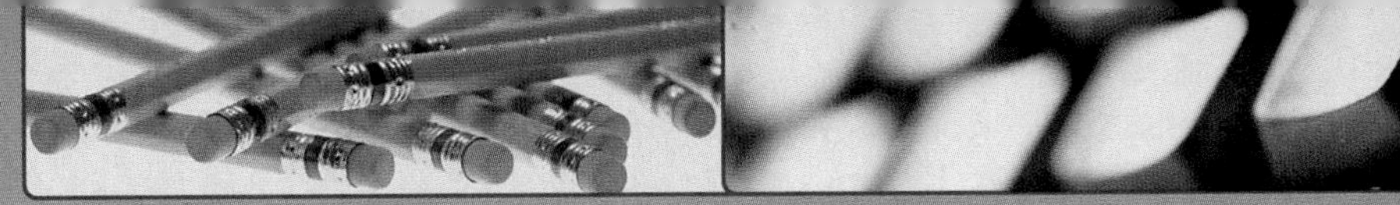

"Whenever you're ready," the coach said. I threw the ball over my head and hit it with all my strength. The ball flew over the net and landed in the back corner of the other side of the gym.

"That was a great hit, Zack!"

I smiled and continued serving balls over the net.

Maintains a consistent point of view

When tryouts were finally over, the coach posted a list of the names and positions of the team. I searched eagerly for mine until I finally saw it. I was the starting server! Before I had time to celebrate, one of the coaches blew a whistle, and everybody walked over.

"All right everyone, now that you know your positions, we have an exhibition game tomorrow at 1 PM before the official season starts. I expect you all to be there and ready to go. We're playing the Tigers at Manhattan Middle School." My heart skipped a beat. Tomorrow I would play against my own school and James.

One o'clock sneaked up on me the next day, and before I knew it, we were warming up in Manhattan's gym. I spotted James on the other side of the court, and when he saw me, he looked stunned.

Finally the ref blew a whistle, starting the game. I got in position and grabbed the ball. I threw it in the air and smacked it across the net. The ball landed out of bounds. My cheeks felt flushed. I was mortified.

Provides details about the characters' thoughts, feelings, and physical characteristics to make them more complex and interesting

The Tigers took the ball and served it over perfectly, but Chris jumped above the net and spiked the ball on the Tigers' side.

The game seemed to drag on and on with the score going back and forth until finally it was 20 to 17 and our ball. The Tigers only needed one more point to win. I set up the ball and hit it over. It landed in the back right corner: ace. I set up again and hit it over. This time it landed in the front left corner: ace. With one more point we could tie the game.

"Keep it up, Zack, you can do it!" Chris yelled. I threw the ball over my head and hit it. This time one of the Tigers returned it. One of our setters just barely tipped it back over the net. Suddenly I saw James jump up and spike the ball straight towards the middle. I dove for it, but it bounced off my hands. The game was over. I wanted to just lie there forever, but one of the guys extended his hand and helped me up.

Builds tension toward a climax

"You did great out there. I've never seen a server play so well," he said, and the rest of the team agreed. After the Tigers were done cheering, James came over and shook my hand.

"I was wrong about you Zack; you really can play."

"Yeah, you did really great too. I couldn't believe that spike."

"I have a feeling this season is going to be the best one yet."

Resolves the conflict and brings the story to a satisfying close

Speaking & Listening Workshop

Giving and Actively Listening to Literary Presentations

You have just written an exciting story, or maybe you have just read an excellent short story or poem. You want to share the passage with another person. You could let that person read it to him or herself. Or you could present the piece of literature aloud. This is called a **literary presentation.**

In this workshop you will learn how to plan and deliver an effective literary presentation. You will also learn how to effectively listen to someone else's presentation. This workshop includes a rubric, a set of standards to use in evaluating either your own presentation or someone else's.

Planning a Literary Presentation

Choose a Piece of Literature You have read a variety of stories and a couple of poems in this unit. You have also written your own short story. Here are a few points to keep in mind when choosing a story for a literary presentation:

- Which story or poem struck you the most? Choose a story or poem that you would like to hear read.
- Read aloud the first few lines. Does the story or poem sound like one you can effectively deliver to an audience?
- Can you give the story or poem the surprise or dramatic reading that it demands?

Identify Your Audience What literature you choose and how you present it will depend partly on who your audience is. Is the audience familiar with the story or poem? Be prepared to answer questions or even accept criticism from your audience.

Review Your Literature Once you have chosen the selection you will present, read it silently. Use the following tips to evaluate if the story or poem is a good one to be read aloud.

- Identify the point of view. Is it told from the first-person point of view? Decide how you will adjust your voice and body language as you present your story.
- How easy or difficult will it be for you to switch character roles in dialogue or become the narrator when necessary?
- Look at the punctuation. Does it suggest emotions or pauses in speech?
- How much emotion is called for, and how much can you deliver?

Word Choice and Sensory Details Sensory details are details that appeal to one of the five senses. If you are reading your own short story, ask yourself: Have I effectively used words to convey emotion or paint a picture of what I want the audience to see in their minds? If you are presenting a story or poem by another writer, consider whether or not you can visualize where and when the story takes place or how a character looks, thinks, or feels. Remember to convey this when you give your presentation to the class.

Evaluating Your Literary Presentation

As with the revision of your writing, a peer reviewer can help improve your presentation. Remember, your reviewer has your best interest in mind when he or she critiques the way you deliver a line or a piece of dialogue. If you are reviewing someone else's presentation, keep in mind that you should give helpful suggestions for improving the presentation. Be respectful in your criticism, and give constructive feedback. Use the rubric on this page to help you evaluate your literary presentation.

Delivering Your Literary Presentation

Nonverbal communication is just as important in giving a literary presentation as speaking is. When you read your story or poem, look at your audience, use facial expressions to convey emotion, and use your body to convey a character's attitude. Remember your pacing, and do not race through a reading, mumble (unless the story calls for it), or read too loudly. Keep your audience interested and focused on the story.

Listen Actively Respect is the key to active listening. Be attentive to the speaker's words, and follow the story's plot. Respond appropriately to funny or surprising parts, and ask questions when appropriate.

Speaking Rubric

Your presentation will be evaluated on these elements:

Content

- ❑ literature is appropriate for audience
- ❑ literature contains vivid sensory details
- ❑ literature uses descriptive words

Delivery and Presentation

- ❑ engaging presentation of dialogue
- ❑ appropriate pacing for tone and purpose of literature
- ❑ effective nonverbal expression

Listening Rubric

As a peer reviewer or audience member, you should do the following:

- ❑ listen quietly and attentively
- ❑ maintain eye contact with speaker
- ❑ ask appropriate questions
- ❑ (as peer reviewer) provide constructive feedback

Test Practice Workshop

Writing Skills

Literary Response

Carefully read the following writing prompt. Before you begin writing, think carefully about what task the assignment is asking you to perform. Then create an outline to help guide your writing.

> In Marta Salinas's short story "The Scholarship Jacket," the main character, Martha, learns that the school principal is going to make her pay money in order to be eligible for the scholarship jacket—an honor awarded to the most academically successful student. When Martha asks her grandfather if he will pay the fifteen-dollar fee, he responds, "Then if you pay for it, Marta, it's not a scholarship jacket, is it? Tell your principal I will not pay the fifteen dollars." Do you believe Martha's grandfather made the right choice?

In your essay, take a position on the grandfather's decision. Use evidence from the story, including direct quotations, in support of your position. As you write, be sure to:

- Organize your essay in a logical and consistent way
- Include introductory and concluding paragraphs
- Introduce your position in the first paragraph
- Support your main idea in each body paragraph

Revising and Editing Skills

In the following excerpt from the first draft of a student's paper, words and phrases are underlined and numbered. Alternatives to the underlined words and phrases appear in the right-hand column. Choose the alternative that best corrects any grammatical or style errors in the original. If you think the original is error-free, choose *NO CHANGE.*

You may also be asked questions about a section of the passage or the entire passage. These questions do not refer to a specific underlined phrase or word and are identified by a number in a box. Record your answers on a separate sheet of paper.

In Gish Jen's story "The White Umbrella" [1] many different things motivate the characters. The story's narrator wants to be like everybody else, and her sister Mona wanted to be happy [2]. Her parents are just trying to provide what's best for she and her sister [3]. Each character's motivation play an important role [4] in the development of the plot and the story's overall mood. [5]

The story's narrator is ashamed that their mother has taken a job working at a grocery store. She wants her mother to stay at home and be "normal." The narrator's feelings are partly the result of how she compares herself to others and of how her parents talk about other families. Early in the story she says [6] "I remembered how sorry my parents had felt for Mrs. Lee when she started waitressing downtown the year before."

1. A. NO CHANGE
   B. "The White Umbrella,"
   C. The White Umbrella
   D. "The White Umbrella;"

2. A. NO CHANGE
   B. Mona wants to be happy
   C. Mona wanted happy
   D. wanted to be happy, Mona

3. A. NO CHANGE
   B. what are best for she and her sister
   C. what's best for her and her sister
   D. what's best for she and she sister

4. A. NO CHANGE
   B. playing an important role
   C. have played an important role
   D. plays an important role

5. Which of the following *best* summarizes the thesis, or main idea, of this essay?
   A. The characters' motivations contribute to the plot and mood.
   B. The characters' motivations are in conflict.
   C. The narrator should pay more attention to her parents.
   D. The plot has the greatest influence on the mood.

6. A. NO CHANGE
   B. she says;
   C. she says,
   D. she said

Reading Skills

Carefully read the following passage. Then, on a separate piece of paper, answer each question.

from "The Ground Is Always Damp" by Luci Tapahonso

One night Leona dreamt that she was sitting outside her parents' home in the bright sunlight. The many trees, the small dusty chickens scratching nearby, and a single cloud above cast sharp dark shadows on the smooth yard. The sudden familiarity of the detailed shadows and clean air startled and awakened her, and later she spoke aloud, addressing her mother who was hundreds of miles away.

"Shimá, my mother, it's cloudy here most of the time. The ground is always damp, and Mom, I don't care to kneel down and sift dirt through my fingers. One day last week, the sun came out for a few hours, and the shadows were soft and furry on the brown grass. That's the way it is here, my mother."

Even though Leona hadn't seen her parents in months, she talked to them silently every day. She imagined that they listened, then responded by explaining things or asking long, detailed questions. Leona did this thoughtfully and felt that they did the same in their daily conversations about her and her children. They wondered what the weather was like and what kind of house Leona and her family lived in. She was certain about this. The difference was that they spoke aloud to each other, or to the various brothers and sisters who lived nearby.

In her dreams, she was always there in New Mexico, driving the winding roads to Taos, watching the harvest dances at Laguna, or maybe selling hay and watermelons with her brothers. In her dreams, she laughed, talking and joking easily in Navajo and English. She woke herself up sometimes because she had laughed aloud, or said, "Aye-e-e"—that old familiar teasing expression.

The New Mexico sky is clear and empty. It is a deep blue, almost turquoise, and Leona's family lives surrounded by the Carriso Mountains in the west, the Sleeping Ute Mountains in the north, the La Plata in the east and the Chuska Mountain range to the southwest. They rely on the distance, the thin, clean air, and the mountains to alert them to rain, thunderstorms, dust storms, and intense heat. At various times, her brothers stand looking across the horizon to see what is in store. They can see fifty miles or more in each direction.

In contrast, when Leona looks to the east most mornings, the sky is gray, the air thick with frost, and the wind blows cold dampness.

"My mother, there are no mountains here, and I can't see very far because the air is thick and heavy with a scent I can't recognize. I haven't been able to smell the arrival of snow here, or to distinguish between the different kinds of rain scent. The rain seems all the same here, except in degree, and it is constant."

1. The sentence that begins in line 2 can best be described as
   A. theme.
   B. description.
   C. tone.
   D. characterization.

2. Who is Shimá?
   A. Leona
   B. Leona's grandmother
   C. Leona's sister
   D. Leona's mother

3. Which of the following *best* describes the paragraph beginning on line 22?
   A. It explains the story's conflict.
   B. It describes the protagonist.
   C. It is filled with sensory details.
   D. It is filled with dialect.

4. Based on the context, what is the meaning of *degree* in line 34?
   A. texture
   B. shape
   C. color
   D. amount

5. From the text, you could infer that Leona is
   A. an adult.
   B. a small child.
   C. an old woman.
   D. an only child.

6. Which of the following *best* describes the tone of the narrator's dialogue?
   A. unsure
   B. humorous
   C. sorrowful
   D. happy

7. The character of the story's narrator can be described as
   A. dynamic.
   B. static.
   C. unreliable.
   D. implied.

8. The conflict in this passage is primarily
   A. internal.
   B. external.
   C. indirect.
   D. resolution.

9. The mood of this passage can best be described as
   A. nostalgic.
   B. excited.
   C. suspenseful.
   D. energetic.

10. This story is written from which point of view?
    A. first-person
    B.. second-person
    C. third-person
    D. limited

Unit 3

Experiencing the World

Nonfiction

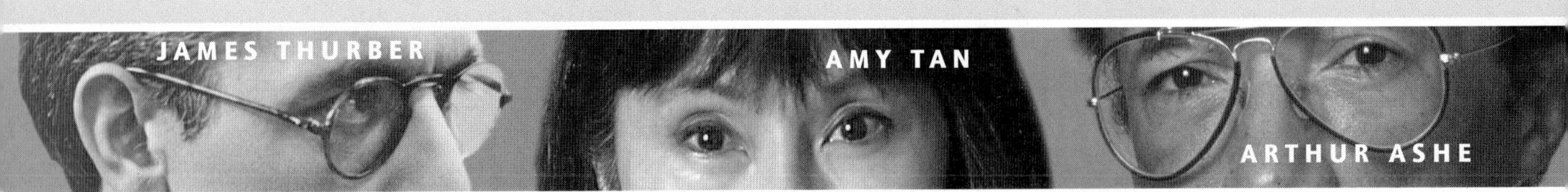

"...my mother said to me, 'You want to be the same as American girls on the outside....But inside you must always be Chinese. You must be proud you are different. Your only shame is to have shame.'"

—AMY TAN, "Fish Cheeks"

Sometimes we feel the need to express an idea, to describe our experiences, or to make a statement about something we believe. In Amy Tan's personal essay "Fish Cheeks," she describes an experience in her youth that helped her to understand the importance of self-acceptance. As you read the nonfiction in this unit, consider what each author is trying to say about him- or herself or the world.

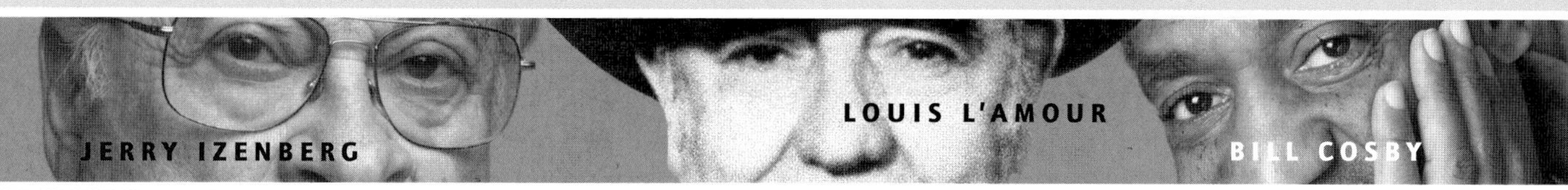

Introduction to Nonfiction

Both of the following passages deal with baseball great Roberto Clemente. How do they differ?

"I am surprised. More than surprised. You are Roberto Clemente, the baseball player?"

"Of course."

"You were lost at sea?"

"Until now."

"There's something not quite right."

"Like what?" says Clemente.

"Like what year do you think this is?"

"When we took off it was 1972, but New Year's Eve. We crashed in the ocean. It must be January fifth or sixth, maybe even the seventh, 1973."

– W. P. KINSELLA, "Searching for January"

"It was almost midnight," recalls Rudy Hernandez, a former teammate of Roberto's.

"We were having this party in my restaurant, and somebody turned on the radio and the announcer was saying that Roberto's plane was feared missing. And then, because my place is on the beach, we saw these giant floodlights crisscrossing the waves, and we heard the sound of the helicopters and the little search planes."

– JERRY IZENBERG, *A Bittersweet Memoir*

Roberto Clemente, outfielder for the Pittsburgh Pirates, in 1964.

Fiction and Nonfiction

These two passages differ in several ways, including writing style. But one very important difference is that Kinsella's re-creation of Clemente in this passage is imaginary, and Izenberg's is an attempt to describe actual events. To put it another way, Kinsella's short story is fiction, and Izenberg's biography is nonfiction.

Fiction is often highly realistic. Kinsella is known for his extensive knowledge of baseball and its history, and he draws on this when writing his fiction, yet his narrative is still invented. On the other hand, Izenberg undertook extensive research and interviews when writing his biography.

In the Introduction to Fiction (page 4), you learned that **fiction** includes any work of prose (writing that is not poetry or drama) that describes an invented or imaginary story. Typical forms of fiction are short stories and novels. **Nonfiction** is writing about real people, places, things, and events. Autobiographies, biographies, journals, essays, histories, and newspaper and magazine articles are all types of nonfiction.

Types of Nonfiction

Among the most common types of nonfiction are autobiography and memoir, biography, and essay.

Autobiography and Memoir

Writing is described as "autobiographical" when the writer presents parts or the whole of his or her own life. There are many types of autobiographical writing, including autobiographies, memoirs, diaries, journals, and letters.

An **autobiography** is told from the *first-person point of view* and is the story of a person's life written by that person. It typically covers the whole of a person's life up to the time of writing. A more focused type of autobiography is the **memoir,** which usually deals with a specific period of a person's life. Annie Dillard's *An American Childhood* (page 257) is a memoir about her childhood.

> The suggestions of adults were uncertain and incoherent. They gave you Nancy Drew with one hand and *Little Women* with the other. They mixed good and bad books together because they could not distinguish between them. Any book which contained children, or short adults, or animals, was felt to be a children's book.

Biography

A **biography** is the story of a person's life told by another person. Milton Meltzer's "Elizabeth I" (page 265) is a biography about one of England's greatest rulers.

> Elizabeth I came to the throne of England in 1558 at the age of twenty-five. It was not a happy time for a young woman to take the responsibility for ruling a kingdom.

Biographies are told from the *third-person point of view,* although writers of biography may also include autobiographical materials, such as letters, diaries, or journals, so that the reader may gain some firsthand knowledge about the person whose life story is being told.

Essay

An **essay** is a short nonfiction work that makes a point about a single subject. The point that the writer is making is the **thesis.** For example, in an essay about school uniforms, the thesis might be that uniforms prevent personal expression.

There are many types of essays. A **personal essay** is a short nonfiction work on a single topic related to the life of the writer. The author of a personal essay may tell a story or an anecdote or reflect on and share thoughts and feelings about something in his or her life.

In an **argumentative essay,** the writer's goal is to persuade the reader to accept a point of view. For example, in "The Eternal Frontier" (page 291), Louis L'Amour tries to make his readers understand the importance of space exploration.

> One might ask—why outer space, when so much remains to be done here? If that had been the spirit of man we would still be hunters and food gatherers, growling over the bones of carrion in a cave somewhere.

Newspaper editorials and petitions are common examples of argumentative writing. Writers of argumentative essays use a variety of techniques to make an argument, including appealing to both logic and emotion, using parallel construction to add force to their statements, and asking rhetorical questions. **Parallelism** is the use of the same grammatical constructions to express ideas of equal importance. A **rhetorical question** is a question asked by an author to reinforce an idea.

Nonfiction Close Reading Model

BEFORE READING

Build Background

You need to apply two types of background to read a piece of nonfiction effectively. One is the selection's historical, scientific, or cultural context. Read the **Build Background** and **Meet the Author** features to get this kind of information. The other type of background is the personal knowledge you bring to your reading.

Set Purpose

A nonfiction writer writes to inform, describe, persuade, or entertain. Read **Set Purpose** to decide what you want to get out of the selection.

Analyze Literature

A nonfiction writer uses different techniques depending on the type of nonfiction he or she is writing. The **Analyze Literature** feature draws your attention to a key literary element.

Use Reading Skills

The **Use Reading Skills** feature will show you skills to help you get the most out of your reading. Learn how to apply skills such as determining author's purpose and using context clues. Identify a graphic organizer that will help you apply the skill before and while you read.

DURING READING

Use Reading Strategies

- **Ask questions** about things that seem significant or interesting.
- **Make predictions** about what's going to happen next. As you read, gather more clues to confirm or change your prediction.
- **Visualize** the information. Form pictures in your mind to help you see what the writer is describing.
- **Make inferences,** or educated guesses, about what is not stated directly.
- **Clarify,** or check that you understand, what you read. Reread any difficult parts.

Analyze Literature

What literary elements stand out? As you read, consider how these elements affect your enjoyment and understanding of the selection.

Make Connections

Notice where connections can be made between the information presented in the selection and your life.

AFTER READING

Find Meaning

Recall the important details of the selection, such as the sequence of events and settings. Use this information to **interpret,** or explain, the meaning of the selection.

Make Judgments

- **Analyze** the text by examining details and deciding what they contribute to the meaning.
- **Evaluate** the text by making judgments about how the author creates meaning.

Analyze Literature

Review how the use of literary elements increased your understanding of the selection. For example, did the author use sensory details? How did they help shape meaning?

Extend

Go beyond the text by exploring the selection's ideas through writing or other creative projects.

from An American Childhood

A Memoir by Annie Dillard

Build Background

Literary Context Annie Dillard is best known as a nature writer. Her Pulitzer Prize–winning collection of essays, *Pilgrim at Tinker Creek* (1974), follows in the tradition of Henry David Thoreau's *Walden* (1854). In her nature writing, Dillard, like Thoreau, combines vivid descriptions of nature with personal reflections on human nature, philosophy, and spirituality. This memoir describes Dillard's early fascination with nature writing.

Reader's Context What do you remember about your first visit to a library?

Set Purpose

Preview the first paragraph to predict what the author will reveal about her thoughts, feelings, and actions.

Analyze Literature

Autobiography An **autobiography** is a work that describes the life of the author, often chronologically. Autobiographies are written from the first-person point of view, using pronouns such as *I* and *me.* One type of autobiographical writing is the **memoir,** in which a writer recalls experiences of a particular time in his or her life. As you read this selection, notice how Dillard uses details to help the reader share her experiences.

Use Reading Skills

Context Clues Preview the vocabulary words from this selection as they are used in the sentences below. Try to unlock the meaning of each word using the context clues provided in the sentences.

1. The first arrow I shot hit the bull's eye, but my subsequent shots missed.
2. Marta wrinkled her nose at the skunk's noisome odor.
3. It is the prerogative of the coach to decide who plays on the team.
4. John's bad attitude and complaining began to exasperate the others.
5. The tedium of fishing always makes Hank doze off.

Meet the Author

Annie Dillard (b. 1945) has written many books and essays about her life, about nature, and about her experiences in nature. She has also written poetry and novels. Dillard grew up in Pittsburgh, Pennsylvania, and taught at Wesleyan College in Middletown, Connecticut. Still a passionate reader, Dillard keeps lists of "Books I Have Read." Dillard says, "I just read, read, read, read. That's all I do."

Preview Vocabulary

sub•se•quent (sʉb´ si kwənt) *adj.,* following in time, order, or place

noi•some (nôi´ səm) *adj.,* offensive smell; objectionable

pre•rog•a•tive (pri räg´ ət iv) *n.,* special power or privilege

ex•as•per•at•ed (ig zas´ pə rāt' ed) *adj.,* irritated

te•di•um (tē´ dē əm) *n.,* boredom

from An American Childhood

Students with Books, 1966. Jacob Lawrence. Private collection.

A Memoir by Annie Dillard

The people of Homewood... they dreamed of ponds and streams.

The Homewood Library had graven across its enormous stone facade: FREE TO THE PEOPLE. In the evenings, neighborhood people—the men and women of Homewood—browsed in the library, and brought their children. By day, the two vaulted rooms, the adults' and children's sections, were almost empty. The kind Homewood librarians, after a trial period, had given me a card to the adult section. This was an enormous silent room with marble floors. Nonfiction was on the left.

Beside the farthest wall, and under leaded windows set ten feet from the floor, so that no human being could ever see anything from them—next to the wall, and at the farthest remove from the idle librarians at their curved wooden counter, and from the oak bench where my mother waited in her camel's-hair coat chatting with the librarians or reading—stood the last and darkest and most obscure of the tall nonfiction stacks: NEGRO HISTORY and NATURAL HISTORY. It was in Natural History, in the cool darkness of a bottom shelf, that I found *The Field Book of Ponds and Streams.*

The Field Book of Ponds and Streams was a small, blue-bound book printed in fine type on thin paper, like *The Book of Common Prayer.* Its third chapter explained how to make sweep nets, plankton nets, glassbottomed buckets, and killing jars. It specified how to mount slides, how to label insects on their pins, and how to set up a freshwater aquarium.

One was to go into "the field" wearing hip boots and perhaps a head net for mosquitoes. One carried in a "rucksack"[1] half a dozen corked test tubes, a smattering of screw-top baby-food jars, a white enamel tray, assorted pipettes[2] and eyedroppers, an artillery of cheesecloth nets, a notebook, a hand lens, perhaps a map, and *The Field Book of Ponds and Streams.* This field—unlike the fields I had seen, such as the field where Walter Milligan played football—was evidently very well watered, for there one could find, and distinguish among, daphniae, planaria, water pennies, stonefly larvae, dragonfly nymphs, salamander larvae, tadpoles, snakes, and turtles, all of which one could carry home.

That anyone had lived the fine life described in Chapter 3 astonished me. Although the title page indicated quite plainly that one Ann Haven Morgan had written *The Field Book of Ponds and Streams,* I nevertheless imagined, perhaps from the authority and freedom of it, that the author was a man. It would be good to write him and assure him that someone had found his book, in the dark near the marble floor in the Homewood Library. I would, in the same letter or in a subsequent one, ask him a question outside the scope of his book, which was where I personally might find a pond, or a stream. But I did not know how to address such a letter, of course, or how to learn if he was still alive.

I was afraid, too, that my letter would disappoint him by betraying my ignorance, which was just beginning to attract my own notice. What, for example, was this noisome sounding substance called cheesecloth, and what do scientists do with it? What, when

DURING READING
Use Reading Skills
Text Organization What kind of organizational pattern does the author use in the first two paragraphs? How effective is this pattern? What do you learn from it?

DURING READING
Analyze Literature
Autobiography What experience is the author sharing with the reader?

DURING READING
Use Reading Skills
Context Clues What are *planaria?* What clues in the text help you determine this?

DURING READING
Use Reading Skills
Context Clues The word *authority* has multiple meanings. Use the surrounding text to identify the meaning of *authority* as it appears in this context.

sub • se • quent (sub´ si kwənt) *adj.,* following in time, order, or place

noi • some (nôi´ səm) *adj.,* offensive smell; objectionable

---

1. **rucksack.** Knapsack
2. **pipettes.** Small tubes for holding fluid

you really got down to it, was enamel? If candy could, notoriously, "eat through enamel," why would anyone make trays out of it? Where—short of robbing a museum—might a fifth-grade student at the Ellis School on Fifth Avenue obtain such a legendary item as a wooden bucket?

DURING READING
Make Connections
How does the admission, at the beginning of this paragraph, that she was afraid affect your feelings about Dillard?

The Field Book of Ponds and Streams was a shocker from beginning to end. The greatest shock came at the end.

When you checked out a book from the Homewood Library, the librarian wrote your number on the book's card and stamped the date on a sheet glued to the book's last page. When I checked out *The Field Book of Ponds and Streams* for the second time, I noticed the book's card. It was almost full. There were numbers on both sides. My hearty author and I were not alone in the world, after all. With us, and sharing our enthusiasm for dragonfly larvae and single-celled plants were, apparently, many Negro adults. Who were these people? Had they, in Pittsburgh's Homewood section, found ponds? Had they found streams? At home, I read the book again; I studied the drawings; I reread Chapter 3; then I settled in to study the due-date slip. People read this book in every season. Seven or eight people were reading this book every year, even during the war.

Every year, I read again *The Field Book of Ponds and Streams.* Often, when I was in the vicinity, I simply visited it. I sat on the marble floor and studied the book's card. There was my number. There was the number of someone else who had checked it out more than once. Might I contact this person and cheer him up? For I assumed that, like me, he had found pickings pretty slim in Pittsburgh.

The people of Homewood, some of whom live in visible poverty, on crowded streets among burned-out houses—they dreamed of ponds and streams. They were saving to buy microscopes. In their bedrooms they fashioned plankton nets. But their hopes were even more vain than mine, for I was a child, and anything might happen; they were adults, living in Homewood. There was neither pond nor stream on the streetcar routes. The Homewood residents whom I knew had little money and little free time. The marble floor was beginning to chill me. It was not fair.

I had been driven into nonfiction against my wishes. I wanted to read fiction, but I had learned to be cautious about it.

"When you open a book," the sentimental library posters said, "anything can happen." This was so. A book of fiction was a bomb.

It was a land mine you wanted to go off. You wanted it to blow your whole day. Unfortunately, hundreds of thousands of books were duds. They had been rusting out of everyone's way for so long that they no longer worked. There was no way to distinguish the duds from the live mines except to throw yourself at them headlong, one by one.

The suggestions of adults were uncertain and incoherent. They gave you Nancy Drew with one hand and *Little Women* with the other. They mixed good and bad books together because they could not distinguish between them. Any book which contained children, or short adults, or animals, was felt to be a children's book. So also was any book about the sea—as though danger or even fresh air were a child's prerogative—or any book by Charles Dickens or Mark Twain. Virtually all British books, actually, were children's books; no one understood children like the British. Suited to female children were love stories set in any century but this one. Consequently one had read, exasperated often to fury, *Pickwick Papers, Désirée, Wuthering Heights, Lad, a Dog, Gulliver's Travels, Gone With the Wind, Robinson Crusoe,* Nordhoff and Hall's *Bounty* trilogy, *Moby-Dick, The Five Little Peppers, Innocents Abroad, Lord Jim, Old Yeller.*

The fiction stacks at the Homewood Library, their volumes alphabetized by author, baffled me. How could I learn to choose a novel? That I could not easily reach the top two shelves helped limit choices a little. Still, on the lower shelves I saw too many books: Mary Johnson, *Sweet Rocket;* Samuel Johnson, *Rasselas;* James Jones, *From Here to Eternity.* I checked out the last because I had heard of it; it was good. I decided to check out books I had heard of. I had heard of *The Mill on the Floss.* I read it, and it was good. On its binding was printed a figure, a man dancing or running; I had noticed this figure before. Like so many children before and after me, I learned to seek out this logo, the Modern Library colophon.[3]

The going was always rocky. I couldn't count on Modern Library the way I could count on, say, *Mad* magazine, which never failed to slay me. *Native Son* was good, *Walden* was pretty good, *The Interpretation of Dreams* was okay, and *The Education of Henry Adams* was awful. *Ulysses*, a very famous book, was also awful. *Confessions* by Augustine, whose title promised so much, was a bust. *Confessions* by Jean-Jacques Rousseau was much better, though it fell apart halfway through.

DURING READING

Analyze Literature

Autobiography How does Dillard feel about the books that adults recommended? Why do you think she feels this way?

pre • rog • a • tive (pri räg´ ət iv) *n.*, special power or privilege

ex • as • per • at • ed (ig zas´ pə rāt' ed) *adj.*, irritated

A book of fiction was a bomb. It was a land mine you wanted to go off.

3. colophon. Publisher's identifying imprint

DURING READING

Analyze Literature

Autobiography How does Dillard support her claim about "most books"? What realization does she have about her taste in books?

te•di•um (tē´ dē əm) *n.*, boredom

In fact, it was a plain truth that most books fell apart halfway through. They fell apart as their protagonists quit, without any apparent reluctance, like idiots diving voluntarily into buckets, the most interesting part of their lives, and entered upon decades of unrelieved tedium. I was forewarned, and would not so bobble my adult life; when things got dull, I would go to sea.

Jude the Obscure was the type case. It starts out so well. Halfway through, its author forgot how to write. After Jude got married, his life was over, but the book went on for hundreds of pages while he stewed in his own juices. The same thing happened in *The Little Shepherd of Kingdom Come,* which Mother brought me from a fair. It was simply a hazard of reading. Only a heartsick loyalty to the protagonists of the early chapters, to the eager children they had been, kept me reading chronological narratives to their bitter ends. Perhaps later, when I had become an architect, I would enjoy the latter halves of books more.

This was the most private and obscure part of life, this Homewood Library; a vaulted marble edifice[4] in a mostly decent Negro neighborhood, the silent stacks of which I pondered in deep concentration for many years. There seemed then, happily, to be an infinitude[5] of books.

I no more expected anyone else on earth to have read a book I had read than I expected someone else to have twirled the same blade of grass. I would never meet those Homewood people who were borrowing *The Field Book of Ponds and Streams;* the people who read my favorite books were invisible or in hiding, underground. Father occasionally raised his big eyebrows at the title of some volume I was hurrying off with, quite as if he knew what it contained—but I thought he must know of it by hearsay, for none of it seemed to make much difference to him. Books swept me away, one after the other, this way and that; I made endless vows according to their lights, for I believed them. ✣

4. **edifice.** Large building
5. **infinitude.** Quality of being infinite or without end

What item or experience from your childhood can unlock a treasure trove of memories for you? What kinds of things can people learn from memories of their childhood?

Find Meaning

1. (a) What information does *The Field Book of Ponds and Streams* contain? (b) Why do you think Dillard is so fascinated by this book?
2. (a) What does Dillard notice about the book's card? (b) What is her reaction? (c) Why does she react this way?
3. (a) What does Dillard say happens to many books of fiction "halfway through"? (b) What do you think she means by this?

Make Judgments

4. (a) What criteria would Dillard use to judge whether or not a book is good? (b) What books would you suggest for Dillard? Explain your answer.
5. (a) What words would you use to describe how Dillard responds to books? (b) Do you think her responses will change as she gets older? Explain.

Analyze Literature

Autobiography How does Annie Dillard help the reader share her experiences? Use a chart to list examples of concrete details and feelings or opinions in *An American Childhood.* Then, in one or two brief paragraphs, summarize the effectiveness of these details, feelings, and opinions in conveying her experiences.

Concrete Details	Feelings/Opinions
The Field Book of Ponds and Streams was printed on thin paper like a prayer book.	reverence; an important book

Extend Understanding

Writing Options

Creative and Informative Writing Imagine that you are a television screenwriter. Write a screenplay based on the excerpt you just read from Annie Dillard's memoir, *An American Childhood.* After you have finished your screenplay, write an essay describing the structural and substantive differences between the excerpt and your screenplay.

Informative Writing An author's voice expresses his or her personality and attitudes. How would you describe Annie Dillard's voice in this passage? Analyze Dillard's voice, or use of language, tone, and sentence structure, in a brief one-page **critical analysis.** Be sure to include a thesis statement and evidence from the text.

Collaborative Learning

Analyze Tone The tone of a selection reflects how the author feels about his or her subject. Think of how you would instruct someone to identify and analyze the tone of the selection. Meet with a partner and take turns giving oral instructions and following oral instructions. Record your work.

Lifelong Learning

Write a Book Summary Select one of the pieces of fiction that Dillard mentions in the selection and research its plot. Write a brief summary of the book's plot for a teacher interested in recommending books to students.

 Go to **www.mirrorsandwindows.com** for more.

Grammar & Style

Phrases

Prepositional Phrases

The kind Homewood librarians, after a trial period, had given me a card....

—ANNIE DILLARD, "An American Childhood"

In this sentence, the independent, or main, clause is broken up by a **phrase.** A phrase is a group of words used as a single part of speech. A phrase lacks a subject, a verb, or both. One of the most common kinds of phrases is the prepositional phrase. A **prepositional phrase** consists of a preposition, its object, and any modifiers of that object. In the above sentence, the word *after* is the preposition; *trial period* is the object.

EXAMPLE

I read in the library's nonfiction section.

A prepositional phrase adds information to a sentence by modifying another word in that sentence. For example, *in the library's nonfiction section* modifies *read.* Prepositional phrases can function as either adjectives or adverbs. The above is an adverb because it modifies a verb. The following example contains a phrase that acts as an adjective, modifying a noun.

EXAMPLE

The shelves in the library were dusty and cluttered.

Participial Phrases

A **participle** is a verb form ending in *-ing, -d,* or *-ed* that acts as an adjective, modifying a noun or pronoun. A **participial phrase** is made up of a participle and all of its modifiers, which may include objects, nouns, adjectives, adverbs, and prepositional phrases. The entire phrase acts as an adjective.

EXAMPLE

Walking in the rows, I was able to find my books.

The participle *walking* and the prepositional phrase *in the rows* make up the participial phrase that modifies *I.*

Be sure to place the participial phrase close to the word it modifies. Otherwise, you may say something you don't mean.

EXAMPLE

I considered the importance of the book standing in the Homewood parking lot.

In this example, the sentence seems to say that the book is standing in the parking lot.

Identifying Phrases

On a separate piece of paper, identify the phrase in each of the following sentences. Then describe the type of phrase it is: prepositional or participial.

1. In the afternoon I hurried home.
2. The librarians gathered in the stacks.
3. Inside *The Field Book of Ponds and Streams,* there were many interesting facts.
4. There were a dozen books beside the card catalog.
5. Kneeling on the library's floor, I was able to find my card.

Apply the Model

BEFORE READING

DURING READING

AFTER READING

GUIDED READING

Elizabeth I

A Biography by Milton Meltzer

Build Background

Historical Context Elizabeth I ruled as queen of England from 1558 until her death in 1603. In the long history of the English monarchy, only five women have held the position of sole ruler of England. Each woman came to the throne because the presiding male ruler or heir had died or because there was no male heir at all. Elizabeth inherited the crown from her father, King Henry VIII. She also inherited the conflict he had created between the English monarchy and the Catholic church.

Reader's Context If you were a queen or king, how would you capture the respect and loyalty of your citizens?

Set Purpose

Preview the first paragraph, and predict how Queen Elizabeth succeeded in making England a great nation. Read to find out how accurate your predictions are.

Analyze Literature

Biography A **biography** is the story of a person's life told by another person. Biographies may be book length or only a few pages. Biographers may interview their subjects, or they may find out about their subjects through research. Most biographers try to convey a balanced picture of a person's life. As you read, decide whether Milton Meltzer presents a fair and objective picture of Elizabeth.

Use Reading Skills

Distinguish Fact from Opinion A *fact* is a statement that can be proven. An *opinion* is a statement that expresses an attitude or desire. Opinions may be supported by facts, but they cannot be proven true or false. Create a chart to record facts and opinions in "Elizabeth I." Put fact statements in the first column. Record opinion statements in the second column.

Fact:	Opinion:
Queen Elizabeth was the daughter of Henry VIII and his second wife, Anne Boleyn.	Queen Elizabeth was one of the most remarkable women who ever lived.

Meet the Author

Milton Meltzer (1915–2009) was born in Worcester, Massachusetts. He is best known for his nonfiction books for young adult readers and for his books on American history. He wrote more than eighty books on such topics as black Americans, Jewish Americans, and the American Revolution.

Preview Vocabulary

pres•tige (pre stēzh´) *n.*, status; standing in general opinion

pros•per•i•ty (prä spər´ ə tē) *n.*, condition of being successful or thriving, especially economic well-being

di•rec•tive (də rek´ tiv) *n.*, order or form of guidance

om•i•nous (äm´ ə nəs) *adj.*, foreboding or foreshadowing evil

for•feit (for´ fət) *v.*, lose or fail to win the right to something by some error, offense, or crime

Elizabeth I

A Biography by Milton Meltzer

"Good Queen Bess" her people called her. But "good" is a tame word for one of the most remarkable women who ever lived. Elizabeth I came to the throne of England in 1558 at the age of twenty-five. It was not a happy time for a young woman to take the responsibility for ruling a kingdom. Religious conflicts, a huge government debt, and heavy losses in a war with France had brought England low. But by the time of Elizabeth's death forty-five years later, England had experienced one of the greatest periods in its long history. Under Elizabeth's leadership, England had become united as a nation; its industry and commerce, its arts and sciences had flourished; and it was ranked among the great powers of Europe.

Elizabeth was the daughter of King Henry VIII and his second wife, Anne Boleyn. At the age of two she lost her mother when Henry had Anne's head chopped off. Not a good start for a child. But her father placed her in the care of one lord or lady after another, and the lively little girl with the reddish-gold hair, pale skin, and golden-brown eyes won everyone's affection.

Almost from her infancy Elizabeth was trained to stand in for ruling men, in case the need should arise. So she had to master whatever they were expected to know and do. Her tutors found the child to be an eager student. She learned history, geography, mathematics, and the elements of astronomy and architecture. She mastered four modern languages—French, Italian, Spanish, and Flemish[1]—as well as classic Greek and Latin. She wrote in a beautiful script that was like a work of art. The earliest portrait painted of her—when she was thirteen—shows a girl with innocent eyes holding a book in her long and delicate hands, already confident and queenly in her bearing.

She was a strong-willed girl who liked to give orders. She loved to be out on horseback, and rode so fast it frightened the men assigned to protect her. She loved dancing too—she never gave it up. Even in her old age she was seen one moonlit night dancing by herself in the garden.

Elizabeth had a half sister, Mary, born of Henry's first wife, Catherine of Aragon. Many years later came Elizabeth, the child of Anne Boleyn, and four years after, her half brother, Edward, the son of Henry's third wife, Jane Seymour. After Henry died, because

And why should she, the absolute ruler of England, allow a man to sit alongside her as king?

DURING READING

Use Reading Strategies
Make Inferences What does this tell you about Elizabeth's father?

DURING READING

Use Reading Strategies
Make Predictions What does this suggest about Elizabeth's future?

---

1. **Flemish.** Language spoken in Flanders, a small region in parts of northern France, Belgium, and the Netherlands

(Opposite page) *Queen Elizabeth I in Coronation Robes,* c. 1559. National Portrait Gallery, London.

"Am I not a queen because God has chosen me to be a queen?"

succession[2] came first through the male, ten-year-old Edward was crowned king. But he lived only another six years. Now Mary took the throne and, soon after, married King Philip II of Spain, a Catholic monarch like herself. He was twenty-seven and she thirty-eight. But they were rarely together, each ruling their own kingdom. Mary died of cancer at the age of forty-two. That made Elizabeth the monarch.

When she came to the throne on November 17, 1558, it was a day to be marked by celebrations, then and long after. As Her Majesty passed down a London street, an astonished housewife exclaimed, "Oh, Lord! The Queen is a woman!" For there were still many who could scarcely believe they were to be ruled by another woman. Elizabeth herself would say with mock modesty that she was "a mere woman." But everyone soon learned she was a very special woman. "Am I not a queen because God has chosen me to be a queen?" she demanded.

DURING READING

Use Reading Strategies

Make Inferences What does this statement of the people's disbelief suggest about the role of women in their society?

As princess and later as queen, Elizabeth lived in various palaces, with much coming and going; each time she moved, she took along her household staff of 120 people. Often the changes were required because there was no sanitation. The smelly palaces had to be emptied so they could be "aired and sweetened."

Even before Elizabeth came of age there was much talk of when she would marry, and whom. Marriages among the nobility and royalty were arranged not for love, but for practical reasons—to add land holdings, to strengthen the prestige and power of families, to cement an alliance of nations against a common enemy.

pres•tige (pre stēzh´) *n.*, status; standing in general opinion

And remember, from the most ancient times, kings claimed that they as men were born to rule by divine right. That is, God had ordained that the crown should pass through the male line of descent. But when the king's wife had no male child, it meant trouble. Who then would rule? That crisis often led to civil war as various factions battled for the power to name a king. Many disputed Elizabeth's right to the throne, and as long as she had neither husband nor successor, her life was in danger.

Ever since Elizabeth was eight, however, she had said again and again, "I will never marry." Did marriage look promising to a girl whose father had six wives, two of whom, including her own mother, he had beheaded? Yet she liked to hear of people who wanted to marry her.

DURING READING

Analyze Literature

Biography Why do you think the biographer asks whether or not marriage looked promising to Elizabeth?

2. **succession.** Order of persons having a right to the throne

And there was no shortage of suitors.[3] She continued to insist she wished to live unmarried. No matter how often she said it, men did not believe it. Understandably, since she often made a prince or duke who had come to court her believe she was finally ready to give in—only at the last moment to back out. Once, to a delegation from Parliament come to beg her to marry, she declared, "I am already bound unto a husband, which is the Kingdom of England."

And why should she, the absolute ruler of England, allow a man to sit alongside her as king? The power of husbands over wives in that century—and even now, in many places of this world—was so

DURING READING

Analyze Literature
Biography What does Elizabeth's statement tell you about her commitments?

---

3. suitors. Men who court or pay loving attention to a woman in order to marry her

Queen Elizabeth I in Procession with Her Courtiers, 1825. Sarah Countess of Essex. Private collection.

great that a husband might snatch the reins of power from her and leave her with the title but not the authority she loved to exercise.

Was it fun to be queen? As monarch, she commanded great wealth, inherited from her father, and people who wanted favors were always enriching her with lavish presents. She was no spendthrift, however. She hated to see money wasted, whether her own or the kingdom's. Early on she began keeping careful household account books, and later she would do the same with the royal accounts. Always she urged her counselors to carry out orders as inexpensively as possible.

DURING READING

Analyze Literature

Biography Why do you think Meltzer includes this information about Elizabeth's spending?

Above everything else, Elizabeth wanted to have her people think well of her. Her deepest desire was to assure them of peace and prosperity. And why not make a grand personal impression upon them at the same time? In her mature years she gave free rein to her love of jewels and staged brilliant displays for the court and the people. Her dresses were decorated with large rubies, emeralds, and diamonds, and she wore jeweled necklaces, bracelets, and rings. In her hair, at her ears, and around her neck she wore pearls—the symbol of virginity.

pros • per • i • ty (prä spər´ ə tē) *n.*, condition of being successful or thriving, especially economic well-being

Above everything else, Elizabeth wanted to have her people think well of her.

During her reign she made many great processions through London, the people wild with excitement, crowding the streets—for the English, like most people, loved spectacle. In the first of them, her coronation, she wore gold robes as she was crowned. Trumpets sounded, pipes and drums played, the organ pealed, bells rang. Then came the state banquet in Westminster Hall. It began at 3:00 P.M., and went on till 1:00 A.M.

Elizabeth was often entertained at house parties. One of them, given by the Earl of Leicester in Kenilworth Castle, lasted for eighteen days in July. Thirty other distinguished guests were invited. The great number of their servants (together with Leicester's) turned the palace into a small town. When darkness fell, candles glittered everywhere, indoors and out, creating a fairyland. Musicians sang and played, the guests danced in the garden, and such a great display of fireworks exploded that the heavens thundered and the castle shook. Then came a pleasure relished in those days: the hideous sport of bear-baiting. A pack of dogs was let loose in an inner courtyard to scratch and bite and tear at thirteen tormented bears. Still, the happy guests retained their appetite for a "most delicious banquet of 300 dishes."

The tremendous festival at Kenilworth was only one of the highlights of Elizabeth's summer festival. She moved from one great house to another all season long, always at the enormous expense of her hosts. They had little to complain of, however, for their wealth was often the product of the queen's generous bestowal[4] of special privileges. In recognition of his high rank and in return for his support, she granted the Duke of Norfolk a license to import carpets from Turkey free of duty. The Earl of Essex was favored with the profitable right to tax imported sweet wines. Other pets[5] got rich from a monopoly on the importation[6] of or taxation of silks, satins, salt, tobacco, starch.

England was a small nation at that time: less than four million people, about as many as live in Arizona today. But the English were a young people, coming to maturity with new worlds opening up to them, in the mind and across the seas. A rebirth of culture—the Renaissance[7]—had begun in the 1400s. With the revival of interest in the literature of the ancient Greek and Roman worlds came the beginning of a great age of discovery. This period marked the transition from medieval to modern times. The arts and sciences were influenced by changes in economic life. All the nation was swept up in the vast tides of change. Merchants, bankers, the gentry,[8] artisans,[9] seamen, miners—men and women of every class and condition—felt themselves part of the national venture.

At the heart of change in England was the queen. But no king or queen rules alone, no matter how authoritative or arrogant they may be. They usually look to others for advice, advice they may follow or reject. Elizabeth appointed ministers to handle the various departments of government, and made Sir William Cecil, then thirty-eight, her principal adviser. He was a brilliant, hardworking master of statecraft, devoted to her and England's well-being, and as ruthless as she and the nation's interests required. When he died in old age, his son Robert replaced him at her side.

So great was the queen's role, however, that her time became known as the Age of Elizabeth. Not only did many fine musicians

DURING READING

Use Reading Strategies

Clarify How does the author support the idea that kings or queens usually look for advice?

4. **bestowal.** Gift
5. **pets.** Persons treated with unusual kindness; favorites
6. **monopoly on the importation.** Exclusive control over the trade in foreign goods
7. **Renaissance** (re' nə sän[t]s´). Revival of art and learning in Europe
8. **gentry.** Upper class of people
9. **artisans.** Artists and craftspeople

flower, but writers too, such as Christopher Marlowe and John Donne and Ben Jonson and Edmund Spenser. And above all, the incomparable William Shakespeare, whose plays were sometimes performed at court. Astronomers, naturalists, mathematicians, geographers, and architects pioneered in their fields.

CULTURAL ▶▶ CONNECTION

The Renaissance Roughly stretching from the fourteenth to the sixteenth century, the Renaissance was a period of rebirth for the arts and sciences in Europe and marks the transition between the Medieval period and the modern world. The Renaissance was also a time of rediscovery of Classical ideas and art from ancient Greece and Rome. Artists such as Leonardo da Vinci and writers such as Shakespeare and Dante created their masterpieces during this fertile time. In part, tolerance of new ideas enabled the arts and sciences to flourish. How do you think Elizabeth influenced the development of the Renaissance in England?

Then, too, there were the daring explorers who pushed English expansion overseas. One of the queen's favorites, Sir Walter Raleigh, planned the colony of Virginia in America and named it for her, the Virgin Queen. The queen herself put money into several of the great voyages, keeping close watch over the plans and their results. She supported Sir Francis Drake on his three-year voyage around the world, profiting mightily from the immense loot he captured from Spanish ships taken in the Pacific.

DURING READING
Use Reading Strategies
Make Predictions How might have her father's actions affected Elizabeth?

For Elizabeth, one of the most urgent problems was the question of religion. Her father had broken with the Catholic church and launched the English Reformation, creating the Church of England, with himself at its head. When Elizabeth's older half sister, Mary (who remained Catholic), married the Catholic king of Spain, Philip II, she reconciled England with the Church of Rome. In Mary's brief reign she persecuted those Protestants who refused to conform, executing some 270 of them.

When Elizabeth became queen upon Mary's death, she said she hoped religion would not prevent her people from living together in peaceful unity. She did not want to pry into people's souls or question their faith. But in 1570, Pope Pius V excommunicated[10] her, denied her right to the throne, and declared her subjects owed her no allegiance. A directive from the pope's office decreed that the assassination of Queen Elizabeth would not be regarded as a sin. The effect of this directive was to turn practicing Catholics—about half of the English, most of them loyal—into potential traitors.

di•rec•tive (də rek´ tiv) *n.*, order or form of guidance

Though Elizabeth had wanted to pursue a middle way of toleration, circumstances threatened to overwhelm her. She had to beware of several Catholic monarchs of Europe who wished to see a Protestant England overthrown. Philip II of Spain sent ambassadors to England to urge Catholics to rise against Elizabeth, put her cousin Mary[11] on the throne, and restore Roman Catholicism as the national faith. The line between power, politics, and religion was becoming very thin.

The line between power, politics, and religion was becoming very thin.

Missionary priests living abroad were sent into England to stir up opposition to the queen. But the English Catholics as a body never rebelled, nor did they ever intend to. Still, missionary priests such as Edmund Campion were convicted of plotting against Elizabeth and executed.

In 1588 a long-threatened invasion of England by Spain was launched by Philip II. He mistakenly believed that the English Catholics were waiting to welcome him. News of his armada[12] of 130 big ships carrying 17,000 soldiers was terrifying. But the queen did not panic. She supervised the high command personally, meanwhile rallying popular support for the defense of the realm and sending troops to protect the coasts while Sir Francis Drake's ships set out to attack the Spanish fleet.

The Spanish Armada was defeated in three battles, its ships dispersed. When the news came of the tremendous victory, the citizens took to the streets, shouting for joy.

DURING READING

Use Reading Skills
Distinguish Fact from Opinion Why is this paragraph's first sentence a statement of fact?

The defeat of the Spanish Armada did not end Spain's aggression against England. The Jesuits[13] in England, who were especially identified with Spain, continued to be persecuted. Richard Topcliffe, a notorious hater of Catholics, was given authority to track down suspects. He examined them under torture to force information about people who had sheltered them. The treatment of them was so vicious and cruel that the victims welcomed death as a release from their agony.

---

10. excommunicated. Excluded from a church or a religious community
11. Mary. Mary Stuart, the Queen of Scotland, not Elizabeth's half sister
12. armada. Large fleet of warships
13. Jesuits. Members of the Roman Catholic Society of Jesus

During Elizabeth's reign several plots to assassinate her were uncovered. Elizabeth managed to give the impression that she was not frightened, but those close to her knew she was. When one of the major plots proved to center around Elizabeth's cousin, Mary Queen of Scots, Elizabeth found it almost intolerable to put to death a crowned queen. Yet she ordered the use of torture on Mary's co-conspirators, and in the end, Mary was beheaded. A song composed by William Byrd at the time suggests how ominous the news of a monarch's execution was:

om•i•nous (äm´ ə nəs) *adj.*, foreboding or foreshadowing evil

The noble famous Queen
who lost her head of late
Doth show that kings as well as clowns
Are bound to fortune's fate,
And that no earthly Prince
Can so secure his crown
But fortune with her whirling wheel
Hath power to pull them down.

When two earls combined forces against her, Elizabeth's troops overcame them. The queen was so enraged she ordered that 800 of the mostly poor rebels be hanged. But she spared the lives of their wealthy leaders so that they might enrich her, either by buying their pardons or by forfeiting their lands.

for•feit (for´ fət) *v.*, lose or fail to win the right to something by some error, offense, or crime

Elizabeth came down hard on writers who criticized her actions. John Stubbs, a zealous[14] Puritan, wrote a pamphlet expressing horror at the possibility the queen might marry a French Catholic. The queen had Stubbs and his publisher tried and convicted for seditious libel.[15] How dare Stubbs say publicly she was too old to marry, and that the much younger French suitor could not possibly be in love with her? Elizabeth was merciless as she invoked the penalty for libel. With a butcher's cleaver, the executioner cut the right hands off Stubbs and his publisher. Not an uncommon punishment.

DURING READING

Analyze Literature
Biography How does this information about these punishments affect your understanding of Elizabeth?

How did Elizabeth learn of all these plots and conspiracies? How did she know what plans Philip II of Spain was devising to invade her kingdom? Spies and secret agents—they were her eyes and ears. Crucial to the flow of information was Sir Francis Walsingham. Trained as a lawyer, he lived on the Continent[16] for years, mastering the languages and the ins and outs of European affairs. Upon his return home, he was asked by Sir William Cecil,

14. zealous. Filled with eagerness in pursuit of something
15. seditious libel. Crime of lying to create opposition to authority
16. Continent. European continent

the queen's right arm, to gather information on the doings and plans of foreign governments. Soon he was made chief of England's secret service. He placed over seventy agents and spies in the courts of Europe. And of course he watched closely the activities of people at home suspected of disloyalty. Letters to and from them were secretly opened, to nip plots in the bud.

Monarchs had absolute power. Elizabeth could arrest anyone, including the topmost ranks of the nobility, and imprison them in the Tower of London even if they had not committed any legal offense. The only thing that held her back was her fear of public opinion. It upset her when a crowd gathered at a public execution and was so disgusted by the butchery that they let out roars of disapproval. Still, like all rulers, Elizabeth said she believed that "born a sovereign princess" she enjoyed "the privilege common to all kings" and was "exempt from human jurisdiction[17] and subject only to the judgement of God."

Elizabeth came down hard on writers who criticized her actions.

Despite her blazing nervous energy, Elizabeth was often sick. Her ailments were anxiously reported and discussed. For the English believed her survival was their only guarantee of freedom from foreign invasion and civil war. Once, suffering a raging toothache for the first time, the queen feared the pain of having an extraction. She had never had a tooth pulled and was terrified. To reassure her, an old friend, the Bishop of London, had her watch while the dental surgeon pulled out one of the bishop's own good teeth. And then she consented to have her own taken out.

DURING READING

Analyze Literature

Biography Why might the author have included this detail about the queen's toothache?

It was commonly believed then that kings and queens had the magical power to cure disease in their subjects. Eager to demonstrate that she too had the sacred power of royalty, Elizabeth prayed intensely before using the royal touch on people with scrofula, a nasty skin disease. Her chaplain said he watched "her exquisite hands, boldly, and without disgust, pressing the sores and ulcers." In one day it was reported that she healed thirty-eight persons. But if she did not feel divinely inspired, she would not try her touch.

Even in the last decade of her life, Elizabeth's energy was astonishing. She was as watchful as always over the affairs of state, though sometimes forgetful. But age made her more irritable; she sometimes shouted at her ladies and even boxed their ears. She was less able to control rival factions out for power, and became so fearful of assassins she rarely left her palaces.

---

17. jurisdiction. Authority to apply the law

A portrait of her done when she was approaching sixty shows her in a great white silk dress studded with aglets[18] of black onyx, coral, and pearl. She wears three ropes of translucent pearls and stands on a map of England, her England. An ambassador reported that at sixty-three she looked old, but her figure was still beautiful, and her conversation was as brilliant and charming as ever.

There was dancing at court every evening, a pastime she still enjoyed. When it came to displays of gallantry by eager young men, she could act a bit vain and foolish, although never letting any hopeful get out of bounds.

DURING READING

Make Connections
Do you agree that Elizabeth was "a rare genius"?

In early 1603 Elizabeth developed a bad cold that led to a serious fever, and then she fell into a stupor[19] for four days. As she lay dying, all of London became strangely silent. On March 24, the life of a rare genius ended. The nation went into mourning.

"Old age came upon me as a surprise, like a frost," she once wrote. ✣

18. aglets. Ornamental pins

19. stupor. State of shock or greatly dulled sense

What are your impressions of Elizabeth? Who in the modern world do you think shares some or many of her traits? How does Elizabeth compare with heads of countries today? What could today's leaders learn from her?

Find Meaning

1. What happened to Elizabeth's mother?
2. (a) What were people's attitudes toward having a female ruler? (b) How did Elizabeth deal with these attitudes?
3. (a) The author suggests some reasons for Elizabeth's refusal to marry. What are these reasons? (b) What did Elizabeth herself declare about this matter to a delegation from Parliament?

Make Judgments

4. Why do you think people were impressed with Elizabeth's grand processions through London?
5. (a) What was at the heart of the religious conflict in England? (b) How did Elizabeth deal with this conflict?
6. Why do you think the author chose Elizabeth as the subject of a biography?

PRIMARY SOURCE ▶▶ CONNECTION

In "Elizabeth I," Milton Meltzer tells of the life of a remarkable English queen. The following selection includes part of a speech Elizabeth gave to the English Parliament, two of her poems, and an excerpt from a letter she wrote to Mary Queen of Scots. As you read, recall what you already know about Elizabeth's life.

Writings by Queen Elizabeth I

from Queen Elizabeth's Speech to Her Last Parliament

Mr. Speaker,

And if my Princely bounty have been abused, and my Grants turned to the hurt of my People contrary to my will and meaning, or if any in Authority under me have neglected, or converted what I have committed unto them, I hope God they will not lay their culps[1] to my charge.

To be a King, and wear a Crown, is a thing more glorious to them that see it, than it is pleasant to them that bear it: for my self, I never was so much enticed with the glorious name of a King, or the royal authority of a Queen, as delighted that god hath made me His Instrument to maintain His Truth and Glory, and to defend this Kingdome from dishonor, damage, tyranny, and oppression....

Thus Mr. Speaker, I commend me to your loyal Loves, and yours to my best care and your further Councils, & I pray you Mr. Controller, & Mr. Secretary, and you of my council, that before these Gentlemen depart into their Countries you bring them all to kiss my Hand. ✣

1. **culps.** Blame

Written with a Diamond on Her Window at Woodstock

Much suspected of me,
Nothing proved can be,
Quoth[2] Elizabeth prisoner. ✤

Written in Her French Psalter[3]

No crooked leg, no bleared[4] eye,
No part deformed out of kind,
Nor yet so ugly half can be
As is the inward suspicious mind. ✤

from Letter to Mary Queen of Scots, 1586

You have in various ways and manners attempted to take my life and to bring my kingdom to destruction by bloodshed. I have never proceeded so harshly against you, but have, on the contrary, protected and maintained you like myself. These treasons will be proved to you and all made manifest.[5] Yet it is my will, that you answer the nobles and peers of the kingdom as if I were myself present. I therefore require, charge, and command that you make answer for I have been well informed of your arrogance. ✤

2. **quoth.** Said
3. **psalter.** Prayer book
4. **bleared.** Watery
5. **manifest.** Evident; clear

TEXT TO TEXT CONNECTION

Both Milton Meltzer's biography and Elizabeth's writings present insights into Elizabeth's life. Compare and contrast what each writer tells. Which selection or selections most reveal Elizabeth's innermost thoughts? Do Elizabeth's writings support the picture of her character as portrayed by Meltzer?

AFTER READING

Analyze Literature

Biography Biographers typically present both facts and opinions about their subjects. Given this selection, what do you think is the biographer's overall opinion of Elizabeth? Do you think he admires her? What evidence from the story supports your answer? Use a web like the one on the right to record words and phrases that indicate whether or not Meltzer admires Elizabeth.

Now review the selection and list any facts that support the biographer's opinion. For example, does Meltzer provide any evidence that Elizabeth was a genius? In a separate list, record any facts that contradict the biographer's opinion. Compare the two lists. Do you think the author's opinion of Elizabeth is fair and accurate? Explain your answer.

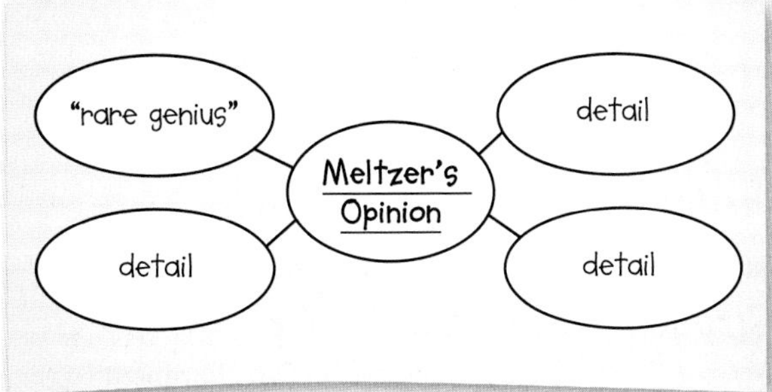

Extend Understanding

Writing Options

Creative Writing Write a one- or two-page **dialogue** between Elizabeth and one of her suitors. Assume that Elizabeth has already said she is not going to marry. Assume also that the suitor is convinced he can change her mind. The suitor should try to persuade Elizabeth by suggesting various logical and emotional advantages to her marriage with him. Elizabeth should respond accordingly. Present your dialogue to the class.

Informative Writing In the excerpt from her last speech to Parliament, Elizabeth says, "To be a King, and wear a Crown, is a thing more glorious to them that see it, than it is pleasant to them that bear it...." In an **informative paragraph,** explain why Elizabeth might have felt this way, given the events of her life. Include a thesis statement and evidence from Meltzer's biography in your paragraph.

Collaborative Learning

Analyze Speech Government leaders are known for giving persuasive speeches. A **policy speech** attempts to persuade listeners to support a change in government policy. These often contain quotations from experts and arguments that address policy issues. In a group, identify and read the text of a contemporary policy speech. Interpret the speaker's purpose by asking questions or making comments about the evidence presented. Finally, analyze the structure of the speech's central argument and identify the different types of evidence used to support the argument. Present your findings to the class.

Critical Literacy

Conduct an Interview Working in pairs, with one person acting as reporter and the other as Elizabeth, conduct an interview. The interview might cover such topics as Elizabeth's views on marriage and government, her leisure activities, and her opinions about religion.

Go to **www.mirrorsandwindows.com** for more.

Vocabulary & Spelling

Greek, Latin, and Anglo-Saxon Roots

She learned history, geography, mathematics, and the elements of astronomy and architecture.

—MILTON MELTZER, "Elizabeth I"

Thousands of common English words are formed from **Latin** and **Greek roots** or base words. In the sentence above, the word *geography* is formed by joining two Greek roots: *geo* meaning "earth" and *graph* meaning "describe." *Architecture* is formed from the Greek roots *arkhi* meaning "chief" and *tekton* meaning "builder."

Anglo-Saxon roots are derived from Old English, which was spoken from the fifth to the twelfth century. The meaning of some modern words is different from the root meaning. For example, *prestige* comes from the Latin word *praestigium*, which meant "deceptive" or "full of tricks." Today, the word means "status," or "standing in general opinion."

Common Roots

Root Word	Meaning	Origin	English Words
alt	"high"	Latin	altitude, altimeter
bio	"life"	Greek	biology, bionic
duc	"lead, bring, take"	Latin	produce, deduce
kno	"skill"	Anglo-Saxon	know, knowledge
nym	"name"	Greek	synonym, antonym
side	"boundary, edge"	Anglo-Saxon	inside, sideline

Root Word	Meaning	Origin	English Words
fare	"go"	Anglo-Saxon	farewell, welfare
spell	"recite"	Anglo-Saxon	spelling, gospel
aster	"star"	Greek	asteroid, asterisk
photo	"light"	Greek	photography, photosynthesis
equi	"equal"	Latin	equilateral, equidistant

Vocabulary Practice

Use a dictionary to find the roots or base words for each of these words from "Elizabeth I." Then write the meaning as it is used in the text.

1. script
2. succession
3. prosperity
4. coronation
5. revival
6. jurisdiction
7. blazing
8. artisans
9. Renaissance
10. armada

Spelling Practice

Words with *ei* or *ie*

A common rule for the vowel combination *ei* or *ie* is the following: "*I* before *e,* except after *c* or when sounded long *a* as in *neighbor* or *weigh.*" However, that saying does not cover every instance. Examine this list of words from "Elizabeth I" to see if they follow this rule.

ancient	foreign	priests
believe	forfeiting	reign
chief	friend	reins
eighteen	medieval	sciences
fields	neither	sovereign

Literary Element

Understanding the Essay

What Is an Essay?

An **essay** is a short nonfiction work that expresses a writer's thoughts about a single subject. A well-written essay clearly presents information and usually has an introduction, body, and conclusion.

Elements of an Essay

Essays all share some common elements.

An **author's purpose** is the goal or aim the writer wants to accomplish with his or her essay. For example, an author might write to inform, to explain, to entertain, to tell a story, or to persuade.

The **audience** is the person or group for whom the author is writing. Audiences affect the way an author writes. For example, an essay intended for an audience unfamiliar with the essay's subject would contain little technical vocabulary.

Tone is the writer's attitude toward the subject or the reader. For example, a writer might use a lighthearted, informal tone when writing about something happy or funny.

Voice is the way a writer uses language to reflect his or her unique personality and attitude toward topic, form, and audience. A writer expresses voice through tone, word choice, and sentence structure.

Point of View is the vantage point from which a story is told. Most essays are written in either the first- or third-person point of view. If a story is told from the first-person point of view, the narrator uses the pronouns *I* and *we* and is a part of the action. When a story is told from a third-person point of view, the narrator is outside the action and uses pronouns such as *he, she, it,* and *they*.

Types of Essays

There are three main types of essays.

A **personal essay** is a short nonfiction work on a single topic related to the life of the writer. A personal essay is written from the author's point of view and often uses the pronouns *I* and *me*.

> *I write to find out what I'm thinking. I write to find out who I am. I write to understand things.*
>
> —JULIA ALVAREZ

An **argumentative essay** presents an argument in order to persuade or convince a reader. The writer supports his or her argument with evidence, such as facts and examples.

An **informative essay** is written to communicate facts. Since the main purpose is to inform, the tone is usually formal. The informative essays that you will encounter in this book appear in Unit 4. For example, Robert Jastrow's "The Size of Things" (page 378) communicates information about the size of the universe.

Apply the Model

BEFORE READING

DURING READING

AFTER READING

GUIDED READING

Names/Nombres

A Personal Essay by Julia Alvarez

Build Background

Historical Context Julia Alvarez was raised in the Dominican Republic, a Spanish-speaking island country in the Caribbean. At the time of Alvarez's birth, the Dominican Republic was ruled by a dictator, Rafael Trujillo. Alvarez's father joined the underground movement that attempted to overthrow Trujillo, but the attempt failed, and in 1960 her family fled to New York City.

Reader's Context How would you feel if everyone suddenly started addressing you by a new name?

Set Purpose

Skim the text to look for unfamiliar terms. Identify and define these terms ahead of time to read without interruption.

Analyze Literature

Personal Essay A short nonfiction work that is written to express the writer's thoughts about a single subject is called a **personal essay.** Personal essays are written from the first-person point of view, using pronouns such as *I* and *we*. Personal essays frequently reveal something about the life of the essay's author and can be written for a variety of purposes.

Use Reading Skills

Identify Author's Purpose Using a graphic organizer can help you determine whether the author's main purpose for writing is to inform, to entertain, or to persuade. Look at the title, skim the selection, and read the footnotes. Then write your observations in the Before Reading section of the chart. Next, read the essay and list the main ideas the author communicates in the During Reading section. Then, in the After Reading section, summarize the author's purpose.

Before Reading	During Reading	After Reading
The author speaks two languages.		

Meet the Author

Julia Alvarez (b. 1950) was ten years old when her family moved back to New York City from the Dominican Republic. Julia worked hard to be proficient in English. She says that having to "pay close attention to each word [was] great training for a writer." She has taught at several colleges and universities and is writer-in-residence at Middlebury College in Vermont. Her works of fiction include *How the Garcia Girls Lost Their Accents* and *Yo!* Alvarez has also published several poetry collections.

Preview Vocabulary

eth•ni•ci•ty (eth ni´ sə tē) *n.,* belonging to a racial, cultural, or national group

spec•i•fy (spe´ sə fī') *v.,* state explicitly

cha•ot•ic (kā ät´ ik) *adj.,* in a state of disorder or confusion

com•mence•ment (kəm men[t]s´ mənt) *adj.,* graduation

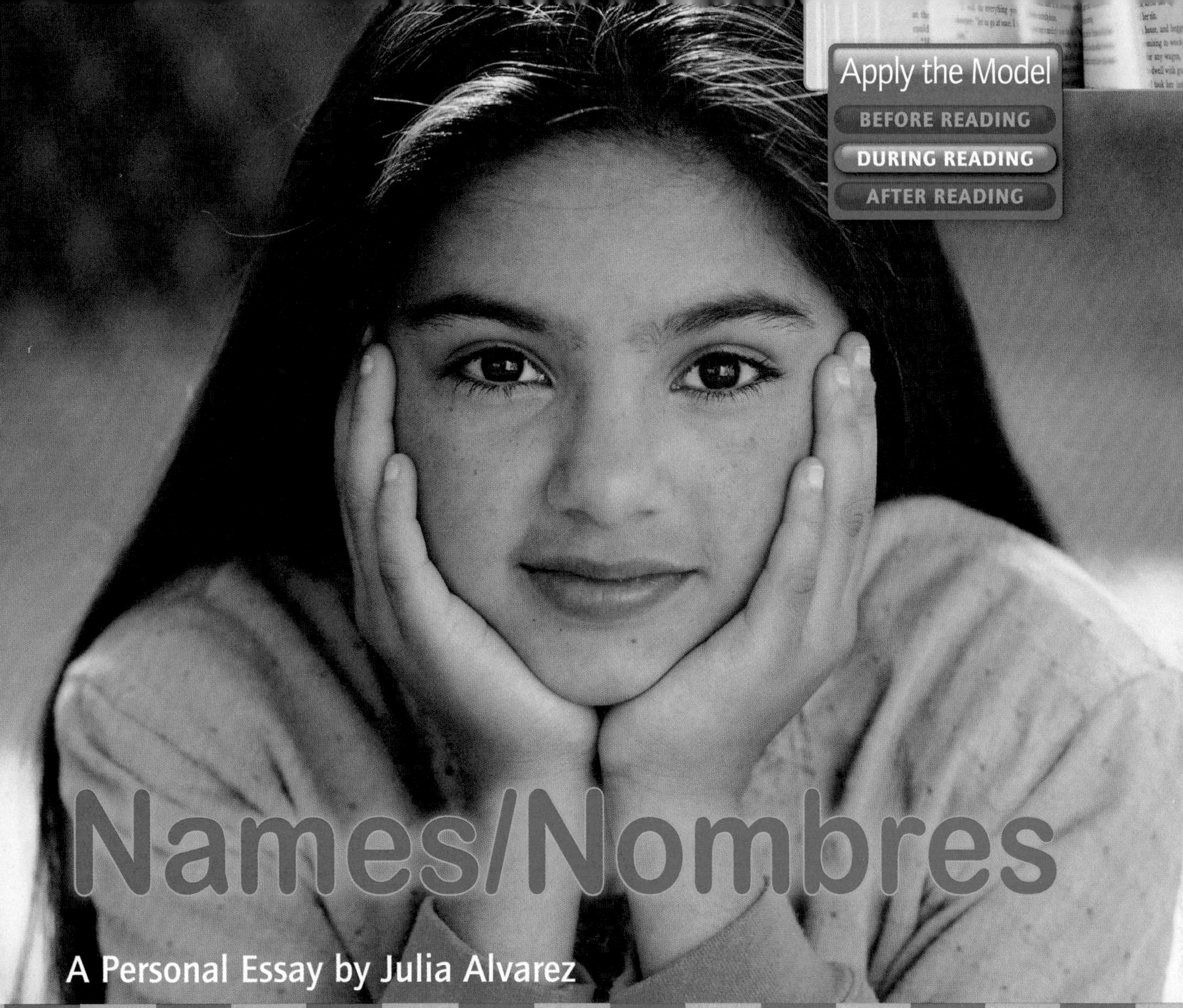

Names/Nombres

A Personal Essay by Julia Alvarez

When we arrived in New York City, our names changed almost immediately. At Immigration, the officer asked my father, *Mister Elbures,* if he had anything to declare. My father shook his head no, and we were waved through.

I was too afraid we wouldn't be let in if I corrected the man's pronunciation, but I said our name to myself, opening my mouth wide for the organ blast of the *a,* trilling my tongue for the drumroll of the *r, All-vah-rrr-es!* How could anyone get *Elbures* out of that orchestra of sound?

At the hotel my mother was *Missus Alburest,* and I was *little girl,* as in, "Hey, little girl, stop riding the elevator up and down. It's *not* a toy."

When we moved into our apartment building, the super called my father *Mister Alberase,* and the neighbors who became mother's

"Say your name in Spanish, oh, please say it!"

JUDY ALCATRAZ, the name on the "Wanted" poster would read.

friends pronounced her name *Jew-lee-ah* instead of *Hoo-lee-ah.* I, her namesake, was known as *Hoo-lee-tah* at home. But at school I was *Judy or Judith,* and once an English teacher mistook me for *Juliet.*

It took a while to get used to my new names. I wondered if I shouldn't correct my teachers and new friends. But my mother argued that it didn't matter. "You know what your friend Shakespeare said, '*A rose by any other name would smell as sweet.*'" My family had gotten into the habit of calling any famous author "my friend" because I had begun to write poems and stories in English class.

By the time I was in high school, I was a popular kid, and it showed in my name. Friends called me *Jules* or *Hey Jude,* and once a group of troublemaking friends my mother forbade me to hang out with called me *Alcatraz.*[1] I was *Hoo-lee-tah* only to Mami and Papi and uncles and aunts who came over to eat *sancocho*[2] on Sunday afternoons—old world folk whom I would just as soon go back to where they came from and leave me to pursue whatever mischief I wanted to in America. *JUDY ALCATRAZ,* the name on the "Wanted" poster would read. Who would ever trace her to me?

DURING READING

Make Connections
Why do you think the name *Judy Alcatraz* is so much more appealing to the author than *"Hoo-lee-tah"*?

My older sister had the hardest time getting an American name for herself because *Mauricia* did not translate into English. Ironically, although she had the most foreign-sounding name, she and I were the Americans in the family. We had been born in New York City when our parents had first tried immigration and then gone back "home," too homesick to stay. My mother often told the story of how she almost changed my sister's name in the hospital.

After the delivery, Mami and some other new mothers were cooing over their newborn sons and daughters and exchanging names, weights and delivery stories. My mother was embarrassed among the Sallys and Janes, Georges and Johns to reveal the rich, noisy name of *Mauricia,* so when her turn came to brag, she gave her baby's name as *Maureen.*

"Why'd ya give her an Irish name with so many pretty Spanish names to choose from?" one of the women asked.

My mother blushed and admitted her baby's real name to the group. Her mother-in-law had recently died, she apologized, and her husband had insisted that the first daughter be named after his mother, *Mauran.* My mother thought it the ugliest name she had

---

1. **Alcatraz.** From the mid-1930s to the mid-1960s, a maximum-security prison for America's toughest criminals
2. ***sancocho*** (san kô´ chō). Caribbean meat stew (Spanish)

ever heard, and talked my father into what she believed was an improvement, a combination of *Mauran* and her own mother's name, *Felicia.*

"Her name is *Mao-ree-shee-ah,*" my mother said to the group of women.

"Why, that's a beautiful name," the other mothers cried. "*Moor-ee-sha, Moor-ee-sha,*" she cooed into the pink blanket. *Moor-ee-sha* it was when we returned to the States eleven years later. Sometimes, American tongues found that mispronunciation tough to say and called her *Maria* or *Marsha* or *Maudy* from her nickname *Maury*. I pitied her. What an awful name to have to transport across borders!

GEOGRAPHY ▶▶ CONNECTION

The Dominican Republic The Dominican Republic occupies two thirds of the island of Hispaniola, which is part of the Greater Antilles chain in the Caribbean Sea. Haiti occupies the remaining third of the island. The Atlantic Ocean is to the north, and the Caribbean Sea is to the south; the island of Puerto Rico is to the east, and Cuba is to the west. The capital city of the Dominican Republic is Santo Domingo. It is a mountainous country, with many rivers and fertile land. The climate is tropical, with a rainy season from May to November. Christopher Columbus landed on Hispaniola in 1492 and founded the first European settlement in America there. Why might it be difficult for Julia to adapt to her new environment?

My little sister, Ana, had the easiest time of all. She was plain *Anne*—that is, only her name was plain, for she turned out to be the pale, blond "American beauty" in the family. The only Hispanic thing about her was the affectionate nicknames her boyfriends sometimes gave her. *Anita*, or, as one goofy guy used to sing to her to the tune of the banana advertisement, *Anita Banana*.

Later, during her college years in the late sixties, there was a push to pronounce Third World[3] names correctly. I remember calling her long distance at her group house and a roommate answering.

"Can I speak to Ana?" I asked, pronouncing her name the American way.

"Ana?" The man's voice hesitated. "Oh! You must mean *Ah-nah!*"

eth • ni • ci • ty (eth ni´ sə tē) *n.*, belonging to a racial, cultural, or national group

Our first few years in the States, though, ethnicity was not yet "in." Those were the blond, blue-eyed, bobby-sock years of junior high and high school before the sixties ushered in peasant blouses, hoop earrings, *sarapes.*[4] My initial desire to be known by my correct Dominican name faded. I just wanted to be Judy and merge with the Sallys and Janes in my class. But, inevitably, my accent and coloring gave me away. "So where are you from, Judy?"

DURING READING

Use Reading Skills

Author's Purpose Compare the anecdotes about the two sisters' names. What point do you think the author is making?

"New York," I told my classmates. After all, I had been born blocks away at Columbia-Presbyterian Hospital.

"I mean, *originally*."

spec • i • fy (spe´ sə fī') *v.*, state explicitly

"From the Caribbean," I answered vaguely, for if I specified, no one was quite sure on what continent our island was located.

"Really? I've been to Bermuda. We went last April for spring vacation. I got the worst sunburn! So, are you from Portoriko?"[5]

"No," I sighed. "From the Dominican Republic."

"Where's that?"

"South of Bermuda."

They were just being curious, I knew, but I burned with shame whenever they singled me out as a "foreigner," a rare, exotic friend.

"Say your name in Spanish, oh, please say it!" I had made mouths drop one day by rattling off my full name, which, according to Dominican custom, included my middle names, Mother's and Father's surnames for four generations back.

---

3. **Third World.** Developing countries of Latin America, Africa, and Asia
4. ***sarapes*** (sə rä´ pēs). Woolen shawls or ponchos (Spanish)
5. **Portoriko.** Puerto Rico

Civil flag of the Dominican Republic.

"Julia Altagracia María Teresa Álvarez Tavares Perello Espaillat Julia Pérez Rochet González." I pronounced it slowly, a name as chaotic with sounds as a Middle Eastern bazaar or market day in a South American village.

My Dominican heritage was never more apparent than when my extended family attended school occasions. For my graduation, they all came, the whole lot of aunts and uncles and the many little cousins who snuck in without tickets. They sat in the first row in order to better understand the Americans' fast-spoken English. But how could they listen when they were constantly speaking among themselves in florid-sounding phrases, rococo[6] consonants, rich, rhyming vowels?

Introducing them to my friends was a further trial to me. These relatives had such complicated names and there were so many of them, and their relationships to myself were so convoluted. There was my Tía[7] Josefina, who was not really an aunt but a much older cousin. And her daughter, Aida Margarita, who was adopted, una hija de crianza.[8] My uncle of affection, Tío José, brought my *madrina*[9] Tía Amelia and her *comadre*[10] Tía Pilar. My friends rarely had more than a "Mom and Dad" to introduce.

DURING READING

Analyze Literature

Personal Essay What does the author want to communicate to the reader about her attitude toward her name?

cha•ot•ic (kā ät´ ik) *adj.*, in a state of disorder or confusion

DURING READING

Use Reading Skills

Meaning of Words Knowing the meaning of foreign words, such as *madrina* and *comadre,* can be helpful. Identify the meaning and origin of the following foreign words and phrases: *que sera sera, eureka,* and *ad nauseam.*

---

6. rococo. Fancy, flamboyant

7. Tía (tē´ ä). Aunt (Spanish); Tío (tē´ ō) is uncle.

8. *una hija de crianza* (ü´ nä ē´ hä de krē än´ sä). An adopted daughter (Spanish)

9. *madrina* (mä drē nä). Godmother (Spanish)

10. *comadre* (kō mä´ drā). Close friend (Spanish)

com • mence • ment (kəm men[t]s´ mənt) *adj.*, graduation

After the commencement ceremony, my family waited outside in the parking lot while my friends and I signed yearbooks with nicknames which recalled our high school good times: "Beans" and "Pepperoni" and "Alcatraz." We hugged and cried and promised to keep in touch.

Our goodbyes went on too long. I heard my father's voice calling out across the parking lot, "*Hoo-lee-tah! Vámonos!*"[11]

Back home, my tíos and tías and primas,[12] Mami and Papi, and *mis hermanas*[13] had a party for me with sancocho and a store-bought *pudín,*[14] inscribed with *Happy Graduation, Julie.* There were many gifts—that was a plus to a large family! I got several wallets and a suitcase with my initials and a graduation charm from my godmother and money from my uncles. The biggest gift was a portable typewriter from my parents for writing my stories and poems.

Someday, the family predicted, my name would be well-known throughout the United States. I laughed to myself, wondering which one I would go by. ✣

DURING READING

Analyze Literature

Personal Essay How does the conclusion of the essay tie back to the beginning?

11. ***Vámonos*** (vä´ mä nōs'). Let's go (Spanish)
12. **primas** (prē´ mäs'). Cousins (Spanish)
13. ***mis hermanas*** (mēs ār mä´ näs). My sisters (Spanish)
14. ***pudín*** (pů dēn´). Pudding (Spanish)

Julia Alvarez, at one point, was willing to change her name to Judy to be more like her classmates. What would you have done in her place? Why do you think people feel the need to fit in?

Find Meaning

1. (a) According to the author, what happens to her family's name at Immigration? (b) Why do you think she repeats the family's name to herself?
2. (a) What does the author's mother advise about correcting the pronunciation of teachers and new friends? (b) Does she follow her mother's advice? Explain.
3. (a) Why does Mrs. Alvarez almost change her daughter's name at the hospital? (b) What conflict does this anecdote foreshadow in the author's life?

Make Judgments

4. Why does Alvarez say that her older sister's name is "an awful name to have to transport across borders"?
5. Although the author says she dislikes being considered "exotic" by her classmates, she takes pleasure in "rattling off" her full name for them. What does this reveal about her feelings?
6. (a) Why does the author describe how her family differs from the families of her classmates? (b) Are these differences really important to her? Explain.
7. (a) What name does the author use when she becomes a professional writer? (b) What does this say about her attitude toward her name?

LITERATURE ▶▶ CONNECTION

In her personal essay, "Names/Nombres," Julia Alvarez reflects on immigration, cultural heritage, and identity. The writer of the following poem, **Janet S. Wong,** was born in the United States to parents who had emigrated from China and Korea. Wong's poetry reflects her cultural heritage and her Asian-American identity. As you read "Face It," think about the significance of the poem's title.

Face It

A Lyric Poem by Janet S. Wong

My nose belongs
to Guangdong, China—
short and round, a Jang family nose.

My eyes belong
to Alsace, France—
wide like Grandmother Hemmerling's.

But my mouth, my big-talking mouth,
belongs
to me, alone. ✤

TEXT ◂TO▸ TEXT CONNECTION

Both Julia Alvarez's essay and Janet Wong's poem explore ideas about cultural heritage and identity. In what ways are the two selections similar? In what ways do they differ? How important is cultural heritage to Alvarez and to the speaker in the poem?

AFTER READING

Analyze Literature

Personal Essay A personal essay is greatly affected by its tone. Tone is the author's attitude toward his or her subject. For example, an author's tone might be humorous, angry, or thoughtful. Use this web to determine the tone of "Names/Nombres." Write details from the essay in the outer ovals. Then write the tone in the center oval.

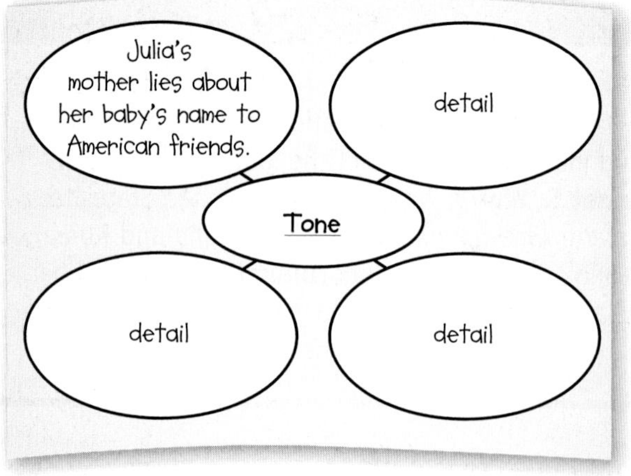

Extend Understanding

Writing Options

Creative Writing Pretend that you are Julia and you want to invite one of your family members to attend your graduation. Write an **invitation** to this family member, stating why you would like the person to come. Note how you feel about the event. Remember to include the date, time, and location of the ceremony.

Informative Writing Is the theme, or central idea, of "Name/Nombres" stated in the essay or is it implied? Write an **informative paragraph** in which you describe the theme. Provide examples from the essay that support your analysis. Share your analysis with the class.

Lifelong Learning

Gather Historical Information Learn more about Alvarez's background by researching the history of the Dominican Republic, where she spent her first ten years. Write a short history of the nation on note cards or in an outline, and then present your findings to the class.

Critical Literacy

Conduct a Panel Discussion What's in a name? Use "Names/Nombres" as a starting point for discussing the importance of names. Do you agree with Shakespeare that "A rose by any other name would smell as sweet"? Can a person's name affect his or her self-image or how others perceive him or her? What do you think parents should consider when they decide on names for their children?

 Go to **www.mirrorsandwindows.com** for more.

Apply the Model

BEFORE READING

DURING READING

AFTER READING

The Eternal Frontier

An Argumentative Essay by Louis L'Amour

GUIDED READING

Build Background

Scientific Context When *Apollo 11* landed on the moon in 1969, extensive space exploration seemed within reach. In the 1970s, satellites were put into orbit, space stations were planned and piloted, and robotic missions were launched. In 1984, the year this essay was written, President Reagan announced plans to build an international space station. This meant that funds were going to be concentrated more on the space station than on sending rockets to explore the solar system.

Reader's Context What do you think is the most important frontier today? The most exciting? The most challenging?

Set Purpose

As you read the essay, pay attention to how the author appeals to both your emotions and logic.

Analyze Literature

Argumentative Essay In an **argumentative essay,** the author expresses a particular viewpoint and attempts to sway the reader to agree with that position. In addition to presenting logical arguments based on reasons and evidence, an author may use persuasive techniques that rely on faulty reasoning or emotional appeals. As you read "The Eternal Frontier," decide what the author's viewpoint is and evaluate the evidence he provides to support that viewpoint.

Use Reading Skills

Analyze Main Idea and Supporting Details To identify the main idea of "The Eternal Frontier," gather details in a main idea map. Then examine the details to determine the author's overall message.

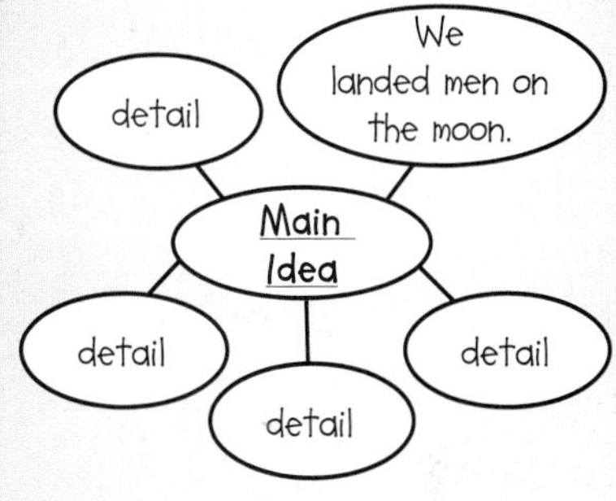

Preview Vocabulary

pre•lim•i•nar•y (pri li´ mə ner' ē) *adj.*, preparing for the main action or event

an•ti•dote (an´ ti dōt') *n.*, remedy

in•cor•po•rate (in kôr´ pə rāt') *v.*, combine into one body

Meet the Author

Louis L'Amour (1908–1988) grew up in North Dakota listening to stories about his grandfather's experiences in the Civil War. L'Amour became an avid reader of history and adventure books. As a young man, L'Amour worked as a lumberjack, a seaman, and a boxer. After serving in World War II, L'Amour began writing Westerns for magazines. By the 1980s, he was a best-selling author. He was the first novelist to be awarded a Congressional gold medal. In 1984, he received the Presidential Medal of Freedom.

The Eternal Frontier

An Argumentative Essay by Louis L'Amour

The question I am most often asked is, "Where is the frontier now?"

The answer should be obvious. Our frontier lies in outer space. The moon, the asteroids, the planets, these are mere stepping stones, where we will test ourselves, learn needful lessons, and grow in knowledge before we attempt those frontiers beyond our solar system. Outer space is a frontier without end, the eternal frontier, an everlasting challenge to explorers not [only] of other planets and other solar systems but also of the mind of man.

All that has gone before was preliminary. We have been preparing ourselves mentally for what lies ahead. Many problems remain, but if we can avoid a devastating[1] war we shall move with a rapidity scarcely to be believed. In the past seventy years we have developed the automobile, radio, television, transcontinental and transoceanic flight, and the electrification of the country, among a multitude of other such developments. In 1900 there were 144 miles of surfaced road in the United States. Now there are over 3,000,000. Paved roads and the development of the automobile have gone hand in hand, the automobile being civilized man's antidote to overpopulation.

pre•lim•i•nar•y (pri li´ mə ner' ē) *adj.*, preparing for the main action or event

an•ti•dote (an´ ti dōt') *n.*, remedy

What is needed now is leaders with perspective; we need leadership on a thousand fronts, but they must be men and women who can take the long view and help to shape the outlines of our future. There will always be the nay-sayers,[2] those who cling to our lovely green planet as a baby clings to its mother, but there will be others like those who have taken us this far along the path to a limitless future.

DURING READING

Analyze Literature
Argumentative Essay How would you paraphrase the argument in this paragraph?

We are a people born to the frontier. It has been a part of our thinking, waking, and sleeping since men first landed on this continent. The frontier is the line that separates the known from the unknown wherever it may be, and we have a driving need to see what lies beyond....

A few years ago we moved into outer space. We landed men on the moon; we sent a vehicle beyond the limits of the solar system, a vehicle still moving farther and farther into that limitless distance.[3]

1. **devastating.** Extremely destructive
2. **nay-sayers.** People who disagree
3. **we sent a vehicle...into that limitless distance.** Reference to *Voyager 1*, an unmanned probe launched in 1977 to explore the far reaches of the universe

DURING READING

Use Reading Skills
Analyze Main Idea and Supporting Details What is the author's main point in this paragraph?

If our world were to die tomorrow, that tiny vehicle would go on and on forever, carrying its mighty message to the stars. Out there, someone, sometime, would know that once we existed, that we had the vision and we made the effort. Mankind is not bound by its atmospheric envelope or by its gravitational field, nor is the mind of man bound by any limits at all.

DURING READING

Make Connections
Does L'Amour provide a logical answer to his question? Do you agree with what he says? Explain.

One might ask—why outer space, when so much remains to be done here? If that had been the spirit of man we would still be hunters and food gatherers, growling over the bones of carrion[4] in a cave somewhere. It is our destiny to move out, to accept the challenge, to dare the unknown. It is our destiny to achieve.

Yet we must not forget that along the way to outer space whole industries are springing into being that did not exist before. The computer age has arisen in part from the space effort, which gave great impetus[5] to the development of computing devices. Transistors, chips, integrated circuits, Teflon, new medicines, new ways of treating diseases, new ways of performing operations, all these and a multitude of other developments that enable man to live and to live better are linked to the space effort. Most of these developments have been so incorporated into our day-to-day life that they are taken for granted, their origin not considered.

in • cor • po • rate (in kôr´ pə rāt') *v.*, combine into one body

If we are content to live in the past, we have no future. And today is the past. ✣

---

4. **carrion.** Dead and decaying flesh
5. **impetus.** Stimulus; force or energy associated with movement

Do you agree with L'Amour's viewpoint? Should humanity be trying to explore space? Why do you think exploration has been such a consistent part of human life for so long?

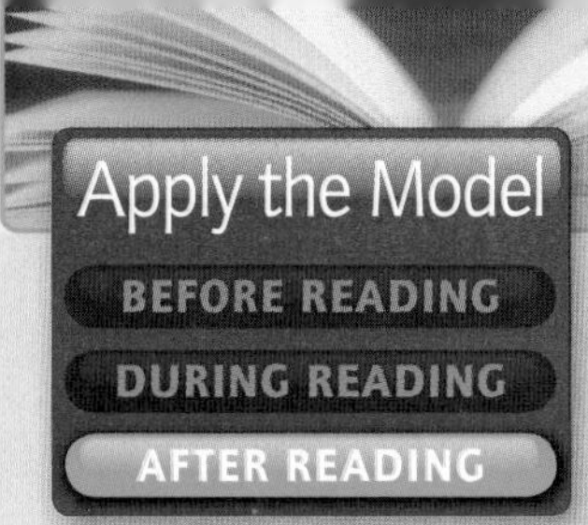

Find Meaning

1. (a) What does Louis L'Amour think is "today's" frontier? (b) Why does he describe the moon, asteroids, and planets as stepping stones?
2. Why does L'Amour include the comparison between the number of paved roads in the United States in 1900 and the number of paved roads now?

Make Judgments

3. When L'Amour recounts the achievements of the moon landing, how does his use of words, phrases, and repetition reveal his opinion of these efforts?
4. Why does L'Amour include a list of the space program's accomplishments?
5. L'Amour says, "If we are content to live in the past, we have no future. And today is the past." What does he mean by this statement?

Analyze Literature

Argumentative Essay What is Louis L'Amour's attitude, or bias, about the topic of this essay? Use a chart to list appeals to logic and appeals to emotion that he uses to persuade readers to agree with his viewpoint. Which appeals are most effective? Which are least effective?

Appeals to Logic	Appeals to Emotion
The developments of the past seventy years show how quickly we can make progress.	Nay-sayers are like babies clinging to their mothers.

Extend Understanding

Writing Options

Creative Writing Imagine that you are a member of the first colony on Mars. Write a **personal letter** to your family describing your experiences. Include some comparisons between life on Mars and life on Earth. Use sensory details and precise language when describing life on Mars.

Informative Writing Imagine that you are an editor putting together an anthology, or collection, of essays and articles about space exploration. Write a **literary response** to "The Eternal Frontier" in which you evaluate the overall effectiveness of this essay. Explain why you will or will not include the essay in your collection.

Collaborative Learning

Identify Facts, Opinions, and Commonplace Assertions *Factual claims* are statements that can be proven, *opinions* are statements that express attitudes or desires, and *commonplace assertions* are claims that are generally considered true. In a small group, complete a three-column chart listing facts, opinions, and commonplace assertions from "The Eternal Frontier." Then read a scientific essay, news article, encyclopedia entry, or other informative text about outer space and complete a fact / opinion / commonplace assertion chart for it.

Media Literacy

Evaluate Media Reports on Space Identify several different websites, newspapers, or magazines that make predictions about the future of space travel. Which is the most persuasive? Why?

 Go to **www.mirrorsandwindows.com** for more.

Grammar & Style

Sentence Types

Sentence Variety

"Where is the frontier now?" The answer should be obvious.

—LOUIS L'AMOUR, "The Eternal Frontier"

Varying your sentences can make your writing more enjoyable to read. You can introduce variety by changing the lengths of your sentences and by using different grammatical constructions. Another method is the use of different sentence types. In the above quotation, the writer asks a question and makes a statement. Questions and statements are two different types of sentences. There are four main types: the declarative, the imperative, the interrogative, and the exclamatory sentence.

Declarative and Imperative Sentences

A **declarative sentence** makes a statement and ends with a period. The declarative is the most common kind of sentence.

EXAMPLES

Space travel is important to the future of humanity.

There will always be new frontiers.

An **imperative sentence** gives a command or makes a request. These kinds of sentences frequently appear in dialogue. Often, the understood subject of these sentences is *you.*

EXAMPLES

Do not allow yourself to be lulled into a sense of satisfaction.

Travel to the moon, to the other planets, and then to the edge of the solar system.

Interrogative and Exclamatory Sentences

An **interrogative sentence** asks a question. Interrogative sentences always end in question marks.

EXAMPLES

What is the future of humanity, if not in space?

How can people deny the importance of exploration?

An **exclamatory sentence** expresses a strong feeling and ends with an exclamation point. Be careful when using exclamatory sentences and the exclamation point; both are frequently overused.

EXAMPLE

We must explore space, now!

Identifying Sentence Types

On a separate sheet of paper, rewrite these sentences with correct end punctuation–a period, question mark, or exclamation point. Next to each sentence, write what kind of sentence it is.

1. Why should we explore space, when Earth is our home
2. If we do not travel to the frontiers, we will betray ourselves
3. Wouldn't humanity still be trapped in the Dark Ages if it hadn't embraced exploration
4. Explore new frontiers
5. Space exploration is the only path that is open to humanity

from OFF THE COURT

An Autobiography by Arthur Ashe

ANCHOR TEXT

DIRECTED READING

BEFORE READING

Build Background

Historical Context From its earliest days, tennis was a sport played mostly by Britain's wealthiest people. As tennis took hold in the United States, private country clubs became the exclusive sites of play. Membership rules at these clubs automatically excluded blacks. In the 1940s and 1950s, when Arthur Ashe was a young boy eager to join the sport, African-American tennis players could only play on courts in black sections of town and were kept out of tournaments in which white athletes played.

Reader's Context Have you ever come face to face with discrimination of any type? How did you handle the situation?

Set Purpose

Use Build Background, the story title, and the first paragraph to preview the excerpt from *Off the Court.* Based on your preview, what do you predict the autobiography will focus on?

Analyze Literature

Description Writing that portrays a character, action, object, or scene is called **description.** Many descriptions use **sensory details,** words and phrases that describe how things look, sound, smell, taste, or feel. As you read the excerpt from *Off the Court,* be aware of how Ashe uses sensory details to bring the reader into his story.

Use Reading Skills

Identify Main Idea The main idea in a piece of nonfiction is often not stated directly. You can use a main idea map to help you find the main idea. Collect the details from the text, and then use these details to determine the main idea of a selection.

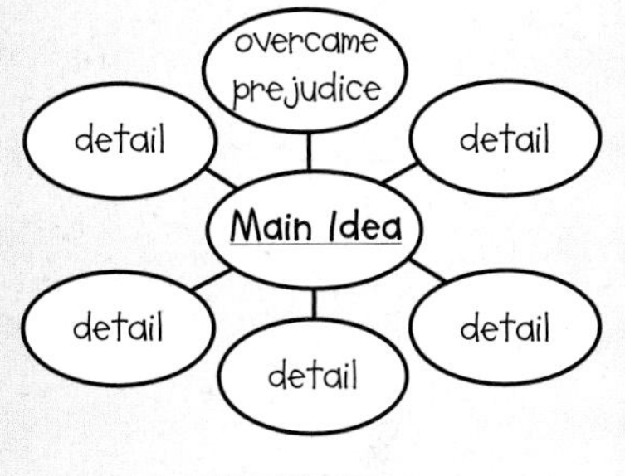

Preview Vocabulary

phys•i•o•log•i•cal•ly (fi' zē ə lä´ ji k[ə]lē) *adv.*, relating to bodily function

dom•i•nant (dä´ mə nənt) *adj.*, having the most control or influence

im•passe (im´ pas') *n.*, situation with no escape

re•press (ri pres´) *v.*, hold in by self-control

re•buff (ri bəf´) *n.*, refusal to meet an advance or offer

Meet the Author

Arthur Ashe was born in 1943 in Richmond, Virginia, and eventually became one of the top junior players in the nation. After college, he won the U.S. Open, and in 1975 he won both the Wimbledon and World Championship Tennis men's singles titles. He died in 1993 of AIDS, contracted from a blood transfusion after open-heart surgery. Arthur Ashe Stadium was dedicated in Flushing Meadows, New York, in 1996, and in 2005, the U.S. Postal Service issued a stamp honoring Ashe.

from

OFF THE COURT

An Autobiography
by Arthur Ashe

Arthur Ashe in 1968 during the Wimbledon Tennis Tournament in London, England.

I WAS TOO SMALL FOR ANY SPORT BUT TENNIS.

You can't compare tennis with baseball, basketball, or football. When Jackie Robinson broke the color line in 1947 with the Brooklyn Dodgers, dozens of good baseball players in the Negro leagues were waiting to follow. When Althea Gibson, the first prominent black in tennis, won national grass-court titles at Forest Hills in 1957 and 1958, there was no reservoir of black talent waiting to walk in if the door ever opened. Blacks had no identification with the sport—on or off the court. Tennis is a difficult game to learn. Very difficult. You have to be a generalist. You can't be a specialist and excel in tennis. You have to become adept in about four or five different sets of exercises, none of which are the same. Physiologically, serving a tennis ball is nothing like hitting a forehand; they're two completely different actions. Hitting a volley is not like hitting an overhead;[1] they too are two completely different functions. You must learn how to do all of them.

I was too small for any sport but tennis. I learned to swim when I was very young, but I was always a bit afraid of water, even if there was no way to avoid Brook Pool on my doorstep. My father wouldn't let me play football because of my size, which was a disappointment, so I tried to make up for it by working harder in other activities. When I wasn't sitting on the front porch of our house buried in a book, I played baseball, basketball, and tennis.

The four tennis courts just outside our side door were used fairly regularly by a handful of black people in Richmond. The all-black Richmond Racquet Club used Brook Field as its home base. As I grew increasingly sensitive to matters of race and color, I noticed that most of the black tennis players came from the educated, well-to-do segment of our community—principals, doctors, dentists, and lawyers. As a seven-year-old trying to find his niche in a complex, segregated society, I found that significant.

The students at Virginia Union also made good use of the courts in the spring. Their campus was just beyond Brook Field and they had just two courts of their own. They practiced at the playground and played teams from other colleges. Ron Charity spent more time on the courts than anyone else. For hours and hours, he hit balls against the wall or served to an empty court. Even my untrained eye could see an unusual grace in his swing, an agility that surpassed most of his opponents.

I watched him play against another school one afternoon. He dominated his opponent and won. His name was whispered around the gaggle of girlfriends, relatives, tennis buffs, and curious bystanders who drifted over from the football fields, baseball diamonds, and basketball courts. Ron Charity, they said, was one of the best black players in the country. I was properly impressed.

The next afternoon, he was out on the courts again, working on his serve. I watched for a while. Finally, he noticed me for the first time.

"What's your name?"

"Arthur Ashe, Junior."

"Your dad runs the playground?"

"Yes, sir."

He nodded and went back to his serve. His wooden racquet flashed high above his head in the late afternoon sun and sliced through the silence. White balls rocketed to

1. **overhead.** Stroke made above the height of the head

phys•i•o•log•i•cal•ly (fi′ zē ə lä′ ji k[ə] lē) *adv.*, relating to bodily function the corners of the opposing court. After a while, he stopped and looked at me again.

"You play tennis?"

I shrugged. I had batted some old tennis balls around with the twelve-dollar nylon-strung racquet that had found its way into the wooden equipment box under my bedroom window.

"You want to learn?"

I nodded. At that age, any sport was a challenge I felt I could master. "You got a racquet. Go get it," he said.

Ron Charity was a patient teacher with an understanding of my strengths and limitations. I weighed about fifty pounds. To get a tennis ball across the net and seventy-eight feet down court with a twenty-seven-inch racquet required a firm grip to withstand the torque from off-center hits.

I grew up aware that I was a Negro, colored, black,...and other less flattering terms.

Ron had me use an Eastern forehand grip, like shaking hands with my racquet. This is the best grip for beginners for three reasons: one, the hand is firmly behind the racquet handle at the moment the ball touches the string—a solid support system; two, it allows the best grip for an all-court attack, either down the line, cross-court, or down the middle; three, as I would learn later, it is a good starting point for future experimentation.

Ron stood on the other side of the net and tossed thousands of balls to me in the year that followed. I concentrated on form, my stroke, and getting the ball over the net. When I was alone and couldn't find someone to hit with me, I played against a backboard. Tennis became something I could do by myself, like reading a book, and I soon found myself absorbed in workouts without worrying about friends.

Pound for pound, I was a good little athlete—not a Lynn Swann or Kurt Thomas[2]—but someone with agility, speed, coordination, and a will to win. If all those elements could produce timing, I was on my way. Timing is the most important element in tennis. It separates players into different levels. John McEnroe, Ilie Nastase, and Evonne Goolagong have it in spades. They were born with it. Some good players have good timing with their hands but not with their feet. John Newcombe had great hands, but his feet were average. Rod Laver's feet were A+, but his hands rated an "A." Billie Jean King had great hands and feet. I would rate my hands and feet at the "B" level.

The eyes also play a vital role in timing. People are right-eyed and left-eyed, just as they are right-handed, and left-handed, right-footed and left-footed. When someone focuses on a tennis ball, one eye—and one eye alone—does the focusing. In turning aside during a backswing, the dominant eye can lose contact with the ball momentarily. At 120 miles an hour, a tennis ball can elude the best eyes. From the beginning, I had no trouble waiting for just the right moment. Because of my lack of size and weight, however, I had to develop a semi-lob off the forehand as a form of survival.

2. **Lynn Swann or Kurt Thomas.** Famous athletes in football and gymnastics, respectively

dom•i•nant (dä´ mə nənt) *adj.*, having the most control or influence

I was aware of the limitations of my height and build and soon accepted the fact that basketball and football were not for me. But baseball was a sport that demanded agility and determination rather than bulk or height. The baseball diamond and tennis court became my homes.

Baseball had special meaning for all colored boys because of Jackie Robinson. Joe Louis was still a big name in boxing, but he was finishing up his career and most of us only heard about his days of glory as heavyweight champion from our parents. As soon as the Brooklyn Dodgers signed Jackie Robinson, every black man, woman, and child in America became a Dodger fan. The New York Yankees had a farm club in Richmond, the Braves, but they were not very popular with blacks because they were so slow to integrate. In 1978, George Steinbrenner, the Yankee owner, offered me a job on his staff. We talked about it over a hamburger at P. J.'s, but I had to turn it down.

One of the highlights of my summers was the baseball school run by Maxie Robinson, the father of the present ABC-TV anchorman.[3] Even in those days, summer camps and schools were big; Mr. Robinson was the football, basketball, and track coach at Armstrong High School, highly respected and a disciplinarian like Daddy. Every day from nine to twelve-thirty, he taught baseball fundamentals. Later in the summer, the school took a trip to Washington to see the Senators[4] play. I could have cared less if they won. I was a Dodger fan.

The trip was fun. It also was a reminder of our segregated world. Contradictions between the slogans of democracy and equality and our reality were sharpened in the District of Columbia. We could not go to certain places. Even where we were not barred, we were not welcome. I grew up aware that I was a Negro, colored, black,... and other less flattering terms.

Heroes also were few—or so I thought. In the South, black heroes who made waves were discouraged. Booker T. Washington was recognized because he stressed self-help and education, and posed no threat to "the natural order of things." Paul Robeson[5] was moderately popular among blacks. His politics, which we didn't fully understand at the time, made us uneasy. Now, he has been elevated to near deity status. Everybody admired Ralph Bunche,[6] especially after he won the Nobel Peace Prize for his Middle East negotiations. George Washington Carver, who made the peanut fashionable long before Jimmy Carter, was highly regarded. I knew about Maggie Walker, president and founder of Consolidated Bank and Trust, Richmond's first black bank. She was the first woman bank president, black or white, in the country.

Like most black children, I held Abe Lincoln in high esteem because I had been taught that he freed the slaves, though for the wrong reasons. My one contemporary white hero was Gene Autry. I liked him because he was the underdog. Roy Rogers was the so-called "king of the cowboys," but Gene Autry was my man. My father took me to see him when I was six years old and I was impressed by the tricks he did with his horse, Champion. Playing cowboys and Indians as a kid, I insisted on being Gene Autry.

---

3. **present ABC-TV anchorman.** Max Robinson, the first black network television anchor, died in 1988.
4. **Senators.** There were two baseball teams by this name in Washington, D.C. The first was moved to Minneapolis-St. Paul in 1961 and renamed the Minnesota Twins. The second team was moved to Arlington in 1971 and renamed the Texas Rangers.
5. **Paul Robeson.** (1898–1976) African-American singer and actor
6. **Ralph Bunche.** (1904–1971) Distinguished African-American diplomat with a long career in the United Nations

In the spring of 1954, Virginia Union hosted the Central Intercollegiate Athletic Association Tennis Tournament. The CIAA was an association of black colleges. I was ten and had been taking lessons from Ron Charity for about three years. During a break in the action, I started hitting some balls on the court that was not in use.

"Somebody wants to meet you," Ron said, approaching the court.

I followed him to a table that was under the tree outside the side door of my house. Seated at the table was the tournament director, recording scores and directing players to the proper courts. Dr. R. W. Johnson was five feet ten inches tall, dark-skinned and handsome, with wavy brown hair and a small scar on his upper lip.

"Dr. Johnson," Ron Charity said, "this is Arthur Ashe, Junior."

He shook my hand and looked me over quizzically. "I understand you're ten years old."

"Yes, sir."

"You've been playing three years."

"Yes, sir."

"You like tennis?"

"Yes, sir."

He nodded, asked a few more questions, and dismissed me. I went back to the empty court, but felt him watching me as I played. When I glanced over, he was talking to Ron. Later that day, he talked to my father for a long time.

After the matches, Daddy spoke to me about this Dr. Johnson. "Arthur Junior," he began. I could tell from the form of address that this was to be a serious conversation. "Dr. Johnson works with young tennis players. He'd like you to come down to his place for a couple of weeks in the summer so you can play against other good players every day. You'll also have a chance to travel to some other tournaments."

If the chance to play against other boys had not been enough, the word "travel" would have done it. Here was a chance to explore the world beyond the pages of my old *National Geographics*. I had been to South Hill in the summer and had traveled to Chicago by train with my grandmother. But Dr. Johnson's offer was almost too good to be true. I had no trouble accepting.

Robert Walter Johnson was born in North Carolina, educated at Lincoln University in Pennsylvania, where he was a black All-American running back. He attended Meharry Medical College in Nashville and was a general practitioner[7] in Lynchburg, Virginia. "Dr. J," as we called him, took up tennis to stay in shape and became a major figure in the American Tennis Association, the black equivalent of the USLTA, until his death in 1971. His obsession was the development of good black junior tennis players.

One year, while driving home from Washington, D.C., he saw a huge sign announcing the "USLTA Inter-Scholastic Championship." He parked his car and watched all those white boys in white tennis uniforms competing against each other. He went to the tournament director and asked if any blacks had ever played. After a long discussion the officials agreed they would accept two black finalists from an all-black qualifying event every year. The first year Dr. Johnson brought players, they lost, 6–0, 6–0, in the first round. He was terribly embarrassed but vowed he would produce a player to win that tournament. I won it in 1961.

Dr. Johnson spent most of his days at his office in the Johnson Medical Building on Fifth Street. He would come home after office hours and play tennis, frequently with some of his cronies. Miss Erdice Creecy, his

7. general practitioner. Family doctor

lifelong secretary and private nurse, supervised his office and three-story house on Pierce Street. The basement of the house was equipped with showers, a recreation room, bar, and a shelf full of books on tennis. I read them all. Dr. Johnson had a tennis court behind his house, a rose garden, and a kennel for his hunting dogs.

> ***I was suddenly exposed to a world of black tennis whose dimensions I had not imagined.***

Almost all our training and practicing was done in the morning and early afternoon so Dr. Johnson could have the court around five o'clock. I spent only two weeks with him that first summer but immediately ran into problems. Ron Charity had been my first teacher, and I patterned my game after him. He had worked for a long time with me on my backhand; I felt I could do anything with it. The key was a very long and early backswing. The ball had to be hit way out in front to allow for as much racquet momentum as possible. My timing on my backhand was very good. But I used a standard backhand grip, and that became the source of my troubles.

Dr. Johnson's son, Bobby, who did a lot of the teaching, wanted to change my backhand the first day I was in Lynchburg.

"Mr. Charity showed me the other way," I protested. I didn't want to change my grip. I felt I could hit all day and not miss.

"I'm your teacher now and I want to change it," Bobby said firmly. I stood my ground.

"Well, if you want Ron Charity to teach you," Bobby said, "why don't you go home?"

We had reached an impasse. Dr. Johnson called my father. Two hours later, the blue Ford screeched to a stop in the driveway. Daddy listened to the explanations of the problem. He turned to me. "Dr. Johnson is teaching you now, Arthur Junior. You do what they say." Daddy then got in his car and drove back to Richmond.

It was that simple. I always obeyed my father. They had no more trouble with me. But to tell the truth, I didn't really change the grip on my backhand that much.

During those two weeks, Dr. Johnson took me to two tournaments, the Southeastern ATA in Durham, North Carolina, and the Mall Tennis Club tournament in Washington. I was suddenly exposed to a world of black tennis whose dimensions I had not imagined. There was black tennis in virtually every major city along the East Coast and in the South, the Midwest, and California.

Because I was the youngest player at Dr. Johnson's, I had the dirtiest jobs. I cleaned his doghouse and weeded his rose gardens. Yet I had acquired these skills from my father, who often had a dozen dogs around Brook Field. I swept sidewalks, made beds, washed dishes, and rolled the tennis court. I didn't enjoy these things, but I understood this as my way of paying back, so I did those chores as quickly as I could.

I also had to use the court when nobody else wanted it so the backboard became my challenge. Sometimes the neighbors would complain about my pounding the backboard at 7 a.m. But by the time breakfast came around, I had put in a good forty-five minutes on the board. Those sessions were fantasy times. I imagined that I was Pancho

im•passe (im´ pas') *n.*, situation with no escape

Gonzales[8] or another famous tennis player in a critical situation, at deuce, set point, match point.[9] In practices, Bobby Johnson would make us run patterns. We had to hit so many down the line, so many cross-court, maybe a cross-court then a down-the-line, come to the net and put away the volley. We had daily contests: who could hit the most forehands without an error, the most forehand returns of serve, deep forehand shots, forehand approach shots, forehand passing shots. Then we ran through the whole series for the backhand.

I noticed early that I had more endurance than the older boys. I was smaller, couldn't hit as hard or serve as fast, but I could last longer. So I would try to go as long as I could in the practice sessions and against the backboard without missing. I also began to learn the standard tennis principles: on approach shots, go down the line, not cross-court; no drop shots from the baseline; when in doubt, hit a semi-lob deep down the middle; get 70 percent of your first serves in.

There were also maxims meant only for little black Southern boys: when in doubt, call your opponent's shot good; if you're serving the game before the change of ends, pick up the balls on your side and hand them to your opponent during the crossover. Dr. Johnson knew we were going into territory that was often hostile and he wanted our behavior to be beyond reproach. It would be years before I understood the emotional toll of repressing anger and natural frustration.

---

8. **Pancho Gonzales.** (1928–1995) Mexican-American tennis player
9. **deuce, set point, match point.** Scores in a tennis match

re•press (ri pres´) *v.*, hold in by self-control

Arthur Ashe playing against Rod Laver of Australia during the 1968 Wimbledon Tennis Tournament.

That summer of '53 was symbolic because it marked the first steps on the road from Richmond. In subsequent years, traveling with Ron Charity and others stressed the importance of camaraderie. Blacks could not eat in restaurants, so we brought our fried chicken, potato salad, and rolls in bags and passed the Thermos around the car. Spending weekends as a guest in someone's house taught me more about social graces than I could have ever learned elsewhere.

I also learned on the court. During a tournament at Barraud Park in Norfolk, I had won the first set against another boy my age and was leading in the second when I started feeling sorry for him. It happens all the time among club players, but not on the prize-money tour anymore. I decided to let my opponent win a few games by making a few intentional errors. I lost the second set, was down, 2–0, in the third, and then began to panic. I tried to come back, but the more I pressed, the more mistakes I made. I lost the third set—and the match. My opponent was elated; I was in tears, angry at myself. It was an important lesson. There would be other occasions when I felt sorry for someone, but I never again let such sympathies affect my game...

My first seventeen years set the stage for the way I view the world. I grew up as an underdog, so I rent from Avis instead of Hertz now. As I played more and more against white juniors, I realized I was fighting assumptions about black inferiorities. Dr. Johnson tried to combat our insecurities by making "the white boys" the ultimate opponent.

"You're not going to beat those white boys playing like that," he would say. "Hit that to a white boy and you'll go home early," was another of his pet phrases.

Knowing that I would not be admitted to certain tournaments protected me from direct rebuffs. O. H. Parrish and some others I played against were terrific guys—period. Some others were too well-mannered to express racism crudely. No player ever refused to appear on court with me. No official ever called me a name. But the indirect rebuffs and innuendoes left their scars.

I noticed early that I had more endurance than the older boys.

The same year that I beat O. H. in the Middle Atlantic Juniors, some kids ransacked the log cabins where we had been housed for the tournament. Officials tried to place the blame on me and phoned Dr. Johnson.

"What do you know about this?" he asked, after I had returned to Lynchburg.

"I don't know anything about it," I said, nervous that I was being implicated and that my future tennis travel could be in jeopardy. "Honest—I don't, Dr. Johnson."

"I believe you, Arthur," he said. "They said they're just investigating, but I wanted to be sure."

Not all of my encounters were harsh. During the National Interscholastics in Charlottesville in 1960, Butch Newman, Cliff Buchholz, and Charlie Pasarell asked me to join them at a movie. I turned them down because I knew I wouldn't get in—but the

re•buff (ri bəf´) *n.*, refusal to meet an advance or offer guys wouldn't take no for an answer. When we got to the theater, the reaction was predictable.

"You can't go in," the woman in the ticket booth said. I wasn't surprised by her statement. But I was slightly elated when Cliff said, "Well, if he can't go in, none of us will go." And all of us left.

I won more than my share of matches by out-thinking opponents.

That summer, Daddy and Dr. Johnson faced their own decision. I had won a number of important regional titles and was ranked among the top junior players in the country. Ever the realist, Daddy knew there were few opportunities for a tennis player to make a living from his sport (this was in the days before open tennis). He knew the obstacles I would face as a black tennis player; yet he felt obliged to give me, as the best young black to come along since Althea Gibson, an opportunity to go as far as I could. My peers, the juniors who had become my friends in many cases, would continue to progress, and the Californians could play all year. To keep up with them, I had to be able to play winter tennis. And there were no such opportunities in Richmond.

The solution was to spend my senior year in high school in St. Louis, Missouri, at the home of Richard Hudlin, a good friend of Dr. Johnson and another tennis buff. The move was practical because each summer I had roamed farther and farther away from home. St. Louis would be the final break with Richmond.

Everybody goes through stages in life when they wish they could change things about themselves or their circumstances. As a sophomore at Maggie Walker, I had made the varsity baseball team and pitched one inning in our first game that spring. The next morning J. Harry Williams, the principal, called me into his office.

"Arthur Junior," he said bluntly. "I'm kicking you off the baseball team."

I was stunned. "Why, Mr. Williams?"

"Arthur, you've got a great future ahead of you as a tennis player. You've gone further than any other black male, and I don't want to risk you getting hurt."

I was deeply disappointed. But the loss was tempered by his acknowledgement that there was something special about my tennis. Spending my senior year in St. Louis gave me the chance not only to change my tennis game but also my personality.

I was always rather shy and studious. I was good in tennis and baseball, but socially I was shy. I came out of my shell in St. Louis, partly because they made such a fuss over me and nobody knew anything about me. I could be a different person, and nobody would ever know the difference. After growing up in a community where everybody knew who I was, either because of my father or because of my tennis, I could be anything I wanted in St. Louis. Because I had a straight-A average and had already taken subjects in Richmond as a junior that were being taught only to seniors at Sumner High School, I was often allowed to study on my own.

It amazed me that I had a higher GPA than anybody else in the school. I would have been valedictorian of my senior class at Sumner, with the highest grade-point average, except that I had been in school only one year and didn't qualify. Still, grades aren't everything.

St. Louis was north of the Mason-Dixon Line, so I thought Sumner would have white students. The city had an integrated school system, but Sumner was in an all-black neighborhood. It was a different sort of neighborhood from Richmond's North Side. The kids were more street-wise, and you had to be tougher to survive. There were more kids in the school, and you didn't get that feeling of community that you did at Maggie Walker. People helped one another out in Richmond, even though there was an unwritten feeling that blacks in the public schools in the South were inferior.

Separate-but-equal was the house line for defending dual school systems in Virginia then. It was really separate and unequal. Many black teachers in the southern public schools had only bachelor's degrees. The amount of public money spent on the black schools per pupil was obviously less than the amount of money spent on the white schools per pupil. Many job opportunities were just closed to blacks, so the curriculum at black public schools was often geared toward the jobs that a black graduate could expect to find when he or she graduated, which wasn't very much. You could drive a truck, teach, become a doctor, lawyer, or undertaker; the best blue-collar job was considered that of a mailman.

Arthur Ashe holds the Wimbledon Gentlemen's Singles Trophy in 1975.

Mr. Hudlin, his wife, and their son welcomed me into their home. Mr. Hudlin was a teacher at Sumner and his wife Jane was a registered nurse. Mr. Hudlin had been the captain of the tennis team at the University of Chicago in 1924 and had a tennis court in the backyard of his home. His son, Dickie, was a ninth-grader, and we got along fairly well. But I think there was an element of jealousy because of the attention my tennis got from his father. Ironically, Mr. Hudlin wanted nothing more than to have his son become a great player, but Dickie just hated tennis.

My game had evolved considerably from the deep lob that was my main weapon at age seven. Aware that junior tennis depended heavily on consistency, Dr. Johnson's plan for my development concentrated on ground strokes. This theory was a serious mistake—but fortunately, one that was correctable.

Dr. J's court at home was clay and few clay-court players, especially juniors, venture to the net. He saw tennis as a game of ground strokes and sound strategy. He believed that a smart player with average strokes could out-think and beat players with better strokes and poor strategy. Up to a point, he was right, and I won more than my share of matches by out-thinking opponents.

But the appearance of California players, with their upbringing on faster hard courts and the serve-and-volley power game, forced a change in my style. At age sixteen, I had to learn to volley in a hurry and make the jump to the eighteen-and-unders. But once I got to St. Louis, I practiced every day at the St. Louis Armory, on a wooden floor. A wooden floor is fast and slick, balls skid off the floor and accelerate after they bounce. I had to shorten my backswing to play well. With my old round-house backswing, the ball would have been in the back fence before I started moving my racquet forward.

A fast wooden floor also gives a player a false sense of confidence about his serve. Even an average serve seems formidable when it skids off a slick floor. It could have lulled me into accepting the shortcomings on my serve, but Mr. Hudlin and Larry Miller, a white pro, told me to lean forward and put more muscle into my service motion.

I started to return serve differently. Usually, I would stand just behind the baseline and wait for the ball. Now I dropped back a yard and a half or so and charged the ball when my opponent served. I had never been comfortable charging the ball because of my clay-court background, but with my new aggressiveness, I developed new techniques to catch the ball on the rise. In the course of some weight-shifting drills suggested by Larry, I developed a topspin backhand, which worked very well for moving the ball cross-court as I charged forward.

I also changed my grip from the Eastern to the Continental. It is a less secure way of holding the racquet for the forehand, but it allows you to hit everything—forehand, backhand, volley[10] or serve—with the same grip. The disadvantage is that flat forehands are very difficult to hit with this grip. I began to observe my opponents' grips to figure out what they could and could not do.

In November 1960 I won my first USLTA national title, the National Junior Indoors. At Christmas, on the way back to St. Louis from the Orange Bowl Juniors in Miami Beach, I stopped off in Richmond to visit my family. While I was at home, I got a telephone call one afternoon.

"Arthur, this is J. D. Morgan," the voice on the telephone said. There was a pause. "I'm the tennis coach at UCLA. We're preparing to offer you a scholarship to come out and play for us."

You could have knocked me over with a feather. I was thrilled beyond belief. I said yes even before he finished his offer. I had no idea that UCLA had any interest in me. I would get offers from Michigan, Michigan State, Arizona, and Hampton Institute later, but every junior player knew that UCLA and USC were the schools for tennis.

My father understood my elation but did not understand the significance of UCLA. He supported my decision to go to California, although he was clearly upset at having me move still farther away from the family.

Mr. Hudlin also realized the importance of my UCLA scholarship, and Dr. Johnson was as thrilled as I was. My senior year capped my long career as a junior player. After fulfilling Dr. Johnson's dream of producing a winner in the Interscholastics, I reached the semifinals of the National Jaycees and the National Juniors. By graduation, I was the fifth-ranked junior in the country and a member of the Junior Davis Cup team that traveled together that summer.

Of course, there was a great deal of fuss about being the "first black" Junior Davis Cup player, the "first black" to get a tennis scholarship to UCLA, the "first black" to win at Charlottesville, etc. Those comments

---

10. volley. Return of a ball before it touches the ground always put me under pressure to justify my accomplishments on racial grounds, as if sports were the cutting edge of our nation's move toward improved race relations. The fact that this kind of accomplishment by a black player got so much attention was an indication that we still had so far to go.

The questions asked in 1960 and 1961 served to remind me of my isolated status in tennis. I played in clubs where the only blacks were waiters, gardeners, and busboys. I knew there was apprehension in some circles about my presence, but I was not about to embarrass myself or anybody else. I was polite, fairly well educated, and I knew which fork to use because I had done some catering with my father.

I was moved into the world of tennis that had little in common with the black experience. The game had a history and tradition I was expected to assimilate, but much of that history and many of those traditions were hostile to me. When I decided to leave Richmond, I left all that Richmond stood for at the time—its segregation, its conservatism, its parochial[11] thinking, its slow progress toward equality, its lack of opportunity for talented black people. I had no intention then of coming back. And I really never would, except to see my family, and for a few tournaments and a Davis Cup match years later.

When I got national recognition as a tennis player in my senior year in high school, it was an important step in my personal campaign to overcome assumptions of inequality. But I also knew that no one in Richmond's white tennis establishment had done anything to help me to get where I was. My memories and experiences about Richmond remain firmly rooted in the 1960s. The support I got—from teachers, relatives, and people like Ron Charity and Dr. Johnson—prepared me for the life I would lead outside the South. ✣

11. **parochial.** Narrow

How would you feel if you were prevented from competing in a sport or going to a public place because of your skin color? What do you think contributed most to Ashe's success? Is success in a given field more a matter of luck or a matter of hard work?

Find Meaning

1. (a) Where did Ashe first learn tennis? (b) How did his physical limitations affect his attraction to tennis?

2. (a) What dispute did Ashe have with Dr. Johnson's son, Bobby? (b) How was the dispute resolved?

3. How did Ashe's personality change in St. Louis?

Make Judgments

4. Ashe says that "traveling with Ron Charity and others stressed the importance of camaraderie," or spirit of friendship. Why was camaraderie important?

5. (a) What social experiences did Ashe have as a result of tennis that he otherwise might not have had? (b) How did these experiences help shape Ashe's view of life and his values?

6. How did Ashe view the discrimination he experienced as a tennis player?

INFORMATIONAL TEXT ▶▶ CONNECTION

After his competitive tennis days were over, **Arthur Ashe** expanded his career to include coaching, fund-raising, and writing. He wrote this editorial for the *New York Times* in 1977. Because of Ashe's fame, newspapers and other organizations valued his views on athletics and education. As you read, notice the sensory details Ashe uses to support his main idea.

A Black Athlete Looks at Education

An Editorial by Arthur Ashe

Since my sophomore year at UCLA, I have become convinced that we blacks spend too much time on the playing fields and too little time in the libraries. Consider these facts: for the major professional sports of hockey, football, basketball, baseball, golf, tennis and boxing, there are roughly only 3170 major league positions available (attributing 200 positions to golf, 200 to tennis and 100 to boxing). And the annual turnover is small.

There must be some way to assure that those who try but don't make it to pro sports don't wind up on street corners or in unemployment lines. Unfortunately, our most widely recognized role models are athletes and entertainers—"runnin'" and "jumpin'" and "singin'" and "dancin'."

Our greatest heroes of the century have been athletes—Jack Johnson, Joe Louis, and Muhammad Ali.[1] Racial and economic discrimination forced us to channel our energies into athletics and entertainment. These were the ways out of the ghetto, the ways to get that Cadillac, those regular shoes, that cashmere sport coat.

Somehow, parents must instill a desire for learning alongside the desire to be Walt Frazier.[2] Why not start by sending black professional athletes into high schools to explain the facts of life?

I have often addressed high school audiences and my message is always the same: "For every hour you spend on the athletic field, spend two in the library. Even if you make it as a pro athlete, your career will be over by the time you are 35. You will need that diploma."

Have these pro athletes explain what happens if you break a leg, get a sore arm, have one bad year or don't make the cut for five or six tournaments. Explain to them the star system, wherein for every star earning millions there are six or seven others making \$15,000 or \$20,000 or \$30,000. Invite a bench-warmer or a guy who didn't make it. Ask him if he sleeps every night. Ask him whether he was graduated. Ask him what he would do if he became disabled tomorrow. Ask him where his old high school athletic buddies are.

We have been on the same roads—sports and entertainment—too long. We need to

1. **Jack Johnson, Joe Louis, and Muhammad Ali.** Twentieth-century African-American boxers
2. **Walt Frazier.** Black basketball player for the New York Knicks (1967–1977) and the Cleveland Cavaliers (1977–1980)

pull over, fill up at the library and speed away to Congress and the Supreme Court, the unions and the business world.

I'll never forget how proud my grandmother was when I graduated from UCLA. Never mind the Davis Cup. Never mind the Wimbledon title. To this day, she still doesn't know what those names mean. What mattered to her was that of her more than thirty children and grandchildren, I was the first to be graduated from college, and a famous college at that. Somehow, that made up for all those floors she scrubbed all those years. ✤

TEXT TO TEXT CONNECTION

The excerpt from Ashe's autobiography and his editorial both deal with being an African-American athlete. Compare and contrast the purpose and content of each selection. Be sure to describe the structural and substantive differences between the two.

AFTER READING

Analyze Literature

Description A writer's use of sensory details helps to portray a character, object, action, or scene. Use a chart to analyze the effect of specific sensory details in the excerpt from *Off the Court*. Then describe the overall mood of the autobiography using two or three key words.

Sensory Detail	Effect
too small for any sport but tennis	

Extend Understanding

Writing Options

Creative Writing Write an **autobiographical essay** about an event in your past. The event should be something that affected you strongly and that you think will interest your readers. Use dialogue and sensory details to create a realistic effect. Share your essay with the class.

Informative Writing Write a one-paragraph **biographical sketch** of Arthur Ashe. Use information from his autobiography, including quotations and paraphrases, and information you gather from the Internet or library. Write as though your sketch will be published in a reference work about famous athletes.

Collaborative Learning

Research a Sport With a partner, research a sport you would like to know more about. Prepare a basic overview of the sport, and present your overview to the class using drawings, photographs, puppets, or demonstrations as supporting visuals.

Critical Literacy

Question and Answer Many famous minority athletes have broken racial and social barriers. Look for information on one or two male or female minority athletes. First, create a set of questions you would like to ask them. Then, research answers to those questions. Report your findings in a question-and-answer format and post your work on the class bulletin board.

Go to **www.mirrorsandwindows.com** for more.

Was Tarzan a Three-Bandage Man?

A Personal Essay by Bill Cosby

DIRECTED READING

BEFORE READING

Build Background

Literary Context The title of this personal essay is a humorous reference to a literary character first created in 1912 by author Edgar Rice Burroughs. *Tarzan of the Apes* was the first book in a series featuring Tarzan, who lived in an African jungle and was known for his strength and courage in the face of danger. Also the title character of several movies, Tarzan was played by various actors over the years.

Reader's Context What do you admire in a person? Is it his or her strength, courage, talent, or something else?

Set Purpose

Based on the title of this essay, do you think it will be serious or humorous?

Analyze Literature

Purpose A writer's **purpose** is his or her goal. For example, people might write to inform, to entertain, or to persuade. Sometimes a writer may have more than one purpose. As you read "Was Tarzan a Three-Bandage Man?" try to determine the author's purpose. Think about how well he achieves this purpose.

Use Reading Skills

Context Clues Preview the vocabulary words from this selection as they are used in the sentences below. Try to unlock the meaning of each word using the context clues in the sentences.

1. Walking backward is a difficult means of locomotion.
2. I tried to emulate my mother's good cooking, but my dishes never tasted the same as hers.
3. We knew Phil had failed his math test because we saw him sitting dejectedly with his head in his hands.

Meet the Author

Bill Cosby was born in 1937 in Philadelphia. He has been called "one of the most influential performers of the second half of the twentieth century." Most Americans recognize Cosby from two popular television shows: *I Spy* and *The Cosby Show*. He has known success as a comedian, actor, and writer, and his books have sold millions of copies. In recent years in his public appearances, he has urged more parental involvement in the lives of young people.

Preview Vocabulary

lo•co•mo•tion (lō' kə mō´ shən) *n.*, power or act of moving from one place to another

em•u•late (em´ yə lāt') *v.*, imitate

de•jec•ted•ly (di jek´ təd lē) *adv.*, sadly; showing lack of confidence

(Opposite page) Sugar Ray Robinson wrapping his hands before a fight in 1956.

Was Tarzan a Three-Bandage Man?

A Personal Essay by
Bill Cosby

"My mother says I gotta stop wearin' a bandage. She wants my whole head to show."

In the days before athletes had learned how to incorporate themselves, they were shining heroes to American kids. In fact, they were such heroes to me and my friends that we even imitated their walks. When Jackie Robinson,[1] a pigeon-toed walker, became famous, we walked pigeon-toed, a painful form of locomotion unless you were Robinson or a pigeon.

"Why you walkin' like that?" said my mother one day.

"This is Jackie *Robinson's* walk," I proudly replied.

"There's somethin' wrong with his shoes?"

"He's the fastest man in baseball."

"He'd be faster if he didn't walk like that. His mother should make him walk right."

A few months later, when football season began, I stopped imitating Robinson and began to walk bowlegged like a player named Buddy Helm.

"Why you always tryin' to change the shape of your legs?" said my mother. "You keep doin' that an' they'll fall off—an' I'm not gettin' you new ones."

Although baseball and football stars inspired us, our real heroes were the famous prize fighters, and the way to emulate a fighter was to walk around with a Band-Aid over one eye. People with acne walked around that way too, but we hoped it was clear that we were worshipping good fists and not bad skin.

The first time my mother saw me being Sugar Ray,[2] not Jackie Robinson, she said, "What's that bandage for?"

"Oh, nuthin'," I replied.

"Now that's a new kinda stupid answer. That bandage gotta be coverin' somethin'—besides your entire brain."

"Well, it's just for show. I wanna look like Sugar Ray Robinson."

"The fastest man in baseball."

"No, that's a different one."

HISTORY ▶▶ CONNECTION

Jackie Robinson Jackie Robinson excelled in most sports in high school and at the University of California, but as an African American, he was often heckled by players on opposing teams. His professional career began when he joined the Kansas City Monarchs of the Negro American League. There, he was spotted by Branch Rickey, president of the Brooklyn Dodgers. Rickey signed Robinson to play for the Montreal Royals. A year later Rickey pulled him from the minor-league affiliate, and Robinson played the 1947 season with the Brooklyn Dodgers. Despite the jeers and insults of some fans and team members, he was named Major League Rookie of the Year. Robinson was inducted into baseball's Hall of Fame in 1962. Why might Robinson have been a hero to young Cosby and his friends?

"You doin' Swiss Family Robinson[3] next?"

"Swiss Family Robinson? They live in the projects?"

"You'd know who they are if you read more books instead of makin' yourself look like an accident. Why can't you try to imitate someone like Booker T. Washington?"[4]

1. **Jackie Robinson.** (1919–1972) First African American in the twentieth century to play in the major leagues
2. **Sugar Ray.** (1921–1989) Ray Robinson, known as "Sugar Ray," was a world champion prize fighter six times.
3. **Swiss Family Robinson.** Story for young people written in 1812 that tells of a family wrecked on a desert island
4. **Booker T. Washington.** (1856–1915) African American born into slavery who became a teacher and founded Tuskegee Institute in Alabama

lo•co•mo•tion (lō' kə mō´ shən) *n.,* power or act of moving from one place to another

em•u•late (em´ yə lāt') *v.,* imitate

"Who does he play for?"

"Bill, let's put it this way: you take off that bandage right now or I'll have your father move you up to stitches."

The following morning on the street, I dejectedly told the boys, "My mother says I gotta stop wearin' a bandage. She wants my whole head to show."

"What's wrong with that woman?" said Fat Albert. "She won't let you do *nuthin'*."

"It's okay, Cos," said Junior, "cause one bandage ain't enough anyway. My brother says the really tough guys wear two."

"One over each eye?" I asked him.

"Or one eye and one nose," he said.

"Man, I wouldn't want to mess with no two-bandage man," said Eddie.

And perhaps the toughest guys of all wore tourniquets around their necks. We were capable of such attire, for we were never more ridiculous than when we were trying to be tough and cool. Most ridiculous, of course, was that our hero worshipping was backwards: we should have been emulating the men who had *caused* the need for bandages. ✣

de • jec • ted • ly (di jek´ təd lē) *adv.*, sadly; showing lack of confidence

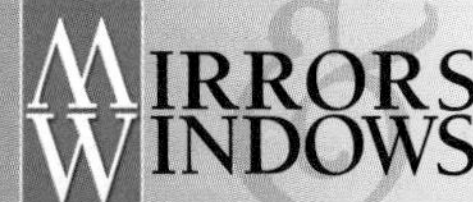

When have you tried to physically emulate one of your heroes? How might a person's attempt to copy a hero be useful? How might it be dangerous?

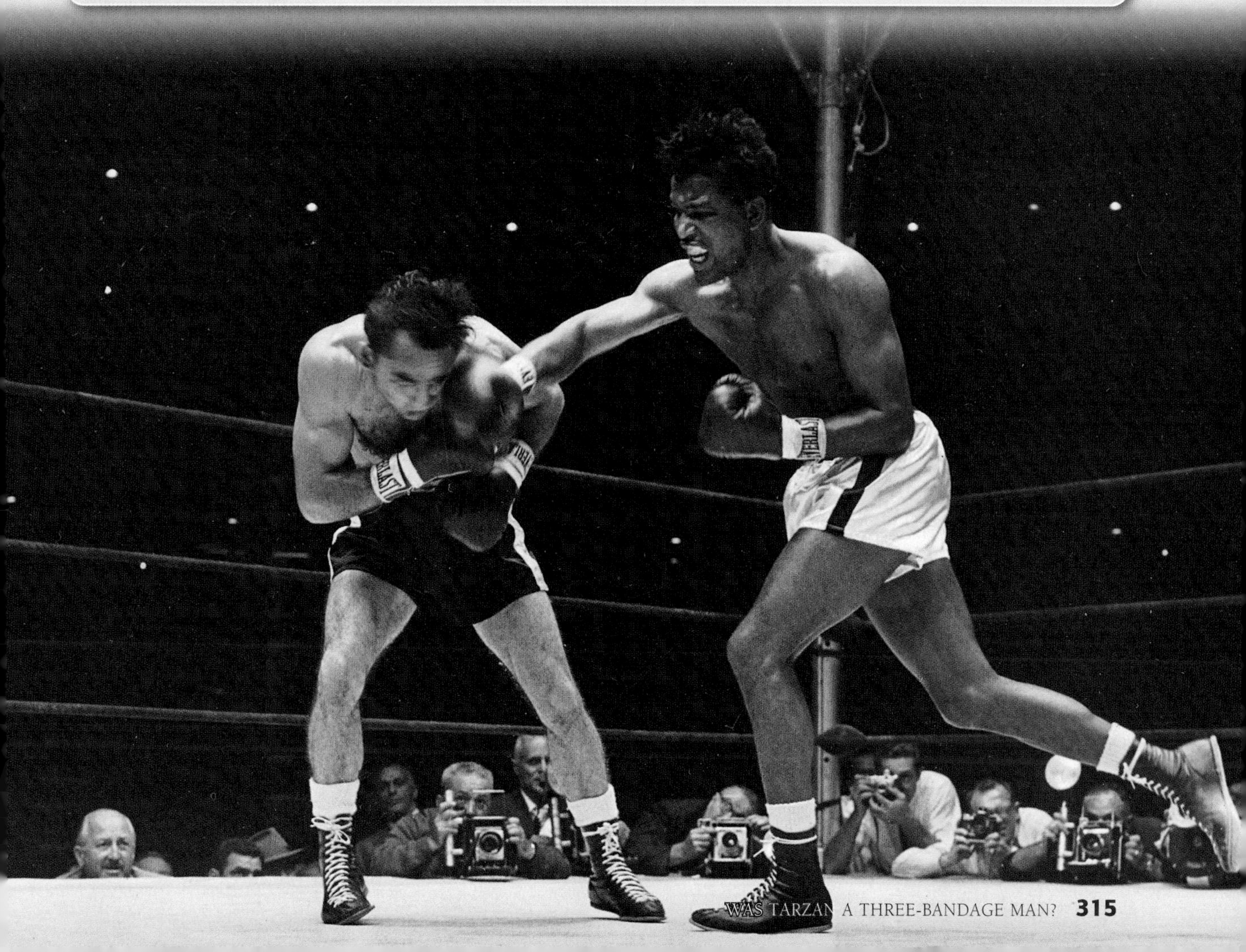

AFTER READING

Find Meaning

1. What do Cosby and his friends do to show that Jackie Robinson is their hero?
2. What does wearing a bandage over one eye indicate about Cosby and his friends?

Make Judgments

3. (a) What is the relationship between Cosby and his mother? (b) How is the tone of this essay affected by the dialogue between Cosby and his mother?
4. How does the author later view his attempts to emulate his heroes?
5. What does this essay tell you about the influence famous people have?

Analyze Literature

Purpose A writer uses specific details to help achieve the purpose of an essay. Use a chart to analyze Cosby's purpose.

Before Reading
Identify the author's purpose, the type of writing he or she uses, and the ideas he or she wants to communicate.
During Reading
Gather ideas that the author communicates to readers.
After Reading
Summarize the ideas the author communicates. Explain how these ideas help fulfill the author's purpose.

Extend Understanding

Writing Options

Creative Writing Think about some funny event that has happened to you or to someone in your family. Write your own humorous anecdote in a **personal letter** that you plan on sending to a close friend. Include as many vivid details as you can.

Argumentative Writing Why is it good (or bad) for young people to admire and copy sports figures? In the introductory sentence of an **argumentative paragraph,** state your answer to this question. Try to appeal to both emotion and logic. In the conclusion, sum up your reasons for feeling as you do. Share your work with the class.

Critical Literacy

Analyze Adaptations Works of nonfiction are often changed or adapted into another medium or genre. Find an adaptation of an autobiography or a diary and describe the structural and substantive differences between the two. An example would be the autobiography *Farewell to Manzanar* by Jeanne Wakatsuki Houston and the 1976 television movie.

Media Literacy

Discuss Humorous Writing In small groups, discuss how the techniques of humorous writing differ from those used in other media, such as movies, comic strips, stand-up comedy, and situation comedies. Create a chart, or other visual aid, in which you show how humor differs in these media.

Go to **www.mirrorsandwindows.com** for more.

FISH CHEEKS

A Personal Essay by Amy Tan

BEFORE READING

Build Background

Cultural Context A traditional Chinese holiday meal may include several kinds of fish (sometimes served whole), tofu, pickled vegetables, and rice. The New Year's holiday, and meal, is perhaps the most important in the Chinese calendar. For Chinese Christians, the Christmas holiday is also very important.

Reader's Context Different cultures in America have different foods and traditions on holidays. What are some traditional holiday foods and customs in your family? Do you think these traditions are important to follow, or will you abandon them when you are older?

Set Purpose

Previewing the title and the first two paragraphs of "Fish Cheeks" will help you to make predictions about what the narrator will experience and how she feels about this experience. Read to determine how accurate your predictions are.

Analyze Literature

Sensory Details Words and phrases that appeal to the five senses are **sensory details.** As you read "Fish Cheeks," notice the details that appeal to sight, sound, touch, taste, and smell.

Meet the Author

Amy Tan's parents came to the San Francisco Bay Area from China, and Tan was born in Oakland, California, in 1952. Although her parents wanted her to become a doctor, she began a writing career instead. Her first of many books, *The Joy Luck Club,* was published in 1989 and was made into a successful film in 1994. She continues to write fiction and nonfiction in San Francisco.

DIRECTED READING

Use Reading Skills

Analyze Text Structure Writing is organized in different ways. Narrative writing is often organized chronologically, in the order or sequence in which events happen. When you read certain types of writing, such as a short story or an account of events in a person's life, keep track of the sequence of events. Use a sequence map to record what happens in "Fish Cheeks." In each box, describe key events in this essay.

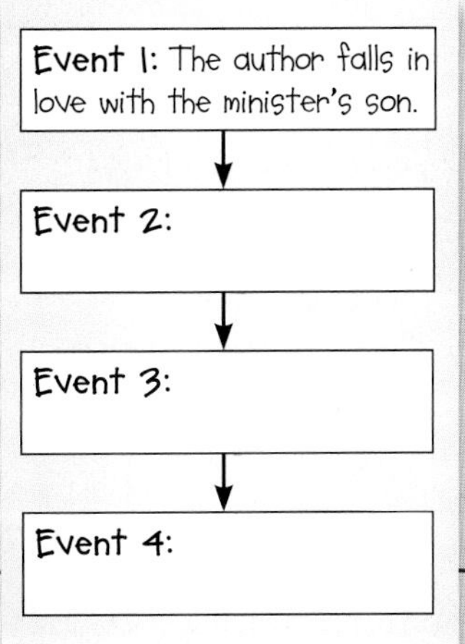

Preview Vocabulary

ap•pall•ing (ə pôl´ iŋ) *adj.,* inspiring disgust

rum•pled (rʉm´ pəld) *adj.,* wrinkled

pluck (plʉk) *v.,* pull off or out

FISH

CHEEKS

A Personal Essay by Amy Tan

I fell in love with the minister's son the winter I turned fourteen. He was not Chinese, but as white as Mary in the manger. For Christmas I prayed for this blond-haired boy, Robert, and a slim new American nose.

When I found out that my parents had invited the minister's family over for Christmas Eve dinner, I cried. What would Robert think of our shabby *Chinese* Christmas? What would he think of our noisy *Chinese* relatives who lacked proper American manners? What terrible disappointment would he feel upon seeing not a roasted turkey and sweet potatoes but *Chinese* food?

On Christmas Eve I saw that my mother had outdone herself in creating a strange menu. She was pulling black veins out of the backs of fleshy prawns.[1] The kitchen was littered with appalling mounds of raw food: A slimy rock cod[2] with bulging fish eyes that pleaded not to be thrown into a pan of hot oil. Tofu, which looked like stacked wedges of rubbery white sponges. A bowl soaking dried fungus back to life. A plate of squid, their backs crisscrossed with knife markings so they resembled bicycle tires.

And then they arrived—the minister's family and all my relatives in a clamor of doorbells and rumpled Christmas packages. Robert grunted hello, and I pretended he was not worthy of existence.

Dinner threw me deeper into despair. My relatives licked the ends of their chopsticks and reached across the table, dipping them into the dozens or so plates of food. Robert and his family waited patiently for platters to be passed to them. My relatives murmured with pleasure when my mother brought out the whole steamed fish. Robert grimaced.[3] Then my father poked his chopsticks just below the fish eye and plucked out the soft meat. "Amy, your favorite," he said, offering me the tender fish cheek. I wanted to disappear.

At the end of the meal my father leaned back and belched loudly, thanking my mother for her fine cooking. "It's a polite Chinese custom to show you are satisfied," explained my father to our astonished guests. Robert was looking down at his plate with a reddened face. The minister managed to muster up a quiet burp. I was stunned into silence for the rest of the night.

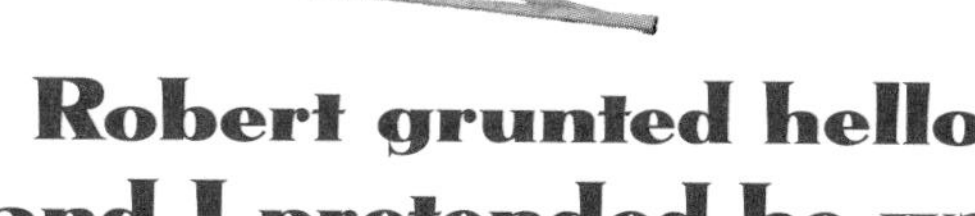

Robert grunted hello, and I pretended he was not worthy of existence.

After everyone had gone, my mother said to me, "You want to be the same as American girls on the outside." She handed me an early gift. It was a miniskirt in beige tweed. "But inside you must always be Chinese. You must be proud you are different. Your only shame is to have shame."

And even though I didn't agree with her then, I knew that she understood how much I had suffered during the evening's dinner. It wasn't until many years later—long after I had gotten over my crush on Robert—that I was able to fully appreciate her lesson and the true purpose behind our particular menu. For Christmas Eve that year, she had chosen all my favorite foods. ✣

---

1. **prawns.** Small shellfish that resemble shrimp
2. **rock cod.** Large, soft-finned fish that lives among rocks
3. **grimaced.** Twisted one's face to show disapproval or disgust

ap•pall•ing (ə pôl´ iŋ) *adj.*, inspiring disgust

rum•pled (rʉm´ pəld) *adj.*, wrinkled

pluck (plʉk) *v.*, pull off or out

What is it like to feel different from others? Would you have felt the way the author feels during dinner? How are those who seem different treated in our society?

AFTER READING

Find Meaning

1. (a) Why does the author say that the mounds of food in the kitchen are appalling?
   (b) What other words express her disgust?
2. Why does she feel deeper despair during dinner?
3. What does the author's mother do to make her daughter feel better?

Make Judgments

4. The author's mother says, "Your only shame is to have shame." What do you think she means?
5. The author says that later she was able to "fully appreciate...the true purpose behind our particular menu." What was that purpose?

Analyze Literature

Sensory Details Amy Tan uses a variety of details that appeal to the senses. Use a chart, like the one to the right, to record the sensory details that Tan uses, beneath the sense to which they appeal.

Sight	Sound	Touch	Taste	Smell
"bulging fish eyes"				

Extend Understanding

Writing Options

Creative Writing Write a **dialogue** between the author as an adult and her mother in which each recalls the Christmas Eve dinner. Be sure to have each woman express her feelings about that time. With a friend, read the dialogue aloud for the class.

Informative Writing Write an **informative essay** in which you describe the problem the author confronts and how she overcomes it. At the end of your essay, tell whether you think the way in which the author overcame this problem is satisfactory. When you are finished, share your essay with the class.

Collaborative Learning

Hold a Small-Group Discussion In a small group, discuss whether or not the structure of Amy Tan's essay is effective. First decide what the structure is. Then think about possible alternative ways the essay could have been organized. Work with the group to plan an agenda that accomplishes your goals within the time allotted and make certain that everyone has a chance to contribute. Finally, organize your thoughts by creating a summary of the text as well as an overview of the material presented.

Lifelong Learning

Conduct Research All cultures have important holidays. Using a variety of sources, research a holiday in a culture different from your own. Create a list with the meaning of the holiday and elements such as food, decorations, displays, music, and celebrations.

Go to **www.mirrorsandwindows.com** for more.

Grammar & Style

Fragments and Run-on Sentences

Fragments

A plate of squid, their backs crisscrossed with knife markings so they resembled bicycle tires.

—AMY TAN, "Fish Cheeks"

A sentence contains a subject and a verb and should express a complete thought. A **sentence fragment** is a phrase or clause that does not express a complete thought but has been punctuated as though it did. The above quote from "Fish Cheeks" is a fragment because it lacks a verb.

FRAGMENTS

Made this the happiest Christmas I can remember.

The fish and slabs of tofu piled on red and green plates.

As a rule, sentence fragments should be avoided. However, for stylistic reasons, authors sometimes include sentence fragments in their work. Novelists and short story writers frequently use sentence fragments to make their characters' dialogue feel more like authentically spoken speech.

Run-on Sentences

A **run-on sentence** is made up of two or more sentences that have been run together as if they were one complete thought. A run-on sentence can confuse the reader about where a thought starts or ends. A run-on sentence is created when no end punctuation is used between two independent clauses.

RUN-ON

I couldn't eat the wonderful dinner I was so embarrassed when my father belched.

This sentence can be corrected by adding appropriate end punctuation or by adding an appropriate conjunction and a comma.

EXAMPLES

I couldn't eat the wonderful dinner. I was so embarrassed when my father belched.

I couldn't eat the wonderful dinner, and I was so embarrassed when my father belched.

You can also correct run-on sentences by inserting a semicolon between two independent clauses. However, only use a semicolon if the two clauses are very closely related.

Sentence Improvement

Identify whether each selection below is a complete sentence, a fragment, or a run-on sentence. Then revise the run-ons and fragments to form one or more complete sentences.

1. The table with dishes, fish, and other seafood.
2. I was happy when my mother gave me the miniskirt.
3. My mother went to the kitchen I started to eat.
4. Across the living room and down the hall.
5. The steam rose from the rice the minister's son did not look up.
6. I learned to be proud of being me.
7. I could not finish eating my dinner.
8. With each plate on the table.
9. Underneath the ribbons and bows and beautiful wrapping paper.
10. My father left the table my mother looked up and smiled.

Comparing Texts

A Bittersweet Memoir

A Biography by Jerry Izenberg

Searching for January

A Short Story by W. P. Kinsella

DIRECTED READING

BEFORE READING

Build Background

Historical Context The subject of both Jerry Izenberg's biography and W. P. Kinsella's short story is Roberto Clemente, who was born in Puerto Rico and joined Major League Baseball in the 1950s. In 1954, he was drafted by the Pittsburgh Pirates and led the team to two World Series victories. He died in 1972 while flying supplies to earthquake victims in Nicaragua.

Reader's Context Who from the past or present do you most admire and why?

Set Purpose

Preview the illustrations and the quotations on the following pages to predict how each text will deal with Clemente's life and death.

Meet the Authors

Jerry Izenberg is a sportswriter and columnist for *The Star-Ledger* in Newark, New Jersey. He was born in 1930. Izenberg's many books include a history of the New York Giants and *Great Latin Sports Figures: Proud People*, from which his memoir of Roberto Clemente is taken.

W. P. Kinsella was born in 1935 in Edmonton, Alberta, a Canadian province. Kinsella has written numerous books about baseball and other topics. His book *Shoeless Joe* was made into the motion picture *Field of Dreams*.

Compare Literature: Characterization

The act of creating or describing a character is called **characterization.** Writers use three major techniques to create characters: showing what characters say, do, and think; showing what other characters say about them; and showing their physical features, dress, and personalities. Use a chart to record examples of characterization.

"A Bittersweet Memoir"	"Searching for January"
He was not a man who made friends casually.	

Preview Vocabulary

de•lin•e•ate (di li´ nē āt') *v.*, describe

brace (brās) *n.*, grove that provides shelter from wind

con•jec•ture (kən jek´ chər) *v.*, predict; guess

lithe•ly (līth´ lē) *adv.*, bending easily

A Bittersweet Memoir

A Biography by Jerry Izenberg

"He was the greatest we ever had...maybe one of the greatest anyone ever had."

Pittsburgh Pirates outfielder Roberto Clemente in 1967.

I saw him play so often. I watched the grace of his movements and the artistry of his reflexes from who knows how many press boxes. None of us really appreciated how pure an athlete he was until he was gone. What follows is a personal retracing of the steps that took Roberto Clemente from the narrow, crowded streets of his native Carolina to the local ball parks in San Juan and on to the major leagues. But it is more. It is a remembrance formed as I stood at the water's edge in Puerto Rico and stared at daybreak into the waves that killed him. It is all the people I met in Puerto Rico who knew him and loved him. It is the way an entire island in the sun and a Pennsylvania city in the smog took his death....

The record book will tell you that Roberto Clemente collected 3,000 hits during his major-league career. It will say that he came to bat 9,454 times, that he drove in 1,305 runs, and played 2,433 games over an eighteen-year span.

But it won't tell you about Carolina, Puerto Rico; and the old square; and the narrow, twisting streets; and the roots that produced him. It won't tell you about the Julio Coronado School and a remarkable woman named María Isabella Casares, whom he called "Teacher" until the day he died and who helped to shape his life in times of despair and depression. It won't tell you about a man named Pedron Zarrilla who found him on a country softball team and put him in the uniform of the Santurce club and who nursed him from promising young athlete to major-league superstar.

And most of all, those cold numbers won't begin to delineate the man Roberto Clemente was. To even begin to understand what this magnificent athlete was all about, you have to work backward. The search begins at the site of its ending.

The car moves easily through the predawn streets of San Juan. A heavy all-night rain has now begun to drive, and there is that post-rain sweetness in the air that holds the promise of a new, fresh, clear dawn. This is a journey to the site of one of Puerto Rico's deepest tragedies. This last says a lot. Tragedy is no stranger to the sensitive emotional people who make this island the human place it is.

Shortly before the first rays of sunlight, the car turns down a bumpy secondary road and moves past small shantytowns, where the sounds of the children stirring for the long

de•lin•e•ate (di liʹ nē āt') *v.*, describe

walk toward school begin to drift out on the morning air. Then there is another turn, between a brace of trees and onto the hardpacked dirt and sand, and although the light has not yet quite begun to break, you can sense the nearness of the ocean. You can hear its waves pounding harshly against the jagged rocks. You can smell its saltiness. The car noses to a stop, and the driver says, "From here you must walk. There is no other way." The place is called Puente Maldonado and the dawn does not slip into this angry place. It explodes in a million lights and colors as the large fireball of the sun begins to nose above the horizon.

"This is the nearest place," the driver tells me. "This is where they came by the thousands on that New Year's Eve and New Year's Day. Out there," he says, gesturing with his right hand, "out there, perhaps a mile and a half from where we stand. That's where we think the plane went down."

He was not a man who made friends casually.

The final hours of Roberto Clemente were like this. Just a month or so before, he had agreed to take a junior-league baseball team to Nicaragua and manage it in an all-star game in Managua. He had met people and made friends there. He was not a man who made friends casually. He had always said that the people you wanted to give your friendship to were the people for whom you had to be willing to give something in return—no matter what the price.

Two weeks after he returned from that trip, Managua, Nicaragua exploded into flames. The earth trembled and people died. It was the worst earthquake anywhere in the Western Hemisphere in a long, long time.

Back in Puerto Rico, a television personality named Luis Vigereaux heard the news and was moved to try to help the victims. He needed someone to whom the people would listen, someone who could say what had to be said and get the work done that had to be done and help the people who had to be helped.

"I knew," Luis Vigereaux said, "Roberto was such a person, perhaps the only such person who would be willing to help."

And so the mercy project, which would eventually claim Roberto's life, began. He appeared on television. But he needed a staging area. The city agreed to give him Sixto Escobar Stadium.

"Bring what you can," he told them. "Bring medicine...bring clothes...bring food... bring shoes...bring yourself and help us load. We need so much. Whatever you bring, we will use."

And the people of San Juan came. They walked through the heat and they drove cars and battered little trucks, and the mound of supplies grew and grew. Within two days, the first mercy planes left for Nicaragua.

Meanwhile, a ship had been chartered and loaded. And as it prepared to steam away, unhappy stories began to drift back from Nicaragua. Not all the supplies that had been flown in, it was rumored, were getting through. Puerto Ricans who had flown the planes had no passports, and Nicaragua was in a state of panic.

"We have people there who must be protected. We have black-market types that must not be allowed to get their hands on these supplies," Clemente told Luis Vigereaux. "Someone must make

brace (brās) *n.*, grove that provides shelter from wind

(Opposite page) San Juan Harbor in Puerto Rico.

sure—particularly before the ship gets there. I'm going on the next plane."

The plane they had rented was an old DC-7. It was scheduled to take off at 4:00 P.M. on December 31, 1972. Long before take-off time, it was apparent that the plane needed more work. It had even taxied onto the runway and then turned back. The trouble, a mechanic who was at the airstrip that day conjectured, had to do with both port [left side] engines. He worked on them most of the afternoon.

The departure time was delayed an hour, and then two, and then three. Across town, a man named Rudy Hernandez, who had been a teammate of Roberto's when they were rookies in the Puerto Rican League and who had later pitched for the Washington Senators, was trying to contact Roberto by telephone. He had just received a five-hundred-dollar donation, and he wanted to know where to send it. He called Roberto's wife, Vera, who told him that Roberto was going on a trip and that he might catch him at the airport. She had been there herself only moments before to pick up some friends who were coming in from the States, and she had left because she was fairly sure that the trouble had cleared and Roberto had probably left already.

"I caught him at the airport and I was surprised," Rudy Hernandez told me. "I said I had this money for Nicaraguan relief and I wanted to know what to do with it. Then I asked him where he was going."

"Nicaragua," Clemente told him.

"It's New Year's Eve, Roberto. Let it wait."

"Who else will go?" Roberto told him. "Someone has to do it."

"Who else will go?" Roberto told him. "Someone has to do it."

At 9 P.M., even as the first stirrings of the annual New Year's Eve celebration were beginning in downtown San Juan, the DC-7 taxied onto the runway, received clearance, rumbled down the narrow concrete strip, and pulled away from the earth. It headed out over the Atlantic and banked toward Nicaragua, and its tiny lights disappeared on the horizon.

Just ninety seconds later, the tower at San Juan International Airport received this message from the pilot: "We are coming back around."

Just that.

Nothing more.

And then there was a great silence.

"It was almost midnight," recalls Rudy Hernandez, a former teammate of Roberto's. "We were having this party in my restaurant, and somebody turned on the radio and the announcer was saying that Roberto's plane was feared missing. And then, because my place is on the beach, we saw these giant floodlights crisscrossing the waves, and we heard the sound of the helicopters and the little search planes."

Drawn by a common sadness, the people of San Juan began to make their way toward the beach, toward Puente Maldonado. A cold rain had begun to fall. It washed their faces and blended with the tears.

They came by the thousands and they watched for three days. Towering waves boiled up and made the search virtually impossible. The U.S. Navy sent a team of expert divers into the area, but the battering of the waves defeated them too. Midway

con•jec•ture (kən jek′ chər) *v.*, predict; guess

through the week, the pilot's body was found in the swift-moving currents to the north. On Saturday bits of the cockpit were sighted.

And then—nothing else.

"I was born in the Dominican Republic," Rudy Hernandez said, "but I've lived on this island for more than twenty years. I have never seen a time or a sadness like that. The streets were empty, the radios silent, except for the constant bulletins about Roberto. Traffic? Forget it. All of us cried. All of us who knew him and even those who didn't, wept that week.

"Manny Sanguillen, the Pittsburgh catcher, was down here playing winter ball, and when Manny heard the news he ran to the beach and he tried to jump into the ocean with skin-diving gear. I told him, man, there's sharks there. You can't help. Leave it to the experts. But he kept going back. All of us were a little crazy that week.

"There will never be another like Roberto."

Who was he...I mean really?

Well, nobody can put together all the pieces of another man's life. But there are so many who want the world to know that it is not as impossible a search as you might think.

He was born in Carolina, Puerto Rico. Today the town has about 125,000 people, but when Roberto was born there in 1934, it was roughly one-sixth its current size.

María Isabella Casares is a schoolteacher. She has taught the children of Carolina for thirty years. Most of her teaching has been done in tenth-grade history classes. Carolina is her home and its children are her children. And among all of those whom she calls her own (who are all the children she taught), Roberto Clemente was something even more special to her.

"His father was an overseer on a sugar plantation. He did not make much money," she explained in an empty classroom at Julio Coronado School. "But then, there are no rich children here. There never have been. Roberto was typical of them. I had known him when he was a small boy because my father had run a grocery store in Carolina, and Roberto's parents used to shop there."

There is this thing that you have to know about María Isabella Casares before we hear more from her. What you have to know is that she is the model of what a teacher should be. Between her and her students even now, as back when Roberto attended her school, there is this common bond of mutual respect. Earlier in the day, I had watched her teach a class in the history of the Abolition Movement in Puerto Rico. I don't speak much Spanish, but even to me it was clear that this is how a class should be, this is the kind of person who should teach, and these are the kinds of students such a teacher will produce.

With this as a background, what she has to say about Roberto Clemente carries much more impact.

"Each year," she said, "I let my students choose the seats they want to sit in. I remember the first time I saw Roberto. He was a very shy boy and he went straight to the back of the room and chose the very last seat. Most of the time he would sit with his eyes down. He was an average student. But there was something very special about him. We would talk after class for hours. He wanted to be an engineer, you know, and perhaps he could have been. But then he began to play softball, and one day he came to me and said, 'Teacher, I have a problem.'

"He told me that Pedron Zarrilla, who was one of our most prominent baseball people, had seen him play, and that Pedron wanted him to sign a professional contract with the Santurce Crabbers. He asked me what he should do.

"I have thought about that conversation many times. I believe Roberto could have been almost anything, but God gave him a gift that few have, and he chose to use that gift. I remember that on that day I told him, 'This is your chance, Roberto. We are poor people in this town. This is your chance to do something. But if in your heart you prefer not to try, then Roberto, that will be your problem—and your decision.'"

There was and there always remained a closeness between this boy-soon-to-be-a-man and his favorite teacher.

"Once, a few years ago, I was sick with a very bad back. Roberto, not knowing this, had driven over from Rio Piedras, where his house was, to see me."

"Where is the teacher?" Roberto asked Mrs. Casares' stepdaughter that afternoon.

"Teacher is sick, Roberto. She is in bed."

"Teacher," Roberto said, pounding on the bedroom door, "get up and put on your clothes. We are going to the doctor whether you want to or not."

"I got dressed," Mrs. Casares told me, "and he picked me up like a baby and carried me in his arms to the car. He came every day for fifteen days, and most days he had to carry me, but I went to the doctor and he treated me. Afterward, I said to the doctor that I wanted to pay the bill.

"'Mrs. Casares,' he told me, 'please don't start with that Clemente, or he will kill me. He has paid all your bills, and don't you dare tell him I have told you.'

"Well, Roberto was like that. We had been so close. You know, I think I was there the day he met Vera, the girl he later married. She was one of my students, too. I was working part-time in the pharmacy and he was already a baseball player by then, and one day Vera came into the store.

"'Teacher,' Roberto asked me, 'who is that girl?'

"'That's one of my students,' I told him. 'Now don't you dare bother her. Go out and get someone to introduce you. Behave yourself.'

"He was so proper, you know. That's just what he did, and that's how he met her, and they were married here in Carolina in the big church on the square."

On the night Roberto Clemente's plane disappeared, Mrs. Casares was at home, and a delivery boy from the pharmacy stopped by and told her to turn on the radio and sit down. "I think something has happened to someone who is very close with you, Teacher, and I want to be here in case you need help."

María Isabella Casares heard the news. She is a brave woman, and months later, standing in front of the empty crypt in the cemetery at Carolina where Roberto Clemente was to have been buried, she said, "He was like a son to me. This is why I want to tell you about him. This is why you must make people—particularly our people, our Puerto Rican children—understand what he was. He was like my son, and he is all our sons in a way. We must make sure that the children never forget how beautiful a man he was."

The next person to touch Roberto Clemente was Pedron Zarrilla, who owned the Santurce club. He was the man who discovered Clemente on the country softball team, and he was the man who signed him for a four-hundred-dollar bonus.

"He was a skinny kid," Pedron Zarrilla recalls, "but even then he had those large powerful hands, which we all noticed right away. He joined us, and he was nervous. But I watched him, and I said to myself, 'this kid can throw and this kid can run, and this kid can hit. We will be patient

Roberto Clemente slides home in a 1971 game against the Montreal Expos.

with him.' The season had been through several games before I finally sent him in to play."

Luis Olmo remembers that game. Luis Olmo had been a major-league outfielder with the Brooklyn Dodgers. He had been a splendid ballplayer. Today he is in the insurance business in San Juan. He sat in his office and recalled very well that first moment when Roberto Clemente stepped up to bat.

"I was managing the other team. They had a man on base and this skinny kid comes out. Well, we had never seen him, so we didn't really know how to pitch to him. I decided to throw him a few bad balls and see if he'd bite.

"He hit the first pitch. It was an outside fast ball, and he never should have been able to reach it. But he hit it down the line for a double. He was the best bad-ball hitter I have ever seen, and if you ask major-league pitchers who are pitching today, they will tell you the same thing. After a while it got so that I just told my pitchers to throw the ball down the middle because he was going to hit it no matter where they put it, and at least if he decided not to swing we'd have a strike on him.

"I played in the big leagues. I know what I am saying. He was the greatest we ever had...maybe one of the greatest anyone ever had. Why did he have to die?"

Once Pedron Zarrilla turned him loose, there was no stopping Roberto Clemente. As Clemente's confidence grew, he began to get better and better. He was the one the crowd came to see out at Sixto Escobar Stadium.

"You know, when Clemente was in the lineup," Pedron Zarrilla says, "there was always this undercurrent of excitement in the ball park. You knew that if he was coming to bat, he would do something spectacular. You knew that if he was on first base, he was going to try to get to second base. You knew that if he was playing right field and there was a man on third base, then that man on third base already knew what a lot of men on third base in the majors were going to find out—you don't try to get home against Roberto Clemente's arm.

"I remember the year that Willie Mays came down here to play in the same outfield with him for the winter season. I remember the wonderful things they did and I remember that Roberto still had the best of it.

"Sure I knew we were going to lose him. I knew it was just a matter of time. But I was only grateful that we could have him if only for that little time."

The major-league scouts began to make their moves. Olmo was then scouting, and he tried to sign him for the Giants. But it was the Dodgers who won the bidding war. The Dodgers had Clemente, but in having him, they had a major problem. He had to be hidden.

This part takes a little explaining. Under the complicated draft rules that baseball used at that time, if the Dodgers were not prepared to bring Clemente up to their major-league team within a year (and because they were winning with proven players, they couldn't), then Clemente could be claimed by another team.

They sent him to Montreal with instructions to the manager to use him as little as possible, to hide him as much as possible, and to tell everyone he had a sore back, a sore arm, or any other excuse the manager could give. But how do you hide a diamond when he's in the middle of a field of broken soda bottles?

In the playoffs that year against Syracuse, they had to use Clemente. He hit two doubles and a home run and threw a man out at home the very first try.

The Pittsburgh Pirates had a man who saw it all. They drafted him at the season's end.

And so Roberto Clemente came to Pittsburgh. He was the finest prospect the club had had in a long, long time. But the Pirates of those days were spectacular losers and even Roberto Clemente couldn't turn them around overnight.

"We were bad, all right," recalls Bob Friend, who later became a great Pirate pitcher. "We lost over a hundred games, and it certainly wasn't fun to go to the ball park under those conditions. You couldn't blame the fans for being noisy and impatient. Branch Rickey, our general manager, had promised a winner. He called it his five-year plan. Actually, it took ten."

When Clemente joined the club, it was Friend who made it his business to try to make him feel at home. Roberto was, in truth, a moody man, and the previous season hadn't helped him any.

"I will never forget how fast he became a superstar in this town," says Bob Friend. "Later he would have troubles because he was either hurt or thought he was hurt, and some people would say that he was loafing. But I know he gave it his best shot and he helped make us winners."

The first winning year was 1960, when the Pirates won the pennant and went on to beat the Yankees in the seventh game of the World Series. Whitey Ford, who pitched against him twice in that Series, recalls that Roberto actually made himself look bad on an outside pitch to encourage Whitey to come back with it. "I did," Ford recalls, "and he unloaded. Another thing I remember is the way he ran out a routine ground ball in the last game and when we were a little slow covering, he beat it out. It was something most people forget but it made the Pirates' victory possible."

The season was over. Roberto Clemente had hit safely in every World Series game. He had batted over .300. He had been a

superstar. But when they announced the Most Valuable Player Award voting, Roberto had finished a distant third.

"I really don't think he resented the fact that he didn't win it," Bob Friend says. "What hurt—and in this he was right—was how few votes he got. He felt that he simply wasn't being accepted. He brooded about that a lot. I think his attitude became one of 'Well, I'm going to show them from now on so that they will never forget.'

"And you know, he sure did."

Roberto Clemente went home and married Vera. He felt less alone. Now he could go on and prove what it was he had to prove. And he was determined to prove it.

"I know he was driven by thoughts like that," explains Buck Canel, a newspaper writer who covers all sports for most of the hemisphere's Spanish language papers. "He would talk with me often about his feelings. You know, Clemente felt strongly about the fact that he was a Puerto Rican and that he was a black man. In each of these things he had pride.

"On the other hand, because of the early language barriers, I am sure that there were times when he *thought* people were laughing at him when they were not. It is difficult for a Latin-American ballplayer to understand everything said around him when it is said at high speed, if he doesn't speak English that well. But, in any event, he wanted very much to prove to the world that he was a superstar and that he could do things that in his heart he felt he had already proven."

In later years, there would be people who would say that Roberto was a hypochondriac (someone who *imagined* he was sick or hurt when he was not). They could have been right, but if they were, it made the things he did even more remarkable. Because I can testify that I saw him throw his body into outfield fences, teeth first, to make remarkable plays. If he thought he was hurt at the time, then the act was even more courageous.

Matty Alou, Manny Mota, Roberto Clemente, and Willie Stargell, members of the 1966 Pittsburgh Pirates.

His moment finally came. It took eleven years for the Pirates to win a World Series berth again, and when they did in 1971, it was Roberto Clemente who led the way. I will never forget him as he was during that 1971 series with the Orioles, a Series that the Pirates figured to lose, and in which they, in fact, dropped the first two games down in Baltimore.

When they got back to Pittsburgh for the middle slice of the tournament, Roberto Clemente went to work and led this team. He was a superhero during the five games that followed. He was the big man in the Series. He was the MVP.[1] He was everything he had ever dreamed of being on a ball field.

1. **MVP.** Most Valuable Player

Most important of all, the entire country saw him do it on network television, and never again—even though nobody knew it would end so tragically soon—was anyone ever to doubt his ability.

The following year, Clemente ended the season by collecting his three-thousandth hit. Only ten other men had ever done that in the entire history of baseball.

"It was a funny thing about that hit," Willie Stargell, his closest friend on the Pirates, explains. "He had thought of taking himself out of the lineup and resting for the playoffs, but a couple of us convinced him that there had to be a time when a man had to do something for himself, so he went on and played and got it. I'm thankful that we convinced him, because, you know, as things turned out, that number three thousand was his last hit.

"When I think of Roberto now, I think of the kind of man he was. There was nothing phony about him. He had his own ideas about how life should be lived, and if you didn't see it that way, then he let you know in so many ways, without words, that it was best you each go your separate ways.

"He was a man who chose his friends carefully. His was a friendship worth having. I don't think many people took the time and the trouble to try to understand him, and I'll admit it wasn't easy. But he was worth it.

"The way he died, you know, I mean on that plane carrying supplies to Nicaraguans who'd been dying in that earthquake, well, I wasn't surprised he'd go out and do something like that. I wasn't surprised he'd go. I just never thought what happened could happen to him.

"But I know this. He lived a full life. And if he knew at that moment what the Lord had decided, well, I really believe he would have said, 'I'm ready.'"

He was thirty-eight years old when he died. He touched the hearts of Puerto Rico in a way that few people ever could. He touched a lot of other hearts, too. He touched hearts that beat inside people of all colors of skin.

He was one of the proudest of The Proud People. ✤

What is your reaction to the life and death of Roberto Clemente? What words would you use to describe him? Many people enjoy reading about famous sports figures in books, magazines, and newspapers. Why do you think this is so?

Find Meaning

1. (a) How did Roberto Clemente die? (b) Why was Clemente going to Nicaragua ?

2. Where did Clemente grow up?

3. (a) Who was María Isabella Casares? (b) What advice did she give Clemente?

Make Judgments

4. (a) What did Clemente's final actions reveal about him? (b) Why did people gather at Puente Maldonado by the thousands?

5. In what ways was Clemente a role model?

6. How well does "A Bittersweet Memoir" give readers an understanding of who Roberto Clemente was and how he changed the world? Explain your answer.

Searching for January

A Short Story by W. P. Kinsella

Is this some local fisherman playing a cruel joke on a tourist?

The sand is white as salt but powdery as icing sugar, cool on my bare feet, although if I push my toes down a few inches, yesterday's heat lurks, waiting to surface with the sun.

It is 6:00 A.M. and I am alone on a tropical beach a mile down from our hotel. The calm ocean is a clear, heart-breaking blue. Fifty yards out a few tendrils of sweet, gray fog laze above the water; farther out the mist, water, and pale morning sky merge.

It appears slowly out of the mist, like something from an Arthurian legend, a large, inflatable life raft, the depressing khaki and olive-drab of military camouflage. A man kneeling in front directs the raft with a paddle. He waves when he sees me, stands up and calls out in an urgent voice, but I can't make it out. As the raft drifts closer I can see that the lone occupant is tall and athletic-looking, dark-skinned, with a long jaw and flashing eyes.

"Clemente!" is the first word I hear clearly. "I am Clemente! The baseball player. My plane went down. Days ago! Everyone must think I am dead."

What he says registers slowly. Clemente! It has been fifteen years. Is this some local fisherman playing a cruel joke on a tourist?

"Yes," I call back, after pausing too long, scanning his features again. There is no question: it is Roberto Clemente. "I believe everyone does think you're dead."

"We crashed on New Year's Eve," he said. "I'm the only one who survived."

He steps <u>lithely</u> into the water, pulls the raft up on the beach, tosses the paddle back into the raft.

"Five days I've been out there," he says. "Give or take a day. I sliced up the other paddle with my pocket knife, made a spear. Caught three fish. Never thought I'd enjoy eating raw fish. But I was so hungry they tasted like they were cooked. By the way, where am I?"

I tell him.

He thinks a minute.

"It's possible. We crashed at night on the way to Managua. The plane was carrying three times the weight it should have, but the need was so great. Supplies for the earthquake victims.

"You look so surprised," he says after a pause. "Have they called off the air search already, given us up for dead?" When I remain silent he continues. "Which way is your hotel? I must call my wife, she'll be so worried."

"I am surprised. More than surprised. You are Roberto Clemente, the baseball player?"

"Of course."

"You were lost at sea?"

"Until now."

"There's something not quite right."

"Like what?" says Clemente.

"Like what year do you think this is?"

"When we took off it was 1972, but New Year's Eve. We crashed in the ocean. It must be January fifth or sixth, maybe even the seventh, 1973. I haven't been gone so long that I'd lose track of the year."

"What if I told you that it was March 1987?"

"I'd laugh. Look at me! I'd be an old man in 1987. I'd be..."

"Fifty two. Fifty three in August."

"How do you know that?"

"I know a little about baseball. I was a fan of yours."

He smiles in spite of himself.

"Thank you. But 1987? Ha! And I don't like the way you said *was. Was* a fan of mine." He touches spread fingers to his chest. "These are the clothes I wore the night we crashed. Do I look like I've been wearing

lithe•ly (līth´ lē) *adv.*, bending easily

them for fifteen years? Is this a fifteen-year growth of beard?" he asks, rubbing a hand across his stubbly chin. "A six-day beard would be my guess."

His eyes study me as if I were an umpire who just called an outside pitch strike three: my pale, tourist's skin, the slight stoop as if the weight of paradise is too much for me.

"Say, what are you doing out here alone at dawn?" Clemente says skeptically. "Are you escaped from somewhere?"

"No. But I think you may be. Believe me, it is 1987."

"Can't be. I can tell. I'm thirty-eight years old. I play baseball. See my World Series ring." He thrusts his hand toward me, the gold and diamonds glitter as the sun blushes above the horizon.

I dig frantically in my wallet. "Look!" I cry. "I'm from Seattle. Here's the 1987 Seattle Mariners schedule." I hold the pocket-sized schedule out for him to look at.

"Seattle doesn't have a team."

"They have a new franchise,[1] since 1977. Toronto came in the same year. Read the schedule."

He studies it for a moment.

"It's crazy, man. I've only been gone a few days."

We sit down on the sand, and I show him everything in my wallet: my credit cards, an uncashed check, my driver's license, coins, and bills.

"Try to remember when your plane went down. Maybe there's a clue there."

We walk slowly in the direction of the hotel, but at the edge of the bay, where we would turn inland, Clemente stops. We retrace our steps.

"It was late in the night. The plane was old. It groaned and creaked like a haunted house. I was sitting back with the cargo—bales of clothes, medical supplies—when the pilot started yelling that we were losing altitude. We must have practically been in the water before he noticed. We hit the ocean a few seconds later, and I was buried under boxes and bales as the cargo shifted. A wooden box bounced off my head, and I was out for...a few seconds or a few minutes." He rubs the top of his head.

"See, I still got the lump. And I bled some, too." He bends toward me so I can see the small swelling, the residue of dried blood clinging around the roots of his sleek, black hair.

"I yelled for the others but I don't know if they were alive or if they heard me."

"When I woke up I was in front of the emergency door, the cargo had rolled over me and I was snug against the exit. The plane must have been more than half submerged. There was this frightening slurping, gurgling sound. Then I realized my clothes were wet. The raft was on the wall right next to the door. I pulled the door open and the ocean flooded in. I set out the raft, inflated it, and took the paddles and the big water canteen off the wall. I yelled for the others but I don't know if they were alive or if they heard me. There was a mountain of cargo between me and the front of the plane.

"I climbed into the raft, paddled a few

1. **franchise.** Right or license granted to a group

yards, and when I looked back the plane was gone. I've been drifting for five or six days, and here I am."

"I don't know where you've been, but you went missing New Year's Eve 1972. They elected you to the Baseball Hall of Fame in 1973, waived the five-year waiting period because you'd died a hero."

"Died?" Clemente begins a laugh, then thinks better of it. "What if I go back with you and call in?"

"You'll create one of the greatest sensations of all time."

"But my wife, my family. Will they all be fifteen years older?"

"I'm afraid so."

"My kids grown up?"

"Yes."

"Maybe my wife has remarried?"

"I don't know, but it's certainly a possibility."

"But, look at me, I'm thirty-eight years old, strong as a bull. The Pirates need me in the outfield."

"I know."

"My teammates?"

"All retired."

"No."

"If I remember right, Bruce Kison was the last to go, retired last year."

"Willie Stargell?"

"Retired in 1982. He's still in baseball but not playing."

"Then I suppose everyone that played at the same time, they're gone too? Marichal? Seaver? Bench? McCovey? Brock? McCarver? Carlton?"

"Carlton's won over three hundred games, but he doesn't know when to quit. He's a marginal player in the American League. So is Don Sutton, though he's also won three hundred. Jerry Reuss is still hanging on, maybe one or two others. Hank Aaron broke Babe Ruth's home-run record, then a guy from Japan named Sadaharu Oh broke Hank Aaron's record."

"And my Pirates?"

"Gone to hell in a handbasket. They won the World Series in '78, Willie Stargell's last hurrah. They've been doormats for several seasons, will be again this year. Attendance is down to nothing; there's talk of moving the franchise out of Pittsburgh."

"They need Roberto Clemente."

"Indeed they do."

"And Nicaragua? The earthquake?"

"The earth wills out," I said. "The will of the people to survive is so strong....The earthquake is history now."

"And Puerto Rico? Is my home a state yet?"

"Not yet."

He looks longingly toward the path that leads to the hotel and town. We sit for a long time in that sand white as a bridal gown. He studies the artifacts of my life. Finally he speaks.

"If I walk up that path, and if the world is as you say—and I think I believe you—I will become a curiosity. The media will swarm

over me unlike anything I've ever known. Religious fanatics will picnic on my blood. If I see one more person, I'll have no choice but to stay here."

"What are your alternatives?"

"I could try to pass as an ordinary citizen who just happens to look like Roberto Clemente did fifteen years ago. But if I become real to the world I may suddenly find myself white-haired and in rags, fifty-three years old."

"What about baseball?"

"I could never play again, I would give myself away. No one plays the game like Clemente."

"I remember watching you play. When you ran for a fly ball it was like you traveled three feet above the grass, your feet never touching. 'He has invisible pillows of angel hair attached to his feet,' my wife said one night, 'that's how he glides across the outfield.'

"Perhaps you could go to the Mexican Leagues," I suggest. "Remember George Brunet, the pitcher? He's still pitching in the badlands and he's nearly fifty."

"I suffer from greed, my friend, from wanting to claim what is mine: my family, my home, my wealth. My choice is all or nothing."

"The nothing being?"

"To continue the search."

"But how?"

"I've searched a few days and already I've found 1987. Time has tricked me some way. Perhaps if I continue searching for January 1973, I'll find it."

"And if you don't?"

"Something closer then, a time I could accept, that would accept me."

"But what if this is all there is? What if you drift forever? What if you drift until you die?"

"I can't leap ahead in time. It's unnatural. I just can't."

"If you came back to baseball, Three Rivers Stadium would be full every night. You could make Pittsburgh a baseball city again. You'd have to put up with the media, the curious, the fanatics. But perhaps it's what you're destined to do."

"I am destined to be found, maybe even on this beach, but fifteen years in your past. I intend to be found. I'll keep searching for January."

He walked a few steps in the direction of the raft.

"Wait. I'll go and bring you supplies. I can be back in twenty minutes."

"No. I don't want to carry anything away from this time. I have five gallons of water, a bale of blankets to warm me at night, the ingenuity to catch food. Perhaps my footprints in the sand are already too much, who knows?"

He is wading in the clear water, already pushing the raft back into the ocean.

"If you find January...if the history I know is suddenly altered, I hope I went to see you play a few times. With you in the line-up the Pirates probably made it into the World Series in '74 and '75. They won their division those years, you know...you would have been the difference..."

I watch him drift. Trapped. Or am I trapped, here in 1987, while he, through some malfunction of the universe, is borne into timelessness? What if I were to accompany him?

"Wait!" I call. "There's something..."

But Clemente has already drifted beyond hearing. I watch as he paddles, his back broad and strong. Just as the mist is about to engulf him, as ocean, fog, and sky merge, he waves his oar once, holding it like a baseball bat, thrusting it at the soft, white sky. ✣

When have you wished to be in another place or time? Why did you feel that way? Why do you think most people have experienced this feeling in their lives?

Comparing Texts

AFTER READING

Find Meaning

1. (a) Who appears out of the mist in front of the narrator? (b) What does this person shout to the narrator?
2. (a) How many years have passed since Clemente's plane went down? (b) How does the narrator prove what year it actually is?

Make Judgments

3. What do Clemente's questions and statements reveal about his values?
4. Why does Clemente decide to go back to his raft?

Compare Literature

Characterization In *direct characterization,* an author or narrator makes direct statements about a character's personality. In *indirect characterization,* the writer reveals a character's personality through the character's words, thoughts, actions, appearance, or the words and thoughts of other characters. Review the descriptions that you recorded in your chart to answer these questions.

1. What did Clemente look like?
2. Find an example of direct and indirect characterization of Clemente from Izenberg's biography or Kinsella's short story.
3. Which selection contains the most examples of Clemente's conversation, regardless of whether this conversation is fictional or not?

Extend Understanding

Writing Options

Creative Writing Imagine that the narrator in "Searching for January" reported his experience on the beach. Assume that you have interviewed the narrator, and write a brief **news article** about the incident. Use quotations from your imaginary interview and information you learned from reading the story.

Informative Writing In an **essay,** compare and contrast Clemente as presented in the biography and in the short story. First, use a graphic organizer to show the features you want to write about, such as appearance, character, achievements, and effect on others. You may organize your work either by examining how Clemente is presented first in one work and then in the other or by discussing each feature in turn. Share your work with the class.

Collaborative Learning

Create a Dialogue Imagine that the narrator of "Searching for January" runs into Clemente once again, after several more years have passed, and Clemente still hasn't changed. Working in pairs, create a dialogue between Clemente and the narrator of "Searching for January." Perform your dialogue for the class.

Media Literacy

Conduct Internet Research Evaluate the home pages of two or three sports organizations. Include in your evaluation how well the home page is organized, how current the information is, how easy it is to find information, and whether you find errors of any kind. Present your findings to the class.

MW Go to **www.mirrorsandwindows.com** for more.

Madam C. J. Walker

A Biography by Jim Haskins

DIRECTED READING

BEFORE READING

Build Background

Historical Context Life for African Americans was very difficult during and just after Reconstruction, the period that followed the Civil War. Many white people refused to hire freed slaves or train them for careers other than farming or manual labor. Many African Americans became sharecroppers. A sharecropper provided farm labor in return for a share in the profits from the crop produced. But sharecroppers had to buy food and equipment from the landowner, and the share of the crop was typically not enough to pay for these things. Often sharecroppers were left with no money or even went into debt.

Reader's Context What goals do you have for your life? What obstacles might you face in achieving these goals?

Set Purpose

Preview the Historical Context and the first page of "Madam C. J. Walker." Predict how Madam Walker might have overcome the obstacles faced by African-American business owners.

Analyze Literature

Introduction and Conclusion An **introduction** to a literary work should capture the reader's attention and present the subject of the work. A **conclusion** should sum up the ideas presented in the piece and present a final analysis of the subject. As you read, pay close attention to the introduction and conclusion of this selection.

Use Reading Skills

Context Clues Unlock the meaning of each word by using the context clues provided in the sentences.

1. Sheri withdrew from the class, with the provision that she could retake it.
2. We protested the decision to segregate students based on race.
3. The coach will try to recruit Gabriel for the basketball team.
4. Mia's ambition is to become a doctor.
5. The ancient Romans held lavish feasts with endless food.
6. The captain made the astute decision to return to port when he saw the storm.

Preview Vocabulary

pro•vi•sion (prə vi´ zhən) *n.*, arrangement made beforehand to deal with a certain need

seg•re•gate (seg´ ri gāt') *v.*, separate a race, class, or ethnic group from the rest of the population; set apart

re•cruit (ri krüt´) *v.*, hire or engage the services

am•bi•tion (am bi´ shən) *n.*, drive to succeed

lav•ish (la´ vish) *adj.*, abundant; rich

as•tute (ə stüt´) *adj.*, possessing practical intelligence and the ability to make good decisions

Meet the Author

Jim Haskins (1941–2005) wrote more than one hundred books in his lifetime. Many of his books tell the stories of famous African Americans, including Rosa Parks, Thurgood Marshall, and Colin Powell. He won the *Washington Post* Children's Book Guild Award for his nonfiction books for young people. Haskins was an English professor at the University of Florida.

Madam C. J. Walker

A Biography by Jim Haskins

Then one night she had a dream.

Madam C. J. Walker was the first American woman to earn a million dollars. There were American women millionaires before her time, but they had inherited their wealth, either from their husbands or from their families. Madam Walker was the first woman to earn her fortune by setting up her own business and proving that women could be financially independent of men. The company she started in the early years of this century is still in operation today.

Madam C. J. Walker was born Sarah Breedlove on December 23, 1867. She grew up in the South under very racist conditions. Her parents, Owen and Minerva Breedlove, had been slaves until President Abraham Lincoln's Emancipation Proclamation and the Union victory in the Civil War had freed the slaves.

Madam C. J. Walker was the first American woman to earn a million dollars.

After the war, few provisions were made to help former slaves become independent. They did not receive money to help them get started in their new lives. They were uneducated, they had few skills except the ability to grow crops, and many were unaware of what freedom meant. Like the majority of former slaves, the Breedloves remained on the Burney family plantation in Delta, Louisiana. They had little choice but to stay on the same land where they had been slaves, only now they were sharecroppers.

Sharecroppers farm land for a landowner. In return, they receive a place to live and part of the crop. But since they must buy what they cannot grow from the landowner, when they harvest the crop they find themselves owing whatever is their share to the landowner anyway.

The Breedloves sharecropped cotton. Like her brothers and sisters, Sarah was working in the cotton fields by the time she was six. By the time she was seven, both her parents were dead, and she moved in with her older sister, Louvenia. A few years later, they moved across the river to Vicksburg, Mississippi.

Sarah had little schooling. Like other sharecroppers' children, she had a chance to go to school only when there were no crops to be planted or harvested, which totaled about four months out of the year. She also had little happiness in her childhood. Not only was she an orphan, but she also suffered at the hands of her sister's cruel husband. Sarah was just fourteen when she married a man named McWilliams to get away from her sister's household.

By the time Sarah got married, conditions in the South for blacks were actually worse than they had been during slavery. This was the time when Jim Crow laws were passed, segregating southern blacks from whites in nearly every area of life. It was the time when white supremacy groups like the Ku Klux Klan achieved their greatest power, and lynchings of blacks were common.

Sarah and her husband lived with the terror of being black as best they could. In

pro • vi • sion (prə vi´ zhən) *n.*, arrangement made beforehand to deal with a certain need

seg • re • gate (seg´ ri gāt') *v.*, separate a race, class, or ethnic group from the rest of the population; set apart

1885 their daughter, Lelia, was born, and her parents dreamed of making a better life for their little girl. Then, when Lelia was two, McWilliams was killed by a lynch mob.[1]

Sarah was a widow at the age of twenty, and the sole support of a two-year-old daughter. She took in laundry to earn a living and was determined to leave the South. With Lelia, she made her way up the Mississippi River and settled in St. Louis, where she worked fourteen hours a day doing other people's laundry. She enrolled Lelia in the St. Louis public schools and was pleased that her daughter would get the education that had been denied to her. But she wanted more for her daughter and for herself.

The Coiffeur. Anne Goldthwaite. The Newark Museum, Newark, New Jersey.

Not long after they moved to St. Louis, Sarah McWilliams realized that her hair was falling out. She did not know why, but it is likely that the practice of braiding her hair too tightly was part of the cause. At the time, few hair-care products were available for black women. The ideal was straight, "white," hair, and to achieve this effect black women divided their hair into sections, wrapped string tightly around each section, and then twisted them. When the hair was later combed out, it was straighter. But this procedure pulled on the scalp and caused the hair to fall out.

Sarah was not the only black woman to suffer from hair loss. But she was one who refused to accept the idea that there was nothing she could do about it. For years she tried every hair-care product available. But nothing worked.

Then one night she had a dream. As she told the story many years later, in her dream "a black man appeared to me and told me what to mix up for my hair. Some of the remedy was grown in Africa, but I sent for it, mixed it, put it on my scalp, and in a few weeks my hair was coming in faster than it had ever fallen out." Sarah never publicly revealed[2] the formula of her mixture.

Sarah's friends remarked on what a full and healthy head of hair she had, and she gave some of her mixture to them. It worked on them, too, so she decided to sell it. She later said that she started her "Hair Grower" business with an investment of $1.50.

She had not been in business long when she received word that a brother who lived in Denver, Colorado, had died, leaving a wife and daughters. Her own daughter, Lelia, was attending Knoxville College, a private black college in Tennessee, and did not need her around all the time. Sarah decided to go to

1. **McWilliams...mob.** No documentation actually proves that he died this way.
2. **revealed.** Showed; made known

Denver to live with her sister-in-law and nieces.

In Denver, Sarah began to sell her special haircare product and did well. But she realized she needed to advertise to get more customers. Six months after arriving in Denver, she married C. J. Walker, a newspaperman who knew a lot about selling by mail order. With his help, she began to advertise her product, first in black newspapers across the state and later in black newspapers nationwide, and to make more money.

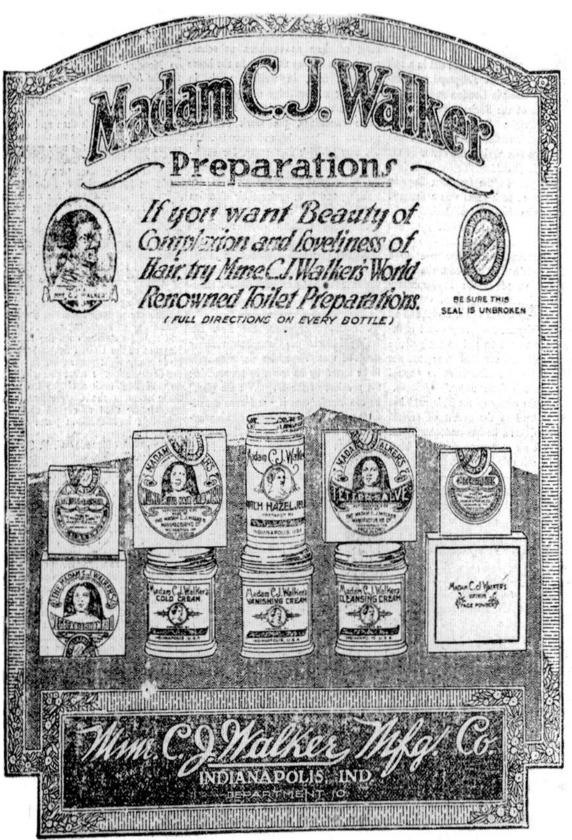

Advertisement showing Madam C. J. Walker's hair and skin products.

But soon her marriage was in trouble. As Sarah Walker later said of her husband, "I had business disagreements with him, for when we began to make ten dollars a day, he thought that amount was enough and that I should be satisfied. But I was convinced that my hair preparations would fill a longfelt want, and when we found it impossible to agree, due to his narrowness of vision, I embarked in business for myself."

In addition to helping her learn about advertising, her marriage gave Sarah Breedlove McWilliams Walker the name she would use for the rest of her life—Madam C. J. Walker. The "Madam" part was an affectation,[3] but Sarah liked the way it sounded. She thought it would be good for her business. By 1906 her business was so well that she was able to stop doing laundry for a living and devote all her time to her hair-care company. Her products by this time included "Wonderful Hair Grower," "Glossine" hair oil, "Temple Grower," and "Tetter Salve" for the scalp.

Madam Walker was very proud of being a woman, and she was convinced that she could make it in the business world without the help of men. Almost from the start she determined that her business would be run by women. In 1906 she put her twenty-one-year-old daughter, Lelia, in charge of her growing mail-order business. She herself started traveling throughout the South and East selling her preparations and teaching her methods of hair care. She was so successful that two years later she and Lelia moved to Pittsburgh, Pennsylvania, and started Lelia College, which taught the Walker System of hair care.

Once again, Lelia ran the business while her mother traveled thousands of miles to spread the word. Madam Walker realized that the normal outlets for her products—white department stores and pharmacies—

3. affectation. Artificial behavior meant to impress others were not open to her. These stores would not stock black products because they did not want black customers. In addition to advertising, mostly in black newspapers, Madam Walker had to depend on the institutions in the black communities, the black churches, and the black women's clubs.

Madam Walker's lectures on hair culture were widely attended. She was an excellent speaker and a commanding woman, nearly six feet tall, who was always beautifully dressed and coiffed.[4] She made a lasting impression wherever she went.

Her travels, and her personality, brought her into contact with many important black people. She joined the National Association of Colored Women and through that organization met the educator Mary McLeod Bethune. She also met Ida B. Wells-Barnett, who worked for the right of women to vote, and against lynching in the South. She formed friendships with these women, who helped her spread the word about her business.

She was an excellent speaker and a commanding woman, nearly six feet tall, who was always beautifully dressed and coiffed.

Although she lacked the formal education that most of these women had, Madam Walker never felt ashamed of her shortcomings[5] in that area. She taught herself as much as she could and was not afraid to ask someone to define a word she did not know or explain something she did not understand.

There were other black hair-care companies in business at this time. A couple of companies were owned by whites. But they stressed hair straightening. Madam Walker emphasized hair care. Most of the products she developed were aimed at producing healthy hair, not straight hair. She did design a steel comb with teeth spaced far enough apart to go through thick hair, but its main purpose was not hair straightening.

Madam Walker also wanted black women to go into business. Why should they toil over hot laundry tubs and clean white people's houses when they could be in business for themselves? Helping other black women also helped the Walker Company, and with this goal in mind Madam Walker recruited and trained scores of women to use and sell Walker products. Many of them set up salons in their own homes. Others traveled door-to-door selling Walker products and demonstrating the Walker System. Madam Walker insisted that her agents sign contracts promising to abide by her strict standards of personal hygiene[6]—long before various states passed similar laws for workers in the cosmetics field. By 1910 the Walker Company had trained around 5,000 black female agents, not just in the United States but in England, France, Italy, and the West Indies. The company itself was taking in $1,000 a day, seven days a week.

That same year, Madam Walker's travels took her to Indianapolis, Indiana, a city that impressed her so much that she decided to

---

4. **coiffed.** Styled, specifically hair
5. **shortcomings.** Less than what is expected or required
6. **hygiene.** Cleanliness and sanitary practices

re•cruit (ri krüt´) *v.*, hire or engage the services

move her headquarters there. She put a man in charge of her operations, which was a departure from her usual philosophy, but Freeman B. Ransom was, in her opinion, an unusual man.

She had met him in her travels when he was working as a train porter summers and during school vacations, while working his way through Columbia University Law School. He impressed her with his ambition and with his vision of progress for blacks. When he finished school, she put him in charge of her Indianapolis headquarters.

In 1913 Lelia moved from Pittsburgh to New York to expand the Walker Company's East Coast operations. Madam Walker built a lavish town house in Harlem at 108–110 West 136th Street and installed a completely equipped beauty parlor.

...Madam Walker insisted that the Madam C. J. Walker Company always be headed by a woman....

Lelia had become an astute businesswoman herself, although she did not have the drive of her mother. Lelia, who changed her name to A'Lelia, liked to enjoy the fruits of their success. The Walker town house soon became the "in" place for parties in Harlem, attended by wealthy and artistic people, black and white.

Madam Walker also enjoyed spending the money she made. In 1917 she built a $250,000 mansion on the Hudson River in upstate New York. She hired the black architect Vertner Tandy to design it and named it Villa Lewaro. She drove around in an electric car, dressed in the finest clothing, and was said to have spent $7,000 on jewelry in a single afternoon.

Madam Walker also gave generously to charity. She had a strong interest in education and took time out of her busy schedule to be tutored by Booker T. Washington, founder of Tuskegee Institute in Alabama. She became an avid reader of literature and American history. She encouraged her friend Mary McLeod Bethune and later gave money to Mrs. Bethune to establish her Daytona Normal and Industrial Institute for Negro Girls in Daytona, Florida. When the National Association of Colored Women decided to pay off the mortgage on the home of the late black abolitionist Frederick Douglass, Madam Walker made the largest single contribution.

Madam Walker did not have much of a private life. She spent her time thinking of new ways to increase her business. The friends she had were people who could help her.

By 1917 the years of traveling and overwork began to take their toll on her. She developed high blood pressure, and in 1918 her doctors warned her that she had to slow down. She turned over her responsibilities in the business to her daughter, to Freeman B. Ransom, and to other trusted associates, and retired to her mansion, Villa Lewaro. There, she tried to relax, but her mind was always on her business. She died quietly of kidney failure resulting from hypertension in May 1919.

am • bi • tion (am bi´ shən) *n.*, drive to succeed

lav • ish (la´ vish) *adj.*, abundant; rich

as • tute (ə stüt´) *adj.*, possessing practical intelligence and the ability to make good decisions

In her will, Madam Walker left the bulk of her estate and the business to her daughter, A'Lelia. But she also provided generously for a variety of educational institutions run by black women, including $5,000 to Dr. Bethune's school. She established a trust fund for an industrial and mission school in West Africa and provided bequests[7] to Negro orphanages, old people's homes, and Negro YWCA branches. In addition, she made bequests to many friends and employees.

Also in her will, Madam Walker insisted that the Madam C. J. Walker Company always be headed by a woman, and her wishes were carried out. Her daughter, A'Lelia, became president of the company after her death and presided at the dedication of the new company headquarters in Indianapolis in 1927, fulfilling a long-held dream of her mother's.

Times have changed greatly since Madam C. J. Walker made her millions. Drugstores and department stores owned by both whites and blacks now stock hair- and skin-care products for black women. Many more companies, white and black, manufacture such products. In the midst of all that competition, the Walker Company is not as active as it once was, although it still sells some of the products Madam developed. The Walker Building is being renovated[8] as part of the rejuvenation of downtown Indianapolis. Now called the Madam Walker Urban Life Center, it houses professional offices and a cultural center.

Madam C. J. Walker, the daughter of former slaves, with little education, overcame the barriers of being black and a woman and succeeded beyond everyone's expectations but her own. ✣

---

7. **bequests.** Things handed down or passed on
8. **renovated.** Replaced worn and broken parts

Madam C. J. Walker helped many African-American women escape poverty and become successful businesswomen. If you could do one thing to help others, what would you choose to do and why?

Find Meaning

1. (a) What inspired Madam Walker to develop her first haircare product? (b) What did she realize she needed to do to get more customers?
2. (a) How did Madam Walker's second husband help her business? (b) Name all the ways that Madam Walker reached possible buyers for her products. Why did she need to use all these methods to sell her products?
3. (a) What did Madam Walker and her second husband disagree about? (b) Why did Madam Walker think her company could do better? (c) What does this suggest about her personality?

Make Judgments

4. (a) What hardships did Madam Walker experience from childhood until the time she started her own business? (b) How did Madam Walker help others who faced similar difficulties? (c) In what ways did she make a difference so that others might not face such a struggle?
5. (a) How did Madam Walker deal with her lack of formal education? (b) What does this behavior say about her?
6. (a) How does the author describe the character of Madam Walker? (b) How did these character traits help her succeed in business?

LITERATURE ▶▶ CONNECTION

In "Madam C. J. Walker," Jim Haskins tells the story of an African-American woman who built a successful business in spite of prejudice and discrimination. The following selection is from *The Sunflower Quilting Bee at Arles,* a story quilt by **Faith Ringgold** (b. 1930). Born in New York City, Ringgold began her career as a painter and is perhaps best known for her painted story quilts, which combine painting, quilted fabric, and storytelling. As you read, consider why the author has chosen to write about this group of women.

The Sunflower Quilting Bee at Arles

A Story Quilt by Faith Ringgold

1. The National Sunflower Quilters Society of America are having quilting bees in sunflower fields around the world to spread the cause of freedom. Aunt Melissa has written to inform me of this and to say: "Go with them to the sunflower fields in Arles.[1] And please take care of them in that foreign country, Willa Marie. These women are our freedom," she wrote.

2. Today the women arrived in Arles. They are Madame Walker, Sojourner Truth, Ida Wells, Fannie Lou Hamer, Harriet Tubman, Rosa Parks, Mary McLeod Bethune and Ella Baker, a fortress of African American women's courage, with enough energy to transform a nation piece by piece.

3. Look what they've done in spite of their oppression: Madame Walker invented the hair straightening comb and became the first self-made American-born woman millionaire. She employed over 3,000 people. Sojourner Truth spoke up brilliantly for women's rights during slavery, and could neither read nor write. Ida Wells made an exposé of the horror of lynching in the South.

4. Fannie Lou Hamer braved police dogs, water hoses, brutal beatings, and jail in order to register thousands of people to vote. Harriet Tubman brought over 300 slaves to freedom in 19 trips from the South on the Underground Railroad during slavery and never lost a passenger. Rosa Parks became the mother of the Civil Rights Movement when she sat down in the front of a segregated bus and refused to move to the back.

5. Mary McLeod Bethune founded Bethune Cookman College and was special advisor to Presidents Harry Truman and Franklin Delano Roosevelt. Ella Baker organized thousands of people to improve the condition of poor housing, jobs, and consumer education. Their trip to Arles was to complete *The Sunflower Quilt,* an international symbol of their dedication to change the world.

---

1. **Arles.** City in France where Vincent van Gogh painted many of his famous sunflower paintings.

6. The Dutch painter, Vincent van Gogh came to see the black women sewing in the sunflower fields. "Who is this strange looking man," they said. "He is un grand peintre," I told them, "though he is greatly troubled in his mind." He held a vase of sunflowers, no doubt une nature morte, a still life, for one of his paintings.

7. "He's the image of the man hit me in the head with a rock when I was a girl," Harriet said. "Make him leave. He reminds me of slavers." But he was not about to be moved. Like one of the sunflowers, he appeared to be growing out of the ground. Sojourner wept into the stitches of her quilting for the loss of her thirteen children mostly all sold into slavery.

8. One of Sojourner's children, a girl, was sold to a Dutch slaver in the West Indies who then took her to Holland. "Was that something this Dutch man might know something about? He should pay for all the pain his people has given us. I am concerned about you, Willa Marie. Is this a natural setting for a black woman?" Sojourner asked.

9. "I came to France to seek opportunity," I said. "It is not possible for me to be an artist in the States." "We are all artists. Piecing is our art. We brought it straight from Africa," they said. "That was what we did after a hard day's work in the fields to keep our sanity and our beds warm and bring beauty into our lives. That was not being an artist. That was being alive."

10. When the sun went down and it was time for us to leave, the tormented little man just settled inside himself and took on the look of the sunflowers in the field as if he were one of them. The women were finished piecing now. "We need to stop and smell the flowers sometimes," they said. "Now we can do our real quilting, our real art: making this world piece up right."

11. "I got to get back to that railroad," Harriet said. "Ain't all us free yet, no matter how many them laws they pass. Sojourner fighting for women's rights. Fannie for voter registration. Ella and Rosa working on civil rights. Ida looking out for mens getting lynch. Mary Bethune getting our young-uns' education, and Madame making money fixing hair and giving us jobs. Lord, we is sure busy."

12. "I am so thankful to my aunt Melissa for sending you wonderful women to me," I said. "Art can never change anything the way you have. But it can make a picture so everyone can see and know our true history and culture from the art. Some day I will make you women proud of me, too. Just wait, you'll see." "We see, Willa Marie," they said. "We see." ✤

TEXT TO TEXT CONNECTION

Jim Haskins's biography and Faith Ringgold's story quilt describe the accomplishments of Madam C. J. Walker and other African-American women. Which of Madam Walker's accomplishments are mentioned in both works? Through these accomplishments, how has Madam Walker contributed to the cause of freedom for African Americans?

AFTER READING

Analyze Literature

Introduction and Conclusion Effective introductions capture the reader's attention and present the subject of the literary work. Effective conclusions sum up the important ideas in a work and present the author's final analysis of the subject. How does Haskins capture the reader's attention in his introduction? What main idea is presented? How are the ideas in the conclusion related to the ideas in the introduction? What is the final point that Haskins makes about Madam Walker's accomplishments? When you are finished, summarize the author's description of Madam Walker's accomplishments. Exchange your summary with a classmate. In a paragraph, evaluate your classmates summary for accuracy of the main ideas, supporting details, and overall meaning of the selection.

Extend Understanding

Writing Options

Creative Writing A **jingle** is a short song or slogan that advertises a product and is easy to remember. Write a jingle to be used in a radio advertisement for one of Madam Walker's haircare products. Your jingle can be spoken or sung. Use concise but catchy language. In small groups, perform your jingle for other group members and vote on the jingle that is the most memorable. Note that advertisements and other media will often influence its audience with words, images, and sounds. When you evaluate your jingles, also evaluate the various ways different types of media influence their audiences. Consider whether the most memorable jingle incorporated any of these same techniques.

Informative Writing Pretend that you are writing a **biography** of someone you admire for a website devoted to great Americans. Choose a person who is currently making important contributions to American society or an important person from American history. Include a summary of the person's life and contributions to American society, and at least one quote in his or her own words.

Critical Literacy

Analyze a Speech A **policy speech** attempts to persuade a listener to support a change in government policy and contains quotations from experts and arguments that address policy issues. Identify and read the text of a contemporary speech that addresses women's rights. Interpret the speaker's purpose by asking questions or making comments about the evidence presented. Finally, analyze the structure of the speech's central argument and identify the different types of evidence used to support the argument.

Media Literacy

Analyze Advertisements Advertising for products has grown immensely on the Internet. Evaluate a variety of product websites that exist as online advertisements. You can enter types of products or specific brand names into any search engine to find ads. What do you learn about the products from the advertisement? What–if any–important information is missing? What methods does the advertisement use to sell the products? Does the ad contain music or sound? If so, how might the sound techniques influence the audience? Report on your findings to your classmates.

Go to **www.mirrorsandwindows.com** for more.

from Barrio Boy

A Memoir by Ernesto Galarza

INDEPENDENT READING

The two of us walked south on Fifth Street one morning to the corner of Q Street and turned right. Half of the block was occupied by the Lincoln School. It was a three-story wooden building, with two wings that gave it the shape of a double-T connected by a central hall. It was a new building, painted yellow, with a shingled roof that was not like the red tile of the school in Mazatlán.[1] I noticed other differences, none of them very reassuring.

We walked up the wide staircase hand in hand and through the door, which closed by itself. A mechanical contraption screwed to the top shut it behind us quietly.

In a matter of seconds I had to decide whether she was a possible friend or a menace.

Up to this point the adventure of enrolling me in the school had been carefully rehearsed. Mrs. Dodson had told us how to find it and we had circled it several times on our walks. Friends in the *barrio*[2] explained that the director was called a principal, and that it was a lady and not a man. They assured us that there was always a person at the school who could speak Spanish.

Exactly as we had been told, there was a sign on the door in both Spanish and

1. **Mazatlán.** Seaport in western Mexico
2. ***barrio.*** Spanish-speaking, urban neighborhood (Spanish)

Ernesto Galarza (1905–1984) began his life near Tepic, Mexico. Due to the instability and social upheaval caused by the Mexican Revolution, Galarza's family migrated to the United States. After settling in Sacramento, California, they worked as farm laborers. Galarza spent much of the rest of his life working with various labor groups to help improve conditions for poor farmhands. In 1979 he was nominated for a Nobel Prize in Literature.

English: "Principal." We crossed the hall and entered the office of Miss Nettie Hopley.

Miss Hopley was at a roll-top desk to one side, sitting in a swivel chair that moved on wheels. There was a sofa against the opposite wall, flanked by two windows and a door that opened on a small balcony. Chairs were set around a table and framed pictures hung on the walls of a man with long white hair and another with a sad face and a black beard.

The principal half turned in the swivel chair to look at us over the pinch glasses crossed on the ridge of her nose. To do this she had to duck her head slightly as if she were about to step through a low doorway.

What Miss Hopley said to us we did not know but we saw in her eyes a warm welcome and when she took off her glasses and straightened up she smiled wholeheartedly, like Mrs. Dodson. We were, of course, saying nothing, only catching the friendliness of her voice and the sparkle in her eyes while she said words we did not understand. She signaled us to the table. Almost tiptoeing across the office, I maneuvered myself to keep my mother between me and the gringo lady. In a matter of seconds I had to decide whether she was a possible friend or a menace. We sat down.

Then Miss Hopley did a formidable thing. She stood up. Had she been standing when we entered she would have seemed tall. But rising from her chair she soared. And what she carried up and up with her was a buxom superstructure,[3] firm shoulders, a straight sharp nose, full cheeks slightly molded by a curved line along the nostrils, thin lips that moved like steel springs, and a high forehead topped by hair gathered in a bun. Miss Hopley was not a giant in body but when she mobilized it to a standing position she seemed a match for giants. I decided I liked her.

She strode to a door in the far corner of the office, opened it and called a name. A boy of about ten years appeared in the doorway. He sat down at one end of the table. He was brown like us, a plump kid with shiny black hair combed straight back, neat, cool, and faintly obnoxious.

Miss Hopley joined us with a large book and some papers in her hand. She, too, sat down and the questions and answers began by way of our interpreter. My name was Ernesto. My mother's name was Henriqueta. My birth certificate was in San Blas. Here was my last report card from the Escuela Municipal Numero 3 para Varones of Mazatlán, and so forth. Miss Hopley put things down in the book and my mother signed a card.

As long as the questions continued, Doña Henriqueta could stay and I was secure. Now that they were over, Miss Hopley saw her to the door, dismissed our interpreter and without further ado took me by the hand and strode down the hall to Miss Ryan's first grade.

Miss Ryan took me to a seat at the front of the room, into which I shrank—the better to survey her. She was, to skinny, somewhat runty me, of a withering height when she patrolled the class. And when I least expected it, there she was, crouching by my desk, her blond radiant[4] face level with mine, her voice patiently maneuvering me over the awful idiocies of the English language.

During the next few weeks, Miss Ryan overcame my fears of tall, energetic teachers

3. buxom superstructure. Large body
4. radiant. Bright; lovely

Tribute to the American Working People (detail), 1951. Honoré D. Sharrer. Smithsonian American Art Museum, Washington, DC.

as she bent over my desk to help me with a word in the pre-primer. Step by step, she loosened me and my classmates from the safe anchorage[5] of the desks for recitations at the blackboard and consultations at her desk. Frequently she burst into happy announcements to the whole class. "Ito can read a sentence," and small Japanese Ito, squint-eyed and shy, slowly read aloud while the class listened in wonder: "Come, Skipper, come, Come and run." The Korean, Portuguese, Italian, and Polish first graders had similar moments of glory, no less shining than mine the day I conquered *butterfly*, which I had been persistently pronouncing in standard Spanish as boo-ter-flee. "Children," Miss Ryan called for attention. "Ernesto has learned how to pronounce butterfly!" And I proved it with a perfect imitation of Miss Ryan. From that celebrated success, I was soon able to match Ito's progress as a sentence reader with "Come, butterfly, come fly with me."

Like Ito and several other first graders who did not know English, I received private lessons from Miss Ryan in the closet, a narrow hall off the classroom with a door at each end. Next to one of these doors Miss Ryan placed a large chair for herself and a small one for me. Keeping an eye on the class through the open door she read with me about sheep in the meadow and a frightened chicken going to see the king, coaching me out of my phonetic rut in words like *pasture, bow-wow-wow, hay,* and *pretty,* which to my Mexican ear and eye had so many unnecessary sounds and letters. She made me watch her lips and then close my eyes as she repeated words I found hard to read. When we came to know each other better, I tried interrupting to tell Miss Ryan how we said it in Spanish. It didn't work. She only said "oh" and went on with *pasture, bow-wow-wow,* and *pretty*. It was as if in that closet we were both discovering together the secrets of the English language and grieving together over the tragedies of Bo-Peep. The main reason I was graduated with honors from the first grade was that I had fallen in love with Miss Ryan. Her radiant, no-nonsense character made us either afraid not to love her or love her so we would not be afraid, I am not sure which. It was not only that we sensed she was with it, but also that she was with us.

Like the first grade, the rest of the Lincoln School was a sampling of the lower part of town where many races made their home. My pals in the second grade were Kazushi, whose parents spoke only Japanese; Matti, a skinny Italian boy; and Manuel, a fat Portuguese who would never get into a fight but wrestled you to the ground and just sat on you. Our assortment of nationalities included Koreans, Yugoslavs, Poles, Irish, and home-grown Americans.

Miss Hopley and her teachers never let us forget why we were at Lincoln: for those who

5. **anchorage.** Place for putting in a ship's anchor; secure place

were alien, to become good Americans; for those who were so born, to accept the rest of us. Off the school grounds we traded the same insults we heard from our elders. On the playground we were sure to be marched up to the principal's office for calling someone a wop, a chink, a dago, or a greaser. The school was not so much a melting pot as a griddle where Miss Hopley and her helpers warmed knowledge into us and roasted racial hatreds out of us.

At Lincoln, making us into Americans did not mean scrubbing away what made us originally foreign. The teachers called us as our parents did, or as close as they could pronounce our names in Spanish or Japanese. No one was ever scolded or punished for speaking in his native tongue on the playground. Matti told the class about his mother's down quilt, which she had made in Italy with the fine feathers of a thousand geese. Encarnación acted out how boys learned to fish in the Philippines. I astounded the third grade with the story of my travels on a stagecoach, which nobody else in the class had seen except in the museum at Sutter's Fort. After a visit to the Crocker Art Gallery and a collection of heroic paintings of the golden age of California, someone showed a silk scroll with a Chinese painting. Miss Hopley herself had a way of expressing wonder over these matters before a class, her eyes wide open until they popped slightly. It was easy for me to feel that becoming a proud American, as she said we should, did not mean feeling ashamed of being a Mexican. ✣

When have you felt like an outsider? How did people make you feel, welcome or unwelcome? Why should people be open to newcomers?

Analyze and Extend

1. Describe some of Miss Ryan's characteristics, including how she looks and behaves. How do these traits affect the narrator?
2. What do you think was the most valuable thing Galarza gained by attending Lincoln School? Support your claim with evidence from the text.
3. Briefly describe Galarza's purpose or purposes. For example, is he writing to entertain, to inform, to persuade, or for a combination of these purposes?

Argumentative Writing Imagine that you are writing a **newspaper editorial** about how centuries of immigration in the United States have influenced the national character. Describe how you think immigrants from all over the world have influenced what it means to be an American. Use direct quotations or paraphrases from *Barrio Boy* as support.

Collaborative Learning With a partner, discuss the importance of a strong education. Create a list of as many main ideas and details in support of your thesis as possible. Then use this list to create a formal outline. Each main idea in your outline should have at least three details that support it. Use your outline to give a presentation to the class.

Go to **www.mirrorsandwindows.com** for more.

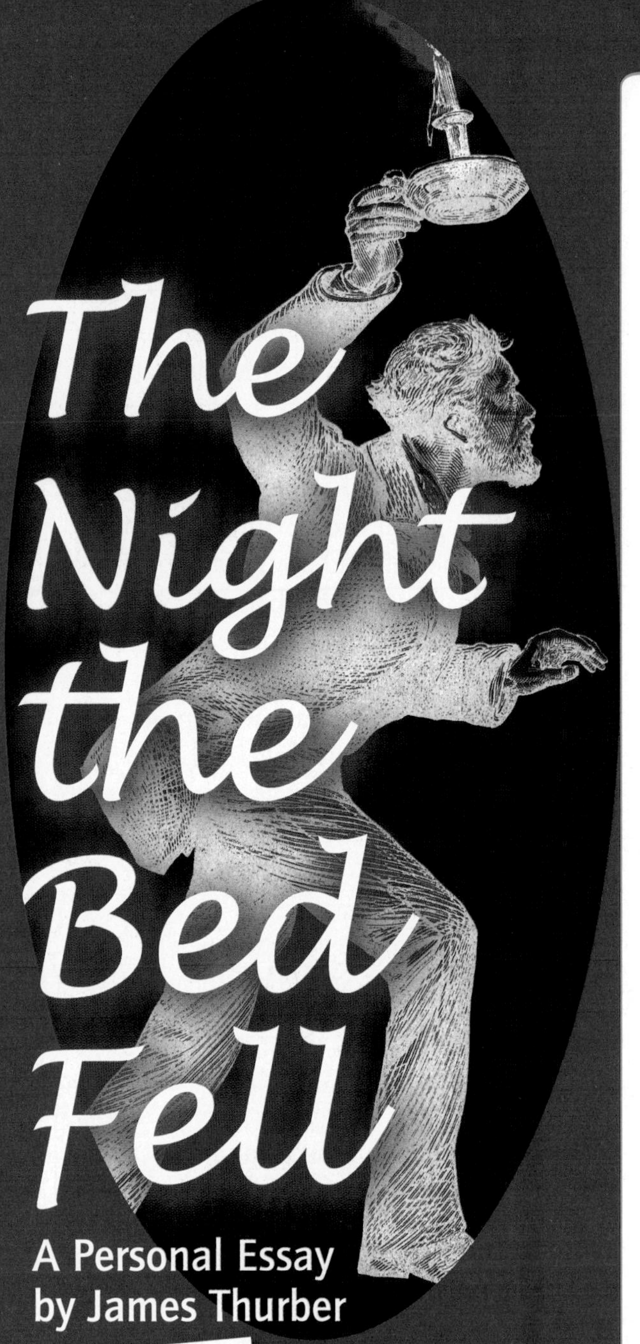

The Night the Bed Fell

A Personal Essay
by James Thurber

The situation was finally put together like a gigantic jigsaw puzzle.

I suppose that the high-water mark of my youth in Columbus, Ohio, was the night the bed fell on my father. It makes a better recitation (unless, as some friends of mine have said, one has heard it five or six times) than it does a piece of writing, for it is almost necessary to throw furniture around, shake doors, and bark like a dog, to lend the proper atmosphere and verisimilitude[1] to what is admittedly a somewhat incredible tale. Still, it did take place.

It happened, then, that my father had decided to sleep in the attic one night, to be away where he could think. My mother opposed the notion strongly because, she said, the old wooden bed up there was unsafe: it was wobbly and the heavy headboard would crash down on father's head in case the bed fell, and kill him. There

1. **verisimilitude.** Appearance of being real

James Thurber (1894–1961) is best known for the humorous stories, essays, and cartoons he wrote and drew for *The New Yorker* magazine. These works are frequently filled with "regular" people who find themselves caught in awkward or improbable situations. Thurber was born in Columbus, Ohio. An accident left him almost completely blind at an early age. His injury prevented him from participating in sports as a young person and later from graduating from college. As a result, Thurber redirected his efforts into his writing. Today he is remembered as one of the greatest American humorists of the twentieth century.

was no dissuading him, however, and at a quarter past ten he closed the attic door behind him and went up the narrow twisting stairs. We later heard ominous creakings as he crawled into bed. Grandfather, who usually slept in the attic bed when he was with us, had disappeared some days before. On these occasions he was usually gone six or eight days and returned growling and out of temper, with the news that the Federal Union was run by a passel[2] of blockheads and that the Army of the Potomac[3] didn't have a chance.

We had visiting us at this time a nervous first cousin of mine named Briggs Beall, who believed that he was likely to cease breathing when he was asleep. It was his feeling that if he were not awakened every hour during the night, he might die of suffocation. He had been accustomed to setting an alarm clock to ring at intervals until morning, but I persuaded him to abandon this. He slept in my room and I told him that I was such a light sleeper that if anybody quit breathing in the same room with me, I would wake instantly. He tested me the first night—which I had suspected he would—by holding his breath after my regular breathing had convinced him I was asleep. I was not asleep, however, and called to him. This seemed to allay[4] his fears a little, but he took the precaution of putting a glass of spirits of camphor[5] on a little table at the head of his bed. In case I didn't arouse him until he was almost gone, he said, he would sniff the camphor, a powerful reviver. Briggs was not the only member of his family who had his crotchets.[6] Old Aunt Melissa Beall (who could whistle like a man, with two fingers in her mouth) suffered under the premonition[7] that she was destined to die on South High Street, because she had been born on South High Street and married on South High Street. Then there was Aunt Sarah Shoaf, who never went to bed at night without the fear that a burglar was going to get in and blow chloroform[8] under

2. **passel.** Large group
3. **Army of the Potomac.** Union Army during the Civil War
4. **allay.** Relieve
5. **spirits of camphor.** Strong-smelling medicinal liquid
6. **crotchets.** Unusual beliefs
7. **premonition.** Strong feeling about the future
8. **chloroform.** Chemical used in early medicine as an anesthetic

her door through a tube. To avert[9] this calamity—for she was in greater dread of anesthetics than of losing her household goods—she always piled her money, silverware, and other valuables in a neat stack just outside her bedroom, with a note reading: "This is all I have. Please take it and do not use your chloroform, as this is all I have." Aunt Gracie Shoaf also had a burglar phobia, but she met it with more fortitude.[10] She was confident that burglars had been getting into her house every night for forty years. The fact that she never missed any thing was to her no proof to the contrary. She always claimed that she scared them off before they could take anything, by throwing shoes down the hallway. When she went to bed she piled, where she could get at them handily, all the shoes there were about her house. Five minutes after she had turned off the light, she would sit up in bed and say "Hark!" Her husband, who had learned to ignore the whole situation as long ago as 1903, would either be sound asleep or pretend to be sound asleep. In either case he would not respond to her tugging and pulling, so that presently she would arise, tiptoe to the door, open it slightly and heave a shoe down the hall in one direction, and its mate down the hall in the other direction. Some nights she threw them all, some nights only a couple of pair.

But I am straying from the remarkable incidents that took place during the night that the bed fell on father. By midnight we were all in bed. The layout of the rooms and the disposition of their occupants is important to an understanding of what later occurred. In the front room upstairs (just under father's attic bedroom) were my mother and my brother Herman, who sometimes sang in his sleep, usually "Marching Through Georgia" or "Onward, Christian Soldiers." Briggs Beall and myself were in a room adjoining[11] this one. My brother Roy was in a room across the hall from ours. Our bull terrier, Rex, slept in the hall.

My bed was an army cot, one of those affairs which are made wide enough to sleep on comfortably only by putting up, flat with the middle section, the two sides which ordinarily hang down like the sideboards of a drop-leaf table. When these sides are up, it is perilous[12] to roll too far toward the edge, for then the cot is likely to tip completely over, bringing the whole bed down on top of one, with a tremendous banging crash. This, in fact, is precisely what happened about two o'clock in the morning. (It was my mother who, in recalling the scene later, first referred to it as "the night the bed fell on your father.")

Always a deep sleeper, slow to arouse (I had lied to Briggs), I was at first unconscious

9. **avert.** Avoid
10. **fortitude.** Strength
11. **adjoining.** Connecting to or positioned next to
12. **perilous.** Dangerous

of what had happened when the iron cot rolled me onto the floor and toppled over on me. It left me still warmly bundled up and unhurt, for the bed rested above me like a canopy. Hence I did not wake up, only reached the edge of consciousness and went back. The racket, however, instantly awakened my mother, in the next room, who came to the immediate conclusion that her worst dread was realized: the big wooden bed upstairs had fallen on father. She therefore screamed, "let's go to your poor father!" It was this shout, rather than the noise of my cot falling, that awakened Herman, in the same room with her. He thought that mother had become, for no apparent reason, hysterical. "You're all right, Mamma!" he shouted, trying to calm her. They exchanged shout for shout for perhaps ten seconds: "Let's go to your poor father!" and "You're all right!" That woke up Briggs. By this time I was conscious of what was going on, in a vague way, but did not yet realize that I was under my bed instead of on it. Briggs, awakening in the midst of loud shouts of fear and apprehension, came to the quick conclusion that he was suffocating and that we were all trying to "bring him out." With a low moan, he grasped the glass of camphor at the head of his bed and instead of sniffing it poured it over himself. The room reeked of camphor. "Ugf, ahfg," choked Briggs, like a drowning man, for he had almost succeeded in stopping his breath under the deluge of pungent spirits. He leaped out of bed and groped toward the open window, but he came up against one that was closed. With his hand, he beat out the glass, and I could hear it crash and tinkle on the alleyway below. It was at this juncture[13] that I, in trying to get up, had the uncanny sensation of feeling my bed above me! Foggy with sleep, I now suspected, in my turn, that the whole uproar was being made in a frantic endeavor to extricate[14] me from what must be an unheard-of and perilous situation. "Get me out of this!" I bawled. "Get me out!" I think I had the nightmarish belief that I was entombed in a mine. "Gugh," gasped Briggs, floundering in his camphor.

By this time my mother, still shouting, pursued by Herman, still shouting, was trying to open the door to the attic, in order to go up and get my father's body out of the wreckage. The door was stuck, however, and wouldn't yield. Her frantic pulls on it only added to the general banging and confusion. Roy and the dog were now up, the one shouting questions, the other barking.

Father, farthest away and soundest sleeper of all, had by this time been awakened by the battering on the attic door. He decided that the house was on fire. "I'm coming, I'm coming!" he wailed in a slow, sleepy voice—it took him many minutes to regain full consciousness. My mother, still believing he was caught under the bed,

13. juncture. Specific point in time

14. extricate. Release a person or thing from a complicated situation detected in his "I'm coming!" the mournful, resigned note of one who is preparing to meet his Maker. "He's dying!" she shouted.

"I'm all right!" Briggs yelled to reassure her. "I'm all right!" He still believed that it was his own closeness to death that was worrying mother. I found at last the light switch in my room, unlocked the door, and Briggs and I joined the others at the attic door. The dog, who never did like Briggs, jumped for him—assuming that he was the culprit in whatever was going on—and Roy had to throw Rex and hold him. We could hear father crawling out of bed upstairs. Roy pulled the attic door open, with a mighty jerk, and father came down the stairs, sleepy and irritable but safe and sound. My mother began to weep when she saw him. Rex began to howl. "What in the name of heaven is going on here?" asked father.

The situation was finally put together like a gigantic jigsaw puzzle. Father caught a cold from prowling around in his bare feet but there were no other bad results. "I'm glad," said mother, who always looked on the bright side of things, "that your grandfather wasn't here." ✣

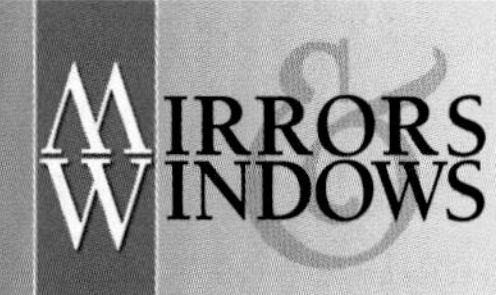

What stories does your family tell about things that happened to them in the past? Are there some stories that are told over and over again? Briefly describe these stories. Why do you think family members repeatedly share the same stories with each other?

Analyze and Extend

1. (a) Do you think Thurber exaggerated some of the events described in this essay? Which events? (b) Why might he have done this?
2. (a) From what point of view is this essay written? (b) How does this point of view affect it?
3. Briefly describe Thurber's purpose or purposes. Do you think he successfully fulfilled his purposes? Explain.

Descriptive Writing Think of a humorous event that has happened in your life. What led up to the event? How was it resolved? Write a brief **descriptive essay** in which you describe the event and the characters involved. Use dialogue, sensory details, and precise language. As you write, be aware of your audience. When you have finished, share your essay with a partner.

Critical Literacy In a small group, create a list of at least five questions you would like to ask Thurber about "The Night the Bed Fell." You might ask questions about specific characters, the events of the night he describes, or if the events actually occurred as he described them. After you have created your list, present your questions to the class.

 Go to **www.mirrorsandwindows.com** for more.

For Your Reading List

The Forbidden Schoolhouse: The True and Dramatic Story of Prudence Crandall and Her Students
by Suzanne Jurmain

In 1831, a school for African-American girls opened in Canterbury, Connecticut. Prudence Crandall, the founder and operator of the school, was sympathetic to the antislavery movement. However, her school met with terrible resistance from the people of Canterbury. This work provides a stirring, and sometimes unsettling, view into a dark corner of America's past.

5,000 Miles to Freedom: Ellen and William Craft's Flight from Slavery
by Dennis Fradin and Judith Fradin

In 1848, Ellen Craft, a light-skinned African American, disguised herself as a white man and escaped with her husband to England. Years later, they returned to America to start their own school. The authors use primary sources, including Ellen's and William's letters and diaries, to enrich the story.

The Kidnapped Prince: The Life of Olaudah Equiano
by Ann Cameron

Olaudah Equiano was kidnapped by slave traders at the age of eleven from his home in Benin, Africa. After spending over ten years as a slave in England, the West Indies, and the United States, Equiano was able to buy his freedom. Cameron's book paints a compelling portrait of Equiano's life.

George Washington, Spymaster: How the Americans Outspied the British and Won the Revolutionary War
by Thomas B. Allen

Spying was a key part of the Revolutionary War, and according to Allen, it may have been central to America's victory over the British. This book includes maps and sample codes and provides a unique perspective from which to view the Revolutionary War.

Big Annie of Calumet: A True Story of the Industrial Revolution
by Jerry Stanley

In 1913, the miners of Calumet, Michigan, went on strike to protest dangerous working conditions and terrible wages. Big Annie Clemenc, the wife of a miner, helped organize a women's group in support of the strike. The strike secured rights for workers in the face of extreme pressure from the mining company.

Bad Boy: A Memoir
by Walter Dean Myers

Walter Dean Myers's depiction of his life growing up in Harlem is exciting, heartbreaking, and vivid. After dropping out of high school and joining the military, he faced a seemingly gloomy future. Although this book describes the many difficult experiences Myers faced, it is, at its core, a celebration of the power to overcome.

Writing Workshop

Informative Writing

Cause-and-Effect Essay

Reading and Writing

In this unit you read personal stories by and about famous people from all areas of life, including sports (Arthur Ashe and Roberto Clemente), entertainment (Bill Cosby), and literature (Julia Alvarez and James Thurber). These people weren't born famous, though they owe their fame in part to their experiences growing up. Our life experiences as young people often greatly affect who we become as adults. This is an example of a cause-and-effect relationship.

In this workshop you will learn how to write a **cause-and-effect essay.** In cause-and-effect writing, you analyze an event and the reasons it occurred, or you consider the relationship between an event and its results. As you approach the assignment, consider your goal and a strategy to help achieve that goal. Pay close attention to the writing rubric, a set of standards by which you judge your work and whether or not your cause-and-effect essay is successful. You will use this rubric in both drafting and revising your essay.

Assignment: Write a cause-and-effect essay in which I examine the causes or results of a specific event.

Goal: To explain a relationship between an event and why it occurred or what happened as a result.

Strategy: To organize my points logically, and to use details and signal words to clearly indicate the cause-and-effect relationship.

Writing Rubric: My cause-and-effect essay should include the following:

- an interesting introduction with a thesis that presents my central idea
- an explanation of the relationship between the effects and their causes
- a clear organizational pattern
- supporting details, facts, and examples
- signal words and phrases
- a strong conclusion that sums up my main points and restates my thesis

What Great Writers Do

Julia Alvarez recalls her life after coming back to the United States with her parents and how that experience influenced her growth as a writer. Note the effects her particular experience caused.

When I'm asked what made me into a writer, I point to the watershed experience of coming to this country. Not understanding the language, I had to pay close attention to each word—great training for a writer. I also discovered the welcoming world of the imagination and books. There, I sunk my new roots.

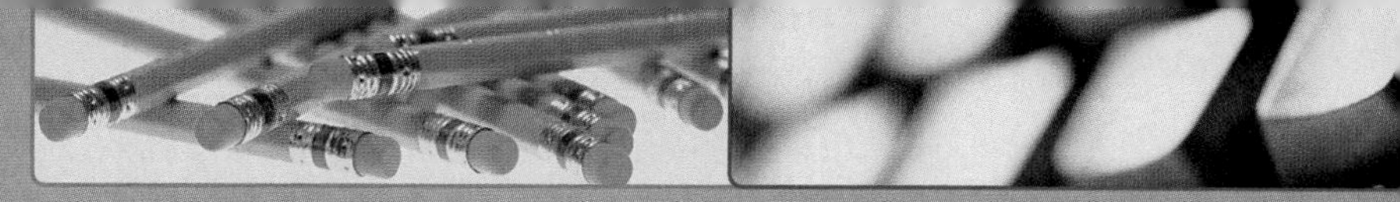

1. PREWRITE

Choosing Your Topic

Begin by brainstorming possible topics that interest you to write about. Consider topics in technology, art, science, nature, and history, to name a few. Then think of a particularly interesting outcome or event and the reasons it occurred or its results. For example, you might choose to write about how an oil spill affected Alaska's ecosystem, what the effects of a large-scale energy blackout were, or how John F. Kennedy's life experiences led to his becoming president. Answer the following questions to spark ideas:

1. What people, places, or events interest you most?
2. What major events have occurred lately? What caused them?
3. What recent events or issues have had surprising or unexpected effects?

Narrow Your Focus Once you decide on a topic, ask yourself if it is too broad to write about. Try to narrow your topic so that it is manageable but you still have enough to write about.

Too broad: How athletes achieve success

Appropriate: How circumstances in Arthur Ashe's life contributed to his success at tennis

Too narrow: How Ashe's height contributed to his success at tennis

Gathering Details

Once you narrow down a topic that interests you, begin gathering the details, facts, and examples that will illustrate your cause-and-effect relationship. A cause-and-effect chart can help you identify the causes that led to an event or outcome. Below is a cause-and-effect chart showing how childhood experiences shaped the life of tennis great Arthur Ashe.

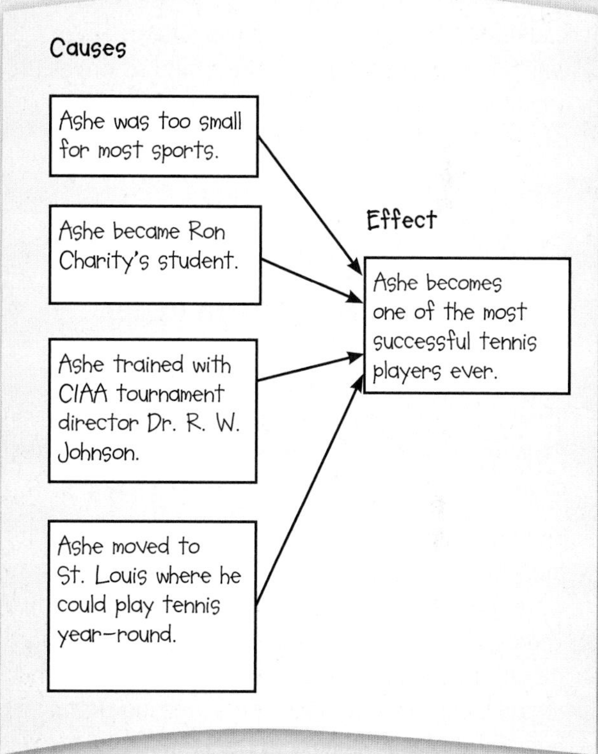

Deciding on Your Purpose

After you gather details about your topic, determine what cause-and-effect relationship you will explain in your essay. State the relationship clearly in a thesis statement.

A series of fortunate circumstances shaped Arthur Ashe's life as a tennis player.

2. DRAFT

Organizing Ideas

When organizing your essay, use **cause-and-effect organization.** Determine which type of cause-and-effect order fits your topic. If you focus on an event and its causes, use effect-to-cause organization. If you focus on an event and its effects, use cause-to-effect organization. Review the organizational models here.

In some cases, a cause-and-effect chain may be the clearest way to organize your essay. Use a cause-and-effect chain if your cause leads to an effect, which in turn causes a new effect, and so on, as in a chain reaction. In a chain, be sure to state the causes and effects in the order they occur.

Effect-to-Cause	Cause-to-Effect
State the Effect	State the Cause
Cause 1	Effect 1
detail	detail
detail	detail
Cause 2	Effect 2
detail	detail
detail	detail
Cause 3	Effect 3
detail	detail
detail	detail

Cause ⟶ Effect (Cause) ⟶ Effect

Putting Your Thoughts on Paper

Like most essays, a cause-and-effect essay has three basic parts: introduction, body, and conclusion. Create a plan for your essay like the one here for an essay on Arthur Ashe. Refer to your cause-and-effect chart to get started.

You may want to draft your essay straight through from the beginning to the end, or you may prefer to write the body paragraphs before the introduction. There is no single way to draft your paper. During the drafting stage, concentrate on the content and organization. You will focus on correcting grammar, punctuation, and spelling at the editing and proofreading stage.

Introduction
- Briefly explain the cause-and-effect relationship between the circumstances of Ashe's life and his tennis achievements.

Body
- Each paragraph should focus on a cause that led to Ashe's achievement.
- Give details to explain the connection between the causes and the effect.

Conclusion
- Restate thesis statement.
- Sum up main points.

Making Connections

In your essay, use transitions and other signal words and phrases to identify cause-and-effect relationships. Be sure to use some variety in your choice of transition words. Here is a list of signal words and phrases that indicate cause-and-effect relationships.

after this	if	then
as a result	in order that	therefore
because	since	thus
consequently	so	while

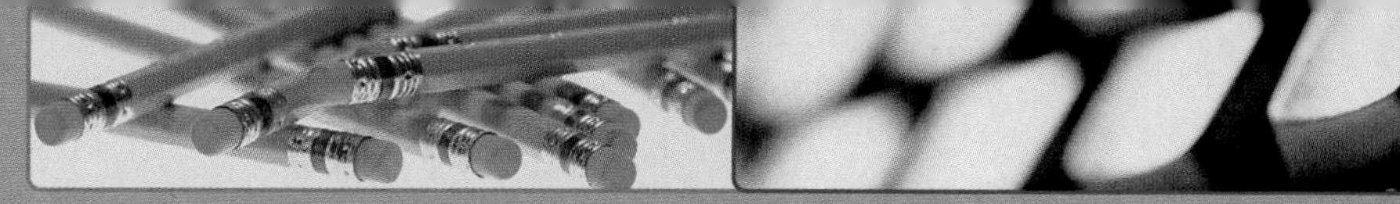

3. REVISE

Evaluating Your Draft

Once your draft is complete, review your writing. First, look over your own paper for strengths and weaknesses. Correct these as best you can. Then, exchange papers with a classmate, and conduct a **peer review.** Discuss ways to improve the drafts.

Below is the first part of an essay about Arthur Ashe. The annotations to the right indicate the reasons for the changes marked in the draft.

Revising Checklist

- ☐ Does the introduction present the cause-and-effect relationship clearly?
- ☐ Is the essay organized in a logical way?
- ☐ Is the relationship between causes and effects explained and supported?
- ☐ Does the essay include signal words?

Arthur Ashe's childhood experiences greatly impacted his life as a professional athlete. From his time on the court under Ron Charity's guidance to winning his first national title, ~~Arthur was surrounded by important people and experiences growing up. He became one of the best tennis players of all time.~~ *a series of fortunate circumstances shaped Arthur Ashe's life as a tennis player.*

Revise introduction to present the cause-and-effect relationship clearly.

Arthur Ashe was a small-framed boy growing up in Richmond, Virginia. *Because* he was so small, his father didn't want him to play contact sports. *So* Arthur spent a lot of time reading, swimming, and playing sports like baseball. As a boy, he used to sit on his back porch and watch the players on the courts outside his house. One player in particular caught Arthur's eye. His name was Ron Charity. Arthur liked watching Ron play, noting the way he hit the ball, how he returned serves and volleys, and how he anticipated shots. *One day, Ron saw Arthur and asked the seven-year-old if he'd like to learn to play tennis. Arthur accepted with an enthusiastic yes, and his career in tennis began.*

Include signal words to indicate a cause-and-effect relationship between events.

Add explanatory sentences to show how the details of the cause led to the effect.

4. EDIT AND PROOFREAD

Focus: Avoiding Wordiness

Wordy sentences make reading unnecessarily confusing and difficult. When you write, use only words necessary to make your meaning clear. To correct wordiness,

1. Replace a group of words with one word.

> *Because* ~~*Due to the fact that*~~ he was so small, his father didn't want him to play contact sports.

2. Delete a group of unnecessary or repetitive words.

> Ron saw Arthur and asked the seven-year-old if he'd like to learn to play ~~the game of~~ tennis.

As you edit your writing for wordiness, consider whether or not the words contribute to the meaning. Note that a long or complicated sentence is not necessarily wordy. Recall that varying sentence length creates rhythm and liveliness in writing.

Focus: Commonly Confused Words

Some common words can be confusing when you are writing. Review carefully your usage of words such as *their, there, they're,* and *excepted* and *accepted* when you revise your draft. If you are confused as to which word is correct, use a dictionary to find out which word has the meaning you're looking for.

> *accepted*
> Arthur ~~excepted~~ with an enthusiastic yes, and his career in tennis began.

Accepted is the correct word in this sentence. It means "agreed to." The word *excepted* means "left out" and would not make sense in the context of the sentence.

Proofreading

Quality Control The purpose of proofreading is to find errors in punctuation, grammar, capitalization, and spelling. You find and fix these errors when you edit your essay. Use proofreader's marks to highlight any errors. (See the Language Arts Handbook, section 4.1, for a list of proofreader's symbols.)

5. PUBLISH AND PRESENT

Final Draft

Final Steps Rewrite your essay to make a final draft. If it is handwritten, make sure the essay is neat and legible. If you are using a word processing program, double-space your paper and use a readable typeface or font. Whether you are submitting your work to your teacher or elsewhere, be sure to check presentation guidelines.

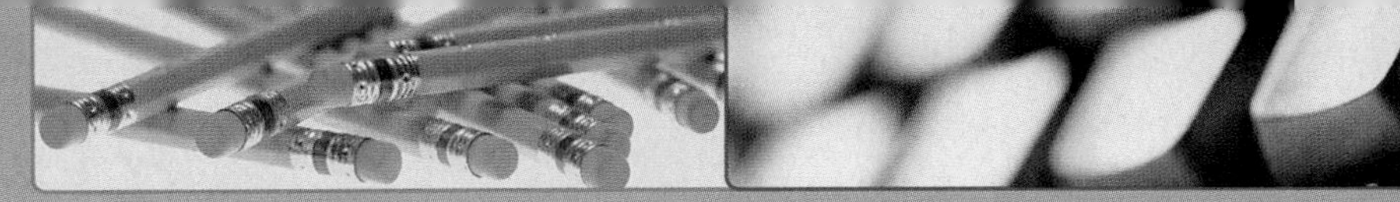

Student Model

Arthur Ashe and His Rise to Star Athlete
by Stewart Anthony

Arthur Ashe's childhood experiences greatly impacted his life as a professional athlete. From his time on the court under Ron Charity's guidance to winning his first national title, a series of fortunate circumstances shaped Arthur Ashe's life as a tennis player.

Presents the cause-and-effect relationship clearly in the introduction

Arthur Ashe was a small-framed boy growing up in Richmond, Virginia. Because he was so small, his father didn't want him to play contact sports. So Arthur spent a lot of time reading, swimming, and playing sports like baseball. As a boy, he used to sit on his back porch and watch the players on the courts outside his house. One player in particular caught Arthur's eye. His name was Ron Charity. Arthur liked watching Ron play, noting the way he hit the ball, how he returned serves and volleys, and how he anticipated shots. One day, Ron saw Arthur and asked the seven-year-old if he'd like to learn to play tennis. Arthur accepted with an enthusiastic yes, and his career in tennis began.

Through Ron Charity, Arthur began learning the basics of tennis. Most of all, Arthur learned timing. "Timing," Arthur would later confirm, "is the most important element in tennis." Ron Charity could only take Arthur so far, however, and he introduced him to his next mentor, Dr. R. W. Johnson.

Dr. Johnson worked with young players, helping them develop their tennis abilities. It was a chance for Arthur to train and play against other good players for two weeks in the summer. Arthur trained with Bobby Johnson, the doctor's son. Arthur learned a lot under the Johnsons, especially the basics of good tennis play and standard tennis principles. He also learned more about the ways of the world at that time, especially the segregated South. Dr. Johnson's support helped Arthur maintain his focus, however, despite the injustices around him.

Dr. Johnson knew that if Arthur were to improve at tennis, he would need to play year round, something he couldn't do in Richmond. Therefore, in his senior year of high school, Arthur moved to St. Louis, Missouri, to live with Mr. Hudlin, Dr. Johnson's friend. There, Arthur could finish high school and continue training on Mr. Hudlin's backyard tennis courts and wooden indoor courts. Arthur's game improved and he eventually earned a scholarship to UCLA, one of the top tennis schools.

Presents causes to explain the effect

Supports the thesis with details, including facts and examples

Highlights the cause-and-effect relationships with signal words and phrases

Avoids unnecessary wordiness

Arthur Ashe went on to become one of the most successful tennis players ever. Arthur seized his opportunities and, through hard work and great mentors, became a champion.

Sums up the main points and restates the thesis

Giving and Actively Listening to Informative Presentations

You have probably explained how to do something, told facts about an event you've witnessed, or given directions to someone. These are all ways of presenting information. In this lesson, you will give an informative presentation to an audience. An effective **informative presentation** delivers factual information in an interesting and lively manner. When you give and actively listen to informative presentations, you share information and exchange ideas with your audience.

Planning an Informative Presentation

Choose a Topic Before you can develop your informative presentation, you must choose a topic. Your topic should be one you are interested in or familiar with. Be sure you can find enough information about your topic to give an effective presentation. You may want to begin with a broad topic and then narrow your topic to a more manageable one. For example, you might begin with a broad topic, such as television, and then narrow it down to the history of television, and then further still to television's early development.

Focus Your Idea Now that you have narrowed your topic, it's time to research and take notes. Use note cards to record your information. Each card should have one main idea and at least three supporting details. Use a highlighter so that you will be able to easily spot the main idea on each note card. Group your notes so that your strongest ideas are presented first.

Identify Your Audience Who will listen to what you have to say? Determine whether or not your audience will be familiar with your topic. This will determine the kind of language you will use. Your choice of using either technical and specialized words or simpler language in your presentation will depend on your audience and its knowledge of the topic. For example, you might avoid using terms such as *photoconductivity* or *cathode ray* when speaking to an audience that knows little about the science of television.

Effective Introductions and Closings From the start, you want to capture your audience's attention. Draw in your audience by making it a part of your presentation. Ask people to imagine, remember, think, or dream. You could open with a statement, such as *Imagine a world without television,* or a question, such as *Have you ever wondered how a television works?* Drawing in an audience makes people more attentive.

You should also be mindful of your closing. An informative presentation should wrap up all the information you have just presented in a clear, clean, and simple way. Draw the audience back in by rephrasing your opening statement or answering the opening question. Leave your audience satisfied with the information you presented.

Evaluating Your Informative Presentation

Work with a partner or a small group and take turns rehearsing what you want to say. After each turn, provide constructive feedback to the speaker. When you give constructive feedback, be respectful, helpful, and polite. Offer praise, but also give ideas for improvement. Use the listening and speaking rubrics on this page to evaluate each informative presentation.

Delivering Your Informative Presentation

Your nonverbal cues are as important as your speaking ability. As you deliver your informative presentation, your main purpose is to deliver factual information. Unless movement is part of your presentation, try to stand still. Maintain eye contact with your audience. If you have charts, graphs, or other visual aids, be sure to present them in the most effective way. Consider how they specifically relate to the text of your presentation.

Listen Actively It is also important to be an active and effective listener. To listen actively and effectively, you should maintain eye contact with the speaker. Remain quiet and attentive, and ask questions when appropriate.

Speaking Rubric

Your informative presentation will be evaluated on the following elements:

Content

- ☐ attention-grabbing introduction and conclusion
- ☐ information organized to achieve a particular purpose and to appeal to a particular audience
- ☐ clear and concise main idea and adequate supporting details

Delivery and Presentation

- ☐ appropriate volume, enunciation, and eye contact
- ☐ effective nonverbal cues
- ☐ appropriate pacing

Listening Rubric

As a peer reviewer or audience member, you should do the following:

- ☐ listen quietly and attentively
- ☐ maintain eye contact with speaker
- ☐ ask appropriate questions
- ☐ (as peer reviewer) provide constructive feedback

Test Practice Workshop

Writing Skills

Informative Essay

Read the following short excerpt and the writing assignment. Before you begin writing, think carefully about what task the assignment is asking you to perform. Then create an outline to help guide your writing.

from *Alone Across the Arctic* by Pam Flowers

The desire to make this expedition didn't just appear suddenly, out of nowhere. When I look back, I can see it was part of a much larger dream that began when I was a kid growing up in Michigan.

I was eleven years old when a scientist came to my school to show slides and talk about Antarctica. I don't remember anything he said. But I clearly recall an image: a photograph of endless snow-covered mountains under a brilliant blue sky.

Immediately I knew I wanted to go to a place like that. The landscape was beautiful, so clean and empty. Best of all, there were no people. To a loner like me, it looked like the most perfect place imaginable.

Even back then, I spent most of my time alone. I didn't fit in well at school. My best friend was my dog, a German shepherd named Lady. Together we wandered the woods near my home, exploring for hours. I imagined ways we could survive in the wilderness—the food I would gather, the shelter I would build. I spent as many hours as possible outside with Lady.

I learned to love that time outdoors, alone with my dog. It became the source of my well-being. But I had no idea that someday I'd explore with my dogs for real in one of the harshest environments on Earth. I didn't expect to grow up to be an Arctic adventurer.

Assignment: What **caused** the narrator to make an expedition alone across the Arctic? Plan and write several paragraphs for an **informative essay** in which you state and support a **thesis** about the **causes** and **effects** of the narrator's decision. Include evidence from the passage to support your thesis.

Revising and Editing Skills

Each blank indicates that a word has been omitted. Beneath the sentence are five words or sets of words. Choose the word or set of words that, when inserted in the sentence, *best* completes the sentence.

1. Disgusted, Mari ___ the ___ meat from the refrigerator and tossed it in the trash.
   A. rebuffed...ominous
   B. plucked...noisome
   C. emulated...chaotic
   D. incorporated...rumpled
   E. forfeited...chaotic

2. The teacher was ___ by George's refusal to follow directions.
   A. forfeited
   B. incorporated
   C. repressed
   D. emulated
   E. exasperated

3. Because they could not come to a compromise, Brad and Roland had reached ___.
   A. a prerogative
   B. an impasse
   C. a conjecture
   D. a prestige
   E. a tedium

4. The vet explained that she had an effective ___ for the dog's troublesome ___ problems.
   A. prerogative...ominous
   B. conjecture...impasse
   C. prosperity...preliminary
   D. antidote...physiological
   E. prestige...chaotic

5. The researchers' ___ that the planet was covered in ice could not be proved.
   A. directive
   B. conjecture
   C. impasse
   D. prestige
   E. antidote

6. The unwanted visitor was ___ as he tried to enter.
   A. plucked
   B. incorporated
   C. emulated
   D. forfeited
   E. rebuffed

7. The team was forced to ___ the game because of unsportsmanlike conduct.
   A. delineate
   B. repress
   C. rebuff
   D. exasperate
   E. forfeit

8. I admire her because she measures ___ in terms of happiness rather than wealth.
   A. impasse
   B. locomotion
   C. tedium
   D. prosperity
   E. prerogative

9. Grace's job was so filled with ___ that she would fall asleep at her desk.
   A. tedium
   B. directive
   C. impasse
   D. conjecture
   E. antidote

Reading Skills

Carefully read the following passage. Then, on a separate piece of paper, answer each question.

from "Flying" by Reeve Lindbergh

I always flew with my father, who had been a pioneer aviator in the 1920s and '30s. I think that he wanted to share his love for the air and for airplanes with his growing family, the way sports-minded fathers took their children to ball games on Saturdays and taught them to play catch afterward. My father took his children to the airport instead and taught them to fly.

Though he was the pilot on these flights, he did not own the airplane. It was a sixty-five-horsepower Aeronca, with tandem cockpits, that he rented from a former bomber pilot whose name was Stanley. Stanley managed the airport, including the huge loaf-shaped hangar that served as a garage for repairs and maintenance to the aircraft, and he leased out the group of small planes tethered near the building like a fleet of fishing boats clustered around a pier.

It was Stanley, most often, who stood in front of the airplane and waited for my father to shout "ConTACT!" from the cockpit window, at which time, Stanley gave the propeller a hefty downward shove that sent it spinning into action and started the plane shaking and shuddering on its way. The job of starting the propeller was simple but perilous. My father had warned us many times about the danger of standing anywhere near a propeller in action. We could list almost as well as he did the limbs that had been severed from the bodies of careless individuals "in a split second" by a propeller's whirling force. Therefore, each time that Stanley started the propeller, I would peer through its blinding whir to catch a glimpse of any pieces of him that might be flying through the air. Each time, I saw only Stanley, whole and smiling, waving us onto the asphalt runway with his cap in his hand and his hair blowing in the wind of our passing—"the propwash" my father called it.

My sister and my three brothers flew on Saturdays too. The older ones were taught to land and take off, to bank and dip, and even to turn the plane over in midair, although my second-oldest brother confessed that he hated this—it made him feel so dizzy. The youngest of my three brothers, only a few years older than me, remembers my father instructing him to "lean into the curve" as the plane made a steep sideways dive toward the ground. My brother was already off balance, leaning away from the curve, and hanging on for dear life. For my sister, our father demonstrated "weightlessness" by having the plane climb steeply and then dive so sharply that for a moment she could feel her body straining upward against her seatbelt, trying to fight free, while our father shouted out from the front seat that one of his gloves was actually floating in midair.

1. Based on the context, which of the following is the *best* definition of the word *pioneer* in line 1?
   A. an early farmer in the western United States
   B. one of the first people to explore a geographic area
   C. one of the first plants to grow in bare land
   D. a person who is one of the first to explore a new activity
   E. a person who traveled west in a covered wagon

2. The narrator's father differs from the fathers of other children because he
   A. doesn't like sports.
   B. doesn't spend time with his children.
   C. teaches his children to fly.
   D. likes football more than baseball.
   E. owns an airplane.

3. The phrase that begins on line 11 "like a fleet of fishing boats clustered around a pier" is an example of
   A. personification.
   B. foreshadowing.
   C. theme.
   D. conflict.
   E. figurative language.

4. Why does the narrator's father shout "ConTACT" in line 13?
   A. It orders Stanley to touch the plane.
   B. It tells Stanley to spin the propeller.
   C. It means the radio is turned on.
   D. It means "I've got the controls."
   E. It tells the narrator to take the controls.

5. In lines 20 and 21, the narrator expected
   A. Stanley to be chopped to pieces.
   B. the plane to shudder and shake.
   C. her father to yell "ConTACT."
   D. the plane to take off.
   E. the plane's engine to start.

6. What can you infer about how the narrator's brothers and sister felt about flying?
   A. They loved everything about it.
   B. They couldn't wait to learn more.
   C. They wanted to fly by themselves.
   D. They hated everything about flying.
   E. They didn't like some parts of it.

7. The protagonist of this passage is
   A. the father.
   B. the narrator.
   C. Stanley.
   D. the narrator's sister.
   E. the narrator's second-oldest brother.

8. What is the overall tone of the passage?
   A. frightened
   B. thrilled
   C. sad
   D. conversational
   E. angry

9. This story is written from which point of view?
   A. first-person
   B. second-person
   C. third-person
   D. third-person limited
   E. third-person omniscient

10. This passage is *best* described as
    A. a literary response.
    B. a biography.
    C. an autobiography or memoir.
    D. an argumentative essay.
    E. a review.

Unit 4

Responding to Nature

Nonfiction

"...imagine that you can see the individual atoms in a kitchen table, and that each atom is the size of a grain of sand. On this scale of enlargement the table will be 2000 miles long."

—ROBERT JASTROW, "The Size of Things"

Have you ever tried to imagine the size of an atom? In his article, scientist Robert Jastrow tries to describe the size of very small things, like the atom, and very large things, like the Milky Way Galaxy. One of the goals of informational texts is to present sometimes complicated information in a straightforward way. As you explore the texts and visuals in this unit, examine how authors and artists present their information.

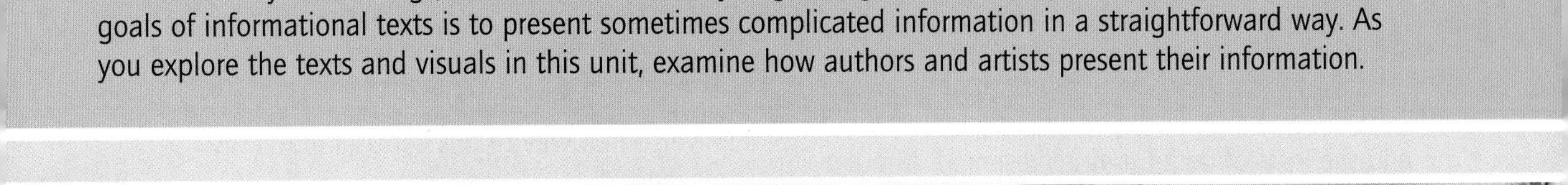

Introduction to Informational Text and Visual Media

Purposes of Nonfiction

In the previous unit, you read several types of nonfiction, including autobiography, biography, and essay. One of the characteristics shared by these types of nonfiction is a subjective approach, an emphasis on the writer's personal response to his or her subject. There are many other types of nonfiction, however, where the writer's approach to the subject is much more objective. To help understand this distinction, read the following passages. Both deal with the importance of space exploration. How do the two passages differ?

> The question I am most often asked is, "Where is the frontier now?" The answer should be obvious. Our frontier lies in outer space. The moon, the asteroids, the planets, these are mere stepping stones, where we will test ourselves, learn needful lessons, and grow in knowledge before we attempt those frontiers beyond our solar system.
>
> —LOUIS L'AMOUR, "The Eternal Frontier"

> Achieving spaceflight enabled humans to begin to explore the solar system and the rest of the universe, to understand the many objects and phenomena that are better observed from a space perspective, and to use for human benefit the resources and attributes of the space environment. All of these activities—discovery, scientific understanding, and the application of that understanding to serve human purposes—are elements of space exploration.
>
> —ENCYCLOPAEDIA BRITANNICA ONLINE, "Space Exploration"

The two passages differ in several ways, including the style of the writing, the tone, and the level of detail that is presented. Another major difference is in the basic purpose of the two passages. Louis L'Amour's essay does far more than simply relate the facts of space exploration. He interprets these facts and uses them to support an idea he is hoping to persuade his reader to accept. By contrast, the basic purpose of the encyclopedia article is to present the facts about space exploration in a straightforward and objective way. An encyclopedia article is one common type of informational text.

Types of Informational Text

An **informational text** is a type of nonfiction whose basic purpose is to inform rather than to entertain or persuade. Among the most common types of informational texts are articles of various kinds. Here are a few of the most familiar.

News Article

A **news article** is an informational text about a particular topic, issue, event, or series of events. News articles can be found in newspapers, in magazines, and on Internet sites. Broadcast news stories on radio and television are also news articles. The main purpose of such articles is to convey information. This is particularly evident in the newspaper story, where the traditional structure is the "inverted pyramid." In a news story using this structure, the most important facts are presented first, followed by less important supporting details.

Science Article

A familiar type of news article is the **science article,** which offers information about a particular theory, scientific observation, or discovery. These articles are sometimes filled with a specialized vocabulary, or *jargon.* Writers who write about science for a mainstream audience, however, usually avoid terms with which most readers would be unfamiliar. Robert Jastrow's "The Size of Things" (page 378), for example, discusses the size of the universe in a way that is concise and easily understood.

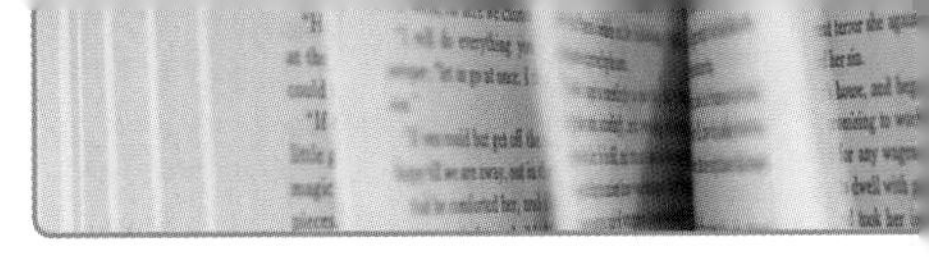

Web Page

A **web page** is the basic unit of the World Wide Web, an organizational structure that includes a large part of what is offered on the Internet. One of the main purposes of web pages is to provide information. Web pages can contain links, or connections to other pages within the site or in completely different sites altogether. These connections are mostly in the form of "hotlinks" or "hyperlinks," which are addresses signaled by underlined or differently colored text.

Types of Visual Media

In addition to written language, information is conveyed through **visual media,** or pictorial or other graphic forms of communication. There is a wide variety of visual media, including photographs, illustrations, charts, diagrams, and maps.

Photograph

A **photograph** is an image typically created by light acting on a sensitive material. Photography is one of the primary visual methods of providing information. Like an informational text, a photograph needs to be "read" carefully. This might include identifying the overall subject, focusing in on specific details, and checking the title, label, caption, or other accompanying text. Photographers take photographs for a purpose. Arthur Rothstein's famous photographs of the Dust Bowl (page 432), for example, were taken to create a historical record and to inform viewers of the plight of poor farmers.

Illustration

An **illustration** is a photograph, drawing, or diagram that serves to make a concept clearer by providing a visual example. The illustrations in Tim Flannery and Peter Schouten's *Astonishing Animals: Extraordinary Creatures and the Fantastic Worlds They Inhabit* (page 443) help readers understand the strange animals that the text describes.

Chart

A **chart** is a visual representation of data that is intended to clarify, highlight, or put a certain perspective on the information presented. There are many types of charts, each with a different purpose. Here are some common examples:

- A *time line* shows the relative order of a series of events, such as dates in a period of history.
- A *flow chart* is a graphic representation of a process. For example, a flow chart might show how a bill becomes a law.
- A *pie chart* or *circle chart* shows the parts that make up the whole of something. For example, a pie chart might show the proportion of the world's fresh water on each continent.

Diagram

A **diagram** is an illustration that serves to explain a concept or process, and the arrangement and relationships among its various parts.

Map

A **map** is a representation, often on a flat surface such as a sheet of paper, of a geographic area that shows various significant features. These features vary with the purpose of the map. For example, a political map includes such features as the boundaries of countries and the locations of cities and towns. The map included in the entry from David Allen Sibley's *The Sibley Guide to Birds* (page 390) shows readers the specific range of a particular bird.

THE SIZE OF THINGS

A Scientific Essay by Robert Jastrow

GUIDED READING

Build Background

Scientific Context This essay deals with the concept of scale—in particular, things so small or so large that scientists must use mathematical formulas to estimate their sizes. Science is forty years advanced from the time Jastrow wrote this essay, but thinking about unimaginable sizes is as challenging today as it was in the 1960s.

Reader's Context Do you ever wonder what you are made of or where the universe ends? Read for some possible answers.

Set Purpose

Preview the essay by skimming it for unfamiliar terms. Skim the words in Preview Vocabulary and the footnotes on each page.

Analyze Literature

Informational Text An **informational text** is a type of nonfiction whose basic purpose is to inform rather than to entertain or persuade. Among the most common types of informational texts are articles and essays of various kinds. "The Size of Things" is a scientific essay, a type of informational text. As you read, discover what information Jastrow is presenting.

Use Reading Skills

Monitor Comprehension The author's purpose in this essay is to inform you, so try to keep track of new information on each page. You can use a note-taking chart like the one here. Record Jastrow's main ideas in the left-hand column, and use the right-hand column to list ideas and terms you would like to understand more fully. When you are done, try summarizing your notes at the bottom of the chart.

Main Ideas	Difficult Ideas and Terms
The electron is very small.	electron microscope

Summary of My Notes:

Meet the Author

Robert Jastrow (1925–2008) joined NASA, the National Aeronautics and Space Administration, when it formed in 1958. He was the first chair of its Lunar Exploration Committee. A theoretical physicist, Jastrow was perfect for the job. Scientists conduct experiments to test their ideas, and theoretical physicists are the scientists who recommend specific experiments for testing theories. At NASA, Jastrow helped establish the scientific goals for the *Apollo* trips to the Moon.

Preview Vocabulary

tes • ti • fy (tes´ tə fī') *v.*, make a statement based on personal knowledge or belief; give evidence

con • clu • sive • ly (kən klü´ siv lē) *adv.*, in a way that ends debate or discussion

de • duce (di düs´) *v.*, infer

dif • fuse (di fyüs´) *adj.*, spread out loosely and widely

void (vôid) *n.*, emptiness

THE SIZE OF THINGS

A Scientific Essay by Robert Jastrow

THE SIZE OF AN ELECTRON IS TO A DUST SPECK AS THE DUST SPECK IS TO THE ENTIRE EARTH.

I once had occasion to testify before the United States Senate Space and Aeronautics Committee on the scientific background of the space program; my talk dealt with the manner in which all substances in the universe are assembled out of neutrons, protons, and electrons[1] as the basic building blocks. After I left the chamber a senior NASA official continued with a summary of the major space science achievements of the last year. Apparently my scholarly presentation had perplexed the senators, although they were anxious to understand the concepts I had presented. However, the NASA official's relaxed manner reassured them, and someone asked him: "How big is the electron? How much smaller is it than a speck of dust?" The NASA official correctly replied that the size of an electron is to a dust speck as the dust speck is to the entire earth.

tes•ti•fy (tes´ tə fī') *v.*, make a statement based on personal knowledge or belief; give evidence

DURING READING

Analyze Literature
Informational Text For whom do you think the author is writing this essay?

1. **neutrons, protons, and electrons.** Three main particles that make up an atom

The electron is indeed a tiny object. Its diameter is one 10-trillionth of an inch, a million times smaller than can be seen with the best electron microscope.[2] Its weight is correspondingly small; 10,000 trillion electrons make up one ounce. How can we be certain that such a small object exists? No one has ever picked up an electron with a pair of forceps[3] and said, "Here is one." The evidence for its existence is all indirect. During the 150 years from the late eighteenth century to the beginning of the twentieth century a great variety of experiments were carried out on the flow of electricity through liquids and gases. The existence of the electron was not proved conclusively by any single one of these experiments. However, the majority of them could be explained most easily if the physicist assumed that the electricity was carried by a stream of small particles, each bearing its own electrical charge. Gradually physicists acquired a feeling, bordering on conviction, that the electron actually exists.

con•clu•sive•ly (kən klü´ siv lē) *adv.*, in a way that ends debate or discussion

DURING READING

Make Connections
Are you convinced that the electron exists, based on this discussion so far? Why or why not?

The question now was, how large is the electron, and how much electric charge does each electron carry? The clearest answer to this question came from an American physicist, Robert Millikan, who worked on the problem at the University of Chicago in the first decades of the twentieth century. Millikan arranged a device, clever for its simplicity, in which an atomizer[4] created a mist of very fine droplets of oil just above a small hole in the top of a container. A small number of the droplets fell through the hole and slowly drifted to the bottom of the container. Millikan could see the motions of these droplets very clearly by illuminating them from the side with a strong light so that they appeared as bright spots against a dark background. Millikan discovered that some of these droplets carried a few extra electrons, which had been picked up in the atomizing process. By applying an electrical force to the droplets and studying their motions in response to this force, he could deduce the amount of electric charge carried by the electrons on each droplet. This charge turned out to be exceedingly minute.[5] As a demonstration of its minuteness, it takes an electric current equivalent to a flow of one million trillion electrons every second to light a 10-watt bulb. All this happened rather recently in the history of science. Millikan's first accurate measurements were completed in 1914.

DURING READING

Use Reading Skills
Monitor Comprehension
What did Millikan want to learn through this experiment?

de•duce (di düs´) *v.*, infer

2. **electron microscope.** Instrument that uses a beam of electrons to make an enlarged image of a very small object
3. **forceps.** Tongs
4. **atomizer.** Instrument that converts a liquid or solid to a fine mist or dust
5. **minute** (mī nüt´). Very small; tiny; infinitesimal

The tiny electron, and two sister particles, are the building blocks out of which all matter in the world is constructed. The sister particles to the electron are the proton and the neutron. They were discovered even more recently than the electron; the proton was identified in 1920 and the neutron was first discovered in 1932. These two particles are massive[6] in comparison with the electron—1840 times as heavy—but still inconceivably light by ordinary standards. The three particles combine in an amazingly simple way to form the objects we see and feel. A strong force of attraction[7] binds neutrons and protons together to form a dense, compact body called the nucleus, whose size is somewhat less than one-trillionth of an inch. Electrons are attracted to the nucleus and circle around it as the planets circle around the sun, forming a solar system in miniature.[8]

THE THREE PARTICLES COMBINE IN AN AMAZINGLY SIMPLE WAY TO FORM THE OBJECTS WE SEE AND FEEL.

Together the electrons and the nucleus make up the atom.

The size of a typical atom is one hundred-millionth of an inch. To get a feeling for the smallness of the atom compared to a macroscopic[9] object, imagine that you can see the individual atoms in a kitchen table, and that each atom is the size of a grain of sand. On this scale of enlargement the table will be 2000 miles long.

DURING READING

Use Reading Skills
Monitor Comprehension
How is an atom different from a grain of sand?

The comparison of the atom with a grain of sand implies that the atom is a solid object. Actually, the atom consists largely of empty space. Each of the atoms that makes up the surface of a table consists of a number of electrons orbiting around a nucleus. The electrons form a diffuse shell around the nucleus, marking the outer boundary of the atom. The size of the atom is 10,000 times as great as the size of the nucleus at the center. If the outer shell of electrons in the atom were the size of the Astrodome that covers the Houston baseball stadium, the nucleus would be a ping-pong ball in the center of the stadium. That is the emptiness of the atom.

dif•fuse (di fyüs´) *adj.*, spread out loosely and widely

If most of the atom is empty space, why does a tabletop offer resistance when you push it with your finger? The reason is that the surface of the table consists of a wall of electrons, the electrons belonging to the outermost layer of atoms in the tabletop; the surface of your finger also consists of a wall of electrons; where they meet,

6. **massive.** Containing a lot of matter or mass; dense
7. **strong force of attraction.** Particles in the nucleus of an atom stick together due to a force known in Jastrow's day as "the strong force." Today scientists know that the protons and neutrons consist of even smaller particles that stay together because of "the strong interaction."
8. **Electrons...forming a solar system in miniature.** This "planetary model" of the atom was popular in the 1960s. Scientists have found it impossible to determine the path of a single electron, so today they say that electrons form a cloud around the nucleus.
9. **macroscopic.** Visible to the naked eye

Palomar Observatory on Palomar Mountain in California.

strong forces of electrical repulsion[10] prevent the electrons in your fingertip from pushing past the outermost electrons in the top of the table into the empty space within each atom. An atomic projectile[11] such as a proton, accelerated to high speed in a cyclotron,[12] could easily pass through these electrons, which are, after all, rather light and unable to hurl back a fast-moving object. But it would take more force than the pressure of the finger can produce to force them aside and penetrate the inner space of the atom.

"IT WAS QUITE THE MOST INCREDIBLE EVENT THAT HAS EVER HAPPENED TO ME IN MY LIFE."

The concept of the empty atom is a recent development. Isaac Newton described atoms as "solid, massy, hard, impenetrable, moveable particles." Through the nineteenth century, physicists continued to regard them as small, solid objects. Lord Rutherford, the greatest experimental physicist of his time, once said, "I was brought up to look at the atom as a nice hard fellow, red or grey in color, according to taste." At the beginning of the twentieth century, J. J. Thomson, a British physicist and one of the pioneers in the investigation of the structure of matter, believed that the atom was a spherical plum pudding of positive electric charge in which negatively charged electrons were embedded like raisins. No one knew that the mass of the atom, and its positive charge, were concentrated in a small, dense nucleus at the center, and that the electrons circled around this nucleus at a considerable distance. But in 1911 Rutherford, acting on a hunch, instructed his assistant, Hans Geiger, and a graduate student named Marsden, to fire a beam of alpha particles[13] into a bit of thin gold foil. These alpha particles are extremely fast-moving atomic projectiles which should have penetrated the gold foil and emerged from the other side. Most of

10. **strong forces of electrical repulsion.** Like charges repel. If you try to join two bar magnets at their negative poles, for example, the poles will push each other apart.
11. **projectile.** Something forcefully propelled, like a bullet
12. **cyclotron.** Instrument that accelerates small particles (like electrons) using electric and magnetic fields
13. **alpha particles.** High-energy particles (radiation) that are ejected from an atomic nucleus at very high speeds

them did, but Geiger and Marsden found that in a very few cases the alpha particles came out of the foil on the same side they had entered. Rutherford said later, "It was quite the most incredible event that has ever happened to me in my life. It was almost as incredible as if you fired a 15-inch shell at a piece of tissue paper and it came back and hit you."

Later Geiger told the story of the occasion on which Rutherford saw the meaning of the experiment. He relates: "One day [in 1911] Rutherford, obviously in the best of spirits, came into my room and told me that he now knew what the atom looked like and how to explain the large deflections[14] of the alpha particles." What had occurred, Rutherford had decided, was that now and then an alpha particle hit a massive object in the foil, which bounced it straight back. He realized that the massive objects must be very small since the alpha particles hit them so rarely. He concluded that most of the mass of the atom is concentrated in a compact body at its center, which he named the nucleus. Rutherford's discovery opened the door to the nuclear era.

DURING READING

Analyze Literature
Informational Text What was Rutherford trying to express with this comparison?

DURING READING

Use Reading Skills
Monitor Comprehension In the phrases "nuclear energy" and "the nuclear era," what does the word *nuclear* mean?

Let us continue with the description of the manner in which the universe is assembled out of its basic particles. Atoms are joined together in groups to form molecules, such as water, which consists of two atoms of hydrogen joined to one atom of oxygen. Large numbers of atoms or molecules cemented together form solid matter. There are a trillion trillion atoms in a cubic inch of an ordinary solid substance, which is roughly the same as the number of grains of sand in all the oceans of the earth.

The earth itself is an especially large collection of atoms bound together in a ball of rock and iron 8000 miles in diameter,[15] weighing six billion trillion tons. It is one of nine planets, which are bound to the sun by the force of gravity. Together the sun and planets form the solar system. The largest of the planets is Jupiter, whose diameter is 86,000 miles; Mercury, the smallest, is 3100 miles across, one-third the size of the earth, and scarcely larger than the moon. All the planets are dwarfed by the sun, whose diameter is one million miles. The weight of the sun is 700 times greater than the combined weight of the nine planets. Like the atom, the solar system consists of a massive central body—the sun—surrounded by small, light objects—the planets—which revolve about it at great distances.

---

14. deflections. Turning or bending of radiation from a straight course
15. diameter. Length of a straight line through the center of a sphere

The sun is only one among 200 billion stars that are bound together by gravity into a large cluster of stars called the galaxy. The stars of the galaxy revolve about its center as the planets revolve about the sun. The sun itself participates in this rotating motion, completing one circuit around the galaxy in 250 million years.

The galaxy is flattened by its rotating motion into the shape of a disk, whose thickness is roughly one-fiftieth of its diameter. Most of the stars in the galaxy are in this disk, although some are located outside it. A relatively small, spherical cluster of stars, called the nucleus of the galaxy,[16] bulges out of the disk at the center. The entire structure resembles a double sombrero[17] with the galactic nucleus as the crown and the disk as the brim. The sun is located in the brim of the sombrero about three-fifths of the way out from the center to the edge. When we look into the sky in the direction of the disk we see so many stars that they are not visible as separate points of light, but blend together into a luminous band stretching across the sky. This band is called Milky Way.

DURING READING

Analyze Literature
Informational Text How does Jastrow help the reader visualize our galaxy?

The stars within the galaxy are separated from one another by an average distance of about 36 trillion miles. In order to avoid the frequent repetition of such awkwardly large numbers, astronomical distances are usually expressed in units of the light year. A light year is defined as the distance covered in one year by a ray of light, which travels at 186,000 miles per second. The distance turns out to be six trillion miles; hence in these units the average distance between stars in the galaxy is five light years, and the diameter of the galaxy is 100,000 light years.

DURING READING

Use Reading Skills
Monitor Comprehension Place these in order from smallest to largest: star, planet, atom, galaxy.

In spite of the enormous size of our galaxy, its boundaries do not mark the edge of the observable universe. The 200-inch telescope on Palomar Mountain[18] has within its range no less than 100 billion other galaxies, each comparable to our own in size and containing a similar number of stars. The average distance between these galaxies is one million light years. The extent of the visible universe, as it can be seen in the 200-inch telescope, is 15 billion light years.

An analogy will help to clarify the meaning of these enormous distances. Let the sun be the size of an orange; on that scale of sizes the earth is a grain of sand circling in orbit around the sun at a

16. **nucleus of the galaxy.** Center of a spiral galaxy like the Milky Way
17. **double sombrero.** The sombrero is a hat with a high crown and a very wide brim. Jastrow is suggesting that the galaxy's shape is like two sombreros placed base to base.
18. **200-inch telescope on Palomar Mountain.** The Hale Telescope on Palomar Mountain near San Diego, California, was the world's largest telescope from 1948 to 1976. It contains a mirror that is 200 inches across.

distance of 30 feet; the giant planet Jupiter, 11 times larger than the earth, is a cherry pit revolving at a distance of 200 feet or one city block; Saturn is another cherry pit two blocks from the sun; and Pluto, the outermost planet,[19] is still another sand grain at a distance of ten city blocks from the sun.

On the same scale the average distance between the stars is 2000 miles. The sun's nearest neighbor, a star called Alpha Centauri, is 1300 miles away. In the space between the sun and its neighbors there is nothing but a thin distribution of hydrogen atoms, forming a vacuum[20] far better than any ever achieved on earth. The galaxy, on this scale, is a cluster of oranges separated by an average distance of 2000 miles, the entire cluster being 20 million miles in diameter.

> **DURING READING**
> **Use Reading Strategies**
> **Clarify** In the model Jastrow proposes, what fruit represents the sun and other stars?

An orange, a few grains of sand some feet away, and then some cherry pits circling slowly around the orange at a distance of a city block. Two thousand miles away is another orange, perhaps with a few specks of planetary matter circling around it. That is the void of space. ✣

void (vôid) *n.*, emptiness

19. Pluto, the outermost planet. In 2006, astronomers decided that Pluto is not a planet.
20. vacuum. Space without any matter at all

If you wanted to know more about either atoms or the universe, whom could you ask? Do you think these topics are good for everyone to study, or just for people who are deeply interested in science?

Find Meaning

1. What does an atom contain?
2. (a) What makes up most of an atom (in terms of its volume)? (b) How is the structure of the universe like the structure of an atom?
3. (a) Why can't the force of your finger push apart the electrons on the top of a table? (b) How can a proton, which is billions of times smaller than a fingertip, push apart those same electrons?

Make Judgments

4. (a) Why do you think Jastrow includes information about people and events in history? (b) What did you learn from this information?
5. Jastrow worked as an astronomer, which is a space scientist. Why do you think he spends so much of this essay talking about atoms?
6. Identify several examples of sensory or descriptive detail in this essay. Explain why you think Jastrow's use of these techniques is or is not effective.
7. What kind of text organizational pattern does Jastrow use in the last seven paragraphs of this essay? Why does he use this pattern? What do you learn from it?

LITERATURE ▶▶ CONNECTION

In "The Size of Things," Robert Jastrow tries to describe objects that are incredibly small and large. He uses descriptions and comparisons to help his readers imagine things they cannot see. **Pattiann Rogers** was born in 1940 in Joplin, Missouri. Her poetry often explores nature and the principles of science. As you read her poem, think about how her purpose and the literary elements she uses compare to those of Jastrow.

Achieving Perspective

A Lyric Poem by Pattiann Rogers

Straight up away from this road,
Away from the fitted particles of frost
Coating the hull of each chick pea,[1]
And the stiff archer bug making its way
In the morning dark, toe hair by toe hair,
Up the stem of the trillium,[2]
Straight up through the sky above this road right now,
The galaxies of the Cygnus A cluster
Are colliding with each other in a massive swarm
Of interpenetrating and exploding catastrophes.
I try to remember that.
And even in the gold and purple pretense
Of evening, I make myself remember
That it would take 40,000 years full of gathering
Into leaf and dropping, full of pulp splitting
And the hard wrinkling of seed, of the rising up
Of wood fibers and the disintegration of forests,
Of this lake disappearing completely in the bodies
Of toad slush and duckweed rock,
40,000 years and the fastest thing we own,
To reach the one star nearest to us.

1. **chick pea.** Seed about the size of a marble; also called garbanzo
2. **trillium.** Spring-blooming three-petalled flower

And when you speak to me like this,
I try to remember that the wood and cement walls
Of this room are being swept away now,
Molecule by molecule, in a slow and steady wind,
And nothing at all separates our bodies
From the vast emptiness expanding, and I know
We are sitting in our chairs
Discoursing[3] in the middle of the blackness of space.
And when you look at me
I try to recall that at this moment
Somewhere millions of miles beyond the dimness
Of the sun, the comet Biela,[4] speeding
In its rocks and ices, is just beginning to enter
The widest arc of its elliptical turn.[5] ✣

3. **Discoursing.** Expressing oneself in conversation
4. **Biela.** Comet discovered by Wilhelm von Biela in 1826
5. **widest arc of its elliptical turn.** An ellipse is an elongated circle. The widest arc would resemble one of the long sides of an oval racetrack.

TEXT ←TO→ TEXT CONNECTION

What feelings does this poem express? Think of how Robert Jastrow might express the same feelings. What perspective do you think Rogers's speaker is trying to achieve? All in all, which presentation is easier to understand, that of Jastrow or Rogers? Be sure to support your opinion with evidence from the texts.

AFTER READING

Analyze Literature

Informational Text Analyze Jastrow's essay with a K-W-L chart. In the first column, put something you already knew about atoms or space. In the center column, write something you want to learn about that topic. Scan the essay to remind yourself of information the article contains, and then, in the third column, write what you learned from the essay. When you are done, summarize what you learned in a single sentence. As a separate activity, write a full summary of the essay and exchange your summary with a classmate. Write an evaluation of their work based on the accuracy of the main ideas, supporting details, and the overall meaning of the essay.

What I Already Know	What I Want to Learn	What I Learned
That atoms are small and the universe is big		

Extend Understanding

Writing Options

Creative Writing Write a **descriptive paragraph** using an analogy. An analogy is a comparison of things that are alike in some ways but different in others. Imagine that you want to describe an atom to one of your state's senators. Then choose what to emphasize–such as the atom's size, its composition, the empty space it contains, or the number of atoms in a common object–and invent an analogy that will convey this to your senator.

Explanatory Writing Jargon is terminology about a specific topic that most people will not understand. Create a **list** of terms from this essay that you believe are jargon. When you have completed your list, draft a definition for each term in your own words. Use a dictionary or other reference material to help you find accurate and complete definitions. Also, using a dictionary, identify the proper syllabication, pronunciation, and part of speech for each word. Finally, consult a thesaurus to identify any alternate word options.

Collaborative Learning

Give Complex Instructions With a partner, take turns giving oral instructions to perform specific tasks, answer questions, or solve problems. Set a time limit for each speaker and switch when your time is up. Focus your instructions on researching or analyzing the selection or the literature connection.

Lifelong Learning

Borrowed Words "Achieving Perspective" uses the phrase "exploding catastrophes." The word *catastrophe* comes from the Greek word *katastrophē* and is one example of foreign words commonly used in the English language. Identify the meaning of the following foreign phrases and acronyms used in English: *bona fide, nemesis,* and *RSVP*. Note any other foreign words that you have encountered.

Go to **www.mirrorsandwindows.com** for more.

Grammar & Style

Adjective and Adverb Clauses

Adjective Clauses

It is one of nine planets, which are bound to the sun by the force of gravity.

—ROBERT JASTROW, "The Size of Things"

In the sentence above, *which are bound to the sun by the force of gravity* is a clause that provides information about the noun *planets*. An **adjective clause** is a dependent clause that modifies a noun or pronoun. Adjective clauses follow the word they modify and are generally introduced with words such as *that, which, who, whom, whose, after, before, since, than, when, why,* and *where.*

When an adjective clause is **essential** to the meaning of a sentence, it should not be set off from the rest of the sentence with commas.

EXAMPLE

This is the method that they used to measure the electron.

When an adjective clause is **nonessential,** it is set off with commas.

EXAMPLE

The senator, who had attended my lecture, asked about the size of an electron.

Adverb Clauses

An **adverb clause** is a dependent clause that functions as an adverb. It modifies a verb, an adjective, or another adverb.

EXAMPLE

The scientists knew the electron existed before they understood its size.

In the sentence above, *before they understood its size* is a clause that modifies the verb *knew*. Adverb clauses often start with a subordinating conjunction such as *after, although, because, before, if, so that, unless, when, whether,* and *while.*

EXAMPLE

Because electrons are so small, they are difficult to measure.

When an adverb clause begins a sentence, it is set off by a comma.

Sentence Improvement

On a separate sheet of paper, correct the punctuation of the clauses in the following sentences. If a sentence has no punctuation errors, write *correct.* Next to each sentence, state whether the clause it contains is an adjective or adverb clause.

1. Millikan was the scientist, who measured the mass of the electron.
2. It was the most incredible event that ever happened to him.
3. Jupiter which has a diameter of 86,000 miles is the largest of the planets.
4. Scientists were unsure of the electron's existence before the experiments.
5. Because of the work of Rutherford and Geiger our understanding of the atom increased.

Apply the Model

BEFORE READING

DURING READING

AFTER READING

from *The Sibley Guide to Birds*

Visual Media by David Allen Sibley

GUIDED READING

Build Background

Scientific Context Ornithologists are scientists who study birds, but there are many more birdwatchers than there are ornithologists. Birdwatchers spend hours looking for birds, and they keep careful records of birds they have seen. Birdwatchers use illustrated manuals called *field guides* to help identify birds. In 2000, ornithologist David Allen Sibley published a field guide that describes over eight hundred species of birds in North America. This entry is about one of those species.

Reader's Context Would you know a wild turkey if you saw one? You probably would. Imagine having this kind of book along with you in the woods and encountering a flock of birds. Study this entry to learn more about them.

Set Purpose

As you read this entry from *The Sibley Guide to Birds,* consider how the author conveys information in words and images. Which do you find more effective?

Analyze Literature

Visual Media In addition to written language, information can be conveyed through **visual media,** pictorial or other graphic forms of communication. There is a wide variety of visual media, including photographs, illustrations, charts, graphs, diagrams, and maps. Field guides, like *The Sibley Guide to Birds,* often contain both text and several different kinds of visual media. As you read this entry, examine how visual media and text interact to provide the reader with information.

Use Reading Skills

Draw Conclusions Use details from the entry to draw a conclusion about what traits can be used to distinguish the wild turkey from other birds. As you study the entry, record details with a web. Put details about the wild turkey in the outer ovals.

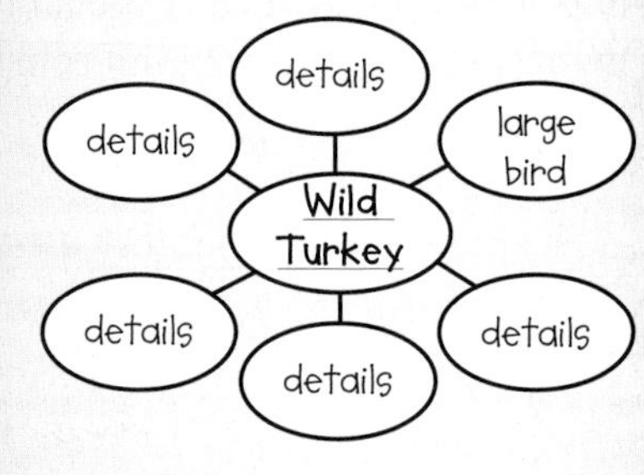

Meet the Author

David Allen Sibley (b. 1962) first started thinking about making a field guide in the 1970s. According to Sibley, "Birds are beautiful, in spectacular as well as subtle ways; their colors, shapes, actions, and sounds are among the most aesthetically pleasing in nature." Sibley lives in Concord, Massachusetts, and continues to write about and paint birds.

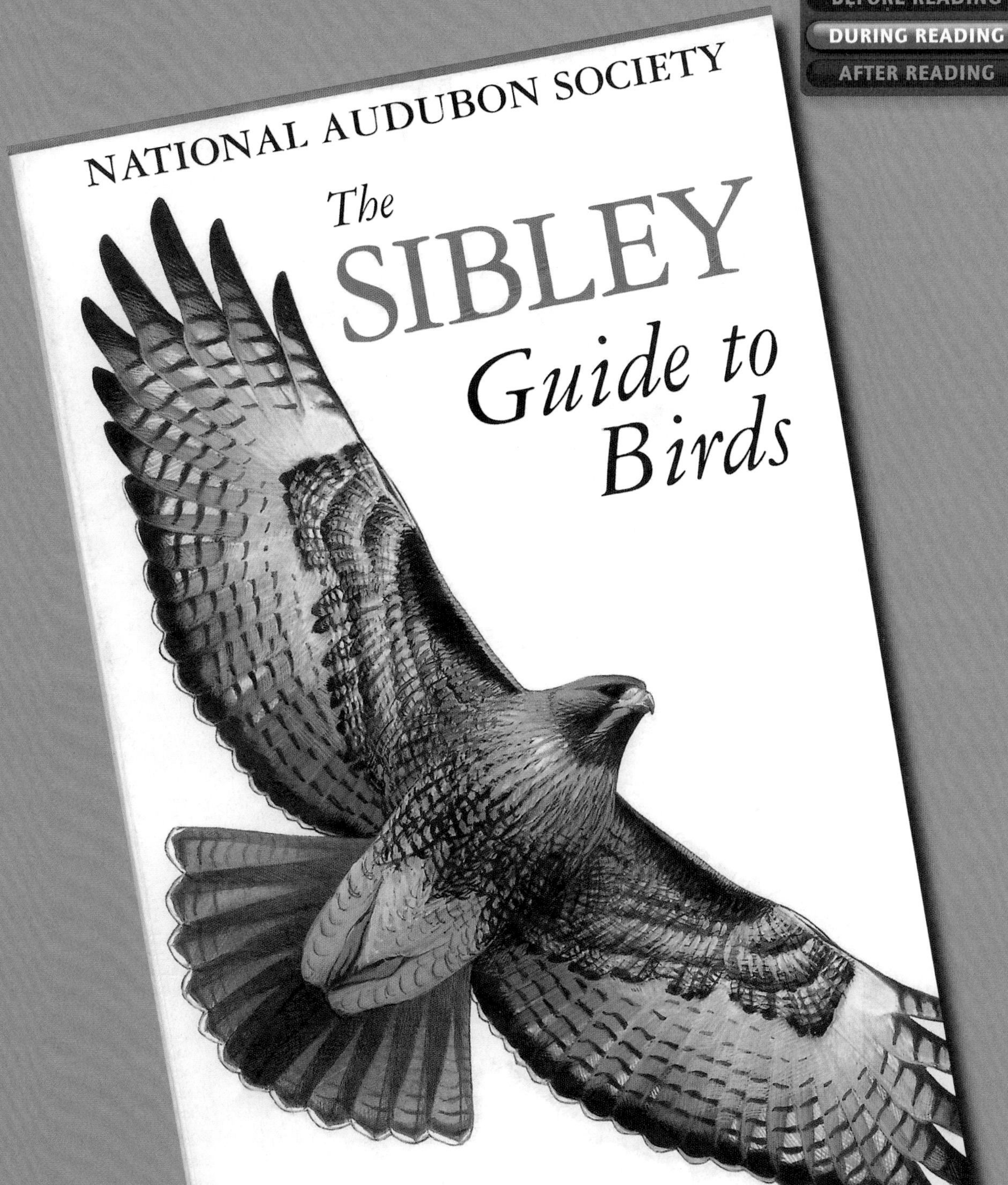

Apply the Model

BEFORE READING

DURING READING

AFTER READING

NATIONAL AUDUBON SOCIETY

The SIBLEY Guide to Birds

Written and illustrated by
DAVID ALLEN SIBLEY

DURING READING

Use Reading Skills

Draw Conclusions What does the word *incongruously* suggest about these birds? Use a dictionary if you need help.

WILD TURKEY

One of our largest birds, Wild Turkey is found in flocks in open woods with fields or clearings, usually in oak or beech woods. It is often seen strolling across open ground in flocks of up to 60.

Wild Turkey

Meleagris gallopavo[1]

♂ L 46" WS 64" WT 16.2 lb (7,400 g)[2]

♀ L 37" WS 50" WT 9.2 lb (4,200 g)

Very large and dark, with heavy, dark body incongruously joined to thin neck, small head, and long legs.

DURING READING

Analyze Literature

Visual Media How can you interpret these drawings to tell a female from a male?

Voice: Male in display gives familiar descending gobble. Female gives loud, sharp *tuk* and slightly longer, whining *yike, yike* . . . repeated in slow series. Both sexes give a variety of other soft clucks and rolling calls.

---

1. ***Meleagris gallopavo.*** Scientific name for the wild turkey species
2. **L, WS, WT.** Abbreviations for *length, wingspan,* and *weight*
3. **♂ ♀.** Symbols for male and female
4. **remiges** (rē´ mi jēz'). Flight feathers, which are attached to wing bones
5. **all feathers...when fresh.** A fresh feather replaces a feather lost during molting.
6. **display.** Action of spreading tail and puffing out the chest to attract a mate

 [7]

Southwestern populations have tail and uppertail coverts[8] tipped pale buffy or whitish, creating a strikingly different appearance than the darker, rufous-tipped Eastern birds, but the change is broadly clinal.[9] Domestic turkeys, often escaped or released, average heavier than Wild Turkey and have white-tipped tail feathers similar to Southwestern birds. Furthermore, birds of mixed ancestry have been widely introduced, and the species is now found farther north and much farther west than ever before. ✤

DURING READING

Use Reading Skills

Draw Conclusions What do you think "birds of mixed ancestry" means?

---

7. (range map.) The color on this map shows where wild turkeys live in North America.

8. coverts (kə´ vərts). Feathers that help streamline and insulate the bird

9. rufous...clinal. *Rufous* (rü´ fəs) refers to a yellowish-pink to orange color; *clinal* (klīn´ əl) is a characteristic, such as color, that changes gradually, usually in relation to a change in environment

When have you taken the time to closely observe something in nature? How did it affect you? Why do you think people like to watch birds?

Find Meaning

1. (a) What are the two main types of wild turkey? (b) How can you tell the difference between them?
2. Which type of bird gobbles and when?
3. Reread the paragraph next to the map. (a) What is a domestic turkey? (b) Based on this paragraph, if you encountered a wild turkey in the woods, would you expect it to look exactly like one of these pictures? Why or why not?

Make Judgments

4. What elements of the description in this entry would help you most when identifying a wild turkey?
5. (a) How do you think Sibley chose the specific details about wild turkeys that appear in this entry? (b) What kinds of topics or pictures do you think he could add if he had more room?
6. This field guide includes advice on identifying birds. Sibley writes: "The first rule is simple: *Look at the bird.* Don't fumble with a book, because by the time you find the right picture, the bird will most likely be gone.... Watch what the bird does, watch it fly away, and only then try to find it in your book." Do you think this is realistic advice? Explain your answer.

INFORMATIONAL TEXT ▶▶ CONNECTION

David Allen Sibley follows in the footsteps of **John James Audubon** (1785–1851). Son of a French sea captain, Audubon came to the United States in 1803 and began to study and paint birds. He eventually published his work in *Birds of America.* Several years later he published *Ornithological Biographies*, from which this excerpt is drawn.

from Wild Turkey

An Essay by John James Audubon

While at Henderson, on the Ohio in Kentucky, I had many wild birds. I had a fine male Turkey that I had raised from its youth, having caught it when it was two or three days old. It became so tame that it would follow any person who called it, and it was the favorite of the little village where I lived. Yet it would never roost with the tame Turkeys, but always slept at night on the roof of the house, where it remained until dawn.

When it was two years old, it began to fly to the woods. There it would remain for most of the day, returning home only when night came on. It kept this up until the following spring, when, several times, I saw it fly from its roosting place in the top of a tall cottonwood tree on the banks of the Ohio. There, after resting a while, it would sail to the opposite shore, where the river was nearly half a mile wide, and return towards night.

One morning I saw it fly off at a very early hour to the woods. I paid little attention. Several days passed, but the bird did not return. I was going towards some lakes near Green River to shoot when I saw a fine large gobbler cross the path before me and move leisurely along. Turkeys were in the best condition for eating at that season. I ordered Juno, my dog, to chase it and flush[1] it into the air. The dog hurried ahead, and, as it drew near the bird, I saw with great surprise that the Turkey did not run off. Juno was about to seize it, when suddenly she stopped and turned her head towards me. I ran to them, and you can guess my surprise when I saw that the creature was my own favorite bird, and discovered that it had recognized the dog and would not fly from it, although it would have run off from a strange dog at once.

A friend of mine who was looking for a deer he had wounded happened to come along. He put my bird on his saddle in front of him and carried it home for me.

The following spring the Turkey was accidentally shot when it was taken for a wild one. It was brought back to me when the hunter saw the red ribbon it wore around its neck.

How shall we explain the way my Turkey knew my dog at sight in the woods, after seeing it at home in the yard and grounds? Was it instinct? Reason? Memory? Or the act of an intelligent mind? ✤

1. **flush.** Force a bird out of hiding

TEXT TO TEXT CONNECTION Sibley's guide provides a lot of visual information, but it also describes the turkey's behavior and voice. How does Sibley's "Wild Turkey" entry help you visualize the turkey Audubon describes?

AFTER READING

Analyze Literature

Visual Media Why do you think Sibley chose to convey some information visually instead of in written form? How might the use of visual media be more effective than language in this context? Create a three-column chart to examine Sibley's use of visual media. In the left column, list examples of illustrations, maps, or symbols. In the middle column, describe the author's purpose for including these. In the right column, briefly describe why this was or was not an effective use of visual media. Finally, write a paragraph that explains the difference between the theme presented in "Wild Turkey" and the author's purpose within "The Sibley Guide to Birds."

Example	Purpose	My Evaluation
illustration of foraging group	useful to bird-watchers in the field; person might actually see this	

Extend Understanding

Writing Options

Creative Writing Imagine that you have a friend who has never seen an image of a wild turkey. Look again at the illustrations of turkeys in this selection. What traits are most prominent? What characteristics do you find most interesting? Use the images and text from this selection to prompt a **descriptive paragraph** for your friend about the wild turkey. Be sure to describe all of the bird's most recognizable traits.

Argumentative Writing Suppose the manager of your local bookstore asks you to recommend some good nature books. Draft a one- or two-paragraph **book review** about *The Sibley Guide to Birds.* Give its purpose and describe any strengths and weaknesses you can name. Then conclude your review by stating whether or not you think the bookstore should carry the book.

Collaborative Learning

Peer Review Exchange your descriptive paragraph about the wild turkey with a partner. Take notes as you read each other's work. Your notes should praise the most effective elements of the paragraph but also specifically suggest how it might be improved. When you are done, share your feedback with your partner.

Lifelong Learning

Identify Birds Find a field guide for wild birds in your region and take it to a wildlife sanctuary, nature park, or other bird habitat. Use the photos and descriptions in the guide to identify as many birds as possible. Take notes on your overall experience and on how useful the guide was. Use your notes to write a one-page review for the publisher of the book. Include comments on the guide's strengths and weaknesses, such as descriptions that were confusing and photos that were particularly helpful. Offer suggestions for improving the guide in its next edition.

Go to **www.mirrorsandwindows.com** for more.

Ships in the Desert

ANCHOR TEXT

An Essay by Al Gore

DIRECTED READING

BEFORE READING

Build Background

Scientific Context "Ships in the Desert" is a nonfiction essay from *Earth in the Balance: Ecology and the Human Spirit,* which Al Gore wrote while serving as a U.S. senator. Gore wanted to raise people's awareness about the environment, its problems, and possible solutions. In a healthy environment, plants, animals, air, soil, and water exist in a balanced relationship.

Reader's Context What environmental problem concerns you? How does it affect you now, or how may it affect you in the future?

Set Purpose

Use Build Background and the first paragraph to preview "Ships in the Desert." Based on your preview, what environmental changes do you think Al Gore will focus on in the essay?

Analyze Literature

Analogy An **analogy** is a comparison of things that are alike in some ways but different in others, for example, a *camel is a ship of the desert.* Writers use analogies to add interest and vitality to their writing, and also to explain difficult ideas in a way that makes them clear and vivid for readers. As you read "Ships in the Desert," think about the analogies Gore uses to describe environmental problems.

Use Reading Skills

Analyze Main Idea and Supporting Details In nonfiction, writers usually have one central thought or message that they want to communicate to readers. All of the facts, details, and examples included in the text are specifically chosen to support and explain that main idea. Identifying supporting details as you read can help you draw conclusions about the writer's main idea. As you read "Ships in the Desert," use a web to keep track of details that can help you find the main idea.

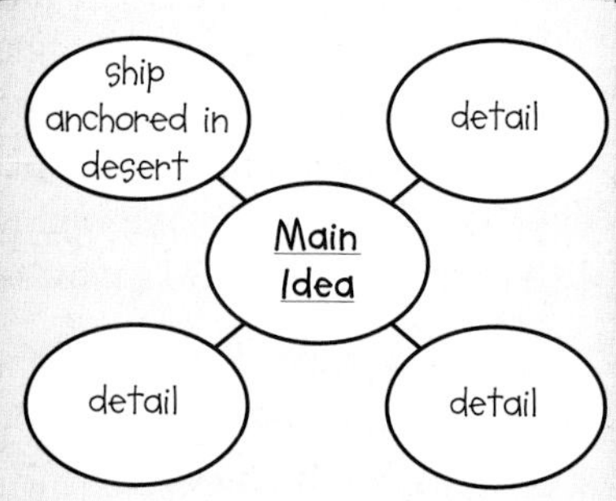

Meet the Author

Al Gore (b. 1948) became vice president of the United States in 1992, the same year that he published *Earth in the Balance: Ecology and the Human Spirit,* from which this essay is taken. As a former U.S. representative and senator, Gore was a leader in environmental awareness. As vice president, Gore worked diligently to fight environmental threats. In 2007, he shared the Nobel Peace Prize for his study of global warming.

Preview Vocabulary

un • pre • ce • dent • ed (ʉn' pre´ sə den' təd) *adj.,* unheard of; new

phe • nom • e • non (fi nä´ mə nän') *n.,* extremely unusual or extraordinary thing or occurrence

per • il (per´ əl) *n.,* danger, exposure to harm

Ships in the Desert

An Essay by Al Gore

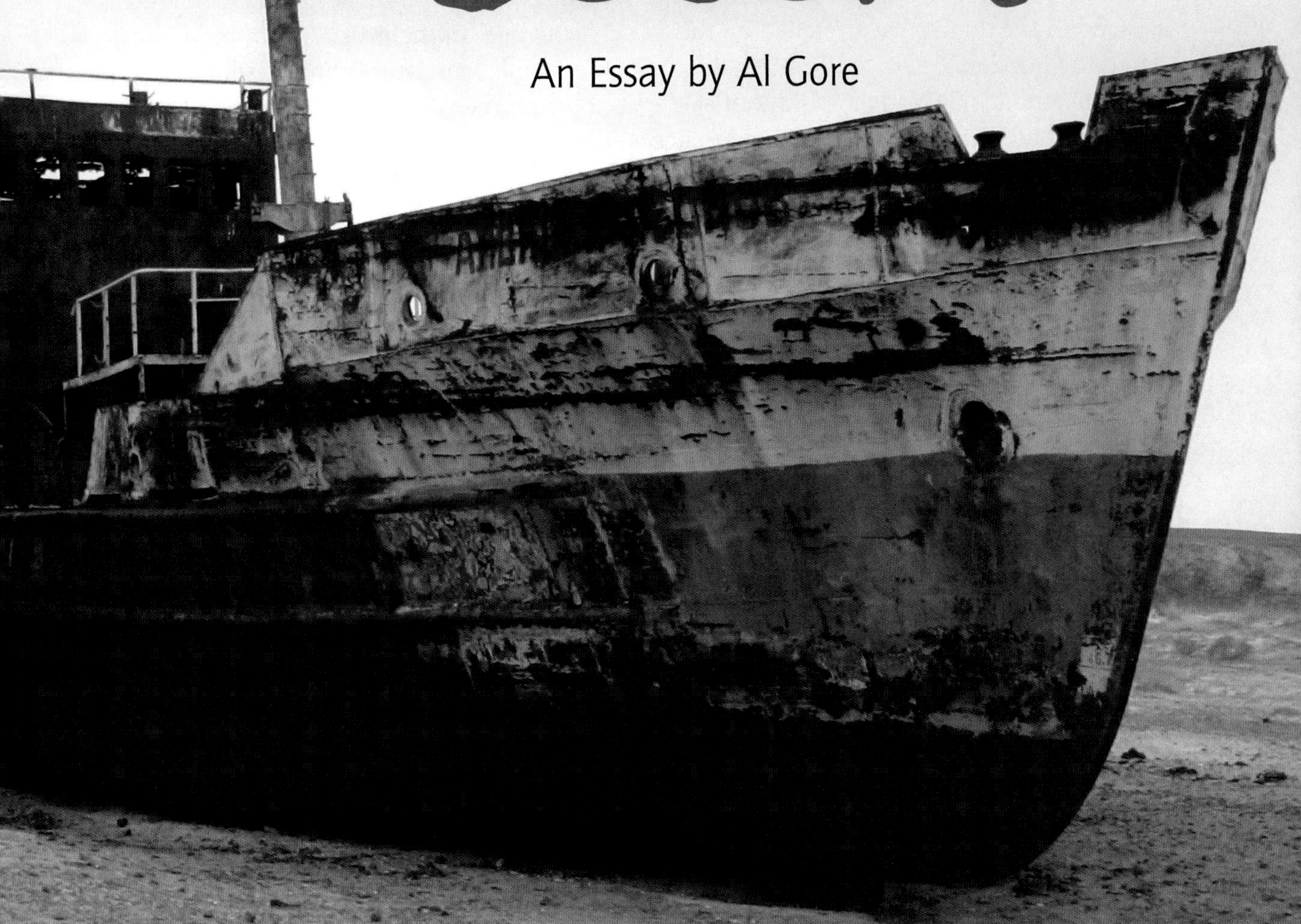

We are creating a world that is hostile to wildness, that seems to prefer concrete to natural landscapes.

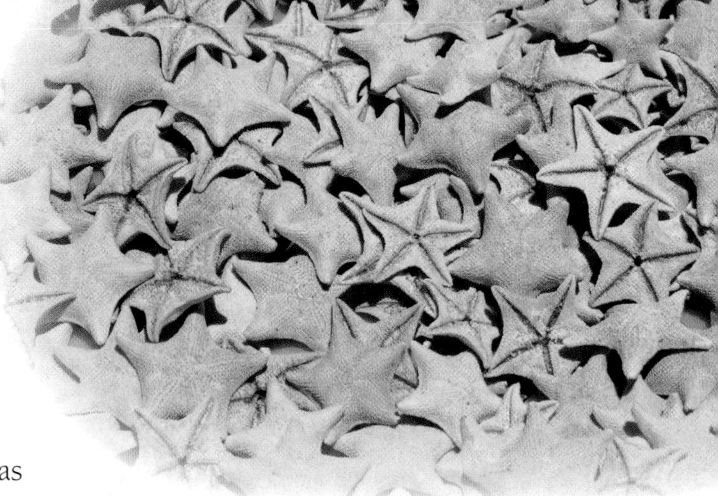

I was standing in the sun on the hot steel deck of a fishing ship capable of processing a fifty-ton catch on a good day. But it wasn't a good day. We were anchored in what used to be the most productive fishing site in all of central Asia, but as I looked out over the bow, the prospects of a good catch looked bleak. Where there should have been gentle blue-green waves lapping against the side of the ship, there was nothing but hot dry sand—as far as I could see in all directions. The other ships of the fleet were also at rest in the sand, scattered in the dunes that stretched all the way to the horizon.

Oddly enough, it made me think of a fried egg I had seen back in the United States on television the week before. It was sizzling and popping the way a fried egg should in a pan, but it was in the middle of a sidewalk in downtown Phoenix. I guess it sprang to mind because, like the ship on which I was standing, there was nothing wrong with the egg itself. Instead, the world beneath it had changed in an unexpected way that made the egg seem—through no fault of its own—out of place. It was illustrating the newsworthy point that at the time Arizona wasn't having an especially good day, either, because for the second day in a row temperatures had reached a record 122 degrees.

As a camel walked by on the dead bottom of the Aral Sea, my thoughts returned to the unlikely ship of the desert on which I stood, which also seemed to be illustrating the point that its world had changed out from underneath it with sudden cruelty. Ten years ago the Aral was the fourth-largest inland sea in the world, comparable to the largest of North America's Great Lakes. Now it is disappearing because the water that used to feed it has been diverted in an ill-considered irrigation scheme to grow cotton in the desert. The new shoreline was almost forty kilometers across the sand from where the fishing fleet was now permanently docked. Meanwhile, in the nearby town of Muynak the people were still canning fish—brought not from the Aral Sea but shipped by rail through Siberia from the Pacific Ocean, more than a thousand miles away.

I had come to the Aral Sea in August 1990 to witness at first hand the destruction taking place there on an almost biblical scale. But during the trip I encountered other images that also alarmed me. For example, the day I returned to Moscow from Muynak, my friend Alexei Yablokov, possibly the leading environmentalist in the Soviet Union, was returning from an emergency expedition to the White Sea, where he had investigated the mysterious and unprecedented death of several *million* starfish, washed up into a knee-deep mass covering many miles of beach. That night, in his apartment, he talked of what it was like for the residents to wade through the starfish in hip boots, trying to explain their death.

Later investigations identified radioactive military waste as the likely culprit in the White Sea deaths. But what about all of the other mysterious mass deaths washing up on beaches around the world? French scientists recently concluded that the explanation for

un•pre•ce•dent•ed (ʉn' pre´ sə den' təd) *adj.*, unheard of; new the growing number of dead dolphins washing up along the Riviera was accumulated environmental stress, which, over time, rendered the animals too weak to fight off a virus. This same phenomenon may also explain the sudden increase in dolphin deaths along the Gulf Coast in Texas as well as the mysterious deaths of 12,000 seals whose corpses washed up on the shores of the North Sea in the summer of 1988. Of course, the oil-covered otters and seabirds of Prince William Sound a year later[1] presented less of a mystery to science, if no less an indictment[2] of our civilization.

As soon as one of these troubling images fades, another takes its place, provoking new questions. What does it mean, for example, that children playing in the morning surf must now dodge not only the occasional jellyfish but the occasional hypodermic needle washing in with the waves? Needles, dead dolphins, and oil-soaked birds—are all these signs that the shores of our familiar world are fast eroding, that we are now standing on some new beach, facing dangers beyond the edge of what we are capable of imagining?

With our backs turned to the place in nature from which we came, we sense an unfamiliar tide rising and swirling around our ankles, pulling at the sand beneath our feet. Each time this strange new tide goes out, it leaves behind the flotsam and jetsam[3] of some giant shipwreck far out at sea, startling images washed up on the sands of our time, each a fresh warning of hidden dangers that lie ahead if we continue on our present course.

My search for the underlying causes of the environmental crisis has led me to travel around the world to examine and study many of these images of destruction. At the very bottom of the earth, high in the Trans-Antarctic Mountains, with the sun glaring at midnight through a hole in the sky, I stood in the unbelievable coldness and talked with a scientist in the late fall of 1988 about the tunnel he was digging through time. Slipping his parka back to reveal a badly burned face that was cracked and peeling, he pointed to the annual layers of ice in a core sample dug from the glacier on which we were standing. He moved his finger back in time to the ice of two decades ago. "Here's where the U.S. Congress passed the Clean Air Act," he said. At the bottom of the world, two continents away from Washington, D.C., even a small reduction in one country's emissions had changed the amount of pollution found in the remotest and least accessible place on earth.

Where there should have been gentle blue-green waves lapping against the side of the ship, there was nothing but hot dry sand...

But the most significant change thus far in the earth's atmosphere is the one that began with the industrial revolution early in the last century and has picked up speed ever since. Industry meant coal, and later oil, and we began to burn lots of it—bringing rising levels of carbon dioxide (CO_2), with its ability to trap more heat in the atmosphere and slowly warm the earth. Fewer than a hundred yards from the South Pole, upwind

1. **oil-covered otters...a year later.** The *Exxon-Valdez* tanker spilled eleven million gallons of oil in Prince William Sound, Alaska, in 1989.
2. **indictment.** Condemnation
3. **flotsam and jetsam.** Floating debris

phe•nom•e•non (fi nä′ mə nän′) *n.*, extremely unusual or extraordinary thing or occurrence from the ice runway where the ski plane lands and keeps its engines running to prevent the metal parts from freeze-locking together, scientists monitor the air several times every day to chart the course of that inexorable change. During my visit, I watched one scientist draw the results of that day's measurements, pushing the end of a steep line still higher on the graph. He told me how easy it is—there at the end of the earth—to see that this enormous change in the global atmosphere is still picking up speed.

Two and a half years later I slept under the midnight sun at the other end of our planet, in a small tent pitched on a twelve-foot-thick slab of ice floating in the frigid Arctic Ocean. After a hearty breakfast, my companions and I traveled by snowmobiles a few miles farther north to a rendezvous[4] point where the ice was thinner—only three and a half feet thick—and a nuclear submarine hovered in the water below. After it crashed through the ice, took on its new passengers, and resubmerged, I talked with scientists who were trying to measure more accurately the thickness of the polar ice cap, which many believe is thinning as a result of global warming. I had just negotiated an agreement between ice scientists and the U.S. Navy to secure the release of previously top secret data from submarine sonar tracks, data that could help them learn what is happening to the north polar cap. Now, I wanted to see the pole itself, and some eight hours after we met the submarine, we were crashing through that ice, surfacing, and then I was standing in an eerily beautiful snowscape, windswept and sparkling white, with the horizon defined by little hummocks, or "pressure ridges" of ice that are pushed up like tiny mountain ranges when separate sheets collide. But here too, CO_2 levels are rising just as rapidly, and ultimately temperatures will rise with them—indeed, global warming is expected to push temperatures up much more rapidly in the polar regions than in the rest of the world. As the polar air warms, the ice here will thin; and since the polar cap plays such a crucial role in the world's weather system, the consequences of a thinning cap could be disastrous.

Considering such scenarios is not a purely speculative exercise. Six months after I returned from the North Pole, a team of scientists reported dramatic changes in the pattern of ice distribution in the Arctic, and a second team reported a still controversial

SCIENCE ▶▶ CONNECTION

Global Warming The greenhouse effect is a naturally occurring process that maintains Earth's warm, life-sustaining temperature. Greenhouse gases (water vapor, carbon dioxide, nitrous oxide, and methane) trap some infrared radiation within the atmosphere. In the last one hundred years, concentrations of greenhouse gases have increased and Earth's temperature has risen by about one degree Fahrenheit. Nearly all scientists believe this is the result of human activities. They also believe that temperatures will continue to rise unless people change their behavior.

4. rendezvouz (rän´ di vü'). Meeting

claim (which a variety of data now suggest) that, overall, the north polar cap has thinned by 2 percent in just the last decade. Moreover, scientists established several years ago that in many land areas north of the Arctic Circle, the spring snowmelt now comes earlier every year, and deep in the tundra[5] below, the temperature of the earth is steadily rising.

As it happens, some of the most disturbing images of environmental destruction can be found exactly halfway between the North and South poles—precisely at the equator in Brazil—where billowing clouds of smoke regularly blacken the sky above the immense but now threatened Amazon rain forest. Acre by acre, the rain forest is being burned to create fast pasture for fast-food beef; as I learned when I went there in early 1989, the fires are set earlier and earlier in the dry season now, with more than one Tennessee's worth of rain forest being slashed and burned each year. According to our guide, the biologist Tom Lovejoy, there are more different species of birds in each square mile of the Amazon than exist in all of North America—which means we are silencing thousands of songs we have never even heard.

But for most of us the Amazon is a distant place, and we scarcely notice the disappearance of these and other vulnerable species. We ignore these losses at our peril, however. They're like the proverbial[6] miners' canaries, silent alarms whose message in this case is that living species of animals and plants are now vanishing around the world *one thousand times faster* than at any time in the past 65 million years.

To be sure, the deaths of some of the larger and more spectacular animal species now under siege do occasionally capture our attention. I have also visited another place along the equator, East Africa, where I encountered the grotesquely horrible image of a dead elephant, its head mutilated by poachers who had dug out its valuable tusks with chain saws. Clearly, we need to change our purely aesthetic[7] consideration of ivory, since its source is now so threatened. To me, its translucent whiteness seems different now, like evidence of the ghostly presence of a troubled spirit, a beautiful but chill apparition, inspiring both wonder and dread.

A similar apparition lies just beneath the ocean. While scuba diving in the Caribbean, I have seen and touched the white bones of a dead coral reef. All over the earth, coral reefs have suddenly started to "bleach" as warmer ocean temperatures put unaccustomed stress on the tiny organisms that normally live in the skin of the coral and give the reef its natural coloration. As these organisms—nicknamed "zooks"—leave the membrane of the coral, the coral itself becomes transparent, allowing its white limestone skeleton to shine through—hence its bleached appearance. In the past, bleaching was almost always an occasional and temporary phenomenon, but repeated episodes can exhaust the coral. In the last few years, scientists have been shocked at the sudden occurrence of extensive worldwide bleaching episodes from which increasing numbers of coral reefs have failed to recover. Though dead, they shine more brightly than before, haunted perhaps by the same ghost that gives spectral[8] light to an elephant's tusk.

But one doesn't have to travel around the world to witness humankind's assault on the earth. Images that signal the distress of our global environment are now commonly seen almost anywhere. A few miles from the

---

5. **tundra.** Flat, frozen, treeless land
6. **proverbial.** Widely referred to
7. **aesthetic.** Relating to beauty
8. **spectral.** Ghostly

per • il (per´ əl) *n.*, danger; exposure to harm

Capitol, for example, I encountered another startling image of nature out of place. Driving in the Arlington, Virginia, neighborhood where my family and I live when the Senate is in session, I stepped on the brake to avoid hitting a large pheasant walking across the street. It darted between the parked cars, across the sidewalk, and into a neighbor's backyard. Then it was gone. But this apparition of wildness persisted in my memory as a puzzle: Why would a pheasant, let alone such a large and beautiful mature specimen, be out for a walk in my neighborhood? Was it a much wilder place than I had noticed? Were pheasants, like the trendy Vietnamese potbellied pigs, becoming the latest fashion in unusual pets? I didn't solve the mystery until weeks later, when I remembered that about three miles away, along the edge of the river, developers were bulldozing the last hundred acres of untouched forest in the entire area. As the woods fell to make way for more concrete, more buildings, parking lots, and streets, the wild things that lived there were forced to flee. Most of the deer were hit by cars; other creatures—like the pheasant that darted into my neighbor's backyard—made it a little farther.

Ironically, before I understood the mystery, I felt vaguely comforted to imagine that perhaps this urban environment, so similar to the one in which many Americans live, was not so hostile to wild things after all. I briefly supposed that, like the resourceful raccoons and possums and squirrels and pigeons, all of whom have adapted to life in the suburbs, creatures as wild as pheasants might have a fighting chance. Now I remember that pheasant when I take my children to the zoo and see an elephant or a rhinoceros. They too inspire wonder and sadness. They too remind me that we are creating a world that is hostile to wildness, that seems to prefer concrete to natural landscapes. We are encountering these creatures on a path we have paved—one that ultimately leads to their extinction. ✤

If you had to give up one thing or change your behavior in one way to save the environment, what would you give up or change? Do you think individual sacrifice and change can make enough of a difference?

Find Meaning

1. (a) Why is the Aral Sea disappearing? (b) What impression of human planning does this create?
2. (a) What effect did passage of the Clean Air Act have on ice core samples dug from polar glaciers? (b) What does this evidence suggest about air pollution?
3. (a) What alarming fact did the author learn about the rain forest on a 1989 visit to the Amazon? (b) Why does the author find this so alarming?

Make Judgments

4. (a) From the examples provided by the author, what conclusions can you draw about human beings' relationship with nature? (b) Why do you think the author provides statistics about the number of species lost each year?
5. (a) What attitudes and behaviors do you think the author would like people to change regarding the environment? (b) Which of these changes will probably be the most difficult for people to make?

INFORMATIONAL TEXT ▶▶ CONNECTION

In "Ships in the Desert," Al Gore bears witness to what he calls "humankind's assault on the earth." The following selection, "I Am a Native of North America," is a personal essay by **Chief Dan George** (1899–1981). Born in North Vancouver, British Columbia, Canada, George was given the tribal name Geswanouth Slaholt. At age sixty-two, after working a variety of odd jobs, George's son encouraged him to take over the part of a Native American character on a Canadian television series. For the next twenty years, George appeared in television, stage, and film productions, including the 1970 film *Little Big Man,* for which he received an Academy Award nomination. As you read, look for details that George uses to explain and support his main idea about modern society's attitudes toward nature.

I Am a Native of North America

A Personal Essay by Chief Dan George

In the course of my lifetime I have lived in two distinct cultures. I was born into a culture that lived in communal houses. My grandfather's house was eighty feet long. It was called a smoke house, and it stood down by the beach along the inlet. All my grandfather's sons and their families lived in this large dwelling. Their sleeping apartments were separated by blankets made of bull rush reeds, but one open fire in the middle served the cooking needs of all. In houses like these, throughout the tribe, people learned to live with one another; learned to serve one another; learned to respect the rights of one another. And children shared the thoughts of the adult world and found themselves surrounded by aunts and uncles and cousins who loved them and did not threaten them. My father was born in such a house and learned from infancy how to love people and be at home with them.

And beyond this acceptance of one another there was a deep respect for everything in nature that surrounded them. My father loved the earth and all its creatures. The earth was his second mother. The earth and everything it contained was a gift from See-see-am[1]...and the way to thank this great spirit was to use his gifts with respect.

I remember, as a little boy, fishing with him up Indian River and I can still see him as the sun rose above the mountain top in the early morning...I can see him standing by the water's edge with his arms raised above his head while he softly moaned..."Thank you, thank you." It left a deep impression on my young mind.

And I shall never forget his disappointment when once he caught me gaffing[2] for fish "just for the fun of it."

1. **See-see-am.** Name of a god in the Salish language
2. **gaffing.** A *gaff* is a pole with a large hook or spear on the end. *Gaffing* involves using a gaff to stab and catch a large fish.

"My Son," he said, "the Great Spirit gave you those fish to be your brothers, to feed you when you are hungry. You must respect them. You must not kill them just for the fun of it."

This then was the culture I was born into and for some years the only one I really knew or tasted. This is why I find it hard to accept many of the things I see around me.

I see people living in smoke houses hundreds of times bigger than the one I knew. But the people in one apartment do not even know the people in the next and care less about them.

It is also difficult for me to understand the deep hate that exists among people. It is hard to understand a culture that justifies the killing of millions in past wars, and is at this very moment preparing bombs to kill even greater numbers. It is hard for me to understand a culture that spends more on wars and weapons to kill, than it does on education and welfare to help and develop.

It is hard for me to understand a culture that not only hates and fights its brothers but even attacks nature and abuses her. I see my white brother going about blotting out nature from his cities. I see him strip the hills bare, leaving ugly wounds on the face of mountains. I see him tearing things from the bosom of mother earth as though she were a monster, who refused to share her treasures with him. I see him throw poison in the waters, indifferent to the life he kills there; and he chokes the air with deadly fumes.

My white brother does many things well for he is more clever than my people but I wonder if he knows how to love well. I wonder if he has ever really learned to love at all. Perhaps he only loves the things that are his own but never learned to love the things that are outside and beyond him. And this is, of course, not love at all, for man must love all creation or he will love none of it. Man must love fully or he will become the lowest of the animals. It is the power to love that makes him the greatest of them all...for he alone of all animals is capable of love.

Love is something you and I must have. We must have it because our spirit feeds upon it. We must have it because without it we become weak and faint. Without love our self-esteem weakens. Without it our courage fails. Without love we can no longer look out confidently at the world. Instead we turn inwardly and begin to feed upon our own personalities and little by little we destroy ourselves.

You and I need the strength and joy that comes from knowing that we are loved. With it we are creative. With it we march tirelessly. With it, and with it alone, we are able to sacrifice for others.

There have been times when we all wanted so desperately to feel a reassuring

hand upon us…there have been lonely times when we so wanted a strong arm around us…I cannot tell you how deeply I miss my wife's presence when I return from a trip. Her love was my greatest joy, my strength, my greatest blessing.

I am afraid my culture has little to offer yours. But my culture did prize friendship and companionship. It did not look on privacy as a thing to be clung to, for privacy builds up walls and walls promote distrust. My culture lived in big family communities, and from infancy people learned to live with others.

My culture did not prize the hoarding of private possessions; in fact, to hoard was a shameful thing to do among my people. The Indian looked on all things in nature as belonging to him and he expected to share them with others and to take only what he needed.

Everyone likes to give as well as receive. No one wishes only to receive all the time. We have taken much from your culture…I wish you had taken something from our culture…for there were some beautiful and good things in it.

Soon it will be too late to know my culture, for integration is upon us and soon we will have no values but yours. Already many of our young people have forgotten the old ways. And many have been shamed of their Indian ways by scorn and ridicule. My culture is like a wounded deer that has crawled away into the forest to bleed and die alone.

The only thing that can truly help us is genuine love. You must truly love us, be patient with us and share with us. And we must love you—with a genuine love that forgives and forgets…a love that forgives the terrible sufferings your culture brought ours when it swept over us like a wave crashing along a beach…with a love that forgets and lifts up its head and sees in your eyes an answering love of trust and acceptance.

This is brotherhood…anything less is not worthy of the name.

I have spoken. ✣

What different details does Al Gore's essay and Chief Dan George's personal essay use to illustrate the causes and effects of human interference with nature? What common message does each writer hope to communicate? Finally, explain the difference between the theme of "I am a Native of North America" and the author's purpose in "Ships in the Desert."

AFTER READING

Analyze Literature

Analogy A writer's use of analogy helps to clarify complicated ideas and enhances the reader's overall understanding and appreciation of the text. Skim "Ships in the Desert," looking for analogies. Use a chart to record analogies you find and tell what the analogies compare. Then explain in one or two sentences how these analogies affect the author's message. As a separate activity, write a full summary of the essay and exchange your summary with a classmate. Write an evaluation of their work based on the accuracy of the main ideas, supporting details, and the overall meaning of the essay.

Example of Analogy	What Is Compared?	Effect
"ghostly presence of a troubled spirit"	ivory to a ghost	

Extend Understanding

Writing Options

Creative Writing Select one of the environmental disasters described in "Ships in the Desert," and write a **letter** to the editor of your local paper calling attention to the problem and stressing why, in your opinion, the problem needs to be resolved. Include in your letter at least one suggestion for how your community can contribute to the solution. Support your claims and opinions with evidence.

Informative Writing Al Gore provides a variety of vivid and startling images that "signal the distress of our global environment." Write a **problem-solution essay** in which you offer a solution to one of the problems he identifies. In the introductory paragraph, state the problem. In the body paragraphs, explain changes people can make to ease or resolve this problem. In the concluding paragraph, suggest what could happen in the future if such changes are not made. Use facts and details from "Ships in the Desert" to support your ideas. Share your work with the class.

Critical Literacy

Write a Proposal In small groups, select an environmental cause that interests you. Imagine that you are going to form a student group working for that cause. Write a proposal to an organization that might be willing to fund your cause, or write a proposal to your school, asking for permission to hold a fund-raiser. When you have finished, share your ideas with the class. You could then agree on volunteer activities to participate in as a class.

Media Literacy

Conduct Internet Research Use a search engine to find websites that discuss environmental issues. Narrow the list to ten websites that address one or two of the environmental problems discussed in "Ships in the Desert." Evaluate each site to determine the author's purpose, tone, bias, and credibility. To assess a site's credibility, distinguish between factual claims, opinions, and commonplace assertions or rhetorical fallacies (untruths or exaggerations).

Go to **www.mirrorsandwindows.com** for more.

Grammar & Style

Simple and Compound Subjects

Simple Subjects

Instead, the world beneath it had changed in an unexpected way....

—AL GORE, "Ships in the Desert"

In a sentence, the **simple subject** is the key word or words in the subject of the independent clause. The simple subject is usually a noun or a pronoun and does not include any modifiers. The simple subject in the quotation above is the noun *world.*

EXAMPLES

The camel is often called the ship of the desert.

He was standing on the deck of a ship in the middle of the desert.

Compound Subjects

Of course, the oil-covered otters and seabirds of Prince William Sound a year later presented less of a mystery to science....

—AL GORE, "Ships in the Desert"

A sentence may have more than one subject. A **compound subject** has two or more simple subjects that have the same predicate. The subjects are joined by the conjunction *and, either, or, neither, nor*, or *but.* In the quotation above, the compound subject is *otters and seabirds.*

If there are three or more subjects, commas should separate each. If there are only two subjects, or if a coordinating conjunction is used between every subject, commas should not be used.

EXAMPLES

Neither my friend nor I contacted the city government about the recycling program.

Juan, Mary Kay, and Jorge are members of the group that the teacher assigned to research environmental problems.

Identifying Simple and Compound Subjects

On a separate sheet of paper, underline once the simple subjects in the following sentences. Underline twice any compound subjects.

1. His thoughts returned to his experiences at the equator.
2. The camels and their drivers kicked up sand as they passed by.
3. Neither scientists nor government officials have the complete picture of global warming.
4. We couldn't believe how much damage had been done.
5. Ten years ago, the Aral was the fourth-largest inland sea in the world.
6. During the trip, the scientists and I encountered other images that alarmed us.
7. They had investigated the mysterious and unusual death of several million starfish.
8. Needles, dead dolphins, and oil-soaked birds are all signs that the shores of our familiar world are fast eroding.
9. The earth's atmosphere began to change.
10. After a hearty breakfast, my companions and I traveled by snowmobile a few miles farther north.

DIRECTED READING

Comparing Texts

Mute Dancers: How to Watch a Hummingbird

A Scientific Essay by Diane Ackerman

The Hummingbird That Lived Through Winter

A Short Story by William Saroyan

BEFORE READING

Build Background

Scientific Context Hummingbirds live only in the Americas. Just sixteen of more than three hundred species appear in the United States. The smallest birds on the planet, hummingbirds are also the only birds that can fly up, down, forward, backward, and sideways.

Reader's Context What lengths would you go to in order to save a sick or wounded animal?

Set Purpose

Preview the title and first few sentences of the essay and the story to make predictions about what you will learn.

Compare Literature: Description

Writing that describes a character, object, or scene using sensory details is called **description.** In this essay and story, the authors use sensory details to help you see, hear, smell, taste, and feel what they are describing. Use a chart to record sensory details and their effects.

Sensory Details	Effect of Details
"fury of iridescence" →	

Meet the Authors

Diane Ackerman (b. 1948) is a naturalist and a writer of poetry, essays, and books. *The Rarest of Rare* and *The Moon by Whale Light* are just two of numerous nonfiction works by Ackerman that delve into the mysteries of the natural world. "Mute Dancers: How to Watch a Hummingbird" was originally published in 1994 in *The New York Times Magazine*.

William Saroyan (1908–1981) was a prolific and versatile writer whose collected works include novels, short stories, plays, and poetry. Saroyan published his first book, *The Daring Young Man on the Flying Trapeze*, at the age of twenty-six. Born in Fresno, California, to Armenian parents, the author attributed much of his inspiration for writing to his Armenian heritage.

Preview Vocabulary

ir•i•des•cence (ir' ə de´ s'n[t]s) *n.*, show of rainbow colors that seem to shimmer and change when viewed from different angles

co•los•sal (kə lä´ səl) *adj.*, of a very large degree or amount

per•pet•u•al (pər pe´ chə wəl) *adj.*, going on forever

be•nign (bi nīn´) *adj.*, posing no threat

trans•for•ma•tion (tran[t]s fər mā´ shən) *n.*, change in composition, structure, or outward form and appearance

The Aztec God Quetzalcoatl with a Hummingbird (manuscript illustration), c. 1500. Aztec artist. Biblioteca Nazionale Centrale, Florence, Italy.

Mute Dancers: How to Watch a Hummingbird

A Scientific Essay
by Diane Ackerman

A lot of hummingbirds die in their sleep. Like a small fury of iridescence, a hummingbird spends the day at high speed, darting and swiveling among thousands of nectar-rich blossoms. Hummingbirds have huge hearts and need colossal amounts of energy to fuel their flights, so they live in a perpetual mania to find food. They tend to prefer red, trumpet-shaped flowers, in which nectar thickly oozes, and eat every 15 minutes or so. A hummingbird drinks with a W-shaped tongue, licking nectar up as a cat might (but faster). Like a tiny drum roll, its heart beats at 500 times a minute. Frighten a hummingbird and its heart can race to over 1,200 times a minute. Feasting and flying, courting and dueling, hummingbirds consume life at a fever pitch. No warm-blooded animal on earth uses more energy, for its size. But that puts them at great peril. By day's end, wrung-out and exhausted, a hummingbird rests near collapse.

Hummingbirds have huge hearts and need colossal amounts of energy to fuel their flights...

In the dark night of the hummingbird, it can sink into a zombielike state of torpor;[1] its breathing grows shallow and its wild heart slows to only 36 beats a minute. When dawn breaks on the fuchsia and columbine, hummingbirds must jump-start their hearts and fire up their flight muscles to raise their body temperature for another all-or-nothing day. That demands a colossal effort, which some can't manage. So a lot of hummingbirds die in their sleep.

1. **torpor.** Hibernation-like state during which there is no movement

ir • i • des • cence (ir' ə de´ s'n[t]s) *n.*, show of rainbow colors that seem to shimmer and change when viewed from different angles

co • los • sal (kə lä´ səl) *adj.*, of a very large degree or amount

per • pet • u • al (pər pe´ chə wəl) *adj.*, going on forever

But most do bestir themselves. This is why, in American Indian myths and legends, hummingbirds are often depicted as resurrection birds, which seem to die and be reborn on another day or in another season. The Aztec[2] god of war was named Huitzilopochtli,[3] a compound word meaning "shining one with weapon like cactus thorn," and "sorcerer that spits fire." Aztec warriors fought, knowing that if they fell in battle they would be reincarnated as glittery, thuglike hummingbirds. The male birds were lionized for their ferocity in battle. And their feathers flashed in the sun like jewel-encrusted shields. Aztec rulers donned ceremonial robes of hummingbird feathers. As they walked, colors danced across their shoulders and bathed them in a supernatural light show.

The feathers were ruffled and there was a bit of blood on the breast, but the bird still looked perky and alive.

While most birds are busy singing a small operetta of who and what and where, hummingbirds are virtually mute. Such small voices don't carry far, so they don't bother much with song. But if they can't serenade a mate, or yell war cries at a rival, how can they perform the essential dramas of their lives? They dance. Using body language, they spell out their intentions and moods just as bees, fireflies or hula dancers do. That means elaborate aerial ballets in which males twirl, joust, sideswipe and somersault. Brazen and fierce, they will take on large adversaries—even cats, dogs or humans.

My neighbor Persis once told me how she'd been needled by hummingbirds. When Persis lived in San Francisco, hummingbirds often attacked her outside her apartment building. From their perspective she was on *their* property, not the other way round, and they flew circles around her to vex her away. My encounters with hummingbirds have been altogether more benign. Whenever I've walked through South American rain forests, with my hair braided and secured by a waterproof red ribbon, hummingbirds have assumed my ribbon to be a succulent flower and have probed my hair repeatedly, searching for nectar. Their touch was as delicate as a sweat bee's. But it was their purring by my ear that made me twitch. In time, they would leave unfed, but for a while I felt like a character in a Li'l Abner[4] cartoon who could be named something like "Hummer." In Portuguese, the word for hummingbird *(Beija flora)* means "flower kisser." It was the American colonists who first imagined the birds humming as they went about their chores.

Last summer, the historical novelist Jeanne Mackin winced to see her cat, Beltane, drag in voles, birds and even baby rabbits. Few things can compete with the blood lust of a tabby cat. But one day Beltane dragged in something rare and shimmery—a struggling hummingbird. The feathers were ruffled and there was a bit of blood on the breast, but the bird still looked perky and alive. So Jeanne fashioned a nest for it out of a small wire basket lined in gauze, and fed it sugar water from an eye dropper. To her

---

2. **Aztec** (az´ tek'). Powerful and highly advanced Native American civilization whose empire was located in central Mexico from the 1400s to the early 1500s
3. **Huitzilopochtli** (wēt' sē lə pōch´ tlē).
4. **Li'l Abner.** Newspaper comic strip created by cartoonist Al Capp in 1934

be•nign (bi nīn´) *adj.,* posing no threat

amazement, as she watched, "it miscarried a little pearl." Hummingbird eggs are the size of coffee beans, and females usually carry two. So Jeanne knew one might still be safe inside. After a quiet night, the hummingbird seemed stronger, and when she set the basket outside at dawn, the tiny assault victim flew away.

It was a ruby-throated hummingbird that she nursed, the only one native to the East Coast. In the winter they migrate thousands of miles over mountains and open water to Mexico and South America. She may well have been visited by a species known to the Aztecs. Altogether, there are 16 species of hummingbirds in North America, and many dozens in South America, especially near the equator, where they can feed on a buffet of blossoms. The tiniest—the Cuban bee hummingbird—is the smallest warm-blooded animal in the world. About two and one-eighth inches long from beak to tail, it is smaller than the toe of an eagle, and its eggs are like seeds.

Hummingbirds are a New World phenomenon. So, too, is vanilla,[5] and their stories are linked. When the early explorers returned home with the riches of the West, they found it impossible, to their deep frustration, to grow vanilla beans. It took ages before they discovered why—that hummingbirds were a key pollinator of vanilla orchids—and devised beaklike splinters of bamboo to do the work of birds.

Now that summer has come at last, lucky days may be spent watching the antics of hummingbirds. The best way to behold them is to stand with the light behind you, so that the bird faces the sun. Most of the trembling colors aren't true pigments, but the result of light staggering through clear cells that act as prisms. Hummingbirds are iridescent for the same reason soap bubbles are. Each feather contains tiny air bubbles separated by dark spaces. Light bounces off the air bubbles at different angles, and that makes blazing colors seem to swarm and leap. All is vanity in the end. The male's shimmer draws a female to mate. But that doesn't matter much to gardeners, watching hummingbirds patrol the impatiens[6] as if the northern lights[7] had suddenly fallen to earth. ✣

---

5. **vanilla.** Fragrant flavoring often used in baking
6. **impatiens.** Plant with many red, pink, or white flowers
7. **northern lights.** Showy display of natural lights that appears in the night sky, also known as the aurora borealis (ə rôr´ ə bôr' ē a´ ləs)

How did this essay make you feel about hummingbirds? What details or descriptions most influenced these feelings? What makes the hummingbird unique?

Find Meaning

1. (a) Why does a hummingbird spend all day eating? (b) How does this affect its condition at night?
2. (a) Why don't hummingbirds sing? (b) According to the author, what do male hummingbirds do to attract mates or assert their power?

Make Judgments

3. (a) How would you describe the narrator's encounters with hummingbirds? (b) What does her description of these encounters suggest about her relationship with nature?
4. (a) Why do you think the author tells how Jeanne Mackin nursed a wounded hummingbird? (b) What do this anecdote and other examples in the essay reveal about the author's attitude toward hummingbirds?

The Hummingbird That Lived Through Winter

A Short Story by William Saroyan

There was a hummingbird once which in the wintertime did not leave our neighborhood in Fresno, California.

I'll tell you about it.

Across the street lived old Dikran, who was almost blind. He was past eighty and his wife was only a few years younger. They had a little house that was as neat inside as it was ordinary outside—except for old Dikran's garden, which was the best thing of its kind in the world. Plants, bushes, trees—all strong, in sweet black moist earth whose guardian was old Dikran. All things from the sky loved this spot in our poor neighborhood, and old Dikran loved *them*.

"It's in your hand. It's dying."

One freezing Sunday, in the dead of winter, as I came home from Sunday School I saw old Dikran standing in the middle of the street trying to distinguish what was in his hand. Instead of going into our house to the fire, as I had wanted to do, I stood on the steps of the front porch and watched the old man. He would turn around and look upward at his trees and then back to the palm of his hand. He stood in the street at least two minutes and then at last he came to me. He held his hand out, and in Armenian[1] he said, "What is this in my hand?"

I looked.

"It is a hummingbird," I said half in English and half in Armenian. Hummingbird I said in English because I didn't know its name in Armenian.

"What is that?" old Dikran asked.

"The little bird," I said. "You know. The one that comes in the summer and stands in the air and then shoots away. The one with the wings that beat so fast you can't see them. It's in your hand. It's dying."

"Come with me," the old man said. "I can't see, and the wife's at church. I can feel its heart beating. Is it in a bad way? Look again once."

I looked again. It was a sad thing to behold. This wonderful little creature of summertime in the big rough hand of the old peasant. Here and pathetic, not suspended in

1. **Armenian.** Language spoken by the people dwelling chiefly in Armenia and in neighboring regions of Turkey and Azerbaijan

a shaft of summer light, not the most alive thing in the world, but the most helpless and heart-breaking.

"It's dying," I said.

The old man lifted his hand to his mouth and blew warm breath on the little thing in his hand which he could not even see. "Stay now," he said in Armenian. "It is not long till summer. Stay, swift and lovely."

We went into the kitchen of his little house, and while he blew warm breath on the bird he told me what to do.

"Put a tablespoon of honey over the gas fire and pour it into my hand, but be sure it is not too hot."

This was done.

After a moment the hummingbird began to show signs of fresh life. The warmth of the room, the vapor of the warm honey—and, well, the will and love of the old man. Soon the old man could feel the change in his hand, and after a moment or two the hummingbird began to take little dabs of the honey.

"It will live," the old man announced. "Stay and watch."

The transformation was incredible. The old man kept his hand generously open, and I expected the helpless bird to shoot upward out of his hand, suspend itself in space, and scare the life out of me—which is exactly what happened. The new life of the little bird was magnificent. It spun about in the little kitchen, going to the window, coming back to the heat, suspending, circling as if it were summertime and it had never felt better in its whole life.

trans • for • ma • tion (tran[t]s fər mā´ shən) *n.*, change in composition, structure, or outward form and appearance

The old man sat on the plain chair, blind but attentive. He listened carefully and tried to see, but of course he couldn't. He kept asking about the bird, how it seemed to be, whether it showed signs of weakening again, what its spirit was, and whether or not it appeared to be restless; and I kept describing the bird to him.

When the bird was restless and wanted to go, the old man said, "Open the window and let it go."

"Will it live?" I asked.

"It is alive now and wants to go," he said. "Open the window."

I opened the window, the hummingbird stirred about here and there, feeling the cold from the outside, suspended itself in the area of the open window, stirring this way and that, and then it was gone.

"Close the window," the old man said.

We talked a minute or two and then I went home.

The old man claimed the hummingbird lived through that winter, but I never knew for sure. I saw hummingbirds again when summer came, but I couldn't tell one from the other.

One day in the summer I asked the old man.

"Did it live?"

"The little bird?" he said.

"Yes," I said. "That we gave the honey to. You remember. The little bird that was dying in the winter. Did it live?"

"Look about you," the old man said. "Do you see the bird?"

"I see humming*birds,*" I said.

"Each of them is our bird," the old man said. "Each of them, each of them," he said swiftly and gently. ✣

When might humans be responsible for helping sick or wounded wild animals? When is it not appropriate to help?

Comparing Texts

AFTER READING

Find Meaning

1. (a) Why does Dikran ask the narrator, "What is this in my hand?" (b) Why doesn't Dikran understand the narrator at first? What does the narrator do to help Dikran understand?
2. (a) How do Dikran and the narrator help the hummingbird? (b) How does the hummingbird's gradual recovery affect the narrator?

Make Judgments

3. (a) Why does Dikran tell the narrator to open the window and let the bird go? (b) What does this reveal about the kind of love Dikran has for birds and nature?
4. (a) What does Dikran mean when he tells the narrator that each of the hummingbirds he sees "is our bird"? (b) Why might it not matter if one of those is the one they saved?

Compare Literature

Description When a writer uses description, he or she uses sensory details to create vivid images that help readers visualize people, places, things, and ideas. Review sensory details in "Mute Dancer: How to Watch a Hummingbird" and "The Hummingbird That Lived Through Winter" that you recorded in your chart to answer these questions.

1. What sensory details does Ackerman use to create a vivid picture of a hummingbird?
2. How does Saroyan evoke a clear image of the hummingbird in his short story?
3. Which details used to describe a hummingbird had the greatest impact on you? Why?

Extend Understanding

Writing Options

Creative Writing Use **dialogue** to write a conversation that old Dikran might have with his wife when she returns home about finding, helping, and releasing the hummingbird. When creating dialogue for Dikran, use details that help him describe what he heard, smelled, and touched as he and the narrator treated the bird. Also have him explain how the experience might have made him feel.

Informative Writing Write a **critical analysis** in which you analyze the first-person point of view used in both "Mute Dancer: How to Watch a Hummingbird" and "The Hummingbird That Lived Through Winter." Explain why this was the most effective point of view to use in the essay and the story. Provide at least one example from the essay and the story to support your ideas. Share your work with the class.

Critical Literacy

Analyze Adaptations Works of nonfiction are often changed or adapted into another medium or genre. Find an adaptation of an autobiography or a diary and describe the structural and substantive differences between the two. Consider comparing Anne Frank's *The Diary of a Young Girl* with a dramatic adaptation (film, play) of the book.

Lifelong Learning

Research Myths and Legends Form a small group to research myths and legends about hummingbirds. Find a myth or legend in which the hummingbird plays a major role. With your group members, decide on a way to retell the myth or legend. You can rewrite the story in your own words and retell it to the class, or you can present the myth or legend as a skit.

Go to **www.mirrorsandwindows.com** for more.

THE FACE OF THE DEEP IS FROZEN

A Historical Essay by Jennifer Armstrong

BEFORE READING

Build Background

Historical Context In August 1914, Ernest Shackleton and twenty-seven men sailed from England toward Antarctica on a mission to cross the barren continent. Their ship became trapped in ice in January of 1915, where it survived the Antarctic winter, but then it sank. The men were forced to camp on the ice and set out on foot. In August 1916, the men were rescued; every member of the expedition survived. This selection is from a book about the harrowing expedition.

Reader's Context Would you like to be an explorer? How would you balance the possible dangers with the potential thrills of doing something remarkable?

Set Purpose

Skim the reading quickly. Based on information in Build Background and the title, predict what will happen in this excerpt. Read to find out how accurate your prediction is.

Analyze Literature

Description An author portrays a character or a scene through **description.** Authors use **sensory details** to describe how things look, sound, smell, taste, or feel. The use of **precise words, imagery,** and **figurative language** in description is important in appealing to the reader's senses. As you read, notice how the author uses these devices to describe.

Meet the Author

Jennifer Armstrong (b. 1961) is an award-winning author of books for young readers. Her book *Shipwreck at the Bottom of the World: The Extraordinary True Story of Shackleton and the Endurance* tells the true tale of an incredible expedition. To write the book, Armstrong conducted months of research, which resulted in vivid descriptions of the explorers and how they survived the trip to Antarctica. Armstrong also writes fiction and science fiction.

Use Reading Skills

Context Clues Preview the vocabulary words from this selection in the sentences below. Try to determine the meaning of each word using the context clues in the sentences.

1. Students referred to the combined offices as the consolidated school district.
2. It can take only a few days of blowing desert sand to entirely erode the surface of a statue.
3. After a few hours in the refrigerator, fat began to congeal on top of the stew.
4. The family had no electricity, and by January their situation was dire.
5. They kept a supply of dried moose meat in a frozen outdoor cache.

DIRECTED READING

Preview Vocabulary

con•sol•i•dat•ed (kən sä´ lə dā təd) *adj.*, joined together; compacted

e•rode (i rōd´) *v.*, wear away, usually through natural forces such as weather

con•geal (kən jēl´) *v.*, change from liquid to solid due to cold temperature

dire (dī´ [ə]r) *adj.*, desperate; horrifying

cache (kash) *n.*, stored supply, often hidden

THE FACE OF THE DEEP IS FROZEN

The ship itself was a mess of snapped rigging and broken spars.

A Historical Essay by Jennifer Armstrong

The Antarctic contains ninety percent of the world's snow and ice, and there are more than eighty kinds of it. There's brash ice, pancake ice, bullet ice, green ice, frazil, nilas, breccia, shuga, slush ice, rotten ice, pressure ice, grease ice, ice dust, shorefast ice, ice flowers, ice haycocks, ice saddles, floes, calf bergs, growlers, and sastrugi, to name just a few. And when it comes to icebergs, there are whole family trees to study. In the family of tabular[1] bergs, there are domed, horizontal, blocky, tilted, and uneven bergs; in the tribe of rounded bergs, there are surrounded, well-rounded, and rounded bergs; and when it comes to irregular bergs, there are tabular remnant, pinnacled, pyramidal, drydock, castellate,[2] jagged, slab, and roof bergs.

Much of the ice on the continent of Antarctica[3] is actually a form of consolidated snow called firn. As snow accumulates, it begins to compact, forcing out the air between the snowflakes. Eventually, all the air is squeezed out, and the snow is a dense, heavy ice. This compression also makes much of the ice blue.

These masses of ice form glaciers that reach the edge of the continent, where every year 5,000 to 10,000 icebergs "calve," or break off, from the ice sheets into the surrounding ocean. Many icebergs are so large that they create their own weather systems. The largest iceberg ever recorded was one the size of Belgium (close to 12,000 square miles), spotted in 1956, and the most northerly iceberg reached twenty-six degrees south latitude in the Atlantic Ocean, in 1894. This is the latitude of Rio de Janeiro, in Brazil, just south of the Tropic of Capricorn.[4] As the icebergs drift, the seawater erodes them from below, until the berg abruptly topples over and continues its journey upside down. The erosion continues until the berg flips again, and then again, and eventually it is eroded and melted away.

As the icebergs calve from the glaciers on the continent, they bring with them mineral deposits scraped up from the ground, and release these nutrients into the water. As they melt, the bergs also release atmospheric nutrients that have been trapped in the ice for centuries. It is this steady deposit of nutrients from icebergs that makes the waters of the Southern Ocean so rich and full of life.

Of course, the ocean around the continent also turns to ice. Salt water freezes at a lower temperature than fresh water, around twenty-seven degrees Fahrenheit, depending on the concentration of salt and other minerals. As the water on the surface cools, it begins to condense, and individual ice crystals act as seeds, causing the water to congeal around them, squeezing the salt out into the water below. On the surface, the water seems to stiffen and turn greasy. This layer of thick, flexible ice is called nilas. If the nilas is disturbed by wind, the ice forms rounded discs called pancakes, which look something like white lily pads with their edges turned up. As the air temperature drops and the water continues to freeze, the pancakes mass together and harden into a single sheet, or ice field. Because the water forces out salt as it freezes, the water below the ice field is saturated with salt and

1. **tabular.** Having a flat surface
2. **castellate.** Built like a castle
3. **the continent of Antarctica.** Surrounding Earth's south pole, this landmass is twice the size of Australia. In winter, ice doubles its size.
4. **twenty-six degrees south latitude...Tropic of Capricorn.** The iceberg traveled very far north, into relatively warm waters.

con • sol • i • dat • ed (kən sä´ lə dā təd) *adj.*, joined together; compacted

e • rode (i rōd´) *v.*, wear away, usually through natural forces such as weather

con • geal (kən jēl´) *v.*, change from liquid to solid due to cold temperature minerals, and the ice itself is clean enough to melt into drinking water.

This process of turning seawater into drinking water is important—it means that a shipwreck on the frozen sea does not *necessarily* mean certain death.

When the exhausted crew of *Endurance* gave up the battle against the pressure and abandoned the ship, the ice field around her was not a sight to inspire confidence. The ship itself was a mess of snapped rigging and broken spars.[5] Beside her on the ice was Dump Camp, a junk pile of most of the stores[6] and equipment the men had. The dogs milled around, straining at their tethers, snapping and snarling at one another. The crew staggered like dead men, utterly beaten from their labors, trying to pitch tents so they could crawl in to sleep. There were only eighteen sleeping bags, originally meant for the overland journey, and the men drew straws to see who would get them. The rest of the men had to make do with wool blankets. Tom Crean was suffering from snow blindness (a temporary condition that often affects polar travelers when they are exposed to the glare of sunlight on snow); he had to be helped into a tent. That night, the ice beneath the tents quivered as whales rubbed up against it from below.

"Though we have been compelled to abandon the ship, which is crushed beyond all hope of ever being righted, we are alive and well, and we have stores and equipment for the task that lies before us. The task is to reach land with all the members of the expedition," Shackleton wrote in his diary the next morning.

There were precious few options available to the Boss. Already the ship had drifted 1,000 miles north and west with the pack ice. The tip of South America was more than 2,000 miles away, and there was no way of reaching it on foot. They had ample food, guns, matches, and dogs. But, after all, they were in the Antarctic, not Hyde Park in London. The circumstances were dire, to say the least.

After a quiet conference with Wild, Shackleton announced his plan to the crew: they would march across the frozen sea with two of the three lifeboats to Paulet Island, 346 miles to the northwest. To the best of Shackleton's knowledge, there was a cache of stores in a hut on Paulet Island from a 1902 Swedish expedition. What they would do once they reached this destination was not specified: it was enough to have a goal. He would plan the next step when they got there. But 346 miles is more than the distance between Boston and New York City, almost as far as from Los Angeles to San Francisco, about the entire width of Iowa. They would have to walk the whole way, hauling their gear and the two boats. The men knew they were doomed without the boats; eventually they would reach open water. They would need the boats, no matter how burdensome they were to drag over the ice. Shackleton gave the men a couple of days' rest. October 30 was the appointed day of departure.

In the meantime, there was much to get ready. Mrs. Chippy, the carpenter's cat, had to be shot, because without the protection of the ship the dogs would have eaten him. The youngest of the puppies, who were too small to pull with a team, also had to be killed. While McNeish and McLeod began fitting the lifeboats onto sledges,[7] the rest of the crew began sorting their equipment. The men were

5. **rigging and spars.** Ropes, wires, and pulleys that support the masts and control a boat's sails, plus the poles that support the rigging
6. **stores.** Supplies
7. **sledges.** Large sleds pulled by animals

dire (dī´ [ə]r) *adj.*, desperate; horrifying

cache (kash) *n.*, stored supply, often hidden

given a two-pound limit on personal gear, which allowed them to keep only the items that were essential for survival—although the Boss did allow them to keep their diaries and their tobacco, and the doctors were allowed their medical supplies. In a dramatic gesture, Shackleton took his gold cigarette case and a handful of gold coins from his pocket and dropped them on the snow. Gold was useless for the task ahead.

He then opened the Bible inscribed to him by Queen Alexandra and ripped out a page from the Book of Job:[8]

Out of whose womb came the ice?

And the hoary frost of Heaven, who hath gendered it?[9]

The waters are hid as with a stone,

And the face of the deep is frozen.

Then he folded the page into a pocket and dropped the heavy Bible on the cigarette case and gold coins, showing the crew the route they must take. If they wanted to survive, they must travel light, harden their hearts against sentimental keepsakes, and trust that they could make do with the bare bones of equipment. Shackleton the improviser[10] believed that it was foolish to burden themselves with equipment for *every* possible emergency. As the day wore on, the pile of discards grew. Extra clothes, books, scientific instruments and specimens, chess sets, flags, lanterns, tools, sewing kits, lucky talismans, razors, barometers, combs, scissors, playing cards, dishes, silverware, photographs—each man added to the heap. Some of the men saved leather suitcases to use for boot repairs later on. Hussey kept his toothbrush, and Shackleton ordered him to keep the banjo, because they would need the comfort of music in the hard months ahead. Each man kept a spoon and a knife.

The journey was ready to begin at 2:00 P.M. on October 30 under heavy gray skies. It had already snowed on and off during the day, and it threatened to continue. That didn't pose much of a problem, but the road ahead did. If they only had to trek across 346 miles of flat ice field, the journey would have been bearable. But stretching ahead of them into the white horizon was a scene of utter devastation and chaos. It was as if a giant hand had smashed down onto the frozen face of the deep and broken it into a million shards.[11] Jagged floes tilted up at all angles. Pressure ridges reared up like wrinkles in a huge white blanket. If the sea had been frozen at the height of a tempest, and every storm-tossed wave locked into place, the scene could not have been more jumbled and uneven. There were 346 miles of *that* to cross—assuming the drift of the pack didn't change course and carry them helplessly in another direction.

On the lead sled went Shackleton, Wordie, Hussey, and Hudson, looking for the best route among the pressure ridges and tumbled ice floes. They were equipped with shovels, picks, and axes to chop a path through the chaos of ice. Behind them came the other dog teams pulling sleds that were each loaded with 900 pounds of stores and gear.

Bringing up the rear was the remainder of the crew pulling the boats on sledge runners. Loaded with food and equipment, the boats weighed in at more than a ton apiece. Fifteen men in harness dragged one boat at a time across the wet snow and over the ice, stopping every quarter mile to rest, before going back to haul the second boat forward. Shackleton was in constant anxiety

8. **Book of Job.** A Hebrew scripture. In the passage Shackleton saved, God is making a long speech to remind the man Job that a person is just one small part of creation.
9. **gendered it.** Given it identity
10. **improviser.** Inventor; one who responds creatively to new situations or makes something out of materials available at the time, without instructions
11. **shards.** Sharp broken pieces

over continuing pressure in the ice. If a crack opened up between one team and another, the result could be disastrous. So he kept the men and sleds and boats close together, relaying forward one agonizing quarter mile at a time. Frequently, one of the dog teams had to be unharnessed from its sled and then hitched to a lifeboat to help the men drag it up and over a hummock or ridge.

After two hours of backbreaking labor, hauling the boats through wet, heavy snow, detouring around piles of broken floe, they were only one mile from *Endurance*. Soaked, and numb with fatigue, the men swallowed a hasty dinner and fell into their tents. It began to snow during the night. When the men resumed their burdens the next day, they had a new layer of heavy, wet slush to trudge through, and more wet snow was falling steadily. After another three hours and only an additional three quarters of a mile, the Boss called a halt. He and Worsley were worried about damaging the boats as they knocked their way across the ice. They were getting nowhere.

At the moment they were on a very large, level floe, more than a half a mile in diameter. There wasn't another good, solid, flat floe in sight, and Shackleton felt they could not do better for a camping place. The men pitched their tents on the wet snow and crawled into their sleeping bags. Shackleton anxiously scouted ahead and found it impossible to advance.

Next morning, he announced that they would stay where they were and let the drifting pack carry them northward into a better position to make for Paulet Island. There was no alternative. Shackleton told Green to start adding large chunks of blubber to the crew's food. The thick seal fat that kept the animals warm would provide valuable calories in the men's diets and keep them from freezing. It was time to get used to it. ✣

Have you ever been in a situation where you "prepared for the worst and hoped for the best"? Why do you think people like Shackleton put themselves in such dangerous situations?

Find Meaning

1. (a) Why do the men abandon their ship? (b) What was the first challenge they faced then?

2. (a) What was the first step in Shackleton's plan? (b) Why did the crew abandon this plan? (c) What new plan did they adopt?

3. (a) What did Shackleton drop into the snow before setting off? (b) Why did some of the men save suitcases?

4. Why did Shackleton have the men pulling the boats keep them so close together?

Make Judgments

5. Why does Armstrong spend so many paragraphs describing ice, icebergs, and seawater?

6. As the crew sets out, Armstrong writes, "What they would do once they reached this destination was not specified: it was enough to have a goal." Why was having a goal enough?

7. (a) What does Shackleton do after the first day and a half on foot? (b) What does this suggest about his qualities as a leader?

LITERATURE ▶▶ CONNECTION

Jennifer Armstrong creates strong images of what it was like to be lost in a frozen world. **Robert Frost** (1874–1963) was a celebrated American poet who spent much of his life in New England. In this poem, the speaker compares fire and ice as ways the world might end. He also equates fire and ice to some particular human emotions. Which one does the speaker find harder to endure? As you read, think about how Frost's imagery compares to the images in "The Face of the Deep Is Frozen."

Fire and Ice

A Lyric Poem by Robert Frost

Some say the world will end in fire,
Some say in ice.
From what I've tasted of desire
I hold with those who favor fire.
But if it had to perish twice,
I think I know enough of hate
To say that for destruction ice
Is also great
And would suffice. ✤

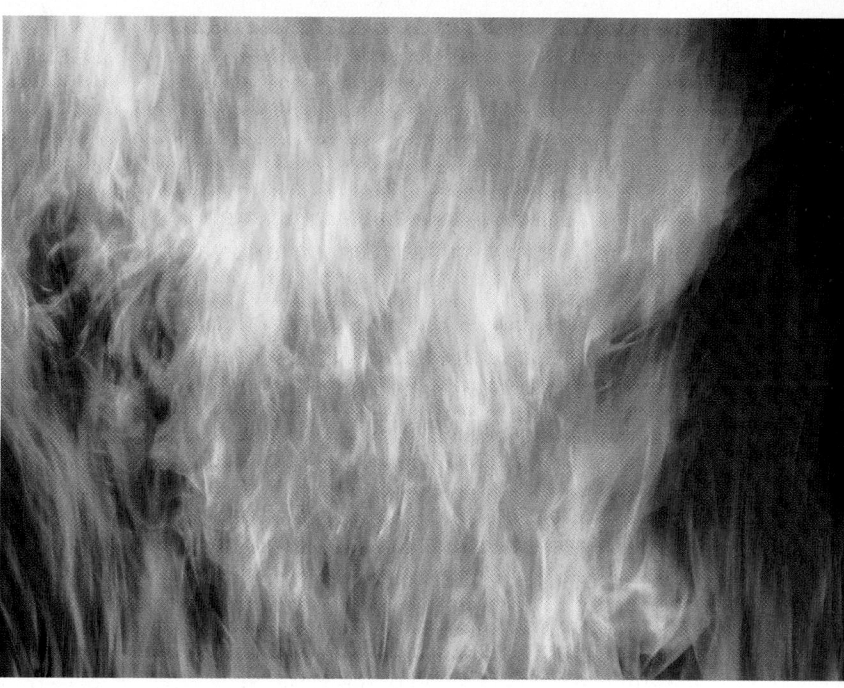

TEXT ←TO→ TEXT CONNECTION

How were the men of Shackleton's expedition prepared for the end of the world? What would they have thought of Frost's poem? Think also about how Frost equates fire with desire and ice with hate. Do you agree with those connections? Finally, explain the difference between the theme of "Fire and Ice" and Jennifer Armstrong's purpose for writing "The Face of the Deep is Frozen." Write your responses in your notebook.

AFTER READING

Analyze Literature

Description A writer's ability to describe events, settings, and characters depends on how well he or she chooses words and images. Make a three-column chart to record some of Armstrong's most effective word choices. Skim the selection, looking for images that affected you strongly. As you notice images, sort them into their proper columns on your chart.

Sensory Details	Precise Words	Figurative Language
Water seems to stiffen and turn greasy.	sentimental keepsakes	"like wrinkles in a huge white blanket"

Extend Understanding

Writing Options

Creative Writing Suppose that you are the leader of a ship's crew facing life or death in Antarctica. Write a one-paragraph **journal entry** about how you feel. Use sensory details, precise words, and figurative language as necessary to express your situation in a limited amount of space. This paper will be sent with the members of your party who are heading off to find help. Reread your paragraph to imagine how seeing it might affect your friends and family as they wait for your return.

Informative Writing How would you describe the mood of "The Face of the Deep Is Frozen"? Think about the setting. Then, in a one-paragraph **literary response,** explain how you think the setting affects the mood of the piece. Recall the author's use of sensory details to evoke the setting, and give an example or two in your paragraph.

Lifelong Learning

Summarize an Incident Use library resources to find out more about the expedition involving Shackleton and the crew of *Endurance*. You could find the book Armstrong wrote about it, encyclopedia articles, and videos or DVDs of dramatizations. Then prepare a poster for display in class that summarizes the incident. Consider using visual devices, such as photographs or time lines, to convey information in your poster.

Critical Literacy

Hold a Debate In a small group, review "The Face of the Deep Is Frozen" to specifically look for decisions that Ernest Shackleton made. Choose one decision that seems most clearly to have involved a difficult choice, and discuss the pros and cons. Then divide into two debate teams and conduct a ten-minute debate, with one side supporting Shackleton's decision and the other side criticizing it. When your debate is over, talk for a minute about why leaders have to make decisions like this one, and what qualities often characterize a good leader.

 Go to **www.mirrorsandwindows.com** for more.

Vocabulary & Spelling

Context Clues

Brazen and fierce, they will take on large adversaries—even cats, dogs or humans.

—DIANE ACKERMAN, "Mute Dancers: How to Watch a Hummingbird"

You can often figure out the meaning of a word from **context clues:** words, phrases, or sentences that provide information about the word. In the quote above, examples of hummingbirds' courage help you define the word *brazen.*

Sometimes you can determine a word's meaning by what it is **compared** to or **contrasted** with.

EXAMPLE

Comparison

The wings are transparent, like glass.

EXAMPLE

Contrast

Some believed hummingbirds were supernatural, and not bound by nature's laws.

You might be able to define a word by a writer's brief **definition** or **description** of it.

EXAMPLE

Definition

The hummingbirds drink nectar, a sweet fluid that comes from plants.

EXAMPLE

Description

Hummingbirds are very small birds that drink from flowers and float soundlessly in the air.

You may also be able to determine a word's meaning by a writer's use of **examples** or his or her **restatement** of the word with a synonym.

EXAMPLE

Example

The bird's coverts, such as the feathers that cover part of its wing, are brightly colored.

EXAMPLE

Restatement

The hummingbird's bill, or beak, is very slender.

Vocabulary Practice

For each of the following sentences, use context clues to define the underlined word.

1. In contrast to the sparrow's drab feathers, the hummingbird's brilliant, colorful feathers were a shock.
2. The verdant jungle was filled with unending lush green plants.
3. The flower's crimson petals were as bright and rich as cherries.
4. The bird's plumule, a kind of soft feather, was nearly colorless.
5. The feathers on the pinion, unlike the feathers on the inner part of the wing, are used to support the bird in flight.

Hmong Storycloth

Visual Media by Mee Vang

BEFORE READING

Build Background

Historical Context The Hmong are an ethnic group from Asia. During the Vietnam War, the U.S. government organized thousands of Hmong soldiers to fight against Lao Communists, or Pathet Lao. In 1975 the Pathet Lao won the war. When they did, all the Hmong who had been fighting against the Communists became refugees. Many of them immigrated to the United States. Today there are large Hmong communities in California, Minnesota, and Wisconsin.

Reader's Context How does your family keep a record of its past? Do your parents keep photographs, paintings you did as a child, or family heirlooms? Why do you think people keep records of the past?

Set Purpose

The pictures in a storycloth can be read from top to bottom much like words on a page. As you look at the storycloth, try to determine the story that is being told.

Analyze Literature

Purpose A visual artist can have a purpose in a way similar to an author. What do you think is the **purpose** of this storycloth? For example, is it meant to inform, educate, persuade, or tell a story? As you look at the storycloth, try to determine the artist's reason for creating it.

Use Reading Skills

Sequence of Events

The order in which events occur is referred to as a *sequence of events.* Fiction and narrative nonfiction are frequently arranged so that the earliest events are described first. As you examine the storycloth, try to determine the sequence of events. Storycloths can be "read" from top to bottom. Use a time line like the one below. List the earliest events at the top of the line.

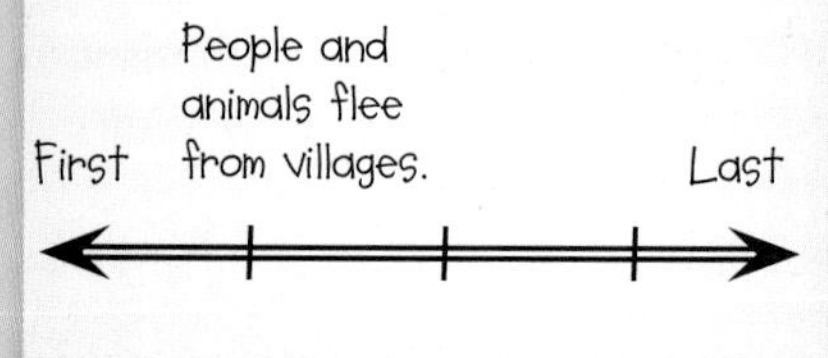

Meet the Artist

This storycloth was created by **Mee Vang**. Vang, like many Hmong women, is skilled in an intricate and ancient form of embroidery known as *paj ntaub* (pronounced pahn-dow), or "flower cloth." Until the 1900s, the Hmong people had no written language and passed along stories either orally or through pictures. Vang's storycloth describes her family's flight from Laos to Thailand and then to the United States.

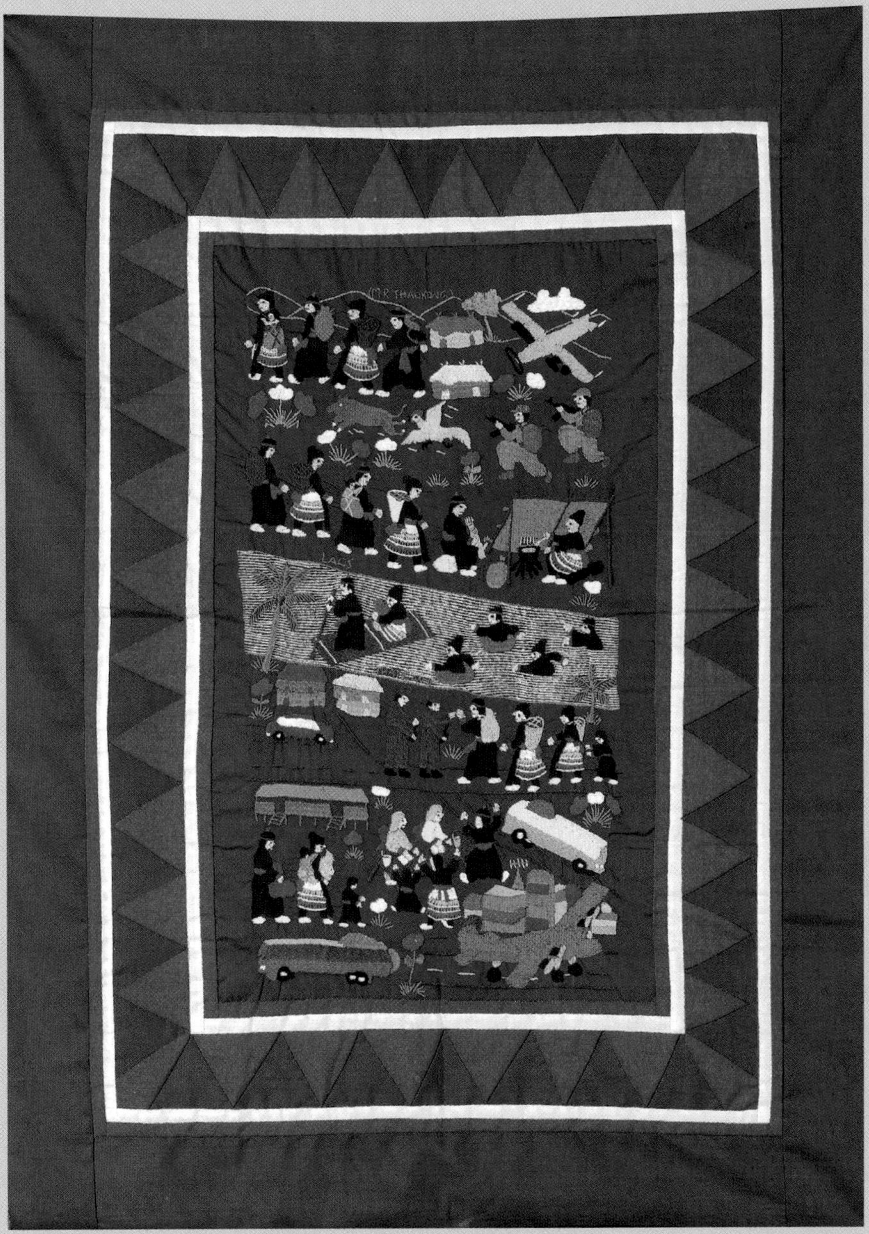

MIRRORS & WINDOWS

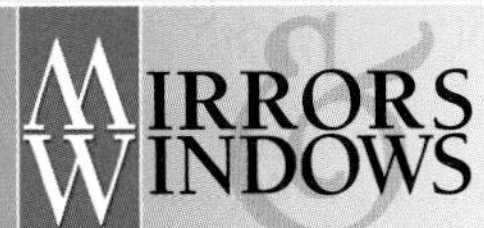

In what way might you try to memorialize an event in your life? Why might it be important to create something, such as a piece of art or writing, about a period of difficulty or struggle?

Find Meaning

1. How do the refugees depicted in this storycloth escape from Laos?
2. What are some of the differences you notice between the ways in which Laos and Thailand are depicted?

Make Judgments

3. Why do you think Vang included images of animals fleeing the village?
4. Who do you think the women sitting at the table near the bottom of the storycloth are?

PRIMARY SOURCE ▶▶ CONNECTION

In her storycloth, Mee Vang re-created her family's escape from Laos and the Pathet Lao. The family of **Maijue Xiong** (b. 1972), a writer and educator who lives in St. Paul, Minnesota, experienced events very similar to those Vang's family experienced. In the following autobiographical essay, Xiong describes how her family fled from Laos under extremely difficult and dangerous circumstances. As you read, compare and contrast Xiong's descriptions with Vang's storycloth.

An Unforgettable Journey

An Autobiography by Maijue Xiong

I was born in a small village called Muong Cha in Laos on April 30, 1972. At the time I was born, my father was a soldier actively fighting alongside the American Central Intelligence Agency against the Communists. Although a war was in progress, life seemed peaceful. We did not think of ever leaving Laos, but one day our lives were changed forever.

We found ourselves without a home or a Country and with a need to seek refuge in another country. This period of relocation involved a lot of changes, adjustments, and adaptations. We experienced changes in our language, customs, traditional values, and social status.[1] Some made the transition quickly; others have never fully adjusted. The changes my family and I experienced are the foundation of my identity today.

After Laos became a Communist country in 1975, my family, along with many others, fled in fear of persecution.[2] Because my father had served as a commanding officer for eleven years with the American Central Intelligence Agency in what is known to the American public as the "Secret War," my family had no choice but to leave immediately. My father's life was in danger, along with those of thousands of others. We were forced to leave loved ones behind, including my grandmother who was ill in bed the day we fled our village. For a month, my family walked through the dense tropical jungles and rice fields, along rugged trails through many mountains, and battled the powerful Mekong River.[3] We traveled in silence at night and slept in the daytime. Children were very hard to keep quiet. Many parents feared the Communist soldiers would hear the cries of their young children; therefore, they drugged the children with opium to keep them quiet. Some parents even left those children who would not stop

1. **social status.** Position of a person in society, whether high, middle, or lower class
2. **persecution.** Act of injuring others or causing them to suffer, usually because of their beliefs
3. **Mekong River.** River in southeast Asia that forms part of the border between Laos and Thailand

crying behind. Fortunately, whenever my parents told my sisters and me to keep quiet, we listened and obeyed.

I do not remember much about our flight, but I do have certain memories that have been imprinted in my mind. It is all so unclear—the experience was like a bad dream: when you wake up, you don't remember what it was you had dreamed about but recall only those bits and pieces of the dream that stand out the most. I remember sleeping under tall trees. I was like a little ant placed in a field of tall grass, surrounded by a dense jungle with trees and bushes all around me—right, left, in the back, and in front of me. I also remember that it rained a lot and that it was cold. We took only what we could carry and it was not much. My father carried a sack of rice, which had to last us the whole way. My mother carried one extra change of clothing for each of us, a few personal belongings, and my baby sister on her back. My older sister and I helped carry pots and pans. My stepuncle carried water, dried meat, and his personal belongings.

From the jungles to the open fields, we walked along a path. We came across a trail of red ants and being a stubborn child, I refused to walk over them. I wanted someone to pick me up because I was scared, but my parents kept walking ahead. They kept telling me to hurry up and to step over the ants, but I just stood there and cried. Finally, my father came back and put me on his shoulders, along with the heavy sack of rice he was carrying. My dad said he carried me on his back practically all the way to Thailand.

I also recall a car accident we had. My father had paid a truckdriver to take my family and relatives to a nearby town. There were about fifteen of us in the truck. My father, along with the driver and my pregnant aunt, sat in front. The rest of us were in the bed of the truck. While going up a steep mountain, the truck got out of control and, instead of going uphill, started sliding downhill and off the road. Everyone was terrified, but with the help of God, the truck was stopped by a tree stump. Everyone panicked and scrambled out, except for my pregnant aunt who was trapped on the passenger's side because the door was jammed. The impact affected her so much that she could not crawl from her seat to the driver's side in order to get out. My father risked his life to save hers. The rest of us stood back and waited breathlessly as he tried to open the jammed door. He managed to free her just as the truck slid down the hill.

Our adventure did not end then—many nights filled with terror were yet to come.

Our adventure did not end then—many nights filled with terror were yet to come. After experiencing many cold days and rainy nights, we finally saw Thailand on the other side of the Mekong River. My parents bribed several fishermen to row us across. The fishermen knew we were desperate, yet, instead of helping us, they took advantage of us. We had to give them all our valuables: silver bars, silver coins, paper money, and my mother's silver wedding necklace, which had cost a lot of money. When it got dark, the fishermen came back

Hmong refugee camp in Thailand.

with a small fishing boat and took us across the river. The currents were high and powerful. I remember being very scared. I kept yelling, "We're going to fall out! We're going to fall into the river!" My mom tried to reassure me but I kept screaming in fear. Finally, we got across safely. My family, along with many other families, were picked up by the Thai police and taken to an empty bus station for the night.

After a whole month at this temporary refugee camp set up in the bus station, during which we ate rice, dried fish, roots we dug up, and bamboo shoots we cut down, and drank water from streams, we were in very poor shape due to the lack of nutrition. Our feet were also swollen from walking. We were then taken to a refugee camp in Nongkhai, where disease was rampant[4] and many people got sick. My family suffered a loss: my baby sister, who was only a few months old, died. She had become very skinny from the lack of milk, and there was no medical care available. The memory of her death still burns in my mind like a flame. On the evening she died, my older sister and I were playing with our cousins outside the building where we stayed. My father came out to tell us the sad news and told us to go find my stepuncle. After we found him, we went inside and saw our mother mourning the baby's death. Fortunately, our family had relatives around to support and comfort us.

Life in the refugee camp was very difficult. Rice, fish, vegetables, and water were delivered to the camp, but the ration for each family was never enough. Many times, the food my family received did not last until the next delivery. My parents went out to work in the fields to earn a little extra money to buy food. As a child, I did not understand why we had to work so hard and live so poorly.

When I left Laos, I was only three years old. I do not remember much of our life there, but my parents have told me that our family had been quite well off. We had our

---

4. rampant. Wild or unrestrained

own house, cattle, rice fields, and a garden where all our vegetables were grown. The money my father received for serving in the army was saved, for there was little need for money. We had enough to eat because we grew our own food. The poor life in the camp is the only life I can remember. I saw my parents' suffering, but I was too young to understand why life was so difficult. Only later did I realize that I and thousands of other young children were victims of a cruel war. Our family remained in Nongkhai for three agonizing years, with our fate uncertain and our future obscure.

Our family life in the camp was very unstable, characterized by deprivation[5] and neglect. My older sister and I were left alone for days while my parents were outside the camp trying to earn money to buy extra food. My parents fought a lot during this period, because we were all under such stress. They knew that if we remained in Thailand, there would be no telling what would become of us. We had to find a better life. Some people in the camp were being sponsored to go to the United States. The news spread that anyone who had served in the military with the CIA could apply to go to America. Since my stepuncle had already gone there two years earlier, he sponsored my family. Because my father had been in the military and we had a sponsor, it took only six months to process our papers when usually it took a year or more.

I can still recall the process of leaving the camp. Our relatives, whom we were leaving behind, walked my family from our house to the bus that was to take us to Bangkok. We boarded the bus with our few belongings. People hung out of the windows to touch loved ones for the last time. They cried, knowing they might never meet again. As the buses slowly made their way through the crowd, people ran after them calling out the names of their relatives. "Have a safe trip to your new home!" they shouted. "Don't forget us who are left behind! Please write and tell us about your new life!" Quickly the camp vanished out of sight...forever. The moments filled with laughter and tears shared with close friends and relatives were now just faint memories.

It took a full day to travel to Bangkok, where we stayed for four nights. The building we stayed in was one huge room. It was depressing and nerve-wracking. I especially remember how, when we got off the bus to go into the building, a small child about my age came up to my family to beg for food. I recall the exact words she said to my father, "Uncle, can you give me some food? I am hungry. My parents are dead and I am here alone." My dad gave her a piece of bread that we had packed for our lunch. After she walked away, my family found an empty corner and rolled out our bedding for the night. That night, the same child came around again, but people chased her away, which made me sad.

In the morning, I ran to get in line for breakfast. Each person received a bowl of rice porridge with a few strips of chicken in it. For four days, we remained in that building, not knowing when we could leave for the United States. Many families had been there for weeks, months, perhaps even years. On the fourth day, my family was notified to be ready early the next morning to be taken to the airport. The plane ride took a long time and I got motion sickness. I threw up a lot. Only when I saw my stepuncle's face after we landed did I know we had come to the end of our journey. We had come in search of a better life in the "land of giants."

On October 2, 1978, my family arrived at Los Angeles International Airport, where

5. **deprivation.** State of being in need

my uncle was waiting anxiously. We stayed with my uncle in Los Angeles for two weeks and then settled in Isla Vista because there were already a few Hmong families there. We knew only one family in Isla Vista, but later we met other families whom my parents had known in their village and from villages nearby. It was in Isla Vista that my life really began. My home life was now more stable. My mother gave birth to a boy a month after we arrived in the United States. It was a joyous event because the first three children she had were all girls. (Boys are desired and valued far more than girls in Hmong culture).

Hmong girl at a refugee camp in Thailand. The sign reads "Dangerous Area."

I entered kindergarten at Isla Vista Elementary School. The first day was scary because I could not speak any English. Fortunately, my cousin, who had been in the United States for three years and spoke English, was in the same class with me. She led me to the playground where the children were playing. I was shocked to see so many faces of different colors. The Caucasian students shocked me the most. I had never seen people with blond hair before. The sight sent me to a bench, where I sat and watched everyone in amazement. In class, I was introduced to coloring. I did not know how to hold a crayon or what it was for. My teacher had to show me how to color. I also soon learned the alphabet. This was the beginning of my lifelong goal to get an education...

Now that I am older, I treasure the long but valuable lessons my parents tried to teach us—lessons that gave me a sense of identity as a Hmong. "Nothing comes easy...," my parents always said. As I attempt to get a college education, I remember how my parents have been really supportive of me throughout my schooling, but because they never had a chance to get an education themselves, they were not able to help me whenever I could not solve a math problem or write an English paper. Although they cannot help me in my schoolwork, I know in my heart that they care about me and want me to be successful so that I can help them when they can no longer help themselves. Therefore, I am determined to do well at the university. I want to become a role model for my younger brother and sisters, for I am the very first member of my family to attend college. I feel a real sense of accomplishment to have set such an example. ✣

TEXT TO TEXT CONNECTION

In "An Unforgettable Journey" Maijue Xiong describes how she and her family encountered and overcame many obstacles, including hunger, sadness, and death. How does her description compare with the depiction of similar events in Vang's storycloth?

AFTER READING

Analyze Literature

Purpose Artists, like authors, often have a purpose or multiple purposes when creating their work. For example, they might wish to inform, educate, or persuade. Re-examine Vang's storycloth and try to determine her purpose or purposes. Create a two-column chart. In the first column, create a list of details from the storycloth. Then, in the second column, list Vang's purpose or purposes.

Detail	Purpose
infants strapped to parents' backs	

Extend Understanding

Writing Options

Creative Writing Imagine that you are an art critic for a newspaper. Write a **descriptive essay** about Vang's storycloth. Describe the storycloth using sensory details and precise language. Be sure to include background information for readers unacquainted with the events depicted in the storycloth.

Informative Writing Using Vang's storycloth, Maijue Xiong's autobiography, and your own research, write a brief **historical essay** about the flight of the Hmong from Laos to Thailand. Describe the dangerous trek through jungles and across the Mekong River. Include details about the situation in the refugee camps and the ability of some refugees to escape to the United States. Use direct quotations from your research and "An Unforgettable Journey." Be sure you distinguish between factual claims, commonplace assertions, and opinions as you do your research. In your own essay, avoid using commonplace assertions, and support your opinions with facts and logical arguments.

Critical Literacy

Analyze a Speech A **policy speech** attempts to persuade a listener to support a change in government policy and contains quotations from experts and arguments that address policy issues. Identify and read the text of a contemporary speech that addresses refugee or immigration policies. Interpret the purpose by asking questions or making comments about the evidence presented. Finally, analyze the structure of the speech's central argument and identify the different types of evidence used to support the argument.

Lifelong Learning

Research Southeast Asia In groups of four or five, research Laos, Vietnam, or Cambodia. Use Internet or library resources to find out about the present political structure of the country you choose, its geography, its population, its languages, and any other important information. Divide tasks between group members and establish an agenda with clear goals and deadlines. Once you have completed your research, present your findings to the class. Be sure to set time limits for speakers and to take notes as other groups present their own research.

Go to **www.mirrorsandwindows.com** for more.

DUST BOWL PHOTOGRAPHS

Visual Media by Arthur Rothstein

DIRECTED READING

BEFORE READING

Build Background

Historical Context As the nation sank into the Great Depression of the 1930s, eight years of drought, combined with misguided farming practices, eroded the Great Plains. When farmers tore out grasses to plant wheat, they removed roots that had held the soil in place. Without water, the topsoil dried out and blew away. The Dust Bowl stretched from Texas to the Dakotas and from Arkansas to Wyoming and New Mexico. It generated huge clouds of grit and eventually displaced over half a million people.

Reader's Context Does your family keep old photographs? Why do you think that is? What can old photographs offer you?

Set Purpose

As you look at the following images of the Dust Bowl, look at the difficulties the people in each photograph faced.

Analyze Literature

Purpose Is there a difference between photographs meant to tell a story—pictures by photojournalists or documentary photographers, for example—and other kinds? What do you think the purpose of these photographs is? For example, are they meant to inform, educate, or persuade? As you look at the photographs, try to determine the photographer's reason for taking them.

Use Reading Skills

Activate Prior Knowledge You probably know something about the Great Depression and the Dust Bowl from studying American history. If you live in a state in the Great Plains or in a state to which Dust Bowl migrants relocated, you may know people who experienced these things firsthand. Before you study Rothstein's photographs, activate your prior knowledge using a K-W-L chart like this one.

What I Already Know	What I Want to Learn	What I Learn
The Dust Bowl destroyed farms.	Did people stay in the Dust Bowl?	

Meet the Photographer

In 1935, **Arthur Rothstein** (1915–1985) joined the Resettlement Administration, which became the Farm Security Administration in 1937. His job was to take photographs of the rural poor. Among Rothstein's most famous photographs are those of Dust Bowl farms and people in Gee's Bend, Alabama. After leaving the government, Rothstein worked for *Look* magazine and as a photographer during World War II.

Playing on Farm, 1936. Arthur Rothstein.

Farmer and Sons Walking in the Face of a Dust Storm, 1936. Arthur Rothstein.

Dust Bowl Farmer Raising a Fence to Keep It from Being Buried under Drifting Sand, 1936. Arthur Rothstein.

Cows Huddling Next to a Windmill in the Dust Bowl, 1936. Arthur Rothstein.

How might a drought—a whole year without rain or snow—affect your region? Is there anything people can do to change the course of a natural disaster like a drought, or are natural disasters something people just have to endure?

Find Meaning

1. In *Farmer and Sons Walking in the Face of a Dust Storm,* what do you think the people are doing?

2. (a) In what ways is the title *Playing on Farm* an inappropriate title for this image? (b) Why do you think Rothstein chose this title?

3. What do the cows in *Cows Huddling Next to a Windmill in the Dust Bowl* suggest about what the land used to be?

Make Judgments

4. In *Dust Bowl Farmer Raising a Fence,* what does the landscape suggest about the challenges the farmer faces?

5. (a) Using sensory details, describe the storm depicted in *Farmer and Sons Walking in the Face of a Dust Storm.* How does the image make you feel? (b) Why do you think the photographer took this picture?

6. Imagine yourself as a member of the intended audience for these pictures in 1936. What would be your response?

INFORMATIONAL TEXT ▶▶ CONNECTION

Arthur Rothstein took pictures of the Dust Bowl. Another prominent photojournalist of the 1930s was **Margaret Bourke-White** (1906–1971). She initially specialized in taking pictures of architecture and industrial operations. As her career developed, she traveled the world. In this essay, she describes a firsthand experience with the Dust Bowl. While you read, try to visualize what she describes.

Dust Changes America

An Essay by Margaret Bourke-White

Vitamin K they call it—the dust which sifts under the door sills, and stings in the eyes, and seasons every spoonful of food. The dust storms have distinct personalities, rising in formation like rolling clouds, creeping up silently like formless fog, approaching violently like a tornado. Where has it come from? It provides topics of endless speculation. Red, it is the topsoil from Oklahoma; brown, it is the fertile earth of western Kansas; the good grazing land of Texas and New Mexico sweeps by as a murky yellow haze. Or, tracing it locally, "My uncle will be along pretty soon," they say; "I just saw his farm go by."

The town dwellers stack their linen in trunks, stuff wet cloths along the window sills, estimate the tons of sand in the darkened air above them, paste cloth masks on their faces with adhesive tape, and try to joke about Vitamin K. But on the farms and ranches there is an attitude of despair.

By coincidence I was in the same parts of the country where last year I photographed the drought. As short a time as eight months ago there was an attitude of false optimism. "Things will get better," the farmers would say. "We're not as hard hit as other states. The government will help out. This can't go on." But this year there is an atmosphere of utter hopelessness. Nothing to do. No use digging out your chicken coops and pigpens after the last "duster" because the next one will be coming along soon. No use trying to keep the house clean. No use fighting off that foreclosure[1] any longer. No use even hoping to give your cattle anything to chew on when their food crops have literally blown out of the ground.

It was my job to avoid dust storms, since I was commissioned by an airplane company to take photographs of its course from the air, but frequently the dust storms caught up with us, and as we were grounded anyway, I started to photograph them. Thus I saw five dust-storm states from the air and from the ground.

In the last several years there have been droughts and sand storms and dusters, but they have been localized, and always one state could borrow from another. But this year the scourge[2] assumes tremendous proportions. Dust storms are bringing

1. **foreclosure.** Taking of property because the person who borrowed money to buy it has not made payments
2. **scourge.** Punishment

distress and death to 300,000 square miles; they are blowing over all of Kansas, all of Nebraska and Wyoming, strips of the Dakotas, about half of Colorado, sections of Iowa and Missouri, the greater part of Oklahoma, and the northern panhandle of Texas, extending into the eastern parts of New Mexico.

Last year I saw farmers harvesting the Russian thistle.[3] Never before had they thought of feeding thistles to cattle. But this prickly fodder[4] became precious for food. This year even the Russian thistles are dying out and the still humbler soap weed[5] becomes as vital to the farmer as the fields of golden grain he tended in the past. Last year's thistle-fed cattle dwindled to skin and bone. This year's herds on their diet of soap weed develop roughened hides, ugly growths around the mouth, and lusterless eyes.

Years of the farmers' and ranchers' lives have gone into the building up of their herds. Their herds were like their families to them. When AAA[6] officials spotted cows and steers for shooting during the cattle-killing days of last summer, the farmers felt as though their own children were facing the bullets. Kansas, a Republican state, has no love for the AAA. This year winds whistled over land made barren by the drought and the crop-conservation program. When Wallace[7] removed the ban on the planting of spring wheat he was greeted by cheers. But the wheat has been blown completely out of the ground. Nothing is left but soap weed, or the expensive cotton-seed cake,[8] and after that—bankruptcy.

The storm comes in a terrifying way. Yellow clouds roll. The wind blows such a gale that it is all my helper can do to hold my camera to the ground. The sand whips into my lens. I repeatedly wipe it away trying to snatch an exposure before it becomes completely coated again. The light becomes yellower, the wind colder. Soon there is no photographic light, and we hurry for shelter to the nearest farmhouse. Three men and a woman are seated around a dust-caked lamp, on their faces grotesque masks of wet cloth. The children have been put to bed with towels tucked over their heads. My host greets us: "It takes grit to live in this country." They are telling stories: A bachelor harnessed the sandblast which ripped through the keyhole by holding his pots and pans in it until they were spick and span. A pilot flying over Amarillo got caught in a sand storm. His motor clogged; he took to his parachute. It took him six hours to shovel his way back to earth. And when a man from the next county was struck by a drop of water, he fainted, and it took two buckets of sand to revive him.

The migrations of the farmer have begun. In many of the worst-hit counties 80 per cent of the families are on relief. In the open farm country one crop failure follows another. After perhaps three successive crop failures the farmer can't stand it any longer. He moves in with relatives and hopes for a job in Arizona or Illinois or some neighboring state where he knows he is not needed. Perhaps he gets a job as a cotton picker, and off he goes with his family, to be turned adrift again after a brief working period.

We passed them on the road, all their household goods piled on wagons, one lucky family on a truck. Lucky, because they had been able to keep their truck when the mortgage was foreclosed. All they owned in the world was packed on it; the children sat

---

3. **Russian thistle.** Prickly plant that American farmers normally treat as a weed
4. **fodder.** Food for livestock
5. **soap weed.** Plant whose leaves release a substance people can use as a detergent
6. **AAA.** Agricultural Adjustment Administration, a crop management program
7. **Wallace.** Henry A. Wallace, secretary of agriculture in the 1930s
8. **cotton-seed cake.** Lump made of cotton seeds after their oil is extracted

HISTORY ▶▶ CONNECTION

The New Deal When Franklin Delano Roosevelt became president in 1933, the national unemployment rate had reached nearly 25 percent. The country was counting on Roosevelt's administration to relieve the economic crisis. During his campaign, Roosevelt promised "a new deal for the American people." In his first one hundred days in office he launched programs to repair the economy. Among them were programs for revitalizing the farm economy. One new agency was the Soil Conservation Service, which offered specific programs to prevent the spread of the Dust Bowl. Why do you think this program was included as part of the New Deal?

Drought Stricken Area, 1934. Alexandre Hogue. Dallas Museum of Art.

on a pile of bureaus topped with mattresses, and the sides of the truck were strapped up with bed springs. The entire family looked like a Ku Klux Klan[9] meeting, their faces done up in masks to protect them from the whirling sand.

Near Hays, Kansas, a little boy started home from school and never arrived there. The neighbors looked for him till ten at night, and all next day a band of two hundred people searched. At twilight they found him, only a quarter of a mile from home, his body nearly covered with silt. He had strangled to death. The man who got lost in his own ten-acre truck garden and wandered around choking and stifling for eight hours before he found his house considered himself lucky to escape with his life. The police and sheriffs are kept constantly busy with calls from anxious parents whose children are lost, and the toll is mounting of people who become marooned and die in the storms.

But the real tragedy is the plight of the cattle. In a rising sand storm cattle quickly become blinded. They run around in circles until they fall and breathe so much dust that they die. Autopsies show their lungs caked with dust and mud. Farmers dread the birth of calves during a storm. The newborn animals will die within twenty-four hours.

And this same dust that coats the lungs and threatens death to cattle and men alike, that ruins the stock of the storekeeper lying unsold on his shelves, that creeps into the gear shifts of automobiles, that sifts through the refrigerator into the butter, that makes housekeeping, and gradually life itself, unbearable, this swirling drifting dust is changing the agricultural map of the United States. It piles ever higher on the floors and beds of a steadily increasing number of deserted farmhouses. A half-buried plowshare, a wheat binder[10] ruffled over with sand, the skeleton of a horse near a dirt-filled water hole are stark evidence of the meager life, the wasted savings, the years of toil that the farmer is leaving behind him. ✤

9. **Ku Klux Klan.** Racist terrorist organization whose members wear pointed white hoods
10. **plowshare...wheat binder.** Farm implements; the plowshare cuts furrows in the soil and the wheat binder bundles cut grain into sheaves.

TEXT ◀ TO ▶ TEXT CONNECTION

In her first paragraph, Margaret Bourke-White says dust storms have personalities. What personality would you give to the storm in Rothstein's *Farmer and Sons Walking in the Face of a Dust Storm?*

AFTER READING

Analyze Literature

Purpose Re-examine Rothstein's photographs and try to determine his purpose or purposes. Create a two-column chart like this one for each photograph. In the first column, create a list of details from the photograph. Then, in the second column, list Rothstein's purpose or purposes.

Detail	Purpose
boy is carefully holding very small puppy	

Extend Understanding

Writing Options

Creative Writing Imagine you want to dramatize the plight of poor farmers to the president of the United States. Think of a short story you could write based on one of Rothstein's photographs. Focus first on determining the central conflict of the story. Then either **outline** the plot of your story, or use a **plot diagram** that shows the exposition, rising action, climax, falling action, and resolution.

Informative Writing Write a list of at least ten **interview questions** you would like to ask one of the people in Rothstein's photographs. Plan to use your interview to write a short article about life in the Dust Bowl. Formulate questions that you think will help you identify how your subject is coping with the effects of the drought and the bad economic situation.

Collaborative Learning

Trace a Migration In a small group, use library resources to research migrations during the Dust Bowl. Start with a specific place affected by the Dust Bowl, such as Oklahoma. Try to learn where people went and what circumstances greeted them in their new homes. Summarize what you learn to share with the class.

Media Literacy

Visit the Library of Congress Rothstein and many other photographers worked for the government during the 1930s and 1940s. Visit the Library of Congress's collection of related photographs online. You can see more pictures of rural America during the Dust Bowl and learn more about the photographers. Choose a page to recommend, and share the web address with the class.

Go to **www.mirrorsandwindows.com** for more.

INDEPENDENT READING

Death in the Open

A Scientific Essay by Lewis Thomas

It is the nature of animals to die alone.

Most of the dead animals you see on highways near the cities are dogs, a few cats. Out in the countryside, the forms and coloring of the dead are strange; these are the wild creatures. Seen from a car window they appear as fragments, evoking memories of woodchucks, badgers, skunks, voles, snakes, sometimes the mysterious wreckage of a deer.

It is always a queer shock, part a sudden upwelling of grief, part unaccountable amazement. It is simply astounding to see an animal dead on a highway. The outrage is more than just the location; it is the impropriety[1] of such visible death, anywhere. You do not expect to see dead animals in the open. It is the nature of animals to die alone, off somewhere, hidden. It is wrong to see them lying out on the highway; it is wrong to see them anywhere.

Everything in the world dies, but we only know about it as a kind of abstraction.[2] If you stand in a meadow, at the edge of a hillside, and look around carefully, almost everything you can catch sight of is in the process of dying, and most things will be dead long before you are. If it were not for

1. **impropriety.** Behavior or conduct considered impolite
2. **abstraction.** Generalized concept, or idea

(Above left) ***Dead Fox Lying in the Undergrowth,*** 1865. Edgar Degas. Musée des Beaux-Arts, Rouen, France.

Lewis Thomas (1913–1993) is one of the best-known science writers of the last fifty years. Thomas had an extraordinary academic career, attending Princeton and Harvard, and he eventually became the dean of Yale Medical School. As a doctor and biologist, Thomas displayed a wide-ranging and keen interest in the world, from the microscopic functions of the cell to the ways in which human society interacts with natural processes. His essays written for the *New England Journal of Medicine,* collected in *The Lives of a Cell,* were awarded the National Book Award in 1974.

the constant renewal and replacement going on before your eyes, the whole place would turn to stone and sand under your feet.

There are some creatures that do not seem to die at all; they simply vanish totally into their own progeny. Single cells do this. The cell becomes two, then four, and so on, and after a while the last trace is gone. It cannot be seen as death; barring mutation, the descendants are simply the first cell, living all over again. The cycles of the slime mold[3] have episodes that seem as conclusive as death, but the withered slug, with its stalk and fruiting body, is plainly the transient tissue of a developing animal; the free-swimming amebocytes use this organ collectively in order to produce more of themselves.

There are said to be a billion billion insects on the earth at any moment, most of them with very short life expectancies by our standards. Someone has estimated that there are 25 million assorted insects hanging in the air over every temperate square mile, in a column extending upward for thousands of feet, drifting through the layers of the atmosphere like plankton.[4] They are dying steadily, some by being eaten, some just dropping in their tracks, tons of them around the earth, disintegrating as they die, invisibly.

Who ever sees dead birds, in anything like the huge numbers stipulated by the certainty of the death of all birds? A dead bird is an incongruity,[5] more startling than an unexpected live bird, sure evidence to the human mind that something has gone wrong. Birds do their dying off somewhere, behind things, under things, never on the wing.

Animals seem to have an instinct for performing death alone, hidden. Even the largest, most conspicuous[6] ones find ways to conceal themselves in time. If an elephant missteps and dies in an open place, the herd will not leave him there; the others will pick him up and carry the body from place to place, finally putting it down in some inexplicably[7] suitable location. When elephants encounter the skeleton of an elephant out in the open, they methodically[8] take up each of the bones and distribute them, in a ponderous[9] ceremony, over neighboring acres.

It is a natural marvel. All of the life of the earth dies, all of the time, in the same volume as the new life that dazzles us each morning, each spring. All we see of this is the odd stump, the fly struggling on the porch floor of the summer house in October, the fragment on the highway. I have lived all my life with an embarrassment of squirrels in my backyard, they are all over the place, all year long, and I have never seen, anywhere, a dead squirrel.

I suppose it is just as well. If the earth were otherwise, and all the dying were done in the open, with the dead there to be looked at, we would never have it out of our minds. We can forget about it much of the time, or think of it as an accident to be avoided, somehow. But it does make the process of dying seem more exceptional than it really is, and harder to engage in at the times when we must ourselves engage.

In our way, we conform as best we can to the rest of nature. The obituary pages tell us of the news that we are dying away, while the birth announcements in finer print, off

---

3. **slime mold.** Protists that can join together to form a slug-like body
4. **plankton.** Organisms that float in bodies of water and serve as food for larger organisms
5. **incongruity.** Inconsistency
6. **conspicuous.** Obvious; noticeable
7. **inexplicably.** Unexplainably
8. **methodically.** Carefully; according to an exact procedure
9. **ponderous.** Slow and awkward

at the side of the page, inform us of our replacements, but we get no grasp from this of the enormity[10] of scale. There are 3 billion of us on the earth, and all 3 billion must be dead, on a schedule, within this lifetime. The vast mortality, involving something over 50 million of us each year, takes place in relative secrecy. We can only really know of the deaths in our households, or among our friends. These, detached in our minds from all the rest, we take to be unnatural events, anomalies,[11] outrages. We speak of our own dead in low voices; struck down, we say, as though visible death can only occur for cause, by disease or violence, avoidably. We send off for flowers, grieve, make ceremonies, scatter bones, unaware of the rest of the 3 billion on the same schedule. All of that immense mass of flesh and bone and consciousness will disappear by absorption into the earth, without recognition by the transient[12] survivors.

Less than a half century from now, our replacements will have more than doubled the numbers. It is hard to see how we can continue to keep the secret, with such multitudes doing the dying. We will have to give up the notion that death is catastrophe, or detestable, or avoidable, or even strange. We will need to learn more about the cycling of life in the rest of the system, and about our connection to the process. Everything that comes alive seems to be in trade for something that dies, cell for cell. There might be some comfort in the recognition of synchrony,[13] in the information that we all go down together, in the best of company. ✤

10. enormity. Great size
11. anomalies. Oddities
12. transient. Disappearing; short-lived
13. synchrony. Occurrences at the same time

Why do you think, so many animals die in private? Do you think animals have an instinct related to this? Do people?

Analyze and Extend

1. What similar attitudes do animals and people share about death? What are some differences in their attitudes?
2. Why do you think elephants act the way that they do about death?
3. Do you agree with Thomas's speculation that in the near future, death will take place in the open? Explain.

Informative Writing In a short essay, write a **literary response** to "Death in the Open." Analyze and evaluate Thomas's main idea and supporting details. In your opening paragraph, state what you believe his main idea to be and whether or not you agree with it. In your body paragraphs, analyze his supporting details and determine whether they effectively support his main idea. Your conclusion should restate your thesis.

Critical Literacy Hold a panel discussion about Thomas's essay in which you share your thoughts about Thomas's essay. Use the literary response that you wrote as the basis for your discussion. Present evidence in support of any claims you make, and listen attentively and respond respectfully to others' ideas.

Go to **www.mirrorsandwindows.com** for more.

Astonishing Animals

Visual Media by Tim Flannery and Peter Schouten

INDEPENDENT READING

Whip dragonfish

(Grammatostomias flagellibarba)

The deeper one ventures in the oceans, the stranger life becomes. Many fish that inhabit the eternally dark ocean depths have highly exaggerated body parts, but none seems as extreme as the whip dragonfish. At twenty centimetres long, it has a barbel or 'beard' that extends a metre and a half from its chin. Just what it uses this pale, brown-speckled 'whip' for is unclear. Perhaps it trawls with its barbel, hoping to attract prey. But if so, how does it reach down with its mouth to swallow it before its prey darts off?

Many deep-sea creatures possess a variety of light-emitting organs known as photophores, and those of the whip dragonfish are peculiar. Only the male has a bright yellow light-emitting organ behind its eyes, the other light-emitting organs being a violet-purple colour in both sexes. These organs produce their light in a complex manner, for it is generated both by the action of particular bacteria that live in the luminescent[1] organs, as well as through chemical reactions produced by the fish itself.

1. **luminescent.** Light producing

Wolftrap seadevil

(Lasiognathus saccostomus)

Also known as 'Regan's strainermouth', the scientific name of this seadevil means 'hairy jaws', and it has one of the worst overbites in nature. The first specimen found was a female just seven centimetres long, which was brought up from the depths of the Caribbean. It is now known to be widespread in the depths of the Pacific and Atlantic oceans. The wolftrap seadevil possesses a strangely raised lateral line system. In fish the lateral line, which runs the length of the body from gills to tail fin, is used to detect changes in water pressure. In this species it may be supersensitive. It also has prominent nostrils, which suggests a fine sense of smell.

The wolftrap seadevil is a true fisherman with a long, articulated fishing pole, line and lure. The lure is illuminated and has two hooked, tooth-like structures that may function as fish-hooks. It evidently snares tiny prey with its lure and hooks and whips them into the cavernous mouth. It may even, like a fly-fisherman, cast its lure towards prey.

Elsman's whipnose

(Gigantactis elsmani)

Gigantactis means 'giant touching device' in Latin, in reference to the extraordinary nose-mounted fishing poles possessed by these curious anglerfish. As recently as 1968 fewer than thirty adult whipnoses of all species (of which there were then ten known) had been collected, and even today these large, predatory deepwater fish are little known. A chance encounter with a Japanese submersible[2] revealed that Elsman's whipnose swims upside down with its lantern in front of it, just above the ocean bottom, perhaps to lure worms from their burrows. It has weak eyes, which may be compensated by an acute sense of smell, the males in particular having prodigious[3] nostrils. ✣

---

2. **submersible.** Small boat or craft that travels underwater
3. **prodigious.** Very large

Tim Flannery (b. 1956) is a museum director, biologist, environmental advocate, and notable science writer. Born and raised in Australia, Flannery holds degrees in English literature, Earth science, and paleontology. He has held teaching positions at numerous universities, including Harvard, where he acted as Visiting Chair in Australian Studies.

Illustrator and painter **Peter Schouten** is a world-renowned wildlife artist. Born in Australia, Schouten was educated as a paleontologist. A self-trained artist, his first book of art led to a position as technical illustrator at the school of zoology at the University of New South Wales. He now works as a freelance wildlife illustrator.

How did you react to the animals depicted in this selection? Describe your reactions, both emotional and intellectual. How do you think most people would react to these animals?

Analyze and Extend

1. For what reason or reasons do you think the whip dragonfish has such a long barbel?
2. (a) What hypothesis is presented regarding the Elsman's whipnose's habit of swimming upside down? (b) Explain why you think this is a reasonable or unreasonable idea.
3. (a) What physical traits do all three fish share? (b) Why do you think they have these traits in common?

Creative Writing Imagine that you are a deep sea explorer. On an undersea mission, you discover one of the animals described and pictured in this selection. Write a **journal entry** about your discovery. Include sensory details and precise language, and list as many specific details about the animal as possible.

Lifelong Learning Using the Internet and the library, further research one of the animals depicted in this selection. Create a list of the facts that you gather, such as the animal's size, diet, and the year in which it was first discovered. Then use this list to create a short informative paragraph about the animal you researched.

 Go to **www.mirrorsandwindows.com** for more.

For Your Reading List

The New Way Things Work
by David Macaulay

David Macaulay's *The New Way Things Work* exposes the secret inner workings of machines. Over the course of a few hundred pages, with drawings and text, Macaulay illustrates and describes how hundreds of machines, from parking meters to zippers, work. His drawings are always clear and often humorous, and his descriptions concise.

Pick Me Up
by Jeremy Leslie and David Roberts

One part puzzle book, one part encyclopedia, *Pick Me Up* is all offbeat. This innovative text combines vivid illustrations, graphic aids, and fascinating tidbits. In the way that individual web pages are linked to hundreds of others, every page is distinct and loaded with cross-references that will send you flipping to other parts of the book.

Photography: An Illustrated History
by Martin W. Sandler

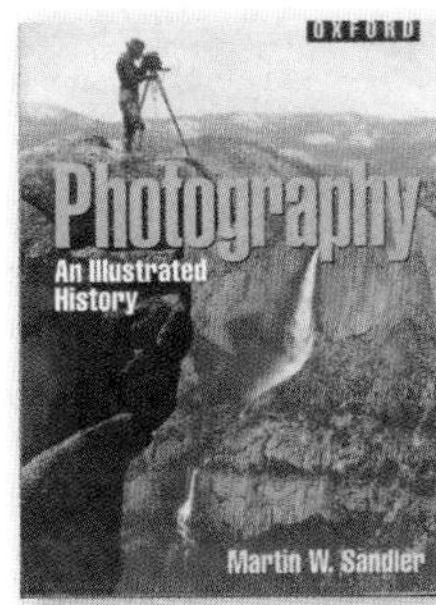

This book is a guide to the technical and creative innovations from the birth of photography to the digital age. From the daguerreotype to moving pictures and computers, every major innovation is accompanied with a photograph that illustrates what is being described in Sandler's thoughtful and extensive text. The book also covers the major fields of the art, such as fashion and war photography.

A Drop of Water
by Walter Wick

In *A Drop of Water*, photographer Walter Wick directs his camera to the study of the science and beauty of water. Through magnification and other techniques, Wick uses his camera to surprise the viewer with a new perspective on something we see every day. Each picture is accompanied by a paragraph describing the scientific principles at work in phenomena from a soap bubble to a droplet of rain.

Raptor! A Kid's Guide to Birds of Prey
by Christyna M. Laubach, René Laubach, and Charles W. G. Smith

In this birding book for young people, the amazing lives of raptors—birds of prey such as owls, hawks, and eagles—are shown up close. Readers learn about the habits, food, behavior, and characteristics of these birds. Each entry includes information that will help with identification in the wild, along with numerous fascinating and informative exercises.

Universe
by Martin Rees (editor)

This nicely illustrated reference text provides a thoughtful and useful guide to the stars. Written by a team of astronomers who simply and carefully explain complicated topics, *Universe* is accessible to even the most science-challenged reader.

Writing Workshop

Descriptive Writing

Descriptive Essay

Assignment: Write a descriptive essay in which I use sensory details and personal thoughts to give a response to nature.

Goal: Convey my impression of a natural subject or event in a vivid way to bring it to life for my audience.

Strategy: Include details that help the audience see, smell, taste, feel, or hear what I am describing, as well as my own thoughts and feelings.

Writing Rubric: My descriptive essay should include the following:

- an introduction that illustrates my impression of a natural subject or event
- a clear organizational pattern appropriate to the subject or event I'm describing
- figurative language and sensory details that create a picture for the reader
- personal thoughts and feelings that help reinforce my overall impression
- strong verbs and active voice
- a conclusion that sums up my impression and adds insight

Reading and Writing

In this unit you have read essays on nature and the natural world. These essays were written by scientists, politicians, and naturalists. The writers described their views of the natural world around them. They wrote about subjects as diverse as the tiniest units of matter to humanity's destructiveness and Earth's resilience.

In this workshop, you will learn how to write a **descriptive essay.** The purpose of a descriptive essay is to present a piece of writing that creates a picture for the reader. Before writing a descriptive essay, determine your goal and a strategy to achieve it. The assignment summary here includes a writing rubric, that is, a set of standards by which you judge your work and whether or not your descriptive essay was successful. You will use this rubric in both drafting and revising your essay.

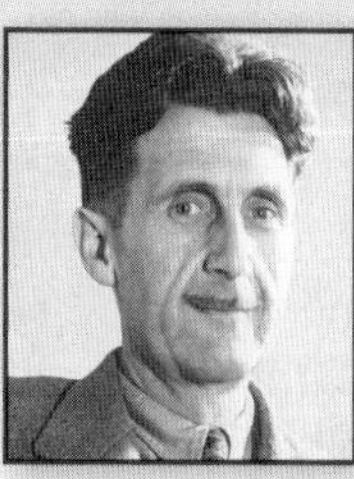

What Great Writers Do

George Orwell (1903–1950) was an essayist, novelist, and satirist. He wrote the novels Animal Farm *and* 1984*.*

Read his passage below about questions a writer should ask. How might this advice pertain to descriptive writing?

A scrupulous writer, in every sentence that he writes, will ask himself at least four questions, thus: What am I trying to say? What words will express it? What image or idiom will make it clearer? Is this image fresh enough to have an effect?

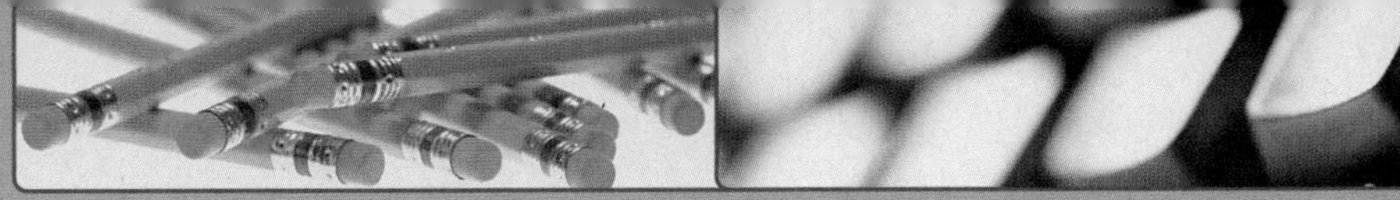

1. PREWRITE

Choosing Your Topic

When you look around at the natural world, you see many things. Think about which subjects from nature fascinate, scare, inspire, or excite you. Specifically, what animals, outdoor spaces, land formations, or types of weather catch your interest? Try to focus on a particular moment or episode in your life when something from the natural world affected you strongly. Once you have a subject in mind, **narrow your focus.**

Below is how one student narrowed her focus. She created an inverted triangle with the broadest subject area first, narrowing it down to a more manageable subject. Keep in mind that any subject can work in a descriptive essay, as long as it is personally meaningful.

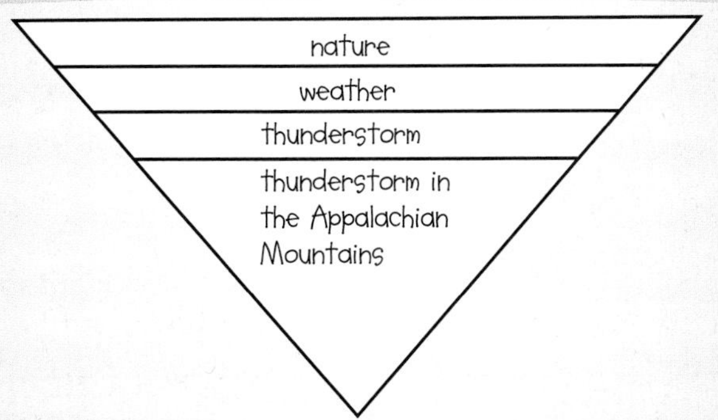

The writer began with the broad subject *nature* and narrowed that down to *weather. Weather* was further narrowed down to *thunderstorm,* and that subject further specified to focus on a *particular* thunderstorm that affected the writer personally.

Gathering Details

After you narrow your subject, begin gathering details. One way to gather sensory details is to create a word web. Here is a word web in which the writer recalls details about an especially frightening thunderstorm she experienced.

These are just a few details that the writer brought to mind about experiencing a thunderstorm. She used her five senses to remember how a specific thunderstorm made her feel.

Deciding on Your Purpose

Once you gather enough details for your essay, decide on your purpose for writing. For a descriptive essay, your purpose is to describe a subject or event with descriptive details and personal thoughts. Your details and thoughts should give your audience a clear picture of the subject or event and how it affected you. Create a thesis statement that reveals your impression of the subject or event. Note the example below.

> A thunderstorm can be one of the scariest and most beautiful things in nature to experience.

2. DRAFT

Organizing Ideas

There are various ways you can organize data for your descriptive essay. You can present your information in one of two major **organizational patterns,** either in chronological order or by spatial order. In **chronological order,** you tell a series of events in the order in which they happened. In **spatial order,** you describe the parts of a scene in order of their location in space. Use spatial order to discuss the physical position or relationship between objects.

Chronological Order	Spatial Order
First Event ↓ Second Event ↓ Third Event ↓ Final Event	1. Top ↕ Bottom 2. Left ←→ Right 3. Near ←→ Far
Signal Words and Phrases first, next, then, after that, before, during, finally	**Signal Words and Phrases** behind, below, above, here, there, on the left, next to, in front of, inside

Putting Your Thoughts on Paper

An essay has three basic parts: an introduction, a body, and a conclusion. Create a plan for writing your descriptive essay like the one on the right. Use your word web.

You may want to write the body of your essay first and then write the introduction and conclusion. You can also write your essay all the way through from the introduction to the conclusion. There is no one correct way to write your essay. Your description should flow from one part to another, however, and be sure to include enough sensory details and personal thoughts to make your impression clear to the reader. For now, concentrate on content and organization. You will focus on grammar, punctuation, and spelling at the editing and proofreading stage.

Introduction
- Introduce the natural subject or event you will describe and your impression.

Body
- Organize by chronological or spatial order.
- Include sensory details in each paragraph.
- Include your personal thoughts and feelings that support your overall impression.

Conclusion
- Summarize your impression and add an insight.

Showing Instead of Telling

Remember that a goal of your descriptive essay is to help your audience picture what you are describing and share in the experience. Add descriptive details, such as sensory images and figurative language, to help your readers feel as if they are there. Consider the example.

Tell:

My brother was afraid.

Show:

My brother glanced at me, and I glanced at him. His face turned pale, and his eyes bulged wide. He clenched his seatbelt like a lifeline. I heard a low whimper as his bottom lip began to quiver.

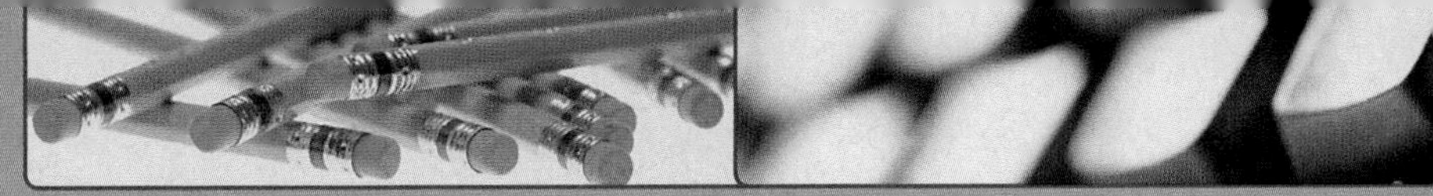

3. REVISE

Evaluating Your Draft

Look over your draft for strengths and weaknesses. Correct weaknesses as best you can. After that, exchange papers with a classmate, and conduct a **peer review.** Then discuss ways you can improve your paper. The following is part of a student's descriptive essay. The annotations to the right indicate the reasons for the changes marked in the draft.

Revising Checklist

- ☐ Does the introduction illustrate my impression of a natural subject or event?
- ☐ Is the essay organized in a logical way?
- ☐ Do I use figurative language, sensory details, and active voice?

The worst thunderstorm I remember happened one summer on a drive back to Pennsylvania from a family trip to Georgia. ~~My grandparents live in Georgia.~~ We were cruising through the Appalachian Mountains when the storm hit. The mountains can be scary even in the best of weather. They are even scarier when you travel through them in a thunderstorm. *A thunderstorm can be one of the scariest and most beautiful things in nature to experience.*

Delete unrelated detail.

State the subject or event you will describe and your impression.

I remember that afternoon. I had fallen asleep in the car when ~~a storm woke me up.~~ *I awoke to the crash of thunder. The air felt thick and moist. It was dark outside, though it was only 3:30 in the afternoon. As I looked out the window, I saw lightning blaze through the shadowy sky, splitting off in random directions like a light show.* If it wasn't so scary, it might have been the most beautiful thing I'd ever seen! The lightning lit up the road and the entire side of the mountain. It felt like the Fourth of July.

Add descriptive details and figurative language to show instead of tell.

A loud clap of thunder ~~was heard~~ *shook the car* as heavy clouds rolled toward us. That's when I knew this was no ordinary rainstorm.

Replace passive voice with strong verbs in the active voice.

4. EDIT AND PROOFREAD

Focus: Passive and Active Voice

Sometimes you may find yourself writing sentences that use the **passive voice.** Passive voice is the act of telling who or what *receives* the action in a sentence rather than showing who or what *performs* the action.

> **Passive Voice:**
>
> The road and the entire side of the mountain were lit up by the lightning.

> In **active voice** the subject performs the action:
>
> The lightning lit up the road and the entire side of the mountain.

Using the passive voice usually makes writing flat and less interesting. It can also create awkward sentences. To recognize passive voice, look for phrases after the action verb that begin with *by* or *by the.* Also watch out for verb phrases that use forms of the verb *be.* Look over your writing and try to rewrite passive sentences so that they are in active voice. Strong verbs in the active voice will make your descriptions clearer and more effective.

Focus: Adjectives and Adverbs

Adjectives and adverbs are descriptive words. Adjectives modify or tell more about nouns. They answer the questions *what kind, how many,* and *which one.* Adverbs modify verbs, adjectives, and other adverbs. They tell *how, when,* or *where* something happens. When you add adjectives and adverbs to your writing, you affect the meaning of the words they modify.

Adding adjectives and adverbs will enhance your descriptive essay and draw in your reader. Be careful not to overuse adjectives and adverbs, however, and lose the meaning of your writing.

> Rain fell.
>
> **Adding adjectives:**
>
> A hard, cold rain fell.
>
> **Adding adverbs:**
>
> Rain fell quickly and steadily.
>
> **Adding adjectives and adverbs:**
>
> A hard, cold rain fell quickly and steadily.

Proofreading

Quality Control The purpose of proofreading is to find errors in punctuation, grammar, capitalization, and spelling. You can always find and fix these errors as you revise your essay, but you should check for these errors specifically in the proofreading stage. Use proofreader's marks to highlight any errors and correct them. (See the Language Arts Handbook, section 4.1, for a list of proofreader's symbols.)

5. PUBLISH AND PRESENT

Final Draft

Rewrite your essay to make a final draft. If you wrote your essay by hand, make sure it is neat and legible. If you used a word processing program, double-space your paper and use a readable typeface or font. Be sure to check about any of your teacher's additional presentation guidelines.

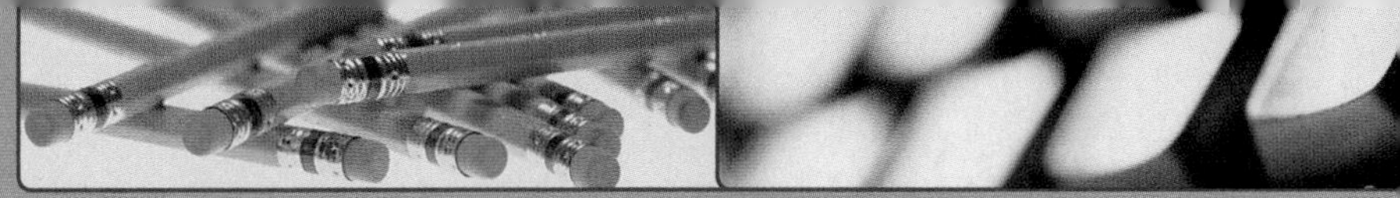

Student Model

A Drive to Remember
by Jamie Lee

The worst thunderstorm I remember happened one summer on a drive back to Pennsylvania from a family trip to Georgia. We were cruising through the Appalachian Mountains when the storm hit. The mountains can be scary even in the best of weather. They are even scarier when you travel through them in a thunderstorm. A thunderstorm can be one of the scariest and most beautiful things in nature to experience.

Introduces the natural event and the writer's impression of that event

I remember that afternoon. I had fallen asleep in the car when I awoke to the crash of thunder. The air felt thick and moist. It was dark outside, though it was only 3:30 in the afternoon. As I looked out the window, I saw lightning blaze through the shadowy sky, splitting off in random directions like a light show. If it wasn't so scary, it might have been the most beautiful thing I'd ever seen! The lightning lit up the road and the entire side of the mountain. It felt like the Fourth of July.

A loud clap of thunder shook the car as heavy clouds rolled toward us. That's when I knew this was no ordinary rainstorm. The deafening sound of thunder made conversation impossible in the car. Yet my brother and I were so fascinated by the show outside our car window that neither of us wanted to talk anyway. Then it started to rain.

Gentle drops fell at first. Suddenly it seemed as though somebody had turned the water on full blast, and the rain crashed down in sheets. A hard, cold rain fell quickly and steadily. My brother glanced at me, and I glanced at him. His face turned pale, and his eyes bulged wide. He clenched his seatbelt like a lifeline. I heard a low whimper as his bottom lip began to quiver. I wondered how my dad could see the road. The rain tap-danced on the roof of the car like a thousand feet at once. Hail smacked against the roof like pelted gravel.

I felt the car slow to a crawl and finally stop along the shoulder of the road. Rain and hail pounded on the car, as if trying to get in with us. My little brother was shaking, and he hid his face inside his sweatshirt. I took his hand and he turned his face into my arm. Finally the noise seemed to ease and float away from us, taking its violence elsewhere. Though it was still raining, the sky wasn't as dark as before, and I knew that the sun was trying to break through the clouds. Dad started the car again, and we headed toward home.

Organized logically, in chronological order

Includes sensory details and figurative language that show instead of tell and help the reader share in the experience

Includes personal thoughts and feelings that support and reinforce the overall impression of the event

Thunderstorms are one of nature's most fascinating and frightening events. They are necessary and natural phenomena, of course, but I plan to be in my own house the next time one hits!

Sums up the writer's impression and adds an insight

Viewing Workshop

Critical Viewing

How are you influenced by images when you watch television or read a web page, newspaper, or magazine? Do you evaluate the effectiveness of photographs, diagrams, illustrations, and charts? When you evaluate an image's meaning, purpose, or effectiveness, you are using **critical viewing** skills. In this workshop you will craft a presentation that uses visual aids to convey information.

Planning a Visual Presentation

Choose an Idea Do you have an interest in something you want to share with others? Might visual aids increase the clarity or effectiveness of your explanation? For example, you may be interested in the preservation of a natural habitat. A strictly verbal presentation may not be enough. Pictures, drawings, and real objects can help convey complicated ideas and bring your topic to life. Be sure to select a topic that will benefit from the use of visual aids.

Select Key Ideas and Visuals Once you select your topic, gather information about it. Use sources such as the Internet, books, magazines, and encyclopedias to begin taking notes. Along with your notes, which will lay the groundwork for the verbal part of your presentation, decide what kinds of visuals you will use to reinforce your main ideas or clarify the most difficult concepts in your presentation. Will photographs, drawings, diagrams, maps, or objects work best? Should you show pictures on poster board, on slides, or as part of a digital presentation? For example, if you were presenting the effects of housing developments on wetlands, you might include before-and-after photographs or illustrations that depict soil erosion.

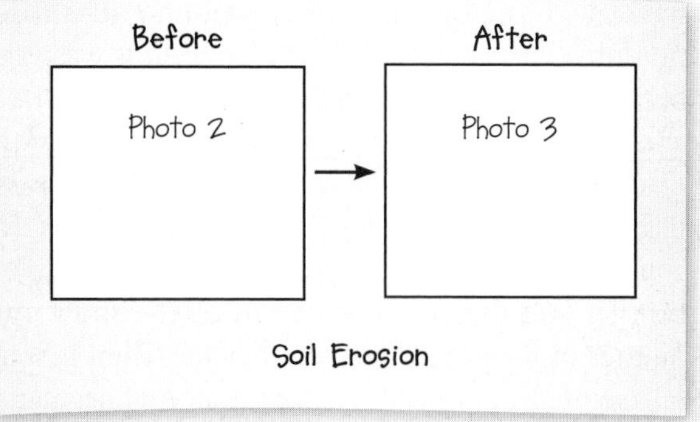

Identify Your Audience What key ideas would you like your audience to learn from your presentation? Are these ideas very complicated? Do they require any special background knowledge or vocabulary? Determine whether your audience will have the background needed to understand any technical information or language. If you are presenting on a topic that requires a good deal of specialized knowledge, consider how you might make this topic accessible to a general audience.

Organize Your Visuals As you gather images, objects, or other visual aids for your presentation, try to determine how to use them in the most effective way. Make sure that you organize your visuals to coincide with your verbal presentation. If you are using photographs or drawings, you may want to set up a storyboard. Key each image to a different main idea in your presentation.

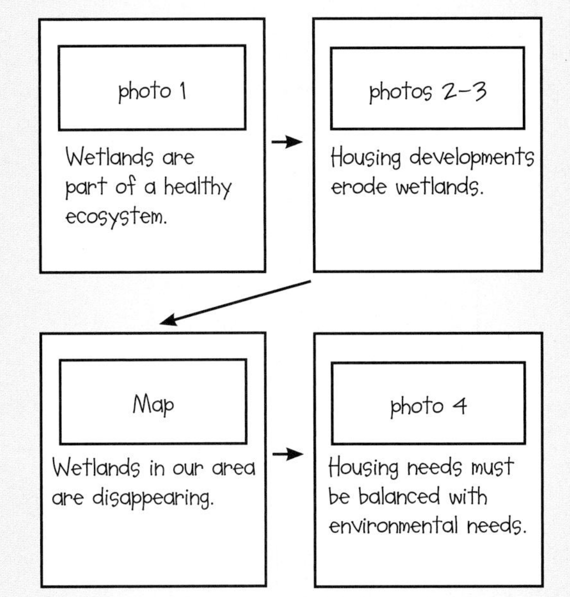

Evaluating Your Presentation

Work with a partner or group on your presentation. Take turns delivering your presentations. Consider how photographs, diagrams, illustrations, and graphs enhance the presentation's impact and improve clarity. Ask yourself: What do these images add? Provide constructive feedback about your peers' use of visual aids. Follow the speaking, listening, and viewing rubric on this page to evaluate the presentation.

Delivering Your Presentation

Insert cues into the notes, outline, or script to prompt you to present your visual aids at the appropriate moment. If you use photographs or art in your presentation, be sure you know the name of the artist or photographer, the title of the piece, and the date it was created. Make sure your visuals are large enough and placed well for your audience to see them. When you refer to your visuals, point to them so that the audience can adjust its attention.

Listen Actively As an active listener, remember to be courteous to the speaker. Do not touch or handle visual aids without the speaker's permission. During the presentation, try to interpret the impact the images have on you. Ask questions when appropriate to clarify anything you find confusing, unclear, or in need of elaboration.

Speaking Rubric

Your presentation will be evaluated on the following elements:

Content

- ☐ visuals enhance appeal of presentation
- ☐ presentation is clear and well organized
- ☐ visuals are effectively used
- ☐ main ideas of presentation are supported with evidence

Delivery and Presentation

- ☐ appropriate volume and pacing
- ☐ appropriate responses to audience questions through clarification and elaboration
- ☐ effective nonverbal communication

Listening and Viewing Rubric

As a peer reviewer or audience member, you should do the following:

- ☐ listen quietly and attentively
- ☐ analyze the images presented
- ☐ ask appropriate questions
- ☐ (as peer reviewer) provide constructive feedback

Test Practice Workshop

Writing Skills

Descriptive Essay

Carefully read the following writing prompt. Before you begin writing, think carefully about what task the assignment is asking you to perform. Then create an outline to help guide your writing.

In his essay "Ships in the Desert," Al Gore uses the analogy of an outgoing tide that leaves behind disturbing images in the sand. These images warn of dangers ahead if humans continue to "turn their backs on nature." What are some ways in which humans ignore nature as they go about their lives? What are some of the dangers that could arise if humans continue to do this?

In your essay, use descriptive and sensory language, as well as analogies, to describe several human actions that are having negative effects on nature. Use examples from Gore's essay, issues you have read or heard about, and evidence from your own life. As you write, be sure to:

- Organize your essay in a logical and consistent way
- Include introductory and concluding paragraphs
- Introduce your position in the first paragraph
- Support your main idea in each body paragraph

Revising and Editing Skills

In the following excerpt from the first draft of a student's paper, words and phrases are underlined and numbered. Alternatives to the underlined words and phrases appear in the right-hand column. Choose the one that *best* corrects any grammatical or style errors in the original. If you think that the original is error free, choose "NO CHANGE."

Some questions might also be asked about a section of the passage or the entire passage. These do not refer to a specific underlined phrase or word and are identified by a number in a box. Record your answers on a separate sheet of paper.

Because tornadoes are unpredictable [1] they are one of the deadliest forces in nature. Like a crazed shopper at a department store sale, a tornado races blindly across the countryside, destroying homes and ending lives. How do I know? I have lived through one. [2]

May 8, 1999, was an evening that I will never forget. The breeze which was thick with moisture [3] carried the pleasant fragrance of freshly turned earth and spring flowers. As we drove through the countryside, my brother Darrell and I were admiring [4] a field of yellow and white daisies, which danced like tiny ballerinas in the soft breeze. The setting sun was brilliant on the western horizon. Then dark clouds and wild winds [5] rolled in like ocean waves approaching the beach. Within minutes, the entire landscape grew silent the dancing daisies were now completely still as rain began to spill from the sky. [6]

1. A. NO CHANGE
   B. Because tornadoes are unpredictable;
   C. Because tornadoes are unpredictable,
   D. Because tornadoes are unpredictable:

2. The first paragraph includes:
   A. visual media.
   B. dialect.
   C. internal conflict.
   D. an analogy.

3. A. NO CHANGE
   B. The breeze, which was thick with moisture,
   C. The breeze. Which was thick with moisture
   D. The breeze; which was thick with moisture;

4. A. NO CHANGE
   B. Darrell and me were admiring
   C. Darrell and me was admiring
   D. Darrell and I was admiring

5. This sentence contains:
   A. a nominative pronoun.
   B. a simple subject.
   C. a compound subject.
   D. the thesis statement.

6. The last sentence of this paragraph is:
   A. the topic sentence.
   B. the thesis.
   C. a fragment.
   D. a run-on.

Reading Skills

Carefully read the following passage. Then, on a separate piece of paper, answer each question.

from "Beastly Behaviors" by Janine Benyus

It was no more than an evolutionary eyeblink ago that our apelike ancestors were crawling on their hands and knees in pursuit of big, dangerous, delicious animals. For five million years (99% of our time on Earth), our survival hinged on finding animals that we could eat. Stalking an animal meant knowing everything about its habits: where it slept, where it drank its daily water, how fast it would run once it caught wind of us. By necessity, we became astute observers of our fellow creatures and learned a respect that comes with intense study of a subject. Although we've stepped further and further from the wild in our last 5,000 years of agriculture and industry, an ancient awe still stirs deep within us. It's that to-the-bone shiver we feel when we see a wolf trot lightly from the woods or hear the thin song of a rising whale.

What is this uncanny ability animals have to amaze, delight, and at times, frighten or repulse us? Part attraction, part fear, and part admiration still make us curious about wild animals even though we no longer need them to fill our stomachs. In this country alone, 115 million people pour through the turnstiles of zoos each year. That's more people than go to all the professional sporting events combined! Worldwide, 357 million people attended the 757 zoos listed in the *1984 International Zoo Yearbook*—the equivalent of all the people in the United States, Canada, France, and the United Kingdom. And it's not just school groups either. For every wide-eyed child, there are three astonished adults rushing to the rail to see the dolphins leap.

These days, animals in zoos represent more than just a shadow of our ancestral past. They are the last ambassadors of a world that is rapidly becoming less and less wild. The red-alert sirens are screaming, and, for the first time in history, we are admitting to our destructiveness and grappling to right the wrongs. Zoos that were once primarily amusement parks are now on the front lines of that fight, working to brighten the future for rare animals in their keeping. To track this sea change in the zoo world, we have to go back thousands of years, to the creation of the very first zoos.

1. According to the author, why did early humans learn about the habits of animals?
   A. They were amazed and delighted by animals.
   B. They wanted to catch them for zoos.
   C. They wanted to catch them for food.
   D. They wanted to know everything about their environment.

2. Judging from the rest of the paragraph, what adjective in the first sentence provides the best clue about why humans were looking for animals?
   A. evolutionary
   B. apelike
   C. dangerous
   D. delicious

3. Based on the context, what is the meaning of *astute* in line 6?
   A. perceptive
   B. fearful
   C. unsure
   D. stupid

4. The sentence that begins in line 10 contains
   A. internal conflict.
   B. external conflict.
   C. dialect.
   D. sensory details.

5. The second paragraph
   A. appeals only to emotion.
   B. contains details that support the main idea.
   C. is mostly dialogue.
   D. uses many analogies.

6. When the author refers to zoos as "the last ambassadors of a world" in line 23, she is
   A. using visual media.
   B. using dialect.
   C. using analogy.
   D. using sensory details.

7. From the sentence in lines 26–28, what can you infer about the present role of zoos?
   A. Without zoos, some rare animals would disappear.
   B. Zoos are out-of-date and dangerous to the survival of animals.
   C. Zoos are more popular than amusement parks.
   D. Without zoos, rare animals would have a much better chance at survival.

8. The purpose of this passage is mainly
   A. to entertain.
   B. to tell a story.
   C. to instruct.
   D. to inform.

9. Based on the last paragraph, you can conclude that
   A. animals should only be kept in zoos.
   B. zoos have changed radically over time.
   C. keeping animals confined in zoos is hurting their survival.
   D. zoos have always had the same purpose.

10. What is the main idea of this passage?
   A. Though their purpose has changed over time, zoos help animals and inspire people.
   B. While zoos are good at inspiring people, they are cruel to animals.
   C. Zoos have always fought to protect animal habitats and the environment.
   D. Today's zoos are little more than amusement parks.

Unit 5

Appreciating Life

Poetry

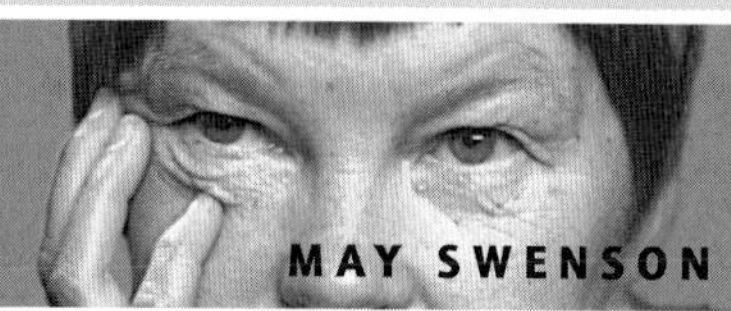

"Summer night—
even the stars
are whispering to each other."

—KOBAYASHI ISSA

Observing the world around you can help you appreciate life. In Kobayashi Issa's haiku–a kind of Japanese poetry–the speaker describes the beauty of the stars on a summer night. As you read the poems in this unit, try to visualize the portraits of the world that the poets create with language. Consider how each poet has a unique perspective on life.

LANGSTON HUGHES

E. E. CUMMINGS

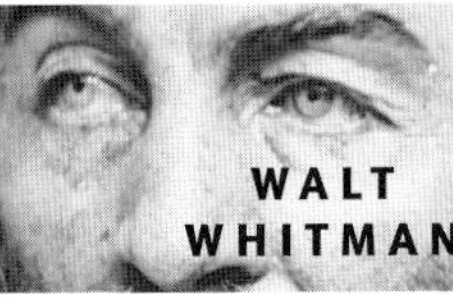

Introduction to Poetry

Don't be polite.

Bite in.

Pick it up with your fingers and lick the juice
that may run down your chin.

It is ready and ripe now, whenever you are.

You don't need a knife or fork or spoon

or plate or napkin or tablecloth.

—EVE MERRIAM, "How to Eat a Poem"

How is this passage different from pieces of literature you have read in previous units? What about its shape and tone makes it unique? The above passage is not prose; it is poetry. The language of **poetry** is musical, and the word choices exact. Poets use imagery, metaphor, simile, and other kinds of figurative language, as well as sound devices such as rhyme and alliteration.

One of the major distinctions between poetry and prose is the use of the line. A **line** of poetry is a single row of words. In prose, sentences are the basic unit with which writers work. Poets, however, work with both the sentence and the line.

Stanzas are made up of lines in the same way that paragraphs are made up of sentences. In a poem, each stanza is separated from the next by a space. The number of lines in a stanza helps to determine the kind of stanza it is. Some of the most common kinds of stanzas include the *couplet,* which is a two-line stanza, the *tercet,* which is a three-line stanza, and the *quatrain,* which is a four-line stanza.

Types of Poetry

Lyric Poems and Narrative Poems

There are two main kinds of poetry: lyric and narrative. A **lyric** poem expresses the emotions of the poem's **speaker,** or narrator. Often lyric poetry focuses on a single moment, image, or idea.

Narrative poetry tells a story and is frequently longer than lyric poetry. Narrative poems can include many of the same literary elements as fiction, such as characters and plot. Edgar Allan Poe's "Annabel Lee" (page 547) and Alfred Noyes's "The Highwayman" (page 551) are both examples of narrative poetry.

Poetic Forms

Within these two broad categories, there are many different poetic forms. A poem's form is determined by its individual elements. Here is a list of some poetic forms:

- **Sonnet:** A sonnet is a fourteen-line poem that usually explores the theme of romantic love. Sonnets are rhymed and use a regular rhythm.
- **Haiku:** Originating in Japan, haikus are short three-line poems that describe a single image or scene from nature. Traditionally, the first and third lines of a haiku have five syllables, whereas the second line has seven.

- **Concrete Poem:** A concrete poem is a poem that is shaped like the thing it describes. For example, if a poem describes a tree, the words on the page would be organized to visually resemble a tree.
- **Free Verse:** Free verse does not use consistent rhymes or rhythms. Free verse can take any shape and address any subject.

Elements of Poetry

Every poem is unique, but most poems use some of the elements listed below. Knowing these elements will help you better understand poetry in general.

Figurative Language and Imagery

Nearly all poems use figurative language and imagery. **Figurative language** is anything written or spoken that is not meant to be taken literally. Figurative language includes metaphors and similes. A **metaphor** is a figure of speech in which one thing is spoken or written about as if it were another. For example, in Diana Rivera's poem "Under the Apple Tree" (page 495), the speaker uses a metaphor to describe a tree: "Branches are suns / that glimmer from within."

A **simile** also compares one thing to another, but it uses the word *like* or *as*. In "Under the Apple Tree," Rivera uses a simile to describe worms: "Earthworms insert themselves into the earth / like glossy, pink pins!"

Other common kinds of figurative language include hyperbole and personification. **Hyperbole** is an exaggeration used for effect or to make a point. **Personification** is a figure of speech in which something not human is described as if it were human. Rivera uses personification to describe apple blossoms: "here, under the apple tree, / where a crowd of petals close their eyes...."

An **image** is a concrete representation of an object or an experience. It is the vivid mental picture created in the reader's mind. When considered together, the images in a literary work are referred to as **imagery.**

Sound Devices

A **sound device** is any element that appeals to the reader's ear. Sound devices make poetry more exciting, more musical, and can affect a poem's meaning. Some of the most common sound devices used in poetry include rhyme, rhythm, and alliteration.

Rhyme is the repetition of sounds at the ends of words. For example, the word *soon* rhymes with *moon*. Sometimes a rhyme is not completely exact, like *step* and *stop*. This is called a **slant rhyme.**

Rhythm is the pattern of beats, or stressed syllables, in a line of poetry. If this pattern is regular, it is called **meter.**

Alliteration is the repetition of consonant sounds at the beginnings of words. For example, the repetition of the *b* sound in *bright blue bottle* is alliteration.

Meaning in Poetry

Finding meaning in poetry is slightly different from finding meaning in short stories or essays. Poems can have many different layers of meaning that make it difficult to identify a single main idea or purpose. In part, this is because poets express their ideas, experiences, and feelings with imagery, figurative language, and symbols. A **symbol** is a thing that stands for itself and something else. Some traditional symbols include doves for peace and owls for wisdom. Symbols can also be unique to a particular piece of literature, author, or culture.

Literary Element

Understanding Imagery and Figurative Language

What Is Imagery?

An **image** is language that creates a concrete representation of an object or an experience. It is the vivid mental picture created in the reader's mind. When considered together, the images in a literary work are referred to as **imagery.**

In the passage on this page from Diana Rivera's poem "Under the Apple Tree," the poet uses sensory details and precise language to create the poem's imagery. For example, "where birds now nestle and sleep," "silver specks," and "fly through the glimmering blue" are all examples of imagery.

Writers can use imagery to create a setting or character, to express an idea or emotion, or to alter the mood or atmosphere of a piece of literature.

What Is Figurative Language?

Figurative language is writing or speech meant to be understood imaginatively instead of literally. Many writers use figures of speech to help readers see things in new ways. Some of the most common kinds of figurative language are metaphor, simile, personification, and hyperbole.

A **metaphor** is a figure of speech in which one thing is spoken or written about as if it were another. Metaphors invite the reader to make a comparison between these two things. A metaphor works because the things being compared have one or more qualities in common. A **simile** is like a metaphor. However, similes use the word *like* or *as* when making a comparison. For example, in the excerpt to the right, Rivera writes that the chirps "rise like tiny bells." The word *like* in this passage compares *chirping* to *tiny bells.*

When a writer uses **personification,** he or she is describing something that is not human as if it were. For example, in "Once by the Pacific" (page 544) Robert Frost describes the waves as if they could think and consciously act.

I like it
here
where birds now nestle and sleep,
where little, high-pitched,
cricketed chirps
rise like tiny bells towards the
ageless moon.

Here,
where insects,—silver specks—
fly through the glimmering blue.

—DIANA RIVERA, "Under the Apple Tree"

Hyperbole is exaggeration. Writers use hyperbole to make a point or to have an effect on the reader. Rivera calls the moon "ageless." This is an example of hyperbole. The moon is not ageless, but Rivera describes it in this way to make the point that the moon is very old.

Poetry Close Reading Model

BEFORE READING

Build Background
You need to apply two different types of background to read a poem effectively. One type is the poem's literary and historical context. Read the **Build Background** and **Meet the Author** features to get this information. The other type of background is the personal knowledge and experience you bring to your reading.

Set Purpose
Read the **Set Purpose** to decide what you want to get out of the poem. Before reading the poem, note how the lines are arranged.

Analyze Literature
Poets use different techniques in writing different poems. The **Analyze Literature** draws your attention to the type of poem or a literary element important to a particular poem.

Use Reading Skills
The **Use Reading Skills** feature will show you skills to help you get the most out of your reading. Learn how to apply skills such as determining author's purpose and using context clues. Identify a graphic organizer that will help you apply the skill before and while you read.

DURING READING

Use Reading Strategies
- **Ask questions** about things that seem significant or interesting.
- **Make predictions** about what's going to happen next. As you read, gather more clues to confirm or change your prediction.
- **Visualize** the images. Form pictures in your mind to help you see who or what the poet is describing.
- **Make inferences,** or educated guesses, about what is not stated directly.
- **Clarify,** or check that you understand, what you read. Reread any difficult parts.

Analyze Literature
What is the purpose of the poem, and what literary elements achieve that purpose? For example, how does imagery or rhyme add to the meaning? Note how these elements affect your understanding of the poem.

Make Connections
Notice where connections can be made between the poem and your life or the world outside the poem. What feelings or thoughts do you have while reading the poem?

AFTER READING

Find Meaning
Recall the important details of the poem, such as the images, figurative language, and rhyme scheme. Use this information to **interpret,** or explain, the poem's meaning.

Make Judgments
- **Analyze** the poem by examining details and deciding what they contribute to the meaning.
- **Evaluate** the poem by making judgments about how the author creates meaning.

Analyze Literature
Review how the use of literary elements increases your understanding of the poem. For example, how might figurative language shape a poem's meaning?

Extend
Go beyond the text by exploring the poem's ideas through writing or other creative projects.

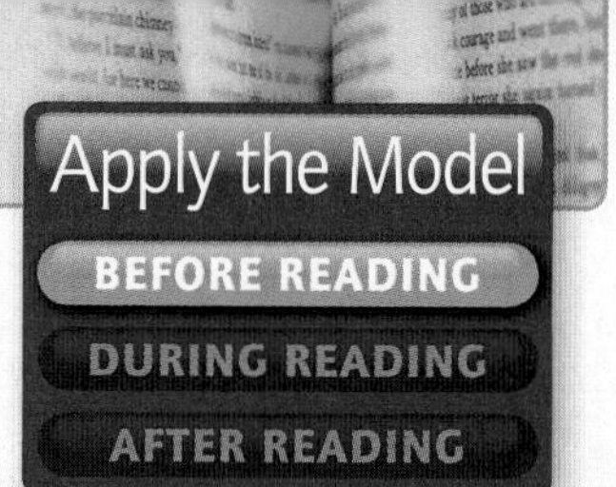

Gold

A Lyric Poem by Pat Mora

GUIDED READING

Build Background

Literary Context Writers who celebrate, in their work, the geography, culture, and traditions of a particular area are known as regional writers. Mexican-American poet Pat Mora is a regional writer who expresses, through her poems and stories, her love of the American Southwest. In the poem "Gold," Mora describes a day in the desert.

Reader's Context Imagine that you are walking in the desert alone. What would you see? What feelings would you have about your surroundings?

Set Purpose

Previewing "Gold" will help you decide how to read and interpret the poem. Look at how the poem is structured, such as the length of the lines and stanzas. Try to determine how these structural elements affect the way in which you read and understand the poem.

Analyze Literature

Imagery The **imagery,** or mental pictures, in a poem often appeal to the reader's senses by describing how things look, sound, feel, taste, or smell. As you read "Gold," think about how the poet uses imagery to help you better visualize the landscape.

Use Reading Skills

Identify Main Idea To identify the main idea of "Gold," gather the details in a main idea map. Then examine the details to determine the overall message the poet wants to convey.

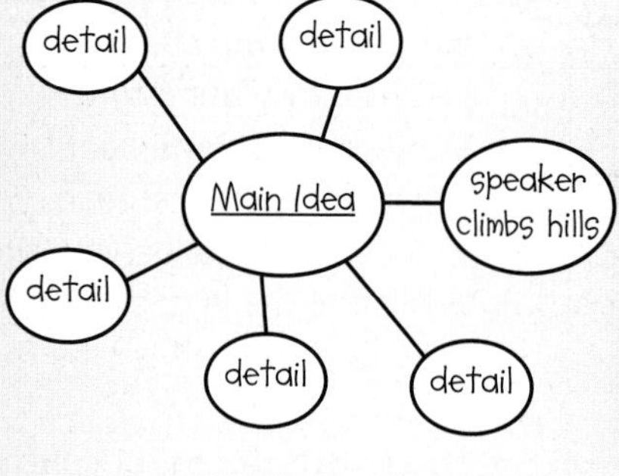

Meet the Author

Pat Mora (b. 1942), born in El Paso, Texas, is a Mexican-American writer of poetry, fiction, and nonfiction for adults and children. She has received many awards for her writing and is an advocate for bilingual literacy. Her writing is marked by strong imagery and often focuses on themes of cultural diversity, the Southwest, native traditions, and universal experiences.

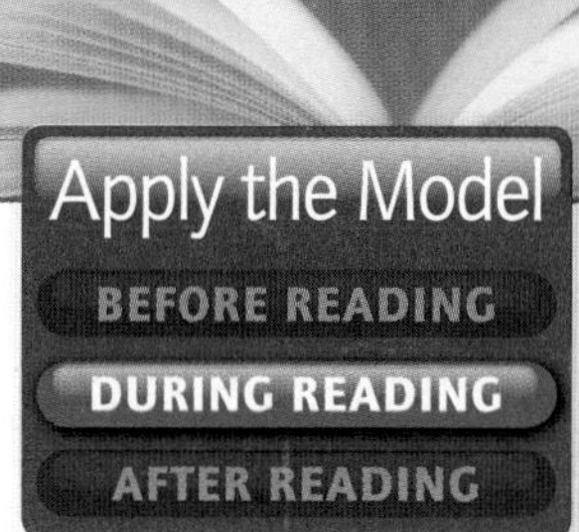

Gold

A Lyric Poem by Pat Mora

When Sun paints the desert
with its gold,
I climb the hills.
Wind runs round boulders, ruffles
my hair. I sit on my favorite rock,
lizards for company, a rabbit,
ears stiff in the shade
of a saguaro.[1]
In the wind, we're all
eye to eye.

Sparrow on saguaro watches
rabbit watch us in the gold
of sun setting.
Hawk sails on waves of light, sees
sparrow, rabbit, lizards, me,
our eyes shining,
watching red and purple sand rivers
stream down the hill.

I stretch my arms wide as the sky
like hawk extends her wings
in all the gold light of this, home. ✤

DURING READING
Analyze Literature
Imagery What do the images in this stanza help you see and feel?

DURING READING
Use Reading Skills
Identify Main Idea What does the third stanza suggest about this poem's main idea?

1. **saguaro** (sə gwär´ ə). Large cactus that grows in the southwestern United States and in northern Mexico

The speaker refers to the desert as "home." "Home" might be a place that makes us feel happy, hopeful, alive, and energized. What is a place that you might call "home"? What kinds of things make people feel most at home?

Find Meaning

1. (a) What is the setting of this poem? (b) What does the fifth line tell you about the speaker's relationship with the setting?
2. What feeling is conveyed by the speaker's word choice in describing the lizards? Explain.
3. What does the speaker call the setting at the end of the poem?

Make Judgments

4. In line 12, the speaker says the rabbit watches "us." In addition to the speaker, who or what is the rabbit watching?
5. (a) What time of day does the second stanza describe? (b) What do you think the speaker is describing in lines 17 and 18?
6. (a) List a simile that the speaker uses in the last stanza. (b) How would you describe the feeling that this simile creates?

Analyze Literature

Imagery Think about how the descriptive words and phrases used in the poem help to create images or mental pictures. List these images in the left column of a two-column chart. Then, in the right column of the chart, write about how each image affects you.

Image	Effect
"Wind runs round boulders, ruffles my hair."	This sounds like a friendly wind.

Extend Understanding

Writing Options

Creative Writing Imagine that you have been asked to submit a **poem** for publication in a school magazine. Select a real or imaginary place where you would like to spend some time. Think about the sights, smells, sounds, textures, and tastes that you associate with this place. Then write a poem about the place you have chosen.

Informative Writing Write a short **critical analysis** in which you describe the main idea of Mora's poem. Examine the use of images, the setting, the speaker's descriptions, and the poem's tone. In the introduction of your analysis, summarize the poem and state what you believe the main idea to be. Then present evidence in support of your claims.

Collaborative Learning

Discuss Author's Purpose With a partner, discuss the author's purpose for writing "Gold." Consider what the poem does for you—does it inform you, entertain you, cause you to reflect on ideas, share a perspective, or persuade you to share a viewpoint? Collect evidence from the poem to support your claims. Then discuss your findings with a larger group.

Lifelong Learning

Report on Desert Life Research one of the desert animals or plants mentioned in "Gold." Use the Internet and library to gather information about your topic. Make an outline to organize your information and create a visual aid. Then, using your outline and visual aid, give a presentation to the class.

Go to **www.mirrorsandwindows.com** for more.

Apply the Model

BEFORE READING

DURING READING

AFTER READING

Feel Like a Bird

A Lyric Poem by May Swenson

GUIDED READING

Build Background

Literary Context May Swenson's poetry is known for its vivid imagery, clever word combinations, and unusual style elements, such as the nontraditional use of capital letters. Swenson once said that poetry is "based in a craving to get through the curtains of things as they appear, to things as they are, and then into the larger, wilder space of things as they are becoming."

Reader's Context Have you ever wanted to be like an animal? What animal?

Set Purpose

Preview the poem, paying attention to its structure; note the length of the lines, the length of the stanzas, and the use of punctuation and capitalization.

Analyze Literature

Metaphor and Simile Poets often use figures of speech to compare one thing to another. A **metaphor** is an unstated comparison between two unlike things that does not use the word *like* or *as*. A **simile** is a stated comparison between two things that uses the word *like* or *as*. As you read "Feel Like a Bird," look for examples of metaphor and simile and think about the effects these figures of speech create.

Use Reading Skills

Monitor Comprehension

Taking notes as you read can help you monitor your comprehension of ideas that are stated in an unusual way. Use a note-taking chart as you read "Feel Like a Bird" to help you understand the meaning of the images that the poet presents.

Before Reading:
Set a purpose.

I am going to determine what the speaker is saying about feeling like a bird.

During Reading:
Take notes.

After Reading:
Reflect on what has been learned.

Meet the Author

May Swenson (1919–1989), born in Logan, Utah, was the oldest of ten children. Because her family spoke Swedish at home, she learned English as a second language. She won many awards for her poetry and was also a critic, editor, translator, and lecturer. Swenson's poems reflect her interest in nature and science. She had a keen eye for observing the world around her and developed a powerful way of describing what she observed.

Preview Vocabulary

snipe (snīp) *v.*, shoot from a hidden position; direct an attack

gid • dy (gi´ dē) *adj.*, feeling dizzy or unsteady

Feel Like a Bird

A Lyric Poem by May Swenson

feel like A Bird
understand
he has no hand

instead A Wing
close-lapped
mysterious thing

in sleeveless coat
he halves The Air
skipping there
like water-licked boat

lands on star-toes
finger-beak in
feather-pocket
finds no Coin

in neat head like
seeds in A Quartered
Apple eyes join
sniping at opposites
stereoscope[1] The Scene
Before

close to floor giddy
no arms to fling
A Third Sail
spreads for calm
his tail

hand better
than A Wing?
to gather A Heap
to count
to clasp A Mate?

or leap
lone-free and mount
on muffled shoulders
to span A Fate? ✣

DURING READING
Analyze Literature
Metaphor and Simile What effect is created by the figures of speech used in lines 8–11?

snipe (snīp) *v.*, shoot from a hidden position; direct an attack

gid • dy (gi´ dē) *adj.*, feeling dizzy or unsteady

DURING READING
Use Reading Skills
Monitor Comprehension
What do you think the speaker is describing in this stanza?

1. **stereoscope.** Instrument with two eyepieces that presents two photographs of a scene at slightly different angles; the combined image creates the illusion of depth so that the scene appears three-dimensional.

Poets and artists often gain inspiration from nature. What feelings and emotions do you associate with nature? Why do you think nature can have such a powerful effect on some people?

Find Meaning

1. (a) In the fifth stanza, what image does the speaker use to describe the bird's eyes? (b) Why do you think Swenson chose this image?
2. (a) What question is the speaker asking in the final two stanzas? (b) How do you think the speaker would answer these questions?

Make Judgments

3. Why do you think the speaker compares birds and people?
4. To what conclusions about birds does the speaker come?

Analyze Literature

Metaphor and Simile How does the poet use metaphor and simile to help you better understand what she is describing? Use the first column of a figurative language chart to list the comparisons you find in the poem. In the second column, write down what is being compared in each example. Then, in the third column, describe what the metaphor or simile helps you envision.

Example of Metaphor or Simile	What Is Compared	What I Envision
in sleeveless coat / he halves The Air	wings to a coat without sleeves	a person in a sleeveless coat flapping their arms

Extend Understanding

Writing Options

Creative Writing Imagine that you want to describe a plant or animal. Write a one-paragraph **descriptive essay** about that plant or animal. Think about how your subject looks, feels, moves, smells, and sounds. Focus on the most striking images that occur to you. Include at least one metaphor or simile.

Informative Writing Lyric poetry describes the emotions of a speaker and does not tell a story. Write a one-page **literary response** to explore what makes "Feel Like a Bird" a lyric poem. Consider these questions: What does this poem reveal about the speaker's emotions? How does the speaker interpret or view the bird's behavior? Then share your work in small groups.

Lifelong Learning

Research Birds Reread "Feel Like a Bird" and try to picture the bird in your mind. What type of bird do you think the poem describes? What clues lead you to this conclusion? Browse through pictures and descriptions in a field guide for ideas. Create a list of three possible candidates.

Media Literacy

Report on Birds in the Media In small groups, brainstorm and make a list of movies, songs, television programs, poems, and stories that feature birds. What do the birds represent in the examples you found? What different emotions do they evoke? Discuss your views on these questions with the group.

Go to **www.mirrorsandwindows.com** for more.

Literary Element

Understanding Sound Devices

What Are Sound Devices?

Sound is one of the most noticeable things that distinguishes poetry from prose. Poetry is often musical, having rhythms, rhymes, and other sound devices. **Sound devices** are elements that writers use to appeal to the ears of listeners or readers. In what ways does the excerpt on this page from "The Village Blacksmith" appeal to your ear?

Sound devices can have a big impact on the mood and tone of a poem. Some sound devices might contribute to a lighthearted or humorous mood or tone. Others might help convey feelings of gloom or sadness. Also, sound devices can influence a poem's meaning by adding strength to a line or by suggesting the way in which a line is meant to be read.

His hair is crisp, and black, and
long,
His face is like the tan;
His brow is wet with honest sweat,
He earns whate'er he can,
And looks the whole world in the
face,
For he owes not any man.

—HENRY WADSWORTH LONGFELLOW
"The Village Blacksmith"

Rhyme

Rhyme is the repetition of sounds at the ends of words. It is one of the most common sound devices used in poetry. For example, the word *tan* at the end of the second line in the excerpt from "The Village Blacksmith" rhymes with the word *can* in the fourth line. Because these words appear at the ends of their lines, the rhyme is referred to as an *end rhyme*. When a poem has a consistent pattern of end rhymes, it is said to have a **rhyme scheme.** You can identify the rhyme scheme by assigning a new letter to each new rhyme. For example:

His hair is crisp, and black, and long,	*a*
His face is like the tan;	*b*
His brow is wet with honest sweat,	*c*
He earns whate'er he can,	*b*

At times, a word in the middle of a line rhymes with either a word at the end of a line or a word in the middle of another line. This is called *internal rhyme*. In "The Village Blacksmith," Longfellow writes: "His brow is wet with honest sweat." Here, the word *wet* rhymes with the word *sweat,* which ends the line.

Also, rhymes are not always completely exact. Sometimes words are used, like the words *step* and *stop,* that only partially rhyme. If a rhyme is close, but not exact, it is called a *slant* or *half rhyme*. For example, in "Father William" (page 475) Lewis Carroll rhymes the word *brain* with *again*. Because this rhyme is not exact, it is a slant rhyme.

(*continued*)

Rhythm

The pattern of stressed and unstressed syllables in a line of poetry is its **rhythm.** Stressed syllables are referred to as beats. A regular and predictable pattern of stressed and unstressed syllables is called **meter.** Reading a poem aloud can help you better hear its rhythm and determine whether or not it is written in meter. For example, read these lines from "The Village Blacksmith" aloud.

His hair is crisp, and black, and long,
  His face is like the tan;

Can you hear the rhythm? Is the pattern of stressed and unstressed syllables regular and predictable? One way to help you determine whether a poem has a regular rhythm is by scanning it. Scanning is the process of marking / over stressed syllables, and ˘ over unstressed syllables.

˘ / ˘ / ˘ / ˘ /
His hair is crisp, and black, and long,

˘ / ˘ / ˘ /
  His face is like the tan;

In this case the pattern is regular. These lines are metered. Every meter is made up of feet. A **foot** is a group of two or more stressed or unstressed syllables. There are different kinds of feet. In the above passage, the poem's meter is made up of feet called *iambs* (ī´ am[b]'z). An iamb contains a single unstressed syllable followed by a single stressed syllable. The first two words in the scanned lines above, *his hair,* make up a single iambic foot.

Onomatopoeia

When a writer uses a word or phrase that sounds like the thing it names, the writer is using **onomatopoeia.** Words like *pow, crash,* and *meow* are all examples of onomatopoeia. This device can add excitement and a layer of sensory experience to description.

Alliteration, Consonance, and Assonance

Writers sometimes repeat the same consonant or vowel sound in two or more nearby words. In Galway Kinnell's poem "Blackberry Eating" (page 481), for example, the *s* sound is repeated several times in a line: "I squeeze, squinch open, and splurge." When a consonant sound is repeated at the beginnings of words, as it is in Kinnell's poem, it is called **alliteration.**

If a consonant sound is repeated at the ends or in the middles of words, it is called **consonance.** When a writer repeats vowel sounds, it is called **assonance.** In "Blackberry Eating," Kinnell writes: "the fat, overripe, icy, black blackberries." In this line, the *i* sound is repeated in the words *overripe* and *icy,* and the *a* sound is repeated in *fat, black,* and *blackberries.*

Apply the Model

BEFORE READING

DURING READING

AFTER READING

Father William

A Humorous Poem by Lewis Carroll

GUIDED READING

Build Background

Historical Context In the 1800s, English schoolchildren were often required to memorize a popular poem by Robert Southey (1774–1843) titled "Old Man's Comforts." In this poem, an old man, Father William, explains that he has good health and a cheerful attitude because he has lived a healthy, virtuous, and moral life. In *Alice's Adventures in Wonderland* (1865), Lewis Carroll poked fun at Southey's poem by having Alice recite "Father William."

Reader's Context How does it feel to be offered bad advice?

Set Purpose

Read "Father William" to determine how the rhyme contributes to the poem's mood.

Analyze Literature

Rhyme The repetition of sounds at the ends of words is called **rhyme.** *Internal rhyme* is the repetition of sounds within lines. *End rhyme* is the repetition of sounds at the ends of lines. A consistent pattern of end rhymes is called a *rhyme scheme.* Identify the rhyme scheme by assigning a new letter to each new rhyme. As you read "Father William," examine the use of rhyme.

Meet the Author

Lewis Carroll (1832–1898) is the pen name of Charles Lutwidge Dodgson, English mathematician, writer, and photographer. His father was a country parson, and he and his seven sisters and three brothers learned to entertain themselves by inventing games and telling stories. In addition to publishing academic works in the field of mathematics, Dodgson used his lively imagination to create humorous poems and stories, the most famous of which is *Alice's Adventures in Wonderland* (1865).

Use Reading Skills

Analyze the Effects of Form on Meaning The *form* of a poem involves its structure, meter, and rhyme scheme. The *structure* is the arrangement of lines and stanzas. The *meter* is the regular pattern of stressed and unstressed syllables in each line. *Rhyme* is the repetition of sounds at the ends of words. Create a two-column chart to help you analyze how each of these elements contributes to the meaning and tone of "Father William."

Form	Effect
Structure: Eight stanzas of four lines each	
Meter:	
Rhyme Scheme:	

Preview Vocabulary

in•ces•sant•ly (in' se´ s'nt lē) *adv.,* constantly

un•com•mon•ly (ən' kä´ mən lē) *adv.,* amazingly

sage (sāj) *n.,* wise man

sup•ple (sʉ´ pəl) *adj.,* flexible

Father William

A Humorous Poem
by Lewis Carroll

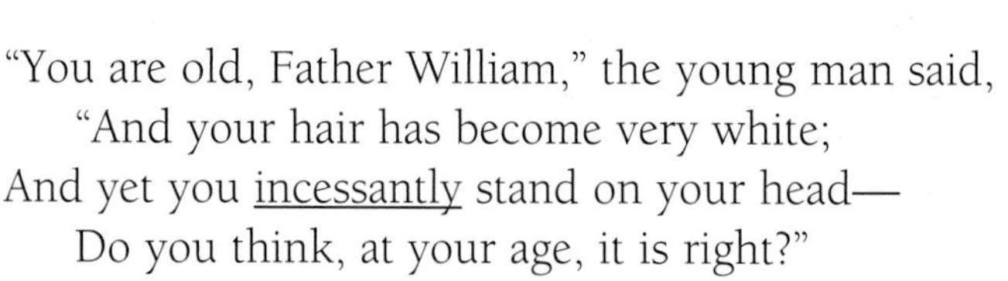

"You are old, Father William," the young man said,
"And your hair has become very white;
And yet you incessantly stand on your head—
Do you think, at your age, it is right?"

in • ces • sant • ly (in' se´ s'nt lē) *adv.*, constantly

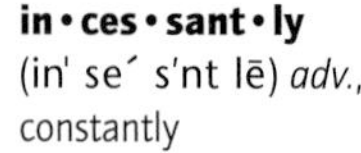

DURING READING

Analyze Literature
Rhyme In this stanza, what words rhyme? What is the rhyme scheme?

"In my youth," Father William replied to his son,
"I feared it might injure the brain;
But, now that I'm perfectly sure I have none,
Why, I do it again and again."

"You are old," said the youth, "as I mentioned before.
And have grown most uncommonly fat;
Yet you turned a back-somersault in at the door—
Pray, what is the reason of that?"

un • com • mon • ly (ən' kä´ mən lē) *adv.*, amazingly

Father William (manuscript illustration), 1865. Lewis Carroll.

"In my youth," said the sage, as he shook his gray locks.
"I kept all my limbs very supple
By the use of this ointment—one shilling[1] the box—
Allow me to sell you a couple?"

"You are old," said the youth, "and your jaws are too weak
For anything tougher than suet;[2]
Yet you finished the goose, with the bones and the beak—
Pray, how did you manage to do it?"

"In my youth," said his father, "I took to the law,
And argued each case with my wife;
And the muscular strength, which it gave to my jaw
Has lasted the rest of my life."

sage (sāj) *n.*, wise man

sup • ple (sʉ´ pəl) *adj.*, flexible

DURING READING

Use Reading Skills
Analyze Effects of Form on Meaning How does repetition work to identify the speaker in each stanza for the reader?

1. **shilling.** British coin
2. **suet.** Fat used in cooking

DURING READING

Make Connections
How do you think most parents would feel about being repeatedly reminded, "You are old"?

"You are old," said the youth, "one would hardly suppose
That your eye was as steady as ever;
Yet you balanced an eel on the end of your nose—
What made you so awfully clever?"

"I have answered three questions, and that is enough,"
Said his father. "Don't give yourself airs!
Do you think I can listen all day to such stuff?
Be off, or I'll kick you downstairs!" ✤

CULTURAL ▶▶ CONNECTION

Alice Liddell photographed by Lewis Carroll.

Wonderland Lewis Carroll's *Alice's Adventures in Wonderland,* originally titled *Alice's Adventures Under Ground,* was first published in 1865. Carroll originally wrote the Alice stories for Alice Liddell, the daughter of the dean of the school at which Carroll taught. Alice's story became so popular that Carroll wrote a sequel, *Through the Looking-Glass, and What Alice Found There.* In the Alice stories, a young girl travels through a strange, illogical fantasy world populated by quirky characters. The story is a rich tapestry of games, riddles, word play, caricatures, parody, jokes, poems, and songs. The book has been translated into more than fifty languages and has been adapted for film and the theater. What do you already know about Alice?

How did you respond to the character of Father William? Did you think he was foolish, intelligent, or strange? What people in the world remind you of Father William?

Find Meaning

1. (a) Who is the speaker in the first stanza? (b) What is surprising about the information he conveys?
2. (a) Who is the speaker in the second stanza? (b) What does he reveal about his personality?
3. (a) What explanation does Father William give for the strength of his jaw? (b) What type of explanation is this? Explain.

Make Judgments

4. What is unusual about the exchanges between father and son?
5. (a) List some of the comical images in "Father William." (b) Why do you think these images are comical?
6. (a) In what way does Father William's response to the last question differ from his other responses? (b) Why do you think he responds in this way?

Analyze Literature

Rhyme To describe a rhyme scheme, each rhyme is assigned a different lowercase letter. For example:

Jack be nimble	a
Jack be quick	b
Jack jump over	c
The candlestick	b

The rhyme scheme of these lines is *abcb*.

Review "Father William," and determine the rhyme scheme of each stanza. On a separate sheet of paper, write out the rhyme scheme. Then discuss how the rhyme scheme affects the mood of the poem.

Extend Understanding

Writing Options

Creative Writing Try to write a **humorous poem** like "Father William." Brainstorm to come up with images, sensory details, metaphors, and similes. When drafting your poem, try to follow the rhyme scheme of "Father William." When you are done, read your poem to the class.

Descriptive Writing Use the poem to write a **character sketch** of Father William. Include details from the poem and at least one direct quotation to support your claims about Father William's character. In your conclusion, be sure to sum up Father William's character in a sentence or two. Then compare your sketch with a partner's sketch.

Collaborative Learning

Discuss Hyperbole With a partner, list examples of hyperbole, or exaggeration, in "Father William." Ask yourself: What purpose does hyperbole serve in this poem? How does hyperbole contribute to the tone? When you are finished, share your list and answers to the above questions with another group.

Critical Literacy

Perform a Role-Play In groups of two, practice reading the dialogue from this poem aloud. One partner should take on the role of Father William, the other of Father William's son. Correct yourself when you make mistakes and provide constructive feedback to your partner.

Go to **www.mirrorsandwindows.com** for more.

Grammar & Style

Personal and Possessive Pronouns

"In my youth," Father William replied
to his son,
"I feared it might injure the brain...."

—LEWIS CARROLL, "Father William"

A **personal pronoun** is used in place of a person or thing. In the quotation above, *my, his, I,* and *it* are all personal pronouns. Personal pronouns may be singular, plural, or possessive.

A **possessive pronoun** shows ownership or possession. Possessive pronouns may be singular or plural.

EXAMPLES

personal pronouns

singular	*I, me, you, he, she, it, him, her*
plural	*we, us, you, they, them*
possessive	*mine, yours, his, hers, ours, theirs, its*

Use personal pronouns to refer to yourself (first person), to refer to people to whom you are speaking (second person), and to refer to other people, places, and things (third person).

EXAMPLES

first person	*I, me, my, mine, we, us, our, ours*
second person	*you, your, yours*
third person	*he, him, his, she, her, hers, it, its, they, them, their, theirs*

Identifying Personal Pronouns in Literature

On a separate sheet of paper, copy and then underline the seven personal pronouns in the following passage.

"In my youth," said the sage, as he shook his gray locks.
"I kept all my limbs very supple
By the use of this ointment—one shilling the box—
Allow me to sell you a couple?"

Sentence Improvement

For each of the following sentences, choose the correct pronoun in parentheses.

1. (Him, His) son said, "(I, me) don't think (your, you) should stand on (your, yours) head."
2. (We, Our) friends think (it, its) makes you look foolish, and I agree with (their, they) opinion.
3. Father William said, "I don't care what (your, them) friends think."
4. (Their, Them) opinions are less important than (us, ours).
5. Arguing with (me, my) wife made my jaw strong, but (I, we) never changed (hers, her) mind about (my, mine) actions.
6. Father William was angry with (his, him) son.
7. (Their, They) were not very impressed with Father William and (his, him) tricks.
8. That is not (your, yours) to take.
9. (We, Our) laughter was very loud in (their, they) house.
10. (You, Your) answer to the question was silly.

Apply the Model

BEFORE READING

DURING READING

AFTER READING

Blackberry Eating

A Lyric Poem by Galway Kinnell

GUIDED READING

Build Background

Scientific Context Several varieties of blackberries grow in the United States. Some are native to North America; others were brought from Europe. Berry breeders and farmers now cultivate many hybrid types of blackberries. Blackberries grow on vinelike bushes, many of which have sharp thorns. Although different varieties of blackberries ripen at different times, many are ready to eat in late summer. Berries ripen earlier in southern climates than they do in the north.

Reader's Context How would you describe the taste of blackberries?

Set Purpose

Preview the poem's first lines to help you determine the tone.

Analyze Literature

Alliteration The repetition of consonant sounds at the beginnings of words is called **alliteration.** Alliteration can have a big impact on a poem's tone and meaning. As you read, watch for examples of alliteration and try to determine the effect that they have.

Use Reading Skills

Identify Author's Perspective An author's perspective is the attitude the author takes toward his or her subject. Authors carefully choose their words to express their perspective. Using a chart can help you determine Galway Kinnell's attitude about eating blackberries. In the first column, write words and phrases from the poem. In the second column, write about the attitudes that these words and phrases reveal.

Word Choices	Attitudes
fat, overripe, icy	

Meet the Author

Galway Kinnell (1927–2014) was born in Providence, Rhode Island. In 1983, he received the Pulitzer Prize for *Selected Poems.* About writing poetry, Kinnell has said, "It's the poet's job to figure out what's happening within oneself, to figure out the connection between the self and the world, and to get it down in words that have a certain shape, that have a chance of lasting."

Preview Vocabulary

un • bid • den (un' bi´ d'n) *adj.*, not asked or invited

splurge (splurj) *v.*, indulge oneself extravagantly or spend a lot of money

Picking Blackberries. William McGeorge. Eaton Gallery, London.

Blackberry Eating

A Lyric Poem by Galway Kinnell

I love to go out in late September
among the fat, overripe, icy, black blackberries
to eat blackberries for breakfast,
the stalks very prickly, a penalty
they earn for knowing the black art
of blackberry-making; and as I stand among them
lifting the stalks to my mouth, the ripest berries
fall almost <u>unbidden</u> to my tongue,
as words sometimes do, certain peculiar words
like *strengths* or *squinched,*
many-lettered, one-syllabled lumps,
which I squeeze, squinch open, and <u>splurge</u> well
in the silent, startled, icy, black language
of blackberry-eating in late September. ✣

un • bid • den (ʉn' bi´ d'n) *adj.,* not asked or invited

DURING READING

Analyze Literature
Alliteration What examples of alliteration do you find in lines 10–14?

splurge (splʉrj) *v.,* indulge oneself extravagantly or spend a lot of money

What is your favorite food? What season, place, or person do you associate with that food? What words would you use to describe this food? Why do you think different people respond differently to foods?

Find Meaning

1. (a) What are the blackberries like in late September? (b) What makes this time of year special for eating blackberries?
2. (a) According to the speaker, what do "certain peculiar words" do? (b) How are these words like blackberries?

Make Judgments

3. What does the phrase "squeeze, squinch open, and splurge" suggest to you? Explain.
4. (a) What sensory details does the writer use in the poem? (b) What overall effect do these details create?

Analyze Literature

Alliteration Alliteration may be used to establish a musical effect, to create a mood, or to emphasize certain words or ideas. Consonance and assonance are sound devices that can be used in similar ways. Reread the poem to identify examples of alliteration, consonance, and assonance. Use a chart to record these examples and to describe the effects of each on the poem.

Sound Device	Effect
alliteration: "black blackberries" ; "squeeze, squinch open"	

Extend Understanding

Writing Options

Narrative Writing Think of a pleasurable experience you have had in nature. Create a list of all of the most important details from this experience. Then use this list to write a **narrative essay** that describes your experience.

Informative Writing Reread "Blackberry Eating" and consider how the first-person point of view influences the effectiveness of the poem's description. Ask yourself: How would this poem be different if the poet had used the third-person point of view? Write a **critical analysis** in which you discuss the effectiveness of the first-person point of view. Share your analysis with a partner once you have finished.

Collaborative Learning

Discuss Alliteration With a partner, discuss the use of sound devices in "Blackberry Eating." Using your sound devices two-column chart, explore the various examples of alliteration, assonance, and consonance that appear in this poem. Discuss the *overall* effect of these sound devices. Then share your findings with the class.

Lifelong Learning

Write a Poem Research three other common fruits or berries. Create a list of descriptive words, sensory details, metaphors, and similes for each. Once you have completed your list, choose the fruit or berry you find the most interesting and write a short poem about it.

Go to **www.mirrorsandwindows.com** for more.

Vocabulary & Spelling

Synonyms and Antonyms

I love to go out in late September
among the fat, overripe, icy, black
blackberries

—GALWAY KINNELL, "Blackberry Eating"

Synonyms are words that have the same, or nearly the same, meaning as another word. For example, the poet might have used the word *cold* or *freezing* in place of the word *icy* in the above lines from "Blackberry Eating." Writers will often choose a specific word instead of its synonym based on that word's connotation, or emotional association.

An **antonym** is a word that means the opposite of another word. In "Blackberry Eating," *early* is an antonym of *late, thin* is an antonym for *fat,* and *outside* is an antonym of *among*.

EXAMPLES

Word	Synonyms	Antonyms
unbidden	*uninvited*	*invited*
	unrequested	*requested*
	unasked	*asked*
	unexpected	*expected*
splurge (v)	*waste*	*save*
	indulge	*conserve*
	gorge	*preserve*
	misuse	*store*

A **thesaurus** is a useful reference for locating synonyms. Antonyms are also sometimes included.

When writing critically or creatively, it can be very useful to consult dictionaries and thesauruses. Finding the right word often involves understanding both denotations, or dictionary definitions, and connotations, or emotional associations. If you are unsure of a word's meaning, consult a dictionary. If you are looking for a word with an appropriate connotation, use a thesaurus.

Vocabulary Practice

Read the following sentences. Then, on a separate sheet of paper, write one synonym and one antonym for every underlined word.

1. The blackberries were juicy and so delicious.
2. There were very few blackberries on the bush; it was a terrible year for blackberries.
3. Last September, my family and I went on a successful blackberry picking expedition.
4. We strolled through the woods on our way to the lake.
5. The sun vanished behind the clouds as we lounged in the field.
6. The water was shimmering in the sunlight.
7. Which berry is the most difficult to pick?
8. That fruit has a very tough skin.
9. Blackberries have a very sweet flavor.
10. The fruit pickers were moving very quickly.

Spelling Practice

Consonant Blends and Digraphs

Consonant blends are clusters of consonants where each letter in the blend maintains its original sound, such as *br* or *cl. Digraphs* are two or three consonants that together make a new sound, such as *sh* or *th*. Be careful when spelling words with consonant blends or digraphs that you remember each letter in the grouping. Identify the consonant blends and digraphs in these words from "Blackberry Eating."

blackberries	splurge
breakfast	squeeze
language	stalks
prickly	strengths

The Village Blacksmith

A Narrative Poem by Henry Wadsworth Longfellow

BEFORE READING

DIRECTED READING

Build Background

Historical Context When Henry Wadsworth Longfellow wrote "The Village Blacksmith" around 1840, blacksmiths played a major role in towns and villages throughout America. The local blacksmith crafted nails, tools, wheels, and other objects made from iron and other metals. One of the blacksmith's most important jobs was making and fitting horseshoes. Since people relied on horses for almost all their transportation, as well as for farming and other heavy work, the blacksmith was a valuable and necessary member of the community.

Reader's Context Whom in your community do you admire for their hard work?

Set Purpose

Preview the number of lines in each stanza to determine how the poem is organized.

Analyze Literature

Rhythm The pattern of stressed syllables, or beats, that you hear when you read a line of poetry is called **rhythm.** Rhythm can give a poem its musical quality. A regular and predictable pattern of stressed and unstressed syllables is called meter. As you read "The Village Blacksmith," notice the number of syllables in each line and which syllables are stressed and unstressed.

Use Reading Skills

Context Clues Preview the vocabulary words from this selection as they are used in the sentences below. Try to unlock the meaning of each word using the context clues provided in the sentences.

1. The wrestler's sinewy neck and arms were signs of his tremendous strength.
2. He went from scrawny to brawny by lifting weights.
3. As the blacksmith's young apprentice pumped the bellows, the fire began to roar.
4. Her life had been wrought by sacrifice and sorrow.

Meet the Author

Henry Wadsworth Longfellow (1807–1882) was an American poet whose simple rhymes and basic American themes made his poetry extremely accessible and popular. Longfellow was among the first American poets to celebrate a young, budding American culture. The spreading chestnut tree and blacksmith shop, from the opening lines of the "The Village Blacksmith," stood along the route that Longfellow took each day to his teaching job at Harvard University in Cambridge, Massachusetts.

Preview Vocabulary

sin•ew•y (sin´ yü' ē) *adj.*, powerful; strong, lean, and clearly displaying muscles and tendons

brawn•y (brô´ nē) *adj.*, muscular, strongly built

bel•lows (be´ lôz') *n.*, device that expands and contracts to draw in and force out air, used to increase the intensity of a fire

wrought (rôt) *v.*, (archaic) past tense of work; created, shaped, or formed through hard work; formed by hammering, as on metal

The Village Blacksmith

A Narrative Poem by Henry Wadsworth Longfellow

Under a spreading chestnut tree
The village smithy[1] stands;
The smith, a mighty man is he,
With large and sinewy hands;
And the muscles of his brawny arms
Are strong as iron bands.

His hair is crisp, and black, and long,
His face is like the tan;
His brow is wet with honest sweat,
He earns whate'er he can,
And looks the whole world in the face,
For he owes not any man.

Week in, week out, from morn till night,
You can hear his bellows blow;
You can hear him swing his heavy sledge,[2]
With measured beat and slow,
Like a sexton[3] ringing the village bell,
When the evening sun is low.

And children coming home from school
Look in at the open door;
They love to see the flaming forge,[4]
And hear the bellows roar,
And catch the burning sparks that fly
Like chaff[5] from a threshing floor.

---

1. **smithy.** Blacksmith's workplace or shop
2. **sledge.** Heavy hammer, held and slung with two hands, used by blacksmiths to pound and shape metal; sledgehammer
3. **sexton.** Person in charge of taking care of a church and performing specific chores, such as ringing the church bell
4. **forge.** Furnace or very hot place where metal is heated so that it can be hammered and shaped; a blacksmith's shop
5. **chaff.** Outer covering or shell of grain seeds that is separated from the grain and discarded

sin•ew•y (sin´ yü' ē) *adj.*, powerful; strong, lean, and clearly displaying muscles and tendons

brawn•y (brô´ nē) *adj.*, muscular, strongly built

bel•lows (be´ lôz') *n.*, device that expands and contracts to draw in and force out air, used to increase the intensity of a fire

(Left) ***The Blacksmith.*** Jefferson David Chalfant. David David Gallery, Philadelphia.

He goes on Sunday to the church,
And sits among his boys;
He hears the parson pray and preach,
He hears his daughter's voice,
Singing in the village choir,
And it makes his heart rejoice.

It sounds to him like her mother's voice,
Singing in Paradise!
He needs must think of her once more,
How in the grave she lies;
And with his hard, rough hand he wipes
A tear out of his eyes.

Toiling—rejoicing—sorrowing,
Onward through life he goes;
Each morning sees some task begin,
Each evening sees it close;
Something attempted, something done,
Has earned a night's repose.

Thanks, thanks to thee, my worthy friend,
For the lesson thou hast taught!
Thus at the flaming forge of life
Our fortunes must be wrought;
Thus on its sounding anvil[6] shaped
Each burning deed and thought. ✣

---

6. anvil. Solid iron block where heated metal is placed to be hammered and shaped

wrought (rôt) *v.*, (archaic) past tense of *work*; created, shaped, or formed through hard work; formed by hammering, as on metal

MIRRORS & WINDOWS

Which of the blacksmith's traits and qualities do you find most admirable? Which of these qualities are most valued in today's world?

AFTER READING

Find Meaning

1. (a) To what does the speaker compare the blacksmith and sound of the sledge in the third stanza? (b) What does this comparison suggest about the speaker's attitude toward the blacksmith?
2. What do the blacksmith's actions in church reveal about him?

Make Judgments

3. (a) What sensory details does the speaker provide in the first two stanzas to help you picture the blacksmith? (b) What do you think the speaker wants readers to understand about the blacksmith from these details?
4. Why does the speaker thank the blacksmith in the last stanza?
5. What do you think the blacksmith symbolizes for the speaker? Explain with examples from the poem.

Analyze Literature

Rhythm Scanning a poem helps you to determine if it has a regular rhythm. Scanning is the process of marking / over stressed syllables and ˘ over unstressed syllables. Read the poem aloud, listening for the rhythm created by stressed and unstressed syllables. Transcribe the first few lines. Then mark the stressed and unstressed syllables. For example, the third line of "The Village Blacksmith" looks like this when scanned.

Line	
3	˘ / ˘ / ˘ / ˘ / The smith, a mighty man is he,

Extend Understanding

Writing Options

Narrative Writing Write a brief **short story** about the village blacksmith described in Longfellow's poem. Introduce a conflict, challenge, or problem for the blacksmith to solve. Reread "The Village Blacksmith" to find details that you can use to help you describe the setting and the blacksmith's character. Use your imagination to introduce additional details that develop the setting and characters.

Informative Writing Write a **critical analysis** that explores Longfellow's use of rhythm and rhyme in the "The Village Blacksmith." Explain the message that Longfellow communicates or reinforces through this use of rhythm and rhyme. Share your work with the class.

Critical Literacy

Conduct a Debate In a small group, conduct a debate about what the speaker means when he says "the lesson thou hast taught." Is the speaker referring to a lesson in blacksmithing? Has the speaker recently learned a specific lesson about life from the blacksmith? Be ready to back up your position with evidence from the poem.

Media Literacy

Do Research With a partner, research the bellows blacksmiths used during Longfellow's time. Use the library, the Internet, or both to find information. Write a description of how to operate this device. If possible, include a labeled sketch that identifies the parts of the bellows and shows how it works.

Go to **www.mirrorsandwindows.com** for more.

Grammar & Style

Nouns: Proper, Plural, Possessive, and Collective

Proper and Plural Nouns

He goes on Sunday to the church,
And sits among his boys;

—HENRY WADSWORTH LONGFELLOW, "The Village Blacksmith"

A **proper noun** names a specific person, place, or thing and begins with a capital letter. In the above quote, *Sunday* is the name of a specific day of the week. Proper nouns include names, dates, places, and things.

If a noun represents more than one thing, it is a **plural noun.** In the lines from "The Village Blacksmith," *boys* is a plural noun formed by adding *-s* to the end of the word. Here are several other rules for forming plural nouns.

Rule	Examples
If a noun ends in *s, sh, ch, x, or z,* add *-es.*	pass/passes, dish/dishes, catch/catches, fox/foxes
If a noun ends in *o* preceded by a consonant, add *-es.*	hero/heroes
If a noun ends in *y* preceded by a consonant, change the *y* to *i* and add *-es.*	berry/berries
For some nouns that end in *f* or *fe,* change the *f* to *v* and add *-es* or *-s.*	loaf/loaves life/lives

Possessive Nouns

Nouns that show ownership are called **possessive nouns.** An apostrophe is used to form the possessive of nouns. To form the possessive of a singular noun, add an apostrophe and an *-s* to the end of the word.

EXAMPLE

The blacksmith's muscles were very strong.

If a plural noun does not end in *s,* add an apostrophe and an *-s* to the end of the word. If the plural noun ends with an *s,* add only an apostrophe.

EXAMPLES

The children's school was only a block away.

The boys' voices carried through the church.

Collective Nouns

Collective nouns name groups that are made up of individuals. A collective noun is considered singular when the group acts together and plural when individuals within the group act independently.

EXAMPLES

singular *The choir sings for the service.*

plural *The choir sing treble, alto, and bass.*

Recognizing Nouns

Rewrite each of the following sentences on a separate sheet of paper. Then underline the nouns in each, and write the kind of noun it is.

1. The blacksmith and his family listen to the children's voices.
2. The townspeople enjoyed discussing the pastor's sermons.
3. Carl Peterson asked the choir to sing a hymn in honor of his mother's birthday.

Mother to Son

A Lyric Poem by Langston Hughes

BEFORE READING

Build Background

Historical Context The Harlem Renaissance of the 1920s and early 1930s was a culturally rich movement, centered in the Harlem district of New York City, where many African-American writers, musicians, and artists had settled. Works of the Harlem Renaissance, such as "Mother to Son," often reflect the struggles faced by African Americans who had fled the rural South searching for prosperity but frequently landed in poverty. At the same time, these works often celebrate the proud heritage of African Americans.

Reader's Context From which member of your family are you most likely to take advice? Why are you willing to listen to this person?

Set Purpose

Preview line lengths, line breaks, capitalization, punctuation, and repetition to see how ideas in the poem are organized. Read to determine how text structure affects the poem's meaning and emotional impact.

Analyze Literature

Repetition The repeated use of a word, group of words, or sound is **repetition.** Poets use repetition to emphasize and connect images, ideas, and feelings. As you read "Mother to Son," note the repeated words and ideas. Consider how this use of repetition unifies the poem and affects your understanding and appreciation of it.

Use Reading Skills

Identify Main Idea

The main idea of a poem is usually implied. Readers have to look at all the details in the poem, including specific word choices, and figure out what these details suggest. As you read "Mother to Son," use a web to keep track of details that can help you identify the main idea.

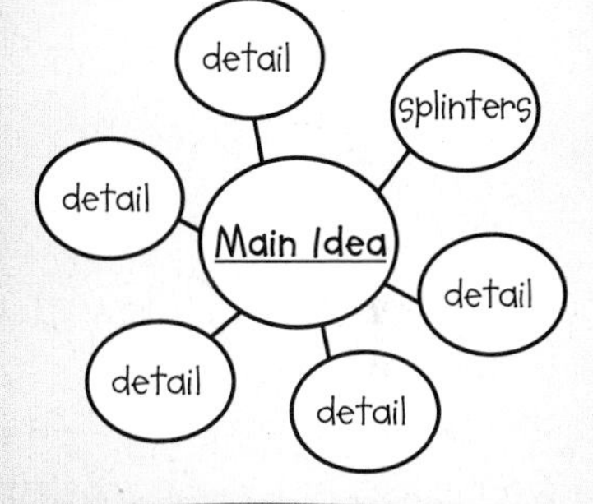

DIRECTED READING

Meet the Author

Langston Hughes (1902–1967), a key figure in the Harlem Renaissance and twentieth-century literature, published his first stories and poems in his high school magazine. Hughes was born in Joplin, Missouri, and was just a toddler when his father left the family. For the remainder of his youth, Hughes was shuffled back and forth between his mother, Carrie, and his grandmother Mary Leary Langston, a proud but poor woman who probably was the inspiration for "Mother to Son."

Mother to Son

A Lyric Poem by Langston Hughes

Mother Courage II, 1974. Charles Wilbert White. National Academy Museum, New York.

Well, son, I'll tell you:
Life for me ain't been no crystal stair.
It's had tacks in it,
And splinters,
And boards torn up,
And places with no carpet on the floor—
Bare.
But all the time
I'se been a-climbin' on,
And reachin' landin's,
And turnin' corners,
And sometimes goin' in the dark
Where there ain't been no light.
So, boy, don't you turn back.
Don't you set down on the steps
'Cause you finds it kinder[1] hard.
Don't you fall now—
For I'se still goin', honey,
I'se still climbin',
And life for me ain't been no crystal stair. ✣

1. **kinder.** Kind of

If you had to ask an adult for advice about life, what person would you ask? What experiences and circumstances make that person the most likely one to offer you sound advice?

AFTER READING

Find Meaning

1. (a) What does the speaker say her life has not been? (b) What does the speaker want her son to understand about her life from this statement?
2. (a) What details does the speaker use in lines 3–7 to explain what her life has been like? (b) What do these details reveal?

Make Judgments

3. (a) What advice is the speaker giving her son in lines 14–17? (b) Is she speaking literally or figuratively when she says "don't you turn back"? Explain.
4. Why do you think the speaker feels the need to give her son advice?
5. (a) What adjectives would you use to describe the speaker's personality? (b) How have her experiences shaped her personality? Use details from the poem in your response.

Analyze Literature

Repetition Repetition in a poem affects its sound and the images that the poem brings to mind. Use a chart to analyze the use of repetition in "Mother to Son," and then briefly state how repetition influences your understanding and appreciation of the poem.

Example	Effect
"Life for me ain't been no crystal stair."	

Extend Understanding

Writing Options

Creative Writing Put yourself in the son's place as you reread "Mother to Son." How do the speaker's words make you feel? Do you agree with everything she says? Do you find her words encouraging and her advice necessary? Would you like to contradict or modify her opinions of you? Write a brief **monologue** in which you respond to the speaker. Tell her how you feel about what she has said and why you feel that way. Deliver your monologue to the class.

Narrative Writing The speaker in "Mother to Son" reminds her son that she has struggled to overcome many obstacles in her life. In a short **personal narrative,** identify a time in your life when you struggled with a serious challenge or difficulty. Explain what you did to face this challenge or difficulty. In your conclusion, explain how this experience changed you, what you learned from it, or both.

Collaborative Learning

Discuss Challenges With a partner, discuss the kinds of challenges the speaker in this poem might have faced. Consider who the speaker is and the setting in which she lived. Think about the indignities that people suffer because of poverty and racial bigotry. Ask yourself what character strengths the speaker had to possess or develop in order to survive her situation. Compare your ideas with those of other students.

Critical Literacy

Dramatic Reading Reading a poem aloud can give you a greater appreciation of its sound and sense. Reading aloud can also offer you an opportunity to dramatize the emotions the poem evokes in you. With a partner, practice reading "Mother to Son" aloud. As you read, self-correct any errors in pronunciation or delivery. When you are ready, perform your reading for the class.

Go to **www.mirrorsandwindows.com** for more.

Under the Apple Tree

A Lyric Poem by Diana Rivera

ANCHOR TEXT

BEFORE READING

Build Background

Scientific Context The speaker in "Under the Apple Tree" has a close-up view of the natural world from under an apple tree. Apple trees belong to the *rosaceae,* or rose, family. In spring, white flowers that look like tiny roses appear on apple trees. Birds and insects pollinate the flowers, causing seeds to grow. The seeds grow into apples in about 140 to 170 days. Apples, like pears, are *pomes*—fleshy fruits consisting of an outer thickened fleshy layer and a central core with five or more seeds.

Reader's Context Where do you like to go to be alone? How do the characteristics of this special place affect your thoughts and view of the world?

Set Purpose

Look at the varied lengths of lines and stanzas in the poem and where sentences begin and end. As you read, decide how this organization affects the rhythm of the poem and the speed at which you read it.

Analyze Literature

Free Verse Poetry that attempts to follow the flow and patterns of regular speech is called **free verse.** Unlike more traditional forms of poetry, free verse does not conform to any strict line structure or to any definite rhyming pattern or meter. As you read "Under the Apple Tree," consider how the free verse form contributes to the poem's meaning.

Use Reading Skills

Identify Multiple Levels of Meaning In poetry, writers frequently use images, metaphors, similes, and sound devices to create multiple levels of meaning. By reading and rereading, you can better understand how these different levels contribute to the poem's overall effect. Use a chart like the one below to help you identify and analyze the effects of these different levels of meaning.

Images	Insects fly through the glimmering blue.
Figurative Language	
Character and Setting	

Meet the Author

Diana Rivera (b. 1954) was born and raised in Puerto Rico. She has studied art in Rome, Italy, and currently resides in Upper Grandview, New York, where she paints and writes. Rivera is the author of *Bird Language,* a collection of poetry published in 1994.

Preview Vocabulary

em•er•ald (em´ rəld) *adj.*, bright green

crev•ice (kre´ vəs) *n.*, narrow opening resulting from a split or crack

trance (trans) *n.*, stunned or dazed state

scrag•gly (skra´ g[ə]lē) *adj.*, uneven or ragged in growth or form

tread (tred) *v.*, walk on, along, or across; **trod** *past tense*

DIRECTED READING

Under the Apple Tree

A Lyric Poem by Diana Rivera

The Apple Tree II, 1916. Gustav Klimt. Private collection.

I like it here,
under the apple tree,
knotty, with its hollow
belly

here
sitting on its branch
above stone fences that separate pastures,

taking life
here
with the sun that strokes
the sides of trees
casting its shadows on emerald hills.

I like it here,
entering the dark crevice of trunks,
studying the butterfly's tiny blue hearts
on powdery wings.

Like horses with their swerved necks,
I concentrate on grass.
Earthworms insert themselves into the earth
like glossy, pink pins!

Against the green, a yellow shrub
furiously sprouts
in a trance of burning stars.

Branches are suns
that glimmer from within
taking life
here, under the apple tree,
where a crowd of petals close their eyes,

em•er•ald (em´ rəld) *adj.*, bright green

crev•ice (kre´ vəs) *n.*, narrow opening resulting from a split or crack

trance (trans) *n.*, stunned or dazed state

where scraggly layers of trunk
seem to slowly come apart.

At sunset the branch I sit
on snaps and coils.
The blue jay hastily darts, and disappears.

I like it
here
where birds now nestle and sleep,
where little, high-pitched, cricketed chirps
rise like tiny bells towards the ageless moon.

Here,
where insects,—silver specks—
fly through the glimmering blue.

Oh, but the mouse hides under the hay and
the cracks.
The horses trod down the pasture,
disappearing
like an impression of veils.

They say this apple tree is very old,
oh, but I like it here,
sitting on its rugged branch

above stone fences that separate
dark, sleepy pastures ✣

scrag•gly (skra´ g[ə]lē) *adj.*, uneven or ragged in growth or form

tread (tred) *v.*, walk on, along, or across; **trod** *past tense*

What part of this experience is similar to an experience in your own life? Is the speaker sharing a purely personal experience, or does the poem also contain a more universal message?

Find Meaning

1. (a) How does the speaker personify, or give human characteristics to, the sun in the third stanza? (b) What does this tell you about how the speaker perceives the sun?
2. (a) What details does the speaker use to describe what happens at sunset? (b) What does the speaker do when sunset comes?

Make Judgments

3. (a) What happens to the horses near the end of the poem? (b) How does the poet use this image to help conclude the poem?
4. (a) How well do you think this poem captures the speaker's experience under the apple tree? (b) What, if anything, does the speaker reveal about herself or himself through the descriptions in this poem?

INFORMATIONAL TEXT ▶▶ CONNECTION

In "Under the Apple Tree," the speaker provides a detailed description of nature as experienced from a perch on the branch of an apple tree. Although the speaker obviously appreciates the apple tree, the speaker never questions how it got there. The following excerpt from *The Botany of Desire: A Plant's-Eye View of the World* is by **Michael Pollan** (b. 1955). Pollan, an award-winning journalist and author of several critically acclaimed books, often writes about the connection between people and their environment. Raised on Long Island in New York, the author currently lives in San Francisco's Bay Area and is a professor of journalism at the University of California, Berkeley. As you read this passage, look for details that provide insight into how apple trees spread across the American landscape.

from The Botany of Desire

An Essay by Michael Pollan

If you happened to find yourself on the banks of the Ohio River on a particular afternoon in the spring of 1806—somewhere just to the north of Wheeling, West Virginia, say—you would probably have noticed a strange makeshift craft drifting lazily down the river. At the time, this particular stretch of the Ohio, wide and brown and bounded on both sides by steep shoulders of land thick with oaks and hickories, fairly boiled with river traffic, as a ramshackle armada[1] of keelboats and barges ferried settlers from the comparative civilization of Pennsylvania to the wilderness of the Northwest Territory.[2]

The peculiar craft you'd have caught sight of that afternoon consisted of a pair of hollowed-out logs that had been lashed together to form a rough catamaran, a sort of canoe plus sidecar.[3] In one of the dugouts lounged the figure of a skinny man of about thirty, who may or may not have been wearing a burlap coffee sack for a shirt and a tin pot for a hat. According to the man in Jefferson County who deemed the scene worth recording, the fellow in the canoe appeared to be snoozing without a care in the world, evidently trusting in the river to take him wherever it was he wanted to go. The other hull, his sidecar, was riding low in the water under the weight of a small mountain of seeds that had been carefully

1. **armada.** Fleet of ships
2. **Northwest Territory.** In the early days of American history, the large expanse of land that became Ohio, Indiana, Illinois, Michigan, Wisconsin, and part of Minnesota
3. **sidecar.** Separate place for a passenger to sit, attached to the side of a vehicle, or in this case, a canoe

blanketed with moss and mud to keep them from drying out in the sun.

The fellow snoozing in the canoe was John Chapman, already well known to people in Ohio by his nickname: Johnny Appleseed. He was on his way to Marietta, where the Muskingum River pokes a big hole into the Ohio's northern bank, pointing straight into the heart of the Northwest Territory. Chapman's plan was to plant a tree nursery along one of that river's as-yet-unsettled tributaries, which drain the fertile, thickly forested hills of central Ohio as far north as Mansfield. In all likelihood, Chapman was coming from Allegheny County in western Pennsylvania, to which he returned each year to collect apple seeds, separating them out from the fragrant mounds of pomace[4] that rose by the back door of every cider mill. A single bushel of apple seeds would have been enough to plant more than three hundred thousand trees; there's no way of telling how many bushels of seed Chapman had in tow that day, but it's safe to say his catamaran was bearing several whole orchards into the wilderness.

The image of John Chapman and his heap of apple seeds riding together down the Ohio has stayed with me since I first came across it a few years ago in an out-of-print biography. The scene, for me, has the resonance[5] of myth—a myth about how plants and people learned to use each other, each doing for the other things they could not do for themselves, in the bargain changing each other and improving their common lot.

Henry David Thoreau once wrote that "it is remarkable how closely the history of the apple tree is connected with that of man," and much of the American chapter of that story can be teased out of Chapman's story. It's the story of how pioneers like him helped domesticate the frontier by seeding it with Old World plants. "Exotics," we're apt to call these species today in disparagement,[6] yet without them the American wilderness might never have become a home. What did the apple get in return? A golden age: untold new varieties and half a world of new habitat.

As an emblem of the marriage between people and plants, the design of Chapman's peculiar craft strikes me as just right, implying as it does a relation of parity[7] and reciprocal[8] exchange between its two passengers. More than most of us do, Chapman seems to have had a knack for looking at the world from the plants' point of view—"pomocentrically,"[9] you might say. He understood he was working for the apples as much as they were working for him. Perhaps that's why he sometimes likened himself to a bumblebee, and why he would rig up his boat the way he did. Instead of towing his shipment of seeds behind him, Chapman lashed the two hulls together so they would travel down the river side by side. ✣

4. **pomace.** Pulpy remains of apples or other fruits after they are smashed and pressed to extract juice
5. **resonance.** Ability to evoke an emotional response
6. **disparagement.** Criticism
7. **parity.** Equality
8. **reciprocal.** Mutual
9. **pomocentrically.** Made-up word meaning "from the fruit's unique viewpoint"

TEXT TO TEXT CONNECTION

What is the main difference between the poem's speaker's relationship with nature and John Chapman's relationship with nature?

AFTER READING

Analyze Literature

Free verse While free verse lacks formal elements, such as a consistent rhyme scheme or meter, that give poetry its traditional structure, free verse is still structured to enhance meaning. In "Under the Apple Tree," consider how the lengths of the lines emphasize the words on those lines. Also, how do sound devices, such as alliteration, assonance, and consonance, affect the poem's rhythm and meaning? Use a two-column chart to determine how these elements affect "Under the Apple Tree."

Element	Effect
Lines made up of the single word here	Emphasizes speaker's attachment to setting

Extend Understanding

Writing Options

Creative Writing A lyric poem expresses the personal feelings and thoughts of a speaker and does not tell a story. Write a **lyric poem** describing a secret hideaway that you have or can imagine. Your poem does not have to rhyme, but it should contain poetic elements, such as alliteration, assonance, consonance, imagery, and figures of speech. Revisit "Under the Apple Tree" and other lyric poems you have read for ideas about how to structure your poem.

Argumentative Writing Write a brief **newspaper editorial** in which you praise an element of nature. Introduce your topic in a lead sentence that will catch a reader's interest. In the body of your editorial, explain or describe your topic. Organize information so that your strongest arguments come first. End your editorial with a "call to action" in which you encourage readers to do or believe something. Share your editorial with the class.

Lifelong Learning

Study Trees Use library resources or the Internet to find information on the relationship between trees and the quality of life in neighborhoods. Keep a log to track the information you find and note sources. Look for answers to questions such as: How do trees affect air and water quality? What resources do trees provide for animals and humans? Use your findings to explain to a group of younger students why we need trees.

Media Literacy

List Poetry Sites Develop a list of at least five kids' amateur poetry sites. Include a review for each site. Critique each site by evaluating elements such as design, content, and ease of use. Finally, rank each site and use that ranking to organize your list. Before searching for the sites, create a list of criteria, or standards, by which to evaluate each element.

Go to **www.mirrorsandwindows.com** for more.

Grammar & Style

Reflexive and Intensive Pronouns

Reflexive Pronouns

Earthworms insert themselves into the
earth
like glossy, pink pins!

—DIANA RIVERA, "Under the Apple Tree"

A **reflexive pronoun** refers back to a noun or pronoun previously used. It indicates that the subject has done something *to* or *for* itself. Reflexive pronouns are formed by adding the suffix *-self* or *-selves* to a pronoun. In the quotation above, *themselves* is a reflexive pronoun that refers back to the noun *earthworms.* Reflexive pronouns may be either singular or plural.

EXAMPLES

myself, herself, himself, ourselves, yourself, yourselves, themselves

The subject of a reflexive pronoun may be implied. A sentence such as "Don't *you* fool yourself" is often written, "Don't fool yourself." The subject (you) is implied. *Yourself* is a reflexive pronoun that refers back to the pronoun *you.*

Intensive Pronouns

Intensive pronouns are used to emphasize a noun or pronoun. In the sentence, "The author herself answered the questions," the word *herself* emphasizes that the author answered the questions rather than having someone else do it. Intensive pronouns don't indicate any action on the part of the noun or pronoun. They are typically added after the word they are intended to emphasize.

EXAMPLES

The boys themselves were offering to help.

I myself am going to send the package.

Occasionally, an intensive pronoun is placed several words away from the noun or pronoun it emphasizes.

EXAMPLE

I prefer sunny days myself.

Identifying Reflexive and Intensive Pronouns

On a separate sheet of paper, rewrite the following sentences. Underline once each reflexive pronoun and the noun or pronoun to which it refers. Underline twice each intensive pronoun and the noun or pronoun to which it refers.

1. I reminded myself to be careful climbing the apple tree.
2. The tree itself provided plenty of shade.
3. Did you paint that picture yourself?
4. The scent of apple blossoms spreads itself across the landscape.
5. The birds hid themselves behind the branches.
6. We ourselves were getting sleepy.
7. You don't have to eat by yourself.
8. We ourselves are unhappy with the work.
9. Johnny Appleseed himself could not have predicted the outcome of his project.
10. He didn't seem capable of just being himself.

THE TROPICS IN NEW YORK

A Lyric Poem by Claude McKay

DIRECTED READING

BEFORE READING

Build Background

Cultural Context The speaker of "The Tropics in New York" is a Jamaican living in New York City in the 1920s. Situated in the Caribbean Sea, in the British West Indies, the island of Jamaica has a hot climate, suitable for growing a variety of tropical fruits and spices. In the early 1900s, Jamaica's economy relied heavily on the export of fruits, especially to the United States. Mangoes, papayas, and guavas would have been unfamiliar to many Americans. Yet, to Jamaican immigrants, these foods would have evoked memories of their tropical island home.

Reader's Context What foods remind you of home? What memories of home do you associate with these foods?

Set Purpose

Before you begin reading, skim the poem to identify the rhyme scheme and stanza lengths.

Analyze Literature

Rhyme Scheme When a rhyme appears at the end of a line of poetry, that rhyme is referred to as an *end rhyme.* When a poem has a consistent pattern of end rhymes, it is said to have a **rhyme scheme.** You can identify the rhyme scheme by assigning a new letter to each new rhyme. As you read "The Tropics in New York," note its rhyme scheme.

Use Reading Skills

Analyze Cause and Effect In poetry, writers use sensory language to describe personal and emotional responses to certain events. The event is the *cause.* The response is the *effect.* Understanding the cause-and-effect relationships in a poem can help you figure out its meaning and message. As you read "The Tropics in New York," use a chart to keep track of causes and effects.

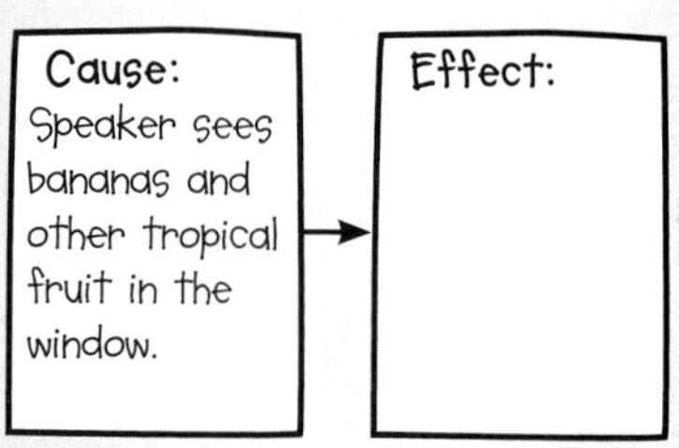

Preview Vocabulary

la•den (lād´ən) *adj.*, weighed down

mys•ti•cal (mis´ ti kəl) *adj.*, having a spiritual quality; mysterious

ben•e•dic•tion (be' nə dik´ shən) *n.*, blessing

Meet the Author

Claude McKay (1890–1948), poet and novelist, lived for many years in the Harlem section of New York City. He was an influential figure in the early days of the Harlem Renaissance in the 1920s. McKay emigrated from Jamaica to the United States in 1912 at a time when racism was prevalent and violence against African Americans was common. While much of McKay's writing reflects the anger and frustration he experienced because of racism, some of his poems, such as "The Tropics in New York," have more wistful themes.

Harvest Scene with Twelve People, c. 20th century. R. Mervilus. Private collection.

THE TROPICS IN NEW YORK

A Lyric Poem by Claude McKay

Bananas ripe and green, and ginger-root,
Cocoa in pods and alligator pears,[1]
And tangerines and mangoes and grapefruit,
Fit for the highest prize at parish[2] fairs,

Set in the window, bringing memories
Of fruit-trees laden by low-singing rills,[3]
And dewy dawns, and mystical blue skies
In benediction over nun-like hills.

My eyes grew dim, and I could no more gaze;
A wave of longing through my body swept,
And, hungry for the old, familiar ways,
I turned aside and bowed my head and wept. ✣

1. **alligator pears.** Avocados; the name given to the fruit by English people living in Jamaica
2. **parish.** One of twelve separate districts in Jamaica, each with its own local government
3. **rills.** Small brooks or streams

la • den (lād´ən) *adj.*, weighed down

mys • ti • cal (mis´ ti kəl) *adj.*, having a spiritual quality; mysterious

ben • e • dic • tion (be' nə dik´ shən) *n.*, blessing

When have you felt homesick for a place or missed someone, such as a relative or close friend? Why do you think homesickness and a longing for the past are frequent themes in literature and art?

AFTER READING

Find Meaning

1. (a) Where does this poem take place? (b) What is the speaker doing?

2. What does the speaker describe in the second stanza?

3. (a) What is the speaker doing at the end of the poem? (b) What caused this situation?

Make Judgments

4. (a) How does the mood of the poem change from the beginning to the end? (b) How do the changes in the mood mirror the changes in the speaker's emotions?

5. In what ways is physical hunger like emotional hunger?

Analyze Literature

Rhyme scheme How does the rhyme scheme in "The Tropics in New York" help to establish tone and convey meaning? Use a chart to identify the rhyme scheme in the poem. Then explain how the rhyme scheme contributes to the poem's tone and meaning.

Lines	Rhyming Words	Rhyme Scheme
1–4	ginger-root grapefruit	
5–8		
9–12		

Extend Understanding

Writing Options

Creative Writing Imagine that you are the speaker in "The Tropics in New York." You grew up among family and friends on a small farm on the lush tropical island of Jamaica. Now you are living in an apartment in New York City. Write a **personal letter** back home. Tell about the fruit and the feelings that it evoked in you, and explain what you miss most about home and why.

Informative Writing Write an **informative essay** comparing and contrasting "Blackberry Eating" (page 481) and "The Tropics in New York." In the introductory paragraph, introduce the poems and their authors and provide a brief summary of each poem. In the body paragraphs, describe the poems' similarities and differences using evidence from each to support your ideas. Be sure to compare form, subject matter, and tone. In the concluding paragraph, restate your main points of comparison. Share your work with the class.

Critical Literacy

Conduct a Television Interview Pretend you are a television reporter and that your assignment is to interview the speaker in "The Tropics in New York." Keep in mind that an experienced reporter knows the importance of gathering background information and preparing a list of questions in advance of an interview. Create a set of questions to use during your interview. Then interview a partner who is pretending to be the speaker of this poem.

Lifelong Learning

Research New Foods Although many of the fruits and spices mentioned in "The Tropics in New York" were once considered new and exotic, today they are found in most supermarkets. Pizza, tacos, and egg rolls are other foods that were fairly recently brought to the United States. Learn about another food new to the United States. Organize the information you find and summarize your findings for the class.

Go to **www.mirrorsandwindows.com** for more.

Comparing Texts

Unfolding Bud

A Lyric Poem by Naoshi Koriyama

How to Eat a Poem

A Lyric Poem by Eve Merriam

DIRECTED READING

BEFORE READING

Build Background

Literary Context Both "Unfolding Bud" and "How to Eat a Poem" are free verse lyric poems. **Free verse** is poetry that does not use a regular rhyme scheme or meter. It originated in the late 1800s among French poets who wanted to use the rhythms of natural speech.

Reader's Context What images would you use to describe your favorite poem or song?

Set Purpose

Skim these poems to predict the authors' purposes. Then read to confirm or change your predictions.

Meet the Authors

Naoshi Koriyama, professor of English at Toyo University in Tokyo, Japan, has studied in the United States and has written some of his best-known work in English rather than in his native Japanese. In addition to writing his own work, he has translated the works of several contemporary Japanese poets into English.

Eve Merriam (1916–1992) was born in Pennsylvania. After college, she lived in New York City, where she wrote for radio. Later, she began teaching and lecturing. Merriam published her first book, *Family Circle,* in 1946. Although poetry was always Merriam's first love, she is also well known as a playwright and fiction writer.

Compare Literature: Metaphor A **metaphor** is a figure of speech in which one thing is spoken or written about as if it were another. The reader is invited to compare the qualities that these two things have in common. As you read the following poems, look for examples of metaphor. Use a two-column chart like the one below to keep track of the metaphors in each poem.

"Unfolding Bud"	"How to Eat a Poem"
poem and water-lily bud	

Unfolding Bud

A Lyric Poem by Naoshi Koriyama

One is amazed
By a water-lily bud
Unfolding
With each passing day,
Taking on a richer color
And new dimensions.

One is not amazed,
At a first glance,
By a poem,
Which is as tight-closed
As a tiny bud.

Yet one is surprised
To see the poem
Gradually unfolding,
Revealing its rich inner self,
As one reads it
Again
And over again. ✤

When have you been unimpressed with something, like a piece of music or literature, and then later learned to love or admire it? Why do you think people's opinions change over time?

Find Meaning

1. (a) What experience is the speaker describing in the first stanza of "Unfolding Bud"? (b) What feelings does the speaker seem to have about this experience?
2. (a) In the second stanza, to what does the speaker compare a poem? (b) What does this description convey about the speaker's attitude toward poetry? Explain.

Make Judgments

3. (a) What experience does the speaker describe in the third stanza? (b) In what way has the speaker's attitude changed?
4. What words seem to tie the ideas in the first and third stanzas together?

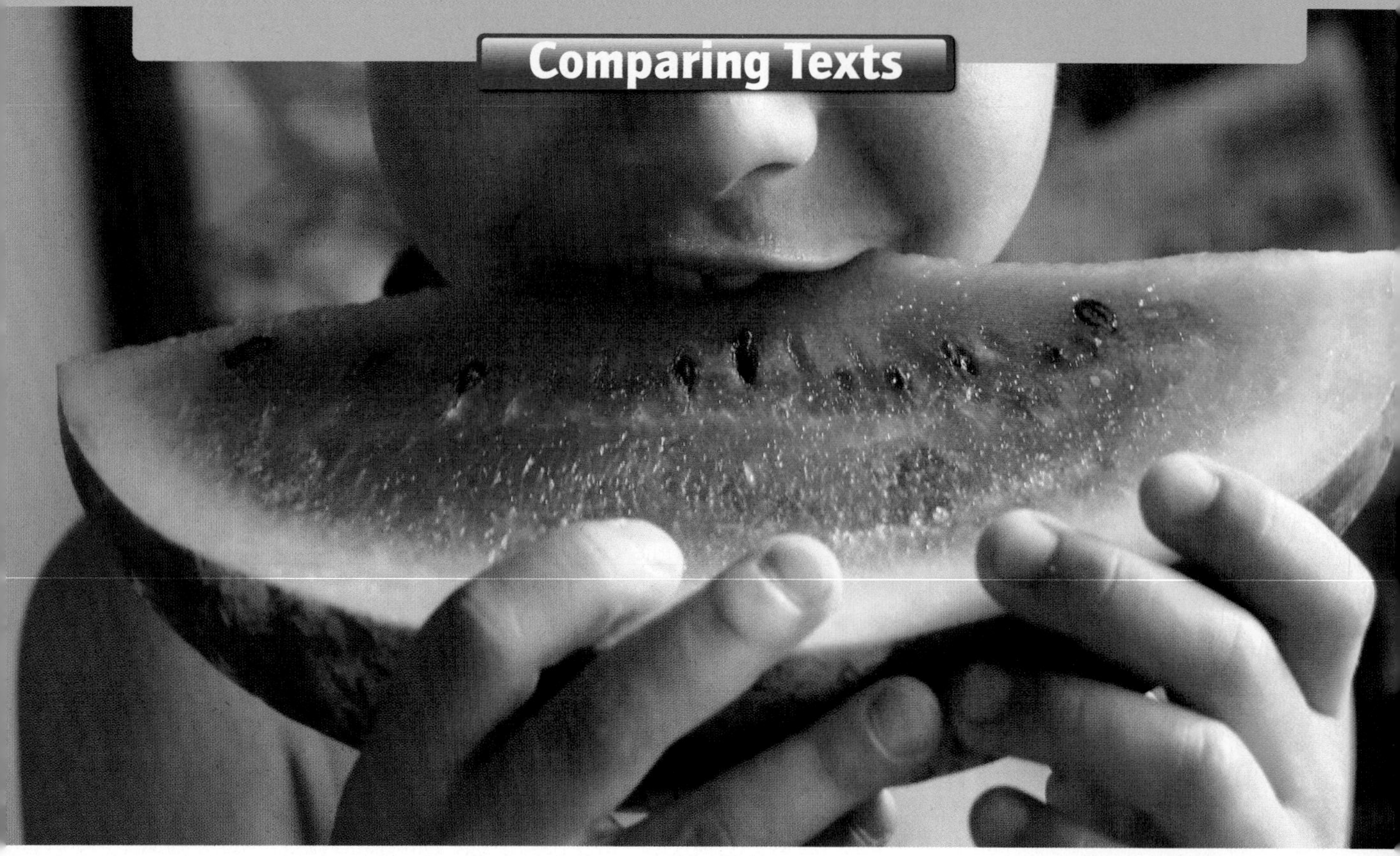

How to Eat a Poem

A Lyric Poem
by Eve Merriam

Don't be polite.
Bite in.
Pick it up with your fingers and lick the juice
that may run down your chin.
It is ready and ripe now, whenever you are.
You do not need a knife or fork or spoon
or plate or napkin or tablecloth.
For there is no core
or stem
or rind
or pit
or seed
or skin
to throw away. ✤

MIRRORS & WINDOWS

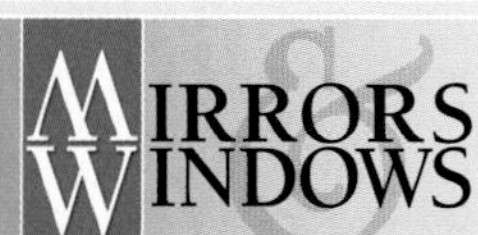

How might a piece of art, like a poem, song, or painting, make you feel liberated? How would you describe this experience? Why do you think the arts can have this effect on people?

AFTER READING

Find Meaning

1. (a) What is unexpected about the title "How to Eat a Poem"? (b) What does the title suggest about the poem?
2. (a) What utensils does the speaker say you do not need while reading a poem? (b) What does not needing special tools or utensils suggest about reading poetry?

Make Judgments

3. To what type of food do you think Merriam is comparing poetry? Explain.
4. (a) What suggestions does Merriam give to a poetry reader? (b) How do these suggestions about "eating" translate into suggestions about "reading"?

Compare Literature

Metaphor An *extended metaphor* in poetry is a comparison between two things that runs throughout a poem. Review the details from "Unfolding Bud" and "How to Eat a Poem" that you recorded in your chart to answer the following questions.

1. What is the extended metaphor in each poem?
2. Based on the metaphor in "Unfolding Bud," how do you think Koriyama thinks people should approach reading poetry? Explain.
3. Based on the metaphor in "How to Eat a Poem," how do you think Merriam wants people to approach reading poetry? Explain.

Extend Understanding

Writing Options

Descriptive Writing Think about an activity such as a sport or a hobby that you enjoy. Write a short **descriptive essay** or a **poem** in which you use an extended metaphor to describe how you feel about the activity. Remember that your metaphor should extend through the entire course of your poem or essay. Once you have finished, share your work with the class.

Argumentative Writing Reread "Unfolding Bud" and "How to Eat a Poem," and evaluate the effectiveness of both poems' use of metaphor. Ask yourself: Which poem uses a more effective metaphor for poetry? Write an **argumentative essay** in which you state your position and defend it with evidence from these texts. Organize your essays so that your strongest evidence and arguments are presented first.

Critical Literacy

Hold a Panel Discussion With your classmates, form a panel to discuss the effectiveness of these two poems' use of metaphor. Always be prepared to clarify any statements you make and to present evidence in support of your claims. Be respectful of others' opinions, and actively listen to their arguments.

Lifelong Learning

Write a Biography Use the Internet and library to research the life of one of the poets in this lesson or another poet from the unit. Then write a brief biography. Include all of the vital details from that poet's life, such as his or her place and year of birth. Also, be sure to give the reader a sense of the poet's writing style.

 Go to **www.mirrorsandwindows.com** for more.

haiku

Haiku by Matsuo Bashō, Yosa Buson, and Kobayashi Issa
translated by Robert Hass

DIRECTED READING

BEFORE READING

Build Background

Historical Context Haiku is a poetic form that originated more than five hundred years ago in Japan. Originally associated with a traditional longer form known as the *tanka,* haiku gained popularity and evolved into its present form as a result of Matsuo Bashō, one of Japan's greatest poets. Many of the haiku that we associate with Bashō, though, are in fact the first three lines from longer poems known as *renga*.

Reader's Context When have you witnessed something startling or beautiful?

Set Purpose

Before you begin reading, examine these poems' structures. What characteristics do all three poems share? In what ways does the structure affect the meaning?

Analyze Literature

Haiku The poetic form known as **haiku** is very short and precise. It has five syllables in the first line, seven in the second line, and five in the third line. A traditional haiku presents a single, powerful image from the natural world. Because these three poems have been translated from Japanese into English, the traditional line lengths have been altered. As you read these poems, try to fully visualize each image.

Use Reading Skills

Compare and Contrast
Compare and contrast the elements in these poems to gain a better understanding of each one. Specifically, compare imagery, tone, structure, and use of figurative language. Use a table like the one below to help you.

	Issa	Bashō	Buson
Imagery			
Tone			
Structure			
Figurative Language			

Meet the Authors

Matsuo Bashō (1644–1694) was a haiku master and a teacher. In 1689 he grew restless, so he sold his house and began to travel. The result was his masterpiece *Narrow Road to the Far North.*

Yosa Buson (1716–1783) was born near Osaka, Japan. He earned his living as a painter but considered himself a poet.

Kobayashi Issa (1763–1827) was born in a small village in the mountains of Japan. Issa's poetry is filled with images of tiny creatures, especially mice, lice, and fleas.

haiku

Haiku by
Matsuo Bashō, Yosa Buson,
and Kobayashi Issa
translated by Robert Hass

Frog and Plum Tree, c. 19th century. Kishi Chikudo.

The old pond—
a frog jumps in,
sound of water. ✤

—Matsuo Bashō

Misty grasses,
quiet waters,
it's evening. ✤

—Yosa Buson

Summer night—
even the stars
are whispering to each other. ✤

—Kobayashi Issa

How did the images in each of these poems affect you? Why do you think artists often use the natural world as a subject and a source of inspiration?

Find Meaning

1. (a) How does the frog alter the setting in the Bashō haiku? (b) Does this change seem surprising, or ordinary? Explain.
2. (a) What time of day does Buson's haiku describe? (b) In what way are the images appropriate to this time of day?

Make Judgments

3. (a) What kind of figurative language appears in Issa's haiku? (b) Describe the effect that this figure of speech has on you.
4. Which haiku made the strongest impression on you? Explain.

INFORMATIONAL TEXT ▶▶ CONNECTION

In these haiku, the poets describe a single moment in the natural world. In the following excerpt from **Steven Harvey**'s book of personal essays, *Lost in Translation,* Harvey discovers how difficult it is to translate haiku. Harvey is a professor of English and the author of *Geometry of Lilies: Life and Death in an American Family.*

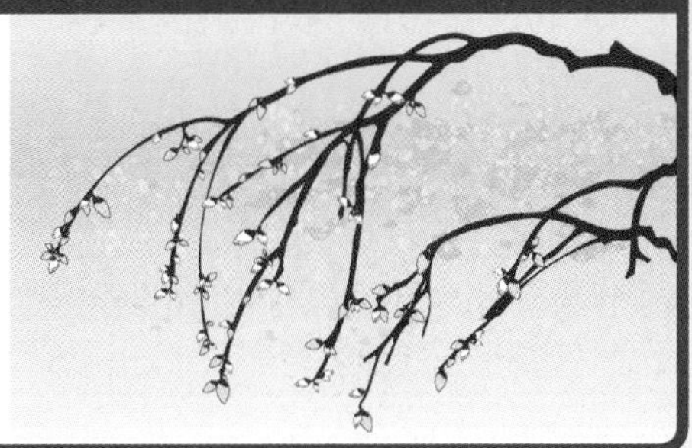

from Lost in Translation

An Essay by Steven Harvey

Armed with my book of Japanese kana[1] and her calculator-like word-finder, Junko and I sat at the dining room table and translated haiku—at least, we tried. I printed a transliterated[2] version of the haiku on the page in front of us and Junko read through it, her hand opening and closing as she counted off the syllables with her fingers.

"Yes, haiku," she said, when her fingers closed into a fist at the end of the five-syllable last line. She scratched the poison ivy under her eye and began writing English words above the Japanese. Over the word *ana* she wrote "hole" and over *ya* she wrote a colon.

"Haiku very boring," she said, opening her eyes wide as she always does when she is excited. "But if you see in your mind—is okay."

Above the syllable *no* she wrote " 's" but stumbled on the word in front of it. "Shoji," she whispered, "how say that." Eyes wide, she typed quickly into her word-finder. "Shoji like sliding door," she mumbled, "but...." Then she showed me the definition on her machine: "A sliding door with a piece of Japanese paper on a lattice."

"Not good for Sam," she added with a giggle. She brought her hand down in a mock karate chop and said, "Bam."

"That's for sure," I said.

She wrote "sliding door" and the word "then" above the long first word in the first line and "milky way" above the last word in the poem.

"Ama-no-gawa," I said in her language, haltingly, like a child—the word, not a word for me, but a plaything on my tongue.

"Mil-ky way," she answered. "Yes."

After a half hour of poking around at this text, our literal translation of Issa's immortal haiku looked like this:

Then:
Sliding door's hole's
Milky Way.

We both examined the sheet for a while, not sure what to do next—this was our first experiment in translating haiku, and the results seemed, well, meager.

"Words and meaning are very different," she said, apologetically. "You must picture."

Despairing of any verbal solution, she drew a stick figure picture of a person under a window with a hole in the shade. Then she

1. **kana.** Japanese writing
2. **transliterated.** Written in the characters of a different alphabet

drew several lines from the hole to the man.

"Moonlight," she said, still drawing the lines—as if the figure were bathed in it. "Moonlight."

I looked back at her, puzzled, and pointed out that there was no mention of moon in the poem.

"Always moon in haiku—if night, always moon. I *sure*." She scratched the poison ivy again just under the rim of her glasses. "Every peoples in Japan know this shoji and this moon," she said. "I *sure*. Must picture moon."

She looked at me and opened her eyes wide again, as if I might look through them and see what she sees. For a moment we shared what is lost in translation. ✣

TEXT TO TEXT CONNECTION

What does Harvey's experience trying to translate haiku from Japanese into English suggest to you about the haiku you have just read?

AFTER READING

Analyze Literature

Haiku Haiku is known for its shortness and use of imagery. These images are intended to elevate the reader to a specific emotional state. What emotions did you experience while reading these three haiku? Use a two-column chart to describe the emotions you experienced.

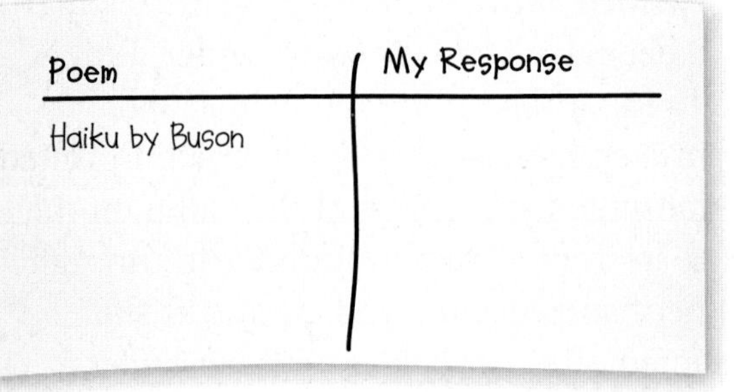

Extend Understanding

Writing Options

Creative Writing Imagine that you are compiling a collection of haiku for a book. In order to make readers aware of your book, you will need to write an **advertisement.** Explain to readers why they should be excited about your collection and what they can expect to encounter in your book.

Explanatory Writing Write **instructions** for a photographer taking snapshots of the things described in one of the three poems. Include time of day, setting, and other elements necessary to capture the mood and content. If possible, exchange instructions with a classmate and try following the steps. Suggest revisions to the instructions based on your experience and results.

Media Literacy

Compare Translations Use the library to find collections of haiku. Look for different versions of the same poems. In what ways do the translations differ? What elements remain the same? Which translation do you like the best? Write down your responses to these questions along with the haiku and the translators of each.

Lifelong Learning

Origins of Haiku Using the library, research the history of haiku. Try to determine the cultural and historical surroundings in which haiku emerged. What was happening in the culture when poets began writing haiku? How has haiku changed over time? Write a summary of your findings.

Go to **www.mirrorsandwindows.com** for more.

A Concrete Poem by E. E. Cummings

BEFORE READING

Build Background

Literary Context One of the best known poets of the twentieth century, E. E. Cummings wrote during a time when literature was changing dramatically. Writers, especially poets, were taking bold new chances in the way they wrote. Cummings himself was known for his unique use of punctuation, spelling, and capitalization.

Reader's Context What have you tried to describe that seemed to resist description? How might figurative language and sensory details help express your ideas?

Set Purpose

Before you begin reading, preview the poem by examining its structure, the use of capitals and punctuation, and the poem's shape on the page. Consider how these elements affect the poem's meaning.

Analyze Literature

Concrete Poetry A **concrete poem,** or shape poem, is a poem with a shape that suggests the thing it describes. For example, the words in a concrete poem about a swan would be set on the page to physically resemble a swan. As you read "the sky was," try to determine what the shape of the poem suggests.

Use Reading Skills

Text Organization In poetry, the way in which a poem is organized is very important. Different kinds of organization are used for different kinds of poetry. In a concrete poem, the text is organized to create a visual effect. As you read the poem, try to determine how its shape influences your interpretation. Use a two-column chart like the one below to record details from the poem and their effects.

Details	Effects
the / sky / was	These lines seem like smoke trailing off.

DIRECTED READING

Meet the Author

Edward Estlin Cummings (1894–1962), the son of a distinguished clergyman, was born in Cambridge, Massachusetts. Cummings attended Harvard University, where he studied literature and classical and modern languages. During World War I, he volunteered to serve as an ambulance driver in France and was imprisoned by French authorities for writing letters that criticized the war. At the time of his death, Cummings was one of the most popular poets in the nation.

Preview Vocabulary

lu • mi • nous (lü´ mə nəs) *adj.,* emitting or reflecting steady, glowing light

spry (sprī) *adj.,* energetic; lively

the sky was

A Concrete Poem by E. E. Cummings

the
  sky
    was
can dy <u>lu</u>
<u>minous</u>
      edible
<u>spry</u>
    pinks shy
lemons
greens coo l choc
olate
s.
    un der,
  a lo
  co
mo
  tive s pout
   ing
     vi
     o
     lets ✤

lu • mi • nous (lü´ mə nəs) *adj.*, emitting or reflecting steady, glowing light

spry (sprī) *adj.*, energetic; lively

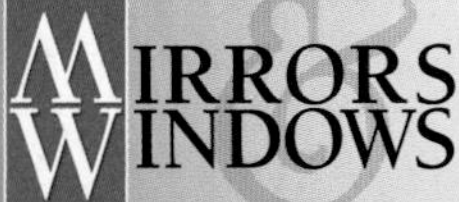

When have you seen a brightly colored or strangely colored sky? How would you describe it? What words would you use? Which things or ideas seem to defy description?

AFTER READING

Find Meaning

1. (a) What appears *edible* to the speaker? (b) What do you think the speaker means by this?
2. (a) What is introduced into the setting after the comma? (b) What is it doing?

Make Judgments

3. What images did you find most compelling in this poem? Explain.
4. In your opinion, how do sensory details affect the poem?

Analyze Literature

Concrete Poetry For a poem to be concrete, it must physically resemble the thing that it describes. Some concrete poems are very precise; others are more abstract. What shape do you think "the sky was" is attempting to imitate? On a separate sheet of paper, draw what you think Cummings's poem is imitating. Then name the object that Cummings's poem resembles. Use a web to help create your drawing. In the outer ovals list details that suggest the object the poem describes.

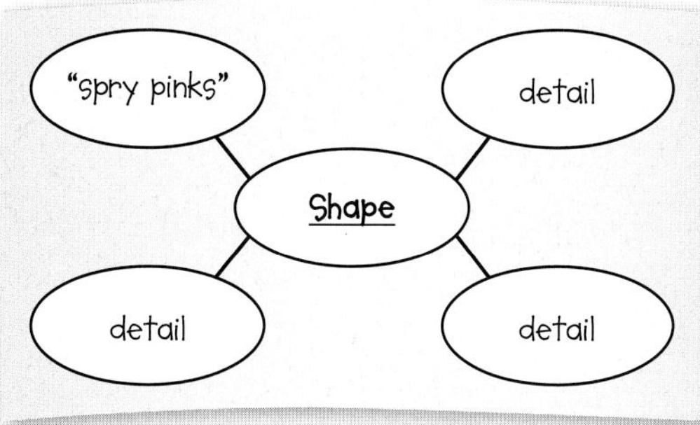

Extend Understanding

Writing Options

Creative Writing Think of an everyday object, such as a pencil or telephone. Think of images, sensory details, and figures of speech that could be used to describe that object. Then write a **concrete poem** about it. Remember, a concrete poem should physically resemble the thing that it describes. Try cutting out a stencil and using that to help guide you in creating your poem.

Argumentative Writing Imagine that you are the literary reviewer for a newspaper and have been asked to write a **review** of Cummings's poem. In your review, describe the elements that make this poem unique, such as its shape, lack of capitalization, and punctuation. Also, give your opinion of the poem. Once you have finished, share your review with a partner.

Collaborative Learning

Discuss Purpose With a partner, discuss Cummings's purpose for creating a poem with this unusual text structure. Ask yourself: What does this structure contribute to the poem's meaning? Does the structure inhibit or aid my understanding of the poem? As you discuss, create a list of your thoughts.

Media Literacy

Concrete Poetry Use the Internet and the library to find other examples of concrete poetry. John Hollander, George Herbert, and Lewis Carroll wrote some of the most famous examples of concrete poetry. Write a short description of at least two concrete poems. Then write a few sentences in which you compare and contrast the poems and state which you like better.

Go to **www.mirrorsandwindows.com** for more.

Two People I Want to Be Like

A Lyric Poem
by Eve Merriam

That man
stuck in traffic
not pounding his fists against the steering
wheel
not trying to shift to the next lane
just
using the time
for a slow steady grin
of remembering
all the good unstuck times

and that woman
clerking in the supermarket
at rush hour
bagging bottles and cartons and boxes and
jars and
cans
punching it all out
slapping it all along
and leveling a smile
at everyone in the line.

I wish they were married to each other.

Maybe it's better they're not,
so they can pass their sweet harmony
around. ✤

Eve Merriam (1916–1992) was born in Pennsylvania. After college, she lived in New York City, where she wrote for radio. Later, she began teaching and lecturing. Merriam published her first book, *Family Circle*, in 1946. Other collections include *It Doesn't Have to Rhyme*, and *If Only I Could Tell You*, from which "Two People I Want to Be Like" was selected. Although poetry was always Merriam's first love, she is also well known as a playwright and fiction writer.

When have you ever admired someone for his or her ability to stay cool under pressure? Why is patience such an admirable trait?

Analyze and Extend

1. (a) What about the two people's actions does the speaker admire? (b) What does the speaker's admiration suggest about him or her?
2. Why does the speaker wish that these two people were married?
3. How do you feel about the speaker's conclusion that it is better for these two people not be married to each other? Explain.

Creative Writing Imagine that you know one of the people described in this poem. Write a short **biography** about this person. Include vital information such as his or her age, occupation, and where he or she lives. Also, describe your subject's personality. Be sure to use some of the information from this poem when writing your biography. Once you have finished, share your biography with a classmate.

Collaborative Learning With a partner, discuss the personality traits of the two people described in this poem. Based on the poem's description, what do you admire about them? Do you think that they always display these traits? Why or why not? Take notes as you hold your discussion. When you are done, use your notes to present your thoughts to the class.

Go to **www.mirrorsandwindows.com** for more.

Miracles

A Lyric Poem by Walt Whitman

INDEPENDENT READING

Why, who makes much of a miracle?
As to me I know of nothing else but miracles,
Whether I walk the streets of Manhattan,
Or dart my sight over the roofs of houses toward the sky,
Or wade with naked feet along the beach just in the edge of the water,
Or stand under trees in the woods,
Or talk by day with any one I love...
Or sit at table at dinner with the rest,
Or look at strangers opposite me riding in the car.
Or watch honey-bees busy around the hive of a summer forenoon,
Or animals feeding in the fields,
Or birds, or the wonderfulness of the sundown, or of stars shining so quiet and bright,
Or the exquisite delicate thin curve of the new moon in spring;
These with the rest, one and all, are to me miracles,
The whole referring, yet each distinct and in its place.

Considered one of the most important American poets, **Walt Whitman** (1819–1892) radically altered how poetry was written and what it was written about. His poetry, typically comprised of long, sprawling free verse lines, often celebrates America's vast spaces, varied experiences, and diverse people. During the Civil War, Whitman served as a nurse, caring for both Confederate and Union soldiers. This experience had a profound impact on Whitman's outlook and his writing.

To me every hour of the light and dark is a miracle,
Every cubic inch of space is a miracle,
Every square yard of the surface of the earth is spread with the same,
Every foot of the interior swarms with the same.

To me the sea is a continual miracle,
The fishes that swim—the rocks—the motion of the waves—the ships with men in them,
What stranger miracles are there? ✣

How is the world full of miracles, both big and small? Do you always feel this way about the world? What makes Whitman's perspective appealing?

Analyze and Extend

1. What do you think Whitman means by his question in the poem's first line: "Why, who makes much of a miracle?"
2. In your opinion, how does the poet's use of repetition affect the poem?
3. The final line of this poem is a rhetorical question, or a question used for effect and for which the answer should be obvious. How do you think Whitman would answer this question? Explain.

Informative Writing What is this poem's main idea? Do you agree with this idea completely? Do you agree partially? Do you disagree? Write a short **literary response** in which you analyze and evaluate the poem's main idea. State what you think the main idea is and provide textual evidence in support of your claim. Then evaluate the main idea, stating why you do or do not agree with it. Present evidence, either textual or otherwise, in support of your position.

Critical Literacy Hold a small-group discussion in which you analyze the form of this poem. Try to describe as many elements as you can. Use terms like *form, line, stanza, rhythm, repetition, lyric poetry,* and *free verse.* Once you have described as many elements as you can, discuss how the poem's form affects its meaning. For example, how do the long line lengths affect the poem's tone?

 Go to **www.mirrorsandwindows.com** for more.

EARLY SONG

A Lyric Poem by Gogisgi

(Right) ***The Navajo,*** c. 20th century. Maynard Dixon. Private collection.

Gogisgi (1927–1997), also known as Carroll Arnett, was born in Oklahoma City, Oklahoma. Of Cherokee and French descent, Gogisgi served in the United States Marines from 1946–1947. After receiving his master's degree from the University of Texas, Gogisgi went on to teach literature and writing. In 1974, he was awarded a National Endowment for the Arts Fellowship in Creative Writing.

As the sun rises
high enough to
warm the frost
off the pine needles,

I rise to make
four prayers of
thanksgiving for
this fine clear day,

for this good brown
earth, for all
brothers and sisters,
for the dark blood

that runs through me
in a great circle
back into this
good brown earth. ✣

How do you show appreciation for the world around you? Why should people show appreciation and respect for nature?

Analyze and Extend

1. Why do you think the speaker performs these prayers in the morning?
2. (a) What do you think the speaker means in the final three lines of this poem? (b) Do you think this is something to be thankful for? Explain.
3. What does the repetition in this poem emphasize?

Creative Writing What are you thankful for? Is it your family, friends, or something simple like the sun or stars? Write a **descriptive paragraph** in which you describe the things that you appreciate most. Use sensory details and figurative language to enhance your description. When you are finished, read your paragraph to the class.

 Go to **www.mirrorsandwindows.com** for more.

For Your Reading List

The Invisible Ladder: An Anthology of Contemporary American Poems for Young Readers

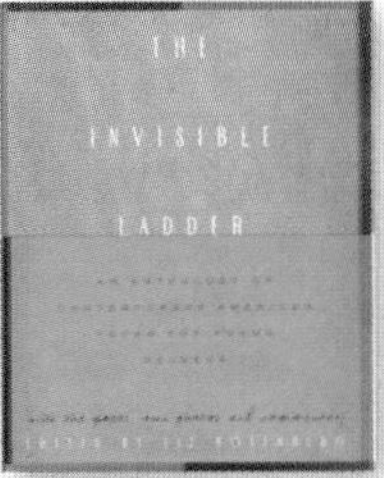

by Liz Rosenberg

In this collection, Rosenberg has assembled a wide range of well-loved poets, such as Galway Kinnell, Nikki Giovanni, and Maxine Kumin. Accompanying each poem are contrasting photos of the poets when they were young and as adults. *The Invisible Ladder* also includes anecdotes from each poet describing how he or she first became interested in the craft.

Becoming Joe DiMaggio

by Maria Testa

This book tells the story of a boy named Joseph Paul and his passion for baseball. Over the course of two dozen brief poems, the reader learns about the challenges Joseph faces and the pleasure he derives from listening to baseball on the radio with his grandfather. As Joseph and his grandfather listen, they follow Joe DiMaggio's budding career, while the reader watches Joseph grow up.

I Am the Darker Brother: An Anthology of Modern Poems by African Americans

by Arnold Adoff

This edition of Adoff's classic collection of African-American verse has been updated to include twenty contemporary writers. Harlem Renaissance poets such as Langston Hughes and Countee Cullen, poets from earlier periods such as Paul Lawrence Dunbar, and later twentieth-century greats such as Gwendolyn Brooks are all represented.

War and the Pity of War

by Neil Philip

In this collection, poets both ancient and modern describe their wartime experiences. Each poem presents a perspective on war and is accompanied by a note that describes the era in which it was written and the war to which it refers. Powerful illustrations accompany each poem. Readers will be fascinated by the depictions of war across such a vast span of time and place.

Ancient Voices

by Kate Hovey

In this unique book, author Kate Hovey gives voice to the gods of Mount Olympus. The poems are divided into four themed sections and appear alongside interesting and often hilarious illustrations. Readers who are familiar with ancient mythology will appreciate the fresh perspective, while those who don't know the stories can find background information about the gods in the appendix.

The Dream on Blanca's Wall

by Jane Medina

This book tells the story of a young girl, Blanca, who decides that she wants to become a teacher. Through twenty-four narrative free verse poems, the reader witnesses the obstacles Blanca faces as well as the support she receives from her teachers and her parents. The book also contains Spanish translations of the poems.

Writing Workshop

Informative Writing

Compare-and-Contrast Essay

Assignment: Write a compare-and-contrast essay in which I examine the similarities and differences between two subjects I choose.

Goal: Make an overall point about these two subjects that will interest my audience.

Strategy: Present evidence for this point by organizing details about my two subjects that clearly show how they are alike and different.

Writing Rubric: My compare-and-contrast essay should include the following:

- an introduction that sparks a reader's interest
- a thesis statement that presents my overall point
- a clear organizational pattern
- transitions that indicate comparisons and contrasts
- an effective conclusion that restates my thesis

Reading and Writing

In this unit, you read a translation of a famous haiku by the Japanese poet Bashō. Here are two more versions.

pond
frog
plop

—JAMES KIRKUP

The old pond
A frog jumped in,
Kerplunk!

—ALLEN GINSBERG

How are the three translations alike and different? To examine their similarities and differences involves making comparisons and contrasts, one of the most basic types of thinking used in studying literature. Much of the critical writing you will do in your literature classes and on standardized tests will ask you to make comparisons and contrasts.

In this workshop you will learn how to write a **compare-and-contrast essay,** a type of informative (or explanatory) writing that analyzes the similarities and differences between two or more related subjects. The following summary shows how you might sum up the assignment for a compare-and-contrast essay—what its goal is and how to go about it. This summary also includes a writing rubric, a set of standards by which to judge whether your compare-and-contrast essay is successful. You will use this rubric both in drafting and in revising your essay.

What Great Writers Do

One approach to the compare-and-contrast essay is to show unexpected similarities. What basic point is Lewis Thomas making about ants and humans?

Ants are so much like human beings as to be an embarrassment. They farm fungi, raise aphids as livestock, launch armies into war, use chemical sprays to alarm and confuse enemies, capture slaves. The families of weaver ants engage in child labor, holding their larvae like shuttles to spin out the thread that sews the leaves together for their fungus gardens....They do everything but watch television.

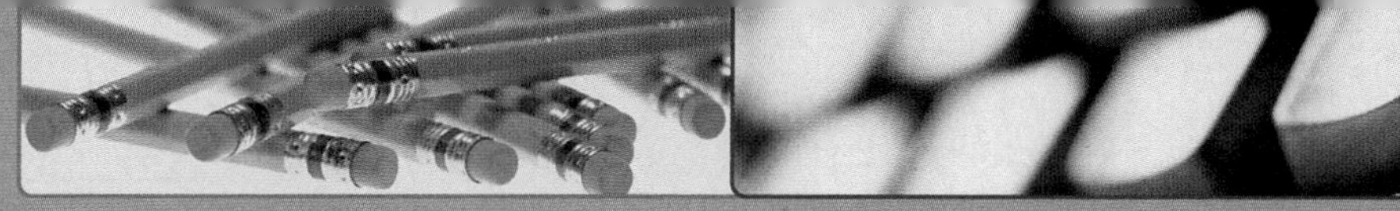

1. PREWRITE

Choosing Your Topic

In everyday life, we are always comparing and contrasting things—people we know, products we own, movies we see. You have material all around you. The point is to choose two subjects that will provide an interesting comparison. When you consider possible subjects, ask yourself if they fall into either of the following categories.

Apples and oranges? It is usually best to choose two subjects that are similar enough to make a fair comparison. Don't choose subjects that are so completely different in kind—such as a baseball team and a coin collection—that any comparison is really a stretch.

Peas in a pod? On the other hand, choose subjects that are different enough to make an interesting comparison. Don't choose subjects that are so alike that few people would be interested in their small differences, such as two different outlets of the same fast-food restaurant chain.

Gathering Details

Once you have chosen two subjects that you think will be interesting to compare and contrast, start organizing details. One way to do this is to make a chart. Here's a chart comparing and contrasting Harper Lee's novel *To Kill a Mockingbird* with the movie based on it. It lists features and details from both the novel and the movie.

Features	Novel	Movie
Plot	two major stories, several minor ones	focuses on two major stories; ignores minor plots
Characters	memorable characters	very fine performances
Setting	effective setting	not filmed on location; movie set seems authentic
Theme	importance of understanding	film expresses the same theme

Deciding on Your Purpose

When you have gathered details about your two subjects, review them to determine what the purpose of your compare-and-contrast essay is. Decide the basic point you are trying to make. This purpose is expressed in your **thesis statement.** An essay comparing and contrasting the book and movie versions of *To Kill a Mockingbird* might start with the following thesis statement:

> A good novel can be turned into a good movie by being faithful to the book's plot, characters, setting, and theme.

2. DRAFT

Organizing Ideas

Once you have chosen your subjects, gathered details, and created your thesis statement, you next need to decide how you want to organize your ideas. There are two basic **organizational patterns** for a compare-and-contrast essay. If you choose the **subject-by-subject** (or block) method, you present all the features of your first subject, then you present those same features about the second subject. If you choose the **point-by-point** method, you present each feature in turn, looking at the first subject, then at the second subject. Here is what these two organizational patterns look like.

Subject-by-Subject	Point-by-Point
novel plot characters setting theme movie plot characters setting theme	plot novel movie characters novel movie setting novel movie theme novel movie

Putting Your Thoughts on Paper

Any essay has three basic parts: an introduction, a body, and a conclusion. Create a plan for your compare-and-contrast essay, such as the one on the right comparing and contrasting the book and movie versions of *To Kill a Mockingbird.*

You might draft your essay straight through from the beginning to the end. Some writers prefer to begin with the body, however, leaving the introduction and conclusion until later. Whichever way you choose, your goal is to get all your ideas down on paper according to the plan you created. At the drafting stage, concentrate on content and organization, not on grammar, punctuation, and spelling. Focus on those details in the revising and proofreading stage.

Introduction
- Identify Harper Lee's novel To Kill a Mockingbird and the film based on it.
- Present my thesis statement.

Body
- Write one paragraph dealing with each feature—plot, character, setting, and theme.
- Compare and contrast the novel's and film's handling of each feature.

Conclusion
- Rephrase my thesis statement.
- Wrap up my essay.

Making Connections

When drafting your essay, make connections by using **transitions,** or words and phrases that clearly indicate comparisons and contrasts. Here are some examples of different types of transitions that can be helpful in a compare-and-contrast essay.

Transitions That Show Comparisons	Transitions That Show Contrasts
also	*although*
as	*but*
both	*however*
each	*in contrast*
just	*yet*
like	*while*

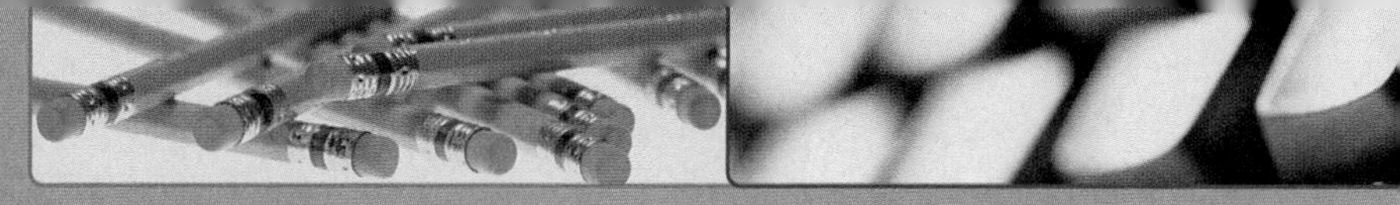

3. REVISE

Evaluating Your Draft

When you revise, you identify strengths and weaknesses in your draft. You can evaluate your own writing. You can also work with a **peer reviewer.** Exchange essays with this partner and evaluate each other's work.

Below is part of a draft of a compare-and-contrast essay. The annotations indicate the reasons for changes.

Revising Checklist

- ❑ Does the introduction engage the reader?
- ❑ Does the thesis present the overall point?
- ❑ Is the essay organized in a logical way?
- ❑ Do I use transitions?

~~Some people think that no movie can be as good as the book it is based on.~~ *Can any movie be as good as the book it is based on? Consider Harper Lee's novel* To Kill a Mockingbird *and the 1962 film version.* The book won the 1961 Pulitzer Prize for fiction, and the movie was nominated for an Academy Award for Best Picture. ~~The movie's music is very good too.~~ A good novel can be turned into a good movie by being faithful to the book's plot, characters, setting, and theme.

Reword opening sentences to sharpen point.

Delete a detail that is off the topic.

Harper Lee's *To Kill a Mockingbird* tells many stories, but her novel has two major plots. The first is how three children, Scout and Jem Finch and their friend Dill Harris, try to find out about their strange neighbor Boo Radley. The second plot is how Jem and Scout's father, the lawyer Atticus Finch, defends a man named Tom Robinson. ~~The~~ *Although the* movie leaves out many stories, it focuses clearly on the two major plots.

Add the transitional word although *to signal a contrast.*

4. EDIT AND PROOFREAD

Focus: Transitions

The effective use of transitional words and phrases is a key element in a successful compare-and-contrast essay. In revising your draft, add transitions where needed to point out similarities and differences.

> Harper Lee created very memorable characters. Atticus Finch and his children, Dill, Boo Radley, Tom Robinson, and the others stay in the reader's memory. ~~The~~ *In the same way, the* actors create very memorable performances.

What Great Writers Do

In the last sentence, what does Bruce Catton indicate with the transitional word each?

So Grant and Lee were in complete contrast, representing two diametrically opposed elements in American life. Grant was the modern man emerging; beyond him, ready to come on the stage, was the great age of steel and machinery, vitality. Lee might have ridden down from the age of chivalry, lance in hand. Each man was the perfect champion of his cause, drawing both his strengths and his weaknesses from the people he led.

Focus: Using Commas

In revising your draft, be aware of common punctuation errors, such as incorrect use of commas to set off words or phrases that interrupt sentences. Use two commas if the word or phrase falls in the middle of the sentence.

> Harper Lee's *To Kill a Mockingbird* tells many stories, and all of them are very interesting, but her novel has two major plots.

Use one comma if the word or phrase falls at the beginning or end of the sentence.

> Lee even calls it a "tired old town," almost like it was a person.

Proofreading

Quality Control The purpose of proofreading is to correct errors in grammar, punctuation, and spelling. You can pick out and fix these errors as you evaluate and revise your essay, but take time to focus on them during the proofreading stage. Use proofreader's marks to highlight any errors you find. (See the Language Arts Handbook, section 4.1, for a list of proofreader's symbols.)

5. PUBLISH AND PRESENT

Publishing and Presenting

Neatness Counts Make the finished version of your essay appealing to read. Handwritten papers should be neat and legible. If you are working on a word processor, double-space the lines of text and use a readable font, or typeface. Whether you are submitting your work to your teacher or elsewhere, be sure to follow any presentation guidelines.

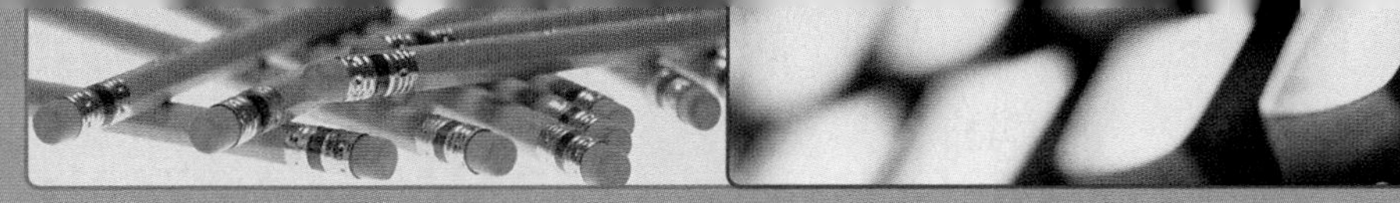

Student Model

Read the Book or See the Movie?
by Kathy Jeffers

Can any movie be as good as the book it is based on? Consider Harper Lee's novel *To Kill a Mockingbird* and the 1962 film version. The book won the 1961 Pulitzer Prize for fiction, and the movie was nominated for an Academy Award for Best Picture. A good novel can be turned into a good movie by being faithful to the book's plot, characters, setting, and theme.

Identifies the specific subjects to be compared and contrasted

Presents the thesis statement

Harper Lee's *To Kill a Mockingbird* tells many stories, and all of them are very interesting, but her novel has two major plots. The first is how three children, Scout and Jem Finch and their friend Dill Harris, try to find out about their strange neighbor Boo Radley. The second plot is how Jem and Scout's father, the lawyer Atticus Finch, defends a man named Tom Robinson. Although the movie leaves out many stories, it focuses clearly on the two major plots.

Harper Lee created very memorable characters. Atticus Finch and his children, Dill, Boo Radley, Tom Robinson, and the others stay in the reader's memory. In the same way, the actors create very memorable performances. Gregory Peck, who played Atticus, won the Oscar for Best Actor. Mary Badham, who played Scout, was nominated for Best Supporting Actress.

Provides details showing similarities and differences

The setting of Harper Lee's novel, the small Alabama town of Maycomb in the 1930s, is a very important part of the effect she creates in her book. Maycomb is practically like a character. Lee even calls it a "tired old town," almost as if it were a person. The film version was not shot in Monroeville, Alabama, the town on which she based Maycomb. However, the movie set looks right.

The theme of *To Kill a Mockingbird* is the importance of understanding other people. As Atticus says, "You never really know a man until you stand in his shoes and walk around in them." In the novel, this theme is expressed through what the children learn about Boo Radley, Tom Robinson, and other people in Maycomb. Although it does not include many of the stories in the novel, the film still makes a powerful statement about the importance of understanding someone.

Although different in some details, the movie faithfully follows the novel's plot, characters, setting, and theme. Seeing the film version of *To Kill a Mockingbird* is not the same as reading the novel, but it is still very satisfying. The movie is as good a film as the book is a novel. So read the book *and* see the movie.

Summarizes the comparison and contrast

Restates the thesis

Giving and Actively Listening to Informative Presentations

Have you ever had something explained to you, such as how to solve a problem, how to operate a device, or the differences between two similar ideas? These are examples of Informative presentations. In an **informative presentation,** you give facts and details about a topic. When you give and actively listen to an informative presentation, you share information about a topic.

There are different kinds of informative presentations. Some examples include *compare-and-contrast, cause-and-effect,* and *problem-and-solution* presentations.

Planning an Informative Presentation

Choose a Topic What will you present? What topics interest you? In an informative presentation, you give facts and details about a subject. What you discuss should be of interest to you and to your audience. Choose a subject that you find interesting and you know others will too. You might present on animals, sports, games, science—anything of your choosing.

Narrow Your Focus Now that you have a topic, narrow it to make it more manageable. You can use a chart to help narrow your topic. For instance, if you decided to discuss sports, you would need to choose a specific sport. Then you would need to narrow your topic further so that a specific aspect of that sport becomes the focus of your presentation. However, avoid narrowing your topic so much that you are left with little to discuss. Your chart might look like this.

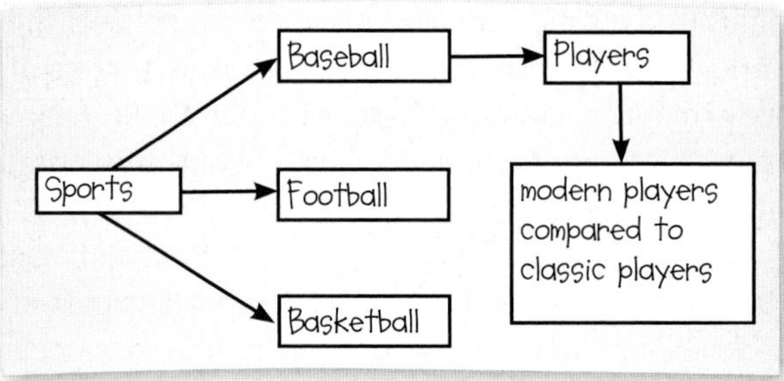

Identify Your Audience Now that you have identified and narrowed your topic, consider your audience. Your audience will determine much of what you say and how you say it. If you know that your audience is very familiar with your topic, try to introduce a new perspective or information with which they may not be familiar. If you know your topic is one your audience knows little about, avoid jargon and technical language.

Organize Your Information How will you organize what you want to say? All presentations should begin with an introduction and end with a conclusion that summarizes all of your main ideas. The kind of order you choose for the body of your presentation depends on your topic. For example, when comparing baseball players of today with those from a century ago, you would probably use **compare-and-contrast order.** To organize using this method, you would present all of the characteristics of one subject, and then those of another. Or you would present a single characteristic of one subject, compare it to that of your other subject, and so on.

Some other kinds of organization that you might find useful include cause-and-effect order, chronological order, and problem-and-solution order. In **cause-and-effect order,** you present one or more causes and one or more effects. In **chronological order,** you present events in the order that they occurred. In **problem-and-solution order,** you present problems and give solutions. Choose the order that best fits what you want to say.

Evaluating Your Informative Presentation

Working with your partner or in a small group, rehearse your presentation. Provide each other with constructive feedback through polite, respectful criticism and praise. Follow the speaking and listening rubrics on this page in your evaluations.

Delivering Your Informative Presentation

Nonverbal communication is an important part of listening and speaking. As you deliver your informative presentation, remember to make eye contact with the audience. In an informative essay, a key purpose is to clearly explain information to the listener. Therefore, speak loudly and clearly.

If you are using visual aids, such as graphs, charts, photographs, or multimedia, try to coordinate these materials with the content of your presentation. Also, avoid any unnecessary movements or gestures that might distract your audience.

Listen Actively It is also important to be an active, involved listener. Listen attentively by making eye contact and maintaining an engaged and respectful posture. Use the information in the presentation to ask relevant questions at the end of the speech or when prompted by the presenter.

Speaking Rubric

Your Informative presentation will be evaluated on these elements:

Content

- ☐ an introduction that draws in the listener
- ☐ ideas clearly, logically, and consistently organized
- ☐ content well-researched and interesting
- ☐ conclusion that summarizes all main ideas

Delivery and Presentation

- ☐ maintains audience involvement
- ☐ good use of voice and nonverbal cues
- ☐ appropriate pacing

Listening Rubric

As a peer reviewer or audience member, you should do the following:

- ☐ listen quietly and attentively
- ☐ analyze any images that are presented
- ☐ ask appropriate questions
- ☐ (as peer reviewer) provide constructive feedback

Test Practice Workshop

Writing Skills

Informative Essay

Read the following short excerpts and the writing assignment that follows. Before you begin writing, think carefully about what task the assignment is asking you to perform. Then create an outline to help guide your writing.

"Song" by Robert Browning

The year's at the spring,
And day's at the morn;
Morning's at seven;
The hill-side's dew-pearled;
The lark's on the wing;
The snail's on the thorn;
God's in his Heaven—
All's right with the world!

"The Gardener" (LXXXV) by Rabindranath Tagore

Who are you, reader, reading my poems an hundred years hence?
I cannot send you one single flower from this wealth of the spring,
one single streak of gold from yonder clouds.
Open your doors and look abroad.
From your blossoming garden gather fragrant memories of the
vanished flowers of an hundred years before.
In the joy of your heart may you feel the living joy that sang one
spring morning, sending its glad voice across a hundred years.

Assignment: What do the two poems have in common? In what ways are they different? Plan and write several paragraphs for an **informative essay** in which you **compare** and **contrast** the poems. Use **transitions** that signal the organization of your essay. Include evidence from the poems to support your thesis.

Revising and Editing Skills

The following sentences test your ability to recognize grammar and usage errors. Each sentence contains either a single error or no error at all. No sentence contains more than one error. The error, if there is one, is underlined and lettered. If the sentence contains an error, select the one underlined part that must be changed to make the sentence correct. If the sentence is correct, select choice E. In choosing answers, follow the requirements of standard written English.

1. The teacher invited my (A) parents and me (B) to the art gallery for (C) a showing of the paintings she (D) had done. No error. (E)

2. The walls (A) of the gym, painted green and trimmed with yellow were (B) so far apart that our voices (C) created echoes (D). No error. (E)

3. The children excused theirselves (A) from the table after they (B) finished eating so they (C) could play with their (D) new toys. No error. (E)

4. Last summer, my parents (A), brother, and I (B) visited the cities (C) of Los Angeles and San Diego. (D) No error. (E)

5. We (A) could not believe (B) how bad the boys (C) behavior had (D) become. No error. (E)

6. The miners (A) faces were covered with soot after the (B) explosion, but their (C) helmets and goggles had protected their (D) heads and eyes from flying debris. No error. (E)

7. While the teacher was (A) explaining Newton's laws (B) of motion, the class were (C) startled when she broke (D) a board with her hand. No error. (E)

8. We ourselves (A) spent almost an hour trying to locate the birds (B) nest so we (C) could put back its (D) egg that had fallen to the ground. No error. (E)

9. The farmer's (A) children (B), in mud-covered overalls were (C) playing in the field with their (D) dog. No error. (E)

10. I (A) am very proud of me (B) because I (C) got straight A's on my (D) report card. No error. (E)

Reading Skills

Carefully read the following passage. Then, on a separate piece of paper, answer each question.

"Silver" by Walter de la Mare

Slowly, silently, now the moon
Walks the night in her silver shoon;
This way, and that, she peers, and sees
Silver fruit upon silver trees;
One by one the casements catch
Her beams beneath the silvery thatch;
Couched in his kennel, like a log,
With paws of silver sleeps the dog;
From their shadowy cote the white breasts peep
Of doves in a silver-feathered sleep;
A harvest mouse goes scampering by,
With silver claws, and a silver eye;
And moveless fish in the water gleam,
By silver reeds in a silver stream.

1. Which of the following sound devices appears in line 1?
   A. onomatopoeia
   B. simile
   C. rhyme scheme
   D. alliteration
   E. internal rhyme

2. Which of the following kinds of figurative language appears in line 3?
   A. simile
   B. onomatopoeia
   C. personification
   D. hyperbole
   E. haiku

3. Which of the following sound devices appears in line 6?
   A. alliteration
   B. onomatopoeia
   C. consonance
   D. rhyme scheme
   E. simile

4. The phrase *like a log* in line 7 is an example of
   A. metaphor.
   B. simile.
   C. personification.
   D. onomatopoeia.
   E. assonance.

5. Which of the following represents the rhyme scheme in the first eight lines?
   A. *abababab*
   B. *aabbccdd*
   C. *abcabcab*
   D. *abbaccdd*
   E. *abbccaab*

6. How many beats, or stressed syllables, appear in line 8?
   A. 1
   B. 2
   C. 3
   D. 4
   E. 5

7. The description in line 14 is an example of
   A. hyperbole.
   B. a simile.
   C. a metaphor.
   D. personification.
   E. imagery.

8. The use of the word *silver* throughout this poem is an example of
   A. hyperbole.
   B. rhyme.
   C. simile.
   D. extended metaphor.
   E. repetition.

9. What is the overall mood of the passage?
   A. frightening
   B. humorous
   C. sad
   D. peaceful
   E. angry

10. Which of the following best describes this poem's point of view?
   A. first-person
   B. second-person
   C. third-person
   D. dynamic
   E. round

Unit 6

Searching Beneath the Surface

Poetry

CARL SANDBURG

ROBERT FROST

ALFRED NOYES

"How dreary—to be—Somebody!
How public—like a Frog— "

—EMILY DICKINSON, "I'm Nobody"

What are authors trying to say with the images, symbols, and language they use? When you analyze a poem, you are searching beneath its surface to find meaning and discover themes. In Emily Dickinson's poem, "I'm Nobody," the author uses a variety of literary devices, including imagery, rhyme, and simile, to praise the privately lived life. As you read the poems in this unit, use your skills to find the meanings that lie just beneath the surface.

Literary Element

Understanding Meaning in Poetry

How Do Poems *Mean?*

Poems frequently challenge readers to imagine something in an unexpected way. Poets accomplish this with figurative language, sound devices, and imagery. Wendy Rose's poem "Loo-Wit" describes Mount Saint Helens, a mountain in southern Washington State that famously erupted in 1980, as if it were an old woman. Why do you think she makes this comparison? How does this comparison affect the way you think about the mountain?

Speaker

In short stories and novels, the voice that tells the story and describes the characters and setting is called the narrator. In poetry, the voice that narrates the poem is referred to as the **speaker.** The speaker sometimes participates in the action of the poem, using the first-person point of view. Other times, as in "Loo-Wit," the speaker narrates from the outside, using the third-person point of view.

The speaker's voice can be very much like the poet's voice, expressing beliefs or describing experiences similar to those of the poet. But you should never assume that a poem's speaker is the same as the poet. Often, the speaker is fictional. A speaker can be a person, an animal, an object, or an idea.

A poem's speaker sometimes explicitly states the theme, or central idea, of the poem. Generally, though, you must infer the theme by examining the tone, mood, description, and figurative language.

Symbolism

A **symbol** is a thing that stands for itself and something else. In "Loo-Wit," Mount Saint Helens is being used as a symbol. The mountain in the poem represents both the real mountain and the violence, beauty, and power of the natural world.

Some symbols are traditional, such as roses for love or doves for peace. Other symbols are unique to a piece of literature or author. In "Loo-Wit" the use of Mount Saint Helens as a symbol is unique.

She crouches
in the north,
her trembling
the source
of dawn.
Light appears
with the shudder
of her slopes,
the movement
of her arm.

—WENDY ROSE, "Loo-Wit"

Symbols can be subjective, having more than one interpretation. It is not always clear how a writer intends a reader to interpret his or her use of a symbol. Always try to determine the theme, and consider how the poet's use of description, figures of speech, and symbols develops the theme.

Theme in Yellow

A Lyric Poem by Carl Sandburg

Build Background

Literary Context "Theme in Yellow" was published in 1916 in *Chicago Poems,* Sandburg's first major collection. Some considered his approach to poetry shocking; others found it refreshing. Most of Sandburg's poems are in the free verse form and use the everyday language of working people. His powerful voice celebrates the raw beauty of industrialism as well as America's landscape, music, and culture.

Reader's Context What is autumn like in your part of the country? What words would you use to describe it?

Set Purpose

Examine the poet's use of imagery. What mental picture does the poem create for you?

Analyze Literature

Speaker The **speaker** is the voice that speaks, or narrates, a poem. The speaker may or may not be the author. Poets often create characters in their poems. As you read "Theme in Yellow," try to determine who the speaker is. Is it a character in the poem, or is the speaker narrating from the outside?

Meet the Author

Carl Sandburg (1878–1967), the son of Swedish immigrants, grew up in Galesburg, Illinois. After the age of thirteen, he pursued his studies on and off while working at a variety of jobs, from bricklaying to house painting. After serving as a soldier during the Spanish-American War (1898), he briefly attended college, worked as a journalist, and became involved in politics. In addition to poetry, Sandburg is known for his biographies of Abraham Lincoln. He was awarded the Pulitzer Prize for *Abraham Lincoln: The War Years* (1939).

Use Reading Skills

Identify Multiple Levels of Meaning In poetry, writers frequently use images, metaphors, similes, and sound devices to create multiple levels of meaning. By reading and rereading, you can better understand how these different levels affect each other and contribute to the poem's overall meaning. Use a chart like the one below to help you identify and analyze the effects of these different levels of meaning.

Images	golden cornfields at dusk
Figurative Language	
Characters, Setting	

Preview Vocabulary

taw•ny (tä´ nē) *adj.,* warm sandy color

dusk (dusk) *n.,* darker stage of twilight

Theme in Yellow

A Lyric Poem by Carl Sandburg

I spot the hills
With yellow balls in autumn.
I light the prairie cornfields
Orange and tawny gold clusters
And I am called pumpkins.
On the last of October
When dusk is fallen
Children join hands
And circle round me
Singing ghost songs
And love to the harvest moon;
I am a jack-o'-lantern
With terrible teeth
And the children know
I am fooling. ✣

DURING READING

Analyze Literature
Speaker Is this poem's speaker the author? Confirm or modify your answer as you read.

taw•ny (tä´ nē) *adj.*, warm sandy color

dusk (dəsk) *n.*, darker stage of twilight

DURING READING

Use Reading Skills
Identify Multiple Levels of Meaning What do the final four lines suggest about the speaker?

What do you like most about autumn? What do you like least about it? In what ways is autumn different from all the other seasons?

Apply the Model

BEFORE READING

DURING READING

AFTER READING

Find Meaning

1. (a) Who or what is this poem's speaker? (b) How does the speaker change by the end of the poem?

2. (a) What colors does the speaker mention in the poem? (b) Why might these colors be the most appropriate for this poem?

Make Judgments

3. (a) What does the speaker claim the children know? (b) In what ways do their actions support this claim?

4. How was the content of this poem surprising? Explain your answer.

Analyze Literature

Speaker In poetry a speaker can be a person, place, or thing and may or may not express the thoughts of the poet. Use a web to determine the attitudes of the speaker. In the center oval, name the speaker. In each outer oval, write a detail that suggests a characteristic of the speaker. Then write a sentence describing the speaker's personality.

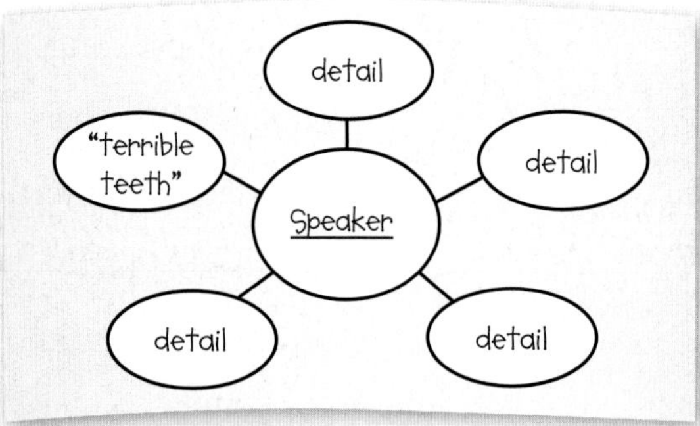

Extend Understanding

Writing Options

Creative Writing Write a **poem** about a favorite place from the perspective of an inanimate object that is a part of that place. Use sensory details and figurative language to help you describe the images and feelings you want your reader to understand.

Informative Writing Think about your reaction to "Theme in Yellow." How does it make you feel? Mood is the feeling or emotion that a writer creates in a work. List some words or phrases that describe the mood of the poem. Consider the speaker's choice of words and images, as well as the speaker's appearance. In a one-page **literary response,** analyze how the speaker affects the mood of "Theme in Yellow."

Collaborative Learning

Discuss Figurative Language Personification is a figure of speech in which an idea, animal, or thing is described as if it were a person. Form a small group, and brainstorm a list of other examples of personification you have encountered. What generalizations can you make about the items on your list?

Lifelong Learning

Research Pumpkins Is a pumpkin a fruit or a vegetable? How long have people been cultivating pumpkins? What are some of the most popular uses of pumpkins? How big do pumpkins grow? Use the Internet or the library to answer these and other questions about pumpkins. Organize your information into an illustrated pamphlet.

Go to **www.mirrorsandwindows.com** for more.

Grammar & Style

Simple, Compound, Complex, and Compound-Complex Sentences

Simple Sentences

I spot the hills
With yellow balls in autumn.

—CARL SANDBURG, "Theme in Yellow"

Sentences are classified according to the types and number of clauses they contain. A **simple sentence** contains one independent clause and no subordinate clauses. Remember that a clause must have both a subject and verb. A simple sentence may have any number of phrases, a compound subject, or a compound verb. The quotation above is a simple sentence.

EXAMPLE

The pumpkins grew all over the hills.

In this simple sentence, the subject is *pumpkins* and the verb is *grew.*

Compound Sentences

I am a jack-o'-lantern
With terrible teeth
And the children know
I am fooling.

—CARL SANDBURG, "Theme in Yellow"

A **compound sentence** consists of two or more independent clauses joined with a comma and a coordinating conjunction, such as *and, but, or, nor, for, yet,* or *so.* In the above quotation, the independent clause *I am a jack-o'-lantern with terrible teeth* is joined to a second independent clause, *the children know I am fooling*, with the coordinating conjunction *and.* The quotation would be a good example of a compound sentence if the poet had used a comma before *and.*

EXAMPLE

Not everyone loves jack-o'-lanterns, but carving them is fun.

In this example, two independent clauses are joined by a comma and the coordinating conjunction *but.*

Complex Sentences

Combining an independent clause with at least one dependent clause makes a **complex sentence.**

EXAMPLE

As the wind began to blow, the sky grew dark.

Compound-Complex Sentences

A **compound-complex sentence** consists of a compound sentence with one or more dependent clauses.

EXAMPLE

As the wind began to blow, the sky grew dark, and we ran for the shelter of the house.

The sky grew dark, and we ran for the shelter of the house is a compound sentence. *As the wind began to blow* is a dependent clause.

Using Different Types of Sentences

Expand each of the following simple sentences into a compound, complex, or compound-complex sentence by adding one or more independent or dependent clauses. Then list the sentence type.

1. Jack-o'-lanterns are made from pumpkins.
2. The children joined hands to form a circle.
3. Jack-o'-lanterns aren't really scary.
4. Molly carved a funny face on her pumpkin.
5. The pumpkins looked like someone painted the hills with orange polka dots.

Apply the Model

BEFORE READING

DURING READING

AFTER READING

GUIDED READING

Once by the Pacific

A Lyric Poem by Robert Frost

Build Background

Literary Context At a time when poets were moving toward free verse and themes of social upheaval, industrial life, and scientific discovery, Frost wrote using traditional poetic forms. He addressed themes of personal relationships, rural life, and nature. Even so, Frost's perspective was that of a modern man. He used simple language in well-crafted lines to express his frequently dark, ironic perspective on nature and society.

Reader's Context When have you ever experienced, firsthand, the fury of nature? In what ways can nature be both creative and destructive?

Set Purpose

Before you begin to read "Once by the Pacific," answer these questions: How many lines are in the poem? How many stanzas? What is the rhyme scheme?

Analyze Literature

Symbolism A **symbol** is a thing that represents itself and something else. As you read "Once by the Pacific," think about the various things being described. What might those things, including the setting, the characters, and their actions, represent?

Use Reading Skills

Analyze Text Organization A *sonnet* is one of the most common poetic forms. A traditional Shakespearean, or English, sonnet is made up of one stanza with fourteen lines organized in three quatrains, or four-line sections, plus a final couplet, or two-line section. The rhyme scheme is *abab cdcd efef gg*. As you read "Once by the Pacific," use a two-column chart to determine how the poem's organization compares with that of a traditional sonnet.

Traditional Sonnet	"Once by the Pacific"
Number of lines:	Number of lines:
Rhyme scheme:	Rhyme scheme:
Stanza structure:	Stanza structure:

Meet the Author

Robert Frost (1874–1963) was born in San Francisco but moved to New England at the age of eleven. He began writing poetry in high school. Frost supported himself and his family through a variety of occupations before achieving success with the publication in 1915 of two poetry collections. While Frost is widely known for poems that celebrate nature's beauty and peacefulness, much of his work, like "Once by the Pacific," is characterized by solemn reflections on life and death.

Preview Vocabulary

din (din) *n.*, loud noise

in•tent (in tent´) *n.*, purpose

Once by the Pacific

A Lyric Poem
by
Robert Frost

Downpour at Etretat, 19th century. Gustave Courbet. Musée des Beaux-Arts, Dijon, France.

The shattered water made a misty din.
Great waves looked over others coming in,
And thought of doing something to the shore
That water never did to land before.
The clouds were low and hairy in the skies,
Like locks blown forward in the gleam of eyes.
You could not tell, and yet it looked as if
The shore was lucky in being backed by cliff,
The cliff in being backed by continent;
It looked as if a night of dark intent
Was coming, and not only a night, an age.
Someone had better be prepared for rage.
There would be more than ocean-water broken
Before God's last *Put out the Light* was spoken. ✣

din (din) *n.,* loud noise

DURING READING
Analyze Literature
Symbolism What might the waves symbolize? Explain.

in • tent (in tent´) *n.,* purpose

DURING READING
Use Reading Skills
Text Organization What is this poem's rhyme scheme?

Would you want to witness the scene being described by the poem's speaker? Why might this scene seem frightening to some people?

Find Meaning

1. (a) According to the speaker, what are the waves doing? (b) What mood does the speaker's description of the waves create?
2. (a) What does the speaker say is coming? (b) What evidence does the speaker offer in support of this prediction?

Make Judgments

3. (a) What image is suggested by the personification in lines 5 and 6? (b) What traits does this image seem to convey? Explain.
4. (a) How does the last couplet refer back to the beginning of the poem? (b) What do the words *"Put out the Light"* suggest?

Analyze Literature

Symbolism How does Frost use symbolism to convey meaning in this poem? Analyze symbols in the poem by listing the symbols in the left column. Then in the right column, write the meaning of the symbols or the ideas that they suggest to you.

Symbol	Meaning
water	

Extend Understanding

Writing Options

Descriptive Writing Refer to the chart you created to analyze the symbolism in "Once by the Pacific." Think about each symbol you identified. What other symbols might represent the same thing? Record details about each new symbol that you imagine. Then choose one of your symbols and use it in a **descriptive paragraph.**

Informative Writing Reread Frost's poem. Try to determine, based on the setting, tone, mood, and other details, what caused the speaker to adopt the perspective in the poem. Write a brief **cause-and-effect essay** in which you state the speaker's outlook and determine the causes for that outlook. Use both direct quotations and paraphrases in support of your claims. At the end of your essay, restate your main idea.

Collaborative Learning

Discuss Responses How does this poem make you feel? Discuss your responses with a partner. Begin by brainstorming a list of adjectives that describe your feelings. What words, rhymes, rhythms, or images specifically influenced your reactions? What mental pictures did you imagine as you read the poem? Summarize the mood and its causes in one or two sentences.

Lifelong Learning

Research the Sonnet The two main types of sonnet are the Shakespearean, or English, sonnet and the Petrarchan, or Italian, sonnet. Research these different forms and collect examples of each type. What are the most common subjects of the sonnets you have collected? Present examples in support of your claims.

Go to **www.mirrorsandwindows.com** for more.

Comparing Texts

Annabel Lee

A Narrative Poem by Edgar Allan Poe

The Highwayman

A Narrative Poem by Alfred Noyes

BEFORE READING

Build Background

Literary Context Poetry that tells a story has ancient roots in the oral tradition. From Greek epics to English ballads, these works were often recited from memory and passed from one generation to another. Some tell exciting tales, such as *The Odyssey,* which relates the adventures of a Greek hero. Other narrative poems relate religious lessons, stories of idealized love, historical events, or personal experiences.

Reader's Context How would you react to a sudden dramatic change in your life?

Set Purpose

Preview these poems' rhyme schemes, rhythms, and text structures. Predict the effects of these elements on each poem.

Compare Literature: Narrative Poetry

A **narrative poem** is a poem that tells a story. Like a short story or a novel, it has characters, setting, plot, and point of view. Use a two-column chart to record the story elements and the poetic elements in "Annabel Lee" and "The Highwayman."

"Annabel Lee"

Poetic Elements	Story Elements
Rhyme Scheme	

Meet the Authors

Edgar Allan Poe (1809–1849) achieved fame as a writer of short stories, poetry, and literary criticism. His haunting poems dwell on melancholy themes and death. "Annabel Lee" was published in 1849, two years after the death of Poe's wife, Virginia.

Alfred Noyes (1880–1958) was born in Wolverhampton, England, and published his first collection of poems at the age of twenty-one. By the age of twenty-eight, he had published five more volumes of poetry. From 1914 to 1923, he taught in the United States.

Preview Vocabulary

bear (ber) *v.*, carry; **bore** *past tense*

peak•ed (pē´ kid) *adj.*, thin and drawn, as from sickness

writhe (rīth) *v.*, twist and turn

re•frain (ri frān´) *n.*, phrase or verse in a song or poem that is repeated throughout

bran•dish (bran´ dish) *v.*, wave threateningly

Found Drowned, 1848–1850. George Frederick Watts. Watts Gallery, Compton, Surrey, Great Britain.

Annabel Lee

A Narrative Poem by Edgar Allan Poe

It was many and many a year ago,
    In a kingdom by the sea.
That a maiden there lived whom you may know
    By the name of Annabel Lee;
And this maiden she lived with no other thought
    Than to love and be loved by me.

I was a child and *she* was a child,
    In this kingdom by the sea;
But we loved with a love that was more than love—
    I and my Annabel Lee—
With a love that the wingèd seraphs of heaven
    Coveted her and me.[1]

And this was the reason that, long ago,
    In this kingdom by the sea,
A wind blew out of a cloud, chilling
    My beautiful Annabel Lee;
So that her highborn kinsmen came
    And bore her away from me,
To shut her up in a sepulcher[2]
    In this kingdom by the sea.

The angels, not half so happy in heaven,
    Went envying her and me—
Yes!—that was the reason (as all men know,
    In this kingdom by the sea)
That the wind came out of a cloud, by night,
    Chilling and killing my Annabel Lee.

But our love it was stronger by far than the love
    Of those who were older than we—
    Of many far wiser than we—
And neither the angels in heaven above
    Nor the demons down under the sea,
Can ever dissever[3] my soul from the soul
    Of the beautiful Annabel Lee:

---

1. **the wingèd seraphs...Coveted her and me.** The angels envied us.
2. **sepulcher.** Tomb or grave
3. **dissever.** Break; sever

bear (ber) *v.*, carry; **bore** *past tense*

For the moon never beams, without bringing me dreams
Of the beautiful Annabel Lee;
And the stars never rise, but I feel the bright eyes
    Of the beautiful Annabel Lee;
And so, all the night-tide, I lie down by the side
Of my darling—my darling—my life and my bride,
    In her sepulcher there by the sea—
    In her tomb by the sounding sea. ✤

CULTURAL ▶▶ CONNECTION

Gothic Literature Edgar Allan Poe wrote during the Victorian Era (1837–1901) and was influenced by the revival of interest in Gothic art, architecture, and literature. The term *Gothic* originally described the heavy, ornate style of art and architecture popular in western Europe during the twelfth through the fifteenth century. *Gothic* later came to be applied to the genre of literature popularized by writers such as Horace Walpole (*The Castle of Otranto,* 1765) and Ann Radcliffe (*The Mysteries of Udolpho,* 1794). The typical Gothic novel is a dark tale of mystery and suspense that features lonely and foreboding settings, evil or mad characters, supernatural elements, and heightened emotion. In what ways does Poe's poem meet these criteria?

Gothic Cathedral Seen through Ruins of a Castle, c. 1852. Carl Gustav Carus. Folkwang Museum, Essen, Germany.

What do you think about the way the speaker in the poem is coping with the death of his loved one? How is his reaction typical or atypical?

Find Meaning

1. (a) At what time in their lives were Annabel Lee and the speaker in love? (b) How much time has passed since then? Explain.

2. (a) What does the speaker say happened to Annabel Lee? (b) Whom does he blame? (c) What do you think really happened to her?

Make Judgments

3. In the fourth stanza, the speaker says, "Yes!–that was the reason...." What impression is created by the poet's use of the exclamation mark? Explain.

4. (a) What does the speaker do at the end of the poem? (b) What do you think he expects to happen?

The Highwaymen, c. 20th century. George Derville Rowlandson. Private collection.

The Highwayman[1]

A Narrative Poem by Alfred Noyes

1. **Highwayman.** Robber who preys on travelers on the highways

PART ONE

The wind was a torrent of darkness among the gusty trees.
The moon was a ghostly galleon[2] tossed upon cloudy seas.
The road was a ribbon of moonlight over the purple moor,[3]
And the highwayman came riding—
    Riding—riding—
The highwayman came riding, up to the old inn door.

He'd a French cocked hat on his forehead, a bunch of lace at his chin,
A coat of the claret[4] velvet, and breeches of brown doeskin.
They fitted with never a wrinkle. His boots were up to the thigh.
And he rode with a jewelled twinkle,
    His pistol butts a-twinkle,
His rapier hilt[5] a-twinkle, under the jewelled sky.

Over the cobbles he clattered and clashed in the dark inn yard,
And he tapped with his whip on the shutters, but all was locked and barred;
He whistled a tune to the window, and who should be waiting there
But the landlord's black-eyed daughter,
    Bess, the landlord's daughter,
Plaiting a dark red love-knot[6] into her long black hair.

And dark in the dark old inn yard a stable wicket[7] creaked
Where Tim the ostler[8] listened. His face was white and <u>peaked</u>.
His eyes were hollows of madness, his hair like mouldy hay,
But he loved the landlord's daughter,
    The landlord's red-lipped daughter,
Dumb[9] as a dog he listened, and he heard the robber say—

"One kiss, my bonny[10] sweetheart, I'm after a prize tonight,
But I shall be back with the yellow gold before the morning light;
Yet, if they press me sharply, and harry[11] me through the day,
Then look for me by moonlight,
    Watch for me by moonlight,
I'll come to thee by moonlight, though hell should bar the way."

---

2. galleon. Large sailing ship
3. moor. Flat, open land
4. claret. Purplish-red color
5. rapier hilt. Sword handle
6. Plaiting a dark red love-knot. Braiding a dark red ribbon
7. wicket. Small door or gate
8. ostler. Person who takes care of horses at an inn
9. dumb. Silent
10. bonny. Pretty; fine
11. harry. Torment; harass

peak • ed (pē´ kid) *adj.*, thin and drawn, as from sickness

He rose upright in the stirrups. He scarce could reach her hand,
But she loosened her hair in the casement.[12] His face burnt like a brand[13]
As the black cascade of perfume came tumbling over his breast;
And he kissed its waves in the moonlight,
(O, sweet black waves in the moonlight!)
Then he tugged at his rein in the moonlight, and galloped away to the west.

PART TWO

He did not come in the dawning. He did not come at noon;
And out of the tawny sunset, before the rise of the moon,
When the road was a gypsy's ribbon, looping the purple moor,
A red coat troop[14] came marching—
Marching—marching—
King George's men came marching, up to the old inn door.

They said no word to the landlord. They drank his ale instead,
But they gagged his daughter, and bound her, to the foot of her narrow bed.
Two of them knelt at her casement, with muskets[15] at their side!
There was death at every window;
And hell at one dark window;
For Bess could see, through her casement, the road that *he* would ride.

---

12. casement. Window frame
13. brand. Burning torch
14. red coat troop. Group of soldiers wearing red coats
15. muskets. Long-barreled firearms

They had tied her up to attention,[16] with many a sniggering jest;[17]
They had bound a musket beside her, with the muzzle beneath her breast!
"Now, keep good watch!" and they kissed her. She heard the doomed man say—
Look for me by moonlight;
    Watch for me by moonlight;
I'll come to thee by moonlight, though hell should bar the way!

She twisted her hands behind her, but all the knots held good!
She writhed her hands till her fingers were wet with sweat or blood!
They stretched and strained in the darkness, and the hours crawled by like years,
Till, now, on the stroke of midnight,
    Cold, on the stroke of midnight,
The tip of one finger touched it! The trigger at last was hers!

The tip of one finger touched it. She strove no more for the rest!
Up, she stood up to attention, with the muzzle beneath her breast.
She would not risk their hearing; she would not strive again;
For the road lay bare in the moonlight;
    Blank and bare in the moonlight;
And the blood of her veins in the moonlight, throbbed to her love's refrain.

Tlot-tlot; tlot-tlot! Had they heard it: The horsehoofs ringing clear;
Tlot-tlot, tlot-tlot, in the distance? Were they deaf that they did not hear?
Down the ribbon of moonlight, over the brow of the hill,
The highwayman came riding—
    Riding—riding—
The red-coats looked to their priming![18] She stood up, straight and still!

Tlot-tlot, in the frosty silence! *Tlot-tlot,* in the echoing night!
Nearer he came and nearer. Her face was like a light.
Her eyes grew wide for a moment; she drew one last deep breath,
Then her finger moved in the moonlight,
    Her musket shattered the moonlight,
Shattered her breast in the moonlight and warned him—with her death.

---

16. tied her up to attention. Tied her to her bedpost, standing upright, with her hands at her sides
17. sniggering jest. Mocking joke
18. looked to their priming. Began to get their muskets ready to fire

writhe (rīth) *v.*, twist and turn

re•frain (ri frān´) *n.*, phrase or verse in a song or poem that is repeated throughout

He turned. He spurred to the westward; he did not know who stood
Bowed, with her head o'er the musket, drenched with her own red blood!
Not till the dawn he heard it, and his face grew grey to hear
How Bess, the landlord's daughter,
    The landlord's black-eyed daughter,
Had watched for her love in the moonlight, and died in the darkness there.

Back, he spurred like a madman, shrieking a curse to the sky,
With the white road smoking behind him and his rapier brandished high.
Blood-red were his spurs in the golden noon, wine-red was his velvet coat;
When they shot him down on the highway,
    Down like a dog on the highway,
And he lay in his blood on the highway, with a bunch of lace at his throat.

And still of a winter's night, they say, when the wind is in the trees,
When the moon is a ghostly galleon tossed upon cloudy seas,
When the road is a ribbon of moonlight over the purple moor,
A highwayman comes riding—
    Riding—riding—
A highwayman comes riding, up to the old inn door.

Over the cobbles he clatters and clangs in the dark inn yard.
He taps with his whip on the shutters, but all is locked and barred.
He whistles a tune to the window, and who should be waiting there
But the landlord's black-eyed daughter,
    Bess, the landlord's daughter,
Plaiting a dark red love-knot into her long black hair. ✤

bran•dish (bran´ dish) *v.*, wave threateningly

Would you describe the actions of the characters in "Annabel Lee" and "The Highwayman" as romantic, tragic, noble, or foolish? Do you think the characters behave like people from real life?

Comparing Texts

AFTER READING

Find Meaning

1. Why do you think the poet divided the poem into two parts?
2. (a) What does the highwayman tell Bess he is going to do? (b) How does Bess feel about the highwayman? How do you know this?
3. (a) What do the red coats do when they arrive at the inn? (b) How do you think they knew the highwayman would come there?

Make Judgments

4. Why do you think the highwayman decides to go back to the inn when he learns what happened to Bess instead of taking the opportunity to escape?
5. What do the last two stanzas suggest about Bess and the highwayman?

Compare Literature

Narrative Poetry Narrative poetry tells a story using rhyme, rhythm, and repetition as well as literary elements common to prose fiction. Review the charts that you created as you read "Annabel Lee" and "The Highwayman" to answer the following questions.

1. In what ways are the characters and settings in "Annabel Lee" and "The Highwayman" alike? In what ways are they different?
2. (a) How would you describe the mood of each poem? (b) What images create this mood?
3. What effect does each poet create through the use of rhyme, rhythm, and repetition?

Extend Understanding

Writing Options

Narrative Writing Think of an exciting incident in your own life or in someone else's that would make a good subject for a **narrative poem.** Before you begin to write your poem, decide what point of view you will use. Would the action be more effectively told from the first- or third-person point of view? Once you have finished, share your poem with the class.

Informative Writing Recall what you know about the character traits of the women depicted in the two poems. What do their actions say about them? Which one would you prefer to meet? In a short **essay,** compare and contrast Annabel Lee and Bess, explaining which one you would choose to meet and why. Then compare your choice with the choices your classmates made.

Critical Literacy

Hold a Panel Discussion Which form of poetry do you prefer—narrative or lyric? With a small group, discuss the merits of each type. In what situations might you prefer to read or listen to a narrative poem? Might some topics, moods, or themes be better suited to lyric poems? Might some be better suited to narrative poems? Be sure to support your claims with evidence.

Lifelong Learning

Write a Literary Critique Research the careers and works of Edgar Allan Poe and Alfred Noyes. Locate and study another poem by each writer. Then write a paragraph that discusses how the poems that you studied fit into the poets' larger bodies of work. Consider each poem's tone, the cultural environment in which it was written, and the author's biography. When you are finished, share your research with the class.

Go to **www.mirrorsandwindows.com** for more.

The Filling Station

A Lyric Poem by Elizabeth Bishop

BEFORE READING

Build Background

Literary Context Elizabeth Bishop published only five volumes of poetry during her lifetime. She tended to devote herself to perfecting each single piece, working and reworking it, rather than quickly moving on to the next poem. The care she took is evident in her precise and detailed observations. She also traveled widely, and her work often reflects her interest in geography. "The Filling Station," which first appeared in her 1965 book *Questions of Travel,* is one such poem.

Reader's Context What can you learn about people by carefully examining the spaces they inhabit?

Set Purpose

Preview the poem's six stanzas, noting the punctuation and the lengths of lines. Consider how these elements influence the way in which you read the poem.

Analyze Literature

Tone A writer's or speaker's attitude toward his or her subject is **tone.** A piece of literature can have many different tones. For example, it could be humorous, serious, angry, or ironic. Elements that contribute to tone include word choice, connotation, figurative language, sentence structure, images, and dialogue. Tone in poetry is also affected by rhyme and rhythm. As you read "The Filling Station," try to determine the poem's tone or tones.

Use Reading Skills

Identify the Main Idea
When reading a poem, it is often necessary to infer the main idea. Pay attention to details, such as the tone, mood, and direct statements made by the speaker. Use a main idea map like the one below to help you determine the main idea in "The Filling Station."

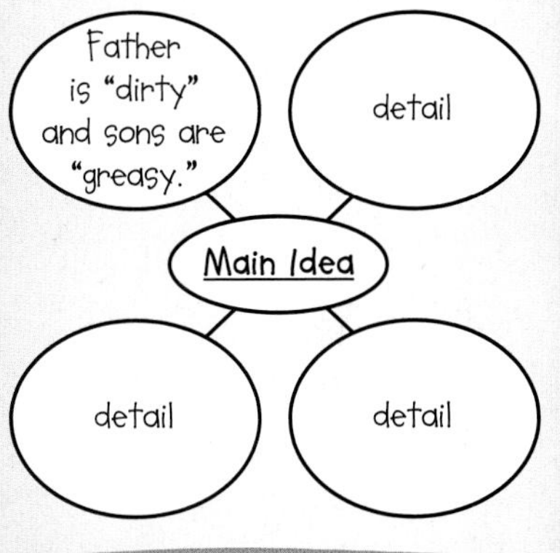

DIRECTED READING

Meet the Author

Elizabeth Bishop (1911–1979) lost her parents at a young age and was raised by relatives in New England and Nova Scotia. After graduating from Vassar College, she traveled in Europe and Africa and then lived in places as varied as Florida, California, Mexico, and Brazil. Bishop won many awards during her lifetime, including the 1956 Pulitzer Prize for Poetry. She also wrote short stories, translated Portuguese literature, and loved to paint.

Preview Vocabulary

trans • lu • cen • cy (tran[t]s lü´ s'nt sē) *n.,* quality of being transparent or allowing some light to pass through

sau • cy (sô sē) *adj.,* bold

ex • tra • ne • ous (ek strā´ nē əs) *adj.,* not essential; not a part of the main idea

cro • chet (krō´shā´) *n.,* needlework made by interlocking loops of thread using a hooked needle

high-strung (hī´ strʉŋ´) *adj.,* nervous; extra sensitive

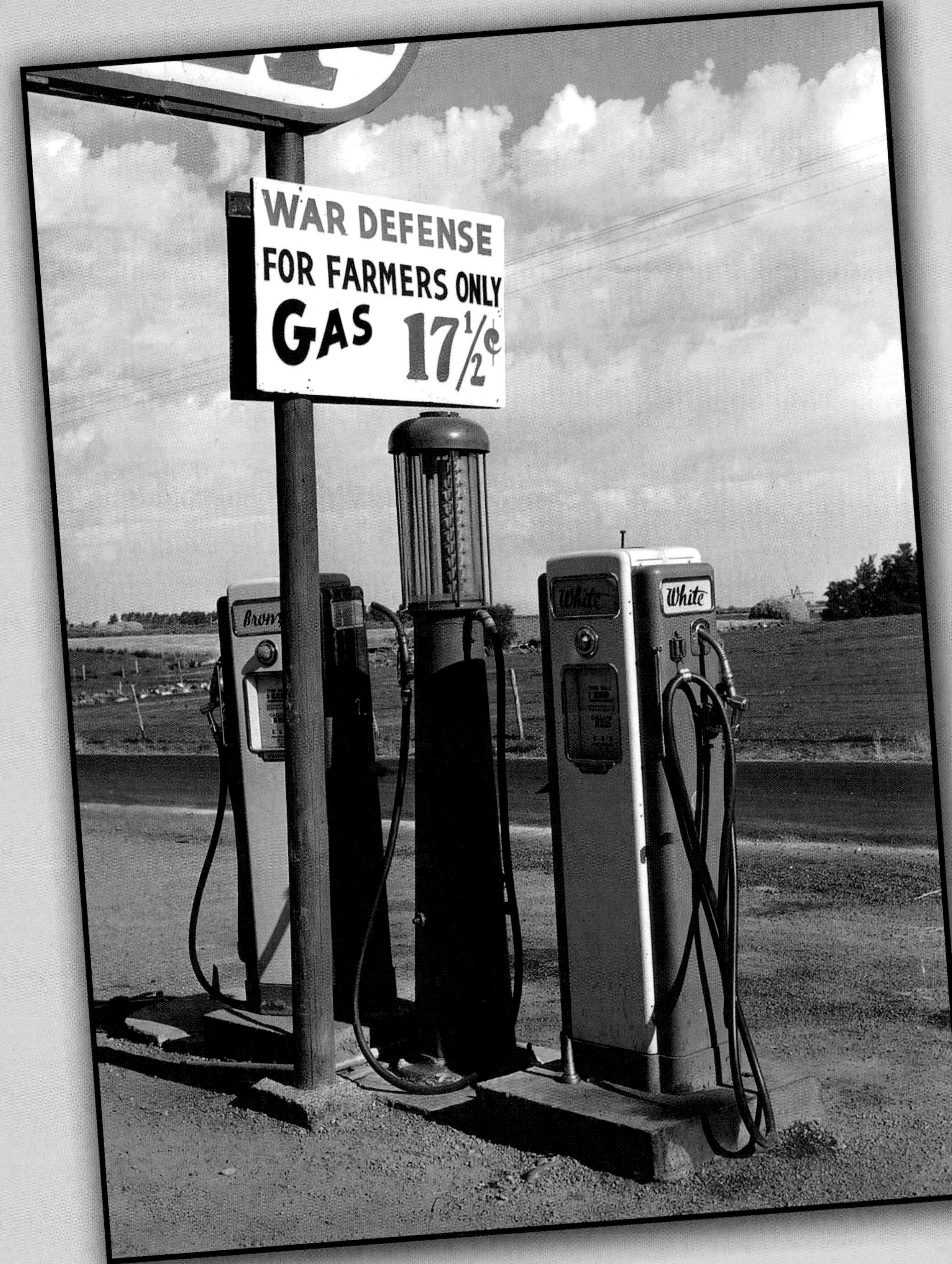
WAR DEFENSE
FOR FARMERS ONLY
GAS 17½¢
White
White

The Filling Station

A Lyric Poem by Elizabeth Bishop

Oh, but it is dirty!
—this little filling station,[1]
oil-soaked, oil-permeated
to a disturbing, over-all
black translucency.
Be careful with that match!

Father wears a dirty,
oil-soaked monkey suit[2]
that cuts him under the arms,
and several quick and saucy
and greasy sons assist him
(it's a family filling station),
all quite thoroughly dirty.

Do they live in the station?
It has a cement porch
behind the pumps, and on it

a set of crushed and grease-
impregnated[3] wickerwork;
on the wicker sofa
a dirty dog, quite comfy.

Some comic books provide
the only note of color—
of certain color. They lie
upon a big dim doily[4]
draping a taboret[5]
(part of the set), beside
a big hirsute begonia.[6]

Why the extraneous plant?
Why the taboret?
Why, oh why, the doily?
(Embroidered in daisy stitch[7]
with marguerites,[8] I think,
and heavy with gray crochet.)
Somebody embroidered the doily.
Somebody waters the plant,
or oils it, maybe. Somebody
arranges the rows of cans
so that they softly say:
ESSO-SO-SO-SO
to high-strung automobiles.
Somebody loves us all. ✤

---

1. **filling station.** Gas station
2. **monkey suit.** Protective overalls worn by mechanics
3. **grease-impregnated.** Filled or saturated with grease
4. **doily.** Small decorative mat
5. **taboret.** Stool or small side table, often shaped like a drum
6. **hirsute begonia.** Type of flowering plant with a hairy stem
7. **daisy stitch.** Stitch used in embroidery, often to create flowers
8. **marguerites.** Daisies; also other flowers that resemble daisies

trans • lu • cen • cy (tran[t]s lü´ s'nt sē) *n.*, quality of being transparent or allowing some light to pass through

sau • cy (sô sē) *adj.*, bold

ex • tra • ne • ous (ek strā´ nē əs) *adj.*, not essential; not a part of the main idea

cro • chet (krō´shā´) *n.*, needlework made by interlocking loops of thread using a hooked needle

high-strung (hī´ strəŋ´) *adj.*, nervous; extra sensitive

How might your initial impression of something change? Do you think a person's willingness to change his or her mind is a good or bad trait?

AFTER READING

Find Meaning

1. (a) What is the only "note of color" in the filling station? (b) How does this note of color compare with the rest of the filling station?
2. (a) What are some of the most frequently repeated words in the poem? (b) What effect does Bishop achieve through this repetition?

Make Judgments

3. Which parts of this poem do you find humorous? Explain.
4. Is the poet's overall attitude toward the scene positive or negative? Explain your answer using examples from the poem.

Analyze Literature

Tone Images, figurative language, and word choice can all help establish tone. Idiom, or language used by a particular class or group, can also influence tone. For example, only a speaker knowledgeable about furniture would choose to say *taboret*; others might just say *stool*. Collect details from the poem that contribute to the tone. Then write a sentence that you think best describes the tone.

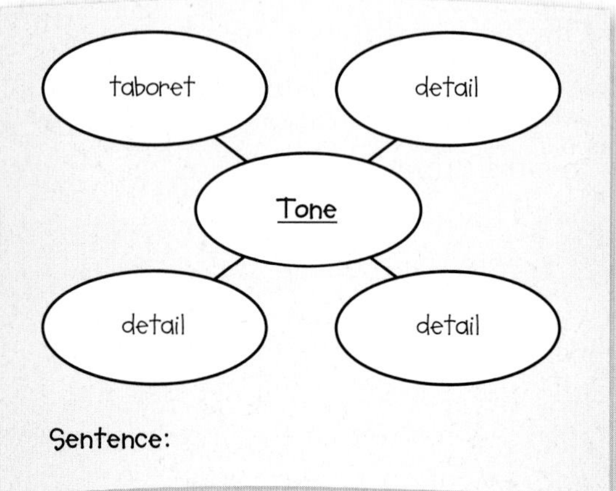

Extend Understanding

Writing Options

Narrative Writing Imagine that you are one of the people Elizabeth Bishop encounters at the filling station. Write a very brief **short story** from that character's point of view, giving your account of the poet's visit to the filling station. Use sensory details to give readers a feeling for how you experience the place, and include dialogue and descriptive details to flesh out the characters. Share your story with the class.

Informative Writing In "The Filling Station," the speaker describes reactions to a filling station, noting the different surprising objects there. In literature, the difference between appearance and reality is referred to as irony. In a short **essay,** analyze the role irony plays in the poem. Provide at least three examples from the poem, explaining why they are ironic and how they express the speaker's feelings or the tone of the piece.

Collaborative Learning

Consider the Author's Perspective Working in a small group, talk about the author's perspective in the poem. As part of the discussion, you may wish to take into account both what you have learned about Bishop's life and the evidence in the poem itself. Be sure to take notes as you discuss. Present your ideas, and the reasons for them, to the class.

Media Literacy

Draw the Images An image is a vivid mental picture created in a reader's mind by language. When considered all together, the images in a literary work are referred to as imagery. Draw some of the images that came to mind as you read "The Filling Station." Exchange your pictures with a classmate. Ask him or her to look at your drawings and to describe the images he or she sees. How are these descriptions like or unlike the images you meant to represent?

Go to **www.mirrorsandwindows.com** for more.

Vocabulary & Spelling

Figurative Language

Somebody
arranges the rows of cans
so that they softly say:
ESSO-SO-SO-SO
to high-strung automobiles.

—ELIZABETH BISHOP, "The Filling Station"

Figurative language is language that expresses more than literal meaning through imaginative or poetic use of words. Poets often use figurative language to help the reader visualize. In the quotation above, Bishop uses an **idiom,** an expression that means something other than what the words literally mean. The expression *high-strung* is an idiom that means "extremely nervous" or "sensitive." *Easy as pie* and *facing the music* are common idioms.

An **analogy** is an extended comparison between two different things. For example, in "The Filling Station," the speaker compares the care someone took in embroidering a doily to demonstrating love.

Two other common types of figurative language are metaphor and simile. A **metaphor** is a comparison between two seemingly unrelated things.

EXAMPLE
The stars were flickering white moths.

A **simile** is a comparison between two seemingly unrelated things that uses the word *like* or *as*.

EXAMPLE
The boys ate like wild animals.

Vocabulary Practice

Identify the type of figurative language in each example from "The Highwayman."

1. The wind was a torrent of darkness among the gusty trees.
2. Her face was like a light.
3. With the white road smoking behind him....
4. Down like a dog on the highway....
5. When the road was a gypsy's ribbon, looping the purple moor....
6. The moon was a ghostly galleon tossed upon cloudy seas.
7. ...his hair like mouldy hay....
8. His face burnt like a brand....
9. ...he spurred like a madman....
10. ...the hours crawled by like years....

Spelling Practice

Words with Vowel Combinations

Vowel combinations can be tricky in spelling because the same pair of letters can be pronounced in different ways. Review this list of spelling words from "The Filling Station" to see different vowel combinations. Try to group the words according to the sound produced by the vowel combination.

automobiles	greasy
certain	heavy
daisy	saucy
embroidered	soaked
extraneous	thoroughly

A Lyric Poem by Phil George

ANCHOR TEXT

DIRECTED READING

BEFORE READING

Build Background

Cultural Context In the late 1800s and early 1900s, the U.S. government forced Native Americans to send their children to church- or government-sponsored schools. These schools required the students to conform to the language, dress, and religion of white people. Native Americans were forced to take English given names. Translations of Native Americans' traditional names were forbidden or strongly discouraged. Government or church officials assigned everyone new names, such as James Peterson and Mary Smith.

Reader's Context To what degree is your name part of who you are? Why?

Set Purpose

Before you begin reading, examine the poem's structure. Watch for patterns in stanza and line length. Consider how these elements influence your interpretation of the poem.

Analyze Literature

Lyric Poetry A **lyric poem** expresses the emotions of the poem's speaker and focuses on a single moment, image, or idea. Lyric poetry is often musical and, unlike narrative poetry, does not tell a story. As you read "Name Giveaway," identify the elements that make this a lyric poem.

Use Reading Skills

Analyze Text Organization A *couplet* is a pair of lines that forms a unit in a poem. In "Name Giveaway," each couplet forms a single stanza. Use a two-column chart to note the idea or emotion expressed in each couplet.

Couplet	Ideas or Emotions
first	
second	
third	

Preview Vocabulary

as•cend (ə send´) *v.*, move upward; rise

Meet the Author

Phil George (1946–2012) was born in Seattle, Washington. He attended Gonzaga University in Spokane, Washington, and the Institute of American Indian Arts in Santa Fe, New Mexico. George's poetry has been published in several anthologies, and he also produced and narrated the video recording *A Season of Grandmothers* for the Public Broadcasting Service. He was a champion Traditional Plateau dancer and a member of the Seven Drums religion.

NAME GIVEAWAY

A Lyric Poem by Phil George

That teacher gave me a new name...again.
She never even had feasts or a giveaway!

Still I do not know what "George" means;
and now she calls me: "Phillip."

TWO SWANS <u>ASCENDING</u> FROM STILL WATERS
must be a name too hard to remember. ✤

as • cend (ə send′) *v.*, move upward; rise

How would you react if you were in the speaker's situation? Would you be angry, sad, or indifferent? How do you think most people would react?

Find Meaning

1. (a) What does the teacher do to the speaker? (b) What does the speaker suggest the teacher should have done?
2. What does the speaker dislike about the name "George"?

Make Judgments

3. (a) What was the speaker's name before the teacher renamed him? (b) How is this name different from "George" or "Phillip"?
4. What feeling do you think the original name inspired in the speaker?

PRIMARY SOURCE ▶▶ CONNECTION

In the lyric poem "Name Giveaway," Phil George muses about how he feels when his teacher gives him a new name. In the following excerpt from a memoir, **Ah-nen-la-de-ni** describes his experiences in a government school for Indians. After he finished school, Ah-nen-la-de-ni became a nurse.

from An Indian Boy's Story

A Memoir by Ah-nen-la-de-ni

When I was thirteen a great change occurred, for the honey-tongued agent of a new Government contract Indian school appeared on the reservation, drumming up boys and girls for his institution. He made a great impression by going from house to house and describing, through an interpreter, all the glories and luxuries of the new place, the good food and teaching, the fine uniforms, the playground and its sports and toys.

All that a wild Indian boy had to do, according to the agent, was to attend this school for a year or two, and he was sure to emerge there from with all the knowledge and skill of the white man....

I had, up to this time, been leading a very happy life, helping with the planting, trapping, fishing, basket making and playing all the games of my tribe—which is famous at lacrosse—but the desire to travel and see new things and the hope of finding an easy way to much knowledge in the wonderful school outweighed my regard for my home and its joys, and so I was one of the twelve boys who in 1892 left our reservation to go to the Government contract school for Indians, situated in a large Pennsylvania city and known as the Institute.

Till I arrived at the school I had never heard that there were any other Indians in the country other than those of our reservation, and I did not know that our tribe was called Mohawk. My people called themselves "Ga-nien-ge-ha-ga," meaning "People of the Beacon Stone," and Indians generally they termed "On-give-hon-we," meaning "Real-men" or "Primitive People."

My surprise, therefore, was great when I found myself surrounded in the school yard by strange Indian boys belonging to tribes of which I had never heard, and when it was said that my people were only the "civilized Mohawks," I at first thought that "Mohawk" was a nickname and fought any boy who called me by it.

I had left home for the school with a great deal of hope, having said to my mother:

"Do not worry. I shall soon return to you a better boy and with a good education!" Little did I dream that that was the last time I would ever see her kind face. She died two years later, and I was not allowed to go to her funeral.

The journey to Philadelphia had been very enjoyable and interesting. It was my first ride on the "great steel horse," as the Indians called the railway train, but my frame of mind changed as soon as my new home was reached.

The first thing that happened to me and to all other freshly caught young redskins when we arrived at the institution was a bath of a particularly disconcerting sort. We were used to baths of the swimming variety, for on the reservation we boys spent a good deal of our time in the water, but this first bath at the institution was different. For one thing, it was accompanied by plenty of soap, and for another thing, it was preceded by a haircut that is better described as a crop.

The little newcomer, thus cropped and delivered over to the untender mercies of larger Indian boys of tribes different from his own, who laughingly attacked his bare skin with very hot water and very hard scrubbing brushes, was likely to emerge from the encounter with a clean skin but perturbed mind. When, in addition, he was prevented from expressing his feelings in the only language he knew, what wonder if some rules of the school were broken.

After the astonishing bath the newcomer was freshly clothed from head to foot, while the raiment in which he came from the reservation was burned or buried. Thereafter he was released by the torturers, and could be seen sidling about the corridors like a lonely crab, silent, sulky, immaculately clean and most disconsolate.

After my bath and reclothing and after having had my name taken down in the records I was assigned to a dormitory, and began my regular school life, much to my dissatisfaction. The recording of my name was accompanied by a change which, though it might seem trifling to the teachers, was very important to me. My name among my own people was "Ah-nen-la-de-ni," which in English means "Turning crowd" or "Turns the crowd," but my family had had the name "La France" bestowed on them by the French some generations before my birth, and at the institution my Indian name was discarded, and I was informed that I was henceforth to be known as Daniel La France.

It made me feel as if I had lost myself. I had been proud of myself and my possibilities as "Turns the crowd," for in spite of their civilized surroundings the Indians of our reservation in my time still looked back to the old warlike days when the Mohawks were great people, but Daniel La France was to me a stranger and a nobody with no possibilities. It seemed as if my prospect of a chiefship had vanished. I was very homesick for a long time. ✣

TEXT ◄TO► TEXT CONNECTION

Both Phil George's poem and Ah-nen-la-de-ni's memoir describe the experience of being given a new name. What does the memoir add to your understanding of the poem? Would the poem serve as a good summary of the experience described in the memoir?

AFTER READING

Analyze Literature

Lyric Poetry A lyric poem expresses the emotions of the poem's speaker, or narrator, and focuses on a single moment, image, or idea. Use a chart to sort out the name changes in "Name Giveaway" and the speaker's feelings about each of his names. In the left column, list, in order, the names given to the speaker. In the right column, write how the speaker felt about each name.

Names	Feelings
George	puzzled

Extend Understanding

Writing Options

Creative Writing The speaker in "Name Giveaway" and Ah-nen-la-de-ni both had strong reactions when their teachers changed their names, yet they went along with the name changes. Imagine that you are a friend of Ah-nen-la-de-ni and that you want to write a **letter** to tell his teacher how he feels about the name change. In the letter, explain why she should stop changing her students' names. Provide solid reasons and examples, and use a polite, knowledgeable tone. Remember to use a business-letter format for your letter.

Informative Writing How do you feel about your own name? What do you like or dislike about it? Would you change it if you could? If so, what would you change it to? Why? Write a brief **personal essay** explaining to your family how you feel about your own name. Give reasons why you would or would not like to change your name. In your concluding paragraph, restate the main idea of your essay.

Critical Literacy

List Questions Imagine that you were given the opportunity to interview Phil George about his life and work. Use the library to research information about him. As you take notes during the research process, record questions you would like to ask the poet. Then meet with a small group to compile the most interesting questions or the questions most necessary for holding a successful interview.

Lifelong Learning

Research History With a partner, research the history of Native American schools. Brainstorm a list of questions about the schools. Where were they located? When were they established? Who ran the schools? What was the reason for having separate schools for Native Americans? Why did Native Americans send their children to these schools? Record the information that you uncover and share your findings with the class.

Go to **www.mirrorsandwindows.com** for more.

Vocabulary & Spelling

Spelling by Syllables

That teacher gave me a new name... again.

—PHIL GEORGE, "Name Giveaway"

How many syllables does the word *again* have? A syllable is a part of a word that contains a single vowel sound. All words have at least one syllable. Understanding how to break words into syllables can help you sound out unfamiliar words and spell them correctly.

There is no single correct way to divide syllables, or syllabicate, and sometimes you will see the same word divided two different ways. There are some general guidelines, however, that will help you syllabicate many words. Here are some of them. *V* stands for vowel and *C* stands for consonant.

Pattern 1: VCV If a word contains a consonant between two vowels, and the first vowel is long, you should break the word after the first vowel. If the vowel is short, break after the consonant.

EXAMPLES

so-lo

cab-in

Pattern 2: VCCV If a word contains two consonants together, you should usually break the word between the two consonants.

EXAMPLE

mud-dy

Pattern 3: VV If a word contains two vowels and both vowels are pronounced, divide the word between the two vowels.

EXAMPLE

cli-ent

Pattern 4: Prefixes A prefix always forms a separate syllable.

EXAMPLE

un-lock

Pattern 5: Suffixes A suffix forms a syllable if it contains a vowel.

EXAMPLE

sense-less

The suffix *-y* follows the VCCV rule.

EXAMPLE

hear-ty

Spelling Practice

Exercise A

Write each of the following words, separating syllables with hyphens. Check your answers by looking up the words in a dictionary. Identify the words' part of speech and pronunciation.

1. billow
2. hammer
3. triumph
4. decline
5. prefer
6. warmly

Exercise B

Determine the meaning of the following words by looking them up and noting where their prefixes and suffixes originated (Greek, Latin, etc.). Then, break the words into their proper syllables.

1. antibody
2. unpublished
3. hyperbole
4. physics
5. universe
6. transfer

Ancestors

A Lyric Poem by Dudley Randall

DIRECTED READING

BEFORE READING

Build Background

Cultural Context Dudley Randall reached the height of his influence during the most active years of the Civil Rights movement. He devoted his career to promoting African-American poets and often wrote about racial themes. His famous poem "The Ballad of Birmingham" is about the racially motivated bombing of an Alabama church. "Ancestors" addresses a less dramatic topic: the genealogical research among people who want to learn about their cultural heritage. In the poem, he pokes gentle fun at people's tendency to claim they descend from nobility.

Reader's Context What do you know about your ancestors?

Set Purpose

Before you begin reading, try to determine whether "Ancestors" is a free verse poem or if it is written in a form you recognize.

Analyze Literature

Author's Purpose An **author's purpose,** or aim, is his or her goal for writing a piece of literature. For example, an author may write to inform, to persuade, or to entertain. Writers may also have multiple purposes. The author's purpose is different from theme, or the work's central idea. As you read "Ancestors," think about why Randall might have written the poem—what was his purpose?

Use Reading Skills

Analyze Main Idea and Supporting Details To identify the main idea of "Ancestors," gather details in a main idea map. Then examine the details to determine the author's overall message.

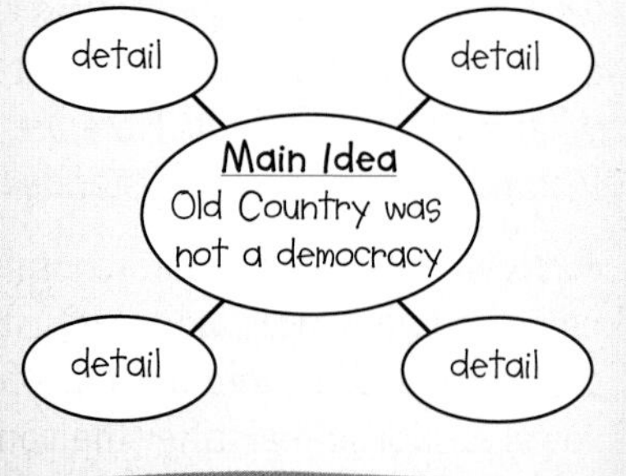

Preview Vocabulary

ar•is•toc•ra•cy (a' rə stä´ krə sē) *n.*, noble or privileged class; government by people who belong to the noble class

by•gone (bī´ gôn') *adj.*, long ago; in the distant past

Meet the Author

A dedicated poet from childhood, **Dudley Randall** (1914–2000) published his first poems at thirteen. Following high school, he supported his writing by working at the Ford Motor Company and then as a mail carrier in Detroit, his hometown. After serving in World War II, he earned a degree and became a librarian. In 1965, Randall founded the Broadside Press and promoted the era's most promising African-American poets. Among other honors, he was named poet laureate of Detroit in 1981.

Ancestors

A Lyric Poem by Dudley Randall

Why are our ancestors
always kings or princes
and never the common people?

Was the Old Country a democracy
where every man was a king?
Or did the slavecatchers
take only the aristocracy
and leave the fieldhands
laborers
streetcleaners
garbage collectors
dishwashers
cooks
and maids
behind?

My own ancestor
(research reveals)
was a swineherd[1]
who tended the pigs
in the Royal Pigstye
and slept in the mud
among the hogs.

Yet I'm as proud of him
as of any king or prince
dreamed up in fantasies
of bygone glory. ✤

1. **swineherd.** Person who tends pigs

ar•is•toc•ra•cy (a' rə stä´ krə sē) *n.*, noble or privileged class; government by people who belong to the noble class

by•gone (bī´ gôn') *adj.*, long ago; in the distant past

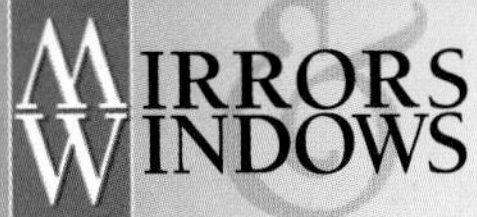

Why is it important to know about your ancestors? How much does it matter to you what kind of people your ancestors were? How do most people feel about their ancestors?

AFTER READING

Find Meaning

1. (a) From where did the speaker's ancestor come? (b) What led you to this conclusion?
2. (a) How did the speaker find out about his or her ancestor? (b) How does the speaker suspect that people have discovered their royal ancestry?

Make Judgments

3. (a) What are some of the occupations the speaker mentions in this poem? (b) In what way does the speaker's use of this list reinforce the poem's main idea?
4. (a) The speaker begins by asking three questions in a row. What effect do these questions create? (b) What sort of answers do you think the speaker expects to receive?

Analyze Literature

Author's Purpose The author's purpose is the reason for writing. The theme is the main message the author hopes to convey to readers. Create a chart identifying the purpose and theme of "Ancestors." Finally, provide an evaluation of how well Dudley Randall succeeded in his goals, from your own point of view as a reader.

Purpose	Theme
persuade	

My Evaluation:

Extend Understanding

Writing Options

Creative Writing Imagine that you have been commissioned to write a **biography** of the speaker's ancestor. Tell the story of the swineherd in chronological order so that the earliest events are told first. Use specific details. For example, be sure to include the place and year of his birth, his occupation, and other vital details. Also include at least one anecdote about the person.

Informative Writing In the last stanza of the poem, the speaker says of his or her ancestor, "I'm as proud of him / as of any king or prince...." Write an **informative paragraph** in which you explain why the speaker might feel this way. Use details from the poem, as well as your own analysis of the issues Randall raises in the poem, to support your thesis.

Critical Literacy

Hold a Panel Discussion Hold a panel discussion to explore the risks and benefits of knowing about ancestry. Agree beforehand who will moderate, or lead the discussion, and decide what points of view the participants will represent. Be sure that you always present evidence in support of your claims, and listen respectfully to other viewpoints.

Lifelong Learning

Research Your Ancestry Investigate your own roots or the roots of someone you admire by doing genealogical research. Talk to your parents, grandparents, and other relatives. Investigate genealogical websites. Use your findings to draw a family tree that goes back at least three generations. Include photos or hand-drawn portraits, as well as brief interesting facts, if desired. Display the family tree in your classroom.

Go to **www.mirrorsandwindows.com** for more.

Grammar & Style

Simple, Complete, and Compound Predicates

Simple and Complete Predicates

My own ancestor…
was a swineherd
who tended the pigs....

—DUDLEY RANDALL, "Ancestors"

The **simple predicate** is the key verb or verb phrase that tells what the subject does, has, or is. The **complete predicate** includes the verb and all the words that modify it. In the quotation above, *was* is the simple predicate and *was a swineherd who tended the pigs* is the complete predicate.

In the following examples, a vertical line separates the subject from the complete predicate. The simple predicate, or verb, is underlined.

EXAMPLES

Ancestors | are people from whom we descend.

All the members of my family | have sung their hearts out.

Compound Predicates

Or did the slavecatchers
take only the aristocracy
and leave the fieldhands....

—DUDLEY RANDALL, "Ancestors"

A **compound predicate** has two or more simple predicates, or verbs, that share the same subject. The verbs are connected by the conjunction *and, or,* or *but.* In the quotation above, *take* and *leave* share the subject, *slavecatchers.*

EXAMPLES

She | traced her ancestors and created a family tree.

My grandfather | met, proposed to, and married my grandmother within a month.

Identifying Simple, Complete, and Compound Predicates

On a separate sheet of paper, rewrite each sentence and draw a vertical line between the complete subject and predicate. Then underline once the simple predicate. Underline twice each compound predicate.

1. One of my ancestors bought land and built houses for all his children.
2. Jamal found addresses for all his cousins and sent them invitations to a family reunion.
3. My grandmother and great-aunt have never agreed.
4. Today would have been my great-grandfather's one hundredth birthday.
5. The first members of our family to arrive here lived, worked, and died within five miles of this house.
6. Many people in my family built their own homes.
7. My father returned from my grandparents' house and told us all about the trip.
8. His youngest sister called home that night.
9. Many of Tom's ancestors lived and worked in Dublin.
10. Carrie walked to the library and spoke with the librarian.

The Lost Parrot

A Narrative Poem by Naomi Shihab Nye

DIRECTED READING

BEFORE READING

Build Background

Scientific Context "The Lost Parrot" is about a boy who is trying to write a poem describing a bird he once had as a pet. *Parrot* is the general term for a varied group of birds, including cockatoos, macaws, and parakeets, that typically live in warm habitats, such as tropical rain forests. More commonly, the term *parrot* is used to refer to large birds with colorful feathers, strong beaks, and fleshy tongues that enable them to mimic words and even sentences.

Reader's Context At some time or other, most of us have lost something or someone we particularly valued. How did you react to your loss at the time?

Set Purpose

Skim through the poem quickly to get a general sense of what it is about. Read to find out who Carlos is and what he is like.

Analyze Literature

Symbol A **symbol** is a thing that stands for both itself and something else. Some traditional symbols include the dove for peace and the lion for courage. Writers also create symbols of their own to represent personal meanings. As you read "The Lost Parrot," decide what the bird might symbolize.

Use Reading Skills

Compare and Contrast
When you compare and contrast, you try to determine what is similar and what is different between two or more things. As you read the poem, compare and contrast the speaker and Carlos. What traits do they share? What makes them different from one another? Use a Venn diagram like the one below.

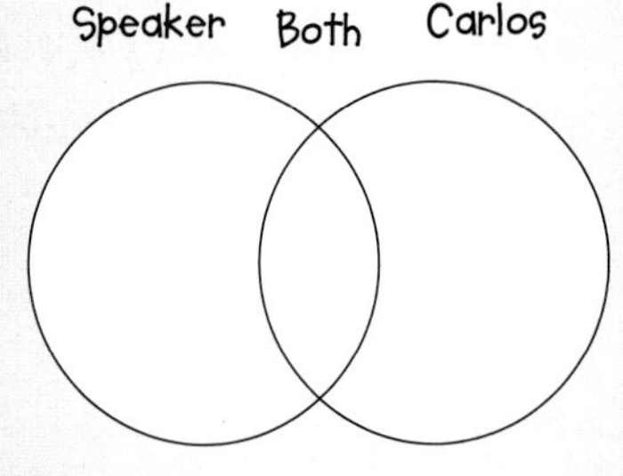

Meet the Author

Naomi Shihab Nye is an award-winning Arab-American poet. Born in 1952 to an American mother and a Palestinian father, she began to write poetry as a child and had her first poems published when she was seven. Her family later moved to San Antonio, which is still her home. After college, she worked as a poet in the schools, encouraging students to explore the material of their own lives through words. "The Lost Parrot" grew out of this experience.

The Lost Parrot

A Narrative Poem
by Naomi Shihab Nye

Carlos bites the end of his pencil
He's trying to write a dream-poem, but waves at me, frowning

I had a parrot

He talks slowly, like his voice travels far
to get out of his body

A dream-parrot?

No, a real parrot!
Write about it

He squirms, looks nervous, everyone else is almost finished
and he hasn't started

It left
What left?
The parrot

He hunches over the table, pencil gripped in fist,
shaping the heavy letters
Days later we will write story-poems, sound-poems,
but always the same subject for Carlos

It left

He will insist on reading it and the class will look puzzled
The class is tired of the parrot

Write more, Carlos
I can't

Why not?

I don't know   where   it went

Each day when I leave he stares at the ceiling
Maybe he is planning an expedition
into the back streets of San Antonio
armed with nets and ripe mangoes
He will find the parrot nesting in a rain gutter
This time he will guard it carefully, make sure it stays

Before winter comes and his paper goes white
in all directions

Before anything else he loves
gets away ✣

When have you tried to use art, such as writing or drawing, to help cope with a loss or a change in your life? Why might creative acts help people deal with loss or change?

AFTER READING

Find Meaning

1. (a) What is Carlos trying to write a poem about? (b) What are the only words he is able to write? (c) Why do you think he is unable to write more?
2. (a) What does the speaker imagine Carlos is planning? (b) Why does the speaker think Carlos wants to do this?

Make Judgments

3. (a) What words and phrases does the speaker use to describe Carlos? (b) How would you sum up the speaker's description of Carlos?
4. What impression of the speaker do you get from this poem?
5. What is being compared in lines 31–32, "Before winter comes and his paper goes white / in all directions"?
6. Why do you think the parrot is so important to Carlos?

Analyze Literature

Symbol Symbols can be either traditional—such as a lamb for innocence—or personal, created by a writer to express some special meaning. In this poem, does the parrot function as a traditional symbol or a personal symbol? What do you think the parrot represents to Carlos? What do you think the bird represents to the speaker? Record your thoughts in a two-column chart.

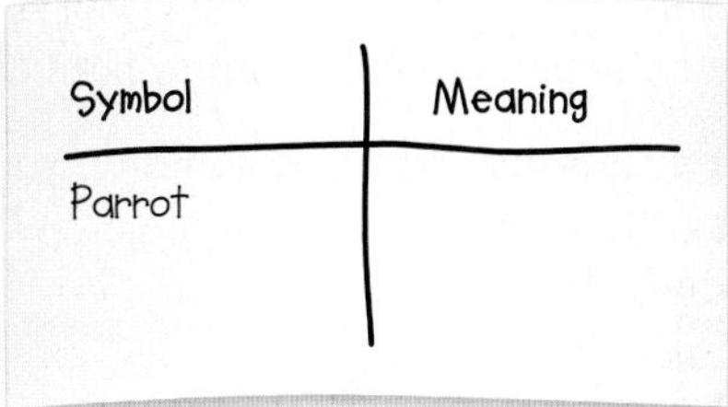

Extend Understanding

Writing Options

Creative Writing According to Naomi Shihab Nye, the images on which a dream poem is based can occur during either sleep or daydreams. She notes, "These can be kooky things, impossible things, wished-for things." She also urges students to "stay in the dream," and not conclude their poems by stating that they woke up. Use Nye's guidelines to write a **dream poem** of your own.

Argumentative Writing Poet William Stafford has described Naomi Shihab Nye as "a champion of the literature of encouragement." Use information from both Meet the Author and "The Lost Parrot" to write an **argumentative paragraph** supporting this view of Nye. Begin your paragraph with a thesis statement, and end it with a summary of all your paragraph's main points. Then exchange your paragraph with a partner.

Collaborative Learning

Speaking and Listening People experience many types of loss throughout life. Family members and friends die; homes and possessions are destroyed by storms, fires, and other disasters. People deal with these losses in very different ways. With other students, have a discussion exploring the effectiveness of various strategies for coping with loss.

Media Literacy

Wild Parrots The award-winning 2003 documentary *The Wild Parrots of Telegraph Hill* presents the fascinating experiences of Mark Bittner, who became the unofficial caretaker of flocks of wild parrots living around San Francisco. Working with a group of classmates, view the film and discuss how the film explores the relationship between Bittner and these birds.

Go to **www.mirrorsandwindows.com** for more.

For My Father

A Narrative Poem by Janice Mirikitani

BEFORE READING

Build Background

Historical Context Near the turn of the twentieth century, many Japanese immigrants made a living as strawberry farmers, especially on the rich farmlands of California, Washington, and Oregon. World War II and the bombing of Pearl Harbor led to the internment of thousands of Japanese Americans and immigrants by the U.S. government. Most Japanese-American strawberry farmers did not return to farming after World War II.

Reader's Context What memories do you have from your early childhood that are impossible to forget? Why are they so vivid in your mind?

Set Purpose

Look at the structure, or the way the words are arranged on the page, in this poem. What can you predict about the poem? Revise your prediction as you read.

Analyze Literature

Hyperbole Exaggeration used for effect is called **hyperbole.** For example, saying someone ate a mountain of spaghetti is an exaggeration. Its effect might be to make someone smile, or to make someone understand that overeating is taking place. As you read "For My Father," identify uses of hyperbole and their effects on you.

Use Reading Skills

Analyze Text Structure
When you read a poem, ask yourself why it takes a particular form or arrangement on the page. Think about how the author may want the poem to be viewed or read and why. As you read "For My Father," use an organizer like this one to sum up the effect of each stanza.

Structure	Effect
stanza 2: four lines	describes child's thoughts

Preview Vocabulary

hack (hak) *v.*, chop or cut forcefully

shield (shēld) *v.*, protect, guard, or defend against

Meet the Author

Janice Mirikitani (b. 1942) spent the first years of her life in an internment camp. Her family, along with thousands of other Japanese Americans, most of whom were U.S. citizens, had been interned against their will after Japan's attack on Pearl Harbor during World War II. In her poetry, Mirikitani often expresses her anger regarding this experience, as well as strong themes of family and her Japanese-American identity.

For My Father

A Narrative Poem by Janice Mirikitani

He came over the ocean
carrying Mt. Fuji[1]
on his back/Tule Lake[2] on his chest
hacked through the brush
of deserts
and made them grow
strawberries

we stole berries
from the stem
we could not afford them
for breakfast

his eyes held
nothing
as he whipped us
for stealing.

the desert had dried
his soul.

wordless
he sold
the rich,
full berries
to hakujines[3]
whose children
pointed at our eyes

they ate fresh
strawberries
with cream.

Father,
I wanted to scream
at your silence.
Your strength
was a stranger
I could never touch.

iron
in your eyes
to shield
the pain
to shield desert-like wind
from patches
of strawberries
grown
from
tears. ✤

---

1. **Mt. Fuji.** Sacred mountain in Japan; a symbol of Japan
2. **Tule Lake.** Camp in Arkansas where Japanese-American people were interned from 1942–1946
3. **hakujines.** Japanese term meaning Caucasians

hack (hak) *v.*, chop or cut forcefully

shield (shēld) *v.*, protect, guard, or defend against

HISTORY ▶▶ CONNECTION

Japanese Internment When Japan bombed Pearl Harbor in Hawaii during World War II, the U.S. government reacted by officially entering the war. The government also began rounding up Japanese Americans in the United States and interning, or imprisoning, them in camps against their will. Tule Lake was the largest of all these internment camps, and life there was harsh. Japanese Americans were crammed into poor housing and received inadequate food and medical care. In addition, like the Japanese Americans who were interned in other camps, they lost everything they had. How does this affect your understanding of the speaker's father?

What kinds of difficulties have your parents faced? How can parents' experiences affect the lives of their children?

AFTER READING

Find Meaning

1. Who is the speaker of this poem?
2. What does the father do that makes the speaker so angry?
3. (a) Who do you think the "we" are in stanza 2? (b) Who are "they" in stanza 6?

Make Judgments

4. (a) Why do you think the father in this poem behaves so harshly to the speaker? (b) How does the speaker feel about it now?
5. In the middle of the poem, the speaker makes a shift in who he or she is addressing. What are the effects of this shift on the reader?
6. This is a short poem—it has just 113 words. How well does the author characterize the father in this short space? Explain.

Analyze Literature

Hyperbole Where did you find hyperbole as you read the poem? What effect did it have on you as a reader? Make a chart like this one to record two or more examples of hyperbole from the poem and to reflect on the emotions or reactions they caused. Then explain how the hyperbole helped you understand the father, the speaker, or the situation better.

Hyperbole	Effect
hacked	sounds angry

Extend Understanding

Writing Options

Creative Writing What would you like to say to a parent or older person about an experience from your past? Write a **personal letter** to someone you are close to about your own experience.

Informative Writing In a few words, sum up your personal response to this poem. Then think about how your response would have been different if the poem had been written in a less emotional tone or with less hyperbole. Write a **literary response** in which you evaluate the difference. Be sure to begin with a clear thesis that states your opinion. Use evidence, such as details, quotes, and examples from the poem to support your opinion.

Lifelong Learning

Research and Report Mt. Fuji is Japan's largest and most majestic mountain. It has been the inspiration of writers, artists, and poets for hundreds of years, and serves as a symbol of Japan throughout the world. Research the mountain, its landscapes, geography, climate, and neighboring inhabitants. Prepare a report for your class, including visual aids.

Critical Literacy

Write a Dialogue Imagine that the father in this poem read the poem and now wants to respond to the speaker. What do you think he might say to the speaker? How might the speaker reply? Create and write the dialogue you imagine taking place between the speaker and the father. Use natural, everyday language and clearly convey the feelings of each person.

Go to **www.mirrorsandwindows.com** for more.

Money Order and Sisters

Poems by Janet S. Wong

BEFORE READING

Build Background

Cultural Context Both of the poems you are about to read use food imagery typical of Asian and Asian-American dishes: rice, fish, tofu, and ginger. Rice is the most important staple of the Asian diet, and variations of fish and rice or salt fish and rice are typical main dishes. Tofu and ginger are common ingredients in the cuisine of China, Korea, and other Asian countries.

Reader's Context Do you have any relatives you have never met? What do you know about them? What do you think they know about you?

Set Purpose

Read the titles of the poems and preview the illustrations that accompany them. What can you predict about the content of each poem? Revise your prediction after you read the first stanza of each poem.

Analyze Literature

Irony The contrast between what is expected and what actually happens is **irony.** Often you can identify irony in literature by noticing outcomes to situations that seem to be the opposite of what you, as a reader, expected. This type of irony is called situational irony. As you read "Money Order" and "Sisters," look for examples of irony.

Use Reading Skills

Evaluate Cause and Effect When you evaluate cause and effect, you are looking for a logical relationship between a cause, or causes, and one or more effects. When you read poetry, you often have to infer causes and effects. As you read "Money Order," use an organizer like this one to identify causes and effects that you can infer from the poem.

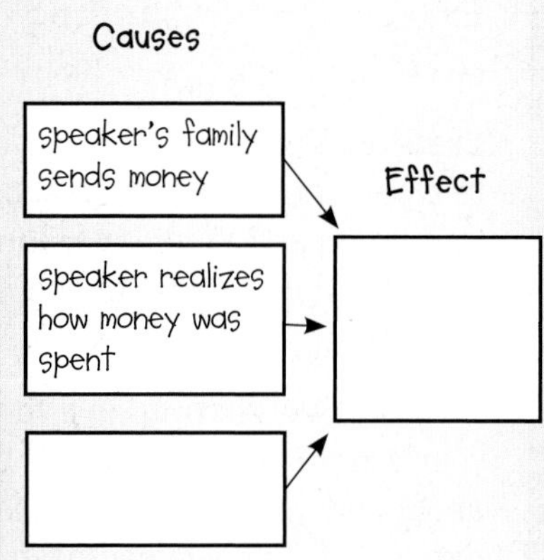

Meet the Author

Janet S. Wong was born in Los Angeles, California, in 1962 to a Korean mother and a Chinese father. Although Wong was educated as an attorney and has practiced law, she has made her reputation as an author of children's poetry. Her poems often use simple words and forms, as well as dashes of humor or irony, to present insight into issues of Asian-American identity. Wong lives on Bainbridge Island, Washington, with her husband and son. The following poems are taken from Wong's collection *A Suitcase of Seaweed and Other Poems.*

Money Order

A Narrative Poem by Janet S. Wong

We eat salt fish[1] and rice,
night after night after night,
to save some money
to send
to cousins
I never have seen

who used our money last year
to buy a color TV,
so they could watch
rich Americans
eating
steak and potatoes. ✣

1. **salt fish.** Fish that has been preserved with salt; salt fish is a cheaper alternative to fresh fish

Sisters

A Lyric Poem by Janet S. Wong

She calls me tofu[1]
because I am so soft,
easily falling apart.

I wish I were tough
and full of fire, like ginger[2]—
like her. ✤

1. **tofu.** White-colored, protein-rich but bland-tasting food made from soybeans
2. **ginger.** Root that is usually sliced, diced, or grated to give a strong, spicy flavor and aroma to a dish

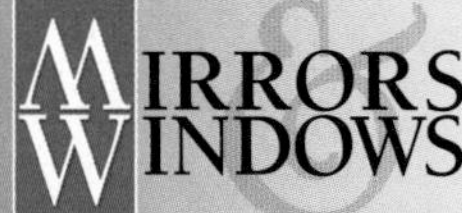

MIRRORS & WINDOWS What feelings are expressed in these poems that you have felt too? Why might these be common feelings?

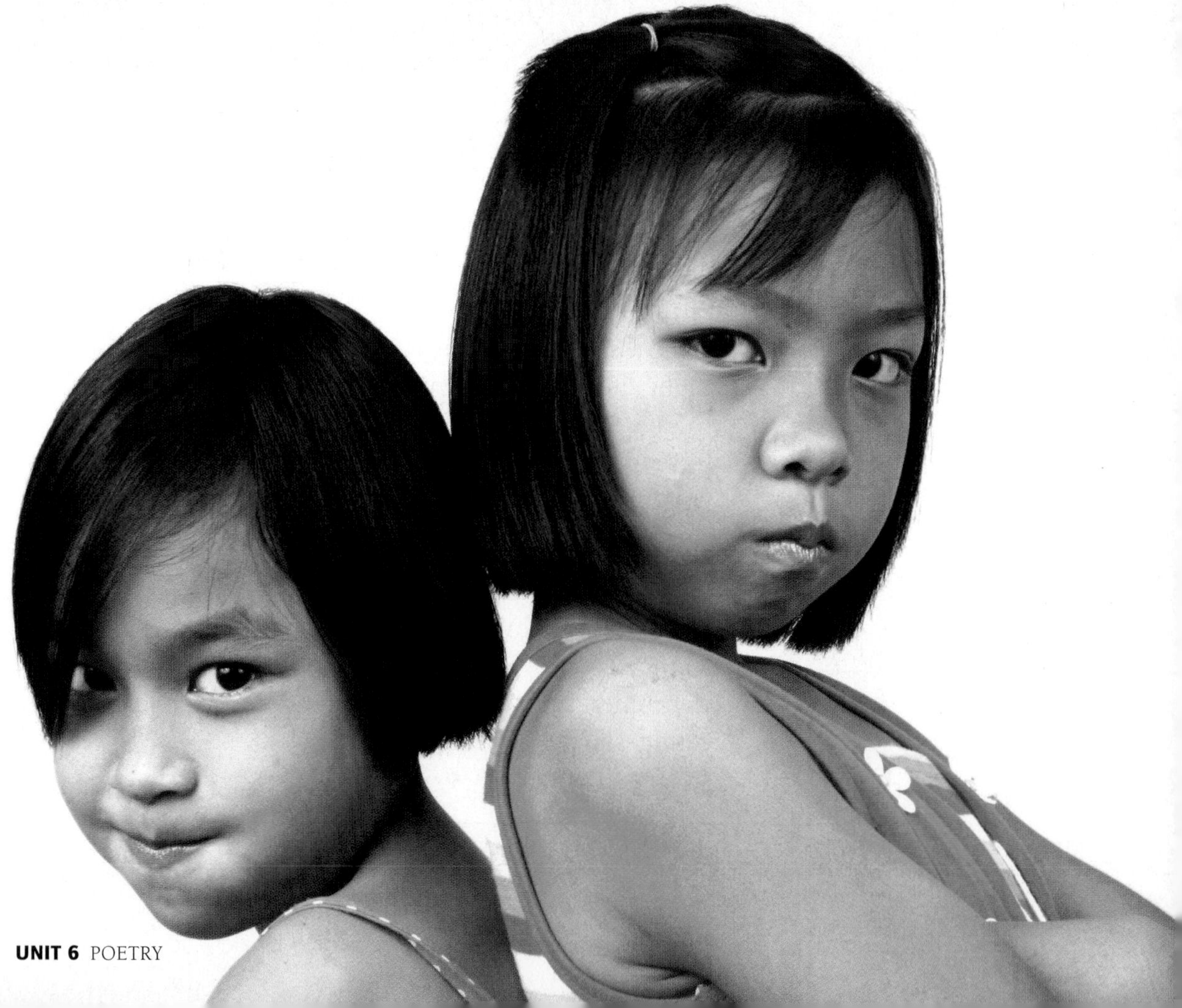

AFTER READING

Find Meaning

1. In "Money Order," who is the speaker referring to with the use of "we"?
2. In "Money Order," where do you think the cousins live?
3. What do you learn about the speaker in "Sisters"?

Make Judgments

4. How does the speaker in "Money Order" feel about sending money to her cousins?
5. (a) What does the title "Money Order" refer to? (b) Why is it a good title for the poem?
6. (a) In "Sisters," how are the sisters different? (b) How are they alike?

Analyze Literature

Irony Several details help create the irony in "Money Order." For example, the cousins probably think of the speaker's family as rich, but what is really true? The cousins may also have a vision of the speaker's family living like the Americans on television live. Use a chart to record details from the poem that are ironic, and explain how they suggest the opposite of what may be true.

Detail	Irony
eating salt fish and rice	

Extend Understanding

Writing Options

Creative Writing Travel brochures often make places seem fabulous—even if the picture they paint is not always accurate. Make a **travel brochure** that tells about your own city or town. Instead of presenting only the best things about your town, however, be as realistic about it as you can. Be as truthful as you would be to good friends or relatives who are thinking about moving there.

Informative Writing What makes you different from other members of your family? What traits do you share with siblings, parents, grandparents, aunts, or uncles? Write a **compare-and-contrast** essay in which you describe the traits that you share with members of your family and the things that make you unique. Be sure to include a thesis statement and support.

Collaborative Learning

Discuss and Speculate The speakers in both "Money Order" and "Sisters" see themselves in comparison to others. In a small group, discuss whether people always define or view themselves, at least in some ways, in comparison with others. Is it possible for us to define ourselves outside the context of those around us? Brainstorm a list of reasons that support your group's decision.

Media Literacy

Contrast Appearance and Reality One reason for the popularity of so-called "reality" television shows may be that many media images are so far from reality. With a partner, discuss the difference between how reality is portrayed in television shows, ads, games, magazines, and so on, and how you see yourself, your own life, and the lives of others around you. Come up with at least three contrasts. Cite specific ads, shows, movies, or other works on which you based each contrast.

Go to **www.mirrorsandwindows.com** for more.

INDEPENDENT READING

La Grande Guerre, 1964.
René Magritte. Private collection.

I'm Nobody

A Lyric Poem
by Emily Dickinson

I'm Nobody! Who are you?
Are you—Nobody—too?
Then there's a pair of us!
Don't tell! they'd banish us—you know!

How dreary—to be—Somebody!
How public—like a Frog—
To tell your name—the livelong June—
To an admiring Bog![1] ✣

1. bog. Marsh or swamp

In her own time, **Emily Dickinson**'s use of punctuation and syntax was considered bizarre. However, she is now considered one of the greatest innovators in American poetry. Dickinson was born in Amherst, Massachusetts, in 1830 and rarely strayed beyond its borders. She was notoriously secretive and published very few poems in her own lifetime. After Dickinson's death in 1886, "corrected" versions of her collected poems appeared, in which her lines were changed to suit the tastes of the day. Not until 1955 were Dickinson's poems finally published in their original unedited state.

When have you felt it was better to be unseen or unnoticed? Why did you feel this way? When might being "somebody" have its disadvantages?

Analyze and Extend

1. In the opening stanza, to whom do you think the speaker is directing these questions? Explain.
2. What do you think the speaker means by the statement, "they'd banish us–you know!"
3. (a) In the second stanza, to what does the speaker compare being "Somebody?"
   (b) What do you think the speaker's attitude toward "Somebodies" is?

Informative Writing Tone is the author's or speaker's attitude toward his or her subject. What do you think the tone of this poem is? Is it humorous? Is it angry? Write a **literary analysis** in which you analyze the poem's tone. Include a thesis statement, and support your claims with evidence from the text. When you are finished, compare your response with that of a partner.

Lifelong Learning Use the library to locate and read more of Emily Dickinson's poetry. *The Poems of Emily Dickinson,* edited by Thomas H. Johnson, contains all 1,775 of her poems. Read several poems and try to locate common themes, topics, and stylistic elements such as rhyme and rhythm. Write a paragraph in which you describe Dickinson's style and her common subjects and themes.

Go to **www.mirrorsandwindows.com** for more.

Provence Kitchen, 20th century. Josephine Trotter. Private collection.

Refugee Ship

A Lyric Poem by Lorna Dee Cervantes

Like wet cornstarch, I slide
past my grandmother's eyes. Bible
at her side, she removes her glasses.
The pudding thickens.
Mama raised me without language,

I'm orphaned from my Spanish name.
The words are foreign, stumbling
on my tongue. I see in the mirror
my reflection: bronzed skin, black hair.

I feel I am a captive
aboard the refugee ship.
The ship that will never dock.
El barco que nunca atraca.[1] ✣

---

1. *El barco...atraca.* The ship that never docks (Spanish)

Lorna Dee Cervantes was born in San Francisco in 1954. When she was a young person, her parents forbade her and her brother from speaking Spanish in the house. Throughout her life, she has been active in civil rights and political movements, including the American Indian Movement. In 1981, she won the American Book Award for *Emplumada,* her first collection of poems. Cervantes has also been awarded grants for poetry from the National Endowment for the Arts, the Paterson Prize for Poetry, and the Latino Literature Award.

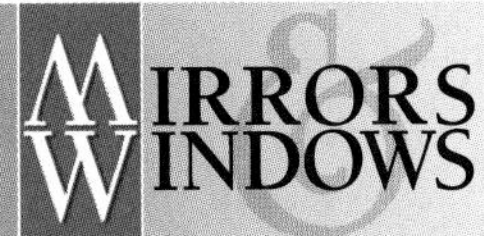

When have you felt cut off from your past or from your family? How did you respond to these feelings? How important is it for people to hold on to their heritage?

Analyze and Extend

1. Explain what you think the speaker means by the comparison made in the opening two lines of the poem.
2. (a) From what is the speaker orphaned? (b) What do you think this means?
3. Is a refugee ship an appropriate symbol for the speaker's situation? Why or why not?

Creative Writing Imagine that you are the speaker in this poem. How would it feel to be in this situation? Write a **diary entry** in the speaker's voice about your feelings. Use information from the poem to help you describe these feelings and your relationship with your mother and grandmother. Title your diary entry "Refugee Ship."

Collaborative Learning Gather in small groups and discuss what the "refugee ship" symbolizes. Does it symbolize the speaker's feelings? Her relationship with her family? Her relationship with her heritage? Be specific. One person in your group should act as secretary and record your discussion and your conclusions about the meaning of this symbol. When you are done, share your thoughts with the class.

 Go to **www.mirrorsandwindows.com** for more.

Loo Wit

A Lyric Poem
by Wendy Rose

The way they do
this old woman
no longer cares
what others think
but spits her black tobacco
any which way
stretching full length
from her bumpy bed.
Finally up
she sprinkles
ashes on the snow,
cold buttes[1]
promising nothing
but the walk
of winter.
Centuries of cedar
have bound her
to earth,
huckleberry ropes
lay prickly
on her neck.
Around her
machinery growls,
snarls and ploughs
great patches
of her skin.
She crouches
in the north,
her trembling
the source
of dawn.

1. **buttes.** Steep hills with flat tops

Wendy Rose was born in California in 1948. Her father was of Hopi descent and her mother was Miwok, a Native American tribe with traditional lands in Northern California. Much of Rose's verse explores issues of tribal identity and Rose's search for her own personal identity. The poem examines a violent natural catastrophe from a distinctly Native American perspective. As Rose has said, "For everything in this universe there is a song to accompany its existence."

Light appears
with the shudder
of her slopes,
the movement
of her arm.
Blackberries unravel,
stones dislodge.
It's not as if
they weren't warned.

She was sleeping
but she heard
the boot scrape,
the creaking floor,
felt the pull of the blanket
from her thin shoulder.
With one free hand
she finds her weapons
and raises them high;
clearing the twigs
from her throat
she sings, she sings,
shaking the sky
like a blanket about her
Loo-Wit[2] sings and sings and sings! ✣

---

2. **Loo-Wit.** Mount Saint Helens; this mountain, situated in southern Washington State, erupted in 1980. It was the most catastrophic volcanic event in the recorded history of North America.

How would you describe a natural disaster? How might figurative language and sensory details enhance your description? When might a straightforward description using facts and figures be more effective?

SCIENCE ▶▶ CONNECTION

Mount Saint Helens Before 1980, Mount Saint Helens had a symmetrical cone that is now largely gone. The eruption was preceded by two months of localized earthquakes and emissions of steam. Then on the morning of May 18, 1980, the volcano erupted for nine hours, beginning with a gigantic lateral explosion that devastated more than 150 square miles, flattening forests and blocking rivers. Mount Saint Helens continued to erupt intermittently for the next three days, destroying vast amounts of wildlife and leaving fifty-seven people dead. Spewed sixteen miles into the air, volcanic ash spread over large areas of the Northwest, bringing midday darkness, disrupting travel, and causing widespread economic damage. In "Loo Wit," the speaker says, "It's not as if they weren't warned." What form might these "warnings" have taken?

Analyze and Extend

1. (a) To what does the speaker compare Loo-Wit? (b) In what ways is this an effective comparison?
2. The speaker claims that around Loo-Wit "machinery growls, / snarls and ploughs / great patches / of her skin." Why do you think the speaker claims that this caused the eruption?
3. What do you think the speaker means by the poem's final line?

Informative Writing This poem uses personification, in which nonhuman things are given human characteristics. How does personification make this poem more effective? Write a **literary analysis** of Rose's use of personification. Be sure to support your claims with evidence from the text. Then exchange your response with a classmate and discuss your reactions.

Lifelong Learning The eruption of Mount Saint Helens was catastrophic. The effects of the blast could be felt around the world. Tons of ash and rock were thrown far into the air. Use a library database to locate books about this eruption and its aftermath. Record the most interesting information you locate. Then use this material to create a poster with images and facts, and present it to the class.

Go to **www.mirrorsandwindows.com** for more.

Canterbury Meadows, 1862. Thomas Sidney Cooper. Art Gallery of New South Wales, Sydney, Australia.

The Pasture

A Lyric Poem by Robert Frost

I'm going out to clean the pasture spring;
I'll only stop to rake the leaves away
(And wait to watch the water clear, I may):
I sha'n't[1] be gone long.—You come too.

I'm going out to fetch the little calf
That's standing by the mother. It's so young,
It totters when she licks it with her tongue.
I sha'n't be gone long.—You come too. ✤

1. **sha'n't.** Shall not

Robert Frost (1874–1963) was born in San Francisco, but he moved to New England at the age of eleven. The quiet, rural landscape of New England profoundly affected his development as a poet. Frost supported himself and his family through a variety of occupations before achieving success with the publication in 1915 of two poetry collections. Frost won four Pulitzer Prizes for Poetry and earned a reputation as one of America's greatest poets.

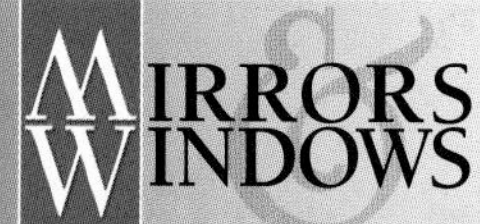

Describe a time when you genuinely enjoyed your work. What kinds of work are particularly fulfilling?

Analyze and Extend

1. (a) What is this poem's rhyme scheme? (b) How does rhyme affect the poem?
2. (a) Describe this poem's tone. (b) In what ways does the tone help you identify the author's purpose?
3. How are the tasks that the speaker describes in this poem similar?

Informative Writing What words or phrases are repeated in this poem? Why do you think these particular words or phrases are repeated? Write a brief **literary analysis** in which you analyze the use of repetition. Before you begin writing, draft a thesis statement that succinctly states the main idea of your analysis. Support your thesis with evidence from the poem.

Collaborative Learning Gather in small groups to discuss the mood of this poem. Try to come to a consensus in your group about what you believe the mood to be. Then try to determine what most contributes to the mood. Also, try to determine to whom the speaker is speaking, and how the speaker influences the mood. Write down your thoughts and your evidence. When you have finished, share your conclusions with the class.

Go to **www.mirrorsandwindows.com** for more.

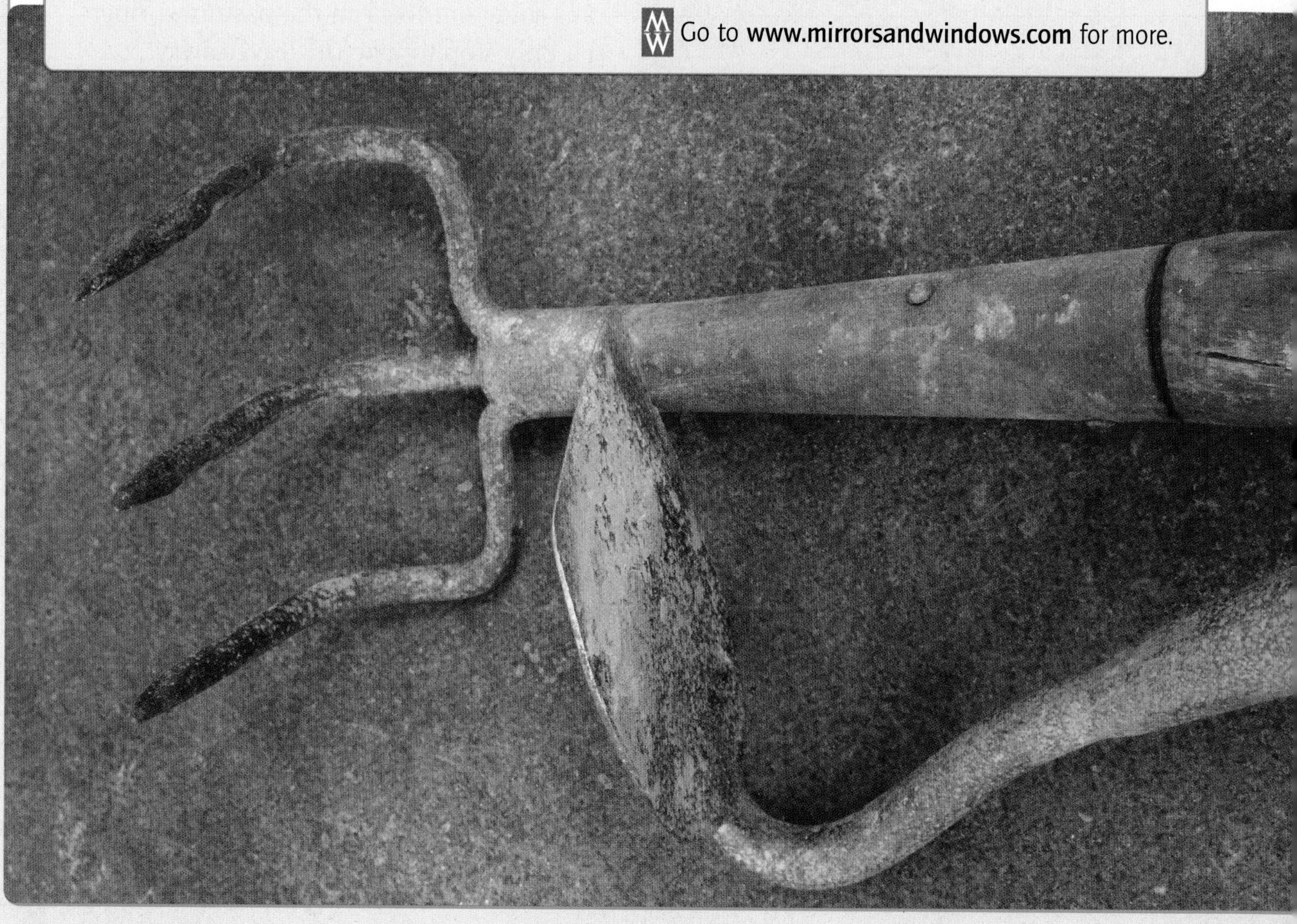

For Your Reading List

Poetry for Young People: William Carlos Williams

by Christopher MacGowan

Many poems in this volume celebrate the unexpected beauty of ordinary things, whether they be a red wheelbarrow, a rotten apple, or broken pieces of green glass. The simple language and clear imagery of Williams's poems transformed American poetry and presented unusual insights into the places and things around us.

Laughing Out Loud, I Fly: Poems in English and Spanish

by Juan Felipe Herrera

Herrera's poems express his memories of the people, places, and foods of his childhood, all in joyful, vivid language: "I am a monkey cartoon or a chile *tamal,* crazy / with paisley patches, infinite flavors cinnamon & / banana ice cream, it's 3 in the afternoon...." His poems, reprinted in Spanish and English, describe the joy and confusion of growing up between two cultures.

I Am Wings: Poems About Love

by Ralph Fletcher

Written from the viewpoint of an infatuated young man, these short, easily understood poems about love form a kind of short story. Moving from attraction at the high school lockers in "First Look" through soaring early love in "I Am Wings" to falling out of love and becoming ready for a new love interest in "Seeds," these thirty-three free verse poems are gentle in tone.

Remember the Bridge: Poems of a People

by Carole Boston Weatherford

Four hundred years of African-American history are represented in these poems by Carole Boston Weatherford, including portraits of Africans who were kidnapped and sold into slavery as well as African-American farmers, craftspeople, storytellers, artists, and civil rights activists. Weatherford's words, along with dramatic drawings and photos of these individuals, immortalize their contributions to African-American freedom.

Poetry for Young People: Walt Whitman

by Jonathan Levin

This collection features some of Whitman's most well-known poems—"I Hear America Singing," "Song of Myself"—and two poems about Abraham Lincoln: "O Captain! My Captain!" and "When Lilacs Last in the Dooryard Bloom'd." This illustrated volume provides a wonderful introduction to the work of a poet who was one of the first truly American voices in poetry.

A Wreath for Emmett Till

by Marilyn Nelson

The death of Emmett Till, a fourteen-year-old black boy who was murdered in Mississippi, inspired Nelson to write a series of sonnets commemorating his life and tragic death. Another inspiration is Shakespeare's *Hamlet*, where Ophelia sadly recites the meanings of various flowers after her father's death. Throughout her poems, Nelson names the flowers she would like to weave into a wreath in memory of Till, whose death helped spark the Civil Rights movement.

Writing Workshop

Narrative Writing

Personal Narrative

Assignment: Write a personal narrative in which I tell about a meaningful event in my life.

Goal: Show the significance of the event to my audience.

Strategy: Include descriptive language as well as my own thoughts and feelings about the event.

Writing Rubric: My personal narrative should include the following:

- an opening that grabs the reader's attention
- important events told in sequence
- descriptive details as well as personal thoughts and feelings
- a compelling conclusion that makes the significance of the event clear to the audience

Reading and Writing

In this unit, you read poems from poets such as Carl Sandburg, Robert Frost, Emily Dickinson, and Dudley Randall about looking beneath the surface. With concise and elegant words, these poets were able to share engaging stories and compelling feelings with their readers.

You will sometimes need to describe an event or series of events from your own life in writing. When you tell a story about yourself, it is important to express your ideas and the events that occurred clearly and in a way that will interest your reader. By using a variety of techniques, such as figurative language, sensory details, characters, and plot, you will be able to tell a compelling story about yourself.

In this workshop you will learn how to write a **personal narrative.** A personal narrative is a true story told by the person it happened to. To complete the assignment, create a goal and determine your strategy to achieve it. This summary includes a writing rubric—a set of standards by which you will judge your work. You will use this rubric in both drafting and revising your essay.

What Great Writers Do

Robert Frost used simple language to reveal deep meaning. In his poetry, he explored the relationship of individuals to each other and to nature. The following is what he said about writing poetry.

A poem begins with a lump in the throat, a home-sickness or a love-sickness. It is a reaching-out toward expression; an effort to find fulfillment. A complete poem is one where the emotion has found its thought and the thought has found the words.

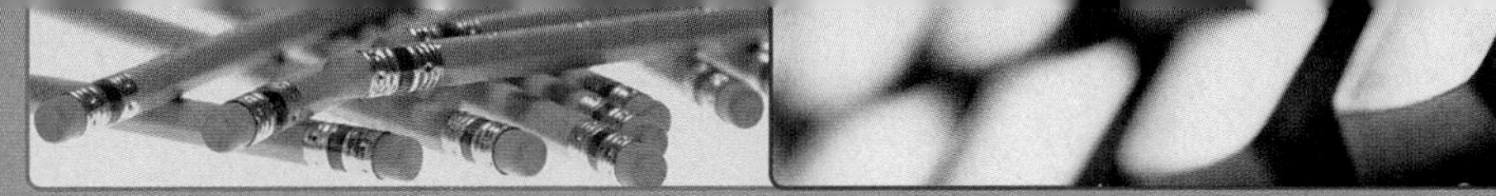

1. PREWRITE

Choosing Your Topic

Since a personal narrative is about an event from your own life, think about events that have affected you strongly. You may want to categorize events using a chart. Look at the chart below created by a student.

Strange	Scary	Exciting	Funny
seeing our town after a tornado	stuck in an elevator	my first roller-coaster ride	playing a trick on my dad
knowing my uncle was getting married before he said so	lost in a store	winning a championship basketball game	learning to square dance
finding a skeleton key that doesn't fit anything	being home alone for the first time	skiing downhill for the first time	sliding down a muddy hill

This student began with four categories: *strange, scary, exciting,* and *funny.* He chose events in his life that could fit into these categories. From these events, he will choose one event to write about in a personal narrative.

Gathering Details

Now that you have chosen an event to write about, it's time to explore it further. Ask yourself key questions about the event: *Who was there? When did it happen? Where did it happen? What time of day was it? Was the weather important? What did I see, hear, taste, touch, or smell? How did I feel about what happened? Why is the event significant or memorable to me?*

Use a word web to further explore the event. Write the event in the center of the web. In the ovals leading from the center, write key words that can help trigger memories of the event.

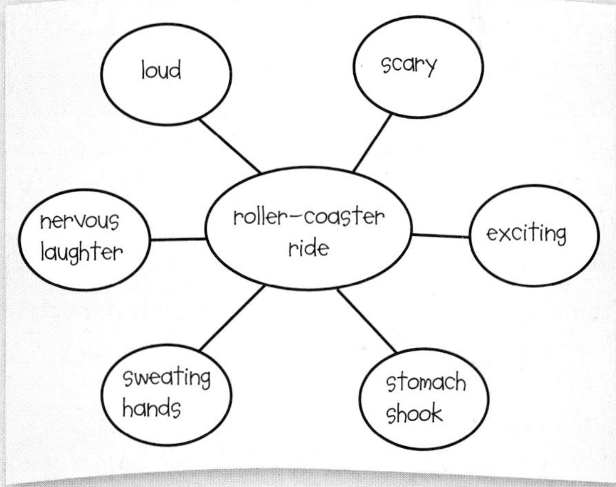

Deciding on Your Purpose

After you choose a topic and gather details, determine your purpose. You might be writing to entertain your audience. You may also want to teach a lesson or give an explanation. Keep in mind that no matter what your topic is, part of your purpose is to show your audience why the event was or is so memorable to you.

2. DRAFT

Organizing Ideas

You will want to organize your writing in an order that is interesting and logical. Most narratives are written in sequence, or **chronological order.** Other possible orders include **cause-effect order** and **problem-and-solution order.** Whichever order you choose, make sure it makes sense for the kind of personal narrative you want to tell.

Chronological Order

1. first event
   details
2. next event
   details
3. final event
   details

Putting Your Thoughts on Paper

A personal narrative should grab a reader's attention right from the beginning. It is your story, so remember to tell what happened from your point of view. Use sensory details so that your reader hears, sees, feels, smells, and tastes everything that you did. Include your own thoughts and feelings as you describe the event. Wrap up your personal narrative with a sentence or two that makes clear the significance or effect of the event.

You may want to write your draft straight through from beginning to end so that you get the story down. At first, concentrate on content and organization. You can then go back and add descriptive and personal details to each part of your draft to help your audience connect with your experience. Mechanical details, such as spelling, grammar, and punctuation, will be the focus of the editing and proofreading stages.

Introduction
- grab the reader's attention with an interesting question or a surprising statement
- hint at the significance or effect of the event

Body
- tell the complete story
- include descriptive language and personal details
- use smooth transitions from one paragraph to the next

Conclusion
- write a compelling ending that wraps up the narrative and tells how things worked out
- explain how the experience affected or changed you and why it is meaningful

Elaborating

Improve your narrative writing by adding details, examples, or transitions to connect ideas. Often a single adjective, sensory detail, or vivid verb can make your description clearer and more colorful.

As you narrate events, you may have a tendency to wander or give details that are irrelevant to your story. Read each sentence carefully. Ask yourself if the sentence is relevant to the story you are trying to tell. If the sentence does not enhance your story, delete it.

3. REVISE

Evaluating Your Draft

Once your draft is complete, review what you have written to determine your narrative's strengths and weaknesses. Check that your organization and ideas are clear. For the best evaluation, have a **peer review.** Exchange papers with a classmate. Have the classmate read what you have written, and then discuss ways to improve your paper. Use the Revising Checklist as a guide. Below is the beginning of a personal narrative. The annotations to the right indicate the reasons for the changes marked in the draft.

Revising Checklist

- ☐ Does the introduction grab the reader and hint at the significance of the event?
- ☐ Are the events told in chronological order?
- ☐ Are descriptive and personal details included?
- ☐ Does the conclusion make the significance of the event clear to the audience?

There is one day in my life that I'll never forget. *That day marked the beginning of a quest for me—to ride every roller coaster in the world! I'm only thirteen now, but I will do it one day.* Here's how it all started.

Hint at the significance of the event in the introduction.

I was only a kid, seven years old, when my brothers Luis and Miguel persuaded my parents that I was old enough (and tall enough) to experience the thrill of the roller coaster called the Monster. I was four when I first saw it. I begged, pleaded, and cried to be allowed to ride it, but my father said no. I clearly was not tall enough at four years old. *Disappointed, I was determined to grow enough by next year.* Next year turned into three years until I was finally tall enough to ride the Monster.

Add personal thoughts and feelings.

I moved slowly along with my brothers in the line that snaked its way closer and closer to the front. *Luis pointed at the triple loops, angles, turns, and steep plunges as the riders screamed and hollered.* Some scared people left the line. ~~I hate waiting in lines.~~ I couldn't wait to be up there! Finally, we reached the front.

Add sensory details.

Take out unnecessary details.

4. EDIT AND PROOFREAD

Focus: Figurative Language

Figurative language brings color and originality to writing. The right figurative language can make an ordinary story or event come alive for the reader. Review the various types of figurative language and examples to make your own writing more effective.

Figurative Language	Examples
A **simile** is a comparison of two unlike things that are alike in at least one way. A simile uses the word *like* or *as* in the comparison.	I was as eager as a race horse.
A **metaphor** is a comparison of two unlike things without use of like or as. A metaphor says something is another thing.	We inched higher up the mountain of steel.
Hyperbole is exaggeration used for effect.	My mouth was open, and my eyes were bulging out of their sockets.
Personification occurs when human traits are used to describe animals, ideas, or inanimate objects.	The Monster beckoned, and I couldn't ignore it.

Focus: Apostrophes

Apostrophes are used to show possession. Pay careful attention to the use of apostrophes in your writing: *Miguel's hat, the boys' laughter.*

Remember these rules about using apostrophes in possessives in your writing.

Rule 1. To form the singular possessive noun, add an apostrophe and the letter *s* to the end of the noun: *Tony's father, the coaster's wheels.*

Rule 2. To form the plural possessive noun, write it in its plural form and add the apostrophe after the *s*: *the girls' hats, the puppies' noses.* For a noun whose plural form does not end in *s*, add an apostrophe and *s* to the end: *children's laughter, men's shoes.*

Apostrophes are also used in contractions, such as *don't, didn't, won't, should've, wouldn't, she's,* and *it's.* Note that the possessive form of *it* is *its; it's* is a contraction for *it is.*

Proofreading

Quality Control The purpose of proofreading is to catch errors in grammar, capitalization, spelling, and punctuation. You can find and fix these errors as you evaluate and revise your narrative. You may also correct these errors as you look for them specifically in a line-by-line reading of your paper. Use proofreader's marks to highlight any errors. See the Language Arts Handbook, section 4.1, for a list of proofreader's marks.

5. PUBLISH AND PRESENT

Final Draft

Now that you have taken your narrative through the revising and editing stages, make a final draft. Make sure your narrative is clean and free of errors. If it is handwritten, make sure the narrative is neat and legible. If you are using a word processing program, double-space your paper and use a readable typeface or font. Be sure to check that you have followed any additional presentation guidelines.

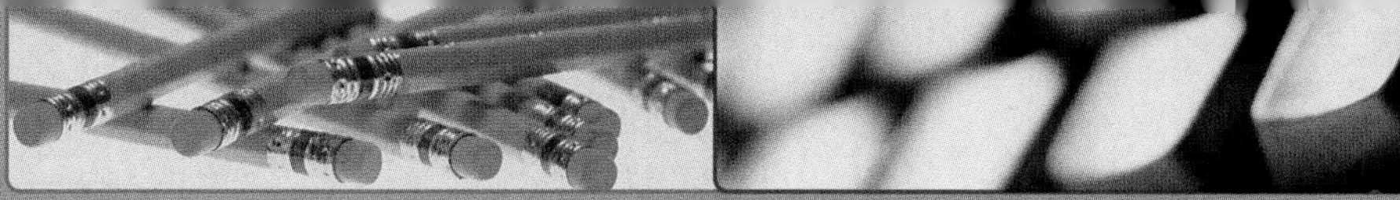

Student Model

A Thrill of a Ride
by Anthony Garcia

There is one day in my life that I'll never forget. That day marked the beginning of a quest for me—to ride every roller coaster in the world! I'm only thirteen now, but I will do it one day. Here's how it all started.

Draws in the reader and introduces the significance of the events

I was only a kid, seven years old, when my brothers Luis and Miguel persuaded my parents that I was old enough (and tall enough) to experience the thrill of the roller coaster called the Monster. I was four when I first saw it. The Monster beckoned, and I couldn't ignore it. I begged, pleaded, and cried to be allowed to ride it, but my father said no. I clearly was not tall enough at four years old. Disappointed, I was determined to grow enough by next year. Next year turned into three years until I was finally tall enough to ride the Monster.

I moved slowly along with my brothers in the line that snaked its way closer and closer to the front. My jaws ached from the grin stuck to my face. Luis pointed at the triple loops, angles, turns, and steep plunges as the riders screamed and hollered. Some scared people left the line. I couldn't wait to be up there! Finally, we reached the front.

As I took the seat next to Miguel, the ride operator stared at me for a moment. I thought he was going to tell me I was still too short to ride on the Monster, but he just shrugged and locked me into my seat. I was as eager as a race horse. I remember Miguel whispering to me, "Okay, little bro?" I just nodded, still grinning, and gripped the bar in front of me. The operator then pushed a handle, and the car jerked forward.

My heart was pounding as we first started rolling. We crept up a small climb and slid down a short drop first. My stomach jumped a little, but it wasn't anything I couldn't handle. Then I was pushed back in the seat as we inched higher up the mountain of steel. I remember every *click-click* of the track as the car continued its climb. When it reached the top, it hesitated only a second, and then we were off. We raced down, climbed back up and whooshed through spins, dips, and curls. My mouth was open and my eyes were bulging out of their sockets, anticipating each new thrill the ride had to offer. After one last corkscrew curl, the car slowed toward the starting block and stopped with a jerk. It was over.

Is organized in chronological order

Elaborates on the events through figurative language, sensory details, and personal thoughts and feelings

My brothers were doubled over with laughter as I, still wide-eyed and opened-mouth, shakily got off the coaster. Then I stopped and looked back at the Monster. My brothers stopped too and looked at me.

I turned to them, grinned, and said, "Let's do it again!"

Wraps up the narrative and reveals the significance of the event to the writer

Speaking & Listening Workshop

Giving and Actively Listening to Narrative Presentations

Have you ever told a story about your life? Have you ever told a story to entertain your friends or family? Have you ever told a story as a means of providing others with information? When you tell a story, you are giving a narrative presentation. In a **narrative presentation,** you describe events from your life or the lives of others. When you give and actively listen to a narrative presentation, you share information about yourself with others.

Planning a Narrative Presentation

Choose a Story To give an effective narrative presentation, you need to first think about a specific event or series of events that you witnessed or in which you participated. Was the event strange, funny, happy, sad, or serious? Brainstorm to come up with a list of possible topics for your narrative presentation. Under each topic, write details related to it, such as the setting, the people involved, and the outcome.

Take Notes Once you have decided on a story to tell, try to jog your memory of the event. Talk to others who were present or perform research to fill in any gaps in your knowledge of the setting or people involved. If you have photographs, you may want to examine them to recall significant details.

Topic:
playing a funny joke on my dad

Details:
fishing in our big green canoe
sunny July afternoon
hooked a fake fish to the end of his line
we laughed the entire ride home

Organize Your Story Narratives are most frequently told in chronological order. When you tell a story in chronological order, you give the events in the order in which they happened. Use a time line to organize your presentation. List all of the most significant events from left to right on the time line.

Identify Your Audience Now that you have identified and organized the story that you are going to tell, consider your audience. Your audience will determine much of what you say and how you say it. If you know that your audience is very familiar with the details of your story, try to introduce a new perspective or information with which they may not be familiar. If you know your story is one with which they are likely to be unfamiliar, try to include as much description and background information as possible.

Evaluating Your Narrative Presentation

Working with a partner or in a small group, rehearse your narrative presentation. Then provide constructive feedback to your partner on what he or she did well and what could be improved. Constructive feedback means that you are respectful and polite whether you give criticism or praise. Follow the listening and speaking rubrics on this page in order to evaluate each oral summary.

Delivering Your Narrative Presentation

Convey dramatic effects through your tone of voice as well as your facial expression. If you are expressing surprise, show surprise in your voice and eyes. If you are expressing fear, show fear in your voice as well as in your movements and facial expressions. Keep your audience interested and entertained. Use gestures as an aid, but do not let them become a distraction from your speech. Remember to speak loudly and clearly. If your story is humorous, pause during moments of laughter.

Listen Actively Listening actively is just as important as being an effective speaker. Pay attention to what the speaker says, and react politely. Do not be a distraction by talking to others during the presentation. Ask questions when appropriate.

Speaking Rubric

Your presentation will be evaluated on these elements:

Content

- ☐ events are ordered chronologically
- ☐ narrative includes characters, setting, and action
- ☐ description used to convey ideas

Delivery and Presentation

- ☐ speaks loud and clear
- ☐ uses effective nonverbal cues
- ☐ uses voice to portray feeling

Listening Rubric

As a peer reviewer or audience member, you should do the following:

- ☐ listen quietly and attentively
- ☐ maintain eye contact with the speaker
- ☐ ask appropriate questions
- ☐ (as peer reviewer) provide constructive feedback

Test Practice Workshop

Writing Skills

Personal Essay

Carefully read the following writing prompt. Before you begin writing, think carefully about what task the assignment is asking you to perform. Then create an outline to help guide your writing.

> In Emily Dickinson's poem "I'm Nobody," the speaker suggests that it's better to be "nobody" than "somebody." What are some of the benefits and drawbacks of being a "nobody" as opposed to a "somebody"? How do you feel about the speaker's claims?

Relate a story from your own life that reflects or challenges the theme of Dickinson's poem. In your narrative, use descriptive, sensory, and figurative language, as well as examples from the poem. Concentrate on writing a compelling opening and closing for your story. As you write, be sure to:

- Organize your narrative in a logical and consistent way
- Include introductory and concluding paragraphs
- Introduce your position in the first paragraph
- Support your main idea in each body paragraph

Revising and Editing Skills

In the following excerpt from the first draft of a student's paper, words and phrases are underlined and numbered. Alternatives to the underlined words and phrases appear in the right-hand column. Choose the one that *best* corrects any grammatical or style errors in the original. If you think that the original is error-free, choose "NO CHANGE."

Some questions might also be asked about a section of the passage or the entire passage. These do not refer to a specific underlined phrase or word and are identified by a number in a box. Record your answers on a separate sheet of paper.

In the words of Archibald MacLeish, "A poem should not mean, but be." What does MacLeish mean? [1] I was hiking in Glacier National Parks forests last summer. (2) I was stunned by a scene that took my breath away. Craggy snow-topped mountains speared the sky and [3] cradled an impossibly smooth lake. The reflections in the lake perfectly mirrored the trees (4) and mountains rising above it. At that moment, I didn't think about what the scene meant. I just experienced it. [5] Similarly, my first thought when reading a good poem is not about its meaning. I simply experience it, letting my minds eye wander along with the poem's (6) images.

1. The second sentence of this paragraph is a
   A. simple sentence.
   B. compound sentence.
   C. complex sentence.
   D. compound-complex sentence.

2. **A.** NO CHANGE
   B. I was hiking, in Glacier National Parks forests, last summer.
   C. I was hiking; in Glacier National Parks forests last summer.
   D. I was hiking in Glacier National Park's forests last summer.

3. The sentence beginning *Craggy snow-topped mountains* has a
   A. simple predicate.
   B. compound predicate.
   C. complex predicate.
   D. compound-complex predicate.

4. **A.** NO CHANGE
   B. lake mirrored perfectly the trees
   C. lake, perfectly mirroring the trees
   D. lake perfectly mirror the trees

5. The sentence *I just experienced it* is a
   A. simple sentence.
   B. compound sentence.
   C. complex sentence.
   D. compound-complex sentence.

6. **A.** NO CHANGE
   B. mind's eye wander along with the poem's
   C. minds eye wander along with the poems
   D. minds eye wander, along with the poem's

Reading Skills

Carefully read the following passage. Then on a separate piece of paper, answer each question.

from *The Song of Hiawatha* by Henry Wadsworth Longfellow

...Gitche Manito, the mighty,
The creator of the nations,
Looked upon them with compassion,
With paternal love and pity;
Looked upon their wrath and wrangling
But as quarrels among children,
But as feuds and fights of children!

Over them he stretched his right hand,
To subdue their stubborn natures,
To allay their thirst and fever,
By the shadow of his right hand;
Spake to them with voice majestic
As the sound of far-off waters,
Falling into deep abysses,
Warning, chiding, spake in this wise:

"O my children! my poor children!
Listen to the words of wisdom,
Listen to the words of warning,
From the lips of the Great Spirit,
From the Master of Life, who made you!

"I have given you lands to hunt in,
I have given you streams to fish in,
I have given you bear and bison,
I have given you roe and reindeer,
I have given you brant and beaver,
Filled the marshes full of wild-fowl,
Filled the rivers full of fishes:
Why then are you not contented?
Why then will you hunt each other?

"I am weary of your quarrels,
Weary of your wars and bloodshed,
Weary of your prayers for vengeance,
Of your wranglings and dissensions;
All your strength is in your union,
All your danger is in discord;
Therefore be at peace henceforward,
And as brothers live together..."

1. Based on the first stanza, the narrator's point of view is:
   A. first-person.
   B. second-person.
   C. third-person limited.
   D. third-person omniscient.

2. Which of the following kinds of figurative language appears in line 5?
   A. symbolism
   B. metaphor
   C. simile
   D. alliteration

3. The sensory language in lines 12–14 mostly contributes to which of the following elements?
   A. rhyme
   B. characterization
   C. plot
   D. conflict

4. Which of the following describes the rhythm of the poem's second stanza?
   A. / ˘ / ˘ / ˘ / ˘
   B. ˘ ˘ ˘ / ˘ ˘ ˘ /
   C. / ˘ ˘ ˘ / ˘ ˘ ˘
   D. ˘ / / / ˘ / / /

5. This passage is an example of which type of poetry?
   A. lyric
   B. concrete
   C. haiku
   D. narrative

6. *Warning* and *chiding* in line 15 contain
   A. alliteration.
   B. metaphor.
   C. onomatopoeia.
   D. consonance.

7. Lines 21–27 contain
   A. metaphor and simile.
   B. analogy and symbolism.
   C. repetition and alliteration.
   D. rhyme and alliteration.

8. Based on the context, what is the most likely meaning of *brant* in line 25?
   A. a Native-American tribe
   B. a type of bird or animal
   C. a type of tree or plant
   D. food and clothing

9. Which of the following literary devices is absent in Longfellow's poem?
   A. rhythm
   B. rhyme
   C. repetition
   D. alliteration

10. What can you infer about the audience to whom Gitche Manito is speaking?
    A. They are warlike and unfriendly toward one other.
    B. They are part of a large family.
    C. They are Gitche Manito's brothers and sisters.
    D. They are all members of the same tribe.

Unit 7

Facing Challenges

Drama

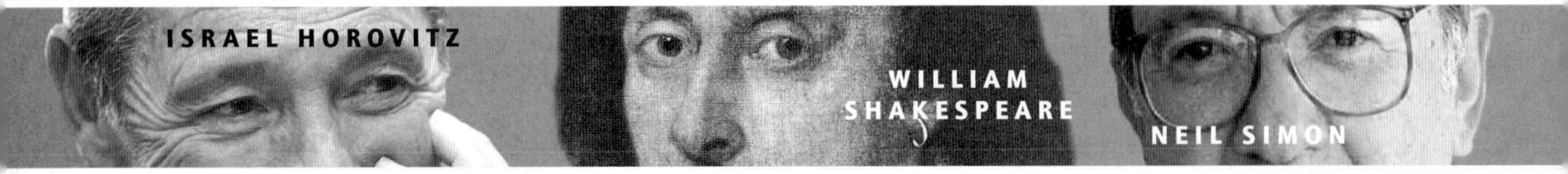

ISRAEL HOROVITZ

"I present him to you: Ebenezer Scrooge....The cold within him freezes his old features, nips his pointed nose, shrivels his cheek...."

—ISRAEL HOROVITZ, *A Christmas Carol: Scrooge and Marley*

Have you ever faced a challenge? In Israel Horovitz's play *A Christmas Carol: Scrooge and Marley*, Ebenezer Scrooge must learn late in life to treat other people with warmth, kindness, and respect. As you read the drama in this unit, consider how the characters face and resolve conflicts. How can you relate their struggles to your own life?

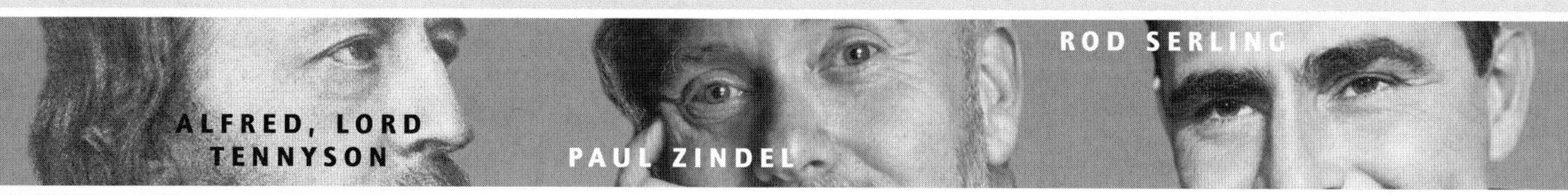

Introduction to Drama

"The bell tolls and I must take my leave. You must stay a while with Scrooge and watch him play out his scroogey life. It is now the story: the once-upon-a-time."

—ISRAEL HOROVITZ, *A Christmas Carol: Scrooge and Marley*

The art of performance has been around since the beginnings of human history. Modern theater can trace its roots back to prehistoric dance rituals, Native American healing ceremonies, African storytellers, and dramatic productions of the ancient Greeks, to name a few. A **drama** is a piece of literature that is written to be performed for an audience.

Dramatic Forms

Plays for the Theater

A play is a type of drama written for the stage. The playwright envisions how the story will take shape and includes specifics such as actors' locations on stage and details about props and sets. Unlike a piece of fiction, a playwright's finished script is not the final step. A director will use the script, in collaboration with actors, to make the story come alive on stage.

Screenplays and Television Scripts

Dramas are not always performed on stage. When you go to the movie theater or watch a sitcom on television, you are watching a different kind of drama. Screenplays and television scripts are dramas written to be acted out on film and shown to an audience on screen. In addition to stage directions dictating how an actor should speak or move, for example, screenplays and television scripts usually state how a scene should be filmed. You will see this in Rod Serling's screenplay, "The Monsters Are Due on Maple Street" (page 694).

Drama versus Fiction

Drama and fiction share many elements, such as plot, characters, dialogue, and setting. However, playwrights are faced with additional challenges. A typical play usually lasts a few hours, and all the action and plot development must take place within that time frame. Playwrights must always be conscious of time, the size of the stage, and an audience's ability to endure and immediately understand what is taking place.

Types of Drama

Most modern Western theater descends from the style of the theatrical productions of the ancient Greeks.

- **Tragedy:** There is usually a heroic protagonist, or main character, who is ultimately destroyed by a tragic flaw within him- or herself.
- **Comedy:** The plot often involves a series of mishaps and humorous situations. Comedies typically have happy endings.

- **Straight Drama:** Most modern plays fall into this category, characterized by realistic characters and situations. Elements of tragedy or comedy may be involved, but usually not in extremes.

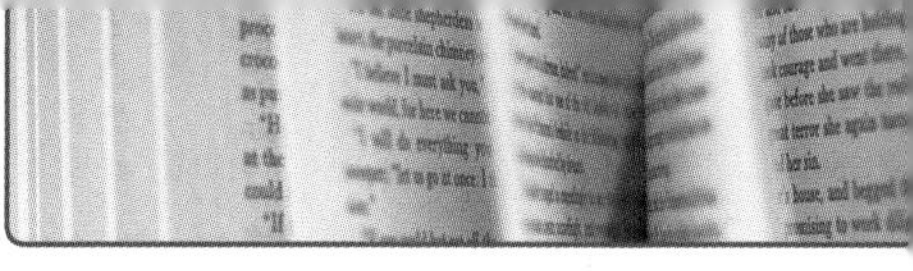

Elements of Drama

A drama, in its simplest form, is a story like any other piece of fiction. Unlike fiction, drama is composed of various theatrical elements that allow the story to be performed and brought to life.

Plot

Just as in novels and short stories, the **plot** introduces a drama's central conflict, or struggle, develops it through rising action, and resolves it after the climax.

Characters

The characters are the individuals who take part in the action of a drama. As in fiction, the **protagonist** is the most important character. Sometimes, another character takes on the role of the **antagonist,** who engages in conflict with the protagonist. Together, all of the characters form the drama's **cast.** The cast is usually listed at the beginning of a script, and it is the actions of and interactions among these characters that reveal the drama's plot.

Dialogue

In a drama, plot is mostly revealed through physical action and **dialogue,** or conversation between characters. Because of the performance format of drama, there is little room for narrative description as there is in most fiction. Thus, the audience learns the thoughts and feelings of characters, as well as the context for the story line, through what the characters do and say to each other. Sometimes, information is presented to the audience through the speech of one character. This is called a **monologue.** William Shakespeare's "St. Crispian's Day Speech" (page 687) from his play *Henry V* is an example of a monologue.

Script

A **script** is a drama's actual text. It includes character names, setting, stage directions, and dialogue. **Stage directions** appear before and after lines of dialogue, and they indicate how a character should say a certain line, what facial expressions to make, what gestures to use, and so on. Directions telling actors how and where to stand, move, or enter and exit the stage usually refer to this grid:

Up Right	Up Center	Up Left
Right Center	Center	Left Center
Down Right	Down Center	Down Left

Audience

The parts of the stage are described from the actors' point of view, looking out at the audience.

Just as a novel is sometimes divided into chapters, a script is usually divided into **acts** and **scenes.** Many plays have two or three acts, and each act is made up of a number of scenes.

Scenery

The scenery of a drama is called the **set.** The set includes the setting of each scene, the stage design, the lighting, and the props, or movable objects used by the characters. The playwright or screenwriter usually includes notes about stage design and the setting of each scene, but it is ultimately up to the production's director to interpret the scenery as he or she wishes.

Interpretations and Culture

A playwright's script may always read the same on paper, but the playwright's words are only the beginning. Each interpretation and performance breathes new life into a drama. Today, the classic plays of the ancient Greeks are still being performed around the world. A drama becomes something new in each theater, with each cast or director, and in each culture or time period in which it is performed and received.

Drama Close Reading Model

BEFORE READING

Build Background
You need to apply two types of background to read a drama effectively. One type is the drama's literary and historical context. Read the **Build Background** and **Meet the Author** features to get this information. The other type of background is the personal knowledge and experience you bring to your reading.

Set Purpose
A playwright presents characters and scenes to say something about life. Read **Set Purpose** to decide what you want to get out of the drama.

Analyze Literature
A playwright uses literary techniques, such as plot and dialogue, to create meaning. The **Analyze Literature** feature draws your attention to a key literary element in the drama.

Use Reading Skills
The **Use Reading Skills** feature will show you skills to help you get the most out of your reading. Learn how to apply skills such as drawing conclusions and summarizing. Identify a graphic organizer that will help you apply the skill before and while you read.

DURING READING

Use Reading Strategies
- **Ask questions** about things that seem significant or interesting.
- **Make predictions** about what's going to happen next. As you read, gather more clues to confirm or change your prediction.
- **Visualize** the drama. Form pictures in your mind to help you see the characters, actions, and settings.
- **Make inferences,** or educated guesses, about what is not stated directly.
- **Clarify,** or check that you understand, what you read. Reread any difficult parts.

Analyze Literature
What literary elements stand out? Are the characters vivid and interesting? Is there a strong central conflict? As you read, consider how these elements affect your enjoyment and understanding of the drama.

Make Connections
Notice where connections can be made between the drama and your life or the world outside the drama. What feelings or thoughts do you have while reading the drama?

AFTER READING

Find Meaning
Recall the important details of the drama, such as the sequence of events and characters' names. Use this information to **interpret,** or explain, the meaning of the drama.

Make Judgments
- **Analyze** the text by examining details and deciding what they contribute to the meaning.
- **Evaluate** the text by making judgments about how the author creates meaning.

Analyze Literature
Review how the use of literary elements increases your understanding of the story. For example, if the author uses monologue, how does it help to shape the drama's meaning?

Extend Understanding
Go beyond the text by exploring the drama's ideas through writing or other creative projects.

A Defenseless Creature

A Drama by Neil Simon, based on a story by Anton Chekhov

GUIDED READING

Build Background

Literary Context "A Defenseless Creature" is from a play entitled *The Good Doctor* by Neil Simon. *The Good Doctor* consists of a series of vignettes adapted from stories written by Russian author Anton Chekhov. Born in 1860, Chekhov began writing comic sketches for humorous journals to support his family and himself as he studied medicine. By 1888, his stories had achieved great popularity. Chekhov went on to become one of Russia's greatest playwrights and was influential in developing the modern short story.

Reader's Context How can persistence convince people to help you even if your request is unreasonable?

Set Purpose

Skim the stage directions in *italic type.* What do you think the mood of the play will be?

Analyze Literature

Drama A story intended to be performed by actors for an audience is called a **drama,** or play. A dramatic script usually includes a cast of characters, a description of the setting, dialogue, and stage directions. As you read "A Defenseless Creature" identify details in the dialogue and stage directions that provide information about the characters.

Use Reading Skills

Identify Cause and Effect As you read a dramatic script, identify cause-and-effect relationships created by stage directions, dialogue, and characters' actions. Determine the reasons, or *causes,* something exists or occurs, as well as the results, or *effects.* Record your ideas in a chart.

Cause	Effect
Kistunov is suffering from gout.	Loud noises bother him.

Preview Vocabulary

in•ca•pac•i•tat•ed (in' kə pa´ sə tāt' ed) *adj.,* unable to engage in normal activities; disabled

com•po•sure (kəm pō´ zhər) *n.,* calmness of mind or appearance

pe•ti•tion (pə ti´ shən) *n.,* formal request

del•i•cate•ly (del´ i kət lē) *adv.,* carefully; cautiously

ar•dent (är´ dənt) *adj.,* warmth of feeling characterized by eager support

prov•o•ca•tion (präv' ə kā´ shən) *n.,* something that calls forth an action or emotion

Meet the Author

Neil Simon (b. 1927) began writing for radio and television comedians while still in his teens. His first play, *Come Blow Your Horn,* was written in 1960. Since then, the prolific author has written dozens of hit Broadway shows and screenplays including *Sweet Charity, Barefoot in the Park,* and *The Odd Couple.* In 1973, *The Good Doctor,* with "A Defenseless Creature" as one of its most popular vignettes, premiered in New York.

A Defenseless Creature

A Drama by Neil Simon, based on a story by Anton Chekhov

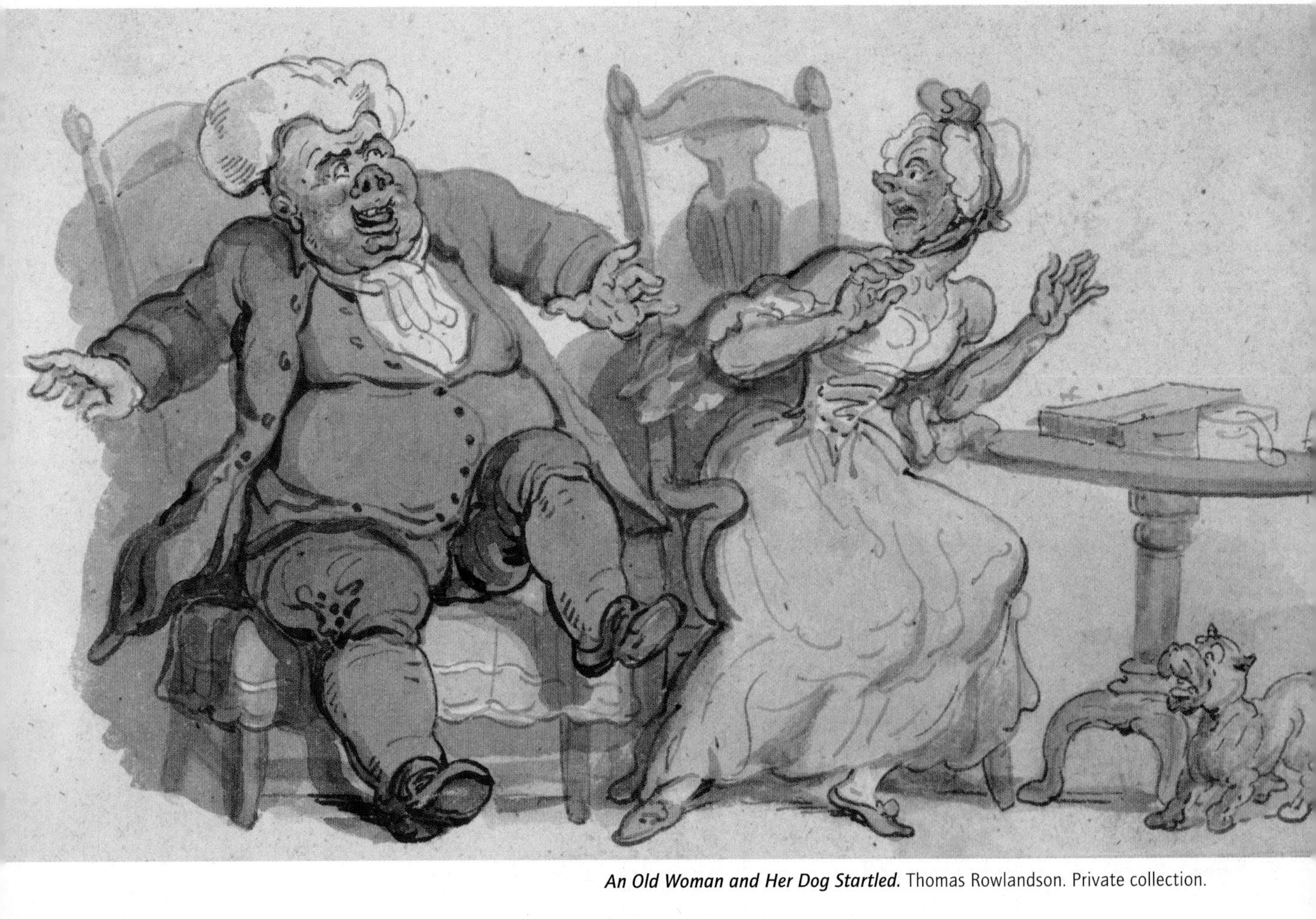

An Old Woman and Her Dog Startled. Thomas Rowlandson. Private collection.

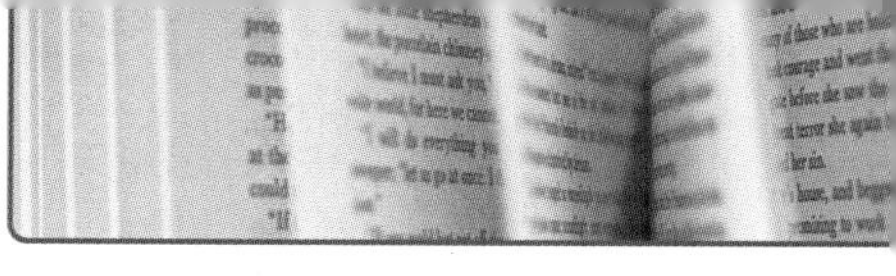

"I'm about to lose my mind. The hair is coming out of my head."

The lights come up on the office of a bank official, Kistunov. *He enters on a crutch; his right foot is heavily encased in bandages, swelling it to three times its normal size. He suffers from the gout*[1] *and is very careful of any mishap which would only intensify his pain. He makes it to his desk and sits. An* Assistant, *rather harried,*[2] *enters.*

> **DURING READING**
> **Analyze Literature**
> **Drama** What do the stage directions demonstrate about Kistunov?

Assistant. [*With volume.*] Good morning, Mr. Kistunov!

Kistunov. Shhh! Please....Please lower your voice.

Assistant. [*Whispers.*] I'm sorry, sir.

Kistunov. It's just that my gout is acting up again and my nerves are like little firecrackers. The least little friction can set them off.

Assistant. It must be very painful, sir.

Kistunov. Combing my hair this morning was agony.

Assistant. Mr. Kistunov.

Kistunov. What is it, Pochatkin?

Assistant. There's a woman who insists on seeing you. We can't make head or tail out of her story, but she insists on seeing the directing manager. Perhaps if you're not well—

> **DURING READING**
> **Use Reading Skills**
> **Identify Cause and Effect** What causes Kistunov to see the woman?

Kistunov. No, no. The business of the bank comes before my minor physical ailments. Show her in, please...quietly. [*The* Assistant *tiptoes out. A* Woman *enters. She is in her late forties, poorly dressed. She is of the working class. She crosses to the desk, a forlorn look on her face. She twists her bag nervously.*] Good morning, madame. Forgive me for not standing, but I am somewhat incapacitated. Please sit down.

in • ca • pac • i • tat • ed (in' kə pa´ sə tāt' ed) *adj.,* unable to engage in normal activities; disabled

Woman. Thank you.

She sits.

Kistunov. Now, what can I do for you?

Woman. You can help me, sir. I pray to God you can help. No one else in this world seems to care....

---

1. **gout.** Condition that causes painful swelling of the joints, especially of the feet and hands
2. **harried.** Overwhelmed by problems

She begins to cry, which in turn becomes a wail—the kind of wail that melts the spine of strong men. KISTUNOV *winces and grits his teeth in pain as he grips the arms of his chair.*

KISTUNOV. Calm yourself, madame. I beg of you. Please calm yourself.

WOMAN. I'm sorry. [*She tries to calm down.*]

KISTUNOV. I'm sure we can sort it all out if we approach the problem sensibly and quietly....Now, what exactly is the trouble?

WOMAN. Well, sir....It's my husband. Collegiate Assessor[3] Schukin. He's been sick for five months....Five agonizing months.

KISTUNOV. I know the horrors of illness and can sympathize with you, madame. What's the nature of his illness?

WOMAN. It's a nervous disorder. Everything grates on his nerves. If you so much as touch him he'll scream out— [*And without warning, she screams a loud bloodcurdling scream that sends* KISTUNOV *almost out of his seat.*] How or why he got it, nobody knows.

DURING READING

Use Reading Skills
Identify Cause and Effect What does Kistunov think causes the husband's nervous disorder?

KISTUNOV. [*Trying to regain his composure.*] I have an inkling....Please go on, a little less descriptively, if possible.

com • po • sure (kəm pō´ zhər) *n.,* calmness of mind or appearance

WOMAN. Well, while the poor man was lying in bed—

KISTUNOV. [*Braces himself.*] You're not going to scream again, are you?

WOMAN. Not that I don't have cause....While he was lying in bed these five months, recuperating, he was dismissed from his job—for no reason at all.

KISTUNOV. That's a pity, certainly, but I don't quite see the connection with our bank, madame.

WOMAN. You don't know how I suffered during his illness. I nursed him from morning till night. Doctored him from night till morning. Besides cleaning my house, taking care of my children, feeding our dog, our cat, our goat, my sister's bird, who was sick....

KISTUNOV. The bird was sick?

WOMAN. My sister! She gets dizzy spells. She's been dizzy a month now. And she's getting dizzier every day.

KISTUNOV. Extraordinary. However—

WOMAN. I had to take care of her children and her house and her cat and her goat, and then her bird bit one of my children, and so our

3. **Collegiate Assessor.** Civil service rank in Imperial Russia

"Yes, well, you've certainly had your pack of troubles, haven't you? But I don't quite see—"

cat bit her bird, so my oldest daughter, the one with the broken arm, drowned my sister's cat, and now my sister wants my goat in exchange, or else she says she'll either drown my cat or break my oldest daughter's other arm—

Kistunov. Yes, well, you've certainly had your pack of troubles, haven't you? But I don't quite see—

Woman. And then, I went to get my husband's pay, they deducted twenty-four rubles[4] and thirty-six kopecks.[5] For what? I asked. Because, they said, he borrowed it from the employees' fund. But that's impossible. He could never borrow without my approval. I'd break his arm....Not while he was sick, of course....I don't have the strength. I'm not well myself, sir. I have this racking cough that's a terrible thing to hear—

She coughs rackingly[6]*—so rackingly that* Kistunov *is about to crack.*

Kistunov. I can well understand why your husband took five months to recuperate. But what is it you want from me, madame?

Woman. What rightfully belongs to my husband—his twenty-four rubles and thirty-six kopecks. They won't give it to me because I'm a woman, weak and defenseless. Some of them have laughed in my face, sir....Laughed! [*She laughs loud and painfully.* Kistunov *clenches*[7] *everything.*] Where's the humor I wonder, in a poor, defenseless creature like myself?

She sobs.

Kistunov. None....I see none at all. However, madame, I don't wish to be unkind, but I'm afraid you've come to the wrong place. Your petition, no matter how justified, has nothing to do with us. You'll have to go to the agency where your husband was employed.

pe•ti•tion (pə ti´ shən) *n.*, formal request

Woman. What do you mean? I've been to *five* agencies already and none of them will even listen to my petition. I'm about to lose my

4. **rubles.** Units of Russian money
5. **kopecks.** Hundredths of a ruble
6. **rackingly.** With heaves of painful effort
7. **clenches.** Holds or grips tightly

"Are you saying you won't believe my husband is sick? Here! Here is a doctor's certificate."

mind. The hair is coming out of my head. [*She pulls out a handful.*] Look at my hair. By the fistful. [*She throws a fistful on his desk.*] Don't tell me to go to another agency!

DURING READING

Analyze Literature

Drama How do the stage directions in this dialogue contribute to the play's mood?

del • i • cate • ly (del´ i kət lē) *adv.*, carefully; cautiously

KISTUNOV. [*Delicately and disgustedly, he picks up her fistful of hair and hands it back to her. She sticks it back in her hair.*] Please, madame, keep your hair in its proper place. Now listen to me carefully. This-is-a-bank. A bank! We're in the banking business. We bank money. Funds that are brought here are banked by us. Do you understand what I'm saying?

WOMAN. What are you saying?

KISTUNOV. I'm saying that I can't help you.

WOMAN. Are you saying you can't help me?

KISTUNOV. [*Sighs deeply.*] I'm trying. I don't think I'm making headway.

WOMAN. Are you saying you won't believe my husband is sick? Here! Here is a doctor's certificate. [*She puts it on the desk and pounds it.*] There's the proof. Do you still doubt that my husband is suffering from a nervous disorder?

KISTUNOV. Not only do I not doubt it, I would swear to it.

WOMAN. Look at it! You didn't look at it!

KISTUNOV. It's really not necessary. I know full well how your husband must be suffering.

WOMAN. What's the point in a doctor's certificate if you don't look at it?! LOOK AT IT!

KISTUNOV. [*Frightened, quickly looks at it.*] Oh, yes....I see your husband is sick. It's right here on the doctor's certificate. Well, you certainly have a good case, madame, but I'm afraid *you've still come to the wrong place*. [*Getting perplexed.*] I'm getting excited.

WOMAN. [*Stares at him.*] You lied to me. I took you as a man of your word and you lied to me.

KISTUNOV. I? LIE? WHEN?

Woman. [*Snatches the certificate.*] When you said you read the doctor's certificate. You couldn't have. You couldn't have read the description of my husband's illness without seeing he was fired unjustly. [*She puts the certificate back on the desk.*] Don't take advantage of me just because I'm a weak, defenseless woman. Do me the simple courtesy of reading the doctor's certificate. That's all I ask. Read it, and then I'll go.

Kistunov. But I read it! What's the point in reading something twice when I've already read it once?

Woman. You didn't read it carefully.

Kistunov. I read it in detail!

Woman. Then you read it too fast. Read it slower.

Kistunov. I don't have to read it slower. I'm a fast reader.

Woman. Maybe you didn't absorb it. Let it sink in this time.

Kistunov. [*Almost apoplectic.*[8]] I absorbed it! It sank in! I could pass a test on what's written here, but it doesn't make any difference because it has nothing to do with our bank!

Woman. [*She throws herself on him from behind.*] Did you read the part where it says he has a nervous disorder? Read that part again and see if I'm wrong.

Kistunov. THAT PART? OH, YES! I SEE YOUR HUSBAND HAS A NERVOUS DISORDER. MY, MY, HOW TERRIBLE! ONLY *I CAN'T HELP YOU! NOW PLEASE GO!* [*He falls back into his chair, exhausted.*]

DURING READING

Analyze Literature
Drama What is the tone of Kistunov's dialogue here? How can you tell?

Woman. [*Crosses to where his foot is resting.*] I'm sorry, Excellency. I hope I haven't caused you any pain.

Kistunov. [*Trying to stop her.*] Please, don't kiss my foot. [*He is too late—she has given his foot a most ardent embrace. He screams in pain.*] Aggghhh! Can't you get this into your balding head? If you would just realize that to come to us with this kind of claim is as strange as your trying to get a haircut in a butcher shop.

ar•dent (är´ dənt) *adj.*, warmth of feeling characterized by eager support

Woman. You can't get a haircut in a butcher shop. Why would anyone go to a butcher shop for a haircut? Are you laughing at me?

Kistunov. Laughing! I'm lucky I'm breathing....Pochatkin!

Woman. Did I tell you I'm fasting? I haven't eaten in three days. I want to eat, but nothing stays down. I had the same cup of coffee

---

8. apoplectic. Bursting with anger

three times today.

Kistunov. [*With his last burst of energy, screams.*] *POCHATKIN!*

prov•o•ca•tion (präv′ ə kā′ shən) *n.,* something that calls forth an action or emotion

Woman. I'm skin and bones. I faint at the least provocation.… Watch. [*She swoons to the floor.*] Did you see? You saw how I just fainted? Eight times a day that happens.

The Assistant *finally rushes in.*

Assistant. What is it, Mr. Kistunov? What's wrong?

Kistunov. [*Screams.*] GET HER OUT OF HERE! Who let her in my office?

Assistant. You did, sir. I asked you and you said, "Show her in."

Kistunov. I thought you meant a human being, not a lunatic with a doctor's certificate.

Woman. [*To* Pochatkin.] He wouldn't even read it. I gave it to him, he threw it back in my face.…You look like a kind person. Have pity on me. You read it and see if my husband is sick or not.

She forces the certificate on Pochatkin.

Assistant. I *read* it, madame. Twice!

Kistunov. Me too. I had to read it twice too.

Assistant. You just showed it to me outside. You showed it to *everyone*. We *all* read it. Even the doorman.

Woman. You just looked at it. You didn't read it.

Kistunov. Don't argue. Read it, Pochatkin. For God's sake, read it so we can get her out of here

Assistant. [*Quickly scans it.*] Oh, yes. It says your husband is sick. [*He looks up; gives it to her.*] Now will you please leave, madame, or I will have to get someone to remove you.

Kistunov. Yes! Yes! Good! Remove her! Get the doorman and two of the guards. Be careful, she's strong as an ox.

Woman. [*To* Kistunov.] If you touch me, I'll scream so loud they'll hear it all over the city. You'll lose all your depositors. No one will come to a bank where they beat weak, defenseless women.…I think I'm going to faint again.…

Kistunov. [*Rising.*] WEAK? DEFENSELESS? You are as defenseless as a charging rhinoceros! You are as weak as the King of the Jungle![9] You are a plague, madame! A plague that wipes out all that crosses

9. King of the Jungle. Lion

"DEFENSELESS? You are as defenseless as a charging rhinoceros!"

your path! You are a raging river that washes out bridges and stately homes! You are a wind that blows villages over mountains! It is women like you who drive men like me to the condition of husbands like yours!

DURING READING

Make Connections
How would you have responded to the Woman?

Woman. Are you saying you're not going to help me?

Kistunov. Hit her, Pochatkin! Strike her! I give you permission to knock her down. Beat some sense into her!

Woman. [*To* Pochatkin.] You hear? You hear how I'm abused? He would have you hit an orphaned mother. Did you hear me cough? Listen to this cough.

She "racks" up another coughing spell.

Assistant. Madame, if we can discuss this in my office—

He takes her arm.

Woman. Get your hands off me....Help! Help! I'm being beaten! Oh, merciful God, they're beating me!

Assistant. I am not beating you. I am just holding your arm.

Kistunov. Beat her, you fool. Kick her while you've got the chance. We'll never get her out of here. Knock her senseless!

He tries to kick her, misses and falls to the floor.

Woman. [*Pointing an evil finger at* Kistunov, *she jumps on the desk and punctuates each sentence by stepping on his desk bell.*] A curse! A curse on your bank! I put on a curse on you and your depositors! May the money in your vaults turn to potatoes! May the gold in your cellars turn to onions! May your rubles turn to radishes, and your kopecks to pickles....

DURING READING

Use Reading Strategies
Make Predictions What do you think the Woman's actions will cause Kistunov to do?

Kistunov. STOP! Stop it, I beg of you!...Pochatkin, give her the money. Give her what she wants. Give her anything—only get her out of here!

Woman. [*To* Pochatkin.] Twenty-four rubles and thirty-six kopecks....Not a penny more. That's all that's due me and that's all I want.

“She’s coming back....She’s coming back....”

Assistant. Come with me, I’ll get you your money.

Woman. And another ruble to get me home. I’d walk but I have very weak ankles.

Kistunov. Give her enough for a taxi, anything, only get her out.

Woman. God bless you, sir. You’re a kind man. I remove the curse. [*With a gesture.*] Curse be gone! Onions to money, potatoes to gold—

Kistunov. [*Pulls on his hair.*] REMOVE HERRRR! Oh, God, my hair is falling out!

He pulls some hair out.

Woman. Oh, there’s one other thing, sir. I’ll need a letter of recommendation so my husband can get another job. Don’t bother yourself about it today. I’ll be back in the morning. God, bless you, sir....

She leaves.

Kistunov. She’s coming back....She’s coming back....[*He slowly begins to go mad and takes his cane and begins to beat his bandaged leg.*] She’s coming back....She’s coming back....

Dim-out. ✤

DURING READING

Analyze Literature
Drama How do the actions indicated in these stage directions help conclude this play?

When has anyone ever caused you to agree to something unreasonable, just because he or she kept nagging you or making your life unpleasant? Why did you agree? Why might most people act in a similar way?

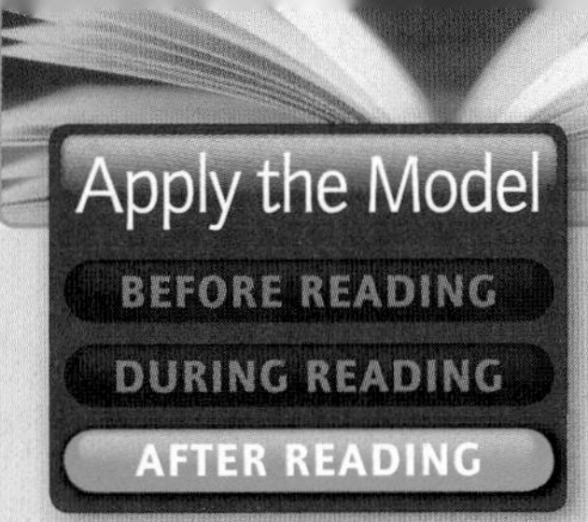

Find Meaning

1. (a) What is the setting of the play? (b) In what way is the setting important to the plot?
2. (a) Why did the Woman come to see Kistunov? (b) Why does Kistunov tell her that she came to the wrong place?
3. Why does Kistunov tell his Assistant to give the Woman the money?

Make Judgments

4. (a) What is the overall mood of the play? (b) What details help establish this mood?
5. (a) What are the Woman's most prominent character traits? (b) How do these traits affect her relationship with Kistunov?
6. (a) Why did the author call this play "A Defenseless Creature"? (b) What title would you give the play? Why?

Analyze Literature

Drama Reading a drama is different from reading a story. Everything you learn about the setting, characters, and plot is revealed through dialogue spoken by the actors, their actions, or details in the stage directions. Use a chart to analyze how the author uses dialogue and stage directions to create humor in the play.

Dialogue	Stage Directions
	Describe funny actions such as pulling out hair and screaming

Extend Understanding

Writing Options

Descriptive Writing Imagine that you are in charge of producing a show for your classmates. Write a brief **scene** for a humorous play. Be sure to include a cast of characters, setting, dialogue, and stage directions. Use "A Defenseless Creature" as a model for your scene.

Informative Writing Write a brief **literary analysis** of "A Defenseless Creature" that focuses on the tone of the play. Begin your analysis with a thesis statement. Use evidence from the play to support your analysis. Describe the effect of the play's tone on the audience.

Media Literacy

Summarize a Play While "A Defenseless Creature" is adapted from a story by Anton Chekhov, Chekhov is best known as a playwright. Locate one of Chekhov's plays in the school library or on the Internet. Use these resources to write a summary of the play.

Collaborative Learning

Analyze a Character In small groups, analyze the character of the defenseless Woman. Use evidence from the play to discuss her characteristics. Then write a short character sketch. Share your sketch with the class.

Go to **www.mirrorsandwindows.com** for more.

Grammar & Style

Verbals: Participles, Gerunds, and Infinitives

Verbals

Verbals are verb forms that act as identifiers or modifiers. There are three different forms of verbals: participles, gerunds, and infinitives.

Participles

"...Scrooge! A squeezing, wrenching, grasping, scraping, clutching, covetous old sinner!"

—ISRAEL HOROVITZ,
A Christmas Carol: Scrooge and Marley

Participles are verb forms that act as adjectives. There are two kinds of participles: *present participles and past participles*. Present participles, such as the ones in the quotation above, end in *-ing*. Most past participles end in *-ed*. Though they are verb forms, participles act as modifiers.

> EXAMPLE
>
> *Scrooge put on his <u>sleeping</u> cap and crawled into bed.*

Gerunds

"What are you doing, Cratchit? Acting cold, are you?"

—ISRAEL HOROVITZ,
A Christmas Carol: Scrooge and Marley

Gerunds are action nouns formed by adding *-ing* to verbs. In the above quotation, the word *acting* is a gerund. Gerunds can act as the subject, direct object, predicate nominative, or object of a preposition in a sentence.

> EXAMPLE
>
> *<u>Eating</u> took time away from business.*

Both participles and gerunds end in *-ing*. To tell whether the word is a participle or a gerund, determine how the word is used in a sentence. When it is used as an adjective, it is a participle. When it is used as a noun, it is a gerund.

Infinitives

"Next you'll be asking to replenish your coal from my coal-box, won't you?"

—ISRAEL HOROVITZ,
A Christmas Carol: Scrooge and Marley

Infinitives are formed by adding the word *to* to a verb. Infinitives can act as nouns, adjectives, or adverbs in a sentence. In the quotation above, *to replenish* is an infinitive.

> EXAMPLE
>
> *Bob wanted <u>to collect</u> what Scrooge owed him.*

Don't confuse infinitives with prepositional phrases beginning with *to*. In a prepositional phrase, *to* is followed by a noun, pronoun, or article rather than a verb.

Identifying Participles, Gerunds, and Infinitives

Write the verbals in the following sentences. Then label each one *participle, gerund,* or *infinitive.*

1. Learning how people really felt about him seemed to change Scrooge.
2. Meeting the beggars, Scrooge explained his unfailing disregard for the poor.
3. His nephew's pleading didn't seem to work on the penny-pinching Scrooge.
4. Bob learned that arriving early was one way to satisfy Scrooge.
5. Placing the roasted goose and cooked vegetables on the table, she invited the guests to eat.

A Christmas Carol: Scrooge and Marley

A Drama by Israel Horovitz

ANCHOR TEXT

DIRECTED READING

BEFORE READING

Build Background

Cultural Context *A Christmas Carol* by Charles Dickens, the novel on which Israel Horovitz based this play, reflects the social and economic conditions that existed in industrialized London in the 1840s. The city then had two separate and distinct personalities. On the one hand, the English upper classes flourished and prospered. On the other hand, the lower classes struggled for survival in the midst of extreme poverty and shameful living and working conditions.

Reader's Context Do you think that wealth automatically brings happiness and that poverty equals misery? Explain.

Set Purpose

Read the title, cast or list of characters, and description of setting. What do you think the mood of the play will be?

Analyze Literature

Plot As with a work of fiction, the **plot** of a drama consists of five parts. These parts include the *exposition,* in which the characters and setting are introduced, the *rising action,* in which the conflict is introduced, the *climax,* which is the story's turning point, the *falling action,* in which the conflict moves toward resolution, and the *resolution.* As you read *A Christmas Carol: Scrooge and Marley,* think about how these plot elements work together to create an interesting and suspenseful story.

Use Reading Skills

Draw Conclusions

When reading a dramatic script, you will encounter dialogue and stage directions. They let readers imagine the setting, characters, and actions. Use the dialogue and stage directions to draw conclusions about the setting, the traits and attitudes of characters, and the nature of the central conflict.

Details	Conclusions
Jacob Marley's ghost speaks in a cackling voice while eerie music plays in the background.	

Meet the Author

Israel Horovitz (b. 1939) had his first play, *The Comeback,* produced when he was eighteen years old. Since then he has written dozens of plays, acclaimed for their diverse subject matter and sharp dialogue. In 1979, the year that *A Christmas Carol* was published, Horovitz founded the prestigious Gloucester Stage Company in Massachusetts, where he was artistic director until 2006.

Preview Vocabulary

bleak (blēk) *adj.,* windy; cold; raw

des•ti•tute (des´ tə tüt') *adj.,* without money or other basic necessities for survival; extremely poor

abun•dance (ə bʉn´ dən[t]s) *n.,* wealth; riches; surplus of money and possessions

world•ly (wʉr[ə]ld´ lē) *adj.,* of or related to this world

lam•en•ta•tion (la' mən tā´ shən) *n.,* expression of sorrow or regret

A Christmas Carol: Scrooge and Marley

A Drama by Israel Horovitz

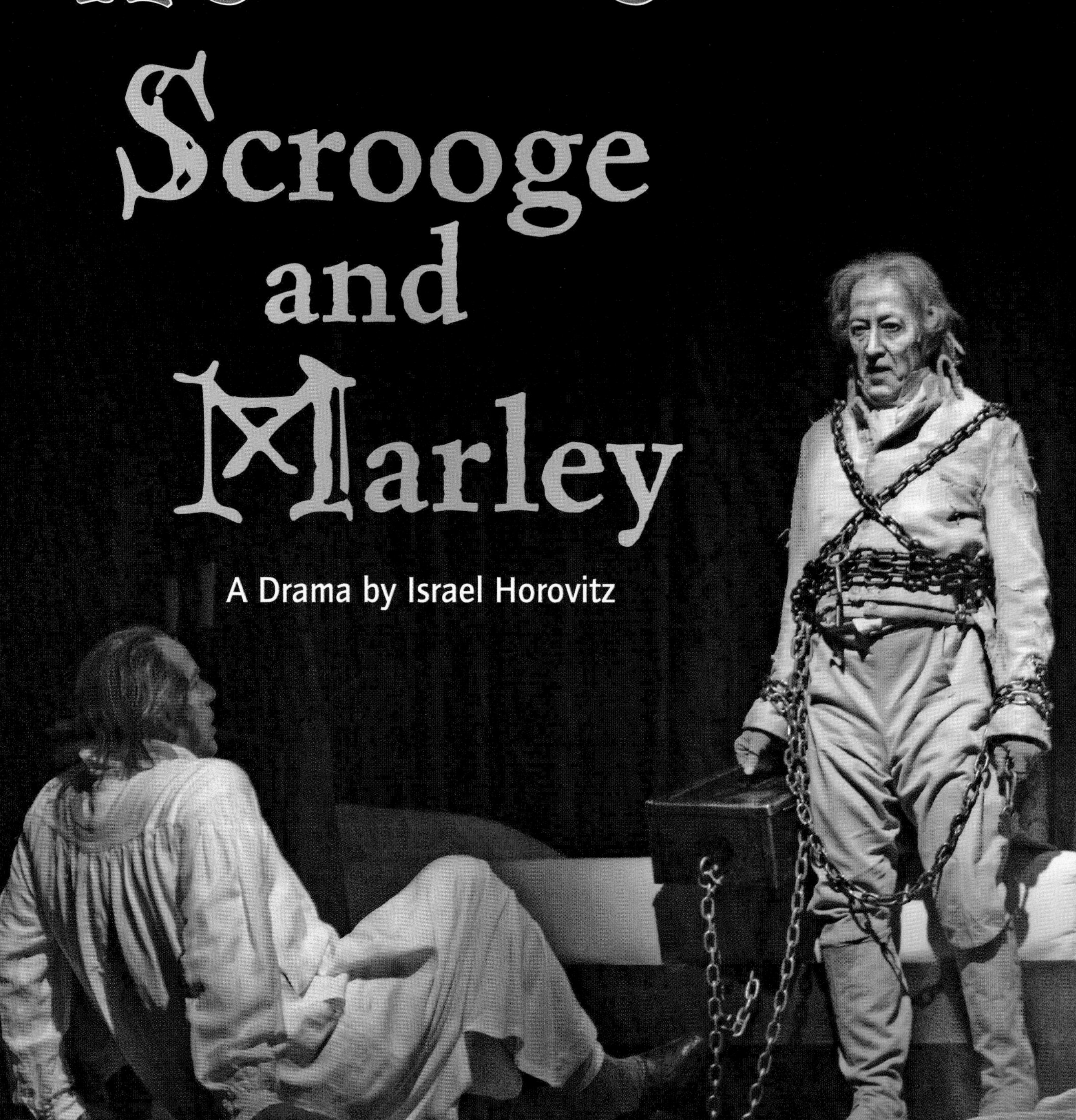

Photos from productions of *A Christmas Carol* by Goodman Theatre, Chicago, 2003–2006.

THE PEOPLE OF THE PLAY

JACOB MARLEY, a spectre[1]
EBENEZER SCROOGE, not yet dead, which is to say still alive
BOB CRATCHIT, Scrooge's clerk
FRED, Scrooge's nephew
THIN DO-GOODERS
PORTLY DO-GOODERS
SPECTRES (various), carrying money-boxes
THE GHOST OF CHRISTMAS PAST
FOUR JOCUND[2] TRAVELERS
A BAND OF SINGERS
A BAND OF DANCERS
LITTLE BOY SCROOGE
YOUNG MAN SCROOGE
FAN, Scrooge's little sister
THE SCHOOLMASTER
SCHOOLMATES
FEZZIWIG, a fine and fair employer
DICK, young Scrooge's co-worker
YOUNG SCROOGE
A FIDDLER
MORE DANCERS
SCROOGE'S LOST LOVE
SCROOGE'S LOST LOVE'S DAUGHTER
SCROOGE'S LOST LOVE'S HUSBAND
THE GHOST OF CHRISTMAS PRESENT
SOME BAKERS
MRS. CRATCHIT, Bob Cratchit's wife
BELINDA CRATCHIT, a daughter
MARTHA CRATCHIT, another daughter
PETER CRATCHIT, a son
TINY TIM CRATCHIT, another son
SCROOGE'S NIECE, Fred's wife
THE GHOST OF CHRISTMAS FUTURE, a mute Phantom
THREE MEN OF BUSINESS
DRUNKS, SCOUNDRELS
WOMEN OF THE STREETS
A CHARWOMAN
MRS. DILBER
JOE, an old second-hand goods dealer
A CORPSE, very like Scrooge
AN INDEBTED FAMILY
ADAM, a young boy
A POULTERER
A GENTLEWOMAN
SOME MORE MEN OF BUSINESS

THE PLACE OF THE PLAY

Various locations in and around the City of London, including SCROOGE'S *Chambers and Offices; the* CRATCHIT *Home;* FRED'S *Home;* SCROOGE'S *School;* FEZZIWIG'S *Offices;* OLD JOE'S *Hide-a-Way.*

THE TIME OF THE PLAY

The entire action of the play takes place on Christmas Eve, Christmas Day, and the morning after Christmas, 1843.

ACT I

— SCENE 1 —

Ghostly mist in auditorium. A single spotlight on JACOB MARLEY. *He is ancient; awful, dead-eyed. He speaks straight out to auditorium.*

MARLEY. [*Cackle-voiced.*] My name is Jacob Marley and I am dead. [*He laughs.*] Oh, no, there's no doubt that I am dead. The register of my burial was signed by the clergyman, the clerk, the undertaker...and by my chief mourner...Ebenezer Scrooge...[*Pause; remembers.*] I am dead as a door-nail.

A spotlight fades up on SCROOGE, *in his counting-house,*[3] *counting.*

Lettering on the window behind SCROOGE *reads:* "SCROOGE AND MARLEY, LTD." *The spotlight is tight on* SCROOGE'S *head and shoulders. We shall not yet see into the offices and setting. Ghostly music continues, under.* MARLEY *looks across at* SCROOGE; *pitifully. After a moment's pause.*

1. **spectre.** Ghost, ghostly presence
2. **jocund.** High-spirited or merry
3. **counting-house.** Office where financial end of a business is handled

Marley. [*Contd.*] I present him to you: Ebenezer Scrooge...England's most tightfisted hand at the grindstone, Scrooge! A squeezing, wrenching, grasping, scraping, clutching, covetous, old sinner! Secret, and self-contained, and solitary as an oyster. The cold within him freezes his old features, nips his pointed nose, shrivels his cheek, stiffens his gait; makes his eyes red, his thin lips blue; and speaks out shrewdly in his grating voice. Look at him. Look at him...

Scrooge *counts and mumbles.*

Scrooge. They owe me money and I will collect. I will have them jailed if I have to. They owe me money and I will collect what is due me.

Marley *moves toward* Scrooge, *two steps. The spotlight stays with him.*

Marley. [*Disgusted.*] He and I were partners for I don't know how many years. Scrooge was my sole executor, my sole administrator, my sole assign, my sole residuary legatee,[4] my sole friend and my sole mourner. But Scrooge was not so cut up by the sad event of my death, but that he was an excellent man of business on the very day of my funeral, and solemnized it with an undoubted bargain. [*Pauses again in disgust.*] He never painted out my name from the window. There it stands, on the window and above the warehouse door: Scrooge and Marley. Sometimes people new to our business call him Scrooge and sometimes they call him Marley. He answers to both names. It's all the same to him. And it's cheaper than painting in a new sign, isn't it? [*Pauses; moves closer to* Scrooge.] Nobody has ever stopped him in the street to say, with gladsome looks, "My dear Scrooge, how are you? When will you come to see me?" No beggars implored him to bestow a trifle,[5] no children ever ask him what it is o'clock, no man or woman now, or ever in his life, not once, inquire the way to such and such a place.

Marley *stands next to* Scrooge *now. They share, so it seems, a spotlight.*

Marley. [*Contd.*] But what does Scrooge care of any of this? It is the very thing he likes! To edge his way along the crowded paths of life, warning all human sympathy to keep its distance.

A ghostly bell rings in the distance. Marley *moves away from* Scrooge *now. As he does, he "takes" the light:* Scrooge *has disappeared into the black void beyond.* Marley *walks, talking directly to the audience. Pauses.*

Marley. [*Contd.*] The bell tolls and I must take my leave. You must stay a while with Scrooge and watch him play out his scroogey life. It is now the story: the once-upon-a-time. Scrooge is in his counting-house. Where else? Christmas eve and Scrooge is busy in his counting-house. It is cold, bleak, biting weather outside: foggy withal:[6] and if you listen closely, you can hear the people in the court go wheezing up and down, beating their hands upon their breasts, and stamping their feet upon the pavement stones to warm them...

The clocks outside strike three.

Marley. [*Contd.*] Only three! and quite dark outside already: it has not been light all day this day.

This ghostly bell rings in the distance again. Marley *looks about him. Music in.* Marley *flies away.*

---

4. **executor...legatee.** Legal terms referring to the person left in charge of a deceased person's estate and carrying out the instructions of the will
5. **bestow a trifle.** Give a small gift
6. **withal.** In addition

bleak (blēk) *adj.*, windy; cold; raw

— SCENE 2 —

Christmas music in, sung by a live chorus, full. At conclusion of song, sound fades under and into distance. Lights up in set: offices of Scrooge and Marley, Ltd. Scrooge *sits at his desk, at work. Near him is a tiny fire.*

His door is open and in his line of vision, we see Scrooge's *clerk,* Bob Cratchit, *who sits in a dismal tank of a cubicle, copying letters. Near* Cratchit *is a fire so tiny as to barely cast a light: perhaps it is one pitifully glowing coal?* Cratchit *rubs his hands together, puts on a white comforter and tries to heat his hands around his candle.* Scrooge's *nephew enters, unseen.*

Scrooge. What are you doing, Cratchit? Acting cold, are you? Next you'll be asking to replenish your coal from my coal-box, won't you? Well, save your breath, Cratchit! Unless you're prepared to find employ elsewhere!

Nephew. [*Cheerfully; surprising* Scrooge.] A Merry Christmas to you, Uncle! God save you!

Scrooge. Bah! Humbug![7]

Nephew. Christmas a "humbug," Uncle? I'm sure you don't mean that.

Scrooge. I do! Merry Christmas? What right do you have to be merry? What reason have you to be merry? You're poor enough!

Nephew. Come, then. What right have you to be dismal? What reason have you to be morose?[8] You're rich enough.

Scrooge. Bah! Humbug!

Nephew. Don't be cross, Uncle.

Scrooge. What else can I be? Eh? When I live in a world of fools such as this? Merry Christmas? What's Christmas time to you but a time of paying bills without any money; a time for finding yourself a year older, but not an hour richer. If I could work my will, every idiot who goes about with "Merry Christmas" on his lips, should be boiled with his own pudding, and buried with a stake of holly through his heart. He should!

Nephew. Uncle!

Scrooge. Nephew! You keep Christmas in your own way and let me keep it in mine.

Nephew. Keep it! But you don't keep it, Uncle.

Scrooge. Let me leave it alone, then. Much good it has ever done you!

Nephew. There are many things from which I have derived good, by which I have not profited, I daresay. Christmas among the rest. But I am sure that I always thought of Christmastime, when it has come round—as a good time: the only time I know of when men and women seem to open their shut-up hearts freely and to think of people below them as if they really were fellow passengers to the grave, and not another race of creatures bound on other journeys. And therefore, Uncle, though it has never put a scrap of gold or silver in my pocket, I believe that it has done me good, and that it will do me good; and I say, God bless it!

The Clerk *in the tank applauds, looks at the furious* Scrooge *and pokes out his tiny fire, as if in exchange for the moment of impropriety.* Scrooge *yells at him.*

Scrooge. [*To the* Clerk.] Let me hear another sound from you and you'll keep your Christmas by losing your situation. [*To the* Nephew.] You're quite a powerful speaker, sir. I wonder you don't go into Parliament.[9]

Nephew. Don't be angry, Uncle. Come! Dine with us tomorrow.

Scrooge. I'd rather see myself dead than see myself with your family!

---

7. **humbug.** Old-fashioned expression meaning "nonsense"
8. **morose.** Negative; bad-tempered
9. **Parliament.** Highest body of the legislature in England made up of the House of Commons and the House of Lords

Nephew. But, why? Why?

Scrooge. Why did you get married?

Nephew. Because I fell in love.

Scrooge. That, sir, is the only thing that you have said to me in your entire lifetime which is even more ridiculous than "Merry Christmas"! [*Turns from* Nephew.] Good afternoon.

Nephew. Nay, Uncle, you never came to see me before I married either. Why give it as a reason for not coming now?

Scrooge. Good afternoon, Nephew!

Nephew. I want nothing from you; I ask nothing of you: why cannot we be friends?

Scrooge. Good afternoon!

Nephew. I am sorry with all my heart, to find you so resolute.[10] But I have made the trial in homage to Christmas, and I'll keep my Christmas humor to the last. So A Merry Christmas, Uncle!

Scrooge. Good afternoon!

Nephew. And A Happy New Year!

Scrooge. Good afternoon!

Nephew. [*He stands facing* Scrooge.] Uncle, you are the most...[*Pauses.*] no, I shan't. My Christmas humor is intact [*Pause.*] God bless you, Uncle...[Nephew *turns and starts for the door, he stops at* Cratchit's *cage.*] Merry Christmas, Bob Cratchit.

Cratchit. Merry Christmas to you, sir, and a very, very happy New Year.

Scrooge. [*Calling across to them.*] Oh, fine, a perfection, just fine...to see the perfect pair of you: husbands, with wives and children to support...my clerk there earning fifteen shillings a week...and the perfect pair of you, talking about a Merry Christmas! [*Pauses.*] I'll retire to Bedlam!

Nephew. [*To* Cratchit.] He's impossible!

---

10. resolute. Determined

Cratchit. Oh, mind him not, sir. He's getting on in years, and he's alone. He's noticed your visit. I'll wager your visit has warmed him.

Nephew. Him? Uncle Ebenezer Scrooge? Warmed? You are a better Christian than I am, sir.

Cratchit. [*Opening the door for* Nephew; *two* Do-Gooders *enter, as* Nephew *exits.*] Good day to you, sir, and God bless.

Nephew. God bless...

One man who enters is portly, the other thin. Both are pleasant.

Cratchit. Can I help you, gentlemen?

Thin Man. [*Carrying papers and books; looks around* Cratchit *to* Scrooge.] Scrooge and Marley's, I believe. Have I the pleasure of addressing Mr. Scrooge, or Mr. Marley?

Scrooge. Mr. Marley has been dead these seven years. He died seven years ago this very night.

Portly Man. We have no doubt his liberality[11] is well represented by his surviving partner...[*Offers his calling card.*]

Scrooge. [*Handing back the card; unlooked at.*] Good afternoon.

Thin Man. This will take but a moment, sir...

Portly Man. At this festive season of the year, Mr. Scrooge, it is more than usually desirable that we should make some slight provision[12] for the poor and destitute, who suffer greatly at the present time. Many thousands are in want of common necessities; hundreds of thousands are in want of common comforts, sir.

Scrooge. Are there no prisons?

Portly Man. Plenty of prisons.

Scrooge. And aren't the Union workhouses still in operation?

Thin Man. They are. Still. I wish that I could say that they are not.

Scrooge. The Treadmill[13] and the Poor Law[14] are in full vigor then?

Thin Man. Both very busy, sir.

Scrooge. Ohhh, I see. I was afraid, from what you said at first that something had occurred to stop them from their useful course. [*Pauses.*] I'm glad to hear it.

Portly Man. Under the impression that they scarcely furnish Christian cheer of mind or body to the multitude, a few of us are endeavoring to raise a fund to buy the Poor some meat and drink and means of warmth. We choose this time, because it is a time, of all others, when Want is keenly felt, and Abundance rejoices. [*Pen in hand; as well as notepad.*] What shall I put you down for, sir?

Scrooge. Nothing!

Portly Man. You wish to be left anonymous?

Scrooge. I wish to be left alone! [*Pauses; turns away; turns back to them.*] Since you ask me what I wish, gentlemen, that is my answer. I help to support the establishments that I have mentioned: they cost enough: and those who are badly off must go there.

Thin Man. Many can't go there; and many would rather die.

Scrooge. If they would rather die, they had better do it, and decrease the surplus

---

11. **liberality.** Generous behavior and attitude; charity
12. **provision.** Thing provided
13. **Treadmill.** Mechanical device used in English prisons on which prisoners were forced to walk at an incline, six to eight hours a day
14. **Poor Law.** England's Old Poor Law, passed in 1601, offered relief to the poor, especially those unable to work because of old age or physical disabilities. The Poor Law Amendment, passed in 1834, made it impossible for people to collect relief outside of workhouses, or poorhouses, which were known for their harsh, shameful conditions.

des•ti•tute (des´ tə tüt') *adj.*, without money or other basic necessities for survival; extremely poor

abun•dance (ə bun´ dən[t]s) *n.*, wealth; riches; surplus of money and possessions population. Besides—excuse me—I don't know that.

Thin Man. But you might know it!

Scrooge. It's not my business. It's enough for a man to understand his own business, and not to interfere with other people's. Mine occupies me constantly. Good afternoon, gentlemen! [Scrooge *turns his back on the gentlemen and returns to his desk.*]

Portly Man. But, sir, Mr. Scrooge...think of the poor.

Scrooge. [*Turns suddenly to them. Pauses.*] Take your leave of my office, sirs, while I am still smiling.

The Thin Man *looks at the* Portly Man. *They are undone. They shrug. They move to door.* Cratchit *hops up to open it for them.*

Thin Man. Good day, sir. [*To* Cratchit.] A Merry Christmas to you, sir...

Cratchit. Yes. A Merry Christmas to both of you...

Portly Man. Merry Christmas...

Cratchit *silently squeezes something into the hand of the* Thin Man.

Thin Man. What's this?

Cratchit. Shhhh...

Cratchit *opens the door; wind and snow whistle into the room.*

Thin Man. Thank you, sir, thank you.

Cratchit *closes the door and returns to his workplace.* Scrooge *is at his own counting table.* He talks to Cratchit *without looking up.*

Scrooge. It's less of a time of year for being merry, and more a time of year for being loony...if you ask me.

Cratchit. Well, I don't know, sir...[*The clock's bell strikes 6 o'clock.*] Well there it is, eh, sir?

Scrooge. Saved by six bells, are you?

Cratchit. I must be going home...[*He snuffs out his candle and puts on his hat.*] I hope you have a...very very lovely day tomorrow, sir.

Scrooge. Hmmm. Oh, you'll be wanting the whole day tomorrow, I suppose?

Cratchit. If quite convenient, sir.

Scrooge. It's not convenient, and it's not fair. If I was to stop half-a-crown for it, you'd think yourself ill-used, I'll be bound?

Cratchit *smiles faintly.*

Cratchit. I don't know, sir...

Scrooge. And yet, you don't think me ill-used, when I pay a day's wages for no work.

Cratchit. It's only but once a year...

Scrooge. A poor excuse for picking a man's pocket every 25th of December! But I suppose you must have the whole day. Be here all the earlier the next morning!

Cratchit. Oh, I will, sir. I will. I promise you. And, sir...

Scrooge. Don't say it, Cratchit.

Cratchit. But let me wish you a...

Scrooge. Don't say it, Cratchit. I warn you...

Cratchit. Sir!

Scrooge. Cratchit!

Cratchit *opens the door.*

Cratchit. All right, then, sir...well... [*Suddenly.*] Merry Christmas, Mister Scrooge!

And he runs out the door, shutting same behind him. Scrooge *moves to his desk; gathering his coat, hat, etc. A* Boy *appears at his window...*

Boy. [*Singing.*] "Away in a manger..."

Scrooge *seizes his ruler and whacks at the image of the* Boy *outside. The* Boy *leaves.*

Scrooge. Bah! Humbug! Christmas! Bah! Humbug! [*He shuts out the light.*]

A NOTE ON THE CROSSOVER, FOLLOWING SCENE 2

Scrooge will walk alone to his rooms from his offices. As he makes a long slow cross of the stage, the scenery should change, Christmas music will be heard, various people will cross by Scrooge, often smiling happily.

There will be occasional pleasant greetings tossed at him. Scrooge, in contrast to all, will grump and mumble. He will snap at passing boys, as might an old horrid hound.

In short, Scrooge's sounds and movements will define him in contrast from all other people who cross the stage: he is the misanthrope, the malcontent, the miser.[15] *He is Scrooge.*

This statement of Scrooge's character, by contrast to all other characters, should seem comical to the audience.

During Scrooge's crossover to his rooms, snow should begin to fall. All passers-by will hold their faces to the sky, smiling, allowing snow to shower them lightly. Scrooge, by contrast, will bat at the flakes with his walking-stick, as might an insomniac swat at a sleep-stopping, middle-of-the-night swarm of mosquitoes. He will comment on the blackness of the night, and, finally, reach his rooms and his encounter with the magical spectre: Marley, his eternal mate.

— SCENE 3 —

Scrooge. No light at all...no moon...that is what is at the center of a Christmas Eve: dead black: void...

Scrooge puts his key in the door's keyhole. He has reached his rooms now. The door knocker changes and is now Marley's face. A musical sound; quickly: ghosty. Marley's image is not at all angry, but looks at Scrooge as did the old Marley look at Scrooge. The hair is curiously stirred; eyes wide open, dead: absent of focus. Scrooge stares wordlessly here. The face, before his very eyes, does deliquesce:[16] *it is a knocker again. Scrooge opens the door and checks the back of same, probably for Marley's pigtail. Seeing nothing but screws and nuts, Scrooge refuses the memory.*

Scrooge. [*Contd.*] Pooh, pooh!

The sound of the door closing resounds throughout the house as thunder. Every room echoes the sound. Scrooge fastens the door and walks across the hall to the stairs, trimming his candle as he goes: and then he goes slowly up the staircase. He checks each room: sitting room, bedroom, lumber-room.[17] *He looks under the sofa, under the table: nobody there. He fixes his evening gruel on the hob;*[18] *changes his jacket. Scrooge sits near the tiny low-flamed fire, sipping his gruel. There are various pictures on the walls: all of them now show likenesses of Marley. Scrooge blinks his eyes.*

Scrooge. [*Contd.*] Bah! Humbug!

Scrooge walks in a circle about the room. The pictures change back into their natural images. He sits down at the table in front of the fire. A bell hangs overhead. It begins to ring, of its own accord. Slowly, surely, begins the ringing of every bell in the house. They continue ringing for nearly half a minute. Scrooge is stunned by the phenomenon. The bells cease their ringing all at once. Deep below Scrooge, in the basement of the house, there is the sound of clanking, of some enormous chain being dragged across the floors; and now up the stairs. We hear doors flying open.

Scrooge. [*Contd.*] Bah still! Humbug still! This is not happening! I won't believe it!

Marley's Ghost enters the room. He is horrible to look at: pigtail, vest, suit as usual, but he drags an enormous chain now, to which is fastened cashboxes, keys, padlocks, ledgers,

15. **misanthrope...miser.** Person who dislikes humanity, is dissatisfied, and is greedy
16. **deliquesce.** Dissolve or melt away
17. **lumber-room.** Spare room
18. **gruel...hob.** Refers to cooking a thin soup over an open fire

deeds, and heavy purses fashioned of steel. He is transparent. If possible, we should now, in faithfulness to Dickens' story, be able to see that MARLEY *has no bowels.* MARLEY *stands opposite the strickened* SCROOGE.

SCROOGE. [*Contd.*] How now! What do you want of me?

MARLEY. Much!

SCROOGE. Who are you?

MARLEY. Ask me who I was.

SCROOGE. Who were you then?

MARLEY. In life, I was your business partner: Jacob Marley.

SCROOGE. I see...can you sit down?

MARLEY. I can.

SCROOGE. Do it then.

MARLEY. I shall. [MARLEY *sits opposite* SCROOGE, *in the chair across the table at the front of the fireplace.*] You don't believe in me.

SCROOGE. I don't.

MARLEY. Why do you doubt your senses?

SCROOGE. Because every little thing affects them. A slight disorder of stomach makes them cheat. You may be an undigested bit of beef, blot of mustard, a crumb of cheese, a fragment of an underdone potato. There's more of gravy than of grave about you, whatever you are!

There is a silence between them. SCROOGE *is made nervous by it. He picks up a toothpick.*

SCROOGE. [*Contd.*] Humbug! I tell you: humbug!

MARLEY *opens his mouth and screams a ghostly, fearful scream. The scream echoes about each room of the house. Bats fly, cats screech, lightning flashes.* SCROOGE *stands and walks backwards against the wall.* MARLEY *stands and screams again. This time, he takes his head and lifts it from his shoulders. His head continues to scream.* MARLEY'S *face again appears on every picture in the room: all screaming.* SCROOGE, *on his knees before* MARLEY.

SCROOGE. [*Contd.*] Mercy! Dreadful apparition,[19] mercy! Why, O! why do you trouble me so?

MARLEY. Man of the worldly mind, do you believe in me, or not?

SCROOGE. I do. I must. But why do spirits such as you walk the earth? And why do they come to me?

MARLEY. It is required of every man that the spirit within him should walk around among his fellow-men, and travel far and wide; and if that spirit goes not forth in life, it is condemned to do so after death [MARLEY *screams again: a tragic scream from his ghosty bones.*] I wear the chain I forged in life. I made it link by link, and yard by yard. Is its pattern strange to you? Or would you know, you, Scrooge, the weight and length of the strong coil you bear yourself? It was full and heavy and long as this, seven Christmas Eves ago. You have labored on it, since. It is a ponderous[20] chain.

Terrified that a chain will appear about his body, SCROOGE *spins and waves the unwanted chain away. None, of course, appears. Sees* MARLEY *watching him dance about the room.* MARLEY *watches* SCROOGE; *silently.*

SCROOGE. Jacob. Old Jacob Marley, tell me more. Speak comfort to me, Jacob.

MARLEY. I have none to give. Comfort comes from other regions, Ebenezer Scrooge, and is conveyed by other ministers, to other kinds of men. A very little more, is all that is permitted to me. I cannot rest, I cannot stay, I cannot linger anywhere...[*He moans again.*] my spirit never walked beyond our counting-house—

---

19. apparition. Ghost-like presence
20. ponderous. Slow and awkward from great weight

world • ly (wɚr[ə]ld´ lē) *adj.,* of or related to this world mark me!—in life my spirit never roved beyond the narrow limits of our money-changing hole; and weary journeys lie before me!

Scrooge. But you were always a good man of business, Jacob.

Marley. [*Screams word "business"; a flashpot explodes with him.*] BUSI-NESS!!! Mankind was my business. The common welfare was my business; charity, mercy, forbearance,[21] benevolence, were, all, my business.

Scrooge *is quaking.*

Marley. [*Contd.*] Hear me, Ebenezer Scrooge! My time is nearly gone!!

Scrooge. I will, but don't be hard upon me. And don't be flowery, Jacob! Pray!

Marley. How is it that I appear before you in a shape that you can see, I may not tell. I have sat invisible beside you many and many a day. That is no light part of my penance. I am here tonight to warn you that you have yet a chance and hope of escaping my fate. A chance and hope of my procuring, Ebenezer.

Scrooge. You were always a good friend to me. Thank'ee!

Marley. You will be haunted by Three Spirits.

Scrooge. Would that be the chance and hope you mentioned, Jacob?

Marley. It is.

Scrooge. I think I'd rather not.

Marley. Without their visits, you cannot hope to shun the path I tread. Expect the first one tomorrow, when the bell tolls one.

Scrooge. Couldn't I take 'em all at once, and get it over, Jacob?

Marley. Expect the second on the next night at the same hour. The third upon the next night when the last stroke of twelve has ceased to vibrate. Look to see me no more. Others may, but you may not. And look that, for your own sake, you remember what has passed between us!

Marley *places his head back upon his shoulders. He approaches the window, and beckons to* Scrooge *to watch. Outside the window, spectres fly by, carrying money-boxes and chains. They make a confused sound of lamentation.* Marley, *after listening a moment, joins into their mournful dirge. He leans to the window and floats out into the bleak, dark night. He is gone.*

Scrooge. [*Rushing to the window.*] Jacob! No, Jacob! Don't leave me! I'm frightened!

He sees that Marley *has gone. He looks outside. He pulls the shutter closed, so that the scene is blocked from his view. All sound stops. After a pause, he re-opens the shutter and all is quiet, as it should be on a Christmas Eve. Carolers carol out of doors, in the distance.* Scrooge *closes the shutter and walks down the stairs. He examines the door by which* Marley *first entered.*

Scrooge. [*Contd.*] No one here at all! Did I imagine all that? Humbug! [*He looks about the room.*] I did imagine it. It only happened in my foulest dream-mind, didn't it? An undigested bit of...

Thunder and lightning in the room, suddenly.

Scrooge. [*Contd.*] Sorry! Sorry!

There is silence again. The lights fade out.

— SCENE 4 —

Christmas music, choral, "Hark the Herald Angels Sing," sung by an onstage choir of children. Above, Scrooge, *in his bed, dead to the world, asleep, in his darkened room. It should appear that the choir is singing somewhere*

21. **forbearance.** Patience

lam•en•ta•tion (la' mən tā´ shən) *n.,* expression of sorrow or regret *outside of the house. When the singing is ended, the choir should fade out of view and* MARLEY *should fade into view, in their place.*

MARLEY. [*Directly to audience.*] From this point forth...I shall be quite visible to you, but invisible to him. [*Smiles.*] He will feel my presence nevertheless, for, unless my senses fail me completely, we are—you and I—witness to the changing of a miser: that one, my partner in life, in business, and in eternity: that one: Scrooge. [*Moves to staircase, below* SCROOGE.] See him now. He endeavors to pierce the darkness with his ferret eyes. [*To audience.*] See him, now. He listens for the hour.

The bells toll. SCROOGE *is awakened and quakes as the hour approaches one o'clock, but the bells stop their sound at the hour of twelve.*

SCROOGE. [*Astonished.*] Midnight! Why this isn't possible. It was past two when I went to bed. An icicle must have gotten into the clock's works! I couldn't have slept through the whole day and far into another night. It isn't possible that anything has happened to the sun, and this is twelve at noon. [*He runs to window; unshutters same; it is night.*] Night, still. Quiet, normal for the season, cold. It is certainly not noon. I cannot in any way afford to lose my days. Securities come due, promissory notes, interest on investments: these are things that happen in the daylight! [*He returns to his bed.*] Was this a dream?

MARLEY *appears in his room. He speaks to the audience.*

MARLEY. You see? He does not, with faith, believe in me fully, even still! Whatever will it take to turn the faith of a miser from money to men?

SCROOGE. Another quarter and it'll be one and Marley's ghosty friends will come. [*Pauses; listens.*] Where's the chime for one?

Ding, dong.

SCROOGE. [*Contd.*] A quarter past!

Repeats.

SCROOGE. [*Contd.*] Half-past!

Repeats.

HISTORY ▶▶ CONNECTION

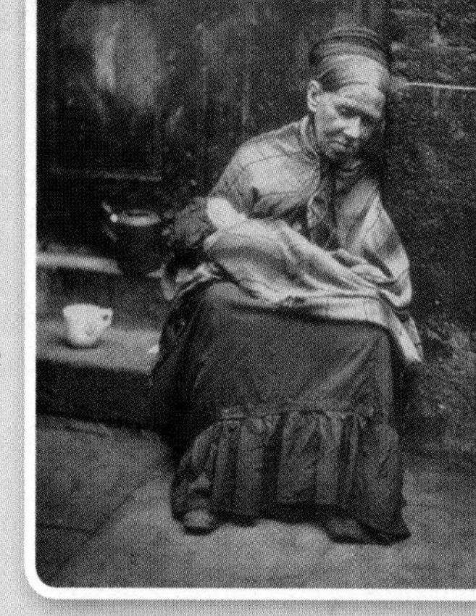

Industry and Reform The Industrial Revolution of the late eighteenth century made England the world's first industrial nation. Factories and textile mills drew huge numbers of peasants to cities in search of work. Without adequate housing or sanitation, however, living conditions were miserable breeding grounds for disease. Factory owners and businesspeople grew wealthy, while the poor, including children, labored long hours for little pay. By the mid-nineteenth century, several reform efforts limited the workday for women and children under thirteen but did little to improve pay or working conditions. How does this information shape your perception of Scrooge?

SCROOGE. [*Contd.*] A quarter to it! But where's the heavy bell of the hour one? This is a game in which I lose my senses! Perhaps, if I allowed myself another short doze.

MARLEY. Doze, Ebenezer, doze.

A heavy bell thuds its one ring: dull and definitely one o'clock. There is a flash of light. SCROOGE *sits up, in a sudden. A hand draws back the curtains by his bed. He sees it.*

SCROOGE. A hand! Who owns it? Hello!

Ghosty music again, but of a new nature to the play. A strange figure stands before SCROOGE*—like a child, yet at the same time like an old man: white hair, but unwrinkled skin; long, muscular arms, but delicate legs and feet. Wears white tunic; lustrous belt cinches waist. Branch of fresh green holly in its hand, but has its dress trimmed with fresh summer flowers. Clear jets of light spring from the crown of its head. Holds cap in hand. The* SPIRIT *is called* PAST.

SCROOGE. [*Contd.*] Are you the Spirit, Sir, whose coming was foretold to me?

PAST. I am.

MARLEY. Does he take this to be a vision of his green grocer?[22]

SCROOGE. Who, and what are you?

PAST. I am the Ghost of Christmas Past.

SCROOGE. Long past?

PAST. Your past.

SCROOGE. May I ask, please, sir, what business you have here with me?

PAST. Your welfare.

SCROOGE. Not to sound ungrateful, sir, and really, please do understand that I am plenty obliged for your concern, but, really, kind spirit, it would have done all the better for my welfare to have been left alone altogether, to have slept peacefully through this night.

PAST. Your reclamation,[23] then. Take heed!

SCROOGE. My what?

PAST. [*Motioning to* SCROOGE *and taking his arm.*] Rise! Fly with me! [*He leads* SCROOGE *to the window.*]

SCROOGE. [*Panicked.*] Fly, but I am a mortal and cannot fly!

PAST. [*Pointing to his heart.*] Bear but a touch of my hand here and you shall be upheld in more than this!

SCROOGE *touches the* SPIRIT'S *heart and the lights dissolve into sparkly flickers. Lovely crystals of music are heard. The scene dissolves into another, Christmas music again.*

— SCENE 5 —

SCROOGE *and the* GHOST OF CHRISTMAS PAST *walk together across an open stage. In the background, we see a field that is open; covered by a soft, downy snow: a country road.*

SCROOGE. Good Heaven! I was bred in this place. I was a boy here!

SCROOGE *freezes, staring at the field beyond.* MARLEY'S *ghost appears beside him; takes* SCROOGE'S face *in his hands, and turns his face to the audience.*

MARLEY. You see this Scrooge: stricken by feeling. Conscious of a thousand odors floating in the air, each one connected with a thousand thoughts, and hopes, and joys, and cares long, long forgotten. [*Pause.*] This one—this—Scrooge—before your very eyes, returns to life, among the living. [*To audience, sternly.*] You'd best pay your most careful attention. I would suggest rapt.

There is a small flash and puff of smoke and MARLEY *is gone again.*

PAST. Your lip is trembling, Mr. Scrooge. And what is that upon your cheek?

SCROOGE. Upon my cheek? Nothing...a blemish on the skin from the eating of overmuch grease...nothing...[*Suddenly.*] Kind Spirit of Christmas Past, lead me where you will, but quickly! To be stagnant[24] in this place is, for me, unbearable!

PAST. You recollect the way?

---

22. green grocer. Person who sells fresh fruits and vegetables
23. reclamation. Recovery
24. stagnant. Unmoving

Scrooge. Remember it! I would know it blindfolded! My bridge, my church, my winding river! [*Staggers about, trying to see it all at once. He weeps again.*]

Past. These are but shadows of things that have been. They have no consciousness of us.

Four jocund travelers enter; singing a Christmas song in four-part harmony—"God Rest Ye Merry Gentlemen."

Scrooge. Listen! I know these men! I know them! I remember the beauty of their song!

Past. But, why do you remember it so happily? It is Merry Christmas that they say to one another! What is Merry Christmas to you, Mr. Scrooge! Out upon Merry Christmas, right? What good has Merry Christmas ever done you, Mr. Scrooge?

Scrooge. [*After a long pause.*] None. No good. None...[*He bows his head.*]

Past. Look, you, sir, a school ahead. The schoolroom is not quite deserted. A solitary child, neglected by his friends, is left there still.

Scrooge *falls to the ground; sobbing as he sees, and we see, a small boy, the* Young Scrooge, *sitting and weeping, bravely, alone at his desk: alone in a vast space, a void.*

Scrooge. I cannot look on him!

Past. You must, Mr. Scrooge, you must.

Scrooge. It's me. [*Pauses; weeps.*] Poor boy. He lived inside his head...alone...[*Pauses; weeps.*] poor boy. [*Pauses; stops his weeping.*] I wish...[*Dries his eyes on his cuff.*] ah! it's too late!

Past. What is the matter?

Scrooge. There was a boy singing a Christmas Carol outside my door last night. I should like to have given him something: that's all.

Past. [*Smiles; waves his hand to* Scrooge.] Come. Let us see another Christmas.

Lights out on little boy. A flash of light. A puff of smoke. Lights up on older boy.

Scrooge. Look! Me, again! Older now! [*Realizes.*] Oh, yes still alone.

The boy—a slightly older Scrooge*—sits alone in a chair, reading. The door to the room opens and a young girl enters. She is much, much younger than this slightly older* Scrooge. *She is, say, six, and he is, say, twelve.* Elder Scrooge *and the* Ghost of Christmas Past *stand watching the scene, unseen.*

Fan. Dear, dear brother, I have come to bring you home.

Boy. Home, little Fan?

Fan. Yes! Home, for good and all! Father is so much kinder than he ever used to be, and home's like heaven! He spoke so gently to me one dear night when I was going to bed that I was not afraid to ask him; once more if you might come home; and he said "yes"...you should; and sent me in a coach to bring you. And you're to be a man and are never to come back here, but first, we're to be together all the Christmas long, and have the merriest time in the world.

Boy. You are quite a woman, little Fan!

Laughing; she drags at Boy, *causing him to stumble to the door with her. Suddenly we hear a mean and terrible voice in the hallway, Off. It is the* Schoolmaster.

Schoolmaster. Bring down Master Scrooge's travel box at once! He is to travel!

Fan. Who is that, Ebenezer?

Boy. O! Quiet, Fan. It is the Schoolmaster, himself!

The door bursts open and into the room bursts with it the Schoolmaster.

Schoolmaster. Master Scrooge?

Boy. Oh, Schoolmaster, I'd like you to meet my little sister, Fan, sir...

Two boys struggle on with Scrooge*'s trunk.*

Fan. Pleased, sir. [*She curtsies.*]

Schoolmaster. You are to travel, Master Scrooge.

Scrooge. Yes, sir. I know, sir...

All start to exit, but Fan *grabs the coattail of the mean old* Schoolmaster.

Boy. Fan!

Schoolmaster. What's this?

Fan. Pardon, sir, but I believe that you've forgotten to say your goodbye to my brother, Ebenezer, who stands still now awaiting it... [*She smiles, curtsies, lowers her eyes.*] Pardon, sir.

Schoolmaster. [*Amazed.*] I...uh...harumph... uhh...well, then...[*Outstretches hand.*] Goodbye, Scrooge.

Boy. Uh, well, goodbye, Schoolmaster...

Lights fade out on all but Boy *looking at* Fan; *and* Scrooge *and* Past *looking at them.*

Scrooge. Oh, my dear, dear little sister, Fan...how I loved her.

Past. Always a delicate creature, whom a breath might have withered, but she had a large heart.

Scrooge. So she had.

Past. She died a woman, and had, as I think, children.

Scrooge. One child.

Past. True. Your nephew.

Scrooge. Yes.

Past. Fine, then. We move on, Mr. Scrooge. That warehouse, there? Do you know it?

Scrooge. Know it? Wasn't I apprenticed[25] there?

Past. We'll have a look.

---

25. apprenticed. Learned a trade by practical experience under a skilled worker

They enter the warehouse. The lights crossfade with them, coming up on an old man in Welsh wig: FEZZIWIG.

SCROOGE. Why, it's old Fezziwig! Bless his heart; it's Fezziwig, alive again!

[FEZZIWIG *sits behind a large, high desk, counting. He lays down his pen; looks at the clock: seven bells sound.*] Quittin' time...

FEZZIWIG. Quittin' time...[*He takes off his waistcoat and laughs; calls off.*] Yo ho, Ebenezer! Dick!

DICK WILKINS *and* EBENEZER SCROOGE*—a young man version—enter the room.* DICK *and* EBENEZER *are* FEZZIWIG'S *apprentices.*

SCROOGE. Dick Wilkins, to be sure! My fellow-'prentice! Bless my soul, yes. There he is. He was very much attached to me, was Dick. Poor Dick! Dear, dear!

FEZZIWIG. Yo ho, my boys. No more work tonight. Christmas Eve, Dick...Christmas, Ebenezer!

They stand at attention in front of FEZZIWIG; *laughing.*

FEZZIWIG. [*Contd.*] Hilli-ho! Clear away, and let's have lots of room here! Hilli-ho, Dick! Chirrup, Ebenezer!

The young men clear the room, sweep the floor, straighten the pictures, trim the lamps, etc. The space is clear now. A FIDDLER *enters, fiddling.*

FEZZIWIG. [*Cont'd.*] Hi-ho, Matthew! Fiddle away...where are my daughters?

The FIDDLER *plays. Three young daughters of* FEZZIWIG, *followed by six young male suitors, are dancing to the music. All employees come in: workers, clerks, housemaids, cousins, the baker, etc. All dance. Full number wanted here. Throughout the dance, food is brought into the feast. It is "eaten" in dance, by the dancers.* EBENEZER *dances with all three of the daughters, as does* DICK. *They compete for the daughters, happily, in the dance.* FEZZIWIG *dances with his daughters.* FEZZIWIG *dances with* DICK *and* EBENEZER. *The music changes:* MRS. FEZZIWIG *enters. She lovingly scolds her husband. They dance. She dances with* EBENEZER, *lifting him and throwing him about. She is enormously fat. When the dance is ended, they all dance off, floating away, as does the music.* SCROOGE *and the* GHOST OF CHRISTMAS PAST *stand alone now. The music is gone.*

PAST. It was a small matter, that Fezziwig made those silly folks so full of gratitude.

SCROOGE. Small!

PAST. Shhh!

Lights up on DICK *and* EBENEZER.

DICK. We are blessed, Ebenezer, truly, to have such a master as Mr. Fezziwig!

YOUNG SCROOGE. He is the best, best, the very and absolute best! If ever I own a firm of my own, I shall treat my apprentices with the same dignity and the same grace. We have learned a wonderful lesson from the master, Dick!

DICK. Ah, that's a fact, Ebenezer. That's a fact!

PAST. Was it not a small matter, really? He spent but a few pounds of his mortal money on your small party. Three or four pounds, perhaps. Is that so much that he deserves such praise as you and Dick so lavish now?

SCROOGE. It isn't that! It isn't that, Spirit. Fezziwig had the power to make us happy or unhappy; to make our service light or burdensome; a pleasure or a toil. The happiness he gave is quite as great as if it cost him a fortune.

PAST. What is the matter?

SCROOGE. Nothing particular.

PAST. Something, I think.

SCROOGE. No, no. I should like to be able to say a word or two to my clerk just now! That's all!

EBENEZER *enters the room and shuts down all the lamps. He stretches and yawns. The* GHOST OF CHRISTMAS PAST *turns to* SCROOGE; *all of a sudden.*

PAST. My time grows short! Quick!

In a flash of light, EBENEZER *is gone, and in his place stands an* OLDER SCROOGE, *this one a man in the prime of his life. Beside him stands a* YOUNG WOMAN *in a mourning dress. She is crying. She says to the* MAN, *with hostility.*

WOMAN. It matters little...to you, very little. Another idol has displaced me.

MAN. What idol has displaced you?

WOMAN. A golden one.

MAN. This is an even-handed dealing of the world. There is nothing on which it is so hard as poverty; and there is nothing it professes to condemn with such severity as the pursuit of wealth!

WOMAN. You fear the world too much. Have I not seen your nobler aspirations fall off one by one, until the master-passion, Gain, engrosses[26] you? Have I not?

SCROOGE. No!

MAN. What then? Even if I have grown so much wiser, what then? Have I changed towards you?

WOMAN. No...

MAN. Am I?

WOMAN. Our contract is an old one. It was made when we were both poor and content to be so. You are changed. When it was made, you were another man.

MAN. I was not another man: I was a boy.

---

26. engrosses. Takes all the attention

Woman. Your own feeling tells you that you were not what you are. I am. That which promised happiness when we were one in heart is fraught[27] with misery now that we are two...

Scrooge. No!

Woman. How often and how keenly I have thought of this, I will not say. It is enough that I have thought of it, and can release you...

Scrooge. [*Quietly.*] Don't release me, madame...

Man. Have I ever sought release?

Woman. In words. No. Never.

Man. In what then?

Woman. In a changed nature; in an altered spirit. In everything that made my love of any worth or value in your sight. If this has never been between us, tell me, would you seek me out and try to win me now? Ah, no!

Scrooge. Ah, yes!

Man. You think not?

Woman. I would gladly think otherwise if I could, heaven knows! But if you were free today, tomorrow, yesterday, can even I believe that you would choose a dowerless[28] girl—you who in your very confidence with her weigh everything by Gain; or, choosing her, do I not know that your repentance and regret would surely follow? I do; and I release you. With a full heart, for the love of him you once were.

Scrooge. Please, I...I...

Man. Please, I...I...

Woman. Please. You may—the memory of what is past half makes me hope you will—have pain in this. A very, very brief time, and you will dismiss the memory of it, as an unprofitable dream, from which it happened well that you awoke. May you be happy in the life that you have chosen for yourself.

Scrooge. No!

Woman. Yourself...alone...

Scrooge. No!

Woman. Goodbye, Ebenezer...

Scrooge. Don't let her go!

Man. Goodbye.

Scrooge. No! [*She exits.* Scrooge *goes to* Younger Man: *himself.*] You fool! Mindless loon! You fool!

---

27. **fraught.** Affected
28. **dowerless.** Lacking a dowry—the gift of goods or money a woman brings to a marriage

Man. [*To exited* Woman.] Fool. Mindless loon. Fool...

Scrooge. Don't say that! Spirit, remove me from this place.

Past. I have told you these were shadows of the things that have been. They are what they are. Do not blame me, Mr. Scrooge.

Scrooge. Remove me! I cannot bear it!

The faces of all who appeared in this scene are now projected for a moment around the stage: enormous, flimsy, silent.

Scrooge. [*Contd.*] Leave me! Take me back! Haunt me no longer!

There is a sudden flash of light: a flare. The Ghost of Christmas Past *is gone.* Scrooge *is, for the moment, alone onstage. His bed is turned down, across the stage. A small candle burns now in* Scrooge*'s hand. There is a child's cap in his other hand. He slowly crosses the stage to his bed, to sleep.* Marley *appears behind* Scrooge*, who continues his long, elderly cross to bed.* Marley *speaks directly to the audience.*

Marley. Scrooge must sleep now. He must surrender to the irresistible drowsiness caused by the recognition of what was. [*Pauses.*] The cap he carries is from ten lives past: his boyhood cap...donned atop a hopeful hairy head...askew, perhaps, or at a rakish angle. Doffed now in honor of regret. Perhaps even too heavy to carry in his present state of weak remorse...

Scrooge *drops the cap. He lies atop his bed. He sleeps. To audience.*

Marley. [*Contd.*] He sleeps. For him, there's even more trouble ahead. [*Smiles.*] For you? The play house tells me there's grog[29] and cider, both hot, as should be your anticipation for the spectres Christmas Present and Future, for I promise you both. [*Smiles again.*] So, I pray you hurry back to your seats refreshed and ready for a miser—to turn his coat of gray into a blazen Christmas holly-red.

A flash of lightning. A clap of thunder. Bats fly. Ghosty music. Marley *is gone.*

CURTAIN

[*Act 2 continues on page 645.*]

---

29. **grog.** Warm drink

Have you ever been miserable when you should have been happy? Why do you think some people are able to maintain a cheerful outlook on life while others, like Scrooge, seem miserable?

Find Meaning

1. (a) Where and when does each of the scenes in Act 1 take place? (b) In what way is the setting important to the plot?
2. (a) Who is Jacob Marley? (b) How does his role change from Scene 1 to Scene 3?
3. Why does Scrooge find it difficult to understand his nephew's enthusiasm for Christmas?

Make Judgments

4. (a) What is the overall mood of Act 1? (b) What details in Scene 1 help to establish this mood?
5. (a) What is Scrooge's most prominent character trait? (b) How does this trait affect his relationships with other characters in the play?
6. Based on Act 1, describe the conflict in this play.

INFORMATIONAL TEXT ▶▶ CONNECTION

The action in *A Christmas Carol: Scrooge and Marley* takes place in London in the mid-1800s. Factories and mills of that time produced a great deal of smoke, and the city was filled with noises and smells associated with horses, unrefrigerated food, and thousands of people going about their daily lives. As you read the description from an essay by **Daniel Pool,** think about what it would have been like for the Cratchits and others living in London at that time.

from What Jane Austen Ate and Charles Dickens Knew

An Essay by Daniel Pool

The fog in London was very real. Just why it was the color it was no one has ever been able to ascertain[1] for sure, but at a certain time of the year—it was worst in November—a great yellowness reigned everywhere, and lamps were lit inside even during the day. In November, December, and January the yellow fog extended out some three or four miles from the heart of the city, causing "pain in the lungs" and "uneasy sensations" in the head. It has been blamed in part on the coal stoves. At eight o'clock in the morning on an average day over London, an observer reported the sky began to turn black with the smoke from thousands of coal fires, presumably for morning fires to warm dining rooms and bedrooms and to cook breakfast. Ladies going to the opera at night with white shawls returned with them gray. It has been suggested that the black umbrella put in its appearance because it did not show the effects of these London atmospherics.[2] The fog was so thick, observed a foreigner at mid-century, that you could take a man by the hand and not be able to see his face, and people literally lost their way and drowned in the Thames. In a very bad week in 1873 more than 700 people above the normal average for the period died in the city, and cattle at an exhibition suffocated to death.

There were problems underfoot as well as in the air. One hundred tons of horse manure dropped on the streets of London each day, and a report to Parliament said that "strangers coming from the country frequently describe the streets of London as smelling of dung like a stable-yard." Originally, many streets were not paved; by mid-century, however, the dust from the pulverized[3] stone with which London streets were paved coated furniture in good weather and turned to mud when it rained. An etiquette book advised gentlemen to walk on the outside of the pavement when accompanying a lady to ensure that they walked on the filthiest part of it, and every major street had a crossing sweeper like Jo in

1. **ascertain.** Find out
2. **atmospherics.** Elements used to create a specific mood
3. **pulverized.** Broken into particles

Bleak House, who for a penny swept the street before you made your way across it on rainy days so your boots did not become impossibly filthy. Nor was the Thames any better. London sewage, some 278,000 tons daily at mid-century, as well as pollutants from the factories along the river's banks, was dumped untreated into the water, presumably helping to fuel the cholera[4] epidemics that swept the city in the early part of the century. The smell was bad enough in the summer of 1858 to cause Parliament to end its session early.

There was what we would surely call noise pollution, too—the incessant sound of wheels and horses' hooves clacking over the pavement, the click of women's pattens[5] on the sidewalks in the rain, the bell of the muffin man, and the cries of the street peddlers selling such items as dolls, matches, books, knives, eels, pens, rat poison, key rings, eggs, and china, to say nothing of the German bands, the itinerant[6] clarinet players, and the hurdy-gurdies.[7] ✤

4. **cholera.** Infectious and often fatal disease
5. **pattens.** Shoes with raised soles
6. **itinerant.** Traveling from place to place
7. **hurdy-gurdies.** Instruments with a droning sound that are played with a crank

TEXT TO TEXT CONNECTION

There is little suggestion of these grim and dirty conditions in *A Christmas Carol: Scrooge and Marley.* How might some of the conditions described in this selection be portrayed in a play? Which would be difficult or impossible to suggest?

Tower Bridge from Cherry Garden Pier, c. 1900. Charles Edward Dixon. Private collection.

AFTER READING

Analyze Literature

Plot The plot in a piece of fiction or drama can be broken up into five parts: *exposition, rising action, climax, falling action,* and *resolution.* Begin a plot diagram for *A Christmas Carol: Scrooge and Marley,* noting the part or parts of the plot that appear in each scene. For each plot part you identify, write the scene number on your diagram; in addition, include a brief description of the action that occurred during that part of the plot. Add to the plot diagram as you read Act 2.

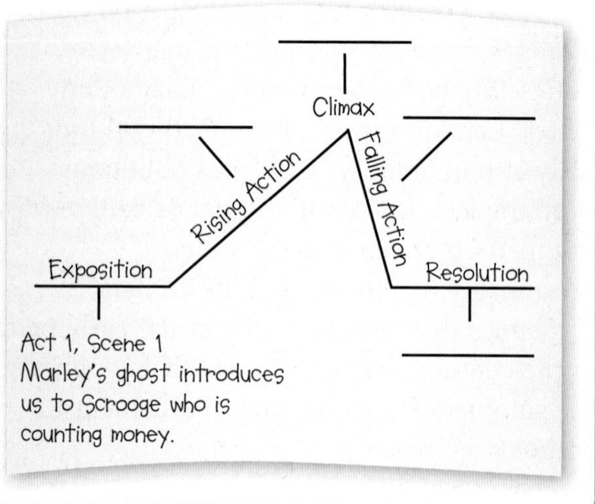

Extend Understanding

Writing Options

Creative Writing Imagine that you are in charge of raising money for a local charity. Write a **business letter** to Scrooge asking for a sizable donation. Be sure to use the proper form for a business letter and appropriately polite language in your letter.

Argumentative Writing Pretend you are a member of the school drama club. Write a **review** of Act 1 of *A Christmas Carol: Scrooge and Marley* for your next meeting. Begin by providing a brief summary of the story and characters. Then evaluate the setting, characterization, mood, dialogue, and stage directions. Use evidence from the play to support your evaluations. Conclude by giving your opinion of the play and telling why you think the drama club should or should not put on this play for the school. Share your work with the class.

Collaborative Learning

Analyze the Story In small groups, discuss why the story of *A Christmas Carol* has remained so popular for so many years. Consider the main themes, the traits and flaws of the characters, and the conflicts that drive the characters and the plot. Prepare for the discussion by reading a summary or watching a film of the original version of *A Christmas Carol* by Charles Dickens.

Critical Literacy

Compare Versions Find and read the first chapter of *A Christmas Carol* by Charles Dickens. Compare and contrast the original story to the dramatic adaptation by Israel Horovitz. Note how each writer reveals characters and conflicts through description, narration, and dialogue. What elements of the story are the same? What elements are different? Create a Venn diagram to show the similarities and differences between the two versions. Then use the diagram to help you explain the reasons for the differences between the versions.

Go to **www.mirrorsandwindows.com** for more.

A Christmas Carol:

Scrooge and Marley

ACT 2

— SCENE 1 —

Lights. Choral music is sung. Curtain. SCROOGE, *in bed; sleeping, in spotlight. We cannot yet see the interior of his room.* MARLEY, *opposite, in spotlight equal to* SCROOGE's. MARLEY *laughs. He tosses his hand in the air and a flame shoots from it, magically, into the air. There is a thunder clap, and then another; a lightning flash, and then another. Ghostly music plays under. Colors change.* MARLEY's *spotlight has gone out and now reappears, with* MARLEY *in it, standing next to the bed and the sleeping* SCROOGE. MARLEY *addresses the audience directly.*

MARLEY. Hear this snoring Scrooge! Sleeping to escape the nightmare that is his waking day. What shall I bring to him now? I'm afraid nothing would astonish old Scrooge now. Not after what he's seen. Not a baby boy, not a rhinoceros, nor anything in between would astonish Ebenezer Scrooge just now. I can think of nothing...[*Suddenly.*] that's it! Nothing! [*He speaks confidentially.*] I'll have the clock strike one and, when he awakes expecting my second messenger, there will be no one...nothing. Then I'll have the bell strike twelve. And then one again…and then nothing. Nothing...[*Laughs.*] nothing will-astonish him. I think it will work.

The bell tolls one. SCROOGE *leaps awake.*

SCROOGE. One! One! This is it: time! [*Looks about the room.*] Nothing!

The bell tolls midnight.

SCROOGE. [*Contd.*] Midnight! How can this be? I'm sleeping backwards.

One again.

SCROOGE. [*Contd.*] Good heavens! One again! I'm sleeping back and forth! [*A pause.* SCROOGE *looks about.*] Nothing! Absolutely nothing!

Suddenly, thunder and lightning. MARLEY *laughs and disappears. The room shakes and glows. There is suddenly spring like music.* SCROOGE *makes a run for the door.*

MARLEY. Scrooge!

SCROOGE. What?

MARLEY. Stay you put!

SCROOGE. Just checking to see if anyone is in here.

Lights and thunder again: more music. MARLEY *is of a sudden gone. In his place sits the* GHOST OF CHRISTMAS PRESENT*—to be called in the stage directions of the play,* PRESENT*—Center of room. Heaped up on the floor to form a kind of throne, are turkeys, geese, game, poultry, brawn,*[1] *great joints of meat, suckling pigs, long wreaths of sausages, mince-pies, plum puddings, barrels of oysters, red hot chestnuts, cherry-cheeked apples, juicy oranges, luscious pears, immense twelfth cakes, and seething bowls of punch, that make the chamber dim with their delicious steam. Upon this throne sits* PRESENT, glorious to see. *He bears a torch, shaped as a Horn of Plenty.*[2] SCROOGE *hops out of the door, and then peeks back again into his bedroom.* PRESENT *calls to* SCROOGE.

PRESENT. Ebenezer Scrooge. Come in, come in! Come in and know me better!

---

1. **brawn.** Pig's or calf's head
2. **Horn of Plenty.** Goat's horn filled with flowers and fruit to suggest prosperity

Scrooge. Hello. How should I call you?

Present. I am the Ghost of Christmas Present. Look upon me.

Present *is wearing a simple green robe. The walls around the room are now covered in greenery, as well. The room seems to be a perfect grove now: leaves of holly, mistletoe and ivy reflect the stage lights. Suddenly, there is a mighty roar of flame in the fireplace and now the hearth burns with a lavish, warming fire. There is an ancient scabbard girdling*[3] *the* Ghost*'s middle, but without sword. The sheath is gone to rust.*

Present. [*Contd.*] You have never seen the like of me before?

Scrooge. Never.

Present. You have never walked forth with younger members of my family; my elder brothers born on Christmases Past?

Scrooge. I don't think I have. I'm afraid I've not. Have you had many brothers, Spirit?

Present. More than eighteen hundred.

Scrooge. A tremendous family to provide for!

Present *stands.*

Scrooge. [*Contd.*] Spirit, conduct me where you will. I went forth last night on compulsion, and learnt a lesson which is working now. Tonight, if you have aught[4] to teach me, let me profit by it.

Present. Touch my robe.

---

3. girdling. Surrounding with a belt
4. aught. Anything

com • pul • sion (kəm pəl´ shən) *n.,* irresistible impulse to perform an act

SCROOGE *walks cautiously to* PRESENT *and touches his robe. When he does lightning flashes, thunder claps, music plays.*

Blackout.

— SCENE 2 —

PROLOGUE

MARLEY *stands spotlit. He speaks directly to the audience.*

MARLEY. My ghostly friend now leads my living partner through the city's streets.

Lights up on SCROOGE *and* PRESENT.

MARLEY. [*Contd.*] See them there and hear the music people make when the weather is severe, as it is now.

Winter music. Choral group behind scrim,[5] sings. When the song is done and the stage is re-set, the lights will fade up on a row of shops, behind the singers. The choral group will hum the song they have just completed and mill about the streets, carrying their dinners to the bakers' shops restaurants. They will, perhaps, sing about being poor at Christmastime, whatever.

PRESENT. These revelers, Mr. Scrooge, carry their own dinners to their jobs, where they will work to bake the meals the rich men and women of this city will eat as their Christmas dinners. Generous people these...to care for the others, so...

PRESENT *walks among the choral group and a sparkling incense falls from his torch on to their baskets, as he pulls the covers off of the baskets. Some of the choral group become angry with each other.*

MAN #1. Hey, you, watch where you're going.

MAN #2. Watch it yourself, mate!

PRESENT *sprinkles them directly, they change.*

MAN #1. I pray go in ahead of me. It's Christmas. You be first!

MAN #2. No, no, I must insist that YOU be first!

MAN #1. All right, I shall be, and gratefully so.

MAN #2. The pleasure is equally mine, for being able to watch you pass, smiling.

MAN #1. I would find it a shame to quarrel on Christmas Day...

MAN #2. As would I.

MAN #1. Merry Christmas then, friend!

MAN #2. And a Merry Christmas straight back to you!

Church bells toll. The choral group enters the buildings; the shops and restaurants; they exit the stage, shutting their doors closed behind them. All sound stops. SCROOGE *and* PRESENT *are alone again.*

SCROOGE. What is it you sprinkle from your torch?

PRESENT. Kindness.

SCROOGE. Do you sprinkle your kindness on any particular people or on all people?

PRESENT. To any person kindly given. And to the very poor most of all.

SCROOGE. Why to the very poor most?

PRESENT. Because the very poor need it most. Touch my heart...here, Mr. Scrooge. We have another journey.

SCROOGE *touches the* GHOST'S *heart and music plays, lights change color, lightning flashes, thunder claps. A choral group appears on the street, singing Christmas carols.*

— SCENE 3 —

MARLEY *stands spotlit in front of a scrim on which is painted the exterior of* CRATCHIT'S *four-roomed house. There is a flash and a clap and*

---

5. scrim. Sheer fabric used on stage to hide a scene until it is lit

MARLEY is gone. The lights shift color again, the scrim flies away, and we are in the interior of the CRATCHIT family home. SCROOGE is there, with the SPIRIT [PRESENT], watching MRS. CRATCHIT set the table, with the help of BELINDA CRATCHIT and PETER CRATCHIT, a baby, pokes a fork into the mashed potatoes on his high-chair's tray. He also chews on his shirt collar.

SCROOGE. What is this place, Spirit?

PRESENT. This is the home of your employee, Mr. Scrooge. Don't you know it?

SCROOGE. Do you mean Cratchit, Spirit? Do you mean this is Cratchit's home?

PRESENT. None other.

SCROOGE. These children are his?

PRESENT. There are more to come presently.

SCROOGE. On his meager earnings! What foolishness!

PRESENT. Foolishness, is it?

SCROOGE. Wouldn't you say so? Fifteen shillings a week's what he gets!

PRESENT. I would say that he gets the pleasure of his family, fifteen time a week times the number of hours in a day! Wait, Mr. Scrooge. Wait, listen and watch. You might actually learn something.

MRS. CRATCHIT. What has ever got your precious father then? And your brother, Tiny Tim? And Martha wasn't as late last Christmas by half an hour!

MARTHA opens the door, speaking to her mother as she does.

MARTHA. Here's Martha, now, Mother!

She laughs. The CRATCHIT CHILDREN squeal with delight.

BELINDA. It's Martha, Mother! Here's Martha!

PETER. Marthmama, Marthmama! Hullo!

BELINDA. Hurrah! Martha! Martha! There's such an enormous goose for us, Martha!

MRS. CRATCHIT. Why, bless your heart alive, my dear, how late you are!

MARTHA. We'd a great deal of work to finish up last night, and had to clear away this morning, Mother.

MRS. CRATCHIT. Well, never mind so long as you are home. Sit ye down before the fire, my dear, and have a warm, Lord bless ye!

BELINDA. No, no! There's Father coming. Hide, Martha, hide!

MARTHA giggles and hides herself.

MARTHA. Where? Here?

PETER. Hide, hide!

BELINDA. Not there! THERE!

MARTHA is hidden. BOB CRATCHIT enters, carrying TINY TIM atop his shoulder. He wears a threadbare and fringeless comforter hanging down in front of him. TINY TIM carries small crutches and his small legs are bound in an iron frame brace.

BOB AND TINY TIM. Merry Christmas.

BOB. Merry Christmas my love, Merry Christmas, Peter; Merry Christmas, Belinda. Why, where is Martha?

MRS. CRATCHIT. Not coming.

BOB. Not coming? Not coming upon Christmas Day?

MARTHA. [*Pokes head out.*] Ohhh, poor Father. Don't be disappointed.

BOB. What's this?

MARTHA. 'Tis I!

BOB. Martha! [*They embrace.*]

TINY TIM. Martha! Martha!

MARTHA. Tiny Tim!

TINY TIM is placed in MARTHA's arms. BELINDA and PETER rush him off-stage.

BELINDA. Come, brother! You must come hear the pudding singing in the copper.

Tiny Tim. The pudding? What flavor have we?

Peter. Plum! Plum!

Tiny Tim. Oh, Mother! I love plum!

The Children *exit the stage, giggling.*

Mrs. Cratchit. And how did little Tim behave?

Bob. As good as gold, and even better. Somehow he gets thoughtful sitting by himself so much, and thinks the strangest things you ever heard. He told me, coming home, that he hoped people saw him in the church, because he was a cripple, and it might be pleasant to them to remember upon Christmas Day, who made lame beggars walk and blind men see. [*Pauses.*] He has the oddest ideas sometimes, but he seems all the while to be growing stronger and more hearty...one would never know.

Hears Tim's *crutch on floor outside door.*

Peter. The goose has arrived to be eaten!

Belinda. Oh, mama, mama, it's beautiful.

Martha. It's a perfect goose, Mother!

Tiny Tim. To this Christmas goose, Mother and Father, I say…[*Yells.*] Hurrah! Hurrah!

Other Children. [*Copying* Tim.] Hurrah! Hurrah!

The family sits round the table. Bob *and* Mrs. Cratchit *serve the trimmings, quickly. All sit; all bow heads, all pray.*

Bob. Thank you, dear Lord, for your many gifts...our dear children; our wonderful meal; our love for one another; and the warmth of our small fire—[*Looks up at all.*] A merry Christmas to us, my dear: God bless us!

All. [*Except* Tim.] Merry Christmas! God bless us!

Tiny Tim. [*In a short silence.*] God bless us every one.

All freeze. Spotlight on Present *and* Scrooge.

Scrooge. Spirit, tell me if Tiny Tim will live.

Present. I see a vacant seat...in the poor chimney corner, and a crutch without an owner, carefully preserved. If these shadows remain unaltered by the future, the child will die.

Scrooge. No, no, kind Spirit! Say he will be spared!

Present. If these shadows remain unaltered by the future, none other of my race will find him here. What then? If he be like to die, he had better do it, and decrease the surplus population.

Scrooge *bows his head. We hear* Bob's *voice speak* Scrooge's *name.*

Bob. Mr. Scrooge...

Scrooge. Huh? What's that? Who calls?

Bob. [*His glass raised in a toast.*[6]] I'll give you Mr. Scrooge, the Founder of the Feast!

Scrooge. Me, Bob? You toast me?

Present. Save your breath, Mr. Scrooge. You can't be seen or heard.

Mrs. Cratchit. The Founder of the Feast, indeed! I wish I had him here, that miser Scrooge. I'd give him a piece of my mind to feast upon, and I hope he'd have a good appetite for it!

Bob. My dear! Christmas Day!

Mrs. Cratchit. It should be Christmas Day, I am sure, on which one drinks the health of such an odious, stingy, unfeeling man as Scrooge...

Scrooge. Oh, Spirit, must I?

Mrs. Cratchit. You know he is, Robert! Nobody knows it better than you do, poor fellow!

---

6. toast. Drink to honor a person

o•di•ous (ō´ dē əs) *adj.*, hateful or disgusting

Bob. This is Christmas Day, and I should like to drink to the health of the man who employs me and allows me to earn my living and our support and that man is Ebenezer Scrooge...

Mrs. Cratchit. I'll drink to his health for your sake and the day's, but not for his sake...a Merry Christmas and a Happy New Year to you, Mr. Scrooge, wherever you may be this day!

Scrooge. Just here, kind madam...out of sight, out of sight...

Bob. Thank you, my dear. Thank you.

Scrooge. Thank you, Bob...and Mrs. Cratchit, too. No one else is toasting me...not now...not ever. Of that I am sure...

Bob. Children...

All. Merry Christmas to Mr. Scrooge.

Bob. I'll pay you six-pence, Tim, for my favorite song.

Tiny Tim. Oh, Father, I'd so love to sing it, but not for pay. This Christmas goose—this feast—you and Mother, my brother and sisters close with me: that's my pay—

Bob. Martha, will you play the notes on the lute, for Tiny Tim's song.

Belinda. May I sing, too, Father?

Bob. We'll all sing.

They sing a song about a tiny child lost in the snow, probably from Wordsworth's[7] *poem.* TIM *sings the lead vocal; all chime in for the chorus. Their song fades under, as the* GHOST OF CHRISTMAS PRESENT *speaks.*

PRESENT. Mark my words, Ebenezer Scrooge. I do not present the Cratchits to you because they are a handsome, or brilliant family. They are not handsome. They are not brilliant. They are not well-dressed, or tasteful to the times. Their shoes are not even water-proofed by virtue of money or cleverness spent. So when the pavement is wet, so are the insides of their shoes and the tops of their toes. These are the Cratchits, Mr. Scrooge. They are not highly special. They are happy, grateful, pleased with one another, contented with the time and how it passes. They don't sing very well, do they? But, nonetheless, they do sing...[*Pauses.*] think of that, Scrooge. 15 shillings a week and they do sing...hear their song until its end.

SCROOGE. I am listening.

The chorus sings full volume now, until...the song ends here.

SCROOGE. [*Contd.*] Spirit, it must be time for us to take our leave. I feel in my heart that it is...that I must think on that which I have seen here...

PRESENT. Touch my robe again...

SCROOGE *touches* PRESENT's *robe. The lights fade out on the* CRATCHITS, *who sit, frozen, at the table.* SCROOGE *and* PRESENT *in a spotlight now. Thunder, lightning, smoke. They are gone.*

— SCENE 4 —

MARLEY *appears in single spotlight. A storm brews. Thunder and lightning.* SCROOGE *and* PRESENT *"fly" past. The storm continues, furiously, and, now and again,* SCROOGE *and* PRESENT *will zip past in their travels.* MARLEY *will speak straight out to the audience.*

MARLEY. The Ghost of Christmas Present, my co-worker in this attempt to turn a miser, flies about now with that very miser, Scrooge, from street to street, and he points out partygoers on their way to Christmas parties. If one were to judge from the numbers of people on their way to friendly gatherings, one might think that no one was left at home to give anyone welcome...but that's not the case, is it? Every home is expecting company and...[*He laughs.*] Scrooge is amazed.

SCROOGE *and* PRESENT *zip past again. The lights fade up around them. We are in the* NEPHEW's *home, in the living room,* PRESENT *and* SCROOGE *stand watching the* NEPHEW: FRED *and his* WIFE, *fixing the fire.*

SCROOGE. What is this place? We've moved from the mines!

PRESENT. You do not recognize them?

SCROOGE. It is my nephew!...and the one he married...

MARLEY *waves his hand and there is a lightning flash. He disappears.*

FRED. It strikes me as sooooo funny, to think of what he said...that Christmas was a humbug, as I live! He believed it!

WIFE. More shame for him, Fred!

FRED. Well, he's a comical old fellow, that's the truth.

WIFE. I have no patience with him.

FRED. Oh, I have! I am sorry for him; I couldn't be angry with him if I tried. Who suffers by his ill whims? Himself, always...

SCROOGE. It's me they talk of, isn't it, Spirit?

FRED. Here, wife, consider this. Uncle Scrooge takes it into his head to dislike us, and he won't come and dine with us. What's the consequence?

---

7. **Wordsworth.** William Wordsworth was a famous English poet of the late eighteenth and early nineteenth centuries.

WIFE. Oh...you're sweet to say what I think you're about to say, too, Fred...

FRED. What's the consequence? He don't lose much of a dinner by it, I can tell you that!

WIFE. Ooooooo, Fred! Indeed, I think he loses a very good dinner...ask my sisters, or your lecherous bachelor friend, Topper...ask any of them. They'll tell you what old Scrooge, your uncle, missed: a dandy meal!

FRED. Well, that's something of a relief, wife. Glad to hear it!

He hugs his WIFE. *They laugh. They kiss.*

FRED. [*Contd.*] The truth is, he misses much yet. I mean to give him the same chance every year, whether he likes it or not, for I pity him. Nay, he is my only uncle and I feel for the old miser...but, I tell you, wife: I see my dear and perfect mother's face on his own wizened[8] cheeks and brow: brother and sister they were, and I cannot erase that from each view of him I take...

WIFE. I understand what you say, Fred, and I am with you in your yearly asking. But he never will accept, you know. He never will.

FRED. Well, true, wife. Uncle may rail at Christmas till he dies. I think I shook him some with my visit yesterday...[*Laughing.*] I refused to grow angry...no matter how nasty he became...[*Whoops.*] It was HE who grew angry, wife!

They both laugh now.

SCROOGE. What he says is true, Spirit.

FRED AND WIFE. Bah humbug!

FRED. [*Embracing his* WIFE.] There is much laughter in our marriage, wife. It pleases me. You please me.

WIFE. And you please me, Fred. You are a good man...

They embrace.

WIFE. [*Contd.*] Come now. We must have a look at the meal...our guests will soon arrive...my sisters, Topper...

FRED. A toast first...[*He hands her a glass.*] A toast to Uncle Scrooge...[*Fill their glasses.*]

WIFE. A toast to him?

FRED. Uncle Scrooge has given us plenty of merriment, I am sure, and it would be ungrateful not to drink to his health. And I say...Uncle Scrooge!

WIFE. [*Laughing.*] You're a proper loon, Fred...and I'm a proper wife to you...[*She raises her glass.*] Uncle Scrooge! [*They drink. They embrace. They kiss.*]

SCROOGE. Spirit, please, make me visible! Make me audible! I want to talk with my nephew and my niece!

Calls out to them. The lights that light the room and FRED *and* WIFE *fade out.* SCROOGE *and* PRESENT *are alone spotlit.*

PRESENT. These shadows are gone to you now, Mr. Scrooge. You may return to them later tonight in your dreams. [*Pauses.*] My time grows short, Ebenezer Scrooge. Look you on me. Do you see how I've aged?

SCROOGE. Your hair has gone grey! Your skin, wrinkled! Are spirits' lives so short?

PRESENT. My stay upon this globe is very brief. It ends tonight.

SCROOGE. Tonight?

PRESENT. At midnight. The time is drawing near! [*Clock strikes 11:45.*] Hear those chimes? In a quarter hour, my life will have been spent! Look, Scrooge, man, look you here.

Two gnarled baby dolls are taken from PRESENT*'s skirts.*

SCROOGE. Who are they?

PRESENT. They are Man's children, and they

---

8. wizened. Shrunken or wrinkled

cling to me, appealing from their fathers. The boy is Ignorance; the girl is Want. Beware them both, and all of their degree,[9] but most of all beware this boy, for I see that written on his brow which is doom, unless the writing is erased.

He stretches out his arms. His voice now amplified: lowly and oddly.

Scrooge. Have they no refuge or resource?

Present. Are there no prisons? Are there no workhouses?

Twelve chimes.

Present. [*Contd.*] Are there no prisons? Are there no workhouses?

A Phantom, *hooded, appears in dim light.*

Present. [*Contd.*] Are there no prisons? Are there no workhouses?

Present *begins to deliquesce.* Scrooge *calls after him.*

Scrooge. Spirit, I'm frightened! Don't leave me! Spirit!

Present. Prisons? Workhouses? Prisons? Workhouses...

He is gone. Scrooge *is alone now with the* Phantom, *who is, of course, the* Ghost of Christmas Future. *The* Phantom *is shrouded in black. Only its outstretched hand is visible from under his ghostly garment.*

Scrooge. Who are you, Phantom? Oh, yes, I think I know you! You are, are you not, the Spirit of Christmas Yet to Come?

No reply.

Scrooge. [*Contd.*] And you are about to show me the shadows of the things that have not yet happened, but will happen in time before us. Is that not so, Spirit?

The Phantom *allows* Scrooge *a look at his face. No other reply wanted here. A nervous giggle here.*

Scrooge. [*Contd.*] Oh, Ghost of the Future, I fear you more than any Spectre I have seen! But, as I know that your purpose is to do me good, and as I hope to live to be another man from what I was, I am prepared to bear you company.

Future *does not reply, but for a stiff arm, hand and finger set, pointing forward.*

Scrooge. [*Contd.*] Lead on, then, lead on. The night is waning fast, and it is precious time to me. Lead on, Spirit!

Future *moves away from* Scrooge *in the same rhythm and motion employed at its arrival.* Scrooge *falls into the same pattern, a considerable space apart from the* Spirit. *In the space between them,* Marley *appears. He looks to* Future *and then to* Scrooge. *He claps his hands. Thunder and lightning.* Three Businessmen *appear, spotlighted singularly. Thus, six points of the stage should now be spotted in light.* Marley *will watch this scene from his position.*

First Businessman. Oh, no, I don't know much about it either way, I only know he's dead.

Second Businessman. When did he die?

First Businessman. Last night, I believe.

Second Businessman. Why, what was the matter with him? [*He uses snuff here; sneezes, etc.*] I thought he'd never die, really...

First Businessman. [*Yawning.*] God knows, God knows...

Third Businessman. What has he done with his money?

Second Businessman. I haven't heard. Have you?

First Businessman. Left it to his Company,

---

9. all of their degree. People of their status or position

wane (wān) *v.,* approach an end

perhaps. Money to Money: you know the expression...

Third Businessman. He hasn't left it to me. That's all I know...

First Businessman. [*Laughing.*] Nor to me... [*Looks at* Second Businessman.] you, then? You got his money???

Second Businessman. [*Laughing.*] Me, me, his money? Nooooo!

They all laugh.

Third Businessman. It's likely to be a cheap funeral, for upon my life, I don't know of a living soul who'd care to venture to it. Suppose we make up a party and volunteer?

Second Businessman. I don't mind going if a lunch is provided, but I must be fed, if I make one.

First Businessman. Well, I am the most disinterested among you, for I never wear black gloves, and I never eat lunch. But I'll offer to go, if anybody else will. When I come to think of it, I'm not all sure that I wasn't his most particular friend; for we used to stop and speak whenever we met. Well, then...bye, bye!

Second Businessman. Bye, bye...

Third Businessman. Bye, bye...

ven•ture (ven[t]´ shər) *v.*, undertake the risks and dangers of an action

They glide offstage in three separate directions. Their lights follow them.

SCROOGE. Spirit, why did you show me this? Why do you show me businessmen from my streets as they take the death of Jacob Marley. That is a thing past. You are future!

JACOB MARLEY *laughs a long, deep laugh. There is a thunder clap and lightning flash, and he is gone.* SCROOGE *faces* FUTURE, *alone on stage now.* FUTURE *wordlessly stretches out his arm-hand-and-finger-set, pointing into the distance. There, above them,* DRUNKS *and* SCOUNDRELS *and* WOMEN OF THE STREETS *"fly" by, half-dressed and slovenly.* [*N.B.*[10] *There could be a dance number here, showing the seamier*[11] *side of London city life.*] *When the scene has passed, a woman enters the playing area. She is almost at once followed by a second woman; and then a man in faded black; and then, suddenly, an old man, who smokes a pipe. The old man scares the other three. They laugh, anxious.*

FIRST WOMAN. Look here, old Joe, here's a chance! If we haven't all three met here without meaning it!

OLD JOE. You couldn't have met in a better place. Come into the parlor. You were made free of it long ago, you know; and the other two an't strangers. [*He stands; shuts a door. Shrieking.*] We're all suitable to our calling. We're well matched. Come into the parlor. Come into the parlor...[*They follow him.* SCROOGE *and* FUTURE *are now in their midst, watching; silent. A truck*[12] *comes in on which is set a small wall with fireplace and a screen of rags, etc. All props for the scene.*] Let me just rake this fire over a bit...[*He does. He trims his lamp with the stem of his pipe. The* FIRST WOMAN *throws a large bundle on to the floor. She sits beside it, crosslegged; defiantly.*]

FIRST WOMAN. What odds then? What odds, Mrs. Dilber? Every person has a right to take care of themselves. HE always did!

MRS. DILBER. That's true indeed! No man more so!

FIRST WOMAN. Why, then, don't stand staring as if you was afraid, woman! Who's the wiser? We're not going to pick holes in each other's coats, I suppose?

MRS. DILBER. No, indeed! We should hope not!

FIRST WOMAN. Very well, then! That's enough. Who's the worse for the loss of a few things like these? Not a dead man, I suppose?

MRS. DILBER. [*Laughing.*] No, indeed!

FIRST WOMAN. If he wanted to keep 'em after he was dead, the wicked old screw, why wasn't he natural in his lifetime? If he had been, he'd have had somebody to look after him when he was struck with Death, instead of lying gasping out his last there, alone by himself.

MRS. DILBER. It's the truest word that was ever spoke. It's a judgment on him.

FIRST WOMAN. I wish it were a heavier one, and it should have been, you may depend on it, if I could have laid my hands on anything else. Open that bundle, old Joe, and let me know the value of it. Speak out plain. I'm not afraid to be the first, nor afraid for them to see it. We knew pretty well that we were helping ourselves; before we met here, I believe. It's no sin. Open the bundle, Joe.

FIRST MAN. No, no, my dear! I won't think of letting you be the first to show what you've... earned...earned from this. I throw in mine. [*He takes a bundle from his shoulder; turns it upside down and empties its contents out on to the floor.*] It's not very extensive, see... seals...a pencil case...sleeve buttons....

---

10. N.B. Abbreviation for *nota bene,* meaning "take special note"

11. seamier. More unpleasant or rough

12. truck. Small cart on which scenery can move onstage and offstage

Mrs. Dilber. Nice sleeve buttons, though...

First Man. Not bad, not bad...a brooch[13] there...

Old Joe. Not really valuable, I'm afraid...

First Man. How much, old Joe?

Old Joe. [*Writing on the wall with chalk.*] A pitiful lot, really. Ten and six and not a sixpence more!

First Man. You're not serious!

Old Joe. That's your account and I wouldn't give another sixpence if I was to be boiled for not doing it. Who's next?

Mrs. Dilber. Me! [*Dumps out contents of her bundle.*] Sheets, towels, silver spoons, silver sugar-tongs...some boots...

Old Joe. [*Writing on wall.*] I always give too much to the ladies. It's a weakness of mine and that's the way I ruin myself. Here's your total comin' up...two pounds-ten...if you asked me for another penny, and made it an open question, I'd repent being so liberal and knock off half a-crown.

First Woman. And now do MY bundle, Joe.

Old Joe. [*Kneeling to open knots on her bundle.*] So many knots, madam...[*He drags out large curtains; dark.*] What do you call this? Bed curtains!

First Woman. [*Laughing.*] Ah, yes, bed curtains!

Old Joe. You don't mean to say you took 'em down, rings and all, with him lying there?

First Woman. Yes, I did, why not?

Old Joe. You were born to make your fortune and you'll certainly do it.

First Woman. I certainly shan't hold my hand, when I can get anything in it by reaching it out, for the sake of such a man as he was, I promise you, Joe. Don't drop that lamp oil on those blankets, now!

Old Joe. His blankets?

First Woman. Whose else's do you think? He isn't likely to catch cold without 'em, I daresay.

Old Joe. I hope that he didn't die of anything catching? Eh?

First Woman. Don't you be afraid of that. I ain't so fond of his company that I'd loiter about him for such things if he did. Ah! You may look through that shirt till your eyes ache, but you won't find a hole in it, nor a threadbare place. It's the best he had, and a fine one, too. They'd have wasted it, if it hadn't been for me.

Old Joe. What do you mean "They'd have wasted it?"

First Woman. Putting it on him to be buried in, to be sure. Somebody was fool enough to do it, but I took it off again [*She laughs, as do they all, nervously.*] If calico[14] ain't good enough for such a purpose, it isn't good enough then for anything. It's quite as becoming to the body. He can't look uglier than he did in that one!

Scrooge. [*A low-pitched moan emits from his mouth; from the bones.*] OOOOOOOooooooO OOOOoooooOOOOOOOOoooooOOOOOO ooooooOO!

Old Joe. One pound six for the lot.

He produces a small flannel bag filled with money. He divvies it out. He continues to pass around the money as he speaks. All are laughing.

Old Joe. [*Contd.*] That's the end of it, you see! He frightened every one away from him while he was alive, to profit us when he was dead! Hah ha ha!

All. HAHAHAHAhahahahahahah!

Scrooge. OOOOOoOOOoooOOOoooOOOo ooOOoooOOoooOOOooo! [*He screams at them.*] Obscene demons! Why not market the

---

13. brooch. Ornament held by a pin and worn near the neck
14. calico. Inexpensive cotton fabric

corpse itself, as sell its trimming??? [*Suddenly.*] Oh, Spirit, I see it, I see it! This unhappy man—this stripped-bare corpse could very well be my own. My life holds parallel! My life ends that way now!

SCROOGE *backs into something in the dark behind his spotlight.* SCROOGE *looks at* FUTURE, *who points to the corpse.* SCROOGE *pulls back the blanket: The corpse is, of course,* SCROOGE, *who screams. He falls aside the bed; weeping.*

SCROOGE. [*Contd.*] Spirit, this is a fearful place. In leaving it, I shall not leave its lesson, trust me. Let us go!

FUTURE *points to the corpse.*

SCROOGE. [*Contd.*] Spirit, let me see some tenderness connected with a death, or that dark chamber, which we just left now, Spirit, will be forever present to me.

FUTURE *spreads his robes again. Thunder and lightning. Lights up in* the CRATCHIT *home setting.* MRS. CRATCHIT *and her daughters, sewing.*

TINY TIM'S VOICE. [*Off.*] And He took a child and set him in the midst of them.

SCROOGE. [*Looking about the room; to* FUTURE.] Huh? Who spoke? Who said that?

MRS. CRATCHIT. [*Puts down her sewing.*] The color hurts my eyes. [*Rubs her eyes.*] That's better. My eyes grow weak sewing by candlelight. I shouldn't want to show your father weak eyes when he comes home...not for the world! It must be near his time...

PETER. [*In corner, reading. Looks up from book.*] Past it, rather. But I think he's been walking a bit slower than usual these last few evenings, Mother.

MRS. CRATCHIT. I have known him walk with...[*Pauses.*] I have known him walk with Tiny Tim upon his shoulder and very fast indeed...

PETER. So have I, Mother! Often!

DAUGHTER. So have I!

MRS. CRATCHIT. But he was very light to carry and his father loved him so, that it was no trouble—no trouble.

BOB, *at door.*

Silent Night, 1891. Viggo Johansen. Hirschsprungske Samling, Copenhagen, Denmark.

MRS. CRATCHIT. [*Contd.*] And there is your father at the door.

BOB CRATCHIT *enters. He wears a comforter. He is cold, forlorn.*

PETER. Father!

BOB. Hello, wife, children...

The DAUGHTER *weeps; turns away from* CRATCHIT.

BOB. [*Contd.*] Children! How good to see you all! And you, wife. And look at this sewing! I've no doubt, with all your industry; we'll have quilt to set down upon our knees in church on Sunday!

MRS. CRATCHIT. You made the arrangements today, then, Robert, for the...service...to be on Sunday.

Bob. The funeral. Oh, well, yes, yes, I did. I wish you could have gone. It would have done you good to see how green a place it is. But you'll see it often, I promised him that I would walk there on Sunday, after the service. [*Suddenly.*] My little, little child! My little child!

All Children. [*Hugging him.*] Oh, Father...

Bob. [*He stands.*] Forgive me. I saw Mr. Scrooge's nephew, who you know I'd just met once before, and he was so wonderful to me, wife...he is the most pleasant-spoken gentleman I've ever met...he said "I am heartily sorry for it and heartily sorry for your good wife. If I can be of service to you in any way, here's where I live." And he gave me this card.

Peter. Let me see it!

Bob. And he looked me straight in the eye, wife, and said, meaningfully, "I pray you'll come to me, Mr. Cratchit, if you need some help. I pray you do." Now it wasn't for the sake of anything that he might be able to do for us, so much as for his kind way. It seemed as if he had known our Tiny Tim and felt with us.

Mrs. Cratchit. I'm sure that he's a good soul.

Bob. You would be surer of it, my dear, if you saw and spoke to him. I shouldn't be at all surprised; if he got Peter a situation.[15]

Mrs. Cratchit. Only hear that, Peter!

Martha. And then, Peter will be keeping company with someone and setting up[16] for himself!

Peter. Get along with you!

Bob. It's just as likely as not, one of these days, though there's plenty of time for that, my dear. But however and whenever we part from one another, I am sure we shall none of us forget poor Tiny Tim—shall we?—or this first parting that was among us?

All Children. Never, Father, never!

Bob. And when we recollect how patient and mild he was, we shall not quarrel easily among ourselves, and forget poor Tiny Tim in doing it.

All Children. No, Father, never!

Little Bob. I am very happy, I am, I am, I am very happy.

Bob *kisses his little son, as does* Mrs. Cratchit, *as do the other children. The family is set now in one sculptural embrace. The lighting fades to a gentle pool of light, tight on them.*

Scrooge. Spectre, something informs me that our parting moment is at hand. I know it, but I know not how I know it.

Future *points to the other side of the stage. Lights out on* Cratchits. Future *moves slowing, gliding.* Scrooge *follows.* Future *points opposite.* Future *leads* Scrooge *to a wall and a tombstone. He points to the stone.*

Scrooge. [*Contd.*] Am *I* that man those ghoulish parasites so gloated over? [*Pauses.*] Before I draw nearer to that stone to which you point, answer me one question. Are these the shadows of things that will lie or, the shadows of things that MAY be, only?

Future *points to the gravestone.* Marley *appears in light. He points to grave as well. Gravestone turns front and grows to ten feet high. Words upon it:* Ebenezer Scrooge. *Much smoke billows now from the grave. Choral music here.* Scrooge *stands looking up at gravestone.* Future *does not at all reply in mortals' words, but points once more to the gravestone. The stone undulates*[17] *and glows. Music plays, beckoning* Scrooge, Scrooge *reeling in terror.*

Scrooge. [*Contd.*] Oh, no, Spirit! Oh, no, no!

---

15. situation. Job

16. keeping company...setting up. Dating and going out on his own

17. undulates. Moves in waves

FUTURE's *finger still pointing.*

SCROOGE. [*Contd.*] Spirit! Hear me! I am not the man I was. I will be the man I would have been but for this intercourse. Why show in this, if I am past all hope?

FUTURE *considers* SCROOGE's *logic. His hand wavers.*

SCROOGE. [*Contd.*] Oh, Good Spirit, I see by your wavering hand that your good nature intercedes for me and pities me. Assure me that I yet may change these shadows that you have shown me by an altered life!

FUTURE's *hand trembles; pointing has stopped.*

SCROOGE. [*Contd.*] I will honor Christmas in my heart and try to keep it all the year. I will live in the Past, the Present, and the Future. The Spirits of all Three shall strive within me. I will not shut out the lessons that they teach. Oh, tell me that I may sponge away the writing that is upon this stone!

SCROOGE *makes a desperate stab at grabbing* FUTURE's *hand. He holds it firm for a moment, but* FUTURE, *stronger than* SCROOGE, *pulls away.* SCROOGE *is on his knees, praying.*

SCROOGE. [*Contd.*] Spirit, dear Spirit, I am praying before you. Give me a sign that all is possible. Give me a sign that all hope for me is not lost. Oh, Spirit, kind Spirit, I beseech thee: give me a sign...

FUTURE *deliquesces, slowly, gently. The* PHANTOM's *hood and robe drop gracefully to the ground in a small heap. Music in. There is nothing in them. They are mortal cloth. The* SPIRIT *is elsewhere.* SCROOGE *has his sign.* SCROOGE *is alone. Tableau.*[18] *The lights fade to black.*

— SCENE 5 —

The end of it. MARLEY, *spotlighted, opposite* SCROOGE, *in his bed, spotlighted.* MARLEY *speaks to audience, directly.*

MARLEY. [*He smiles at* SCROOGE.] The firm of Scrooge and Marley is doubly blessed: two misers turned; one, alas, in Death, too late; but the other miser turned in Time's penultimate[19] nick. Look you on my friend, Ebenezer Scrooge...

SCROOGE. [*Scrambling out of bed; reeling in delight.*] I will live in the Past, in the Present, and in the Future! The Spirits of all Three shall strive within me!

MARLEY. [*He points and moves closer to* SCROOGE's *bed.*] Yes, Ebenezer, the bedpost is your own. Believe it! Yes, Ebenezer, the room is your own. Believe it!

SCROOGE. Oh, Jacob Marley! Wherever you are, Jacob, know ye that I praise you for this! I praise you...and heaven...and Christmas time! [*Kneels facing away from* MARLEY.] I say it to ye on my knees, old Jacob, on my knees! [*He touches his bed curtains.*] Not torn down. My bed curtains are not at all torn down! Rings and all, here they are! They are here: I am here: the shadows of things that would have been, may now be dispelled. They will be, Jacob! I know they will be! [*He chooses clothing for the day. He tries different pieces of clothing and settles, perhaps, on a dress suit, plus a cape of the bed clothing: something of color.*] I am light as a feather, I am happy as an angel, I am as merry as a schoolboy. I am as giddy as a drunken man! [*Yells out window and then out to audience.*] Merry Christmas to everybody! Merry Christmas to everybody! A Happy New Year to all the world! Hallo here! Whoop! Whoop! Hallo! Hallo! I don't know what day of the month it is! I don't care! I don't know anything! I'm quite a baby! I don't care! I don't care a fig! I'd much rather

---

18. tableau. Motionless person or group

19. penultimate. Next to the last–the last being death

in•ter•cede (in' tər sēd') *v.,* come between to cause a change be a baby than be an old wreck like me or Marley! (Sorry, Jacob, wherever ye be!) Hallo! Hallo there!

Church bells chime in Christmas Day. A small boy, named ADAM, *is seen now as a light fades up on him.*

SCROOGE. [*Contd.*] Hey, you, boy! What's today? What day of the year is it?

ADAM. Today, sir? Why, it's Christmas Day!

SCROOGE. It's Christmas Day, is it? Whoop! Well, I haven't missed it after all, have I? The Spirits did all they did in one night. They can do anything they like, right? Of course they can! Of course they can!

ADAM. Excuse me, sir?

SCROOGE. Huh? Oh, yes, of course, what's your name, lad?

SCROOGE *and* ADAM *will play their scene from their own spotlights.*

ADAM. Adam, sir.

SCROOGE. Adam! What a fine, strong name! Do you know the poulterer's[20] in the next street but one, at the corner?

ADAM. I certainly should hope I know him, sir!

SCROOGE. A remarkable boy! An intelligent boy! Do you know whether the poulterer's have sold the prize turkey that was hanging up there? I don't mean the little prize turkey, Adam, I mean the big one!

ADAM. What, do you mean the one they've got that's as big as me?

SCROOGE. I mean, the turkey the size of Adam: that's the bird!

ADAM. It's hanging there now, sir.

SCROOGE. It is? Go and buy it! No, no, I am absolutely in earnest and buy it and tell 'em to bring it here, so that I may give them directions to where I want it delivered, as a gift. Come back here with the man, Adam, and I'll give you a shilling. Come back here with him in less than five minutes, and I'll give you half-a-crown!

ADAM. Oh, my, sir! Don't let my brother in on this.

ADAM *runs offstage.* MARLEY *smiles.*

MARLEY. An act of kindness is like the first green grape of summer: one leads to another and another and another. It would take a queer man indeed to not follow an act of kindness with an act of kindness. One simply whets the tongue for more...the taste of kindness is too too sweet. Gifts—goods—are lifeless. But the gift of goodness one feels in the giving is full of life. It...is...a...wonder.

Pauses; moves closer to SCROOGE, *who is totally occupied with his dressing and arranging of his room and his day. He is making lists, etc.* MARLEY *reaches out to* SCROOGE.

ADAM. [*Calling, off.*] I'm here! I'm here!

ADAM *runs on with a man, who carries an enormous turkey.*

ADAM. [*Contd.*] Here I am, sir. Three minutes flat! A world record! I've got the poultryman and he's got the poultry! [*He pants, out of breath.*] I have earned my prize, sir, if I live...

He holds his heart, playacting. SCROOGE *goes to him and embraces him.*

SCROOGE. You are truly a champion, Adam...

MAN. Here's the bird you ordered, sir.

SCROOGE. Oh, my, MY!!! Look at the size of that turkey, will you! He never could have stood upon his legs, that bird! He would have snapped them off in a minute, like sticks of sealingwax! Why you'll never be able to carry that bird to Camden-Town.[21] I'll give you money for a cab...

MAN. Camden-Town's where it's goin', sir?

---

20. poulterer. Person who sells chickens, turkeys, and geese
21. Camden-Town. Area of North London

Scrooge. Oh, I didn't tell you? Yes, I've written the precise address down just here on this...[*Hands paper to him.*] Bob Cratchit's house. Now he's not to know who sends him this. Do you understand me? Not a word... [*Handing out money and chuckling.*]

Man. I understand, sir, not a word.

Scrooge. Good. There you go then...this is for the turkey...[*Chuckle.*] and this is for the taxi. [*Chuckle.*]...and this is for your world-record run, Adam.

Adam. But I don't have change for that, sir.

Scrooge. Then keep it, my lad. It's Christmas!

Adam. [*He kisses* Scrooge*'s cheek, quickly.*] Thank you, sir. Merry, Merry Christmas! [*He runs off.*]

Man. And you've given me a bit overmuch here, too, sir...

Scrooge. Of course I have, sir. It's Christmas!

Man. Oh, well, thanking you, sir, I'll have this bird to Mr. Cratchit and his family in no time, sir. Don't you worry none about that. Merry Christmas to you, sir, and a very happy New Year, too...

The man exits. Scrooge *walks in a large circle about the stage, which is now gently lit. A chorus sings Christmas music far in the distance. Bells chime as well, far in the distance. A* GENTLEWOMAN *enters and passes.* SCROOGE *is on the streets now.*

SCROOGE. Merry Christmas, madam...

WOMAN. Merry Christmas, sir...

The PORTLY BUSINESSMAN *from the first act enters.*

SCROOGE. Merry Christmas, sir.

PORTLY MAN. Merry Christmas, sir.

SCROOGE. Oh, you! My dear sir! How do you do? I do hope that you succeeded yesterday! It was very kind of you. A Merry Christmas.

PORTLY MAN. Mr. Scrooge?

SCROOGE. Yes, Scrooge is my name though I'm afraid you may not find it very pleasant. Allow me to ask your pardon. And will you have the goodness to— [*He whispers into the man's ear.*]

PORTLY MAN. Lord bless me! My dear Mr. Scrooge, are you serious!?!

SCROOGE. If you please. Not a farthing less. A great many back-payments are included in it, I assure you. Will you do me that favor?

PORTLY MAN. My dear sir, I don't know what to say to such munifi—[22]

SCROOGE. [*Cutting him off.*] Don't say anything, please. Come and see me. Will you?

PORTLY MAN. I will! I will! Oh, I will, Mr. Scrooge! It will be my pleasure!

SCROOGE. Thank'ee, I am much obliged to you. I thank you fifty times. Bless you!

PORTLY MAN *passes offstage.* SCROOGE *now comes to the room of his* NEPHEW *and* NIECE. *He stops at the door, begins to knock on it, loses his courage, tries again, loses his courage again, tries again, fails again, and then backs off and runs at the door, causing a tremendous bump against it. The* NEPHEW *and* NIECE *are startled.* SCROOGE, *poking head into room.*

SCROOGE. Fred!

NEPHEW. Why, bless my soul! Who's that?

NEPHEW AND NIECE. [*Together.*] How now? Who goes?

SCROOGE. It's I. Your Uncle Scrooge.

NIECE. Dear heart alive!

SCROOGE. I have come to dinner. May I come in, Fred?

NEPHEW. May you come in???!!! With such pleasure for me you may, Uncle!!! What a treat!

NIECE. What a treat, Uncle Scrooge! Come in, come in!

They embrace a shocked and delighted SCROOGE. FRED *calls into the other room.*

NEPHEW. Come in here, everybody, and meet my Uncle Scrooge! He's come for our Christmas party!

Music in. Lighting here indicates that day has gone to night and gone day again. It is early, early morning. SCROOGE *walks alone from the party exhausted, to his offices, opposite side of the stage. He opens his offices. The offices are as they were at the start of the play.* SCROOGE *seats himself with his door wide open so that he can see into the tank, as he awaits* CRATCHIT, *who enters, head down, full of guilt.* CRATCHIT *starts writing almost before he sits.*

SCROOGE. What do you mean by coming in here at this time of day, a full eighteen minutes late, Mr. Cratchit? Hallo, sir? Do you hear me?

BOB. I am very sorry, sir. I am behind my time.

SCROOGE. You are? Yes, I certainly think you are. Step this way, sir, if you please...

BOB. It's only but once a year, sir...it shall not be repeated. I was making rather merry yesterday and into the night.

---

22. munifi—. Short for *munificence,* which means "great generosity"

Scrooge. Now, I'll tell you what, Cratchit. I am not going to stand this sort of thing any longer. And therefore...[*He stands and pokes his finger into* Bob's *chest.*] I am...about...to... raise...your salary.

Bob. Oh, no, sir, I...[*Realizes.*] what did you say, sir?

Scrooge. A Merry Christmas, Bob...[*He claps* Bob's *back.*] A merrier Christmas, Bob, my good fellow than I have given you for many a year. I'll raise your salary and endeavor to assist your struggling family and we will discuss your affairs this very afternoon over a bowl of smoking bishop,[23] Bob! Make up the fires and buy another coal scuttle before you dot another i, Bob. It's too damned cold in this place! We need warmth and cheer, Bob Cratchit! Do you hear me? DO...YOU... HEAR...ME?

Bob Cratchit *stands, smiles at* Scrooge. Bob Cratchit *faints.* Blackout. *As the main lights black out, a spotlight appears on* Scrooge, *another on* Marley. *He talks directly to the audience.*

Marley. Scrooge was better than his word. He did it all and infinitely more; and to Tiny Tim, who did NOT die, he was a second father. He became as good a friend, as good a master, as good a man, as the good old city knew, or any other good old city, town, or borough in the good old world. And it was always said of him that he knew how to keep Christmas well, if any man alive possessed the knowledge. [*Pauses.*] May that be truly said of us, and all of us: And so, as Tiny Tim observed...

Tiny Tim. [*Atop* Scrooge's *shoulder.*] God Bless Us, Every One...

Lights up on chorus, singing final Christmas Song. Scrooge *and* Marley *and all spirits and other characters of the play join in.*

The play has ended. ✤

23. **smoking bishop.** Warm drink made with wine and citrus fruit

Have you, like Scrooge, ever found great happiness in helping others or in changing your attitude toward life and other people? In what ways can others be helped without money or material things?

Find Meaning

1. (a) What does Present sprinkle from his torch? (b) Who receives Present's gift?
2. (a) How does Fred feel about his uncle? (b) What does Fred's wife say that Scrooge missed?
3. (a) Whose death does Scrooge think the three businessmen are discussing? (b) How does he find out about his own death?

Make Judgments

4. (a) How does Present make Scrooge think about the way he has acted in the past? (b) Why do you think seeing Tiny Tim changes the way Scrooge feels?
5. (a) How did Mrs. Dilber and the other people get the goods they are selling to Old Joe? (b) Why were they able to do this? Explain your answer.
6. What is the theme of *A Christmas Carol: Scrooge and Marley?* Use details to support your answer.

PRIMARY SOURCE ▶▶ CONNECTION

Dickens wrote and personally published *A Christmas Carol: A Ghost Story of Christmas* because his earlier works were not selling well, he was in debt, and his wife was expecting their fifth child. Dickens's expectations of quick revenue were not realized, however, because he had commissioned **John Leech,** a well-known London artist, to illustrate the book with hand-colored etchings and wood engravings.

from A Christmas Carol

Illustrations by John Leech

Marley's Ghost, 1843. John Leech. Dickens House Museum, London.

Scrooge's Third Visitor, 1843. John Leech. Dickens House Museum, London.

The Last of the Visitors, 1843. John Leech. Dickens House Museum, London.

TEXT TO TEXT CONNECTION

In what ways do these illustrations accurately reflect the way you imagined the characters and setting of this play? In what ways do they enhance your understanding of the play?

AFTER READING

Analyze Literature

Plot Return to the plot diagram you began at the end of Act 1. What part or parts of the plot took place in Act 2? For each plot part you identify, write the act and scene number on your diagram. In addition, include a brief description of the action that occurred during that part of the plot.

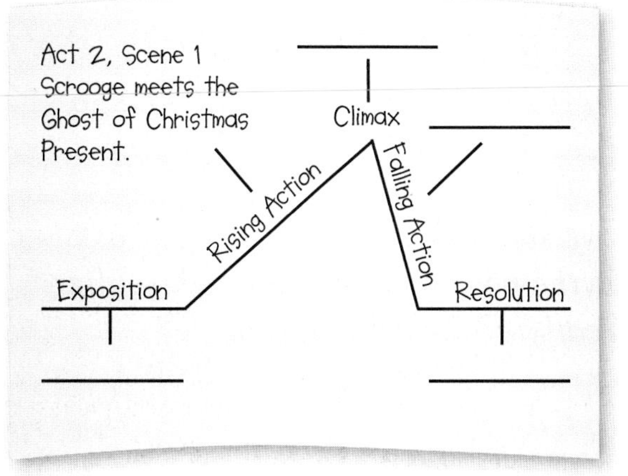

Extend Understanding

Writing Options

Creative Writing Write a **diary entry** as if you were Scrooge. Describe a key event of the past few days. Include sensory information about what you saw, heard, touched, and smelled. As you write, match Scrooge's tone, mood, and attitude about life, money, and people.

Informative Writing In a play, you can learn about a character from stage directions as well as from what characters say and do. In a short **informative essay,** compare and contrast the characters of Scrooge and Marley. State your main point in your thesis, and support it with evidence from the play. Include information about Scrooge's and Marley's physical appearance, attitude, and other aspects of their personalities.

Lifelong Learning

Research Religious Holidays Use the Internet or library resources to research the history and practices associated with holidays from different cultures, such as Ramadan or Passover. Share your findings with the class in an oral report. Use visuals, examples, or other nonverbal media to enliven your presentation.

Critical Literacy

Perform a Scene In small groups, practice and perform a scene from Act 2 of *A Christmas Carol: Scrooge and Marley*. Carefully read the stage directions and gather any props or set decorations. Choose one group member to be the "director." Hold a few rehearsals before performing the scene for the class.

 Go to **www.mirrorsandwindows.com** for more.

Vocabulary & Spelling

Using Dictionaries and Thesauruses

...we should make some slight provision for the poor and destitute, who suffer greatly at the present time.

—ISRAEL HOROVITZ, *A Christmas Carol: Scrooge and Marley*

Context clues suggest the meaning of the word *destitute* in the above quotation. However, to learn the exact definition of the word, you can look in a dictionary.

A **dictionary** is a reference source that provides one or more **definitions,** or meanings, of a word. Dictionaries also provide the **pronunciation** of the word—or the way the word is usually spoken—and a word's etymology. A word's **etymology** is its history or origin, including the root or base words from which it is formed. Etymology is usually provided for the simplest present-tense form of the word.

EXAMPLE

des · ti · tute (des´ tə tüt) *adj.* without money or other basic necessities for survival; extremely poor

[Latin *destituere* meaning "to abandon, deprive"]

A **thesaurus** is a reference source that contains synonyms rather than definitions. Synonyms are words that have the same, or nearly the same, meaning as another word. Synonyms are clues to a word's meaning.

EXAMPLE

destitute: *adj.* PENNILESS: poor, impoverished, distressed

Review the Terms

dictionary: a reference source that provides meanings and other information about words

definition: the meaning of a word

pronunciation: the way a word is usually spoken

etymology: the history or origin of a word

thesaurus: a reference containing synonyms for many words

Vocabulary Practice

Use a dictionary to list the meaning of each word below from *A Christmas Carol: Scrooge and Marley*. Then use a thesaurus to list two synonyms for each word.

1. bleak
2. abundance
3. worldly
4. lamentation
5. lavish
6. compulsion
7. odious
8. venture
9. intercede
10. undulate

Spelling Practice

Silent Letters

Silent letters can pose a problem in spelling unless you are familiar with the word or can recognize a common form. For instance, if you know that the *b* in *comb* is silent, you will know how to pronounce *lamb* when you see it and may be able to remember to spell it with the silent letter. Group these words from the excerpt from *A Christmas Carol* by patterns in their silent letters.

answers	doubt	lightly
assign	fastens	listen
business	indebted	whistle
daughter	knocker	wrenching

Let Me Hear You Whisper

A Drama by Paul Zindel

BEFORE READING

Build Background

Scientific Context Dolphins fascinate humans, and as a result, the field of scientific research on dolphins is large. Researchers study dolphin intelligence as well as their complex social relationships and their communication system. Some of this research is aimed at training dolphins for useful tasks such as locating and retrieving objects. However, much of today's research is aimed at conservation of the species and its habitat.

Reader's Context Think of a time you felt a connection with an animal. What were your feelings? What about the animal caused them?

Set Purpose

Read the play's cast of characters and its setting. Predict what types of tasks Helen may have to do in her new job.

Analyze Literature

Dialogue Conversation involving two or more characters is called **dialogue.** Plays are mostly made up of dialogue and stage directions. In fiction, narration helps tell the story. In a play, there is usually no narration, so dialogue and characters' actions are the tools the playwright uses to tell the story. Stage directions tell how the character is supposed to speak and what he or she should be doing while delivering the lines.

Use Reading Skills

Distinguish Between Major and Minor Details Authors include many details to make their writing rich and believable. Major details are the keys to understanding a story. Minor details enhance a story but are not necessarily important to remember. You can use a chart to help you distinguish between these two types. When you complete the chart, consider how these details fit together.

Major Details:	Minor Details:
Helen has a new job in a lab.	The reception desk is in the hall.

DIRECTED READING

Meet the Author

Paul Zindel (1936–2003) was interested in both science and writing as a child. He wrote his first play in high school. As a college student, he majored in chemistry but was also inspired by his creative writing teacher. Zindel taught high school science before becoming a full-time writer. As a writer, he created numerous plays and young adult novels. His first young adult novel was *The Pigman.*

Preview Vocabulary

a • nal • y • sis (ə na´ lə səs) *n.,* act of separating something into its parts to examine them

com • pul • so • ry (kəm pu̇l´ sə rē) *adj.,* required by a law or rule

ap • pre • hen • sive • ly (a' pri hen[t]´ siv lē) *adv.,* in a way that shows fear or caution

ter • mi • nate (tu̇r´ mə nāt') *v.,* end

Let Me Hear You Whisper

A Drama by Paul Zindel

"You will do best not to become fond of the subject animals."

CHARACTERS

Helen *A little old cleaning lady who lives alone in a one-room apartment and spends most of her spare time feeding stray cats and dogs. She has just been hired to scrub floors in a laboratory that performs rather strange experiments with dolphins.*

Miss Moray *A briskly efficient custodial supervisor who has to break Helen in to her new duties at the laboratory. She has a face that is so uptight she looks like she either throws stones at pigeons or teaches Latin.*

Dr. Crocus *The dedicated man of science who devises and presides over the weird experiments.*

Mr. Fridge *Assistant to Dr. Crocus. He is so loyal and uncreative that if Dr. Crocus told him to stick his head in the mouth of a shark, he'd do it.*

Dan *A talky janitor, also under Miss Moray's control, who at every chance ducks out of the Manhattan laboratory for a beer at the corner bar.*

A Dolphin *The subject of an experiment being performed by Dr. Crocus.*

SETTING: *The action takes place in the hallway, laboratory and specimen room of a biology experimentation association located in Manhattan near the Hudson River.*

TIME: *The action begins with the night shift on Monday and ends the following Friday.*

ACT 1

SCENE 1

Dr. Crocus *and* Mr. Fridge *are leaving the laboratory where they have completed their latest experimental tinkering with a dolphin, and they head down a corridor to the elevator. The elevator door opens and* Miss Moray *emerges with* Helen.

Miss Moray. Dr. Crocus. Mr. Fridge. I'm so glad we've run into you. I want you to meet Helen.

Helen. Hello.

Dr. Crocus *and* Mr. Fridge *nod and get on elevator.*

Miss Moray. Helen is the newest member of our Custodial Engineering Team.

Miss Moray *and* Helen *start down the hall.*

Miss Moray. Dr. Crocus is the guiding heart here at the American Biological Association Development for the Advancement of Brain Analysis. For short, we call it "Abadaba."

Helen. I guess you have to.

They stop at a metal locker at the end of the hall.

Miss Moray. This will be your locker and your key. Your equipment is in this closet.

Helen. I have to bring in my own hangers, I suppose.

Miss Moray. Didn't you find Personnel pleasant?

Helen. They asked a lot of crazy questions.

Miss Moray. Oh, I'm sorry. [*Pause.*] For instance.

Helen. They wanted to know what went on in my head when I'm watching television in my living room and the audience laughs. They asked if I ever thought the audience was laughing at *me*.

Miss Moray. [*Laughing.*] My, oh my! [*Pause.*] What did you tell them?

Helen. I don't have a TV.

Miss Moray. I'm sorry.

Helen. I'm not.

Miss Moray. Yes. Now, it's really quite simple. That's our special soap solution. One tablespoon to a gallon of hot water, if I may suggest.

a•nal•y•sis (ə na´ lə səs) *n.*, act of separating something into its parts to examine them

HELEN *is busy running water into a pail which fits into a metal stand on wheels.*

MISS MORAY. I'll start you in the laboratory. We like it done first. The specimen room is next, and finally the hallway. By that time we'll be well toward morning, and if there are a few minutes left, you can polish the brass strip. [*She points to brass strip which runs around the corridor, halfway between ceiling and floor.*] Ready? Fine.

They start down the hall, MISS MORAY *thumbing through papers on a clipboard.*

MISS MORAY. You were with one concern for fourteen years, weren't you? Fourteen years with Metal Climax Building. That's next to the Radio City Music Hall, isn't it, dear?

HELEN. Uh-huh.

MISS MORAY. They sent a marvelous letter of recommendation. My! Fourteen years on the seventeenth floor. You must be very proud. Why did you leave?

HELEN. They put in a rug.

MISS MORAY *leads* HELEN *into the laboratory, where* DAN *is picking up.*

MISS MORAY. Dan, Helen will be taking Marguerita's place. Dan is the night porter[1] for the fifth through ninth floors.

DAN. Hiya!

HELEN. Hello. [*She looks around.*]

MISS MORAY. There's a crock on nine you missed, and the technicians on that floor have complained about the odor.

HELEN *notices what appears to be a large tank of water with a curtain concealing its contents.*

HELEN. What's that?

MISS MORAY. What? Oh, that's a dolphin, dear. But don't worry about anything except the floor. Dr. Crocus prefers us not to touch either the equipment or the animals.

HELEN. Do you keep him cramped up in that all the time?

MISS MORAY. We have a natatorium for it to exercise in, at Dr. Crocus's discretion.[2]

HELEN. He looks really cramped.

MISS MORAY *closes a curtain which hides the tank.*

MISS MORAY. Well, you must be anxious to begin. I'll make myself available at the reception desk in the hall for a few nights in case any questions arise. Coffee break at two and six A.M. Lunch at four A.M. All clear?

HELEN. I don't need a coffee break.

MISS MORAY. Helen, we all need Perk-You-Ups. All of us.

HELEN. I don't want one.

MISS MORAY. They're compulsory. [*Pause.*] Oh, Helen, I know you're going to fit right in with our little family. You're such a nice person. [*She exits.*] [HELEN *immediately gets to work, moving her equipment into place and getting down on her hands and knees to scrub the floor.* DAN *exits.* HELEN *gets in a few more rubs, glances at the silhouette of the dolphin's tank behind the curtain, and then continues. After a pause, a record begins to play.*]

RECORD. "Let me call you sweetheart,

I'm in love with you.

Let me hear you whisper

That you love me, too."

HELEN'S *curiosity makes her open the curtain and look at the dolphin. He looks right back at her. She returns to her work, singing "Let Me Call You Sweetheart" to herself, missing a word here and there; but her eyes return to the dolphin. She*

---

1. **porter.** Janitor
2. **discretion.** Freedom to choose or make a decision

com • pul • so • ry (kəm pʉl´ sə rē) *adj.*, required by a law or rule

Faraday's Magnetic Laboratory, 1852. Harriet Jane Moore. The Royal Institution, London.

becomes uncomfortable under his stare and tries to ease her discomfort by playing peek-a-boo with him. There is no response and she resumes scrubbing and humming. The dolphin lets out a bubble or two and moves in the tank to bring his blowhole to the surface.

Dolphin. Youuuuuuuuuuu.

Helen *hears the sound, assumes she is mistaken, and goes on with her work.*

Dolphin. Youuuuuuuuuuu.

Helen *has heard the sound more clearly this time. She is puzzled, contemplates a moment, and then decides to get up off the floor. She closes the curtain on the dolphin's tank and leaves the laboratory. She walks the length of the hall to* Miss Moray, *who is sitting at a reception desk near the elevator.*

Miss Moray. What is it, Helen?

Helen. The fish is making some kinda funny noise.

Miss Moray. Mammal, Helen. It's a mammal.

Helen. The mammal's making some kinda funny noise.

Miss Moray. Mammals are supposed to make funny noises.

Helen. Yes, Miss Moray.

Helen *goes back to the lab. She continues scrubbing.*

Dolphin. Youuuuuuuuuuu.

She apprehensively approaches the curtain and

ap • pre • hen • sive • ly (a' pri hen[t]´ siv lē) *adv.*, in a way that shows fear or caution *opens it. Just then* DAN *barges in. He goes to get his reaching pole, and* HELEN *hurriedly returns to scrubbing the floor.*

DAN. Bulb out on seven.

HELEN. What do they have that thing for?

DAN. What thing?

HELEN. That.

DAN. Yeah, he's something, ain't he? [*Pause.*] They're tryin' to get it to talk.

HELEN. Talk?

DAN. Uh-huh, but he don't say nothing. They had one last year that used to laugh. It'd go "heh heh heh heh heh heh heh." Then they got another one that used to say "Yeah, it's four o'clock." Everybody took pictures of that one. All the magazines and newspapers.

HELEN. It just kept saying "Yeah, it's four o'clock"?

DAN. Until it died of pneumonia. They talk outta their blowholes, when they can talk that is. Did you see the blowhole?

HELEN. No.

DAN. Come on and take a look.

HELEN. I don't want to look at any blowhole.

DAN. Miss Moray's at the desk. She won't see anything.

HELEN *and* DAN *go to the tank. Their backs are to the lab door and they don't see* MISS MORAY *open the door and watch them.*

DAN. This one don't say anything at all. They been playing the record every seven minutes for months, and it can't even learn a single word. Don't even say "Polly want a cracker."

MISS MORAY. Helen?

HELEN *and* DAN *turn around.*

MISS MORAY. Helen, would you mind stepping outside a moment?

HELEN. Yes, Miss Moray.

DAN. I was just showing her something.

MISS MORAY. Hadn't we better get on with our duties?

DAN. All right, Miss Moray.

MISS MORAY *guides* HELEN *out into the hall, and puts her arm around her as though taking her into her confidence.*

MISS MORAY. Helen, I called you out here because…well, frankly, I need your help.

HELEN. He was just showing me…

MISS MORAY. Dan is an idle-chatter breeder. How many times we've told him, "Dan, this is a scientific atmosphere you're employed in and we would appreciate a minimum of subjective[3] communication." So—if you can help, Helen—and I'm sure you can, enormously—we'd be so grateful.

HELEN. Yes, Miss Moray.

MISS MORAY *leads* HELEN *back to the lab.*

MISS MORAY. Now, we'll just move directly into the specimen room. The working conditions will be ideal for you in here.

HELEN *looks ready to gag as she looks around the specimen room. It is packed with specimen jars of all sizes. Various animals and parts of animals are visible in their formaldehyde baths.*

MISS MORAY. Now, you will be responsible not only for the floor area but the jars as well. A feather duster—here—is marvelous.

MISS MORAY *smiles and exits. The sound of music and voice from beyond the walls floats over.*

RECORD. "Let me call you sweetheart…"

HELEN *gasps as her eyes fall upon one particular jar in which is floating a preserved human brain. The lights go down, ending Act 1, Scene 1.*

---

3. **subjective.** Based on personal feelings and opinions rather than facts

SCENE 2

It is the next evening. HELEN *pushes her equipment into the lab. She opens the curtain so she can watch the dolphin as she works. She and the dolphin stare at each other.*

HELEN. Youuuuuuuuuuu. [*She pauses, watches for a response.*] Youuuuuuuuuuu. [*Still no response. She turns her attention to her scrubbing for a moment.*] Polly want a cracker? Polly want a cracker? [*She wrings out a rag and resumes work.*] Yeah, it's four o'clock. Yeah, it's four o'clock. Polly want a cracker at four o'clock?

She laughs at her own joke, then goes to the dolphin's tank and notices how sad he looks. She reaches her hand in and just touches the top of his head. He squirms and likes it.

HELEN. Heh heh heh heh heh heh heh heh heh.

MISS MORAY *gets off the elevator and hears the peculiar sounds coming from the laboratory. She puts her ear against the door.*

HELEN. Heh heh heh heh heh...

MISS MORAY. [*Entering.*] Look how nicely the floor's coming along! You must have a special rinsing technique.

HELEN. Just a little vinegar in the rinse water.

MISS MORAY. You brought the vinegar yourself. Just so the floors...they are sparkling, Helen. Sparkling! [*She pauses—looks at the dolphin, then at* HELEN.] It's marvelous, Helen, how well you've adjusted.

HELEN. Thank you, Miss Moray.

MISS MORAY. Helen, the animals here are used for experimentation, and....Well, take Marguerita. She had fallen in love with the mice. All three hundred of them. She seemed shocked when she found out Dr. Crocus was...using...them at the rate of twenty or so a day in connection with electrode implanting. She noticed them missing after a while and when I told her they'd been decapitated, she seemed terribly upset.

HELEN. What do you want with the fish—mammal?

MISS MORAY. Well, dolphins may have an intelligence equal to our own. And if we can teach them our language—or learn theirs—we'll be able to communicate.

HELEN. I can't understand you.

MISS MORAY. [*Louder.*] Communicate! Wouldn't it be wonderful?

HELEN. Oh, yeah....They chopped the heads off three hundred mice? That's horrible.

MISS MORAY. You're so sensitive, Helen. Every laboratory in the country is doing this type of work. It's quite accepted.

HELEN. Every laboratory cutting off mouse heads!

MISS MORAY. Virtually....

HELEN. How many laboratories are there?

MISS MORAY. I don't know. I suppose at least five thousand.

HELEN. Five thousand times three hundred... that's a lot of mouse heads. Can't you just have one lab chop off a couple and then spread the word?

MISS MORAY. Now, Helen—this is exactly what I mean. You will do best not to become fond of the subject animals. When you're here a little longer you'll learn...well...there are some things you just have to accept on faith.

MISS MORAY *exits, leaving the lab door open for* HELEN *to move her equipment out.*

DOLPHIN. Whisper....[HELEN *pauses a moment.*] Whisper to me. [*She exits as the lights go down, ending the scene.*]

SCENE 3

It is the next evening. HELEN *goes from her locker to the laboratory.*

DOLPHIN. Hear....

HELEN. What?

DOLPHIN. Hear me....

DAN *barges in with his hamper, almost frightening* HELEN *to death. He goes to the dolphin's tank.*

DAN. Hiya fella! How are ya? That reminds me. Gotta get some formaldehyde jars set up by Friday. If you want anything just whistle.

He exits. HELEN *goes to the tank and reaches her hand out to pet the dolphin.*

HELEN. Hear. [*Pause.*] Hear.

DOLPHIN. Hear.

HELEN. Hear me.

DOLPHIN. Hear me.

HELEN. That's a good boy.

DOLPHIN. Hear me....

HELEN. Oh, what a pretty fellow. Such a pretty fellow.

MISS MORAY *enters.*

MISS MORAY. What are you doing, Helen?

HELEN. I...uh....

MISS MORAY. Never mind. Go on with your work.

MISS MORAY *surveys everything, then sits on a stool.* DAN *rushes in with large jars on a wheeled table.*

DAN. Scuse me, but I figure I'll get this formaldehyde set up tonight.

MISS MORAY. Very good, Dan.

HELEN. [*Noticing the dolphin is stirring.*] What's the formaldehyde for?

MISS MORAY. The experiment series on...the dolphin will...terminate on Friday. That's why it has concerned me that you've apparently grown...fond...of the mammal.

HELEN. They're gonna kill it?

DAN. Gonna sharpen the handsaws now. Won't have any trouble getting through the skull on this one, no, sir. [*He exits.*]

HELEN. What for? Because it didn't say anything? Is that what they're killing it for?

MISS MORAY. Helen, no matter how lovely our intentions, no matter how lonely we are and how much we want people or animals... to like us...we have no right to endanger the genius about us. Now, we've spoken about this before.

HELEN *is dumbfounded as* MISS MORAY *exits.* HELEN *gathers her equipment and looks at the dolphin, which is staring desperately at her.*

DOLPHIN. Help. [*Pause.*] Please help me.

HELEN *is so moved by the cries of the dolphin she looks ready to burst into tears as the lights go down, ending Act 1.*

ACT 2

The hall. It is the night that the dolphin is to be dissected. Elevator doors open and HELEN *gets off, nods, and starts down the hall.* MISS MORAY *comes to* HELEN *at closet.*

MISS MORAY. I hope you're well this evening.

HELEN. When they gonna kill it?

MISS MORAY. Don't say kill, Helen. You make it sound like murder. Besides, you won't have to go into the laboratory at all this evening.

HELEN. How do they kill it?

MISS MORAY. Nicotine mustard, Helen. It's very humane. They inject it.

HELEN. Maybe he's a mute.

ter•mi•nate (tʉr´ mə nāt') *v.*, end

Miss Moray. Do you have all your paraphernalia?[4]

Helen. Some human beings are mute, you know. Just because they can't talk we don't kill them.

Miss Moray. It looks like you're ready to open a new box of steel wool.

Helen. Maybe he can type with his nose. Did they try that?

Miss Moray. Now, now, Helen—

Helen. Miss Moray, I don't mind doing the lab.

Miss Moray. Absolutely not! I'm placing it off limits for your own good. You're too emotionally involved.

Helen. I can do the lab, honest. I'm not emotionally involved.

Miss Moray. [*Motioning her to the specimen-room door.*] Trust me, Helen. Trust me.

Helen. [*Reluctantly disappearing through the door.*] Yes, Miss Moray.

Miss Moray *stations herself at the desk near the elevator and begins reading her charts.* Helen *slips out of the specimen room and into the laboratory without being seen. The lights in the lab are out and moonlight from the window casts eerie shadows.*

Dolphin. Help.

Helen *opens the curtain. The dolphin and she look at each other.*

Dolphin. Help me.

Helen. You don't need me. Just say something to them. Anything. They just need to hear you say something.…You want me to tell 'em? I'll tell them. I'll just say I heard you say "Help." [*Pauses, then speaks with feigned cheerfulness.*] I'll go tell them.

Dolphin. Noooooooooooooo.

Helen *stops. Moves back toward tank.*

Helen. They're gonna kill you!

Dolphin. Plaaaaan.

Helen. What?

Dolphin. Plaaaaaaaan.

Helen. Plan? What plan?

Dan *charges through the door and snaps on the light.*

Dan. Uh-oh. Miss Moray said she don't want you in here.

Helen *goes to* Dr. Crocus's *desk and begins to look at various books on it.*

Helen. Do you know anything about a plan?

Dan. She's gonna be mad. What plan?

Helen. Something to do with.…[*She indicates the dolphin.*]

Dan. Hiya, fella!

Helen. About the dolphin.…

Dan. They got an experiment book they write in.

Helen. Where?

Dan. I don't know.

Helen. Find it and bring it to me in the animals' morgue.[5] Please.

---

4. **paraphernalia.** Assorted pieces of equipment used for a specific purpose
5. **morgue.** Place where bodies are kept

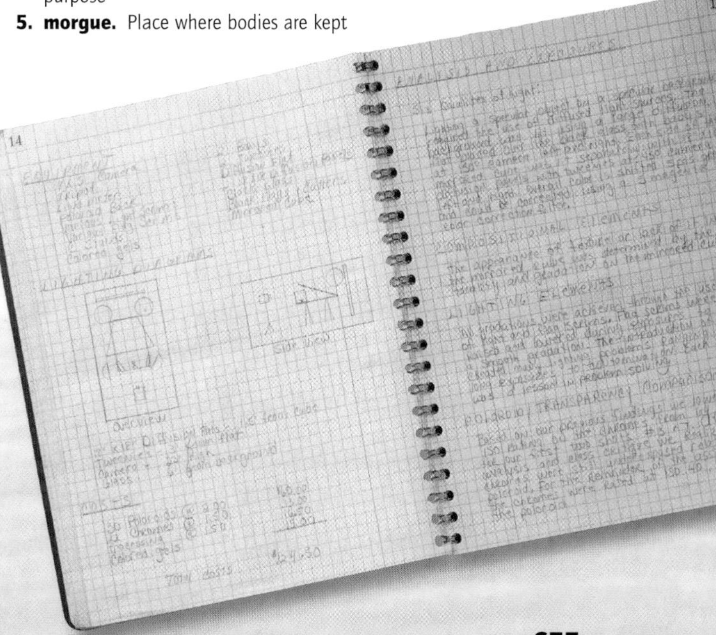

Dan. I'll try. I'll try, but I got other things to do, you know.

Helen *slips out the door and makes it safely back into the specimen room.* Dan *rummages through the desk and finally finds the folder. He is able to sneak into the specimen room.*

Dan. Here.

Helen *grabs the folder and starts going through it.* Dan *turns and is about to go back out into the hall when he sees that* Miss Moray *has stopped reading.* Helen *skims through more of the folder. It is a bulky affair. She stops at a page discussing uses of dolphins.* Miss Moray *gets up from the desk and heads for the specimen-room door.*

"I don't like lazy selfish people, mammals or animals."

Dan. She's coming.

Helen. Maybe you'd better hide. Get behind the table. Here, take the book.

Dan *ducks down behind one of the specimen tables, and* Helen *starts scrubbing away.* Miss Moray *opens the door.*

Miss Moray. Perk-You-Up time, Helen. Tell Dan, please. He's in the laboratory.

Helen *moves to the lab door, opens it, and calls into the empty room.*

Helen. Perk-You-Up time.

Miss Moray. Tell him we have ladyfingers.[6]

Helen. We have ladyfingers.

Miss Moray. Such a strange thing to call a confectionery, isn't it? It's almost macabre.

Helen. Miss Moray….

Miss Moray. Yes, Helen?

Helen. I was wondering why they wanna talk with….

Miss Moray. Now now now!

Helen. I mean, supposing dolphins *did* talk?

Miss Moray. Well, like fishing, Helen. If we could communicate with dolphins, they might be willing to herd fish for us. The fishing industry would be revolutionized.

Helen. Is that all?

Miss Moray. All? Heavens, no. They'd be a blessing to the human race. A blessing. They would be worshipped in oceanography. Checking the Gulf Stream…taking water temperatures, depth, salinity readings. To say nothing of the contributions they could make in marine biology, navigation, linguistics![7] Oh, Helen, it gives me the chills.

Helen. It'd be good if they talked.

Miss Moray. God's own blessing.

Dan *opens the lab doors and yells over* Helen's *head to* Miss Moray.

Dan. I got everything except the head vise. They can't saw through the skull bone without the head vise.

Miss Moray. Did you look on five? They had it there last week for…what they did to the St. Bernard.

From the laboratory, music drifts out. They try to talk over it.

Dan. I looked on five.

Miss Moray. You come with me. It must have been staring you in the face.

6. **ladyfingers.** Small finger-shaped cakes
7. **linguistics.** Study of languages

DAN *and* MISS MORAY *get on the elevator.*

MISS MORAY. We'll be right back, Helen.

The doors close and HELEN *hurries into the laboratory. She stops just inside the door, and it is obvious that she is angry.*

DOLPHIN. Boooooooooook.

HELEN. I looked at your book. I looked at your book all right!

DOLPHIN. Boooooooooook.

HELEN. And you want to know what I think? I don't think much of you, that's what I think.

DOLPHIN. Boooooooooook.

HELEN. Oh, shut up. Book book book book book. I'm not interested. You eat yourself silly—but to get a little fish for hungry humans is just too much for you. Well. I'm going to tell 'em you can talk.

The dolphin moves in the tank, lets out a few warning bubbles.

HELEN. You don't like that, eh? Well, I don't like lazy selfish people, mammals or animals.

The dolphin looks increasingly desperate and begins to make loud blatt and beep sounds. He struggles in the tank.

HELEN. Cut it out—you're getting water all over the floor.

DOLPHIN. Boooooooooook!

HELEN *looks at the folder on the desk. She picks it up, opens it, closes it, and sets it down again.*

HELEN. I guess you don't like us. I guess you'd die rather than help us....

DOLPHIN. Hate.

HELEN. I guess you do hate us....

She returns to the folder.

HELEN. [*Reading.*] Military implications... war...plant mines in enemy waters...deliver atomic warheads...war...nuclear torpedoes... attach bombs to submarines...terrorize enemy waters...war....They're already thinking about ways to use you for war. Is that why you can't talk to them? [*Pause.*] What did you talk to me for? [*Pause.*] You won't talk to them, but you...you talk to me because...you want something...there's something...I can do?

DOLPHIN. Hamm....

HELEN. What?

DOLPHIN. Hamm....

HELEN. Ham? I thought you ate fish.

DOLPHIN. [*Moving with annoyance.*] Ham... purrrr.

HELEN. Ham...purrrr? I don't know what you're talking about.

DOLPHIN. [*Even more annoyed.*] Ham...purrrr.

HELEN. Ham...purrrr. What's a purrrr?

Confused and scared, she returns to scrubbing the hall floor just as the doors of the elevator open, revealing MISS MORAY, DAN, *and* MR. FRIDGE. DAN *pushes a dissection table loaded with shiny instruments toward the lab.*

MISS MORAY. Is the good doctor in yet?

MR. FRIDGE. He's getting the nicotine mustard on nine. I'll see if he needs assistance.

MISS MORAY. I'll come with you. You'd better leave now, Helen. It's time. [*She smiles and the elevator doors close.*]

DAN. [*Pushing the dissection table through the lab doors.*] I never left a dirty head vise. She's trying to say I left it like that.

HELEN. Would you listen a minute? Ham... purrrr. Do you know what a ham...purrrr is?

DAN. The only hamper I ever heard of is out in the hall. [HELEN *darts to the door, opens it, and sees the hamper at the end of the hall.*]

HELEN. The hamper!

Dan. Kazinski left the high-altitude chamber dirty once, and I got blamed for that, too. [*He exits.*]

Helen. [*Rushing to the dolphin.*] You want me to do something with the hamper. What? To get it? To put…you want me to put you in it? But what'll I do with you? Where can I take you?

Dolphin. Sea….

Helen. See? See what?

Dolphin. Sea….

Helen. I don't know what you're talking about. They'll be back in a minute. I don't know what to do!

Dolphin. Sea…sea….

Helen. See?…The sea! That's what you're talking about! The river…to the sea!

She darts into the hall and heads for the hamper. Quickly she pushes it into the lab, and just as she gets through the doors unseen, Miss Moray *gets off the elevator.*

Miss Moray. Helen? [*She starts down the hall. Enters the lab. The curtain is closed in front of the tank.*]

Miss Moray. Helen? Are you here? Helen?

She sees nothing and is about to leave when she hears movement behind the curtain. She looks down and sees Helen's *shoes.* Miss Moray *moves to the curtain and pulls it open. There is* Helen *with her arms around the front part of the dolphin, lifting it a good part of the way out of the water.*

Miss Moray. Helen, what do you think you're hugging?

Helen *drops the dolphin back into the tank.*

Mr. Fridge. [*Entering.*] Is anything wrong, Miss Moray?

Miss Moray. No…nothing wrong. Nothing at all. Just a little spilled water.

Helen *and* Miss Moray *grab sponges from the lab sink and begin to wipe up the water around the tank.* Dr. Crocus *enters and begins to fill a hypodermic syringe while* Mr. Fridge *expertly gets all equipment into place.* Dan *enters.*

Mr. Fridge. Would you like to get an encephalogram[8] during the death process, Dr. Crocus?

Dr. Crocus. Why not?

Mr. Fridge *begins to implant electrodes in the dolphin's head. The dolphin commences making high-pitched distress signals.*

Miss Moray. Come, Helen. I'll see you to the elevator.

Miss Moray *leads her out to the hall.* Helen *gets on her coat and kerchief.*

Miss Moray. Frankly, Helen, I'm deeply disappointed. I'd hoped that by being lenient with you—and heaven knows I have been—you'd develop a heightened loyalty to our team.

Helen. [*Bursting into tears and going to the elevator.*] Leave me alone.

Miss Moray. [*Softening as she catches up to her.*] You really are a nice person, Helen. A very nice person. But to be simple and nice in a world where great minds are giant-stepping the micro- and macrocosms, well—one would expect you'd have the humility to yield in unquestioning awe. I truly am very fond of you, Helen, but you're fired. Call Personnel after nine A.M.

As Miss Moray *disappears into the laboratory, the record starts to play.*

Record. "Let me call you sweetheart, I'm in love with you. Let me hear you whisper…."

The record is roughly interrupted. Instead of getting on the elevator, Helen *whirls around and barges into the lab.*

---

8. encephalogram. X-ray picture of the brain

Helen. Who do you think you are? [*Pause.*] Who do you think you *are?* [*Pause.*] I think you're a pack of killers, that's what I think.

Miss Moray. Doctor. I assure you this is the first psychotic outbreak she's made. She did the entire brass strip....

Helen. I'm tired a being a nice person, Miss Moray. I'm going to report you to the ASPCA,[9] or somebody, because...I've decided I don't like you cutting the heads off mice and sawing through skulls of St. Bernards... and if being a nice person is just not saying anything and letting you pack of butchers run around doing whatever you want, then I don't want to be nice anymore. [*Pause.*] You gotta be very stupid people to need an animal to talk before you know just from looking at it that it's saying something...that it knows what pain feels like. I'd like to see you all with a few electrodes in your heads. Being nice isn't any good. [*Looking at dolphin.*] They just kill you off if you do that. And that's being a coward. You gotta talk back. You gotta speak up against what's wrong and bad, or you can't ever stop it. At least you've gotta try. [*She bursts into tears.*]

Miss Moray. Nothing like this has ever happened with a member of the Custodial Engineering....Helen, dear....

Helen. Get your hands off me. [*Yelling at the dolphin.*] You're a coward, that's what you are. I'm going.

Dolphin. Loooooooooveeeeeeeee.

Everyone turns to stare at the dolphin.

Dolphin. Love.

Dr. Crocus. Get the recorder going.

---

9. ASPCA. American Society for the Prevention of Cruelty to Animals

HELEN *pats the dolphin, exits. The laboratory becomes a bustle of activity.*

DOLPHIN. Love....

DR. CROCUS. Is the tape going?

MR. FRIDGE. Yes, Doctor.

DOLPHIN. Love.

DR. CROCUS. I think that woman's got something to do with this. Get her back in here.

MISS MORAY. Oh, I fired her. She was hugging the mammal...and....

DOLPHIN. Love.

DR. CROCUS. Just get her. [*To* MR. FRIDGE.] You're sure the machine's recording?

MISS MORAY. Doctor, I'm afraid you don't understand. That woman was hugging the mammal....

DR. CROCUS. Try to get another word out of it. One more word....

MISS MORAY. The last thing in the world I want is for our problem in Custodial Engineering to....

DR. CROCUS. [*Furious.*] Will you shut up and get that washwoman back in here?

MISS MORAY. Immediately, Doctor.

She hurries out of the lab. HELEN *is at the end of the hall waiting for the elevator.*

MISS MORAY. Helen? Oh, Helen? Don't you want to hear what the dolphin has to say. He's so cute! Dr. Crocus thinks that his talking might have something to do with you. Wouldn't that be exciting? [*Pause.*] Please, Helen. The doctor....

HELEN. Don't talk to me, do you mind?

MISS MORAY. It was only in the heat of argument that I...of course, you won't be discharged. All right? Please, Helen, you'll embarrass me....

The elevator doors open and HELEN *gets on to face* MISS MORAY. *She looks at her a moment and then lifts her hand to press the button for the ground floor.*

MISS MORAY. Don't you dare...Helen, the team needs you, don't you see? You've done so well—the brass strip, the floors. The floors have never looked so good. Ever. Helen, please. What will I do if you leave?

HELEN. Why don't you get a rug?

HELEN *helps slam the elevator doors in* MISS MORAY'S *face as the lights go down, ending the play.* ✤

Imagine you have a job that requires you to do something you do not believe is right or that makes you uncomfortable. How would you handle the situation? When is it acceptable to refuse an order?

Find Meaning

1. (a) What is Helen's opinion about the way animals are treated in the lab? (b) How might Dr. Crocus respond to her opinion?
2. How do Helen and Miss Moray differ?
3. (a) How are Helen and the dolphin alike? (b) How are they different?

Make Judgments

4. Is Miss Moray a good supervisor? Explain.
5. Do you think Helen is a good employee? Why or why not?
6. Is Helen right to leave her job at the end of the play? Why or why not?

INFORMATIONAL TEXT ▶▶ CONNECTION

Let Me Hear You Whisper is about a dolphin that speaks. While the selection is fiction, it is true that dolphins have a language of whistles that they use to communicate with each other. Other animals also use language. In fact, some apes have been taught to use a form of human language. The following article, "Going Ape Over Language," by **Natalie Rosinsky** describes how a chimpanzee named Washoe learned to communicate with humans. As you read the article, think about the differences between the treatment of animals in the play and in the article.

from Going Ape Over Language

An Article by Natalie Rosinsky

Humans talking with apes? Such conversations were once found only in fables, or in science fiction like *Planet of the Apes.* But, since the 1960s, scientists have "gone ape" over other methods of interspecies communication.

Great apes physically cannot produce the consonants or some vowel sounds of human speech. So, instead of spoken language, researchers are using American Sign Language (ASL) and technology to teach human language to other primates.

A Chimpanzee Named Washoe

In 1966, Dr. Allen Gardner and his wife, Beatrix, began teaching ASL to a year-old female chimpanzee named Washoe. They taught Washoe by "cross-fostering" her—that is, treating her like a deaf human child. Washoe had a stimulating[1] environment filled with toys and attentive human companions who used ASL to "discuss" daily activities. In those first years, one important topic of conversation was—of course—potty training! Dr. Roger Fouts, an early companion, and his wife, Debbi, have now spent more than 30 years with "Project Washoe." In 1992, the Foutses founded the Chimpanzee and Human Communication Institute at Central Washington University, where Washoe lives with an adoptive family of four other ASL-using chimpanzees.

Washoe is the most "talkative" member of this group, with an ASL vocabulary of 240 signs. She often "translates" spoken words she understands into ASL. Washoe signs correctly even when an object is out of sight—signaling "DOG," for example, whenever she hears canine barking. She also accurately puts together short "sentences"—signing "ROGER TICKLE WASHOE" when this is what has occurred. If she does not know the sign for an item, Washoe creatively yet logically "renames" it. She called her first candy bar a "CANDY BANANA?"

Yet emotion, not just logic, has filled some of Washoe's most memorable conversations with humans. Washoe had

1. **stimulating.** Causing a feeling of interest or excitement

Claudine Andre, director of the "Lola ya bonobo" park in the Democratic Republic of the Congo, plays with bonobos.

already had two unsuccessful pregnancies when she learned that a caregiver's baby had died. The chimpanzee looked groundward, then directly into the woman's eyes, and signed "CRY" while touching the woman's cheek just below her eye. Later that day, Washoe wouldn't let her caregiver go home without further consolation,[2] signing "PLEASE PERSON HUG."

Researchers are also excited by the chimpanzees' use of ASL among themselves. Washoe, her adoptive son Loulis, and other family members have been videotaped having ASL conversations on their own about games, food, and "housecleaning." Birthday parties and holiday celebrations are other "hot" topics of conversation. The chimpanzees have even been observed "talking to themselves," much as a human might mutter under her breath. When Loulis mischievously ran away with one of her favorite magazines, an annoyed Washoe signed "BAD, BAD, BAD" to herself.

It is Loulis's use of ASL, though, that may be most significant. In a planned experiment, researchers avoided signing in Loulis's presence during his first five years. Yet Loulis—like deaf human childen—learned ASL by watching and imitating his adoptive mother and other family members! Chimpanzees, it seems, not only can learn human language, but also can transmit it to others.

A Gorilla Named Koko

Koko, a female lowland gorilla, began learning ASL in 1972, when she was one year old. Her teacher, Dr. Francine Patterson, provided her with a gorilla companion in 1976, when three-year-old Michael joined them at the official start of the Gorilla Foundation.

Koko has a working vocabulary of 1,000 signs and understands 2,000 spoken words. Michael—before his unexpected death last year—used 600 signs to communicate. Both gorillas, like Washoe, have shown creativity and logic in naming unknown objects. It was obvious to Koko that a face mask is an "EYE HAT," while Michael had no difficulty at all in titling his painting (yes, gorillas paint) of a bouquet of flowers "STINK"! Koko has even used ASL to "talk" herself out of trouble. When a trainer caught her eating a crayon, Koko signed "LIP" and pretended to be applying lipstick! Koko also likes to joke using ASL, calling herself an "ELEPHANT" after pointing to a long tube held out in front of her like that animal's trunk.

2. consolation. Comfort expressed to someone who is upset or sad

Koko has also used ASL to express sadness and some complex ideas. She mourned the death of her kitten, named All Ball, by repeatedly signing "SAD." When asked when gorillas die, Koko signed "TROUBLE OLD." When she was then asked what happens to gorillas after they die, Koko answered "COMFORTABLE HOLE." With Dr. Patterson as an interpreter, Koko has even participated in on-line, computerized "chats"!

A Bonobo Named Kanzi

Kanzi, a male bonobo[3] born in 1980, speaks a different human language than Washoe and Koko. He communicates in "Yerkish," a visual code invented by researchers at Georgia State University and the Yerkes Primate Research Center. "Yerkish" is a set of several hundred geometric symbols called "lexigrams," each representing a verb, noun, or adjective. These lexigrams are placed on an adapted computer keyboard, which bonobos learn to use while learning the meanings of the lexigrams. Kanzi communicates by computer! (Outdoors, Kanzi points to lexigrams on a carry-around tagboard.)

Kanzi, who also understands more than 1,000 spoken English words, first learned Yerkish by watching humans train his mother. Like a silent toddler who astonishes parents by first speaking in complete sentences, two-year-old Kanzi amazed researchers on the day he first "spoke" Yerkish by using most of the lexigrams taught to his mother. By the age of six, he had a Yerkish vocabulary of 200 lexigrams. According to Dr. Sue Savage-Rumbaugh, Kanzi and other bonobos construct logical sentences in Yerkish and even use the lexigram for "later" to discuss future activities.

Aping Their Betters?

Linguist Noam Chomsky insists that human beings are the only primates neurologically capable of language. Some other scientists, including MIT's Dr. Steven Pinker, share this view. They conclude that "Project Washoe" and similar research prove only that apes can be trained, and that they will imitate the behavior of trainers just for rewards or approval. These critics maintain that investigators, along with animal rights activists, have misinterpreted the results of these researchers because they want to believe that apes can "talk."

But there are answers to these objections. The private signing done by chimpanzees is evidence that apes use language for more than rewards or approval. And the technology used to teach "Yerkish" to bonobos lessens the possibly questionable element of imitation in this and similar research. Furthermore, as Dr. Sue Savage-Rumbaugh notes, comprehension and visual cues between humans are themselves part of a broader definition of language. It may be unfair to define language for apes only in the narrowest sense. Lastly, current research into how apes communicate among themselves in the wild is reshaping our views of them. Geographically separated groups of bonobos have their own "dialects" of communicative gestures and sounds. And bonobos already may communicate symbolically among themselves, smashing plants and placing them at particular angles as "road signs." ✣

---

3. **bonobo.** Ape that looks and behaves much like a chimpanzee

TEXT ↔ TO ↔ TEXT CONNECTION

Both Zindel's play and Rosinsky's article address scientists who study animal language. How does the form of communication differ between the two selections? What are the differences between the use of animals? Contrast the purposes for study in the two selections. Do you think Helen's character would have been willing to work for the Gardners?

AFTER READING

Analyze Literature

Dialogue Paul Zindel uses dialogue to reveal the traits of the characters in the play. Revisit some of the lines of dialogue spoken by Helen, Miss Moray, and Dan. Decide what the characters' words show about them. Use a chart to record your findings and interpretations. Use the ideas in your chart to write a summary statement about each character.

Character	What the Character Says	What the Dialogue Shows about the Character
Helen	"Some human beings are mute, you know. Just because they can't talk we don't kill them."	

Extend Understanding

Writing Options

Creative Writing Recall your thoughts from Build Background about a connection you have had with an animal. Use the experience of reading the previous selections to help you think more deeply about your connection to that animal. Write a **journal entry** about this connection. Include factual information and personal thoughts and feelings.

Informative Writing Analyze how Paul Zindel used dialogue in *Let Me Hear You Whisper.* Revisit the play to get more ideas about how dialogue reveals character traits and motives. Also, analyze how Zindel uses dialogue to advance the plot. Write a **critical analysis** of Zindel's use of dialogue. Include a thesis statement, and give examples from the play to support your points.

Lifelong Learning

Write a Research Report Use books, science magazines, and the Internet to research what scientists have learned about the intelligence of dolphins. What can dolphins do? What can't they do? Compare and contrast their intelligence with that of other animals. How are their abilities similar to human abilities? Try to include some visuals such as charts, tables, or graphic organizers in your report.

Critical Literacy

Perform Reader's Theater In small groups, choose a scene from the play to perform, and assign a role to each group member. Be creative in your interpretation of the characters, setting, and props. Rehearse your scene repeatedly as a group, and perform it for the class.

Go to **www.mirrorsandwindows.com** for more.

Comparing Texts

St. Crispian's Day Speech

A Dramatic Monologue by William Shakespeare

The Charge of the Light Brigade

A Narrative Poem by Alfred, Lord Tennyson

BEFORE READING

Build Background

Historical Context Shakespeare's "St. Crispian's Day Speech," from the play *Henry V*, recalls the battle in the French village of Agincourt. There King Henry V, who ruled England from 1413 to 1422, staged a victorious battle in 1415. "The Charge of the Light Brigade" by Alfred, Lord Tennyson memorializes the 1854 Battle of Balaklava during the Crimean War.

Reader's Context What traits do successful leaders share?

Set Purpose

Skim both texts to help make predictions about the purpose and attitude of the speaker in each selection.

Meet the Authors

William Shakespeare (1564–1616) was born and educated in the small village of Stratford-on-Avon. Shakespeare moved to London where he worked as an actor and a playwright. He became part owner of London's famed Globe Theater in 1599, at which *Henry V* was performed.

Alfred, Lord Tennyson (1809–1892) was appointed England's poet laureate by Queen Victoria in 1850. In "The Charge of the Light Brigade," which contains some of the most frequently quoted lines of his poetry, Tennyson recounts the story of a poorly planned military attack that cost hundreds of British soldiers their lives.

Compare Literature: Diction

In literature, **diction** is part of a writer's overall style. It refers to the writer's word choice. The diction in a piece of literature can be formal or informal, ornate or plain, outdated or modern, and so on. To help you identify and describe the diction of each text, use a chart to record examples of words and phrases that suggest a specific diction.

"St. Crispian's Day Speech"	Effect of Diction
ne'er	
a-bed	

Preview Vocabulary

blun•der (blun´ dər) *v.*, make a serious error in judgment; make a thoughtless mistake

reel (rēl) *v.*, stumble as the result of a hard hit

St. Crispian's Day Speech

A Dramatic Monologue
by William Shakespeare

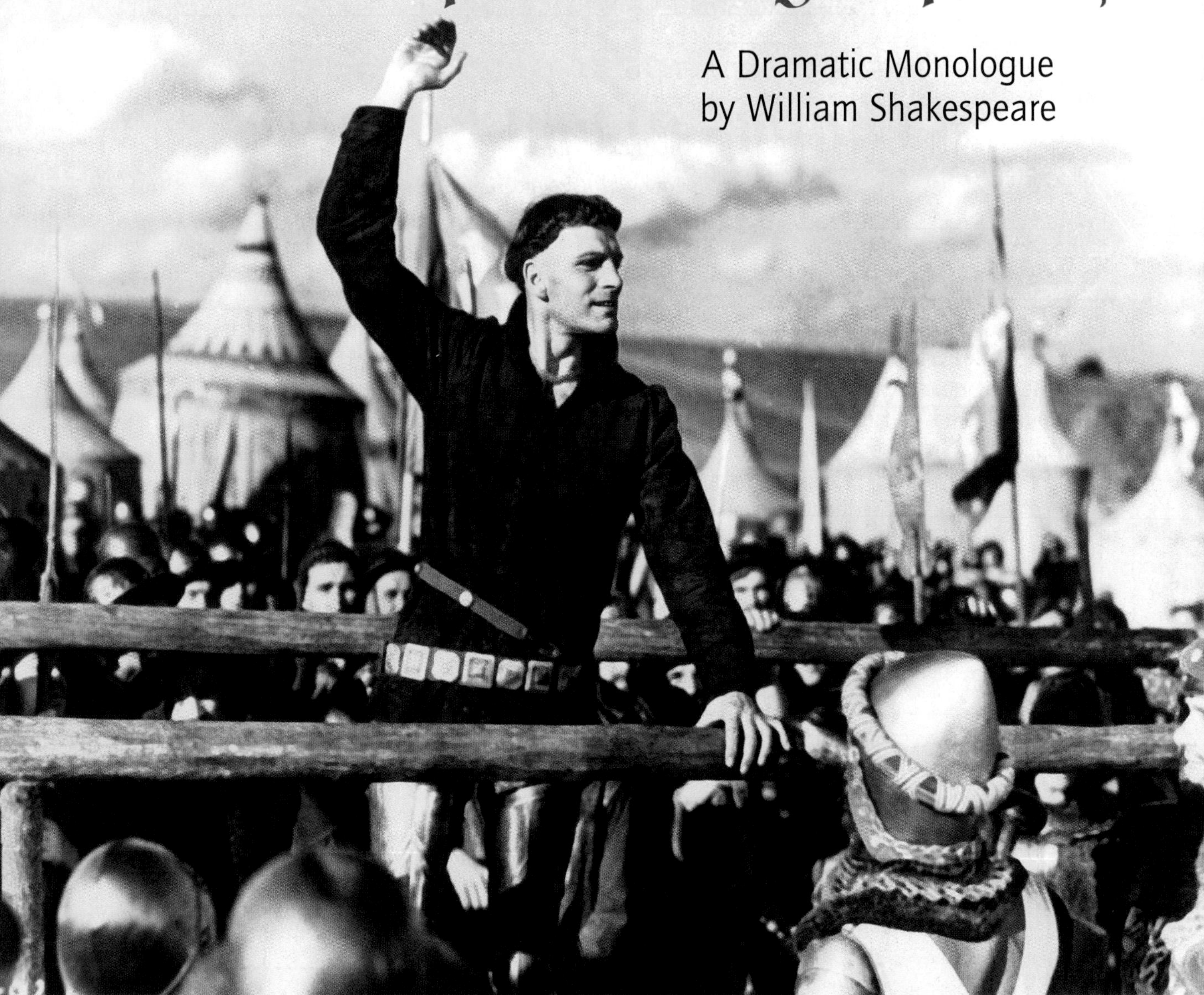

Sir Laurence Olivier as Henry V in a 1944 film version of Shakespeare's play.

This day is call'd the feast of Crispian:[1]
He that outlives this day, and comes safe home,
Will stand a' tiptoe when this day is named,
And rouse him at the name of Crispian.
He that shall live this day, and see old age,

1. **feast of Crispian.** Christian holiday celebrated on October 25, honoring Crispin and Saint Crispian, two brothers martyred for their religious beliefs in the third century

Will yearly on the vigil feast his neighbors,
And say, "To-morrow is Saint Crispian."
Then will he strip his sleeve and show his scars,
And say, "These wounds I had on Crispin's day."
Old men forget; yet all shall be forgot,
But he'll remember with advantages
What feats he did that day. Then shall our names,
Familiar his mouth as household words,
Harry the King, Bedford and Exeter,
Warwick and Talbot, Salisbury and Gloucester,[2]
Be in their flowing cups freshly rememb'red.
This story shall the good man teach his son;
And Crispin Crispian shall ne'er go by,
From this day to the ending of the world,
But we in it shall be remembered—
We few, we happy few, we band of brothers;
For he to-day that sheds his blood with me
Shall be my brother; be he ne'er so vile,
This day shall gentle his condition;
And gentlemen in England, now a-bed,
Shall think themselves accurs'd they were not here;
And hold their manhoods cheap whiles any speaks
That fought with us upon Saint Crispin's day. ✤

---

2. **Bedford...Gloucester.** Bedford, Exeter, Warwick, Talbot, Salisbury, and Gloucester were English nobility and members of King Henry's entourage.

If you had doubts about engaging in a battle, what effect would an inspirational speech such as Henry's have on you? Is it fair of military leaders to urge troops into battle when they know their chances of success are slim?

Find Meaning

1 (a) When does Henry give the St. Crispian's Day speech? (b) What is his main purpose for giving this speech?

2. (a) What does Henry believe the men who survive the battle will say and feel on the anniversary of the battle? (b) What can you infer about Henry's understanding of human nature from these remarks?

Make Judgments

3. (a) Why do you think Henry mentions his own name and the names of several English noblemen? (b) In your opinion, is this a wise tactic?

4. Of all the reasons Henry gives for joining him in battle, which one would you have found most convincing? Why?

The Charge of the Light Brigade

A Narrative Poem by Alfred, Lord Tennyson

1

Half a league,[1] half a league,
Half a league onward,
All in the valley of Death
Rode the six hundred.
"Forward, the Light Brigade![2]
Charge for the guns!" he said:
Into the valley of Death
Rode the six hundred.

2

"Forward, the Light Brigade!"
Was there a man dismayed?
Not though the soldier knew
Someone had blundered:
Theirs not to make reply,
Theirs not to reason why,
Theirs but to do and die,
Into the valley of Death
Rode the six hundred.

3

Cannon to right of them,
Cannon to left of them,
Cannon in front of them
Volleyed[3] and thundered;
Stormed at with shot and shell,
Boldly they rode and well,
Into the jaws of Death,
Into the mouth of Hell
Rode the six hundred.

1. **league.** Measure of distance equal to about three miles
2. **Light Brigade.** A *brigade* is a unit of troops. The term *light* was assigned to the British brigade because the soldiers carried only swords into battle.
3. **volleyed.** Fired or discharged (weapons) all at once

blun • der (blʉn´ dər) *v.*, make a serious error in judgment; make a thoughtless mistake

(Above) ***Balaclava, 1889,*** c. 19th century. John Charlton. Blackburn Museum and Art Gallery, Lancashire, United Kingdom.

CULTURAL ▶▶ CONNECTION

Crimean War During the Crimean War (1853–1856), the allied forces of Great Britain, France, Turkey, and Sardinia fought against the forces of the Russian Empire. Much of the fighting took place on Crimea, a peninsula in the Black Sea that is now the Ukraine. On October 25, 1854, a British brigade of more than six hundred soldiers staged a brave but futile assault on a Russian encampment near the town of Balaklava. The British cavalry, moving under confused and mistaken orders from two rival British officers, was bombarded by cannon fire on three sides. When the skirmish ended, nearly two hundred and fifty English soldiers were dead or wounded. The battle itself had no major significance to the outcome of the war.

4

Flashed all their sabers bare,
Flashed as they turned in air,
Sab'ring the gunners there,
Charging an army, while
    All the world wondered:
Plunged in the battery smoke
Right through the line they broke:
Cossack[4] and Russian
Reeled from the saber stroke
    Shattered and sundered.
Then they rode back, but not,
    Not the six hundred.

5

Cannon to right of them,
Cannon to left of them,
Cannon behind them
    Volleyed and thundered;
Stormed at with shot and shell,
While horse and hero fell,
They that had fought so well
Came through the jaws of Death,
Back from the mouth of Hell,
All that was left of them,
    Left of six hundred.

6

When can their glory fade?
O the wild charge they made!
    All the world wondered.
Honor the charge they made!
Honor the Light Brigade,
    Noble six hundred! ✤

4. Cossack. Soldier in the Russian cavalry unit known as Cossacks

reel (rēl) *v.*, stumble as the result of a hard hit

What is your opinion of the British soldiers, knowing that the orders to charge were a mistake? Do soldiers really have no right "to make reply" or "to reason why," and no choice but "to do and die"?

Comparing Texts

AFTER READING

Find Meaning

1. (a) What is the meaning of the lines "Into the valley of Death / Rode the six hundred"? (b) Why are these lines repeated at the ends of the first, second, and third stanzas and echoed at the ends of the remaining stanzas?
2. (a) How do the troops feel as they ride into battle? (b) Aware of the probable outcome, why do the members of the Light Brigade continue the assault?

Make Judgments

3. (a) How does the speaker feel about the British soldiers who participated in this battle? (b) How does the speaker think the rest of the world will feel about them?
4. Tennyson may have begun writing this poem to attack the mistake made by the commanding officers at Balaklava. In the end, what do you think Tennyson's goal was?

Compare Literature

Diction Diction is a part of a writer's overall style. It refers to the writer's word choice. When choosing words, writers consider how the words will sound and what images the words will evoke in the reader's mind. Review the words and phrases from "St. Crispian's Day Speech" and "The Charge of the Light Brigade" that you recorded in your diction chart to answer the following questions.

1. What words and phrases in "St. Crispian's Day Speech" most helped you to describe the diction?
2. What words and phrases in "The Charge of the Light Brigade" most helped you to describe the diction?
3. Describe the diction in both texts. How does each poem's diction compare?

Extend Understanding

Writing Options

Narrative Writing Write a **narrative poem** that uses the same subject as Tennyson's poem. Do research to learn more about the events surrounding the Battle of Balaklava and the people involved. Consider writing your poem from a new point of view, for example, from the point of view of one of the soldiers or perhaps one of the leaders.

Informative Writing Write an **informative paragraph** comparing and contrasting the speakers in "St. Crispian's Day Speech" and "The Charge of the Light Brigade." Discuss similarities and differences in the speakers' tone and purposes. Provide examples to support your claims.

Lifelong Learning

Research Shakespeare To understand the context of "St. Crispian's Day Speech," learn more about the play from which it is taken. Use the library to research the plot, characters, and notable scenes from *Henry V.* Present your findings to the class as an oral report.

Critical Literacy

Recite a Monologue With a partner, practice reciting Shakespeare's "St. Crispian's Day Speech." Provide feedback about your partner's delivery, including tone of voice, clarity, and facial expressions. When you feel you are ready, perform the monologue for the class.

Go to **www.mirrorsandwindows.com** for more.

Grammar & Style

Punctuation: Dashes, Semicolons, and Colons

Dashes

But we in it shall be remembered—

We few, we happy few, we band of brothers

—WILLIAM SHAKESPEARE, "St. Crispian's Day Speech"

A **dash,** like the one that ends the first line in the quotation above, is used to show a sudden break or change in thought. Note that a dash is longer than a hyphen. Dashes sometimes replace other marks of punctuation, such as periods, semicolons, or commas. In the quotation above, the dash provides a dramatic pause.

EXAMPLE

Today, you will fight a great battle—a battle that will be remembered forever.

Semicolons

Old men forget; yet all shall be forgot....

—WILLIAM SHAKESPEARE, "St. Crispian's Day Speech"

A **semicolon** joins two closely related independent clauses. The semicolon signals a pause that is longer than a comma's pause but shorter than that of a period.

EXAMPLE

The soldiers are preparing themselves; they will be ready for battle.

Conjunctions such as *and, but, so, or, nor, for,* and *yet* can also be used to combine two related independent clauses. A semicolon can be used in place of the comma and the conjunction. Using a semicolon instead of a comma and a coordinating conjunction adds emphasis to the second clause.

EXAMPLES

The opposing army is much larger, <u>and</u> it will probably defeat Henry and his troops.

The opposing army is much larger; it will probably defeat Henry and his troops.

Colons

A **colon** introduces a list of items. Colons are also used between numbers that tell hours and minutes and after the greeting in a business letter.

EXAMPLE

You will be remembered for three things: your courage, your boldness, and your bravery.

Understanding Dashes, Semicolons, and Colons

Rewrite the following sentences, correcting the punctuation where necessary. If no changes are needed, write *correct.*

1. This is your greatest challenge; my band of brothers.
2. People often forget: you will not be forgotten.
3. The story blends these elements drama, adventure, and excitement.
4. We shall be remembered–we few, we happy few.
5. The battle draws close we are prepared.
6. Everyone will honor you; those who shed their blood with me shall be my brothers.
7. His troops were ready with their weapons; swords, shields, and spears.

The Monsters Are Due on Maple Street

A Screenplay by Rod Serling

CHARACTERS

NARRATOR
FIGURE ONE
FIGURE TWO

RESIDENTS OF MAPLE STREET

STEVE BRAND
CHARLIE'S WIFE
MRS. GOODMAN
MRS. BRAND
TOMMY
WOMAN
DON MARTIN
SALLY *(Tommy's Mother)*
MAN ONE
MAN TWO
PETE VAN HORN
CHARLIE
LES GOODMAN

-ACT 1-

Fade in on a shot of the night sky. The various nebulae and planet bodies stand out in sharp, sparkling relief, and the camera begins a slow pan across the Heavens.

NARRATOR'S VOICE. There is a fifth dimension beyond that which is known to man. It is a dimension as vast as space, and as timeless as infinity. It is the middle ground between light and shadow—between science and

Rod Serling (1924–1975) is one of the best-known television writers of all time. His sometimes frightening, often strange, and always amazing program *The Twilight Zone* changed the face of prime-time television. Born in Syracuse, New York, Serling served as a paratrooper in World War II. Soon after his discharge from the military, Serling attended Antioch College in Ohio, where he studied literature and worked part time as a scriptwriter. By the age of thirty-one, Serling had already won an Emmy for his work in television. The following screenplay originally aired on March 4, 1960, during the first season of *The Twilight Zone.*

superstition. And it lies between the pit of man's fears and the summit of his knowledge. This is the dimension of imagination. It is an area which we call The Twilight Zone.

The camera has begun to pan down until it passes the horizon and is on a sign which reads "Maple Street." Pan down until we are shooting down at an angle toward the street below. It's a tree-lined, quiet residential American street, very typical of the small town. The houses have front porches on which people sit and swing on gliders, conversing across from house to house. STEVE BRAND *polishes his car parked in front of his house. His neighbor,* DON MARTIN, *leans against the fender watching him. A Good Humor man rides a bicycle and is just in the process of stopping to sell some ice cream to a couple of kids. Two women gossip on the front lawn. Another man waters his lawn.*

NARRATOR'S VOICE. Maple Street, U.S.A., late summer. A tree-lined little world of front porch gliders, hop scotch, the laughter of children, and the bell of an ice cream vendor.

There is a pause and the camera moves over to a shot of the Good Humor man and two small boys who are standing alongside, just buying ice cream.

NARRATOR'S VOICE. At the sound of the roar and the flash of light it will be precisely 6:43 P.M. on Maple Street.

At this moment one of the little boys, TOMMY, *looks up to listen to a sound of a tremendous screeching roar from overhead. A flash of light plays on both their faces and then it moves down the street past lawns and porches and rooftops and then disappears.*

Various people leave their porches and stop what they're doing to stare up at the sky. STEVE BRAND, *the man who's been polishing his car, now stands there transfixed, staring upwards. He looks at* DON MARTIN, *his neighbor from across the street.*

STEVE. What was that? A meteor?

DON. [*Nods.*] That's what it looked like. I didn't hear any crash though, did you?

STEVE. [*Shakes his head.*] Nope. I didn't hear anything except a roar.

MRS. BRAND. [*From her porch.*] Steve? What was what?

STEVE. [*Raising his voice and looking toward porch.*] Guess it was a meteor, honey. Came awful close, didn't it?

MRS. BRAND. Too close for my money! Much too close.

The camera pans across the various porches to people who stand there watching and talking in low tones.

NARRATOR'S VOICE. Maple Street. Six-forty-four P.M. on a late September evening. [*A pause.*] Maple Street in the last calm and reflective moment...before the monsters came!

The camera slowly pans across the porches again. We see a man screwing a light bulb on a front porch, then getting down off the stool to flick the switch and finding that nothing happens.

Another man is working on an electric power mower. He plugs in the plug, flicks on the switch of the power mower, off and on, with nothing happening.

Through the window of a front porch, we see a woman pushing her finger back and forth on the dial hook. Her voice is indistinct and distant, but intelligible and repetitive.

WOMAN. Operator, operator, something's wrong on the phone, operator!

MRS. BRAND *comes out on the porch and calls to* STEVE.

MRS. BRAND. [*Calling.*] Steve, the power's off. I had the soup on the stove and the stove just stopped working.

WOMAN. Same thing over here. I can't get anybody on the phone either. The phone seems to be dead.

We look down on the street as we hear the voices creep up from below, small, mildly disturbed voices highlighting these kinds of phrases:

VOICES.

Electricity's off.

Phone won't work.

Can't get a thing on the radio.

My power mower won't move, won't work at all.

Radio's gone dead!

PETE VAN HORN, *a tall, thin man, is seen standing in front of his house.*

VAN HORN. I'll cut through the back yard… See if the power's still on on Floral Street. I'll be right back!

He walks past the side of his house and disappears into the back yard.

The camera pans down slowly until we're looking at ten or eleven people standing around the street and overflowing to the curb and sidewalk. In the background is STEVE BRAND'S *car.*

STEVE. Doesn't make sense. Why should the power go off all of a sudden, and the phone line?

DON. Maybe some sort of an electrical storm or something.

CHARLIE. That don't seem likely. Sky's just as blue as anything. Not a cloud. No lightning. No thunder. No nothing. How could it be a storm?

WOMAN. I can't get a thing on the radio. Not even the portable.

The people again murmur softly in wonderment and question.

CHARLIE. Well, why don't you go downtown and check with the police, though they'll probably think we're crazy or something. A little power failure and right away we get all flustered and everything.

STEVE. It isn't just the power failure, Charlie. If it was, we'd still be able to get a broadcast on the portable.

There's a murmur of reaction to this. STEVE *looks from face to face and then over to his car.*

STEVE. I'll run downtown. We'll get this all straightened out.

He walks over to the car, gets in it, turns the key. Looking through the open car door, we see the crowd watching him from the other side. STEVE *starts the engine. It turns over sluggishly*[1] *and then just stops dead. He tries it again and this time he can't get it to turn over. Then, very slowly and reflectively, he turns the key back to "off" and slowly gets out of the car.*

The people stare at STEVE. *He stands for a moment by the car, then walks toward the group.*

STEVE. I don't understand it. It was working fine before…

---

1. **sluggishly.** Inactively; slowly moving

Don. Out of gas?

Steve. [*Shakes his head.*] I just had it filled up.

Woman. What's it mean?

Charlie. It's just as if…as if everything had stopped. [*Then he turns toward* Steve.] We'd better walk downtown. [*Another murmur of assent*[2] *at this.*]

Steve. The two of us can go, Charlie. [*He turns to look back at the car.*] It couldn't be the meteor. A meteor couldn't do this.

He and Charlie *exchange a look, then they start to walk away from the group.*

We see Tommy, *a serious-faced fourteen-year-old in spectacles who stands a few feet away from the group. He is halfway between them and the two men, who start to walk down the sidewalk.*

Tommy. Mr. Brand…you better not!

Steve. Why not?

Tommy. They don't want you to.

Steve *and* Charlie *exchange a grin, and* Steve *looks back toward the boy.*

Steve. Who doesn't want us to?

Tommy. [*Jerks his head in the general direction of the distant horizon.*] Them!

Steve. Them?

Charlie. Who are them?

Tommy. [*Very intently.*] Whoever was in that thing that came by overhead.

Steve *knits his brows for a moment, cocking his head questioningly. His voice is intense.*

Steve. What?

Tommy. Whoever was in that thing that came over. I don't think they want us to leave here.

Steve *leaves* Charlie *and walks over to the boy. He kneels down in front of him. He forces his voice to remain gentle. He reaches out and holds the boy.*

Steve. What do you mean? What are you talking about?

Tommy. They don't want us to leave. That's why they shut everything off.

Steve. What makes you say that? Whatever gave you that idea?

Woman. [*From the crowd.*] Now isn't that the craziest thing you ever heard?

Tommy. [*Persistently but a little intimidated by the crowd.*] It's always that way, in every story I ever read about a ship landing from outer space.

Woman. [*To the boy's mother,* Sally, *who stands on the fringe of the crowd.*] From outer space, yet! Sally, you better get that boy of yours up to bed. He's been reading too many comic books or seeing too many movies or something.

Sally. Tommy, come over here and stop that kind of talk.

Steve. Go ahead, Tommy. We'll be right back. And you'll see. That wasn't any ship or anything like it. That was just a…a meteor or something. Likely as not—[*He turns to the group, now trying to weight his words with an optimism he obviously doesn't feel but is desperately trying to instill in himself as well as the others.*] No doubt it did have something to do with all this power failure and the rest of it. Meteors can do some crazy things. Like sunspots.

---

2. assent. Agreement

201

Don. [*Picking up the cue.*] Sure. That's the kind of thing—like sunspots. They raise Cain[3] with radio reception all over the world. And this thing being so close—why, there's no telling the sort of stuff it can do. [*He wets his lips, smiles nervously.*] Go ahead, Charlie. You and Steve go into town and see if that isn't what's causing it all.

Steve *and* Charlie *again walk away from the group down the sidewalk. The people watch silently.*

Tommy *stares at them, biting his lips, and finally calling out again.*

Tommy. *Mr. Brand!*

The two men stop again. Tommy *takes a step toward them.*

Tommy. Mr. Brand...please don't leave here.

Steve *and* Charlie *stop once again and turn toward the boy. There's a murmur in the crowd, a murmur of irritation and concern as if the boy were bringing up fears that shouldn't be brought up; words which carried with them a strange kind of validity that came without logic but nonetheless registered and had meaning and effect. Again we hear a murmur of reaction from the crowd.*

Tommy *is partly frightened and partly defiant as well.*

Tommy. You might not even be able to get to town. It was that way in the story. Nobody could leave. Nobody except—

Steve. Except who?

Tommy. Except the people they'd sent down ahead of them. They looked just like humans. And it wasn't until the ship landed that—

The boy suddenly stops again, conscious of the parents staring at them and of the sudden hush of the crowd.

Sally. [*In a whisper, sensing the antagonism*[4] *of the crowd.*] Tommy, please son...honey, don't talk that way—

Man One. That kid shouldn't talk that way...and we shouldn't stand here listening to him. Why this is the craziest thing I ever heard of. The kid tells us a comic book plot and here we stand listening—

Steve *walks toward the camera, stops by the boy.*

Steve. Go ahead, Tommy. What kind of story was this? What about the people that they sent out ahead?

Tommy. That was the way they prepared things for the landing. They sent four people. A mother and a father and two kids who looked just like humans...but they weren't.

There's another silence as Steve *looks toward the crowd and then toward* Tommy. *He wears a tight grin.*

Steve. Well, I guess what we'd better do then is to run a check on the neighborhood and see which ones of us are really human.

There's laughter at this, but it's a laughter that comes from a desperate attempt to lighten the atmosphere. It's a release kind of laugh. The people look at one another in the middle of their laughter.

Charlie. There must be somethin' better to do than stand around makin' bum jokes about it. [*Rubs his jaw nervously.*] I wonder if

---

3. **raise Cain.** Cause trouble
4. **antagonism.** Hostility; open opposition

Floral Street's got the same deal we got. [*He looks past the houses.*] Where is Pete Van Horn anyway? Didn't he get back yet?

Suddenly there's the sound of a car's engine starting to turn over.

We look across the street toward the driveway of LES GOODMAN'S *house. He's at the wheel trying to start the car.*

SALLY. Can you get it started, Les? [*He gets out of the car, shaking his head.*]

GOODMAN. No dice.

He walks toward the group. He stops suddenly as behind him, inexplicably and with a noise that inserts itself into the silence, the car engine starts up all by itself. GOODMAN *whirls around to stare toward it.*

The car idles roughly, smoke coming from the exhaust, the frame shaking gently. GOODMAN'S *eyes go wide, and he runs over to his car.*

The people stare toward the car.

MAN ONE. He got the car started somehow. He got his car started!

The camera pans along the faces of the people as they stare, somehow caught up by this revelation and somehow, illogically, wildly, frightened.

WOMAN. How come his car just up and started like that?

SALLY. All by itself. He wasn't anywheres near it. It started all by itself.

DON *approaches the group, stops a few feet away to look toward* GOODMAN'S *car and then back toward the group.*

DON. And he never did come out to look at that thing that flew overhead. He wasn't even interested. [*He turns to the faces in the group, his face taut and serious.*] Why? Why didn't he come out with the rest of us to look?

CHARLIE. He always was an oddball. Him and his whole family. Real oddball.

DON. What do you say we ask him?

The group suddenly starts toward the house. In this brief fraction of a moment they take the first step toward performing a metamorphosis[5] *that changes people from a group into a mob. They begin to head purposefully across the street toward the house at the end.* STEVE *stands in front of them. For a moment their fear almost turns their walk into a wild stampede, but* STEVE'S *voice, loud, incisive, and commanding, makes them stop.*

STEVE. Wait a minute…wait a minute! Let's not be a mob!

The people stop as a group, seem to pause for a moment, and then much more quietly and slowly start to walk across the street. GOODMAN *stands alone facing the people.*

GOODMAN. I just don't understand it. I tried to start it and it wouldn't start. You saw me. All of you saw me.

And now, just as suddenly as the engine started, it stops and there's a long silence that is gradually intruded upon by the frightened murmuring of the people.

GOODMAN. I don't understand. I swear…I don't understand. What's happening?

DON. Maybe you better tell us. Nothing's working on this street. Nothing. No lights, no power, no radio. [*And then meaningfully.*] Nothing except one car—yours!

---

5. metamorphosis. Change in form or nature

The people pick this up and now their murmuring becomes a loud chant filling the air with accusations and demands for action. Two of the men pass DON *and head toward* GOODMAN, *who backs away, backing into his car and now at bay.*

GOODMAN. Wait a minute now. You keep your distance—all of you. So I've got a car that starts by itself—well, that's a freak thing, I admit it. But does that make me some kind of a criminal or something? I don't know why the car works—it just does!

This stops the crowd momentarily and now GOODMAN, *still backing away, goes toward his front porch. He goes up the steps and then stops to stand facing the mob.*

We see a long shot of STEVE *as he comes through the crowd.*

STEVE. [*Quietly.*] We're all on a monster kick, Les. Seems that the general impression holds that maybe one family isn't what we think they are. Monsters from outer space or something. Different than us. Fifth columnists[6] from the vast beyond. [*He chuckles.*] You know anybody that might fit that description around here on Maple Street?

GOODMAN. What is this, a gag or something? This a practical joke or something?

We see a close-up of the porch light as it suddenly goes out. There's a murmur from the group.

GOODMAN. Now I suppose that's supposed to incriminate[7] me! The light goes on and off. That really does it, doesn't it? [*He looks around the faces of the people.*] I just don't understand this—[*He wets his lips, looking from face to face.*] Look, you all know me. We've lived here five years. Right in this house. We're no different from any of the rest of you! We're no different at all. Really...this whole thing is just...just weird—

WOMAN. Well, if that's the case, Les Goodman, explain why—[*She stops suddenly, clamping her mouth shut.*]

GOODMAN. [*Softly.*] Explain what?

STEVE. [*Interjecting.*] Look, let's forget this—

CHARLIE. [*Overlapping him.*] Go ahead, let her talk. What about it? Explain what?

WOMAN. [*A little reluctantly.*] Well... sometimes I go to bed late at night. A couple of times...a couple of times I'd come out on the porch and I'd see Mr. Goodman here in the wee hours of the morning standing out in front of his house...looking up at the sky. [*She looks around the circle of faces.*] That's right, looking up at the sky as if...as if he were waiting for something. [*A pause.*] As if he were looking for something.

There's a murmur of reaction from the crowd again.

We cut suddenly to a group shot. As GOODMAN *starts toward them, they back away frightened.*

GOODMAN. You know really...this is for laughs. You know what I'm guilty of? [*He laughs.*] I'm guilty of insomnia. Now what's the penalty for insomnia? [*At this point the laugh, the humor, leaves his voice.*] Did you

---

6. Fifth columnists. Citizens who support the goals of an invading army

7. incriminate. Show proof of involvement in a crime

hear what I said? I said it was insomnia. [*A pause as he looks around, then shouts.*] I said it was insomnia! You fools. You scared, frightened rabbits, you. You're sick people, do you know that? You're sick people—all of you! And you don't even know what you're starting because let me tell you...let me tell you—this thing you're starting—that should frighten you. As God is my witness...you're letting something begin here that's a nightmare!

–ACT 2–

We see a medium shot of the GOODMAN *entry hall at night. On the side table rests an unlit candle.* MRS. GOODMAN *walks into the scene, a glass of milk in hand. She sets the milk down on the table, lights the candle with a match from a box on the table, picks up the glass of milk, and starts out of scene.*

MRS. GOODMAN *comes through her porch door, glass of milk in hand. The entry hall, with table and lit candle, can be seen behind her.*

Outside, the camera slowly pans down the sidewalk, taking in little knots of people who stand around talking in low voices. At the end of each conversation they look toward LES GOODMAN'S *house. From the various houses we can see candlelight but no electricity, and there's an all-pervading quiet that blankets the whole area, disturbed only by the almost whispered voices of the people as they stand around. The camera pans over to one group where* CHARLIE *stands. He stares across at* GOODMAN'S *house.*

We see a long shot of the house. Two men stand across the street in almost sentry-like poses. Then we see a medium shot of a group of people.

SALLY. [*A little timorously.*[8]] It just doesn't seem right, though, keeping watch on them. Why...he was right when he said he was one of our neighbors. Why, I've known Ethel Goodman ever since they moved in. We've been good friends—

CHARLIE. That don't prove a thing. Any guy who'd spend his time lookin' up at the sky early in the morning—well, there's something wrong with that kind of person. There's something that ain't legitimate. Maybe under normal circumstances we could let it go by, but these aren't normal circumstances. Why, look at this street! Nothin' but candles. Why, it's like goin' back into the dark ages or somethin'!

STEVE *walks down the steps of his porch, walks down the street over to* LES GOODMAN'S *house, and then stops at the foot of the steps.* GOODMAN *stands there, his wife behind him, very frightened.*

GOODMAN. Just stay right where you are, Steve. We don't want any trouble, but this time if anybody sets foot on my porch, that's what they're going to get—trouble!

STEVE. Look Les—

GOODMAN. I've already explained to you people. I don't sleep very well at night sometimes. I get up and I take a walk and I look up at the sky. I look at the stars!

MRS. GOODMAN. That's exactly what he does. Why this whole thing, it's...it's some kind of madness or something.

STEVE. [*Nods grimly.*] That's exactly what it is—some kind of madness.

---

8. timorously. Shyly

Charlie's Voice. [*Shrill, from across the street.*] You best watch who you're seen with, Steve! Until we get all this straightened out, you ain't exactly above suspicion yourself.

Steve. [*Whirling around toward him.*] Or you, Charlie. Or any of us, it seems. From age eight on up!

Woman. What I'd like to know is—what are we gonna do? Just stand around here all night?

Charlie. There's nothin' else we can do! [*He turns back looking toward* Steve *and* Goodman *again.*] One of 'em'll tip their hand.[9] They got to.

Steve. [*Raising his voice.*] There's something you can do, Charlie. You could go home and keep your mouth shut. You could quit strutting around like a self-appointed hanging judge and just climb into bed and forget it.

Charlie. You sound real anxious to have that happen, Steve. I think we better keep our eye on you too!

Don. [*As if he were taking the bit in his teeth, takes a hesitant step to the front.*] I think everything might as well come out now. [*He turns toward* Steve.] Your wife's done plenty of talking, Steve, about how odd you are!

Charlie. [*Picking this up, his eyes widening.*] Go ahead, tell us what she's said.

We see a long shot of Steve *as he walks toward them from across the street.*

Steve. Go ahead, what's my wife said? Let's get it all out. Let's pick out every idiosyncrasy[10] of every single man, woman, and child on the street. And then we might as well set up some kind of kangaroo court.[11] How about a firing squad at dawn, Charlie, so we can get rid of all the suspects? Narrow them down. Make it easier for you.

Don. There's no need gettin' so upset, Steve. It's just that...well...Myra's talked about how there's been plenty of nights you spent hours down in your basement workin' on some kind of radio or something. Well, none of us have ever seen that radio—

By this time Steve *has reached the group. He stands there defiantly close to them.*

Charlie. Go ahead, Steve. What kind of "radio set" you workin' on? I never seen it. Neither has anyone else. Who you talk to on that radio set? And who talks to you?

Steve. I'm surprised at you, Charlie. How come you're so dense all of a sudden? [*A pause.*] Who do I talk to? I talk to monsters from outer space. I talk to three-headed green men who fly over here in what look like meteors.

Steve's *wife steps down from the porch, bites her lip, calls out.*

Mrs. Brand. Steve! Steve, please. [*Then looking around, frightened, she walks toward the group.*] It's just a ham radio[12] set, that's all. I bought him a book on it myself. It's just a ham radio set. A lot of people have them. I can show it to you. It's right down in the basement.

Steve. [*Whirls around toward her.*] Show them nothing! If they want to look inside our house—let them get a search warrant.

---

9. **tip their hand.** Expose themselves; accidentally reveal information
10. **idiosyncrasy.** Odd character trait
11. **kangaroo court.** Unjust or unofficial court
12. **ham radio.** Noncommercial two-way radio

CHARLIE. Look, buddy, you can't afford to—

STEVE. [*Interrupting.*] Charlie, don't tell me what I can afford! And stop telling me who's dangerous and who isn't and who's safe and who's a menace. [*He turns to the group and shouts.*] And you're with him, too—all of you! You're standing here all set to crucify—all set to find a scapegoat[13]—all desperate to point some kind of a finger at a neighbor! Well now look, friends, the only thing that's gonna happen is that we'll eat each other up alive—

He stops abruptly as CHARLIE *suddenly grabs his arm.*

CHARLIE. [*In a hushed voice.*] That's not the only thing that can happen to us.

Cut to a long shot looking down the street. A figure has suddenly materialized in the gloom and in the silence we can hear the clickety-clack of slow, measured footsteps on concrete as the figure walks slowly toward them. One of the women lets out a stifled cry. The young mother grabs her boy as do a couple of others.

TOMMY. [*Shouting, frightened.*] It's the monster! It's the monster!

Another woman lets out a wail and the people fall back in a group, staring toward the darkness and the approaching figure.

We see a medium group shot of the people as they stand in the shadows watching. DON MARTIN *joins them, carrying a shotgun. He holds it up.*

DON. We may need this.

STEVE. A shotgun? [*He pulls it out of* DON's *hand.*] Good Lord—will anybody think a thought around here? Will you people wise up? What good would a shotgun do against—

Now CHARLIE *pulls the gun from* STEVE's *hand.*

CHARLIE. No more talk, Steve. You're going to talk us into a grave! You'd let whatever's out there walk right over us, wouldn't yuh? Well, some of us won't!

He swings the gun around to point it toward the sidewalk. The dark figure continues to walk toward them.

---

13. scapegoat. Person, group, or thing that is unfairly blamed

The group stands there, fearful, apprehensive, mothers clutching children, men standing in front of wives. CHARLIE *slowly raises the gun. As the figure gets closer and closer he suddenly pulls the trigger. The sound of it explodes in the stillness. There is a long angle shot looking down at the figure, who suddenly lets out a small cry, stumbles forward onto his knees and then falls forward on his face.* DON, CHARLIE, *and* STEVE *race forward over to him.* STEVE *is there first and turns the man over. Now the crowd gathers around them.*

STEVE. [*Slowly looks up.*] It's Pete Van Horn.

DON. [*In a hushed voice.*] Pete Van Horn! He was just gonna go over to the next block to see if the power was on—

WOMAN. You killed him, Charlie. You shot him dead!

CHARLIE. [*Looks around at the circle of faces, his eyes frightened, his face contorted.*] But…but I didn't know who he was. I certainly didn't know who he was. He comes walkin' out of the darkness—how am I supposed to know who he was? [*He grabs* STEVE.] Steve—you know why I shot! How was I supposed to know he wasn't a monster or something? [*He grabs* DON *now.*] We're all scared of the same thing. I was just tryin' to…tryin' to protect my home, that's all! Look, all of you, that's all I was tryin' to do. [*He looks down wildly at the body.*] I didn't know it was somebody we knew! I didn't know—

There's a sudden hush and then an intake of breath. We see a medium shot of the living room window of CHARLIE'*s house. The window is not lit, but suddenly the house lights come on behind it.*

WOMAN. [*In a very hushed voice.*] Charlie... Charlie…the lights just went on in your house. Why did the lights just go on?

DON. What about it, Charlie? How come you're the only one with lights now?

GOODMAN. That's what I'd like to know. [*A pause as they all stare toward* CHARLIE.]

GOODMAN. You were so quick to kill, Charlie, and you were so quick to tell us who we had to be careful of. Well, maybe you had to kill. Maybe Peter there was trying to tell us something. Maybe he'd found out something and came back to tell us who there was amongst us we should watch out for—

CHARLIE backs away from the group, his eyes wide with fright.

CHARLIE. No...no...it's nothing of the sort! I don't know why the lights are on. I swear I don't. Somebody's pulling a gag or something.

He bumps against STEVE, who grabs him and whirls him around.

STEVE. *A gag?* A gag? Charlie, there's a dead man on the sidewalk and you killed him! Does this thing look like a gag to you?

CHARLIE breaks away and screams as he runs toward his house.

CHARLIE. No! No! Please!

A man breaks away from the crowd to chase CHARLIE.

We see a long angle shot looking down as the man tackles CHARLIE and lands on top of him. The other people start to run toward them. CHARLIE is up on his feet, breaks away from the other man's grasp, lands a couple of desperate punches that push the man aside. Then he forces his way, fighting, through the crowd to once again break free, jumps up on his front porch. A rock thrown from the group smashes a window alongside of him, the broken glass flying past him. A couple of pieces cut him. He stands there perspiring, rumpled, blood running down from a cut on the cheek. His wife breaks away from the group to throw herself into his arms. He buries his face against her. We can see the crowd converging on the porch now.

VOICES.

It must have been him.

He's the one.

We got to get Charlie.

Another rock lands on the porch. Now CHARLIE pushes his wife behind him, facing the group.

CHARLIE. Look, look I swear to you...it isn't me...but I do know who it is...I swear to you, I do know who it is. I know who the monster is here. I know who it is that doesn't belong. I swear to you I know.

GOODMAN. [*Shouting.*] What are you waiting for?

WOMAN. [*Shouting.*] Come on, Charlie, come on.

MAN ONE. [*Shouting.*] Who is it, Charlie, tell us!

DON. [*Pushing his way to the front of the crowd.*] All right, Charlie, let's hear it!

CHARLIE's eyes dart around wildly.

CHARLIE. It's...it's...

MAN TWO. [*Screaming.*] Go ahead, Charlie, tell us.

CHARLIE. It's...it's the kid. It's Tommy. He's the one!

There's a gasp from the crowd as we cut to a shot of SALLY holding her son TOMMY. The boy at first doesn't understand and then, realizing the eyes are all on him, buries his face against his mother.

SALLY. [*Backs away.*] That's crazy! That's crazy! He's a little boy.

WOMAN. But he knew! He was the only one who knew! He told us all about it. Well, how did he know? How could he have known?

The various people take this up and repeat the question aloud.

VOICES.

How could he know?

Who told him?

Make the kid answer.

Don. It was Charlie who killed old man Van Horn.

Woman. But it was the kid here who knew what was going to happen all the time. He was the one who knew!

We see a close-up of Steve.

Steve. Are you all gone crazy? [*Pause as he looks about.*] Stop.

A fist crashes at Steve's *face, staggering him back out of the frame of the picture.*

There are several close camera shots suggesting the coming of violence. A hand fires a rifle. A fist clenches. A hand grabs the hammer from Van Horn's *body, etc. Meanwhile, we hear the following lines.*

Don. Charlie has to be the one—Where's my rifle—

Woman. Les Goodman's the one. His car started! Let's wreck it.

Mrs. Goodman. What about Steve's radio—He's the one that called them—

Mrs. Goodman. Smash the radio. Get me a hammer. Get me something.

Steve. Stop—Stop—

Charlie. Where's that kid—Let's get him.

Man One. Get Steve—Get Charlie—They're working together.

The crowd starts to converge around the mother, who grabs the child and starts to run with him. The crowd starts to follow, at first walking fast, and then running after him.

We see a full shot of the street as suddenly Charlie's *lights go off and the lights in another house go on. They stay on for a moment, then from across the street other lights go on and then off again.*

Man One. [*Shouting.*] It isn't the kid...it's Bob Weaver's house.

Woman. It isn't Bob Weaver's house. It's Don Martin's place.

Charlie. I tell you it's the kid.

Don. It's Charlie. He's the one.

We move into a series of close-ups of various people as they shout, accuse, scream, interspersing these shots with shots of houses as the lights go on and off, and then slowly in the middle of this nightmarish morass[14] *of sight and sound the camera starts to pull away, until once again we've reached the opening shot looking at the Maple Street sign from high above.*

The camera continues to move away until we dissolve to a shot looking toward the metal side of a space craft, which sits shrouded in darkness. An open door throws out a beam of light from the illuminated interior. Two figures silhouetted against the bright lights appear. We get only a vague feeling of form, but nothing more explicit than that.

Figure One. Understand the procedure now? Just stop a few of their machines and radios and telephones and lawn mowers...throw them into darkness for a few hours, and then you just sit back and watch the pattern.

Figure Two. And this pattern is always the same?

Figure One. With few variations. They pick the most dangerous enemy they can find... and it's themselves. And all we need do is sit back...and watch.

Figure Two. Then I take it this place...this

14. morass. Complicated or bewildering situation

Maple Street…is not unique.

FIGURE ONE. [*Shaking his head.*] By no means. Their world is full of Maple Streets. And we'll go from one to the other and let them destroy themselves. One to the other…one to the other…one to the other…one to the other—

Now the camera pans up for a shot of the starry sky and over this we hear the NARRATOR'S VOICE.

NARRATOR'S VOICE. The tools of conquest do not necessarily come with bombs and explosions and fallout. There are weapons that are simply thoughts, attitudes, prejudices—to be found only in the minds of men. For the record, prejudices can kill and suspicion can destroy and a thoughtless frightened search for a scapegoat has a fallout all its own for the children…and the children yet unborn. [*A pause.*] And the pity of it is… that these things cannot be confined to…The Twilight Zone! ❖

How do you think the characters felt being unfairly judged or threatened? Why do people sometimes reach unfair or dangerous conclusions?

Analyze and Extend

1. (a) Why is Les Goodman singled out in the first act? (b) What does this suggest?
2. (a) In what ways would you have acted differently from the residents of Maple Street? (b) In what ways would you have acted or felt the same?
3. Serling often incorporated social and political commentary into his work. Describe the social or political comment that this screenplay makes.

Informative Writing What is the effect of the ending of this screenplay? Does it lessen or enhance the overall impact of the screenplay? How does it affect the theme? Write a short **literary analysis** of "The Monsters Are Due on Maple Street" in which you analyze and evaluate the conclusion. Be sure to include a thesis statement and evidence from the text in support of your claims. When you are finished, present your paper to the class.

Critical Literacy Gather into small groups to role-play characters from the screenplay. One member should act as a reporter, while others should choose the characters they would like to play. As a group, generate a list of questions that the reporter will ask. Then act out interviews based on these questions.

Go to **www.mirrorsandwindows.com** for more.

For Your Reading List

The Jumbo Book of Drama

by Deborah Dunleavy

This book is an introduction to all aspects of the theater, including drama, comedy, and tragedy. Dunleavy has broken the book up into four "Acts." Act 1 introduces physical movement; Act 2 focuses on the uses of the voice; Act 3 investigates comedy and tragedy; and Act 4 looks at other aspects of the theater, such as directing, lights, set design, and costumes. Dunleavy has also included many engaging activities, exercises, and scripts for young actors.

Plays from Hispanic Tales

by Barbara Winther

These one-act plays are based on Hispanic folk tales and legends, including trickster tales, a ghost story, and tales on the themes of honor and honesty. These clever and lively tales come from Aztec and Mayan culture, South and Central America, Spain, and the Caribbean. An introduction to each play gives background information on the story and how it fits into Hispanic folklore.

Shakespeare's Theater

by Jacqueline Morley

Full-color illustrations of Shakespeare's Globe Theatre dominate this book about the origins of English theater. Key elements in each picture are magnified with inset illustrations. Quotes from Shakespeare's plays and detailed color artwork throughout enhance this fascinating look at Elizabethan theater.

Plays of Black Americans: The Black Experience in America, Dramatized for Young People

by Sylvia E. Kamerman

This collection of eleven plays, including plays about Martin Luther King, Jr., Langston Hughes, Abraham Lincoln, and the abolitionist movement, focuses on important moments in African-American history. These short plays offer a creative and unusual way of presenting the contributions of famous individuals to American history.

Greek Theatre

by Stewart Ross

This introduction to ancient Greek theater opens with the preparations for a performance of *Oedipus the King*. A description of the early history of Greek drama follows and includes theater festivals, set design, actors and choruses, and biographical sketches of Greek playwrights. Color photographs of ancient sites and artifacts illustrate the text.

Seattle Children's Theatre: Six Plays for Young Audiences

by Marisa Smith

These plays focus on young people searching for their places in the world. Plays include a work based on the memoirs of Joyce Simmons—a Native American woman who was forced to leave her family and attend an off-reservation boarding school—and an adaptation of the classic story *Anne of Green Gables*.

Writing Workshop

Argumentative Writing

Argumentative Essay

Assignment: Write an argumentative essay in which I try to win others to my point of view.

Goal: To present my topic clearly and convincingly to my audience.

Strategy: Present evidence for my point of view through persuasive techniques.

Writing Rubric: My argumentative essay should include the following:

- an introduction that grabs the reader's attention, that includes a question or a quotation, or that connects to a common human experience
- a thesis statement in the introduction that clearly presents my argument or point of view
- a clear and logical organizational pattern
- evidence, such as reasons, facts, and examples, to support my thesis
- an effective conclusion that restates my thesis and adds a final insight

Reading and Writing

In Shakespeare's "St. Crispian's Day Speech," King Henry tries to persuade his troops that they will be seen as heroes for their participation in the battle of Agincourt. In your own life, you have probably tried to persuade parents, family members, teachers, or friends to agree with a point of view or to take a specific action.

In this workshop, you will learn how to write an argumentative essay. This is an expository essay in which you try to convince your audience to do or believe something. In an **argumentative essay,** you can appeal to the logic and emotion of your audience, use persuasive techniques, and address opposing viewpoints in a counterargument. The following summary includes a rubric, that is, a set of standards by which you judge your work to determine whether or not you were successful in the final product. You will use the rubric in both drafting and revising your essay.

What Great Writers Do

William Shakespeare, (1564–1616), was a well-known English dramatist and the author of plays such as Romeo and Juliet, Hamlet, *and* Othello. *Many sayings are attributed to him. Here is what he said about the power of words to influence. How might this saying apply to your own argumentative writing?*

"Strong words make strong reasons."

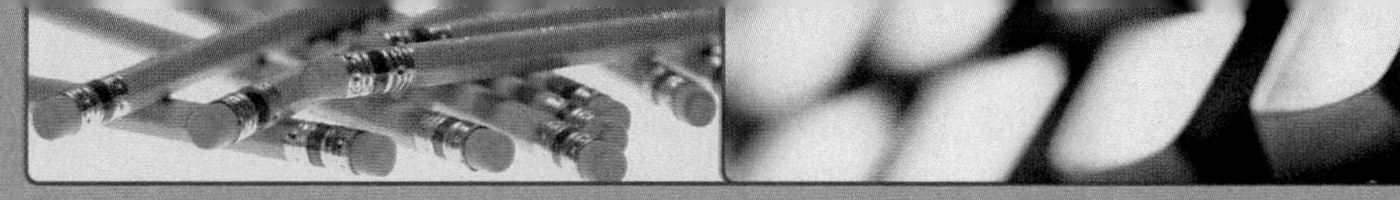

1. PREWRITE

Choosing Your Topic

An argumentative essay should be on a topic about which you feel strongly. Consider your school or community. What kinds of local issues affect you? What would you change? Is there something that might change that you would want to remain the same? Ask yourself questions to choose an appropriate and interesting topic for your argumentative essay.

1. Does this topic interest a lot of people?
2. How do I feel about this topic?
3. Can I find enough information on the topic?
4. Is this topic debatable?

The answers to these questions will help you determine if you can and should write about a particular topic. Use the questions to explore a variety of topics.

Gathering Information

Once you have your topic, gather details about it. For instance, if your topic is on the use of cell phones in school, gather facts and examples to support your position. Finding out as much information as possible on your topic will help strengthen your position and help you anticipate counterarguments. Note that your original position on the topic may change as you gather more and more information. This is acceptable. Just be sure that you have enough evidence to support your position. You may want to use a graphic organizer like this one to help you write.

Cell Phones in School

Pros	Cons
• helpful in an emergency	• distracting
• keeps parents informed of students' whereabouts	• some students use them to play games or cheat
• convenient	•
•	

Keep in mind that if your pros and cons are nearly equal in number, you may not be able to make a strong argument. Revise your topic as necessary to make sure you can argue convincingly for one side or the other.

Determining Your Thesis Statement

Once you choose a topic and gather enough information, determine your thesis. Your purpose is to persuade your audience of your position, so be sure your thesis is an opinion statement that can be supported logically. See the example below.

It is important that students be allowed to have cell phones in school, as long as they use them responsibly.

2. DRAFT

Organizing Ideas

Review the information you gathered to write your essay. Organize your ideas to make your meaning clear and to present a convincing argument to your audience. A logical organization pattern for an argumentative essay is **order of importance.** For example, you might state your most important point first to draw in your reader. Or you might choose to begin with a less important point and save your strongest point for the end. Stating your most important point last leaves your audience with a strong impression of your argument. Determine which order better fits your argument.

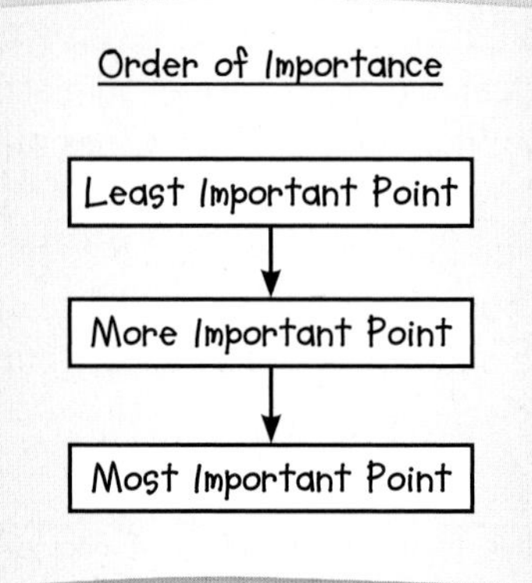

Putting Your Thoughts on Paper

An essay has three basic parts: an introduction, a body, and a conclusion. Create a plan for your argumentative essay like the one on the right. Use your organizational plan as you begin drafting.

Begin with an effective introduction. Remember, you want to grab your reader's attention right away. The opening of your essay should make your reader want to pay close attention to what you have written about the topic. As you draft your essay, remember it is only the first draft. Write your thoughts and refine them later. Record your main ideas and supporting evidence and organize these ideas in a logical and effective way. You can fix errors in grammar, spelling, and punctuation later.

Introduction

- Grab the reader's attention right away with an interesting opener.
- State the position in a clear thesis.

Body

- In the topic sentence of each body paragraph, state a reason or main point.
- In supporting sentences, give supporting evidence.
- Anticipate and respond to counterarguments.

Conclusion

- Restate the thesis in a new way.
- Add an insight.

Addressing Counterarguments

In argumentative essays, writers use various techniques to convince an audience of their point of view or position on a topic. One method is to anticipate potential counterarguments and to respond to them. When a writer does this, he or she shows that both sides of the argument have been considered. The writer should show through supportive facts and details why his or her point of view should be seen as the correct one.

When addressing a counterargument, keep your audience in mind. Try to anticipate opposing points, address them, and point out the flaws in those arguments. Keep your tone respectful, but make your position clear. Your goal is to show your audience that your position is the most logical one.

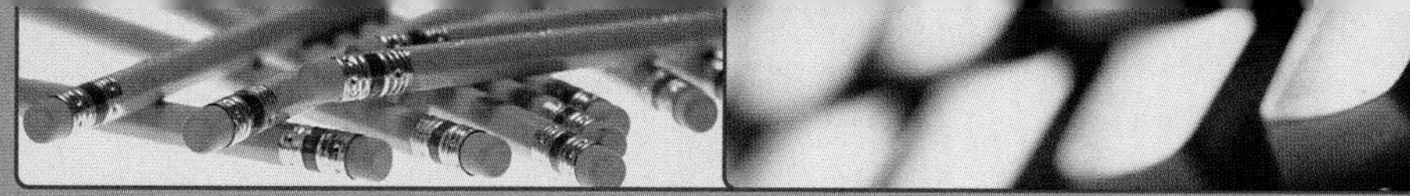

3. REVISE

Evaluating Your Draft

Read over your draft and note strengths and weaknesses. Correct these as best you can. To get a better evaluation, conduct a **peer review** with a classmate. Have him or her look over what you have written and discuss ways you can improve your paper. Use the Revising Checklist.

Below is part of a draft. The annotations to the right indicate the reasons for the revisions.

Revising Checklist

- ☐ Does the introduction grab the reader's attention?
- ☐ Does the thesis present the argument?
- ☐ Is there a clear organizational pattern?
- ☐ Is the thesis supported with evidence?

Imagine you are at school after hours. Practice ran long, and the last bus has gone. You have no phone. No one has a phone. The school is locked and it's getting late. What do you do? By now, most of the school knows about the new rule the school board is considering that would ban all cell phone use for students. If passed, this decision would make the school less safe for students. The school board is making a ~~ridiculous~~ *hasty* decision based on a few minor incidents. *It is important that students be allowed to have cell phones in school, as long as they use them responsibly.*

Grab the audience's attention in the introduction.

Maintain a respectful tone.

Include a clear thesis statement.

Many students are involved in after-school activities. Though the school has a reliable bus service, sometimes activities run long. The buses run on a schedule, and if students miss the final bus, they are stuck. *With a cell phone, students can call a parent or other adult to pick them up or give them permission to go to a friend's house.* Cell phones offer that convenience and that added protection. Parents feel better knowing that their children can keep in touch.

Use reasons and evidence to support the argument.

4. EDIT AND PROOFREAD

Focus: Parallel Structure

When sentences or parts of a sentence are **parallel,** they have the same grammatical structure. For example, all verbs are in the same tense. Parallel structure makes ideas clearer and can add impact or emphasis to your writing. Note the correction below.

Not parallel:
Whether a student walks to school, rides the bus, or will get a ride, a cell phone can come in handy.

Corrected:
Whether a student walks to school, rides the bus, or gets a ride, a cell phone can come in handy.

Reread your draft and edit it to make like ideas parallel. In argumentative writing, parallel structure is an effective way to emphasize points and help make them memorable to your audience.

Focus: Comparative and Superlative

There are three forms of adjectives and adverbs: positive, comparative, and superlative. The form of an adjective or adverb is often changed to show the degree to which a certain quality is present.

In the sentence *Cell phones are an important part of life,* the word *important* is used in the **positive form.** It focuses on one thing—cell phones—without comparing them to anything else.

To use the **comparative form,** two things need to be compared, as in *Cell phones are more important than gym shoes.* Cell phones and gym shoes are being compared. The word *more* is used with the word *important* to show this comparison.

The **superlative form** compares three or more things, such as in *Cell phones are the most important items a student can carry.* The use of the word *most* with the word *important* compares cell phones with everything else a student can carry.

Most adjectives and adverbs that have one syllable, and some that have two syllables, form their comparative and superlative degrees by adding *-er* or *-est.* Other two-syllable modifiers and all modifiers of more than two syllables use *more* and *most.*

Proofreading

Correct Final Errors The purpose of proofreading is to find errors you have made in punctuation, grammar, capitalization, and spelling. Use proofreader's marks to highlight any errors. (See the Language Arts Handbook, section 4.1, for a list of proofreader's symbols.)

5. PUBLISH AND PRESENT

Final Draft

Submit Your Work Rewrite your essay to make a final draft. If it is handwritten, make sure the essay is neat and legible. If you are using a word processing program, double-space your paper and use a readable font or typeface. Whether you are submitting your work to your teacher or someone else, be sure to check about presentation guidelines.

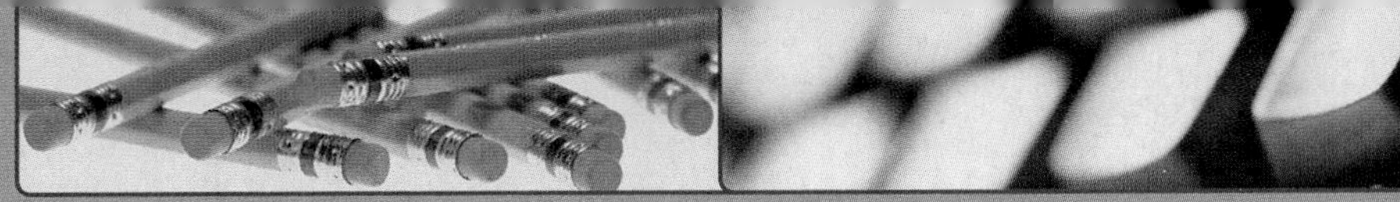

Student Model

Cell Phones for Students
by Kyla Weatherspoon

Imagine you are at school after hours. Practice ran long, and the last bus has gone. You have no phone. No one has a phone. The school is locked and it's getting late. What do you do? By now, most of the school knows about the new rule the school board is considering that would ban all cell phone use for students. If passed, this decision would make the school less safe for students. The school board is making a hasty decision based on a few minor incidents. Cell phones are important to our health and welfare. It is important that students be allowed to have cell phones in school, as long as they use them responsibly.

Includes an attention-grabbing opener

States the position in a clear thesis

Many students are involved in after-school activities. Though the school has a reliable bus service, sometimes activities run long. The buses run on a schedule, and if students miss the final bus, they are stuck. With a cell phone, students can call a parent or other adult to pick them up or give them permission to go to a friend's house. Cell phones offer that convenience and that added protection. Parents feel better knowing that their children can keep in touch.

Cell phones are also good to have in case of an emergency. Whether a student walks to school, rides the bus, or gets a ride, a cell phone can come in handy. Things can happen when you least expect them. We live in a state that gets a lot of snow in the winter. Sometimes buses get stuck or break down due to the weather. Having a cell phone allows students to call for help or let a parent or guardian know they will not be returning home on time. If there is a problem at school, many parents appreciate a call from their children telling them that they are okay. If there is an emergency at home, parents can leave a text or voice message for their children and let them know any change of plans.

States main points in a logical order

Includes reasons, facts, and examples to support the argument

Cell phones can be distracting during class, and some students use them to play games or even cheat on tests. Yet, instead of banning cell phone use entirely, the school board could make and enforce rules regarding when and where cell phones can be used. This would prevent the negative uses of cell phones, while allowing them to keep students safe.

Responds to a counterargument

Maintains a respectful tone

Banning cell phones altogether seems like the wrong direction to take. If used responsibly, cell phones can keep students safe. Before the school board makes a decision that could have negative consequences, it should consider a plan that works for everyone.

Sums up main points and adds additional insight

Giving and Actively Listening to Persuasive Presentations

Think of a time when you discussed a controversial issue with a friend or family member. Did you take a position that others disagreed with? How did you try to convince others that your position was correct? In a **persuasive presentation,** you try to influence an audience's beliefs about an issue. When you give and actively listen to persuasive presentations, you participate in an exchange of ideas and attempt to gain support for your perspective.

Planning a Persuasive Presentation

Choose a Topic What particular topic do you feel strongly about? Is there more than one perspective on this topic or issue? Is it controversial? Take time to think through a topic you would like to discuss with an audience. For example, do you feel strongly about the building of a new gymnasium? Should a dog park be built in your neighborhood? Do you think your district should have year-round school or a shorter school week? Select a topic that is of interest to you and about which you can present evidence in support of your claims.

Examine Both Sides Once you select an issue to present, consider as many different perspectives on the issue as possible. Try to anticipate objections to your position that others may raise when you give your presentation. These objections are known as **counterarguments.** Once you have established some counterarguments, consider how you will address them. It may be helpful to make a chart. For example, look at this chart on the issue of a new park.

The Need for a Park

Counterargument	Response
Too many kids in area	Young people good for the community
Dangerous activity	Safe place to play
Young children on equipment	Minimum age limit
Park not regulated	Rules and regulations enforced

Evaluate Evidence and Audience During your presentation, you must appear knowledgeable about your topic. Introduce facts, anecdotes, quotations, and other research in support of your opinions. As you present this information, avoid jargon, or specialized vocabulary with which your audience may not be familiar. Be prepared to answer questions about the information you present.

Avoid Fallacies A **fallacy** is an untruth, an exaggeration of the truth, or an example of faulty logic. A persuasive presentation may present facts, but it is your opinion and interpretation of those facts that you use to convince others. Be careful of using generalizations. When you use words such as *all, everyone, no one,* and *anybody*, you are making a generalization. Generalizations are often misleading. Examine your presentation prior to delivering it and eliminate these kinds of statements.

Evaluating Your Persuasive Presentation

Work with a partner or a peer group to evaluate your persuasive presentations. Provide feedback to each other on what was done well and what still needs work. Continue to be constructive in your comments, offering helpful criticism in a polite and respectful way. Follow the listening and speaking rubrics on this page in order to evaluate each persuasive presentation.

Delivering Your Persuasive Presentation

Begin your presentation with a strong opener. You might begin with a question, a quotation, a visual demonstration, or an interesting anecdote or fact. Sometimes the repetition of a key word or phrase can help keep your audience involved with the main idea of your presentation.

Close with a brief powerful statement to leave your audience something to think about long after you have ended your presentation. You want your point of view to become the point of view of your audience.

Active Listening Active listening is just as important as effective speaking. Pay attention to what the speaker says and react politely, asking questions when appropriate.

Speaking Rubric

Your presentation will be evaluated on these elements:

Content

- ☐ ideas were clearly presented
- ☐ viewpoint was easily understood
- ☐ valid arguments were presented
- ☐ strong opening and closing were included

Delivery and Presentation

- ☐ convincing persuasive techniques
- ☐ effective nonverbal expression
- ☐ appropriate volume and pacing

Listening Rubric

As a peer reviewer or audience member, you should do the following:

- ☐ listen quietly and attentively
- ☐ maintain eye contact with speaker
- ☐ ask appropriate questions
- ☐ (as peer reviewer) provide constructive feedback

Test Practice Workshop

Writing Skills

Argumentative Essay

Read the following short excerpt and the writing assignment that follows. Before you begin writing, think carefully about what task the assignment is asking you to perform. Then create an outline to help guide your writing.

from *Braille: The Early Life of Louis Braille* by Lola H. and Coleman A. Jennings

CHARACTERS: LOUIS BRAILLE, a young blind boy who wants to learn to read
BARBIER: Inventor of sonography, a system that represents sounds with dots and dashes punched in paper

LOUIS. I am honored to meet the inventor of sonography.
BARBIER. Ahhh! Then, you have learned my system...and you find it helpful?
LOUIS. *[Hesitantly.]* I think it is a good beginning, Captain...You have done the blind a great service with your invention. But it's very complicated...Each sound is written with too many dots and dashes. It's hard to feel them. And when you write, punching so many dots makes writing very slow...
BARBIER. *[Getting angry.]* This is a note-making system. You don't need periods, commas, and question marks when you write short messages.
LOUIS. But sir, we need a system that we can use for books, too.
BARBIER. Since when have the blind needed to read books? *[Crossing to* PIGNIER.*]* Are these the hopes you encourage in this school, Headmaster Pignier? I thought you were here to teach trades to the blind. *[To Louis.]* Is there anything else?
LOUIS. *[Reluctantly.]* I...can't find a way to write numbers so we can do arithmetic.
BARBIER. *[Exploding.]* I suppose now you want to be bookkeepers! Foolish child, you do sums in your head. Any number too large for that is not for the blind to be concerned with. Good day, young man! *[Starts to exit.]*

Assignment: Barbier believed that the blind should accept their limitations and not aspire to the same things "normal" people do. Plan and write an **argumentative essay** in which you state and support a **thesis** about the value of encouraging all people to succeed. Include **persuasive techniques** and **rhetorical devices,** as well as **counterarguments.**

Revising and Editing Skills

The following passage is a draft of a student's essay. The passage contains grammatical and other errors that require correction. Some questions require you to correct specific sentences. Others ask you to identify parts of the essay or to improve the overall organization. Answer each question on a separate sheet of paper.

(1) Drama is a literary form involve dialogue that characters perform. (2) A script contains dialogue spoken by the characters, as well as stage directions. (3) The written text of a drama is called a *script*. (4) One purpose of a script's stage directions is to state clearly what actors should do. (5) Stage directions often include descriptions of the setting; descriptions of the characters' appearance; and directions on how a character should act or move. (6) Stage directions are useful for three things—to visualize a scene, to stage a drama, and to instruct actors. (7) There are two main types of drama. (8) Comedies are humorous plays that end happily. (9) Tragedies, in which the central characters meet an unhappy or disastrous end.

1. Which of the following is the *best* revision of sentence 1?

- **A.** Drama is a literary form; involve dialogue that characters perform.
- **B.** Drama is a literary form involving dialogue that characters perform.
- **C.** Drama is a literary form, involve dialogue that characters perform.
- **D.** Drama is a literary form to involve dialogue that characters perform.
- **E.** Drama is a literary form: involve dialogue that characters perform.

2. What change should be made to sentence 2 to improve the paragraph's organization?

- **A.** Sentence 2 could be moved to the end of the paragraph.
- **B.** Sentence 2 could be removed.
- **C.** Sentence 2 could be moved after sentence 3.
- **D.** Sentence 2 could be moved after sentence 6.
- **E.** Sentence 2 could be moved to the start of the paragraph.

3. The semicolons in sentence 5 should be replaced with

- **A.** hyphens.
- **B.** periods.
- **C.** dashes.
- **D.** commas.
- **E.** colons.

4. The dash in sentence 6 should be replaced with a

- **A.** hyphen.
- **B.** period.
- **C.** semicolon.
- **D.** question mark.
- **E.** colon.

5. What error appears in sentence 9?

- **A.** The sentence is a run-on.
- **B.** The sentence is a fragment.
- **C.** The sentence uses incorrect end punctuation.
- **D.** The sentence lacks a semicolon.
- **E.** The sentence lacks subject-verb agreement.

6. What change could be made to improve the overall organization of the paragraph?

- **A.** Move sentence 5 to a separate paragraph.
- **B.** Move sentence 1 to the end of the paragraph.
- **C.** Move sentence 2 to a separate paragraph.
- **D.** Remove sentence 3.
- **E.** Move sentences 7, 8, and 9 to a separate paragraph.

Reading Skills

Carefully read the following passage. Then on a separate piece of paper, answer each question.

from *The Ugly Duckling* by A. A. Milne

CHARACTERS
THE KING
THE QUEEN
THE PRINCESS CAMILLA
THE CHANCELLOR
DULCIBELLA
PRINCE SIMON
CARLO

[The scene is the Throne Room of the Palace; a room of many doors, or, if preferred, curtain-openings: simply furnished with three thrones for Their Majesties and Her Royal Highness the PRINCESS CAMILLA*—in other words, with three handsome chairs. At each side is a long seat: reserved, as it might be, for His Majesty's Council (if any), but useful, as today, for other purposes. The* KING *is asleep on his throne with a handkerchief over his face. He is a king of any country from any storybook, in whatever costume you please. But he should be wearing his crown.]*

A VOICE. *[Announcing.]* His Excellency the Chancellor! *[The* CHANCELLOR*, an elderly man in hornrimmed spectacles, enters, bowing. The* KING *wakes up with a start and removes the handkerchief from his face.]*

KING. *[With simple dignity.]* I was thinking.

CHANCELLOR. *[Bowing.]* Never, Your Majesty, was greater need for thought than now.

KING. That's what I was thinking. *[He struggles into a more dignified position.]* Well, what is it? More trouble?

CHANCELLOR. What we might call the old trouble, Your Majesty.

KING. It's what I was saying last night to the Queen. "Uneasy lies the head that wears a crown," was how I put it.

CHANCELLOR. A profound and original thought, which may well go down to posterity.

KING. You mean it may go down well with posterity. I hope so. Remind me to tell you some time of another little thing I said to Her Majesty: something about a fierce light beating on a throne. Posterity would like that, too. Well, what is it?

CHANCELLOR. It is in the matter of Her Royal Highness's wedding.

KING. Oh...yes.

CHANCELLOR. As Your Majesty is aware, the young Prince Simon arrives today to seek Her Royal Highness's hand in marriage. He has been traveling in distant lands and, as I understand, has not—er—has not—

KING. You mean he hasn't heard anything.

CHANCELLOR. It is a little difficult to put this tactfully, Your Majesty.

KING. Do your best, and I will tell you afterwards how you got on.

CHANCELLOR. Let me put it this way. The Prince Simon will naturally assume that Her Royal Highness has the customary—so customary as to be, in my own poor opinion, slightly monotonous—has what one might call the inevitable—so inevitable as to be, in my opinion again, almost mechanical—will assume, that she has the, as I think of it, faultily faultless, icily regular, splendidly—

KING. What you are trying to say in the fewest words possible is that my daughter is not beautiful.

CHANCELLOR. Her beauty is certainly elusive, Your Majesty.

1. Lines 1–8 are an example of
   A. plot.
   B. setting.
   C. cast list.
   D. stage directions.
   E. dialogue.
2. Lines 9–21 are an example of
   A. setting.
   B. monologue.
   C. dialogue.
   D. stage directions.
   E. cast list.
3. What is the tone of the exchange between the King and the Chancellor in lines 27–33?
   A. humorous
   B. angry
   C. serious
   D. sad
   E. solemn
4. Lines 33–40 are an example of
   A. setting.
   B. monologue.
   C. dialogue.
   D. stage directions.
   E. cast list.
5. Based on the context, what does the word *posterity* in line 40 mean?
   A. the past
   B. future generations
   C. books
   D. present day
   E. friends
6. What is the tone of lines 50–55?
   A. jolly
   B. peaceful
   C. self-assured
   D. angry
   E. hesitant
7. Based on the context, what does the word *tactfully* in line 57 mean?
   A. quiet
   B. full of confusion
   C. full of humor
   D. showing meanness
   E. showing sensitivity
8. What conflict is introduced in this passage?
   A. the Chancellor's anger
   B. the King's restlessness
   C. the Princess's disappearance
   D. the arrival of the Prince
   E. the Chancellor's plot against the King
9. This excerpt is most likely drawn from the
   A. exposition.
   B. rising action and resolution.
   C. rising action and climax.
   D. climax.
   E. falling action and resolution.
10. Which of the following *best* describes this play?
   A. tragedy
   B. Shakespearean drama
   C. comedy
   D. straight drama
   E. Greek tragedy

Unit 8

Seeking Wisdom

Folk Literature

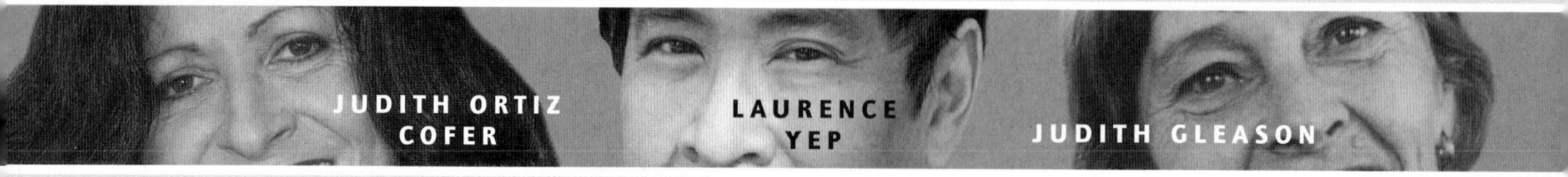

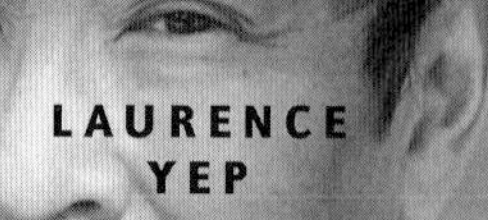

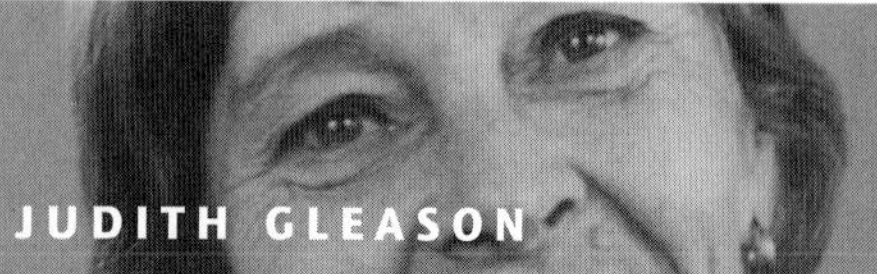

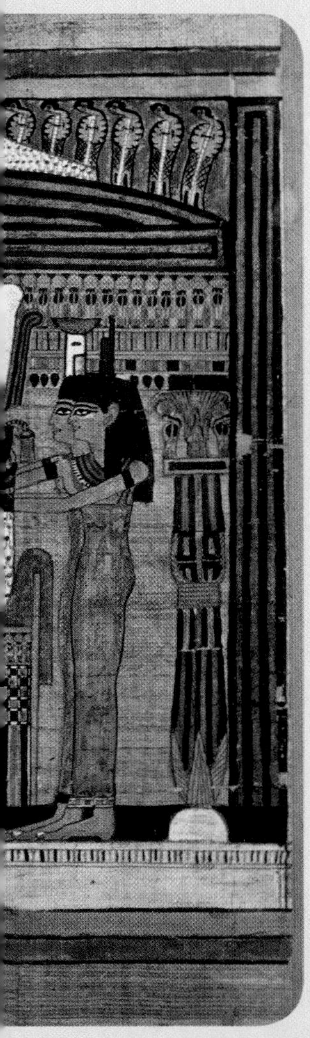

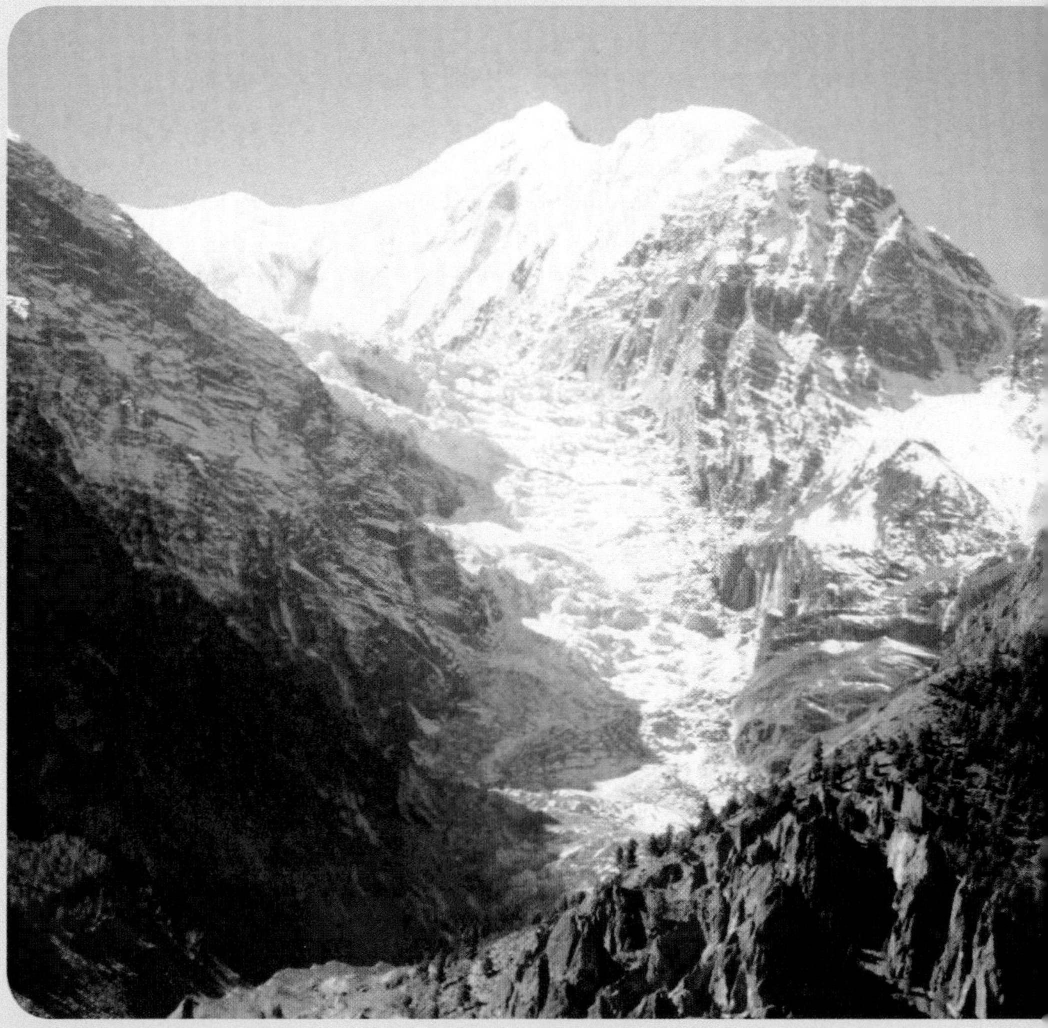

"He could never bear to be beaten, even if he must risk his life in some rash way to win."

—OLIVIA E. COOLIDGE, "Phaëthon, Son of Apollo"

Think of some of your favorite stories. What lessons do they teach? In Olivia E. Coolidge's retelling of the Greek myth "Phaëthon, Son of Apollo," Phaëthon insists on driving his father's chariot, even though he is not ready. Phaëthon's pride leads to disaster. As you read the tales, fables, and myths in this unit, try to determine what wisdom each story offers.

JOSEPH CAMPBELL
ZORA NEALE HURSTON
R. K. NARAYAN

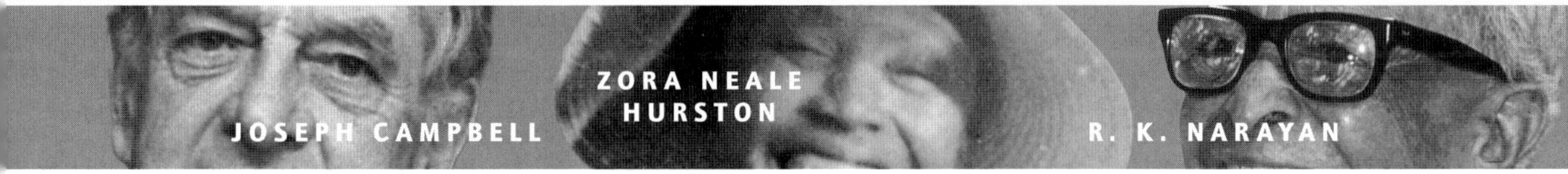

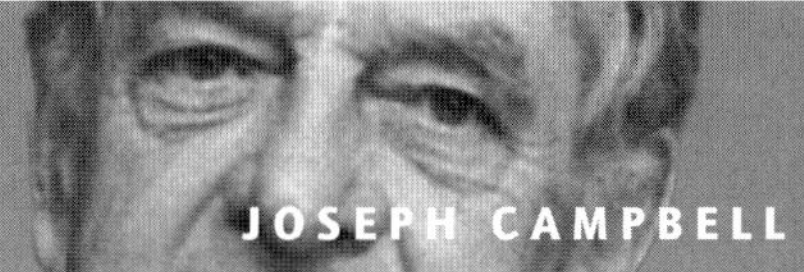

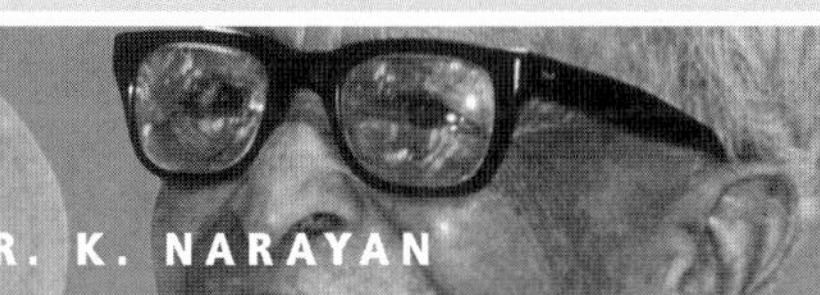

Introduction to Folk Literature

Long before people invented writing, they were telling stories, reciting poetry, and singing songs about their beliefs, dreams, and experiences. Much of this material formed part of the **folk literature,** the works, ideas, or customs of a culture passed by word of mouth from generation to generation. Eventually, many of these stories, poems, and songs were written down and have become part of world literature. Works in folk literature or the *oral traditions* of peoples around the world include myths, legends, folk tales, fairy tales, and fables.

Myths

What is happening in the following passage?

> Demeter ran about searching for her lost daughter, and all nature grieved with her. Flowers wilted, trees lost their leaves, and the fields grew barren and cold. In vain did the plow cut through the icy ground; nothing could sprout and nothing could grow while the goddess of the harvest wept. People and animals starved and the gods begged Demeter again to bless the earth. But she refused to let anything grow until she had found her daughter.
>
> — INGRI AND EDGAR PARIN D'AULAIRE, "Persephone and Demeter"

In this passage, nothing will grow because the goddess of the harvest has lost her child. The passage is part of a Greek myth. A **myth** is a traditional story that usually presents supernatural events involving gods and heroes.

The myths of the classical world, which includes both the Greeks and the Romans, are usually the most well known to Western audiences. However, nearly all cultures have created their own body of myths, gods, and goddesses.

Types of Myths

There are many kinds of myths. Three common and widespread types are creation myths, origin myths, and hero myths. A *creation myth* tells how the world and human beings came to exist. An *origin myth,* or nature myth, is a story that explains objects or events in the natural world. Ingri and Edgar Parin d'Aulaire's "Persephone and Demeter" (page 727) is a Greek origin myth. A *hero myth* tells of the deeds and adventures of a hero. The plots of hero myths often involve battles with monsters and the adventurous journeys known as *quests.* Olivia Coolidge's "Phaëthon, Son of Apollo" (page 770) is a Greek hero myth. A type of story related to the myth is the legend. A *legend* is a traditional story that is popularly thought of as historical but lacks evidence to verify that the events occurred. Stories about the Trojan War and King Arthur are legends.

Replica of the legendary Trojan Horse. During the Trojan War, Greek soldiers hid in the horse to enter the city of Troy secretly.

Many legends begin as *oral histories,* or stories that are passed from generation to generation orally. Oral histories are not written down and may change with time, often gaining or losing plot or other story elements. "Tsali of the Cherokees" (page 747) is an example of oral history.

The Value of Myths

Every early culture around the world created its own myths. Learning about these myths can help you better understand the cultures that produced them. Examining myths provides an effective way to compare and contrast the beliefs and values of different cultures. Understanding myths can also help you better understand your own culture. Characters, events, and ideas from myths often appear in contemporary literature. Words derived from mythological characters and places also appear in modern English. Becoming familiar with myths from around the world will help you identify these references in other works and in everyday life.

The Little Mermaid (illustration), c. 1900. Eddie J. Andrews.

Folk Tales and Fables

Folk tales are stories passed by word of mouth from generation to generation. Although the term *folk tale* is often used to refer to any type of story in folk literature, it also refers specifically to stories that could have taken place anywhere and at any time and that are considered anonymous (created by an unknown person). "Hansel and Gretel" and "Little Red Riding Hood" are two well-known folk tales. Folk tales, like myths, can be filled with supernatural events and creatures. Often, seemingly regular people will encounter magical beings or go on adventures that introduce them to otherworldly places and characters.

Trickster Tales

One common type of folk tale is the **trickster tale.** The trickster character, which can be a human or an animal with speech and other human traits, has two sides. Tricksters frequently cause trouble, but they are also clever and creative. Judith Gleason's "Eshu" (page 733), a Yoruban folk tale, is an example of a trickster tale. Like myths, folk tales sometimes offer explanations for features of the natural world. Zora Neale Hurston's retelling of the African-American folk tale, "How the Snake Got Poison" (page 803), is an example of such a folk tale.

Fables

A **fable** is a brief story that frequently includes animal characters and a moral. The stories of the ancient Greek writer known as Aesop are the most famous fables in Western literature. "The Fox and the Crow" (page 765) is one of Aesop's fables.

Little Red Riding Hood (illustration), c. 19th century. Charles Robinson.

Folk Literature Close Reading Model

BEFORE READING

Build Background
Apply two types of background to read myths, fables, and folk tales effectively. One type is the story's literary and cultural context. Read the **Build Background** and **Meet the Author** features to get this information. The other type of background is the personal knowledge and experience you bring to your reading.

Set Purpose
Folk literature presents characters and actions to say something about life. Read **Set Purpose** to decide what you want to get out of the story.

Analyze Literature
Folk literature includes literary techniques, such as plot and setting, to create meaning. The **Analyze Literature** feature draws your attention to key literary elements.

Use Reading Skills
The **Use Reading Skills** feature will show you skills to help you get the most out of your reading. Identify a graphic organizer to help you apply the skill before and while you read.

DURING READING

Use Reading Strategies
- **Ask questions** about things that seem significant or interesting.
- **Make predictions** about what's going to happen next. As you read, gather more clues to confirm or change your prediction.
- **Visualize** the story. Form pictures in your mind to help you see the characters, actions, and settings.
- **Make inferences,** or educated guesses, about what is not stated directly.
- **Clarify,** or check that you understand, what you read. Reread any difficult parts.

Analyze Literature
What literary elements stand out? Are the characters vivid and interesting? Is there a lesson or moral? As you read, consider how these elements affect your enjoyment and understanding of the story.

Make Connections
Notice where connections can be made between the story and your life or another story, myth, or legend. What feelings or thoughts do you have while reading the story?

AFTER READING

Find Meaning
Recall the important details of the story, such as the sequence of events and character traits. Use this information to help **interpret**, or explain, the meaning of the story.

Make Judgments
- **Analyze** the text by examining details and deciding what they contribute to the meaning.
- **Evaluate** the text by making judgments about how the author creates meaning.

Analyze Literature
Review how the use of literary elements increases your understanding of the story. For example, if the story includes dialogue, how does it help shape the story's meaning?

Extend Understanding
Go beyond the text by exploring the story through writing or other creative projects.

Apply the Model

BEFORE READING

DURING READING

AFTER READING

Persephone and Demeter

A Greek Myth retold by Ingri and Edgar Parin d'Aulaire

GUIDED READING

Build Background

Cultural Context As long as nine thousand years ago, civilizations existed in the lands around the Aegean Sea, in present-day Greece and Turkey. Architecture and arts such as sculpture, pottery, and music flourished in these societies. The literature of that time was passed on by word of mouth, and many stories were told about the Greek pantheon of gods and goddesses.

Reader's Context Think about your own relationships. What friend or family member cheers you up? What qualities make that person so special?

Set Purpose

Preview the vocabulary words and footnotes. Then skim for other unfamiliar words and look them up.

Analyze Literature

Myth A traditional story that usually presents supernatural events involving gods and heroes is called a **myth.** There are many different kinds of myths. An *origin myth,* like "Persephone and Demeter," is a story that explains the existence of things or events in the natural world. As you read "Persephone and Demeter," determine what real-world phenomena it explains.

Use Reading Skills

Monitor Comprehension
One good method for monitoring your comprehension is to pose questions about the text. As you read, ask yourself: What have I learned about Greek myth? To what characters, events, settings, and ideas have I been introduced? Use a K-W-L chart to record your ideas.

What I Know	What I Want to Know	What I Learned
Persephone and Demeter were Greek goddesses.		

Meet the Authors

Authors and illustrators **Ingri d'Aulaire** (1904–1980) and **Edgar Parin d'Aulaire** (1898–1986) met in Germany. Ingri was from a large Norwegian family. Edgar, the son of two artists, grew up in Switzerland. The couple moved to the United States in 1929 and collaborated on their first children's book two years later. The collections of Greek and Norse myths that they published in the 1960s remain popular today.

Preview Vocabulary

yawn•ing (yô´ niŋ) *adj.,* wide open

root (rüt) *v.,* dig in the ground

cleft (kleft) *n.,* space made when something breaks open

a•veng•ing (ə venj´ iŋ) *adj.,* taking revenge or punishing someone for something

bar•ren (ber´ ən) *adj.,* unable to reproduce or bear fruit; desolate

ra•di•ant (rā´ dē ənt) *adj.,* shining bright

Persephone and Demeter

The Rape of Persephone by Hades, c. 19th century. English School. Bibliothèque des Arts Décoratifs, Paris.

A Greek Myth retold by Ingri and Edgar Parin d'Aulaire

At the reins stood grim Hades.

Persephone grew up on Olympus[1] and her gay laughter rang through the brilliant halls. She was the daughter of Demeter, goddess of the harvest, and her mother loved her so dearly she could not bear to have her out of her sight. When Demeter sat on her golden throne her daughter was always on her lap; when she went down to earth to look after her trees and fields, she took Persephone. Wherever Persephone danced on her light feet, flowers sprang up. She was so lovely and full of grace that even Hades,[2] who saw so little, noticed her and fell in love with her. He wanted her for his queen, but he knew that her mother would never consent to part with her, so he decided to carry her off.

DURING READING

Use Reading Skills
Monitor Comprehension
Why does Hades decide to kidnap Persephone?

One day as Persephone ran about in the meadow gathering flowers, she strayed away from her mother and the attending nymphs.[3] Suddenly, the ground split open and up from the yawning crevice came a dark chariot drawn by black horses. At the reins stood grim Hades. He seized the terrified girl, turned his horses, and plunged back into the ground. A herd of pigs rooting in the meadow tumbled into the cleft, and Persephone's cries for help died out as the ground closed again as suddenly as it had opened. Up in the field, a little swineherd[4] stood and wept over the pigs he had lost, while Demeter rushed wildly about in the meadow, looking in vain for her daughter, who had vanished without leaving a trace.

yawn • ing (yô´ niŋ) *adj.*, wide open

root (rüt) *v.*, dig in the ground

cleft (kleft) *n.*, space made when something breaks open

With the frightened girl in his arms, Hades raced his snorting horses down away from the sunlit world. Down and down they sped on the dark path to his dismal underground palace. He led weeping Persephone in, seated her beside him on a throne of black marble, and decked her with gold and precious stones. But the jewels brought her no joy. She wanted no cold stones. She longed for warm sunshine and flowers and her golden-tressed[5] mother.

DURING READING

Make Connections
How does Persephone feel about Hades's riches? How would you feel if you were in her place?

Dead souls crowded out from cracks and crevices to look at their new queen, while ever more souls came across the Styx[6] and Persephone watched them drink from a spring under dark poplars. It was the spring of Lethe,[7] and those who drank from its waters forgot who they were and what they had done on earth.

---

1. **Olympus.** Mountain in what is now Thessaly, Greece, where the ancient Greeks believed most gods lived
2. **Hades.** God of the underworld; sometimes the name *Hades* is used for the underworld itself
3. **nymphs.** Minor female goddesses who live in natural spots like forests or trees, rivers, and streams
4. **swineherd.** Person who keeps or tends pigs
5. **golden-tressed.** Having golden hair (tresses); blond
6. **Styx.** Main river of the underworld, which surrounds it and separates it from the world of the living
7. **Lethe.** River of forgetfulness

a•veng•ing (ə venj´ iŋ) *adj.*, taking revenge or punishing someone for something

bar•ren (ber´ ən) *adj.*, unable to reproduce or bear fruit; desolate

DURING READING

Use Reading Skills
Monitor Comprehension Why does Demeter's grief have an effect on nature?

DURING READING

Use Reading Skills
Monitor Comprehension How does Demeter find out what happened to Persephone?

Rhadamanthus, a judge of the dead, dealt out punishment to the souls of great sinners. They were sentenced to suffer forever under the whips of the avenging Erinyes.[8] Heroes were led to the Elysian fields,[9] where they lived happily forever in never-failing light.

Around the palace of Hades there was a garden where whispering poplars and weeping willows grew. They had no flowers and bore no fruit and no birds sang in their branches. There was only one tree in the whole realm of Hades that bore fruit. That was a little pomegranate[10] tree. The gardener of the underworld offered the tempting pomegranates to the queen, but Persephone refused to touch the food of the dead.

Wordlessly she walked through the garden at silent Hades' side and slowly her heart turned to ice.

Above, on earth, Demeter ran about searching for her lost daughter, and all nature grieved with her. Flowers wilted, trees lost their leaves, and the fields grew barren and cold. In vain did the plow cut through the icy ground; nothing could sprout and nothing could grow while the goddess of the harvest wept. People and animals starved and the gods begged Demeter again to bless the earth. But she refused to let anything grow until she had found her daughter.

Bent with grief, Demeter turned into a gray old woman. She returned to the meadow where Persephone had vanished and asked the sun if he had seen what had happened, but he said no, dark clouds had hidden his face that day. She wandered around the meadow and after a while she met a youth whose name was Triptolemus. He told her that his brother, a swineherd, had seen his pigs disappear into the ground and had heard the frightened screams of a girl.

Demeter now understood that Hades had kidnapped her daughter, and her grief turned to anger. She called to Zeus[11] and said that she would never again make the earth green if he did not command Hades to return Persephone. Zeus could not let the world

---

8. Erinyes. Three spirits of punishment
9. Elysian fields. Paradise
10. pomegranate. Round, red fruit with a hard rind
11. Zeus. King of the Greek gods

perish and he sent Hermes[12] down to Hades, bidding him to let Persephone go. Even Hades had to obey the orders of Zeus, and sadly he said farewell to his queen.

Joyfully, Persephone leaped to her feet, but as she was leaving with Hermes, a hooting laugh came from the garden. There stood the gardener of Hades, grinning. He pointed to a pomegranate from which a few of the kernels were missing. Persephone, lost in thought, had eaten the seeds, he said.

Then dark Hades smiled. He watched Hermes lead Persephone up to the bright world above. He knew that she must return to him, for she had tasted the food of the dead.

When Persephone again appeared on earth, Demeter sprang to her feet with a cry of joy and rushed to greet her daughter. No longer was she a sad old woman, but a radiant goddess. Again she blessed her fields and the flowers bloomed anew and the grain ripened.

ra•di•ant (rā´ dē ənt) *adj.,* shining bright

"Dear child," she said, "never again shall we be parted. Together we shall make all nature bloom." But joy soon was changed to sadness, for Persephone had to admit that she had tasted the food of the dead and must return to Hades. However, Zeus decided that mother and daughter should not be parted forever. He ruled that Persephone had to return to Hades and spend one month in the underworld for each seed she had eaten.

Every year, when Persephone left her, Demeter grieved, nothing grew, and there was winter on earth. But as soon as her daughter's light footsteps were heard, the whole earth burst into bloom. Spring had come. As long as mother and daughter were together, the earth was warm and bore fruit.

DURING READING

Analyze Literature
Myth What is one natural phenomenon this myth attempts to explain?

Demeter was a kind goddess. She did not want mankind to starve during the cold months of winter when Persephone was away. She lent her chariot, laden with grain, to Triptolemus, the youth who had helped her to find her lost daughter. She told him to scatter her golden grain over the world and teach men how to sow it in spring and reap it in fall and store it away for the long months when again the earth was barren and cold. ✣

12. Hermes. Messenger god

When have you, like Demeter, experienced an emotion that changed your outlook on life? Was the emotion positive or negative? In what ways can emotions be both destructive and constructive?

Apply the Model

BEFORE READING

DURING READING

AFTER READING

Find Meaning

1. (a) What is it like in the underworld? (b) How is this different from the world above?
2. According to the myth, what happens to great sinners after they die? To heroes?
3. (a) How does Demeter react when Persephone is kidnapped? (b) In what ways is this similar to how a human mother would react?

Make Judgments

4. What do you think Hades's decision to kidnap Persephone says about his personality?
5. (a) Does Persephone's schedule at the end of the story seem fair to you? (b) How would you have settled the problem if you were Zeus?

Analyze Literature

Myth What aspects of the natural world and human experience are explained in the myth "Persephone and Demeter"? Create a two-column chart to document your ideas. In the first column, write the questions people might have had about their world, and in the second, write the details from the story that help to answer those questions.

Real-world Question	Myth's Explanation
What makes plants grow?	

Extend Understanding

Writing Options

Narrative Writing Imagine that you are a storyteller and you must recite the story of Persephone and Demeter. Write a **retelling** of the myth using modern characterizations, language, and imagery. Add dialogue to develop the characters. Recite your modernized myth to your classmates.

Argumentative Writing In "Persephone and Demeter," the goddess Demeter must appeal to Zeus to help save her daughter. Put yourself in Demeter's place and write a short **persuasive speech** to deliver to Zeus. A successful persuasive argument begins with a statement of the writer's position, followed by three or more reasons supporting that position.

Lifelong Learning

Find a Myth Choose an aspect of nature that is explained in "Persephone and Demeter." Then find a myth from another culture that explains the same thing. What are the similarities? The differences? Share your findings with the class.

Critical Literacy

Greek Myth Prepare a presentation about another Greek myth. Choose a myth that has something in common with "Persephone and Demeter." For example, you may wish to choose a myth that features Persephone. You could also focus on a different retelling of the same story. In your presentation, describe traits common to both myths. Which story do you prefer? Why?

Go to **www.mirrorsandwindows.com** for more.

Eshu

A Yoruban Folk Tale retold by Judith Gleason

Build Background

Cultural Context The Yoruba people live primarily in southwestern Nigeria, an area they settled about a thousand years ago. According to Yoruban tradition, Earth and heavens were created by a supreme being, Oludumare. Below him were several hundred minor deities, or Orisha, and among the most powerful of those was Eshu. He was not only a trickster—a traditional figure of mischief—but also the messenger who carried news from Earth to Oludumare.

Reader's Context When has a foolish argument threatened one of your friendships? How did you resolve the situation?

Set Purpose

Preview "Eshu," looking for unfamiliar terms. Write down any words and phrases you would like to investigate further.

Analyze Literature

Folk Tale Stories passed by word of mouth from generation to generation are **folk tales.** They often depict everyday activities and the adventures of common people. In addition, folk tales sometimes include gods and other supernatural characters. As you read, think about how "Eshu" depicts daily life in this community.

Use Reading Skills

Identify the Main Idea The main idea, or theme, is what the author wants you to know or think after reading a work. The main idea is often not stated outright. Readers need to examine supporting details of the dialogue, tone, description, plot, and characterization to identify the main idea. Create a main idea map to help you determine the main idea of "Eshu."

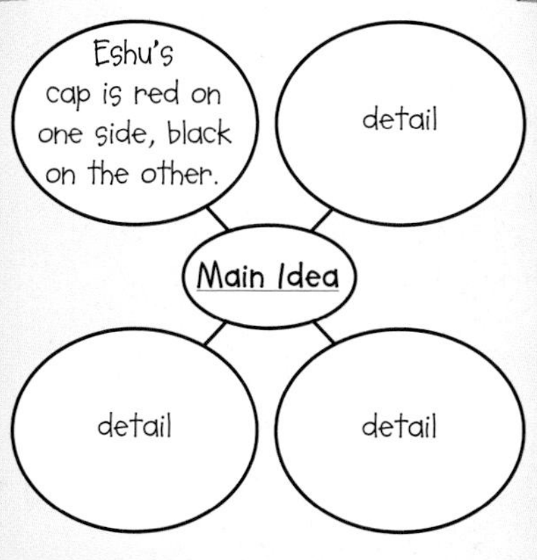

Meet the Author

Anthropologist **Judith Gleason** (1929–2012) was an expert in Yoruba culture. Since 1960, she was a practitioner of Santeria—a religion that evolved among Yoruban slaves in Cuba. Her books include the novel *Agotime: Her Legend* and an anthology of African praise poems, *Leaf and Bone.* The story of Eshu appeared in Orisha: *The Gods of Yorubaland.*

Preview Vocabulary

cour•te•ous (kʉr´ tē əs) *adj.*, polite; well mannered

re•tal•i•ate (ri ta´ lē āt') *v.*, respond to an action by doing a similar thing back, usually in a negative sense, such as repaying one injury by inflicting another

as•ton•ish•ing (ə stä´ ni shiŋ) *adj.*, amazing; very surprising

Eshu

A Yoruban Folk Tale
retold by
Judith Gleason

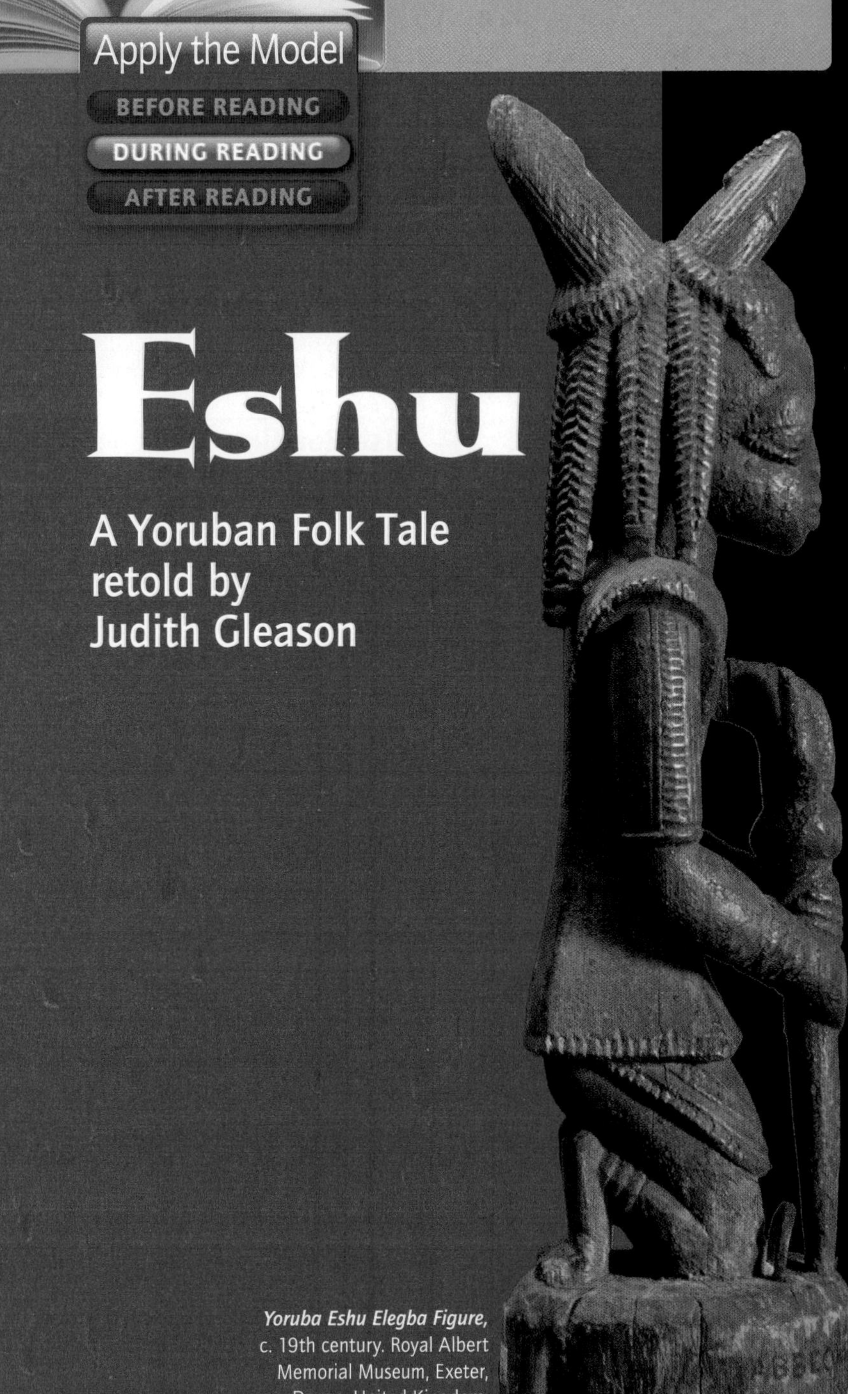

Yoruba Eshu Elegba Figure, c. 19th century. Royal Albert Memorial Museum, Exeter, Devon, United Kingdom.

There were two friends who loved each other like yam porridge and pepper soup.

> **DURING READING**
> **Use Reading Strategies**
> **Visualize** Picture the two friends' work plots. How are they arranged?

There were two friends who loved each other like yam porridge and pepper soup. Whenever they went out, they wore identical cloths. Their farm plots, thanks to the chief's respect for their friendship, were adjoining. The path to and from the village was all that divided them as they worked, and all day long they called across courteous greetings:

cour•te•ous (kʉr´ tē əs) *adj.*, polite; well mannered

"Good-day my very special friend, I hope the sun is not beating too hard upon your shoulders."

"Not at all, my dear age-mate; I salute you for working so steadily in the heat."

"May your soil yield even finer crops than mine."

"My compliments upon your new wife; may she bring forth sons to commend your industry."

"Salutations on the coming cool of the evening."

"May the sun not deceive you into lingering too late in the field."

And so on, as weaver bird[1] converses with weaver bird, these friends continued to embroider their amity.[2]

Until one day an old man walked down the path between them. It was Eshu. He was wearing a pointed cap, black on one side and red on the other. He held his pipe to the nape of his neck[3] and slung his stick over his shoulder so that it dangled down his back instead of over his chest as he usually carried it. The two friends answered his greeting, then went on with their work and thought no more about him until, late in the afternoon as they prepared to go home, one of them said, "I wonder what business that old man had in our village?"

"Whatever it was, he must have completed it quickly," said the other.

"How do you know?"

"Because he left before noon, don't you remember? Long before our wives brought out our dinners."

"True, he passed by midmorning," said the other, "but he was heading into the village, not out of it."

"Nonsense," said his friend, "he was going in the opposite direction, up country, not towards the village as you said. Perhaps you've confused him with another. This traveler was an old, old man with a stick slung over his shoulder. You know, the one who used to wear a black cap."

"Don't take that tone with me. I know precisely who he is, and today he looked exactly the same and, as always, his face was following his pipe bowl into our village."

"You looked at his pipe, but I saw his feet. For all we know, he may have been puffing through a hole in the back of his neck; but this much is clear: That old man in his brand new red hat was leaving our village farther and farther behind him."

DURING READING

Analyze Literature

Folk Tale What have you learned so far about daily life in this setting?

"I wonder what business that old man had in our village?"

---

1. **weaver bird.** Type of bird known for being very social and for making elaborate hanging nests by interweaving grasses and other fibers
2. **embroider their amity.** Increase their friendship
3. **nape of his neck.** Back of his neck

"How absurd to talk about backwards pipe-smoking. You're just trying to throw me off the track."

"Not at all. There are infinite possibilities in this world, which only a clod like you would fail to consider. For example, it's perfectly possible, although unlikely, that the sun won't set this evening. What I saw I saw, without error, and you, too stubborn to admit your lack of observation, your lack of imagination, retaliate by accusing me of playing with the facts just to get a wedge under your bulk. Why shouldn't a man buy a hat of a different color? And why shouldn't he invent a new way of smoking? I've half a mind to cut a hole in the back of my neck just to show you it can be done."

re•tal•i•ate (ri ta´ lē āt') *v.*, respond to an action by doing a similar thing back, usually in a negative sense, such as repaying one injury by inflicting another

DURING READING

Use Reading Skills
Identify the Main Idea What does this friend's claim that he always thought the other was "a little mad" suggest about the main idea?

"And stop the sun, I suppose. I've always thought you a little mad, and now I'm convinced of it. Some witch is eating you. You ought to go to a doctor—"

"So that's it! I don't care what you think. You're impossible. I can't imagine why I ever found you good company. Your stupid face revolts me. I can't stop myself," he said, hitting his friend over the head with his hoe.

"So you admit you're mad, mad enough to pick a fight with me. Well I accept the challenge. Crazy or not, there's but one way to deal with unreasonable aggressors." And with that he threw his one-time friend flat on his back.

"Crude, evil-tempered man," said the other, "flat-footed rhinoceros, illegitimate offspring of a mortar and pestle.[4] Begone. I don't care how late it is. I wouldn't walk home at midnight with you. Our friendship is finished. Dead. No words will ever pass between us again."

When the chief heard of the astonishing quarrel between these two whose loyalty he had always supposed more durable than that of other men, he sighed deeply and went off to perform a sacrifice to Eshu. The next time village council met, he reallocated[5] the land so that henceforth the former friends would work at opposite corners of the communal tract. Then, holding up an old hoe for all to see, he said, mysteriously, "The sacrifice that iron refused to make is what's eating him." ✤

as•ton•ish•ing (ə stä´ ni shiŋ) *adj.*, amazing; very surprising

DURING READING

Use Reading Strategies
Make Inferences What does the chief's response to the quarrel tell you about his character?

4. **mortar and pestle.** Device for pulverizing herbs
5. **reallocated.** Reassigned

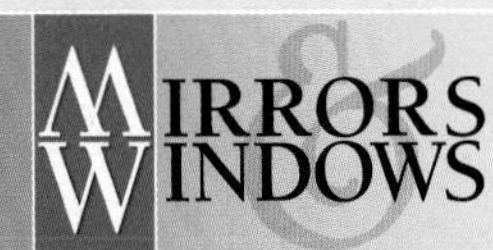

Think of a time when you had a quarrel with a close friend or family member. What caused this conflict? Why are some friendships stronger than others?

Find Meaning

1. (a) How exactly does Eshu trick the two friends? (b) What does his success suggest about their friendship?
2. What does the chief say at the end of the tale?

Make Judgments

3. Why do you think Eshu acts the way he does?
4. (a) Which parts of the folk tale do you find funny? (b) How might humor help convey the main idea?

Analyze Literature

Folk Tale Folk tales often depict everyday activities and the adventures of common people. These stories offer insights into the culture from which they come. What have you learned about Yoruban culture and everyday life from this folk tale? Create a list of details from the folk tale that help paint a picture of Yoruban culture. Then write a sentence that summarizes what you know.

Yoruban Culture

1. Agricultural community

2.

3.

My Summary:

Extend Understanding

Writing Options

Creative Writing Imagine that you are gardening in one of the plots right next to the two friends in "Eshu." Concerned about the harm Eshu can cause, you decide to write a **flyer** to give passersby, warning them about his tricks. Use library resources or the Internet to find other Yoruban stories that feature the trickster god Eshu. Distribute copies of the flyer to classmates.

Informative Writing Can you think of a better solution than the one the chief devised? Write a brief **critical analysis** about the problem solving that occurs in "Eshu." Begin by stating your opinion of the chief's actions. Then briefly describe and discuss the problems the characters face and suggest your own solutions.

Collaborative Learning

Discuss the Role of the Trickster Working in a small group, discuss why Eshu behaves the way he does in the folk tale. What motivates him? You may wish to read folk tales and myths from other traditions that feature tricksters, for example, Anansi the spider in Ashanti folklore and Loki in Norse mythology.

Lifelong Learning

Research the History of Nigeria Research Nigeria's history. Begin by consulting a general reference work. Then, as a class, brainstorm specific topics related to the country's history. Choose a topic that interests you and research it in greater depth. Create a multimedia presentation, and present your report to the class.

Go to **www.mirrorsandwindows.com** for more.

The Secret Name of Ra

An Egyptian Myth retold by Geraldine Harris

DIRECTED READING

BEFORE READING

Build Background

Cultural Context While ancient Egyptians worshipped a large number of gods, the sun god, Ra, was the most important. He was both creator and sustainer of the world. As an agricultural people, the Egyptians worshipped the power of the sun to make crops flourish. Each day Ra traveled across the sky in his bark canoe, and at night he traveled through the underworld, where he vanquished a giant serpent before emerging on the other side of the world.

Reader's Context When have you given your trust to someone you should not have? What was the outcome?

Set Purpose

Preview Build Background, as well as the vocabulary, footnotes, and artwork with the reading. Try to predict what this story will be about.

Analyze Literature

Motivation A force that moves a character to think, feel, or behave a certain way is called a **motivation.** You might expect the gods in "The Secret Name of Ra" to have very different reasons for their actions than humans. However, Egyptian gods possess many human qualities. As you read, try to determine the motivations of both Isis and Ra.

Use Reading Skills

Analyze Cause and Effect A *cause* is an action or event that makes something else happen. Any action or event that results from a cause is an *effect.* By analyzing the causes and effects, you will better understand the plot, characters, and theme of a story. As you read, create a cause-and-effect chart for "The Secret Name of Ra."

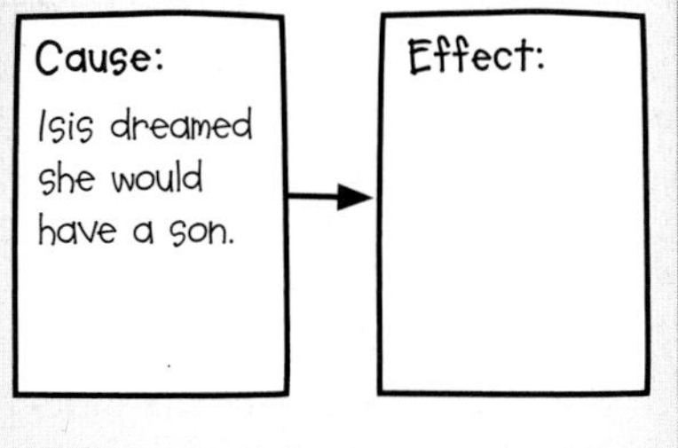

Preview Vocabulary

sole (sōl) *adj.*, only

ex • alt • ed (ig zōlt´ ed) *adj.*, held in high regard

cun • ning (kʉ´ niŋ) *adj.*, clever or tricky

de • i • ty (dē´ə tē) *n.*, god or goddess

driv • el (driv´ əl) *v.*, drool

a • byss (ə bis´) *n.*, bottomless pit; something too deep to measure

Meet the Author

Geraldine Harris (b. 1951) teaches Egyptology at Oxford University in England and has published both fiction and nonfiction. Her creative writing, which includes the four-novel Seven Citadels series for young readers, is strongly influenced by her knowledge of folklore and mythology. Harris has also published a number of books about ancient Egyptian mythology and culture.

The Secret Name of Ra

Detail depicting the deceased led by Horus before Osiris, c. 1250 BC. British Museum, London.

An Egyptian Myth retold by Geraldine Harris

Ra gave a scream that was heard through all creation.

Ra, the Sole Creator was visible to the people of Egypt as the disc of the sun, but they knew him in many other forms. He could appear as a crowned man, a falcon or a man with a falcon's head and, as the scarab beetle[1] pushes a round ball of dung in front of it, the Egyptians pictured Ra as a scarab pushing the sun across the sky. In caverns deep below the earth were hidden another seventy-five forms of Ra: mysterious beings with mummified bodies[2] and heads consisting of birds or snakes, feathers or flowers. The names of Ra were as numerous as his forms; he was the Shining One, The Hidden One, The Renewer of the Earth, The Wind in the Souls, The Exalted One, but there was one name of the Sun God which had not been spoken since time began. To know this secret name of Ra was to have power over him and over the world that he had created.

Isis longed for such a power. She had dreamed that one day she would have a marvellous falcon-headed son called Horus and she wanted the throne of Ra to give to her child. Isis was the Mistress of Magic, wiser than millions of men, but she knew that nothing in creation was powerful enough to harm its creator. Her only chance was to turn the power of Ra against himself and at last Isis thought of a cruel and cunning plan. Every day the Sun God walked through his kingdom, attended by a crowd of spirits and lesser deities, but Ra was growing old. His eyes were dim, his step no longer firm and he had even begun to drivel.

One morning Isis mingled with a group of minor goddesses and followed behind the King of the Gods. She watched the face of Ra until she saw his saliva drip onto a clod of earth. When she was sure that no-one was taking any notice of her, she scooped up the earth and carried it away. Isis mixed the earth with the saliva of Ra to form clay and modelled a wicked-looking serpent. Through the hours of darkness she whispered spells over the clay serpent as it lay lifeless in her hands. Then the cunning goddess carried it to a crossroads on the route which the Sun God always took. She hid the serpent in the long grass and returned to her palace.

The next day Ra came walking through his kingdom with the spirits and lesser deities crowding behind him. When he approached the crossroads, the spells of Isis began to work and the clay serpent quivered into life. As the Sun God passed, it bit him in the ankle and crumbled back into earth. Ra gave a scream that was heard through all creation.

His jaws chattered and his limbs shook as the poison flooded through him like a rising Nile. "I have been wounded by something deadly," whispered Ra. "I know that in my heart, though my eyes cannot see it. Whatever it was, I, the Lord of Creation, did not make it. I am sure that none of you would have done such a terrible thing to me, but I have never felt such pain! How can this have happened to me? I am the Sole Creator, the child of the watery abyss. I am the god with a thousand names, but my secret name was only spoken once, before time began. Then it was hidden in my body so that no-one should ever learn it and be able to

1. **scarab beetle.** Dung beetle; this insect was held sacred by ancient Egyptians, who saw it as a symbol both of the sun god and of the continued existence of the soul after death.
2. **mummified bodies.** Bodies that have been preserved for burial by removing the internal organs, treating them with special substances, and wrapping them in cloth to keep them from decaying

sole (sōl) *adj.*, only

ex • alt • ed (ig zōlt´ ed) *adj.*, held in high regard

cun • ning (kʉ´ niŋ) *adj.*, clever or tricky

de • i • ty (dē´ə tē) *n.*, god or goddess

driv • el (driv´ əl) *v.*, drool

a • byss (ə bis´) *n.*, bottomless pit; something too deep to measure work spells against me. Yet as I walked through my kingdom something struck at me and now my heart is on fire and my limbs shake. Send for the Ennead![3] Send for my children! They are wise in magic and their knowledge pierces heaven."

Satis his daughter. Cunning Thoth and wise Seshat, goddess of writing; virile Min and snake-headed Renenutet, goddess of the harvest, kindly Meskhenet and monstrous Taweret, goddesses of birth—all of them were summoned to the side of Ra.

The gods and goddesses gathered around the Sun God, weeping and wailing, afraid that he was going to die. Isis stood among them beating her breast and pretending to be as distressed and bewildered as all the other frightened deities.

"Father of All," she began, "whatever is the matter? Has some snake bitten you? Has some wretched creature dared to strike at his Creator? Few of the gods can compare with me in wisdom and I am the Mistress of Magic. If you will let me help you, I'm sure that I can cure you."

HISTORY ▶▶ CONNECTION

Ancient Egypt Although most of North Africa is desert, the fertile lands of the Nile River valley made it possible for a thriving civilization to develop in ancient Egypt during the third millennium BC. Sustained by increasingly sophisticated agricultural practices, Egyptians were free to explore architecture, the arts, and the sciences. Much of what they achieved can still be seen today. During most of its history, ancient Egypt was ruled by a series of all-powerful kings called pharaohs. A pharaoh, as the earthly embodiment of a god, was responsible for maintaining *ma'at,* or "divine order," in the kingdom. What role do you think this concept of *ma'at* plays in "The Secret Name of Ra"?

Messengers hurried to the great gods and from the four pillars of the world came the Ennead: Shu and Tefenet, Geb and Nut, Seth and Osiris, Isis and Nephthys. Envoys traveled the land and the sky and the watery abyss to summon all the deities created by Ra. From the marshes came frog-headed Heket, Wadjet the cobra goddess and the fearsome god, crocodile-headed Sobek. From the deserts came fiery Selkis, the scorpion goddess, Anubis the jackal, the guardian of the dead and Nekhbet the vulture goddess. From the cities of the north came warlike Neith, gentle cat-headed Bastet, fierce lion-headed Sekhmet and Ptah the god of crafts. From the cities of the south came Onuris, the divine huntsman and ram-headed Khnum with Anukis his wife and

Ra was grateful to Isis and told her all that had happened. "Now I am colder than water and hotter than fire," complained the Sun God. "My eyes darken. I cannot see the sky and my body is soaked by the sweat of fever."

"Tell me your full name," said cunning Isis. "Then I can use it in my spells. Without that knowledge the greatest of magicians cannot help you."

"I am the maker of heaven and earth," said Ra. "I made the heights and the depths,

3. **Ennead.** Literally, a group of nine; in Egyptian mythology, the most ancient group of nine gods

I set horizons at east and west and established the gods in their glory. When I open my eyes it is light; when I close them it is dark. The mighty Nile floods at my command. The gods do not know my true name but I am the maker of time, the giver of festivals. I spark the fire of life. At dawn I rise as Khepri, the scarab and sail across the sky in the Boat of Millions of Years.[4] At noon I blaze in the heavens as Ra and at evening I am Ra-atum, the setting sun."

"We know all that," said Isis. "If I am to find a spell to drive out this poison, I will have to use your secret name. Say your name and live."

"My secret name was given to me so that I could sit at ease," moaned Ra, "and fear no living creature. How can I give it away?"

Isis said nothing and knelt beside the Sun God while his pain mounted. When it became unbearable, Ra ordered the other gods to stand back while he whispered his secret name to Isis. "Now the power of the secret name has passed from my heart to your heart," said Ra wearily. "In time you can give it to your son, but warn him never to betray the secret!"

"My secret name was given to me so that I could sit at ease... and fear no living creature. How can I give it away?"

Isis nodded and began to chant a great spell that drove the poison out of the limbs of Ra and he rose up stronger than before. The Sun God returned to the Boat of Millions of Years and Isis shouted for joy at the success of her plan. She knew now that one day Horus her son would sit on the throne of Egypt and wield the power of Ra. ✤

4. **Boat of Millions of Years.** Name often used in Egyptian texts for the boat in which Ra sailed across the sky during the day and through the underworld at night

Think of a time you tricked someone in order to get something you wanted very badly. How did you justify your actions to yourself or others? Is there ever a time when it is acceptable to trick others?

Find Meaning

1. (a) What are some of the names of Ra? (b) What do these names suggest about his place in ancient Egyptian religious life?

2. (a) What is Isis's plan for learning Ra's secret name? (b) What does her plan reveal about her character?

3. (a) What does Isis create to harm Ra? (b) Why is this object able to hurt him?

Make Judgments

4. Why did Ra trust Isis?

5. (a) Egyptian deities have both human and divine qualities. What human qualities do Ra and Isis have? (b) Why might these gods exhibit human traits?

LITERATURE ▶▶ CONNECTION

In "The Secret Name of Ra," the sun god has become a failing old man and Isis plots to replace him. The hymn, or song of praise, excerpted here comes from a time when an Egyptian pharaoh attempted something similar. Akhenaton and his queen Nefertiti ruled Egypt during the fourteenth century BC. They ordered their people to abandon the old gods. Instead, they were to worship a single sun god, the formerly minor deity Aton. In the end, the change didn't catch on. The people returned to their old ways after Akhenaton's death. It is unlikely that Akhenaton wrote the hymn himself, although it is sometimes attributed to him.

from Akhenaton's Hymn to the Sun

A Hymn translated by John A. Wilson

When thou settest[1] in the western horizon,
The land is in darkness as if in death.
Men sleep in a room with heads wrapped up,
And no eye sees another.
Though all their goods under their heads be stolen,
Yet would they not perceive it.
Every lion comes forth from his den,
And all creeping things sting.
Darkness is a shroud[2] and the earth is still,
For he who made them rests in his horizon.

At daybreak, when thou risest[3] on the horizon,
When thou shinest as the sun disk by day,
Thou drivest away darkness and givest thy rays;
Then the Two Lands[4] are in daily festivity:
Men awake and stand upon their feet,
For thou hast[5] raised them up.
They wash their bodies and take their clothing,
Their arms raised in praise at thy appearing.
And all the world, they do their work....

1. **thou settest.** You set
2. **shroud.** Cloth used to wrap a body before burial
3. **thou risest.** You rise
4. **Two Lands.** Upper and Lower Egypt, regions that were at war for centuries, until they were united around 3,000 BC by a king named Menes
5. **thou hast.** You have

How manifold[6] it is,
What thou hast made!
It is hidden from the face of man.
Thou sole god, without thy like,
Thou didst create the world after thy desire,
Whilst[7] thou wert alone:
All mankind, cattle and wild beasts,
Whatever goes by foot upon the earth,
Whatever flies on high with wings....
The world came into being by thy hand,
According as thou didst make them all.
When thou hast risen they live,
When thou settest then they die.
Thou art lifetime thy own self,
For we live only through thee.
Eyes are fixed on beauty until thou settest,
All work is laid aside when thou settest in the west.
But when thou risest again,
Then everything is made to flourish.... ✣

---

6. manifold. Having many different forms, features, or parts
7. whilst. While

TEXT ⟷ TO ⟷ TEXT CONNECTION

Although "The Secret Name of Ra" and "Akhenaton's Hymn to the Sun" feature different sun gods, both provide a sense of how much ancient Egyptians revered the sun. Based on details from both works, why do you think this is so?

AFTER READING

Analyze Literature

Motivation When you read, analyzing characters' motivations gives you a deeper understanding of the story and a better sense of the people the writer has worked to portray. Make a three-column chart in which you track the motivations of Ra and Isis and relate that information to their personality traits and behaviors.

Character	Traits and Behaviors	Motivation
Ra	getting old	

Extend Understanding

Writing Options

Narrative Writing Use what you learned from reading "The Secret Name of Ra" to create your own short Egyptian **myth.** Use Geraldine Harris's retelling as your model. Include characters, settings, and themes that appear in her myth.

Informative Writing A summary retells the main ideas of a text. A summary should be shorter than the original and use different words. Write a **summary** of "The Secret Name of Ra." Cover all the key details of the plot, setting, and characters. When you are done, read your summary to the class.

Collaborative Learning

Examine Motivation With a partner, discuss why Ra would have a secret name that held such power over him. Skim "The Secret Name of Ra" to look for possible answers to this question. Seek out other versions of the same myth to see if they provide additional guidance. Present your ideas to the class and solicit more ideas.

Lifelong Learning

Learn About the Nile Research the Nile to learn how the river affected the lives of the ancient Egyptians. Possible topics to investigate include the agricultural practices that evolved along its shores, gods and goddesses that were associated with the Nile, and the settlements built near it. Prepare and deliver a presentation on your findings for the class.

Go to **www.mirrorsandwindows.com** for more.

Vocabulary & Spelling

Homographs, Homophones, and Homonyms

Isis mixed the earth with the saliva of Ra to form clay....

—GERALDINE HARRIS, "The Secret Name of Ra"

English contains many words that are spelled alike but pronounced differently—such as *lead* (to guide) and *lead* (the metal). It also includes words that are pronounced alike but spelled differently—such as *hear* and *here*—and words that are both spelled and pronounced alike but have completely different meanings. For example, *form* in the above quotation can mean "an appearance," "a category," "a printed document," or the verb "to shape." These types of easily confused words are known as homographs, homophones, and homonyms.

Homographs and Homophones

Homographs are words that have the same spelling but have different meanings and different pronunciations.

EXAMPLE

produce (prə düs´) *v.*, make

produce (prō´ düs) *n.*, products grown on a farm, especially fruit and vegetables

Homophones are words that are pronounced the same but differ in spelling and meaning.

EXAMPLE

bare (ber) *adj.*, without covering

bear (ber) *v.*, support; hold up

Other common examples include *to, two,* and *too;* and *their, they're,* and *there.*

Homonyms

Homonyms are words that are both homographs and homophones—that is, they are spelled and pronounced alike but have different and unrelated meanings. For example, the word *fine* can refer to a penalty or to a feeling of well being.

Use context clues to determine the meaning of multiple meaning words. First, determine the word's part of speech. Then, decide which meaning makes sense in context.

Vocabulary Practice

On a separate sheet of paper, choose the correct spelling to complete each sentence.

1. ...the Sun God walked (threw, through) his kingdom....
2. ...all of them were summoned to the (side, sighed) of Ra.
3. They are wise in magic and (there, their, they're) knowledge pierces heaven.

Spelling Practice

Homophones

The following words from "The Secret Name of Ra" have homophones, or words that sound the same, but have different spellings and meanings. Write a homophone for each word in the list below.

for	sail	through
great	so	to
knew	sole	warn
know	son	
or	there	

ANCHOR TEXT

Tsali of the Cherokees

An Oral History by Norah Roper, as told to Alice Lee Marriott

BEFORE READING

Build Background

Historical Context The Trail of Tears is a prominent, painful episode in Cherokee history. In the mid-1800s, thousands of Cherokee from the southeastern United States were dispossessed of their land by the U.S. government and forced to march to a region called Indian Territory. There they joined similarly relocated Choctaw, Chickasaw, Creek, and Seminole tribes.

Reader's Context Imagine what it would feel like if strangers arrived and forced your family from its property. Read to learn about a time when that was a common experience for Native Americans.

Set Purpose

As you read, try to determine how oral histories differ from legends and myths. What elements might oral histories and these other genres share?

Analyze Literature

Motivation A force that moves a character to think, feel, or behave in a certain way is called a **motivation.** A character's motivations can often be determined by analyzing his or her actions. As you read "Tsali of the Cherokees," try to determine what motivates the major and the minor characters and how these motivations affect the plot.

Use Reading Skills

Identify Author's Purpose An author's purpose is his or her reason for writing. For example, writers may write to inform, to entertain, or to persuade. A writer may also have more than one purpose. As you read this oral history, try to identify the author's purpose for recording and retelling this story. Use a two-column chart to help.

Details	Author's Purpose
Chiefs acted unfairly	

DIRECTED READING

Meet the Author

Alice Lee Marriott (1910–1992) was an ethnologist, or a person who studies cultural history and practices such as rituals and medicine. Ethnologists often collect oral histories, which are unwritten stories recounted by the descendants of people who originally experienced the events. Alice Lee Marriott was a longtime resident of Oklahoma and recorded this oral history from a Cherokee named Norah Roper, granddaughter of Tsali.

Preview Vocabulary

en•croach•ing (in krōch´ iŋ) *adj.*, trespassing; creeping slowly into a territory with the object of stealing it

mis•sion•ary (mi´ shə ner' ē) *n.*, person sent to other countries or remote areas to spread a religion and, sometimes, to care for people

sulk•i•ly (sʉl´ kə lē) *adv.*, moodily silent

mi•li•tia (mə li´ shə) *n.*, citizens' army

a•skew (ə skyü´) *adj.*, out of line; crooked

Reenactment of the Trail of Tears 150 years after the forced relocation of the Cherokee.

Tsali of the Cherokees

An Oral History by Norah Roper, as told to Alice Lee Marriott

They knew that their tribal chiefs traveled back and forth to the white man's place called Washington more often than they used to do. They knew that when the chiefs came back from that place, there were quarrels in the tribal council.

Up in the hills and the back country, where the *Ani Keetoowah*—the true Cherokees—lived, word of the changes came more slowly than the changes themselves came to the valley Cherokees. Many of the hill people never left their farm lands, and those who did went only to the nearest trading post and back. Few travelers ever came into the uplands, where the mists of the Smokies[1] shut out the encroaching world.

So, when the news came that some of the chiefs of the Cherokees had touched the pen, and put their names or their marks on a paper, and agreed by doing so that this was no longer Cherokee country, the *Ani Keetoowah* could not believe what they heard. Surely, they said to each other, this news must be false. No Cherokee—not even a mixed-blood—would sign away his own and his people's lands. But that was what the chiefs had done.

Then the word came that the chiefs were even more divided among themselves and that not all of them had touched the pen. Some were not willing to move away to the

1. **Smokies.** Great Smoky Mountains, part of the Appalachian range in North Carolina and Tennessee

en•croach•ing (in krōch′ iŋ) *adj.*, trespassing; creeping slowly into a territory with the object of stealing it new lands across the Mississippi and settle in the hills around Fort Gibson, Oklahoma.

"Perhaps we should hang on," the *Ani Keetoowah* said to one another. "Perhaps we will not have to go away after all." They waited and hoped, although they knew in their hearts that hope is the cruelest curse on mankind.

One of the leaders of the *Ani Keetoowah* was Tsali. The white men had trouble pronouncing his name, so they called him "Charley" or "Dutch." Tsali was a full blood, and so were his wife and their family. They were of the oldest *Keetoowah* Cherokee blood and would never have let themselves be ashamed by having half-breed relatives.

Tsali and his four sons worked two hillsides and the valley between them, in the southern part of the hill country. Tsali and his wife and their youngest son lived in a log house at the head of the hollow. The others had their own homes, spread out along the hillsides. They grew corn and beans, a few English peas, squashes and pumpkins, tobacco and cotton, and even a little sugar cane and indigo.[2] Tsali's wife kept chickens in a fenced run away from the house.

The women gathered wild hemp[3] and spun it; they spun the cotton, and the wool from their sheep. Then they wove the thread into cloth, and sometimes in winter when their few cattle and the sheep had been cared for and the chickens fed and there was not much else to do, the men helped at the looms,[4] which they had built themselves. The women did all the cutting and the making of garments for the whole family.

Tsali and his family were not worldly rich, in the way that the chiefs and some of the Cherokees of the valley towns were rich. They had hardly seen white man's metal money in their lives. But Tsali's people never lacked for food, or good clothing, or safe shelter.

The missionaries seldom came into the uplands then. Tsali took his sons and their wives, and his own wife, to the great dance ground where the seven *Keetoowah* villages gathered each month at the time of the full moon. There they danced their prayers in time to the beating of the women's terrapin-shell[5] leg rattles, around and around the mound of packed white ashes on top of which bloomed the eternal fire that was the life of all the Cherokees.

"There's no hope this time. The lands have all been sold. . . . You'll have to go west."

The occasional missionaries fussed over the children. They gave them white men's names, so that by Tsali's time everyone had an Indian name and an English one. The Cherokees listened to the missionaries politely, for the missionaries were great gossips, and the Cherokees heard their news and ignored the rest of their words.

"You will have to go soon," said one white preacher to Tsali. "There's no hope this time. The lands have all been sold, and the Georgia troopers are moving in. You'll have to go west."

"We'll never leave," Tsali answered. "This is our land and we belong to it. Who could take it from us—who would want it? It's hard even for us to farm here, and we're used to

---

2. **indigo.** Plant used to make a blue dye
3. **hemp.** Plant with tough stems whose fibers can be woven into rope and cloth
4. **looms.** Machines for weaving fabric from fibers or threads
5. **terrapin-shell.** Turtle shell

mis•sion•ary (mi´ shə ner' ē) *n.*, person sent to other countries or remote areas to spread a religion and, sometimes, to care for people hill farming. The white men wouldn't want to come here—they'll want the rich lands in the valleys, if the lowland people will give them up."

"They want these hills more than any other land," the missionary said. He sounded almost threatening. "Don't you see, you poor ignorant Indian? They are finding gold—gold, man, gold—downstream in the lower *Keetoowah* country. That means that the source of the gold is in the headwaters of the rivers that flow from here down into the valleys. I've seen gold dust in those streams myself."

"Gold?" asked Tsali. "You mean this yellow stuff?" And he took a buckskin pouch out of the pouch that hung from his sash, and opened it. At the sight of the yellow dust the pouch contained, the missionary seemed to go a little crazy.

"That's it!" he cried. "Where did you get it? How did you find it? You'll be rich if you can get more."

"We find it in the rivers, as you said," Tsali replied. "We gather what we need to take to the trader. I have this now because I am going down to the valley in a few days, to get my wife some ribbons to trim her new dress."

"Show me where you got it," the missionary begged. "We can all be rich. I'll protect you from the other white men, if you make me your partner."

"No, I think I'd better not," said Tsali thoughtfully. "My sons are my partners, as I was my father's. We do not need another partner, and, as long as we have our old squirrel guns, we do not need to be protected. Thank you, but you can go on. We are better off as we are."

The missionary coaxed and threatened, but Tsali stood firm. In the end, the white man went away, without any gold except a pinch that Tsali gave him, because the missionary seemed to value the yellow dust even more than the trader did.

Then it was time to go to the trading post. When Tsali came in the store, the trader said to him, "Well, Chief, glad to see you. I hear you're a rich man these days."

"I have always been a rich man," Tsali answered. "I have my family and we all have our good health. We have land to farm, houses to live in, food on our tables, and enough clothes. Most of all, we have the love in our hearts for each other and our friends. Indeed, you are right. We are very rich."

"That's one way of looking at it," said the trader, "but it isn't what I was thinking about. From what I hear, there's gold on your land. You've got a gold mine."

"A gold man?" repeated Tsali. "I never heard of a gold man."

"No!" shouted the trader. "A gold mine, I said. A place where you can go and pick up gold."

"Oh, that!" Tsali exclaimed. "Yes, we have some places like that on our land. Here's some of the yellow dust we find there."

And he opened the pouch to show the trader. The trader had seen pinches of Tsali's gold dust before, and taken it in trade, without saying much about it. Now he went as crazy as the missionary. "Don't tell anybody else about this, Charley," he whispered, leaning over the counter. "We'll just keep it to ourselves. I'll help you work it out, and I'll keep the other white men away. We'll all be rich."

"Thank you," said Tsali, "but I don't believe I want to be rich that way. I just want enough of this stuff to trade you for ribbons and sugar."

"Oh, all right," answered the trader sulkily, "have it your own way. But don't blame me if you're sorry afterwards."

sulk•i•ly (sʉl´ kə lē) *adv.*, moodily silent

"I won't blame anybody," said Tsali, and bought his ribbon.

A month later, when the Georgia militia came riding up the valley to Tsali's house, the missionary and the trader were with them. The men all stopped in front of the house, and Tsali's wife came out into the dogtrot, the open-ended passage that divided the two halves of the house and made a cool breezeway where the family sat in warm weather. She spoke to the men.

"Won't you come in and sit down?"

"Where's the old man?" the militia captain asked.

"Why, he's working out in the fields," said Amanda. "Sit down and have a cool drink of water while I send the boy for him."

"Send the boy quickly," the captain ordered. "We'll wait in our saddles and not trouble to get down."

"All right, if you'd rather not," Amanda said. "Do you mind telling me why you're here?"

"We're here to put you off this place," said the captain. "Haven't you heard? This isn't Cherokee land any more; the chiefs signed it over to the government, and now it's open for settlement. One or the other of these two gentlemen will probably claim it."

"They can't do that!" Amanda protested. "It's our land—nobody else's. The chiefs had no right to sign it away. My husband's father worked this place, and his father before him. This is our home. This is where we belong."

"No more," said the captain. "You belong in the removal camps[6] down by the river, with the rest of the Indians. They're going to start shipping the Cherokees west tomorrow morning."

Amanda sat down on the bench in the dogtrot with her legs trembling under her. "All of us?" she asked.

"Every one of you."

"Let me call my son and send him for his daddy," Amanda said.

"Hurry up!"

Amanda went into the house, calling to the boy, who was just fourteen and had been

SOCIAL STUDIES ▶▶ CONNECTION

Indian Removal From almost the moment they arrived on this continent, white settlers regularly took and traded Native American lands. As Native Americans were displaced by ever larger numbers of white settlers, the U.S. government began to forcibly remove tribes to "Indian Territory"—what is now the state of Oklahoma. Today, Oklahoma has the highest Native American population of any state. This population includes members of the Choctaw, Creek, Seminole, Cherokee, and Chickasaw tribes. How does this information affect your understanding of Tsali?

6. **removal camps.** Temporary residences for people forced from their own property

mi • li • tia (mə li´ shə) *n.,* citizens' army

standing, listening, behind the door. She gave him his father's old squirrel gun, and he sneaked his own blowgun and darts and slid out the back of the house. Amanda went back to the dogtrot and sat and waited. She sat there and waited, while the missionary, the trader, and the captain quarreled about which of their wives should cook in her kitchen. She let them quarrel and hoped her men were all right.

Tsali and his older sons were working the overhill corn field, when the boy came panting up and told them what had happened.

"Is your mother all right?" Tsali asked.

"She was when I left," the boy answered.

"We'll hide in the woods till they're gone," Tsali told his older sons. "If they find us, they'll have to kill us to put us off this land."

"What about the women?" the oldest son asked.

"They'll be all right," Tsali answered. "Your mother's a quick-thinking woman; she'll take care of them. If we can hide in the caves by the river till dark, we'll go back then and get them."

They slipped away into the woods, downhill to the river, taking the boy with them, although he offered to go back and tell the white men he couldn't find his father.

All afternoon Amanda waited. Her daughters-in-law saw the strange men and horses in front of the big house and came to join her. At dusk, the captain gave up and ordered his men to make camp in the front yard. "We'll wait here until the men come back," he said.

With the white men camped all around the house, the women went into the kitchen and barred all the doors. It was a long time before the campfires made from the fence pickets ceased to blaze and began to smolder. It was a longer time until the women heard it—a scratch on the back door, so soft and so light that it would have embarrassed a mouse. Amanda slid back the bar, and Tsali and his sons slipped into the darkened room. There was just enough moonlight for them to make out each other's shapes.

"We came to get you," Tsali said. "Come quickly. Leave everything except your knives. Don't wait a minute."

Amanda and her daughters-in-law always wore their knives at their belts, so they were ready. One at a time, Tsali last, the whole family crept out of their home and escaped into the woods.

They slipped away into the woods, downhill to the river, taking the boy with them. . . .

In the morning, when the white men stretched and scratched and woke, the *Ani Keetoowah* were gone.

It was spring, and the weather was warm, but the rain fell and soaked the Cherokees. They had brought no food, and they dared not fire a gun. One of the daughters-in-law was pregnant, and her time was close. Amanda was stiff and crippled with rheumatism.[7] They gathered wild greens, for it was too early for berries or plums, and the men and boy trapped small animals and birds in string snares the women made by pulling out their hair and twisting it.

Day by day, for four weeks, the starving family listened to white men beating through the woods. The Cherokees were tired and cold and hungry, but they were silent. They even began to hope that in time the white men would go away and the Indians would be safe.

---

7. rheumatism. Chronic, painful joint inflammation

It was not to be. One trooper brought his dog, and the dog caught the human scent. So the dog, with his man behind him, came sniffing into the cave, and Tsali and his family were caught before the men could pick up their loaded guns.

The militiamen shouted, and other white men came thudding through the woods. They tied the Cherokee men's hands behind them and bound them all together along a rope. The militiamen pushed Tsali and his sons through the woods. The women followed, weeping.

At last they were back at their own house, but they would not have recognized it. The troopers had plundered the garden and trampled the plants they didn't eat. The door from the kitchen into the dogtrot hung askew, and the door to the main room had been wrenched off its hinges. Clothes and bedding lay in filthy piles around the yard. What the militiamen could not use, they ruined.

Cherokee woman carrying her child in Raleigh, North Carolina, in 1946.

"Oh, my garden!" cried Amanda, and, when she saw the scattered feathers, "Oh, my little hens!"

"What are you going to do with us?" Tsali demanded.

"Take you down to the river. The last boat is loading today. There's still time to get you on it and out of here."

"I—will—not—go," Tsali said quietly. "You—nor you—nor you—nobody can make me go."

"Our orders are to take all the Cherokees. If any resist, shoot them."

"Shoot me, then!" cried Tsali. The captain raised his rifle.

"Stop!" Amanda screamed. She stepped over beside her husband. "If you shoot, shoot us both," she ordered. "Our lives have been one life since we were no older than our boy here. I don't want to go on living without my husband. And I cannot leave our home any more than he can. Shoot us both."

The four sons stepped forward. "We will die with our parents," the oldest one said. "Take our wives to the boat, if that is the only place where they can be safe, but we stay here." He turned to his wife and the other young women.

"That is my order as your husband," Tsali's son said. "You must go away to the west and make new lives for yourselves while

a•skew (ə skyü´) *adj.*, out of line; crooked

you are still young enough to do so." The wives sobbed and held out their arms, but the husbands turned their backs on the women. "We will stay with our parents," all the young men said.

The young boy, too, stood with his brothers, beside his father. "Let this boy go," Tsali said to the white men. "He is so young. A man grows, and plants his seed, and his seed goes on. This is my seed. I planted it. My older sons and I have had our chances. They will leave children, and their names will never be forgotten. But this boy is too young. His seed has not ripened for planting yet. Let him go, to care for his sisters, on the way to the west."

"Very well," said the captain. "He can't do much harm if he does live." He turned to two militiamen. "Take the boy and the young women away," he ordered. "Keep them going till they come to the boats, and load them on board."

The young women and the boy, stunned and silenced, were driven down the road before they could say goodbye, nor would the trooper let them look back. Behind them, as they started on the long main road, they heard the sound of the shots. ✣

When was the last time your family had to relocate? Should families define themselves by where they have lived in past generations, or should they identify themselves only with where they live today?

Find Meaning

1. (a) What is Tsali's attitude about the gold on his land? (b) How does his attitude differ from the attitudes of the missionary and the trader? (c) What does this difference suggest?
2. (a) What do the Cherokee chiefs do? (b) How does Tsali respond to their actions?
3. (a) Why does Tsali refuse to go west? (b) What is the result of his refusal?

Make Judgments

4. What do the soldiers' actions suggest about their feelings for the Cherokee?
5. What is your opinion about Tsali's sons' decision to stay with their parents?
6. Describe your feelings about Tsali's decision to stay on his land.

INFORMATIONAL TEXT ▶▶ CONNECTION

In "Tsali of the Cherokees," Alice Lee Marriott retells the story of one family's experience during the removal of the Cherokee from Georgia. In the following article by history and social studies writer **Christine Graf,** the reasons for this removal and its effects on the Cherokee are described. As you read, use the information this article presents to better understand the story of Tsali.

(Above) ***The Trail of Tears,*** 1942. Robert Lindneux. The Granger Collection, New York.

Moving West: A Native American Perspective

A Magazine Article by Christine Graf

Wouldn't it be wonderful to discover gold on your land? Well, when gold was discovered on land where Cherokee Indians lived in Georgia, it wasn't wonderful at all—at least, not for them.

By the 1800s, white settlers had already taken most of the Cherokee land. The Cherokees were left with only a small section of western Georgia. When gold was discovered there in 1828, whites wanted this last part of Cherokee land, too. Through an act of Congress called the Indian Removal Act, President Andrew Jackson ordered the Cherokees to leave. Dozens of other American Indian tribes had already been forced from their land.

In May 1838, army troops began forcing the Cherokees from their homes. The Cherokees were imprisoned in forts, then forced to walk almost 1,000 miles into Oklahoma. This terrible, forced migration became known as the Trail of Tears. Four thousand Cherokees died as a result.

American Indians faced other difficulties as more and more settlers moved west. Contact with white people meant exposure to new diseases. In 1837 alone, tens of thousands of Indians died of smallpox, a disease carried into Indian land by white fur traders.

In many parts of the West, settlers took over traditional Indian hunting and farming lands. They killed most of the buffalo the Indians needed for food, clothes, tipis, and more. "When the buffalo went away, the hearts of my people fell to the ground, and they could not lift them up again," said Crow Indian Plenty Coups.

By the late 1800s, thousands of tribes had been forced by the government to give up their land. Some fought back against army attacks. Sadly, they were no match for the United States Army and couldn't save their land. Instead, they were forced to live on reservations (land set aside for them). Their lives were never the same. ✤

TEXT ⟷ TO ⟷ TEXT CONNECTION

Some Cherokee agreed to sell their land to the white settlers, but most did not. Was it wise for them to sell their land? How does reading this account affect the way you interpret "Tsali of the Cherokees"?

AFTER READING

Analyze Literature

Motivation What motivated Tsali? What motivated his wife and sons? What motivated the soldiers, the missionary, and the trader? Use a two-column chart to record details about each of the characters to determine what motivated their actions.

Details	Motivation
"missionary seemed to go a little crazy"	Tsali's gold

Extend Understanding

Writing Options

Creative Writing It is the winter of 1839, and you are a budding writer in northern Alabama. You have been hearing about a forced march of Cherokees, something the federal government has ordered so that white people can search for gold on native land. Investigate and write a **news article** about the forced march in three or four paragraphs. Each paragraph should have just two or three sentences. When you are done, exchange articles with a classmate and act as each other's editor.

Informative Writing Write a **literary analysis** of Tsali's character. Use the chart you created to analyze character motivation in "Tsali of the Cherokees" to help you form and support your thesis. Ask yourself: Why did Tsali choose to stay on his land? What does he value? How does he interact with others? At the end of your analysis, be sure to restate your thesis. When you are finished, share your analysis with the class.

Lifelong Learning

Dig Into History The Indian Removal Act of 1830 was just one of many government actions that affected Native Americans. Find out more about President Jackson's life and political career, the laws and treaties related to native people during Jackson's presidency, and the national mood that permitted Jackson to order relocation of the tribes. Summarize what you learn with a poster you could display in class.

Critical Literacy

Plan an Interview Suppose you had an opportunity to meet a survivor who walked the Trail of Tears. Prepare some interview questions you can ask this person as part of an oral history of the migration. With no more than ten questions, try to draw out stories about what the experience was like. Write your questions in a way that will allow you to learn both facts and feelings from the person you interview.

Go to **www.mirrorsandwindows.com** for more.

We Are All One

A Chinese Folk Tale retold by Laurence Yep

BEFORE READING

Build Background

Literary Context Like folk tales everywhere, Chinese folk tales began as part of folk literature. These stories were told by parents and grandparents to reinforce the values and traditions of their culture while also providing entertainment. A popular theme in both folk tales and myths is the quest, in which the main character goes on a journey to solve a problem. Along the way, the character encounters obstacles and is either helped or hindered by characters or animals that have magical powers.

Reader's Context How does it make you feel to do a favor for someone with no expectation of reward? Have you ever reaped an unexpected reward from doing a good deed?

Set Purpose

Before you begin, read the title of the selection and consider the selection's genre. Use these clues to predict what will happen in the folk tale.

Analyze Literature

Conflict The **conflict** in a piece of fiction is the struggle between a character and him- or herself, another character, society, or nature. As you read "We Are All One," identify the central conflict of the story, and note the other obstacles that the main character overcomes along the way.

Use Reading Skills

Sequence of Events
Using a graphic organizer can help you keep track of the sequence of events, or the order in which things happen, in a story. As you read "We Are All One," use a time line to keep track of the key events in the story.

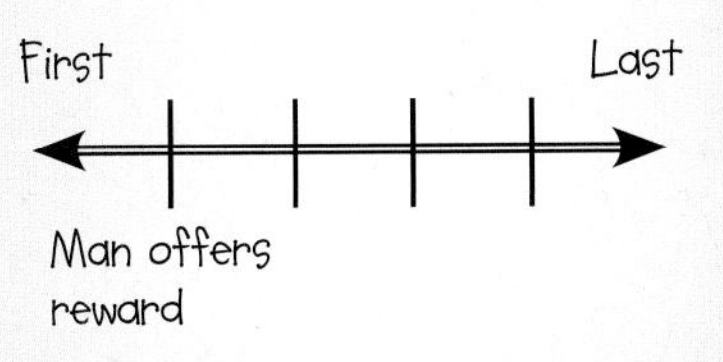

Preview Vocabulary

lar•va (lär´ və) *n.*, early wingless form of a newly hatched insect; **larvae** (lär´ vī) *n. pl.*

re•gret•ful•ly (ri gret´ fə lē) *adv.*, with a sense of loss or sorrow

o•men (ō´ mən) *n.*, prophetic sign

dis•solve (di zälv´) *v.*, melt; reduce to liquid form

wea•ri•ly (wir´ ə lē) *adv.*, tiredly

Meet the Author

Laurence Yep (b. 1948) grew up in San Francisco. As a boy, he enjoyed reading fantasy and science fiction stories about children who traveled to strange places. Yep writes for children and young adults and has won many awards for his novels and story collections. Books he has written include *Dragonwings, Child of the Owl,* and *Sea Glass.*

DIRECTED READING

We Are All One

A Chinese Folk Tale retold by Laurence Yep

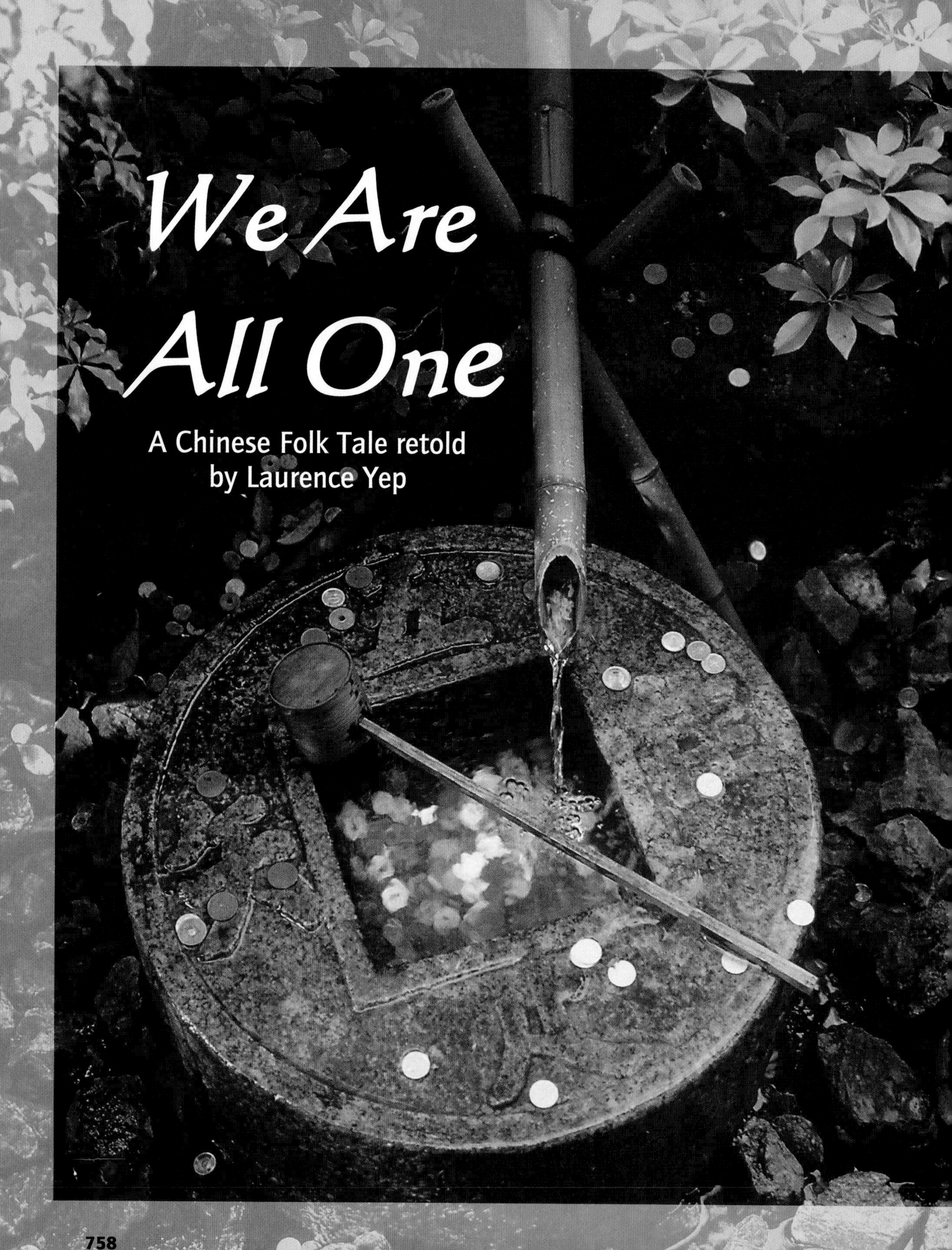

...he gave away as much as he sold, so he was always poor.

Long ago there was a rich man with a disease in his eyes. For many years, the pain was so great that he could not sleep at night. He saw every doctor he could, but none of them could help him.

"What good is all my money?" he groaned. Finally, he became so desperate that he sent criers[1] through the city offering a reward to anyone who could cure him.

Now in that city lived an old candy peddler. He would walk around with his baskets of candy, but he was so kind-hearted that he gave away as much as he sold, so he was always poor.

When the old peddler heard the announcement, he remembered something his mother had said. She had once told him about a magical herb that was good for the eyes. So he packed up his baskets and went back to the single tiny room in which his family lived.

When he told his plan to his wife, she scolded him, "If you go off on this crazy hunt, how are we supposed to eat?"

Usually the peddler gave in to his wife, but this time he was stubborn. "There are two baskets of candy," he said. "I'll be back before they're gone."

The next morning, as soon as the soldiers opened the gates, he was the first one to leave the city. He did not stop until he was deep inside the woods. As a boy, he had often wandered there. He had liked to pretend that the shadowy forest was a green sea and he was a fish slipping through the cool waters.

As he examined the ground, he noticed ants scurrying about. On their backs were larvae like white grains of rice. A rock had fallen into a stream, so the water now spilled into the ant's nest.

"We're all one," the kind-hearted peddler said. So he waded into the shallow stream and put the rock on the bank. Then with a sharp stick, he dug a shallow ditch that sent the rest of the water back into the stream.

Without another thought about his good deed, he began to search through the forest. He looked everywhere; but as the day went on, he grew sleepy. "Ho-hum. I got up too early. I'll take just a short nap," he decided, and lay down in the shade of an old tree, where he fell right asleep.

In his dreams, the old peddler found himself standing in the middle of a great city. Tall buildings rose high overhead. He couldn't see the sky even when he tilted back his head. An escort of soldiers marched up to him with a loud clatter of their black lacquer armor. "Our queen wishes to see you," the captain said.

The frightened peddler could only obey and let the fierce soldiers lead him into a shining palace. There, a woman with a high crown sat upon a tall throne. Trembling, the old peddler fell to his knees and touched his forehead against the floor.

But the queen ordered him to stand. "Like the great Emperor Yü of long ago, you tamed the great flood. We are all one now.

1. **criers.** People who shouted news throughout the town

lar•va (lär´ və) *n.*, early wingless form of a newly hatched insect; **larvae** (lär´ vī) *n. pl.*

You have only to ask, and I or any of my people will come to your aid."

The old peddler cleared his throat. "I am looking for a certain herb. It will cure any disease of the eyes."

The queen shook her head regretfully. "I have never heard of that herb. But you will surely find it if you keep looking for it."

And then the old peddler woke. Sitting up, he saw that in his wanderings he had come back to the ants' nest. It was there he had taken his nap. His dream city had been the ants' nest itself.

"This is a good omen," he said to himself, and he began searching even harder. He was so determined to find the herb that he did not notice how time had passed. He was surprised when he saw how the light was fading. He looked all around then. There was no sight of his city—only strange hills. He realized then that he had searched so far he had gotten lost.

Night was coming fast and with it the cold. He rubbed his arms and hunted for shelter. In the twilight, he thought he could see the green tiles of a roof.

He stumbled through the growing darkness until he reached a ruined temple. Weeds grew through cracks in the stones and most of the roof itself had fallen in. Still, the ruins would provide some protection.

As he started inside, he saw a centipede[2] with bright orange skin and red tufts of fur along its back. Yellow dots covered its sides like a dozen tiny eyes. It was also rushing into the temple as fast as it could, but there was a bird swooping down toward it.

The old peddler waved his arms and shouted, scaring the bird away. Then he put down his palm in front of the insect. "We are all one, you and I." The many feet tickled his skin as the centipede climbed onto his hand.

Inside the temple, he gathered dried leaves and found old sticks of wood and soon he had a fire going. The peddler even picked some fresh leaves for the centipede from a bush near the temple doorway. "I may have to go hungry, but you don't have to, friend."

He wanted to run from the temple, but he couldn't even get up.

Stretching out beside the fire, the old peddler pillowed his head on his arms. He was so tired that he soon fell asleep, but even in his sleep he dreamed he was still searching in the woods. Suddenly he thought he heard footsteps near his head. He woke instantly and looked about, but he only saw the brightly colored centipede.

"Was it you, friend?" The old peddler chuckled and, lying down, he closed his eyes again. "I must be getting nervous."

"We are one, you and I," a voice said faintly—as if from a long distance. "If you go south, you will find a pine tree with two trunks. By its roots, you will find a magic bead. A cousin of mine spat on it years ago. Dissolve that bead in wine and tell the rich man to drink it if he wants to heal his eyes."

The old peddler trembled when he heard the voice, because he realized that the centipede was magical. He wanted to run

2. **centipede.** Wormlike insect that has numerous body segments, each with a pair of legs

re•gret•ful•ly (ri gret´ fə lē) *adv.*, with a sense of loss or sorrow

o•men (ō´ mən) *n.*, prophetic sign

dis•solve (di zälv´) *v.*, melt; reduce to liquid form

from the temple, but he couldn't even get up. It was as if he were glued to the floor.

But then the old peddler reasoned with himself: If the centipede had wanted to hurt me, it could have long ago. Instead, it seems to want to help me.

So the old peddler stayed where he was, but he did not dare open his eyes. When the first sunlight fell through the roof, he raised one eyelid cautiously. There was no sign of the centipede. He sat up and looked around, but the magical centipede was gone.

He followed the centipede's instructions when he left the temple. Traveling south, he kept a sharp eye out for the pine tree with two trunks. He walked until late in the afternoon, but all he saw were normal pine trees.

Wearily he sat down and sighed. Even if he found the pine tree, he couldn't be sure that he would find the bead. Someone else might even have discovered it a long time ago.

But something made him look a little longer. Just when he was thinking about turning back, he saw the odd tree. Somehow his tired legs managed to carry him over to the tree, and he got down on his knees. But the ground was covered with pine needles and his old eyes were too weak. The old peddler could have wept with frustration, and then he remembered the ants.

He began to call, "Ants, ants, we are all one."

wea•ri•ly (wir´ ə lē) *adv.*, tiredly

Almost immediately, thousands of ants came boiling out of nowhere. Delighted, the old man held up his fingers. "I'm looking for a bead. It might be very tiny."

Then, careful not to crush any of his little helpers, the old man sat down to wait. In no time, the ants reappeared with a tiny bead. With trembling fingers, the old man took the bead from them and examined it. It was colored orange and looked as if it had yellow eyes on the sides.

There was nothing very special about the bead, but the old peddler treated it like a fine jewel. Putting the bead into his pouch, the old peddler bowed his head. "I thank you and I thank your queen," the old man said. After the ants disappeared among the pine needles, he made his way out of the woods.

The next day, he reached the house of the rich man. However, he was so poor and ragged that the gatekeeper only laughed at him. "How could an old beggar like you help my master?"

The old peddler tried to argue. "Beggar or rich man, we are all one."

"Beggar or rich man, we are all one."

But it so happened that the rich man was passing by the gates. He went over to the old peddler. "I said anyone could see me. But it'll mean a stick across your back if you're wasting my time."

The old peddler took out the pouch. "Dissolve this bead in some wine and drink it down." Then, turning the pouch upside down, he shook the tiny bead onto his palm and handed it to the rich man.

The rich man immediately called for a cup of wine. Dropping the bead into the wine, he waited a moment and then drank it down. Instantly the pain vanished. Shortly after that, his eyes healed.

The rich man was so happy and grateful that he doubled the reward. And the kindly old peddler and his family lived comfortably for the rest of their lives. ✤

How might you reflect the peddler's belief that "We are all one" in your own life? How would the world be different if everyone practiced this philosophy?

AFTER READING

Find Meaning

1. (a) What is the setting of this story? (b) How is the setting important to the plot?

2. (a) What does the old candy peddler decide to do to help the rich man? (b) Why do you think he decides to do this?

3. (a) What good deed does the peddler perform for the ants? (b) What does he say as he does this? (c) What does he mean by this?

Make Judgments

4. Why does the peddler think his dream of the ants' nest is a good omen?

5. Why is the peddler more frightened by the centipede than by the ants?

6. (a) How do the ants help the peddler? (b) What inspires the peddler to ask the ants for help?

Analyze Literature

Conflict As the peddler goes on his journey, he encounters several obstacles that prevent him from completing his task. List each obstacle the peddler encounters, and note how the problem was solved. Then review all the obstacles and determine the story's main conflict.

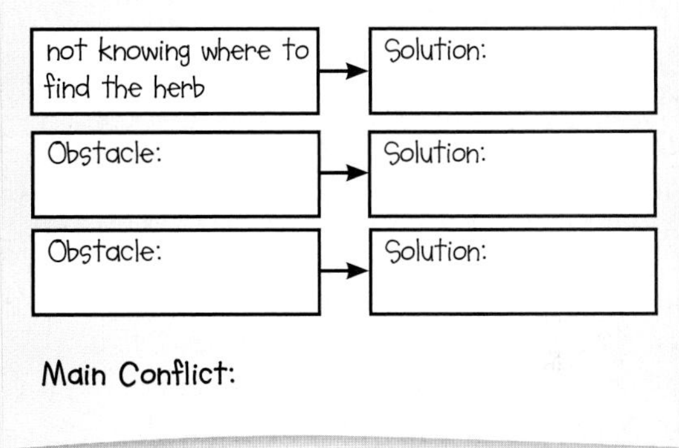

Extend Understanding

Writing Options

Descriptive Writing Review the dream sequence in which the ants are described as soldiers in shining black armor. Using this passage as a model, write a **descriptive paragraph** in which you personify an animal. Use the animal's habitat and natural appearance as the basis for your imagined humanlike description.

Informative Writing Write a **literary response** in which you analyze and evaluate the theme of "We Are All One." First, describe the theme, restating it in your own words. Then, provide evidence that supports your claim. Finally, state whether or not you agree with the theme of the folk tale.

Critical Literacy

Hold a Debate As a class, debate the notion that "we are all one." Do you agree with it or disagree with it? If a national government adopted this concept as a guiding principle, what kinds of policies might the government implement? How would the world be different if everyone believed that "we are all one"?

Lifelong Learning

Magical Animals Animals that have magical or unusual powers are fairly common in folk tales. In a small group, brainstorm a list of other stories in which the main character encounters magical animals. Do some animals appear more frequently in these tales than others? If so, what might explain this? How do they interact with humans? Present your findings to the class.

Go to **www.mirrorsandwindows.com** for more.

Grammar & Style

Misplaced Modifiers

When the old peddler heard the announcement, he remembered something his mother had said.

—LAURENCE YEP, "We Are All One"

Misplaced modifiers are phrases and clauses that confuse the meaning of a sentence. A **misplaced modifier** is located so far from the word it should modify that it appears to be modifying an inappropriate word.

For example, in the quotation above, the phrase *When the old peddler heard the announcement* modifies the verb *remembered*. Consider the following reworking of the above quotation.

INCORRECT

He remembered something his mother had said when the old peddler heard the announcement.

Now the placement of the phrase *when the old peddler heard the announcement* makes it appear to modify the verb *said.*

To correct misplaced modifiers, move the modifier closer to the word it modifies.

INCORRECT

He noticed ants scurrying around when he examined the ground.

In this example, it sounds as if the ants scurried because he examined the ground. To correct this error, move the modifier.

CORRECT

When he examined the ground, he noticed ants scurrying around.

Correcting Misplaced Modifiers

Rewrite each sentence so that the underlined phrase or clause modifies the underlined word.

1. The old peddler pillowed his head on his arms lying beside the fire.
2. Dissolve the bead in the wine that you find near a pine tree.
3. The peddler saw a bird swooping toward a caterpillar looking up.
4. A small fire burned in the cave that the peddler had built.
5. The peddler saw the odd tree as it was getting dark.
6. The announcement included information about the rich man posted on the wall.
7. The ants looked up at the peddler crawling from their nest.
8. The queen spoke with the peddler in her crown.
9. The rich man waited for the peddler at his table.
10. When the peddler asked for help, the queen called her army from her throne.
11. A bird flew over the peddler's head watching the earth.
12. The rich man yelled at his guard drinking his wine.
13. Pine trees glimmered in the sunlight dropping needles to the ground.
14. An ant crawled up the peddler's leg clenching a bead in its mouth.
15. The magic centipede moved around the temple speaking to the peddler.

Ant and Grasshopper
The Fox and the Crow
The Lion and the Statue

Greek Fables by Aesop

BEFORE READING

Build Background

Historical Context Fables are an ancient form of folk tale that spread from India and Greece into western Europe around the fourth century BC. In the first or second century AD, fables attributed to Aesop were recorded in verse by the Greek poet Babrius and also by the Roman poet Phaedrus. In the following centuries, the fable became a popular genre in world literature. In the seventeenth century, the French writer Jean de La Fontaine used the fable genre to write satires. Later writers of fables in English include Ambrose Bierce, George Orwell, and James Thurber.

Reader's Context How can old tales that feature animals as characters teach lessons that are useful in today's world?

Set Purpose

Think about what you know about the fable genre to help you determine what to expect from the selections and how to read them.

Analyze Literature

Fable A brief story, written in prose or verse, that conveys a moral or lesson is called a **fable.** The characters in a fable are usually animals that are given human characteristics. As you read these three selections, think about the message, or moral, that each one conveys.

Use Reading Skills

Identify Author's Purpose An author's purpose is his or her reason for writing. After reading each fable, consider what you think the author was attempting to accomplish. Use a two-column chart, like the one below, to help determine the author's purpose for each fable.

Details	Author's Purpose
The ant gathers grain all summer, "grain by grain."	

Meet the Author

Aesop (620?–560? BC) may or may not have actually existed. There are several different stories about the background of this man, whose name is always linked with animal fables from the Greek oral tradition. Some say that Aesop was a freed slave; others say that he was an adviser to King Croesus of Lydia or a riddle-solver for King Lycurgus of Babylon. It is also possible that ancient storytellers simply attributed these animal fables to an imaginary author.

The Ant and the Grasshopper, c. 20th century. Edward Bawden. Chelmsford Museums, Essex, United Kingdom.

Ant and Grasshopper

Aesop's Fable retold by James Reeves

All summer the ant had been working hard, gathering a store of corn for the winter. Grain by grain she had taken it from the fields and stowed it away in a hole in the bank, under a hawthorn bush.

One bright, frosty day in winter Grasshopper saw her. She was dragging out a grain of corn to dry it in the sun. The wind was keen, and poor Grasshopper was cold.

"Good morning, Ant," said he. "What a terrible winter it is! I'm half dead with hunger. Please give me just one of your corn grains to eat. I can find nothing, although I've hopped all over the farmyard. There isn't a seed to be found. Spare me a grain, I beg."

"Why haven't you saved anything up?" asked Ant. "I worked hard all through the summer, storing food for the winter. Very glad I am too, for as you say, it's bitterly cold."

"I wasn't idle last summer, either," said Grasshopper.

"And what did you do, pray?"

"Why, I spent the time singing," answered Grasshopper. "Every day from dawn till sunset I jumped about or sat in the sun, chirruping to my heart's content."

"Oh you did, did you?" replied Ant. "Well, since you've sung all summer to keep yourself cheerful, you may dance all winter to keep yourself warm. Not a grain will I give you!"

And she scuttled off into her hole in the bank, while Grasshopper was left cold and hungry. ✣

Fox and Crow. Bibliothèque Nationale, Paris.

The Fox and the Crow

Aesop's Fable retold by Joseph Jacobs

A Fox once saw a Crow fly off with a piece of cheese in its beak and settle on a branch of a tree. "That's for me, as I am a Fox," said Master Reynard, and he walked up to the foot of the tree.

"Good day, Mistress Crow," he cried. "How well you are looking today: how glossy your feathers; how bright your eye. I feel sure your voice must surpass that of other birds, just as your figure does; let me hear but one song from you that I may greet you as the Queen of Birds."

The Crow lifted up her head and began to caw her best, but the moment she opened her mouth the piece of cheese fell to the ground, only to be snapped up by Master Fox. "That will do," said he. "That was all I wanted. In exchange for your cheese I will give you a piece of advice for the future—

Do not trust flatterers." ✤

The Lion and the Statue

Aesop's Fable retold by Joseph Jacobs

A Man and a Lion were discussing the relative strength of men and lions in general. The Man contended that he and his fellows were stronger than lions by reason of their greater intelligence. "Come now with me," he cried, "and I will soon prove that I am right." So he took him into the public gardens and showed him a statue of Hercules overcoming the Lion and tearing his mouth in two.

"That is all very well," said the Lion, "but proves nothing, for it was a man who made the statue." ✣

Emperor Commodus as Hercules, AD 191–192. Unknown artist. Musei Capitolini, Rome.

How have you applied a moral lesson from one of these fables? Which fable offers the most useful advice for people today? Why is it important advice?

AFTER READING

Find Meaning

1. (a) Why does Ant refuse to help Grasshopper? (b) Do you agree with Ant's decision? Why or why not?
2. (a) In "The Fox and the Crow," what goal does the Fox achieve? (b) How does the Fox achieve this goal?
3. (a) What do the characters argue about in "The Lion and the Statue"? (b) Why does the man want the Lion to see the statue?

Make Judgments

4. What human character trait does the Crow exhibit that causes her to be tricked by the Fox?
5. In "Ant and Grasshopper," what adjectives would you use to describe the character traits of each animal?
6. In your own words, describe the moral of "The Lion and the Statue."

Analyze Literature

Fable How well do the events in each fable support the moral? How do the characters and the events help you remember and understand the lesson conveyed? Use a chart to paraphrase, or restate in your own words, the moral of each fable. Then write a brief evaluation of that moral.

	Moral	My Evaluation
"Ant and Grasshopper"	The fruits of labor only go to those who work hard for them.	
"The Fox and the Crow"		
"The Lion and the Statue"		

Extend Understanding

Writing Options

Narrative Writing Write a modern **fable** for young children. Remember that a fable should convey a straightforward moral lesson. Decide on a lesson that you think is important for young children to learn, and think of a plot that might teach that lesson. Be sure to include animal characters that have human traits. State the moral at the end of your fable.

Argumentative Writing Write an **editorial** to post on a class website. In your editorial, support one of the morals from the fables. Choose the moral that you think is the most useful. Determine why you think this lesson is relevant. Then use these reasons to back up your claims.

Critical Literacy

Create a Drama With a partner, select one of these fables to rewrite as a short drama. Make a list of the characters; write descriptions of the set, costumes, and props; and write the dialogue and stage directions. Rehearse your play several times before you perform it for your class.

Lifelong Learning

Research Fables Use the library or the Internet to find fables from a variety of cultures. On note cards, write brief summaries of at least four fables. Include the moral of each fable. Present your summaries to the class. Then, as a class, compare the fables and morals you have collected. Discuss similarities and differences. Post the note cards in a class display, organizing them according to culture.

Go to **www.mirrorsandwindows.com** for more.

Phaëthon, Son of Apollo

A Greek Myth retold by Olivia E. Coolidge

DIRECTED READING

BEFORE READING

Build Background

Cultural Context The heroes of ancient Greece were highly revered. A hero might have one parent who was a god and one who was a human, or a hero might simply be a person with exceptional attributes, such as beauty or strength. Many heroes were known for their bold and daring exploits. Both gods and heroes had character flaws similar to those of ordinary humans, and these flaws often led to their downfall.

Reader's Context When have you done something that others warned was dangerous? Why did you do it?

Set Purpose

Before you begin to read, look at the artwork that accompanies the story, think about the title and genre, and use these clues to predict the theme or message that the myth conveys.

Analyze Literature

Allegory A story that has a symbolic meaning in addition to its literal meaning is an **allegory.** Often, allegorical stories offer moral lessons. As you read "Phaëthon, Son of Apollo," think about the underlying meanings related to the characters and events.

Use Reading Skills

Draw Conclusions

Allegories convey truths or generalizations about human behavior or experience. As you read "Phaëthon, Son of Apollo," use a two-column chart to collect evidence and draw conclusions about the theme or message of the allegory.

Evidence	Conclusion
Phaëthon always had to be the first and best at everything, and he would take any risk to win.	

Meet the Author

Olivia E. Coolidge (1908–2006) was born in London, England. She graduated from Oxford University in 1931 and went on to earn a master's degree. The first book she published was *Greek Myths* in 1949, which she wrote for children and young adults. She later published collections of Roman and Egyptian myths as well as biographies and historical fiction. Coolidge is acclaimed for her accurate portrayals of historical subjects and for her ability to bring ancient and mythical worlds to life.

Preview Vocabulary

def•er•ence (de´ fə rən[t]s) *n.*, respectful yielding

im•plore (im plōr´) *v.*, beg

dis•suade (di swād´) *v.*, deter a person from a course of action by persuasion

pre•cip•i•tous (pri si´ pə təs) *adj.*, very steep

am•ber (am´ bər) *adj.*, yellowish red; *n.*, hardened sap

Phaëthon, Son of Apollo

The Chariot of Apollo, 1907–1910. Odilon Redon. Fitzwilliam Museum, University of Cambridge, United Kingdom.

A Greek Myth retold by Olivia E. Coolidge

Phaëthon loved to boast of his divine father as he saw the golden chariot riding high through the air.

"Let me drive the chariot of the sun

Though Apollo always honored the memory of Daphne she was not his only love. Another was a mortal, Clymene,[1] by whom he had a son named Phaëthon.[2] Phaëthon grew up with his mother, who, since she was mortal, could not dwell in the halls of Olympus[3] or in the palace of the sun. She lived not far from the East in the land of Ethiopia, and as her son grew up, she would point to the place where Eos,[4] goddess of the dawn, lighted up the sky and tell him that there his father dwelt. Phaëthon loved to boast of his divine father as he saw the golden chariot riding high through the air. He would remind his comrades of other sons of gods and mortal women who, by virtue of their great deeds, had themselves become gods at last. He must always be first in everything, and in most things this was easy, since he was in truth stronger, swifter, and more daring than the others. Even if he were not victorious, Phaëthon always claimed to be first in honor. He could never bear to be beaten, even if he must risk his life in some rash way to win.

Most of the princes of Ethiopia willingly paid Phaëthon honor, since they admired him greatly for his fire and beauty. There was one boy, however, Epaphos,[5] who was rumored to be a child of Zeus[6] himself. Since this was not certainly proved, Phaëthon chose to disbelieve it and to demand from Epaphos the deference that he obtained from all others. Epaphos was proud too, and one day he lost his temper with Phaëthon and turned on him, saying, "You are a fool to believe all that your mother tells you. You are all swelled up with false ideas about your father."

Crimson with rage, the lad rushed home to his mother and demanded that she prove to him the truth of the story that she had often told. "Give me some proof," he implored her, "with which I can answer this insult of Epaphos. It is a matter of life and death to me, for if I cannot, I shall die of shame."

"I swear to you," replied his mother solemnly, "by the bright orb of the sun itself that you are his son. If I swear falsely, may I never look on the sun again, but die before the next time he mounts the heavens. More than this I cannot do, but you, my child, can go to the eastern palace of Phoebus Apollo—it lies not far away—and there speak with the god himself."

The son of Clymene leaped up with joy at his mother's words. The palace of Apollo was indeed not far. It stood just below the eastern horizon, its tall pillars glistening with bronze and gold. Above these it was white with gleaming ivory, and the great doors were flashing silver, embossed with pictures of earth, sky, and sea, and the gods that dwelt therein. Up the steep hill and the bright steps climbed Phaëthon, passing unafraid through the silver doors, and stood in the presence of the sun. Here at last he was forced to turn away his face, for Phoebus sat in state on his golden throne. It gleamed with emeralds and precious stones, while on the head of the god was a brilliant diamond crown upon which no eye could look undazzled.

Phaëthon hid his face, but the god had recognized his son, and he spoke kindly,

1. **Clymene** (klim´ ə nē).
2. **Phaëthon** (fā´ ə tän).
3. **Olympus.** In Greek mythology, the home of the gods
4. **Eos** (e´ äs).
5. **Epaphos** (ep´ ə fəs).
6. **Zeus.** Ruler of the gods, associated with the thunderbolt; he controlled thunder, lightning, and rain.

def•er•ence (de´ fə rən[t]s) *n.*, respectful yielding

im•plore (im plōr´) *v.*, beg

across the heavens for one day," he said.

asking him why he had come. Then Phaëthon plucked up courage and said, "I come to ask you if you are indeed my father. If you are so, I beg you to give me some proof of it so that all may recognize me as Phoebus'[7] son."

SCIENCE ▶▶ CONNECTION

Solar Models While ancient peoples told myths such as the story of Phaëthon to help explain the rising and setting of the sun, ancient astronomers were carefully observing the movements of the celestial bodies and forming theories about the universe. About AD 150, Egyptian scientist Claudius Ptolemy theorized that the Earth was at the center of the universe. According to Ptolemy's model, the Earth is stationary and the planets, sun, and moon move slowly around it. However, this Earth-centered, or *geocentric,* theory left many questions unanswered. It wasn't until the sixteenth century that Polish astronomer Nicolaus Copernicus began to establish the basis for the sun-centered, or *heliocentric,* universe. Though stories such as "Phaëthon, Son of Apollo" are scientifically unsound, why might they still be useful?

(Above) ***Portrait of Polish Astronomer Nicolas Copernicus,*** c. 1933.

The god smiled, being well pleased with his son's beauty and daring. He took off his crown so that Phaëthon could look at him, and coming down from his throne, he put his arms around the boy, and said, "You are indeed my son and Clymene's, and worthy to be called so. Ask of me whatever thing you wish to prove your origin to men, and you shall have it."

Phaëthon swayed for a moment and was dizzy with excitement at the touch of the god. His heart leaped; the blood rushed into his face. Now he felt that he was truly divine, unlike other men, and he did not wish to be counted with men any more. He looked up for a moment at his radiant father. "Let me drive the chariot of the sun across the heavens for one day," he said.

Apollo frowned and shook his head. "I cannot break my promise, but I will dissuade you if I can," he answered. "How can you drive my chariot, whose horses need a strong hand on the reins? The climb is too steep for you. The immense height will make you dizzy. The swift streams of air in the upper heaven will sweep you off your course. Even the immortal gods could not drive my chariot. How then can you? Be wise and make some other choice."

The pride of Phaëthon was stubborn, for he thought the god was merely trying to frighten him. Besides, if he could guide the sun's chariot, would he not have proved his right to be divine rather than mortal? For that he would risk his life. Indeed, once he had seen Apollo's splendor, he did not wish to go back and live among men. Therefore, he insisted on his right until Apollo had to give way.

When the father saw that nothing else would satisfy the boy, he bade the Hours

---

7. Phoebus (fē´ bəs). Another name for Apollo

dis • suade (di swād´) *v.,* deter a person from a course of action by persuasion bring forth his chariot and yoke the horses. The chariot was of gold and had two gold-rimmed wheels with spokes of silver. In it there was room for one man to stand and hold the reins. Around the front and sides of it ran a rail, but the back was open. At the end of a long pole there were yokes for the four horses. The pole was of gold and shone with precious jewels: the golden topaz, the bright diamond, the green emerald, and the flashing ruby. While the Hours were yoking the swift, pawing horses, rosy-fingered Dawn hastened to the gates of heaven to draw them open. Meanwhile Apollo anointed his son's face with a magic ointment, that he might be able to bear the heat of the fire-breathing horses and the golden chariot. At last Phaëthon mounted the chariot and grasped the reins, the barriers were let down, and the horses shot up into the air.

At first the fiery horses sped forward up the accustomed trail, but behind them the chariot was too light without the weight of the immortal god. It bounded from side to side and was dashed up and down. Phaëthon was too frightened and too dizzy to pull the reins, nor would he have known anyway whether he was on the usual path. As soon as the horses felt that there was no hand controlling them, they soared up, up with fiery speed into the heavens till the earth grew pale and cold beneath them. Phaëthon shut his eyes, trembling at the dizzy, precipitous height. Then the horses dropped down, more swiftly than a falling stone, flinging themselves madly from side to side in panic because they were masterless. Phaëthon dropped the reins entirely and clung with all his might to the chariot rail. Meanwhile as they came near the earth, it dried up and cracked apart. Meadows were reduced to white ashes, cornfields smoked and shriveled, cities perished in flame. Far and wide on the wooded mountains the forests were ablaze, and even the snowclad Alps were bare and dry. Rivers steamed and dried to dust. The great North African plain was scorched until it became the desert that it is today. Even the sea shrank back to pools and caves, until dried fishes were left baking upon the white-hot sands. At last the great earth mother called upon Zeus to save her from utter destruction, and Zeus hurled a mighty thunderbolt at the unhappy Phaëthon, who was still crouched in the chariot, clinging desperately to the rail. The dart cast him out, and he fell flaming in a long trail through the air. The chariot broke in pieces at the mighty blow, and the maddened horses rushed snorting back to the stable of their master, Apollo.

Unhappy Clymene and her daughters wandered over the whole earth seeking the body of the boy they loved so well. When they found him, they took him and buried him. Over his grave they wept and could not be comforted. At last the gods in pity for their grief changed them into poplar trees, which weep with tears of amber in memory of Phaëthon. ✣

pre•cip•i•tous (pri si´ pə təs) *adj.*, very steep

am•ber (am´ bər) *adj.*, yellowish red; *n.*, hardened sap

Think of a time when you overestimated your abilities. What happened? Why do you think people misjudge themselves in this way?

AFTER READING

Find Meaning

1. What does Phaëthon's behavior with his friends reveal about his character?

2. (a) Who is Phaëthon's father? (b) Why does Phaëthon want everyone to know who his father is?

3. (a) What does Phaëthon request of his father? (b) Why does he ask for this?

Make Judgments

4. (a) Why does Apollo agree to Phaëthon's request? (b) Should he have refused? Why or why not?

5. (a) At what point would most people have recognized the danger involved in driving the chariot? (b) Why do you think Phaëthon failed to recognize this?

Analyze Literature

Allegory Allegories typically present a moral lesson. What is the theme, or message, of "Phaëthon, Son of Apollo"? Use a theme map to gather details from this story. List the main characters and their traits, the story's central conflict, and the way this conflict is resolved. Then think about what these details suggest about the story's theme.

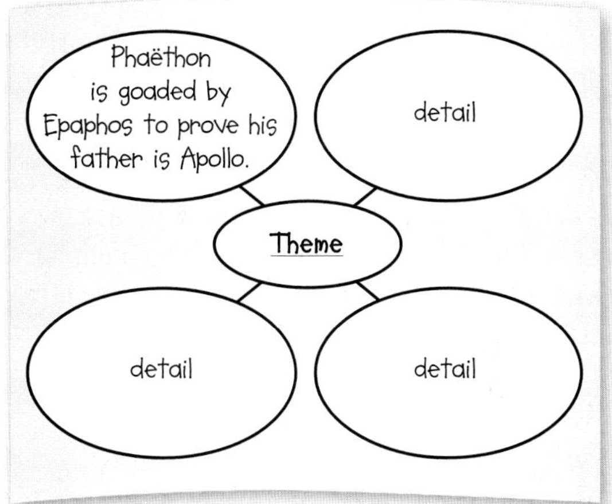

Extend Understanding

Writing Options

Creative Writing Imagine that your crops were lost as a result of Phaëthon's ride. Write a **business letter** to Apollo to complain about his management of the sun. Cite reasons for your dissatisfaction. Offer some suggestions for how to correct the problem. Be sure to use an appropriate and respectful tone.

Informative Writing Using your theme map, write a brief **literary analysis** of "Phaëthon, Son of Apollo." At the start of your analysis, state the theme of this myth in a thesis. Then support your claims with reasons and evidence from the text. At the end of your response, restate what you believe the theme to be, and sum up your main points.

Critical Literacy

Write a Character Sketch In small groups, collect and discuss information about Phaëthon's personality. Begin by listing his reasons for wanting to drive his father's chariot. Then determine what this list suggests about his character. Use the information you collect to write a brief character sketch of Phaëthon.

Lifelong Learning

Compare Myths Use library resources or the Internet to locate another retelling of this myth. Compare and contrast the two retellings. Do they both express the same theme? In what ways are the retellings alike? In what ways are they different? Create a Venn diagram to show how these retellings are both similar and different.

Go to **www.mirrorsandwindows.com** for more.

Grammar & Style

Dangling Modifiers

Crimson with rage, the lad rushed home to his mother....

—OLIVIA E. COOLIDGE, "Phaëthon, Son of Apollo"

Dangling modifiers confuse the reader. A **dangling modifier** seems to modify nothing because the word it should modify does not appear in the sentence.

A reader assumes that an introductory phrase or clause will modify the first noun after the comma. For example, imagine a sentence similar to the quotation above.

INCORRECT

Crimson with rage, the fence kept him away from us.

The sentence is confusing because it appears that *the fence* was crimson with rage.

To correct dangling modifiers, reword the sentence. The sentence often becomes clear when the modified word or words is added.

CORRECT

Crimson with rage, he was kept away from us by the fence.

By expanding the dangling phrase into a full subordinate clause, you can also eliminate dangling modifiers.

INCORRECT

Falling toward the earth, many fields were burned.

CORRECT

As Phaëthon fell toward the earth, he burned many fields.

By changing the dangling phrase *Falling toward the earth* into the full subordinate clause *As Phaëthon fell toward the earth,* the dangling modifier is eliminated.

Understanding Dangling Modifiers

On a separate sheet of paper, revise each sentence to correct the dangling modifier.

1. Receiving answers from his mother, questions about his father remained.
2. Poorly behaved, it was easy to guess that something would happen to him.
3. Anointing his face with a magic ointment, the sun wouldn't burn Phaëthon.
4. Diving and soaring, the sky was filled with light.
5. Falling near the earth, meadows were reduced to white ashes.
6. Acting superior to other children, a terrible end was endured.
7. Crying out in fear, the chariot fell to earth.
8. After leaving his home, the sun grabbed his attention.
9. While speaking with his mother, laughter of the other children could be heard.
10. Calling to the horses, the chariot rose and fell.

Comparing Texts

The Instruction of Indra

A Hindu Myth retold by Joseph Campbell with Bill Moyers

SUCH PERFECTION

A Short Story by R. K. Narayan

DIRECTED READING

BEFORE READING

Build Background

Cultural Context Hindu tradition holds that everything cycles through the stages of birth, order, and destruction. The stages of this cycle are presided over by the deities Brahma, Vishnu, and Shiva, respectively. According to the doctrine of karma, one's search for enlightenment extends through many lifetimes. A person's deeds determine the quality of that person's next life.

Reader's Context What often happens to boastful people?

Set Purpose

Scan each selection to identify unfamiliar words. Then use a dictionary to determine the meanings of these words.

Meet the Authors

Joseph Campbell (1904–1987) gained an international reputation as a scholar of mythology and comparative religion. He studied at universities in the United States and in Europe. Broadcast journalist Bill Moyers produced a television series and a book based on interviews with Campbell called *The Power of Myth*.

R. K. Narayan (1906–2001), born in Madras, India, has been called India's greatest twentieth-century writer in English. Best known for his novels, he also wrote short stories and stories based on Hindu mythology. Narayan's long writing career spanned more than fifty years.

Compare Literature: Symbolism

A **symbol** is something that stands for or represents both itself and something else. Use a chart like this one to list the symbols and what they stand for in "The Instruction of Indra" and "Such Perfection."

	"The Instruction of Indra"	"Such Perfection"
Symbol	Indra's palace	
What Symbol Stands for		

Preview Vocabulary

drought (draůt) *n.*, period of dry weather; lack of rain

cos•mic (käz´ mik) *adj.*, relating to the universe as a whole

gran•di•ose (gran´ dē ōs') *adj.*, magnificent; grand

dis•il•lu•sioned (dis' ə lü´ zhənd) *adj.*, disappointed; dissatisfied

man•i•fes•ta•tion (ma' nə fə stā´ shən) *n.*, example; instance

The Instruction of Indra

A Hindu Myth retold by Joseph Campbell with Bill Moyers

"Indras before you. I have seen them come and go, come and go."

There is a wonderful story in one of the Upanishads[1] about the god Indra.[2] Now, it happened at this time that a great monster had enclosed all the waters of the earth, so there was a terrible drought, and the world was in a very bad condition. It took Indra quite a while to realize that he had a box of thunderbolts and that all he had to do was drop a thunderbolt on the monster and blow him up. When he did that, the waters flowed, and the world was refreshed and Indra said, "What a great boy am I."

So, thinking, "What a great boy am I," Indra goes up to the cosmic mountain, which is the central mountain of the world, and decides to build a palace worthy of such as he. The main carpenter of the gods goes to work on it, and in very quick order he gets the palace into pretty good condition.

Engraving of Indra mounted on his elephant, c. 1880.

But every time Indra comes to inspect it, he has bigger ideas about how splendid and grandiose the palace should be. Finally, the carpenter says, "My god, we are both immortal, and there is no end to his desires. I am caught for eternity." So he decides to go to Brahma, the creator god, and complain.

Brahma sits on a lotus,[3] the symbol of divine energy and divine grace. The lotus grows from the navel of Vishnu, who is the sleeping god, whose dream is the universe. So the carpenter comes to the edge of the great lotus pond of the universe and tells his story to Brahma. Brahma says, "You go home. I will fix this up." Brahma gets off his lotus and kneels down to address sleeping Vishnu. Vishnu just makes a gesture and says something like, "Listen, fly, something is going to happen."

Next morning, at the gate of the palace that is being built, there appears a beautiful blue-black boy with a lot of children around him, just admiring his beauty. The porter at the gate of the new palace goes running to Indra, and Indra says, "Well, bring in the boy." The boy is brought in, and Indra, the king god, sitting on his throne, says, "Young man, welcome. And what brings you to my palace?"

"Well," says the boy with a voice like thunder rolling on the horizon, "I have been told that you are building such a palace as no Indra before you ever built."

And Indra says, "Indras before me, young man—what are you talking about?"

The boy says, "Indras before you. I have seen them come and go, come and go. Just think, Vishnu sleeps in the cosmic ocean, and the lotus of the universe grows from his navel. On the lotus sits Brahma, the creator.

1. **Upanishads.** Indian philosophical and religious writings
2. **Indra.** Chief god of ancient India
3. **lotus.** Pink or white water lily used as a religious symbol in Hinduism

drought (draůt) *n.*, period of dry weather; lack of rain

cos • mic (käz´ mik) *adj.*, relating to the universe as a whole

gran • di • ose (gran´ dē ōs') *adj.*, magnificent; grand

God with Three Faces, Brahma, c. 11th century. Musée Guimet, Paris.

And so the boy points to the ants and says, "Former Indras all. Through many lifetimes they rise from the lowest conditions to highest illumination.[4] And then they drop their thunderbolt on a monster, and they think, 'What a good boy am I.' And down they go again."

While the boy is talking, a crotchety old yogi[5] comes into the palace with a banana leaf parasol. He is naked except for a loincloth,[6] and on his chest is a little disk of hair, and half the hairs in the middle have all dropped out.

The boy greets him and asks him just what Indra was about to ask. "Old man, what is your name? Where do you come from? Where is your family? Where is your house? And what is the meaning of this curious constellation of hair on your chest?"

"Well," says the old fella, "my name is Hairy. I don't have a house. Life is too short for that. I just have this parasol. I don't have a family. I just meditate on Vishnu's feet, and think of eternity, and how passing time is. You know, every time an Indra dies, a world disappears—these things just flash by like that. Every time an Indra dies, one hair drops out of this circle on my chest. Half the hairs are gone now. Pretty soon they will all be gone. Life is short. Why build a house?"

Then the two disappear. The boy was Vishnu, the Lord Protector,[7] and the old yogi

Brahma opens his eyes, and a world comes into being, governed by an Indra. Brahma closes his eyes, and a world goes out of being. The life of a Brahma is four hundred and thirty-two thousand years. When he dies, the lotus goes back, and another lotus is formed, and another Brahma. Then think of the galaxies beyond galaxies in infinite space, each a lotus, with a Brahma sitting on it, opening his eyes, closing his eyes. And Indras? There may be wise men in your court who would volunteer to count the drops of water in the oceans of the world or the grains of sand on the beaches, but no one would count those Brahmin, let alone those Indras."

While the boy is talking, an army of ants parades across the floor. The boy laughs when he sees them, and Indra's hair stands on end, and he says to the boy, "Why do you laugh?"

The boy answers, "Don't ask unless you are willing to be hurt."

Indra says, "I ask. Teach." (That, by the way, is a good Oriental idea: you don't teach until you are asked. You don't force your mission down people's throats.)

4. **illumination.** Highest level of spiritual understanding
5. **yogi.** Hindu holy man, one who practices a spiritual path, or yoga
6. **loincloth.** Cloth worn about the waist and upper thighs
7. **Vishnu, the Lord Protector.** In Hindu belief, one of the appearances of Vishnu on Earth was as Krishna, frequently pictured as a beautiful blue-black youth

was Shiva, the creator and destroyer of the world, who had just come for the instruction of Indra, who is simply a god of history but thinks he is the whole show.

Indra is sitting there on the throne, and he is completely disillusioned, completely shot. He calls the carpenter and says, "I'm quitting the building of this palace. You are dismissed." So the carpenter got his intention. He is dismissed from the job, and there is no more house building going on.

Indra decides to go out and be a yogi and just meditate on the lotus feet of Vishnu. But he has a beautiful queen named Indrani. And when Indrani hears of Indra's plan, she goes to the priest of the gods and says, "Now he has got the idea in his head of going out to become a yogi."

"Well," says the priest, "come in with me, darling, and we will sit down, and I will fix this up."

So they sit down before the king's throne, and the priest says, "Now, I wrote a book for you many years ago on the art of politics. You are in the position of the king of the gods. You are a manifestation of the mystery of Brahma in the field of time. This is a high privilege. Appreciate it, honor it, and deal with life as though you were what you really are. And besides, now I am going to write you a book on the art of love so that you and your wife will know that in the wonderful mystery of the two that are one, the Brahma is radiantly present also."

And with this set of instructions, Indra gives up his idea of going out and becoming a yogi and finds that, in life, he can represent the eternal as a symbol, you might say, of the Brahma.

So each of us is, in a way, the Indra of his own life. You can make a choice, either to throw it all off and go into the forest to meditate, or to stay in the world, both in the life of your job, which is the kingly job of politics and achievement, and in the love life with your wife and family. Now, this is a very nice myth, it seems to me. ✣

dis•il•lu•sioned (dis' ə lü´ zhənd) *adj.*, disappointed; dissatisfied

man•i•fes•ta•tion (ma' nə fə stā´ shən) *n.*, example; instance

In your own words, explain the lessons that Indra learned. How important are such lessons in your own life? How are these lessons relevant to people living in today's world?

Find Meaning

1. (a) What problem does Indra solve by using a thunderbolt? (b) What might you infer about Indra from the fact that it took him "quite a while to realize" that he could use the thunderbolts?

2. (a) Why does Indra decide to build a palace? (b) Based on Indra's actions, what do you think of him?

Make Judgments

3. In what ways do you find the arguments of the beautiful blue-black boy and the old yogi compelling?

4. (a) Why does Indrani go to see the priest? (b) Do you agree with the priest's advice to Indra? Explain.

SUCH PERFECTION

A Short Story by R. K. Narayan

A sense of great relief filled Soma as he realized that his five years of labor were coming to an end. He had turned out scores of images in his lifetime, but he had never done any work to equal this. He often said to himself that long after the Deluge[1] had swept the earth this Nataraja[2] would still be standing on His pedestal.

No other human being had seen the image yet. Soma shut himself in and bolted all the doors and windows and plied[3] his chisel[4] by the still flame of a mud lamp, even when there was a bright sun outside. It made him perspire unbearably, but he did not mind it so long as it helped him to keep out prying eyes. He worked with a fierce concentration and never encouraged anyone to talk about it.

After all, his labors had come to an end. He sat back, wiped the perspiration off his face and surveyed his handiwork with great satisfaction. As he looked on he was overwhelmed by the majesty of this image. He fell prostrate[5] before it, praying, "I have taken five years to make you. May you reside in our temple and bless all human beings!" The dim mud flame cast subtle shadows on the image and gave it an undertone of rippling life. The sculptor stood lost in this vision. A voice said, "My friend, never take this image out of this room. It is too perfect...." Soma trembled with fear. He looked round. He saw a figure crouching in a dark corner of the room—it was a man. Soma dashed forward and clutched him by the throat. "Why did you come here?" The other writhed under the grip and replied, "Out of admiration for you. I have always loved your work. I have waited for five years...."

"How did you come in?"

"With another key while you were eating inside...."

Soma gnashed his teeth. "Shall I strangle you before this God and offer you as sacrifice?" "By all means," replied the other, "if it will help you in any way...but I doubt it. Even with a sacrifice you cannot take it

1. **Deluge.** In Hindu mythology, every 4,320,000 years humanity is destroyed by a flood and is then re-created.
2. **Nataraja.** Form of the Hindu god Shiva, also known as Lord of the Dance, whose dancing sets in motion the destruction of the world
3. **plied.** Worked with
4. **chisel.** Wedgelike tool used for shaping wood or stone
5. **prostrate.** Stretched out with face on the ground in humility

out. It is too perfect. Such perfection is not for mortals." The sculptor wept. "Oh, do not say that. I worked in secrecy only for this perfection. It is for our people. It is a God coming into their midst. Don't deny them that." The other prostrated before the image and prayed aloud, "God give us the strength to bear your presence...."

This man spoke to people and the great secret was out. A kind of dread seized the people of the village. On an auspicious[6] day, Soma went to the temple priest and asked, "At the coming full moon my Nataraja must be consecrated.[7] Have you made a place for him in the temple?" The priest answered, "Let me see the image first...." He went over to the sculptor's house, gazed on the image and said, "This perfection, this God, is not for mortal eyes. He will blind us. At the first chance of prayer before him, he will dance...and we shall be wiped out...." The sculptor looked so unhappy that the priest added, "Take your chisel and break a little toe or some other part of the image, and it will be safe...." The sculptor replied that he would sooner crack the skull of his visitor. The leading citizens of the village came over and said, "Don't mistake us. We cannot give your image a place in our temple. Don't be angry with us. We have to think of the safety of all the people in the village....Even now if you are prepared to break a small finger..."

"Get out, all of you," Soma shouted. "I don't care to bring this Nataraja to your temple. I will make a temple for him where he is. You will see that it becomes the greatest temple on earth...." Next day he pulled down a portion of the wall of the room and constructed a large doorway opening on the street. He called Rama, the tom-tom beater, and said, "I will give you a silver coin for your trouble. Go and proclaim in all nearby villages that this Nataraja will be consecrated at the full moon. If a large crowd turns up, I will present you with a lace shawl."

At the full moon, men, women and children poured in from the surrounding villages. There was hardly an inch of space vacant anywhere. The streets were crammed with people. Vendors of sweets and toys and flowers shouted their wares, moving about in the crowd. Pipers and drummers, groups of persons chanting hymns, children shouting in joy, men greeting each other—all this created a mighty din. Fragrance of flowers and incense hung over the place. Presiding over all this there was the brightest moon that ever shone on earth.

The screen which had covered the image parted. A great flame of camphor was waved in front of the image, and bronze bells rang. A silence fell upon the crowd. Every eye was fixed upon the image. In the flame of the circling camphor Nataraja's eyes lit up. His limbs moved, his ankles jingled. The crowd was awe-stricken. The God pressed one foot on earth and raised the other in dance. He destroyed the universe under his heel, and smeared the ashes over his body, and the same God rattled the drum in his hand and by its rhythm set life in motion again....Creation, Dissolution and God attained a meaning now; this image brought it out...the bells rang louder every second. The crowd stood stunned by this vision vouchsafed[8] to them.

At this moment a wind blew from the east. The moon's disc gradually dimmed. The wind gathered force, clouds blotted out the moon; people looked up and saw only pitchlike darkness above. Lightning flashed, thunder roared and fire poured down from the sky. It

---

6. **auspicious.** Giving promise of success or good fortune
7. **consecrated.** Made sacred; dedicated
8. **vouchsafed.** Granted

was a thunderbolt striking a haystack and setting it ablaze. Its glare illuminated the whole village. People ran about in panic, searching for shelter. The population of ten villages crammed in that village. Another thunderbolt hit a house. Women and children shrieked and wailed. The fires descended with a tremendous hiss as a mighty rain came down. It rained as it had never rained before. The two lakes, over which the village road ran, filled, swelled and joined over the road. Water flowed along the streets. The wind screamed and shook the trees and the homes. "This is the end of the world!" wailed the people through the storm.

The whole of the next day it was still drizzling. Soma sat before the image, with his head bowed in thought. Trays and flowers and offerings lay scattered under the image, dampened by rain. Some of his friends came wading in water, stood before him and asked, "Are you satisfied?" They stood over him like executioners and repeated the question and added, "Do you want to know how many lives have been lost, how many homes washed out and how many were crushed by the storm?"

"No, no, I don't want to know anything," Soma replied. "Go away. Don't stand here and talk."

"God has shown us only a slight sign of his power. Don't tempt Him again. Do something. Our lives are in your hands. Save us, the image is too perfect."

After they were gone he sat for hours in the same position, ruminating.[9] Their words still troubled him. "Our lives are in your hands." He knew what they meant. Tears gathered in his eyes. "How can I mutilate this image? Let the whole world burn, I don't care. I can't touch this image." He lit a lamp before the God and sat watching. Far off the sky rumbled. "It is starting again. Poor human beings, they will all perish this time." He looked at the toe of the image. "Just one neat stroke with the chisel, and all troubles will end." He watched the toe, his hands trembled. "How can I?" Outside, the wind began to howl. People were gathering in front of his house and were appealing to him for help.

Soma prostrated before the God and went out. He stood looking at the road over which the two lakes had joined. Over the eastern horizon a dark mass of cloud was rolling up. "When that cloud comes over, it will wash out the world. Nataraja! I cannot mutilate your figure, but I can offer myself as a sacrifice if it will be any use...." He shut his eyes and decided to jump into the lake. He checked himself. "I must take a last look at the God before I die." He battled his way through the oncoming storm. The wind shrieked. Trees shook and trembled. Men and cattle ran about in panic.

He was back just in time to see a tree crash on the roof of his house. "My home," he cried, and ran in. He picked up his Nataraja from amidst splintered tiles and rafters. The image was unhurt, except for a little toe which was found a couple of yards off, severed by a falling splinter.

"God himself has done this to save us!" people cried.

The image was installed with due ceremonies at the temple on the next full moon. Wealth and honors were showered on Soma. He lived to be ninety-five, but he never touched his mallet and chisel again. ✣

9. **ruminating.** Meditating or reflecting

If you were in Soma's place, would you destroy the statue? Why do you think destroying a beautiful thing might be difficult?

Comparing Texts

AFTER READING

Find Meaning

1. Why do people fear Nataraja?
2. (a) What does the priest suggest that Soma should do to his image of Nataraja? (b) Why does he want Soma to do this?

Make Judgments

3. Why do you think Soma refuses to change his sculpture of Nataraja?
4. (a) When does the god finally decide to save the people? (b) What do you think caused him to make this decision?

Compare Literature

Symbolism Writers use symbolism to convey a message that is greater than the literal meaning contained in a story. Review the symbolism in "The Instruction of Indra" and "Such Perfection" and answer the following questions.

1. In "The Instruction of Indra," what do the ants symbolize?
2. What does the disk on the yogi's chest symbolize?
3. In "Such Perfection," what different things does the statue symbolize?

Extend Understanding

Writing Options

Creative Writing In this story, Indra learns some lessons. Imagine that you are **taking notes** for him so that he will not forget what he has learned. Jot down the lessons that he should draw from his experiences. Also, write down meaningful and relevant quotations from the different characters Indra encounters.

Informative Writing Write an **informative paragraph** in which you compare and contrast the symbols in "The Instruction of Indra" and "Such Perfection." Refer to the chart you made at the start of this lesson. In what ways are the symbols alike? In what ways do they differ? Share your paragraph with the class.

Collaborative Learning

Discuss Meaning In small groups, discuss your ideas about the theme of "The Instruction of Indra." What generalizations can you make about the character of Indra? What lessons can the reader learn from this story? How might these lessons relate to your own life? After discussing the story, write down your interpretation of its theme. Support your claims with evidence from the text.

Lifelong Learning

Compare Hinduism and Buddhism India is the birthplace of two major Eastern religions, Hinduism and Buddhism. With a partner, research the history of these religions. What geographic locations are associated with Hinduism? With Buddhism? What are the main principles and beliefs of each religion? In what ways are they similar and different? Organize your information and prepare a brief written report that compares and contrasts the two religions.

Go to **www.mirrorsandwindows.com** for more.

Amaterasu

A Japanese Myth retold by Carolyn Swift

DIRECTED READING

BEFORE READING

Build Background

Historical Context Japan's mountainous geography led to the development of small independent villages. In the years around AD 150, a priestess named Himiko united many of these villages under her rule and established contact and trade with China. Around AD 200, the Yamato people of central Japan gained control over most of the country. The Yamato rulers claimed to be descended from the sun goddess, Amaterasu, a claim that Japanese emperors continued to make into the twentieth century.

Reader's Context How do you react when you feel that someone has been unfair to you?

Set Purpose

Previewing the images and quotes that accompany "Amaterasu" will help you make predictions about the setting, characters, and mood. Read to determine how accurate your predictions are.

Analyze Literature

Characterization The act of creating or describing a character is called **characterization.** Writers use three major techniques to create a character: showing what characters say, do, and think; showing what other characters say about them; and showing what physical features, dress, and personality the characters display. As you read, note how these elements help to develop the characters in "Amaterasu."

Use Reading Skills

Draw Conclusions As you read, gather evidence to draw conclusions about the myth's characters. What motivates them? How are they influenced by the setting and other characters? Do they represent something other than themselves? Use a two-column chart to record details from the story and your conclusions.

Details	My Conclusions
Susanoo complains about everything, even when he is made god of the sea.	

Preview Vocabulary

grum•ble (grəm´ bəl) *v.*, mumble unhappily

fond•ness (fän[d]´ nəs) *n.*, affection; having a liking

Meet the Author

Carolyn Swift (1923–2002) was born in London and moved to Ireland in 1946, where she cofounded the Pike Theatre. She was an actor and a director before she began writing full-time. In addition to writing plays, Swift wrote many books for young people, including two series of novels known as the Bugsy and Robbers series. She has also written many retellings of myths.

Amaterasu

A Japanese Myth retold by Carolyn Swift

Amaterasu Appearing from the Cave, 1882. Taiso Yoshitoshi. Private collection.

Without the sun's heat the land became very cold and nothing grew in field or forest.

...he found himself facing the drawn bow of a fierce-looking warrior.

Back in the mists of time there lived a boy called Susanoo. His father and mother were the first people on earth, but then his father became Lord of the Heavens and his mother Lady of the Underworld.

Susanoo himself lived with his brothers and sisters on the bridge which linked heaven and earth, but he was always complaining. He complained about not being able to visit his mother, even though his father explained to him that if he once went to the underworld he would never be able to come back, and he complained even more when his sister Amaterasu was given the jewelled necklace of heaven and made goddess of the sun, while he was given only corals and made god of the sea. Finally his father became sick of his constant moanings and groanings.

"I don't want to see your face around Heaven any more," he told him. "You have the whole earth and sea to play around in so there's no need for you to make all our lives a misery up here."

"Oh, all right," Susanoo grumbled, "but first I must say goodbye to Amaterasu."

So off he stumped to look for her. Being in a bad mood, he shook every mountain he passed so that rocks crashed down the slopes, and he stamped his feet so that the earth quaked. Hearing all the noise, Amaterasu was frightened. She took up her bow and arrow so that, when her younger brother arrived, he found himself facing the drawn bow of a fierce-looking warrior.

"You can put that thing down," he told her. "I come in peace."

"Prove it," she said suspiciously, not taking her eyes off him.

Susanoo handed her his sword. She took it from him and broke it into three pieces. Then, before he could complain, she blew on them and turned them into three beautiful little girls.

"One day these three little daughters of mine will bring new life into the world," she told him, "while your sword could only have brought death."

"I can do better than that!" Susanoo boasted. "Give me the necklaces you're wearing."

So Amaterasu unclasped the five necklaces and gave them to her brother. Then he blew on them and turned them into five little boys.

...the world was suddenly plunged into darkness.

"Now I have five sons," he said.

"They were made out of my necklaces so they should be my sons!" Amaterasu snapped.

"But your daughters were made from my sword," Susanoo argued.

"That's different!" Amaterasu told him.

At that Susanoo lost his temper. He tore

grum•ble (grum´ bəl) *v.*, mumble unhappily

up all the rice fields that Amaterasu had been carefully ripening and caused such destruction that the frightened goddess ran and hid in a cave, blocking the entrance with a large stone.

Because Amaterasu was the sun goddess, this meant that the world was suddenly plunged into darkness. Without the sun's heat the land became very cold and nothing grew in field or forest. Worse still, the evil spirits took advantage of the darkness to get up to all sorts of wickedness. It was a disaster. Something had to be done, so all the good spirits gathered together in a dry river bed to try to decide what to do.

"We must tempt Amaterasu to come out of the cave," said one.

"And block up the entrance the minute she does, so she can't go back into it again," added another.

"But what would tempt her to come out?" asked a third.

"We must put everything she likes most outside," replied the first.

"And what does she like most?" the third asked.

"Seeing her sunny face reflected in the lake," answered a fourth.

"But we can't bring the lake up to the cave!" objected the third.

"Then we must make something that will reflect her face the way the lake does and put that outside the cave," suggested a fifth.

"I don't know what we could make that would do that," the third grumbled, "and anyway, how will she know it's there unless we can get her to come out of the cave in the first place?"

At that they all looked thoughtful. No one spoke for a while.

"I know!" the second suddenly shouted in triumph. "She always used to come out every morning as soon as she heard the cock crow. We must get all the cocks to crow outside the cave."

So they all put their heads together to try to think what would reflect the sun like the waters of the lake. After trying all sorts of

CULTURAL ▶▶ CONNECTION

Shintoism In Shinto, the ancient native religion of Japan, Amaterasu is the goddess of the sun. Until 1946, Japanese emperors were considered to be gods descended from Amaterasu. It is said that when the first emperor, Jimmu, took power in 660 BC, Amaterasu gave him holy relics known as the Imperial Regalia as proof of his divine authority. The Imperial Regalia include the sacred mirror, the sacred sword, and the curved jewels. The mirror and the jewels were used to lure Amaterasu from the cave where she hid from her brother's rage. The sword was presented to Amaterasu by Susanoo to acknowledge his submission. Today, the mirror is believed to be in Amaterasu's shrine in Ise, Japan, and the jewels are kept at the Imperial Palace in Tokyo. The sword was lost in battle in 1185. How does this information affect your reading of the myth?

Amaterasu's shrine in Ise, Japan.

things in vain, they finally managed to invent a mirror, or looking-glass. This they hung from the branch of a japonica tree[1] immediately opposite the cave and, knowing Amaterasu's <u>fondness</u> for jewellery, they hung jewelled necklaces from the other branches.

"If Susanoo had stayed out of heaven when his father told him to, this would never have happened!"

When all was ready, they gathered outside the cave with every cock they could find. First they chanted prayers. Then they gave the signal and all the cocks began to crow. Not satisfied with that, everyone present began to sing and dance, led by the goddess Ama no Uzume[2] doing a tap-dance on an upturned tub.

Wondering what all the noise was about, Amaterasu peeped out of the cave and at once saw her own face reflected in the mirror. She had never seen a looking-glass before, so she thought the people must have found another sun to replace her and ran from the cave in a rage. The others immediately stretched ropes across the mouth of the cave to stop her from going back into it again, but there was no need. By then she had discovered that it was her own shining face looking back at her. She was delighted by this and by the necklaces, as well as the singing and dancing for, truth to tell, she had begun to feel lonely in her cave. So once more the sun's bright rays lit the earth and the trees and flowers and rice began to grow again in its heat. Then everyone suddenly remembered the cause of all the trouble.

"If Susanoo had stayed out of heaven when his father told him to, this would never have happened!" they shouted angrily, and went off in a body to look for him. When they found him, they cut off his pigtail as punishment and threw him out of heaven by force. ✤

---

1. **japonica tree.** Any tree, shrub, or plant associated with the Far East
2. **Ama no Uzume.** Goddess of dawn and mirth

fond • ness (fän[d]´ nəs) *n.*, affection; having a liking

MIRRORS & WINDOWS If you were in Susanoo's place, how would you feel about being chosen as god of the sea rather than god of the sun? In what ways can jealousy ruin friendships?

AFTER READING

Find Meaning

1. (a) What does Susanoo complain about? (b) Why do you think Susanoo complains so much?
2. (a) What does Amaterasu do with Susanoo's sword? (b) What does her action indicate about her character?
3. (a) Why does Amaterasu hide in the cave? (b) Why are the good spirits concerned about Amaterasu's staying in the cave?

Make Judgments

4. What do Susanoo's actions indicate about his character?
5. (a) What plan do the good spirits develop to draw Amaterasu out of the cave? (b) Why does Amaterasu not mind being tricked?
6. What natural phenomenon might this story attempt to explain?

Analyze Literature

Characterization How does the writer create the character of Amaterasu? Remember that characterization makes use of direct description, words, actions, and the character's internal states. Use a web to organize what you have learned about the goddess. In each outer circle, list a detail from the myth that helps you understand Amaterasu's character.

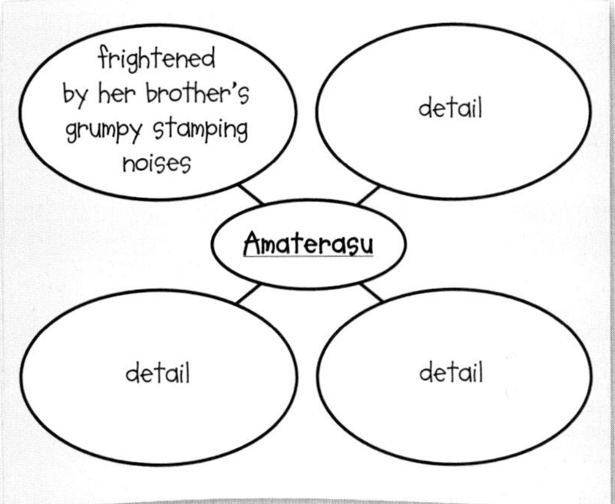

Extend Understanding

Writing Options

Informative Writing Imagine that you have been asked to write a brief **biography** of Amaterasu. Use the library or Internet to supplement the information you have learned about her from this myth. Maintain a consistent third-person point of view, and relate her biography in chronological order.

Explanatory Writing When Susanoo frightened Amaterasu, she fled into a cave and hid, causing disaster in the world. Imagine that Amaterasu has fled into the cave again. If she isn't persuaded to come out, crops won't grow and people will starve. Write a set of logically ordered **instructions** for how to lure Amaterasu out again.

Lifelong Learning

Summarize Stories In this myth, the good spirits trick Amaterasu into coming out of the cave. What happens after that? Use the Internet to read more stories about Amaterasu. Write summaries of the end of this myth and of one of the stories you find. Share one of your summaries with the class.

Media Literacy

Evaluate Websites Locate and review several websites that provide information about Japanese culture and history. Evaluate the websites for reliability and quality, explaining the criteria on which you based your evaluation. For example, does the information seem accurate, complete, current, and well written? Write a brief paragraph for each website you visit.

Go to **www.mirrorsandwindows.com** for more.

Aunty Misery

A Puerto Rican Folk Tale retold by Judith Ortiz Cofer

DIRECTED READING

BEFORE READING

Build Background

Literary Context The folk tales of Puerto Rico are heavily influenced by Spanish culture, which has dominated the island for hundreds of years. Like the fables popularized by Aesop, "Aunty Misery" includes elements of magic, trickery, and a stated lesson or moral. Details such as setting and character names reflect the island culture of Puerto Rico.

Reader's Context If you could have just one wish granted, what would it be?

Set Purpose

Preview the title and skim the text to learn the setting. Read to determine the lesson the folk tale conveys.

Analyze Literature

Simile A **simile** is a comparison between two unlike things that uses *like* or *as*. Writers use similes to create vivid images and to stimulate the reader's imagination. As you read "Aunty Misery," look for the author's use of similes and pay attention to how they help you visualize what is being described.

Use Reading Skills

Analyze Cause and Effect A *cause* is an action or event that makes something else happen. Any action or event that results from a cause is an *effect*. One cause may have several effects, and an effect may become the cause of other events. Use a chart to keep track of causes and effects in "Aunty Misery."

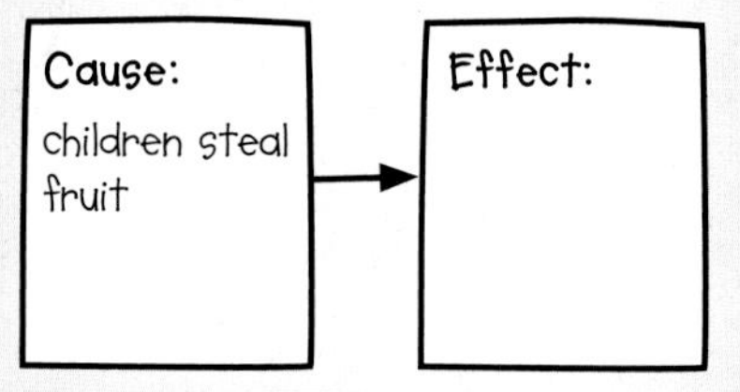

Meet the Author

Judith Ortiz Cofer (b. 1952) was born in Puerto Rico. Although her family moved to the United States in 1956, they kept close ties with Puerto Rico. The award-winning writer credits her *abuela*, grandmother, for her storytelling gifts. "When my abuela sat us down to tell a story, we learned something from it, even though we always laughed." Cofer's poetry, essays, and novels frequently explore themes related to Puerto Rican culture.

Preview Vocabulary

taunt (tänt) *v.*, mock; jeer at

gnarled (när[ə]ld) *adj.*, misshapen

in•ev•i•ta•ble (i ne´ və tə bəl) *n.*, unavoidable situation

Study of Three Pears, c. 20th century. Ashton Hinrichs. Private collection.

Aunty Misery

A Puerto Rican Folk Tale retold by Judith Ortiz Cofer

This is a story about an old, a very old woman who lived alone in her little hut with no other company than a beautiful pear tree that grew at her door. She spent all her time taking care of this tree. The neighborhood children drove the old woman crazy by stealing her fruit. They would climb her tree, shake its delicate limbs, and run away with armloads of golden pears, yelling insults at *la Tía Miseria*, Aunty Misery, as they called her.

They would climb her tree, shake its delicate limbs, and run away with armloads of golden pears....

One day, a traveler stopped at the old woman's hut and asked her for permission to spend the night under her roof. Aunty Misery saw that he had an honest face and bid the pilgrim come in. She fed him and made a bed for him in front of her hearth. In the morning the stranger told her that he would show his gratitude for her hospitality by granting her one wish.

"There is only one thing that I desire," said Aunty Misery.

"Ask, and it shall be yours," replied the stranger, who was a sorcerer in disguise.

"I wish that anyone who climbs up my pear tree should not be able to come back down until I permit it."

"Your wish is granted," said the stranger, touching the pear tree as he left Aunty Misery's house.

And so it happened that when the children came back to taunt the old woman and to steal her fruit, she stood at her window watching them. Several of them shimmied up the trunk of the pear tree and immediately got stuck to it as if with glue. She let them cry and beg her for a long time before she gave the tree permission to let them go on the condition that they never again steal her fruit, or bother her.

Time passed and both Aunt Misery and her tree grew bent and gnarled with age. One day another traveler stopped at her door. This one looked untrustworthy to her, so before letting him into her home the old woman asked him what he was doing in her village. He answered her in a voice that was dry and hoarse, as if he had swallowed a desert: "I am Death, and I have come to take you with me."

Thinking fast Aunty Misery said, "All right, but before I go I would like to pluck some pears from my beloved tree to remember how much pleasure it brought me in this life. But I am a very old woman and cannot climb to the tallest branches where the best fruit is. Will you be so kind as to do it for me?"

"*I am Death, and I have come to take you with me.*"

With a heavy sigh like wind through a tomb, Señor Death climbed the pear tree. Immediately he became stuck to it as if with glue. And no matter how much he cursed and threatened, Aunty Misery would not allow the tree to release Death.

Many years passed and there were no deaths in the world. The people who make their living from death began to protest loudly. The doctors claimed no one bothered to come in for examinations or treatments anymore, because they did not fear dying; the pharmacists' business suffered too because medicines are, like magic potions, bought to prevent or postpone the inevitable; priests and undertakers were unhappy with the situation also, for obvious reasons. There were also many old folks tired of life who wanted to pass on to the next world to rest from miseries of this one.

La Tía Miseria was blamed by these people for their troubles, of course. Not wishing to be unfair, the old woman made a deal with her prisoner, Death: if he promised not ever to come for her again, she would give him his freedom. He agreed. And that is why there are two things you can always count on running into in this world: Misery and Death: *La miseria y la muerte.* ✤

taunt (tänt) *v.*, mock; jeer at

gnarled (när[ə]ld) *adj.*, misshapen

in•ev•i•ta•ble (i neˊ və tə bəl) *n.*, unavoidable situation

For what reasons would you appreciate Aunty Misery's actions? Why might they upset you? Do you think that a world without death would be a good or bad thing?

Find Meaning

1. (a) What do the children do to annoy the old woman? (b) Why do you think they call her Aunty Misery?

2. (a) Why does the sorcerer grant a wish to Aunty Misery? (b) What does Aunty Misery's wish reveal about her?

Make Judgments

3. What does Aunty Misery's behavior toward the first traveler reveal about her?

4. What lesson about life does this folk tale convey?

Analyze Literature

Simile How do the similes in this selection help to create mental images? Use the first column of a chart to list the similes that you find in "Aunty Misery." In the second column, write down the comparison being made by the simile. In the third column, describe the effect of the simile or what it adds to the story.

Simile	Comparison	Effect
"stuck to it as if with glue"	compares the children stuck in the tree to things stuck with glue	

Extend Understanding

Writing Options

Creative Writing Themes explored in prose can also be explored in poetry. Write a **poem** about Aunty Misery, her pear tree, and Death. You may wish simply to retell the story, or you may want to express your own feelings about the story. Use simile, metaphor, and sensory language in your poem.

Informative Writing A story's theme, or message, often gives readers new insights about life or human nature. Write a brief **informative paragraph** to explore the theme of "Aunty Misery." Describe the theme in your own words, and evaluate its effectiveness. Is "Aunty Misery" a story you would enjoy telling to a friend? What truth does this story reveal? Explain.

Collaborative Learning

Discuss the Message Is the message of "Aunty Misery" optimistic, or hopeful, or is it pessimistic, or gloomy? Discuss this question in small groups, citing examples from the story to support your opinion. Share your thoughts with the class.

Critical Literacy

Hold a Panel Discussion Did Aunty Misery make a good decision or a bad decision when she let Death out of the pear tree? List the effects of each course of action. Hold a panel discussion to consider the question and try to reach a general consensus on this topic. Present evidence in support of your opinions and be respectful of other points of view.

Go to **www.mirrorsandwindows.com** for more.

Taos Countryside, 1999. Patti Mollica. Private collection.

The Force of Luck

A Southwestern Folk Tale retold by Rudolfo A. Anaya

Once two wealthy friends got into a heated argument. One said that it was money which made a man prosperous, and the other maintained that it wasn't money, but luck, which made the man. They argued for some time and finally decided that if only they could find an honorable man then perhaps they could prove their respective points of view.

One day while they were passing through a small village they came upon a miller who was grinding corn and wheat. They paused to ask the man how he ran his business. The miller replied that he worked for a master and that he earned only four bits a day, and with that he had to support a family of five.

The friends were surprised. "Do you mean to tell us you can maintain a family of five on only fifteen dollars a month?" one asked.

"I live modestly to make ends meet," the humble miller replied.

The two friends privately agreed that if they put this man to a test perhaps they could resolve their argument.

"I am going to make you an offer," one of them said to the miller. "I will give you two hundred dollars and you may do whatever you want with the money."

"But why would you give me this money when you've just met me?" the miller asked.

"Well, my good man, my friend and I have a long standing argument. He contends that it is luck which elevates a man to high position,

Rudolfo A. Anaya (b. 1937) often draws on the themes and settings of the American Southwest to create his stories. His works, including short stories, plays, and novels, offer insights into the Hispanic cultural life of this region. Born in Pastura, New Mexico, Anaya moved throughout the state during his youth. "The Force of Luck" is a retelling of a traditional oral folk tale of the American Southwest.

"The first fish my husband catches will be yours."

and I say it is money. By giving you this money perhaps we can settle our argument. Here, take it, and do with it what you want!"

So the poor miller took the money and spent the rest of the day thinking about the strange meeting which had presented him with more money than he had ever seen. What could he possibly do with all this money? Be that as it may, he had the money in his pocket and he could do with it whatever he wanted.

When the day's work was done, the miller decided the first thing he would do would be to buy food for his family. He took out ten dollars and wrapped the rest of the money in a cloth and put the bundle in his bag. Then he went to the market and bought supplies and a good piece of meat to take home.

On the way home he was attacked by a hawk that had smelled the meat which the miller carried. The miller fought off the bird but in the struggle he lost the bundle of money. Before the miller knew what was happening the hawk grabbed the bag and flew away with it. When he realized what had happened he fell into deep thought.

"Ah," he moaned, "wouldn't it have been better to let that hungry bird have the meat! I could have bought a lot more meat with the money he took. Alas, now I'm in the same poverty as before! And worse, because now those two men will say I am a thief! I should have thought carefully and bought nothing. Yes, I should have gone straight home and this wouldn't have happened!"

So he gathered what was left of his provisions[1] and continued home, and when he arrived he told his family the entire story.

When he was finished telling his story his wife said, "It has been our lot[2] to be poor, but have faith in God and maybe someday our luck will change."

The next day the miller got up and went to work as usual. He wondered what the two men would say about his story. But since he had never been a man of money he soon forgot the entire matter.

Three months after he had lost the money to the hawk, it happened that the two wealthy men returned to the village. As soon as they saw the miller they approached him to ask if his luck had changed. When the miller saw them he felt ashamed and afraid that they would think that he had squandered the money on worthless things. But he decided to tell them the truth and as soon as they had greeted each other he told his story. The men believed him. In fact, the one who insisted that it was money and not luck which made a man prosper took out another two hundred dollars and gave it to the miller.

"Let's try again," he said, "and let's see what happens this time."

The miller didn't know what to think. "Kind sir, maybe it would be better if you put this money in the hands of another man," he said.

"No," the man insisted, "I want to give it to you because you are an honest man, and if we are going to settle our argument you have to take the money!"

The miller thanked them and promised to do his best. Then as soon as the two men left he began to think what to do with the money so that it wouldn't disappear as it had the first time. The thing to do was to take the money

1. **provisions.** Food or supplies
2. **lot.** Fate

straight home. He took out ten dollars, wrapped the rest in a cloth, and headed home.

When he arrived his wife wasn't at home. At first he didn't know what to do with the money. He went to the pantry where he had stored a large earthenware jar filled with bran. That was as safe a place as any to hide the money, he thought, so he emptied out the grain and put the bundle of money at the bottom of the jar, then covered it up with the grain. Satisfied that the money was safe he returned to work.

That afternoon when he arrived home from work he was greeted by his wife.

"Look, my husband, today I bought some good clay with which to whitewash[3] the entire house."

"And how did you buy the clay if we don't have any money?" he asked.

"Well, the man who was selling the clay was willing to trade for jewelry, money, or anything of value," she said. "The only thing we had of value was the jar full of bran, so I traded it for the clay. Isn't it wonderful, I think we have enough clay to whitewash these two rooms!"

The man groaned and pulled his hair.

"Oh, you crazy woman! What have you done? We're ruined again!"

"But why?" she asked, unable to understand his anguish.

"Today I met the same two friends who gave me the two hundred dollars three months ago," he explained. "And after I told them how I lost the money they gave me another two hundred. And I, to make sure the money was safe, came home and hid it inside the jar of bran—the same jar you have traded for dirt! Now we're as poor as we were before! And what am I going to tell the two men? They'll think I'm a liar and a thief for sure!"

"Let them think what they want," his wife said calmly. "We will only have in our lives what the good Lord wants us to have. It is our lot to be poor until God wills it otherwise."

So the miller was consoled and the next day he went to work as usual. Time came and went, and one day the two wealthy friends returned to ask the miller how he had done with the second two hundred dollars. When the poor miller saw them he was afraid they would accuse him of being a liar and a spendthrift.[4] But he decided to be truthful and as soon as they had greeted each other he told them what had happened to the money.

"That is why poor men remain honest," the man who had given him the money said. "Because they don't have money they can't get into trouble. But I find your stories hard to believe. I think you gambled and lost the money. That's why you're telling us these wild stories."

"Either way," he continued, "I still believe that it is money and not luck which makes a man prosper."

"Well, you certainly didn't prove your point by giving the money to this poor miller," his friend reminded him. "Good evening, you luckless man," he said to the miller.

"Thank you, friends," the miller said.

"Oh, by the way, here is a worthless piece of lead I've been carrying around. Maybe you can use it for something," said the man who believed in luck. Then the two men left, still debating their points of view on life.

Since the lead was practically worthless, the miller thought nothing of it and put it in his jacket pocket. He forgot all about it until he arrived home. When he threw his jacket

---

3. whitewash. Paint with a mixture used to whiten walls

4. spendthrift. Person who is wasteful with money

on a chair he heard a thump and he remembered the piece of lead. He took it out of the pocket and threw it under the table. Later that night after the family had eaten and gone to bed, they heard a knock at the door.

"Who is it? What do you want?" the miller asked.

"It's me, your neighbor," a voice answered. The miller recognized the fisherman's wife. "My husband sent me to ask you if you have any lead you can spare. He is going fishing tomorrow and he needs the lead to weight down the nets."

The miller remembered the lead he had thrown under the table. He got up, found it, and gave it to the woman.

"Thank you very much, neighbor," the woman said. "I promise you the first fish my husband catches will be yours."

"Think nothing of it," the miller said and returned to bed. The next day he got up and went to work without thinking any more of the incident. But in the afternoon when he returned home he found his wife cooking a big fish for dinner.

"Since when are we so well off we can afford fish for supper?" he asked his wife.

"Don't you remember that our neighbor promised us the first fish her husband caught?" his wife reminded him. "Well this was the fish he caught the first time he threw his net. So it's ours, and it's a beauty. But you should have been here when I gutted him! I found a large piece of glass in his stomach!"

"And what did you do with it?"

"Oh, I gave it to the children to play with," she shrugged.

When the miller saw the piece of glass he noticed it shone so brightly it appeared to illuminate the room, but because he knew nothing about jewels he didn't realize its value and left it to the children. But the bright glass was such a novelty that the children were soon fighting over it and raising a terrible fuss.

Now it so happened that the miller and his wife had other neighbors who were jewelers. The following morning when the miller had gone to work the jeweler's wife visited the miller's wife to complain about all the noise her children had made.

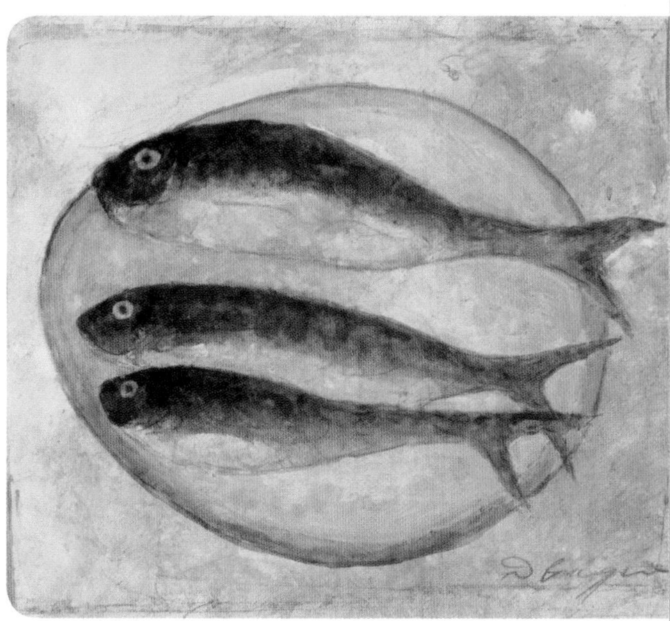

Three Fishes, 1997. David Brayne. Private collection.

"We couldn't get any sleep last night," she moaned.

"I know, and I'm sorry, but you know how it is with a large family," the miller's wife explained. "Yesterday we found a beautiful piece of glass and I gave it to my youngest one to play with and when the others tried to take it from him he raised a storm."

The jeweler's wife took interest. "Won't you show me that piece of glass?" she asked.

"But of course. Here it is."

"Ah, yes, it's a pretty piece of glass. Where did you find it?"

"Our neighbor gave us a fish yesterday and when I was cleaning it I found the glass in its stomach."

"Why don't you let me take it home for just a moment. You see, I have one just like it and I want to compare them."

"Yes, why not? Take it," answered the miller's wife.

So the jeweler's wife ran off with the glass to show it to her husband. When the jeweler saw the glass he instantly knew it was one of the finest diamonds he had ever seen.

"It's a diamond!" he exclaimed.

"I thought so," his wife nodded eagerly. "What shall we do?"

"Go tell the neighbor we'll give her fifty dollars for it, but don't tell her it's a diamond!"

"No, no," his wife chuckled, "of course not." She ran to her neighbor's house. "Ah yes, we have one exactly like this," she told the miller's wife. "My husband is willing to buy it for fifty dollars—only so we can have a pair, you understand."

"I can't sell it," the miller's wife answered. "You will have to wait until my husband returns from work."

That evening when the miller came home from work his wife told him about the offer the jeweler had made for the piece of glass.

"But why would they offer fifty dollars for a worthless piece of glass?" the miller wondered aloud. Before his wife could answer they were interrupted by the jeweler's wife.

"What do you say, neighbor, will you take fifty dollars for the glass?" she asked.

"No, that's not enough," the miller said cautiously. "Offer more."

"I'll give you fifty thousand!" the jeweler's wife blurted out.

"A little bit more," the miller replied.

"Impossible!" the jeweler's wife cried, "I can't offer any more without consulting my husband." She ran off to tell her husband how the bartering was going, and he told her he was prepared to pay a hundred thousand dollars to acquire the diamond.

He handed her seventy-five thousand dollars and said, "Take this and tell him that tomorrow, as soon as I open my shop, he'll have the rest."

When the miller heard the offer and saw the money he couldn't believe his eyes. He imagined the jeweler's wife was jesting with him, but it was a true offer and he received the hundred thousand dollars for the diamond. The miller had never seen so much money, but he still didn't quite trust the jeweler.

"I don't know about this money," he confided to his wife. "Maybe the jeweler plans to accuse us of robbing him and thus get it back."

"Oh no," his wife assured him, "the money is ours. We sold the diamond fair and square—we didn't rob anyone."

"I think I'll still go to work tomorrow," the miller said. "Who knows, something might happen and the money will disappear, then we would be without money and work. Then how would we live?"

So he went to work the next day, and all day he thought about how he could use the money. When he returned home that afternoon his wife asked him what he had decided to do with their new fortune.

"I think I will start my own mill," he

answered, "like the one I operate for my master. Once I set up my business we'll see how our luck changes."

The next day he set about buying everything he needed to establish his mill and to build a new home. Soon he had everything going.

Six months had passed, more or less, since he had seen the two men who had given him the four hundred dollars and the piece of lead. He was eager to see them again and to tell them how the piece of lead had changed his luck and made him wealthy.

"Once I set up my business we'll see how our luck changes."

Time passed and the miller prospered. His business grew and he even built a summer cottage where he could take his family on vacation. He had many employees who worked for him. One day while he was at his store he saw his two benefactors[5] riding by. He rushed out into the street to greet them and ask them to come in. He was overjoyed to see them, and he was happy to see that they admired his store.

"Tell us the truth," the man who had given him the four hundred dollars said. "You used that money to set up this business."

The miller swore he hadn't, and he told them how he had given the piece of lead to his neighbor and how the fisherman had in return given him a fish with a very large diamond in its stomach. And he told them how he had sold the diamond.

"And that's how I acquired this business and many other things I want to show you," he said. "But it's time to eat. Let's eat first then I'll show you everything I have now."

The men agreed, but one of them still doubted the miller's story. So they ate and then the miller had three horses saddled and they rode out to see his summer home. The cabin was on the other side of the river where the mountains were cool and beautiful. When they arrived the men admired the place very much. It was such a peaceful place that they rode all afternoon through the forest. During their ride they came upon a tall pine tree.

"What is that on top of the tree?" one of them asked.

"That's the nest of a hawk," the miller replied.

"I have never seen one; I would like to take a closer look at it!"

"Of course," the miller said, and he ordered a servant to climb the tree and bring down the nest so his friend could see how it was built. When the hawk's nest was on the ground they examined it carefully. They noticed that there was a cloth bag at the bottom of the nest. When the miller saw the bag he immediately knew that it was the very same bag he had lost to the hawk which fought him for the piece of meat years ago.

"You won't believe me, friends, but this is the very same bag in which I put the first two hundred dollars you gave me," he told them.

"If it's the same bag," the man who had doubted him said, "then the money you said the hawk took should be there."

5. benefactors. People who provide financial support

"No doubt about that," the miller said. "Let's see what we find."

The three of them examined the old, weatherbeaten bag. Although it was full of holes and crumbling, when they tore it apart they found the money intact. The two men remembered what the miller had told them and they agreed he was an honest and honorable man. Still, the man who had given him the money wasn't satisfied. He wondered what had really happened to the second two hundred he had given the miller.

They spent the rest of the day riding in the mountains and returned very late to the house.

As he unsaddled their horses, the servant in charge of grooming and feeding the horses suddenly realized that he had no grain for them. He ran to the barn and checked, but there was no grain for the hungry horses. So he ran to the neighborhood granary and there he was able to buy a large clay jar of bran. He carried the jar home and emptied the bran into a bucket to wet it before he fed it to the horses. When he got to the bottom of the jar he noticed a large lump which turned out to be a rag covered package. He examined it and felt something inside. He immediately went to give it to his master who had been eating dinner.

"Master," he said, "look at this package which I found in an earthenware jar of grain which I just bought from our neighbor!"

The three men carefully unraveled the cloth and found the other one hundred and ninety dollars which the miller had told them he had lost. That is how the miller proved to his friends that he was truly an honest man.

And they had to decide for themselves whether it had been luck or money which had made the miller a wealthy man! ✤

How is luck important in your life? How has luck helped you get to where you are today? For most people, how might luck play a role in their lives?

Analyze and Extend

1. (a) In what ways is the hawk attack an unlucky event? (b) How is it lucky?
2. (a) What effect does the piece of lead have on the miller? (b) Why is this surprising?
3. In your opinion, was it luck or money that made the miller a wealthy man? Explain.

Informative Writing In literature, something is considered ironic if it defies the expectations of the reader. Write a brief **critical analysis** of the use of irony in "The Force of Luck." Which events are ironic? How does the use of irony affect your appreciation of the story? How does the use of irony affect the theme? State your position in a thesis, and support it with evidence.

Critical Literacy Gather into small groups, and hold a debate about "The Force of Luck." Was it luck or money that had the greatest impact on the miller's fate? Half of the group should adopt one position, and half should adopt the other. Present evidence from the story in support of your claims. Be respectful of others' opinions.

 Go to **www.mirrorsandwindows.com** for more.

How the Snake Got Poison

An African-American Folk Tale retold by Zora Neale Hurston

INDEPENDENT READING

Well, when God made de snake he put him in de bushes to ornament de ground. But things didn't suit de snake so one day he got on de ladder and went up to see God. "Good mawnin', God."

"How do you do, Snake?"

"Ah ain't so many, God, you put me down there on my belly in de dust and everything trods upon me and kills off my generations. Ah ain't got no kind of protection at all."

But things didn't suit de snake so one day he got on de ladder and went up to see God.

God looked off towards immensity and thought about de subject for a while, then he said, "Ah didn't mean for nothin' to be stompin' you snakes lak dat.

"You got to have some kind of a protection. Here, take dis poison and put it in yo' mouf and when they tromps on you, protect yo'self."

So de snake took de poison in his mouf and went on back.

So after awhile all de other varmints went up to God.

"Good evenin', God."

"How you makin' it, varmints?"

"God, please do somethin' 'bout dat snake. He' layin' in de bushes there wid

Zora Neale Hurston (1891–1960) retold a number of traditional African-American folk tales, like "How the Snake Got Poison," in books such as *Mules and Men* and *Go Gator and Muddy the Water*. Throughout her life, Hurston also wrote many other works, including short stories, novels, plays, and essays. She is perhaps best known for her novel *Their Eyes Were Watching God.*

poison in his mouf and he's strikin' everything dat shakes de bush. He's killin' up our generations. Wese skeered to walk de earth."

So God sent for de snake and tole him:

"Snake, when Ah give you dat poison, Ah didn't mean for you to be hittin' and killin' everything dat shake de bush. I give you dat poison and tole you to protect yo'self when they tromples on you. But you killin' everything dat moves. Ah didn't mean for you to do dat."

De snake say, "Lawd, you know Ah'm down here in de dust. Ah ain't got no claws to fight wid, and Ah ain't got no feets to git me out de way. All Ah kin see is feets comin' to tromple me. Ah can't tell who my enemy is and who is my friend. You gimme dis protection in my mouf and Ah uses it."

"When you hear feets comin' you ring yo' bell and if it's yo' friend, he'll be keerful."

God thought it over for a while then he says:

"Well, snake, I don't want yo' generations all stomped out and I don't want you killin' everything else dat moves. Here take dis bell and tie it to yo' tail. When you hear feets comin' you ring yo' bell and if it's yo' friend, he'll be keerful. If it's yo' enemy, it's you and him."

So dat's how de snake got his poison and dat's how come he got rattles.

Biddy, biddy, bend my story is end.
Turn loose de rooster and hold de hen. ✤

When have you felt that you needed a slight advantage over others? In what ways was the situation fair or unfair? Why should everyone have an equal opportunity to succeed?

Analyze and Extend

1. (a) Why does the snake ask God for help? (b) What happens as a result of its request?
2. What do the varmints' complaints suggest about the difficulties associated with fairness?
3. (a) In what ways is God's solution at the end of the story a good one? (b) In what ways might it be a bad one?

Informative Writing Write a brief **critical analysis** of the tone, dialect, and content of this story. How do these elements relate to or reflect the culture from which this folk tale is derived? As you write, present evidence from the story in support of your claims. At the end of your analysis, restate the main idea and sum up the most important points.

Lifelong Learning Using the Internet, identify and research a kind of poisonous snake. Learn as much information as you can, focusing on the most vital details, such as its life span, diet, and the region in which it lives. Also, try to determine the threat level it poses to humans. Then present your findings to the class.

Go to **www.mirrorsandwindows.com** for more.

INDEPENDENT READING

The Rabbits Who Caused All the Trouble

A Fable by James Thurber

Within the memory of the youngest child there was a family of rabbits who lived near a pack of wolves. The wolves announced that they did not like the way the rabbits were living. (The wolves were crazy about the way they themselves were living, because it was the only way to live.) One night several wolves were killed in an earthquake and this was blamed on the rabbits, for it is well known that rabbits pound on the ground with their hind legs and cause earthquakes. On another night one of the wolves was killed by a bolt of lightning and this was also blamed on the rabbits, for it well known that lettuce-eaters cause lightning. The wolves threatened to civilize the rabbits if they didn't behave, and the rabbits decided to run away to a desert island. But the other animals, who lived at a great distance, shamed them, saying, "You must stay where you are and be brave. This is no world for escapists.[1]

If the wolves attack you, we will come to your aid, in all probability." So the rabbits continued to live near the wolves and one day there was a terrible flood which drowned a great many wolves. This was blamed on the rabbits, for it is well known that carrot-

1. escapists. Those who wish to escape from reality

American wit **James Thurber** (1894–1961) is well known for his cartoons and humorous stories, including fables like this one. (See page 356 for more about Thurber.) **"The Rabbits Who Caused All the Trouble"** appeared in *The New Yorker* magazine in 1939. In 1940, it was included in his book *Fables for Our Time*. At the time Thurber wrote his tale, the Nazi party, led by Adolf Hitler, had risen to power in Germany by blaming Jewish people for many of the nation's problems. Jews all over Europe were being forced into ghettos and concentration camps and killed in massacres called pogroms. More than six million Jews died before the Allied nations, including U.S., Russian, and British forces, defeated Hitler in 1945. As you read, decide whether Thurber intended his fable as a comment on Nazism in Europe.

nibblers with long ears cause floods. The wolves descended on the rabbits, for their own good, and imprisoned them in a dark cave, for their own protection.

When nothing was heard about the rabbits for some weeks, the other animals demanded to know what had happened to them. The wolves replied that the rabbits had been eaten and since they had been eaten the affair was a purely internal matter. But the other animals warned that they might possibly unite against the wolves unless some reason was given for the destruction of the rabbits. So the wolves gave them one. "They were trying to escape," said the wolves, "and, as you know, this is no world for escapists."

Moral: Run, don't walk, to the nearest desert island. ❖

Why do you think others choose not to become involved when they see that a person or group of people is being mistreated?

Analyze and Extend

1. (a) What do the wolves dislike about the rabbits? What troubles do the wolves blame on the rabbits? (b) What reasons do the wolves give for blaming the rabbits?
2. (a) What happens to the rabbits? (b) What blame do the other animals have in what happens to the rabbits, and why?
3. **Satire** is humorous writing intended to point out human failings. (a) What makes this fable satirical? (b) What type of human behavior is Thurber criticizing?

Narrative Writing A fable is a tale with a moral, or lesson. Reread the story "The Rabbits Who Caused All the Trouble" and come up with several alternative morals to the story. Share your ideas with others in your class.

Collaborative Learning Form groups to discuss Thurber's fable and how it relates to history and/or current events. Who might the wolves represent in human society past and present? Who might the rabbits represent? You may conduct research to find examples.

Go to **www.mirrorsandwindows.com** for more.

RABBIT and the TUG of WAR

As told by Michael Thompson with art by Jacob Warrenfeltz

It is told that one day Rabbit was going along his usual way...

...when he spied two Buffalo lying on opposite sides of a dusty hill...

...and he got an idea.

Michael Thompson is a high-school English teacher from the Mvskoke (Muskogee) Creek people of Oklahoma. **Jacob Warrenfeltz** is a comic book artist who lives in Maryland. They collaborated to create this graphic version of **"Rabbit and the Tug of War,"** a Native American trickster tale, for the book *Trickster: Native American Tales*. The rabbit is a trickster figure in the folklore of many Native American groups. This story was taken from the Mvskoke tradition. It is an old tale which was first written down in the early 1900s by ethnographer John Swanton.

"Hensci, Brother Buffalo. I don't know why people always brag about your strength. I may be small, but I believe I'm stronger than you."
"Let's see which of us is stronger," Rabbit persisted. "Let's have a pulling contest."
The Buffalo gave a little snort to show what he thought of that.
At first the Buffalo said, "I don't bother with little things like you," but finally, after Rabbit had pestered him and pestered him, he agreed to pull against him in a tug-of-war.
Then Rabbit went around the hill to the other Buffalo and made the same agreement.

Next he got a big strong grapevine...
...and carried it across the hill, first to one Buffalo, then to the other, and he positioned himself at the center.
When he was ready, he gave a loud whoop...
...and the two Buffalo began to pull hard against each other.

First one Buffalo would drag his opponent nearly to the top of the hill in a great cloud of dust...

...with Rabbit making a loud "Whoop!" in the middle every little while...

...and then the other would do the same to him...

...until he finally got tired of whooping and went home laughing to himself.

After a long time, when the two Buffalo were both nearly worn out and all the
whooping had stopped, they began to think that something was wrong...

...so they walked around the hill and met.

They said, "Rabbit has made big fun of us. Because of this, we will no longer let him drink at our waterhole. Let him die of thirst, for all we care."

Rabbit heard about what the Buffalo had decided.
And soon, of course, Rabbit got a terrible thirst.
But then he happened to meet a very pretty young Deer and he got another idea.
He asked her to loan her shoes.
Then he put them on and went down to the waterhole where the Buffalo were.

"I heard that you have forbidden Rabbit to drink water here," he said to them, "but I suppose you won't mind if I do."

Not having very good eyesight, the Buffalo only looked at the tracks that Rabbit made...

...and seeing they were those of the Deer, they said, "Oh, Sister, it's only Rabbit we have forbidden because he played a trick on us."

"But you're welcome to drink all you want."

Recall a funny trick you played on a friend or family member, or a time when a trick was played on you. How did you feel in each case?

Analyze and Extend

1. (a) What trick does the Rabbit play on the two Buffalo? How does he trick them a second time? (b) Why do you think the Buffaloes fall for Rabbit's tricks?
2. Tricksters are common figures in folklore. On the one hand they cause trouble, but they are also clever and creative. Do you see the Rabbit as a hero or a villain in this tale? Explain.
3. A **graphic tale** is one that is told through pictures. How do the pictures add to the story?

Narrative Writing A **trickster tale** is a tale that involves a human or animal that plays tricks on others. Common tricksters include the rabbit, the fox, and the spider of African folklore. Find other examples of trickster tales. Then write your own original trickster tale. You may use an unexpected person or animal as your trickster.

Lifelong Learning Conduct research to find out more about the Mvskoke Creek people. Where is their homeland? What types of animals did they hunt? Create a map showing the major Native American groups in each part of the continental U.S.

Go to **www.mirrorsandwindows.com** for more.

from

Ella Enchanted

A Novel by Gail Carson Levine

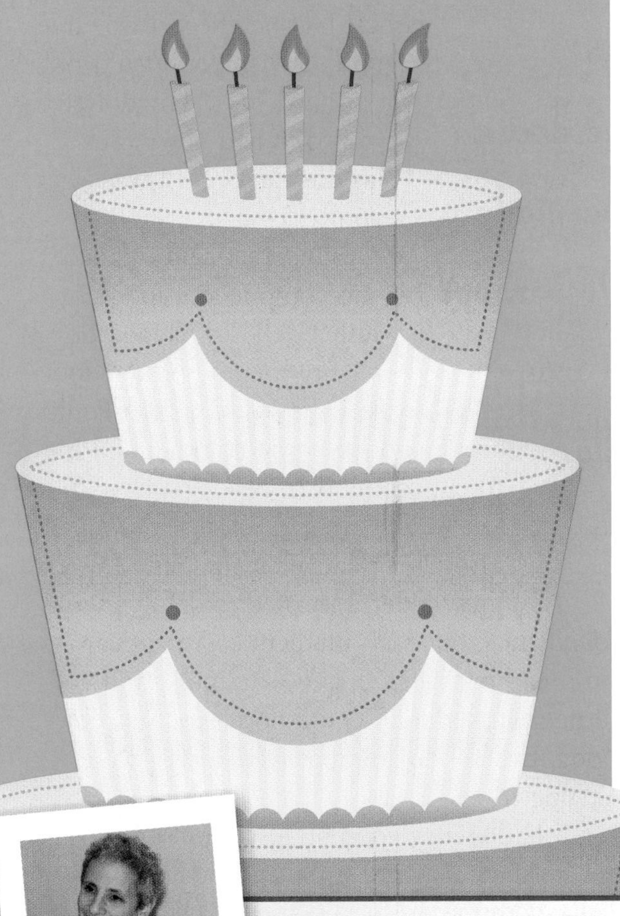

Chapter One

"My gift is obedience. Ella will always be obedient. Now stop crying, child."

That fool of a fairy Lucinda did not intend to lay a curse on me. She meant to bestow a gift. When I cried inconsolably through my first hour of life, my tears were her inspiration. Shaking her head sympathetically at Mother, the fairy touched my nose. "My gift is obedience. Ella will always be obedient. Now stop crying, child."

I stopped.

Father was away on a trading expedition as usual, but our cook, Mandy, was there. She and Mother were horrified, but no matter how they explained it to Lucinda, they couldn't make her understand the terrible things she'd done to me. I could picture the argument: Mandy's freckles standing out sharper than usual, her frizzy gray hair in disarray, and her double chin shaking with anger; Mother still and intense, her brown curls damp from labor, the laughter gone from her eyes.

I couldn't imagine Lucinda. I didn't know what she looked like.

American author **Gail Carson Levine** (b. 1947) grew up in Manhattan, New York. She worked as a welfare administrator for many years before becoming a successful writer of books for young adults. *Ella Enchanted,* first published in 1997, was Levine's first book. The novel is based on the popular fairy tale *Cinderella,* but with lots of humorous twists. *Ella Enchanted* received a Newbery Honor in 1998 and was made into a movie in 2004.

She wouldn't undo the curse.

My first awareness of it came on my fifth birthday. I seem to remember that day perfectly, perhaps because Mandy told the tale so often.

" For your birthday," she'd start, "I baked a beautiful cake. Six layers."

Bertha, our head maid, had sewn a special gown for me. "Blue as midnight with a white sash. You were small for your age even then, and you looked like a china doll, with a white ribbon in your black hair and your cheeks red from excitement."

In the middle of the table was a vase filled with flowers that Nathan, our manservant, had picked.

We all sat around the table. (Father was away again.) I was thrilled. I had watched Mandy bake the cake and Bertha sew the gown and Nathan pick the flowers.

Mandy cut the cake. When she handed me my piece, she said without thinking, "Eat."

The first bite was delicious. I finished the slice happily. When it was gone, Mandy cut another. That one was harder. When it was gone, no one gave me more, but I knew I had to keep eating. I moved my fork into the cake itself.

"Ella, what are you doing?" Mother said.

"Little piggy." Mandy laughed. "It's her birthday, Lady. Let her have as much as she wants." She put another slice on my plate.

I felt sick, and frightened. Why couldn't I stop eating?

Instead of making me docile, Lucinda's curse made a rebel of me. Or perhaps I was that way naturally.

Swallowing was a struggle. Each bite weighed on my tongue and felt like a sticky mass of glue as I fought to get it down. I started crying while I ate.

Mother realized first. "Stop eating, Ella," she commanded.

I stopped.

Anyone could control me with an order. It had to be a direct command, such as "Put on a shawl," or "You must go to bed now." A wish or a request had no effect. I was free to ignore "I wish you would put on a shawl," or "Why don't you go to bed now?" But against an order I was powerless.

If someone told me to hop on one foot for a day and a half, I'd have to do it. And hopping on one foot wasn't the worst order I could be given. If you commanded me to cut off my own head, I'd have to do it.

I was in danger at every moment.

As I grew older, I learned to delay my obedience, but each moment cost me dear—in breathlessness, nausea, dizziness, and other complaints. I could never hold out for long. Even a few minutes were a desperate struggle.

I had a fairy godmother, and Mother asked her to take the curse away. But my fairy godmother said Lucinda was the only one who could remove it. However, she also said it might be broken someday without Lucinda's help.

But I didn't know how. I didn't even know who my fairy godmother was.

Instead of making me docile,[1] Lucinda's curse made a rebel of me. Or perhaps I was that way naturally.

Mother rarely insisted I do anything. Father knew nothing of my curse and saw me too infrequently to issue many commands. But Mandy was bossy, giving orders almost as often as she drew breath. Kind orders or for-your-own-good orders. "Bundle up, Ella." Or "Hold this bowl while I beat the eggs, sweet."

I disliked these commands, harmless as they were. I'd hold the bowl, but move my feet so she would have to follow me around the kitchen. She'd call me minx[2] and try to hem me in with more specific instructions, which I would find new ways to evade. Often, it was a long business to get anything done between us, with Mother laughing and egging each of us on by turn.

We'd end happily—with me finally choosing to do what Mandy wanted, or with Mandy changing her order to a request.

When Mandy would absentmindedly give me an order I knew she didn't mean, I'd say, "Do I have to?" And she'd reconsider.

When I was eight, I had a friend, Pamela, the daughter of one of the servants. One day she and I were in the kitchen, watching Mandy make marchpane.[3] When Mandy sent me to the pantry for more almonds, I returned with only two. She ordered me back with more exact instructions, which I followed exactly, while still managing to frustrate her true wishes.

Later, when Pamela and I retreated to the garden to devour the candy, she asked why I hadn't done what Mandy wanted straight off.

"I hate when she's bossy," I answered.

Pamela said smugly, "I always obey my elders."

"That's because you don't have to."

"I do have to, or Father will slap me."

"It's not the same as for me. I'm under a

1. **docile.** Easily taught or directed; obedient
2. **minx.** A girl or young woman who is considered overly bold
3. **marchpane.** Marzipan, a candy made from almond paste

spell." I enjoyed the importance of the words. Spells are rare. Lucinda was the only fairy rash enough to cast them on people.

"Like Sleeping Beauty?"

"Except I won't have to sleep for a hundred years."

"What's your spell?"

I told her.

"If anybody gives you an order, you have to obey? Including me?"

I nodded.

"Can I try it?"

"No." I hadn't anticipated this. I changed the subject. "I'll race you to the gate."

"All right, but I command you to lose the race."

"Then I don't want to race."

"I command you to race, and I command you to lose."

We raced. I lost.

We picked berries. I had to give Pamela the sweetest, ripest ones. We played princesses and ogres. I had to be the ogre.

An hour after my admission, I punched her. She screamed, and blood poured from her nose.

Our friendship ended that day. Mother found Pamela's mother a new situation far from our town of Frell.

After punishing me for using my fist, Mother issued one of her infrequent commands: never to tell anyone about my curse. But I wouldn't have anyway. I had learned caution. ✣

When is it a good idea to disobey an order?

Analyze and Extend

1. (a) What "gift" does Ella receive from the fairy Lucinda? (b) Why is this gift really a curse?
2. (a) What problems does the curse create for Ella? (b) How does she learn to deal with the curse?
3. A **parody** is a piece of writing that imitates another work in order to make fun of it. Explain why this selection can be considered a parody of fairy tales. What elements of a fairy tale does it have, and how does it put a humorous twist on fairy tales?

Informative Writing Heroines in fairy tales are usually presented to be beautiful, sweet-tempered, and obedient. Write a **critical essay** examining Ella's character. How is she similar and/or different from the typical fairy tale heroine?

Critical Literacy In small groups, choose a scene from the story to perform in front of the class. You may use the dialogue from the story and ad lib your own lines as you wish. Alternately, you may create an original skit showing problems Ella might encounter in life as a result of her curse.

Go to **www.mirrorsandwindows.com** for more.

For Your Reading List

Horse Hooves and Chicken Feet: Mexican Folktales

by Neil Philip

The folk tales in this collection describe a fascinating world of magical creatures and supernatural events, where a boy outsmarts a great magician, a witch transforms seven brothers into seven blue oxen, and a mysterious shadow rescues a man from drowning. The collection includes colorful, vibrant illustrations inspired by Mexican folk art.

Beowulf

by Michael Morpurgo

The epic of Beowulf, Britain's oldest epic poem, tells the story of a courageous young warrior who battles dreadful creatures, including the monster Grendel and a powerful dragon. The poem was composed around AD 800. Battles and action scenes are illustrated throughout with bold and dramatic paintings by Michael Foreman.

The Four Corners of the Sky

by Steve Zeitlin

This collection of stories from many different cultures describes ancient beliefs about the creation of the world. Stories include Egyptian, Greek, Hebrew, Incan, Indian, and Chinese accounts of creation, with background information about each culture and its beliefs. Also included are illustrations of designs and artifacts from each culture.

Peace Walker: The Legend of Hiawatha and Tekanawita

by C. J. Taylor

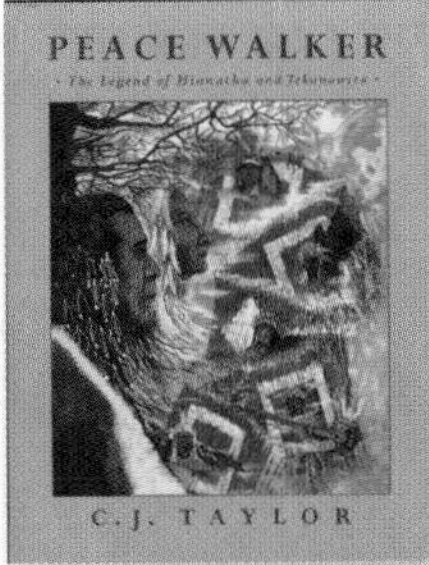

Author C. J. Taylor draws upon her Mohawk ancestry to present the story of the Iroquois Confederacy, one of the world's great democracies, and the peace walker, Hiawatha. The legend describes how Chief Hiawatha and Chief Tekanawita united to defeat the cruel Chief Atotahara, bringing peace and unity to their nations.

The Legend of Lord Eight Deer: An Epic of Ancient Mexico

by John M. D. Pohl

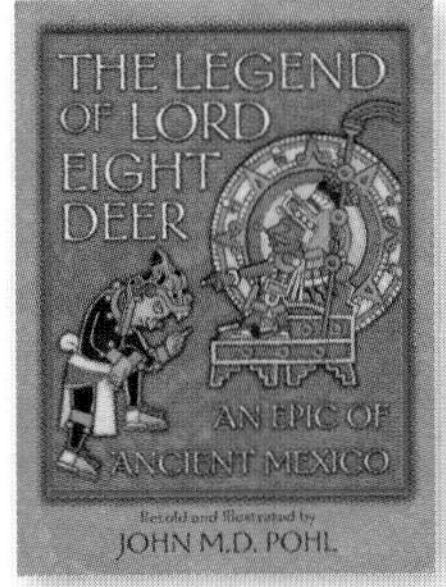

This epic story of the Mixtec people of Mexico describes the journey of Lord Eight Deer to the gates of the Sun God. The story was recorded in pictographs more than five hundred years ago. The author's bold and powerful illustrations are based on the images in the original Mixtec source. This dramatic story presents a picture of one of the last great civilizations of early Mexico.

The Story of King Arthur and His Knights

by Howard Pyle

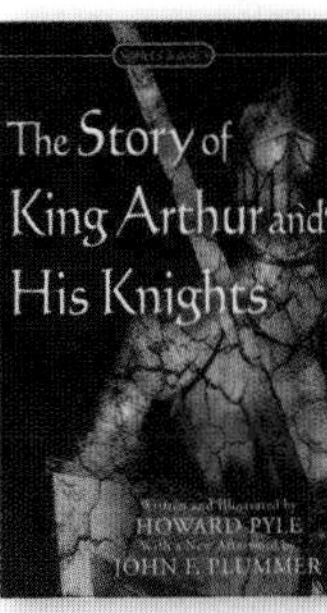

Master storyteller Howard Pyle retells the legend of King Arthur, the knights of the round table, and the court of Camelot in a lively and accessible style. Discover the legend that inspired great works of literature by many famous authors, including Alfred, Lord Tennyson; Sir Thomas Malory; and T. H. White.

Writing Workshop

Informative Writing

Research Report

Assignment: Write an effective research report on a topic of my choosing.

Goal: Thoroughly research my topic and write an interesting report that answers my questions about the topic.

Strategy: Use a variety of sources to research the topic and present my information to an audience in a clear and logically organized way.

Writing Rubric: My research report should include the following:

- an introduction that clearly states my purpose and thesis
- a clear organizational pattern with effective transitions
- quoted, paraphrased, and summarized information from multiple sources that supports my thesis
- an effective conclusion that sums up my main points
- a list of sources cited in my report

Reading and Writing

In this unit, you have read myths and folk tales. In earlier times, myths and folk tales were created to explain mysteries of nature or how something came to be. Today, we do research to find out about the world around us, past and present.

In this unit, you will learn how to write an effective **research report.** In a research report, a writer uses multiple sources to find out information about a topic. You may sum up the assignment by creating a goal and deciding how to go about writing. Use the writing rubric, or set of standards by which you will judge your work, as a guide and to determine whether or not you were successful. You will use this rubric in both drafting and revising your report.

What Great Writers Do

Gail Gibbons is a writer of children's nonfiction books. In an interview, she gave the following advice to teachers about assigning topics for student writers. Consider Gibbons's advice as you consider topics of your own.

Tell [students] to write what they find exciting and interesting in their lives or something they're really curious about themselves. If they don't follow that route, they're going to write a very boring thing.

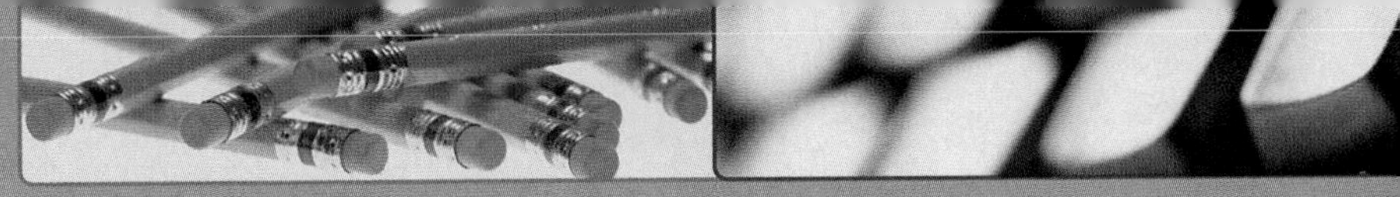

1. PREWRITE

Choosing and Narrowing Your Topic

You have read many different forms of literature about varied topics from varied time periods in this book. Which selections or issues caused you to see your world in a different way? What sparked your interest or made you curious? Did any particular topic or issue leave you wanting to know more? Perhaps you have questions that haven't yet been answered. Use your questions and curiosity to guide you in selecting a topic and conducting your research.

First, brainstorm topics of interest. Use a cluster chart to narrow your topic. State your general topic in the center of the cluster chart, and identify interesting aspects of the topic in the outer parts. Then, decide on the aspect you find most engaging.

Remember to narrow your focus so that it is manageable for a research paper, but do not make it so narrow that you won't be able to find enough information to write about.

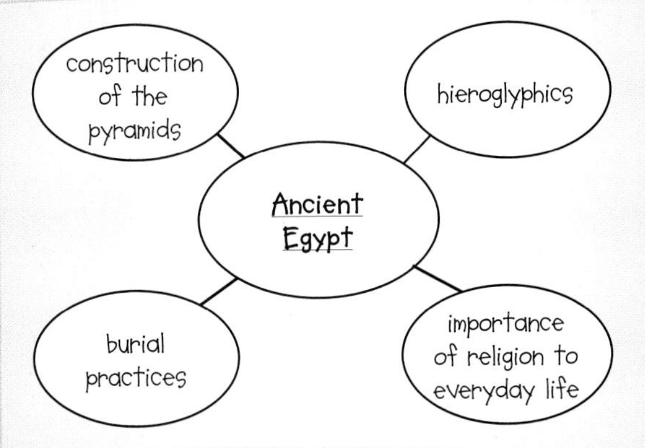

Gathering Information

Primary and Secondary Sources Use at least four different sources of information in your report. Try to include both primary and secondary sources for the most comprehensive and accurate perspective on your topic. **Primary sources** are firsthand accounts recorded by people who personally witnessed an event or situation. Primary sources include letters, journals, and historical documents. **Secondary sources** are accounts that explain or give information about a person, event, or topic but that rely on material from other sources rather than firsthand accounts. Secondary sources include encyclopedias, newspaper articles, and most books.

Evaluate Sources When researching material, make sure your information is accurate and current. Are your facts and statistics up to date? Check that Internet articles come from reputable sources and can be verified. Use information from several different types of sources and be sure that the authors are experts or professionals in their fields.

Make a list of questions you want to answer about your topic to guide your research. Use your questions to keep your research focused. Consider one student's questions about how religion affected everyday life of the ancient Egyptians.

1. What was the purpose of religion in Egyptian life?
2. How did the ancient Egyptians view death?
3. How did religion affect Egyptian daily life?

Deciding On Your Purpose

Use your questions to develop a thesis stating your topic and perspective. You may wish to do some research before settling on a thesis. See the example below.

For the ancient Egyptians, religion was a part of their everyday lives.

2. DRAFT

Organizing Your Information

Organize Sources Keep track of your research and sources using note cards. Use a different note card for each source you use. Write the source information on the card. In the upper right or left corner, number each card. This will help you keep track of which information came from which sources, and it will help you later in writing your Works Cited list.

1

Jim R. Eddy, Ancient Egypt, Thomson Gale, Farmington Hills, 2005.

1

What is the purpose of religion?

Eddy, Ancient Egypt

p. 26 "Religious duties and responsibilities were at the heart of the Egyptian life and civilization. Each community and region in Egypt had its own god or set of gods."

Take Notes As you research your sources and take notes, write the main idea or guiding question at the top of each note card. Then quote the supporting detail exactly (using quotation marks) or paraphrase it in your own words, listing the page number or numbers where you found it. Write the number on the upper corner of the card that corresponds to the number on the source card. Use a new card for each new piece of information.

Putting Your Thoughts on Paper

Before you begin writing, sort your note cards by main idea. Consider the best order for presenting your ideas. You might choose **chronological order, cause-and-effect order,** or **comparison-and-contrast order,** to name a few. Make sure the order you choose makes sense for the ideas you are presenting. Use transitions that make your organization clear to your audience and your ideas easy to follow.

Create an outline to organize your main ideas and research into manageable chunks. Make sure to include your introduction, body, and main ideas. Make sure each body paragraph has a main idea and support. For more complex ideas, you may need several body paragraphs. Nonetheless, make sure each paragraph has a main idea and support. The main ideas and details in your outline will become your topic sentences and supporting sentences in your draft.

From your outline, you can begin writing your report. Use your notes and outline to write a first draft. Concentrate on content and organization.

The Ancient Egyptians and Their Gods

I. Introduction: Religion was a part of everyday life for the ancient Egyptians.

II. The Beginnings
  A. Where Egypt is located
  B. Records of ancient life

III. Land of the Gods
  A. Major gods and goddesses
    1. Ra
    2. Osiris and Isis
  B. Minor gods
    1. Bes
    2. Tawaret

IV. Life on Earth
  A. Pharaohs
  B. The Nile River

V. Conclusion: Ancient Egyptians lived their religion every day.

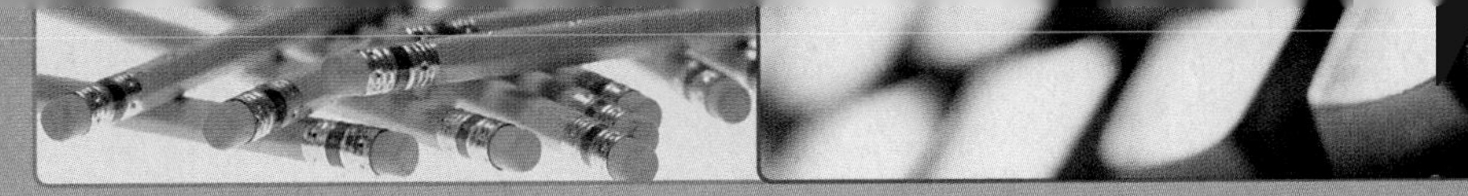

3. REVISE

Evaluating Your Draft

Once your draft is complete, review what you have written for strengths and weaknesses. Correct errors as best you can, revising the organization or adding details. Then conduct a **peer review.** Exchange papers with a classmate and have him or her review your draft and discuss ways to improve it. Use the Revising Checklist as a guide.

Below is part of a research report on ancient Egypt. The annotations to the right indicate the reasons for the changes marked in the draft.

Revising Checklist

- ❑ Does the introduction clearly state the purpose and thesis of the report?
- ❑ Is there a clear organizational pattern?
- ❑ Is the thesis supported with information from multiple sources?
- ❑ Are sources clearly cited?

Egypt has one of the oldest civilizations in the world. The ancient Egyptians believed in many gods and goddesses. *While we may worship on Fridays, Saturdays, or Sundays in accordance with our religious beliefs, for the ancient Egyptians, religion was a part of their everyday lives.*

Add a thesis statement to give the paper a purpose.

Beginnings

Ancient Egypt rose out of the desert along the Nile River. While other tribal groups were still in the hunter-gatherer stage of existence, the ancient Egyptians found no need to move about or follow prey in order to survive. The Nile River gave them everything they needed *(Eddy 7)*. Yet, as with most ancient cultures, the ways of the world were a mystery to the ancient Egyptians. Why did the sun rise and set? Why were there sandstorms? Made the river flood? Who made them? *Ancient Egyptians contemplated and tried to explain these and other questions about their existence.*

Cite the source for paraphrased information.

Add a sentence to explain how information relates to the thesis.

4. EDIT AND PROOFREAD

Focus: Paraphrasing and Summarizing

As you gather research, you will need to quote, paraphrase, or summarize the information from other sources in your report. Whether you quote the material directly or restate the ideas in your own words, give credit to the original source.

Direct Quotation: Quote the author's exact words when the phrasing is particularly effective.

Paraphrase: To paraphrase is to restate someone else's ideas. A paraphrase can include both main ideas and supporting details. Most of your research will be paraphrased.

Summarize: To summarize, you only state someone else's main ideas in your own words. You may wish to summarize a complicated idea to provide your readers with basic information.

Look at the example below to see how a student paraphrased ideas about hieroglyphics.

> The ancient scribes wrote in a picture style called hieroglyphics. Without a code, this writing was almost impossible to understand. It wasn't until 1822 when a Frenchman named Jean Champollion broke the code and the history of the ancient Egyptian people was revealed (Caselli 4).

Note how a citation immediately follows the paraphrased material and precedes the end punctuation. Full source information is listed in a Works Cited list at the end of the report.

Focus: Conjunctions

Your sentences should flow smoothly in your paragraphs. Use conjunctions to combine sentences to make your writing smoother. Review the three kinds of conjunctions.

Coordinating conjunctions are *and, but, or, nor, so, for,* and *yet.* Use them to combine subjects, predicates, and simple sentences of *equal* importance.

Correlative conjunctions are words used in pairs to join parts of a sentence. *Both/and, either/or, neither/nor,* and *not only/but also* are common correlative conjunctions. Both parts of the sentence must be of *equal* importance and structure.

Subordinating conjunctions introduce dependent clauses in sentences. These clauses cannot stand alone. That is, they do not make a complete thought by themselves. Subordinating conjunctions connect them to independent clauses.

> **While** the ancient Egyptians had major gods, they also had minor or local gods.

Proofreading

Quality Control The purpose of proofreading is to find errors you have made in the mechanics and grammar of your paper. You can find and fix these errors as you evaluate and revise your report. You should also look for them specifically at the proofreading stage. Use proofreader's marks to highlight any errors. (See the Language Arts Handbook, section 4.1, for a list of proofreader's symbols.)

5. PUBLISH AND PRESENT

Final Draft

Now that you have edited and proofread your report, rewrite it to make a final draft for presentation. If you are using a word processing program, double-space your paper and use a readable typeface or font. Be sure to check any guidelines for presenting the final paper. Make sure any quoted, paraphrased, or summarized information is properly cited.

Student Model

The Ancient Egyptians and Their Gods
by Randy Scott

Egypt has one of the oldest civilizations in the world. The ancient Egyptians believed in many gods and goddesses. While we may worship on Fridays, Saturdays, or Sundays in accordance with our beliefs, for the ancient Egyptians, religion was a part of their everyday lives.

States topic and purpose clearly in the introduction

Beginnings

Includes titles to serve as transitions for each section and point out the main ideas

Ancient Egypt rose out of the desert along the Nile River. While other tribal groups were still in the hunter-gatherer stage of existence, the ancient Egyptians found no need to move about or follow prey in order to survive. The Nile River gave them everything they needed (Eddy 7). Yet, as with most ancient cultures, the ways of the world were a mystery to the ancient Egyptians. Why did the sun rise and set? Why were there sandstorms? Who made the river flood? Who made them? Ancient Egyptians contemplated and tried to explain these and other questions about their existence.

Once the Egyptians figured out a system of writing, they began to keep records of their legends, myths, and beliefs about life. The ancient scribes wrote in a picture style called hieroglyphics. Without a code, this writing was almost impossible to understand. It wasn't until 1822 when a Frenchman named Jean Champollion broke the code and the history of the ancient Egyptian people was revealed (Caselli 4).

Paraphrases information from sources and includes proper citation

Land of the Gods

The ancient Egyptians believed in many gods. Some were personal house gods, but there were also major gods that everyone knew about. Some of these principal gods included Ra, the sun god who became the most important god. He was also known as Atum (Ra-Atum) and Amun (Amun-Ra), the creator god. Ra was the father of Shu, the air, and Tefnut, the moon goddess and wife of Shu. To the ancient Egyptians, intermarriage between gods and goddesses was acceptable. For example, Shu and Tefnut had two children, Nut, the sky goddess, and Geb, the Earth. It was Shu's job to keep Nut and Geb apart, but Nut and Geb loved each other and together had four children, Osiris, Isis, Seth (or Set), and Nephthys. Isis and Osiris had a son, Horus.

The gods of the ancient Egyptians had specific forms that signified their roles in Egyptian society. Usually the gods were shown with the head or body of an animal to represent their power, such as a falcon,

Student Model CONTINUED

hawk, or ibis head, the body of a lion or a hippopotamus, or even the head of a crocodile. Anything the image of a god carried or wore was a part of that god's power.

States the main idea in a topic sentence followed by supporting sentences

For the ancient Egyptians, the gods did not live in far-off places and look down upon them. Their gods were a part of their everyday existence. In some stories, Ra was the first pharaoh. In these ancient tales, he took the form of a man and ruled over the land of Egypt. In other stories, Ra's grandson Osiris was the true first pharaoh. It was he who taught the ancient Egyptians how to farm and cultivate their fields. He later became ruler of heaven and the underworld (McCall 16). Isis, Osiris's sister and wife, was the most powerful goddess. When Osiris was killed through the treachery of his brother Seth, Isis made sure that her son Horus—and not the evil Seth—would become the next pharaoh after Osiris (Ardagh 19).

While the ancient Egyptians had major gods, they also had minor or local gods. One of these was Bes, protector of the home and god of family life. He was also the god of children, pleasure, music, and dance (Broyles 27). Tawaret was a god who protected women in childbirth. Ancient Egyptians usually kept shrines in their homes to honor these minor gods and seek their blessings.

Ancient Egyptians were deeply concerned about the afterlife. They created elaborate tales of what happened to a body and its spirit after a person died. If you go to modern Egypt today, you can see monuments to their strong beliefs in the afterlife. Pyramids, tombs, and temples all concern the transition between life on earth and life after death. A person's life was judged once he or she left earth and traveled to the underworld. The Egyptians learned the art of mummification and removed the important organs, such as the heart and liver, from the body before burial. These organs were put into jars, and the judge of the underworld, the god Anubis, would weigh a person's heart against a feather on the scales on Ma'at, the god of balance and order. This idea reflects the ancient Egyptian belief in the sense of balance. The ancient Egyptians believed a person needed to live a good life on earth in order to enjoy a pleasant afterlife.

Life on Earth

The central figure in the everyday life of ancient Egyptians was the pharaoh. For the everyday Egyptian, the pharoah symbolized god on earth. In fact, he was regarded as a god, and to the people of Egypt, he became Horus, their greatest pharaoh. It was through him that the land

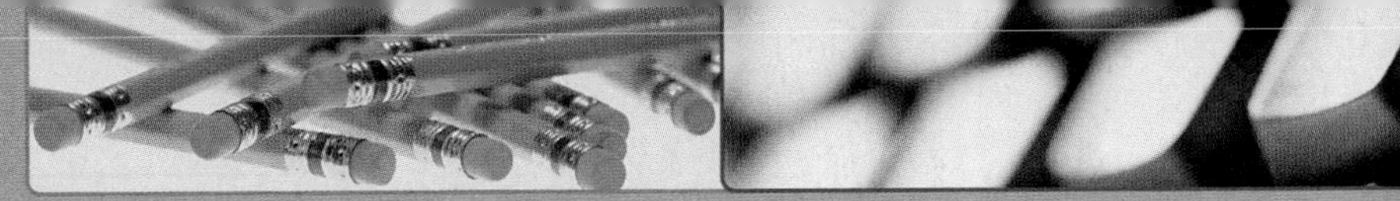

would be rewarded with the ability to sustain itself, and that ability came from the inundation, or flooding, of the Nile River (Watson 7).

Egypt is surrounded by desert. Rain rarely falls there, and the life of ancient Egyptians depended on the flooding from the Nile River. When it flooded, rich soil would wash up on the shores, allowing the people to plant crops and sustain themselves. The flooding had to be just right, though. Too much water and the crops could not be planted at the right time of year. Too little flooding and the people would have a poor yield or no crops at all. The main job of the pharaoh was to make sure the flooding happened on time and just right. He had to please the gods to make sure his people did not starve in times of need.

Unlike many modern people, the Egyptians lived their religion every day through their devotion to their gods and goddesses. Their daily lives depended on the life-giving waters of the Nile River and the power of the pharaoh. To the ancient Egyptian, life and death were closely linked, and what one did on the earth mattered greatly once one left it.

Sums up main ideas and restates thesis in the conclusion

Works Cited

Ardagh, Philip. *Ancient Egyptian Myths and Legends.* Chicago: World Book, Vol. 2, 2002. Print.

Broyles, Janell. *Egyptian Mythology.* New York: The Rosen Publishing Group, 2006. Print.

Caselli, Morley. *Egyptian Myths.* Lincolnwood: Peter Bedrick Books, 1999. Print.

Eddy, Jim R. *Ancient Egypt.* Farmington Hills: Thomson Gale, 2005. Print.

McCall, Henrietta. *Gods and Goddesses in the Daily Life of Ancient Egyptians.* Columbus: McGraw-Hill Children's Publishing, 2002. Print.

Watson, John. "An Overview of the Ancient Egyptian Religion." Web. 13 June 2009. <http://www.touregypt.net/featurestories/religion.htm>.

Includes Works Cited with sources in alphabetical order and in correct form

Speaking & Listening Workshop

Giving and Actively Listening to Research Presentations

Throughout your academic career, you will be asked to give presentations that require research. This research may be done at the library, online, or through interviews. In a **research presentation,** you orally present information you have gathered about a specific topic. When you give and actively listen to a research presentation, you share the information you learned with others.

Planning a Research Presentation

Prepare Your Topic When selecting a topic on which to present, consider the kinds of sources that will be available to you. Ask yourself: Is this topic too narrow? Too broad? Will I be able to find an adequate number of reliable sources to support my claims? However, you may be using a research paper as the basis of your presentation. If this is the case, you should not simply give a reading of your paper. Look it over and decide which points you want to stress in your presentation.

Select Key Points If you are using a written report, make a summary of what you want to say. Review the outline you made or notes you took during the prewriting stage of your paper. If you are beginning from scratch, use several different sources. Incorporate paraphrased information and direct quotations from these sources. Be sure to cite sources as you present.

Make note cards on which you list all of the key points you want to make during your presentation. Use these note cards as a guide. For example, the following is a set of partial notes that one student made. Notice that the student indicates where to present visual aids.

Facts on Frogs

Introduction

- Found on every continent except Antarctica
- At least 3,900 species of frogs in the world
- Frogs and toads closely related

Life Cycle (diagram A)

- begins life as fertilized egg
- tadpole
- tadpole with legs
- froglet
- frog

Identify Your Audience Even though your audience may know something about your topic, it is unlikely that they have done as much research as you. Consider the different ways you can expand on what they already know. Also, make sure that your topic is appropriate and the information you present is clear and reliable. Be prepared to answer questions about your topic.

Organize Your Speech Remember, you are giving an oral presentation of your research. You are not reading word for word from a research paper you have written. Organize your notes in a way that fits your research and is comfortable for you. If you are describing a series of events, chronological order will suit your presentation best. If you are giving facts, organize your presentation point by point. You may also want to consider cause-and-effect order, problem-and-solution order, or comparison-and-contrast order. Find an order that best suits the materials you are presenting.

Evaluating Your Research Presentation

Work with a partner or small group to evaluate your research presentations. Offer constructive feedback on the subject, organization, and delivery of the material. Remember to be helpful and respectful in your criticism and praise. Follow the speaking and listening rubrics on this page to evaluate each research presentation.

Delivering Your Research Presentation

Prior to your presentation, organize any pictures, objects, or other visual media you want to include. Make sure you have marked in your notes when to show these pictures or objects. Remember to maintain eye contact with your audience. Refer to your notes, but don't read them word for word. Avoid unnecessary movements if they are not part of what you are trying to say. Speak loudly and clearly enough to be heard and understood.

Active Listening When listening to a research presentation, be a considerate and courteous audience member. Give the speaker your undivided attention. Remain quiet and respectful, and ask questions at the appropriate time.

Speaking Rubric

Your presentation will be evaluated on these elements:

Contents

- ☐ clear organization of material
- ☐ strong introduction and conclusion
- ☐ in-depth presentation of material
- ☐ ideas supported with evidence

Delivery and Presentation

- ☐ appropriate volume and pacing
- ☐ appropriate use of photographs or objects
- ☐ good eye contact with audience
- ☐ effective use of nonverbal expression

Listening Rubric

As a peer reviewer or audience member, you should do the following:

- ☐ listen quietly and attentively
- ☐ maintain eye contact with speaker
- ☐ ask appropriate questions
- ☐ (as peer reviewer) provide constructive feedback

Test Practice Workshop

Writing Skills

Research Report

Carefully read the following writing prompt. Before you begin writing, think carefully about what task the assignment is asking you to perform. Then create an outline to help guide your writing.

> In this unit, you have read several myths about Greek gods, such as Persephone, Demeter, and Apollo. In many cultures, gods are wise beings. However, many of the gods in Greek myths show human failings such as foolishness and envy. How do the gods that you have read about demonstrate human failings?

Write a research report in which you examine the personalities of gods from the myths in this unit. Discuss the qualities present in their personalities and the ways these characters are like or unlike humans. Gather your information from at least three myths. In your essay, use both paraphrases and direct quotations. As you write, be sure to:

- Organize your report in a logical and consistent way
- Include introductory and concluding paragraphs
- Introduce your main idea in the first paragraph
- Support your main idea in each body paragraph

Revising and Editing Skills

In the following excerpt from the first draft of a student's paper, words and phrases are underlined and numbered. Alternatives to the underlined words and phrases appear in the right-hand column. Choose the one that *best* corrects any grammatical or style errors in the original. If you think that the original is error-free, choose "NO CHANGE."

Some questions might also focus on a section of the passage or the entire passage. These do not refer to a specific underlined phrase or word and are identified by a number in a box. Record your answers on a separate sheet of paper.

Greek myths evolved over many centuries, culture influenced their development. [1] The gods, goddesses, and heroes that populate these myths also mirror cultural beliefs. Having great authority, the people saw them as all-powerful. (2) The most important figures in early Greek myths was (3) very powerful males, such as Uranos and Kronos. The best-known leader of the Greek gods was Zeus, who threw (4) thunderbolts across the sky to demonstrate his power. Although goddesses with some godlike powers also lived on Mount Olympus they (5) often got the better of their male counterparts through guile or deceit. [6]

1. Which of the following errors appears in the first sentence?
   A. run-on sentence
   B. misplaced modifier
   C. dangling modifier
   D. lack of subject-verb agreement

2. A. NO CHANGE
   B. Because the gods had great authority, the people saw them as all-powerful.
   C. People, having great authority, were all-powerful.
   D. Having great authority; the people saw them as all-powerful.

3. A. NO CHANGE
   B. figures in early Greek myths were
   C. figure in early Greek myths was
   D. figure in early Greek myths were

4. A. NO CHANGE
   B. Greek gods were Zeus, who threw
   C. Greek gods was Zeus, who throws
   D. Greek gods was Zeus who threw

5. A. NO CHANGE
   B. also lived on Mount Olympus; they
   C. also lived on Mount Olympus—they
   D. also lived on Mount Olympus, they

6. The last sentence in this passage is:
   A. a simple sentence.
   B. a compound sentence.
   C. a complex sentence.
   D. a compound-complex sentence.

Reading Skills

Carefully read the following passage. Then, on a separate piece of paper, answer each question.

from "Why the Owl Has Big Eyes"

Raweno, the Everything-Maker, was busy creating various animals. He was working on Rabbit, and Rabbit was saying: "I want nice long legs and long ears like a deer, and sharp fangs and claws like a panther."

"I do them up the way they want to be; I give them what they ask for," said Raweno. He was working on Rabbit's hind legs, making them long, the way Rabbit had ordered.

Owl, still unformed, was sitting on a tree nearby and waiting his turn. He was saying: "Whoo, whoo, I want a nice long neck like Swan's, and beautiful red feathers like Cardinal's, and a nice long beak like Egret's, and a nice crown of plumes like Heron's. I want you to make me into the most beautiful, the fastest, the most wonderful of all birds."

Raweno said: "Be quiet. Turn around and look in another direction. Even better, close your eyes. Don't you know that no one is allowed to watch me work?" Raweno was just then making Rabbit's ears very long, the way Rabbit wanted them.

Owl refused to do what Raweno said. "Whoo, whoo," he replied, "Nobody can forbid me to watch. Nobody can order me to close my eyes. I like watching you, and watch I will."

Then Raweno became angry. He grabbed Owl, pulling him down from his branch, stuffing his head deep into his body, shaking him until his eyes grew big with fright, pulling at his ears until they were sticking up at both sides of his head.

"There," said Raweno, "that'll teach you. Now you won't be able to crane your neck to watch things you shouldn't watch. Now you have big ears to listen when someone tells you what not to do. Now you have big eyes—but not so big that you can watch me, because you'll be awake only at night, and I work by day. And your feathers won't be red like cardinal's but gray like this"—and Raweno rubbed Owl all over with mud—"as punishment for your disobedience." So Owl flew off, pouting: "Whoo, whoo, whoo."

Then Raweno turned back to finish Rabbit, but Rabbit had been so terrified by Raweno's anger, even though it was not directed at him, that he ran off half done. As a consequence, only Rabbit's hind legs are long, and he has to hop about instead of walking and running. Also, because he took fright then, Rabbit has remained afraid of most everything....

1. In line 3, what is the rabbit's most likely motivation for asking for sharp fangs and claws like a panther?
   A. It wanted to be able to defend itself.
   B. It wanted to attack humans.
   C. It wanted to attack the owl.
   D. It wanted to fight a panther.

2. What does the quotation that begins in line 4 suggest about Raweno's character?
   A. He is cruel.
   B. He is unpredictable.
   C. He is generous.
   D. He is mischievous.

3. Lines 12–17 contribute mainly to which literary element?
   A. setting
   B. conflict
   C. simile
   D. theme

4. Based on the context, the word *crane* in line 21 is used as a:
   A. noun.
   B. adjective.
   C. verb.
   D. adverb.

5. Which word *best* describes Owl's character?
   A. curious
   B. wise
   C. arrogant
   D. grateful

6. Which of the following *best* describes the theme of this story?
   A. It is best to avoid discussion.
   B. Do not be arrogant.
   C. Owls are curious animals.
   D. Rabbits are afraid of everything.

7. This story is told from which of the following points of view?
   A. first-person
   B. second-person
   C. third-person limited
   D. third-person omniscient

8. Based on the story, why is Rabbit frightened of everything?
   A. He is ashamed of the way he looks.
   B. He is smaller than all the other animals.
   C. He thinks Owl might still be around.
   D. He does not have claws and fangs.

9. Which of the following *best* describes the genre of this story?
   A. drama
   B. myth
   C. fable
   D. epic poem

10. Which of the following *best* describes the character Raweno?
   A. He is a god.
   B. He is a trickster.
   C. He is a symbol.
   D. He is an allegory.

Language Arts Handbook

1	**Reading Strategies & Skills**	835
2	**Vocabulary & Spelling**	850
3	**Grammar & Style**	866
4	**Writing**	902
5	**Research & Documentation**	912
6	**Applied English**	923
7	**Speaking & Listening**	926
8	**Test-Taking Skills**	935

1.1 The Reading Process

The reading process begins before you actually start to read. All readers use a reading process, even if they don't think about it. By becoming aware of this process, you can learn to read closely to become a more effective reader. The reading process can be broken down into three stages: before reading, during reading, and after reading.

BEFORE READING

BUILD BACKGROUND

- Think about the **context** you as a reader bring to the selection based on your knowledge and experiences. What do you know about the topic? What do you want to know?

SET PURPOSE

- **Preview** the text to set a purpose for reading. Skim the first few paragraphs and glance through the selection to figure out what it's about and who the main characters are. What can you learn from the art or photos?

USE READING SKILLS

- Apply **reading skills** such as determining the author's purpose, analyzing text structure, and previewing new vocabulary.

DURING READING

USE READING STRATEGIES

- **Ask questions** about things that seem unusual or interesting, like why a character might have behaved in an unexpected way.
- **Visualize** by forming pictures in your mind to help you see the characters or actions.
- **Make predictions** about what's going to happen next. As you read, gather more clues that will either confirm or change your predictions.
- **Make inferences**, or educated guesses, about what is not stated directly. Things may be implied or hinted at, or they may be left out altogether.
- **Clarify** your understanding of what you read by rereading any difficult parts.

ANALYZE LITERATURE

- Determine what **literary elements** stand out as you read the selection. Ask whether the characters are engaging and lifelike. Determine if there is a strong central conflict or theme.

MAKE CONNECTIONS

- Notice where there are **connections** between the story and your life or the world beyond the story. Be aware of feelings or thoughts you have while reading the story.

AFTER READING

REFER TO TEXT

- Think about the facts. **Remember details** like characters' names, locations or settings, and any other things that you can recall.
- Determine the **sequence of events** or the order in which things happened.
- **Reread** the story to pick up any details you may have missed the first time around.
- Try to **summarize** the story in a sentence or two based on the events.

REASON WITH TEXT

- **Analyze** the text by breaking down information into smaller pieces and figuring out how those pieces fit into the story as a whole. Your knowledge of literary tools can help you analyze the author's technique.
- **Evaluate** the text. **Synthesize** and **draw conclusions** by bringing together what you have read and using it to make a decision or form an opinion. Decide if you agree with the author's views.

Framework for Reading

BEFORE READING

ASK YOURSELF

- ❑ What's my purpose for reading this?
- ❑ What is this going to be about?
- ❑ How is this information organized?
- ❑ What do I already know about the topic?
- ❑ How can I apply this information to my life?

DURING READING

ASK YOURSELF

- ❑ What is the best way to accomplish my purpose for reading?
- ❑ What do I want or need to find out while I'm reading?
- ❑ What is the essential information presented here?
- ❑ What is the importance of what I am reading?
- ❑ Do I understand what I just read?
- ❑ What can I do to make the meaning more clear?

AFTER READING

ASK YOURSELF

- ❑ What did I learn from what I have read?
- ❑ What is still confusing?
- ❑ What do I need to remember from my reading?
- ❑ What effect did this text have on me?
- ❑ What else do I want to know about this topic?

1.2 Using Reading Strategies

Reading closely means thinking about what you are reading as you read it. A **reading strategy**, or plan, helps you read closely and get more from your reading. The following strategies can be applied at each stage of the reading process: before, during, and after reading.

Reading Strategies

- Build Background
- Set Purpose
- Ask Questions
- Visualize
- Make Predictions
- Make Inferences
- Clarify
- Make Connections

BUILD BACKGROUND

Each reader brings his or her own context to a selection based on prior knowledge and experiences. What do you know about the topic? What do you want to know? Before and during reading, think about what you already know about the topic or subject matter. By connecting to your prior knowledge, you will increase your interest in and understanding of what you read. Fill in the first two columns of a K-W-L Chart before you read. Fill in the last column after you finish reading.

K-W-L Chart

What I *Know*	What I *Want* to Learn	What I Have *Learned*
Queen Elizabeth I was the queen of England a long time ago and never married.	Why didn't she marry?	Elizabeth I was the daughter of King Henry VIII who had six wives. Her father had her mother beheaded.

SET PURPOSE

Before you begin reading, think about your reason for reading the material. You might be reading from a textbook to complete a homework assignment, skimming a magazine for information about one of your hobbies, or reading a novel for your own enjoyment. Know why you are reading and what information you seek. Decide on your purpose for reading as clearly as you can. Be aware that the purpose of your reading may change as you read.

Preview the text to set a purpose for reading. Skim the first few paragraphs and glance through the selection to figure out what it's about and who the main characters are. What can you learn from the art or photos? Fill in a Reader's Purpose Chart at each stage of reading to set a purpose for reading and to help you attain it.

Reader's Purpose Chart

Before Reading
Set a purpose for reading I want to read "Seventh Grade" because it could be a story about people my age and I could see if they are like me.
During Reading
Take notes on what you learn
After Reading
Reflect on your purpose and what you learned

ASK QUESTIONS

Think and reflect by asking questions to further your understanding of what you are reading. Asking questions helps you to pinpoint parts of the text that are confusing. You can ask questions in your head, or you may write them down. Ask questions about things that seem unusual or interesting, like why a character might have behaved in an unexpected way. What do you wonder about as you read the text? Use a Generate Questions Bookmark like the following to record your questions as you read.

Generate Questions Bookmark

Page #	What I Wonder About
214	How does Victor think he's going to make Teresa be his girl?

VISUALIZE

Reading is more than simply sounding out words. It is an active process that requires you to use your imagination. When you visualize, you form a picture or an image in your mind of the action and descriptions in a text. Each reader's images will be different based on his or her prior knowledge and experiences. Keep in mind that there are no "right" or "wrong" visualizations. Visualize by forming pictures in your mind to help you see the characters or actions. Use a Visualization Map to draw pictures that represent key events in a selection. Write a caption under each box that explains each event. Draw the events in the order they occur.

Visualization Map

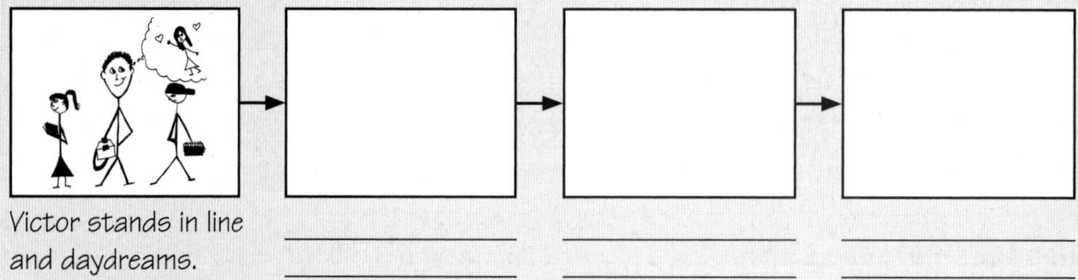

Victor stands in line and daydreams.

MAKE PREDICTIONS

When you **make predictions** during reading, you are making guesses about what the reading is going to be about or what might happen next. Before you read, make predictions based on clues from the page and from what you already know about the topic. As you read, gather more clues that will either confirm or change your predictions.

Prediction Chart

Guesses	Reasons	Evidence
The portrait salesman is going to steal Don Mateo's money.	The picture Don Mateo gives him is his only picture of his son, so I'm guessing something will go wrong with it.	The salesman keeps talking about how his new manager wants payment in cash. The salesman also seems frightened and timid and says it will take a month to deliver the picture.

MAKE INFERENCES

Making an inference means putting together the clues given in the text with your own prior knowledge. Make inferences, or educated guesses, about what is not stated directly. Things may be implied or hinted at, or they may be left out altogether. By paying close attention to what you read, you will be able to make inferences about what the writer is trying to communicate. Use an Inference Chart to document your conclusions.

Inference Chart

Text	What I Infer
In "Papa's Parrot," the parrot says, "Where's Harry?"	Harry's father has been lonely, saying "Where's Harry?" so many times that the parrot learned how to say it.
Detail from Text	**Conclusions**

CLARIFY

Check that you understand what you read and identify text that is confusing or unclear. If you encounter problems or lose focus, it may be helpful to use **Fix-Up Ideas,** such as rereading difficult parts, reading in shorter chunks, going back and reading aloud, or changing your reading rate. (See Monitor Comprehension on page 834 for more information.)

MAKE CONNECTIONS

Notice where there are **connections** between the story and your life or the world beyond the story. Be aware of feelings or thoughts you have while reading the story.

Connections Chart

Page #	Event	Reminds Me of
392	The Sibley Guide to Birds describes wild turkeys.	I've eaten turkey at Thanksgiving dinner.

1.3 Using Reading Skills

Using the following skills as you read helps you to read closely and become an independent, thoughtful, and active reader who can accomplish tasks evaluated on tests, particularly standardized tests.

Reading Skills

- Identify Author's Purpose and Approach
- Skim and Scan
- Find the Main Idea
- Determine Importance of Details
- Understand Literary Elements
- Meaning of Words
- Use Context Clues
- Take Notes
- Analyze Text Organization
- Identify Sequence of Events
- Compare and Contrast
- Evaluate Cause and Effect
- Classify and Reorganize Information
- Distinguish Fact from Opinion
- Identify Multiple Levels of Meaning
- Interpret Visual Aids
- Monitor Comprehension
- Summarize
- Draw Conclusions

IDENTIFY AUTHOR'S PURPOSE AND APPROACH

Author's Purpose

A writer's **purpose** is his or her aim or goal. Being able to figure out an author's purpose, or purposes, is an important reading skill. An author may write with one or more of the purposes listed in the following chart. A writer's purpose corresponds to a specific mode, or type, of writing. A writer can choose from a variety of forms while working within a mode.

Purposes of Writing

Mode of Writing	Purpose	Examples
informative	to inform	news article, research report
narrative	to express thoughts or ideas, or to tell a story	personal account, memoir
descriptive	to portray a person, place, object, or event	travel brochure, personal profile
argumentative	to convince people to accept a position and respond in some way	editorial, petition

Once you identify what the author is trying to do, you can evaluate, or judge, how well the author achieved that purpose. For example, you may judge that the author of an argumentative essay made a good and convincing argument. Or, you may decide that the novel you are reading has a boring plot.

Before Reading
Identify the author's purpose, the type of writing he or she uses, and the ideas he or she wants to communicate.
During Reading
Gather ideas that the author communicates to the readers.
After Reading
Summarize the ideas the author communicates. Explain how these ideas help fulfill the author's purpose.

Author's Approach

The literary elements, the terms and techniques used in literature, make up the **author's approach** to conveying his or her main idea or theme. Understanding the author's approach in fiction involves recognizing literary elements such as *point of view, tone,* and *mood.* What perspective, or way of looking at things, does the author have? What is his or her attitude toward the subject? Is the writing serious or playful in nature? What emotions is the writer trying to evoke in the reader? (See Understand Literary Elements on page 828.)

SKIM AND SCAN

When you **skim**, you glance through material quickly to get a general idea of what it is about. Skimming is an excellent way to get a quick overview of material. It is useful for previewing a chapter in a textbook, for surveying material to see if it contains information that will be useful to you, and for reviewing material for a test or an essay.

When you **scan**, you look through written material quickly to locate particular information. Scanning is useful when, for example, you want to find an entry in an index or a definition in a textbook chapter. To scan, simply run your eye down the page, looking for a key word. When you find the key word, slow down and read carefully.

To **skim** a text, preview the following:	When you **scan** a text, you may be looking for the following:
• titles • headings • bold or colored type • topic sentences • first/last paragraphs of sections • summaries • graphics	• specific information • key words • main ideas • answers to questions

FIND THE MAIN IDEA

The **main idea** is a brief statement of what you think the author wants you to know, think, or feel after reading the text. In some cases, the main idea will actually be stated. Check the first and last paragraphs for a sentence that sums up the entire passage. The author may not tell you what the main idea is, and you will have to infer it.

In general, nonfiction texts have main ideas; literary texts (poems, short stories, novels, plays, and personal essays) have themes. Sometimes, however, the term *main idea* is used to refer to the theme of a literary work, especially an essay or a poem. Both deal with the central idea in a written work.

A good way to find the main or overall idea of a whole selection (or part of a selection) is to gather important details into a Main Idea Map like the one below. Use the details to determine the main or overall thought or message.

Main Idea Map

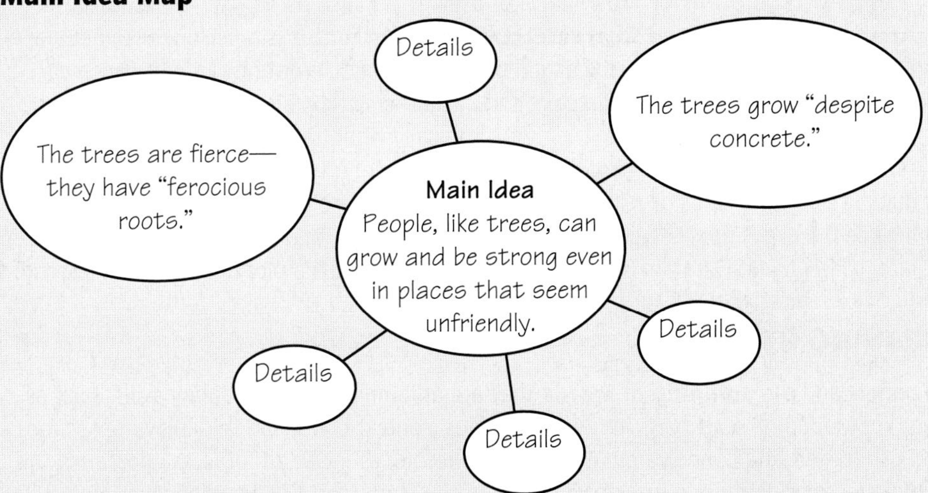

DETERMINE IMPORTANCE OF DETAILS

The main ideas are what the selection is about; the minor ideas and details provide support for the main ones. To identify supporting details, you need to do the following:

- **Locate basic facts**, such as names, dates, and events.
- **Determine the importance** of those facts to the understanding of the piece. Some facts or details will be more important than others.

- **Interpret** subtly stated details. These details can help clarify the author's stance or purpose, or they may give fuller meaning to the basic facts.
- **Understand the function** of a part of a passage. Is the author providing information, supporting a previously made point, presenting a conflicting argument, building suspense? Pay attention to how your understanding of a topic or your feelings toward it change as you read.
- **Make inferences**, or educated guesses, about how the author uses the supporting details to achieve his or her desired result. Put together clues from the text with your known prior knowledge to make inferences. A Main Idea Map or an Inference Chart can help you keep track of your ideas.

UNDERSTAND LITERARY ELEMENTS

Literary elements are the terms and techniques that are used in literature. When you read literature, you need to be familiar with the literary terms and reading skills listed below. These literary elements are explained in more detail in the Introduction to Fiction on page 4.

- **Recognize Mood and Tone** The atmosphere or emotion conveyed by a literary work is called **mood.** A writer creates mood by using concrete details to describe the setting, characters, or events. **Tone** is the writer's attitude toward the subject or toward the reader of a work. Examples of different tones that a work may have include familiar, ironic, playful, sarcastic, serious, and sincere.
- **Understand Point of View** The vantage point, or perspective, from which a story or narrative is told is referred to as **point of view**. Stories are typically written from the following points of view:
  first-person point of view: narrator uses words such as *I* and *we*
  second-person point of view: narrator uses *you*
  third-person point of view: narrator uses words such as *he, she, it,* and *they*
- **Analyze Character and Characterization** A **character** is a person (or sometimes an animal) who takes part in the action of a story. Characterization is the literary techniques writers use to create characters and make them come alive.
- **Examine Plot Development** The plot is basically what happens in a story. A **plot** is a series of events related to a central conflict, or struggle. A typical plot involves the introduction of a conflict, its development, and its eventual resolution. The elements of plot include the exposition, rising action, climax, falling action, and resolution. A graphic organizer called a Plot Diagram (page 6) can be used to chart the plot of a literature selection.

MEANING OF WORDS

To understand the **meaning of words** that are unfamiliar, use vocabulary skills, such as prior knowledge of word parts and word families, context clues (see the following section), and denotation and connotation. Other helpful resources include footnotes, glossaries, and dictionaries. For more information, refer to the Language Arts Handbook, section 2, Vocabulary & Spelling, page 836.

USE CONTEXT CLUES

You can often figure out the meaning of an unfamiliar word by using context clues. **Context clues** are words and phrases near a difficult word that provide hints about its meaning. The context in which a word is used may help you guess what it means without having to look it up in the dictionary.

Different types of context clues include the following:

- **comparison clue:** shows a comparison, or how the unfamiliar word is like something that might be familiar to you
- **contrast clue:** shows that something contrasts, or differs in meaning, from something else
- **restatement clue:** uses different words to express the same idea
- **examples clue:** gives examples of other items to illustrate the meaning of something
- **cause-and-effect clue:** tells you that something happened as a result of something else

TAKE NOTES

Taking or making notes helps you pay attention to the words on a page and remember important ideas. *Paraphrase,* or write in your own words, what you have read and put it into notes you can read later. Taking or making notes is also a quick way for you to retell what you have just read. Since you cannot write in, mark up, or highlight information in a textbook or library book, make a response bookmark like the one that follows and use it to record your thoughts and reactions. As you read, ask yourself questions, make predictions, react to ideas, identify key points, and/or write down unfamiliar words.

Response Bookmark

Page #	Questions, Predictions, Reactions, Key Points, and Unfamiliar Words
319	Will Robert be as horrified by the Chinese dinner as the narrator thinks he will?

Making notes in **graphic organizers** helps you organize ideas as you read. For instance, if you are reading an essay that compares two authors, you might use a Venn Diagram to collect information about each author. If you are reading about an author's life, you may construct a Time Line. As you read a selection, create your own method for gathering and organizing information. You might use your own version of a common graphic organizer or invent a new way to show what the selection describes.

Common Graphic Organizers

Cause-and-Effect Chart, page 831
Classification Chart, page 832
Connections Chart, page 825
Drawing Conclusions Log, page 835
Fact from Opinion Chart, page 832
Generate Questions Bookmark, page 824
Inference Chart, page 825
K-W-L Chart, page 823
Levels of Meaning Chart, page 833
Main Idea Map, page 827
Prediction Chart, page 824
Pro and Con Chart, page 831
Reader's Purpose Chart, page 823
Response Bookmark, above
Sequence Map, page 830
Summary Chart, page 835
Time Line, page 830
Venn Diagram, page 831
Visualization Map, page 824

ANALYZE TEXT ORGANIZATION

Text organization refers to the different ways a text may be presented or organized. If you are aware of the ways different texts are organized, you will find it easier to understand what you read. For example, familiarity with typical plot elements—the exposition, rising action, climax, falling action, and resolution—is important for understanding the events in a short story or novel. Focusing on signal words and text patterns is important for understanding nonfiction and informational text. For instance, transition words, such as *first, second, next, then,* and *finally,* might indicate that an essay is written in chronological, or time, order. Common methods of organization are shown in the following chart.

Methods of Organization

Chronological Order	Events are given in the order they occur.
Order of Importance	Details are given in order of importance or familiarity.
Comparison and Contrast Order	Similarities and differences of two things are listed.
Cause and Effect Order	One or more causes are presented followed by one or more effects.

IDENTIFY SEQUENCE OF EVENTS

Sequence refers to the order in which things happen. When you read certain types of writing, such as a short story, a novel, a biography of a person's life, or a history book, keep track of the sequence of events. You might do this by making a Time Line or a Sequence Map.

Time Line

To make a Time Line, draw a line and divide it into equal parts like the one below. Label each part with a date or a time. Then add key events at the right places along the Time Line.

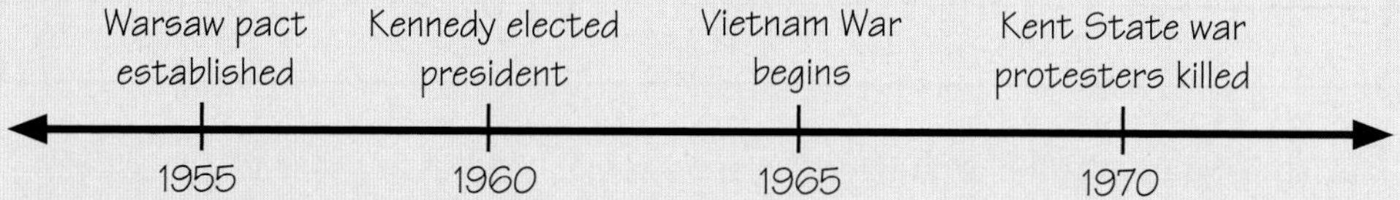

Sequence Map

In each box, draw pictures that represent key events in a selection. Then write a caption under each box that explains each event. Draw the events in the order in which they occur.

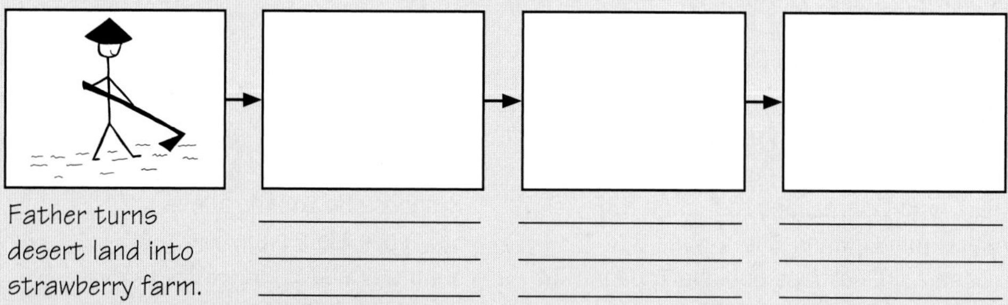

Father turns desert land into strawberry farm.

COMPARE AND CONTRAST

Comparing and contrasting are closely related processes. When you **compare** one thing to another, you describe similarities between the two things; when you **contrast** two things, you describe their differences. To compare and contrast, begin by listing the features of each subject. Then go down both lists and check whether each feature is shared or not. You can also show similarities and differences in a *Venn Diagram.* A Venn Diagram uses two slightly overlapping circles. The outer part of each circle shows what aspects of two things are different from each other. The inner, or shared, part of each circle shows what aspects the two things have in common.

Venn Diagram

Another method for comparison and contrast is to use a Pro and Con Chart like the one below to take notes on both sides of an argument.

Pro and Con Chart

Arguments in Favor of Exploring Outer Space (PRO)	Arguments Against Exploring Outer Space (CON)
Argument 1: We must continue to explore outer space. **Support:** The space effort has a history of creating scientific discoveries such as Teflon and transistors.	**Argument 1:** **Support:**

EVALUATE CAUSE AND EFFECT

When you evaluate **cause and effect,** you are looking for a logical relationship between a cause or causes and one or more effects. A writer may present one or more causes followed by one or more effects, or one or more effects followed by one or more causes. Transitional, or signal, words and phrases that indicate cause and effect include *one cause, another effect, as a result, consequently,* and *therefore.* As a reader, you determine whether the causes and effects in a text are reasonable. A graphic organizer like the one below will help you to recognize relationships between causes and effects. Keep track of what happens in a story and why in a chart like the one below. Use cause-and-effect signal words to help you identify causes and their effects.

Cause-and-Effect Chart

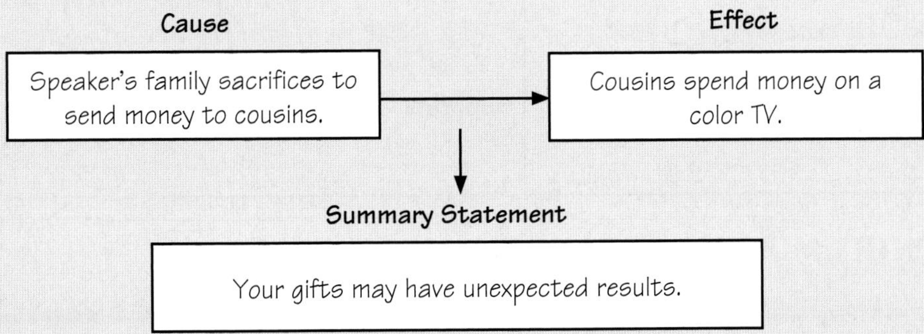

CLASSIFY AND REORGANIZE INFORMATION

To **classify** is to put into classes or categories. Items in the same category should share one or more characteristics. A writer may group things to show similarities and name the categories to clarify how one group is similar or different from another. For example, whales can be classified by their method of eating as *baleen* or *toothed*. Classifying or reorganizing the information into categories as you read increases your understanding.

The key step in classifying is choosing categories that fit your purpose. Take classification notes in a chart like the one that follows to help you organize separate types or groups and sort their characteristics.

Classification Chart

Category 1 Electron	Category 2 Nucleus	Category 3 Atom
Items in Category	Items in Category	Items in Category
Details and Characteristics	Details and Characteristics	Details and Characteristics

DISTINGUISH FACT FROM OPINION

A **fact** is a statement that can be proven by direct observation. Every statement of fact is either true or false. The following statement is an example of fact:

> Many Greek myths deal with human emotion. (This statement is a fact that can be proven by examining the content of Greek myths.)

An **opinion** is a statement that expresses an attitude or a desire, not a fact about the world. One common type of opinion statement is a *value statement*. A value statement expresses an attitude toward something.

> Ancient Greece produced some **beautiful** and **inspiring** myths. (The adjectives used to describe myths express an attitude or opinion toward something that cannot be proven.)

Fact from Opinion Chart

Fact: The Endurance was shipwrecked, but the crew survived on the ice of the Antarctic. Proof: Historical records, Shackleton's diary	Opinion: Support:

IDENTIFY MULTIPLE LEVELS OF MEANING

There is often more than one purpose to a story or nonfiction work. Though there is always a main idea or theme, other levels of meaning are nonetheless important in understanding the overall meaning of the selection. As you read, take note of the multiple levels of meaning, and record them in a Levels of Meaning Chart like the one on the following page.

Levels of Meaning Chart

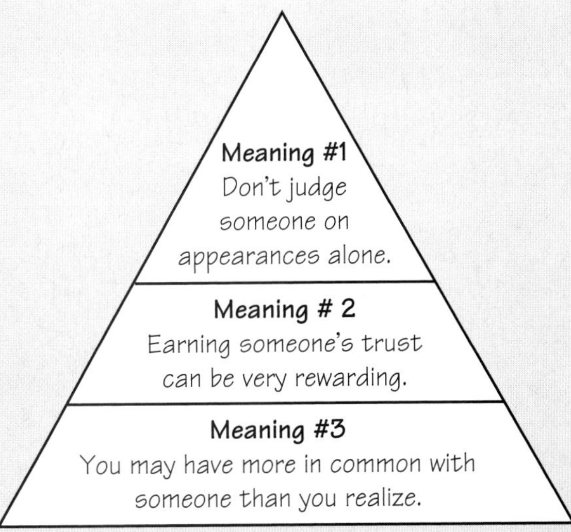

READING STRATEGIES & SKILLS

INTERPRET VISUAL AIDS

Visual aids are charts, graphs, pictures, illustrations, photos, maps, diagrams, spreadsheets, and other materials that present information. Many writers use visual aids to present data in understandable ways. Information visually presented in tables, charts, and graphs can help you find data, see trends, discover facts, and uncover patterns.

Pie Chart

A **pie chart** is a circle that stands for a whole group or set. The circle is divided into parts to show the divisions of the whole. When you look at a pie chart, you can see the relationships of the parts to one another and to the whole.

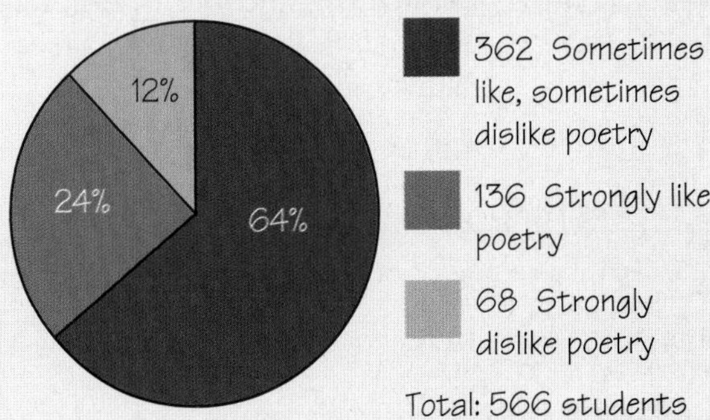

Bar Graph

A **bar graph** compares amounts of something by representing the amounts as bars of different lengths. In the bar graph shown on the next page, each bar represents the value in dollars of canned goods donated by several communities to a food drive. To read the graph, simply imagine a line drawn from the edge of the bar to the bottom of the graph. Then read the number. For example, the bar graph on the next page shows that the community of Russell Springs donated $600 worth of goods during the food drive.

DOLLAR VALUE OF DONATED GOODS TO CANNED FOOD DRIVE

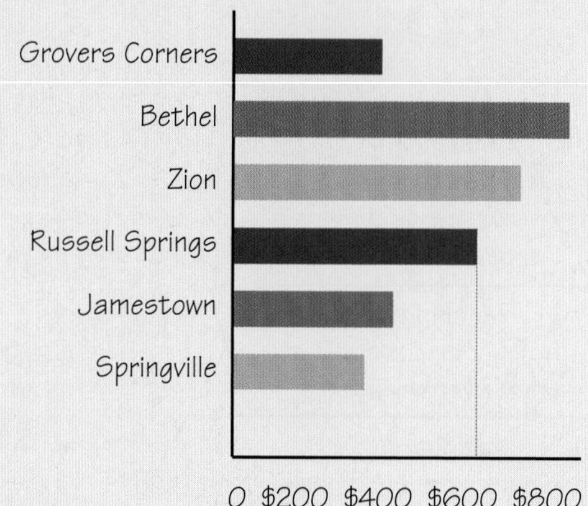

Map

A **map** is a representation, usually on a surface such as paper or a sheet of plastic, of a geographic area showing various significant features of that area.

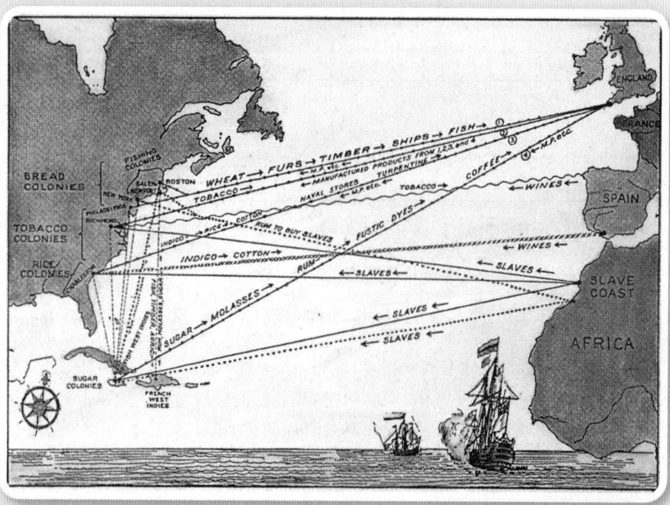

MONITOR COMPREHENSION

All readers occasionally have difficulty as they read. As you read, you should always **monitor,** or pay attention to, your progress, stopping frequently to check how well you are understanding what you are reading. If you encounter problems or lose focus, use a **fix-up idea** to get back on track. The following **fix-up ideas** can help you "fix up" any confusion or lack of attention you experience as you read. You probably use many of these already.

- **Reread** If you don't understand a sentence, paragraph, or section the first time through, go back and reread it. Each time you reread a text, you understand and remember more.
- **Read in shorter chunks** Break a long text into shorter chunks. Read through each "chunk." Then go back and make sure you understand that section before moving on.

- **Read aloud** If you are having trouble keeping your focus, try reading aloud to yourself. Go somewhere private and read aloud, putting emphasis and expression in your voice. Reading aloud also allows you to untangle difficult text by talking your way through it.
- **Ask questions** As you read, stop and ask yourself questions about the text. These questions may help you pinpoint things that are confusing you or things that you want to come back to later. You can ask questions in your head, or jot them down in the margins or on a piece of paper.
- **Change your reading rate** Your reading rate is how fast or slow you read. Good readers adjust their rate to fit the situation. In some cases, when you just need to get the general idea or main points of a reading, or if the reading is simple, you will want to read through it quickly and not get bogged down. Other times, such as when a text is difficult or contains a lot of description, you will need to slow down and read carefully.

SUMMARIZE

Summarizing is giving a shortened version of something that has been said or written, stating its main points. When you summarize a selection, you are **paraphrasing,** or restating something using other words in order to make it simpler or shorter. Summarizing what you have read will help you identify, understand, and remember the main and supporting points in the text. Read and summarize short sections of a selection at a time. Then write a summary of the entire work. Use a Summary Chart like the one below.

Summary Chart

Summary Chart
Summary of Section 1: The village blacksmith is a mighty, strong man.
Summary of Section 2: He makes an honest living and doesn't owe any man.
Summary of Section 3: He works long hard days every day of the week.
Summary of Section 4: The children love to watch him work at the forge and bellows.
Summary of the Selection: The village blacksmith is a valuable member of the community.

DRAW CONCLUSIONS

When you **draw conclusions,** you are gathering pieces of information and then deciding what that information means. Drawing conclusions is an essential part of reading. It may be helpful to use a graphic organizer such as a chart or log to keep track of the information you find while you are reading and the conclusions you draw.

Drawing Conclusions Log

Key Idea	Key Idea	Key Idea
Eshu was trying to trick the farmers to ruin their friendship. **Supporting Points** Eshu wore a cap that was black on one side and red on the other.	 **Supporting Points**	 **Supporting Points**
Overall Conclusion Eshu wore his cap that way so that the friends would have seen different things.		

2 Vocabulary & Spelling

2.1 Using Context Clues

You can often figure out the meaning of an unfamiliar word by using context clues. Context clues, or hints you gather from the words and sentences around the unfamiliar word, prevent you from having to look up every unknown word in the dictionary. The chart below defines the types of context clues and gives you an example of each. It also lists words that signal each type of clue.

Context Clues	
comparison clue	shows a comparison, or how the unfamiliar word is like something that might be familiar to you
signal words	*and, like, as, just as, as if, as though*
EXAMPLE Joan was as nimble as a mountain goat as she hiked along the steep, rocky trail. (A mountain goat is extremely agile and sure on its feet. Nimble must mean "agile.")	
contrast clue	shows that something contrasts, or differs in meaning, from something else
signal words	*but, nevertheless, on the other hand, however, although, though, in spite of*
EXAMPLE Hsuan is very reflective, but his friend Ku Min is known for jumping into things without thinking about them. (The word *but* signals a contrast between Hsuan's and Ku Min's ways of doing things. If Ku Min jumps in without thinking, Hsuan must think things through more thoroughly. *Reflective* must mean "thoughtful, meditative.")	
restatement clue	uses different words to express the same idea
signal words	*that is, in other words, or*
EXAMPLE I know Kayesha will prevail in the student council election; I have no doubt that she's going to win! (As the information after the semicolon indicates, *prevail* means "win.")	
examples clue	gives examples of other items to illustrate the meaning of something
signal words	*including, such as, for example, for instance, especially, particularly*
EXAMPLE Trevor has always been interested in celestial bodies such as planets, stars, and moons. (If you know enough about the examples listed, you can tell that celestial bodies are visible bodies in the sky.)	
cause-and-effect clue	tells you that something happened as a result of something else
signal words	*if/then, when/then, thus, therefore, because, so, as a result of, consequently*
EXAMPLE I hadn't planned on going to the party, but the host invited me in such a cordial way that I felt welcome. (If the host's cordial invitation helped the speaker feel welcome, you can guess that *cordial* means "friendly.")	

2.2 Breaking Words Into Base Words, Word Roots, Prefixes, and Suffixes

Many words are formed by adding prefixes and suffixes to main word parts called base words (if they can stand alone) or word roots (if they can't). A prefix is a letter or group of letters added to the beginning of a word to change its meaning. A suffix is a letter or group of letters added to the end of a word to change its meaning.

Word Part	Definition	Example
base word	main word part that can stand alone	form
word root	main word part that can't stand alone	struc
prefix	letter or group of letters added to the beginning of the word	pre–
suffix	letter or group of letters added to the end of the word	–tion

Common Prefixes		
Prefix	**Meaning**	**Examples**
anti–/ant–	against; opposite	antibody, antacid
bi–	two	bicycle, biped
circum–	around; about	circumnavigate, circumstance
co–/col–/com–/con–/cor–	together	cooperate, collaborate, commingle, concentrate, correlate
counter–	contrary; complementary; opposite	counteract, counterpart
de–	opposite; remove; reduce	decipher, defrost, devalue
dia–	through; apart	dialogue, diaphanous
dis–	not; opposite of	dislike, disguise
dys–	abnormal; difficult; bad	dysfunctional, dystopia
ex–	out of; from; away	explode, export, extend
extra–/extro–	outward; outside; beyond	extraordinary, extrovert
hyper–	too much, too many, extreme; above	hyperbole, hyperactive
hypo–	under	hypodermic, hypothermic
il–, im–, in–, ir–	not	illogical, impossible, inoperable, irrational
	in; within; toward; on	illuminate, imperil, infiltrate, irrigate
inter–	among; between	international, intersect
intra–/intro–	into; within; inward	introvert, intramural
mis–	wrongly	mistake, misfire
non–	not	nonsense, nonsmoker

Common Prefixes		
Prefix	**Meaning**	**Examples**
out–	in a manner that goes beyond	outrun, outmuscle
over–	excessive	overdone, overkill
post–	after; later	postgame, postpone
pre–	before	prefix, premature
pro–	before; forward	proceed, prologue
re–	again; back	redo, recall
retro–	back	retrospect, retroactive
semi–	half; partly	semicircle, semidry
sub–/sup–	under	substandard, subfloor, support
super–	above; over; exceeding	superstar, superfluous
trans–	across; beyond	transatlantic, transfer, transcend
ultra–	too much; too many; extreme	ultraviolet, ultrasound
un–	not	unethical, unhappy
under–	below; short of a quantity or limit	underestimate, understaffed
uni–	one	unicorn, universe

Common Suffixes		
Noun Suffixes	**Meaning**	**Examples**
–ance/–ancy/–ence/–ency	quality; state	defiance, independence, emergency
–age	action; process	marriage, voyage
–ant/–ent	one who	defendant, assistant, resident
–ar/–er/–or	one who	lawyer, survivor, liar
–dom	state; quality of	freedom, boredom
–ion/–tion	action; process	revolution, occasion
–ism	act; state; system of belief	plagiarism, barbarism, Buddhism
–ist	one who does or believes something	ventriloquist, idealist
–itude, –tude	quality of; state of	multitude, magnitude
–ity/–ty	state of	longevity, piety
–ment	action or process; state or quality; product or thing	development, government, amusement, amazement, ointment, fragment
–ness	state of	kindness, happiness

Common Suffixes		
Adjective Suffixes	**Meaning**	**Examples**
–able/–ible	capable of	attainable, possible
–al	having characteristics of	personal, governmental
–er	more	higher, calmer, shorter
–est	most	lowest, craziest, tallest
–ful	full of	helpful, gleeful, woeful
–ic	having characteristics of	scientific, chronic
–ish	like	childish, reddish
–ive	performs; tends toward	creative, pensive
–less	without	hapless, careless
–ous	possessing the qualities of	generous, joyous
–y	indicates description	happy, dirty, flowery
Adverb Suffixes	**Meaning**	**Examples**
–ly	in such a way	quickly, studiously, invisibly
–ward, –ways, –wise	in such a direction	toward, sideways, crosswise
Verb Suffixes	**Meaning**	**Examples**
–ate	make or cause to be	fixate, activate
–ed	past tense of verb	walked, acted, fixed
–ify/–fy	make or cause to be	magnify, glorify
–ing	indicates action in progress (present participle); can also be a noun (gerund)	running, thinking, being
–ize	bring about; cause to be	colonize, legalize

Common Word Roots		
Word Root	**Meaning**	**Examples**
act	do	actor, reaction
ann/annu/enni	year	annual, bicentennial
aqu	water	aquarium, aquatic
aster, astr	star	asteroid, astronomy
aud	hear	audition, auditorium
bene	good	beneficial, benefactor
bibl, bibli	book	Bible, bibliography
chron	time	chronic, chronological
cred	believe; trust	credit, credible
cycl	circle	bicycle, cyclone

Common Word Roots		
Word Root	**Meaning**	**Examples**
dem/demo	people	democracy, demagogue
derm	skin	dermatologist, hypodermic
dic/dict	say	dictate, dictionary
fer	carry	transfer, refer
fin	end	finish, infinite
flect/flex	bend	deflect, reflex, flexible
hydra, hydro	water	hydrate, hydrogen
ign	fire	ignite, ignition, igneous
ject	throw	projector, eject
lect/leg	read; choose	lecture, election, legible
liber	free	liberate, liberal
log/logue	word; speech; discourse	logic, monologue
luc/lumin	shine; light	lucid, luminous
mal	bad	malevolent, malodorous
man/manu	hand	manufacture, manual
metr	measure	metric, metronome
ped	foot; child	pedal, pediatrics
phon/phony	sound; voice; speech	symphony, microphone
phot	light	photography, photon
physi	nature	physical, physics
pop	people	popular, populate
port	carry	transport, portable
psych	mind; soul	psychology, psychic
reg	rule	register, regulate
rupt	break	disrupt, interruption, rupture
scrib/script	write	describe, prescription
spec/spect/spic	look	speculate, inspect, specimen
ter/terr	earth	inter, terrestrial, terrain
therm	heat	thermal, hypothermia
vid/vis	see	video, visual
vol/volv	turn	evolution, revolve

2.3 Using a Dictionary

When you can't figure out a word using the strategies already described, or when the word is important to the meaning of the text and you want to make sure you have it right, use a dictionary. There are many parts to a dictionary entry.

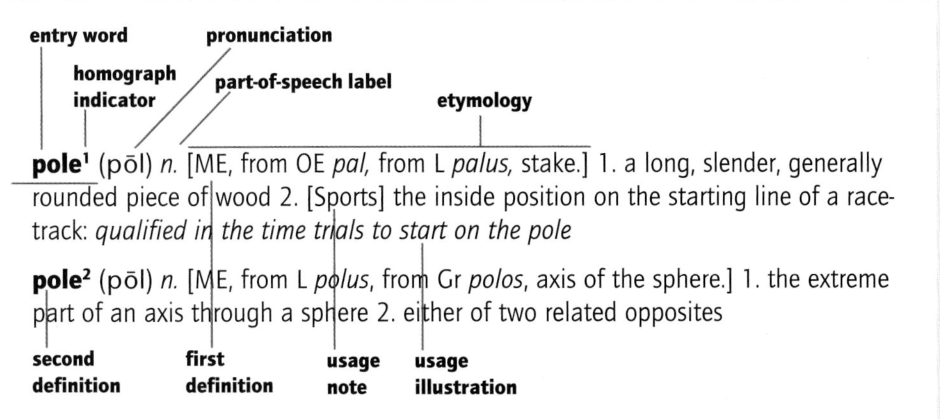

The **pronunciation** is given immediately after the entry word. The dictionary's table of contents will tell you where you can find a complete key to pronunciation symbols. In some dictionaries, a simplified pronunciation key is provided at the bottom of each page.

An abbreviation of the **part of speech** usually follows the pronunciation. This label tells how the word can be used. If a word can be used as more than one part of speech, a separate entry is provided for each part of speech.

An **etymology** is the history of the word. In the first entry, the word *pole* can be traced back through Middle English (ME) and Old English (OE) to the Latin (L) word *palus,* which means "stake." In the second entry, the word *pole* can be traced back through Middle English to the Latin word *polus,* which comes from the Greek (Gr) word *polos,* meaning "axis of the sphere."

Sometimes the entry will include a list of **synonyms,** or words that have the same or very similar meanings. The entry may also include a **usage illustration,** which is an example of how the word is used in context.

2.4 Exploring Word Origins and Word Families

The English language expands constantly and gathers new words from many different sources. Understanding the source of a word can help you unlock its meaning.

One source of new words is the names of people and places associated with the thing being named. Words named for people and places are called **eponyms.**

EXAMPLES

hamburger Originally known as "Hamburg steak," the hamburger takes its name from the German city Hamburg.

spoonerism The slip of the tongue whereby the beginning sounds of words are switched is named after the Rev. William A. Spooner, who was known for such slips. For example, after a wedding, he told the groom, "It is kisstomary to cuss the bride."

VOCABULARY & SPELLING

Another source for new words is **acronyms.** Acronyms are words formed from the first letter or letters of the major parts of terms.

EXAMPLES

sonar, from sound navigation ranging

NATO, from North American Treaty Organization

Some words in the English language are borrowed from other languages.

EXAMPLES

deluxe (French), **Gesundheit** (German), **kayak** (Inuit)

Many words are formed by shortening longer words.

EXAMPLES

ad, from advertisement

lab, from laboratory

stereo, from stereophonic

Brand names are often taken into the English language. People begin to use these words as common nouns, even though most of them are still brand names.

EXAMPLES

Scotch tape **Xerox** **Rollerblade**

2.5 Understanding Multiple Meanings

Each definition in the entry gives a different meaning of the word. When a word has more than one meaning, the different definitions are numbered. The first definition in an entry is the most common meaning of the word, but you will have to choose the meaning that fits the context in which you have found the word. Try substituting each definition for the word until you find the one that makes the most sense. If you come across a word that doesn't seem to make sense in context, consider whether that word might have another, lesser known meaning. Can the word be used as more than one part of speech, for example, as either a noun or a verb? Does it have a broader meaning than the one that comes to your mind?

Keep in mind that some words not only have multiple meanings but also different pronunciations. Words that are spelled the same but are pronounced differently are called **homographs.**

2.6 Understanding Denotation and Connotation

The **denotation** of a word is its dictionary definition. Sometimes, in order to understand a passage fully, it is helpful to know the connotations of the words as well. A **connotation** of a word is an emotional association the word has in addition to its literal meaning. For example, the words *cheap* and *thrifty* both denote "tending to spend less money," but *cheap* has a negative connotation similar to "stingy," whereas *thrifty* has a positive connotation involving being responsible with money. The best way to learn the connotation of a word is to pay attention to the context in which the word appears or to ask someone more familiar with the word.

Connotation Chart

Negative	Neutral	Positive
weird	unusual	unique
freakish	different	remarkable
bizarre	uncommon	extraordinary
abnormal	rare	unequaled
mob	group	congregation

2.7 Spelling

SPELLING RULES

Always check your writing for spelling errors, and try to recognize the words that give you more trouble than others. Use a dictionary when you find you have misspelled a word. Keep a list in a notebook of words that are difficult for you to spell. Write the words several times until you have memorized the correct spelling. Break down the word into syllables and carefully pronounce each individual syllable.

Some spelling problems occur when adding prefixes or suffixes to words or when making nouns plural. Other spelling problems occur when words follow certain patterns, such as those containing *ie/ei*. The following spelling rules can help you spell many words correctly.

PREFIXES AND SUFFIXES

Prefixes

A **prefix** is a letter or a group of letters added to the beginning of a word to change its meaning. When adding a prefix, do not change the spelling of the word itself.

EXAMPLES

mis– + perception = misperception
im– + possible = impossible
in– + conceivable = inconceivable
anti– + social = antisocial
al– + mighty = almighty

Suffixes

A **suffix** is a letter or a group of letters added to the end of a word to change its meaning.

The spelling of most words is not changed when the suffix *–ness* or *–ly* is added.

EXAMPLES

shy + –ness = shyness
forgive + –ness = forgiveness
eager + –ness = eagerness
strange + –ly = strangely
bad + –ly = badly
splendid + –ly = splendidly

If you are adding a suffix to a word that ends with *y* following a vowel, usually leave the *y* in place.

EXAMPLES

employ	employs	employing	employed
defray	defrays	defraying	defrayment
buoy	buoys	buoying	buoyancy

If you are adding a suffix to a word that ends with *y* following a consonant, change the *y* to *i* before adding any ending except *–ing*.

EXAMPLES

bury	buried	burying
copy	copied	copying
supply	supplied	supplying
magnify	magnified	magnifying

Double the final consonant before adding a suffix beginning with a vowel (such as *–ed, –en, –er, –ing, –ence, –ance,* or *–y*) in words ending in a single consonant preceded by a single vowel if the word is either a single syllable or ends in a stressed syllable.

EXAMPLES

regret	regrettable	regretting
quit	quitter	quitting
fan	fanned	fanning
refer	referred	referring
plot	plotted	plotting
deter	deterrence	deterring
rot	rotten	rotting

If you are adding a suffix that begins with a vowel to a word that ends with a silent *e*, usually drop the *e.*

EXAMPLES

tune	tuning
oblige	obligation
pursue	pursuable
grieve	grievous

If you are adding a suffix that begins with a consonant to a word that ends with a silent *e*, usually leave the *e* in place.

EXAMPLES

spite	spiteful
achieve	achievement
state	stately
lame	lameness

EXCEPTIONS

awe	awful
wise	wisdom
nine	ninth
due	duly

If the word ends in a soft *c* sound (spelled *ce*) or a soft *g* sound (spelled *ge*), keep the *e* when adding the suffixes *–able* or *–ous.*

EXAMPLES

acknowledge	acknowledgeable
enforce	enforceable
outrage	outrageous

PLURAL NOUNS

Plural Nouns

Most noun plurals are formed by simply adding *–s* to the end of the word.

EXAMPLES

surface + –s = surfaces
mouthful + –s = mouthfuls
platelet + –s = platelets
refrigerator + –s = refrigerators

The plural of nouns that end in *o, s, x, z, ch,* or *sh* should be formed by adding *–es.*

EXAMPLES

tomato + –es = tomatoes
loss + –es = losses
fox + –es = foxes
buzz + –es = buzzes
inch + –es = inches
flash + –es = flashes

The exception to the rule above is that musical terms and certain other words that end in *o* are usually made plural by adding *–s.* Check a dictionary if you aren't sure whether to add *–s* or *–es.*

EXAMPLES

piano + –s = pianos
solo + –s = solos
soprano + –s = sopranos
vibrato + –s = vibratos

Form the plural of nouns that end in *y* following a consonant by changing the *y* to an *i* and adding *–es.*

EXAMPLES

democracy	democracies
fairy	fairies
fallacy	fallacies
fifty	fifties
filly	fillies

Nouns that end in *f* or *fe* must be modified, changing the *f* or *fe* to *v,* before adding *–es* to the plural form.

EXAMPLES

shelf	shelves
knife	knives
scarf	scarves
leaf	leaves
calf	calves

SPELLING PATTERNS

The ie/ei Spelling Pattern

A word spelled with the letters *i* and *e* and has a long *e* sound is usually spelled *ie* except after the letter *c.*

EXAMPLES

belief	conceive
piece	receive
field	deceit

EXCEPTIONS

leisure	either

VOCABULARY & SPELLING

Use *ei* when the sound is not long *e.*

EXAMPLES

forfeit surfeit foreign height

EXCEPTIONS

science mischief sieve

If the vowel combination has a long *a* sound (as in *eight*), always spell it with *ei.*

EXAMPLES

weight reign vein

When two vowels are pronounced separately in a word, spell them in the order of their pronunciation.

EXAMPLES

siesta patio diode transient

The "Seed" Sound Pattern

The "seed" ending sound has three spellings: *–sede, –ceed,* and *–cede.*

EXAMPLES

Only one word ends in *–sede: supersede*

Three words end in *–ceed: proceed, succeed, exceed*

All other words end in *–cede: accede, concede, recede, precede, secede*

Silent Letters

Some spelling problems result from letters written but not heard when a word is spoken. Becoming familiar with the patterns in letter combinations containing silent letters will help you identify other words that fit the patterns.

- Silent *b* usually occurs with *m.*

EXAMPLES

dumb bomb climb lamb

- Silent *b* also appears in *debt* and *doubt.*
- Silent *c* often appears with *s.*

EXAMPLES

scissors scent scenic science

- Silent *g* often appears with *n.*

EXAMPLES

design resign gnome foreign

- Silent *gh* often appears at the end of a word, either alone or in combination with *t (–ght).*

EXAMPLES

fright freight sought wrought

- Silent *h* appears at the beginning of some words.

EXAMPLES

hourly heir honestly honor

- Silent *h* also appears in a few other words, as in *rhythm* and *ghost.*
- Silent *k* occurs with *n.*

EXAMPLES

knack knight knot kneecap knapsack

- Silent *n* occurs with *m* at the end of some words.

EXAMPLES

condemn solemn column autumn

- Silent *p* occurs with *s* at the beginning of some words.

EXAMPLES

psyche psychosis psoriasis

- Silent *s* occurs with *l* in some words.

EXAMPLES

island islet aisle

- Silent *t* occurs with *s* in a few words.

EXAMPLES

listen hasten nestle

- Silent *w* occurs at the beginnings of some words.

EXAMPLES

wreak wrong wraith wrapper

- Silent *w* also occurs with *s* in a few words, such as *sword* and *answer.*

Letter Combinations

Some letter combinations have a different pronunciation when combined and can cause spelling problems.

- The letters *ph* produce the *f* sound.

EXAMPLES

sphinx photograph alphanumeric phosphate

- The letters *gh* produce the *f* sound usually at the end of a word. (Otherwise, they are silent.)

EXAMPLES

cough enough neigh weigh

- The letter combination *tch* sounds the same as *ch*.

EXAMPLES

sketch pitch snitch hatch
such hunch grouch torch

If the letters *c* and *g* have soft sounds (of *s* and *j*), they will usually be followed by *e, i,* or *y.*

EXAMPLES

cyclone circle regent
giant cent gyroscope
outrageous region

VOCABULARY & SPELLING

If the letters *c* and *g* have hard sounds (of *k* and *g*), they will usually be followed by *a, o,* or *u*.

EXAMPLES

candid	gasket	conjugate
congeal	garland	gun
convey	argument	cunning

Spelling Patterns of Borrowed Words

Many words borrowed from other languages follow the spelling patterns of the original language. For example, some English words borrowed from French, Spanish, and Italian follow letter patterns of the language of origin.

- The final *t* is silent in many words borrowed from French.

EXAMPLES

croquet   ballet

- The letter combinations *eur* and *eau* appear at the end of many words with French origin.

EXAMPLES

amateur	bureau	grandeur
chauffeur	plateau	tableau

- The letter combination *oo* appears in many words borrowed from the Dutch language.

EXAMPLES

roost   cooper   toot

Many plural Italian words end in *i*.

EXAMPLES

ravioli   manicotti   linguini

Many words of Spanish origin end in *o*.

EXAMPLES

machismo   tomato   patio

Compound Nouns

A **compound noun** consists of two or more nouns used together to form a single noun. Sometimes they are written as one word *(football, uptown);* other times they are written separately *(picnic table, tennis shoes)*. Some compound nouns are connected with hyphens *(great-grandfather, fly-by-night).* Consult a good dictionary when you are not sure of the form of compounds.

Numerals

Spell out numbers of *one hundred* or less and all numbers rounded to hundreds. Larger round numbers such as *seven thousand* or *three million* should also be spelled out.

EXAMPLES

Joe Morgan hit more than **twenty** home runs and stole at least **thirty** bases in the same season **four** times in his career.

Joe DiMaggio was the first baseball player to receive an annual salary of more than **a hundred thousand** dollars.

Use a hyphen to separate compound numbers from twenty-one through ninety-nine.

EXAMPLES

forty-two birds
seventy-four candles
one hundred soldiers
sixty thousand dollars

Use a hyphen in a fraction used as a modifier, but not in a fraction used as a noun.

EXAMPLES

The glass is **two-fifths full** of water.

After an hour, I had mowed **three fourths** of the backyard.

Use Arabic numerals for numbers greater than one hundred that are not rounded numbers.

EXAMPLES

Our company sent out **493,745** mailings in just **145** days this year.

My uncle boasted that he has read **1,323** books thus far in his life.

If a number appears at the beginning of a sentence, spell it out or rewrite the sentence.

EXAMPLES

incorrect
356 years ago, my ancestors moved to North America.
correct
Three hundred fifty-six years ago, my ancestors moved to North America.
correct
My ancestors moved to North America **356** years ago.

Use words to write the time unless you are writing the exact time (including the abbreviation AM or PM). When the word *o'clock* is used for time of day, express the number in words.

EXAMPLES

Our meeting will start at **a quarter after ten.**

At **eight-thirty,** the show will begin.

I was born at **5:22 PM** on a Monday.

You have until **three o'clock** to finish the proposal.

Use numerals to express dates, street numbers, room numbers, apartment numbers, telephone numbers, page numbers, exact amounts of money, scores, and percentages. Spell out the word *percent.* Round dollar or cent amounts of only a few words may be expressed in words.

EXAMPLES

May 27, 1962 — three hundred dollars
(402) 555-1725 — Apartment 655
5219 Perret Street — 38 percent
pages 49–73 — $1.6 billion (or $1,600,000,000)
seventy cents — $2,634

When you write a date, do not add *–st, –nd,* or *–th.*

EXAMPLES

incorrect
August 17th, 1968 — November 5th
correct
August 17, 1968 — November 5 or the fifth of November

COMMON SPELLING ERRORS

Pronunciation is not always a reliable guide for spelling because words are not always spelled the way they are pronounced. However, by paying attention to both letters that spell sounds and letters that are silent, you can improve some aspects of your spelling. Always check a dictionary for the correct pronunciations and spellings of words that are new to your experience.

Extra Syllables

Sometimes people misspell a word because they include an extra syllable. For example, *arthritis* is easily misspelled if it is pronounced *artheritis,* with four syllables instead of three. Pay close attention to the number of syllables in these words.

EXAMPLES

two syllables

foundry   carriage   lonely

three syllables

privilege   boundary   separate

Omitted Sounds

Sometimes people misspell a word because they do not sound one or more letters when pronouncing the word. Be sure to include the underlined letters of these words even if you don't pronounce them.

EXAMPLES

barb<u>a</u>rous   can<u>d</u>idate   drown<u>e</u>d   mischi<u>e</u>vous   soph<u>o</u>more
gra<u>ti</u>tude   gov<u>er</u>nor   groc<u>e</u>ry   quan<u>t</u>ity   liter<u>a</u>ture

Homophones

Words that have the same pronunciation but different spellings and meanings are called **homophones.** An incorrect choice can be confusing to your readers. Knowing the spelling and meaning of these groups of words will improve your spelling.

EXAMPLES

allowed/aloud
sole/soul
hear/here
ascent/assent
threw/through
night/knight
brake/break
weak/week
coarse/course
alter/altar
some/sum
lead/led
bear/bare
wait/weight
pair/pear
compliment/complement
site/sight/cite
plain/plane
capital/capitol
who's/whose
peace/piece
buy/bye/by

Commonly Confused Words

Some other groups of words are not homophones, but they are similar enough in sound and spelling to create confusion. Knowing the spelling and meaning of these groups of words will also improve your spelling.

EXAMPLES

access/excess
accept/except
formally/formerly
literal/literally
farther/further
principle/principal
passed/past
desert/dessert
nauseous/nauseated
stationary/stationery
alternate/alternative
loose/lose

COMMONLY MISSPELLED WORDS

Some words are often misspelled. Here is a list of 150 commonly misspelled words. If you master this list, you will avoid many errors in your spelling.

absence
abundant
academically
accessible
accidentally
accommodate
accurate
acknowledgment
acquaintance
adequately
adolescent
advantageous
advisable
ancient
annihilate
anonymous
answer
apparent
article
attendance
bankruptcy
beautiful
beggar
beginning
behavior
biscuit
breathe
business
calendar
camouflage
catastrophe
cellar
cemetery
changeable
clothes
colossal
column
committee
conceivable
conscientious
conscious
consistency
deceitful
descendant
desirable
disastrous
discipline
efficiency
eighth
embarrass
enormous
enthusiastically
environment
exhaust
existence
fascinating
finally
forfeit
fulfill
guerrilla
guidance
hindrance
hypocrite
independent
influential
ingenious
institution
interference
irrelevant
irresistible
judgment
league
leisure
license
lightning
liquefy
magnificent
manageable
maneuver
meadow
mediocre
miniature
mischievous
misspell
mortgage
mysterious
naïve
necessity
nickel
niece
noticeable
nucleus
nuisance
nutritious
obedience
occasionally
occurrence
orchestra
outrageous
pageant
parallel
pastime
peasant
permanent
persistent
phenomenon
physician
pneumonia
prestige
privilege
procedure
prophesy
prove
receipt
referred
rehearsal
relieve
resistance
resources
responsibility
rhythm
schedule
seize
separate
sergeant
siege
significance
souvenir
sponsor
succeed
surprise
symbol
synonymous
temperature
tomorrow
transparent
twelfth
undoubtedly
unmistakable
unnecessary
vacuum
vehicle
vengeance
villain
vinegar
weird
whistle
withhold
yacht
yield

3.1 The Sentence

THE SENTENCE

In the English language, the sentence is the basic unit of meaning. A **sentence** is a group of words that expresses a complete thought. Every sentence has two basic parts: a subject and a predicate. The **subject** tells whom or what the sentence is about. The **predicate** tells information about the subject.

EXAMPLE

sentence
The old professor | read the dusty manuscript.
(subject) **(predicate)**

A group of words that does not have both a subject and a predicate is called a **sentence fragment.** A sentence fragment does not express a complete thought.

EXAMPLES

sentence fragment The baker.
(The fragment does not have a predicate. The group of words does not answer the question *What did the baker do?*)
sentence fragment Frosted the chocolate cake.
(The fragment does not have a subject. The group of words does not answer the question *Who frosted the chocolate cake?*)
sentence fragment In his kitchen.
(The fragment does not have a subject or predicate. The group of words does not tell what the sentence is about or tell what the subject does.)
complete sentence The baker frosted the chocolate cake in his kitchen.

FUNCTIONS OF SENTENCES

There are four different kinds of sentences: *declarative, interrogative, imperative,* and *exclamatory*. Each kind of sentence has a different purpose. You can vary the tone and mood of your writing by using the four different sentence types.

- A **declarative sentence** makes a statement. It ends with a period.

EXAMPLE

Your cat would like to eat her supper now.

- An **interrogative sentence** asks a question. It ends with a question mark.

EXAMPLE

When will your cat eat her supper?

- An **imperative sentence** gives an order or makes a request. It ends with a period or an exclamation point. An imperative sentence has an understood subject, most often *you.*

EXAMPLES

(You) Please feed your cat.
(You) Look in the cupboard for the cat food.

- An **exclamatory sentence** expresses strong feeling. It ends with an exclamation point.

EXAMPLE

Your cat is really hungry!

SIMPLE AND COMPLETE SUBJECTS AND PREDICATES

In a sentence, the **simple subject** is the key word or words in the subject. The simple subject is usually a noun or a pronoun and does not include any modifiers. The **complete subject** includes the simple subject and all the words that modify it.

The **simple predicate** is the key verb or verb phrase that tells what the subject does, has, or is. The **complete predicate** includes the verb and all the words that modify it.

In the following sentence, a vertical line separates the complete subject and complete predicate. The simple subject is underlined once. The simple predicate is underlined twice.

EXAMPLE

(complete subject) **(complete predicate)**
The large black umbrella | shielded my brother and sister from the rain.

Sometimes, the simple subject is also the complete subject, and the simple predicate or verb is also the complete predicate.

EXAMPLE

Jesse Owens | ran.

To find the simple subject and simple predicate in a sentence, first break the sentence into its two basic parts: complete subject and complete predicate. Then, identify the simple predicate by asking yourself, "What is the action of this sentence?" Finally, identify the simple subject by asking yourself, "Who or what is performing the action?" In the following sentences, the complete predicate is in parentheses. The simple predicate, or verb, appears in boldface.

EXAMPLES

one-word verb Three energetic monkeys (**climbed** up the tree.)
two-word verb Three energetic monkeys (**are climbing** up the tree.)
three-word verb Three energetic monkeys (**have been climbing** up the tree.)
four-word verb Three energetic monkeys (**might have been climbing** up the tree.)

COMPOUND SUBJECTS AND PREDICATES

A sentence may have more than one subject or predicate. A **compound subject** has two or more simple subjects that have the same predicate. The subjects are joined by the conjunction *and, or,* or *but.*

A **compound predicate** has two or more simple predicates, or verbs, that share the same subject. The verbs are connected by the conjunction *and, or,* or *but.*

EXAMPLES

compound subject
Ice and snow | make travel difficult in the winter.
compound predicate
Some teachers | show videos and play CDs during their classes.

The conjunctions *either* and *or* and *neither* and *nor* can also join compound subjects or predicates.

EXAMPLES

compound subject
Either Peter *or* Paul | sings the national anthem before each game.
Neither yesterday *nor* today | seemed like a good time to start the project.
compound predicate
Her dogs | *either* heard *or* smelled the intruder in the basement.
The police inspector | *neither* visited *nor* called last night.

A sentence may also have a compound subject and a compound predicate.

EXAMPLE

compound subject and compound predicate
John and Diane | drove to the lake and fished all afternoon.

SENTENCE STRUCTURES

A **simple sentence** consists of one independent clause and no subordinate clauses. It may have a compound subject and a compound predicate. It may also have any number of phrases. A simple sentence is sometimes called an independent clause because it can stand by itself.

EXAMPLES

Three bears emerged from the forest.

They spotted the campers and the hikers and decided to pay a visit.

The three bears enjoyed eating the campers' fish, sandwiches, and candy bars.

A **compound sentence** consists of two sentences joined by a semicolon or by a coordinating conjunction and a comma. Each part of the compound sentence has its own subject and verb. The most common coordinating conjunctions are *and, or, nor, for, but, so,* and *yet.*

EXAMPLES

compound sentence
Grover Cleveland served as president from 1885 to 1889**;** he served a second term in the White House from 1893 to 1897.
compound sentence
An economic downturn gripped the nation during Cleveland's second term**, and** his popularity with Americans dwindled.

A **complex sentence** consists of one independent clause and one or more subordinate clauses. The subordinate clauses in the examples below are underlined.

EXAMPLES

When you finish your report, remember to print it out on paper that contains 25 percent cotton fiber.

Jim will water the lawn after he returns home from the baseball game.

3.2 The Parts of Speech

IDENTIFYING THE PARTS OF SPEECH

Each word in a sentence performs a basic function or task. Words perform four basic tasks; they name, modify, express action or state of being, or link.

There are eight different parts of speech. Each part of speech is defined in the following chart.

Part of Speech	Definition	Example
noun	A **noun** names a person, place, thing, or idea.	**Apples, oranges,** and **potato chips** were the only **items** on the **list.**
pronoun	A **pronoun** is used in place of a noun.	Fanny whispered to **her** friend as **they** waited for **their** new teacher.
verb	A **verb** expresses action or a state of being.	Playful fox cubs **tumbled** out of the den and **chased** one another across the field.
adjective	An **adjective** modifies a noun or pronoun. The most common adjectives are the articles *a, an,* and *the.*	**Tattered** curtains hung in the **dark** windows of the **gray, sagging** house.
adverb	An **adverb** modifies a verb, an adjective, or another adverb.	**Sharply** turning to the left, the bicyclist **nearly** caused an accident.
preposition	A **preposition** shows the relationship between its object—a noun or a pronoun—and another word in a sentence. Common prepositions include *after, around, at, behind, beside, off, through, until, upon,* and *with.*	**During** winter, we often sit **by** the fireplace **in** the evening.
conjunction	A **conjunction** joins words or groups of words. Common conjunctions are *and, but, for, nor, or, so,* and *yet.*	**Neither** Grant **nor** Felix felt tired after two miles, **so** they ran another mile.
interjection	An **interjection** is a word used to express emotion. Common interjections are *oh, ah, well, hey,* and *wow.*	**Wow!** Did you see the dive he took from the high jump?

3.3 Nouns

NOUNS

A **noun** is a part of speech that names a person, place, idea, or thing. In this unit, you'll learn about the different kinds of nouns and what they name.

EXAMPLES

people Sidney, teacher, mother, photographer

places city, Wrigley Field, Kentucky

ideas admiration, addition, relief, plan

things checkerboard, butterfly, flight, ring

Types of Nouns	Definition	Examples
common noun	names a person, place, idea, or thing	mother, garage, plan, flower
proper noun	names a specific person, place, or thing; begins with capital letter	John Adams, New York City, Monroe Doctrine
concrete noun	names a thing that can be touched, seen, heard, smelled, or tasted	ruler, mirror, giggle, garbage, banana
abstract noun	names an idea, a theory, a concept, or a feeling	approval, philosophy, faith, communism
singular noun	names one person, place, idea, or thing	governor, tree, thought, shoe
plural noun	names more than one thing	governors, trees, thoughts, shoes
possessive noun	shows ownership or possession of things or qualities	Jan's, Mrs. Wilson's, women's, intern's
compound noun	made up of two or more words	staircase, picnic table, brother-in-law
collective noun	names groups	organization, platoon, team

3.4 Pronouns

PRONOUNS

A **pronoun** is used in place of a noun. Sometimes a pronoun refers to a specific person or thing.

Pronouns can help your writing flow more smoothly. Without pronouns, your writing can sound awkward and repetitive.

The most commonly used pronouns are *personal pronouns*, *reflexive and intensive pronouns*, *demonstrative pronouns*, *indefinite pronouns*, *interrogative pronouns*, and *relative pronouns.*

Types of Pronouns	Definition	Examples
personal pronoun	used in place of the name of a person or thing	I, me, we, us, he, she, it, him, her, you, they, them
indefinite pronoun	points out a person, place, or thing, but not a specific or definite one	one, someone, anything, other, all, few, nobody
reflexive pronoun	refers back to a noun previously used; adds –self and –selves to other pronoun forms	myself, herself, yourself, themselves, ourselves
intensive pronoun	emphasizes a noun or a pronoun	me myself, he himself, you yourself, they themselves, we ourselves
interrogative pronoun	asks a question	who, whose, whom, what, which
demonstrative pronoun	points out a specific person, place, idea, or thing	this, these, that, those
relative pronoun	introduces an adjective clause	that, which, who, whose, whom
singular pronoun	used in place of the name of one person or thing	I, me, you, he, she, it, him, her
plural pronoun	used in place of more than one person or thing	we, us, you, they, them
possessive pronoun	shows ownership or possession	mine, yours, his, hers, ours, theirs

PRONOUNS AND ANTECEDENTS

The word that a pronoun stands for is called its **antecedent.** The antecedent clarifies the meaning of the pronoun. The pronoun may appear in the same sentence as its antecedent or in a following sentence.

EXAMPLES

Where is **Michael? He** is at the library.
(*Michael* is the antecedent of *He.*)

Amy's black **dog** barks loudly because **he** is hungry.
(*Dog* is the antecedent of *he.*)

A pronoun should agree in both number (singular or plural) and gender (masculine, feminine, or neutral) with its antecedent.

EXAMPLES

number

singular	**Robert Frost** wrote many poems. "Stopping by Woods on a Snowy Evening" is perhaps **his** most well-known poem.
plural	The visiting **poets** were asked if **they** would give a reading on Saturday night.

gender

masculine	**Robert Frost** was born in California, but **he** was raised in Massachusetts and New Hampshire.
feminine	**Toni Morrison** begins **her** writing day before dawn.
neutral	The **poem** is titled "Birches," and **it** is one of my favorites.

Singular pronouns are used with some nouns that are plural in form but singular in meaning, such as *economics, electronics, gymnastics, linguistics, mathematics, measles, news,* and *physics.*

EXAMPLES

My younger brother has the **measles.** I hope I don't catch **it.**
Would you like to try **gymnastics? It** is excellent exercise.

Plural pronouns are used with some nouns that are plural in form but refer to single items, such as *pliers, eyeglasses, pants, scissors,* and *shorts.*

EXAMPLES

I can't find my **eyeglasses.** Have you seen **them?**
The **pants** fit you well, but **they** need hemming.

Agreement between a relative pronoun—*who, whom, whose, which,* and *that*—and its antecedent is determined by the number of the antecedent.

EXAMPLES

Marie, who has always enjoyed **her** rural life, has surprisingly decided to move to the city. (*Who* is singular because it refers to the singular noun *Marie. Her* is used to agree with *who.*)

All who wish to vote by absentee ballot should complete **their** ballots and mail **them** to the county clerk's office. (*Who* is plural because it refers to the plural pronoun *All. Their* is used to agree with *who. Them* is used to agree with *ballots.*)

PRONOUN CASES

Personal pronouns take on different forms—called *cases*—depending on how they are used in sentences. Personal pronouns can be used as subjects, direct objects, indirect objects, and objects of prepositions. In the English language, there are three case forms for personal pronouns: *nominative, objective,* and *possessive*. The following chart organizes personal pronouns by case, number, and person.

Personal Pronouns

	Nominative Case	Objective Case	Possessive Case
Singular			
first person	I	me	my, mine
second person	you	you	your, yours
third person	he, she, it	him, her, it	his, her, hers, its
Plural			
first person	we	us	our, ours
second person	you	you	your, yours
third person	they	them	their, theirs

Indefinite Pronouns

An **indefinite pronoun** points out a person, place, or thing, but not a particular or definite one. The indefinite pronouns are listed below.

Singular	Plural	Singular or Plural
another	both	all
anybody	few	any
anyone	many	more
anything	others	most
each	several	none
each other		some
either		
everybody		
everyone		
everything		
much		
neither		
nobody		
no one		
nothing		
one		
one another		
somebody		
someone		
something		

EXAMPLES

singular
Something makes a ticking noise in the night.

Everyone is welcome to join us at the picnic.

plural
Many are eager to participate in the summer festival.

Several were missing the necessary information.

3.5 Verbs

VERBS—PREDICATES

Every sentence can be divided into two parts: the **subject** and the **predicate.** The following sentence is divided between the complete subject and the complete predicate.

EXAMPLE

The barn **owl** | **glided** slowly over the cornfield.

The subject of a sentence names whom or what the sentence is about. The predicate tells what the subject does, is, or has. A **verb** is the predicate without any complements, linkers, or modifiers. In other words, the verb is the simple predicate.

Verbs are the **expressers** of the English language. Verbs are used to express action or a state of being. They tell whether the action is completed, continuing, or will happen in the future. Verbs also express all kinds of conditions for the action. Verbs in the English language can be from one to four words long. When a main verb is preceded by one or more helping verbs, it is called a **verb phrase.**

EXAMPLES

Dale **mows** his neighbors' lawns.

Dale **is mowing** his neighbors' lawns.

Dale **has been mowing** his neighbors' lawns.

Dale **might have been mowing** his neighbors' lawns.

The following chart lists the different types of verbs and their functions, along with examples of how they are used.

Type of Verb	Definition	Examples
action verb	names an action	howl, wobble, skitter, flutter, fly
helping verb	helps a main verb express action or a state of being	My dogs will howl when a siren sounds. A butterfly has been fluttering above the daisies.
linking verb	connects a noun with another noun, pronoun, or adjective that describes or identifies it; the most common linking verbs are formed from the verb *to be*	The butterfly is a monarch. It seems to float in the breeze.
transitive verb	has a direct object	The scientist remembered the secret code.
intransitive verb	does not have a direct object	My brother snores.
irregular verb	has a different past tense form and spelling	forget/forgot think/thought write/wrote

VERB TENSES

The Simple Tenses

Verbs have different forms, called **tenses,** which are used to tell the time in which an action takes place. The **simple tenses** of the verb are **present, past,** and **future.**

The **present tense** tells that an action happens now—in present time.

EXAMPLES

present tense singular	The green frog **jumps** into the pond.
present tense plural	The green frogs **jump** into the pond.
present tense singular	The teacher **walks** down the hall.
present tense plural	The teachers **walk** down the hall.

The **past tense** tells that an action happened in the past—prior to the present time. The past tense of a regular verb is formed by adding *–d* or *–ed* to the present verb form.

EXAMPLES

past tense singular	The green frog **jumped** into the pond.
past tense plural	The green frogs **jumped** into the pond.
past tense singular	The teacher **walked** down the hall.
past tense plural	The teachers **walked** down the hall.

The **future tense** tells that an action will happen in the future. The future tense is formed by adding the word *will* or *shall* before the present verb form.

EXAMPLES

future tense singular	The green frog **will jump** into the pond.
future tense plural	The green frogs **will jump** into the pond.
future tense singular	The teacher **shall walk** down the hall.
future tense plural	The teachers **shall walk** down the hall.

The Perfect Tenses

The **perfect tenses** of verbs also express present, past, and future time, but they show that the action continued and was completed over a period of time or that the action will be completed in the present or future. The perfect tense is formed by using *has, have,* or *had* with the past participle.

EXAMPLES

present perfect singular	Vera **has baked** the birthday cake. The birthday cake **has been baked** by Vera.
present perfect plural	Vera and Hans **have baked** the birthday cake. (have or has + past participle)
past perfect singular	Vera **had baked** the birthday cake. The birthday cake **had been baked** by Vera.
past perfect plural	Vera and Hans **had baked** the birthday cake. (had + past participle)
future perfect singular	Vera **will have baked** the birthday cake. The birthday cake **will have been baked** by Vera.
future perfect plural	Vera and Hans **will have baked** the birthday cake. (will have or shall have + past participle)

3.6 Complements

COMPLEMENTS FOR ACTION VERBS

A sentence must have a subject and a verb to communicate its basic meaning. In the following sentences, the subject and verb express the total concept. There is no receiver of the verb's action.

EXAMPLES

We talked.

I never lose.

The tree fell.

Many sentences that include action verbs, however, need an additional word or group of words to complete the meaning.

EXAMPLES

The soldiers climbed.

The soldiers climbed the wall.

The group of words *The musicians tuned* contains a subject *(musicians)* and a verb *(tuned).* Although the group of words may be considered a sentence, it does not express a complete thought. The word *instruments* completes the meaning expressed by the verb *tuned*. Therefore, *instruments* is called a **complement** or a completing word. The *completers* for action verbs are **direct objects** and **indirect objects.**

Direct Objects

A **direct object** receives the action in the sentence. It usually answers the question *what?* or *whom?* To find the direct object, find the action verb in the sentence. Then ask *what?* or *whom?* about the verb.

EXAMPLES

I **found** a **coin** in the pond. (*Found* is the action verb. What did I find? *Coin* is the direct object.)

The dog **jumped** the **fence.** (*Jumped* is the action verb. What did the dog jump? *Fence* is the direct object.)

Remember to use object pronouns for a direct object.

singular me, you, him, her, it
plural us, you, them

EXAMPLES

Betty told **us** to drive west.

Evan questioned **him** about the wallet.

Indirect Objects

Sometimes the direct object is received by someone or something. This receiver is called the **indirect object.** It comes before the direct object and tells *to whom* the action is directed or *for whom* the action is performed. Only verbs that have direct objects can have indirect objects.

EXAMPLE

Seth **sold** Karl a **car.** (*Sold* is the action verb. *Car* is the direct object because it tells what Seth sold. *Karl* is an indirect object. It tells to whom Seth sold a car.)

To identify the indirect object: (1) Look for a noun or a pronoun that precedes the direct object. (2) Determine whether the word you think is a direct object seems to be the understood object of the preposition *to* or *for.*

COMPLEMENTS FOR LINKING VERBS

A **linking verb** connects a subject with a noun, a pronoun, or an adjective that describes it or identifies it. Linking verbs do not express action. Instead, they express state of being and need a noun, a pronoun or an adjective to complete the sentence meaning.

In each of the following sentences, the subject and verb would not be complete without the words that follow them.

EXAMPLES

The chocolate cake **was** rich.
(The verb *was* connects the subject *cake* with a word that describes it—*rich.*)

The wind and rain **are** cold.
(The verb *are* connects the compound subject *wind and rain* with a word that describes it—*cold.*)

Most linking verbs are forms of the verb *to be,* including *am, are, is, was,* and *been.* Other words that can be used as linking verbs include *appear, feel, grow, smell, taste, seem, sound, look, stay, feel, remain,* and *become*. When *to be* verbs are part of an action verb, they are helpers.

3.7 Agreement

SUBJECT AND VERB AGREEMENT

A **singular** noun describes or stands for *one* person, place, thing, or idea. A **plural noun** describes or stands for *more than one* person, place, thing, or idea.

EXAMPLES

singular nouns	book	apple	rose	mouse	child
plural nouns	books	apples	roses	mice	children

In a sentence, a verb must be singular if its subject is singular and plural if its subject is plural. In other words, a verb must agree in number with its subject.

EXAMPLES

singular subject and verb	The apple seems ripe.
plural subject and verb	The apples seem ripe.
singular subject and verb	A rose smells lovely in the evening.
plural subject and verb	The roses smell lovely in the evening.
singular subject and verb	A mouse runs across the room.
plural subject and verb	The mice run across the room.

COMPOUND SUBJECT AND VERB AGREEMENT

A **compound subject** consists of two or more subjects that share the same verb.

EXAMPLE

Frank and Wyatt ride horses in the corral. (The compound subject—*Frank and Wyatt*—shares the verb *ride.*)

A compound subject must have either a singular or a plural verb, depending on how the parts of the subject are connected.

Use a singular verb:
- when the compound subject is made up of singular nouns or pronouns connected by *either/or* or *neither/nor.*

EXAMPLES

singular verb
Either Tom or Jesse **looks** like a good choice to start the game.

Neither sword nor axe **prevents** me from finishing this quest.

Use a plural verb:
- when the compound subject is connected by the coordinating conjunction *and.*
- when the compound subject is formed from plural nouns or pronouns.

EXAMPLES

plural
Cars and trucks **park** in the field.

Either cats or dogs **provide** good companionship.

When a compound subject consists of a singular subject and a plural subject connected by *or* or *nor,* use a verb that agrees in number with the subject that is closer to it in the sentence.

EXAMPLES

Either Kevin or his sisters **watch** the children in the park. (*sisters watch*—plural)

Neither the players nor their coach **endorses** the statement of the owner. (*coach endorses*—singular)

INDEFINITE PRONOUN AND VERB AGREEMENT

An **indefinite pronoun** does not refer to a specific person, place, or thing. Some indefinite pronouns are always singular and take singular verbs: *anybody, anyone, anything, each, either, everybody, everyone, everything, much, neither, nobody, no one, nothing, one, somebody, someone, something.*

EXAMPLES

singular
Nobody knows the size of the universe.

Something occurs at noon every day.

Some indefinite pronouns are always plural and take plural verbs: *both, few, many, others, several.*

EXAMPLES

plural
Many of our presidents **were** military officers.

Both understand that this must never happen again.

3.8 Modifiers

ADJECTIVES

Adjectives modify nouns by telling specific details about them.

EXAMPLES

noun	a car
a little more specific	an orange car
more specific yet	the fast orange car
even more specific	a sporty, fast orange car

Some adjectives tell *how many* or *what kind* about the nouns or pronouns they modify.

EXAMPLES

There were **several** cars in the lot.

They chose the car with the **tinted** windows.

Other adjectives tell *which one* or *which ones*.

EXAMPLES

Our car has rust spots.

Those cars in the junkyard were once very expensive.

The **articles** *a, an,* and *the* are the most commonly occurring adjectives. *A* and *an* refer to any person, place, or thing in general. *The* refers to a specific person, place, or thing.

EXAMPLES

A fence can be made of wood or metal. (*A* refers to a fence in general.)

The gate on **the** fence is open. (*The* refers to a specific gate on a specific fence.)

A **proper adjective** is formed from a proper noun. Proper adjectives are capitalized and often end in *–n, –an, –ian, –ese,* or *–ish.*

EXAMPLES

African mahogany trees are valued for their hard, reddish brown wood.

Furniture and ships are often built with durable **Asian** teakwood.

Type of Adjective	Definition	Examples
adjective	modifies nouns and pronouns; answers the questions *what kind? which one? how many?* and *how much?*	**shiny** pennies **hieroglyphic** inscription **dozen** roses **one** mistake
article	*a* and *an* refer to an unspecified person, place, thing, or idea; *the* refers to a specific person, place, thing, or idea	**A** problem has developed. I peeled **an** orange. **The** tomatoes are ripe.
proper adjective	is formed from proper nouns; is capitalized; often ends in *–n, –an, –ian, –ese,* or *–ish*	**Serbian** restaurant **Victorian** England **Chinese** calendar **Jewish** tradition

ADVERBS

Adverbs modify verbs, adjectives, or other adverbs. Many times adverbs will tell us *how, when, where, why* or *to what extent.*

EXAMPLES

adverbs modify verbs
The children sing **cheerfully.** (*Cheerfully* tells how they sing.)

Eagles **usually** fly **high** in the summer sky. (*Usually* tells when they fly in the sky; high tells where they fly.)

adverbs modify adjectives
These noble birds are **especially** graceful. (*Especially* tells to what extent they are graceful.)

Some rare birds are **nearly** extinct. (*Nearly* tells to what extent the birds are extinct.)

adverbs modify adverbs
The eagles swoop down on their prey **very** quickly. (*Very* tells to what extent they swoop down on their prey quickly.)

The birds grip **so** strongly, few animals can escape their clutches. (*So* tells how strongly they grip.)

POSITION OF ADVERBS

An adverb can be placed before or after a verb it modifies. Sometimes an adverb can be separated from a verb by another word or words.

EXAMPLES

The coin collector **carefully examined** the rare silver coin.

Eager to find out when it was minted, he **looked carefully** through the magnifying glass.

He **polished** the coin **carefully** to reveal the embossed date.

Note, however, in the following examples, how changing the position of an adverb changes the meaning of the sentence.

EXAMPLES

He **only** worried about money. (He did nothing else but worry about money.)

He worried **only** about money. (He worried about nothing else but money.)

3.9 Prepositions and Conjunctions

PREPOSITIONS AND CONJUNCTIONS

Prepositions and conjunctions are the linkers of the English language. They are used to join words and phrases to the rest of a sentence. They also show the relationships between ideas. Prepositions and conjunctions help writers vary their sentences by connecting sentence parts in different ways.

A **preposition** is used to show how its object, a noun or a pronoun, is related to other words in the sentence. Some commonly used prepositions include *above, after, against, among, around, at, behind, beneath, beside, between, down, for, from, in, on, off, toward, through, to, until, upon,* and *with.*

GRAMMAR & STYLE

EXAMPLES

A whale swam **under** our boat.

We had to crawl **through** the tunnel **between** the two buildings.

A **conjunction** is a word used to link related words, groups of words, or sentences. Like a preposition, a conjunction shows the relationship between the words it links. Some of the most commonly used conjunctions are *and, but, for, nor, or, yet, so, if, after, because, before, although, unless, while,* and *when.* Some conjunctions are used in pairs, such as *both/and, neither/nor,* and *not only/but also.*

EXAMPLES

I found leaves **and** twigs in the yard.

He stopped running **after** he twisted his ankle.

Neither the plaintiffs **nor** the defendants understand the ruling.

3.10 Interjections

An **interjection** is a part of speech that expresses feeling, such as surprise, joy, relief, urgency, pain, or anger. Common interjections include *ah, aha, alas, bravo, dear me, goodness, great, ha, help, hey, hooray, hush, indeed, mercy, of course, oh, oops, ouch, phooey, really, say, see, ugh,* and *whew.*

EXAMPLES

Hey, that's not fair!

Goodness, you don't need to get so upset.

Hush! You'll wake the baby.

Why, of course! Please do join us for dinner.

3.11 Phrases

A **phrase** is a group of words used as a single part of speech. A phrase lacks a subject, a verb, or both; therefore, it cannot be a sentence. There are three common kinds of phrases: prepositional phrases, verbal phrases, and appositive phrases.

PREPOSITIONAL PHRASES

A **prepositional phrase** consists of a preposition, its object, and any modifiers of that object. A prepositional phrase adds information to a sentence by relating its object to another word in the sentence. It may function as an adjective or an adverb.

EXAMPLES

adjectives

Ted bought a car **with a sunroof.** (The prepositional phrase *with a sunroof* tells what kind of car Ted bought. The phrase is an adjective, modifying the noun *car.*)

adverbs

The fog drifted **over the hill.** (The prepositional phrase *over the hill* tells where the fog drifted. The phrase is an adverb, modifying the verb *drifted.*)

VERBAL PHRASES

Verbals are verb forms that act as namers or modifiers.

A **participle** is a verb form ending in *–ing, –d,* or *–ed* that acts as an adjective, modifying a noun or a pronoun. A **participial phrase** is made up of a participle and all of the words related to the participle, which may include objects, modifiers, and prepositional phrases. The entire phrase acts as an adjective.

EXAMPLES

Climbing carefully up the tree, Elijah was able to reach the cat. (The participle *climbing*, the adverb *carefully,* and the prepositional phrase *up the tree* make up the participial phrase that modifies *Elijah.*)

Jim came up with the idea for the mural **painted on the building.** (The participle *painted* and the prepositional phrase *on the building* make up the participial phrase that modifies *mural.*)

A **gerund phrase** is a phrase made up of a gerund (a verb form ending in *–ing*) and all of its modifiers and complements. The entire phrase functions as a noun.

EXAMPLES

Waiting for the bus is boring for Tracy. (The gerund phrase functions as the subject of the sentence.)

Tracy hates **waiting for the bus** at the corner. (The gerund phrase functions as the direct object of the sentence.)

Sometimes the *to* of an infinitive phrase is left out; it is understood.

EXAMPLES

Jerry helped **[to]** paint the house.

I'll go **[to]** feed the cat.

APPOSITIVE PHRASES

An **appositive phrase** is a group of words made up of an appositive and all its modifiers. The phrase renames or identifies a noun or a pronoun.

EXAMPLES

Dr. George, **the former football coach,** is our new professor. (The appositive phrase renames the noun *Dr. George.*)

The television show ***Let's Make a Deal*** used to be very popular. (The appositive phrase identifies which show used to be very popular.)

The first example above, *the former football coach,* is a **nonessential,** or **nonrestrictive, appositive phrase.** It is not necessary to the meaning of the sentence; it is not needed to identify Dr. George, since we already know that he is our new professor. Therefore, it is set off with commas.

The second example, *Let's Make a Deal,* is an **essential,** or **restrictive, appositive phrase.** It is necessary for understanding the sentence because it identifies which particular television show, since we do not already know which one. This appositive phrase is not set off with commas.

3.12 Clauses

A **clause** is a group of words that contains a subject and a verb and that functions as one part of speech. There are two types of clauses—independent and subordinate.

An **independent clause,** sometimes called a *main clause,* has a subject and a verb and expresses a complete thought. Since it can stand alone as a sentence, it is called *independent.*

EXAMPLE

Abraham Lincoln is often called the "Great Emancipator."

A **subordinate clause** or *dependent clause* has a subject and a verb, but it doesn't express a complete thought. It can't stand alone. It must be attached to or inserted into an independent clause. When you combine subordinate clauses with independent clauses, you form complete sentences.

EXAMPLES

When the bell rang, the students ran out of the room. (The subordinate clause *when the bell rang* is attached to an independent clause.)

The dog **that barked all night** slept throughout the day. (The subordinate clause *that barked all night* is inserted into the independent clause *The dog slept throughout the day.*)

3.13 Common Usage Problems

INCORRECT SUBJECT-VERB AGREEMENT

A subject and its verb must agree in number. Use singular verb forms with singular subjects and plural verb forms with plural subjects.

Intervening Words

A prepositional phrase that comes between a subject and a verb does not determine whether the subject is singular or plural.

EXAMPLES

The **captain** on the bridge **gazes** across the sea. (*captain gazes,* singular)

The **detective,** in addition to the police, **looks** for clues at the house. (*detective looks,* singular)

The **players** on the team **practice** diligently. (*players practice,* plural)

The **books** in the back of the store **are** only half price. (*books are,* plural)

In some cases, the *object* of the preposition controls the verb.

EXAMPLES

Jim and his brother **plan** strategy before each game.

Cars, trucks, and motorcycles **roar** past our house.

Compound Subjects

Use a plural verb with most compound subjects connected by *and.*

EXAMPLES

Charlotte and her boss **review** the budget once a month.

Otters, beavers, and alligators **live** near bodies of water.

INCORRECT USE OF APOSTROPHES

Use an apostrophe to replace letters that have been left out in a contraction.

EXAMPLES

it's = it is   don't = do not   I'll = I will

Use an apostrophe to show possession.

Singular Nouns

Use an apostrophe and an *s* (*'s*) to form the possessive of a singular noun, even if it ends in *s*, *x*, or *z*.

EXAMPLES

Rachel's notebook	Frank's lizard	Conan's ring
lynx's paw	jazz's history	boss's desk

Plural Nouns

Use an apostrophe and an *s* (*'s*) to form the possessive of a plural noun that does not end in *s*.

EXAMPLES

women's shirts   children's books   people's candidate

Use an apostrophe alone to form the possessive of a plural noun that ends in *s*.

EXAMPLES

rodents' food   the boys' locker room   the ships' sails

Do not add an apostrophe or *'s* to possessive personal pronouns: *mine, yours, his, hers, its, ours,* or *theirs.* They already show ownership.

EXAMPLES

Our cars are painted; **theirs** are still rusty.

The shark opened **its** mouth.

DOUBLE NEGATIVES

Make sure that you use only one of the following negatives in each sentence: *not, nobody, none, nothing, hardly, can't, doesn't, won't, isn't, aren't.* A **double negative** is the use of two negative words together when only one is needed. Correct double negatives by removing one of the negative words or by replacing one of the negative words with a positive word.

EXAMPLES

double negative
We won't hardly make it in time.

corrected sentence
We will hardly make it in time. We won't make it in time.

double negative
Nell wasn't never able to win the big prize.

corrected sentence
Nell was never able to win the big prize. Nell wasn't ever able to win the big prize.

DANGLING AND MISPLACED MODIFIERS

A **dangling modifier** has nothing to modify because the word it would logically modify is not present in the sentence. In the following sentence, the modifying phrase has no logical object. The sentence says that a whale was flying.

EXAMPLE
Flying above the ocean, a whale was spotted.

You can eliminate dangling modifiers by rewriting the sentence so that an appropriate word is provided for the modifier to modify. You can also expand a dangling phrase into a full subordinate clause.

EXAMPLES
Flying above the ocean, we saw a whale.

As we flew above the ocean, we spotted a whale.

A **misplaced modifier** is located too far from the word it should modify.

EXAMPLE
I found a penny during my morning jog on a park bench.

You can revise a misplaced modifier by moving it closer to the word it modifies.

EXAMPLES
I found a penny on a park bench during my morning jog.

On a park bench I found a penny during my morning jog.

During my morning jog, I found a penny on a park bench.

FORMS OF *WHO* AND *WHOM*

Who and *whom* can be used to ask questions and to introduce subordinate clauses. Knowing what form of *who* to use can sometimes be confusing. The case of the pronoun *who* is determined by the pronoun's function in a sentence.

nominative case	who, whoever
objective case	whom, whomever

EXAMPLES
Who wrote the novel *One Hundred Years of Solitude?* (Because *who* is the subject in the sentence, the pronoun is in the nominative case.)

Did you say **who** called? (Because *who* is the subject of the subordinate clause, the pronoun is in the nominative case.)

Whoever returns my wallet will receive a reward. (Because *whoever* is the subject in the sentence, the pronoun is in the nominative case.)

Whom did you visit? (Because *whom* is the direct object in the sentence, the pronoun is in the objective case.)

3.14 Commonly Misused Words

The following chart contains an alphabetic list of words and phrases that often cause usage problems.

Word/Phrases	Correct Use	Examples
a, an	Use *a* before words beginning with a consonant sound. Use *an* before words beginning with a vowel sound, including a silent *h*.	While walking in the woods, Jonah saw **a** coyote. **An** orangutan has a shaggy, reddish brown coat and very long arms. It is hard to find **an** honest politician in this town.
accept, except	*Accept* is a verb meaning "to receive willingly" or "to agree." *Except* is a preposition that means "leaving out" or "but."	I wish you would **accept** this token of my appreciation. Everyone has apologized for the misunderstanding **except** the mayor.
affect, effect	*Affect* is a verb that means "to influence." The noun *effect* means "the result of an action." The verb *effect* means "to cause" or "to bring about."	You can't let the audience **affect** your concentration. We saw the **effect** of last night's storm throughout the town. Peter will **effect** the proposed reorganization when he takes office.
ain't	This word is nonstandard English. Avoid using it in speaking and writing.	**nonstandard:** I ain't going to study English this semester. **standard:** I **am not** going to study English this semester.
all ready, already	*All ready* means "entirely ready or prepared." *Already* means "previously."	Speaking with each team member, I determined that they were **all ready** to play. Sandy **already** finished her homework before soccer practice.
all right	*All right* means "satisfactory," "unhurt," "correct," or "yes, very well." The word *alright* is not acceptable in formal written English.	**All right,** let's begin the meeting. Is your ill father going to be **all right?**
a lot	*A lot* means "a great number or amount" and is always two words. Because it is imprecise, you should avoid it except in informal usage. *Alot* is not a word.	We found **a lot** of seashells on the beach. Your brother had **a lot** of help planning the surprise party.
altogether, all together	*Altogether* is an adverb meaning "thoroughly." Something done *all together* is done as a group or mass.	He was **altogether** embarrassed after tripping on the sidewalk. The family members were **all together** when they heard the good news.
anywheres, everywheres, somewheres, nowheres	Use these words and others like them without the *s: anywhere, everywhere, somewhere, nowhere.*	The little gray dog was **nowhere** to be found. Yolanda never goes **anywhere** without her cell phone.
at	Don't use this word after *where.*	Where are your brothers hiding?
bad, badly	*Bad* is always an adjective, and *badly* is always an adverb. Use *bad* after linking verbs.	I developed a **bad** cold after shoveling the heavy, wet snow. Tom feels **bad** about losing your favorite CD. We **badly** need to find another relief pitcher.

GRAMMAR & STYLE

Word/Phrases	Correct Use	Examples
beside, besides	*Beside* means "next to." *Besides* means "in addition to." *Besides* can also be an adverb meaning "moreover."	The yellow plant is sitting **beside** the purple vase. I bought socks and shoes **besides** a new shirt and jacket. There is nothing worth watching on TV tonight; **besides,** I have to study for a test.
between, among	Use *between* when referring to two people or things. Use *among* when you are discussing three or more people or things.	While on vacation, I divided my time **between** Paris and Brussels. The thoughtful pirate divided the loot **among** his shipmates.
bring, take	Use *bring* when you mean "to carry to." It refers to movement toward the speaker. Use *take* when you mean "to carry away." It refers to movement away from the speaker.	You need to **bring** your backpack home. Don't forget to **take** the garbage out to the curb tonight.
bust, busted	Do not use these nonstandard words as verbs to substitute for *break* or *burst.*	**nonstandard:** I busted my leg sliding into third base. The barrel busted after the extra batch was added. **standard:** I **broke** my leg sliding into third base. The barrel **burst** after the extra batch was added.
can, may	The word *can* means "able to do something." The word *may* is used to ask or give permission.	**Can** you speak a foreign language? You **may** borrow my red sweater.
choose, chose	*Choose* is the present tense, and *chose* is the past tense.	I **choose** to start work at 6:00 AM each day. Randy **chose** to quit his job after working only three days.
could of	Use the helping verb *have* (which may sound like *could of*) with *could, might, must, should, ought,* and *would.*	**nonstandard:** We could of won the game in overtime. **standard:** We **could have** won the game in overtime.
doesn't, don't	*Doesn't* is the contraction of *does not.* It is used with singular nouns and the pronouns *he, she, it, this,* and *that. Don't* is the contraction of *do not.* Use it with plural nouns and the pronouns *I, we, they, you, these,* and *those.*	Jason **doesn't** know what to make for lunch. We **don't** answer the phone during dinner.
farther, further	Use *farther* to refer to physical distance. Use *further* to refer to greater extent in time or degree or to mean "additional."	I walked **farther** today than I did yesterday. The board members will discuss this issue **further** at the meeting. The essay requires **further** revision before it can be published.
fewer, less	Use *fewer,* which tells "how many," to refer to things that you can count individually. *Fewer* is used with plural words. Use *less* to refer to quantities that you cannot count. It is used with singular words and tells "how much."	I see **fewer** fans coming out to the ballpark each year. Jasmine has more experience and thus needs **less** training than Phil.
good, well	*Good* is always an adjective. *Well* is an adverb meaning "ably" or "capably." *Well* is also a predicate adjective meaning "satisfactory" or "in good health." Don't confuse *feel good,* which means "to feel happy or pleased," with *feel well,* which means "to feel healthy."	Charles was a **good** pilot during the war. Leslie felt **good** [pleased] after bowling three strikes in a row. Shirley paints **well** for someone with no formal training. Not feeling **well,** Samuel stayed home from school today.

Word/Phrases	Correct Use	Examples
had ought, hadn't ought	The verb *ought* should never be used with the helping verb *had.*	**nonstandard:** Ted had ought to find another route into town. **standard:** Ted **ought** to find another route into town. **nonstandard:** She hadn't ought climb that tree. **standard:** She **ought** not climb that tree.
hardly, scarcely	Since both of these words have negative meanings, do not use them with other negative words such as *not, no, nothing*, and *none.*	**nonstandard:** That music is so loud I can't hardly hear myself think. **standard:** That music is so loud I can **hardly** hear myself think. **nonstandard:** Shane hadn't scarcely enough gas to make it back home. **standard:** Shane had **scarcely** enough gas to make it back home.
he, she, they	Do not use these pronouns after a noun. This error is called a double subject.	**nonstandard:** Jed's brother he is a famous actor. **standard:** Jed's brother is a famous actor.
hisself, their-selves	These are incorrect forms. Use *himself* and *themselves.*	**nonstandard:** Paul talks to hisself when mowing the lawn. **standard:** Paul talks to **himself** when mowing the lawn. **nonstandard:** The panel talked among theirselves about the Holy Roman Empire. **standard:** The panel talked among **them-selves** about the Holy Roman Empire.
how come	Do not use in place of *why.*	**nonstandard: How come** you didn't call me last night? **standard: Why** didn't you call me last night?
in, into	Use *in* to mean "within" or "inside." Use *into* to suggest movement toward the inside from the outside.	The children were **in** the kitchen. The children raced **into** the kitchen.
its, it's	*Its* is a possessive pronoun. *It's* is the contraction for *it is.*	The radio station held **its** annual fundraiser. **It's** too late tonight to start another game.
kind, sort, type	Use *this* or *that* to modify the singular nouns *kind, sort*, and *type.* Use *these* and *those* to modify the plural nouns *kinds, sorts*, and *types. Kind* should be singular when the object of the preposition following it is singular. It should be plural when the object of the preposition is plural.	This **kind** of ice cream is my favorite. These **types** of problems are difficult to solve.
kind of, sort of	Do not use these terms to mean "somewhat" or "rather."	**nonstandard:** He feels kind of sluggish today. **standard:** He feels rather sluggish today.
lay, lie	*Lay* means "to put" or "to place." *Lay* usually takes a direct object. *Lie* means "to rest" or "to be in a lying position." *Lie* never takes a direct object. (Note that the past tense of *lie* is *lay.*)	Please **lay** the blanket on the bed. I **laid** the blanket on the bed. **Lie** down on the bed and take a nap. Mary **lay** down on the bed and took a nap.
learn, teach	*Learn* means "to gain knowledge." *Teach* means "to give knowledge." Do not use them interchangeably.	Betty took lessons to **learn** how to fly a small airplane. I would like to find someone to **teach** me how to sew.

Word/Phrases	Correct Use	Examples
like, as	*Like* is usually a preposition followed by an object. It generally means "similar to." *As, as if,* and *as though* are conjunctions used to introduce subordinate clauses. *As* is occasionally a preposition: *He worked as a farmer.*	The alligator was motionless **like** a rock on the riverbank. The spider spun its web **as** the unsuspecting fly flew into the silky trap. Roger looks **as though** he's not feeling well.
of	This word is unnecessary after the prepositions *inside, outside,* and *off.*	The feather pillow slid **off** the bed. People gathered **outside** the stadium before the game. Please put the chattering parrot **inside** its cage.
precede, proceed	*Precede* means "to go or come before." *Proceed* means "to go forward."	The calf-roping competition will **precede** the bull-riding event. If you hear the alarm, **proceed** down the stairs and out the exit.
quiet, quite	Although these words sound alike, they have different meanings. *Quiet* is an adjective that means "making little or no noise"; *quite* is an adverb meaning "positively" or "completely."	The house became **quiet** after the baby finally fell asleep. Unfortunately, our bill for the car repairs was **quite** large.
real, really	*Real* is an adjective meaning "actual." *Really* is an adverb meaning "actually" or "genuinely." Do not use *real* to mean "very" or "extremely."	The table is very sturdy because it is made of **real** oak. Heather was **really** (not *real*) excited about trying out for the play.
reason...because	*Reason is because* is both wordy and redundant. Use *reason is that* or simply *because.*	**nonstandard:** The reason I am in a good mood is because today is Friday. **standard:** The reason for my good mood is that it is Friday. **standard:** The reason for my good mood is that today is Friday. **standard:** I am in a good mood because today is Friday.
regardless, irre-gardless	Use *regardless, unmindful, heedless,* or *anyway. Irregardless* is a double negative and should never be used.	**nonstandard:** Irregardless of the rain, the concert will still be held as scheduled. **standard: Regardless** of the rain, the concert will still be held as scheduled.
rise, raise	*Rise* is an intransitive verb that means "to move upward." It is an irregular verb that does not take a direct object. *Raise* is a transitive verb that means "to lift or make something go upward." It is a regular verb that takes a direct object.	The sun **rises** and sets every day. Perry **raised** his hand to ask a question.
scratch, itch	*Scratch* means "to scrape lightly to relieve itching." *Itch* means "to feel a tingling of the skin, with the desire to scratch."	Please do not **scratch** the mosquito bites. The mosquito bites on my leg still **itch.**
set, sit	*Set* is a transitive verb meaning "to place something." It always takes a direct object. *Sit* is an intransitive verb meaning "to rest in an upright position." It does not take a direct object.	Please **set** the pitcher of milk on the table. Let's **sit** outside on the back deck.
some, somewhat	*Some* is an adjective meaning "a certain unspecified quantity." *Somewhat* is an adverb meaning "slightly." Do not use *some* as an adverb.	**nonstandard:** The pressure on her schedule has eased some. **standard:** The pressure on her schedule has eased **somewhat.** **standard:** I need to find **some** index cards before starting my report.

Word/Phrases	Correct Use	Examples
than, then	*Than* is a conjunction used in comparisons. *Then* is an adverb that shows a sequence of events.	Hank's lawn is greener **than** Dale's lawn is. We went to the post office and **then** drove to the mall.
that	*That* is used to refer either to people or things. Use it to introduce essential, or restrictive, clauses that refer to things or groups of people. Do not use a comma before *that* when it introduces an essential clause.	The tree **that** fell in the storm was more than one hundred years old. An automobile **that** never needs repairs is rare.
their, there, they're	*Their* is the possessive form of *they*. *There* points out a place or introduces an independent clause. *They're* is the contracted form of *they are*.	Our neighbors inspected **their** roof after the hailstorm. When you arrive at the airport, I will be **there** waiting. I don't think **they're** going to be visiting us this summer.
them	*Them* is a pronoun. It should never be used as an adjective. Use *those*.	**nonstandard:** Remember to return them books to the library. **standard:** Remember to return **those** books to the library.
this here, that there	Do not use. Simply say *this* or *that*.	**nonstandard:** This here is the best coffee shop in town. **standard: This** is the best coffee shop in town. **nonstandard:** That there is an antique rocking chair. **standard: That** is an antique rocking chair.
to, too, two	*To* is a preposition that can mean "in the direction of." *Too* is an adverb that means both "extremely, overly" and "also." *Two* is the spelling for the number 2.	Please carry the luggage **to** the car. Leah has **too** many boxes in the attic. Tony and Liz are excellent students, **too.** I bought **two** pairs of blue jeans.
try and	Use *try to* instead.	**nonstandard:** Try and find the umbrella before you leave. **standard: Try to** find the umbrella before you leave.
use to, used to	Be sure to add the *–d* to *use* to form the past participle.	**nonstandard:** Rory use to enjoy singing in the choir. **standard:** Rory **used to** enjoy singing in the choir.
way, ways	Do not use *ways* for *way* when referring to distance.	**nonstandard:** We traveled a long ways from home. **standard:** We traveled a long **way** from home.
when, where	When you define a word, don't use *when* or *where*.	**nonstandard:** A *perfect game* is when a bowler throws twelve strikes resulting in a score of 300. **standard:** A *perfect game* is twelve strikes resulting in a score of 300.
where, that	Do not use *where* to mean "that."	**nonstandard:** I read where school will start a week earlier in August. **standard:** I read **that** school will start a week earlier in August.

Word/Phrases	Correct Use	Examples
which, that, who, whom	*Which* is used to refer only to things. Use it to introduce nonessential, or nonrestrictive, clauses that refer to things or to groups of people. Always use a comma before *which* when it introduces a nonessential clause.	Our garage, **which** was built last year, is already showing signs of wear. The panel, **which** was assembled to discuss the election, will publish its conclusions.
who, whom	*Who* or *whom* is used to refer only to people. Use *who* or *whom* to introduce essential and nonessential clauses. Use a comma only when the pronoun introduces a nonessential clause.	Lyle is the man **who** rescued us from the fire. Abraham Lincoln, **whom** many admired, issued the Emancipation Proclamation.
who's, whose	*Who's* is a contraction for *who is* or *who has*. *Whose* is the possessive form of *who*.	**Who's** going to make dinner tonight? **Whose** pig is running loose in my garden?
without, unless	Do not use the preposition *without* in place of the conjunction *unless*.	**nonstandard:** I am not leaving without I have your endorsement. **standard:** I am not leaving **without** your endorsement. **standard:** I am not leaving **unless** I have your endorsement.
your, you're	*Your* is a possessive pronoun. *You're* is a contraction for the words *you are*.	Ron repaired **your** leaky kitchen faucet. **You're** very skilled at repairing things!

3.15 Punctuation

EDITING FOR PUNCTUATION ERRORS

When editing your work, correct all punctuation errors. Several common punctuation errors to avoid are the incorrect use of end marks, commas, semicolons, and colons.

Punctuation Reference Chart

Punctuation	Function	Examples
End Marks	tell the reader where a sentence ends and show the purpose of the sentence; periods are also used for abbreviations.	Our next-door neighbor is Mrs**.** Ryan**.**
Periods	with **declarative** sentences	The weather forecast predicts rain tonight**.**
	with **abbreviations**	
	personal names	**N.** Scott Momaday, **W. W.** Jacobs, Ursula **K.** Le Guin
	titles	**Mr.** Bruce Webber, **Mrs.** Harriet Cline, **Ms.** Steinem, **Dr.** Duvall, **Sen.** Hillary Clinton, **Gov.** George Pataki, **Capt.** Horatio Hornblower, **Prof.** Klaus
	business names	Tip Top Roofing **Co.**, Green **Bros.** Landscaping, Gigantic **Corp.**
	addresses	Oak **Dr.**, Grand **Blvd.**, Main **St.**, Kennedy **Pkwy.**, Prudential **Bldg.**
	geographical terms	Kensington, **Conn.**, San Francisco, **Calif.**, Canberra, **Aus.**
	time	2 **hrs.** 15 **min., Thurs.** morning, **Jan.** 20, 21st **cent.**

Punctuation	Function	Examples
	units of measurement	3 **tbsp.** olive oil 1/2 **c.** peanut butter 8 **oz.** milk 5 **ft.** 4 **in.** 20 **lbs.**
	exceptions: metric measurements, state names in postal addresses, or directional elements	**metric measurements** cc, ml, km, g, L **state postal codes** MN, WI, IA, NE, CA, NY **compass points** N, NW, S, SE
Question Marks	with **interrogative** sentences	May I have another serving of spaghetti**?**
Exclamation Points	with **exclamatory** sentences	Hey, be careful**!**
Commas	to separate words or groups of words within a sentence; to tell the reader to pause at certain spots in the sentence	Casey was confident he could hit a home run**,** but he struck out.
	to separate items in a series	The magician's costume included a **silk scarf, black satin hat,** and **magic wand.**
	to combine sentences using *and, but, or, nor, yet, so,* or *for*	An infestation of beetles threatened the summer squash and zucchini crops**, yet** the sturdy plants thrived. I'll apply an organic insecticide**, or** I'll ignore the garden pest problem.
	after an introductory word, phrase, or clause	**Surprisingly,** fashions from the 1970s are making a comeback. **Frayed and tight-fitting,** denim bellbottoms remain a fashion hit.
	to set off words or phrases that interrupt sentences	Harpers Ferry**, a town in northeastern West Virginia,** was the site of John Brown's raid in 1859. The violent raid**, however,** frightened people in the North and South. **An abolitionist leader,** Brown was captured during the raid and later executed.
	between two or more adjectives that modify the same noun and that could be joined by *and*	A **warm,** [and] **spicy** aroma enticed us to enter the kitchen. Steaming bowls of chili satisfied the **tired,** [and] **hungry** travelers.
	to set off names used in direct address	**Olivia,** the zinnias and daisies need to be watered. Please remember to turn off the back porch light**, John.**
	to separate parts of a date	The United States Stock Exchange collapsed on October **28, 1929.** The stock market crash in October 1929 precipitated a severe economic crisis.
	to separate items in addresses	Gabriel García Márquez was born in **Aracataca, Colombia.** My brother will be moving to **1960 Jasmine Avenue, Liberty, Missouri 64068.**
Semicolons	to join two closely related sentences	It was a beautiful summer morning**;** we took advantage of it by going on a picnic.
	to join the independent clauses of a compound sentence if no coordinating conjunction is used	Marjory Stoneman Douglas was a pioneer conservationist. She formed a vigorous grassroots campaign to protect and restore the Everglades. Marjory Stoneman Douglas was a pioneer conservationist**;** she formed a vigorous grassroots campaign to protect and restore the Everglades.

Punctuation	Function	Examples
	between independent clauses joined by a conjunction if either clause contains commas	Douglas was a writer, editor, publisher, and tireless advocate for the protection of the Everglades**;** and President Clinton awarded her the Medal of Freedom in 1993 for her work.
	between items in a series if the items contain commas	Members of Friends of the Everglades **wrote petitions; contacted local groups, political organizations, and governmental agencies; and gathered public support** for the restoration of the Everglades.
	between independent clauses joined by a conjunctive adverb or a transitional phrase	**conjunctive adverb** Starting in 1948, the Central and Southern Florida Project ditched and drained the Everglades**; consequently,** the four million acre wetland was reduced by half. **transitional phrase** Douglas knew that restoration of the Everglades would be a daunting task**; in other words,** she knew that it would take the combined efforts of local, state, and federal groups working in unison.
Colons	to mean "note what follows"	Make sure you have all your paperwork in order**:** passport, visa, and tickets.
	to introduce a list of items	*The Tragedy of Romeo and Juliet* explores **these dominant themes:** civil strife, revenge, love, and fate. The main characters in the play are **as follows:** Romeo, Juliet, Paris, Mercutio, Tybalt, and Friar Lawrence. The role of Juliet has been played by **the following actresses:** Norma Shearer, Susan Shentall, and Olivia Hussey.
	to introduce a long or formal statement or a quotation	Shakespeare's prologue to *Romeo and Juliet* begins with **these memorable lines:** Two households, both alike in dignity, In fair Verona, where we lay our scene, From ancient grudge break to new mutiny, Where civil blood makes civil hands unclean. John Dryden made **the following remark about Shakespeare:** "He was the man who of all modern, and perhaps ancient poets, had the largest and most comprehensive soul." Nearly everyone recognizes **this line by Shakespeare:** "All the world's a stage."
	between two independent clauses when the second clause explains or summarizes the first clause	Shakespeare deserves the greatest of praise**:** his work has influenced and inspired millions of people over the centuries. For Romeo and Juliet, their love is star-crossed**:** If they tell their feuding parents of their love, they will be forbidden from seeing each other. On the other hand, by keeping their love secret, they follow a path that leads, tragically, to their deaths.
	between numbers that tell hours and minutes, after the greeting in a business letter, and between chapter and verse of religious works	Our English class meets Tuesdays and Thursdays from **9:00** AM to **10:00** AM Dear Juliet**:** Please meet me on the balcony at midnight. Ecclesiastes **3:1–8**

Punctuation	Function	Examples
	not after a verb, between a preposition and its object(s), or after *because* or *as*	**after a verb** **incorrect** Three of Shakespeare's most famous plays are: *Romeo and Juliet, Macbeth,* and *Hamlet.* **correct** These are three of Shakespeare's most famous plays: *Romeo and Juliet, Macbeth,* and *Hamlet.* **between a preposition and its object(s)** **incorrect** I have seen performances of Shakespeare's plays in: London, New York, and Chicago. **correct** I have seen performances of Shakespeare's plays in the following cities: London, New York, and Chicago. **after *because* or *as*** **incorrect** Shakespeare was a great playwright because: he had an extraordinary skill in depicting human nature and the universal struggles all people experience. **correct** Shakespeare was a great playwright because he had an extraordinary skill in depicting human nature and the universal struggles all people experience.
Ellipsis Points	to show that material from a quotation or a quoted passage has been left out	"Doing something does not require discipline**...**it creates its own discipline."
	if material is left out at the beginning of a sentence or passage	**...**The very thought of hard work makes me queasy.
	if material is left out in the middle of a sentence	The very thought**...**makes me queasy.
	if material is left out at the end of a sentence	It's hard work, doing something with your life**....**I'd rather die in peace. Here we are, all equal and alike and none of us much to write home about**....**
Apostrophes	to form the possessive case of a singular or plural noun	the **window's** ledge, **Carlos's** father, **jazz's** beginnings, **wolves'** howls, twenty-five **cents'** worth, **countries'** treaties, **students'** textbooks
	to show joint or separate ownership	**Zack and Josh's** experiment, **Lisa and Randall's** cabin, **Sarah's** and **Jason's** schedules, **Steve's and John's** trumpets
	to form the possessive of an indefinite pronoun	**anyone's** guess, **each other's** notes, **everybody's** dream
	to form a contraction to show where letters, words, or numerals have been omitted	**I'm** = I am **you're** = you are **she's** = she is **o'clock** = of the clock **they're** = they are
	to form the possessive of only the last word in a compound noun, such as the name of an organization or a business	brother-in-**law's** sense of humor; Teller, Teller, and **Teller's** law firm; Volunteer Nursing **Association's** office
	to form the possessive of an acronym	**NASA's** flight plan, **NATO's** alliances, **UNICEF's** contributions
	to form the plural of letters, numerals, and words referred to as words	two **A's**, **ABC's**, three **7's**, twelve **yes's**
	to show the missing numbers in a date	drought of **'02**, class of **'06**

GRAMMAR & STYLE

Punctuation	Function	Examples
Underlining and Italics	with titles of books, plays, long poems, periodicals, works of art, movies, radio and television series, videos, computer games, comic strips, and long musical works and recordings	**books:** *To Kill a Mockingbird, Silent Spring, Black Elk Speaks* **plays:** *The Tragedy of Romeo and Juliet, The Monsters Are Due on Maple Street* **long poems:** *Metamorphoses, The Odyssey* **periodicals:** *Sports Illustrated, Wall Street Journal, The Old Farmer's Almanac* **works of art:** *The Acrobat, In the Sky, The Teacup* **movies:** *Il Postino, North by Northwest, Cast Away* **radio/television series:** *Fresh Air, West Wing, Friends, Animal Planet* **videos:** *Yoga for Strength, Cooking with Julia, Wizard of Oz* **computer games:** *Empire Earth, Age of Wonders II* **comic strips:** *Zits, Foxtrot, Overboard* **long musical works/recordings:** *Requiem, Death and the Maiden, La Traviata*
	with the names of trains, ships, aircraft, and spacecraft	**trains:** *Sunset Limited* **ships:** *Titanic* **aircraft:** *Air Force One* **spacecraft:** *Apollo 13*
	with words, letters, symbols, and numerals referred to as such	The word ***filigree*** has a Latin root. People in western New York pronounce the letter ***a*** with a harsh, flat sound. The children learned that the symbol ***+*** is used in addition. Your phone number ends with four ***7***'s.
	to set off foreign words or phrases that are not common in English	Did you know the word ***amor*** means "love"? The first Italian words I learned were ***ciao*** and ***pronto***.
	to place emphasis on a word	Why is the soup ***blue***? You're not going to borrow ***my*** car.
Quotation Marks	at the beginning and end of a direct quotation	**"**Do you want to ride together to the concert?**"** asked Margaret. **"**Don't wait for me,**"** sighed Lillian. **"**I'm running late as usual.**"**
	to enclose the titles of short works such as short stories, poems, articles, essays, parts of books and periodicals, songs, and episodes of TV series	**short stories: "**Gwilan's Harp,**" "**Everyday Use**"** **poems: "**Hanging Fire,**" "**Mirror**"** **articles: "**Where Stars Are Born,**" "**Ghost of Everest**"** **essays: "**Thinking Like a Mountain,**" "**It's Not Talent; It's Just Work**"** **parts of books: "**The Obligation to Endure,**" "**Best Sky Sights of the Next Century**"** **songs: "**At the Fair,**" "**Johnny's Garden**"** **episodes of TV series: "**The Black Vera Wang,**" "**Isaac and Ishmael**"**
	to set off slang, technical terms, unusual expressions, invented words, and dictionary definitions	We nicknamed our dog **"Monkey"** because he moves quickly and loves to play tricks. My mother says that **"groovy"** and **"cool"** were the slang words of her generation. Did you know that the word *incident* means **"a definite, distinct occurrence"**?

Punctuation	Function	Examples
Hyphens	to make a compound word or compound expression	**compound nouns:** great-grandfather Schaefer, great-uncle Tom **compound adjectives used before a noun:** best-known novel, down-to-earth actor, real-life adventure **compound numbers:** ninety-nine years, twenty-five cents **spelled-out fractions:** one-half inch, three-fourths cup
	to divide an already hyphenated word at the hyphen	Finally, after much coaxing, our **great-** **grandfather** told his stories.
	to divide a word only between syllables	**incorrect:** After hiking in the woods, the novice ca- mpers became tired and hungry. **correct:** After hiking in the woods, the novice **camp-** **ers** became tired and hungry.
	with the prefixes *all-, ex-, great-, half-* and *self-,* and with all prefixes before a proper noun or proper adjective	**all-**purpose, **ex-**husband, **pre-**Industrial age, **great-**grandparent, **half-**baked, **self-**expression
	with the suffixes *-free, -elect,* and *-style*	fragrance-**free** detergent, mayor-**elect** Kingston, Southern-**style** hospitality
Dashes	to show a sudden break or change in thought	"I say it did," replied the other. "There was no thought about it; I had just**—**What's the matter?"
	to mean *namely, that is,* or *in other words*	Our puppy knows only two commands**—***sit* and *stay.* The hotel rates were surprisingly reasonable**—**less than a hundred dollars**—**for a double room.
Parentheses and Brackets	around material added to a sentence but not considered of major importance	Toni Cade Bambara **(**1939–1995**)** grew up in Harlem and Brooklyn, New York. The Taj Mahal **(**a majestic site!**)** is one man's tribute of love to his departed, beloved wife. More grocery stores are stocking natural food ingredients **(**for example, whole grains, soy products, and dried fruits**)**.
	to punctuate a parenthetical sentence contained within another sentence.	When the quilt is dry **(**it shouldn't take long**)**, please fold it and put it in the linen closet. The piping-hot funnel cakes **(**they were covered with powdered sugar!**)** just melted in our mouths. The vitamin tablets **(**aren't you supposed to take one every morning?**)** provide high doses of vitamins A and E.
	to enclose words or phrases that interrupt the sentence and are not considered essential to meaning.	They took pasta salad and fruit **(**how could we have forgotten dessert?**)** to the summer concert.
	to enclose information that explains or clarifies a detail in quoted material	A literary critic praised the author's new book, "She **[**Martha Grimes**]** never fails to delight her devoted fans with witty dialogue, elegant prose, and a cast of characters we'd like to consider our friends." Another literary critic wrote, "**[**Martha**]** Grimes is the queen of the mystery genre."

3.16 Capitalization

EDITING FOR CAPITALIZATION ERRORS

To avoid capitalization errors, check your draft for proper nouns and proper adjectives; geographical names, directions, and historical names; and titles of artworks and literary works.

Capitalization Reference Chart

Category/Rule	Examples
Proper Nouns and Proper Adjectives	
Proper Nouns	
Names of people	**S**ojourner **T**ruth, **F**ranklin **D. R**oosevelt, **M**artin **L**uther **K**ing **J**r.
Months, days, and holidays	**O**ctober, **W**ednesday, **M**emorial **D**ay
Names of religions, languages, races, and nationalities	**B**aptist, **C**atholicism, **C**hilean, **B**uddhism, **F**rench, **H**ispanic, **G**reek, **A**frican **A**merican
Names of clubs, organization, businesses, and institutions	**L**ittle **L**eague, **A**merican **H**eart **A**ssociation, **P**ratt-**R**ead **C**ompany, **W**ebster **B**ank
Names of awards, prizes, and medals	**E**mmy **A**ward, **N**obel **P**eace **P**rize, **P**urple **H**eart, **P**ulitzer **P**rize
Proper Adjectives	
Proper adjectives formed from proper nouns	**J**apanese gardening, **E**nglish class, **C**aribbean music, **A**laskan oil drilling
Proper nouns used as adjectives	**S**enate bill, **A**gatha **C**hristie masterpiece, **C**alifornia coast, **F**ranklin stove
I and First Words	
The pronoun *I*.	Next week **I** will leave on my trip to Yellowstone National Park.
First word of each sentence.	**T**he oldest of the U.S. national parks is noted for its beauty, wildlife, and geysers.
First word of a direct quotation.	"**T**hat mountain stands taller than any other in the state," the guide reported with pride to his group of tourists.
First lines of most poetry. (Follow the capitalization of the original poem.)	**A**nd far as the eye of God could see **D**arkness covered everything, **B**lacker than a hundred midnights **D**own in a cypress swamp.
First word in a letter salutation and the name or title of the person addressed.	**D**ear **D**ad, **M**y dear **A**unt **N**ola, **D**ear **M**adam
First word in letter closings.	**S**incerely yours, **Y**ours truly, **F**ondly, **W**arm wishes
Family Relationships and Titles of Persons	
Capitalize the titles or abbreviations that come before the names of people.	**A**dmiral Michael Chase, **M**s. Gloria Steinem, **S**enator Dodd, **M**r. and **M**rs. Douglas, **D**r. Watson, **C**hief **J**ustice Oliver Wendell Holmes
Person's title as a proper noun.	Can you meet us on Tuesday, **R**abbi? It's time to start rounds, **D**octor.
Words showing family relationships when used as titles or as substitutes for a name.	**U**ncle Fred, **G**randmother Parker, **F**ather, **C**ousin Sam
Abbreviations	
Social titles after a name.	My teacher is named **Mr.** Franks. Can't you ask **Prof.** Pardoe to help us in the soup kitchen?
Abbreviate the titles of organizations.	Northeastern **Mfg.** Connecticut Yard Workers **Assoc.**

Category/Rule	Examples
Parts of government, and business, with the initials of each word in the title.	**NATO** (North Atlantic Treaty Organization) **USMC** (United States Marine Corps) **IBM** (International Business Machines) **SNET** (Southern New England Telephone)
Abbreviate address titles.	Stoughton **St.**, Fort **Rd.**, Park **Ave.**
Time Designations	
Time abbreviations BCE (BC), CE (AD), AM, and PM	Hatshepsut, who lived from 1503 to 1482 **BCE**, was one of five women to reign as Queen of Egypt. The cruel Caligula ruled Rome until **CE** 41. My appointment was for 9:30 **AM**, and I'm not happy about waiting. We have a 7:00 **PM** dinner reservation at my favorite restaurant.
Geographical Names, Directions, and Historical Names	
Names of cities, states, countries, islands, and continents	**cities:** **H**onolulu, **M**oscow, **G**uatemala **C**ity **states:** **G**eorgia, **I**owa, **N**ew **M**exico **countries:** **Z**imbabwe, **B**elgium, **E**cuador **islands:** **T**ahiti, **C**ayman **I**slands, **C**yprus **continents:** **N**orth **A**merica, **E**urope, **A**frica
Names of bodies of water and geographical features	**B**lack **S**ea, **S**nake **R**iver, **S**ahara **D**esert, **M**ount **M**cKinley
Names of buildings, monuments, and bridges	**W**oolsey **H**all, **E**mpire **S**tate **B**uilding, **V**ietnam **V**eterans **M**emorial, **G**olden **G**ate **B**ridge
Names of streets and highways	**R**ailroad **A**venue, **N**ew **E**ngland **T**urnpike, **P**alm **D**rive, **R**oute 153
Sections of the country	the **S**unbelt, the **P**acific **C**oast, the **S**outheast, the **M**idwest
Names of historical events, special events, documents, and historical periods	**historical events:** **B**attle of the **B**ulge, **W**orld **W**ar **I** **special events:** **S**ummerfest, **B**oston **M**arathon **documents:** **M**agna **C**arta, **D**eclaration of **I**ndependence **historical periods:** **R**econstruction, **I**ndustrial **A**ge
Titles of Artworks and Literary Works	
First and last words and all important words in the titles of artworks and literary works, including books, magazines, short stories, poems, songs, movies, plays, paintings, and sculpture	*Transworld Skateboarding* (magazine), ***T**oo **C**lose to the **F**alls* (book), "**T**he **C**ask of **A**montillado" (short story), **B**irches at **S**unrise (painting), "**P**olka **D**ots and **M**oonbeams" (song), ***T**he **L**ion in **W**inter* (movie)
Titles of religious works	**H**ebrew **B**ible, **K**oran, **O**ld **T**estament

GRAMMAR & STYLE

3.17 Writing Effective Sentences

SENTENCE FRAGMENTS

A sentence contains a subject and a verb and should express a complete thought. A **sentence fragment** is a phrase or clause that does not express a complete thought but that has been punctuated as though it did.

EXAMPLES

complete sentence The gray fox ran across the field.

sentence fragment Ran across the field. (The subject is missing.)

sentence fragment The gray fox. (The verb is missing.)

sentence fragment Across the field. (The subject and verb are missing.)

RUN-ON SENTENCES

Take a look at the following examples of run-on sentences. In the first run-on, no punctuation mark is used between the run-on sentences. In the second run-on, a comma is used incorrectly.

EXAMPLES

The umpire watched the two teams warm up before the game his headache had gone away.

At the start of the American Revolution, about three million people lived in the thirteen colonies, about one third of them supported the British government.

You can correct a run-on by dividing it into two separate sentences. Mark the end of each idea with a period, question mark, or exclamation point. Capitalize the first word of each new sentence.

EXAMPLE

The umpire watched the two teams warm up before the game. His headache had gone away.

You can also correct a run-on by using a semicolon. The second part of the sentence is not capitalized. Use a semicolon to join two sentences only if the thoughts are closely related.

EXAMPLE

At the start of the American Revolution, about three million people lived in the thirteen colonies; about one third of them supported the British government.

SENTENCE COMBINING AND EXPANDING

A series of short sentences in a paragraph can make your writing sound choppy and uninteresting. The reader might also have trouble understanding how your ideas are connected. By **combining and expanding sentences,** you can connect related ideas, make sentences longer and smoother, and make a paragraph more interesting to read.

One way to combine sentences is to take a key word or phrase from one sentence and insert it into another sentence.

EXAMPLES

short, choppy sentences
The girl rode a bicycle. It was pink.

combined sentence (with key word)
The girl rode a pink bicycle.

short, choppy sentences
We took a trip in the summer. We went to the Texas coast.

combined sentence (with key phrase)
We took a summer trip to the Texas coast.

Another way of combining sentences is to take two related sentences and combine them by using a coordinating conjunction—*and, but, or, so, for, yet,* or *nor.* By using a coordinating conjunction, you can form a compound subject, a compound verb, or a compound sentence. Be sure to use a comma before the coordinating conjunction that links two sentences.

EXAMPLES

two related sentences
Stephen lived close to the ocean. He often sailed on his boat in the summer.

combined sentence
Stephen lived close to the ocean, **and** he often sailed on his boat in the summer. (compound sentence)

two related sentences
Dandelions sprang up in the backyard. There were also broadleaf weeds.

combined sentence
Dandelions **and** broadleaf weeds sprang up in the backyard. (compound subject)

two related sentences
Rain beat down upon the trail. It drenched the weary travelers.

combined sentence
Rain beat down upon the trail **and** drenched the weary travelers. (compound verb)

VARYING SENTENCE STRUCTURE

Just as you probably wouldn't like to eat the same thing for breakfast every morning, your readers don't enjoy reading the same sentence pattern in every paragraph. By **varying sentence beginnings** you can give your sentences rhythm, create variety, and keep your readers engaged. Sentences often begin with a subject. To vary sentence beginnings, start some sentences with a one-word modifier, a prepositional phrase, a participial phrase, or a subordinate clause.

EXAMPLES

subject
She usually finishes her test before the rest of the class.

one-word modifier
Usually, she finishes her test before the rest of the class.

prepositional phrase
Before lunch he plans the following day's activities.

participial phrase
Humming a lively tune, the warden reviewed the parole cases.

subordinate clause
Since it rarely rains where he lives, Jeff leaves the top down on his convertible.

WORDY SENTENCES

A **wordy sentence** includes extra words and phrases that can be difficult, confusing, or repetitive to read. When you write, use only words necessary to make your meaning clear. Revise and edit your sentences so that they are not unnecessarily wordy or complicated.

Replace a group of words with one word.

EXAMPLES

wordy
I quit my job **because of the fact that** the company wanted me to work overtime each week.

revised
I quit my job **because** the company wanted me to work overtime each week.

Replace a clause with a phrase.

EXAMPLES

wordy
When the batter hit the ball over the fence into the stands, the crowd cheered wildly.

revised
When the batter hit the ball over the fence, the crowd cheered wildly.

Delete a group of unnecessary or repetitive words.

EXAMPLES

wordy
What I think is your book will appeal to children in grade school.

revised
I think your book will appeal to grade school children.

wordy
Joe suffers from insomnia, **and he doesn't sleep well at night.**

revised
Joe suffers from insomnia.

USING PARALLELISM

A sentence has **parallelism** when the same forms are used to express ideas of equal—or parallel—importance. Parallelism can add emphasis, balance, and rhythm to a sentence. Words, phrases, and clauses that have the same form and function in a sentence are called **parallel.**

EXAMPLES

not parallel
The singers **took** the stage, **dazzled** the crowd, and then **had returned** to their dressing rooms. (The highlighted verbs are not in the same tense.)

parallel
The singers **took** the stage, **dazzled** the crowd, and **returned** to their dressing rooms.

not parallel
The performers are **talented, lively,** and **dance.** (The three highlighted words include two adjectives and one verb.)
parallel
The performers are **talented, lively,** and **energetic** dancers.

MAKING PASSIVE SENTENCES ACTIVE

A verb is **active** when the subject of the verb performs the action. It is **passive** when the subject of the verb receives the action.

EXAMPLES
active
Lenny bought Rachel a scarf.

passive
A scarf was bought for Rachel by Lenny.

USING COLORFUL LANGUAGE

When you write, use words that tell your readers exactly what you mean. **Colorful language**—such as precise and lively nouns, verbs, and modifiers—tells your readers exactly what you mean and makes your writing more interesting.

Precise nouns give your reader a clear picture of who or what is involved in the sentence.

EXAMPLES
original sentence
The cat walked into the building.

revised sentence
The Siamese cat walked into the grocery **store.**

Colorful, vivid verbs describe the specific action in the sentence.

EXAMPLES
original sentence
Her brother ran across the yard.

revised sentence
Her brother darted across the yard.

Modifiers—adjectives and adverbs—describe the meanings of other words and make them more precise. Colorful or surprising modifiers can make your writing come alive for your readers.

EXAMPLES
original sentence
The tired farmer planted the last row of corn.

revised sentence
The exhausted farmer wearily planted the last row of corn.

WRITING

4 Writing

4.1 The Writing Process

All writers—whether they are beginning writers, famous published writers, or somewhere in between—go through a process that leads to a complete piece of writing. The specifics of each writer's process may be unique, but for every writer, writing is a series of steps or stages.

The Writing Process	
Stage	**Tasks**
1. Prewriting	Plan your writing: choose a topic, audience, purpose, and form; gather ideas; arrange them logically.
2. Drafting	Get your ideas down on paper.
3. Revising	Evaluate, or judge, the writing piece and suggest ways to improve it. Judging your own writing is called self-evaluation. Judging a classmate's writing is called peer evaluation. Work to improve the content, organization, and expression of your ideas. Proofread your writing for errors in spelling, grammar, capitalization, and punctuation. Correct these errors, make a final copy of your paper, and proofread it again.
Writing Follow-Up: Publish and Present	Share your work with an audience.
Reflect	Think through the writing process to determine what you learned as a writer, what you accomplished, and what you would like to strengthen the next time you write.

While writing moves through these stages, it is also a continuing cycle. You might need to go back to a previous stage before going on to the next step. Returning to a previous stage will strengthen your final work. Note also that you can take time to reflect on your writing between any of the other stages. The more you reflect on your writing, the better your writing will become.

1 PREWRITE

In the prewriting stage of the writing process, you decide on a purpose, audience, topic, and form. You also begin to discover your voice and gather and organize ideas.

Prewriting Plan	
Set Your Purpose	A **purpose,** or aim, is the goal that you want your writing to accomplish.
Identify Your Audience	An **audience** is the person or group of people intended to read what you write.
Find Your Voice	**Voice** is the quality of a work that tells you that one person wrote it.
Select Your Topic	A **topic** is simply something to write about. For example, you might write about a sports hero or about a cultural event in your community.
Select a Writing Form	A **form** is a kind of writing. For example, you might write a paragraph, an essay, a short story, a poem, or a news article.

Set Your Purpose

When you choose your mode and form of writing, think about what purpose or aim you are trying to accomplish. Your purpose for writing might be to inform, to tell a story, to describe something, or to convince others to see your viewpoint. Your writing might have more than one purpose. For example, a piece of writing might inform your readers about an important event while persuading them to respond in a specific way.

Mode of Writing	Purpose	Form
informative	to inform	news article, research report
narrative	to express thoughts or ideas, or to tell a story	personal account, memoir, short story
descriptive	to portray a person, place, object, or event	travel brochure, personal profile, poem
argumentative	to convince people to accept a position and respond in some way	editorial, petition, political speech

Identify Your Audience

An **audience** is the person or group of people intended to read what you write. For example, you might write for yourself, a friend, a relative, or your classmates. The best writing usually is intended for a specific audience. Choosing a specific audience before writing will help you make important decisions about your work. For an audience of young children, for example, you would use simple words and ideas. For an audience of your peers in an athletic group, you would use jargon and other specialized words that your peers already know. For an adult audience, you would use more formal language.

Use the following questions to help identify your audience.

- Who will be most interested in my topic?
- What are their interests and values?
- How much do they already know about the topic?
- What background information do they need in order to understand my ideas and point of view?
- What words, phrases, or concepts will I need to define for my audience?
- How can I capture my audience's interest from the very start?

Use Appropriate Language

Formal Versus Informal English To write effectively, you must choose your language according to your audience, purpose, and the occasion or situation. **Formal English** contains carefully constructed, complete sentences; avoids contractions; follows standard English usage and grammar; uses a serious tone; and uses sophisticated vocabulary. **Informal English** contains everyday speech and popular expressions, uses contractions, and may include sentence fragments.

Formal English is appropriate for school essays, oral or written reports, interviews, and debates. Informal English is appropriate for communication with friends, personal letters or notes, and journal entries.

WRITING

EXAMPLES

formal English
I am very pleased that I received a perfect score on the math exam.

informal English
I'm so pumped that I aced that math exam!

Find Your Voice

Voice is the quality of a work that tells you that one person wrote it. Voice makes a person's writing unique. In your writing, you should strive to develop your own voice, not to imitate the voices of others. Be true to your own voice, and your experience will speak directly to the experience of others.

Select Your Topic

A **topic** is simply something to write about. For example, you might write about a sports hero or about a cultural event in your community. Here are some ideas that may help you find interesting writing topics:

Ways to Find a Writing Topic	
Check your journal	Search through your journal for ideas that you jotted down in the past. Many professional writers get their ideas from their journals.
Think about your experiences	Think about people, places, or events that affected you strongly. Recall experiences that taught you important lessons or that you felt strongly about.
Look at reference works	Reference works include printed or computerized dictionaries, atlases, almanacs, and encyclopedias.
Browse in a library	Libraries are treasure houses of information and ideas. Simply looking around in the stacks of a library can suggest good ideas for writing.
Use mass media	Newspapers, magazines, radio, television, and films can suggest good topics for writing. For example, a glance at listings for public television programs might suggest topics related to the arts, to history, or to nature.
Search the Internet	Search key words in a search engine or web browser to expand on your ideas. Make sure to keep your work original and avoid plagiarizing from websites.

Select a Writing Form

Another important decision that a writer needs to make is what form his or her writing will take. A form is a kind of writing. Once you've identified your topic, your purpose for writing, and your audience, a particular form of writing may become immediately obvious as the perfect one to convey your ideas. But, sometimes, an unexpected choice of form may be even more effective in presenting your topic. The following chart lists some of the many different forms of writing.

Forms of Writing

adventure	brochure	directions	fantasy
advertisement	character sketch	editorial	history
advice column	children's story	epitaph	human interest story
agenda	comedy	essay	instructions
apology	consumer report	eulogy	interview questions
autobiography	debate	experiment	itinerary
biography	detective story	fable	journal entry
book review	dialogue	family history	letter

magazine article	obituary	proposal	speech
memorandum	parable	radio or tv spot	sports story
minutes	paraphrase	recommendation	statement of belief
movie review	petition	research report	summary
mystery	play	résumé	tall tale
myth	police/accident report	science fiction	tour guide
narrative	poster	short story	want ad
newspaper article		song lyrics	

WRITING

Gather Ideas

After you have identified your purpose, audience, topic, and form, the next step in the prewriting stage is to gather ideas. There are many ways to gather ideas for writing.

- **Brainstorm** When you **brainstorm,** you think of as many ideas as you can, as quickly as you can, without stopping to evaluate or criticize them. Anything goes—no idea should be rejected in the brainstorming stage.
- **Freewrite** **Freewriting** is simply taking a pencil and paper and writing whatever comes into your mind. Try to write for several minutes without stopping and without worrying about spelling, grammar, usage, or mechanics.
- **Question** Ask the **reporting questions** *who, what, where, when, why,* and *how* about your topic. This questioning strategy is especially useful for gathering information about an event or for planning a story.
- **Create a Graphic Organizer** A good way to gather information is to create a **graphic organizer,** such as a Venn Diagram, Sensory Details Chart, Time Line, Story Map, or Pro-and-Con Chart. For examples, see the Language Arts Handbook, section 1, Reading Strategies and Skills, page 821.

Organize Your Ideas

Writing Paragraphs After you have gathered ideas for a piece of writing, the next step is to organize these ideas in a useful and reader-friendly way. The most basic organization of ideas occurs in forming paragraphs. A good paragraph is a carefully organized unit of writing. It develops a sequence in narrative writing or develops a particular topic in informational or argumentative writing.

Paragraphs with Topic Sentences Many paragraphs include a topic sentence that presents a main idea. The topic sentence can be placed at the beginning, middle, or end of the paragraph. Topic sentences usually appear early on in the paragraph and are commonly followed by one or more supporting sentences. Often these supporting sentences begin with transitions that relate them to the other sentences or to the topic sentence. This type of paragraph may end with a clincher sentence, which sums up what has been said in the paragraph.

EXAMPLE

> Whether it's rock or Bach, music that's played too loud can put more than a temporary damper on your hearing. At most rock concerts and many night clubs, the sound intensity is high enough to cause irreversible damage to the delicate sensor cells lining the inner ear. Car and home stereo equipment and headphones can also harm your hearing when the volume is cranked up too high.
>
> from "Hearing Under Seige"
> by Bob Ludlow

Paragraphs Without Topic Sentences Most paragraphs do not have topic sentences. In a narrative piece of writing, many paragraphs state a series of events, and no sentence in the paragraph sums up the events. In good narrative writing, the sequence of events appears in chronological order. Descriptive writing may contain paragraphs organized spatially—in the order in which the speaker or narrator sees, hears, feels, smells, and tastes things in a given situation.

Write Your Thesis Statement

One way to start organizing your writing, especially if you are writing an informative or argumentative essay, is to identify the main idea of what you want to say. Present this idea in the form of a sentence or two called a thesis statement. A **thesis statement** is simply a sentence that presents the main idea or the position you will take in your essay.

Example thesis for an argumentative essay

The development at Rice Creek Farm should be stopped because it will destroy one of the best natural areas near the city.

Example thesis for an informative essay

Wilma Rudolph was an athlete who succeeded in the elite sport of tennis before the world was willing to recognize her.

Methods of Organization

The ideas in your writing should be ordered and linked in a logical and easily understandable way. You can organize your writing in the following ways:

Methods of Organization	
Chronological Order	Events are given in the order they occur.
Order of Importance	Details are given in order of importance or familiarity.
Comparison-and-Contrast Order	Similarities and differences of two things are listed.
Cause-and-Effect Order	One or more causes are presented followed by one or more effects.

To link your ideas, use connective words and phrases. In informational or argumentative writing, *for example, as a result, finally, therefore,* and *in fact* are common connectives. In narrative and descriptive writing, words like *first, then, suddenly, above, beyond, in the distance,* and *there* are common connectives. In comparison-contrast organization, common phrases include *similarly, on the other hand,* and *in contrast.* In cause-and-effect organization, linkers include *one cause, another effect, as a result, consequently, finally,* and *therefore.*

Create an Outline An **outline** is an excellent framework for highlighting main ideas and supporting details. To create a rough outline, simply list your main ideas in some logical order. Under each main idea, list the supporting details set off by dashes.

EXAMPLE

What Is Drama?
Definition of Drama
—Tells a story
—Uses actors to play characters
—Uses a stage, properties, lights, costumes, makeup, and special effects
Types of Drama
—Tragedy
—Definition: A play in which the main character meets a negative fate

— Examples: *Antigone, Romeo and Juliet, Death of a Salesman*

— Comedy

— Definition: A play in which the main character meets a positive fate

— Examples: *A Midsummer Night's Dream, Cyrano de Bergerac, The Odd Couple*

2 DRAFT

After you have gathered your information and organized it, the next step in writing is to produce a draft. A **draft** is simply an early attempt at writing a paper. Different writers approach drafting in different ways. Some prefer to work slowly and carefully, perfecting each part as they go. Others prefer to write a discovery draft, getting all their ideas down on paper in rough form and then going back over those ideas to shape and focus them. When writing a discovery draft, you do not focus on spelling, grammar, usage, and mechanics. You can take care of those details during revision.

Draft Your Introduction

The purpose of an introduction is to capture your reader's attention and establish what you want to say. An effective introduction can start with a quotation, a question, an anecdote, an intriguing fact, or a description that hooks the reader to keep reading. An effective introduction can open with a quotation, question, anecdote, fact, or description.

EXAMPLES

"That's one small step for man, one giant leap for mankind." With these words, Neil Armstrong signaled his success as the first man to set foot on the moon...

What would it be like if all the birds in the world suddenly stopped their singing?

When my brother was nineteen, he volunteered in a homeless shelter making sure people had a safe place to spend the night. He told me once that he would never forget the time he met...

Draft Your Body

When writing the body of an essay, refer to your outline. Each heading in your outline will become the main idea of one of your paragraphs. To move smoothly from one idea to another, use transitional words or phrases. As you draft, include evidence from documented sources to support the ideas that you present. This evidence can be paraphrased, summarized, or quoted directly. For information on proper documentation, see the Language Arts Handbook 5.5, Documenting Sources, page 904.

Draft Your Conclusion

In the conclusion, bring together the main ideas you included in the body of your essay and create a sense of closure to the issue you raised in your thesis. There is no single right way to conclude a piece of writing. Possibilities include:

- Making a generalization
- Restating the thesis and major supporting ideas in different words
- Summarizing the points made in the rest of the essay
- Drawing a lesson or moral
- Calling on the reader to adopt a view or take an action
- Expanding on your thesis or main idea by connecting it to the reader's own interests
- Linking your thesis to a larger issue or concern

3 REVISE

Evaluate Your Draft

Self- and Peer Evaluation When you evaluate something, you examine it carefully to find its strengths and weaknesses. Evaluating your own writing is called **self-evaluation.** A **peer evaluation** is an evaluation of a piece of writing done by classmates, or peers. The following tips can help you to become a helpful peer reader, to learn to give and receive criticism, and to improve your writing.

Tips for evaluating writing

- **Check for content** Is the content, including the main idea, clear? Have any important details been left out? Do unimportant or unrelated details confuse the main point? Are the main idea and supporting details clearly connected to one another?
- **Check for organization** Are the ideas in the written work presented in a logical order?
- **Check the style and language** Is the language appropriately formal or informal? Is the tone appropriate for the audience and purpose? Have any key or unfamiliar terms been defined?

Tips for delivering helpful criticism

- **Be focused** Concentrate on content, organization, and style. At this point, do not focus on proofreading matters such as spelling and punctuation; they can be corrected during the proofreading stage.
- **Be positive** Respect the writer's feelings and genuine writing efforts. Tell the writer what you like about his or her work. Answer the writer's questions in a positive manner, tactfully presenting any changes you are suggesting.
- **Be specific** Give the writer concrete ideas for improving his or her work.

Tips for benefiting from helpful criticism

- **Tell your peer evaluator your specific concerns and questions.** If you are unsure whether you've clearly presented an idea, ask the evaluator how he or she might restate the idea.
- **Ask questions to clarify comments that your evaluator makes.** When you ask for clarification, you make sure you understand your evaluator's comments.
- **Accept your evaluator's comments graciously.** Criticism can be helpful, but you don't have to use any or all of the suggestions.

Revise for Content, Organization, and Style

After identifying weaknesses in a draft through self-evaluation and peer evaluation, the next step is to revise the draft. Here are four basic ways to improve meaning and content:

- **Adding or Expanding** Sometimes writing can be improved by adding details, examples, or transitions to connect ideas. Often a single added adjective, for example, can make a piece of writing clearer or more vivid.

EXAMPLE

draft Wind whistled through the park.

revised The **bone-chilling** wind whistled through the park.

- **Cutting or Condensing** Often writing can be improved by cutting unnecessary or unrelated material.

EXAMPLE

draft Will was firmly determined to find the structure of the DNA molecule.

revised Will was determined to find the structure of the DNA molecule.

EXAMPLE

draft Several things had been bothering Tanya.

revised Several personal problems had been bothering Tanya.

- **Moving** Often you can improve the organization of your writing by moving part of it so that related ideas appear near one another.

After you've revised the draft, ask yourself a series of questions. Think of these questions as your "revision checklist."

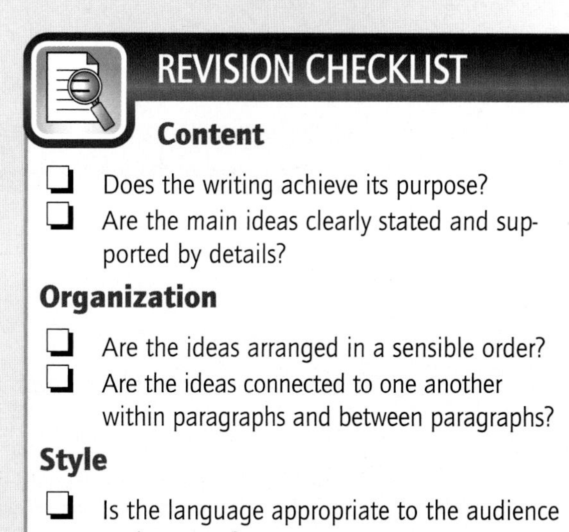

REVISION CHECKLIST

Content

- ❑ Does the writing achieve its purpose?
- ❑ Are the main ideas clearly stated and supported by details?

Organization

- ❑ Are the ideas arranged in a sensible order?
- ❑ Are the ideas connected to one another within paragraphs and between paragraphs?

Style

- ❑ Is the language appropriate to the audience and purpose?
- ❑ Is the mood appropriate to the purpose of the writing?

WRITING

Proofread for Errors

When you proofread your writing, you read it through to look for errors and to mark corrections. When you mark corrections, use the standard proofreading symbols as shown in the following chart.

Proofreader's Symbols

Symbol and Example	Meaning of Symbol	Symbol and Example	Meaning of Symbol
The very first time	Delete (cut) this material.	gebril	Change the order of these letters.
dog life	Insert (add) something that is missing.	end. "Watch out," she yelled.	Begin a new paragraph.
Geor/e	Replace this letter or word.	Love conquers all	Put a period here.
All the horses king's	Move this word to where the arrow points.	Welcome friends.	Put a comma here.
		Getthe stopwatch	Put a space here.
french toast	Capitalize this letter.	Dear Madam	Put a colon here.
the vice-President	Lowercase this letter.	She walked he rode.	Put a semicolon here.
housse	Take out this letter and close up space.	name brand products	Put a hyphen here.
		cats meow	Put an apostrophe here.
book keeper	Close up space.	cat's cradle stet	Let it stand. (Leave as it is.)

WRITING

After you have revised your draft, make a clean copy of it and proofread it for errors in spelling, grammar, and punctuation. Use the following proofreading checklist.

Proofreading Checklist

Spelling

- ❑ Are all words, including names, spelled correctly?

Grammar

- ❑ Does each verb agree with its subject?
- ❑ Are verb tenses consistent and correct?
- ❑ Are irregular verbs formed correctly?
- ❑ Are there any sentence fragments or run-ons?
- ❑ Have double negatives been avoided?
- ❑ Have frequently confused words, such as *affect* and *effect*, been used correctly?

Punctuation

- ❑ Does every sentence end with an end mark?
- ❑ Are commas used correctly?
- ❑ Do all proper nouns and proper adjectives begin with capital letters?

WRITING FOLLOW-UP

Publish and Present

Some writing is done just for oneself—journal writing, for example. Most writing, however, is meant to be shared with others. Here are several ways in which you can publish your writing or present it to others:

- Submit your work to a local publication, such as a school literary magazine, school newspaper, or community newspaper.
- Submit your work to a regional or national publication.
- Enter your work in a contest.
- Read your work aloud to classmates, friends, or family members.
- Collaborate with other students to prepare a publication—a brochure, online literary magazine, anthology, or newspaper.
- Prepare a poster or bulletin board, perhaps in collaboration with other students, to display your writing.
- Make your own book by typing or word processing the pages and binding them together.
- Hold an oral reading of student writing as a class or school-wide project.
- Share your writing with other students in a small writers' group.

Reflect

After you've completed your writing, think through the writing process to determine what you learned as a writer, what you learned about your topic, how the writing process worked or didn't work for you, and what skills you would like to strengthen.

Reflection can be done on a self-evaluation form, in small-group discussion, or simply in silent reflection. By keeping a journal, however, you'll be able to keep track of your writing experience and pinpoint ways to make the writing process work better for you. Here are some questions to ask as you reflect on the writing process and yourself as a writer:

- Which part of the writing process did I enjoy most and least? Why? Which part of the writing process was most difficult? least difficult? Why?
- What would I change about my approach to the writing process next time?
- What have I learned in writing about this topic?
- What have I learned by using this form?
- How have I developed as a writer while writing this piece?
- What strengths have I discovered in my work?
- What aspects of my writing do I want to strengthen? How can I strengthen them?

4.2 Modes and Purposes of Writing

Types of writing generally fall within four main classifications or modes: informative, narrative, descriptive, and argumentative. Each of these modes has a specific purpose. See the Mode of Writing Chart on page 826.

Informative Writing

The purpose of **informative writing** is to inform, to present or explain an idea or a process. News articles and research reports are examples of informative, or expository, writing. One function of informative writing is to define, since a definition explains what something is. Another function of informative writing is to analyze and interpret. For example, a book review is writing that analyzes and interprets a piece of literature to inform an audience about its worth. Similarly, a movie review evaluates and judges for its viewing audience how well a movie accomplishes its purpose.

Narrative Writing

Narrative writing tells a story or relates a series of events. It can be used to entertain, to make a point, or to introduce a topic. Narrating an event involves the dimension of action over time.

Narratives are often used in essays, reports, and other nonfiction forms because stories are entertaining and fun to read. Just as important, they are a good way to make a point. Biographies, autobiographies, and family histories are also forms of narrative writing.

Descriptive Writing

The purpose of **descriptive writing** is to entertain, enrich, and enlighten by using a form such as fiction or poetry to share a perspective. Descriptive writing is used to describe something, to set a scene, to create a mood, to appeal to the reader's senses. Descriptive writing is often creative and uses visual and other sensual details, emotional responses, and imagery. Poems, short stories, and plays are examples of descriptive writing.

Argumentative Writing

The purpose of **argumentative writing** is to persuade readers or listeners to respond in some way, such as to agree with a position, change a view on an issue, reach an agreement, or perform an action. Argumentative writing uses evidence to support an argument and convince the audience to adopt a point of view. Examples of argumentative writing are editorials, petitions, political speeches, and essays.

5.1 Research Skills

Learning is a lifelong process, one that extends far beyond school. Both in school and on your own, it is important to remember that your learning and growth are up to you. One good way to become an independent lifelong learner is to master research skills. Research is the process of gathering ideas and information. One of the best resources for research is the library.

How Library Materials Are Organized

Each book in a library is assigned a unique number, called a call number. The call number is printed on the spine (edge) of each book. The numbers serve to classify books as well as to help the library keep track of them. Libraries commonly use one of two systems for classifying books. Most school and public libraries use the Dewey Decimal System.

Dewey Decimal System

Call Numbers	Subjects
000–099	Reference and General Works
100–199	Philosophy, Psychology
200–299	Religion
300–399	Social Studies
400–499	Language
500–599	Science, Mathematics
600–699	Technology
700–799	Arts
800–899	Literature
900–999	History, Geography, Biography[1]

1. Biographies (920s) are arranged alphabetically by the name of the person whose life is treated in each biography.

How to Locate Library Materials

If you know the call number of a book or the subject classification number you want, you can usually go to the bookshelves, or stacks, to obtain the book. Use the signs at the ends of the rows to locate the section you need. Then find the particular shelf that contains call numbers close to yours.

Library collections include many other types of publications besides books, such as magazines, newspapers, audio and video recordings, and government documents. Ask a librarian to tell you where to find the materials you need. To find the call numbers of books that will help you with your research, use the library's catalog. The catalog lists all the books in the library (or a group of libraries if it is part of a larger system).

Internet Libraries It is also possible to visit the Internet Public library online at **http://www.ipl.org/.** The Internet Public Library is the first public library of the Internet. This site provides library services to the Internet community by finding, evaluating, selecting, organizing, describing, and creating quality information resources; teaches what librarians have to contribute in a digital environment; and promotes the importance of libraries.

Computerized Catalogs Many libraries today use computerized catalogs. Systems differ from library to library, but most involve using a computer terminal to search through the library's collection. You can usually search by author, title, subject, or key word.

EXAMPLE COMPUTERIZED CATALOG SEARCHES

Search By	Example	Hints
Author	gould, stephen j	Type last name first. Type as much of the name as you know.
Title	mismeasure of man	Omit articles such as *a, an,* or *the* at the beginning of titles.
Subject	intelligence tests; ability-testing	Use the list of subjects provided by the library.
Key words	darwin; intelligence; craniology	Use related topics if you can't find anything in your subject.

If your library has a computerized catalog, you will need to learn how to use your library's particular system. A librarian can help you to master the system. The following is a sample book entry screen from a computerized catalog.

Author	Wallace, David Rains, 1945–
Title	The Quetzal and the Macaw: The Story of Costa Rica's National Parks
Publication info.	Sierra Club Books, 1992
No. of pages/size	xvi, 222 p. : maps : 24 cm.
ISBN	ISBN 0-87156-585-4
Subjects	National parks and reserves–Costa Rica–History
	Costa Rica. Servicio de Parques
	Nacionales–History
	Nature conservation–Costa Rica–History
Dewey call number	333.78

Interlibrary Loans Many libraries are part of larger library networks. In these libraries, the computerized catalog covers the collections of several libraries. If you want a book from a different library, you will need to request the book at the library's request desk or by using its computer. Ask your librarian to help you if you have questions. He or she will be able to tell you when the book will be shipped to your library.

Using Reference Works

Most libraries have an assortment of reference works in which knowledge is collected and organized so that you can find it easily. Usually, reference works cannot be checked out of the library.

Types of Dictionaries You will find many types of dictionaries in the library reference section. The most common is a dictionary of the English language. Examples include *Merriam Webster's Collegiate Dictionary,* the *American Heritage Dictionary,* and the multi-volume *Oxford English Dictionary*. Other word dictionaries focus on slang, abbreviations and acronyms, English/foreign language translation, and spelling. Biographical, historical, scientific, and world language dictionaries are also some of the works you will find in the reference section.

Using a Thesaurus A thesaurus is a reference book that groups synonyms, or words with similar meanings. Suppose that you are writing an essay and have a word that means almost but not quite what you want, or perhaps you find yourself using the same word over and over. A thesaurus can give you fresh and precise words to use. For example, if you look up the word *sing* in a thesaurus, you might find the following synonyms listed:

sing (v.) carol, chant, croon, hum, vocalize, warble, yodel

Using Almanacs, Yearbooks, and Atlases **Almanacs** and **yearbooks** are published each year. An almanac provides statistics and lists, often related to recent events. In an almanac you can find facts about current events, countries of the world, famous people, sports, entertainment, and many other subjects. An overview of the events of the year can be found in a yearbook. Some of the more widely used almanacs and yearbooks are *The Guinness Book of World Records;* the *Information Please, Almanac, Atlas, and Yearbook;* the *World Almanac and Book of Facts;* and the *World Book Yearbook of Events.*

An **atlas** is a collection of maps and other geographical information. Some atlases show natural features such as mountains and rivers; others show political features such as countries and cities. If you need to locate a particular feature on a map in an atlas, refer to the gazetteer, an index that lists every item shown on the map.

Using Biographical References and Encyclopedias A **biographical reference** contains information on the lives of famous people. Examples include *Who's Who,* the *Dictionary of American Biography,* and *Contemporary Authors.*

Encyclopedias provide a survey of knowledge. General encyclopedias, such as *World Book,* contain information on many different subjects. Specialized encyclopedias, such as the *LaRousse Encyclopedia of Mythology,* contain information on one particular area of knowledge. The topics in an encyclopedia are treated in articles, which are usually arranged in alphabetical order. If you look up a topic and do not find it, check the index (usually in the last volume). The index will tell you where in the encyclopedia your topic is covered.

Using Indexes, Appendices, and Glossaries An **index** lists in alphabetical order the subjects mentioned in a book or collection of periodicals and pages where these subjects are treated. Indexes help you locate possible sources of information about your topic. An index can be at the back of a book of nonfiction, or it can be a published book itself. Indexes are available as bound books, on microfilm, and online on the Internet.

An **appendix** provides additional material, often in chart or table form, at the end of a book or other writing.

A **glossary** lists key words in a book and their definitions.

Primary and Secondary Sources

Primary sources are the original unedited materials created by someone directly involved in an event or speaking directly for a group. They may include firsthand documents such as diaries, interviews, works of fiction, artwork, court records, research reports, speeches, letters, surveys, and so on.

Secondary sources offer commentary or analysis of events, ideas, or primary sources. They are often written significantly later and may provide historical context or attempt to describe or explain primary sources. Examples of secondary sources include dictionaries, encyclopedias, textbooks, and books and articles that interpret or review original works.

	Primary Source	**Secondary Source**
Art	Painting	Article critiquing the artist's technique
History	Prisoner's diary	Book about World War II internment camps
Literature	Poem	Literary criticism on a particular form of poetry
Science	Research report	Analysis of results

See the Language Arts Handbook 5.3, Media Literacy, page 902, for information on using newspapers, periodicals, and other forms of media to document your research.

5.2 Internet Research

The Internet is an enormous collection of computer networks that can open a whole new world of information. With just a couple of keystrokes, you can access libraries, government agencies, high schools and universities, nonprofit and educational organizations, museums, user groups, and individuals around the world.

Keep in mind that the Internet is not regulated and everything you read online may not be verified or accurate. Confirm facts from the Internet against another source. In addition, to become a good judge of Internet materials, do the following:

- **Consider the domain name of the resource.** Be sure to check out the sites you use to see if they are commercial (.com or .firm), educational (.edu), governmental (.gov), or organizational (.org or .net). Ask yourself questions like these: What bias might a commercial site have that would influence its presentation of information? Is the site sponsored by a special-interest group that slants or spins information to its advantage?

Key to Internet Domains	
.com	commercial entity
.edu	educational institution
.firm	business entity
.gov	government agency or department
.org or .net	organization

- **Consider the author's qualifications.** Regardless of the source, ask these questions: Is the author named? What expertise does he or she have? Can I locate other online information about this person? Evaluate the quality of information.
- **How accurate is the information?** Does it appear to be reliable and without errors? Is the information given without bias?
- **Check the date posted.** Is the information timely? When was the site last updated?

Keep Track of Your Search Process

- ❑ Write a brief statement of the topic of your research.
- ❑ Write key words or phrases that will help you search for this information.
- ❑ Note the search engines that you will use.
- ❑ As you conduct a search, note how many "hits" or Internet sites the search engine has accessed. Determine whether you need to narrow or expand your search. Write down new key words and the results of each new search.
- ❑ Write down all promising sites. As you access them, evaluate the source and nature of the information and jot down your assessment.
- ❑ As you find the information you need, document it carefully according to the directions in Citing Internet Sources, page 906.
- ❑ Keep a list of favorite websites, either in your research journal or in your browser software. This feature may be called bookmark or favorites. You can click on the name of the site in your list and return to that page without having to retype the URL (Uniform Resource Locator).

Search Tools

A number of popular and free search engines allow you to find topics of interest. Keep in mind that each service uses slightly different methods of searching, so you may get different results using the same key words.

Aol	www.aol.com
Ask	www.ask.com
Bing	www.bing.com
Google	www.google.com
Wow	www.wow.com
WebCrawler	www.webcrawler.com
Yahoo	www.yahoo.com

Search Tips

- To make searching easier, less time consuming, and more directed, narrow your subject to a key word or a group of key words. These key words are your search terms. Key search connectors, or Boolean commands, can help you limit or expand the scope of your topic.

  AND (or +) narrows a search by retrieving documents that include both terms—for example: Ulysses Grant AND Vicksburg.

  OR broadens a search by retrieving documents that include any of the terms—for example: Ulysses Grant OR Vicksburg OR Civil War.

  NOT narrows a search by excluding documents containing certain words—for example: Ulysses Grant NOT Civil War.

- If applicable, limit your search by specifying a geographical area by using the word *near*—for example, golf courses near Boulder, Colorado.
- When entering a group of key words, present them in order, from the most important to the least important key word.
- If the terms of your search are not leading you to the information you need, try using synonyms. For example, if you were looking for information about how to care for your garden, you might use these terms: *compost, pest control,* and *watering*.
- Avoid opening the link to every page in your results list. Search engines typically present pages in descending order of relevancy or importance. The most useful pages will be located at the top of the list. However, skimming the text of lower order sites may give you ideas for other key words.
- If you're not getting the desired results, check your input. Common search mistakes include misspelling search terms and mistyping URLs. Remember that URLs must be typed exactly as they appear, using the exact capital or lowercase letters, spacing, and punctuation.

For information on citing Internet sources, see the Language Arts Handbook 5.6, Documenting Sources.

5.3 Media Literacy

The term **media,** in most applications, is used as a plural of *medium,* which means a channel or system of communication, information, or entertainment. *Mass media* refers specifically to means of communication, such as newspapers, radio, or television, which are designed to reach the mass of the people. *Journalism* is the gathering, evaluating, and disseminating, through various media, of news and facts of current interest. Originally, journalism encompassed only such printed matter as newspapers and periodicals. Today, however, it includes other media used to distribute news, such as radio, television, documentary or newsreel films, the Internet, and computer news services.

Newspapers are publications usually issued on a daily or weekly basis, the main function of which is to report the news. Newspapers also provide commentary on the news, advocate various public policies, furnish special information and advice to readers, and sometimes include features such as comic strips, cartoons, and serialized books.

Periodicals are publications released at regular intervals, such as journals, magazines, or newsletters. Periodicals feature material of special interest to particular audiences. The contents of periodicals can be unrelated to current news stories—however, when dealing with the news, periodicals tend to do so in the form of commentaries or summaries.

Technical writing refers to scientific or process-oriented instructional writing that is of a technical or mechanical nature. Technical writing includes instruction manuals, such as computer software manuals, how-to instructional guides, and procedural memos.

Electronic media include online magazines and journals, known as webzines or e-zines; computer news services; and many web-based newspapers that are available on the Internet. The web is by far the most widely used part of the Internet.

Multimedia is the presentation of information using the combination of text, sound, pictures, animation, and video. Common multimedia computer applications include games, learning software, presentation software, reference materials, and web pages. Most multimedia applications include links that enable users to switch between media elements and topics. The connectivity provided by these links transforms multimedia from static presentations with pictures and sound into a varied and informative interactive experience.

Visual media, such as fine art, illustrations, and photographs, are used extensively in today's visually stimulating world to enhance the written word. Visual arts offer insights into our world in a different way than print does. Critical viewing or careful examination of a painting or photograph can help you to comprehend its meaning and be able to compare and contrast the visual image with a literary work or other piece of writing.

5.4 Evaluating Sources

To conduct your research efficiently, you need to evaluate your sources and set priorities among them. Ideally, a source will be:

- **Unbiased** When an author has a personal stake in what people think about a subject, he or she may withhold or distort information. Investigate the author's background to see if she or he is liable to be biased. Using loaded language and overlooking obvious counterarguments are signs of author bias.
- **Authoritative** An authoritative source is reliable and trustworthy. An author's reputation, especially among others who conduct research in the same field, is a sign of authority. Likewise, periodicals and publishers acquire reputations for responsible or poor editing and research.
- **Timely** Information about many subjects changes rapidly. An astronomy text published last year may already be out of date. In other fields—for instance, algebra—older texts may be perfectly adequate. Consult with your teacher and your librarian to decide how current your sources must be.
- **Available** Borrowing through interlibrary loan, tracing a book that is missing, or recalling a book that has been checked out to another person takes time. Make sure to allow enough time for these materials.
- **Appropriate for your level** Find sources that present useful information that you can understand. Materials written for "young people" may be too simple to be helpful.

Books written for experts may presume knowledge that you do not have. Struggling with a difficult text is often worth the effort, but if you do so, monitor your time and stay on schedule.

5.5 Documenting Sources

As you use your research in your writing, you must document your sources of information.

- Credit the sources of all ideas and facts that you use.
- Credit original ideas or facts that are expressed in text, tables, charts, and other graphic information.
- Credit all artistic property, including works of literature, song lyrics, and ideas.

Keeping a Research Journal A research journal is a notebook, electronic file, or other means to track the information you find as you conduct research. A research journal can include the following:

- A list of questions you want to research. (Such questions can be an excellent source of writing topics.)

EXAMPLES

How did the Vietnam Veterans Memorial come to be? Why is it one of the most visited memorials in America?

Where can I find more artwork by Faith Ringgold?

Why was Transcendentalism such an important literary movement in America but not in Europe?

Avoiding Plagiarizing **Plagiarism** is taking someone else's words or thoughts and presenting them as your own. Plagiarism is a very serious problem and has been the downfall of many students and professionals. Whenever you use someone else's writing to help you with a paper or a speech, you must be careful either to **paraphrase,** put the ideas in your own words; **summarize** the main ideas; or to use **quotation marks.** In any case, you must document your sources and give credit to the person whose ideas you are using. As you do research, make sure to include paraphrases, summaries, and direct quotations in your notes.

Informal and Formal Note-Taking

Informal Note-Taking Take informal notes when you want information for your own use only, and when you will not need to quote or document your sources. You would take informal notes when preparing materials to use in studying, for instance, as you watch a film or listen to a lecture.

Informal note-taking is similar to outlining. Use important ideas as headings, and write relevant details below. You will not be able to copy every word, nor is there any need to. Write phrases instead of sentences. You will also want to record information about the event or performance, including the date, time, place, speaker, and title, as applicable.

EXAMPLE

quotation
"Jerzy Kosinski came to the United States in 1957, and in 1958 he was awarded a Ford Foundation fellowship."
notes
Jerzy Kosinski

—came to US 1957
—Ford Foundation fellowship 1958

Formal Note-Taking Take formal notes when you may need to quote or document your sources. When you are keeping formal notes for a project—for instance, for a debate or a research paper—you should use 4" x 6" index cards.

Preparing Note Cards

1. Identify the source at the top right corner of the card. (Use the source numbers from your bibliography cards.)
2. Identify the subject or topic of the note on the top line of the card. (This will make it easier to organize the cards later.)
3. Use a separate card for each fact or quotation. (This will make it easier to organize the cards later.)
4. Write the pertinent source page number or numbers after the note.

EXAMPLE

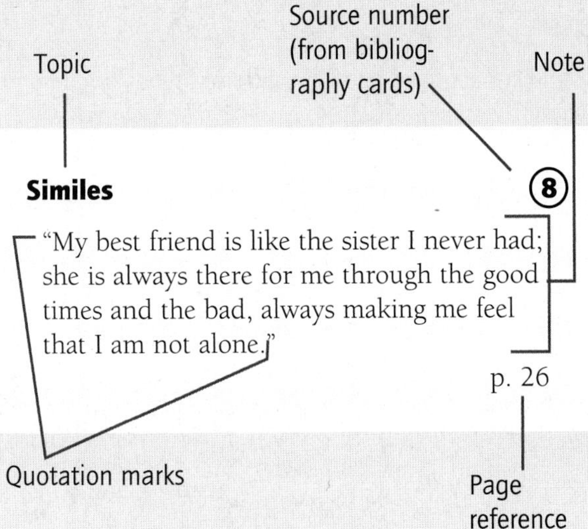

Bibliographies and Bibliography Cards

If you are writing a research paper, your teacher will ask you to include a bibliography to tell where you got your information. A bibliography is a list of sources that you used for your writing. A source is a book, a magazine, a film, or any other written or audiovisual material that you use to get information. As you work on your paper, you should be writing down on note cards the information for each source that you use.

EXAMPLE

2

Van Lawick-Goodall, Jane.

In the Shadow of Man

Boston: Houghton, 1971.

Peabody Institute Library

599.8

For each source used, prepare an index card with complete bibliographical information. Include all of the information in the following chart when preparing your cards.

Information to Include on a Bibliography Card	
Author(s)	Write the complete name(s) of all author(s), editor(s), and translator(s).
Title	Write the complete title. If the piece is contained in a larger work, include the title of the larger work. (For example, write the name of the encyclopedia as well as the name of the article you used.)
Publisher	Write exactly as it appears on the title page.
Place and date of publication	Copy this information from the title page or copyright page of a book. For a magazine, write the date of the issue that you used.
Location and call number	Note where you found the book. If it is in a library collection, write the call number.
Card number	Give each bibliography card that you prepare a number. Write that number in the top right-hand corner of the card and circle it. When you take notes from the source, include this number on each note card so that you will be able to identify the source of the note later on.

The following chart shows the correct form for citing different types of bibliography entries, following the *Modern Language Association (MLA) Style Manual.* Note that all citations should include the medium of the publication, such as *print*, *film*, or *Web*.

MLA Forms for Works Cited

Book	Douglass, Frederick. *Escape from Slavery: The Boyhood of Frederick Douglass in His Own Words.* New York: Alfred A. Knopf, 1994. Print.
Magazine article	Reston, James, Jr. "Orion: Where Stars Are Born." *National Geographic.* December 1995: 90–101. Print.
Encyclopedia entry	"Lewis and Clark Expedition." *Encyclopedia Americana*. Jackson, Donald. 1995 ed. Print.
Interview	Campbell, Silas. Personal interview. 6 February 2007.
Film	*The Big Heat.* Dir. Fritz Lang. With Glenn Ford and Gloria Grahame. Writ. Sidney Boehm. Based on the novel of the same title by William P. McGiven. 90 min. Columbia, 1953. Film.

Citing Internet Sources

To document your Internet sources, use your research journal to record each site you visit (See the Language Arts Handbook, 5.2 Internet Research, page 879) or make bibliography cards as you search. An Internet source entry should include the following general pieces of information:

- Name of the author, if available, last name first, followed by a period.
- Title of the source, document, file, or page in quotation marks, followed by a period.
- Date of the material if available, followed by a period.
- Name of the database or online source, underlined or italicized, and followed by a period.
- Medium of publication (Web).
- Date the source was accessed (day, month, year).

- Provide an electronic address, URL, only when needed to locate the source or if required by your instructor. Enclose the URL in angle brackets (< >), followed by a period. Avoid showing network and e-mail addresses as underlined hyperlinks. Note that when line length forces you to break a Web address, always break it after a slash mark.

The *Modern Language Association Style Manual* acknowledges that all source tracking information on the Internet may not be obtainable. Therefore, the manual recommends that if you cannot find some of this information, cite what is available.

EXAMPLES

Armstrong, Mark. "That's 'Sir' Mick Jagger to You." 17 June 2002. E! Online, Inc. Web. 17 June 2009 <http://www.eonline.com/News/Items/0,1,10110,00.html>.

For sites with no name of the database or online source:

Chachich, Mike. "Letters from Japan Vol 1" 30 March 1994. Web. 17 June 2009 <http://www.chachich.com/cgi-bin/catlfj?1>.

For sites with no author:

"The Science Behind the Sod." 13 June 2002. *MSU News Bulletin*. Web. 17 June 2009 <http://www.newsbulletin.msu.edu/june13/sod.html>.

For e-mail messages:

Daniel Akaka (senator@akaka.senate.gov). "Oceanic Exploration Grant." E-mail to Al Franken (senator@franken.senate.gov). 17 June 2009.

Parenthetical Documentation Parenthetical documentation is currently the most widely used form of documentation. To use this method to document the source of a quotation or an idea, you place a brief note identifying the source in parentheses immediately after the borrowed material. This type of note is called a parenthetical citation, and the act of placing such a note is called citing a source.

The first part of a parenthetical citation refers the reader to a source in your List of Works Cited or Works Consulted. For the reader's ease in finding the source in your bibliography, you must cite the work according to how it is listed in the bibliography.

EXAMPLES

For works listed by title, use an abbreviated title.

Sample bibliographic entry

"History." *Encyclopedia Britannica: Macropædia*. 1992 ed. Print.

Sample citation

Historians go through three stages in textual criticism ("History" 615).

For works listed by author or editor, use the author's or editor's last name.

Sample bibliographic entry

Brown, Dee. *Bury My Heart at Wounded Knee: An Indian History of the American West*. New York: Holt, 1970. Print.

Sample citation

"Big Eyes Schurz agreed to the arrest" (Brown 364).

When the listed name or title is stated in the text, cite only the page number.

Brown states that Big Eyes Schurz agreed to it (364).

For works of multiple volumes, use a colon after the volume number.

Sample bibliographic entry
Pepys, Samuel. *The Diary of Samuel Pepys.* Eds. Robert Latham and William Matthews. 10 vols. Berkeley: University of California Press, 1972. Print.

Sample citation
On the last day of 1665, Pepys took the occasion of the new year to reflect, but not to celebrate (6: 341–2).

For works quoted in secondary sources, use the abbreviation "qtd. in."

Sample citation
According to R. Bentley, "reason and the facts outweigh a hundred manuscripts" (qtd. in "History" 615).

For classic works that are available in various editions, give the page number from the edition you are using, followed by a semicolon; then identify the section of the work to help people with other editions find the reference.

Footnotes and Endnotes

In addition to parenthetical documentation, footnoting and endnoting are two other accepted methods.

Footnotes Instead of putting citations in parentheses within the text, you can place them at the bottom or foot of the page; hence the term *footnote.* In this system, a number or symbol is placed in the text where the parenthetical citation would otherwise be, and a matching number or symbol at the bottom of the page identifies the citation. This textbook, for example, uses numbered footnotes in its literature selections to define obscure words and to provide background information.

Endnotes Many books use endnotes instead of footnotes. Endnotes are like footnotes in that a number or symbol is placed within the text, but the matching citations are compiled at the end of the book, chapter, or article rather than at the foot of the page. Footnote and endnote entries begin with the author's (or editor's) name in its usual order (first name, then last) and include publication information and a page reference.

EXAMPLES

Book with one author
[1]Jean Paul-Sartre, *Being and Nothingness* (New York: The Citadel Press, 1966) 149–151. Print.

Book with one editor and no single author
[2]Shannon Ravenel, ed., *New Stories from the South: The Year's Best, 1992* (Chapel Hill, NC: Algonquin Books, 1992) 305. Print.

Magazine article
[3]Andrew Gore, "Road Test: The Apple Powerbook," *MacUser,* December 1996: 72. Print.

6.1 Workplace and Consumer Documents

Applied English is English in the world of work or business, or *practical* English. Entering a new school, writing a professional letter, applying for a job, reading an instructional manual—these are but a few of the many situations you may encounter that involve **workplace and consumer documents.** You can apply English skills to many real-world situations, using your reading, writing, speaking, and listening abilities to help you be successful in any field or occupation you choose to pursue.

6.2 Writing a Step-by-Step Procedure

A **step-by-step procedure** is a how-to or process piece that uses directions to teach someone something new. Written procedures include textual information and sometimes graphics. Spoken procedures can be given as oral demonstrations. They can include textual and graphic information and other props. Examples of step-by-step procedures include an oral demonstration of how to saddle a horse; instructions on how to treat a sprained ankle; a video showing how to do the perfect lay-up in basketball; and an interactive Internet site allowing the user to design and send a bouquet of flowers.

Guidelines for Writing a Step-by-Step Procedure

- Demonstrate the steps. If you are showing how to make something, create several different samples to show each step of the procedure. For example, if you are showing how to make a wooden basket, you might want to display the raw materials, the started basket, the basket halfway finished, and then the finished product.
- Be prepared. The best way to prevent problems is to anticipate and plan for them. Rehearse an oral demonstration several times. If you are preparing the procedure in written form, go through your directions as if you knew nothing about the process. Anticipate what it would be like to learn this procedure for the first time. See if you can follow your own directions, or have a friend work through the procedure and offer suggestions for improvement.
- Acknowledge mistakes. If you are sharing a procedure "live" as an oral demonstration and you can't talk around or correct a mistake, tell your audience what has gone wrong, and why. If you handle the situation in a calm, direct way, the audience may also learn from your mistake.
- Know your topic. The better you know it, the better you will be able to teach others.

6.3 Writing a Business Letter

A **business letter** is usually addressed to someone you do not know personally. Therefore, a formal tone is appropriate for such a letter. Following appropriate form is especially important when writing business letters. If you follow the correct form and avoid errors in spelling, grammar, usage, and mechanics, your letter will sound professional and make a good impression. Above the salutation, a business letter should contain the name and title of the person to whom you are writing and the name and address of that person's company or organization (see the model on the following page).

One common form for a business letter is the block form. In the **block form,** each part of the letter begins at the left margin. The parts are separated by line spaces.

Begin the salutation with the word *Dear,* followed by the courtesy or professional title used in the inside address, such as Ms., Mr., or Dr., and a colon. If you are not writing to a specific person, you may use a general salutation such as *Dear Sir or Madam.*

In the body of your letter, use a polite, formal tone and standard English. Make your points clearly, in as few words as possible.

End with a standard closing such as *Sincerely, Yours truly,* or *Respectfully yours.* Capitalize only the first word of the closing. Type your full name below the closing, leaving three or four blank lines for your signature. Sign your name below the closing in blue or black ink (never in red or green). Proofread your letter before you send it. Poor spelling, grammar, or punctuation can ruin an otherwise well-written business letter.

One of the most frequently used types of business letters is an **application letter,** which you would write to apply to a school or for a job. In an application letter, it is important to emphasize your knowledge about the business and the skills that you can bring to the position.

Guidelines for Writing a Business Letter

- Outline your main points before you begin.
- Word process your letter, if at all possible. Type or print it on clean 8 1/2" x 11" white or off-white paper. Use only one side of the paper.
- Use the block form or another standard business letter form.
- Single space, leaving a blank line between each part, including paragraphs.
- Use a standard salutation and a standard closing.
- Stick to the subject. State your main idea clearly at the beginning of the letter. Keep the letter brief and informative.
- Check your spelling, grammar, usage, and punctuation carefully.

6.4 Writing a Proposal

A **proposal** outlines a project that a person wants to complete. It presents a summary of an idea, the reasons why the idea is important, and an outline of how the project would be carried out. Because the proposal audience is people who can help carry out the proposal, a proposal is both informative and argumentative.

EXAMPLES

- You want funding for an art project that would benefit your community.
- Your student council proposes a clothing drive for disaster relief.
- You and a group of your friends want to help organize a summer program for teens your age.

Guidelines for Writing a Proposal

- Keep the tone positive, courteous, and respectful.
- State your proposal and rationale briefly and clearly.
- Give your audience all necessary information. A proposal with specific details makes it clear what you want approved, and why your audience—often a committee or someone in authority—should approve it.
- Use standard, formal English.
- Format your proposal with headings, lists, and schedules to make your proposed project easy to understand and approve.

6.5 Writing a Public Service Announcement

A **public service announcement,** or **PSA,** is a brief, informative article intended to be helpful to the community. PSAs are written by nonprofit organizations and concerned citizens for print in local newspapers, for broadcast by television and radio stations, and for publication on the Internet.

EXAMPLES

- an article by the American Cancer Society outlining early warning signs of cancer
- an announcement promoting Safety Week
- an informative piece telling coastal residents what to do during a hurricane

Guidelines for Writing a Public Service Announcement

- Know your purpose. What do you want your audience to know from reading or hearing your piece?
- State your information as objectively as possible.
- As with most informative writing, use the 5 *Ws* and an *H—who, what, where, why, when,* and *how*—questioning strategy to get your important information at the beginning of your story.
- Keep your announcement brief. Local media are more likely to publish or broadcast your piece if it is short and to the point.
- Include contact information in case the media representative has any questions. You might also include contact information in the PSA itself.
- Key or type your PSA in conventional manuscript form. Make sure the text is double-spaced and that you leave margins of at least an inch on all sides of the page.
- At the end of the PSA, key "END" to designate the end of the announcement.
- Be aware of print and broadcast deadlines and make sure your material is sent on time.

7.1 Verbal and Nonverbal Communication

When a person expresses meaning through words, he or she is using verbal communication. When a person expresses meaning without using words, for example by standing up straight or shaking his or her head, he or she is using nonverbal communication. When we speak to another person, we usually think that the meaning of what we say comes chiefly from the words we use. However, as much as sixty percent of the meaning of a message may be communicated nonverbally.

Elements of Verbal Communication

Element	Description	Guidelines for Speakers
Volume	Loudness or softness	Vary your volume, but make sure that you can be heard.
Melody, Pitch	Highness or lowness	Vary your pitch. Avoid speaking in a monotone (at a single pitch).
Pace	Speed	Vary the speed of your delivery to suit what you are saying.
Tone	Emotional quality	Suit your tone to your message, and vary it appropriately as you speak.
Enunciation	Clearness with which words are spoken	When speaking before a group, pronounce your words more precisely than you would in ordinary conversation.

Elements of Nonverbal Communication

Element	Description	Guidelines for Speakers
Eye contact	Looking audience members in the eye	Make eye contact regularly with people in your audience. Try to include all audience members.
Facial expression	Using your face to show your emotions	Use expressions to emphasize your message—raised eyebrows for a question, pursed lips for concentration, eyebrows lowered for anger, and so on.
Gesture	Meaningful motions of the arms and hands	Use gestures to emphasize points. Be careful, however, not to overuse gestures. Too many can be distracting.
Posture	Position of the body	Keep your spine straight and head high, but avoid appearing stiff. Stand with your arms and legs slightly open, except when adopting other postures to express particular emotions.
Proximity	Distance from audience	Keep the right amount of distance between yourself and the audience. You should be a comfortable distance away, but not so far away that the audience cannot hear you.

7.2 Listening Skills

Active Versus Passive Listening

Active listening requires skill and concentration. The mind of a good listener is focused on what a speaker is trying to communicate. In other words, an effective listener is an active listener. Ineffective listeners view listening as a passive activity, something that simply "happens" without any effort on their part. **Passive listening** is nothing more than hearing sounds. This type of listening can cause misunderstanding and miscommunication.

ADAPTING LISTENING SKILLS

Just as different situations require different types of listening, different tasks or goals may also require different listening strategies and skills.

Listening for Comprehension

Listening for comprehension means listening for information or ideas communicated by other people. For example, you are listening for comprehension when you try to understand directions to a friend's house or your teacher's explanation of how to conduct a classroom debate.

When listening for comprehension, your goal is to reach understanding, so it is important to recognize and remember the key information or ideas presented. Concentrate on getting the **main points or major ideas** of a message rather than all the supporting details. This can prevent you from becoming overwhelmed by the amount of information presented.

You might also use a technique called **clarifying and confirming** to help you better remember and understand information. This technique involves paraphrasing or repeating back to the speaker in your own words the key information presented to make sure that you have understood correctly. If the situation prevents you from using the technique—for instance, if there is no opportunity for you to respond directly to the speaker—it can still be helpful to rephrase the information in your own words in your head to help you remember and understand it.

Listening Critically

Listening critically means listening to a message in order to comprehend and evaluate it. When listening for comprehension, you usually assume that the information presented is true. Critical listening, on the other hand, includes **comprehending and judging** the arguments and appeals in a message in order to decide whether to accept or reject them. Critical listening is most useful when you encounter a persuasive message such as a sales pitch, advertisement, campaign speech, or news editorial.

When evaluating a persuasive message, you might consider the following:

- Is the speaker trustworthy and qualified to speak about this subject?
- Does the speaker present logical arguments supported by solid facts?
- Does the speaker use unproven assumptions to make a case?
- Does the speaker use questionable motivational appeals, such as appeals to fear or to prejudice?

These questions can help you decide whether or not to be convinced by a persuasive message.

Listening to Learn Vocabulary

Listening to learn vocabulary involves a very different kind of listening because the focus is on learning new words and how to use them properly. For instance, you have a conversation with someone who has a more advanced vocabulary and use this as an opportunity to learn new words. The key to listening in order to learn vocabulary is to **pay attention to how words are used in context.** Sometimes it is possible to figure out what an unfamiliar word means based simply on how the word is used in a sentence.

Once you learn a new word, try to use it several times so it becomes more familiar and you become comfortable using it. Also be sure to look up the word in a dictionary to find out whether it has other meanings or connotations of which you are not aware.

Listening for Appreciation

Listening for appreciation means listening purely for enjoyment or entertainment. You might listen appreciatively to a singer, a comedian, a storyteller, an acting company, or a humorous speaker. Appreciation is a very individual matter and there are no rules about how to appreciate something. However, as with all forms of listening, listening for appreciation requires attention and concentration.

7.3 Collaborative Learning and Communication

Collaboration is the act of working with one or more other people to achieve a goal. Many common learning situations involve collaboration.

- Participating in a small-group discussion
- Doing a small-group project
- Tutoring another student or being tutored
- Doing peer evaluation

Guidelines for Group Discussion

- **Listen actively.** Maintain eye contact with the speakers. Make notes on what they say. Mentally translate what they say into your own words. Think critically about whether you agree or disagree with each speaker, and why.
- **Be polite.** Wait for your turn to speak. Do not interrupt others. If your discussion has a group leader, ask to be recognized before speaking by raising your hand.
- **Participate in the discussion.** At appropriate times, make your own comments or ask questions of other speakers.
- **Stick to the discussion topic.** Do not introduce unrelated or irrelevant ideas.
- **Assign roles.** For a formal dicussion, choose a group leader to guide the discussion and a secretary to record the minutes (the main ideas and proposals made by group members). Also draw up an agenda before the discussion, listing items to be discussed.

Guidelines for Projects

- **Choose a group leader** to conduct the meetings of your project group.
- **Set a goal** for the group. This goal should be some specific outcome or set of outcomes that you want to bring about.
- **Make a list of tasks** that need to be performed.
- **Make a schedule** for completing the tasks, including dates and times for completion of each task.
- **Make an assignment sheet.** Assign certain tasks to particular group members. Be fair in distributing the work to be done.

- **Set times for future meetings** You might want to schedule meetings to evaluate your progress toward your goal as well as meetings to actually carry out specific tasks.
- **Meet to evaluate** your overall success when the project is completed. Also look at the individual contributions of each group member.

7.4 Asking and Answering Questions

There are many situations in which you will find it useful to ask questions of a speaker, or in which you will be asked questions about a presentation. Often a formal speech or presentation will be followed by a question-and-answer period. Keep the following guidelines in mind when asking or answering questions.

Guidelines for Asking and Answering Questions

- **Wait to be recognized.** In most cases, it is appropriate to raise your hand if you have a question and to wait for the speaker or moderator to call on you.
- **Make questions clear and direct.** The longer your question, the less chance a speaker will understand it. Make your questions short and to the point.
- **Do not debate or argue.** If you disagree with a speaker, the question-and-answer period is not the time to hash out an argument. Ask to speak with the speaker privately after the presentation is over, or agree on a later time and place to meet.
- **Do not take others' time.** Be courteous to other audience members and allow them time to ask questions. If you have a follow-up question, ask the speaker if you may proceed with your follow up.
- **Do not give a speech.** Sometimes audience members are more interested in expressing their own opinion than in asking the speaker a question. Do not give in to the temptation to present a speech of your own.
- **Come prepared for a question-and-answer period.** Although you can never predict the exact questions that people will ask you, you can anticipate many questions that are likely to be asked. Rehearse aloud your answers to the most difficult questions.
- **Be patient.** It may take some time for audience members to formulate questions in response to your speech. Give the audience a moment to do so. Don't run back to your seat the minute your speech is over, or if there is an awkward pause after you invite questions.
- **Be direct and succinct.** Be sure to answer the question directly as it has been asked, and to provide a short but clear answer.

7.5 Conducting an Interview

In an interview, you meet with someone and ask him or her questions. Interviewing experts is an excellent way to gain information about a particular topic. For example, if you are interested in writing about the art of making pottery, you might interview an art teacher, a professional potter, or the owner of a ceramics shop.

When planning an interview, you should do some background research on your subject and think carefully about questions you would like to ask. Write out a list of questions, including some about the person's background as well as about your topic. Other questions might occur to you as the interview proceeds, but it is best to be prepared. For guidelines on being a good listener, see Language Arts Handbook 7.2, Listening Skills, page 913. Guidelines for interviewing appear on the following page:

Guidelines for Conducting an Interview

- **Set up a time in advance.** Don't just try to work questions into a regular conversation. Set aside time to meet in a quiet place where both you and the person you are interviewing can focus on the interview.
- **Explain the purpose** of the interview. Be sure the person you are interviewing knows what you want to find out and why you need to know it. This will help him or her to answer your questions in a way that is more useful and helpful to you.
- **Ask mostly open-ended questions.** These are questions that allow the person you are interviewing to express a personal point of view. They cannot be answered with a simple "yes" or "no" nor a brief statement of fact. The following are all examples of open-ended questions:

  "Why did you become a professional potter?"
  "What is the most challenging thing about owning your own ceramics shop?"
  "What advice would you give to a beginning potter?"

  One of the most valuable questions to ask at the end of the interview is, "What would you like to add that I haven't asked about?" This can provide some of the most interesting or vital information of all.
- **Tape-record the interview** (if possible). Then you can review the interview at your leisure. Be sure to ask the person you are interviewing whether or not you can tape-record the session. If the person refuses, accept his or her decision.
- **Take notes** during the interview, whether or not you are also tape-recording it. Write down the main points and some key words to help you remember details. Record the person's most important statements word for word.
- **Clarify spelling and get permission** for quotations. Be sure to get the correct spelling of the person's name and to ask permission to quote his or her statements.
- **End the interview on time.** Do not extend the interview beyond the time limits of your appointment. The person you are interviewing has been courteous enough to give you his or her time. Return this courtesy by ending the interview on time, thanking the person for his or her help, and leaving.
- **Write up the results** of the interview as soon as possible after you conduct it. Over time, what seemed like a very clear note may become unclear or confusing. If you are unclear of something important that the person said, contact him or her and ask for clarification.
- **Send a thank-you note** to the person you interviewed as a follow-up.

7.6 Public Speaking

The nature of a speech, whether formal or informal, is usually determined by the situation or context in which it is presented. **Formal speeches** usually call for a greater degree of preparation, might require special attire such as a suit or dress, and are often presented to larger groups who attend specifically to hear the presentation. A formal speech situation might exist when presenting an assigned speech to classmates, giving a presentation to a community group or organization, or presenting a speech at an awards ceremony. **Informal speeches** are more casual and might include telling a story among friends, giving a pep talk to your team at halftime, or presenting a toast at the dinner table.

Types of Speeches

The following are four common types of speeches:

- **Extemporaneous:** a speech in which the speaker refers to notes occasionally and that has a specific purpose and message. An example would be a speech given at a city council meeting.

- **Informative:** a speech used to share new and useful information with the audience. Informative speeches are based on fact, not opinion. Examples would include a speech on how to do something or a speech about an event.
- **Persuasive:** a speech used to convince the audience to side with an opinion and adopt a plan. The speaker tries to persuade the audience to believe something, do something, or change their behavior. Persuasive speeches use facts and research to support, analyze, and sell an opinion and plan. Martin Luther King's famous "I Have a Dream" speech and Nelson Mandela's "Glory and Hope" speech are examples of persuasive speeches.
- **Commemorative:** a speech that honors an individual for outstanding accomplishments and exemplary character. Examples would be a speech honoring a historical figure, leader, teacher, athlete, relative, or celebrity.

Guidelines for Giving a Speech

A speech should always include a beginning, a middle, and an end. The **beginning,** or introduction, of your speech should spark the audience's interest, present your central idea, and briefly preview your main points. The **middle,** or body, of your speech should expand upon each of your main points in order to support the central idea. The **end,** or conclusion, of your speech should be memorable and should give your audience a sense of completion.

- **Be sincere and enthusiastic.** Feel what you are speaking about. Apathy is infectious and will quickly spread to your audience.
- **Maintain good but relaxed posture.** Don't slouch or lean. It's fine to move around a bit; it releases normal nervous tension. Keep your hands free to gesture naturally instead of holding on to note cards, props, or the podium so much that you will "tie up" your hands.
- **Speak slowly.** Oral communication is more difficult than written language and visual images for audiences to process and understand. Practice pausing. Don't be afraid of silence. Focus on communicating with the audience. By looking for feedback from the audience, you will be able to pace yourself appropriately.
- **Maintain genuine eye contact.** Treat the audience as individuals, not as a mass of people. Look at individual faces.
- **Speak in a genuine, relaxed, conversational tone.** Don't act or stiffen up. Just be yourself.
- **Communicate.** Focus on conveying your message, not "getting through" the speech. Focus on communicating with the audience, not speaking at or to it.
- **Use strategic pauses.** Pause briefly before proceeding to the next major point, before direct quotations, and to allow important or more complex bits of information to sink in.
- **Remain confident and composed.** Remember that listeners are generally "for you" while you are speaking, and signs of nervousness are usually undetectable. To overcome initial nervousness, take two or three deep breaths as you are stepping up to speak.

7.7 Oral Interpretation

Oral interpretation is the process of presenting a dramatic reading of a literary work or group of works. The presentation should be sufficiently dramatic to convey to the audience a sense of the particular qualities of the work. Here are the steps you need to follow to prepare and present an oral interpretation:

Guidelines for Oral Interpretation

1. **Choose a cutting,** which may be a single piece; a selection from a single piece; or several short, related pieces on a single topic or theme.
2. **Write** the introduction and any necessary transitions. The introduction should mention the name of each piece, the author, and, if appropriate, the translator. It should also present the overall topic or theme of the interpretation. Transitions should introduce and connect the parts of the interpretation.
3. **Rehearse,** using appropriate variations in volume, pitch, pace, stress, tone, gestures, facial expressions, and body language. If your cutting contains different voices (a narrator's voice and characters' voices, for example), distinguish them. Try to make your verbal and nonverbal expression mirror what the piece is saying. However, avoid movement—that's for drama. Practice in front of an audience or mirror, or use a video camera or tape recorder.
4. **Present** your oral interpretation. Before actually presenting your interpretation, relax and adopt a confident attitude. If you begin to feel stage fright, try to concentrate on the work you are presenting and the audience, not on yourself.

Interpreting Poetry

Here are some additional considerations as you prepare to interpret a poem. The way you prepare your interpretation of a poem will depend on whether the poem you have chosen is a lyric poem, a narrative poem, or a dramatic poem.

- A **lyric poem** has a single speaker who reports his or her own emotions.
- A **narrative poem** tells a story. Usually a narrative poem has lines belonging to the narrator, or person who is telling the story. The narrator may or may not take part in the action.
- A **dramatic poem** contains characters who speak. A dramatic poem may be lyrical, in which characters simply report emotions, or narrative, which tells a story. A dramatic monologue presents a single speaker at a moment of crisis or self-revelation and may be either lyrical or narrative.

Before attempting to dramatize any poem, read through the poem carefully several times. Make sure that you understand it well. To check your understanding, try to paraphrase the poem, or restate its ideas, line by line, in your own words.

7.8 Telling a Story

A story or narrative is a series of events linked together in some meaningful fashion. We use narratives constantly in our daily lives: to make a journal entry, to tell a joke, to report a news story, to recount a historical event, to record a laboratory experiment, and so on. When creating a narrative, consider all of the following elements:

Guidelines for Storytelling

- **Decide on your purpose.** Every story has a point or purpose. It may be simply to entertain or to share a personal experience, but it may have a moral or lesson.
- **Select a focus.** The focus for your narrative will depend largely on your purpose in telling it.
- **Choose your point of view.** The storyteller or narrator determines the point of view from which the story will be told. You can choose to speak in the *first person,* either as a direct participant in the events or as an observer (real or imagined) who witnessed the events firsthand, or in the *third person* voice to achieve greater objectivity.

- **Determine sequence of events.** The sequence of events refers to the order in which they are presented. Although it might seem obvious that stories should "begin at the beginning," this is not always the best approach. Some narratives begin with the turning point of the story to create a sense of drama and to capture the listeners' interest. Others begin at the end of the story and present the events leading up to this point in hindsight. Wherever you choose to begin the story, your narrative should present events in a logical fashion and establish a clear sense of direction for your listeners.
- **Determine duration of events.** Duration refers to how long something lasts. Everyone has experienced an event that seemed to last for hours, when in reality it only took minutes to occur. A good storyteller can likewise manipulate the duration of events in order to affect the way listeners experience them.
- **Select details carefully.** Make them consistent with your focus and make sure they are necessary to your purpose. A well-constructed story should flow smoothly, and should not get bogged down by irrelevant or unnecessary detail. Details can also establish the tone and style of the story and affect how listeners react to the events being described.
- **Choose characters.** All stories include characters who need to be developed so that they become real for listeners. Try to provide your listeners with vivid, concrete descriptions of the mental and physical qualities of important characters in the story. Remember that listeners need to understand and relate to the characters in order to appreciate their behavior.
- **Create dialogue.** Although it is possible to tell a story in which the characters do not speak directly, conversation and dialogue help to add life to a story. As with detail, dialogue should be used carefully. It is important that dialogue sound authentic, relate to the main action of the story, and advance the narrative.

7.9 Participating in a Debate

A debate is a contest in which two people or groups of people defend opposite sides of a proposition in an attempt to convince a judge or an audience to agree with their views. Propositions are statements of fact, value, or policy that usually begin with the word "resolved." The following are examples of typical propositions for debate:

RESOLVED	That lie detector tests are inaccurate. (proposition of fact)
RESOLVED	That imagination is more important than knowledge. (proposition of value)
RESOLVED	That Congress should prohibit the sale of handguns to private citizens. (proposition of policy)

The two sides in a debate are usually called the affirmative and the negative. The affirmative takes the "pro" side of the debate and argues in favor of the proposition, whereas the negative takes the "con" side and argues against the proposition. Using a single proposition to focus the debate ensures that the two sides argue or clash over a common topic. This allows the participants in the debate to develop their logic and ability to argue their positions persuasively.

Guidelines for Participating in a Debate

- **Be prepared.** In a debate, it will never be possible to anticipate all the arguments your opponent might make. However, by conducting careful and thorough research on both sides of the issue, you should be able to prepare for the most likely arguments you will

SPEAKING & LISTENING

encounter. You can prepare briefs or notes on particular issues in advance of the debate to save yourself preparation time during the debate.

- **Be organized.** Because a debate involves several speeches that concern the same basic arguments or issues, it is important that you remain organized during the debate. When attacking or refuting an opponent's argument, or when advancing or defending your own argument, be sure to follow a logical organizational pattern to avoid confusing the audience or the other team.
- **Take notes** by turning a long sheet of paper sideways. Draw one column for each speaker, taking notes on each speech going down one column, and recording notes about a particular argument or issue across the page as it is discussed in each successive speech.
- **Be audience-centered.** In arguing with your opponent, it is easy to forget the goal of the debate: to persuade your audience that your side of the issue is correct.
- **Prepare in advance** for the most likely arguments your opponents, will raise. Use time sparingly to organize your materials and think of responses to unanticipated arguments. Save time for the end of the debate, during rebuttal speeches, when it will be more valuable.

7.10 Preparing a Multimedia Presentation

Whether you use a simple overhead projector and transparencies or a PowerPoint presentation that involves graphics, video, and sound, multimedia technology can add an important visual element to a presentation. Consider the following guidelines to create a multimedia presentation:

Guidelines for a Multimedia Presentation

- **Use effective audiovisuals** that enhance understanding. The multimedia elements should add to the verbal elements, not distract from them. Be sure the content of the presentation is understandable, and that the amount of information—both verbal and visual—will not overwhelm audience members.
- **Make sure the presentation is clearly audible and visible.** Video clips or graphics may appear blurry on a projection screen or may not be visible to audience members in the back or on the sides of the room. Audio clips may sound muffled or may echo in a larger room or a room with different acoustics. When creating a multimedia presentation, be sure the presentation can be easily seen and heard from all parts of the room.
- **Become familiar with the equipment.** Well before the presentation, be sure you know how to operate the equipment you will need, that you know how to troubleshoot if the equipment malfunctions, and that the equipment you will use during the presentation is the same as that which you practiced with.
- **Check the room** to be sure it can accommodate your needs. Once you know where you will make your presentation, be sure the necessary electrical outlets and extension cords are available, that lights can be dimmed or turned off as needed, that the room can accommodate the equipment you will use, and so on.
- **Rehearse with the equipment.** Make sure that you can operate the equipment while speaking at the same time. Be sure that the multimedia elements are coordinated with other parts of your presentation. If you will need to turn the lights off in the room, make sure you can operate the equipment in the dark and can still see your note cards.

8.1 Preparing for Tests

Tests are a common part of school life. You take tests in your classes to show what you have learned in each class. In addition, you might have to take one or more standardized tests each year. Standardized tests measure your skills against local, state, or national standards and may determine whether you graduate, what kind of job you can get, or which college you can attend. Learning test-taking strategies will help you succeed on the tests you are required to take.

The following guidelines will help you to prepare for and take tests on the material you have covered in class.

Preparing for a Test

- **Know what will be covered on the test.** If you have questions about what will be covered, ask your teacher.
- **Make a study plan** to allow yourself time to go over the material. Avoid last-minute cramming.
- **Review the subject matter.** Use the graphic organizers and notes you made as you read as well as notes you took in class. Review any study questions given by your teacher.
- **Make lists** of important names, dates, definitions, or events. Ask a friend or family member to quiz you on them.
- **Try to predict questions** that may be on the test. Make sure you can answer them.
- **Get plenty of sleep** the night before the test. Eat a nutritious breakfast on the morning of the test.

Taking a Test

- **Survey the test** to see how long it is and what types of questions are included.
- **Read all directions and questions carefully.** Make sure you know exactly what to do.
- **Plan your time.** Answer easy questions first. Allow extra time for complicated questions. If a question seems too difficult, skip it and go back to it later. Work quickly, but do not rush.
- **Save time for review.** Once you have finished, look back over the test. Double-check your answers, but do not change answers too readily. Your first responses are often correct.

8.2 Strategies for Taking Standardized Tests

Standardized tests are given to large groups of students in a school district, a state, or a country. Statewide tests measure how well students are meeting the learning standards the state has set. Other tests, such as the SAT (Scholastic Aptitude Test) or ACT (American College Test), are used to help determine admission to colleges and universities. Others must be taken to enter certain careers. These tests are designed to measure overall ability or skills acquired so far. Learning how to take standardized tests will help you to achieve your goals.

You can get better at answering standardized test questions by practicing the types of questions that will be on the test. Use the Test Practice Workshop questions in this book and other sample questions your teacher gives you to practice. Think aloud with a partner or small group about how you would answer each question. Notice how other students tackle the questions and learn from what they do.

In addition, remember these points:

- **Rule out some choices** when you are not sure of the answer. Then guess from the remaining possibilities.
- **Skip questions that seem too difficult** and go back to them later. Be aware, however, that most tests allow you to go back only within a section.
- **Follow instructions exactly.** The test monitor will read instructions to you, and instructions may also be printed in your test booklet. Make sure you know what to do.

8.3 Answering Objective Questions

An **objective question** has a single correct answer. The following chart describes the kinds of questions you may see on objective tests. It also gives you strategies for tackling each kind of question.

Description	Guidelines
True/False You are given a statement and asked to tell whether the statement is true or false.	• If any part of a statement is false, then the statement is false. • Words like *all, always, never,* and *every* often appear in false statements. • Words like *some, usually, often,* and *most* often appear in true statements. • If you do not know the answer, guess. You have a 50/50 chance of being right.
Matching You are asked to match items in one column with items in another column.	• Check the directions. See if each item is used only once. Also check to see if some are not used at all. • Read all items before starting. • Match those items you know first. • Cross out items as you match them.
Short Answer You are asked to answer the question with a word, phrase, or sentence.	• Read the directions to find out if you are required to answer in complete sentences. • Use correct spelling, grammar, punctuation, and capitalization. • If you cannot think of the answer, move on. Something in another question might remind you of the answer.

8.4 Answering Multiple-Choice Questions

On many standardized tests, questions are multiple choice and have a single correct answer. The guidelines below will help you answer these kinds of questions effectively.

- **Read each question carefully.** Pay special attention to any words that are bolded, italicized, written in all capital letters, or otherwise emphasized.
- **Read all choices** before selecting an answer.
- **Eliminate** any answers that do not make sense, that disagree with what you remember from reading a passage, or that seem too extreme. Also, if two answers have exactly the same meaning, you can eliminate both.
- **Beware of distractors.** These are incorrect answers that look attractive because they are partially correct. They might contain a common misunderstanding, or they might apply the right information in the wrong way. Distractors are based on common mistakes students make.
- **Fill in circles completely** on your answer sheet when you have selected your answer.

8.5 Answering Reading Comprehension Questions

Reading comprehension questions ask you to read a passage and answer questions about it. These questions measure how well you perform the essential reading skills. Many of the Reading Assessment questions that follow each literature selection in this book are reading comprehension questions. Use them to help you learn how to answer these types of questions correctly. Work through each question with a partner using a "think aloud." Say out loud how you are figuring out the answer. Talk about how you can eliminate incorrect answers and determine the correct choice. You may want to make notes as you eliminate answers. By practicing this thinking process with a partner, you will be more prepared to use it silently when you have to take a standardized test.

The following steps will help you answer the reading comprehension questions on standardized tests.

- **Preview the passage and questions** and predict what the text will be about.
- **Use the reading strategies** you have learned to read the passage. Mark the text and make notes in the margins.
- **Reread the first question carefully.** Make sure you know exactly what it is asking.
- **Read the answers.** If you are sure of the answer, select it and move on. If not, go on to the next step.
- **Scan the passage** to look for key words related to the question. When you find a key word, slow down and read carefully.
- **Answer the question** and go on to the next one. Answer each question in this way.

8.6 Answering Synonym and Antonym Questions

Synonym or antonym questions give you a word and ask you to select the word that has the same meaning (for a synonym) or the opposite meaning (for an antonym). You must select the best answer even if none is exactly correct. For this type of question, you should consider all the choices to see which is best. Always notice whether you are looking for a synonym or an antonym. You will usually find both among the answers.

8.7 Answering Sentence Completion Questions

Sentence completion questions present you with a sentence that has one or two words missing. You must select the word or pair of words that best completes the sentence. The key to questions with two words missing is to make sure that both parts of the answer you have selected work well in the sentence.

8.8 Answering Constructed-Response Questions

In addition to multiple-choice questions, many standardized tests include **constructed-response questions** that require you to write essay answers in the test booklet. Constructed-response questions might ask you to identify key ideas or examples from the text by writing a sentence about each. In other cases, you will be asked to write a paragraph in response to a question about the selection and to use specific details from the passage to support your answer.

Other constructed-response questions ask you to apply information or ideas from a text in a new way. Another question might ask you to use information from the text in a particular imaginary situation. As you answer these questions, remember that you are being evaluated based on your understanding of the text. Although these questions may offer opportunities to be creative, you should still include ideas, details, and examples from the passage you have just read.

The following tips will help you answer constructed-response questions effectively:

- **Skim the questions first.** Predict what the passage will be about.
- **Use reading strategies** as you read. Underline information that relates to the questions and make notes. After you have finished reading, you can decide which of the details you have gathered to use in your answers.
- **List the most important points** to include in each answer. Use the margins of your test booklet or a piece of scrap paper.
- **Number the points** you have listed to show the order in which they should be included.
- **Draft your answer to fit** in the space provided. Include as much detail as possible in the space you have.
- **Revise and proofread** your answers as you have time.

8.9 Answering Essay Questions

An essay question asks you to write an answer that shows what you know about a particular subject. A simplified writing process like the one below will help you tackle questions like this.

1. Analyze the Question

Essay questions contain clues about what is expected of you. Sometimes you will find key words that will help you determine exactly what is being asked. See the chart below for some typical key words and their meanings.

Key Words for Essay Questions	
analyze; identify	break into parts, and describe the parts and how they are related
compare	tell how two or more subjects are similar; in some cases, also mention how they are different
contrast	tell how two or more subjects are different from each other
describe	give enough facts about or qualities of a subject to make it clear to someone who is unfamiliar with it
discuss	provide an overview and analysis; use details for support
evaluate; argue	judge an idea or concept, telling whether you think it is good or bad, or whether you agree or disagree with it
explain	make a subject clearer, providing supporting details and examples
interpret	tell the meaning and importance of an event or concept
justify	explain or give reasons for decisions; be persuasive
prove	provide factual evidence or reasons for a statement
summarize	state only the main points of an event, concept, or debate

2. Plan Your Answer

As soon as the essay prompt is clear to you, collect and organize your thoughts about it. First, gather ideas using whatever method is most comfortable for you. If you don't immediately have ideas, try freewriting for five minutes. When you **freewrite,** you write whatever comes into your head without letting your hand stop moving. You might also gather ideas in a cluster chart like the one below. Then, organize the ideas you came up with. A simple outline or chart can help.

3. Write Your Answer

Start with a clear thesis statement in your opening paragraph. Your **thesis statement** is a single sentence that sums up your answer to the essay question. Then follow your organizational plan to provide support for your thesis. Devote one paragraph to each major point of support for your thesis. Use plenty of details as evidence for each point. Write quickly and keep moving. Don't spend too much time on any single paragraph, but try to make your answer as complete as possible. End your essay with a concluding sentence that sums up your major points.

4. Revise Your Answer

Make sure you have answered all parts of the question and included everything you were asked to include. Check to see that you have supplied enough details to support your thesis. Check for errors in grammar, spelling, punctuation, and paragraph breaks. Make corrections to your answer.

ACT. An **act** is a major division of a play. There are two acts in Israel Horowitz's *A Christmas Carol* (Unit 7).

ALLEGORY. An **allegory** is a work in which characters, events, or settings symbolize, or represent, something else. Olivia E. Coolidge's retelling of the Greek myth "Phaëthon, Son of Apollo" (Unit 8) is an allegory.

ALLITERATION. **Alliteration** is the repetition of initial consonant sounds. Though alliteration usually refers to sounds at the beginnings of words, it can also be used to refer to sounds within words. In Galway Kinnell's poem "Blackberry Eating" (Unit 5), for example, the s sound is repeated several times:

> I squeeze, squinch open, and splurge.
> in the silent, startled, icy, black language
> of blackberry-eating in late September.

ALLUSION. An **allusion** is a reference to a well-known person, event, object, or work from history or literature. For example, the title of Borden Deal's story "Antaeus" (Unit 2) is a literary allusion to the Greek myth of Antaeus, a giant who was extremely powerful as long as his feet touched the earth, but became weak once he was lifted off the ground.

ANALOGY. An **analogy** is a comparison of two things that are alike in some ways but otherwise quite different. Often an analogy explains or describes something unfamiliar by comparing it to something more familiar.

ANECDOTE. An **anecdote** is usually a short account of an interesting, amusing, or biographical incident. Anecdotes are sometimes used in nonfiction writing as examples to help support an idea or opinion. In "Names/Nobres" (Unit 3), Julia Alveraz tells several anecdotes to underscore the idea that a person's name can be important to his or her identity.

ANTAGONIST. An **antagonist** is a character or force in a literary work that is in conflict with a main character, or protagonist. The antagonist of Tomás Rivera's story "The Portrait" (Unit 1), is the portrait salesman who has cheated everyone out of their money. *See* Character.

ARTICLE. An **article** is an informational piece of writing about a particular topic, issue, events, or series of events. Articles usually appear in newspapers, professional journals, or magazines, or on websites. An *editorial* is an article meant to give an opinion. A *review* is an article that is a critical evaluation of a work, such as a book, play, movie, or musical performance. "The Size of Things" by Robert Jastrow (Unit 4) is an example of a familiar type of news—a science article.

ASSONANCE. **Assonance** is the repetition of vowel sounds in stressed syllables. An example is the repetition of the long *i* sound and the short *a* sound in the following line from Galway Kinnell's poem "Blackberry Eating" (Unit 5):

> the fat, overripe, icy, black blackberries.

ATMOSPHERE. *See* Mood.

AUTOBIOGRAPHY. An **autobiography** is the story of a person's life, written by that person. *Off the Court* by Arthur Ashe (Unit 3) is an example of an autobiography. *See* Biography *and* Memoir.

BALLAD. A **ballad** is a poem that tells a story and is written in four- to six-line stanzas, usually meant to be sung. Most ballads have regular rhythms and rhyme schemes and feature a refrain, or repetition of lines.

BIAS. **Bias** is a personal judgment about something, or a mental leaning in one direction or another.

BIOGRAPHY. A **biography** is the story of a person's life, told by someone other than that person. Milton Meltzer's "Elizabeth I" (Unit 3) is a biography. *See* Autobiography.

CHARACTER. A **character** is an individual that takes part in the action of a literary work. A character is usually a person but may also be a personified plant, animal, object, or imaginary creature. The main character, or protagonist, has the central role in a work and is in conflict with the antagonist.

Characters can also be classified in other ways. *Major characters* play significant roles in a work, and *minor characters* play lesser roles. A *flat character* shows only one quality, or character trait. Tokubei, the wealthy merchant, in *The Inn of Lost Time* by Lensey Namioka (Unit 1) is a flat character. A *round character* shows the multiple character traits of a real person. A *static character* does not change during the course of the action. A *dynamic character* does change.

CHARACTERIZATION. **Characterization** is the act of creating or describing a character. Writers create characters using three major techniques: showing what characters say, do, or think; showing what other characters say or think about them; and describing what physical features, dress, and personalities the characters display. The first two methods may be considered examples of *indirect characterization,* in which the writer *shows* what a character is like and allows the reader to judge the character. The third technique is considered *direct characterization,* in which the writer *tells* what the character is like. *See* Character.

CHORUS. In drama, a **chorus** is a group of actors who speak directly to the audience between scenes, commenting on the action of the play. In classical Greek drama, the chorus conveyed its message through a series of *odes,* or serious poems, which it sang throughout the play.

CHRONOLOGICAL ORDER. When telling a story in **chronological order,** the writer unfolds events in the order in which they occurred.

CLIMAX. The **climax** is the high point of interest and suspense in a literary work. The term also is sometimes used to describe the turning point of the action in a story or play, the point at which the rising action ends and the falling action begins. The climax in Ernest Hemingway's "A Day's Wait" (Unit 1) occurs when the narrator comes home to find Schatz causing a commotion. He refuses to let anyone into his room and asks his father how long he has to live. *See* Plot.

COMEDY. A **comedy** is any lighthearted or humorous literary work with a happy ending, especially one prepared for the stage or the screen. Comedy is often contrasted with tragedy, in which the hero meets an unhappy fate. Comedies typically show characters with human limitations, faults, and misunderstandings. The action in a comedy usually progresses from initial order to a humorous misunderstanding or confusion and back to order again. Standard elements of comedy include mistaken identities, word play, satire, and exaggerated characters and events. "A Defenseless Creature" by Neil Simon (Unit 7) is a comedy. *See* Tragedy.

CONFLICT. A **conflict** is a struggle between two forces in a literary work. A plot introduces a conflict, develops it, and eventually resolves it. There are two types of conflict: external and internal. In an *external conflict,* the main character struggles against another character, against the forces of nature, against society or social norms, or against fate. In an *internal conflict,* the main character struggles against some element within himself or herself. In Ray Bradbury's "The Foghorn" (Unit 1), the conflict is external, between the main characters and a force of nature, a strange sea creature attracted by the sound of the foghorn. *See* Plot.

CONNOTATION. The **connotation** of a word is the set of ideas or emotional associations it suggests, in addition to its actual meaning. For example, the word *inexpensive* has a positive connotation, whereas the word *cheap* has a negative connotation, even though both words refer to "low cost." *See* Denotation.

CONSONANCE. **Consonance** is a kind of rhyme in which the consonant sounds of two words match, but the preceding vowel sounds do not, as in the words *wind* and *sound.* In Diana Rivera's poem "Under the Apple Tree" (Unit 5) the author repeats the "ks" sound in the words "trunks," "necks," "strokes," and "specks."

CONTEXT. The conditions under which a literary work occurs make up its **context.** Context is closely related to setting, but focuses more on the environment of the time and place. Two common types of context include historical and cultural.

COUPLET. A **couplet** is two lines of verse that rhyme. These lines from Robert Frost's "Once by the Pacific" (Unit 6) provide an example:

> There would be more than ocean-water
> broken
> Before God's last *Put out the Light* was
> spoken.

A *closed couplet* is a pair of rhyming lines that present a complete statement. A pair of rhyming iambic pentameter lines is also known as a *heroic couplet.*

DENOTATION. The **denotation** of a word is its dictionary meaning without any emotional associations. For example, the words *dirt* and *soil* share a common denotation. However, dirt has a negative connotation of uncleanliness, whereas soil does not. *See* Connotation.

DÉNOUEMENT. *See* Plot.

DESCRIPTION. A **description** is a picture in words. *Descriptive writing* is used to portray a character, an object, or a scene. Descriptions include *sensory details*—words and phrases that describe how things look, sound, smell, taste, or feel. In her poem "How to Eat a Poem" (Unit 5), Eve Merriam appeals to the sense of touch when she compares reading a poem to eating something juicy:

> Pick it up with your fingers and
> lick the juice
> that may run down your chin.

DIALECT. A **dialect** is a version of a language spoken by the people of a particular place, time, or social group. A *regional dialect* is one spoken in a particular place. A *social dialect* is one spoken by members of a particular social group or class. The following is an example of dialect from Toni Cade Bambara's story "The War of the Wall" (Unit 1):

> "Watcha got there, sweetheart?" he asked the twin with the plate.
> "Suppah," she said all soft and countrylike.

DIALOGUE. **Dialogue** is conversation between two or more people or characters. Plays are made up of dialogue and stage directions. Fictional works are made up of dialogue, narration, and description. When dialogue is included in fiction or nonfiction, the speaker's words are enclosed in quotation marks.

DICTION. **Diction,** when applied to writing, refers to the author's choice of words. Much of a writer's style is determined by his or her diction, the types of words that he or she chooses. *See* Style.

DRAMA. A **drama** is a story told through characters played by actors. Dramas are divided into segments called *acts.* The script of a drama is made up of dialogue spoken by the characters and stage directions. Because it is meant to be performed before an audience, drama features elements such as lighting, costumes, makeup, properties, set pieces, music, sound effects, and the movements and expressions of actors. Two major types of drama are comedy and tragedy. *See* Comedy, Dialogue, Stage Directions, *and* Tragedy.

DRAMATIC IRONY. *See* Irony.

DRAMATIC MONOLOGUE. A **dramatic monologue** is a poem written in the form of a speech of a single character to an imaginary audience.

DRAMATIC POEM. A **dramatic poem** relies heavily on literary devices such as *monologue* (speech by a single character) or *dialogue* (conversation involving two or more characters). Often dramatic poems tell stories. Types of dramatic poetry include the dramatic monologue and the soliloquy. *See* Dramatic Monologue *and* Soliloquy.

EPIC. An **epic** is a long story, often told in verse, involving heroes and gods. Grand in length and scope, an epic provides a portrait of an entire culture, of the legends, beliefs, values, laws, arts, and ways of life of a people. *The Odyssey* and *Beowulf* are examples of epics.

EPIPHANY. An **epiphany** is a moment of sudden insight in which the nature of a person, thing, or situation is revealed.

ESSAY. An **essay** is a short nonfiction work that presents a single main idea, or *thesis,* about a particular topic.

- An *informative*, or *expository*, *essay* explores a topic with the goal of informing or enlightening the reader.
- An *argumentative*, or *persuasive*, *essay* aims to persuade the reader to accept a certain point of view. Louis L'Amour's "The Eternal Frontier" (Unit 3) is an example of an argumentative essay.
- A *personal essay* explores a topic related to the life or interests of the writer. Personal essays are characterized by an intimate and informal style or tone. "Fish Cheeks" (Unit 3) is a personal essay by Amy Tan.

EXPOSITION. In a plot, the **exposition** provides background information, often about the characters, setting, or conflict. Exposition is also another word for *informative*, or *expository*, *writing,* the type of writing that aims to inform or explain. *See* Plot.

EXTENDED METAPHOR. An **extended metaphor** is a point-by-point presentation of one thing as though it were another. The description is meant as an implied comparison, inviting the reader to associate the thing being described with something that is quite different from it.

FABLE. **Fables** are brief stories, often with animal characters, told to express morals. Famous fables include those of Aesop retold by James Reeves and Joseph Jacobs in Unit 8.

FALLING ACTION. *See* Plot.

FANTASY. A fantasy is a literary work that contains highly unrealistic elements. Included as fantasy are stories that resemble fairy tales, involve the supernatural, or have imaginary characters and settings. Joan Aiken's "The Serial Garden" (Unit 1) contains elements of fantasy. *See* Magical Realism *and* Science Fiction.

FAIRY TALES. **Fairy tales** are stories that deal with mischievous spirits and other supernatural occurrences, often in medieval settings.

FICTION. **Fiction** is any work of prose that tells an invented or imaginary story. The primary forms of fiction are the novel and the short story. *See* Novel *and* Short Story.

FIGURATIVE LANGUAGE. **Figurative language** is writing or speech meant to be understood imaginatively instead of literally. Many writers, especially poets, use figurative language to help readers to see things in new ways. Types of figurative language, or **figures of speech,** include *hyperbole, metaphor, personification, simile,* and *understatement.*

FIGURES OF SPEECH. *See* Figurative Language.

FLASHBACK. A **flashback** interrupts the chronological sequence of a literary work and presents an event that occurred earlier. Writers use flashbacks most often to provide background information about characters or situations. In the short story "The Inn of Lost Time" by Lensey Namioka (Unit 1), Zenta remembers the time when he and the wealthy merchant Tokubei stopped their journey at an inn where the innkeeper tried to swindle the merchant. This flashback helps explain Zenta's wariness toward his current hosts.

FOLK LITERATURE. **Folk literature,** or *folklore,* refers to a body of cultural knowledge and beliefs passed from one generation to the next, both orally and in writing. Much of folk literature originated as part of the *oral tradition,* or the passing of a work, an idea, or a custom by word of mouth from generation to generation.

FOLK TALE. A **folk tale** is a brief story passed by word of mouth from generation to generation. Types of folk tales include fairy tales, tall tales, parables, and fables. Zora Neale Hurston's retelling of the African-American folk tale "How the Snake Got Poison" (Unit 8) is an example of a folk tale that offers an explaination for a feature in the natural world.

FOOT. *See* Meter.

FORESHADOWING. **Foreshadowing** is the act of presenting hints to events that will occur later in a story. In Joseph Bruchac's "Jed's Grandfather" (Unit 2), the main character's dreams suggest coming difficulties.

FREE VERSE. **Free verse** is poetry that does not use regular rhyme, meter, or stanza division. Free verse may contain irregular line breaks and sentence fragments and tends to mimic the rhythm of ordinary speech. Most contemporary poetry is written in free verse. "Unfolding Bud" by Naoshi Koriyama (Unit 5) is an example of poem written in free verse.

GENRE. A **genre** (zhän′ rə) is a type or category of literary composition. Major genres of literature include fiction, nonfiction, poetry, and drama. *See* Drama, Fiction, Poetry, *and* Prose.

HAIKU. A **haiku** is a traditional Japanese three-line poem containing five syllables in the first line, seven in the second, and five again in the third. The syllable pattern is often lost when a haiku is translated into English. A haiku presents a single vivid image, often of nature or the seasons, intended to evoke in the reader a specific emotional or spiritual response.

HERO. A **hero** is a character whose actions are inspiring and courageous. In early literature, a hero was often part divine and had remarkable abilities, such as magical power, superhuman strength, or great courage. Phaëthon in Olivia Coolidge's "Phaëthon, Son of Apollo" (Unit 8) is one such hero. In contemporary literature, the term *hero* often refers to any main character. The mongoose Rikki-Tikki-Tavi is the hero of Rudyard Kipling's story "Rikki-Tikki-Tavi" (Unit 1).

HYPERBOLE. A **hyperbole** (hī pür′ bə lē′) is an overstatement, or exaggeration, used for dramatic effect.

IAMB. *See* Meter.

IAMBIC PENTAMETER. *See* Meter.

IDIOM. An **idiom** is an expression that cannot be understood from the meanings of its separate words but must be learned as whole.

IMAGE. An **image** is a picture formed in the mind of a reader.

IMAGERY. **Imagery** is language that creates pictures by appealing to the senses of sight, sound, touch, taste, and smell. *See* Description *and* Figurative Language.

INFORMATIONAL TEXT. An **informational text** is a form of nonfiction that aims to convey or explain information. Examples of informational texts include reference materials, articles, editorials, and how-to writing.

IRONY. **Irony** is the difference between appearance and reality—in other words, what seems to be and what really is. Types of irony include the following:

dramatic irony, in which something is known by the reader or audience but unknown to the characters; *verbal irony,* in which a character says one thing but means another; and *irony of situation,* in which an event occurs that violates the expectations of the characters, the reader, or the audience. In Elizabeth Bishop's "The Filling Station" (Unit 6), the station and its workers are dirty and greasy, but we learn by the poet's descriptions of details of extraneous items of decoration that the station is quite cared for and loved.

LEGEND. A **legend** is a story that is passed down through generations and is often based on real events or characters from the past. Unlike myths, legends are usually considered to be historical; however, they may contain elements that are fantastic or unverifiable.

LYRIC POEM. A **lyric poem** is a highly musical type of poetry that expresses the emotions of a speaker. Lyric poems are often contrasted with narrative poems, which have storytelling as their main purpose. "Gold" by Pat Mora (Unit 5) is a lyric poem. *See* Poetry.

MEMOIR. A **memoir** is a type of autobiography that focuses on one incident or period in a person's life. Annie Dillard's *An American Childhood* (Unit 3) is a memoir about her childhood. *See* Autobiography.

METAPHOR. A **metaphor** is a comparison in which one thing is spoken or written about as if it were another. This figure of speech invites the reader to make a comparison between the writer's actual subject, the *tenor* of the metaphor, and another thing to which the subject is likened, the *vehicle* of the metaphor. In "Feel Like a Bird" (Unit 5), May Swenson uses the following metaphors to describe a bird by comparing it to a person:

lands on star-toes
finger-beak in
feather-pocket
finds no Coin

See Extended Metaphor *and* Figurative Language.

METER. **Meter** is a regular rhythmic pattern in poetry. This pattern is determined by the number of beats, or stresses, in each line. Stressed and unstressed syllables are divided into rhythmical units called *feet.* Feet commonly used in poetry are as follows:

Type of Foot	Stress Pattern	Example
iamb (iambic)	an unstressed syllable followed by a stressed syllable	in**sist**
trochee (trochaic)	a stressed syllable followed by an unstressed syllable	**free**dom
anapest (anapestic)	two unstressed syllables followed by one stressed syllable	unim**pressed**
dactyl (dactylic)	one stressed syllable followed by two unstressed syllables	**fe**verish
spondee (spondaic)	two stressed syllables	**baseball**

Terms used to describe the number of feet in a line include the following:

monometer for a one-foot line
dimeter for a two-foot line
trimeter for a three-foot line
tetrameter for a four-foot line
pentameter for a five-foot line
hexameter, or Alexandrine, for a six-foot line
heptameter for a seven-foot line
octameter for an eight-foot line

A complete description of the meter of a line includes both the term for the type of foot used most often in the line and the term for the number of feet in the line. The most common meters are iambic tetrameter and iambic pentameter. The following are examples of each:

iambic tetrameter

˘ / ˘ / ˘ / ˘ /
O slow | ly, slow | ly rose | she up

iambic pentameter

˘ / ˘ / ˘ / ˘ / ˘ /
The cur | few tolls | the knell | of part | ing day

MOOD. **Mood,** or atmosphere, is the emotion created in the reader by part or all of a literary work. The writer can evoke in the reader an emotional response—such as fear, discomfort, longing, or anticipation—by working carefully with descriptive language and sensory details. "The Foghorn" by Ray Bradbury (Unit 1) has a lonely, mysterious mood.

MORAL. A **moral** is a lesson that relates to the principles of right and wrong and is intended to be drawn from a story or other work of literature.

MOTIF. A **motif** is any element that appears in one or more works of literature or art. Examples of common folk tale motifs found in oral traditions throughout the world include granting of three wishes, the trial or quest, and the magical metamorphosis, or transformation of one thing into another. "Cinderella," "The Ugly Duckling," and the Arthurian "Sword in the Stone" are examples of the transformation motif, in which persons or creatures of humble station are revealed to be exceptional. Much can be revealed about a literary work by studying the motifs within it.

MOTIVATION. A **motivation** is a force that moves a character to think, feel, or behave in a certain way. Lester Simons, in "The 11:59" by Patricia McKissack (Unit 1), is motivated by fear of death to try to escape the 11:59.

MYTH. A **myth** is a traditional story, rooted in a particular culture, that deals with gods, goddesses, and other supernatural beings, as well as human heroes. Myths often embody religious beliefs and values and explain natural phenomena. Every early culture around the globe has produced its own myths. Ingri and Edgar Parin d'Aulaire's "Persephone and Demeter" (Unit 8) is a Greek origin myth.

NARRATION. **Narration** is a type of writing that tells a story, or describes events.

NARRATIVE POEM. A **narrative poem** is one that tells a story. Edgar Allan Poe's "Annabel Lee" (Unit 6) is an example of a narrative poem. *See* Poetry.

NARRATOR. A **narrator** is a character or speaker who tells a story. The writer's choice of narrator is important to the story and determines how much and what kind of information readers will be given about events and other characters. The narrator in a work of fiction may be a major or minor character or simply someone who witnessed or heard about the events being related. A *reliable narrator* gives a trustworthy account of events. An *unreliable narrator* cannot be trusted because he or she comments on and offers opinions about events. *See* Point of View *and* Speaker.

NONFICTION. **Nonfiction** writing explores real people's lives, places, things, events, and ideas. Essays, autobiographies, biographies, and news articles are all types of nonfiction. *See* Prose.

NOVEL. A **novel** is a long work of fiction. Often novels have involved plots, many characters, and numerous settings.

ODE. An **ode** is a poem to honor or praise someone or something.

ONOMATOPOEIA. **Onomatopoeia** is the use of words or phrases that sound like the things to which they refer. Examples of onomatopoeia include words such as buzz, click, and pop. In "The Highwayman" by Alfred Noyes (Unit 6), *tlot-tlot, tlot-tlot* is an example of onomatopoeia.

ORAL TRADITION. The **oral tradition** is the passing of a work, an idea, or a custom by word of mouth from generation to generation. Common works found in the oral traditions of peoples around the world include folk tales, fables, fairy tales, tall tales, nursery rhymes, proverbs, legends, myths, parables, riddles, charms, spells, and ballads. *See* Folk Tale, Legend, Myth, *and* Parable.

PARALLELISM. **Parallelism** is a rhetorical device in which a writer emphasizes the equal value or weight of two or more ideas by expressing them in the same grammatical form. *See* Rhetorical Device.

PERSONIFICATION. **Personification** is a figure of speech in which an animal, a thing, a force of nature, or an idea is described as if it were human or is given human characteristics. For example, in the poem "Under the Apple Tree" (Unit 5) Diana Rivera uses personification to describe apple blossoms:

> here, under the apple tree,
> where a crowd of petals close their
> eyes...."

PERSUASION. **Persuasion,** or *argumentative writing,* is intended to change or influence the way a reader thinks or feels about a particular issue or idea.

PLOT. A **plot** is the series of events related to a central conflict, or struggle. A plot typically introduces a conflict, develops it, and eventually resolves it. A plot often contains the following elements, although it may not include all of them and they may not appear in precisely this order:

- The **exposition,** or introduction, sets the tone or mood, introduces the characters and setting, and provides necessary background information.
- The **rising action** is where the conflict is developed and intensified.

- The **climax** is the high point of interest or suspense.
- The **falling action** consists of all the events that follow the climax.
- The **resolution,** or dénouement (dā' nü män´), is the point at which the central conflict is ended, or resolved.

POETRY. **Poetry** is a major type of literature. It features imaginative and musical language carefully chosen and arranged to communicate experiences, thoughts, or emotions. It differs from prose in that it compresses meaning into fewer words and often uses meter, rhyme, and imagery. Poetry is usually arranged in lines and stanzas as opposed to sentences and paragraphs, and it can be more free in the ordering of words and the use of punctuation. Types of poetry include narrative, dramatic, and lyric. *See* Dramatic Poem, Lyric Poem, Meter, Narrative Poem, *and* Rhyme.

POINT OF VIEW. **Point of view** is the vantage point, or perspective, from which the story is told—in other words, who is telling the story. In **first-person** point of view, the story is told by someone who participates in or witnesses the action; this person, called the narrator, uses words such as *I* and *we* in telling the story. **Second-person** point of view uses the word *you* and addresses the reader directly, positioning the reader in the story. In **third-person** point of view, the narrator usually stands outside the action and observes; the narrator uses words such as *he, she, it,* and *they.* There are two types of third-person point of view: limited and omniscient. In *limited point of view,* the thoughts of only the narrator or a single character are revealed. In *omniscient point of view,* the thoughts of all the characters are revealed. Piri Thomas's "Amigo Brothers" (Unit 2) is told from a third-person omniscient point of view. *See* Narrator.

PRIMARY SOURCE. *See* Source.

PROSE. **Prose** is the broad term used to describe all writing that is not drama or poetry, including fiction and nonfiction. Types of prose writing include novels, short stories, essays, and news stories. Most biographies, autobiographies, and letters are written in prose.

PROSE POEM. A **prose poem** is a passage of prose that makes such extensive use of poetic language that the line between prose and poetry becomes blurred.

PROTAGONIST. A **protagonist** has the central role in a literary work. In Tomás Rivera's "The Portrait" (Unit 1), Don Mateo is the protagonist. *See* Antagonist.

PROVERBS. **Proverbs,** or *adages,* are traditional sayings, such as "You can lead a horse to water, but you can't make it drink."

PURPOSE. A writer's **purpose** is his or her aim, or goal. People usually write with one or more of the following purposes: to inform or explain *(informative writing);* to portray a person, place, object, or event *(descriptive writing);* to convince people to accept a position and respond in some way *(argumentative writing);* and to express thoughts or ideas, or to tell a story *(narrative writing).*

QUATRAIN. A **quatrain** is a stanza of poetry containing four lines. *See* Stanza.

REFRAIN. A **refrain** is a line or group of lines repeated in a poem or song. Many ballads contain refrains.

REPETITION. **Repetition** is a writer's intentional reuse of a sound, word, phrase, or sentence. Writers often use repetition to emphasize ideas or, especially in poetry, to create a musical effect. *See* Rhetorical Device.

RESOLUTION. *See* Plot.

RHETORICAL DEVICE. A **rhetorical device** is a technique used by a speaker or writer to achieve a particular effect, especially to persuade or influence. Common rhetorical devices include parallelism, repetition, and rhetorical questions. *See* Parallelism, Repetition, *and* Rhetorical Question.

RHETORICAL QUESTION. A **rhetorical question** is a question asked for effect but not meant to be answered. In the essay "Ships in the Desert" (Unit 4), Al Gore asks the rhetorical question: "What does it mean . . . that children playing in the morning surf must now dodge not only the occasional jellyfish but the occasional hypodermic needle washing in with the waves?"

RHYME. **Rhyme** is the repetition of sounds in words. Types of rhyme include the following:

- *end rhyme* (the use of rhyming words at the ends of lines)
- *internal rhyme* (the use of rhyming words within lines)
- *exact rhyme* (in which the rhyming words end with the same sound or sounds, as in *moon* and *June*)
- *slant rhyme* (in which the rhyming sounds are similar but not identical, as in *rave* and *rove*)

- *sight rhyme* (in which the words are spelled similarly but pronounced differently, as in *lost* and *ghost* or *give* and *thrive*)

RHYME SCHEME. A **rhyme scheme** is the pattern of end rhymes designated by assigning a different letter of the alphabet to each rhyme. In the following verse from "The Village Blacksmith" by Henry Wadsworth Longfellow (Unit 5), the rhyme scheme is *abcb.*

> His hair is crisp, and black, and long,
> His face is like the tan;
> His brow is wet with honest sweat,
> He earns whate'er he can,

RHYTHM. **Rhythm** is the pattern of beats, or stresses, in a line poetry. Rhythm can be regular or irregular. A regular rhythmic pattern in a poem is called a *meter. See* Meter.

RISING ACTION. *See* Plot.

ROMANCE. **Romance** is a term used to refer to the following four types of literature:

- medieval stories about the adventures and loves of knights
- novels and other fiction involving exotic locations and extraordinary or mysterious events and characters
- nonrealistic fiction in general
- in popular, modern usage, love stories of all kinds

SATIRE. **Satire** is humorous writing or speech intended to point out errors, falsehoods, foibles, or failings. It is written for the purpose of reforming human behavior or human institutions.

SCENE. A **scene** is a short section of a play that usually marks changes of time and place.

SCIENCE FICTION. **Science fiction** is highly imaginative fiction containing fantastic elements based on scientific principles, discoveries, or laws. Rod Serling's drama "The Monsters Are Due on Maple Street" (Unit 7) is an example of science fiction.

SENSORY DETAILS. *See* Description.

SETTING. The **setting** of a literary work is the time and place in which it occurs, together with all the details used to create a sense of a particular time and place. Writers create setting by various means. In drama, the setting is often revealed by the stage set and the costumes, though it may be revealed through what the characters say about their environs. In fiction, setting is most often revealed by means of description of such elements as landscape, scenery, buildings, furniture, clothing, the weather, and the season. It can also be revealed by how characters talk and behave. The setting of Lensey Namioka's "The Inn of Lost Time" (Unit 1) includes both the geographic location of Japan and the eighteenth century—the time period in which the story takes place.

SHORT STORY. A **short story** is a brief work of fiction. Short stories are typically crafted carefully to develop a plot, a conflict, characters, a setting, a mood, and a theme, all within relatively few pages. *See* Fiction *and* Genre.

SIMILE. A **simile** is a comparison of two seemingly unlike things using the word "like" or "as." Alfred Noyes uses this figure of speech in "The Highwayman" (Unit 6):

> His eyes were hollows of madness, his hair like
> mouldy hay,

SONNET. A **sonnet** is a fourteen-line poem, usually in iambic pentameter, that follows one of a number of different rhyme schemes. The *English, Elizabethan,* or *Shakespearean* sonnet is divided into four parts: three quatrains and a final couplet. The rhyme scheme of such a sonnet is *abab cdcd efef gg.* The *Italian* or *Petrarchan* sonnet is divided into two parts: an octave and a sestet. The rhyme scheme of the octave is *abbaabba.* The rhyme scheme of the sestet can be *cdecde, cdcdcd,* or *cdedce.* Robert Frosts's "Once by the Pacific" (Unit 6) is a sonnet. *See* Stanza *and* Rhyme Scheme.

SOURCE. A **source** is evidence of an event, an idea, or a development. A *primary source* is direct evidence, or proof that comes straight from those involved. Primary sources include official documents as well as firsthand accounts, such as diaries, letters, photographs, and paintings done by witnesses or participants.

SPEAKER. The **speaker** is the character who speaks in, or narrates, a poem—the voice assumed by the writer. The speaker and the writer of a poem are not necessarily the same person. The speaker in Edna St. Vincent Millay's poem "The Courage That My Mother Had" (Unit 2) wishes she had inherited her mother's courage. *See* Narrator.

SPEECH. A **speech** is a public address that was original delivered orally. "Queen Elizabeth's Speech to Her Last Parliament" (Unit 3) is an example of a speech.

SPIRITUALS. **Spirituals** are religious songs from the African-American folk tradition.

STAGE DIRECTIONS. **Stage directions** are notes included in a play, in addition to the dialogue, for the purpose of describing how something should be performed on stage. Stage directions describe setting, lighting, music, sound effects, entrances and exits, properties, and the movements of characters. They are usually printed in italics and enclosed in brackets or parentheses.

STANZA. A **stanza** is a group of lines in a poem. The following are some types of stanza:

two-line stanza	couplet
three-line stanza	triplet or tercet
four-line stanza	quatrain
five-line stanza	quintain or quintet
six-line stanza	sestet
seven-line stanza	septet
eight-line stanza	octave

STEREOTYPE. A **stereotype** is an overgeneralization about a group of people based on a lack of knowledge and experience.

STYLE. **Style** is the manner in which something is said or written. A writer's style is characterized by such elements as word choice (or *diction*), sentence structure and length, and other recurring features that distinguish his or her work from that of another. One way to think of a writer's style is as his or her written personality.

SUSPENSE. **Suspense** is a feeling of expectation, anxiousness, or curiosity created by questions raised in the mind of a reader or viewer.

SYMBOL. A **symbol** is anything that stands for or represents both itself and something else. Writers use two types of symbols—conventional, and personal or idiosyncratic. A *conventional symbol* is one with traditional, widely recognized associations. Such symbols include doves for peace; the color green for jealousy; winter, evening, or night for old age; wind for change or inspiration. A *personal* or *idiosyncratic symbol* is one that assumes its secondary meaning because of the special use to which it is put by a writer. In Sandra Cisneros's "Four Skinny Trees" (Unit 2), the trees are symbols of the narrator's experience growing up in the city.

TALL TALE. A **tall tale** is a story, often lighthearted or humorous, that contains highly exaggerated, unrealistic elements. Stories about Paul Bunyan are tall tales.

TANKA. A **tanka** is a traditional Japanese poem consisting of five lines, with five syllables in the first and third lines and seven syllables in the other lines (5-7-5-7-7). The syllable pattern is often lost when a tanka is translated into English. Tanka uses imagery to evoke emotions in the reader, but its images are often more philosophical and less immediate than those in a haiku. See Haiku.

THEME. A **theme** is a central message or perception about life that is revealed through a literary work. Themes may be stated or implied. A *stated theme* is presented directly, whereas an *implied theme* must be inferred. Most works of fiction do not have a stated theme but rather several implied themes. A *universal theme* is a message about life that can be understood by people of most cultures. A stated theme of Marta Salinas's "The Scholarship Jacket" (Unit 2) is that earning something is different from buying something. An implied theme is that it is important to stand up for what you believe.

THESIS. A **thesis** is a main idea that is supported in a work of nonfiction. The thesis of "The Eternal Frontier" by Louis L'Amour (Unit 3) is that it is humankind's destiny to explore outer space.

TONE. **Tone** is the emotional attitude toward the reader or toward the subject implied by a literary work. Examples of the different tones that a work may have include familiar, ironic, playful, sarcastic, serious, and sincere. In the short story "The War of the Wall" (Unit 1), Toni Cade Bambara employs a combative tone.

TRAGEDY. A **tragedy** is a work of literature, particularly a drama, that tells the story of the fall of a person of high status. It celebrates the courage and dignity of a tragic hero in the face of inevitable doom. Sometimes that doom is made inevitable by a tragic flaw. Today, the term *tragedy* is used more loosely to mean any work that has an unhappy ending. *See* Comedy, Tragic Hero, *and* Tragic Flaw.

TRAGIC FLAW. A **tragic flaw** is a weakness of personality that causes the tragic hero to make unfortunate choices.

TRAGIC HERO. A **tragic hero** is the main character in a tragedy.

TRICKSTER. The **trickster,** who is either an animal or a shape-shifter, is more than an annoyance to the mythical gods: He or she is often responsible for bringing important gifts to humanity, such as fire. Judith Gleason's "Eshu" (Unit 8), a Yoruban folk tale, is an example of a trickster tale.

VOICE. **Voice** is the way a writer uses language to reflect his or her unique personality and attitude toward topic, form, and audience. A writer expresses voice through tone, word choice, or diction, and sentence structure. *See* Diction *and* Tone.

Glossary of Vocabulary Words

Pronunciation Key

Vowel Sounds

a	h**a**t	i	s**i**t	ü	bl**ue,** st**ew**	ə	extr**a**
ā	pl**a**y	ī	m**y**	oi	b**oy**		und**er**
ä	st**a**r			ou	w**ow**		civ**il**
		ō	g**o**				hon**or**
e	th**e**n	ô	p**aw**, b**o**rn	u	**u**p		bog**us**
ē	m**e**	u̇	b**oo**k, p**u**t	ʉ	b**u**rn		

Consonant Sounds

b	**b**ut	j	**j**ump	p	**p**op	th	**th**e
ch	wa**tch**	k	bri**ck**	r	**r**od	v	**v**alley
d	**d**o	l	**l**ip	s	**s**ee	w	**w**ork
f	**f**udge	m	**m**oney	sh	**sh**e	y	**y**ell
g	**g**o	n	o**n**	t	si**t**	z	plea**s**ure
h	**h**ot	ŋ	so**ng**, si**n**k	th	wi**th**		

A

ab • sent • mind • ed • ly (ab' sənt mīn´ dəd lē) *adv.*, lost in thought; unaware

a • bund • ance (ə bʉn´ dən[t]s) *n.*, wealth; riches; surplus of money and possessions

a • byss (ə bis´) *n.*, bottomless pit; something too deep to measure

am • ber (am´ bər) *adj.*, yellowish red; *n.*, hardened sap

am • bi • tion (am bi´ shən) *n.*, drive to succeed

a • nal • y • sis (ə na´ lə səs) *n.*, act of separating something into its parts to examine them

an • ti • dote (an´ ti dōt') *n.*, remedy

ap • pall • ing (ə pôl´ iŋ) *adj.*, inspiring disgust

ap • pre • hen • sive • ly (a' pri hen[t]´ siv lē) *adv.*, in a way that shows fear or caution

ar • dent (är´ dənt) *adj.*, warmth of feeling characterized by eager support

ar • is • toc • ra • cy (a' rə stä´ krə sē) *n.*, noble or privileged class; government by people who belong to the noble class

as • cend (ə send´) *v.*, move upward; rise

a • skew (ə skyü´) *adj.*, out of line; crooked

as • ton • ish • ing (ə stä´ ni shiŋ) *adj.*, amazing; very surprising

as • tute (ə stüt´) *adj.*, possessing practical intelligence and the ability to make good decisions

a • veng • ing (ə venj´ iŋ) *adj.*, taking revenge or punishing someone for something

B

bar • rage (bə räzh´) *n.*, outpouring of many things at once

bar • ren (ber´ ən) *adj.*, unable to reproduce or bear fruit; desolate

bear (ber) *v.*, carry; bore (past tense)

bel • lows (be´ lôz') *n.*, device that expands and contracts to draw in and force out air, used to increase the intensity of a fire

ben • e • dic • tion (be' nə dik´ shən) *n.*, blessing

be • nign (bi nīn´) *adj.*, posing no threat

bleak (blēk) *adj.*, windy; cold; raw

blun • der (blʉn´ dər) *v.*, make a serious error in judgment; make a thoughtless mistake

brace (brās) *n.*, grove that provides shelter from wind

bran • dish (bran´ dish) *v.*, wave threateningly

brawn • y (brô´ nē) *adj.*, muscular, strongly built

brood (brüd) *v.*, dwell on a gloomy subject; worry

by • gone (bī´ gôn') *adj.*, long ago; in the distant past

C

cache (kash) *n.*, stored supply, often hidden

cha • ot • ic (kā ät´ ik) *adj.*, in a state of disorder or confusion

chide (chīd) *v.*, express mild disapproval

cleft (kleft) *n.*, space made when something breaks open

co • los • sal (kə lä´ səl) *adj.*, of a very large degree or amount

co • in • ci • dence (kō in[t]´ sə den[t]s) n., chance occurrence

com • mence • ment (kəm men[t]s´ mənt) *adj.*, graduation

com • pen • sate (käm´ pən sāt') *v.*, balance, offset, repay

com • po • sure (kəm pō´ zhər) *n.*, calmness of mind or appearance

com • pul • sion (kəm pəl´ shən) *n.*, irresistible impulse to perform an act

com • pul • so • ry (kəm pʉl´ sə rē) *adj.*, required by a law or rule
con • clu • sive • ly (kən klü´ siv lē) *adv.*, in a way that ends debate or discussion
con • geal (kən jēl´) *v.*, change from liquid to solid due to cold temperature
con • jec • ture (kən jek´ chər) *v.*, predict; guess
con • sol • i • dat • ed (kən sä´ lə dā təd) *adj.*, joined together; compacted
con • vic • tion (kən vik´ shən) *n.*, belief; self-confidence; boldness
cos • mic (käz´ mik) *adj.*, relating to the universe as a whole
cour • te • ous (kʉr´ tē əs) *adj.*, polite; well mannered
cow • er (kaů´ [ə]r) *v.*, shrink and tremble as from anger, threats, or blows
cred • i • bil • i • ty (kre' də bi´ lə tē) *n.*, believability; ability to inspire belief
crev • ice (kre´ vəs) *n.*, narrow opening resulting from a split or crack
cro • chet (krō´shā´) *n.*, needle-work made by interlocking loops of thread using a hooked needle
cul • ti • va • ted (kʉl´ tə vāt' əd) *adj.*, prepared for growing plants
cun • ning (kʉ´ niŋ) *adj.*, clever or tricky

D

de • duce (di düs´) *v.*, infer
def • er • ence (de´ fə rən[t]s) *n.*, respectful yielding
de • i • ty (dē´ə tē) *n.*, god or goddess
de • jec • ted • ly (di jek´ təd lē) *adv.*, sadly; showing lack of confidence
del • i • cate • ly (del´ i kət lē) *adv.*, carefully; cautiously
de • lin • e • ate (di li´ nē āt') *v.*, describe
des • e • crate (des´ i krāt') *v.*, treat with disrespect
des • o • late (de´ sə lət) *adj.*, lonely, sad
des • ti • tute (des´ tə tüt') *adj.*, without money or other basic necessities for survival; extremely poor
dev • a • stat • ing (de´ və stā' tiŋ) *adj.*, overwhelming
dif • fuse (di fyüs´) *adj.*, spread out loosely and widely
din (din) *n.*, loud noise
dire (dī´ [ə]r) *adj.*, desperate; horrifying
di • rec • tive (də rek´ tiv) *n.*, order or form of guidance
dis • il • lu • sioned (dis' ə lü´ zhənd) *adj.*, disappointed; dissatisfied
dis • may (dis mā´) *n.*, sudden loss of courage; shock
dis • pel (di spel´) *v.*, break up; make vanish
dis • solve (di zälv´) *v.*, melt; reduce to liquid form
dis • suade (di swād´) *v.*, deter a person from a course of action by persuasion
do • main (dō mān´) *n.*, land that a person owns; rightful territory
dom • i • nant (dä´ mə nənt) *adj.*, having the most control or influence
driv • el (dri´ vəl) *v.*, drool
drought (draůt) *n.*, period of dry weather; lack of rain
dub (dʉb) *v.*, give a nickname
dusk (dʉsk) *n.*, darker stage of twilight

E

e • go • tism (ē´ gə' ti zəm) *n.*, large sense of self-importance; conceit
em • er • ald (em´ rəld) *adj.*, bright green
em • u • late (em´ yə lāt') *v.*, imitate
en • croach • ing (in krōch´ iŋ) *adj.*, trespassing; creeping slowly into a territory with the object of stealing it
ep • i • dem • ic (e' pə de´ mik) *n.*, outbreak of contagious disease that spreads rapidly
e • rode (i rōd´) *v.*, wear away, usually through natural forces such as weather
eth • ni • ci • ty (eth ni´ sə tē) *n.*, belonging to a racial, cultural, or national group
ex • alt • ed (ig zōlt´ ed) *adj.*, held in high regard
ex • as • per • at • ed (ig zas´ pə rāt' ed) *adj.*, irritated
ex • tra • ne • ous (ek strā´ nē əs) *adj.*, not essential; not a part of the main idea

F

fe • roc • i • ty (fə räs´ ət ē) *n.*, fierceness or intensity
flail (flāl) *v.*, swing
flour • ish (flʉr´ ish) *v.*, grow luxuriously
flush (flʉsh) *adj.*, having a red color to the skin
fond • ness (fän[d]´ nəs) *n.*, affection; having a liking
for • feit (for´ fət) *v.*, lose or fail to win the right to something by some error, offense, or crime
for • lorn (fər lôrn´) *adj.*, sad; lonely; hopeless

G

gid • dy (gi´ dē) *adj.*, feeling dizzy or unsteady
gnarled (när[ə]ld) *adj.*, misshapen
gran • di • ose (gran´ dē ōs') *adj.*, magnificent; grand
grum • ble (grʉm´ bəl) *v.*, mumble unhappily

H

ha • bit • u • al (hə´ bi ch [ə] wel) *adj.*, behaving in a certain manner by habit
hack (hak) *v.*, chop or cut forcefully

high-strung (hī´ strʉŋ´) *adj.*, nervous; extra sensitive

I

im • passe (im´ pas') *n.*, situation with no escape
im • plore (im plōr´) *v.*, beg
in • ca • pac • i • tat • ed (in' kə pa´ sə tāt' ed) *adj.*, unable to engage in normal activities; disabled
in • ces • sant • ly (in' se´ sənt lē) *adv.*, constantly
in • cor • po • rate (in kôr´ pə rāt') *v.*, combine into one body
in • ert (i nʉrt´) *adj.*, still; unmoving
in • ev • i • ta • ble (i ne´ və tə bəl) *n.*, unavoidable situation
in • flu • en • za (in' flu['] en´ zə) *n.*, viral disease characterized by fever, muscular aches, and respiratory distress
in • tent (in tent´) *n.*, purpose
in • ter • cede (in' tər sēd´) *v.*, come between to cause a change
in • tri • cate (in´ tri kət) *adj.*, elaborate
ir • i • des • cence (ir' ə de´ sən[t]s) *n.*, show of rainbow colors that seem to shimmer and change when viewed from different angles

K

kind • ling (kin´ [d] liŋ) *n.*, material used to start a fire, often dry sticks

L

la • bor • i • ous (lə bôr´ ē əs) *adj.*, produced by hard work
la • den (lād´ən) *adj.*, weighed down
lam • en • ta • tion (la' mən tā´ shən) *n.*, expression of sorrow or regret
lar • va (lär´ və) *n.*, early wingless form of a newly hatched insect; larvae (lär´ vī) *n. pl.*
lav • ish (la´ vish) *adj.*, abundant; rich
lib • er • a • tion (li' bə rā´ shən) *n.*, state of being free or of achieving civil rights
lithe • ly (līth´ lē) *adv.*, bending easily
lo • co • mo • tion (lō' kə mō´ shən) *n.*, power or act of moving from one place to another
lu • mi • nous (lü´ mə nəs) *adj.*, emitting or reflecting steady, glowing light

M

man • i • fes • ta • tion (ma' nə fə stā´ shən) *n.*, example; instance
ma • nip • u • late (mə nip´ yə lāt') *v.*, treat or operate with the hands in a skillful manner
mas • ter • piece (mas´ tər pēs') *n.*, artist's greatest work
mea • ger (mē´ gər) *adj.*, lacking in quantity or quality
mes • mer • ize (mez´ mə rīz') *v.*, fascinate, spellbind
mi • li • tia (mə li´ shə) *n.*, citizens' army
mis • sion • ary (mi´ shə ner' ē) *n.*, person sent to other countries or remote areas to spread a religion and, sometimes, to care for people
mys • ti • cal (mis´ ti kəl) *adj.*, having a spiritual quality; mysterious

N

noi • some (nôi´ səm) *adj.*, offensive smell; objectionable

O

ob • sessed (əb sest´) *adj.*, preoccupied
o • di • ous (ō´ dē əs) *adj.*, hateful or disgusting
o • men (ō´ mən) *n.*, prophetic sign
om • i • nous (äm´ ə nəs) *adj.*, foreboding or foreshadowing evil

P

peak • ed (pē´ kid) *adj.*, thin and drawn, as from sickness
per • il (per´ əl) *n.*, danger; exposure to harm
per • pet • u • al (pər pe´ chə wəl) *adj.*, going on forever
pe • ti • tion (pə ti´ shən) *n.*, formal request
phe • nom • e • non (fi nä´ mə nän') *n.*, extremely unusual or extraordinary thing or occurrence
phys • i • o • log • i • cal • ly (fi' zē ə lä´ ji k[ə] lē) *adv.*, relating to bodily function
pluck (plʉk) *v.*, pull off or out
poi • gnant (poi´ nyənt) *adj.*, deeply affecting or touching; somber
pre • cip • i • tous (pri si´ pə təs) *adj.*, very steep
pred • a • tor (pred´ at ər) *n.*, animal that gets food by capturing and eating other animals
pre • lim • i • nar • y (pri li´ mə ner' ē) *adj.*, preparing for the main action or event
pre • rog • a • tive (pri räg´ ət iv) *n.*, special power or privilege
pres • tige (pre stēzh´) *n.*, status; standing in general opinion
pri • me • val (prī mē´ vəl) *adj.*, from the earliest ages
pros • per • i • ty (prä spər´ ə tē) *n.*, condition of being successful or thriving, especially economic well-being
prov • i • dence (präv´ əd əns) *n.*, valuable gift; godsend
pro • vi • sion (prə vi´ zhən) *n.*, arrangement made beforehand to deal with a certain need
prov • o • ca • tion (präv' ə kā´ shən) *n.*, something that calls forth an action or emotion

R

ra • di • ant (rā´ dē ənt) *adj.*, shining bright

rapt (rapt) *adj.,* mentally engrossed or absorbed

rav • en • ous (ra´ və nəs) *adj.,* very eager for food

re • buff (ri bəf´) *n.,* refusal to meet an advance or offer

re • cruit (ri krüt´) *v.,* hire or engage the services

reel (rēl) *v.,* stumble as the result of a hard hit

re • frain (ri frān´) *n.,* phrase or verse in a song or poem that is repeated throughout

re • gret • ful • ly (ri gret´ fə lē) *adv.,* with a sense of loss or sorrow

re • press (ri pres´) *v,.* hold in by self-control

re • tal • i • ate (ri ta´ lē āt') *v.,* respond to an action by doing a similar thing back, usually in a negative sense, such as repaying one injury by inflicting another

rev • e • la • tion (re' və lā´ shən) *n.,* act of revealing or showing, usually something astonishing or enlightening

root (rüt) *v.,* dig in the ground

rum • pled (rʉm´ pəld) *adj.,* wrinkled

S

sage (sāj) *n.,* wise man

sau • cy (sô sē) *adj.,* bold

scav • en • ger (scav´ ən jər) *n.,* animal that gets food by eating the dead bodies of other animals

scep • ter (sep´ tər) *n.,* tall staff or baton that a ruler carries as a symbol of authority

scowl (skau̇[ə]l) *v.,* lower the eyebrows, as if squinting or frowning

scrag • gly (skra´ g[ə]lē) *adj.,* uneven or ragged in growth or form

seg • re • gate (seg´ ri gāt') *v.,* separate a race, class, or ethnic group from the rest of the population; set apart

shield (shēld) *v.,* protect, guard, or defend against

sin • ew • y (sin´ yü' ē) *adj.,* powerful; strong, lean, and clearly displaying muscles and tendons

snipe (snīp) *v.,* shoot from a hidden position; direct an attack

sole (sōl) *adj.,* only

spec • i • fy (spe´ sə fī') *v.,* state explicitly

spec • ter (spek´ tər)

splurge (splʉrj) *v.,* indulge oneself extravagantly or spend a lot of money

spry (sprī) *adj.,* energetic; lively

staunch • est (stônch´ est) *adj.,* most loyal or committed

stu • pen • dous (stu̇ pen´ dəs) *adj.,* marvelous; awe-inspiring

sub • se • quent (sʉb´ si kwənt) *adj.,* following in time, order, or place

sulk • i • ly (sʉl´ kə lē) *adv.,* moodily silent

sup • ple (sʉ´ pəl) *adj.,* flexible

surge (sʉrj) *v.,* rise and move forward

swag • ger (swa´ gər) *n.,* walk with an insolent air; strut

T

taunt (tänt) *v.,* mock; jeer at

taw • ny (tä´ nē) *adj.,* warm sandy color

te • di • um (tē´ dē əm) *n.,* boredom

ter • mi • nate (tʉr´ mə nāt') *v.,* end

tes • ti • fy (tes´ tə fī') *v.,* make a statement based on personal knowledge or belief; give evidence

teth • er (te´ th̲ər) *n.,* rope or chain that allows an animal to move in a limited area

trance (tran[t]s) *n.,* state of detachment from one's physical surroundings; stunned or dazed state

trans • for • ma • tion (tran[t]s fər mā´ shən) *n.,* change in composition, structure, or outward form and appearance

trans • lu • cen • cy (tran[t]s lü´ sənt sē) *n.,* quality of being transparent or allowing some light to pass through

tread (tred) *v.,* walk on, along, or across; trod (past tense)

trough (trôf) *n.,* long, shallow container

trudge (trʉj´) *v.,* walk heavily; plod

U

un • bid • den (ʉn' bi´ dən) *adj.,* not asked or invited

un • com • mon • ly (ən' kä´ mən lē) *adv.,* amazingly

un • pre • ce • dent • ed (ʉn' pre´ sə den' təd) *adj.,* unheard of; new

V

ven • ture (ven[t]´ shər) *v.,* undertake the risks and dangers of an action

ver • i • fy (ver´ ə fī') *v.,* test or check for correctness

void (vôid) *n.,* emptiness

W

wane (wān) *v.,* approach an end

war • y (wer´ ē) *adj.,* cautious

wea • ri • ly (wir´ ə lē) *adv.,* tiredly

with • drawn (wit̲h̲ drôn´) *adj.,* introverted; unresponsive

world • ly (wʉr[ə]ld´ lē) *adj.,* of or related to this world

wor • ri • some (wʉr´ ē səm) *adj.,* causing worry

writhe (rīth) *v.,* twist and turn

wrought (rôt) *v.,* (archaic) past tense of *work;* created, shaped, or formed through hard work; formed by hammering, as on metal

Y

yawn • ing (yô´ niŋ) *adj.,* wide open

Literary Acknowledgments

Bret Adams Limited. "Hollywood and the Pits" by Cherylene Lee from *American Dragons: Twenty-Five Asian American Voices*, edited by Laurence Yep, 1992. Reprinted by permission of Bret Adams Limited.

Arizona State University. "The Scholarship Jacket" by Marta Salinas from *Nosotras: Latina Literature Today* (1986) by Maria del Carmen Boza, Beverly Silva, and Carmen Valle, eds. Reprinted by permission of Bilingual Press/Editorial Bilingüe at Arizona State University, Tempe, AZ.

Arté Publico Press. "The Portrait" by Tomás Rivera and translated by Evangeline Vigil-Pinon published in *And the Earth Did Not Devour Him*. Reprinted by permission of Arté Publico Press. "Refugee Ship" by Lorna Dee Cervantes. Reprinted by permission of Arté Publico Press.

Elizabeth Barnett. "The Courage That My Mother Had" by Edna St. Vincent Millay. From *Collected Poems.* Copyright © 1954, 1982 by Norma Millay Ellis. Reprinted by permission of Elizabeth Barnett, Literary Executor, the Millay Society.

Janine M. Benyus. "Our Love Affair with Animals" from *Beastly Behaviors: A Zoo Lover's Companion* by Janine M. Benyus. Copyright © 1992 by Janine M. Benyus. Reprinted by permission of Janine M. Benyus.

Susan Bergholz Literary Services. "Four Skinny Trees" from *The House on Mango Street* by Sandra Cisneros. Copyright © 1984 by Sandra Cisneros. Published by Vintage Books, a division of Random House, Inc. and in hardcover by Alfred A. Knopf in 1994. Reprinted by permission of Susan Bergholz Literary Services, New York, NY and Lamy, NM. All rights reserved. "Names/Nombres" by Julia Alvarez, first published in *Nuestro, March 1985.* Reprinted by permission of Susan Bergholz Literary Services, New York, NY and Lamy, NM.

BOA Editions. "in the inner city" copyright © 1987 by Lucille Clifton. Reprinted from from *Good Woman: Poems and a Memoir, 1969–1980* by Lucille Clifton. Reprinted by permission of BOA Editions.

Brandt & Hochman Literary Agents, Inc. "The Serial Garden" from *Armitage, Armitage, Fly Away Home* by Joan Aiken. Copyright © 1966 by McMillan and Company, Ltd. Copyright © 1994 by Joan Aiken. Reprinted by permission of Brandt & Hochman Literary Agents, Inc. All rights reserved.

Curtis Brown, Ltd. "Gold" by Pat Mora. Copyright © 1998 by Pat Mora. First appeared in *Home: A Journey Through America*, published by Silver Whistle Books. Reprinted by permission of Curtis Brown, Ltd. From *The Ugly Duckling* by A. A. Milne. Copyright © 1941 by A. A. Milne. Reprinted by permission of Curtis Brown, London.

The Christian Science Monitor. "Unfolding Bud" by Naoshi Koriyama. Reproduced with permission from the July 3, 1957 issue of *The Christian Science Monitor* (www.scmonitor.com) © 1957 *The Christian Science Monitor.* All rights reserved.

Cobblestone Publishing. "Going Ape Over Language" from *Odyssey's* October 2001 issue: *Passionate About Primates* © 2001, Cobblestone Publishing, 30 Grove Street, Suite C, Peterborough, NH 03458. All rights reserved. Used by permission of Carus Publishing Company. "Moving West: A Native American Perspective" by Chrisine Graf. From *AppleSeeds'* February 2005 issue: *Growing Up on the Frontier*, © 2005, Carus Publishing Company, published by Cobblestone Publishing, 30 Grove Street, Suite C, Peterborough, NH 03458. All rights reserved. Used by permission of the publisher.

Judith Ortiz Cofer. "Aunty Misery: A Folktale from Puerto Rico" by Judith Ortiz Cofer. Reprinted by permission of the author.

Ruth Cohen, Inc. "The Inn of Lost Time" by Lensey Namioka, copyright © 1989, from *Connections: Short Stories by Outstanding Writers for Young Adults*, edited by Donald R. Gallo. Reprinted by permission of Lensey Namioka. All rights are reserved by the author.

Don Congdon Associates. "The Foghorn" from *The Saturday Evening Post* June 23, 1951 by Ray Bradbury. Copyright © 1951 by The Curtis Publishing Company, renewed 1979 by Ray Bradbury. Reprinted by permission of Don Congdon Associates, Inc.

The Curtis Publishing Company From *The Snow Goose* by Paul Gallico. Copyright © 1940 by The Curtis Publishing Company. Copyright renewed 1968 by Paul Gallico. Reprinted by permission of The Curtis Publishing Company.

Sandra Dijkstra Literary Agency. "Fish Cheeks" by Amy Tan. Copyright © 1989 by Amy Tan. First appeared in *Seventeen Magazine.* Reprinted by permission of the author and the Sandra Dijkstra Literary Agency.

Dunham Literary, Inc. "Flying" by Reeve Lindbergh from *When I Was Your Age: Original Stories About Growing Up*, edited by Amy Ehrlich. Copyright ©

1996 by Reeve Lindbergh. Originally published by Candlewick Press. Reprinted by the permission of Dunham Literary as agents for the author.

Farrar, Straus & Giroux, Inc. "Filling Station" from The *Complete Poems 1927–1979* by Elizabeth Bishop. Copyright © 1979, 1983 by Alice Helen Methfessel. Reprinted by permission of Farrar, Straus and Giroux, LLC. "The Green Mamba" by Roald Dahl. Reprinted by permission of Farrar, Straus & Giroux, Inc.

Judith Gleason. "Eshu" from *Orisha: The Gods of Yorubaland* by Judith Gleason. Reprinted by permission of the author.

Fulcrum Books. "The Rabbit and the Tug of War" by Michael Thompson and Jacob Warrenfeltz from Trickster. Reprinted by permission of Fulcrum Books.

Graphic Arts Center Publishing Company. An excerpt from *Alone across the Artic* by Pam Flowers. Reprinted by permission of Graphic Arts Center Publishing Company.

Maxine Groffsky Literary Agency. "The White Umbrella" by Gish Jen. Copyright © 1984 by Gish Jen. First published in *The Yale Review*. From the collection *Who's Irish?* By Gish Jen published in 1999 by Alfred A. Knopf. Reprinted by permission of the author.

Grove Atlantic, Inc. "Astonishing Animals: Extraordinary Creatures and the Fantastic Worlds They Inhabit" by Tim Flannery and Peter Schouten. Copyright © 2007 by Tim Flannery. Used by permission Grove/Atlantic, Inc.

Hancock House Publishers. "I Am a Native of North America" by Chief Dan George, from *My Heart Soars.* Copyright © 1974 by Clarke Irwin. Used by permission of Hancock House Publishers. www.HancockHouse.com

Harcourt, Inc. "The Hummingbird that Lived Through Winter" from *My Kind of Crazy, Wonderful People: Seventeen Stories and a Play* by William Saroyan. Copyright © 1944 and renewed 1972 by William Saroyan, reprinted by permission of Harcourt, Inc. This material may not be reproduced in any form or by any means without the prior written permission of the publisher. "Seventh Grade" from *Baseball in April and Other Stories* by Gary Soto. Copyright © 1990 by Gary Soto. Reprinted by permission of Harcourt, Inc.

HarperCollins Publishers, Inc. "An American Childhood" by Anne Dillard. Copyright © 1987 by Anne Dillard. Reprinted by permission of HarperCollins Publishers, Inc. "How the Snake Got Poison" pp. 131–132, from *Mules and Men* by Zora Neale Hurston, copyright © 1935 by Zora Neale Hurston, renewed © 1963 by John C. Hurston and Joel Hurston. Reprinted by permission of HarperCollins Publishers. "Searching for January" from *The Dixon Corn Belt League and Other Baseball Stories* by W. P. KINSELLA. Copyright 1993 by W. P. Kinsella. Reprinted by permission of HarperCollins Publishers, Inc. "We Are All One" from *The Rainbow People* by Laurence Yep. Text copyright © 1989 by Laurence Yep. Reprinted by permission of HarperCollins Publishers, Inc. from *Ella Enchanted* by Gail Carson Levine. Reprinted by permission of HarperCollins Publishers, Inc.

Harvard University Press. "I'm Nobody! Who are you?" by Emily Dickinson. Reprinted by permission of the publishers and the Trustees of Amherst College from *The Poems of Emily Dickinson*, Ralph W. Franklin, ed., Cambridge, Mass.: The Belknap Press of Harvard University Press, Copyright © 1998 by the President and Fellows of Harvard College. Copyright © 1951, 1955, 1979, 1983 by the President and Fellows of Harvard College. "Tsali of the Cherokees" as told to Alice Marriott by Norah Roper (pp. 147–54) from *American Indian Mythology* by Alice Marriott and Carol K. Rachlin.

Barbara Hogenson Agency. "The Night The Bed Fell" by James Thurber from *My Life and Hard Times.* Reprinted by permission of Barbara Hogenson Agency. "The Rabbits Who Caused All the Trouble" from *Fables for Our Time & Famous Poems*, illustrated by James Thurber. Copyright © 1940 by Rosemary A. Thurber. Reprinted by arrangement with Rosemary A. Thurber and The Barbara Hogenson Agency, Inc. All rights reserved. To read more about James Thurber, go to www.ThurberHouse.org.

Henry Holt and Company. "Fire and Ice" from *The Poetry of Robert Frost* edited by Edward Connery Lathem. Copyright 1923, 1969 by Henry Holt and Company. Copyright 1951 by Robert Frost. Reprinted by permission of Henry Holt and Company, LLC. "Once By the Pacific" by Robert Frost. From *The Poetry of Robert Frost* edited by Edward Connery Lathem. Copyright © 1928, copyright 1969 by Henry Holt and Co., Copyright © 1956 by Robert Frost. Reprinted by permission of Henry Holt and Company, LLC. "The Pasture" by Robert Frost from *The Poetry of Robert Frost* edited by Edward Connery Lathem. Copyright © 1939, 1967, 1969 by Henry Holt and Company. Reprinted by permission of Henry Holt and Company, LLC.

Holy Cow! Press. "Jed's Grandfather" from *Turtle Meat and Other Stories* by Joseph Bruchac. Reprinted by permission of Holy Cow! Press.

Houghton Mifflin Company. "The Aqualung" from *The New Way Things Work* by David Macaulay. Compilation copyright © 1988, 1998 Dorling Kindersley Ltd., London. Text copyright © 1988, 1998 David Macaulay, Neil Ardley. Illustrations copyright © 1988, 1998 David Macaulay. Reprinted by permission of Houghton Mifflin Co. All rights reserved. "Blackberry Eating" from *Mortal Acts, Mortal Words* by Galway Kinnell, copyright © 1980 by Galway Kinnell. Reprinted by permission of Houghton Mifflin Company. All rights reserved. "Phaethon, Son of Apollo" from *Greek Myths* by Olivia E. Coolidge. Copyright © 1949 by Olivia E. Coolidge; copyright renewed © 1977 by Olivia E. Coolidge. Adapted by permission of Houghton Mifflin Company. All rights reserved. "Ships in the Desert" from *Earth in the Balance* by Al Gore. Copyright © 1992 by Senator Al Gore. Reprinted by permission of Houghton Mifflin Company. All rights reserved. "St. Crispian's Day Speech" from *Henry V* by William Shakespeare, edited by G. Blakemore Evans, The Riverside Shakespeare. Copyright © 1974 by Houghton Mifflin Co.

Jerry Izenberg. "Roberto Clemente: A Bittersweet Memoir" from *Great Latin Sport Figures* by Jerry Izenberg. Reprinted by permission of the author.

Coleman A. Jennings. Excerpt from "Braille: The Early Life of Louis Braille" from *Theater for Children*, edited by Coleman A. Jennings. Copyright © 2005 by Coleman A. Jennings. Reprinted by permission of Coleman A. Jennings.

Liveright Publishing Corporation. "the/ sky/ was," copyright © 1925, 1953, E.E. Cummings, copyright © 1991 by the Trustees for the E.E. Cummings Trust. Copyright © 1976 by George James Firmage, from *Complete Poems: 1904–1962* by E.E. Cummings, edited by George J. Firmage. Reprinted by permission of Liveright Publishing Corporation.

Carol Mann Agency. "The Size of Things" by Robert Jastrow, copyright © 1990 by Robert Jastrow, published by W. W. Norton. Reprinted with permission from Carol Mann Agency.

MBA Literary Agency. "The Smallest Dragonboy" by Anne McCaffrey from *A Gift of Dragons* is reprinted by kind permission of the author.

Milkweed Editions. "Achieving Perspective" from *Firekeeper: Selected Poems* by Pattiann Rogers, Minneapolis: Milkweed Editions, 2005. Copyright © 2005 by Pattiann Rogers. Reprinted with permission from Milkweed Editions.

William Morris Agency, LLC. "A Christmas Carol: Scrooge and Marley" by Israel Horowitz. Copyright © 1994 by Fountain Pen, LLC. All rights reserved. Reprinted by permission of William Morris Agency, LLC on behalf of the author. *Let me Hear You Whisper* by Paul Zindel. Copyright © 1974 by Paul Zindel. Used in electronic form by permission of William Morris Agency, LLC on behalf of the author.

Ashley Matin Moss. "Antaeus" by Borden Deal. Reprinted by permission of Ashley Matin Moss.

Museum of New Mexico Press. "The Force of Luck" by Rudolfo A. Anaya from *Cuentos*. Reprinted by permission of Museum of New Mexico Press.

The Nation. "Dust Changes America" by Margaret Bourke-White. From *The Nation*, May 22, 1935. Reprinted with permission of *The Nation.*

National Audubon Society. "Wild Turkey" from *The Bird Biographies of John James Audubon* selected and edited by Alice Ford. Copyright © 1957 by Alice Ford. Reprinted by permission of National Audubon Society.

The New York Times. "A Black Athlete Looks At Education" by Arthur Ashe from *The New York Times*, February 5, © 1977 The New York Times. All rights reserved. Used by permission and protected by the copyright laws of the United States. The printing, copying, redistribution, or retransmission of the material without express written permission is prohibited.

Naomi Shihab Nye. "The Lost Parrot" from *Hugging the Jukebox* by Naomi Shihab Nye. Reprinted by permission of the author.

Fifi Oscard Agency. Excerpt from *Off the Court* by Arthur Ashe. Reprinted by permission of Fifi Oscard Agency.

Penguin Books Ltd. From *The Narrow Road to the Deep North and Other Travel Sketches* by Matsuo Basho, translated with an introduction by Nobuyuki Yuasa (Penguin Classics, 1966). Copyright © Nobuyuki Yuasa, 1966. Reprinted by permission of Penguin Books Ltd.

Penguin Group (USA) Inc. "Death in the Open," from *The Lives of a Cell* by Lewis Thomas. Copyright © 1973 by The Massachusetts Medical Society. Used by permission of Viking Penguin, a division of Penguin Group (USA) Inc. "Elizabeth I," from *Ten Queens: Portraits of Women of Power* by Milton Meltzer, copyright © 1998 by Milton Meltzer, text. Used by permission of Dutton Children's Books, A Division of Penguin Young Readers Group, a Member of Penguin Group (USA), 345 Hudson Street, New York, NY 10014. All rights reserved. "Such Perfection" from *Malgudi Days* by R.K. Narayan, copyright © 1972, 1975, 1978, 1980, 1981, 1982 by R.K. Narayan. Used by permission of Viking Penguin, a division of Penguin Group (USA) Inc. "Was Tarzan a Three-Bandaged Man" from *Childhood* by Bill Cosby. Copyright © 1991 by William H. Cosby. Reprinted by pernission of Viking Penguin, a division of Penguin Gour (USA) Inc.

Poolbeg Press Ltd. "Amaterasu" from *World Myths and Tales* by Carolyn Swift. Reprinted by permission of Poolbeg Press Ltd.

Random House, Inc. "The 11:59" From *The Dark Thirty: Southern Tales of the Supernatural* by Patricia C. McKissack. Text copyright 1992 by Patricia C. McKissack. Reprinted by permission of Alfred A. Knopf Children's Books, Inc., a division of Random House, Inc. From *Botany of Desire* by Michael Pollan, copyright © 2001 by Michael Pollan. Used by permission of Random house, Inc. From *D'Aulaires Book of Greek Myths* by Ingri & Edgar Parin D'Aulaire, copyright © 1962 by Ingri and Edgar Parin D'Aulaire. Used by permission of Random House Children's Books, a division of Random House, Inc. "The Face of the Deep Is Frozen" from *Shipwreck at the Bottom of the World* by Jennifer M. Armstrong. Copyright © 1998 by Jennifer M. Armstrong. Reprinted by permission of Crown Children's Books, a division of Random House, Inc. From *Frontier* by Louis L' Amour, photographs by David Muench, copyright © 1984 by Louis L' Amour Enterprises, Inc. Used by permission of Bantam Books, a division of Random House, Inc. "Mother to Son" by Langston Hughes. Copyright © 1994 by the Estate of Langston Hughes from *The Collected Poems of Langston Hughes* by Langston Hughes, edited by Arnold Rampersad with David Roessel, Associate Editor. Used by permission of Alfred A. Knopf, a division of Random House, Inc. "Mute Dancers: How to Watch a Hummingbird from *A Slender Thread* by Diane Ackerman, copyright © 1996 by Diane Ackerman. Used by permission of Random House, Inc. From *The Power of Myth* by Joseph Campbell & Bill Moyers, copyright © 1988 by Apostrophe S Productions, Inc. and Bill Moyers and Alfred Van der march Editions, Inc. for itself and the estate of Joseph Campbell. Used by permission of Doubleday, a division of Random House, Inc. From *The Sibley Guide to Birds* by David Allen Sibley. Copyright © 2000 by Chanticlear Press, Inc. Reprinted by permission of Random House, Inc. "Silver" from *The Complete Poems of Walter de la Mare.* Copyright © 1969 by the literary trustees of Walter de la Mare. Reprinted by permission of Alfred Knopf, a division of Random House, Inc. "The War of the Wall" from *Deep Sightings and Rescue Missions* by Toni Cade Bambara, copyright © 1996 by The Estate of Toni Cade Bambara. Used by permission of Pantheon Books a division of Random House, Inc. "Why the Owl Has Big Eyes" (Iroquois myth) from *American Indian Myths and Legends*, edited by Richard Erdoes and Alfonso Ortiz. Copyright © 1984 by Richard Erdoes and Alfonso Ortiz. Reprinted by permission of Pantheon Books, a division of Random House, Inc.

Marian Reiner, Literary Agent. "How to Eat a Poem" from *A Sky Full of Poems* by Eve Merriam. Copyright © 1964, 1970, 1973, 1986 by Eve Merriam. All Rights Reserved. Used by permission of Marian Reiner. "Two People I Want to Be Like" from *If Only I Could Tell You* by Eve Merriam. Copyright © 1983 Eve Merriam. All Rights Reserved. Reprinted by permission of Marian Reiner.

Faith Ringgold. "The Sunflower Quilting Bee at Arles" by Faith Ringgold. Reprinted by permission of the author.

Diana Rivera. "Under the Apple Tree" from *The Invisible Ladder* by Diana Rivera. Reprinted by permission of the author.

Kenneth Rosen. "Name Giveaway" from *Voices of the Rainbow* by Phil George, edited by Kenneth Rosen. Reprinted with permission by Kenneth Rosen.

Scholastic, Inc. From *The Greatest: Muhammad Ali* by Walter Dean Myers. Copyright © 2001 by Walter Dean Myers. Reprinted by permission of Scholastic, Inc. "Madam C.J. Waler" from *One More River to Cross: The Stories of Twelve Black Americans* by Jim Haskins. Copyright © by Jim Haskins. Reprinted by permission of Scholastic Inc.

Seaver Books. "Uncle Tony's Goat" reprinted from *Storyteller* by Leslie Marmon Silko. Copyright © 1981 by Leslie Marmon Silko. Published and reprinted by Seaver Books, New York, New York.

The Rod Serling Trust. "Monsters Are Due on Maple Street" by Rod Serling. Reprinted by permission of the Rod Serling Trust.

Neil Simon. "A Defenseless Creature" from *The Good Doctor* by Neil Simon. Copyright © 1974 by Neil Simon. Copyright renewed 2002 by Neil Simon. Professionals and amateurs are hereby warned that *The Good Doctor* is fully protected under the Berne Convention and the Universal Copyright Convention and is subject to royalty. All rights, including without limitation professional, amateur, motion picture, television, radio, recitation, lecturing, public reading and foreign translation rights, computer media rights and the right of reproduction, and electronic storage or retrieval, in whole or in part and in any form, are strictly reserved and none of these rights can be exercised or used without written permission from the copyright owner. Inquiries for stock and amateur performances should be addressed to Samuel French, Inc., 45 West 25th Street, New York, NY 10010. All other inquiries should be addressed to Gary N. DaSilva, 111 N. Sepulveda Blvd., Suite 250, Manhattan Beach, CA 90266-6850.

Simon & Schuster, Inc. "A Day's Wait" from *The Short Stories of Ernest Hemingway*. Copyright 1933 by Charles Scribner's Sons. Copyright renewed 1961 by Mary Hemingway. Reprinted with permission of Scribner, a Division of Simon & Schuster. "Face It" from *A Suitcase of Seaweed and Other Poems* by Janet S. Wong. Copyright © 1996 Janet S. Wong. Reprinted with the permission of Margaret K. McElderry Books, an imprint of Simon & Schuster Children's Publishing Division. "Money Order" & "Sisters" from *A Suitcase of Seaweed and Other Poems* by Janet S. Wong. Copyright © 1996 Janet S. Wong. Reprinted with the permission of Margaret K. McElderry Books, an imprint of Simon & Schuster Children's Publishing Division. "Papa's Parrot" from *Every Living Thing* by Cynthia Rylant. Copyright © 1985 Cynthia Rylant. Reprinted with the permission of Atheneum Books for Young Readers, an imprint of Simon & Schuster Children's Publishing Division. "The Lion and the Statue" from The *Fables of Aesop: Selected, Told Anew and Their History Traced* by Joseph Jacobs. Copyright © 1964 Macmillan Publishing Company. Reprinted with the permission of Simon & Schuster Books for Young Readers, an imprint of Simon & Schuster Children's Publishing Division. An excerpt from *What Jane Austen Ate and Charles Dickens Knew, from Fox Hunting to Whist: The Facts of Daily Life in Nineteenth-Century England* by Daniel Pool. Copyright © 1993 by Daniel Pool. Reprinted with the permission of Simon & Schuster Adult Publishing Group. All rights reserved.

The Society of Authors. "Silver" from *The Complete Poems of Walter de la Mare.* Copyright © 1969 by the literary trustees of Walter de la Mare. Reprinted by permission of Alfred Knopf, a division of Random House, Inc.

Literary Estate of May Swenson. "Feel Like a Bird" from *Nature* by May Swenson. Reprinted by permission of the Literary Estate of May Swenson.

Temple University Press. "An Unforgettable Journey" from *Hmong Means Free: Life in Laos and America* by Maijue Xiong. Reprinted by permission of Temple University Press.

Piri Thomas. "Amigo Brothers" from *Stories from the Barrio* by Piri Thomas. Reprinted by permission of the author.

University of Arizona Press. From "The Ground is always Damp" from *Blue Horses Rush In* by Luci Tapahonso. Copyright © 1997 Luci Tapahonso. Reprinted by permission of the University of Arizona Press.

University of Chicago Press. Excerpt from *Akhenaton's Hymn to the Sun* translated by John A. Wilson. Reprinted by permission of University of Chicago Press.

University of Georgia Press. From *Lost In Translation* by Steven Harvey. Copyright © 1997 by Steven Harvey. Reprinted by permission of University of Georgia Press.

University of Notre Dame Press. From *Barrio Boy* by Ernesto Galarza. Copyright © 1971 by University of Notre Dame Press. Used by permission.

Walker & Company. From *A Long Hard Journey: A Story of the Pullman Porter* by Patricia and Frederick McKissack. Copyright © 1989 by Patricia and Frederick McKissack. Reprinted by permission of Walker & Company.

West End Press. From *Loo-Wit* by Wendy Rose. Reprinted by permission of West End Press.

Rhoda Weyr Literary Agency. "Flying" by Reeve Lindbergh from *When I Was Your Age: Original Stories About Growing Up*, edited by Amy Ehrlich. Copyright © 1966 by Reeve Lindbergh. Permission granted by The Rhoda Weyr Agency, New York.

Art and Photo Credits

Cover Andrei Dragomir/Moment/Thinkstock; **iii** Andrei Dragomir/Moment/Thinkstock; **viii** (top and bottom) PhotoDisc; (middle) © SHAMIL ZHUMATOV/Reuters/Corbis; **ix** (top) © Raymond Gehman/CORBIS; (middle) Media Bakery; (bottom left) © age fotostock/SuperStock; (bottom right) PhotoDisc; **x** (top) © Getty Images; (middle) Jupiter Images; (bottom left) iStock photo; **xi** (top) © Austin J. Stevens/Animals Animals–Earth Scenes—All rights reserved; (middle) Jupiter Images; **xii** (top and bottom right) iStockphoto; (left) PhotoDisc; **xiii** (top) © Raymond Gehman/CORBIS; (middle) PhotoDisc; (bottom) Jupiter Images; **xiv** (top and middle) PhotoDisc; (bottom) Jupiter Images; **xv** (top) Royalty-Free/Corbis; (middle) PhotoDisc; (bottom) iStockphoto; **xvi** (middle) Jupiter Images; (bottom) © SHAMIL ZHUMATOV/Reuters/Corbis; **xvii** © CORBIS; **xviii** Shutterstock; **xix** (top) Shutterstock; (middle) PhotoDisc; (bottom) © age fotostock/SuperStock; **xx** Jupiter Images; **xxi** (top) Media Bakery; (bottom) PhotoDisc; **xxii** Macduff Everton/Getty Images; **xxiii** (top) Jupiter Unlimited; (middle) Media Bakery; (bottom) Shutterstock; **xxiv** Yoruba Eshu Elegba Figure, Abeokuta, Southwest Nigeria, mid 19th century (carved wood)/© Royal Albert Memorial Museum, Exeter, Devon, UK/The Bridgeman Art Library; **xxv** (top) Shutterstock; (middle) The Rattle Snake (w/c on paper), Bartram, William (1739–1823)/© The Right Hon. Earl of Derby/The Bridgeman Art Library; (bottom) © Bettmann/CORBIS.

Unit 1

2 (top) Jupiter Images; (bottom left) Courtesy of JFK Presidential Library and Museum; (bottom middle) © Bettmann/CORBIS; (bottom right) Courtesy of Lensey Namioka; **3** (top) © Ralph A. Clevenger/CORBIS; (bottom left) Courtesy of Library of Congress; (bottom middle) Courtesy of Leslie Marmon Silko; (bottom right) Courtesy of Library of Congress; **4** © Bettmann/CORBIS; **5** Courtesy of Library of Congress; **6** © 2007 PunchStock; **9** Courtesy of Library of Congress; **10** © Geoffrey Clements/CORBIS; **12** Jupiter Images; **13** © Getty Images; **17** (all) Jupiter Images; **18** Courtesy of JFK Presidential Library and Museum; **19** Jupiter Images; **21** Courtesy of Library of Congress; **26** Courtesy of Library of Congress; **27** The Granger Collection, New York; **29** Jupiter Images; **30** Courtesy of Lensey Namioka; **31** Jupiter Images; **33** © Christie's Images/CORBIS; **37** iStock photo; **39** © Condé Nast Archive/CORBIS; **40** © Asian Art & Archaeology, Inc./CORBIS; **49** Courtesy of Tomás Rivera; **50** Courtesy of the United States Marine Corps; **52** © Bettmann/CORBIS; **57** Courtesy of Library of Congress; **58** © Wolfgang Flamisch/zefa/Corbis; **59** Jupiter Images; **61** Courtesy of NASA; **63** © William J. Weber; **63–71** (border) © IBID photo; **64** © David Butow/CORBIS SABA; **67** Jupiter Images; **68** Photodisc; **69** © Flip Schulke/CORBIS; **73** © Bettmann/CORBIS; **74** © Ralph A. Clevenger/CORBIS; **78** The Loch Ness Monster, illustration, c. 1935 (litho), D'Achille, Gino (20th century)/Private Collection/The Bridgeman Art Library; **79** AP Images; **85** (all) Courtesy of Library of Congress; **86** Rikki-Tikki-Tavi, illustration from The Jungle Book by Rudyard Kipling (1865–1936) published in Paris, 1937 (colour litho), Collot, Andre (d. 1976)/Bibliotheque Nationale, Paris, France, Archives Charmet/The Bridgeman Art Library; **89** Jupiter Images; **93** Rikki-Tikki-Tavi, illustration from The Jungle Book by Rudyard Kipling (1865–1936) published in Paris, 1930 (colour litho), Soulas, Louis Joseph (1905–1954)/Bibliotheque Nationale, Paris, France, Archives Charmet/The Bridgeman Art Library; **98** © Austin J. Stevens/Animals Animals–Earth Scenes—All rights reserved; **101** © age footstock/SuperStock; **103** Copyright © AUSTIN J. STEVENS/Animals Animals–Earth Scenes—All rights reserved; **105** (top) © Jason Hosking/zefa/Corbis; (bottom) Courtesy of Leslie Marmon Silko; **108** © Kevin Fleming/CORBIS; **109** © C3066 Hinrich Baesemann/dpa/Corbis; **110** © Peter Turnley/CORBIS; **111** (top) Jupiter Images; (bottom) Courtesy of Joan Aiken; **113** Courtesy of Dover Flowers; **114** Jupiter Images; **116** Courtesy of Dover Flowers; **117** Jupiter Images; **118** Royalty-Free/Corbis; **122** Jupiter Images; **125** Jacket cover from Tuck Everlasting by Natalie Babbitt. Jacket design copyright © 1975 by Natalie Babbitt. Reprinted by permission of Farrar, Straus and Giroux, LLC; Jacket cover Eragon by Christopher Raolini. Copyright © 2003 by John Jude Palencar, from Eragon (Book Inheritance) by Christopher Paolini. Used by permission of Alfred A. Knopf, an imprint of Random House Children's Books, a division of Random House, Inc.; Cover from Zazoo by Richard Mosher (Boston: Graphia, 2004.); **126** (left) Jupiter Images; (right) © Bettmann/CORBIS; **127** Jupiter Images; **132** Eileen Ryan Photography.

Unit 2

138 (top) © Ashley Cooper/Corbis; (bottom left) © Ulf Andersen/Getty Images; (bottom middle) Courtesy of Gary Soto; (bottom right) Courtesy of Cherylene Lee; **139** (top) Smithsonian American Art Museum, Washington, DC/Art Resource, NY; (bottom left) Time & Life Pictures/Getty Images; (bottom middle) Courtesy of Piri Thomas; (bottom right) © Time & Life Pictures/Getty Images; **140** (top) © Benelux/zefa/Corbis; (bottom) © Patrick Bennett/CORBIS; **141** (top) © Getty Images/Marvin E. Newman; (bottom) Courtesy of Cherylene Lee; **142** © Getty Images/Marvin E. Newman; **145** © Cherylene Lee; **147** © SOQUI TED/CORBIS SYGMA; **148** © Louie Psihoyos/CORBIS; **150** © Vince Streano/CORBIS; **152** Shutterstock; **153** (left) iStockphoto; (right) © Blue Lantern Studio/CORBIS; **155** iStockphoto; **158** © Michael S. Lewis/CORBIS; **161** Royalty-Free/Corbis; **163** Courtesy of Piri Thomas; **164** *The Big Fight* (oil on canvas on wood), Crook, P. J. (b. 1945)/Private Collection/The Bridgeman Art Library; **166–167** Image Source; **169** PhotoDisc; **170** *Boxer Right* (acrylic on canvas), Tatham, Carol (Contemporary Artist)/Private Collection/The Bridgeman Art Library; **173** AP Images; **174** AP Images; **177** © Ulf Andersen/Getty Images; **178** Royalty-Free/Corbis; **179** iStockphoto; **181** Time & Life Pictures/Getty Images; **182** Jupiter Images; **184** Royalty-Free/Corbis; **185–189** PhotoDisc; **191** (top) © Martin Benjamin 2007; (bottom) Time & Life Pictures/Getty Images; **192** © Raymond Gehman/CORBIS; **195** © Michael & Patricia Fogden/CORBIS; **196** PhotoDisc; **197** PhotoDisc; **199** (top) Smithsonian American Art Museum, Washington, DC/Art Resource, NY; (bottom) Photo by Marcia Corbino; (background) Jupiter Images; **200** Jupiter Images; **201** Smithsonian American Art Museum, Washington, DC/Art Resource, NY; **203** Courtesy of Library of Congress; **204** iStockphoto; **207** Courtesy of Library of Congress; **209** iStockphoto; **210** (top) © Patrick Bennett/Corbis; (bottom) © Ashley Cooper/CORBIS; **212** Courtesy of Gary Soto; **213** © Tim Pannell/CORBIS; **215** Jupiter Images; **220** (top) Jupiter Images; (bottom) Courtesy of Cynthia Rylant; **221** PhotoDisc; **222** Jupiter Unlimited; **224** (top) iStockphoto; (bottom) Creative Commons Attribution Sharealike 2.0 License; **227** iStockphoto; **230** *Ms Fr 2810 f.55v Dragons and other beasts* (vellum), Boucicaut Master, (fl.1390–1430) (and workshop)/Bibliotheque Nationale, Paris, France/The Bridgeman Art Library; **233** © Gary Bell/zefa/Corbis; **237** *The Outcasts of 19 Schuyler Place* by E.L. Konigsburg. Jacket illustration © 2004 E.L. Konigsburg. Reprinted with the permission of Atheneum Books for Young Readers, an imprint of Simon & Schuster Children's Publishing Division from *The Outcasts of 19 Schuyler Place* by E.L. Konigsburg; *Al Capone Does My Shirts* by Gennifer Choldenko. Copyright © 2004 by Gennifer Choldenko. Reprinted by permission of Penguin Group (USA), Inc.; Jacket design by Philomena Tuosto from *Holes* by Louis Sachar. Jacket design copyright © 1998 by Pilomena Tuosto. Reprinted by permission of Farrar, Straus and Giroux, LLC; *Romiette and Julio* by Sharon Draper. Copyright © 1999 by Sharon Draper. Reprinted by permission of FPG/Getty Image; Jacket Cover from *Pictures of Hollis Woods* by Patricia Reilly Giff. Used by permission of Random House Children's Books, a division of Random House, Inc.; Book cover *The Chosen*, copyright © 1967, from *The Chosen* by Chaim Potok. Used by permission of Ballantine Books, a division of Random House, Inc.; **238** (left) Jupiter Images; (right) Courtesy of The Anacostia Museum Archives, Smithsonian Institution; **240** Jupiter Images; **246** Eileen Ryan Photography.

Unit 3

252 (top) The Jacob and Gwendolyn Lawrence Foundation/Art Resource, NY; (bottom left) © Bettmann/CORBIS; (bottom middle) AP Images; (bottom right) © Getty Images; **253** (top) © Bridgeman Art Library/National Portrait Gallery, London, UK; (bottom left) AP Images; (bottom middle) AP Images; (bottom right) © Lynn Goldsmith/CORBIS; **254** (left) PhotoDisc; (right) © Bettmann/CORBIS; **255** PhotoDisc; **257** G. Richard Howard/Time & Life Pictures/Getty Images; **258** The Jacob and Gwendolyn Lawrence Foundation/Art Resource, NY; **260** PhotoDisc; **262** PhotoDisc; **265** Courtesy of Milton Meltzer; **266** © Bridgeman Art Library/National Portrait Gallery, London, UK; **269** *Queen Elizabeth I in procession with her Courtiers* (c. 1600–1603) from *Memoirs of the Court of Queen Elizabeth* after an oil attributed to Robert Peake (c. 1592–1667) at Sherborne Castle, published in 1825 (w/c and gouache on paper), Essex, Sarah Countess of (d. 1838)/Private Collection, The Stapleton Collection/The Bridgeman Art Library; **272** G.11631.B.L. Title Page with a Portrait of Shakespeare, from *Mr. William Shakespeare's Comedies, Histories and Tragedies*, edited by J. Heminge and H. Condell, engraving by Droeshout, 1623/British Library, London, UK,

© British Library Board. All Rights Reserved/The Bridgeman Art Library; **277** © Roy Rainford/Robert Harding World Imagery/Corbis; **278** Shutterstock; **281** Royalty-Free/Corbis; **282** AP Images; **283** Media Bakery; **285** © Robert Harding Picture Library Ltd/Alamy; **287** Jupiter Images; **289** © IBID Photo; **291** AP Images; **292** Royalty-Free/Corbis; **294** PhotoDisc; **297** © Getty Images; **298** © Jerry Cooke/CORBIS; **304** © Bettmann/CORBIS; **307** Associated Press; **310** Jupiter Images; **312** © Lynn Goldsmith/CORBIS; **313** © Bettmann/CORBIS; **314** © Getty Images; **315** AP Images; **317** AP Images; **318** © Phil Schermeister/CORBIS; **319** PhotoDisc; **322** (top) © Star Ledger; (bottom) AP Images; **323** © Bettmann/CORBIS; **324** iStockphoto; **329** © Bettmann/CORBIS; **331** © Bettmann/CORBIS; **333–336** Jupiter Images; **337** Shutterstock; **340** Bloomsbury USA/Walker & Co.; **341** The Granger Collection, New York; **343** The Newark Museum/Art Resource, NY; **344** Courtesy of Library of Congress; **348** iStockphoto; **349** © Faith Ringgold; **352** Courtesy of Library of Congress; **354** Sharrer, Honore D. (1920–) © Smithsonian American Art Museum, Washington, DC/Art Resource, NY; **356** (top) PhotoDisc; (bottom) © Bettmann/CORBIS; **357–359** PhotoDisc; **361** Cover from *The Forbidden Schoolhouse* by Suzanne Jurmain. Copyright © 2005 by Suzanne Jurmain. Jacket cover photo © Doug Mindell. Reprinted by permission of Houghton Mifflin Company. All rights reserved; Cover from *George Washington, Spymaster; How the Americans Outspied the British and Won the Revolutionary War* by Thomas B. Allen. Reprinted by permission of National Geographic Society; Cover from *5,000 Miles to Freedom: Ellen and William Craft's Flight from Slavery* by Dennis and Judith Fradin. Reprinted by permission of National Geographic Society; Jacket cover from *Big Annie of Calumet* by Jerry Stanley. Used by permission of Crown Publishers, a division of Random House, Inc.; From *The Kidnapped Prince: The Life of Olaudah Equiano* adapted by Ann Cameron, copyright © 1995 by Ann Cameron. Jacket illustration copyright © 1995 by Dan Andreasen. Used by permission of Alfred A. Knopf, an imprint of Random House Children's Books, a division of Random House, Inc.; *Bad Boy: A Memoir* by Walter Dean Myers. Reprinted by permission of HarperCollins Publishers; **362** (left) Jupiter Images; (right) AP Images; **363** Jupiter Images; **368** Eileen Ryan Photography.

Unit 4

374 (top) © Corbis; (bottom left) Courtesy of Jennifer Armstrong; (bottom middle) Time & Life Pictures/Getty Images; (bottom right) AP Images; **375** (top) *Drought Stricken Area*, 1934 (oil on canvas), Hogue, Alexandre (1898–1994)/Dallas Museum of Art, Texas, USA/The Bridgeman Art Library; (bottom left) © Robert Maass/CORBIS; (bottom middle) © Carolynne Bailey (bottom right) Time & Life Pictures/Getty Images; **376** Jupiter Images; **377** PhotoDisc; **378** Time & Life Pictures/Getty Images; **379** © CORBIS; **382** © Roger Ressmeyer/CORBIS; **386** © STScI/NASA/Corbis; **387** © Aaron Horowitz/CORBIS; **390** © Carolynne Bailey; **394** Jupiter Images; **396** © Robert Maass/CORBIS; **396–397** © SHAMIL ZHUMATOV/Reuters/Corbis; **398** iStockphoto; **400** Royalty-Free/Corbis; **403** © Canadian Museum of Civilization/CORBIS; **404–405** Shutterstock; **408** (top) Time & Life Pictures/Getty Images; (bottom) AP Images; **409** *Quetzalcoatl, the plumed serpent, god of the wind, learning and the priesthood, master of life, creator and civiliser, patron of every art and inventor of metallurgy* (manuscript)/Biblioteca Nazionale Centrale, Florence, Italy/The Bridgeman Art Library; **412** Jupiter Images; **415** Courtesy of Jennifer Armstrong; **416** © Hulton-Deutsch Collection/CORBIS; **421** (all) PhotoDisc; **425** Storycloth, Mee Vang; Private collection; **426** © Dave Bartruff/CORBIS; **428** AP Images; **430** © Reuters/Corbis; **432** Courtesy of Library of Congress; **433–436** © 1936 Arthur Rothstein; **438** *Drought Stricken Area*, 1934 (oil on canvas), Hogue, Alexandre (1898–1994)/Dallas Museum of Art, Texas, USA/The Bridgeman Art Library; **440** (top) *Dead fox lying in the Undergrowth*, 1865 (oil on canvas), Degas, Edgar (1834–1917)/Musée des Beaux-Arts, Rouen, France, Peter Willi/The Bridgeman Art Library; (bottom) © Bettmann/CORBIS; **446** AFP/Getty Images; **447** Cover from *The New Way Things Work* by David Macaulay. Compilation copyright © 1988, 1998 Dorling Kindersley Ltd., London. Illustrations copyright © 1988, 1998 David Macaulay. Reprinted by permission of Houghton Mifflin Company. All rights reserved; *A Drop of Water* by Walter Wick. Text and photographs copyright © 1997 by Walter Wick. Reprinted by permission of Scholastic Inc.; *Pick Me Up* by David Roberts and Jeremy Leslie. Reprinted by permission of John Brown Publishing Ltd.; *Raptor! A Kid's Guide to Birds of Prey* by Chirstyna and René Lauback, and Charles W. G. Smith. Copyright © 2002 by Christyna Lauback, René Lauback, and Charles W. G. Smith. Reprinted by permission of Storey Publishing; *Photography: An Illustrated History* by Martin W. Sandler. Copyright © 2002 by Martin W. Sandler. Reprinted by permission of Oxford University Press; *Universe* edited by Martin Rees. Copyright © 2005 Dorling Kindersley Limited. Reprinted by permission of DK Publishing; **448** (left) Shutterstock; (right) AP Images; **449** Jupiter Unlimited; **454** Eileen Ryan Photography.

Unit 5

460 (top) © Shutterstock; (bottom left) © Oscar White/CORBIS; (bottom middle) © Corbis; (bottom right) © Oscar White/CORBIS; **461** (top) *Mother Courage II*, 1974 (oil on canvas), White, Charles Wilbert (1918–1979)/National Academy Museum, New York, USA/The Bridgeman Art Library; (bottom left) Courtesy of Library of Congress; (bottom middle) © Bettmann/CORBIS; (bottom right) Courtesy of Library of Congress; **462** © Edmond Van Hoorick/SuperStock; **463** Superstock; **464** Shutterstock; **466** Courtesy of Pat Mora; **467** Shutterstock; **469** © Oscar White/CORBIS; **470** Shutterstock; **473** © age fotostock/SuperStock; **474** © age fotostock/SuperStock; **475** Courtesy of Library of Congress; **478** The Pierpont Morgan Library/Art Resource, NY; **481** © Oscar White/CORBIS; **482** Fine Art Photographic Library, London/Art Resource, NY; **485** Courtesy of Library of Congress; **486** © David David Gallery/SuperStock; **488** Shutterstock; **491** Courtesy of Library of Congress; **492** *Mother Courage II*, 1974 (oil on canvas), White, Charles Wilbert (1918–1979)/National Academy Museum, New York, USA/The Bridgeman Art Library; **496** *The Apple Tree II*, 1916 (oil on canvas), Klimt, Gustav (1862–1918)/Private Collection/The Bridgeman Art Library; **498** *Johnny Appleseed* (1774–1847) (colored engraving), American School, (19th century)/Private Collection, Peter Newark American Pictures/The Bridgeman Art Library; **502** © CORBIS; **503** © Edmond Van Hoorick/SuperStock; **505** Eve Merriam: Photo by Bachrach; **506–508** Shutterstock; **511** © Christie's Images/CORBIS; **513** iStockphoto; **515** © Bettmann/CORBIS; **516** © Eddi Böhnke/zefa/Corbis; **518** (top) Jupiter Images; (bottom) Eve Merriam: Photo by Bachrach; **519** PhotoDisc; **520** Courtesy of Library of Congress; **521** iStockphoto; **522** *The Navajo* (oil on canvas), Dixon, Maynard (1875–1946)/Private Collection, Photo © Christie's Images/The Bridgeman Art Library; **523** *The Invisible Ladder: An Anthology of Contemporary American Poems for Young Readers* edited by Liz Rosenberg. Compilation copyright © 1996 by Liz Rosenberg. Reprinted by permission of Henry Holt & Company; Cover from *War and the Pity of War*, edited by Neil Philip. Jacket illustrations copyright © 1998 by Michael McCurdy. Reprinted by permission of Clarion Books, an imprint of Houghton Mifflin Company. All rights reserved; *Becoming Joe DiMaggio* by Maria Testa. Text copyright © 2002 by Maria Testa, illustration copyright © 2002 by Scott Hunt. Reprinted by permission of Candlewick Press, Inc.; *Ancient Voices* by Kate Hovey. Jacket illustration © 2004 Murray Kimber. Reprinted with the permission of Margaret K. McElderry Books, an imprint of Simon & Schuster Children's Publishing Division from *Ancient Voices* by Kate Hovey, illustrated by Murray Kimber; *I Am the Darker Brother: An Anthology of Modern Poems by African Americans* edited by Arnold Adoff. Reprinted by permission of James Ransome; *The The Dream on Blanca's Wall: Poems in English and Spanish* by Jane Medina, illustration by Robert Casilla. (Wordsong, an imprint of Boyds Mills Press, 2004.) Reprinted by permission of Boyds Mills Press, Inc.; **524** (left) PhotoDisc; (right) © Bettmann/CORBIS; **525** (all) Jupiter Images; **528** Time & Life Pictures/Getty Images; **530** InspireStock Images.

Unit 6

536 (top) Media Bakery; (bottom left and middle) Courtesy of Library of Congress; (bottom right) Time & Life Pictures/Getty Images; **537** (top) Art Resource, NY; (bottom left) © Bettmann/CORBIS; (bottom middle) Courtesy of Library of Congress; (bottom right) © Bettmann/CORBIS; **538** Jupiter Images; **539** (bottom) Courtesy of Library of Congress; (background) Media Bakery; **540–541** Media Bakery; **544** Courtesy of Library of Congress; **545** *Downpour at Etretat* (oil on canvas), Courbet, Gustave (1819–1877)/Musée des Beaux-Arts, Dijon, France, Giraudon/The Bridgeman Art Library; **547** (top) Courtesy of Library of Congress; (bottom) Time & Life Pictures/Getty Images; **548** *Found Drowned*, 1848–1850 (oil on canvas), Watts, George Frederick (1817–1904)/© Trustees of the Watts Gallery, Compton, Surrey, UK/The Bridgeman Art Library; **550** Erich Lessing/Art Resource, NY; **551** *The Highwaymen* (oil on canvas), Rowlandson, George Derville (1861–1930)/Private Collection, Haynes Fine Art at the Bindery Galleries, Broadway/The Bridgeman Art Library; **553** Jupiter Images; **557** © Bettmann/CORBIS; **558** Courtesy of Library of Congress; **563** Courtesy of Library of

Congress; **564** © University of Virginia; **568** Courtesy of the African American Registry; **569** Courtesy of Library of Congress; **572** Courtesy of Naomi Shihab Nye; **573** iStockphoto; **576** Getty Images; **577** (foreground) © SuperStock, Inc./SuperStock; (background) Courtesy of Library of Congress; **578** Courtesy of Library of Congress; **580** ANNELINDSAY Photography; **581** © Thomas Holton/Getty; **582** Shutterstock; **584** (top) Art Resource, NY; (bottom) © Bettmann/CORBIS; **585** PhotoDisc; **586** (top) © Josephine Trotter/SuperStock; (bottom) © Bryce Milligan; **587** PhotoDisc; **588** © CORBIS; **590** iStockphoto; **591** (top) *Canterbury Meadows*, 1862 (oil on panel), Cooper, Thomas Sidney (1803–1902)/Art Gallery of New South Wales, Sydney, Australia, Gift of W. A. Little 1928/The Bridgeman Art Library; (bottom) Courtesy of Library of Congress; **592** PhotoDisc; **593** *Poetry for Young People* by William Carlos Williams edited by Christopher McGowan. Text copyright © 2004 by Chistopher McGowan, Illustration copyright © by Robert Crockett. Reprinted by permission of Sterling Publishing Co., Inc.; *Remember the Bridge: Poems of a People* by Carole Boston Weatherford. Text copyright © 2002 by Carole Boston Weatherford; Book cover *Laughing Out Loud, I Fly: Poems in English and Spanish* by Juan Felipe Herrera. Used by permission of HarperCollins Publishers; *Poetry for Young People* by Walt Whitman, edited by Jonathan Levin. Text © 1997 by Jonathan Levin. Illustration © 1997 by Jim Burke. Reprinted by permission of Sterling Publishing Co.; *I am Wings: Poems About Love* by Ralph Fletcher. Text copyright © 1994 by Ralph Fletcher. Photographs copyright © 1994 by Joe Baker. Reprinted by permission of Joe Baker; Cover from *A Wreath for Emmett Till* by Marilyn Nelson, illustrated by Philippe Lardy. Jacket painting © 2005 by Philippe Lardy. Reprinted by permission of Houghton Mifflin Company. All rights reserved; **594** Courtesy of Library of Congress; **595** Jupiter Images; **600** Jupiter Images.

Unit 7

606 (top) Macduff Everton/Getty Images; (bottom left) AFP/Getty Images; (bottom middle) Courtesy of the Library of Congress; (bottom right) AP Images; **607** (top) © Michael Brosilow; (bottom left) Courtesy of Library of Congress; (bottom middle) © Roger Ressmeyer/CORBIS; (bottom right) © Bettmann/CORBIS; **608** Media Bakery; **611** AP Images; **612** *An Old Woman and her Dog Startled by Male Company* (pen & ink and w/c on paper), Rowlandson, Thomas (1756–1827)/Private Collection, © Chris Beetles, London, U.K./The Bridgeman Art Library; **620** Shutterstock; **623** AFP/Getty Images; **624** © Michael Brosilow; **628** © Michael Brosilow; **634** *The Crawlers* (Woodbury type), Thomson, John (1837–1921)/Victoria & Albert Museum, London, UK/The Bridgeman Art Library; **636** © Michael Brosilow; **638** © Michael Brosilow; **640** © Michael Brosilow; **642** Shutterstock; **643** *Tower Bridge from Cherry Garden Pier*, c. 1900 (w/c on paper), Dixon, Charles Edward (1872–1934)/Private Collection, Bourne Gallery, Reigate, Surrey/The Bridgeman Art Library; **646** © Michael Brosilow; **650** © Michael Brosilow; **654** © Michael Brosilow; **657** *Silent Night*, 1891 (oil on canvas) by Viggo Johansen (1851–1935), © Hirschsprungske Samling, Copenhagen, Denmark/The Bridgeman Art Library, Nationality/copyright status: Danish/out of copyright; **661** © Michael Brosilow; **663** © Michael Brosilow; **665** (top) Jupiter Images; (bottom) *Marley's Ghost*, 1843. John Leech. Dickens House Museum, London; **666** (left) *Scrooge's Third Visitor*, 1843. John Leech. Dickens House Museum, London; (right) *The Last of the Visitors*, 1843. John Leech. Dickens House Museum, London; **669** © Roger Ressmeyer/CORBIS; **670** Jupiter Unlimited; **673** *Faraday's Magnetic Laboratory*, 1852 (w/c on paper), Moore, Harriet Jane (1801–1884)/The Royal Institution, London, UK/The Bridgeman Art Library; **681** Jupiter Unlimited; **683** Shutterstock; **684** ISSOUF SANOGO/AFP/Getty Images; **687** (all) Courtesy of Library of Congress; **688** Courtesy of Photofest, Sir Lawrence Olivier as Henry V in a 1944 film version of Shakespeare's play; **690** *Balaclava*, 1889 (oil on canvas), Charlton, John (1849–1917)/© Blackburn Museum and Art Gallery, Lancashire, UK/The Bridgeman Art Library; **691** Helmet, c. 1855 (gilt metal), English School, (19th century)/Courtesy of the Council, National Army Museum, London, UK/The Bridgeman Art Library; **694** (top) © Macduff Everton/Getty Images; (bottom) © Bettmann/CORBIS; **698** © H. Armstrong Roberts/CORBIS; **704–705** © Digital Art/CORBIS; **709** Cover from *The Jumbo Book of Drama* written by Deborah Dunleavy and illustrated by Jane Kurisu, is used by permission of Kids Can Press Ltd., Toronto. Text © 2004 Deborah Dunleavy. Illustrations © 2004 Jane Kurisu; *Plays of Black Americans: the Black Experience in America, Dramatized for Young People* edited by Sylvia E. Kamerman. Copyright © 1987, 1994 by Sylvia K. Burrack. Reprinted by permission of Plays, Inc.; *Plays from Hispanic Tales* by Barbara Winther. Copyright © 1998 by Barbara Winther. Reprinted by permission of

Plays, Inc.; *Greek Theatre* by Stewart Ross. Copyright © 1996 by Wayland Publishers Limited. Reprinted by permission of Contemporary Publishing Group, Inc.; *Shakespeare's Theater* by Jacqueline Morley and John James. Reprinted by permission of Simon & Schuster; *Seattle Children's Theatre: Six Plays for Young Readers* by Marisa Smith. Reprinted by permission of Smith and Kraus Publishers, Inc.; **710** Courtesy of Library of Congress; **711** © Royalty-Free/Corbis; **716** Radius Images.

Unit 8

722 (top) Detail depicting the deceased led by Horus before Osiris, c. 1250 BC (painted papyrus), Egyptian, 19th Dynasty (c. 1297–1185 BC)/British Museum, London, UK/The Bridgeman Art Library; (bottom left) Courtesy of Judith Ortiz Cofer; (bottom middle) © Joanne Ryder/Writer Pictures; (bottom right) Courtesy of Judith Gleason; **723** (top) Jupiter Images; (bottom left) Writers Pictures/@Joseph Campbell Foundation; (bottom middle) Courtesy of Library of Congress; (bottom right) AFP/Getty Images; **724** © Dennis Degnan/CORBIS; **725** (all) © Blue Lantern Studio/CORBIS; **727** Courtesy of D'Aulaire; **728** The Rape of Persephone by Hades (colour litho), English School, (19th century)/Bibliotheque des Arts Decoratifs, Paris, France, Archives Charmet/The Bridgeman Art Library; **730** © Sal Maimone/SuperStock; **733** Courtesy of Judith Gleason; **734** Yoruba Eshu Elegba Figure, Abeokuta, Southwest Nigeria, mid 19th century (carved wood)/© Royal Albert Memorial Museum, Exeter, Devon, UK/The Bridgeman Art Library; **738** Courtesy of Geraldine Harris; **739** (background) © Rosemary Calvert/SuperStock; **739** (foreground) Detail depicting the deceased led by Horus before Osiris, c. 1250 BC (painted papyrus), Egyptian, 19th Dynasty (c. 1297–1185 BC)/British Museum, London, UK/The Bridgeman Art Library; **741** SuperStock; **743** © Christine Osborne/CORBIS; **744** Shutterstock; **748** Time & Life Pictures/Getty Images; **753** © Bettmann/CORBIS; **754** PhotoDisc; **755** The Trail of Tears, 1942. Robert Lindneux. The Granger Collection, New York; **757** (bottom) © Joanne Ryder/Writer Pictures; (background) Jupiter Images; **758** Jupiter Images; **761** iStockphoto; **765** Aesop, 1640 (oil on canvas), Velasquez, Diego Rodriguez de Silva y (1599–1660)/Prado, Madrid, Spain, Giraudon/The Bridgeman Art Library; **766** The Ant and the Grasshopper from 'Aesop's Fables' series (offset from linocut), Bawden, Edward (1903–1989)/© Chelmsford Museums, Essex, UK/The Bridgeman Art Library; **767** The Art Archive/Bibliothèque Nationale Paris/Marc Charmet; **768** © Araldo de Luca/CORBIS; **771** The Chariot of Apollo, 1907–1910 (oil on canvas), Redon, Odilon (1840–1916)/Fitzwilliam Museum, University of Cambridge, UK/The Bridgeman Art Library; **773** © Bettmann/CORBIS; **777** (top) Writers Pictures/© Joseph Campbell Foundation; (bottom) AFP/Getty Images; **778** Jupiter Images; **779** Jupiter Unlimited Images; **780** © Art Archive; **782** iStockphoto; **786** Kunak McGann, The O'Brien Press; **787** © Asian Art & Archaeology, Inc./CORBIS; **789** Roof of the Naiku, Shinto shrine, dedicated to Amaterasu, the sun goddess, Ise. Ise, Japan, Photo Credit: Werner Forman/Art Resource, NY; **790** Shutterstock; **792** Courtesy of Judith Ortiz Cofer; **793** © Leslie Hinrichs/SuperStock; **796** (top) © Patti Mollica/SuperStock; **796** (bottom) AP Images; **799** © The Grand Design/SuperStock; **803** (top) The Rattle Snake (w/c on paper), Bartram, William (1739–1823)/© The Right Hon. Earl of Derby/The Bridgeman Art Library; (bottom) Courtesy of Library of Congress; **805** Cover from Horse Hooves and Chicken Feet: Mexican Folktales, edited by Neil Philip. Jacket illustrations copyright © 2003 by Jaqueline Mair. Reprinted by permission of Clarion Books, an imprint of Houghton Mifflin Company. All rights reserved; Peace Walker: The Legend of Hiawatha and Takenawita by Carrie J. Taylor. Reprinted by permission of Tundra Books of Northern New York; Beowulf by Michael Morpurgo ISBN: 978-1-58049-348-2. Copyright © 2005 Prestwick House. Reprinted by permission of Prestwick House Inc.; The Legend of Lord Eight Deer: An Epic of Mexico retold and illustrated by John M.D. Pohl. Copyright © 2002 by John M.D. Pohl. Reprinted by permission of Oxford University Press; The Four Corners of the Sky by Steve Zeitlin. Text copyright © 2000 by Steve Zeitlin and illustration copyright © 2000 by Chris Raschka. Reprinted by permission of Henry Holt & Company; From The Story of King Arthur and His Knights by Howard Pyle, copyright © 1986 by New American Library. Used by permission of Signet, an imprint of Penguin Group (USA) Inc.; **807** Image courtesy of Michael Thompson **809** Jupiter Images; **815** (Top) © Carrie Wendel/iStockphoto LP; (bottom) Image by Larry D. Moore, used under a Creative Commons License. **817** © powerlines/iStockphoto LP; **828** Eileen Ryan Photography. **834** (top left) Shutterstock; (top right) iStockphoto; (bottom left) © Bettmann/CORBIS; (bottom right) Royalty-Free/Corbis.

Index of Skills

Reading Strategies & Skills/Literary Elements

act, 609
adaptions, 316, 414
allegory, 770, 775
alliteration, 463, 474, 481, 482, 483
allusion, 211
analogy, 396, 406
analyze, 8, 256, 316, 414, 431, 465, 610, 644, 726, 835
antagonist, 5, 7, 17, 609
argumentative essay, 255, 281, 291, 293, 295
argumentative writing, 840
ask questions, 8, 256, 351, 465, 610, 726, 835, 838, 849
assonance, 474
author's approach, 840
author's perspective, 560
author's purpose, 152, 282, 286, 481, 568, 570, 747, 765, 840
autobiography, 255, 257, 259, 261, 262, 263
bar chart, 847–848
biography, 255, 265, 268, 269, 270, 274, 275
build background, 8, 256, 465, 610, 726, 835, 837
cast, 609
cause and effect, 9, 12, 49, 63, 141, 144, 147, 149, 151, 502, 580, 611, 613, 614, 738, 792, 845
cause-and-effect chart, 845
cause-and-effect clue, 843
cause-and-effect order, 844
character, 5, 17, 18, 19, 20, 22, 23, 25, 28, 212, 218, 609, 621, 842
characterization, 17, 322, 339, 786, 791
chart, 377
chronological order, 7, 844
clarify, 8, 256, 271, 385, 465, 610, 726, 835, 839
classification chart, 846
classify, 846
climax, 6, 9, 49
comedy, 608
compare and contrast, 181, 386, 510, 572, 775, 844–845
compare translations, 514
compare versions, 644
comparison clue, 843
comparison-and-contrast order, 844
comprehension, 378, 380, 381, 383, 384, 469, 471, 727, 728, 730
conclusions, 340, 351
concrete poem, 462, 515, 517
conflict, 7, 9, 49, 57, 62, 199, 211, 757, 763
connections, 8, 276, 619, 729
connections chart, 839
consonance, 474
context, 835
context clues, 73, 154, 160, 199, 257, 259, 312, 340, 415, 485, 842–843
contrast appearance and reality, 583
contrast clue, 843
creation myths, 724
description, 297, 311, 386, 408, 414, 415, 422, 426
descriptive writing, 840
determine importance, 841–842
diagram, 377
dialect, 63, 71
dialogue, 609, 669, 686
diction, 687, 692
distinguish fact from opinion, 265, 273, 295
drama, 606, 610, 613, 616, 617, 621
draw conclusions, 57, 163, 390, 392, 393, 623, 770, 786, 835, 849
drawing conclusions log, 849
dynamic characters, 17
effects of form on meaning, 475, 477
end rhyme, 473
essay, 255, 281
evaluate, 8, 256, 465, 610, 726, 791, 835
examples clue, 843
exposition, 6
external conflict, 7
fable, 725, 765, 769
fact, 846
fact from opinion chart, 295, 846
fact vs. opinion, 846
facts and opinions, 2
falling action, 6
fantasy, 4
fiction, 4, 5
figurative language, 415, 463, 464
film, 575
first-person point of view, 842
fix-up ideas, 839, 848–849
flashback, 7
flat character, 17
folk literature, 722, 724, 757
folk tale, 725, 733, 735
foot, 474
foreshadowing, 7
framework for reading, 836
free verse, 462, 495, 500
generate questions bookmark, 838
graphic organizers, 843
Greek myth, 732
haiku, 462, 510, 514
half rhyme, 473
hero myth, 724
horror, 4
hyperbole, 463, 464, 576, 579
ideas, 355
illustration, 377
image, 463, 464, 560
imagery, 415, 421, 463, 464, 466, 467, 468
implied theme, 153
inference chart, 839
inferences, 8, 11, 150, 256, 267, 268, 465, 610, 726, 736
informational text, 376, 378, 379, 383, 384, 388
informative essay, 281
informative writing, 840
internal conflict, 7
internal rhyme, 473

interpret, 8, 256, 465, 609, 610, 726, 842
introductions, 340, 351
irony, 580, 583
judgments, 8, 256, 465, 610, 726
K-W-L chart, 837
legend, 724
levels of meaning chart, 847
line, 462
literary elements, 835, 842
literary fiction, 4
locate basic facts, 841
lyric poem, 462, 562, 566
main character, 18, 212
main idea, 841
main idea map, 841
main ideas and supporting details, 177, 291, 294, 297, 396, 466, 467, 491, 568, 557, 733, 736
major and minor details, 669
major characters, 5, 17
make connections, 835, 839
make inferences, 835, 839, 842
make predictions, 835, 838
map, 377, 848
meaning, 8, 256, 465, 495, 538, 539, 541, 726
meaning of words, 842
meet author, 8, 256, 465, 610, 726
memoir, 255, 257
metaphor, 463, 464, 469, 471, 472, 505, 509
meter, 463, 474
minor characters, 5, 17, 212
monitor comprehension, 848–849
monologue, 609
mood, 29, 84, 181, 189, 842
motivation, 17, 738, 745, 747, 756
mystery, 4
myth, 724, 727, 731, 732
narrative, 462
narrative poem, 547, 556
narrative writing, 840
nature myth, 724
news article, 376
nonfiction, 255, 376
note taking, 843
novel, 4
onomatopoeia, 474
opinion, 846
oral histories, 724
oral traditions, 724, 747
order of importance, 844
organization, 7
origin myth, 724
parallelism, 255
paraphrase, 849
personal essay, 255, 281, 282, 287, 288, 290
personification, 85, 104, 463, 464
photograph, 377
pie chart, 847
plot, 5, 6, 7, 9, 11, 14, 15, 49, 55, 199, 609, 623, 644, 667, 842
poetry, 460, 500, 585
point of view, 5, 140, 141, 142, 152, 281, 842
popular fiction, 4
precise words, 415
prediction chart, 838
predictions, 8, 12, 14, 22, 256, 267, 272, 465, 610, 619, 726
preview, 835, 837
prior knowledge, 432
pro and con chart, 845
protagonist, 5, 17, 18, 609
purpose, 312, 316, 424, 431, 432, 439, 840
quests, 724
read aloud, 849
read in shorter chunks, 848
reader's purpose chart, 837
reading process, 835–836
reading rate, 849
reading skills, 835, 839–849
reading strategy, 836–839
recall, 8, 256, 465, 610, 726
remember details, 835
repetition, 491, 494
reread, 835, 848
resolution, 6, 9, 49
respond, 8, 23, 38, 145, 147, 260, 284, 294, 380, 478
response bookmark, 843
restatement clue, 843
rhetorical question, 255
rhyme, 463, 473, 475, 476, 479
rhyme scheme, 473, 502, 504
rhythm, 463, 474, 485, 489
rising action, 6
round characters, 17
scan, 840–841
scene, 84, 609
scenery, 609
science article, 376
science fiction, 4
screenplay, 608
script, 609
second-person point of view, 842
sensory details, 297, 317, 320, 415
sequence, 844
sequence map, 844
sequence of events, 30, 34, 38, 41, 44, 45, 46, 212, 424, 757, 835
set, 609
set purpose, 8, 256, 465, 610, 726, 835, 835, 837
setting, 5, 29, 30, 32, 33, 34, 35, 36, 39, 40, 42, 46, 47, 55
short story, 4
simile, 463, 464, 469, 471, 472, 792, 793
skim, 840–841
slant rhyme, 463, 473
sonnet, 462
sound devices, 463, 473
speaker, 462, 538, 539, 541, 542
stage directions, 609
stanza, 462
stated theme, 153
static characters, 17
straight drama, 608
summarize, 422, 621, 791, 835, 849
summary chart, 849
symbol, 463, 538, 544, 572, 575
symbolism, 189, 544, 545, 546, 777, 785
synthesize, 835
taking notes, 18, 19, 23, 395, 843
television scripts, 608
text organization, 515, 544, 545, 562, 843–844
text structure, 317, 576
theme, 5, 153, 154, 156, 157, 158, 159, 161

thesis, 255
third-person point of view, 842
time line, 844
tone, 191, 263, 281, 557, 560, 842
topic, 153
tragedy, 608
trickster tale, 725
understand function, 842
understanding, 726
Venn diagram, 845
visual aids, 847–848
visual media, 377, 390, 392, 395
visualization map, 838
visualize, 8, 256, 465, 610, 726, 734, 835, 838
voice, 281
web page, 377
western, 4

Vocabulary Skills

acronyms, 856
analogy, 561
Anglo-Saxon roots, 280
antonyms, 484
borrowed words, 388, 856, 862
base word, 851
brand names, 842
cause-and-effect clue, 850
commonly confused words, 864
commonly misspelled words, 865
comparison, 423
comparison clue, 850
compound nouns, 862
connotation, 16, 856–857
connotation chart, 857
context clues, 423, 850
contrast, 423
contrast clue, 850
definitions, 423, 668
denotation, 856–857
description, 423
dictionaries, 855
eponyms, 855
etymology, 682, 855
example, 423
examples clue, 850,
extra syllables, 864
figurative language, 561
Greek roots, 280
homographs, 856
homonyms, 746
homophones, 746, 864
idiom, 561
ie/ei spelling pattern, 859–860
Latin roots, 280
letter combinations, 861–862
metaphor, 561
near synonyms, 16
numerals, 862–863
omitted sounds, 864
part of speech, 855
plural nouns, 859
prefixes, 176, 567, 835, 851–852, 857
pronunciations, 668, 855
restatement, 423
restatement clue, 850
roots, 176
seed sound pattern, 860
signal words, 850
silent letters, 860–861
simile, 561
spelling errors, 864
spelling rules, 857
suffixes, 176, 567, 851, 852–853, 857–858
syllables, 567
synonyms, 16, 484, 855
thesaurus, 484, 668
usage illustration, 855
word families, 855–856
word origins, 855–856
word root, 851, 853–854

Grammar & Style

abbreviations, 896–897
abstract noun, 870
action verb, 859
active voice, 901
adjective clauses, 190, 389
adjectives, 869, 878
adverb clauses, 190, 389
adverbs, 869, 879
agreement, 857, 876–877,882–883
antecedent, 871
antecedent-pronoun agreement, 56
apostrophe, 883, 893
appositive phrase, 881
article, 878
bracket, 895
capitalization, 896–897
case, 872
clauses, 190, 389, 859, 881
collective nouns, 490, 870
colons, 693, 892–893
colorful language, 901
combined sentences, 898–899
commas, 162, 528, 891
common noun, 870
complement, 875–876
complete predicates, 571, 867
complete subject, 867
complex sentences, 543, 868
compound noun, 870
compound predicates, 571,867–868
compound sentences, 162, 543, 868
compound subjects, 407, 867–868, 877, 882
compound subject-verb agreement, 877
compound-complex sentences, 543
concrete noun, 870
conjunction, 869, 879–880
coordinating conjunctions, 824
correlative conjunctions, 824
dangling modifier, 884
dashes, 693, 895
declarative sentences, 296, 866
demonstrative pronoun, 870
dependent clauses, 190
direct object, 875
double negative, 883
ellipsis point, 893
end marks, 890–891
essential clauses, 389
exclamation point, 891
exclamatory sentence, 867
expressers, 873
family relationships, 896
future tense, 852, 874
gender agreement, 56
geographical directions, 897
geographical names, 897
gerund phrase, 881
gerunds, 622
helping verb, 873

historical names, 897
hyphen, 895
I and first words, 896
imperative sentences, 296, 866
indefinite pronoun, 870, 872, 877–878
indefinite pronoun-verb agreement, 877–878
independent clauses, 190, 881
indirect object, 875–876
infinitives, 622
intensive pronouns, 501, 848, 870
interjection, 869, 879
interrogative pronoun, 870
interrogative sentences, 296, 866
intervening words, 882
intransitive verb, 873
irregular verb, 873
italics, 894
linking verb, 873, 876
literary words, 897
misplaced modifiers, 764, 884
misused words, 885–890
modifiers, 878–879
nominative case, 872
nominative pronouns, 72
nonessential clauses, 389
nouns, 490, 869–870
objective case, 872
objective pronouns, 72
parallelism, 900–901
parentheses, 895
participial phrases, 264, 881
participles, 264, 622, 881
passive voice, 901
past tense, 874
perfect tense, 874
period, 890–891
personal pronouns, 480, 870, 872
phrases, 264, 880–881
plural nouns, 490, 870, 876
plural pronoun, 870
possessive case, 872
possessive noun, 870
possessive pronouns, 480
predicate nominative case, 72
predicates, 571, 866–868, 873
preposition, 869, 879–880
prepositional phrases, 264, 880
present tense, 859–874
pronoun agreement, 871
pronoun-antecedent agreement, 56
pronouns, 72, 501, 869, 870–872
proper adjectives, 878, 896
proper nouns, 490, 870, 896
punctuation, 693, 890–895
question mark, 891
quotation mark, 894
reflexive pronouns, 501, 870
relative pronoun, 870
run-on sentences, 321, 898
semicolons, 693, 891–892
sentence fragments, 321, 866, 898
sentence structure, 899–900
sentence types, 296
sentence variety, 296
sentences, 543, 866–868, 898–901
simple predicates, 571, 867
simple sentences, 543, 868
simple subjects, 407, 867
simple tenses, 883–874
singular noun, 870, 876
singular pronoun, 870
subject-verb agreement, 48, 876, 882–883
subjects, 407, 866–868
subordinate clause, 882
subordinating conjunctions, 824
tense, 873–874
time designations, 897
titles of art, 897
transitive verb, 873
unclear antecedents, 56
underlining, 894
usage problems, 882–884verb phrase, 873
verb tense, 873–874
verbal phrase, 881
verbals, 622
verbs, 869, 873
verb-subject agreement, 48
verb tense, 219
who and *whom*, 884
wordy sentence, 900

Writing

active voice, 452
adjectives, 452
adverbs, 452
apostrophes, 598
argumentative essay, 509, 710, 718
argumentative paragraph, 316, 575
argumentative speech, 732
argumentative techniques, 718
audience, 902, 903
autobiographical essay, 311
biographical sketch, 311
biography, 71, 351, 388, 509, 519, 570, 791
book review, 236, 395
book summary, 263
brainstorm, 905
cause-and-effect essay, 362, 546
cause-and-effect order, 364, 596, 808
cause-and-effect organization, 906
character sketch, 479, 775
chronological order, 240, 450, 596, 808
chronological organization, 906
commonly confused words, 366
comparative form, 714
compare-and-contrast essay, 104, 198, 524, 583
comparison-and-contrast order, 808
comparison-and-contrast organization, 906
conclusion, 907
concrete poem, 517
counterarguments, 718, 712
critical analysis, 263, 414, 468, 483, 489, 686, 737, 802, 804
description, 180
descriptive essay, 180, 263, 431, 448, 456, 472, 509
descriptive paragraph, 47, 388, 395, 522, 546, 763
descriptive writing, 903, 911
dialogue, 28, 71, 175, 279, 320, 414, 579
diary entry, 110, 189, 587, 667
draft, 907
drama, 769
dream poem, 575
editorial, 62, 769
essay, 124, 339, 556, 560
fable, 769
figurative language, 598

flyer, 737
form, 902, 904–905
formal English, 903–904
freewrite, 905
gather ideas, 905
graphic organizer, 905
historical essay, 431
humorous poem, 479
informal English, 903–904
informative essay, 15, 175, 218, 320, 370, 504, 532, 667
informative paragraph, 161, 189, 279, 290, 570, 692, 785, 795
informative writing, 362, 524, 806, 903, 911
interview questions, 439
introduction, 907
invitation, 290
jingle, 351
journal entry, 152, 223, 422, 446, 686
letter, 15, 62, 104, 406, 566
list, 388
literary analysis, 47, 585, 590, 592, 621, 708, 756, 775
literary critique, 556
literary response, 134, 152, 180, 211, 248, 295, 422, 442, 472, 521, 542, 579, 763
lyric poem, 500
monologue, 494
myth, 745
narrative essay, 483
narrative poem, 556, 692
narrative writing, 238, 903, 911
neatness, 528
newspaper editorial, 355, 500
order of importance, 712
order of importance organization, 906
organization, 128, 450, 526, 906–907
outline, 439, 906–907
paragraph, 28, 84
parallel structure, 714
paraphrasing, 810
passive voice, 452
peer evaluation, 908
personal essay, 360, 566, 602
personal letter, 295, 316, 504, 579
personal narrative, 494, 594
persuasive writing, 62, 84, 903, 911
plot diagram, 439
poem, 198, 468, 483, 509, 542, 795
point-by-point organization, 526
point of view, 242
positive form, 714
prewrite, 902–907
problem-and-solution essay, 406
problem-and-solution order, 596
proofread, 909–910
publish and present, 910
punctuating dialogue, 242
propose, 902, 903
questions, 47, 218, 360, 566
quotations, 242
reflect, 910–911
reporting question, 905
research essay, 71
research report, 686, 806, 830
response to piece of literature, 126
response to short story, 126
retelling of myth, 732
review, 263
review of play, 644
review of poem, 517
revise, 908–910
rhetorical devices, 718
scene, 621
screenplay, 263
script, 175
self-evaluation, 908
sentence variety, 130
short story, 218, 238, 489, 560
spatial order, 450
speech, 161, 351
story summary, 55
subject-by-subject organization, 526
summary, 745, 824
superlative form, 714
taking notes, 785
thesis, 718
thesis statement, 525, 906
tone, 128, 240
topic, 902, 904
topic sentence, 128, 905–906
transitions, 526, 528
travel brochure, 583
voice, 902, 904
wordiness, 366
writing process, 902–911

Research & Documentation

advertisements, 351
African-American athletes, 316
African-American sports heroes, 310
ancestry, 570
Ancient Egypt, 741
animal languages, 683
animals, 446
aqualung, 83
archaeological site details, 152
attitudes toward nature, 403
biography, 279
birds, 394, 395, 472
blacksmith's bellows, 489
changing names, 564
chart, 28
chart of Fahrenheit and Celsius equivalents, 62
city living, 210
civil rights, 69
Crimean War, 691
cultural identity, 289
description, 177, 180
desert life, 468
divine order in kingdom, 741
documenting sources
  bibliographies and bibliography cards, 919–920
  citing Internet sources, 920–921
  formal note-taking, 919
  informal note-taking, 918–919
  note cards, 919
  parenthetical documentation, 921–922
  plagiarism, 918
  quotation marks, 918
  research journal, 918
  summarize, 918
Dominican Republic, 285
dragons, 236
dreams, 198
Egyptian sun god, 743
England, industry and reform in, 634

environment, 406, 498
fables, 769
famous awards, 161
figurative language, 177
Franklin Roosevelt's New Deal, 438
freedom rides, 69
geocentric theory, 773
geologic time, 148
giant squid, 79
global warming, 400
Golden Gloves tournament, 175
gothic literature, 550
heliocentric theory, 773
Hinduism and Buddhism, 785
Hispanic Americans in Korean War, 55
historical information, 290
holidays, 320
illustrations for "A Christmas Carol," 665
imagery, 177
Indian removal, 751
Indian Removal Act, 756
Industrial Revolution, 634
Internet research
- key domains, 915
- search tips, 916
- search tools, 916
- tracking search process, 915

interviews, 15
Jackie Robinson, 314
Japanese American internment in World War II, 578
Library of Congress, 439
London in mid-1894s, 642
magical animals in folk tales, 763
media literacy
- electronic media, 917
- multimedia, 917
- newspapers, 917
- periodicals, 917
- technical writing, 917
- visual media, 917

mimics, 223
mood, 73
Mount Saint Helens, 590
Mt. Fuji, 579
myths and legends, 395, 414, 732
NASA on Mars space mission, 61
Native American schools, 566
Native Americans in Oklahoma, 751
Native languages, 198
new foods, 504
Nigeria's history, 737
Nile River, 745
nonfiction, 173
personification, 177
photography, 436
point of view, 163, 175
poisonous snakes, 804
police work, 15
President Jackson's life, 756
Ptolemy, 773
Pullman porters' union, 26
pumpkins, 542
Queen Elizabeth I, 277
religious holidays, 667
removal of Cherokees from Georgia, 755
Renaissance, 272
researching skills
- almanacs, yearbooks, atlases, 914
- appendix, 914
- biographical reference, 914
- computerized catalogs, 913
- Dewey Decimal System, 912
- dictionaries, 913
- glossary, 914
- index, 914
- interlibrary loan, 913
- Internet libraries, 912
- library material organization, 90452–913
- locating library materials, 913–914
- primary source, 914
- reference materials, 913–914
- secondary source, 914
- thesaurus, 913

romance, 218
sea creatures, 79
sensory details, 177
Shakespeare, 692
Shintoism, 789
solar models, 773
sonnet form, 546
source evaluation, 917–918
Southeast Asia, 431
sports, 311, 339
story quilts, 348
time line, 28
trace migration, 439
trees, 180, 500
underwater creatures, 84
unit conversion, 62
urban murals, 71
victory gardens, 203
western green mamba and king cobra snakes, 104
Wonderland, 478

Applied English

advertisement, 514
advertising jingle, 124
application letter, 924
business letter, 211, 644, 775, 923–924
instructions, 180, 388, 514, 791
job description, 84
news article, 339, 756
news report, 55
proposal, 406, 924
public service announcement, 925
step-by-step procedure, 923
workplace and consumer documents, 923

Speaking & Listening

Speaking and Listening, 133, 279, 575
active listening, 369, 455, 531, 601, 927
answering questions, 929
asking questions, 929
avoid fallacies, 716
cause-and-effect order, 531
chronological order, 531
collaborative learning, 928
commemorative speech, 931
communicating by computer, 161
compare-and-contrast order, 531
counterarguments, 716
debate, 422, 489, 763, 933–934
dialogue, 339
discussion, 47, 211, 246, 316, 468, 479, 483, 494, 517, 519, 521, 542, 546, 583, 737, 785, 795
dramatic poem, 932

dramatic reading, 494
enunciation, 926
extemporaneous, 930
eye contact, 926
facial expression, 926
formal speech, 930–931
gesture, 926
group discussion, 928
group projects, 928–929
informal speech, 930–931
informative presentation, 368, 530
informative speech, 931
interviews, 279, 504, 756, 929–930
key ideas, 454
listening skills
  active vs. passive listening, 927
  clarifying and confirming, 927
  comprehending and judging, 279, 927
  comprehension, 927
  critical listening, 279, 431, 927
  for appreciation, 928
  main points, 927
  to learn vocabulary, 928
literary presentation, 246
lyric poem, 932
main point, 927
major ideas, 927
melody, 926
monologue, 692
multimedia presentation, 934
narrative poem, 932
narrative presentation, 600
nonverbal communication, 926
oral interpretation, 931–932
oral presentation of poem, 931–932
oral summary, 132
organization, 531
pace, 926
panel discussion, 104, 290, 442, 509, 556, 570, 795
passive listening, 927
perform scene, 667
persuasive presentation, 716
persuasive speech, 931
pitch, 926
posture, 926
problem-and-solution order, 531
proximity, 926
public speaking, 930–931
reader's theater, 686
research presentation, 814
role-play, 479, 708
sensory details, 246
small group debate, 802
small group discussion, 110, 320, 587, 592
speeches, 930–931
storytelling, 932–933
tone, 926
verbal communication, 926
viewing, 454
visuals, 454, 455
volume, 926
word choice, 246

Test-Taking Skills

antonym questions, 937
constructed-response questions, 937–938
essay questions, 938–939
multiple-choice questions, 936
objective questions, 936
preparing for test, 935
reading comprehension questions, 937
standardized test strategies, 935–936
synonym questions, 937

Index of Titles & Authors

A

"Achieving Perspective" (Rogers), 386
Ackerman, Diane, 408
Aesop, 765
"After Twenty Years" (Henry), 10, 16
Ah-nen-la-de-ni, 564
Aiken, Joan, 111
"Akhenaton's Hymn to the Sun" (Wilson), 743
"Alone Across the Arctic" (Flowers), from, 370
Alvarez, Julia, 282, 362
"Amaterasu" (Swift), 787
American Childhood, An (Dillard), from, 258
"Amigo Brothers" (Thomas), 164
Anaya, Rudolfo A., 796
"Ancestors" (Randall), 568
"Annabel Lee" (Poe), 549
"Ant and Grasshopper: Aesop's Fable (Reeves), 768
"Antaeus" (Deal), 139, 200
"Aqualung, The," 83
Armstrong, Jennifer, 415
Ashe, Arthur, 297, 310
"Astonishing Animals" (Flannery & Schouten), 443
Audobon, John James, 394
"Aunty Misery," (Cofer) 783
Avi, 134

B

Bambera, Toni Cade, 63
Barrio Boy (Galarza), from, 352
Bashō, Matsuo, 510
"Beastly Behaviors" (Benyus), from, 458
Benyus, Janine, 458
Bishop, Elizabeth, 557
"Bittersweet Memoir, A" (Izenberg), 323
"Black Athlete Looks at Education, A" (Ashe), 310
"Blackberry Eating" (Kinnell), 482
"Botany of Desire, The" (Pollan), from, 498
Bourke-White, Margaret, 436
Bradbury, Ray, 3, 73, 126
Braille: The Early Life of Louis Braille (Jennings & Jennings), from, 718
Browning, Robert, 532
Bruchac, Joseph, 191
Buson, Yosa, 510

C

Campbell, Joseph, 777
Carroll, Lewis, 475, 478
Catton, Bruce, 528
Cervantes, Lorna Dee, 586
"Charge of the Light Brigade, The" (Tennyson), 690
Chekov, Anton, 612
"Christmas Carol, A" (Leech), from, 665
"Christmas Carol, A: Scrooge and Marley" (Horovitz), 624
Cisneros, Sandra, 177
Clifton, Lucille, 210
Cofer, Judith Ortiz, 782
Coolidge, Olivia E., 770
Cosby, Bill, 312
"Courage My Mother Had, The" (Millay), 197
Cummings, Edward Estlin, 515

D

Dahl, Roald, 98
d'Aulaire, Edgar Parin, 727
d'Aulaire, Ingri, 727
"Day's Wait, A" (Hemingway), 58
de la Mare, Walter, 534
Deal, Borden, 199
"Death in the Open" (Thomas), 440
"Defenseless Creature, A" (Simon), 612
Dickinson, Emily, 537, 584
Dillard, Annie, 257
"Dinner Party, The" (Gardner), 136
"Dust Bowl Photographs" (Rothstein), 433
"Dust Changes America" (Bourke-White), 436

E

"Early Song" (Gogisgi), 522
"11:59, The" (McKissack), 4, 17, 19
Elizabeth I (Meltzer), 266
Ella Enchanted, from, 815
"Eshu: A Yoruban Folk Tale Retold" (Gleason), 734
"Eternal Frontier, The" (L'Armour), 293, 376

F

"Face It" (Wong), 289
"Face of the Deep Is Frozen, The" (Armstrong), 416
"Father William" (Carroll), 476
"Feel Like a Bird" (Swenson), 471
"Filling Station, The" (Bishop), 559
"Fire and Ice" (Frost), 421
"Fish Cheeks" (Tan), 253, 318
Flannery, Tim, 446
Flowers, Pam, 370
"Flying" (Lindbergh), from, 372
"Foghorn, The" (Bradbury), 3, 74
"For My Father" (Mirikitani), 577, 578
"Force of Luck, The" (Anaya), 796
"Four Skinny Trees" (Cisneros), 178
"Fox and the Crow, The: Aesop's Fable" (Jacobs), 765
Frost, Robert, 421, 544, 591, 594

G

Galarza, Ernesto, 352
"Gardener, The" (Tagore), 532
Gardner, Mona, 136
George, Chief Dan, 403
George, Phil, 562
Gibbons, Gail, 806
Gleason, Judith, 733
Gogisgi, 522
"Going Ape Over Language" (Rosinsky), from, 683
"Gold" (Mora), 467
Gore, Al, 396
Graf, Christine, 755
Greatest, The: Muhammad Ali (Myers), from, 174

"Green Mamba, The" (Dahl), 98
"Ground Is Always Damp, The" (Tapahonso), 250

H

haiku, 511, 512
Harris, Geraldine, 738
Harvey, Steven, 513
Haskins, Jim, 340
Hemingway, Ernest, 57
Henry, O., 9
"Highwayman, The" (Noyes), 551, 552
"Hmong Storycloth" (Vang), 425
"Hollywood and the Pits" (Lee), 142
Horovitz, Israel, 623
"How the Snake Got Poison" (Hurston), 803
"How to Eat a Poem" (Merriam), 462, 508
Hughes, Langston, 491
"Hummingbird That Lived Through Winter, The" (Saroyan), 412
Hurston, Zora Neale, 803

I

"I Am a Native of North America" (George), 403
"I'm Nobody" (Dickinson), 537, 584
"in the inner city" (Clifton), 210
"Indian Boy's Story, An" (Ah-nen-la-de-ni), from, 564
"Inn of Lost Time, The" (Namioka), 29, 31
"Instruction of Indra, The" (Campbell & Moyers), 778
Issa, Kobayashi, 510
Izenberg, Jerry, 322

J

Jacobs, Joseph, 765, 770
Jastrow, Robert, 378
"Jed's Grandfather" (Bruchac), 140, 192
Jen, Gish, 181
Jennings, Coleman A., 718
Jennings, Lois H., 718

K

Kinnell, Galway, 481
Kinsella, W.P., 333
Kipling, Rudyard, 85
Koriyama, Naoshi, 505

L

L'Amour, Louis, 291
Lee, Cherylene, 141
Leech, John, 665
"Let Me Hear You Whisper" (Zindel), 670
"Letter to Mary Queen of Scots, 1586" (Queen Elizabeth I), from, 278
Levine, Gail Carson, 815
Liddell, Alice, 478
Lindbergh, Reeve, 372
"Lion and the Statue, The: Aesop's Fable (Jacobs), 770
"Long Hard Journey, A: The Story of Pullman Porter" (McKissack & McKissack), from, 26
Longfellow, Henry Wadsworth, 473, 485, 604
"Loo-Wit" (Rose), 538, 586
"Lost in Translation" (Harvey), from, 513
"Lost Parrot, The" (Nye), 573

M

Macaulay, David, 83
"Madam C.J. Walker" (Haskins), 341
Marriott, Alice Lee, 747
"Mars Climate Orbiter Team Finds Likely Cause of Loss" (NASA), 61
McCaffrey, Anne, 224
McKay, Claude, 502
McKissack, Fredrick, 26
McKissack, Patricia, 4, 18, 26
Meltzer, Milton, 265
Merriam, Eve, 503, 518
Millay, Edna St. Vincent, 191
Milne, A.A., 720
"Miracles" (Whitman), 520
Mirikitani, Janice, 576
"Money Order" (Wong), 580
"Monsters Are Due on Maple Street, The" (Serling), 694
Mora, Pat, 466
"Mother to Son" (Hughes), 493
"Moving West: A Native American Perspective" (Graf), 755
"Mute Dancers: How to Watch a Hummingbird" (Ackerman), 409
Myers, Walter Dean, 173, 238

N

"Name Giveaway" (George), 563
"Names/Nombres" (Alvarez), 283
Namioka, Lensey, 30
Narayan, R.K., 777
New Way Things Work, The (Macaulay), 83
"Night the Bed Fell, The" (Thurber), 356
Noyes, Alfred, 547
Nye, Naomi Shihab, 572

O

O. Henry, 9
Off the Court (Ashe), from, 299
"Once by the Pacific" (Frost), 545

P

"Papa's Parrot" (Rylant), 220
"Pasture, The" (Frost), 591
"Persephone and Demeter" (d'Aulaire & d'Aulaire), 728
"Pets" (Avi), from, 134
"Phaethon, Son of Apollo" (Coolidge), 771
Poe, Edgar Allan, 547
Pollan, Michael, 498
Pool, Daniel, 642
"Portrait, The" (Rivera), 50

Q

"Queen Elizabeth's Speech to Her Last Parliament" (Queen Elizabeth I), from, 277
Queen Elizabeth I, 277, 278

R

"Rabbit and the Tug of War, (Thompson and Warrenfeltz), 809
"Rabbits Who Caused All the Trouble, The" (Thurber), 805
Randall, Dudley, 568
Reeves, James, 768
"Refugee Ship" (Cervantes), 586
"Rikki-Tikki-Tavi" (Kipling), 86
Ringgold, Faith, 348
Rivera, Diana, 495
Rivera, Tomás 49
Rogers, Pattiann, 386
Rose, Wendy, 588
Rosinsky, Natalie, 683
Rothstein, Arthur, 432
Rylant, Cynthia, 220

S

Salinas, Marta, 154
Sandburg, Carl, 539
Saroyan, William, 408
"Scholarship Jacket, The" (Salinas), 155, 162
Schouten, Peter, 446
"Searching for January" (Kinsella), 254, 333
"Secret Name of Ra, The" (Harris), 739
"Serial Garden, The" (Aiken), 111
Serling, Rod, 694
"Seventh Grade" (Soto), 212
Shakespeare, William, 687, 710
"Ships in the Desert" (Gore), 397
Sibley, David Allen, 390
Sibley Guide to Birds, The (Sibley), from, 391
Silko, Leslie Marmon, 105
"Silver" (de la Mare), 534
Simon, Neil, 611
"Sisters" (Wong), 582
"Size of Things, The" (Jastrow), 375, 379
"sky was, the" (Cummings), 516
"Smallest Dragonboy, The" (McCaffrey), 224
"Song" (Browning), 532
"Song of Hiawatha, The" (Longfellow), from, 604
Soto, Gary, 212
"St. Crispian's Day Speech" (Shakespeare), 688
Student Model: "After Twenty Years" (Mendoza), 131
"Such Perfection" (Narayan), 782
"Sunflower Quilting Bee at Arles, The" (Ringgold), 348
Swenson, May, 469
Swift, Carolyn, 786

T

Tagore, Rabindranath, 532
Tan, Amy, 317
Tapahonso, Luci, 250
Tennyson, Alfred, 687
"Theme in Yellow" (Sandburg), 541, 543
Thomas, Lewis, 440, 524
Thomas, Piri, 163
Thompson, Michael, 807
Thurber, James, 356, 805
"Tropics in New York, The" (McKay), 503
"Tsali of the Cherokees" (Marriott), 748
"Two People I Want to Be Like" (Merriam), 518

U

"Ugly Duckling, The" (Milne), from, 720
"Uncle Tony's Goat" (Silko), 105
"Under the Apple Tree" (Rivera), 464, 496
"Unfolding Bird" (Koriyama), 507
"Unforgettable Journey, An" (Xiong), 426

V

Vang, Mee, 424
"Village Blacksmith, The" (Longfellow), 473, 487

W

"War of the Wall, The" (Bambara), 64, 72
Warrenfeltz, Jacob, 807
"Was Tarzan a Three-Bandage Man?" (Cosby), 313
"We Are All One" (Yep), 758
"What Jane Austen Ate and Charles Dickens Knew" (Pool), from, 642
"White Umbrella, The" (Jen), 182, 190
Whitman, Walt, 520
"Why the Owl Has Big Eyes," from, 818
"Wild Turkey" (Audubon), from, 394
Wilson, John A., 743
Wong, Janet S., 289, 580, 582
"Written in Her French Psalter" (Queen Elizabeth I), 278
"Written with a Diamond on Her Window at Woodstock" (Queen Elizabeth I), 278

X

Xiong, Maijue, 426

Y

Yep, Laurence, 757

Z

Zindel, Paul, 669

For Your Reading List

5,000 Miles To Freedom: Ellen and William Craft's Flight from Slavery (Fradin & Fradin), 361
Al Capone Does My Shirts (Choldenko), 237
Ancient Voices (Hovey), 523
Bad Boy: A Memoir (Myers), 361
Becoming Joe DiMaggio (Testa), 523
Beowulf (Morpurgo), 805
Big Annie of Calumet: A True Story of the Industrial Revolution (Stanley), 361
Bradbury Series: 100 of His Most Celebrated Tales (Bradbury), 125
Chosen, The (Potok), 237
Devil's Arithemetic, The (Yolen), 125

Dream of Blancha's Wall, The (Medina), 523
Drop of Water, A (Wick), 447
Eragon (Paolini), 125
Forbidden Schoolhouse: The True and Dramatic Story of Prudence Crandall and Her Students, The (Jurmain), 361
Four Corners of the Sky, The (Zeitlin), 805
George Washington, Spymaster: How the Americans Outspied the British and Won the Revolutionary War (Allen), 361
Greek Theatre (Ross), 709
Holes (Sachar), 237
Horse Hooves and Chicken Feet: Mexican Folktales (Philip), 805
I Am the Darker Brother: An Anthology of Modern Poems by African Americans (Adoff), 523
I Am Wings: Poems About Love (Fletcher), 593
Invisible Ladder: An Anthology of Contemporary American Poems for Young Readers, The (Rosenberg), 523
Jumbo Book of Drama, The (Dunleavy), 709
Kidnapped Prince: The Life of Olaudah Equiano, The (Cameron), 361
Laughing Out Loud, I Fly: Poems in English and Spanish (Herrera), 593
Legend of Lord Eight Deer: An Epic of Ancient Mexico, The (Pohl), 805
New Way Things Work, The (Macauley), 447
Outcasts of 19 Schuyler Place, The (Konigsburg), 237
Peace Walker: The Legend of Hiawatha and Tekanawita (Taylor), 805
Photography: An Illustrated History (Sandler), 447
Pick Me Up (Leslie & Roberts), 447
Pictures of Hollis Woods (Giff), 237
Plays From Hispanic Tales (Winther), 709
Plays of Black Americans: The Black Experience in America, Dramatized for Young People (Kamerman), 709
Poetry for Young People: Walt Whitman (Levin), 593
Poetry for Young People: William Carlos Williams (MacGowan), 593
Raptor! A Kid's Guide to Birds of Prey (Laubach, Laubach, & Smith), 447
Remember the Bridge: Poems of A People (Weatherford), 593
Romiette and Julio (Draper), 237
Seattle Children's Theatre: Six Plays for Young Audiences (Smith), 709
Shakespeare's Theater (Morley), 709
Story of King Arthur and His Knights, The (Pyle), 805
Tuck Everlasting (Babbitt), 125
Universe (Rees), 447
War and the Pity of War (Philip), 523
Wreath for Emmett Till, A (Nelson), 593
Wrinkle in Time, A (L'Engle), 125
Zazoo (Mosher), 125